# OXFORD TAKE OFF IN SPANISH DICTIONARY

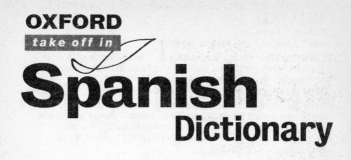

# OXFORD
## *take off in*
# Spanish
## Dictionary

SPANISH–ENGLISH
ENGLISH–SPANISH

ESPAÑOL–INGLÉS
INGLÉS–ESPAÑOL

*Christine Lea*

# OXFORD
### UNIVERSITY PRESS

# OXFORD
### UNIVERSITY PRESS

*Great Clarendon Street, Oxford* OX2 6DP

*Oxford University Press is a department of the University of Oxford.*
*It furthers the University's objective of excellence in research, scholarship,*
*and education by publishing worldwide in*

*Oxford  New York*

*Athens  Auckland  Bangkok  Bogotá  Buenos Aires  Calcutta*
*Cape Town  Chennai  Dar es Salaam  Delhi  Florence  Hong Kong  Istanbul*
*Karachi  Kuala Lumpur  Madrid  Melbourne  Mexico City  Mumbai*
*Nairobi  Paris  São Paulo  Singapore  Taipei  Tokyo  Toronto  Warsaw*
*with associated companies in  Berlin  Ibadan*

*Oxford is a registered trade mark of Oxford University Press*
*in the UK and in certain other countries*

*Library of Congress Cataloging in Publication Data*
*Data available*

*British Library Cataloguing in Publication Data*
*Data available*
*ISBN 0–19–860333–9*

10 9 8 7 6 5 4 3 2 1

*Printed in Great Britain*
*by Mackays of Chatham plc*
*Chatham, Kent*

# Contents · Índice

# Preface

This dictionary has been written with speakers of both English and Spanish in mind and contains the most useful words and expressions of the English and Spanish languages of today. Wide coverage of culinary and motoring terms has been included to help the tourist.

Common abbreviations, names of countries, and other useful geographical names are included.

English pronunciation is given by means of the International Phonetic Alphabet. It is shown for all headwords and for those derived words whose pronunciation is not easily deduced from that of a headword. The rules for pronunciation of Spanish are given on page x.

I should like to thank particularly Mary-Carmen Beaven whose comments have been invaluable. I would also like to acknowledge the help given me unwittingly by Dr M. Janes and Mrs J. Andrews, whose French and Italian Minidictionaries have served as models for the present work.

C.A.L.

# Prefacio

Este diccionario de Oxford se escribió tanto para los hispanohablantes como para los angloparlantes y contiene las palabras y frases más corrientes de ambas lenguas de hoy. Se incluyen muchos términos culinarios y de automovilismo que pueden servir al turista.

Las abreviaturas más corrientes, los nombres de países, y otros términos geográficos figuran en este diccionario.

La pronunciación inglesa sigue el Alfabeto Fonético Internacional. Se incluye para cada palabra clave y todas las derivadas cuya pronunciación no es fácil de deducir a partir de la palabra clave. Las reglas de la pronunciación española se encuentran en la página x.

Quisiera reconocer la ayuda de Mary-Carmen Beaven cuyas observaciones me han sido muy valiosas. También quiero agradecerles al Dr. M. Janes y a la Sra. J. Andrews cuyos minidiccionarios del francés y del italiano me han servido de modelo para el presente.

C.A.L.

# Introduction

The swung dash (~) is used to replace a headword or that part of a headword preceding the vertical bar (|). In both English and Spanish only irregular plurals are given. Normally Spanish nouns and adjectives ending in an unstressed vowel form the plural by adding *s* (e.g. *libro, libros*). Nouns and adjectives ending in a stressed vowel or a consonant add *es* (e.g. *rubí, rubíes; pared, paredes*). An accent on the final syllable is not required when *es* is added (e.g. *nación, naciones*). Final *z* becomes *ces* (e.g. *vez, veces*). Spanish nouns and adjectives ending in *o* form the feminine by changing the final *o* to *a* (e.g. *hermano, hermana*). Most Spanish nouns and adjectives ending in anything other than final *o* do not have a separate feminine form with the exception of those denoting nationality etc; these add *a* to the masculine singular form (e.g. *español, española*). An accent on the final syllable is then not required (e.g. *inglés, inglesa*). Adjectives ending in *án, ón*, or *or* behave like those denoting nationality with the following exceptions: *inferior, mayor, mejor, menor, peor, superior* where the feminine has the same form as the masculine. Spanish verb tables will be found in the appendix.

## The Spanish alphabet

In Spanish *ch, ll* and *ñ* are considered separate letters and in the Spanish–English section, therefore, they will be found after *cu, lu* and *ny* respectively.

# Introducción

La tilde (∼) se emplea para substituir a la palabra cabeza de artículo o aquella parte de tal palabra que precede a la barra vertical (|). Tanto en inglés como en español se dan los plurales solamente si son irregulares. Para formar el plural regular en inglés se añade la letra *s* al sustantivo singular, pero se añade *es* cuando se trata de una palabra que termina en *ch*, *sh*, *s*, *ss*, *us*, *x*, o *z* (p.ej. *sash*, *sashes*). En el caso de una palabra que termina en *y* precedida por una consonante, la *y* se cambia en *ies* (p.ej. *baby*, *babies*). Para formar el tiempo pasado y el participio pasado se añade *ed* al infinitivo de los verbos regulares ingleses (p.ej. *last*, *lasted*). En el caso de los verbos ingleses que terminan en *e* muda se añade sólo la *d* (p.ej. *move*, *moved*). En el caso de los verbos ingleses que terminan en *y* hay que cambiar la *y* en *ied* (p.ej. *carry*, *carried*). Los verbos irregulares se encuentran en el diccionario por orden alfabético remitidos al infinitivo, y también en la lista en el apéndice.

# Pronunciation of Spanish

**Vowels:**

a    is between pronunciation of *a* in English *cat* and *arm*

e    is like *e* in English *bed*

i    is like *ee* in English *see* but a little shorter

o    is like *o* in English *hot* but a little longer

u    is like *oo* in English *too*

y    when a vowel is as Spanish **i**

**Consonants:**

b    1) in initial position or after nasal consonant is like English *b*
     2) in other positions is between English *b* and English *v*

c    1) before **e** or **i** is like *th* in English *thin*
     2) in other positions is like *c* in English *cat*

ch    is like *ch* in English *chip*

d    1) in initial position, after nasal consonants and after **l** is like English *d*
     2) in other positions is like *th* in English *this*

f    is like English *f*

g    1) before **e** or **i** is like *ch* in Scottish *loch*
     2) in initial position is like *g* in English *get*
     3) in other positions is like 2) but a little softer

h    is silent in Spanish but see also **ch**

j    is like *ch* in Scottish *loch*

k    is like English *k*

l    is like English *l* but see also **ll**

ll    is like *lli* in English *million*

m    is like English *m*

n    is like English *n*

ñ    is like *ni* in English *opinion*

p    is like English *p*

q    is like English *k*

r    is rolled or trilled

s    is like *s* in English *sit*

t    is like English *t*

v    1) in initial position or after nasal consonant is like English *b*
     2) in other positions is between English *b* and English *v*

w is like Spanish **b** or **v**
x is like English *x*
y is like English *y*
z is like *th* in English *thin*

# Pronunciación Inglesa

**Símbolos fonéticos**

**Vocales y diptongos**

| | | | | |
|---|---|---|---|---|
| iː | see | ə | ago |
| ɪ | sit | eɪ | page |
| e | ten | əʊ | home |
| æ | hat | aɪ | five |
| ɑː | arm | aɪə | fire |
| ɒ | got | aʊ | now |
| ɔː | saw | aʊə | flour |
| ʊ | put | ɔɪ | join |
| uː | too | ɪə | near |
| ʌ | cup | eə | hair |
| ɜː | fur | ʊə | poor |

**Consonantes**

| | | | | |
|---|---|---|---|---|
| p | pen | s | so |
| b | bad | z | zoo |
| t | tea | ʃ | she |
| d | dip | ʒ | measure |
| k | cat | h | how |
| g | got | m | man |
| tʃ | chin | n | no |
| dʒ | June | ŋ | sing |
| f | fall | l | leg |
| v | voice | r | red |
| θ | thin | j | yes |
| ð | then | w | wet |

# Abbreviations · Abreviaturas

| | | |
|---|---|---|
| adjective | *a* | adjetivo |
| abbreviation | *abbr/abrev* | abreviatura |
| administration | *admin* | administración |
| adverb | *adv* | adverbio |
| American | *Amer* | americano |
| anatomy | *anat* | anatomía |
| architecture | *archit/arquit* | arquitectura |
| definite article | *art def* | artículo definido |
| indefinite article | *art indef* | artículo indefinido |
| astrology | *astr* | astrología |
| motoring | *auto* | automóvil |
| auxiliary | *aux* | auxiliar |
| aviation | *aviat/aviac* | aviación |
| biology | *biol* | biología |
| botany | *bot* | botánica |
| commerce | *com* | comercio |
| conjunction | *conj* | conjunción |
| cookery | *culin* | cocina |
| electricity | *elec* | electricidad |
| school | *escol* | enseñanza |
| Spain | *Esp* | España |
| feminine | *f* | femenino |
| familiar | *fam* | familiar |
| figurative | *fig* | figurado |
| philosophy | *fil* | filosofía |
| photography | *foto* | fotografía |
| geography | *geog* | geografía |
| geology | *geol* | geología |
| grammar | *gram* | gramática |
| humorous | *hum* | humorístico |
| interjection | *int* | interjección |
| interrogative | *inter* | interrogativo |
| invariable | *invar* | invariable |
| legal, law | *jurid* | jurídico |
| Latin American | *LAm* | latinoamericano |
| language | *lang* | lengua(je) |
| masculine | *m* | masculino |
| mathematics | *mat(h)* | matemáticas |
| mechanics | *mec* | mecánica |
| medicine | *med* | medicina |
| military | *mil* | militar |
| music | *mus* | música |
| mythology | *myth* | mitología |
| noun | *n* | nombre |
| nautical | *naut* | náutica |
| oneself | *o.s.* | uno mismo, se |
| proprietary term | *P* | marca registrada |

| | | |
|---|---|---|
| pejorative | *pej* | peyorativo |
| philosophy | *phil* | filosofía |
| photography | *photo* | fotografía |
| plural | *pl* | plural |
| politics | *pol* | política |
| possessive | *poss* | posesivo |
| past participle | *pp* | participio de pretérito |
| prefix | *pref* | prefijo |
| preposition | *prep* | preposición |
| present participle | *pres p* | participio de presente |
| pronoun | *pron* | pronombre |
| psychology | *psych* | psicología |
| past tense | *pt* | tiempo pasado |
| railway | *rail* | ferrocarril |
| relative | *rel* | relativo |
| religion | *relig* | religión |
| school | *schol* | enseñanza |
| singular | *sing* | singular |
| slang | *sl* | argot |
| someone | *s.o.* | alguien |
| something | *sth* | algo |
| technical | *tec* | técnico |
| television | *TV* | televisión |
| university | *univ* | universidad |
| auxiliary verb | *v aux* | verbo auxiliar |
| verb | *vb* | verbo |
| intransitive verb | *vi* | verbo intransitivo |
| pronominal verb | *vpr* | verbo pronominal |
| transitive verb | *vt* | verbo transitivo |
| transitive & intransitive verb | *vti* | verbo transitivo e intransitivo |

## Proprietary terms

This dictionary includes some words which are, or are asserted to
  be, proprietary names or trade marks. Their inclusion does not
  imply that they have acquired for legal purposes a
  non-proprietary or general significance, nor is any other
  judgement implied concerning their legal status. In cases where
  the editor has some evidence that a word is used as a
  proprietary name or trade mark this is indicated by the letter
  (P), but no judgement concerning the legal status of such words
  is made or implied thereby.

## Marcas registradas

Este diccionario incluye algunas palabras que son o pretenden
  ser marcas registradas. No debe atribuirse ningún valor
  jurídico ni a la presencia ni a la ausencia de tal designación.

# ESPAÑOL-INGLÉS
# SPANISH-ENGLISH

# A

**a** *prep* in, at; (*dirección*) to; (*tiempo*) at; (*hasta*) to, until; (*fecha*) on; (*más tarde*) later; (*medio*) by; (*precio*) for, at. **~ 5 km** 5 km away. **¿~ cuántos estamos?** what's the date? **~l día siguiente** the next day. **~ la francesa** in the French fashion. **~ las 2** at 2 o'clock. **~ los 25 años** (*edad*) at the age of 25; (*después de*) after 25 years. **~ no ser por** but for. **~ que** I bet. **~ 28 de febrero** on the 28th of February

**ábaco** *m* abacus

**abad** *m* abbot

**abadejo** *m* (*pez*) cod

**abad|esa** *f* abbess. **~ía** *f* abbey

**abajo** *adv* (*down*) below; (*dirección*) down(wards); (*en casa*) downstairs. ● *int* down with. **calle ~** down the street. **el ~ firmante** the undersigned. **escaleras ~** downstairs. **la parte de ~** the bottom part. **los de ~** those at the bottom. **más ~** below.

**abalanzarse** [10] *vpr* rush towards

**abalorio** *m* glass bead

**abanderado** *m* standard-bearer

**abandon|ado** *adj* abandoned; (*descuidado*) neglected; ⟨*personas*⟩ untidy. **~ar** *vt* leave ⟨*un lugar*⟩; abandon ⟨*personas, cosas*⟩. ● *vi* give up. **~arse** *vpr* give in; (*descuidarse*) let o.s. go. **~o** *m* abandonment; (*estado*) abandon

**abani|car** [7] *vt* fan. **~co** *m* fan. **~queo** *m* fanning

**abarata|miento** *m* reduction in price. **~r** *vt* reduce. **~rse** *vpr* ⟨*precios*⟩ come down

**abarca** *f* sandal

**abarcar** [7] *vt* put one's arms around, embrace; (*comprender*) embrace; (*LAm, acaparar*) monopolize

**abarquillar** *vt* warp. **~se** *vpr* warp

**abarrotar** *vt* overfill, pack full

**abarrotes** *mpl* (*LAm*) groceries

**abast|ecer** [11] *vt* supply. **~ecimiento** *m* supply; (*acción*) supplying. **~o** *m* supply. **dar ~o a** supply

**abati|do** *a* depressed. **~miento** *m* depression. **~r** *vt* knock down, demolish; (*fig, humillar*) humiliate. **~rse** *vpr* swoop (**sobre** on); (*ponerse abatido*) get depressed

**abdica|ción** *f* abdication. **~r** [7] *vt* give up. ● *vi* abdicate

**abdom|en** *m* abdomen. **~inal** *a* abdominal

**abec|é** *m* (*fam*) alphabet, ABC. **~edario** *m* alphabet

**abedul** *m* birch (tree)

**abej|a** *f* bee. **~arrón** *m* bumble-bee. **~ón** *m* drone. **~orro** *m* bumble-bee; (*insecto coleóptero*) cockchafer

**aberración** *f* aberration

**abertura** *f* opening

**abet|al** *m* fir wood. **~o** *m* fir (tree)

**abierto** *pp véase* **abrir.** ● *a* open

**abigarra|do** *a* multi-coloured; (*fig, mezclado*) mixed. **~miento** *m* variegation

**abigeato** *m* (*Mex*) rustling

**abism|al** *a* abysmal; (*profundo*) deep. **~ar** *vt* throw into an abyss; (*fig, abatir*) humble. **~arse** *vpr* be absorbed (**en** in), be lost (**en** in). **~o** *m* abyss; (*fig, diferencia*) world of difference

**abizcochado** *a* spongy

**abjura|ción** *f* abjuration. **~r** *vt* forswear. ● *vi*. **~r de** forswear

**ablanda|miento** *m* softening. **~r** *vt* soften. **~rse** *vpr* soften

**ablución** *f* ablution

**abnega|ción** *f* self-sacrifice. **~do** *a* self-sacrificing

**aboba|do** *a* silly. **~miento** *m* silliness

**aboca|do** *a* ⟨*vino*⟩ medium. **~r** [7] *vt* pour out

**abocetar** *vt* sketch

**abocinado** *a* trumpet-shaped

**abochornar** *vt* suffocate; (*fig, avergonzar*) embarrass. **~se** *vpr* feel embarrassed; ⟨*plantas*⟩ wilt

**abofetear** *vt* slap

**aboga|cía** *f* legal profession. **~do** *m* lawyer; (*notario*) solicitor; (*en el tribunal*) barrister, attorney (*Amer*). **~r** [12] *vi* plead

**abolengo** *m* ancestry

**aboli|ción** *f* abolition. **~cionismo** *m* abolitionism. **~cionista** *m* & *f* abolitionist. **~r** [24] *vt* abolish

**abolsado** *a* baggy

**abolla|dura** *f* dent. **~r** *vt* dent

**abomba|do** *a* convex; (*Arg, borracho*) drunk. **~r** *vt* make convex. **~rse** *vpr* (*LAm, corromperse* ) start to rot, go bad

**abomina|ble** *a* abominable. **~ción** *f* abomination. **~r** *vt* detest. ● *vi.* **~r de** detest

**abona|ble** *a* payable. **~do** *a* paid. ● *m* subscriber

**abonanzar** *vi* ⟨*tormenta*⟩ abate; ⟨*tiempo*⟩ improve

**abon|ar** *vt* pay; (*en agricultura*) fertilize. **~aré** *m* promissory note. **~arse** *vpr* subscribe. **~o** *m* payment; (*estiércol*) fertilizer; (*a un periódico*) subscription

**aborda|ble** *a* reasonable; ⟨*persona*⟩ approachable. **~je** *m* boarding. **~r** *vt* tackle ⟨*un asunto*⟩; approach ⟨*una persona*⟩; (*naut*) come alongside

**aborigen** *a* & *m* native

**aborrascarse** [7] *vpr* get stormy

**aborrec|er** [11] *vt* hate; (*exasperar*) annoy. **~ible** *a* loathsome. **~ido** *a* hated. **~imiento** *m* hatred

**aborregado** *a* ⟨*cielo*⟩ mackerel

**abort|ar** *vi* have a miscarriage. **~ivo** *a* abortive. **~o** *m* miscarriage; (*voluntario*) abortion; (*fig, monstruo*) abortion. **hacerse ~ar** have an abortion

**abotaga|miento** *m* swelling. **~rse** [12] *vpr* swell up

**abotonar** *vt* button (up)

**aboveda|do** *a* vaulted. **~r** *vt* vault

**abra** *f* cove

**abracadabra** *m* abracadabra

**abrasa|dor** *a* burning. **~r** *vt* burn; (*fig, consumir*) consume. **~rse** *vpr* burn

**abrasi|ón** *f* abrasion; (*geología*) erosion. **~vo** *a* abrasive

**abraz|adera** *f* bracket. **~ar** *vt* [10] embrace; (*encerrar*) enclose. **~arse**

*vpr* embrace. **~o** *m* hug. **un fuerte ~o de** (*en una carta*) with best wishes from

**abrecartas** *m* paper-knife

**ábrego** *m* south wind

**abrelatas** *m invar* tin opener (*Brit*), can opener

**abreva|dero** *m* watering place. **~r** *vt* water ⟨*animales*⟩. **~rse** *vpr* ⟨*animales*⟩ drink

**abrevia|ción** *f* abbreviation; (*texto abreviado*) abridged text. **~do** *a* brief; ⟨*texto*⟩ abridged. **~r** *vt* abbreviate; abridge ⟨*texto*⟩; cut short ⟨*viaje etc*⟩. ● *vi* be brief. **~tura** *f* abbreviation

**abrig|ada** *f* shelter. **~adero** *m* shelter. **~ado** *a* ⟨*lugar*⟩ sheltered; ⟨*personas*⟩ well wrapped up. **~ar** [12] *vt* shelter; cherish ⟨*esperanza*⟩; harbour ⟨*duda, sospecha*⟩. **~arse** *vpr* (take) shelter; (*con ropa*) wrap up. **~o** *m* (over)coat; (*lugar*) shelter

**abril** *m* April. **~eño** *a* April

**abrillantar** *vt* polish

**abrir** [*pp* **abierto**] *vt/i* open. **~se** *vpr* open; (*extenderse*) open out; ⟨*el tiempo*⟩ clear

**abrocha|dor** *m* buttonhook. **~r** *vt* do up; (*con botones*) button up

**abrojo** *m* thistle

**abroncar** [7] *vt* (*fam*) tell off; (*abuchear*) boo; (*avergonzar*) shame. **~se** *vpr* be ashamed; (*enfadarse*) get annoyed

**abroquelarse** *vpr* shield o.s.

**abruma|dor** *a* overwhelming. **~r** *vt* overwhelm

**abrupto** *a* steep; (*áspero*) harsh

**abrutado** *a* brutish

**absceso** *m* abscess

**absentismo** *m* absenteeism

**ábside** *m* apse

**absintio** *m* absinthe

**absolución** *f* (*relig*) absolution; (*jurid*) acquittal

**absolut|amente** *adv* absolutely, completely. **~ismo** *m* absolutism. **~ista** *a* & *m* & *f* absolutist. **~o** *a* absolute. **~orio** *a* of acquittal. **en ~o** (*de manera absoluta*) absolutely; (*con sentido negativo*) (not) at all

**absolver** [2, *pp* **absuelto**] *vt* (*relig*) absolve; (*jurid*) acquit

**absor|bente** *a* absorbent; (*fig, interesante*) absorbing. **~ber** *vt* absorb. **~ción** *f* absorption. **~to** *a* absorbed

**abstemio** *a* teetotal. ● *m* teetotaller

**absten|ción** *f* abstention. **~erse** [40] *vpr* abstain, refrain (**de** from)

**abstinen|cia** *f* abstinence. **~te** *a* abstinent

**abstra|cción** *f* abstraction. **~cto** *a* abstract. **~er** [41] *vt* abstract. **~erse** *vpr* be lost in thought. **~ído** *a* absent-minded

**abstruso** *a* abstruse

**absuelto** *a* (*relig*) absolved; (*jurid*) acquitted

**absurdo** *a* absurd. ● *m* absurd thing

**abuche|ar** *vt* boo. **~o** *m* booing

**abuel|a** *f* grandmother. **~o** *m* grandfather. **~os** *mpl* grandparents

**ab|ulia** *f* lack of willpower. **~úlico** *a* weak-willed

**abulta|do** *a* bulky. **~miento** *m* bulkiness. **~r** *vt* enlarge; (*hinchar*) swell; (*fig, exagerar*) exaggerate. ● *vi* be bulky

**abunda|ncia** *f* abundance. **~nte** *a* abundant, plentiful. **~r** *vi* be plentiful. **nadar en la ~ncia** be rolling in money

**aburguesa|miento** *m* conversion to a middle-class way of life. **~rse** *vpr* become middle-class

**aburri|do** *a* (*con estar*) bored; (*con ser*) boring. **~miento** *m* boredom; (*cosa pesada*) bore. **~r** *vt* bore. **~rse** *vpr* be bored, get bored

**abus|ar** *vi* take advantage. **~ar de la bebida** drink too much. **~ivo** *a* excessive. **~o** *m* abuse. **~ón** *a* (*fam*) selfish

**abyec|ción** *f* wretchedness. **~to** *a* abject

**acá** *adv* here; (*hasta ahora*) until now. **~ y allá** here and there. **de ~ para allá** to and fro. **de ayer ~** since yesterday

**acaba|do** *a* finished; (*perfecto*) perfect; (*agotado*) worn out. ● *m* finish. **~miento** *m* finishing; (*fin*) end. **~r** *vt/i* finish. **~rse** *vpr* finish; (*agotarse*) run out; (*morirse*) die. **~r con** put an end to. **~r de** (+ *infinitivo*) have just (+ *pp*). **~ de llegar** he has just arrived. **~r por** (+ *infinitivo*) end up (+ *gerundio*). **¡se acabó!** that's it!

**acabóse** *m*. **ser el ~** be the end, be the limit

**acacia** *f* acacia

**acad|emia** *f* academy. **~émico** *a* academic

**acaec|er** [11] *vi* happen. **~imiento** *m* occurrence

**acalora|damente** *adv* heatedly. **~do** *a* heated. **~miento** *m* heat. **~r** *vt* warm up; (*fig, excitar*) excite. **~rse** *vpr* get hot; (*fig, excitarse*) get excited

**acallar** *vt* silence

**acampanado** *a* bell-shaped

**acampar** *vi* camp

**acanala|do** *a* grooved. **~dura** *f* groove. **~r** *vt* groove

**acantilado** *a* steep. ● *m* cliff

**acanto** *m* acanthus

**acapara|r** *vt* hoard; (*monopolizar*) monopolize. **~miento** *m* hoarding; (*monopolio*) monopolizing

**acaracolado** *a* spiral

**acaricia|dor** *a* caressing. **~r** *vt* caress; (*rozar*) brush; ⟨*proyectos etc*⟩ have in mind

**ácaro** *m* mite

**acarre|ar** *vt* transport; ⟨*desgracias etc*⟩ cause. **~o** *m* transport

**acartona|do** *a* ⟨*persona*⟩ wizened. **~rse** *vpr* (*ponerse rígido*) go stiff; ⟨*persona*⟩ become wizened

**acaso** *adv* maybe, perhaps. ● *m* chance. **~ llueva mañana** perhaps it will rain tomorrow. **al ~** at random. **por si ~** in case

**acata|miento** *m* respect (**a** for). **~r** *vt* respect

**acatarrarse** *vpr* catch a cold, get a cold

**acaudalado** *a* well off

**acaudillar** *vt* lead

**acceder** *vi* agree; (*tener acceso*) have access

**acces|ibilidad** *f* accessibility. **~ible** *a* accessible; ⟨*persona*⟩ approachable. **~o** *m* access, entry; (*med, ataque*) attack; (*llegada*) approach

**accesorio** *a & m* accessory

**accidenta|do** *a* ⟨*terreno*⟩ uneven; (*agitado*) troubled; ⟨*persona*⟩ injured

**accident|al** *a* accidental. **~arse** *vpr* have an accident. **~e** *m* accident

**acci|ón** *f* (*incl jurid*) action; (*hecho*) deed. **~onar** *vt* work. ● *vi* gesticulate. **~onista** *m & f* shareholder

**acebo** *m* holly (tree)

**acebuche** *m* wild olive tree

**acecinar** *vt* cure ⟨*carne*⟩. **~se** *vpr* become wizened

**acech|ar** *vt* spy on; (*aguardar*) lie in wait for. **~o** *m* spying. **al ~o** on the look-out

**acedera** f sorrel

**acedía** f (pez) plaice; (acidez) heartburn

**aceit|ar** vt oil; (culin) add oil to. ~**e** m oil; (de oliva) olive oil. ~**era** f oil bottle; (para engrasar) oilcan. ~**ero** a oil. ~**oso** a oily

**aceitun|a** f olive. ~**ado** a olive. ~**o** m olive tree

**acelera|ción** f acceleration. ~**damente** adv quickly. ~**dor** m accelerator. ~**r** vt accelerate; (fig) speed up, quicken

**acelga** f chard

**ac|émila** f mule; (como insulto) ass (fam). ~**emilero** m muleteer

**acendra|do** a pure. ~**r** vt purify; refine (metales)

**acensuar** vt tax

**acent|o** m accent; (énfasis) stress. ~**uación** f accentuation. ~**uar** [21] vt stress; (fig) emphasize. ~**uarse** vpr become noticeable

**aceña** f water-mill

**acepción** f meaning, sense

**acepta|ble** a acceptable. ~**ción** f acceptance; (aprobación) approval. ~**r** vt accept

**acequia** f irrigation channel

**acera** f pavement (Brit), sidewalk (Amer)

**acerado** a steel; (fig, mordaz) sharp

**acerca** de prep about

**acerca|miento** m approach; (fig) reconciliation. ~**r** [7] vt bring near. ~**rse** vpr approach

**acería** f steelworks

**acerico** m pincushion

**acero** m steel. ~ **inoxidable** stainless steel

**acérrimo** a (fig) staunch

**acert|ado** a right, correct; (apropiado) appropriate. ~**ar** [1] vt hit (el blanco); (adivinar) get right, guess. ● vi get right. ~**ar a** happen to. ~**ar con** hit on. ~**ijo** m riddle

**acervo** m pile; (bienes) common property

**acetato** m acetate

**acético** a acetic

**acetileno** m acetylene

**acetona** f acetone

**aciago** a unlucky

**aciano** m cornflower

**ac|íbar** m aloes; (planta) aloe; (fig, amargura) bitterness. ~**ibarar** vt add aloes to; (fig, amargar) embitter

**acicala|do** a dressed up, overdressed. ~**r** vt dress up. ~**rse** vpr get dressed up

**acicate** m spur

**acid|ez** f acidity. ~**ificar** [7] vt acidify. ~**ificarse** vpr acidify

**ácido** a sour. ● m acid

**acierto** m success; (idea) good idea; (habilidad) skill

**aclama|ción** f acclaim; (aplausos) applause. ~**r** vt acclaim; (aplaudir) applaud

**aclara|ción** f explanation. ~**r** vt lighten (colores); (explicar) clarify; (enjuagar) rinse. ● vi (el tiempo) brighten up. ~**rse** vpr become clear. ~**torio** a explanatory

**aclimata|ción** f acclimatization, acclimation (Amer). ~**r** vt acclimatize, acclimate (Amer). ~**rse** vpr become acclimatized, become acclimated (Amer)

**acné** m acne

**acobardar** vt intimidate. ~**se** vpr get frightened

**acocil** m (Mex) freshwater shrimp

**acod|ado** a bent. ~**ar** vt (doblar) bend; (agricultura) layer. ~**arse** vpr lean on (en on). ~**o** m layer

**acog|edor** a welcoming; (ambiente) friendly. ~**er** [14] vt welcome; (proteger) shelter; (recibir) receive. ~**erse** vpr take refuge. ~**ida** f welcome; (refugio) refuge

**acogollar** vi bud. ~**se** vpr bud

**acolcha|do** a quilted. ~**r** vt quilt, pad

**acólito** m acolyte; (monaguillo) altar boy

**acomet|edor** a aggressive; (emprendedor) enterprising. ~**er** vt attack; (emprender) undertake; (llenar) fill. ~**ida** f attack. ~**ividad** f aggression; (iniciativa) enterprise

**acomod|able** a adaptable. ~**adizo** a accommodating. ~**ado** a well off. ~**ador** m usher. ~**adora** f usherette. ~**amiento** m suitability. ~**ar** vt arrange; (adaptar) adjust. ● vi be suitable. ~**arse** vpr settle down; (adaptarse) conform. ~**aticio** a accommodating. ~**o** m position

**acompaña|do** a accompanied; (concurrido) busy. ~**miento** m accompaniment. ~**nta** f companion. ~**nte** m companion; (mus) accompanist. ~**r** vt accompany; (adjuntar) enclose. ~**rse** vpr (mus) accompany o.s.

**acompasa|do** *a* rhythmic. **~r** *vt* keep in time; (*fig*, *ajustar*) adjust

**acondiciona|do** *a* equipped. **~miento** *m* conditioning. **~r** *vt* fit out; (*preparar*) prepare

**acongojar** *vt* distress. **~se** *vpr* get upset

**acónito** *m* aconite

**aconseja|ble** *a* advisable. **~do** *a* advised. **~r** *vt* advise. **~rse** *vpr* take advice. **~rse con** consult

**aconsonantar** *vt/i* rhyme

**acontec|er** [11] *vi* happen. **~imiento** *m* event

**acopi|ar** *vt* collect. **~o** *m* store

**acopla|do** *a* coordinated. **~miento** *m* coupling; (*elec*) connection. **~r** *vt* fit; (*elec*) connect; (*rail*) couple

**acoquina|miento** *m* intimidation. **~r** *vt* intimidate. **~rse** *vpr* be intimidated

**acoraza|do** *a* armour-plated. ● *m* battleship. **~r** [10] *vt* armour

**acorazonado** *a* heart-shaped

**acorcha|do** *a* spongy. **~rse** *vpr* go spongy; (*parte del cuerpo*) go to sleep

**acord|ado** *a* agreed. **~ar** [2] *vt* agree (upon); (*decidir*) decide; (*recordar*) remind. **~e** *a* in agreement; (*mus*) harmonious. ● *m* chord

**acorde|ón** *m* accordion. **~onista** *m* & *f* accordionist

**acordona|do** *a* (*lugar*) cordoned off. **~miento** *m* cordoning off. **~r** *vt* tie, lace; (*rodear*) surround, cordon off

**acorrala|miento** *m* (*de animales*) rounding up; (*de personas*) cornering. **~r** *vt* round up (*animales*); corner (*personas*)

**acorta|miento** *m* shortening. **~r** *vt* shorten; (*fig*) cut down

**acos|ar** *vt* hound; (*fig*) pester. **~o** *m* pursuit; (*fig*) pestering

**acostar** [2] *vt* put to bed; (*naut*) bring alongside. ● *vi* (*naut*) reach land. **~se** *vpr* go to bed; (*echarse*) lie down; (*Mex, parir*) give birth

**acostumbra|do** *a* (*habitual*) usual. **~do a** used to, accustomed to. **~r** *vt* get used. **me ha acostumbrado a levantarme por la noche** he's got me used to getting up at night. ● *vi.* **~r (a)** be accustomed to. **acostumbro comer a la una** I usually have lunch at one o'clock. **~rse** *vpr* become accustomed, get used

**acota|ción** *f* (*nota*) marginal note; (*en el teatro*) stage direction; (*cota*) elevation mark. **~do** *a* enclosed. **~r** *vt* mark out (*terreno*); (*anotar*) annotate

**ácrata** *a* anarchistic. ● *m* & *f* anarchist

**acre** *m* acre. ● *a* (*olor*) pungent; (*sabor*) sharp, bitter

**acrecenta|miento** *m* increase. **~r** [1] *vt* increase. **~rse** *vpr* increase

**acrec|er** [11] *vt* increase. **~imiento** *m* increase

**acredita|do** *a* reputable; (*pol*) accredited. **~r** *vt* prove; accredit (*representante diplomático*); (*garantizar*) guarantee; (*autorizar*) authorize. **~rse** *vpr* make one's name

**acreedor** *a* worthy (**a** of). ● *m* creditor

**acribillar** *vt* (*a balazos*) riddle (**a** with); (*a picotazos*) cover (**a** with); (*fig*, *a preguntas etc*) pester (**a** with)

**acrimonia** *f* (*de sabor*) sharpness; (*de olor*) pungency; (*fig*) bitterness

**acrisola|do** *a* pure; (*fig*) proven. **~r** *vt* purify; (*confirmar*) prove

**acritud** *f* (*de sabor*) sharpness; (*de olor*) pungency; (*fig*) bitterness

**acr|obacia** *f* acrobatics. **~obacias aéreas** aerobatics. **~óbata** *m* & *f* acrobat. **~obático** *a* acrobatic. **~obatismo** *m* acrobatics

**acrónimo** *m* acronym

**acróstico** *a* & *m* acrostic

**acta** *f* minutes; (*certificado*) certificate

**actinia** *f* sea anemone

**actitud** *f* posture, position; (*fig*) attitude, position

**activ|ación** *f* speed-up. **~amente** *adv* actively. **~ar** *vt* activate; (*acelerar*) speed up. **~idad** *f* activity. **~o** *a* active. ● *m* assets

**acto** *m* act; (*ceremonia*) ceremony. **en el ~** immediately

**act|or** *m* actor. **~riz** *f* actress

**actuación** *f* action; (*conducta*) behaviour; (*theat*) performance

**actual** *a* present; (*asunto*) topical. **~idad** *f* present. **~idades** *fpl* current affairs. **~ización** *f* modernization. **~izar** [10] *vt* modernize. **~mente** *adv* now, at the present time. **en la ~idad** nowadays

**actuar** [21] *vt* work. ● *vi* act. **~ como**, **~ de** act as

**actuario** *m* clerk of the court. ~ **(de seguros)** actuary

**acuarel|a** *f* watercolour. **~ista** *m & f* watercolourist

**acuario** *m* aquarium. **A~** Aquarius

**acuartela|do** *a* quartered. **~miento** *m* quartering. **~r** *vt* quarter, billet; (*mantener en cuartel*) confine to barracks

**acuático** *a* aquatic

**acuci|ador** pressing. **~ar** *vt* urge on; (*dar prisa a*) hasten. **~oso** *a* keen

**acuclillarse** *vpr* crouch down, squat down

**acuchilla|do** *a* slashed; ⟨*persona*⟩ stabbed. **~r** *vt* slash; stab ⟨*persona*⟩; (*alisar*) smooth

**acudir** *vi*. ~ **a** go to, attend; keep ⟨*una cita*⟩; (*en auxilio*) go to help

**acueducto** *m* aqueduct

**acuerdo** *m* agreement. ● *vb véase* **acordar.** ¡**de** ~! OK! **de** ~ **con** in accordance with. **estar de** ~ agree. **ponerse de** ~ agree

**acuesto** *vb véase* **acostar**

**acuidad** *f* acuity, sharpness

**acumula|ción** *f* accumulation. **~dor** *a* accumulative. ● *m* accumulator. **~r** *vt* accumulate. **~rse** *vpr* accumulate

**acunar** *vt* rock

**acuña|ción** *f* minting, coining. **~r** *vt* mint, coin

**acuos|idad** *f* wateriness. **~o** *a* watery

**acupuntura** *f* acupuncture

**acurrucarse** [7] *vpr* curl up

**acusa|ción** *f* accusation. **~do** *a* accused; (*destacado*) marked. ● *m* accused. **~dor** *a* accusing. ● *m* accuser. **~r** *vt* accuse; (*mostrar*) show; (*denunciar*) denounce. **~rse** *vpr* confess; (*notarse*) become marked. **~torio** *a* accusatory

**acuse** *m*. ~ **de recibo** acknowledgement of receipt

**acus|ica** *m & f* (*fam*) telltale. **~ón** *a & m* telltale

**acústic|a** *f* acoustics. **~o** *a* acoustic

**achacar** [7] *vt* attribute

**achacoso** *a* sickly

**achaflanar** *vt* bevel

**achantar** *vt* (*fam*) intimidate. **~se** *vpr* hide; (*fig*) back down

**achaparrado** *a* stocky

**achaque** *m* ailment

**achares** *mpl* (*fam*). **dar** ~ make jealous

**achata|miento** *m* flattening. **~r** *vt* flatten

**achica|do** *a* childish. **~r** [7] *vt* make smaller; (*fig, empequeñecer, fam*) belittle; (*naut*) bale out. **~rse** *vpr* become smaller; (*humillarse*) be humiliated

**achicopalado** *a* (*Mex*) depressed

**achicoria** *f* chicory

**achicharra|dero** *m* inferno. **~nte** *a* sweltering. **~r** *vt* burn; (*fig*) pester. **~rse** *vpr* burn

**achispa|do** *a* tipsy. **~rse** *vpr* get tipsy

**achocolatado** *a* (chocolate-)brown

**achuch|ado** *a* (*fam*) hard. **~ar** *vt* jostle, push. **~ón** *m* shove, push

**achulado** *a* cocky

**adagio** *m* adage, proverb; (*mus*) adagio

**adalid** *m* leader

**adamascado** *a* damask

**adapta|ble** *a* adaptable. **~ción** *f* adaptation. **~dor** *m* adapter. **~r** *vt* adapt; (*ajustar*) fit. **~rse** *vpr* adapt o.s.

**adecentar** *vt* clean up. **~se** *vpr* tidy o.s. up

**adecua|ción** *f* suitability. **~damente** *adv* suitably. **~do** *a* suitable. **~r** *vt* adapt, make suitable

**adelant|ado** *a* advanced; ⟨*niño*⟩ precocious; ⟨*reloj*⟩ fast. **~amiento** *m* advance(ment); (*auto*) overtaking. **~ar** *vt* advance, move forward; (*acelerar*) speed up; put forward ⟨*reloj*⟩; (*auto*) overtake. ● *vi* advance, go forward; ⟨*reloj*⟩ gain, be fast. **~arse** *vpr* advance, move forward; ⟨*reloj*⟩ gain; (*auto*) overtake. **~e** *adv* forward. ● *int* come in!; (¡*siga!*) carry on! **~o** *m* advance; (*progreso*) progress. **más ~e** (*lugar*) further on; (*tiempo*) later on. **pagar por ~ado** pay in advance.

**adelfa** *f* oleander

**adelgaza|dor** *a* slimming. **~miento** *m* slimming. **~r** [10] *vt* make thin. ● *vi* lose weight; (*adrede*) slim. **~rse** *vpr* lose weight; (*adrede*) slim

**ademán** *m* gesture. **ademanes** *mpl* (*modales*) manners. **en** ~ **de** as if to

**además** *adv* besides; (*también*) also. ~ **de** besides

**adentr|arse** *vpr*. ~ **en** penetrate into; study thoroughly ⟨*tema etc*⟩. **~o** *adv* in(side). **mar ~o** out at sea. **tierra ~o** inland

**adepto** *m* supporter

**aderez|ar** [10] *vt* flavour ‹*bebidas*›; (*condimentar*) season; dress ‹*ensalada*›. **~o** *m* flavouring; (*con condimentos*) seasoning; (*para ensalada*) dressing

**adeud|ar** *vt* owe. **~o** *m* debit

**adhe|rencia** *f* adhesion; (*fig*) adherence. **~rente** *a* adherent. **~rir** [4] *vt* stick on. ● *vi* stick. **~rirse** *vpr* stick; (*fig*) follow. **~sión** *f* adhesion; (*fig*) support. **~sivo** *a* & *m* adhesive

**adici|ón** *f* addition. **~onal** *a* additional. **~onar** *vt* add

**adicto** *a* devoted. ● *m* follower

**adiestra|do** *a* trained. **~miento** *m* training. **~r** *vt* train. **~rse** *vpr* practise

**adinerado** *a* wealthy

**adiós** *int* goodbye!; (*al cruzarse con alguien*) hello!

**adit|amento** *m* addition; (*accesorio*) accessory. **~ivo** *m* additive

**adivin|ación** *f* divination; (*por conjeturas*) guessing. **~ador** *m* fortune-teller. **~anza** *f* riddle. **~ar** *vt* foretell; (*acertar*) guess. **~o** *m* fortune-teller

**adjetivo** *a* adjectival. ● *m* adjective

**adjudica|ción** *f* award. **~r** [7] *vt* award. **~rse** *vpr* appropriate. **~tario** *m* winner of an award

**adjunt|ar** *vt* enclose. **~o** *a* enclosed; (*auxiliar*) assistant. ● *m* assistant

**adminículo** *m* thing, gadget

**administra|ción** *f* administration; (*gestión*) management. **~dor** *m* administrator; (*gerente*) manager. **~dora** *f* administrator; manageress. **~r** *vt* administer. **~tivo** *a* administrative

**admira|ble** *a* admirable. **~ción** *f* admiration. **~dor** *m* admirer. **~r** *vt* admire; (*asombrar*) astonish. **~rse** *vpr* be astonished. **~tivo** *a* admiring

**admi|sibilidad** *f* admissibility. **~sible** *a* acceptable. **~sión** *f* admission; (*aceptación*) acceptance. **~tir** *vt* admit; (*aceptar*) accept

**adobar** *vt* (*culin*) pickle; (*fig*) twist

**adobe** *m* sun-dried brick. **~ra** *f* mould for making (sun-dried) bricks

**adobo** *m* pickle

**adocena|do** *a* common. **~rse** *vpr* become common

**adoctrinamiento** *m* indoctrination

**adolecer** [11] *vi* be ill. **~ de** suffer with

**adolescen|cia** *f* adolescent. **~te** *a* & *m* & *f* adolescent

**adonde** *conj* where

**adónde** *adv* where?

**adop|ción** *f* adoption. **~tar** *vt* adopt. **~tivo** *a* adoptive; ‹*patria*› of adoption

**adoqu|ín** *m* paving stone; (*imbécil*) idiot. **~inado** *m* paving. **~inar** *vt* pave

**adora|ble** *a* adorable. **~ción** *f* adoration. **~dor** *a* adoring. ● *n* worshipper. **~r** *vt* adore

**adormec|edor** *a* soporific; ‹*droga*› sedative. **~er** [11] *vt* send to sleep; (*fig, calmar*) calm, soothe. **~erse** *vpr* fall asleep; (*un miembro*) go to sleep. **~ido** *a* sleepy; ‹*un miembro*› numb. **~imiento** *m* sleepiness; (*de un miembro*) numbness

**adormidera** *f* opium poppy

**adormilarse** *vpr* doze

**adorn|ar** *vt* adorn (con, de with). **~o** *m* decoration

**adosar** *vt* lean (a against)

**adqui|rido** *a* acquired. **~rir** [4] *vt* acquire; (*comprar*) buy. **~sición** *f* acquisition; (*compra*) purchase. **~sitivo** *a* acquisitive. **poder** *m* **~sitivo** purchasing power

**adrede** *adv* on purpose

**adrenalina** *f* adrenalin

**adscribir** [*pp* **adscrito**] *vt* appoint

**aduan|a** *f* customs. **~ero** *a* customs. ● *m* customs officer

**aducir** [47] *vt* allege

**adueñarse** *vpr* take possession

**adul|ación** *f* flattery. **~ador** *a* flattering. ● *m* flatterer. **~ar** *vt* flatter

**ad|ulteración** *f* adulteration. **~ulterar** *vt* adulterate. ● *vi* commit adultery. **~ulterino** *a* adulterous. **~ulterio** *m* adultery. **~últera** *f* adulteress. **~últero** *a* adulterous. ● *m* adulterer

**adulto** *a* & *m* adult, grown-up

**adusto** *a* severe, harsh

**advenedizo** *a* & *m* upstart

**advenimiento** *m* advent, arrival; (*subida al trono*) accession

**adventicio** *a* accidental

**adverbi|al** *a* adverbial. **~o** *m* adverb

**advers|ario** *m* adversary. **~idad** *f* adversity. **~o** *a* adverse, unfavourable

**advert|encia** *f* warning; (*prólogo*) foreword. **~ido** *a* informed. **~ir** [4] *vt* warn; (*notar*) notice

**adviento** *m* Advent

**advocación** *f* dedication

**adyacente** *a* adjacent

**aéreo** *a* air; (*photo*) aerial; ⟨*ferrocarril*⟩ overhead; (*fig*) flimsy

**aeróbica** *f* aerobics

**aerodeslizador** *m* hovercraft

**aerodinámic|a** *f* aerodynamics. **~o** *a* aerodynamic

**aeródromo** *m* aerodrome, airdrome (*Amer*)

**aero|espacial** *a* aerospace. **~faro** *m* beacon. **~lito** *m* meteorite. **~nauta** *m & f* aeronaut. **~náutica** *f* aeronautics. **~náutico** *a* aeronautical. **~nave** *f* airship. **~puerto** *m* airport. **~sol** *m* aerosol

**afab|ilidad** *f* affability. **~le** *a* affable

**afamado** *a* famous

**af|án** *m* hard work; (*deseo*) desire. **~anar** *vt* (*fam*) pinch. **~anarse** *vpr* strive (**en, por** to). **~anoso** *a* laborious

**afea|miento** *m* disfigurement. **~r** *vt* disfigure, make ugly; (*censurar*) censure

**afección** *f* disease

**afecta|ción** *f* affectation. **~do** *a* affected. **~r** *vt* affect

**afect|ísimo** *a* affectionate. **~ísimo amigo** (*en cartas*) my dear friend. **~ividad** *f* emotional nature. **~ivo** *a* sensitive. **~o** *m* (*cariño*) affection. ● *a*. **~o** *a* attached to. **~uosidad** *f* affection. **~uoso** *a* affectionate. **con un ~uoso saludo** (*en cartas*) with kind regards. **suyo ~ísimo** (*en cartas*) yours sincerely

**afeita|do** *m* shave. **~dora** *f* electric razor. **~r** *vt* shave. **~rse** *vpr* (have a) shave

**afelpado** *a* velvety

**afemina|do** *a* effeminate. ● *m* effeminate person. **~miento** *m* effeminacy. **~rse** *vpr* become effeminate

**aferrar** [1] *vt* grasp

**afgano** *a & m* Afghan

**afianza|miento** *m* (*reforzar*) strengthening; (*garantía*) guarantee. **~rse** [10] *vpr* become established

**afic|ión** *f* liking; (*conjunto de aficionados*) fans. **~onado** *a* keen (**a** on), fond (**a** of). ● *m* fan. **~onar** *vt* make fond. **~onarse** *vpr* take a liking to. **por ~ón** as a hobby

**afila|do** *a* sharp. **~dor** *m* knifegrinder. **~dura** *f* sharpening. **~r** *vt*

sharpen. **~rse** *vpr* get sharp; (*ponerse flaco*) grow thin

**afilia|ción** *f* affiliation. **~do** *a* affiliated. **~rse** *vpr* become a member (**a** of)

**afiligranado** *a* filigreed; (*fig*) delicate

**afín** *a* similar; (*próximo*) adjacent; ⟨*personas*⟩ related

**afina|ción** *f* refining; (*auto, mus*) tuning. **~do** *a* finished; (*mus*) in tune. **~r** *vt* refine; (*afilar*) sharpen; (*acabar*) finish; (*auto, mus*) tune. ● *vi* be in tune. **~rse** *vpr* become more refined

**afincarse** [7] *vpr* settle

**afinidad** *f* affinity; (*parentesco*) relationship

**afirma|ción** *f* affirmation. **~r** *vt* make firm; (*asentir*) affirm. **~rse** *vpr* steady o.s.; (*confirmar*) confirm. **~tivo** *a* affirmative

**aflic|ción** *f* affliction. **~tivo** *a* distressing

**afligi|do** *a* distressed. ● *m* afflicted. **~r** [14] *vt* distress. **~rse** *vpr* grieve

**afloja|miento** *m* loosening. **~r** *vt* loosen; (*relajar*) ease. ● *vi* let up

**aflora|miento** *m* outcrop. **~r** *vi* appear on the surface

**aflu|encia** *f* flow. **~ente** *a* flowing. ● *m* tributary. **~ir** [17] *vi* flow (**a** into)

**af|onía** *f* hoarseness. **~ónico** *a* hoarse

**aforismo** *m* aphorism

**aforo** *m* capacity

**afortunado** *a* fortunate, lucky

**afrancesado** *a* francophile

**afrent|a** *f* insult; (*vergüenza*) disgrace. **~ar** *vt* insult. **~oso** *a* insulting

**África** *f* Africa. **~ del Sur** South Africa

**africano** *a & m* African

**afrodisíaco** *a & m*, **afrodisiaco** *a & m* aphrodisiac

**afrontar** *vt* bring face to face; (*enfrentar*) face, confront

**afuera** *adv* out(side). **¡~!** out of the way! **~s** *fpl* outskirts

**agachar** *vt* lower. **~se** *vpr* bend over

**agalla** *f* (*de los peces*) gill. **~s** *fpl* (*fig*) guts

**agarrada** *f* row

**agarrader|a** *f* (*LAm*) handle. **~o** *m* handle. **tener ~as** (*LAm*), **tener ~os** have influence

**agarr|ado** *a* (*fig, fam*) mean. **~ador** *a* (*Arg*) ⟨*bebida*⟩ strong. **~ar** *vt* grasp; (*esp LAm*) take, catch. ● *vi* ⟨*plantas*⟩ take root. **~arse** *vpr* hold on; (*reñirse, fam*) fight. **~ón** *m* tug; (*LAm, riña*) row

**agarrota|miento** *m* tightening; (*auto*) seizing up. **~r** *vt* tie tightly; ⟨*el frío*⟩ stiffen; garotte ⟨*un reo*⟩. **~rse** *vpr* go stiff; (*auto*) seize up

**agasaj|ado** *m* guest of honour. **~ar** *vt* look after well. **~o** *m* good treatment

**ágata** *f* agate

**agavilla|dora** *f* (*máquina*) binder. **~r** *vt* bind

**agazaparse** *vpr* hide

**agencia** *f* agency. **~ de viajes** travel agency. **~ inmobiliaria** estate agency (*Brit*), real estate agency (*Amer*). **~r** *vt* find. **~rse** *vpr* find (out) for o.s.

**agenda** *f* notebook

**agente** *m* agent; (*de policía*) policeman. **~ de aduanas** customs officer. **~ de bolsa** stockbroker

**ágil** *a* agile

**agilidad** *f* agility

**agita|ción** *f* waving; (*de un líquido*) stirring; (*intranquilidad*) agitation. **~do** *a* ⟨*el mar*⟩ rough; (*fig*) agitated. **~dor** *m* (*pol*) agitator

**agitanado** *a* gypsy-like

**agitar** *vt* wave; shake ⟨*botellas etc*⟩; stir ⟨*líquidos*⟩; (*fig*) stir up. **~se** *vpr* wave; ⟨*el mar*⟩ get rough; (*fig*) get excited

**aglomera|ción** *f* agglomeration; (*de tráfico*) traffic jam. **~r** *vt* amass. **~rse** *vpr* form a crowd

**agn|osticismo** *m* agnosticism. **~óstico** *a* & *m* agnostic

**agobi|ador** *a* ⟨*trabajo*⟩ exhausting; ⟨*calor*⟩ oppressive. **~ante** *a* ⟨*trabajo*⟩ exhausting; ⟨*calor*⟩ oppressive. **~ar** *vt* weigh down; (*fig, abrumar*) overwhelm. **~o** *m* weight; (*cansancio*) exhaustion; (*opresión*) oppression

**agolpa|miento** *m* (*de gente*) crowd; (*de cosas*) pile. **~rse** *vpr* crowd together

**agon|ía** *f* death throes; (*fig*) agony. **~izante** *a* dying; ⟨*luz*⟩ failing. **~izar** [10] *vi* be dying

**agor|ar** [16] *vt* prophesy. **~ero** *a* of ill omen. ● *m* soothsayer

**agostar** *vt* wither

**agosto** *m* August. **hacer su ~** feather one's nest

**agota|do** *a* exhausted; ⟨*libro*⟩ out of print. **~dor** *a* exhausting. **~miento** *m* exhaustion. **~r** *vt* exhaust. **~rse** *vpr* be exhausted; ⟨*libro*⟩ go out of print

**agracia|do** *a* attractive; (*que tiene suerte*) lucky. **~r** *vt* make attractive

**agrada|ble** *a* pleasant, nice. **~r** *vi* please. **esto me ~** I like this

**agradec|er** [11] *vt* thank ⟨*persona*⟩; be grateful for ⟨*cosa*⟩. **~ido** *a* grateful. **~imiento** *m* gratitude. **¡muy ~ido!** thanks a lot!

**agrado** *m* pleasure; (*amabilidad*) friendliness

**agrandar** *vt* enlarge; (*fig*) exaggerate. **~se** *vpr* get bigger

**agrario** *a* agrarian, land; ⟨*política*⟩ agricultural

**agrava|miento** *m* worsening. **~nte** *a* aggravating. ● *f* additional problem. **~r** *vt* aggravate; (*aumentar el peso*) make heavier. **~rse** *vpr* get worse

**agravi|ar** *vt* offend; (*perjudicar*) wrong. **~arse** *vpr* be offended. **~o** *m* offence

**agraz** *m*. **en ~** prematurely

**agredir** [24] *vt* attack. **~ de palabra** insult

**agrega|do** *m* aggregate; (*funcionario diplomático*) attaché. **~r** [12] *vt* add; (*unir*) join; appoint ⟨*persona*⟩

**agremiar** *vt* form into a union. **~se** *vpr* form a union

**agres|ión** *f* aggression; (*ataque*) attack. **~ividad** *f* aggressiveness. **~ivo** *a* aggressive. **~or** *m* aggressor

**agreste** *a* country

**agria|do** *a* (*fig*) embittered. **~r** [*regular, o raramente* 20] *vt* sour. **~rse** *vpr* turn sour; (*fig*) become embittered

**agr|ícola** *a* agricultural. **~icultor** *a* agricultural. ● *m* farmer. **~icultura** *f* agriculture, farming

**agridulce** *a* bitter-sweet; (*culin*) sweet-and-sour

**agriera** *f* (*LAm*) heartburn

**agrietar** *vt* crack. **~se** *vpr* crack; ⟨*piel*⟩ chap

**agrimens|or** *m* surveyor. **~ura** *f* surveying

**agrio** *a* sour; (*fig*) sharp. **~s** *mpl* citrus fruits

**agronomía** *f* agronomy

**agropecuario** *a* farming

**agrupa|ción** *f* group; (*acción*) grouping. **~r** *vt* group. **~rse** *vpr* form a group

**agua** *f* water; (*lluvia*) rain; (*marea*) tide; (*vertiente del tejado*) slope. **~ abajo** downstream. **~ arriba** upstream. **~ bendita** holy water. **~ caliente** hot water. **estar entre dos ~s** sit on the fence. **hacer ~** (*naut*) leak. **nadar entre dos ~s** sit on the fence

**aguacate** *m* avocado pear; (*árbol*) avocado pear tree

**aguacero** *m* downpour, heavy shower

**agua f corriente** running water

**aguachinarse** *vpr* (*Mex*) (*cultivos*) be flooded

**aguada** *f* watering place; (*naut*) drinking water; (*acuarela*) water-colour

**agua f de colonia** eau-de-Cologne

**aguad|o** *a* watery. **~ucho** *m* refreshment kiosk

**agua: ~ dulce** fresh water. **~fiestas** *m & f invar* spoil-sport, wet blanket. **~ fría** cold water. **~fuerte** *m* etching

**aguaje** *m* spring tide

**agua: ~mala f, ~mar** *m* jellyfish

**aguamarina** *f* aquamarine

**agua: ~miel** *m* mead. **~ mineral con gas** fizzy mineral water. **~ mineral sin gas** still mineral water. **~nieve** *f* sleet

**aguanoso** *a* watery; (*tierra*) waterlogged

**aguant|able** *a* bearable. **~aderas** *fpl* patience. **~ar** *vt* put up with, bear; (*sostener*) support. **●** *vi* hold out. **~arse** *vpr* restrain o.s. **~e** *m* patience; (*resistencia*) endurance

**agua: ~pié** *m* watery wine. **~ potable** drinking water. **~r** [15] *vt* water down. **~ salada** salt water.

**aguardar** *vt* wait for. **●** *vi* wait

**agua: ~rdiente** *m* (cheap) brandy. **~rrás** *m* turpentine, turps (*fam*). **~turma** *f* Jerusalem artichoke. **~zal** *m* puddle

**agud|eza** *f* sharpness; (*fig, perspicacia*) insight; (*fig, ingenio*) wit. **~izar** [10] *vt* sharpen. **~izarse** *vpr* (*enfermedad*) get worse. **~o** *a* sharp; (*ángulo, enfermedad*) acute; (*voz*) high-pitched

**agüero** *m* omen. **ser de buen ~** augur well

**aguij|ada** *f* goad. **~ar** *vt* (*incl fig*) goad. **~ón** *m* point of a goad. **~onazo** *m* prick. **~onear** *vt* goad

**águila** *f* eagle; (*persona perspicaz*) astute person

**aguileña** *f* columbine

**aguil|eño** *a* aquiline. **~ucho** *m* eaglet

**aguinaldo** *m* Christmas box

**aguja** *f* needle; (*del reloj*) hand; (*arquit*) steeple. **~s** *fpl* (*rail*) points

**agujer|ear** *vt* make holes in. **~o** *m* hole

**agujetas** *fpl* stiffness. **tener ~** be stiff

**agujón** *m* hairpin

**agusanado** *a* full of maggots

**agutí** *m* (*LAm*) guinea pig

**aguza|do** *a* sharp. **~miento** *m* sharpening. **~r** [10] *vt* sharpen

**ah** *int* ah!, oh!

**aherrojar** *vt* (*fig*) oppress

**ahí** *adv* there. **de ~ que** so that. **por ~** over there; (*aproximadamente*) thereabouts

**ahija|da** *f* god-daughter, godchild. **~do** *m* godson, godchild. **~r** *vt* adopt

**ahínco** *m* enthusiasm; (*empeño*) insistence

**ahíto** *a* full up

**ahog|ado** *a* (*en el agua*) drowned; (*asfixiado*) suffocated. **~ar** [12] *vt* (*en el agua*) drown; (*asfixiar*) suffocate; put out (*fuego*). **~arse** *vpr* (*en el agua*) drown; (*asfixiarse*) suffocate. **~o** *m* breathlessness; (*fig, angustia*) distress; (*apuro*) financial trouble

**ahondar** *vt* deepen; **●** *vi* go deep. **~ en** (*fig*) examine in depth. **~se** *vpr* get deeper

**ahora** *adv* now; (*hace muy poco*) just now; (*dentro de poco*) very soon. **~ bien** but. **~ mismo** right now. **de ~ en adelante** from now on, in future. **por ~** for the time being

**ahorca|dura** *f* hanging. **~r** [7] *vt* hang. **~rse** *vpr* hang o.s.

**ahorita** *adv* (*fam*) now. **~ mismo** right now

**ahorquillar** *vt* shape like a fork

**ahorr|ador** *a* thrifty. **~ar** *vt* save. **~arse** *vpr* save o.s. **~o** *m* saving; (*cantidad ahorrada*) savings. **~os** *mpl* savings

**ahuecar** [7] *vt* hollow; fluff up (*colchón*); deepen (*la voz*); (*marcharse, fam*) clear off (*fam*)

**ahuizote** m (Mex) bore

**ahulado** m (LAm) oilskin

**ahuma|do** a (culin) smoked; (de colores) smoky. ~r vt (culin) smoke; (llenar de humo) fill with smoke. ● vi smoke. ~rse vpr become smoky; ⟨comida⟩ acquire a smoky taste; (emborracharse, fam) get drunk

**ahusa|do** a tapering. ~rse vpr taper

**ahuyentar** vt drive away; banish ⟨pensamientos etc⟩

**airado** a annoyed

**aire** m air; (viento) breeze; (corriente) draught; (aspecto) appearance; (mus) tune, air. ~ **acondicionado** air-conditioned. ~ar vt air; (ventilar) ventilate; (fig, publicar) make public. ~arse vpr. **salir para** ~**arse** go out for some fresh air. **al ~ libre** in the open air. **darse** ~s give o.s. airs

**airón** m heron

**airos|amente** adv gracefully. ~o a draughty; (fig) elegant

**aisla|do** a isolated; (elec) insulated. ~dor a (elec) insulating. ● m (elec) insulator. ~miento m isolation; (elec) insulation. ~nte a insulating. ~r [23] vt isolate; (elec) insulate

**ajajá** int good! splendid!

**ajar** vt crumple; (estropear) spoil

**ajedre|cista** m & f chess-player. ~z m chess. ~zado a chequered, checked

**ajenjo** m absinthe

**ajeno** a (de otro) someone else's; (de otros) other people's; (extraño) alien

**ajetre|arse** vpr be busy. ~o m bustle

**ají** m (LAm) chilli; (salsa) chilli sauce

**aj|iaceite** m garlic sauce. ~ilimójili m piquant garlic sauce. ~illo m garlic. **al** ~**illo** cooked with garlic. ~o m garlic. ~o-a-rriero m cod in garlic sauce

**ajorca** f bracelet

**ajuar** m furnishings; (de novia) trousseau

**ajuma|do** a (fam) drunk. ~rse vpr (fam) get drunk

**ajust|ado** a right; ⟨vestido⟩ tight. ~ador m fitter. ~amiento m fitting; (adaptación) adjustment; (acuerdo) agreement; (de una cuenta) settlement. ~ar vt fit; (adaptar) adapt; (acordar) agree; settle ⟨una cuenta⟩;

(apretar) tighten. ● vi fit. ~arse vpr fit; (adaptarse) adapt o.s.; (acordarse) come to an agreement. ~e m fitting; (adaptación) f adjustment; (acuerdo) agreement; (de una cuenta) settlement

**ajusticiar** vt execute

**al** = **a;el**

**ala** f wing; (de sombrero) brim; (deportes) winger

**alaba|ncioso** a boastful. ~nza f praise. ~r vt praise. ~rse vpr boast

**alabastro** m alabaster

**álabe** m (paleta) paddle; (diente) cog

**alabe|ar** vt warp. ~arse vpr warp. ~o m warping

**alacena** f cupboard (Brit), closet (Amer)

**alacrán** m scorpion

**alacridad** f alacrity

**alado** a winged

**alambi|cado** a distilled; (fig) subtle. ~camiento m distillation; (fig) subtlety. ~car [7] vt distil. ~que m still

**alambr|ada** f wire fence; (de alambre de espinas) barbed wire fence. ~ar vt fence. ~e m wire. ~e de espinas barbed wire. ~era f fireguard

**alameda** f avenue; (plantío de álamos) poplar grove

**álamo** m poplar. ~ **temblón** aspen

**alano** m mastiff

**alarde** m show. ~ar vi boast

**alarga|dera** f extension. ~do a long. ~dor m extension. ~miento m lengthening. ~r [12] vt lengthen; stretch out ⟨mano etc⟩; (dar) give, pass. ~rse vpr lengthen, get longer

**alarido** m shriek

**alarm|a** f alarm. ~ante a alarming. ~ar vt alarm, frighten. ~arse vpr be alarmed. ~ista m & f alarmist

**alba** f dawn

**albacea** m executor. ● f executrix

**albacora** (culin) tuna(-fish)

**albahaca** f basil

**albanés** a & m Albanian

**Albania** f Albania

**albañal** m sewer, drain

**albañil** m bricklayer. ~ería f (arte) bricklaying

**albarán** m delivery note

**albarda** f packsaddle; (Mex) saddle. ~r vt saddle

**albaricoque** m apricot. ~ro m apricot tree

**albatros** m albatross

**albedrío** m will. **libre** ~ free will

**albéitar** *m* veterinary surgeon (*Brit*), veterinarian (*Amer*), vet (*fam*)

**alberca** *f* tank, reservoir

**alberg|ar** [12] *vt* (*alojar*) put up; ‹*viviendas*› house; (*dar asilo*) shelter. **~arse** *vpr* stay; (*refugiarse*) shelter. **~ue** *m* accommodation; (*refugio*) shelter. **~ue de juventud** youth hostel

**albóndiga** *f* meatball, rissole

**albor** *m* dawn. **~ada** *f* dawn; (*mus*) dawn song. **~ear** *vi* dawn

**albornoz** *m* (*de los moros*) burnous; (*para el baño*) bathrobe

**alborot|adizo** *a* excitable. **~ado** *a* excited; (*aturdido*) hasty. **~ador** *a* rowdy. ● *m* trouble-maker. **~ar** *vt* disturb, upset. ● *vi* make a racket. **~arse** *vpr* get excited; ‹*el mar*› get rough. **~o** *m* row, uproar

**alboroz|ado** *a* overjoyed. **~ar** [10] *vt* make laugh; (*regocijar*) make happy. **~arse** *vpr* be overjoyed. **~o** *m* joy

**albufera** *f* lagoon

**álbum** *m* (*pl* **~es** *o* **~s**) album

**alcachofa** *f* artichoke

**alcald|e** *m* mayor. **~esa** *f* mayoress. **~ía** *f* mayoralty; (*oficina*) mayor's office

**álcali** *m* alkali

**alcalino** *a* alkaline

**alcance** *m* reach; (*de arma, telescopio etc*) range; (*déficit*) deficit

**alcancía** *f* money-box

**alcantarilla** *f* sewer; (*boca*) drain

**alcanzar** [10] *vt* (*llegar a*) catch up; (*coger*) reach; catch ‹*un autobús*›; ‹*bala etc*› strike, hit. ● *vi* reach; (*ser suficiente*) be enough. **~ a** manage

**alcaparra** *f* caper

**alcaucil** *m* artichoke

**alcayata** *f* hook

**alcazaba** *f* fortress

**alcázar** *m* fortress

**alcoba** *f* bedroom

**alcoh|ol** *m* alcohol. **~ol desnaturalizado** methylated spirits, meths (*fam*). **~ólico** *a* & *m* alcoholic. **~olímetro** *m* breathalyser (*Brit*). **~olismo** *m* alcoholism. **~olizarse** [10] *vpr* become an alcoholic

**Alcorán** *m* Koran

**alcornoque** *m* cork-oak; (*persona torpe*) idiot

**alcuza** *f* (olive) oil bottle

**aldaba** *f* door-knocker. **~da** *f* knock at the door

**alde|a** *f* village. **~ano** *a* village; (*campesino*) rustic, country. **~huela** *f* hamlet

**alea|ción** *f* alloy. **~r** *vt* alloy

**aleatorio** *a* uncertain

**alecciona|dor** *a* instructive. **~miento** *m* instruction. **~r** *vt* instruct

**aledaños** *mpl* outskirts

**alega|ción** *f* allegation; (*Arg, Mex, disputa*) argument. **~r** [12] *vt* claim; (*jurid*) allege. ● *vi* (*LAm*) argue. **~to** *m* plea

**aleg|oría** *f* allegory. **~órico** *a* allegorical

**alegr|ar** *vt* make happy; (*avivar*) brighten up. **~arse** *vpr* be happy; (*emborracharse*) get merry. **~e** *a* happy; (*achispado*) merry, tight. **~emente** *adv* happily. **~ía** *f* happiness. **~ón** *m* sudden joy, great happiness

**aleja|do** *a* distant. **~miento** *m* removal; (*entre personas*) estrangement; (*distancia*) distance. **~r** *vt* remove; (*ahuyentar*) get rid of; (*fig, apartar*) separate. **~rse** *vpr* move away

**alela|do** *a* stupid. **~r** *vt* stupefy. **~rse** *vpr* be stupefied

**aleluya** *m* & *f* alleluia

**alemán** *a* & *m* German

**Alemania** *f* Germany. **~ Occidental** (*historia*) West Germany. **~ Oriental** (*historia*) East Germany

**alenta|dor** *a* encouraging. **~r** [1] *vt* encourage. ● *vi* breathe

**alerce** *m* larch

**al|ergia** *f* allergy. **~érgico** *a* allergic

**alero** *m* (*del tejado*) eaves

**alerón** *m* aileron

**alerta** *adv* alert, on the alert. ¡**~**! look out! **~r** *vt* alert

**aleta** *f* wing; (*de pez*) fin

**aletarga|do** *a* lethargic. **~miento** *m* lethargy. **~r** [12] *vt* make lethargic. **~rse** *vpr* become lethargic

**alet|azo** *m* (*de un ave*) flap of the wings; (*de un pez*) flick of the fin. **~ear** *vi* flap its wings, flutter. **~eo** *m* flapping (of the wings)

**aleve** *a* treacherous

**alevín** *m* young fish

**alevos|ía** *f* treachery. **~o** *a* treacherous

**alfab|ético** *a* alphabetical. **~etizar** [10] *vt* alphabetize; teach to read

and write ⟨a uno⟩. ~**eto** m alphabet.
~**eto Morse** Morse code
**alfalfa** f lucerne (Brit), alfalfa
(Amer)
**alfar** m pottery. ~**ería** f pottery.
~**ero** m potter
**alféizar** m window-sill
**alferecía** f epilepsy
**alférez** m second lieutenant
**alfil** m (en ajedrez) bishop
**alfile|r** m pin. ~**razo** m pinprick.
~**tero** m pin-case
**alfombr|a** f (grande) carpet;
(pequeña) rug, mat. ~**ar** vt carpet.
~**illa** f rug, mat; (med) German
measles
**alforja** f saddle-bag
**algas** fpl seaweed
**algarabía** f (fig, fam) gibberish,
nonsense
**algarada** f uproar
**algarrob|a** f carob bean. ~**o** m carob
tree
**algazara** f uproar
**álgebra** f algebra
**algebraico** a algebraic
**álgido** a (fig) decisive
**algo** pron something; (en frases
interrogativas) anything. ● adv
rather. ¿~ **más?** is there anything
else? ¿**quieres tomar algo?** (de beber)
would you like a drink?; (de comer)
would you like something to eat?
**algod|ón** m cotton. ~**ón de azúcar**
candy floss (Brit), cotton candy
(Amer). ~**onero** a cotton. ● m cotton plant. ~**ón hidrófilo** cotton
wool
**alguacil** m bailiff
**alguien** pron someone, somebody;
(en frases interrogativas) anyone,
anybody
**alguno** a (delante de nombres mas-
culinos en singular **algún**) some; (en
frases interrogativas) any; (pospuesto al nombre en frases negativas) at all. **no tiene idea alguna** he
hasn't any idea at all. ● pron one;
(en plural) some; (alguien)
someone. **alguna que otra vez** from
time to time. **algunas veces, alguna
vez** sometimes
**alhaja** f piece of jewellery; (fig) treasure. ~**r** vt deck with jewels; (amueblar) furnish
**alharaca** f fuss
**alhelí** m wallflower
**alheña** f privet
**alhucema** f lavender

**alia|do** a allied. ● m ally. ~**nza** f alli-
ance; (anillo) wedding ring. ~**r** [20]
vt combine. ~**rse** vpr be combined;
(formar una alianza) form an
alliance
**alias** adv & m alias
**alicaído** a (fig, débil) weak; (fig, abatido) depressed
**alicates** mpl pliers
**aliciente** m incentive; (de un lugar)
attraction
**alien|ado** a mentally ill. ~**ista** m & f
psychiatrist
**aliento** m breath; (ánimo) courage
**aligera|miento** m lightening; (ali-
vio) alleviation. ~**r** vt make lighter;
(aliviar) alleviate, ease; (apresurar)
quicken
**alij|ar** vt (descargar) unload;
smuggle ⟨contrabando⟩. ~**o** m
unloading; (contrabando) contraband
**alimaña** f vicious animal
**aliment|ación** f food; (acción) feed-
ing. ~**ar** vt feed; (nutrir) nourish.
● vi be nourishing. ~**arse** vpr feed
(con, de on). ~**icio** a nourishing.
~**o** m food. ~**os** mpl (jurid)
alimony. **productos** mpl ~**icios**
foodstuffs
**alimón. al** ~ adv jointly
**alinea|ción** f alignment; (en
deportes) line-up. ~**r** vt align, line
up
**aliñ|ar** vt (culin) season. ~**o** m
seasoning
**alioli** m garlic sauce
**alisar** vt smooth
**alisios** apl. **vientos** mpl ~ trade
winds
**aliso** m alder (tree)
**alista|miento** m enrolment. ~**r** vt
put on a list; (mil) enlist. ~**rse** vpr
enrol; (mil) enlist
**aliteración** f alliteration
**alivi|ador** a comforting. ~**ar** vt
lighten; relieve ⟨dolor, etc⟩; (hurtar,
fam) steal, pinch (fam). ~**arse** vpr
⟨dolor⟩ diminish; ⟨persona⟩ get
better. ~**o** m relief
**aljibe** m tank
**alma** f soul; (habitante) inhabitant
**almac|én** m warehouse; (LAm,
tienda) grocer's shop; (de un arma)
magazine. ~**enes** mpl department
store. ~**enaje** m storage; (derechos)
storage charges. ~**enamiento** m
storage; (mercancías almacenadas)
stock. ~**enar** vt store; stock up with

⟨*provisiones*⟩. **~enero** *m* (*Arg*) shopkeeper. **~enista** *m* & *f* shopkeeper
**almádena** *f* sledge-hammer
**almanaque** *m* almanac
**almeja** *f* clam
**almendr|a** *f* almond. **~ado** *a* almond-shaped. **~o** *m* almond tree
**almiar** *m* haystack
**alm|íbar** *m* syrup. **~ibarado** *a* syrupy. **~ibarar** *vt* cover in syrup
**almid|ón** *m* starch. **~onado** *a* starched; (*fig, estirado*) starchy
**alminar** *m* minaret
**almirant|azgo** *m* admiralty. **~e** *m* admiral
**almirez** *m* mortar
**almizcle** *m* musk
**almohad|a** *f* cushion; (*de la cama*) pillow; (*funda*) pillowcase. **~illa** *f* small cushion; (*acerico*) pincushion. **~ón** *m* large pillow, bolster. **consultar con la ~a** sleep on it
**almorranas** *fpl* haemorrhoids, piles
**alm|orzar** [2 & 10] *vt* (*a mediodía*) have for lunch; (*desayunar*) have for breakfast. ● *vi* (*a mediodía*) have lunch; (*desayunar*) have breakfast. **~uerzo** *m* (*a mediodía*) lunch; (*desayuno*) breakfast
**alocado** *a* scatter-brained
**alocución** *f* address, speech
**aloja|do** *m* (Mex) lodger, guest. **~miento** *m* accommodation. **~r** *vt* put up. **~rse** *vpr* stay
**alondra** *f* lark
**alpaca** *f* alpaca
**alpargat|a** *f* canvas shoe, espadrille. **~ería** *f* shoe shop
**Alpes** *mpl* Alps
**alpin|ismo** *m* mountaineering, climbing. **~ista** *m* & *f* mountaineer, climber. **~o** *a* Alpine
**alpiste** *m* birdseed
**alquil|ar** *vt* (*tomar en alquiler*) hire ⟨*vehículo*⟩, rent ⟨*piso, casa*⟩; (*dar en alquiler*) hire (out) ⟨*vehículo*⟩, rent (out) ⟨*piso, casa*⟩. **~arse** *vpr* ⟨*casa*⟩ be let; ⟨*vehículo*⟩ be on hire. **se alquila** to let (*Brit*), for rent (*Amer*). **~er** *m* (*acción de alquilar un piso etc*) renting; (*acción de alquilar un vehículo*) hiring; (*precio por el que se alquila un piso etc*) rent; (*precio por el que se alquila un vehículo*) hire charge. **de ~er** for hire
**alquimi|a** *f* alchemy. **~sta** *m* alchemist
**alquitara** *f* still. **~r** *vt* distil

**alquitr|án** *m* tar. **~anar** *vt* tar
**alrededor** *adv* around. **~ de** around; (*con números*) about. **~es** *mpl* surroundings; (*de una ciudad*) outskirts
**alta** *f* discharge
**altamente** *adv* highly
**altaner|ía** *f* (*orgullo*) pride. **~o** *a* proud, haughty
**altar** *m* altar
**altavoz** *m* loudspeaker
**altera|bilidad** *f* changeability. **~ble** *a* changeable. **~ción** *f* change, alteration. **~do** *a* changed, altered; (*perturbado*) disturbed. **~r** *vt* change, alter; (*perturbar*) disturb; (*enfadar*) anger, irritate. **~rse** *vpr* change, alter; (*agitarse*) get upset; (*enfadarse*) get angry; ⟨*comida*⟩ go off
**alterca|do** *m* argument. **~r** [7] *vi* argue
**altern|ado** *a* alternate. **~ador** *m* alternator. **~ante** *a* alternating. **~ar** *vt/i* alternate. **~arse** *vpr* take turns. **~ativa** *f* alternative. **~ativo** *a* alternating. **~o** *a* alternate
**alteza** *f* height. **A~** (*título*) Highness
**altibajos** *mpl* (*de terreno*) unevenness; (*fig*) ups and downs
**altiplanicie** *f* high plateau
**altísimo** *a* very high. ● *m*. **el A~** the Almighty
**altisonante** *a*, **altísono** *a* pompous
**altitud** *f* height; (*aviat, geog*) altitude
**altiv|ez** *f* arrogance. **~o** *a* arrogant
**alto** *a* high; ⟨*persona*⟩ tall; ⟨*voz*⟩ loud; (*fig, elevado*) lofty; (*mus*) ⟨*nota*⟩ high(-pitched); (*mus*) ⟨*voz, instrumento*⟩ alto; ⟨*horas*⟩ early. **tiene 3 metros de ~** it is 3 metres high. ● *adv* high; (*de sonidos*) loud(ly). ● *m* height; (*de un edificio*) high floor; (*viola*) viola; (*voz*) alto; (*parada*) stop. ● *int* halt!, stop! **en lo ~ de** on the top of
**altoparlante** *m* (*esp LAm*) loudspeaker
**altruis|mo** *m* altruism. **~ta** *a* altruistic. ● *m* & *f* altruist
**altura** *f* height; (*altitud*) altitude; (*de agua*) depth; (*fig, cielo*) sky. **a estas ~s** at this stage. **tiene 3 metros de ~** it is 3 metres high
**alubia** *f* French bean
**alucinación** *f* hallucination
**alud** *m* avalanche

**aludi|do** *a* in question. **darse por ~do** take it personally. **no darse por ~do** turn a deaf ear. **~r** *vi* mention

**alumbra|do** *a* lit; (*achispado, fam*) tipsy. ● *m* lighting. **~miento** *m* lighting; (*parto*) childbirth. **~r** *vt* light. ● *vi* give birth. **~rse** *vpr* (*emborracharse*) get tipsy

**aluminio** *m* aluminium (*Brit*), aluminum (*Amer*)

**alumno** *m* pupil; (*univ*) student

**aluniza|je** *m* landing on the moon. **~r** [10] *vi* land on the moon

**alusi|ón** *f* allusion. **~vo** *a* allusive

**alverja** *f* vetch; (*LAm, guisante*) pea

**alza** *f* rise. **~cuello** *m* clerical collar, dog-collar (*fam*). **~da** *f* (*de caballo*) height; (*jurid*) appeal. **~do** *a* raised; (*persona*) fraudulently bankrupt; (*Mex, soberbio*) vain; (*precio*) fixed. **~miento** *m* raising; (*aumento*) rise, increase; (*pol*) revolt. **~r** [10] *vt* raise, lift (up); raise (*precios*). **~rse** *vpr* rise; (*ponerse en pie*) stand up; (*pol*) revolt; (*quebrar*) go fraudulently bankrupt; (*apelar*) appeal

**allá** *adv* there. **¡~ él!** that's his business. **~ fuera** out there. **~ por el 1970** around about 1970. **el más ~** the beyond. **más ~** further on. **más ~ de** beyond. **por ~** over there

**allana|miento** *m* levelling; (*de obstáculos*) removal. **~miento de morada** burglary. **~r** *vt* level; remove ‹*obstáculos*›; (*fig*) iron out ‹*dificultades etc*›; burgle ‹*una casa*›. **~rse** *vpr* level off; (*hundirse*) fall down; (*ceder*) submit (**a** to)

**allega|do** *a* close. ● *m* relation. **~r** [12] *vt* collect

**allí** *adv* there; (*tiempo*) then. **~ donde** wherever. **~ fuera** out there. **por ~** over there

**ama** *f* lady of the house. **~ de casa** housewife. **~ de cría** wet-nurse. **~ de llaves** housekeeper

**amab|ilidad** *f* kindness. **~le** *a* kind; (*simpático*) nice

**amado** *a* dear. **~r** *m* lover

**amaestra|do** *a* trained; (*en circo*) performing. **~miento** *m* training. **~r** *vt* train

**amag|ar** [12] *vt* (*amenazar*) threaten; (*mostrar intención de*) show signs of. ● *vi* threaten; ‹*algo bueno*› be in the offing. **~o** *m* threat; (*señal*) sign; (*med*) sympton

**amalgama** *f* amalgam. **~r** *vt* amalgamate

**amamantar** *vt* breast-feed

**amancebarse** *vpr* live together

**amanecer** *m* dawn. ● *vi* dawn; (*persona*) wake up. **al ~** at dawn, at daybreak

**amanera|do** *a* affected. **~miento** *m* affectation. **~rse** *vpr* become affected

**amanezca** *f* (*Mex*) dawn

**amansa|dor** *m* tamer. **~miento** *m* taming. **~r** *vt* tame; break in ‹*un caballo*›; soothe ‹*dolor etc*›. **~rse** *vpr* calm down

**amante** *a* fond. ● *m & f* lover

**amañ|ar** *vt* arrange. **~o** *m* scheme

**amapola** *f* poppy

**amar** *vt* love

**amara|je** *m* landing on the sea; (*de astronave*) splash-down. **~r** *vt* land on the sea; (*astronave*) splash down

**amarg|ado** *a* embittered. **~ar** [12] *vt* make bitter; embitter ‹*persona*›. **~arse** *vpr* get bitter. **~o** *a* bitter. ● *m* bitterness. **~ura** *f* bitterness

**amariconado** *a* effeminate

**amarill|ear** *vi* go yellow. **~ento** *a* yellowish; (*tez*) sallow. **~ez** *f* yellow; (*de una persona*) paleness. **~o** *a & m* yellow

**amarra** *f* mooring rope. **~s** *fpl* (*fig, fam*) influence. **~do** *a* (*LAm*) mean. **~r** *vt* moor; (*atar*) tie. ● *vi* (*empollar, fam*) study hard, swot (*fam*)

**amartillar** *vt* cock (*arma de fuego*)

**amas|ar** *vt* knead; (*fig, tramar, fam*) concoct, cook up (*fam*). **~ijo** *m* dough; (*acción*) kneading; (*fig, mezcla, fam*) hotchpotch

**amate** *m* (*Mex*) fig tree

**amateur** *a & m & f* amateur

**amatista** *f* amethyst

**amazona** *f* Amazon; (*mujer varonil*) mannish woman; (*que monta a caballo*) horsewoman

**Amazonas** *m*. **el río ~** the Amazon

**ambages** *mpl* circumlocutions. **sin ~** in plain language

**ámbar** *m* amber

**ambarino** *a* amber

**ambici|ón** *f* ambition. **~onar** *vt* strive after. **~onar ser** have an ambition to be. **~oso** *a* ambitious. ● *m* ambitious person

**ambidextro** *a* ambidextrous. ● *m* ambidextrous person

**ambient|ar** *vt* give an atmosphere to. **~arse** *vpr* adapt o.s. **~e** *m* atmosphere; (*medio*) environment

**ambig|uamente** *adv* ambiguously.
~**üedad** *f* ambiguity. ~**uo** *a*
ambiguous; (*fig, afeminado, fam*)
effeminate

**ámbito** *m* ambit

**ambos** *a & pron* both. ~ **a dos** both
(of them)

**ambulancia** *f* ambulance; (*hospital
móvil*) field hospital

**ambulante** *a* travelling

**ambulatorio** *m* out-patients' department

**amedrentar** *vt* frighten, scare. ~**se**
*vpr* be frightened

**amén** *m* amen. ● *int* amen! **en un
decir** ~ in an instant

**amenaza** *f* threat. ~**dor** *a*, ~**nte** *a*
threatening. ~**r** [10] *vt* threaten

**amen|idad** *f* pleasantness. ~**izar**
[10] *vt* brighten up. ~**o** *a* pleasant

**América** *f* America. ~ **Central** Cent-
ral America. ~ **del Norte** North
America. ~ **del Sur** South America.
~ **Latina** Latin America

**american|a** *f* jacket. ~**ismo** *m*
Americanism. ~**ista** *m & f* Amer-
icanist. ~**o** *a* American

**amerindio** *a & m & f* Amerindian,
American Indian

**ameriza|je** *m* landing on the sea; (*de
astronave*) splash-down. ~**r** [10] *vt*
land on the sea; (*astronave*) splash
down

**ametralla|dora** *f* machine-gun. ~**r**
*vt* machine-gun

**amianto** *m* asbestos

**amig|a** *f* friend; (*novia*) girl-friend;
(*amante*) lover. ~**able** *a* friendly.
~**ablemente** *adv* amicably. ~**rse**
[12] *vpr* live together

**am|ígdala** *f* tonsil. ~**igdalitis** *f*
tonsillitis

**amigo** *a* friendly. ● *m* friend; (*novio*)
boy-friend; (*amante*) lover. **ser** ~ **de**
be fond of. **ser muy** ~**s** be good
friends

**amilanar** *vt* frighten, scare. ~**se** *vpr*
be frightened

**aminorar** *vt* lessen; slow down
⟨*velocidad*⟩

**amist|ad** *f* friendship. ~**ades** *mpl*
friends. ~**osamente** *adv* amicably.
~**oso** *a* friendly

**amnesia** *f* amnesia

**amnist|ía** *f* amnesty. ~**iar** [20] *vt*
grant an amnesty to

**amo** *m* master; (*dueño*) owner; (*jefe*)
boss; (*cabeza de familia*) head of the
family

**amodorra|miento** *m* sleepiness.
~**rse** *vpr* get sleepy

**amojonar** *vt* mark out

**amola|dor** *m* knife-grinder. ~**r** [2] *vt*
sharpen; (*molestar, fam*) annoy

**amoldar** *vt* mould; (*acomodar*) fit

**amonedar** *vt* coin, mint

**amonesta|ción** *f* rebuke, rep-
rimand; (*de una boda*) banns. ~**r** *vt*
rebuke, reprimand; (*anunciar la
boda*) publish the banns

**amoníaco** *m*, **amoníaco** *m*
ammonia

**amontillado** *m* Amontillado, pale
dry sherry

**amontona|damente** *adv* in a heap.
~**miento** *m* piling up. ~**r** *vt* pile up;
(*fig, acumular*) accumulate. ~**rse**
*vpr* pile up; ⟨*gente*⟩ crowd together;
(*amancebarse, fam*) live together

**amor** *m* love. ~**es** *mpl* (*relaciones
amorosas*) love affairs. **con mil** ~**es**,
**de mil** ~**es** with (the greatest of)
pleasure. **hacer el** ~ make love. **por
(el)** ~ **de Dios** for God's sake

**amorata|do** *a* purple; (*de frío*) blue.
~**rse** *vpr* go black and blue

**amorcillo** *m* Cupid

**amordazar** [10] *vt* gag; (*fig*) silence

**amorfo** *a* amorphous, shapeless

**amor:** ~**ío** *m* affair. ~**oso** *a* loving;
⟨*cartas*⟩ love

**amortajar** *vt* shroud

**amortigua|dor** *a* deadening. ● *m*
(*auto*) shock absorber. ~**miento** *m*
deadening; (*de la luz*) dimming. ~**r**
[15] *vt* deaden ⟨*ruido*⟩; dim ⟨*luz*⟩;
cushion ⟨*golpe*⟩; tone down ⟨*color*⟩

**amortiza|ble** *a* redeemable. ~**ción** *f*
(*de una deuda*) repayment; (*recuperación*) redemption. ~**r** [10] *vt*
repay ⟨*una deuda*⟩

**amoscarse** [7] *vpr* (*fam*) get cross,
get irritated

**amostazarse** [10] *vpr* get cross

**amotina|do** *a & m* insurgent, rebel-
lious. ~**miento** *m* riot; (*mil*)
mutiny. ~**r** *vt* incite to riot. ~**rse**
*vpr* rebel; (*mil*) mutiny

**ampar|ar** *vt* help; (*proteger*) protect.
~**arse** *vpr* seek protection; (*de la
lluvia*) shelter. ~**o** *m* protection; (*de
la lluvia*) shelter. **al** ~**o de** under
the protection of

**amperio** *m* ampere, amp (fam)

**amplia|ción** *f* extension; (*photo*)
enlargement. ~**r** [20] *vt* enlarge,
extend; (*photo*) enlarge

**amplifica|ción** f amplification. ~dor m amplifier. ~r [7] amplify
**ampli|o** a wide; (espacioso) spacious; ‹ropa› loose-fitting. ~tud f extent; (espaciosidad) spaciousness; (espacio) space
**ampolla** f (med) blister; (frasco) flask; (de medicamento) ampoule, phial
**ampuloso** a pompous
**amputa|ción** f amputation; (fig) deletion. ~r vt amputate; (fig) delete
**amueblar** vt furnish
**amuinar** vt (Mex) annoy
**amuralla|do** a walled. ~r vt build a wall around
**anacardo** m (fruto) cashew nut
**anaconda** f anaconda
**anacr|ónico** a anachronistic. ~onismo m anachronism
**ánade** m & f duck
**anagrama** m anagram
**anales** mpl annals
**analfabet|ismo** m illiteracy. ~o a & m illiterate
**analgésico** a & m analgesic, pain-killer
**an|álisis** m invar analysis. ~álisis de sangre blood test. ~alista m & f analyst. ~alítico a analytical. ~alizar [10] vt analyze
**an|alogía** f analogy. ~álogo a analogous
**ananás** m pineapple
**anaquel** m shelf
**anaranjado** a orange
**an|arquía** f anarchy. ~árquico a anarchic. ~arquismo m anarchism. ~arquista a anarchistic. ● m & f anarchist
**anatema** m anathema
**anat|omía** f anatomy. ~ómico a anatomical
**anca** f haunch; (parte superior) rump; (nalgas, fam) bottom. ~s fpl de rana frogs' legs
**ancestral** a ancestral
**anciano** a elderly, old. ● m elderly man, old man; (relig) elder. los ~s old people
**ancla** f anchor. ~dero m anchorage. ~r vi anchor, drop anchor. echar ~s anchor. levar ~s weigh anchor
**áncora** f anchor; (fig) refuge
**ancho** a wide; ‹ropa› loose-fitting; (fig) relieved; (demasiado grande) too big; (ufano) smug. ● m width; (rail) gauge. **a mis anchas, a sus**

**anchas etc** comfortable, relaxed. **quedarse tan ancho** behave as if nothing has happened. **tiene 3 metros de ~** it is 3 metres wide
**anchoa** f anchovy
**anchura** f width; (medida) measurement
**andaderas** fpl baby-walker
**andad|or** a good at walking. ● m baby-walker. ~ura f walking; (manera de andar) walk
**Andalucía** f Andalusia
**andaluz** a & m Andalusian
**andamio** m platform. ~s mpl scaffolding
**andar** [25] vt (recorrer) cover, go. ● vi walk; ‹máquina› go, work; (estar) be; (moverse) move. ● m walk. ¡anda! go on! come on! ~iego a fond of walking; (itinerante) wandering. ~ por be about. ~se vpr (marcharse) go away
**andén** m platform; (de un muelle) quayside; (LAm, acera) pavement (Brit), sidewalk (Amer)
**Andes** mpl Andes
**andino** a Andean
**Andorra** f Andorra
**andrajo** m rag. ~so a ragged
**andurriales** mpl (fam) out-of-the-way place
**anduve** vb véase **andar**
**anécdota** f anecdote
**anega|dizo** a subject to flooding. ~r [12] vt flood. ~rse vpr be flooded, flood
**anejo** a attached. ● m annexe; (de libro etc) appendix
**an|emia** f anaemia. ~émico a anaemic
**anest|esia** f anaesthesia. ~ésico a & m anaesthetic. ~esista m & f anaesthetist
**anex|ión** f annexation. ~ionar vt annex. ~o a attached. ● m annexe
**anfibio** a amphibious. ● m amphibian
**anfiteatro** m amphitheatre; (en un teatro) upper circle
**anfitri|ón** m host. ~ona f hostess
**ángel** m angel; (encanto) charm
**angelical** a, **angélico** a angelic
**angina** f. ~ de pecho angina (pectoris). tener ~s have tonsillitis
**anglicano** a & m Anglican
**anglicismo** m Anglicism
**anglófilo** a & m Anglophile
**anglo|hispánico** a Anglo-Spanish. ~sajón a & m Anglo-Saxon

**angosto** *a* narrow

**anguila** *f* eel

**angula** *f* elver, baby eel

**angular** *a* angular

**ángulo** *m* angle; (*rincón, esquina*) corner; (*curva*) bend

**anguloso** *a* angular

**angusti|a** *f* anguish. **~ar** *vt* distress; (*inquietar*) worry. **~arse** *vpr* get distressed; (*inquietarse*) get worried. **~oso** *a* anguished; (*que causa angustia*) distressing

**anhel|ante** *a* panting; (*deseoso*) longing. **~ar** *vt* (+ *nombre*) long for; (+ *verbo*) long to. ● *vi* pant. **~o** *m* (*fig*) yearning. **~oso** *a* panting; (*fig*) eager

**anidar** *vi* nest

**anill|a** *f* ring. **~o** *m* ring. **~o de boda** wedding ring

**ánima** *f* soul

**anima|ción** *f* (*de personas*) life; (*de cosas*) liveliness; (*bullicio*) bustle; (*en el cine*) animation. **~do** *a* lively; ‹*sitio etc*› busy. **~dor** *m* compère, host

**animadversión** *f* ill will

**animal** *a* animal; (*fig, torpe, fam*) stupid. ● *m* animal; (*fig, idiota, fam*) idiot; (*fig, bruto, fam*) brute

**animar** *vt* give life to; (*dar ánimo*) encourage; (*dar vivacidad*) liven up. **~se** *vpr* (*decidirse*) decide; (*ponerse alegre*) cheer up. ¿te animas a venir al cine? do you fancy coming to the cinema?

**ánimo** *m* soul; (*mente*) mind; (*valor*) courage; (*intención*) intention. ¡**~**! come on!, cheer up! **dar ~s** encourage

**animosidad** *f* animosity

**animoso** *a* brave; (*resuelto*) determined

**aniquila|ción** *f* annihilation. **~miento** *m* annihilation. **~r** *vt* annihilate; (*acabar con*) ruin. **~rse** *vpr* deteriorate

**anís** *m* aniseed; (*licor*) anisette

**aniversario** *m* anniversary

**ano** *m* anus

**anoche** *adv* last night, yesterday evening

**anochecer** [11] *vi* get dark; ‹*persona*› be at dusk. **anochecí en Madrid** I was in Madrid at dusk. ● *m* nightfall, dusk. **al ~** at nightfall

**anodino** *a* indifferent

**an|omalía** *f* anomaly. **~ómalo** *a* anomalous

**an|onimato** *m* anonymity. **~ónimo** *a* anonymous; ‹*sociedad*› limited. ● *m* anonymity; (*carta*) anonymous letter

**anormal** *a* abnormal; (*fam*) stupid, silly. **~idad** *f* abnormality

**anota|ción** *f* noting; (*acción de poner notas*) annotation; (*nota*) note. **~r** *vt* (*poner nota*) annotate; (*apuntar*) make a note of

**anquilosa|miento** *m* paralysis. **~r** *vt* paralyze. **~rse** *vpr* become paralyzed

**ansi|a** *f* anxiety, worry; (*anhelo*) yearning. **~ar** [20 *o regular*] *vt* long for. **~edad** *f* anxiety. **~oso** *a* anxious; (*deseoso*) eager

**antag|ónico** *a* antagonistic. **~onismo** *m* antagonism. **~onista** *m* & *f* antagonist

**antaño** *adv* in days gone by

**antártico** *a* & *m* Antarctic

**ante** *prep* in front of, before; (*en comparación con*) compared with; (*frente a peligro, enemigo*) in the face of; (*en vista de*) in view of. ● *m* (*piel*) suede. **~anoche** *adv* the night before last. **~ayer** *adv* the day before yesterday. **~brazo** *m* forearm

**ante...** *pref* ante...

**antece|dente** *a* previous. ● *m* antecedent. **~dentes** *mpl* history, background. **~dentes penales** criminal record. **~der** *vt* precede. **~sor** *m* predecessor; (*antepasado*) ancestor

**antedicho** *a* aforesaid

**antelación** *f* advance. **con ~** in advance

**antemano** *adv* **de ~** beforehand

**antena** *f* antenna; (*radio, TV*) aerial

**anteojeras** *fpl* blinkers

**anteojo** *m* telescope. **~s** *mpl* (*gemelos*) opera glasses; (*prismáticos*) binoculars; (*LAm, gafas*) glasses, spectacles

**ante: ~pasados** *mpl* forebears, ancestors. **~pecho** *m* rail; (*de ventana*) sill. **~poner** [34] *vt* put in front (**a** of); (*fig*) put before, prefer. **~proyecto** *m* preliminary sketch; (*fig*) blueprint. **~puesto** *a* put before

**anterior** *a* previous; (*delantero*) front, fore. **~idad** *f*. **con ~idad** previously. **~mente** *adv* previously

**antes** *adv* before; (*antiguamente*) in days gone by; (*mejor*) rather; (*primero*) first. **~ de** before. **~ de ayer**

the day before yesterday. ~ **de que** + *subj* before. ~ **de que llegue** before he arrives. **cuanto** ~, **lo** ~ **posible** as soon as possible

**antesala** *f* anteroom; (*sala de espera*) waiting-room. **hacer** ~ wait (to be received)

**anti...** *pref* anti...

**anti:** ~**aéreo** *a* anti-aircraft. ~**biótico** *a* & *m* antibiotic. ~**ciclón** *m* anticyclone

**anticip|ación** *f* anticipation. **con** ~**ación** in advance. **con media hora de**~**ación** half an hour early. ~**adamente** *adv* in advance. ~**ado** *a*. **por** ~**ado** in advance. ~**ar** *vt* bring forward; advance (*dinero*). ~**arse** *vpr* be early. ~**o** *m* (*dinero*) advance; (*fig*) foretaste

**anti:** ~**concepcional** *a* & *m* contraceptive. ~**conceptivo** *a* & *m* contraceptive. ~**congelante** *m* antifreeze

**anticua|do** *a* old-fashioned. ~**rio** *m* antique dealer. ~**rse** *vpr* go out of date

**anticuerpo** *m* antibody

**antídoto** *m* antidote

**anti:** ~**estético** *a* ugly. ~**faz** *m* mask. ~**gás** *a invar.* **careta** ~**gás** gas mask

**antig|ualla** *f* old relic. ~**uamente** *adv* formerly; (*hace mucho tiempo*) long ago. ~**üedad** *f* antiquity; (*objeto*) antique; (*en un empleo*) length of service. ~**uo** *a* old, ancient. **chapado a la** ~**ua** old-fashioned

**antílope** *m* antelope

**Antillas** *fpl* West Indies

**antinatural** *a* unnatural

**antip|atía** *f* dislike; (*cualidad de antipático*) unpleasantness. ~**ático** *a* unpleasant, unfriendly

**anti:** ~**semita** *m* & *f* anti-Semite. ~**semítico** *a* anti-Semitic. ~**semitismo** *m* anti-Semitism. ~**séptico** *a* & *m* antiseptic. ~**social** *a* antisocial

**antítesis** *f invar* antithesis

**antoj|adizo** *a* capricious. ~**arse** *vpr* fancy. **se le** ~**a un caramelo** he fancies a sweet. ~**o** *m* whim; (*de embarazada*) craving

**antología** *f* anthology

**antorcha** *f* torch

**antro** *m* cavern; (*fig*) dump, hole. ~ **de perversión** den of iniquity

**antropófago** *m* cannibal

**antrop|ología** *f* anthropology. ~**ólogo** *m* & *f* anthropologist

**anual** *a* annual. ~**lidad** *f* annuity. ~**lmente** *adv* yearly. ~**rio** *m* yearbook

**anudar** *vt* tie, knot; (*fig, iniciar*) begin; (*fig, continuar*) resume. ~**se** *vpr* get into knots. ~**se la voz** get a lump in one's throat

**anula|ción** *f* annulment, cancellation. ~**r** *vt* annul, cancel. ● *a* (*dedo*) ring. ● *m* ring finger

**Anunciación** *f* Annunciation

**anunci|ante** *m* & *f* advertiser. ~**ar** *vt* announce; advertise (*producto comercial*); (*presagiar*) be a sign of. ~**arse** *vpr* promise to be. ~**o** *m* announcement; (*para vender algo*) advertisement, advert (*fam*); (*cartel*) poster

**anzuelo** *m* (fish)hook; (*fig*) bait. **tragar el** ~ be taken in, fall for it

**añadi|do** *a* added. ~**dura** *f* addition. ~**r** *vt* add. **por** ~**dura** besides

**añejo** *a* (*vino*) mature; (*jamón etc*) cured

**añicos** *mpl* bits. **hacer** ~ (*romper*) smash (to pieces); (*dejar cansado*) wear out

**añil** *m* indigo

**año** *m* year. ~ **bisiesto** leap year. ~ **nuevo** new year. **al** ~ per year, a year. **¿cuántos** ~**s tiene? tiene 5** ~**s** how old is he? he's 5 (years old). **el** ~ **pasado** last year. **el** ~ **que viene** next year. **entrado en** ~**s** elderly. **los** ~**s 60** the sixties

**añora|nza** *f* nostalgia. ~**r** *vt* miss. ● *vi* pine

**apabullar** *vt* crush; (*fig*) intimidate

**apacentar** [1] *vt* graze. ~**se** *vpr* graze

**apacib|ilidad** *f* gentleness; (*calma*) peacefulness. ~**le** *a* gentle; (*tiempo*) mild

**apacigua|dor** *a* pacifying. ~**miento** *m* appeasement. ~**r** [15] *vt* pacify; (*calmar*) calm; relieve (*dolor etc*). ~**rse** *vpr* calm down

**apadrina|miento** *m* sponsorship. ~**r** *vt* sponsor; be godfather to (*a un niño*); (*en una boda*) be best man for

**apaga|dizo** *a* slow to burn. ~**do** *a* extinguished; (*color*) dull; (*aparato eléctrico*) off; (*persona*) lifeless; (*sonido*) muffled. ~**r** [12] *vt* put out (*fuego, incendio*); turn off, switch off (*aparato eléctrico*); quench (*sed*); muffle (*sonido*). ~**rse** *vpr* (*fuego*) go out; ‹*luz*› go out; ‹*sonido*› die away; (*fig*) pass away

**apagón** *m* blackout

**apalabrar** *vt* make a verbal agreement; (*contratar*) engage. ~**se** *vpr* come to a verbal agreement

**apalanca|miento** *m* leverage. ~**r** [7] *vt* (*levantar*) lever up; (*abrir*) lever open

**apalea|miento** *m* (*de grano*) winnowing; (*de alfombras, frutos, personas*) beating. ~**r** *vt* winnow ‹*grano*›; beat ‹*alfombras, frutos, personas*›; (*fig*) be rolling in ‹*dinero*›

**apantallado** *a* (*Mex*) stupid

**apañ|ado** *a* handy. ~**ar** *vt* (*arreglar*) fix; (*remendar*) mend; (*agarrar*) grasp, take hold of. ~**arse** *vpr* get along, manage. ¡**estoy** ~**ado!** that's all I need!

**aparador** *m* sideboard

**aparato** *m* apparatus; (*máquina*) machine; (*teléfono*) telephone; (*rad, TV*) set; (*ostentación*) show, pomp. ~**samente** *adv* ostentatiously; (*impresionante*) spectacularly. ~**si-dad** *f* ostentation. ~**so** *a* showy, ostentatious; ‹*caída*› spectacular

**aparca|miento** *m* car park (*Brit*), parking lot (*Amer*). ~**r** [7] *vt/i* park

**aparea|miento** *m* pairing off. ~**r** *vt* pair off; mate ‹*animales*›. ~**rse** *vpr* match; ‹*animales*› mate

**aparecer** [11] *vi* appear. ~**se** *vpr* appear

**aparej|ado** *a* ready; (*adecuado*) fitting. **llevar** ~**ado**, **traer** ~**ado** mean, entail. ~**o** *m* preparation; (*avíos*) equipment

**aparent|ar** *vt* (*afectar*) feign; (*parecer*) look. ● *vi* show off. ~**a 20 años** she looks like she's 20. ~**e** *a* apparent; (*adecuado, fam*) suitable

**apari|ción** *f* appearance; (*visión*) apparition. ~**encia** *f* appearance; (*fig*) show. **cubrir las** ~**encias** keep up appearances

**apartad|ero** *m* lay-by; (*rail*) siding. ~**o** *a* separated; (*aislado*) isolated. ● *m* (*de un texto*) section. ~**o** (*de correos*) post-office box, PO box

**apartamento** *m* flat (*Brit*), apartment

**apart|amiento** *m* separation; (*LAm, piso*) flat (*Brit*), apartment; (*aislamiento*) seclusion. ~**ar** *vt* separate; (*quitar*) remove. ~**arse** *vpr* leave; abandon ‹*creencia*›; (*quitarse*

*de en medio*) get out of the way; (*aislarse*) cut o.s. off. ~**e** *adv* apart; (*por separado*) separately; (*además*) besides. ● *m* aside; (*párrafo*) new paragraph. ~**e de** apart from. **dejar** ~**e** leave aside. **eso** ~**e** apart from that

**apasiona|do** *a* passionate; (*entusiasta*) enthusiastic; (*falto de objetividad*) biassed. ● *m* lover (**de** of). ~**miento** *m* passion. ~**r** *vt* excite. ~**rse** *vpr* get excited (**de, por** about), be mad (**de, por** about); (*ser parcial*) become biassed

**ap|atía** *f* apathy. ~**ático** *a* apathetic

**apea|dero** *m* (*rail*) halt. ~**r** *vt* fell ‹*árbol*›; (*disuadir*) dissuade; overcome (*dificultad*); sort out ‹*problema*›. ~**rse** *vpr* (*de un vehículo*) get off

**apechugar** [12] *vi* push (with one's chest). ~ **con** put up with

**apedrear** *vt* stone

**apeg|ado** *a* attached. ~**o** *m* (*fam*) affection. **tener** ~**o a** be fond of

**apela|ción** *f* appeal. ~**r** appeal; (*recurrir*) resort (**a** to)

**apelmazar** [10] *vt* compress

**apellid|ar** *vt* call. ~**arse** *vpr* be called. ¿**cómo te apellidas?** what's your surname? ~**o** *m* surname

**apenar** *vt* pain. ~**se** *vpr* grieve

**apenas** *adv* hardly, scarcely; (*enseguida que*) as soon as. ~ **si** (*fam*) hardly

**ap|éndice** *m* (*med*) appendix; (*fig*) appendage; (*de un libro*) appendix. ~**endicitis** *f* appendicitis

**apercibi|miento** *m* warning. ~**r** *vt* warn (**de** of, about); (*amenazar*) threaten. ~**rse** *vpr* prepare; (*percatarse*) provide o.s. (**de** with)

**apergaminado** *a* ‹*piel*› wrinkled

**aperitivo** *m* (*bebida*) aperitif; (*comida*) appetizer

**aperos** *mpl* agricultural equipment

**apertura** *f* opening

**apesadumbrar** *vt* upset. ~**se** *vpr* be upset

**apestar** *vt* stink out; (*fastidiar*) pester. ● *vi* stink (**a** of)

**apet|ecer** [11] *vt* long for; (*interesar*) appeal to. ¿**te** ~**ece una copa?** do you fancy a drink? do you feel like a drink?. ● *vi* be welcome. ~**ecible** *a* attractive. ~**ito** *m* appetite; (*fig*) desire. ~**itoso** *a* tempting

**apiadarse** *vpr* feel sorry (**de** for)

**ápice** *m* (*nada, en frases negativas*) anything. **no ceder un** ~ not give an inch

**apicult|or** *m* bee-keeper. ~**ura** *f* bee-keeping

**apilar** *vt* pile up

**apiñar** *vt* pack in. ~**se** *vpr* ⟨*personas*⟩ crowd together; ⟨*cosas*⟩ be packed tight

**apio** *m* celery

**apisonadora** *f* steamroller

**aplacar** [7] *vt* placate; relieve ⟨*dolor*⟩

**aplanar** *vt* smooth. ~**se** *vpr* become smooth; ⟨*persona*⟩ lose heart

**aplasta|nte** *a* overwhelming. ~**r** *vt* crush. ~**rse** *vpr* flatten o.s.

**aplatanarse** *vpr* become lethargic

**aplau|dir** *vt* clap, applaud; (*fig*) applaud. ~**so** *m* applause; (*fig*) praise

**aplaza|miento** *m* postponement. ~**r** [10] *vt* postpone; defer ⟨*pago*⟩

**aplebeyarse** *vpr* lower o.s.

**aplica|ble** *a* applicable. ~**ción** *f* application. ~**do** *a* ⟨*persona*⟩ diligent. ~**r** [7] *vt* apply; (*fijar*) attach. ~**rse** *vpr* apply o.s.

**aplom|ado** *a* self-confident; (*vertical*) vertical. ~**o** *m* (self-) confidence, aplomb; (*verticalidad*) verticality

**apocado** *a* timid

**Apocalipsis** *f* Apocalypse

**apocalíptico** *a* apocalyptic

**apoca|miento** *m* diffidence. ~**r** [7] *vt* belittle ⟨*persona*⟩. ~**rse** *vpr* feel small

**apodar** *vt* nickname

**apodera|do** *m* representative. ~**r** *vt* authorize. ~**rse** *vpr* seize

**apodo** *m* nickname

**apogeo** *m* (*fig*) height

**apolilla|do** *a* moth-eaten. ~**rse** *vpr* get moth-eaten

**apolítico** *a* non-political

**apología** *f* defence

**apoltronarse** *vpr* get lazy

**apoplejía** *f* stroke

**apoquinar** *vt/i* (*fam*) fork out

**aporrear** *vt* hit, thump; beat up ⟨*persona*⟩

**aporta|ción** *f* contribution. ~**r** *vt* contribute

**aposent|ar** *vt* put up, lodge. ~**o** *m* room, lodgings

**apósito** *m* dressing

**aposta** *adv* on purpose

**apostar**¹ [2] *vt/i* bet

**apostar**² *vt* station. ~**se** *vpr* station o.s.

**apostilla** *f* note. ~**r** *vt* add notes to

**apóstol** *m* apostle

**apóstrofo** *m* apostrophe

**apoy|ar** *vt* lean (**en** against); (*descansar*) rest; (*asentar*) base; (*reforzar*) support. ~**arse** *vpr* lean, rest. ~**o** *m* support

**apreci|able** *a* appreciable; (*digno de estima*) worthy. ~**ación** *f* appreciation; (*valoración*) appraisal. ~**ar** *vt* value; (*estimar*) appreciate. ~**ativo** *a* appreciative. ~**o** *m* appraisal; (*fig*) esteem

**aprehensión** *f* capture

**apremi|ante** *a* urgent, pressing. ~**ar** *vt* urge; (*obligar*) compel; (*dar prisa a*) hurry up. ● *vi* be urgent. ~**o** *m* urgency; (*obligación*) obligation

**aprender** *vt/i* learn. ~**se** *vpr* learn (by heart)

**aprendiz** *m* apprentice. ~**aje** *m* apprenticeship

**aprensi|ón** *f* apprehension; (*miedo*) fear. ~**vo** *a* apprehensive, fearful

**apresa|dor** *m* captor. ~**miento** *m* capture. ~**r** *vt* seize; (*prender*) capture

**aprestar** *vt* prepare. ~**se** *vpr* prepare

**apresura|damente** *adv* hurriedly, in a hurry. ~**do** *a* in a hurry; (*hecho con prisa*) hurried. ~**miento** *m* hurry. ~**r** *vt* hurry. ~**rse** *vpr* hurry

**apret|ado** *a* tight; (*difícil*) difficult; (*tacaño*) stingy, mean. ~**ar** [1] *vt* tighten; press ⟨*botón*⟩; squeeze ⟨*persona*⟩; (*comprimir*) press down. ● *vi* be too tight. ~**arse** *vpr* crowd together. ~**ón** *m* squeeze. ~**ón de manos** handshake

**aprieto** *m* difficulty. **verse en un** ~ be in a tight spot

**aprisa** *adv* quickly

**aprisionar** *vt* imprison

**aproba|ción** *f* approval. ~**r** [2] *vt* approve (of); pass ⟨*examen*⟩. ● *vi* pass

**apropia|do** *a* appropriate. ~**rse** *vpr*. ~**rse de** appropriate, take

**aprovecha|ble** *a* usable. ~**do** *a* (*aplicado*) diligent; (*ingenioso*) resourceful; (*egoísta*) selfish; (*económico*) thrifty. ~**miento** *m* advantage; (*uso*) use. ~**r** *vt* take advantage of; (*utilizar*) make use of. ● *vi* be useful. ~**rse** *vpr* make the

most of it. ~rse de take advantage
of. ¡que aproveche! enjoy your
meal!
**aprovisionar** vt supply (con, de
with)
**aproxima|ción** f approximation;
(proximidad) closeness; (en la lotería) consolation prize. ~damente
adv roughly, approximately. ~do a
approximate, rough. ~r vt bring
near; (fig) bring together (personas). ~rse vpr come closer,
approach
**apt|itud** f suitability; (capacidad)
ability. ~o a (capaz) capable; (adecuado) suitable
**apuesta** f bet
**apuesto** m smart. ● vb véase **apostar**
**apunta|ción** f note. ~do a sharp.
~dor m prompter
**apuntalar** vt shore up
**apunt|amiento** m aiming; (nota)
note. ~ar vt aim (arma); (señalar)
point at; (anotar) make a note of,
note down; (sacar punta) sharpen;
(en el teatro) prompt. ~arse vpr put
one's name down; score (triunfo,
tanto etc). ~e m note; (bosquejo)
sketch. tomar ~s take notes
**apuñalar** vt stab
**apur|adamente** adv with difficulty.
~ado a difficult; (sin dinero) hard
up; (agotado) exhausted; (exacto)
precise, carefully done. ~ar vt
exhaust; (acabar) finish; drain
(vaso etc); (fastidiar) annoy;
(causar vergüenza) embarrass.
~arse vpr worry; (esp LAm, apresurarse) hurry up. ~o m tight spot,
difficult situation; (vergüenza)
embarrassment; (estrechez) hardship, want; (esp LAm, prisa) hurry
**aquejar** vt trouble
**aquel** a (f **aquella**, mpl **aquellos**, fpl
**aquellas**) that; (en plural) those;
(primero de dos) former
**aquél** pron (f **aquélla**, mpl **aquéllos**,
fpl **aquéllas**) that one; (en plural)
those; (primero de dos) the former
**aquello** pron that; (asunto) that
business
**aquí** adv here. de ~ from here. de ~
a 15 días in a fortnight's time. de ~
para allí to and fro. de ~ que so that.
hasta ~ until now. por ~ around
here
**aquiescencia** f acquiescence
**aquietar** vt calm (down)

**aquí**: ~ fuera out here. ~ mismo
right here
**árabe** a & m & f Arab; (lengua)
Arabic
**Arabia** f Arabia. ~ saudita, ~ saudí
Saudi Arabia
**arábigo** a Arabic
**arado** m plough. ~r m ploughman
**Aragón** m Aragon
**aragonés** a & m Aragonese
**arancel** m tariff. ~ario a tariff
**arandela** f washer
**araña** f spider; (lámpara)
chandelier
**arañar** vt scratch
**arar** vt plough
**arbitra|je** m arbitration; (en
deportes) refereeing. ~r vt/i arbit-
rate; (en fútbol etc) referee; (en tenis
etc) umpire
**arbitr|ariedad** f arbitrariness.
~ario a arbitrary. ~io m (free) will;
(jurid) decision, judgement
**árbitro** m arbitrator; (en fútbol etc)
referee; (en tenis etc) umpire
**árbol** m tree; (eje) axle; (palo) mast
**arbol|ado** m trees. ~adura f rigging.
~eda f wood
**árbol**: ~ genealógico family tree. ~
de navidad Christmas tree
**arbusto** m bush
**arca** f (caja) chest. ~ de Noé Noah's
ark
**arcada** f arcade; (de un puente)
arches; (náuseas) retching
**arca|ico** a archaic. ~ísmo m
archaism
**arcángel** m archangel
**arcano** m mystery. ● a mysterious,
secret
**arce** m maple (tree)
**arcén** m (de autopista) hard shoulder; (de carretera) verge
**arcilla** f clay
**arco** m arch; (de curva) arc; (arma,
mus) bow. ~ iris m rainbow
**archipiélago** m archipelago
**archiv|ador** m filing cabinet. ~ar vt
file (away). ~o m file; (de documentos históricos) archives
**arder** vt/i burn; (fig, de ira) seethe.
~se vpr burn (up). **estar que arde**
be very tense. **y va que arde** and
that's enough
**ardid** m trick, scheme
**ardiente** a burning. ~mente adv
passionately
**ardilla** f squirrel

**ardor** m heat; (fig) ardour. ~ **del estómago** m heartburn. ~**oso** a burning

**arduo** a arduous

**área** f area

**arena** f sand; (en deportes) arena; (en los toros) (bull)ring. ~**l** m sandy area

**arenga** f harangue. ~**r** [12] vt harangue

**aren|isca** f sandstone. ~**isco** a, ~**oso** a sandy

**arenque** m herring. ~ **ahumado** kipper

**argamasa** f mortar

**Argel** m Algiers. ~**ia** f Algeria

**argelino** a & m Algerian

**argentado** a silver-plated

**Argentina** f. la ~ Argentina

**argentin|ismo** m Argentinism. ~**o** a silvery; (de la Argentina) Argentinian, Argentine. ● m Argentinian

**argolla** f ring

**argot** m slang

**argucia** f sophism

**argüir** [19] vt (deducir) deduce; (probar) prove, show; (argumentar) argue; (echar en cara) reproach. ● vi argue

**argument|ación** f argument. ~**ador** a argumentative. ~**ar** vt/i argue. ~**o** m argument; (de libro, película etc) story, plot; (resumen) synopsis

**aria** f aria

**aridez** f aridity, dryness

**árido** a arid, dry. ● m. ~**s** mpl dry goods

**Aries** m Aries

**arisco** a (persona) unsociable; (animal) vicious

**arist|ocracia** f aristocracy. ~**ócrata** m & f aristocrat. ~**ocrático** a aristocratic

**aritmética** f arithmetic

**arma** f arm, weapon; (sección) section. ~**da** f navy; (flota) fleet. ~ **de fuego** firearm. ~**do** a armed (de with). ~**dura** f armour; (de gafas etc) frame; (tec) framework. ~**mento** m arms, armaments; (acción de armar) armament. ~**r** vt arm (de with); (montar) put together. ~**r un lío** kick up a fuss. **La A~da Invencible** the Armada

**armario** m cupboard; (para ropa) wardrobe. ~ **ropero** wardrobe

**armatoste** m monstrosity, hulk (fam)

**armazón** m & f frame(work)

**armer|ía** f gunsmith's shop; (museo) war museum. ~**o** m gunsmith

**armiño** m ermine

**armisticio** m armistice

**armonía** f harmony

**armónica** f harmonica, mouth organ

**armoni|oso** harmonious. ~**zación** f harmonizing. ~**zar** [10] vt harmonize. ● vi harmonize; (personas) get on well (con with); (colores) go well (con with)

**arnés** m armour. **arneses** mpl harness

**aro** m ring, hoop; (Arg, pendiente) ear-ring

**arom|a** m aroma; (de vino) bouquet. ~**ático** a aromatic. ~**atizar** [10] vt perfume; (culin) flavour

**arpa** f harp

**arpado** a serrated

**arpía** f harpy; (fig) hag

**arpillera** f sackcloth, sacking

**arpista** m & f harpist

**arp|ón** m harpoon. ~**onar** vt, ~**onear** vt harpoon

**arque|ar** vt arch, bend. ~**arse** vpr arch, bend. ~**o** m arching, bending

**arque|ología** f archaeology. ~**ológico** a archaeological. ~**ólogo** m archaeologist

**arquería** f arcade

**arquero** m archer; (com) cashier

**arqueta** f chest

**arquetipo** m archetype; (prototipo) prototype

**arquitect|o** m architect. ~**ónico** a architectural. ~**ura** f architecture

**arrabal** m suburb; (LAm, tugurio) slum. ~**es** mpl outskirts. ~**ero** a suburban; (de modales groseros) common

**arracima|do** a in a bunch; (apiñado) bunched together. ~**rse** vpr bunch together

**arraiga|damente** adv firmly. ~**r** [12] vi take root. ~**rse** vpr take root; (fig) settle

**arran|cada** f sudden start. ~**car** [7] vt pull up (planta); extract (diente); (arrebatar) snatch; (auto) start. ● vi start. ~**carse** vpr start. ~**que** m sudden start; (auto) start; (de emoción) outburst

**arras** fpl security

**arrasa|dor** a overwhelming, devastating. ~**r** vt level, smooth; raze to the ground (edificio etc); (llenar) fill to the brim. ● vi (el cielo) clear.

~**rse** *vpr* ‹*el cielo*› clear; ‹*los ojos*› fill with tears; (*triunfar*) triumph

**arrastr|ado** *a* (*penoso*) wretched. ~**ar** *vt* pull; (*rozar contra el suelo*) drag (along); give rise to ‹*consecuencias*›. ● *vi* trail on the ground. ~**arse** *vpr* crawl; (*humillarse*) grovel. ~**e** *m* dragging; (*transporte*) haulage. **estar para el** ~**e** (*fam*) have had it, be worn out. **ir** ~**ado** *de* hard up

**arrayán** *m* myrtle

**arre** *int* gee up! ~**ar** *vt* urge on; give ‹*golpe*›

**arrebañar** *vt* scrape together; scrape clean ‹*plato etc*›

**arrebat|ado** *a* enraged; (*irreflexivo*) impetuous; ‹*cara*› flushed. ~**ar** *vt* snatch (away); ‹*el viento*› blow away; (*fig*) win (over); captivate ‹*corazón etc*›. ~**arse** *vpr* get carried away. ~**o** *m* (*de cólera etc*) fit; (*éxtasis*) extasy

**arrebol** *m* red glow

**arreciar** *vi* get worse, increase

**arrecife** *m* reef

**arregl|ado** *a* neat; (*bien vestido*) well-dressed; (*moderado*) moderate. ~**ar** *vt* arrange; (*poner en orden*) tidy up; sort out ‹*asunto, problema etc*›; (*reparar*) mend. ~**arse** *vpr* (*ponerse bien*) improve; (*prepararse*) get ready; (*apañarse*) manage, make do; (*ponerse de acuerdo*) come to an agreement. ~**árselas** manage, get by. ~**o** *m* (*incl mus*) arrangement; (*acción de reparar*) repair; (*acuerdo*) agreement; (*orden*) order. **con** ~**o a** according to

**arrellanarse** *vpr* lounge, sit back

**arremangar** [12] *vt* roll up ‹*mangas*›; tuck up ‹*falda*›. ~**se** *vpr* roll up one's sleeves

**arremet|er** *vt/i* attack. ~**ida** *f* attack

**arremolinarse** *vpr* mill about

**arrenda|dor** *m* (*que da en alquiler*) landlord; (*que toma en alquiler*) tenant. ~**miento** *m* renting; (*contrato*) lease; (*precio*) rent. ~**r** [1] *vt* (*dar casa en alquiler*) let; (*dar cosa en alquiler*) hire out; (*tomar en alquiler*) rent. ~**tario** *m* tenant

**arreos** *mpl* harness

**arrepenti|miento** *m* repentance, regret. ~**rse** [4] *vpr*. ~**rse de** be sorry, regret; repent ‹*pecados*›

**arrest|ar** *vt* arrest, detain; (*encarcelar*) imprison. ~**o** *m* arrest; (*encarcelamiento*) imprisonment

**arriar** [20] *vt* lower ‹*bandera, vela*›; (*aflojar*) loosen; (*inundar*) flood. ~**se** *vpr* be flooded

**arriba** *adv* (up) above; (*dirección*) up(wards); (*en casa*) upstairs. ● *int* up with; (*¡levántate!*) up you get!; (*¡ánimo!*) come on! ¡~ **España!** long live Spain! ~ **mencionado** aforementioned. **calle** ~ up the street. **de** ~ **abajo** from top to bottom. **de 100 pesetas para** ~ more than 100 pesetas. **escaleras** ~ upstairs. **la parte de** ~ the top part. **los de** ~ those at the top. **más** ~ above

**arribar** *vi* ‹*barco*› reach port; (*esp LAm, llegar*) arrive

**arribista** *m* & *f* self-seeking person, arriviste

**arribo** *m* (*esp LAm*) arrival

**arriero** *m* muleteer

**arriesga|do** *a* risky. ~**r** [12] *vt* risk; (*aventurar*) venture. ~**rse** *vpr* take a risk

**arrim|ar** *vt* bring close(r); (*apartar*) move out of the way ‹*cosa*›; (*apartar*) push aside ‹*persona*›. ~**arse** *vpr* come closer, approach; (*apoyarse*) lean (a on). ~**o** *m* support. **al** ~**o de** with the support of

**arrincona|do** *a* forgotten. ~**rse** *vt* put in a corner; (*perseguir*) corner; (*arrumbar*) put aside; (*apartar a uno*) leave out, ignore. ~**rse** *vpr* become a recluse

**arriscado** *a* ‹*terreno*› uneven

**arrobar** *vt* entrance. ~**se** *vpr* be enraptured

**arrocero** *a* rice

**arrodillarse** *vpr* kneel (down)

**arrogan|cia** *f* arrogance; (*orgullo*) pride. ~**te** *a* arrogant; (*orgulloso*) proud

**arrogarse** [12] *vpr* assume

**arroj|ado** *a* brave. ~**ar** *vt* throw; (*dejar caer*) drop; (*emitir*) give off, throw out; (*producir*) produce. ● *vi* (*esp LAm, vomitar*) be sick. ~**arse** *vpr* throw o.s. ~**o** *m* courage

**arrolla|dor** *a* overwhelming. ~**r** *vt* roll (up); (*atropellar*) run over; ‹*ejército*› crush; ‹*agua*› sweep away; (*tratar sin respeto*) have no respect for

**arropar** *vt* wrap up; (*en la cama*) tuck up; (*fig, amparar*) protect. ~**se** *vpr* wrap (o.s.) up

**arroy|o** *m* stream; (*de una calle*) gutter; (*fig, de lágrimas*) flood; (*fig, de sangre*) pool. **poner en el ～o** throw into the street. **～uelo** *m* small stream

**arroz** *m* rice. **～al** *m* rice field. **～ con leche** rice pudding

**arruga** *f* (*en la piel*) wrinkle, line; (*en tela*) crease. **～r** [12] *vt* wrinkle; crumple ⟨*papel*⟩; crease ⟨*tela*⟩. **～rse** *vpr* ⟨*la piel*⟩ wrinkle, get wrinkled; ⟨*tela*⟩ crease, get creased

**arruinar** *vt* ruin; (*destruir*) destroy. **～se** *vpr* ⟨*persona*⟩ be ruined; ⟨*edificio*⟩ fall into ruins

**arrullar** *vt* lull to sleep. ● *vi* ⟨*palomas*⟩ coo. **～se** *vpr* bill and coo

**arrumaco** *m* caress; (*zalamería*) flattery

**arrumbar** *vt* put aside

**arsenal** *m* (*astillero*) shipyard; (*de armas*) arsenal; (*fig*) store

**arsénico** *m* arsenic

**arte** *m en singular, f en plural* art; (*habilidad*) skill; (*astucia*) cunning. **bellas ～s** fine arts. **con ～** skilfully. **malas ～s** trickery. **por amor al ～** for nothing, for love

**artefacto** *m* device

**arter|amente** *adv* artfully. **～ía** *f* cunning

**arteria** *f* artery; (*fig, calle*) main road

**artero** *a* cunning

**artesan|al** *a* craft. **～ía** *f* handicrafts. **～o** *m* artisan, craftsman. **objeto** *m* **de ～ía** hand-made article

**ártico** *a & m* Arctic

**articula|ción** *f* joint; (*pronunciación*) articulation. **～damente** *adv* articulately. **～do** *a* articulated; ⟨*lenguaje*⟩ articulate. **～r** *vt* articulate

**articulista** *m & f* columnist

**artículo** *m* article. **～s** *mpl* (*géneros*) goods. **～ de exportación** export commodity. **～ de fondo** editorial, leader

**artificial** *a* artificial

**artificiero** *m* bomb-disposal expert

**artificio** *m* (*habilidad*) skill; (*dispositivo*) device; (*engaño*) trick. **～so** *a* clever; (*astuto*) artful

**artilugio** *m* gadget

**artiller|ía** *f* artillery. **～o** *m* artilleryman, gunner

**artimaña** *f* trap

**art|ista** *m & f* artist; (*en espectáculos*) artiste. **～ísticamente** *adv* artistically. **～ístico** *a* artistic

**artr|ítico** *a* arthritic. **～itis** *f* arthritis

**arveja** *f* vetch; (*LAm, guisante*) pea

**arzobispo** *m* archbishop

**as** *m* ace

**asa** *f* handle

**asad|o** *a* roast(ed). ● *m* roast (meat), joint. **～o a la parrilla** grilled. **～o al horno** (*sin grasa*) baked; (*con grasa*) roast. **～or** *m* spit. **～ura** *f* offal

**asalariado** *a* salaried. ● *m* employee

**asalt|ante** *m* attacker; (*de un banco*) robber. **～ar** *vt* storm ⟨*fortaleza*⟩; attack ⟨*persona*⟩; raid ⟨*banco etc*⟩; (*fig*) ⟨*duda*⟩ assail; (*fig*) ⟨*idea etc*⟩ cross one's mind. **～o** *m* attack; (*en boxeo*) round

**asamble|a** *f* assembly; (*reunión*) meeting; (*congreso*) conference. **～ísta** *m & f* member of an assembly

**asapán** *m* (*Mex*) flying squirrel

**asar** *vt* roast; (*fig, acosar*) pester (a with). **～se** *vpr* be very hot. **～ a la parrilla** grill. **～ al horno** (*sin grasa*) bake; (*con grasa*) roast

**asbesto** *m* asbestos

**ascendencia** *f* descent

**ascend|ente** *a* ascending. **～er** [1] *vt* promote. ● *vi* go up, ascend; ⟨*cuenta etc*⟩ come to, amount to; (*ser ascendido*) be promoted. **～iente** *m & f* ancestor; (*influencia*) influence

**ascens|ión** *f* ascent; (*de grado*) promotion. **～ional** *a* upward. **～o** *m* ascent; (*de grado*) promotion. **día** *m* **de la A～ión** Ascension Day

**ascensor** *m* lift (*Brit*), elevator (*Amer*). **～ista** *m & f* lift attendant (*Brit*), elevator operator (*Amer*)

**asc|eta** *m & f* ascetic. **～ético** *a* ascetic

**asco** *m* disgust. **dar ～** be disgusting; (*fig, causar enfado*) be infuriating. **estar hecho un ～** be disgusting. **hacer ～s de algo** turn up one's nose at sth. **me da ～ el ajo** I can't stand garlic. **¡qué ～!** how disgusting! **ser un ～** be a disgrace

**ascua** *f* ember. **estar en ～s** be on tenterhooks

**asea|damente** *adv* cleanly. **～do** *a* clean; (*arreglado*) neat. **～r** *vt* (*lavar*) wash; (*limpiar*) clean; (*arreglar*) tidy up

**asedi|ar** *vt* besiege; (*fig*) pester. **～o** *m* siege

**asegura|do** *a & m* insured. **～dor** *m* insurer. **～r** *vt* secure, make safe; (*decir*) assure; (*concertar un seguro*)

insure; (*preservar*) safeguard. ∼**rse**
*vpr* make sure

**asemejarse** *vpr* be alike

**asenta|da** *f*. **de una** ∼**da** at a sitting.
∼**do** *a* situated; (*arraigado*) established. ∼**r** [1] *vt* place; (*asegurar*)
settle; (*anotar*) note down. ● *vi* be
suitable. ∼**rse** *vpr* settle; (*estar situado*) be situated

**asenti|miento** *m* consent. ∼**r** [4] *vi*
agree (**a** to). ∼**r con la cabeza** nod

**aseo** *m* cleanliness. ∼**s** *mpl* toilets

**asequible** *a* obtainable; (*precio*)
reasonable; (*persona*) approachable

**asesin|ar** *vt* murder; (*pol*) assassinate. ∼**ato** *m* murder; (*pol*) assassination. ∼**o** *m* murderer; (*pol*)
assassin

**asesor** *m* adviser, consultant. ∼**amiento** *m* advice. ∼**ar** *vt* advise.
∼**arse** *vpr*. ∼**arse con/de** consult.
∼**ía** *f* consultancy; (*oficina*) consultant's office

**asestar** *vt* aim (*arma*); strike (*golpe
etc*); (*disparar*) fire

**asevera|ción** *f* assertion. ∼**r** *vt*
assert

**asfalt|ado** *a* asphalt. ∼**ar** *vt* asphalt.
∼**o** *m* asphalt

**asfixia** *f* suffocation. ∼**nte** *a* suffocating. ∼**r** *vt* suffocate. ∼**rse** *vpr*
suffocate

**así** *adv* so; (*de esta manera*) like this,
like that. ● *a* such. ∼ ∼, ∼ **asado** so-so. ∼ **como** just as. ∼...
**como** both... and. ∼ **pues** so. ∼ **que**
so; (*enseguida*) as soon as. ∼ **sea** so
be it. ∼ **y todo** even so. **aun** ∼ even
so. **¿no es** ∼**?** isn't that right? **y** ∼
**(sucesivamente)** and so on

**Asia** *f* Asia

**asiático** *a* & *m* Asian

**asidero** *m* handle; (*fig, pretexto*)
excuse

**asidu|amente** *adv* regularly. ∼**idad**
*f* regularity. ∼**o** *a* & *m* regular

**asiento** *m* seat; (*situación*) site. ∼
**delantero** front seat. ∼ **trasero**
back seat. **tome Vd** ∼ please take a
seat

**asigna|ción** *f* assignment; (*sueldo*)
salary. ∼**r** *vt* assign; allot (*porción,
tiempo etc*)

**asignatura** *f* subject. ∼ **pendiente**
(*escol*) failed subject; (*fig*) matter
still to be resolved

**asil|ado** *m* inmate. ∼**ado político**
refugee. ∼**o** *m* asylum; (*fig*) shelter;

(*de ancianos etc*) home. ∼**o de huérfanos** orphanage. **pedir** ∼**o político**
ask for political asylum

**asimétrico** *a* asymmetrical

**asimila|ción** *f* assimilation. ∼**r** *vt*
assimilate. ∼**rse** *vpr* be assimilated. ∼**rse a** resemble

**asimismo** *adv* in the same way,
likewise

**asir** [45] *vt* grasp. ∼**se** *vpr* grab hold
(**a, de** of)

**asist|encia** *f* attendance; (*gente*)
people (present); (*en un teatro etc*)
audience; (*ayuda*) assistance. ∼**encia médica** medical care. ∼**enta** *f*
assistant; (*mujer de la limpieza*)
charwoman. ∼**ente** *m* assistant.
∼**ente social** social worker. ∼**ido** *a*
assisted. ∼**ir** *vt* assist, help; (*un
médico*) treat. ● *vi*. ∼**ir a** attend, be
present at

**asm|a** *f* asthma. ∼**ático** *a* & *m*
asthmatic

**asn|ada** *f* (*fig*) silly thing. ∼**o** *m* donkey; (*fig*) ass

**asocia|ción** *f* association; (*com*) partnership. ∼**do** *a* associated; (*miembro etc*) associate. ● *m* associate.
∼**r** *vt* associate; (*com*) take into
partnership. ∼**rse** *vpr* associate;
(*com*) become a partner

**asolador** *a* destructive

**asolar**[1] [1] *vt* destroy. ∼**se** *vpr* be
destroyed

**asolar**[2] *vt* dry up (*plantas*)

**asoma|da** *f* brief appearance. ∼**r** *vt*
show. ● *vi* appear, show. ∼**rse** *vpr*
(*persona*) lean out (**a, por** of); (*cosa*)
appear

**asombr|adizo** *a* easily frightened.
∼**ar** *vt* (*pasmar*) amaze; (*sorprender*) surprise. ∼**arse** *vpr* be
amazed; (*sorprenderse*) be
surprised. ∼**o** *m* amazement, surprise. ∼**osamente** *adv* amazingly.
∼**oso** *a* amazing, astonishing

**asomo** *m* sign. **ni por** ∼ by no means

**asonada** *f* mob; (*motín*) riot

**aspa** *f* cross, X-shape; (*de molino*)
(windmill) sail. ∼**do** *a* X-shaped

**aspaviento** *m* show, fuss. ∼**s** *mpl*
gestures. **hacer** ∼**s** make a big fuss

**aspecto** *m* look, appearance; (*fig*)
aspect

**aspereza** *f* roughness; (*de sabor etc*)
sourness

**áspero** *a* rough; (*sabor etc*) bitter

**aspersión** *f* sprinkling

**aspiración** f breath; (*deseo*) ambition

**aspirador** a suction. ~a f vacuum cleaner

**aspira|nte** m candidate. ~r vt breathe in; ‹*máquina*› suck up. ● vi breathe in; ‹*máquina*› suck. ~r a aspire to

**aspirina** f aspirin

**asquear** vt sicken. ● vi be sickening. ~se vpr be disgusted

**asqueros|amente** adv disgustingly. ~idad f filthiness. ~o a disgusting

**asta** f spear; (*de la bandera*) flagpole; (*mango*) handle; (*cuerno*) horn. **a media ~** at half-mast. ~do a horned

**asterisco** m asterisk

**astilla** f splinter. ~s fpl firewood. ~r vt splinter. **hacer ~s** smash. **hacerse ~s** shatter

**astillero** m shipyard

**astringente** a & m astringent

**astro** m star

**astr|ología** f astrology. ~ólogo m astrologer

**astrona|uta** m & f astronaut. ~ve f spaceship

**astr|onomía** f astronomy. ~onómico a astronomical. ~ónomo m astronomer

**astu|cia** f cleverness; (*ardid*) cunning. ~to a astute; (*taimado*) cunning

**asturiano** a & m Asturian

**Asturias** fpl Asturias

**asueto** m time off, holiday

**asumir** vt assume

**asunción** f assumption. **A~** Assumption

**asunto** m subject; (*cuestión*) matter; (*de una novela*) plot; (*negocio*) business. ~s mpl **exteriores** foreign affairs. **el ~ es que** the fact is that

**asusta|dizo** a easily frightened. ~r vt frighten. ~rse vpr be frightened

**ataca|nte** m & f attacker. ~r [7] vt attack

**atad|ero** m rope; (*cierre*) fastening; (*gancho*) hook. ~ijo m bundle. ~o a tied; (*fig*) timid. ● m bundle. ~ura f tying; (*cuerda*) string

**ataj|ar** vi take a short cut. ~o m short cut; (*grupo*) bunch. **echar por el ~o** take the easy way out

**atalaya** f watch-tower; (*fig*) vantage point

**atañer** [22] vt concern

**ataque** m attack; (*med*) fit, attack. ~ **al corazón** heart attack. ~ **de nervios** hysterics

**atar** vt tie (up). ~se vpr get tied up

**atardecer** [11] vi get dark. ● m dusk. **al ~** at dusk

**atarea|do** a busy. ~rse vpr work hard

**atasc|adero** m (*fig*) stumbling block. ~ar [7] vt block; (*fig*) hinder. ~arse vpr get stuck; ‹*tubo etc*› block. ~o m obstruction; (*auto*) traffic jam

**ataúd** m coffin

**atav|iar** [20] vt dress up. ~iarse vpr dress up, get dressed up. ~ío m dress, attire

**atemorizar** [10] vt frighten. ~se vpr be frightened

**Atenas** fpl Athens

**atenazar** [10] vt (*fig*) torture; ‹*duda, miedo*› grip

**atención** f attention; (*cortesía*) courtesy, kindness; (*interés*) interest. **¡~!** look out! ~ a beware of. **llamar la ~** attract attention, catch the eye. **prestar ~** pay attention

**atender** [1] vt attend to; heed ‹*consejo etc*›; (*cuidar*) look after. ● vi pay attention

**atenerse** [40] vpr abide (**a** by)

**atentado** m offence; (*ataque*) attack. ~ **contra la vida de uno** attempt on s.o.'s life

**atentamente** adv attentively; (*con cortesía*) politely; (*con amabilidad*) kindly. **le saluda ~** (*en cartas*) yours faithfully

**atentar** vi commit an offence. ~ **contra la vida de uno** make an attempt on s.o.'s life

**atento** a attentive; (*cortés*) polite; (*amable*) kind

**atenua|nte** a extenuating. ● f extenuating circumstance. ~r [21] vt attenuate; (*hacer menor*) diminish, lessen. ~rse vpr weaken

**ateo** a atheistic. ● m atheist

**aterciopelado** a velvety

**aterido** a frozen (stiff), numb (with cold)

**aterra|dor** a terrifying. ~r vt terrify. ~rse vpr be terrified

**aterriza|je** m landing. ~je **forzoso** emergency landing. ~r [10] vt land

**aterrorizar** [10] vt terrify

**atesorar** vt hoard

**atesta|do** a packed, full up. ● m sworn statement. ~r vt fill up, pack; (*jurid*) testify

**atestiguar** [15] *vt* testify to; *(fig)* prove

**atiborrar** *vt* fill, stuff. **~se** *vpr* stuff o.s.

**ático** *m* attic

**atilda|do** *a* elegant, neat. **~r** *vt* put a tilde over; *(arreglar)* tidy up. **~rse** *vpr* smarten o.s. up

**atina|damente** *adv* rightly. **~do** *a* right; *(juicioso)* wise, sensible. **~r** *vt/i* hit upon; *(acertar)* guess right

**atípico** *a* exceptional

**atiplado** *a* high-pitched

**atirantar** *vt* tighten

**atisb|ar** *vt* spy on; *(vislumbrar)* make out. **~o** *m* spying; *(indicio)* hint, sign

**atizar** [10] *vt* poke; give *(golpe)*; *(fig)* stir up; arouse, excite *(pasión etc)*

**atlántico** *a* Atlantic. **el (océano) A~** the Atlantic (Ocean)

**atlas** *m* atlas

**atl|eta** *m & f* athlete. **~ético** *a* athletic. **~etismo** *m* athletics

**atm|ósfera** *f* atmosphere. **~osférico** *a* atmospheric

**atolondra|do** *a* scatter-brained; *(aturdido)* bewildered. **~miento** *m* bewilderment; *(irreflexión)* thoughtlessness. **~r** *vt* bewilder; *(pasmar)* stun. **~rse** *vpr* be bewildered

**atolladero** *m* bog; *(fig)* tight corner

**at|ómico** *a* atomic. **~omizador** *m* atomizer. **~omizar** [10] *vt* atomize

**átomo** *m* atom

**atónito** *m* amazed

**atonta|do** *a* bewildered; *(tonto)* stupid. **~r** *vt* stun. **~rse** *vpr* get confused

**atormenta|dor** *a* tormenting. ● *m* tormentor. **~r** *vt* torture. **~rse** *vpr* worry, torment o.s.

**atornillar** *vt* screw on

**atosigar** [12] *vt* pester

**atracadero** *m* quay

**atracador** *m* bandit

**atracar** [7] *vt (amarrar)* tie up; *(arrimar)* bring alongside; rob *(banco, persona)*. ● *vi (barco)* tie up; *(astronave)* dock. **~se** *vpr* stuff o.s. **(de** with)

**atracci|ón** *f* attraction. **~ones** *fpl* entertainment, amusements

**atrac|o** *m* hold-up, robbery. **~ón** *m*. **darse un ~ón** stuff o.s.

**atractivo** *a* attractive. ● *m* attraction; *(encanto)* charm

**atraer** [41] *vt* attract

**atragantarse** *vpr* choke *(con* on). **la historia se me atraganta** I can't stand history

**atranc|ar** [7] *vt* bolt *(puerta)*; block up *(tubo etc)*. **~arse** *vpr* get stuck; *(tubo)* get blocked. **~o** *m* difficulty

**atrapar** *vt* trap; *(fig)* land *(empleo etc)*; catch *(resfriado)*

**atrás** *adv* behind; *(dirección)* back- (wards); *(tiempo)* previously, before. ● *int* back! **dar un paso ~** step backwards. **hacia ~, para ~** backwards

**atras|ado** *a* behind; *(reloj)* slow; *(con deudas)* in arrears; *(país)* backward. **llegar ~ado** arrive late. **~ar** *vt* slow down; *(retrasar)* put back; *(demorar)* delay, postpone. ● *vi (reloj)* be slow. **~arse** *vpr* be late; *(reloj)* be slow; *(quedarse atrás)* be behind. **~o** *m* delay; *(de un reloj)* slowness; *(de un país)* backwardness. **~os** *mpl* arrears

**atravesa|do** *a* lying across; *(bizco)* cross-eyed; *(fig, malo)* wicked. **~r** [1] *vt* cross; *(traspasar)* go through; *(poner transversalmente)* lay across. **~rse** *vpr* lie across; *(en la garganta)* get stuck, stick; *(entrometerse)* interfere

**atrayente** *a* attractive

**atrev|erse** *vpr* dare. **~erse con** tackle. **~ido** *a* daring, bold; *(insolente)* insolent. **~imiento** *m* daring, boldness; *(descaro)* insolence

**atribución** *f* attribution. **atribuciones** *fpl* authority

**atribuir** [17] *vt* attribute; confer *(función)*. **~se** *vpr* take the credit for

**atribular** *vt* afflict. **~se** *vpr* be distressed

**atribut|ivo** *a* attributive. **~o** *m* attribute; *(símbolo)* symbol

**atril** *m* lectern; *(mus)* music stand

**atrincherar** *vt* fortify with trenches. **~se** *vpr* entrench (o.s.)

**atrocidad** *f* atrocity. **decir ~es** make silly remarks. **¡qué ~!** how terrible!

**atrochar** *vi* take a short cut

**atrojarse** *vpr (Mex)* be cornered

**atrona|dor** *a* deafening. **~r** [2] *vt* deafen

**atropell|adamente** *adv* hurriedly. **~ado** *a* hasty. **~ar** *vt* knock down, run over; *(empujar)* push aside; *(maltratar)* bully; *(fig)* outrage, insult. **~arse** *vpr* rush. **~o** *m (auto)* accident; *(fig)* outrage

**atroz** *a* atrocious; (*fam*) huge. ～**mente** *adv* atrociously, awfully

**atuendo** *m* dress, attire

**atufar** *vt* choke; (*fig*) irritate. ～**se** *vpr* be overcome; (*enfadarse*) get cross

**atún** *m* tuna (fish)

**aturdi|do** *a* bewildered; (*irreflexivo*) thoughtless. ～**r** *vt* bewilder, stun; 〈*ruido*〉 deafen. ～**rse** *vpr* be stunned; (*intentar olvidar*) try to forget

**atur(r)ullar** *vt* bewilder

**atusar** *vt* smooth; trim 〈*pelo*〉

**auda|cia** *f* boldness, audacity. ～**z** *a* bold

**audib|ilidad** *f* audibility. ～**le** *a* audible

**audición** *f* hearing; (*concierto*) concert

**audiencia** *f* audience; (*tribunal*) court

**auditor** *m* judge-advocate; (*de cuentas*) auditor

**auditorio** *m* audience; (*sala*) auditorium

**auge** *m* peak; (*com*) boom

**augur|ar** *vt* predict; 〈*cosas*〉 augur. ～**io** *m* omen. ～**ios** *mpl*. con nuestros ～**ios para** with our best wishes for

**augusto** *a* august

**aula** *f* class-room; (*univ*) lecture room

**aulaga** *f* gorse

**aull|ar** [23] *vi* howl. ～**ido** *m* howl

**aument|ar** *vt* increase; put up 〈*precios*〉; magnify 〈*imagen*〉; step up 〈*producción, voltaje*〉. ● *vi* increase. ～**arse** *vpr* increase. ～**ativo** *a & m* augmentative. ～**o** *m* increase; (*de sueldo*) rise

**aun** *adv* even. ～ **así** even so. ～ **cuando** although. **más** ～ even more. **ni** ～ not even

**aún** *adv* still, yet. ～ **no ha llegado** it still hasn't arrived, it hasn't arrived yet

**aunar** [23] *vt* join. ～**se** *vpr* join together

**aunque** *conj* although, (even) though

**aúpa** *int* up! **de** ～ wonderful

**aureola** *f* halo

**auricular** *m* (*de teléfono*) receiver. ～**es** *mpl* headphones

**aurora** *f* dawn

**ausen|cia** *f* absence. ～**tarse** *vpr* leave. ～**te** *a* absent. ● *m & f* absentee; (*jurid*) missing person. **en** ～ **de** in the absence of

**auspicio** *m* omen. **bajo los** ～**s de** sponsored by

**auster|idad** *f* austerity. ～**o** *a* austere

**austral** *a* southern. ● *m* (*unidad monetaria argentina*) austral

**Australia** *m* Australia

**australiano** *a & m* Australian

**Austria** *f* Austria

**austriaco, austríaco** *a & m* Austrian

**aut|enticar** [7] authenticate. ～**enticidad** *f* authenticity. ～**éntico** *a* authentic

**auto** *m* sentence; (*auto, fam*) car. ～**s** *mpl* proceedings

**auto...** *pref* auto...

**auto|ayuda** *f* self-help. ～**biografía** *f* autobiography. ～**biográfico** *a* autobiographical. ～**bombo** *m* self-glorification

**autobús** *m* bus. **en** ～ by bus

**autocar** *m* coach (*Brit*), (long-distance) bus (*Amer*)

**aut|ocracia** *f* autocracy. ～**ócrata** *m & f* autocrat. ～**ocrático** *a* autocratic

**autóctono** *a* autochthonous

**auto: ～determinación** *f* self-determination. ～**defensa** *f* self-defence. ～**didacto** *a* self-taught. ● *m* autodidact. ～**escuela** *f* driving school. ～**giro** *m* autogiro

**autógrafo** *m* autograph

**automación** *f* automation

**autómata** *m* robot

**autom|ático** *a* automatic. ● *m* press-stud. ～**atización** *f* automation. ～**atizar** [10] *vt* automate

**automotor** *a* (*f* **automotriz**) self-propelled. ● *m* diesel train

**autom|óvil** *a* self-propelled. ● *m* car. ～**ovilismo** *m* motoring. ～**ovilista** *m & f* driver, motorist

**aut|onomía** *f* autonomy. ～**onómico** *a*, ～**ónomo** *a* autonomous

**autopista** *f* motorway (*Brit*), freeway (*Amer*)

**autopsia** *f* autopsy

**autor** *m* author. ～**a** *f* author(ess)

**autori|dad** *f* authority. ～**tario** *a* authoritarian. ～**tarismo** *m* authoritarianism

**autoriza|ción** *f* authorization. ～**damente** *adv* officially. ～**do** *a* authorized, offical; 〈*opinión etc*〉 authoritative. ～**r** [10] *vt* authorize

**auto:** ~**rretrato** *m* self-portrait. ~**servicio** *m* self-service restaurant. ~**stop** *m* hitch-hiking. **hacer** ~**stop** hitch-hike

**autosuficien|cia** *f* self-sufficiency. ~**te** *a* self-sufficient

**autovía** *f* dual carriageway

**auxili|ar** *a* assistant; ⟨*servicios*⟩ auxiliary. ● *m* assistant. ● *vt* help. ~**o** *m* help. ¡~**o**! help! ~**os espirituales** last rites. **en** ~**o de** in aid of. **pedir** ~**o** shout for help. **primeros** ~**os** first aid

**Av.** *abrev* (*Avenida*) Ave, Avenue

**aval** *m* guarantee

**avalancha** *f* avalanche

**avalar** *vt* guarantee

**avalorar** *vt* enhance; (*fig*) encourage

**avance** *m* advance; (*en el cine*) trailer; (*balance*) balance; (*de noticias*) early news bulletin. ~ **informativo** publicity hand-out

**avante** *adv* (*esp LAm*) forward

**avanza|do** *a* advanced. ~**r** [10] *vt* move forward. ● *vi* advance

**avar|icia** *f* avarice. ~**icioso** *a*, ~**iento** *a* greedy; (*tacaño*) miserly. ~**o** *a* miserly. ● *m* miser

**avasalla|dor** *a* overwhelming. ~**r** *vt* dominate

**Avda.** *abrev* (*Avenida*) Ave, Avenue

**ave** *f* bird. ~ **de paso** (*incl fig*) bird of passage. ~ **de presa**, ~ **de rapiña** bird of prey

**avecinarse** *vpr* approach

**avecindarse** *vpr* settle

**avejentarse** *vpr* age

**avellan|a** *f* hazel-nut. ~**o** *m* hazel (tree)

**avemaría** *f* Hail Mary. **al** ~ at dusk

**avena** *f* oats

**avenar** *vt* drain

**avenida** *f* (*calle*) avenue; (*de río*) flood

**avenir** [53] *vt* reconcile. ~**se** *vpr* come to an agreement

**aventaja|do** *a* outstanding. ~**r** *vt* surpass

**aventar** [1] *vt* fan; winnow ⟨*grano etc*⟩; (*viento*) blow away

**aventur|a** *f* adventure; (*riesgo*) risk. ~**a amorosa** love affair. ~**ado** *a* risky. ~**ar** *vt* risk. ~**arse** *vpr* dare. ~**a sentimental** love affair. ~**ero** *a* adventurous. ● *m* adventurer

**avergonza|do** *a* ashamed; (*embarazado*) embarrassed. ~**r** [10 & 16] *vt* shame; (*embarazar*) embar-

rass. ~**rse** *vpr* be ashamed; (*embarazarse*) be embarrassed

**aver|ía** *f* (*auto*) breakdown; (*daño*) damage. ~**iado** *a* broken down; ⟨*fruta*⟩ damaged, spoilt. ~**iar** [20] *vt* damage. ~**iarse** *vpr* get damaged; ⟨*coche*⟩ break down

**averigua|ble** *a* verifiable. ~**ción** *f* verification; (*investigación*) investigation; (*Mex, disputa*) argument. ~**dor** *m* investigator. ~**r** [15] *vt* verify; (*enterarse de*) find out; (*investigar*) investigate. ● *vi* (*Mex*) quarrel

**aversión** *f* aversion (**a, hacia, por** for)

**avestruz** *m* ostrich

**aviación** *f* aviation; (*mil*) air force

**aviado** *a* (*Arg*) well off. **estar** ~ be in a mess

**aviador** *m* (*aviat*) member of the crew; (*piloto*) pilot; (*Arg, prestamista*) money-lender; (*Arg, de minas*) mining speculator

**aviar** [20] *vt* get ready, prepare; (*arreglar*) tidy; (*reparar*) repair; (*LAm, prestar dinero*) lend money; (*dar prisa*) hurry up. ~**se** *vpr* get ready. ¡**aviate**! hurry up!

**av|ícula** *a* poultry. ~**icultor** *m* poultry farmer. ~**icultura** *f* poultry farming

**avidez** *f* eagerness, greed

**ávido** *a* eager, greedy

**avieso** *a* (*maligno*) wicked

**avinagra|do** *a* sour. ~**r** *vt* sour; (*fig*) embitter. ~**rse** *vpr* go sour; (*fig*) become embittered

**avío** *m* preparation. ~**s** *mpl* provisions; (*utensilios*) equipment

**avi|ón** *m* aeroplane (*Brit*), airplane (*Amer*). ~**oneta** *f* light aircraft

**avis|ado** *a* wise. ~**ar** *vt* warn; (*informar*) notify, inform; call ⟨*medico etc*⟩. ~**o** *m* warning; (*anuncio*) notice. **estar sobre** ~**o** be on the alert. **mal** ~**ado** ill-advised. **sin previo** ~**o** without notice

**avisp|a** *f* wasp. ~**ado** *a* sharp. ~**ero** *m* wasps' nest; (*fig*) mess. ~**ón** *m* hornet

**avistar** *vt* catch sight of

**avitualla|miento** *m* supplying. ~**r** *vt* provision

**avivar** *vt* stoke up ⟨*fuego*⟩; brighten up ⟨*color*⟩; arouse ⟨*interés, pasión*⟩; intensify ⟨*dolor*⟩. ~**se** *vpr* revive; (*animarse*) cheer up

**axila** *f* axilla, armpit

**axiom|a** *m* axiom. **~ático** *a* axiomatic

**ay** *int* (*de dolor*) ouch!; (*de susto*) oh!; (*de pena*) oh dear! **~ de** poor. **¡~ de ti!** poor you!

**aya** *f* governess, child's nurse

**ayer** *adv* yesterday. ● *m* past. **antes de ~** the day before yesterday. **~ por la mañana** yesterday morning. **~ (por la) noche** last night

**ayo** *m* tutor

**ayote** *m* (*Mex*) pumpkin

**ayuda** *f* help, aid. **~ de cámara** valet. **~nta** *f*, **~nte** *m* assistant; (*mil*) adjutant. **~nte técnico sanitario (ATS)** nurse. **~r** *vt* help

**ayun|ar** *vi* fast. **~as** *fpl*. **estar en ~as** have had no breakfast; (*fig, fam*) be in the dark. **~o** *m* fasting

**ayuntamiento** *m* town council, city council; (*edificio*) town hall

**azabache** *m* jet

**azad|a** *f* hoe. **~ón** *m* (large) hoe

**azafata** *f* air hostess

**azafrán** *m* saffron

**azahar** *m* orange blossom

**azar** *m* chance; (*desgracia*) misfortune. **al ~** at random. **por ~** by chance

**azararse** *vpr* go wrong; (*fig*) get flustered

**azaros|amente** *adv* hazardously. **~o** *a* hazardous, risky; (*persona*) unlucky

**azoga|do** *a* restless. **~rse** [12] *vpr* be restless

**azolve** *m* (*Mex*) obstruction

**azora|do** *a* flustered, excited, alarmed. **~miento** *m* confusion, embarrassment. **~r** *vt* embarrass; (*aturdir*) alarm. **~rse** *vpr* get flustered, be alarmed

**Azores** *fpl* Azores

**azot|aina** *f* beating. **~ar** *vt* whip, beat. **~e** *m* whip; (*golpe*) smack; (*fig, calamidad*) calamity

**azotea** *f* flat roof. **estar mal de la ~** be mad

**azteca** *a* & *m* & *f* Aztec

**az|úcar** *m* & *f* sugar. **~ucarado** *a* sweet. **~ucarar** *vt* sweeten. **~ucarero** *m* sugar bowl

**azucena** *f* (white) lily

**azufre** *m* sulphur

**azul** *a* & *m* blue. **~ado** *a* bluish. **~ de lavar** (washing) blue. **~ marino** navy blue

**azulejo** *m* tile

**azuzar** *vt* urge on, incite

# B

**bab|a** *f* spittle. **~ear** *vi* drool, slobber; (*niño*) dribble. **caerse la ~a** be delighted

**babel** *f* bedlam

**babe|o** *m* drooling; (*de un niño*) dribbling. **~ro** *m* bib

**Babia** *f*. **estar en ~** have one's head in the clouds

**babieca** *a* stupid. ● *m* & *f* simpleton

**babor** *m* port. **a ~** to port, on the port side

**babosa** *f* slug

**babosada** *f* (*Mex*) silly remark

**babos|ear** *vt* slobber over; (*niño*) dribble over. **~eo** *m* drooling; (*de niño*) dribbling. **~o** *a* slimy; (*LAm, tonto*) silly

**babucha** *f* slipper

**babuino** *m* baboon

**baca** *f* luggage rack

**bacaladilla** *f* small cod

**bacalao** *m* cod

**bacon** *m* bacon

**bacteria** *f* bacterium

**bache** *m* hole; (*fig*) bad patch

**bachillerato** *m* school-leaving examination

**bada|jazo** *m* stroke (of a bell). **~o** *m* clapper; (*persona*) chatterbox

**bagaje** *m* baggage; (*animal*) beast of burden; (*fig*) knowledge

**bagatela** *f* trifle

**Bahamas** *fpl* Bahamas

**bahía** *f* bay

**bail|able** *a* dance. **~ador** *a* dancing. ● *m* dancer. **~aor** *m* Flamenco dancer. **~ar** *vt/i* dance. **~arín** dancer. **~arina** *f* dancer; (*de baile clásico*) ballerina. **~e** *m* dance. **~e de etiqueta** ball. **ir a ~ar** go dancing

**baja** *f* drop, fall; (*mil*) casualty. **~ por maternidad** maternity leave. **~da** *f* slope; (*acto de bajar*) descent. **~mar** *m* low tide. **~r** *vt* lower; (*llevar abajo*) get down; bow (*la cabeza*). **~r la escalera** go downstairs. ● *vi* go down; (*temperatura, precio*) fall. **~rse** *vpr* bend down. **~r(se) de** get out of (*coche*); get off (*autobús, caballo, tren, bicicleta*). **dar(se) de ~** take sick leave

**bajeza** *f* vile deed

**bajío** *m* sandbank

**bajo** *a* low; (*de estatura*) short, small; ⟨*cabeza, ojos*⟩ lowered; (*humilde*) humble, low; (*vil*) vile, low; ⟨*color*⟩ pale; ⟨*voz*⟩ low; (*mus*) deep. ● *m* lowland; (*bajío*) sandbank; (*mus*) bass. ● *adv* quietly; ⟨*volar*⟩ low. ● *prep* under; (*temperatura*) below. ~ **la lluvia** in the rain. **los ~s fondos** the low district. **por lo ~** under one's breath; (*fig*) in secret

**bajón** *m* drop; (*de salud*) decline; (*com*) slump

**bala** *f* bullet; (*de algodón etc*) bale. ~ **perdida** stray bullet. **como una ~** like a shot

**balada** *f* ballad

**baladí** *a* trivial

**baladrón** *a* boastful

**baladron|ada** *f* boast. ~**ear** *vi* boast

**balan|ce** *m* swinging; (*de una cuenta*) balance; (*documento*) balance sheet. ~**cear** *vt* balance. ● *vi* hesitate. ~**cearse** *vpr* swing; (*vacilar*) hesitate. ~**ceo** *m* swinging. ~**za** *f* scales; (*com*) balance

**balar** *vi* bleat

**balaustrada** *f* balustrade, railing(s); (*de escalera*) banisters

**balay** *m* (*LAm*) wicker basket

**balazo** *m* (*disparo*) shot; (*herida*) bullet wound

**balboa** *f* (*unidad monetaria panameña*) balboa

**balbuc|ear** *vt/i* stammer; ⟨*niño*⟩ babble. ~**eo** *m* stammering; (*de niño*) babbling. ~**iente** *a* stammering; ⟨*niño*⟩ babbling. ~**ir** [24] *vt/i* stammer; ⟨*niño*⟩ babble

**balc|ón** *m* balcony. ~**onada** *f* row of balconies. ~**onaje** *m* row of balconies

**balda** *f* shelf

**baldado** *a* disabled, crippled; (*rendido*) shattered. ● *m* disabled person, cripple

**baldaquín** *m*, **baldaquino** *m* canopy

**baldar** *vt* cripple

**balde** *m* bucket. **de ~** free (of charge). **en ~** in vain. ~**ar** *vt* wash down

**baldío** *a* ⟨*terreno*⟩ waste; (*fig*) useless

**baldosa** *f* (floor) tile; (*losa*) flagstone

**balduque** *m* (*incl fig*) red tape

**balear** *a* Balearic. ● *m* native of the Balearic Islands. **las Islas** *fpl* **B~es** the Balearics, the Balearic Islands

**baleo** *m* (*LAm, tiroteo*) shooting; (*Mex, abanico*) fan

**balido** *m* bleat; (*varios sonidos*) bleating

**ball|ín** *m* small bullet. ~**ines** *mpl* shot

**balística** *f* ballistics

**baliza** *f* (*naut*) buoy; (*aviat*) beacon

**balneario** *m* spa; (*con playa*) seaside resort. ● *a*. **estación** *f* **balnearia** spa; (*con playa*) seaside resort

**balompié** *m* football (*Brit*), soccer

**ball|ón** *m* ball, football. ~**oncesto** *m* basketball. ~**onmano** *m* handball. ~**volea** *m* volleyball

**balotaje** *m* (*LAm*) voting

**balsa** *f* (*de agua*) pool; (*plataforma flotante*) raft

**bálsamo** *m* balsam; (*fig*) balm

**balsón** *m* (*Mex*) stagnant water

**baluarte** *m* (*incl fig*) bastion

**balumba** *f* mass, mountain

**ballena** *f* whale

**ballesta** *f* crossbow

**ballet** /ba'le/ (*pl* **ballets** uba'le/) *m* ballet

**bambole|ar** *vi* sway; ⟨*mesa etc*⟩ wobble. ~**arse** *vpr* sway; ⟨*mesa etc*⟩ wobble. ~**o** *m* swaying; (*de mesa etc*) wobbling

**bambú** *m* (*pl* **bambúes**) bamboo

**banal** *a* banal. ~**idad** *f* banality

**banan|a** *f* (*esp LAm*) banana. ~**o** *m* (*LAm*) banana tree

**banast|a** *f* large basket. ~**o** *m* large round basket

**banc|a** *f* banking; (*en juegos*) bank; (*LAm, asiento*) bench. ~**ario** *a* bank, banking. ~**arrota** *f* bankruptcy. ~**o** *m* (*asiento*) bench; (*com*) bank; (*bajío*) sandbank. **hacer ~arrota, ir a la ~arrota** go bankrupt

**banda** *f* (*incl mus, radio*) band; (*grupo*) gang, group; (*lado*) side. ~**da** *f* (*de aves*) flock; (*de peces*) shoal. ~ **de sonido,** ~ **sonora** sound-track

**bandeja** *f* tray; (*LAm, plato*) serving dish. **servir algo en** ~ **a uno** hand sth to s.o. on a plate

**bandera** *f* flag; (*estandarte*) banner, standard

**banderill|a** *f* banderilla. ~**ear** *vt* stick the banderillas in. ~**ero** *m* banderillero

**banderín** *m* pennant, small flag, banner

**bandido** *m* bandit

**bando** m edict, proclamation; (*partido*) faction. ∼s mpl banns. **pasarse al otro** ∼ go over to the other side

**bandolero** m bandit

**bandolina** f mandolin

**bandoneón** m large accordion

**banjo** m banjo

**banquero** m banker

**banqueta** f stool; (*LAm, acera*) pavement (*Brit*), sidewalk (*Amer*)

**banquete** m banquet; (*de boda*) wedding reception. ∼ar vt/i banquet

**banquillo** m bench; (*jurid*) dock; (*taburete*) footstool

**bañ|ado** m (*LAm*) swamp. ∼ador m (*de mujer*) swimming costume; (*de hombre*) swimming trunks. ∼ar vt bathe, immerse; bath ⟨*niño*⟩; (*culin, recubrir*) coat. ∼arse vpr go swimming, have a swim; (*en casa*) have a bath. ∼era f bath, bath-tub. ∼ero m life-guard. ∼ista m & f bather. ∼o m bath; (*en piscina, mar etc*) swim; (*bañera*) bath, bath-tub; (*capa*) coat(ing)

**baptisterio** m baptistery; (*pila*) font

**baquet|a** f (*de fusil*) ramrod; (*de tambor*) drumstick. ∼ear vt bother. ∼eo m nuisance, bore

**bar** m bar

**barahúnda** f uproar

**baraja** f pack of cards. ∼r vt shuffle; juggle, massage ⟨*cifras etc*⟩. ● vi argue (con with); (*enemistarse*) fall out (con with). ∼s fpl argument. **jugar a la** ∼ play cards. **jugar a dos** ∼s, **jugar con dos** ∼s be deceitful, indulge in double-dealing

**baranda** f, **barandal** m, **barandilla** f handrail; (*de escalera*) banisters

**barat|a** f (*Mex*) sale. ∼ija f trinket. ∼illo m junk shop; (*géneros*) cheap goods. ∼o a cheap. ● m sale. ● adv cheap(ly). ∼ura f cheapness

**baraúnda** f uproar

**barba** f chin; (*pelo*) beard. ∼do a bearded

**barbacoa** f barbecue; (*Mex, carne*) barbecued meat

**bárbaramente** adv savagely; (*fig*) tremendously

**barbari|dad** f barbarity; (*fig*) outrage; (*mucho, fam*) awful lot (*fam*). **¡qué** ∼**dad!** how awful! ∼e f barbarity; (*fig*) ignorance. ∼smo m barbarism

**bárbaro** a barbaric, cruel; (*bruto*) uncouth; (*estupendo, fam*) terrific (*fam*). ● m barbarian. **¡qué** ∼**!** how marvellous!

**barbear** vt (*afeitar*) shave; (*Mex, lisonjear*) fawn on

**barbecho** m fallow

**barber|ía** f barber's (shop). ∼o m barber; (*Mex, adulador*) flatterer

**barbi|lampiño** a beardless; (*fig*) inexperienced, green. ∼lindo m dandy

**barbilla** f chin

**barbitúrico** m barbiturate

**barbo** m barbel. ∼ **de mar** red mullet

**barbot|ar** vt/i mumble. ∼ear vt/i mumble. ∼eo m mumbling

**barbudo** a bearded

**barbullar** vi jabber

**barca** f (small) boat. ∼ **de pasaje** ferry. ∼je m fare. ∼za f barge

**Barcelona** f Barcelona

**barcelonés** a of Barcelona, from Barcelona. ● m native of Barcelona

**barco** m boat; (*navío*) ship. ∼ **cisterna** tanker. ∼ **de vapor** steamer. ∼ **de vela** sailing boat. **ir en** ∼ go by boat

**bario** m barium

**barítono** m baritone

**barman** m (*pl* **barmans**) barman

**barniz** m varnish; (*para loza etc*) glaze; (*fig*) veneer. ∼ar [10] vt varnish; glaze ⟨*loza etc*⟩

**bar|ométrico** a barometric. ∼ómetro** m barometer

**bar|ón** m baron. ∼onesa f baroness

**barquero** m boatman

**barra** f bar; (*pan*) French bread; (*de oro o plata*) ingot; (*palanca*) lever. ∼ **de labios** lipstick. **no pararse en** ∼s stop at nothing

**barrabasada** f mischief, prank

**barraca** f hut; (*vivienda pobre*) shack, shanty

**barranco** m ravine, gully; (*despeñadero*) cliff, precipice

**barre|dera** f road-sweeper. ∼dura f rubbish. ∼minas m invar mine-sweeper

**barren|a** f drill, bit. ∼ar vt drill. ∼o m large (mechanical) drill. **entrar en** ∼a ⟨*avión*⟩ go into a spin

**barrer** vt sweep; (*quitar*) sweep aside

**barrera** f barrier. ∼ **del sonido** sound barrier

**barriada** f district

**barrica** f barrel

**barricada** f barricade

**barrido** m sweeping

**barrig|a** f (pot-)belly. ~**ón** a, ~**udo** a pot-bellied

**barril** m barrel. ~**ete** m keg, small barrel

**barrio** m district, area. ~**bajero** a vulgar, common. ~**s bajos** poor quarter, poor area. **el otro** ~ (fig, fam) the other world

**barro** m mud; (arcilla) clay; (arcilla cocida) earthenware

**barroco** a Baroque. • m Baroque style

**barrote** m heavy bar

**barrunt|ar** vt sense, have a feeling. ~**e** m, ~**o** m sign; (presentimiento) feeling

**bartola** f. **tenderse a la** ~, **tumbarse a la** ~ take it easy

**bártulos** mpl things. **liar los** ~ pack one's bags

**barullo** m uproar; (confusión) confusion. **a** ~ galore

**basa** f, **basamento** m base; (fig) basis

**basar** vt base. ~**se** vpr. ~**se en** be based on

**basc|a** f crowd. ~**as** fpl nausea. ~**osidad** f filth. **la** ~**a** the gang

**báscula** f scales

**bascular** vi tilt

**base** f base; (fig) basis, foundation. **a** ~ **de** thanks to; (mediante) by means of; (en una receta) as the basic ingredient(s). **a** ~ **de bien** very well. **partiendo de la** ~ **de**, **tomando como** ~ on the basis of

**básico** a basic

**basílica** f basilica

**basilisco** m basilisk. **hecho un** ~ furious

**basta** f tack, tacking stitch

**bastante** a enough; (varios) quite a few, quite a lot of. • adv rather, fairly; (mucho tiempo) long enough; (suficiente) enough; (Mex, muy) very

**bastar** vi be enough. ¡**basta**! that's enough! **basta decir que** suffice it to say that. **basta y sobra** that's more than enough

**bastardilla** f italics. **poner en** ~ italicize

**bastardo** m bastard; (fig, vil) mean, base

**bastidor** m frame; (auto) chassis. ~**es** mpl (en el teatro) wings. **entre** ~**es** behind the scenes

**bastión** f (incl fig) bastion

**basto** a coarse. ~**s** mpl (naipes) clubs

**bast|ón** m walking stick. **empuñar el** ~**ón** take command. ~**onazo** m blow with a stick

**basur|a** f rubbish, garbage (Amer); (en la calle) litter. ~**ero** m dustman (Brit), garbage collector (Amer); (sitio) rubbish dump; (recipiente) dustbin (Brit), garbage can (Amer). **cubo** m **de la** ~**a** dustbin (Brit), garbage can (Amer)

**bata** f dressing-gown; (de médico etc) white coat. ~ **de cola** Flamenco dress

**batall|a** f battle. ~**a campal** pitched battle. ~**ador** a fighting. • m fighter. ~**ar** vi battle, fight. ~**ón** m battalion. • a. **cuestión** f **batallona** vexed question. **de** ~**a** everyday

**batata** f sweet potato

**bate** m bat. ~**ador** m batter; (cricket) batsman

**batería** f battery; (mus) percussion. ~ **de cocina** kitchen utensils, pots and pans

**batido** a beaten; (nata) whipped. • m batter; (bebida) milk shake. ~**ra** f beater. ~**ra eléctrica** mixer

**batín** m dressing-gown

**batir** vt beat; (martillar) hammer; mint (monedas); whip (nata); (derribar) knock down. ~ **el récord** break the record. ~ **palmas** clap. ~**se** vpr fight

**batuta** f baton. **llevar la** ~ be in command, be the boss

**baúl** m trunk; (LAm, auto) boot (Brit), trunk (Amer)

**bauti|smal** a baptismal. ~**smo** m baptism, christening. ~**sta** a & m & f Baptist. ~**zar** [10] vt baptize, christen

**baya** f berry

**bayeta** f (floor-)cloth

**bayoneta** f bayonet. ~**zo** m (golpe) bayonet thrust; (herida) bayonet wound

**baza** f (naipes) trick; (fig) advantage. **meter** ~ interfere

**bazar** m bazaar

**bazofia** f leftovers; (basura) rubbish

**beat|itud** f (fig) bliss. ~**o** a blessed; (de religiosidad afectada) sanctimonious

**bebé** m baby

**beb|edero** m drinking trough; (sitio) watering place. ~**edizo** a drinkable. ● *m* potion; (*veneno*) poison. ~**edor** *a* drinking. ● *m* heavy drinker. ~**er** *vt/i* drink. **dar de** ~**er a uno** give s.o. a drink. ~**ida** *f* drink. ~**ido** *a* tipsy, drunk

**beca** *f* grant, scholarship. ~**rio** *m* scholarship holder, scholar

**becerro** *m* calf

**befa** *f* jeer, taunt. ~**r** *vt* scoff at. ~**rse** *vpr*. ~**rse de** scoff at. **hacer** ~ **de** scoff at

**beige** /beis, bes/ *a* & *m* beige

**béisbol** *m* baseball

**beldad** *f* beauty

**belén** *m* crib, nativity scene; (*barullo*) confusion

**belga** *a* & *m* & *f* Belgian

**Bélgica** *f* Belgium

**bélico** *a*, **belicoso** *a* warlike

**beligerante** *a* belligerent

**bella|co** *a* wicked. ● *m* rogue. ~**quear** *vi* cheat. ~**quería** *f* dirty trick

**bell|eza** *f* beauty. ~**o** *a* beautiful. ~**as artes** *fpl* fine arts

**bellota** *f* acorn

**bemol** *m* flat. **tener (muchos)** ~**es** be difficult

**bencina** *f* (*Arg, gasolina*) petrol (*Brit*), gasoline (*Amer*)

**bend|ecir** [46 *pero imperativo* **bendice**, *futuro, condicional y pp regulares*] *vt* bless. ~**ición** *f* blessing. ~**ito** *a* blessed, holy; (*que tiene suerte*) lucky; (*feliz*) happy

**benefactor** *m* benefactor. ~**a** *f* benefactress

**benefic|encia** *f* (*organización pública*) charity. ~**iar** *vt* benefit. ~**iarse** *vpr* benefit. ~**iario** *m* beneficiary; (*de un cheque etc*) payee. ~**io** *m* benefit; (*ventaja*) advantage; (*ganancia*) profit, gain. ~**ioso** *a* beneficial, advantageous

**benéfico** *a* beneficial; (*de beneficencia*) charitable

**benemérito** *a* worthy

**beneplácito** *m* approval

**ben|evolencia** *f* benevolence. ~**évolo** *a* benevolent

**bengala** *f* flare. **luz** *f* **de B**~ flare

**benign|idad** *f* kindness; (*falta de gravedad*) mildness. ~**o** *a* kind; (*moderado*) gentle, mild; (*tumor*) benign

**beodo** *a* drunk

**berberecho** *m* cockle

**berenjena** *f* aubergine (*Brit*), eggplant. ~**l** *m* (*fig*) mess

**bermejo** *a* red

**berr|ear** *vi* (*animales*) low, bellow; (*niño*) howl; (*cantar mal*) screech. ~**ido** *m* bellow; (*de niño*) howl; (*de cantante*) screech

**berrinche** *m* temper; (*de un niño*) tantrum

**berro** *m* watercress

**berza** *f* cabbage

**besamel(a)** *f* white sauce

**bes|ar** *vt* kiss; (*rozar*) brush against. ~**arse** *vpr* kiss (each other); (*tocarse*) touch each other. ~**o** *m* kiss

**bestia** *f* beast; (*bruto*) brute; (*idiota*) idiot. ~ **de carga** beast of burden. ~**l** *a* bestial, animal; (*fig, fam*) terrific. ~**lidad** *f* bestiality; (*acción brutal*) horrid thing

**besugo** *m* sea-bream. **ser un** ~ be stupid

**besuquear** *vt* cover with kisses

**betún** *m* bitumen; (*para el calzado*) shoe polish

**biberón** *m* feeding-bottle

**Biblia** *f* Bible

**bíblico** *a* biblical

**bibliografía** *f* bibliography

**biblioteca** *f* library; (*librería*) bookcase. ~ **de consulta** reference library. ~ **de préstamo** lending library. ~**rio** *m* librarian

**bicarbonato** *m* bicarbonate. ~ **sódico** bicarbonate of soda

**bici** *f* (*fam*) bicycle, bike (*fam*). ~**cleta** *f* bicycle. **ir en** ~**cleta** go by bicycle, cycle. **montar en** ~**cleta** ride a bicycle

**bicolor** *a* two-colour

**bicultural** *a* bicultural

**bicho** *m* (*animal*) small animal, creature; (*insecto*) insect. ~ **raro** odd sort. **cualquier** ~ **viviente, todo** ~ **viviente** everyone

**bidé** *m*, **bidet** *m* bidet

**bidón** *m* drum, can

**bien** *adv* (*mejor*) well; (*muy*) very, quite; (*correctamente*) right; (*de buena gana*) willingly. ● *m* good; (*efectos*) property; (*provecho*) advantage, benefit. ¡~! fine!, OK!, good! ~... **(o)** ~ either... or. ~ **que** although. ¡**está** ~! fine! alright! **más** ~ rather. ¡**muy** ~! good! **no** ~ as soon as. ¡**qué** ~! marvellous!, great! (*fam*) **si** ~ although

**bienal** *a* biennial

**bien**~**aventurado** *a* fortunate. ~**estar** *m* well-being. ~**hablado** *a* well-spoken. ~**hechor** *m* benefactor.

~**hechora** f benefactress. ~**intencionado** a well-meaning

**bienio** m two years, two year-period

**bien:** ~**quistar** vt reconcile. ~**quistarse** vpr become reconciled. ~**quisto** a well-liked

**bienvenid|a** f welcome. ~**o** a welcome. ¡~**o!** welcome! **dar la** ~**a a uno** welcome s.o.

**bife** m (Arg), **biftek** m steak

**bifurca|ción** f fork, junction. ~**rse** [7] vpr fork

**b|igamia** f bigamy. ~**ígamo** a bigamous. ● m & f bigamist

**bigot|e** m moustache. ~**udo** a with a big moustache

**bikini** m bikini; (culin) toasted cheese and ham sandwich

**bilingüe** a bilingual

**billar** m billiards

**billete** m ticket; (de banco) note (Brit), bill (Amer). ~ **de banco** banknote. ~ **de ida y vuelta** return ticket (Brit), round-trip ticket (Amer). ~ **sencillo** single ticket (Brit), one-way ticket (Amer). ~**ro** m, ~**ra** f wallet, billfold (Amer)

**billón** m billion (Brit), trillion (Amer)

**bimbalete** m (Mex) swing

**bi|mensual** a fortnightly, twice-monthly. ~**mestral** a two-monthly. ~**motor** a twin-engined. ● m twin-engined plane

**biodegradable** a biodegradable

**bi|ografía** f biography. ~**ográfico** a biographical. ~**ógrafo** m biographer

**bi|ología** f biology. ~**ológico** a biological. ~**ólogo** m biologist

**biombo** m folding screen

**biopsia** f biopsy

**bioquímic|a** f biochemistry; (persona) biochemist. ~**o** m biochemist

**bípedo** m biped

**biplano** m biplane

**biquini** m bikini

**birlar** vt (fam) steal, pinch (fam)

**birlibirloque** m. **por arte de** ~ (as if) by magic

**Birmania** f Burma

**birmano** a & m Burmese

**biromen** m (Arg) ball-point pen

**bis** m encore. ● adv twice. ¡~**!** encore! **vivo en el 3** ~ I live at 3A

**bisabuel|a** f great-grandmother. ~**o** m great-grandfather. ~**os** mpl great-grandparents

**bisagra** f hinge

**bisar** vt encore

**bisbise|ar** vt whisper. ~**o** m whisper(ing)

**bisemanal** a twice-weekly

**bisiesto** a leap. **año** m ~ leap year

**bisniet|a** f great-granddaughter. ~**o** m great-grandson. ~**os** mpl great-grandchildren

**bisonte** m bison

**bisté** m, **bistec** m steak

**bisturí** m scalpel

**bisutería** f imitation jewellery, costume jewellery

**bizco** a cross-eyed. **quedarse** ~ be dumbfounded

**bizcocho** m sponge (cake); (Mex, galleta) biscuit

**bizquear** vi squint

**blanc|a** f white woman; (mus) minim. ~**o** a white; ‹tez› fair. ● m white; (persona) white man; (intervalo) interval; (espacio) blank; (objetivo) target. ~**o de huevo** white of egg, egg-white. **dar en el** ~**o** hit the mark. **dejar en** ~**o** leave blank. **pasar la noche en** ~**o** have a sleepless night. ~**o y negro** black and white. ~**ura** f whiteness. ~**uzco** a whitish

**blandir** [24] vt brandish

**bland|o** a soft; ‹carácter› weak; (cobarde) cowardly; ‹palabras› gentle, tender. ~**ura** f softness. ~**uzco** a softish

**blanque|ar** vt whiten; white-wash ‹paredes›; bleach ‹tela›. ● vi turn white; (presentarse blanco) look white. ~**cino** a whitish. ~**o** m whitening

**blasfem|ador** a blasphemous. ● m blasphemer. ~**ar** vi blaspheme. ~**ia** f blasphemy. ~**o** a blasphemous. ● m blasphemer

**blas|ón** m coat of arms; (fig,) honour, glory. ~**onar** vt emblazon. ● vi boast (**de** of, about)

**bledo** m nothing. **me importa un** ~, **no se me da un** ~ I couldn't care less

**blinda|je** m armour. ~**r** vt armour

**bloc** m (pl **blocs**) pad

**bloque** m block; (pol) bloc. ~**ar** vt block; (mil) blockade; (com) freeze. ~**o** m blockade; (com) freezing. **en** ~ en bloc

**blusa** f blouse

**boato** m show, ostentation

**bob|ada** f silly thing. **~alicón** a stupid. **~ería** f silly thing. **decir ~adas** talk nonsense

**bobina** f bobbin, reel; (foto) spool; (elec) coil

**bobo** a silly, stupid. ● m idiot, fool

**boca** f mouth; (fig, entrada) entrance; (de cañón) muzzle; (agujero) hole. **~ abajo** face down. **~ arriba** face up. **a ~ de jarro** point-blank. **con la ~ abierta** dumbfounded

**bocacalle** f junction. **la primera ~ a la derecha** the first turning on the right

**bocad|illo** m sandwich; (comida ligera, fam) snack. **~o** m mouthful; (mordisco) bite; (de caballo) bit

**boca: ~jarro. a ~jarro** point-blank. **~manga** f cuff

**bocanada** f puff; (de vino etc) mouthful

**bocaza** f invar, **bocazas** f invar big-mouth

**boceto** m outline, sketch

**bocina** f horn. **~zo** m toot, blast. **tocar la ~** sound one's horn

**bock** m beer mug

**bocha** f bowl. **~s** fpl bowls

**bochinche** m uproar

**bochorno** m sultry weather; (fig, vergüenza) embarrassment. **~so** a oppressive; (fig) embarrassing. **¡qué ~!** how embarrassing!

**boda** f marriage; (ceremonia) wedding

**bodeg|a** f cellar; (de vino) wine cellar; (almacén) warehouse; (de un barco) hold. **~ón** m cheap restaurant; (pintura) still life

**bodoque** m pellet; (tonto, fam) thickhead

**bofes** mpl lights. **echar los ~** slog away

**bofet|ada** f slap; (fig) blow. **dar una ~ada a uno** slap s.o. in the face. **darse de ~adas** clash. **~ón** m punch

**boga** m & f rower; (hombre) oarsman; (mujer) oarswoman; (moda) fashion. **estar en ~** be in fashion, be in vogue. **~da** f stroke (of the oar). **~dor** rower, oarsman. **~r** [12] vt row. **~vante** m (crustáceo) lobster

**Bogotá** f Bogotá

**bogotano** a from Bogotá. ● m native of Bogotá

**bohemio** a & m Bohemian

**bohío** m (LAm) hut

**boicot** m (pl **boicots**) boycott. **~ear** vt boycott. **~eo** m boycott. **hacer el ~** boycott

**boina** f beret

**boîte** /bwat/ m night-club

**bola** f ball; (canica) marble; (naipes) slam; (betún) shoe polish; (mentira) fib; (Mex, reunión desordenada) rowdy party. **~ del mundo** (fam) globe. **contar ~s** tell fibs. **dejar que ruede la ~** let things take their course. **meter ~s** tell fibs

**bolas** fpl (LAm) bolas

**boleada** f (Mex) polishing of shoes

**boleadoras** (LAm) fpl bolas

**bolera** f bowling alley

**bolero** m (baile, chaquetilla) bolero; (fig, mentiroso, fam) liar; (Mex, limpiabotas) bootblack

**boletín** m bulletin; (publicación periódica) journal; (escolar) report. **~ de noticias** news bulletin. **~ de precios** price list. **~ informativo** news bulletin. **~ meteorológico** weather forecast

**boleto** m (esp LAm) ticket

**boli** m (fam) Biro (P), ball-point pen

**boliche** m (juego) bowls; (bolera) bowling alley

**bolígrafo** m Biro (P), ball-point pen

**bolillo** m bobbin; (Mex, panecillo) (bread) roll

**bolívar** m (unidad monetaria venezolana) bolívar

**Bolivia** f Bolivia

**boliviano** a Bolivian. ● m Bolivian; (unidad monetaria de Bolivia) boliviano

**bolo** m skittle

**bolsa** f bag; (monedero) purse; (LAm, bolsillo) pocket; (com) stock exchange; (cavidad) cavity. **~ de agua caliente** hot-water bottle

**bolsillo** m pocket; (monedero) purse. **de ~** pocket

**bolsista** m & f stockbroker

**bolso** m (de mujer) handbag

**boll|ería** f baker's shop. **~ero** m baker. **~o** m roll; (con azúcar) bun; (abolladura) dent; (chichón) lump; (fig, jaleo, fam) fuss

**bomba** f bomb; (máquina) pump; (noticia) bombshell. **~ de aceite** (auto) oil pump. **~ de agua** (auto) water pump. **~ de incendios** fire-engine. **pasarlo ~** have a marvellous time

**bombach|as** fpl (LAm) knickers, pants. **~o** m (esp Mex) baggy trousers, baggy pants (Amer)

**bombarde|ar** vt bombard; (mil) bomb. **~o** m bombardment; (mil) bombing. **~ro** m (avión) bomber

**bombazo** m explosion

**bombear** vt pump; (mil) bomb

**bombero** m fireman. **cuerpo** m **de ~s** fire brigade (Brit), fire department (Amer)

**bombilla** f (light) bulb; (LAm, para maté) pipe for drinking maté; (Mex, cucharón) ladle

**bombín** m pump; (sombrero, fam) bowler (hat) (Brit), derby (Amer)

**bombo** m (tambor) bass drum. **a ~ y platillos** with a lot of fuss

**bomb|ón** m chocolate. **ser un ~ón** be a peach. **~ona** f container. **~onera** f chocolate box

**bonachón** a easygoing; (bueno) good-natured

**bonaerense** a from Buenos Aires. ● m native of Buenos Aires

**bonanza** f (naut) fair weather; (prosperidad) prosperity. **ir en ~** (naut) have fair weather; (fig) go well

**bondad** f goodness; (amabilidad) kindness. **tenga la ~ de** would you be kind enough to. **~osamente** adv kindly. **~oso** a kind

**bongo** m (LAm) canoe

**boniato** m sweet potato

**bonito** a nice; (mono) pretty. **¡muy ~!**, **¡qué ~!** that's nice!, very nice!. ● m bonito

**bono** m voucher; (título) bond. **~ del Tesoro** government bond

**boñiga** f dung

**boqueada** f gasp. **dar las ~s** be dying

**boquerón** m anchovy

**boquete** m hole; (brecha) breach

**boquiabierto** a open-mouthed; (fig) amazed, dumbfounded. **quedarse ~** be amazed

**boquilla** f mouthpiece; (para cigarillos) cigarette-holder; (filtro de cigarillo) tip

**borboll|ar** vi bubble. **~ón** m bubble. **hablar a ~ones** gabble. **salir a ~ones** gush out

**borbot|ar** vt bubble. **~ón** m bubble. **hablar a ~ones** gabble. **salir a ~ones** gush out

**bordado** a embroidered. ● m embroidery. **quedar ~**, **salir ~** come out very well

**bordante** m (Mex) lodger

**bordar** vt embroider; (fig, fam) do very well

**bord|e** m edge; (de carretera) side; (de plato etc) rim; (de un vestido) hem. **~ear** vt go round the edge of; (fig) border on. **~illo** m kerb. **al ~e de** on the edge of; (fig) on the brink of

**bordo** m board. **a ~** on board

**borinqueño** a & m Puerto Rican

**borla** f tassel

**borra** f flock; (pelusa) fluff; (sedimento) sediment

**borrach|era** f drunkenness. **~ín** m drunkard. **~o** a drunk. ● m drunkard; (temporalmente) drunk. **estar ~o** be drunk. **ni ~o** never in a million years. **ser ~o** be a drunkard

**borrador** m rough copy; (libro) rough notebook

**borradura** f crossing-out

**borrajear** vt/i scribble

**borrar** vt rub out; (tachar) cross out

**borrasc|a** f storm. **~oso** a stormy

**borreg|o** m year-old lamb; (fig) simpleton; (Mex, noticia falsa) hoax. **~uil** a meek

**borric|ada** f silly thing. **~o** m donkey; (fig, fam) ass

**borrón** m smudge; (fig, imperfección) blemish; (de una pintura) sketch. **~ y cuenta nueva** let's forget about it!

**borroso** a blurred; (fig) vague

**bos|caje** m thicket. **~coso** a wooded. **~que** m wood, forest. **~quecillo** m copse

**bosquej|ar** vt sketch. **~o** m sketch

**bosta** f dung

**bostez|ar** [10] vi yawn. **~o** m yawn

**bota** f boot; (recipiente) leather wine bottle

**botadero** m (Mex) ford

**botánic|a** f botany. **~o** a botanical. ● m botanist

**botar** vt launch. ● vi bounce. **estar que bota** be hopping mad

**botarat|ada** f silly thing. **~e** m idiot

**bote** m bounce; (golpe) blow; (salto) jump; (sacudida) jolt; (lata) tin, can; (vasija) jar; (en un bar) jar for tips; (barca) boat. **~ salvavidas** lifeboat. **de ~ en ~** packed

**botell|a** f bottle. **~ita** f small bottle

**botica** f chemist's (shop) (Brit), drugstore (Amer). **~rio** m chemist (Brit), druggist (Amer)

**botija** f, **botijo** m earthenware jug

**botín** m half boot; (despojos) booty; (LAm, calcetín) sock

**botiquín** *m* medicine chest; (*de primeros auxilios*) first aid kit

**bot|ón** *m* button; (*yema*) bud. **~onadura** *f* buttons. **~ón de oro** buttercup. **~ones** *m invar* bellboy (*Brit*), bellhop (*Amer*)

**botulismo** *m* botulism

**boutique** /buˈtik/ *m* boutique

**bóveda** *f* vault

**boxe|ador** *m* boxer. **~ar** *vi* box. **~o** *m* boxing

**boya** *f* buoy; (*corcho*) float. **~nte** *a* buoyant

**bozal** *m* (*de perro etc*) muzzle; (*de caballo*) halter

**bracear** *vi* wave one's arms; (*nadar*) swim, crawl

**bracero** *m* labourer. **de ~** (*fam*) arm in arm

**braga** *f* underpants, knickers; (*cuerda*) rope. **~dura** *f* crotch. **~s** *fpl* knickers, pants. **~zas** *m invar* (*fam*) henpecked man

**bragueta** *f* flies

**braille** /breil/ *m* Braille

**bram|ar** *vi* roar; (*vaca*) moo; (*viento*) howl. **~ido** *m* roar

**branquia** *f* gill

**bras|a** *f* hot coal. **a la ~a** grilled. **~ero** *m* brazier; (*LAm, hogar*) hearth

**Brasil** *m*. **el ~** Brazil

**brasile|ño** *a & m* Brazilian. **~ro** *a & m* (*LAm*) Brazilian

**bravata** *f* boast

**bravío** *a* wild; ‹*persona*› coarse, uncouth

**brav|o** *a* brave; ‹*animales*› wild; ‹*mar*› rough. ¡**~!** *int* well done! bravo! **~ura** *f* ferocity; (*valor*) courage

**braz|a** *f* fathom. **nadar a ~a** do the breast-stroke. **~ada** *f* waving of the arms; (*en natación*) stroke; (*cantidad*) armful. **~ado** *m* armful. **~al** *m* arm-band. **~alete** *m* bracelet; (*brazal*) arm-band. **~o** *m* arm; (*de animales*) foreleg; (*rama*) branch. **~o derecho** right-hand man. **a ~o** by hand. **del ~o** arm in arm

**brea** *f* tar, pitch

**brear** *vt* ill-treat

**brécol** *m* broccoli

**brecha** *f* gap; (*mil*) breach; (*med*) gash. **estar en la ~** be in the thick of it

**brega** *f* struggle. **~r** [12] *vi* struggle; (*trabajar mucho*) work hard, slog away. **andar a la ~** work hard

**breña** *f*, **breñal** *m* scrub

**Bretaña** *f* Brittany. **Gran ~** Great Britain

**breve** *a* short. **~dad** *f* shortness. **en ~** soon, shortly. **en ~s momentos** soon

**brez|al** *m* moor. **~o** *m* heather

**brib|ón** *m* rogue, rascal. **~onada** *f*, **~onería** *f* dirty trick

**brida** *f* bridle. **a toda ~** at full speed

**bridge** /britʃ/ *m* bridge

**brigada** *f* squad; (*mil*) brigade. **general de ~** brigadier (*Brit*), brigadier-general (*Amer*)

**brill|ante** *a* brilliant. ● *m* diamond. **~antez** *f* brilliance. **~ar** *vi* shine; (*centellear*) sparkle. **~o** *m* shine; (*brillantez*) brilliance; (*centelleo*) sparkle. **dar ~o, sacar ~o** polish

**brinc|ar** [7] *vi* jump up and down. **~o** *m* jump. **dar un ~o** jump. **estar que brinca** be hopping mad. **pegar un ~o** jump

**brind|ar** *vt* offer. ● *vi*. **~ar por** toast, drink a toast to. **~is** *m* toast

**br|ío** *m* energy; (*decisión*) determination. **~ioso** *a* spirited; (*garboso*) elegant

**brisa** *f* breeze

**británico** *a* British. ● *m* Briton, British person

**brocado** *m* brocade

**bróculi** *m* broccoli

**brocha** *f* paintbrush; (*para afeitarse*) shaving-brush

**broche** *m* clasp, fastener; (*joya*) brooch; (*Arg, sujetapapeles*) paperclip

**brocheta** *f* skewer

**brom|a** *f* joke. **~a pesada** practical joke. **~ear** *vi* joke. **~ista** *a* fun-loving. ● *m & f* joker. **de ~a, en ~a** in fun. **ni de ~a** never in a million years

**bronca** *f* row; (*represión*) telling-off

**bronce** *m* bronze. **~ado** *a* bronze; (*por el sol*) tanned, sunburnt. **~ar** *vt* tan ‹*piel*›. **~arse** *vpr* get a suntan

**bronco** *a* rough

**bronquitis** *f* bronchitis

**broqueta** *f* skewer

**brot|ar** *vi* ‹*plantas*› bud, sprout; (*med*) break out; ‹*líquido*› gush forth; ‹*lágrimas*› well up. **~e** *m* bud, shoot; (*med*) outbreak; (*de líquido*) gushing; (*de lágrimas*) welling-up

**bruces** *mpl*. **de ~** face down(wards). **caer de ~** fall flat on one's face

**bruj|a** f witch. ● a (Mex) penniless. **~ear** vi practise witchcraft. **~ería** f witchcraft. **~o** m wizard, magician; (LAm) medicine man

**brújula** f compass

**brum|a** f mist; (fig) confusion. **~oso** a misty, foggy

**bruñi|do** m polish. **~r** [22] vt polish

**brusco** a (repentino) sudden; ⟨persona⟩ brusque

**Bruselas** fpl Brussels

**brusquedad** f abruptness

**brut|al** a brutal. **~alidad** f brutality; (estupidez) stupidity. **~o** a (estúpido) stupid; (tosco) rough, uncouth; ⟨peso, sueldo⟩ gross

**bucal** a oral

**buce|ar** vi dive; (fig) explore. **~o** m diving

**bucle** m curl

**budín** m pudding

**budis|mo** m Buddhism. **~ta** m & f Buddhist

**buen** véase bueno

**buenamente** adv easily; (voluntariamente) willingly

**buenaventura** f good luck; (adivinación) fortune. **decir la ~ a uno, echar la ~ a uno** tell s.o.'s fortune

**bueno** a (delante de nombre masculino en singular **buen**) good; (apropiado) fit; (amable) kind; ⟨tiempo⟩ fine. ● int well!; (de acuerdo) OK!, very well! **¡buena la has hecho!** you've gone and done it now! **¡buenas noches!** good night! **¡buenas tardes!** (antes del atardecer) good afternoon!; (después del atardecer) good evening! **¡~s días!** good morning! **estar de buenas** be in a good mood. **por las buenas** willingly

**Buenos** Aires m Buenos Aires

**buey** m ox

**búfalo** m buffalo

**bufanda** f scarf

**bufar** vi snort. **estar que bufa** be hopping mad

**bufete** m (mesa) writing-desk; (despacho) lawyer's office

**bufido** m snort; (de ira) outburst

**buf|o** a comic. **~ón** a comical. ● m buffoon. **~onada** f joke

**bugle** m bugle

**buharda** f, **buhardilla** f attic; (ventana) dormer window

**búho** m owl

**buhoner|ía** f pedlar's wares. **~o** m pedlar

**buitre** m vulture

**bujía** f candle; (auto) spark(ing)-plug

**bula** f bull

**bulbo** m bulb

**bulevar** m avenue, boulevard

**Bulgaria** f Bulgaria

**búlgaro** a & m Bulgarian

**bulo** m hoax

**bulto** m (volumen) volume; (tamaño) size; (forma) shape; (paquete) package; (protuberancia) lump. **a ~** roughly

**bulla** f uproar; (muchedumbre) crowd

**bullicio** m hubbub; (movimiento) bustle. **~so** a bustling; (ruidoso) noisy

**bullir** [22] vt stir, move. ● vi boil; (burbujear) bubble; (fig) bustle

**buñuelo** m doughnut; (fig) mess

**BUP** abrev (Bachillerato Unificado Polivalente) secondary school education

**buque** m ship, boat

**burbuj|a** f bubble. **~ear** vi bubble; ⟨vino⟩ sparkle. **~eo** m bubbling

**burdel** m brothel

**burdo** a rough, coarse; ⟨excusa⟩ clumsy

**burgu|és** a middle-class, bourgeois. ● m middle-class person. **~esía** f middle class, bourgeoisie

**burla** f taunt; (broma) joke; (engaño) trick. **~dor** a mocking. ● m seducer. **~r** vt trick, deceive; (seducir) seduce. **~rse** vpr. **~rse de** mock, make fun of

**burlesco** a funny

**burlón** a mocking

**bur|ocracia** f civil service. **~ócrata** m & f civil servant. **~ocrático** a bureaucratic

**burro** m donkey; (fig) ass

**bursátil** a stock-exchange

**bus** m (fam) bus

**busca** f search. **a la ~ de** in search of. **en ~ de** in search of

**busca: ~pié** m feeler. **~pleitos** m invar (LAm) trouble-maker

**buscar** [7] vt look for. ● vi look. **buscársela** ask for it. **ir a ~ a uno** fetch s.o.

**buscarruidos** m invar trouble-maker

**buscona** f prostitute

**busilis** m snag

**búsqueda** f search

**busto** m bust

**butaca** f armchair; (en el teatro etc) seat

**butano** m butane

**buzo** m diver

**buzón** m postbox (Brit), mailbox (Amer)

# C

**Cu** abrev (Calle) St, Street, Rd, Road

**cabal** a exact; (completo) complete. **no estar en sus ~es** not be in one's right mind

**cabalga|dura** f mount, horse. **~r** [12] vt ride. ● vi ride, go riding. **~ta** f ride; (desfile) procession

**cabalmente** adv completely; (exactamente) exactly

**caballa** f mackerel

**caballada** f (LAm) stupid thing

**caballeresco** a gentlemanly. **literatura** f **caballeresca** books of chivalry

**caballer|ía** f mount, horse. **~iza** f stable. **~izo** m groom

**caballero** m gentleman; (de orden de caballería) knight; (tratamiento) sir. **~samente** adv like a gentleman. **~so** a gentlemanly

**caballete** m (del tejado) ridge; (de la nariz) bridge; (de pintor) easel

**caballito** m pony. **~ del diablo** dragonfly. **~ de mar** sea-horse. **los ~s** (tiovivo) merry-go-round

**caballo** m horse; (del ajedrez) knight; (de la baraja española) queen. **~ de vapor** horsepower. **a ~** on horseback

**cabaña** f hut

**cabaret** /kaba're/ m (pl **cabarets** /kaba're/) night-club

**cabece|ar** vi nod; (para negar) shake one's head. **~o** m nodding, nod; (acción de negar) shake of the head

**cabecera** f (de la cama, de la mesa) head; (en un impreso) heading

**cabecilla** m leader

**cabell|o** m hair. **~os** mpl hair. **~udo** a hairy

**caber** [28] vi fit (**en** into). **los libros no caben en la caja** the books won't fit into the box. **no cabe duda** there's no doubt

**cabestr|illo** m sling. **~o** m halter

**cabeza** f head; (fig, inteligencia) intelligence. **~da** f butt; (golpe recibido) blow; (saludo, al dormirse) nod. **~zo** m butt; (en fútbol) header. **andar de ~** have a lot to do. **dar una ~da** nod off

**cabida** f capacity; (extensión) area. **dar ~ a** leave room for, leave space for

**cabina** f (de avión) cabin, cockpit; (electoral) booth; (de camión) cab. **~ telefónica** telephone box (Brit), telephone booth (Amer)

**cabizbajo** a crestfallen

**cable** m cable

**cabo** m end; (trozo) bit; (mil) corporal; (mango) handle; (geog) cape; (naut) rope. **al ~** eventually. **al ~ de una hora** after an hour. **de ~ a rabo** from beginning to end. **llevar(se) a ~** carry out

**cabr|a** f goat. **~a montesa** f mountain goat. **~iola** f jump, skip. **~itilla** f kid. **~ito** m kid

**cabrón** m cuckold

**cabuya** f (LAm) pita, agave

**cacahuate** m (Mex), **cacahuete** m peanut

**cacao** m (planta y semillas) cacao; (polvo) cocoa; (fig) confusion

**cacare|ar** vt boast about. ● vi ⟨gallo⟩ crow; ⟨gallina⟩ cluck. **~o** m (incl fig) crowing; (de gallina) clucking

**cacería** f hunt

**cacerola** f casserole, saucepan

**caciqu|e** m cacique, Indian chief; (pol) cacique, local political boss. **~il** a despotic. **~ismo** m caciquism, despotism

**caco** m pickpocket, thief

**cacof|onía** f cacophony. **~ónico** a cacophonous

**cacto** m cactus

**cacumen** m acumen

**cacharro** m earthenware pot; (para flores) vase; (coche estropeado) wreck; (cosa inútil) piece of junk; (chisme) thing. **~s** mpl pots and pans

**cachear** vt frisk

**cachemir** m, **cachemira** f cashmere

**cacheo** m frisking

**cachetada** f (LAm), **cachete** m slap

**cachimba** f pipe

**cachiporra** f club, truncheon. **~zo** m blow with a club

**cachivache** m thing, piece of junk

**cacho** m bit, piece; (LAm, cuerno) horn; (miga) crumb

**cachondeo** m (fam) joking, joke

**cachorro** m (perrito) puppy; (de otros animales) young

**cada** *a invar* each, every. **~ uno** each one, everyone. **uno de ~ cinco** one in five

**cadalso** *m* scaffold

**cadáver** *m* corpse. **ingresar ~** be dead on arrival

**cadena** *f* chain; (*TV*) channel. **~ de fabricación** production line. **~ de montañas** mountain range. **~ perpetua** life imprisonment

**cadencia** *f* cadence, rhythm

**cadera** *f* hip

**cadete** *m* cadet

**caduc|ar** [7] *vi* expire. **~idad** *f*. **fecha** *f* **de ~idad** sell-by date. **~o** *a* decrepit

**cae|dizo** *a* unsteady. **~r** [29] *vi* fall. **~rse** *vpr* fall (over). **dejar ~r** drop. **estar al ~r** be about to happen. **este vestido no me ~ bien** this dress doesn't suit me. **hacer ~r** knock over. **Juan me ~ bien** I get on well with Juan. **su cumpleaños cayó en Martes** his birthday fell on a Tuesday

**café** *m* coffee; (*cafetería*) café. ● *a*. **color ~** coffee-coloured. **~ con leche** white coffee. **~ cortado** coffee with a little milk. **~ (solo)** black coffee

**cafe|ína** *f* caffeine. **~tal** *m* coffee plantation. **~tera** *f* coffee-pot. **~tería** *f* café. **~tero** *a* coffee

**caíd|a** *f* fall; (*disminución*) drop; (*pendiente*) slope. **~o** *a* fallen; (*abatido*) dejected. ● *m* fallen

**caigo** *vb véase* **caer**

**caimán** *m* cayman, alligator

**caj|a** *f* box; (*grande*) case; (*de caudales*) safe; (*donde se efectúan los pagos*) cash desk; (*en supermercado*) check-out. **~a de ahorros** savings bank. **~a de caudales**, **~a fuerte** safe. **~a postal de ahorros** post office savings bank. **~a registradora** till. **~ero** *m* cashier. **~etilla** *f* packet. **~ita** *f* small box. **~ón** *m* large box; (*de mueble*) drawer; (*puesto de mercado*) stall. **ser de ~ón** be a matter of course

**cal** *m* lime

**cala** *f* cove

**calaba|cín** *m* marrow; (*fig, idiota, fam*) idiot. **~za** *f* pumpkin; (*fig, idiota, fam*) idiot

**calabozo** *m* prison; (*celda*) cell

**calado** *a* soaked. ● *m* (*naut*) draught. **estar ~ hasta los huesos** be soaked to the skin

**calamar** *m* squid

**calambre** *m* cramp

**calami|dad** *f* calamity, disaster. **~toso** *a* calamitous, disastrous

**calar** *vt* soak; (*penetrar*) pierce; (*fig, penetrar*) see through; sample (*fruta*). **~se** *vpr* get soaked; (*zapatos*) leak; (*auto*) stall

**calavera** *f* skull

**calcar** [7] *vt* trace; (*fig*) copy

**calceta** *f*. **hacer ~** knit

**calcetín** *m* sock

**calcinar** *vt* burn

**calcio** *m* calcium

**calco** *m* tracing. **~manía** *f* transfer. **papel** *m* **de ~** tracing-paper

**calcula|dor** *a* calculating. **~dora** *f* calculator. **~dora de bolsillo** pocket calculator. **~r** *vt* calculate; (*suponer*) reckon, think

**cálculo** *m* calculation; (*fig*) reckoning

**caldea|miento** *m* heating. **~r** *vt* heat, warm. **~rse** *vpr* get hot

**calder|a** *f* boiler; (*Arg, para café*) coffee-pot; (*Arg, para té*) teapot. **~eta** *f* small boiler

**calderilla** *f* small change, coppers

**calder|o** *m* small boiler. **~ón** *m* large boiler

**caldo** *m* stock; (*sopa*) soup, broth. **poner a ~ a uno** give s.o. a dressing-down

**calefacción** *f* heating. **~ central** central heating

**caleidoscopio** *m* kaleidoscope

**calendario** *m* calendar

**caléndula** *f* marigold

**calenta|dor** *m* heater. **~miento** *m* heating; (*en deportes*) warm-up. **~r** [1] *vt* heat, warm. **~rse** *vpr* get hot, warm up

**calentur|a** *f* fever, (high) temperature. **~iento** *a* feverish

**calibr|ar** *vt* calibrate; (*fig*) measure. **~e** *m* calibre; (*diámetro*) diameter; (*fig*) importance

**calidad** *f* quality; (*función*) capacity. **en ~ de** as

**cálido** *a* warm

**calidoscopio** *m* kaleidoscope

**caliente** *a* hot, warm; (*fig, enfadado*) angry

**califica|ción** *f* qualification; (*evaluación*) assessment; (*nota*) mark. **~r** [7] *vt* qualify; (*evaluar*) assess; mark (*examen etc*). **~r de** describe as, label. **~tivo** *a* qualifying. ● *m* epithet

**caliz|a** f limestone. **~o** a lime
**calm|a** f calm. ¡**~a!** calm down!
**~ante** a & m sedative. **~ar** vt calm,
soothe. ● vi ⟨viento⟩ abate. **~arse**
vpr calm down; ⟨viento⟩ abate.
**~oso** a calm; ⟨flemático, fam⟩
phlegmatic. **en ~a** calm. **perder la**
**~a** lose one's composure
**calor** m heat, warmth. **hace ~** it's
hot. **tener ~** be hot
**caloría** f calorie
**calorífero** m heater
**calumni|a** f calumny; ⟨oral⟩ slander;
⟨escrita⟩ libel. **~ar** vt slander; ⟨por
escrito⟩ libel. **~oso** a slanderous;
⟨cosa escrita⟩ libellous
**caluros|amente** adv warmly. **~o** a
warm
**calv|a** f bald patch. **~ero** m clearing.
**~icie** f baldness. **~o** a bald; ⟨te-
rreno⟩ barren
**calza** f ⟨fam⟩ stocking; ⟨cuña⟩ wedge
**calzada** f road
**calza|do** a wearing shoes. ● m foot-
wear, shoe. **~dor** m shoehorn. **~r**
[10] vt put shoes on; ⟨llevar⟩ wear.
● vi wear shoes. ● vpr put on. ¿**qué**
**número calza Vd?** what size shoe do
you take?
**calz|ón** m shorts; ⟨ropa interior⟩
knickers, pants. **~ones** mpl shorts.
**~oncillos** mpl underpants
**calla|do** a quiet. **~r** vt silence; keep
⟨secreto⟩; hush up ⟨asunto⟩. ● vi be
quiet, keep quiet, shut up ⟨fam⟩.
**~rse** vpr be quiet, keep quiet, shut
up ⟨fam⟩. ¡**cállate!** be quiet! shut up!
⟨fam⟩
**calle** f street, road; ⟨en deportes, en
autopista⟩ lane. **~ de dirección**
**única** one-way street. **~ mayor** high
street, main street. **abrir ~** make
way
**callej|a** f narrow street. **~ear** vi wan-
der about the streets. **~ero** a street.
● m street plan. **~ón** m alley. **~uela**
f back street, side street. **~ón sin**
**salida** cul-de-sac
**call|ista** m & f chiropodist. **~o** m
corn, callus. **~os** mpl tripe. **~oso** a
hard, rough
**cama** f bed. **~ de matrimonio** double
bed. **~ individual** single bed. **caer en**
**la ~** fall ill. **guardar ~** be confined
to bed
**camada** f litter; ⟨fig, de ladrones⟩
gang
**camafeo** m cameo
**camaleón** m chameleon

**cámara** f room; ⟨de reyes⟩ royal
chamber; ⟨fotográfica⟩ camera; ⟨de
armas, pol⟩ chamber. **~ fotográfica**
camera. **a ~ lenta** in slow motion
**camarada** f colleague; ⟨amigo⟩
companion
**camarer|a** f chambermaid; ⟨de
restaurante etc⟩ waitress; ⟨en casa⟩
maid. **~o** m waiter
**camarín** m dressing-room; ⟨naut⟩
cabin
**camarón** m shrimp
**camarote** m cabin
**cambi|able** a changeable; ⟨com etc⟩
exchangeable. **~ante** a variable.
**~ar** vt change; ⟨trocar⟩ exchange.
● vi change. **~ar de idea** change
one's mind. **~arse** vpr change. **~o**
m change; ⟨com⟩ exchange rate;
⟨moneda menuda⟩ (small) change.
**~sta** m & f money-changer. **en ~o**
on the other hand
**camelia** f camellia
**camello** m camel
**camilla** f stretcher; ⟨sofá⟩ couch
**camina|nte** m traveller. **~r** vt cover.
● vi travel; ⟨andar⟩ walk; ⟨río,
astros etc⟩ move. **~ta** f long walk
**camino** m road; ⟨sendero⟩ path,
track; ⟨dirección, medio⟩ way. **~ de**
towards, on the way to. **abrir ~**
make way. **a medio ~, a la mitad**
**del ~** half-way. **de ~** on the way.
**ponerse en ~** set out
**cami|ón** m lorry; ⟨Mex, autobús⟩
bus. **~onero** m lorry-driver.
**~oneta** f van
**camis|a** f shirt; ⟨de un fruto⟩ skin. **~a**
**de dormir** nightdress. **~a de fuerza**
strait-jacket. **~ería** f shirt shop.
**~eta** f T-shirt; ⟨ropa interior⟩ vest.
**~ón** m nightdress
**camorra** f ⟨fam⟩ row. **buscar ~** look
for trouble, pick a quarrel
**camote** m ⟨LAm⟩ sweet potato
**campamento** m camp
**campan|a** f bell. **~ada** f stroke of a
bell; ⟨de reloj⟩ striking. **~ario** m bell
tower, belfry. **~eo** m peal of bells.
**~illa** f bell. **~udo** a bell-shaped;
⟨estilo⟩ bombastic
**campaña** f countryside; ⟨mil, pol⟩
campaign. **de ~** ⟨mil⟩ field
**campe|ón** a & m champion. **~onato**
m championship
**campes|ino** a country. ● m peasant.
**~tre** a country
**camping** /'kampin/ m ⟨pl **campings**
/'kampin/⟩ camping; ⟨lugar⟩
campsite. **hacer ~** go camping

**campiña** f countryside

**campo** m country; (*agricultura, fig*) field; (*de tenis*) court; (*de fútbol*) pitch; (*de golf*) course. **~santo** m cemetery

**camufla|do** a camouflaged. **~je** m camouflage. **~r** vt camouflage

**cana** f grey hair, white hair. **echar una ~ al aire** have a fling. **peinar ~s** be getting old

**Canadá** m. **el ~** Canada

**canadiense** a & m Canadian

**canal** m (*incl TV*) channel; (*artificial*) canal; (*del tejado*) gutter. **~ de la Mancha** English Channel. **~ de Panamá** Panama Canal. **~ón** m (*horizontal*) gutter; (*vertical*) drain-pipe

**canalla** f rabble. ● m (*fig, fam*) swine. **~da** f dirty trick

**canapé** m sofa, couch; (*culin*) canapé

**Canarias** fpl. **(las islas) ~** the Canary Islands, the Canaries

**canario** a of the Canary Islands. ● m native of the Canary Islands; (*pájaro*) canary

**canast|a** f (large) basket. **~illa** f small basket; (*para un bebé*) layette. **~illo** m small basket. **~o** m (large) basket

**cancela** f gate

**cancela|ción** f cancellation . **~r** vt cancel; write off ⟨*deuda*⟩; (*fig*) forget

**cáncer** m cancer. **C~** Cancer

**canciller** m chancellor; (*LAm, ministro de asuntos exteriores*) Minister of Foreign Affairs

**canci|ón** f song. **~ón de cuna** lullaby. **~onero** m song-book. **¡siempre la misma ~ón!** always the same old story!

**cancha** f (*de fútbol*) pitch, ground; (*de tenis*) court

**candado** m padlock

**candel|a** f candle. **~ero** m candlestick. **~illa** f candle

**candente** a (*rojo*) red-hot; (*blanco*) white-hot; (*fig*) burning

**candidato** m candidate

**candidez** f innocence; (*ingenuidad*) naïvety

**cándido** a naïve

**candil** m oil-lamp; (*Mex, araña*) chandelier. **~ejas** fpl footlights

**candinga** m (*Mex*) devil

**candor** m innocence; (*ingenuidad*) naïvety. **~oso** a innocent; (*ingenuo*) naïve

**canela** f cinnamon. **ser ~** be beautiful

**cangrejo** m crab. **~ de río** crayfish

**canguro** m kangaroo; (*persona*) baby-sitter

**can|íbal** a & m cannibal. **~ibalismo** m cannibalism

**canica** f marble

**canijo** m weak

**canino** a canine. ● m canine (tooth)

**canje** m exchange. **~ar** vt exchange

**cano** a grey-haired

**canoa** f canoe; (*con motor*) motor boat

**canon** m canon

**can|ónigo** m canon. **~onizar** [10] vt canonize

**canoso** a grey-haired

**cansa|do** a tired. **~ncio** m tiredness. **~r** vt tire; (*aburrir*) bore. ● vi be tiring; (*aburrir*) get boring. **~rse** vpr get tired

**cantábrico** a Cantabrian. **el mar ~** the Bay of Biscay

**canta|nte** a singing. ● m singer; (*en óperas*) opera singer. **~or** m Flamenco singer. **~r** vt/i sing. ● m singing; (*canción*) song; (*poema*) poem. **~rlas claras** speak frankly

**cántar|a** f pitcher. **~o** m pitcher. **llover a ~os** pour down

**cante** m folk song. **~ flamenco, ~ jondo** Flamenco singing

**cantera** f quarry

**cantidad** f quantity; (*número*) number; (*de dinero*) sum. **una ~ de** lots of

**cantilena** f, **cantinela** f song

**cantimplora** f water-bottle

**cantina** f canteen; (*rail*) buffet

**canto** m singing; (*canción*) song; (*borde*) edge; (*de un cuchillo*) blunt edge; (*esquina*) corner; (*piedra*) pebble. **~ rodado** boulder. **de ~** on edge

**cantonés** a Cantonese

**cantor** a singing. ● m singer

**canturre|ar** vt/i hum. **~o** m humming

**canuto** m tube

**caña** f stalk, stem; (*planta*) reed; (*vaso*) glass; (*de la pierna*) shin. **~ de azúcar** sugar-cane. **~ de pescar** fishing-rod

**cañada** f ravine; (*camino*) track

**cáñamo** m hemp. **~ índio** cannabis

**cañ|ería** f pipe; (*tubería*) piping. **~o** m pipe, tube; (*de fuente*) jet. **~ón** m pipe, tube; (*de órgano*) pipe; (*de* *chimenea)* flue; *(arma de fuego)* cannon; *(desfiladero)* canyon. **~onazo** *m* gunshot. **~onera** *f* gunboat

**caoba** *f* mahogany

**ca|os** *m* chaos. **~ótico** *a* chaotic

**capa** *f* cloak; *(de pintura)* coat; *(culin)* coating; *(geol)* stratum, layer

**capacidad** *f* capacity; *(fig)* ability

**capacitar** *vt* qualify, enable; *(instruir)* train

**caparazón** *m* shell

**capataz** *m* foreman

**capaz** *a* capable, able; *(espacioso)* roomy. **~ para** which holds, with a capacity of

**capazo** *m* large basket

**capcioso** *a* sly, insidious

**capellán** *m* chaplain

**caperuza** *f* hood; *(de pluma)* cap

**capilla** *f* chapel; *(mus)* choir

**capita** *f* small cloak, cape

**capital** *a* capital, very important. ● *m* *(dinero)* capital. ● *f* *(ciudad)* capital; *(LAm, letra)* capital (letter). **~ de provincia** county town

**capitali|smo** *m* capitalism. **~sta** *a* & *m* & *f* capitalist. **~zar** [10] *vt* capitalize

**capit|án** *m* captain. **~anear** *vt* lead, command; *(un equipo)* captain

**capitel** *m* *(arquit)* capital

**capitulaci|ón** *f* surrender; *(acuerdo)* agreement. **~ones** *fpl* marriage contract

**capítulo** *m* chapter. **~s matrimoniales** marriage contract

**capó** *m* bonnet *(Brit)*, hood *(Amer)*

**capón** *m* *(pollo)* capon

**caporal** *m* chief, leader

**capota** *f* *(de mujer)* bonnet; *(auto)* folding top, sliding roof

**capote** *m* cape

**Capricornio** *m* Capricorn

**capricho** *m* whim. **~so** *a* capricious, whimsical. **a ~** capriciously

**cápsula** *f* capsule

**captar** *vt* harness ⟨agua⟩; grasp ⟨sentido⟩; hold ⟨atención⟩; win ⟨confianza⟩; *(radio)* pick up

**captura** *f* capture. **~r** *vt* capture

**capucha** *f* hood

**capullo** *m* bud; *(de insecto)* cocoon

**caqui** *m* khaki

**cara** *f* face; *(de una moneda)* obverse; *(de un objeto)* side; *(aspecto)* look, appearance; *(descaro)* cheek. **~ a** towards; *(frente a)* facing. **~ a ~** face to face. **~ o cruz** heads or tails.

**dar la ~** face up to. **hacer ~ a** face. **no volver la ~ atrás** not look back. **tener ~ de** look, seem to be. **tener ~ para** have the face to. **tener mala ~** look ill. **volver la ~** look the other way

**carabela** *f* caravel, small light ship

**carabina** *f* rifle; *(fig, señora, fam)* chaperone

**Caracas** *m* Caracas

**caracol** *m* snail; *(de pelo)* curl. **¡~es!** Good Heavens! **escalera *f* de ~** spiral staircase

**carácter** *m* *(pl* **caracteres)** character. **con ~ de, por su ~ de** as

**característic|a** *f* characteristic; *(LAm, teléfonos)* dialling code. **~o** *a* characteristic, typical

**caracteriza|do** *a* characterized; *(prestigioso)* distinguished. **~r** [10] *vt* characterize

**cara: ~ dura** cheek, nerve. **~dura** *m* & *f* cheeky person, rotter *(fam)*

**caramba** *int* good heavens!, goodness me!

**carámbano** *m* icicle

**caramelo** *m* sweet *(Brit)*, candy *(Amer)*; *(azúcar fundido)* caramel

**carancho** *m* *(Arg)* vulture

**carapacho** *m* shell

**caraqueño** *a* from Caracas. ● *m* native of Caracas

**carátula** *f* mask; *(fig, teatro)* theatre; *(Mex, esfera del reloj)* face

**caravana** *f* caravan; *(fig, grupo)* group; *(auto)* long line, traffic jam

**caray** *int* *(fam)* good heavens!, goodness me!

**carb|ón** *m* coal; *(papel)* carbon (paper); *(para dibujar)* charcoal. **~oncillo** *m* charcoal. **~onero** *a* coal. ● *m* coal-merchant. **~onizar** [10] *vt* *(fig)* burn (to a cinder). **~ono** *m* carbon

**carburador** *m* carburettor

**carcajada** *f* burst of laughter. **reírse a ~s** roar with laughter. **soltar una ~** burst out laughing

**cárcel** *m* prison, jail; *(en carpintería)* clamp

**carcel|ario** *a* prison. **~ero** *a* prison. ● *m* prison officer

**carcom|a** *f* woodworm. **~er** *vt* eat away; *(fig)* undermine. **~erse** *vpr* be eaten away; *(fig)* waste away

**cardenal** *m* cardinal; *(contusión)* bruise

**cárdeno** *a* purple

**cardiaco**, **cardíaco** a cardiac, heart.
● m heart patient
**cardinal** a cardinal
**cardiólogo** m cardiologist, heart
specialist
**cardo** m thistle
**carear** vt bring face to face ⟨per-
sonas⟩; compare ⟨cosas⟩
**carecer** [11] vi. ~ **de** lack. ~ **de sentido** not to make sense
**caren|cia** f lack. ~**te** a lacking
**carero** a expensive
**carestía** f (precio elevado) high price;
(escasez) shortage
**careta** f mask
**carey** m tortoiseshell
**carga** f load; (fig) burden; (acción)
loading; (de barco) cargo; (obli-
gación) obligation. ~**do** a loaded;
(fig) burdened; ⟨tiempo⟩ heavy;
⟨hilo⟩ live; ⟨pila⟩ charged. ~**mento**
m load; (acción) loading; (de un
barco) cargo. ~**nte** a demanding.
~**r** [12] vt load; (fig) burden; (mil,
elec) charge; fill ⟨pluma etc⟩; (fig,
molestar, fam) annoy. ● vi load. ~**r
con** pick up. ~**rse** vpr (llenarse) fill;
⟨cielo⟩ become overcast; (enfadarse,
fam) get cross. **llevar la ~ de algo**
be responsible for sth
**cargo** m load; (fig) burden; (puesto)
post; (acusación) accusation,
charge; (responsabilidad) charge. **a
~ de** in the charge of. **hacerse ~ de**
take responsibility for. **tener a su ~**
be in charge of
**carguero** m (Arg) beast of burden;
(naut) cargo ship
**cari** m (LAm) grey
**cariacontecido** a crestfallen
**caria|do** a decayed. ~**rse** vpr decay
**caribe** a Caribbean. **el mar** m **C~** the
Caribbean (Sea)
**caricatura** f caricature
**caricia** f caress
**caridad** f charity. ¡**por ~**! for goodness sake!
**caries** f invar (dental) decay
**carilampiño** a clean-shaven
**cariño** m affection; (caricia) caress.
~ **mío** my darling. ~**samente** adv
tenderly, lovingly; (en carta) with
love from. ~**so** a affectionate. **con
mucho ~** (en carta) with love from.
**tener ~ a** be fond of. **tomar ~ a** take
a liking to. **un ~** (en carta) with love
from
**carism|a** m charisma. ~**ático** a
charismatic

**caritativo** a charitable
**cariz** m look
**carlinga** f cockpit
**carmesí** a & m crimson
**carmín** m (de labios) lipstick; (color)
red
**carnal** a carnal; ⟨pariente⟩ blood,
full. **primo ~** first cousin
**carnaval** m carnival. ~**esco** a carnival. **martes** m **de ~** Shrove
Tuesday
**carne** f (incl de frutos) flesh; (para
comer) meat. ~ **de cerdo** pork. ~ **de
cordero** lamb. ~ **de gallina** goose-
flesh. ~ **picada** mince. ~ **de ternera**
veal. ~ **de vaca** beef. **me pone la ~
de gallina** it gives me the creeps. **ser
de ~ y hueso** be only human
**carné** m card; (cuaderno) notebook.
~ **de conducir** driving licence
(Brit), driver's license (Amer). ~ **de
identidad** identity card.
**carnero** m sheep; (culin) lamb
**carnet** /kar'ne/ m card; (cuaderno)
notebook. ~ **de conducir** driving
licence (Brit), driver's license
(Amer). ~ **de identidad** identity
card
**carnicer|ía** f butcher's (shop); (fig)
massacre. ~**o** a carnivorous; (fig,
cruel) cruel, savage. ● m butcher;
(animal) carnivore
**carnívoro** a carnivorous. ● m
carnivore
**carnoso** a fleshy
**caro** a dear. ● adv dear, dearly.
**costar ~ a uno** cost s.o. dear
**carpa** f carp; (tienda) tent
**carpeta** f file, folder. ~**zo** m. **dar
~zo a** shelve, put on one side
**carpinter|ía** f carpentry. ~**o** m
carpinter, joiner
**carraspe|ar** vi clear one's throat.
~**ra** f. **tener ~ra** have a frog in one's
throat
**carrera** f run; (prisa) rush; (concurso) race; (recorrido, estudios)
course; (profesión) profession,
career
**carreta** f cart. ~**da** f cart-load
**carrete** m reel; (película) 35mm film
**carretera** f road. ~ **de circunvalación** bypass, ring road. ~
**nacional** A road (Brit), highway
(Amer). ~ **secundaria** B road (Brit),
secondary road (Amer)
**carret|illa** f trolley; (de una rueda)
wheelbarrow; (de bebé) baby-
walker. ~**ón** m small cart

**carril** _m_ rut; (_rail_) rail; (_de autopista etc_) lane

**carrillo** _m_ cheek; (_polea_) pulley

**carrizo** _m_ reed

**carro** _m_ cart; (_LAm, coche_) car. ∼ **de asalto**, ∼ **de combate** tank

**carrocería** _f_ (_auto_) bodywork; (_taller_) car repairer's

**carroña** _f_ carrion

**carroza** _f_ coach, carriage; (_en desfile de fiesta_) float

**carruaje** _m_ carriage

**carrusel** _m_ merry-go-round

**carta** _f_ letter; (_documento_) document; (_lista de platos_) menu; (_lista de vinos_) list; (_geog_) map; (_naipe_) card. ∼ **blanca** free hand. ∼ **de crédito** credit card

**cartearse** _vpr_ correspond

**cartel** _m_ poster; (_de escuela etc_) wall-chart. ∼**era** _f_ hoarding; (_en periódico_) entertainments. ∼**ito** _m_ notice. **de** ∼ celebrated. **tener** ∼ be a hit, be successful

**cartera** _f_ wallet; (_de colegial_) satchel; (_para documentos_) briefcase

**cartería** _f_ sorting office

**carterista** _m & f_ pickpocket

**cartero** _m_ postman, mailman (_Amer_)

**cartílago** _m_ cartilage

**cartilla** _f_ first reading book. ∼ **de ahorros** savings book. **leerle la** ∼ **a uno** tell s.o. off

**cartón** _m_ cardboard

**cartucho** _m_ cartridge

**cartulina** _f_ thin cardboard

**casa** _f_ house; (_hogar_) home; (_empresa_) firm; (_edificio_) building. ∼ **de correos** post office. ∼ **de huéspedes** boarding-house. ∼ **de socorro** first aid post. **amigo de la** ∼ family friend. **ir a** ∼ go home. **salir de** ∼ go out

**casad|a** _f_ married woman. ∼**o** _a_ married. ● _m_ married man. **los recién** ∼**os** the newly-weds

**casamentero** _m_ matchmaker

**casa|miento** _m_ marriage; (_ceremonia_) wedding. ∼**r** _vt_ marry. ● _vi_ get married. ∼**rse** _vpr_ get married

**cascabel** _m_ small bell. ∼**eo** _m_ jingling

**cascada** _f_ waterfall

**cascado** _a_ broken; ⟨_voz_⟩ harsh

**cascanueces** _m invar_ nutcrackers

**cascar** [7] _vt_ break; crack ⟨_frutos secos_⟩; (_pegar_) beat. ● _vi_ (_fig, fam_) chatter, natter (_fam_). ∼**se** _vpr_ crack

**cáscara** _f_ (_de huevo, frutos secos_) shell; (_de naranja_) peel; (_de plátano_) skin

**casco** _m_ helmet; (_de cerámica etc_) piece, fragment; (_cabeza_) head; (_de barco_) hull; (_envase_) empty bottle; (_de caballo_) hoof; (_de una ciudad_) part, area

**cascote** _m_ rubble

**caserío** _m_ country house; (_conjunto de casas_) hamlet

**casero** _a_ home-made; (_doméstico_) domestic, household; (_amante del hogar_) home-loving; ⟨_reunión_⟩ family. ● _m_ owner; (_vigilante_) caretaker

**caseta** _f_ small house, cottage. ∼ **de baño** bathing hut

**caset(t)e** _m & f_ cassette

**casi** _adv_ almost, nearly; (_en frases negativas_) hardly. ∼ ∼ very nearly. ∼ **nada** hardly any. ¡∼ **nada!** is that all! ∼ **nunca** hardly ever

**casilla** _f_ small house; (_cabaña_) hut; (_de mercado_) stall; (_en ajedrez etc_) square; (_departamento de casillero_) pigeon-hole

**casillero** _m_ pigeon-holes

**casimir** _m_ cashmere

**casino** _m_ casino; (_sociedad_) club

**caso** _m_ case; (_atención_) notice. ∼ **perdido** hopeless case. ∼ **urgente** emergency. **darse el** ∼ **(de) que** happen. **el** ∼ **es que** the fact is that. **en** ∼ **de** in the event of. **en cualquier** ∼ in any case, whatever happens. **en ese** ∼ in that case. **en todo** ∼ in any case. **en último** ∼ as a last resort. **hacer** ∼ **de** take notice of. **poner por** ∼ suppose

**caspa** _f_ dandruff

**cáspita** _int_ good heavens!, goodness me!

**casquivano** _a_ scatter-brained

**cassette** _m & f_ cassette

**casta** _f_ (_de animal_) breed; (_de persona_) descent

**castaña** _f_ chestnut

**castañet|a** _f_ click of the fingers. ∼**ear** _vi_ ⟨_dientes_⟩ chatter

**castaño** _a_ chestnut, brown. ● _m_ chestnut (tree)

**castañuela** _f_ castanet

**castellano** _a_ Castilian. ● _m_ (_persona_) Castilian; (_lengua_) Castilian, Spanish. ∼**parlante** _a_ Castilian-speaking, Spanish-speaking. **¿habla Vd** ∼**?** do you speak Spanish?

**castidad** *f* chastity

**castig|ar** [12] *vt* punish; (*en deportes*) penalize. **~o** *m* punishment; (*en deportes*) penalty

**Castilla** *f* Castille. **~ la Nueva** New Castille. **~ la Vieja** Old Castille

**castillo** *m* castle

**cast|izo** *a* true; ⟨*lengua*⟩ pure. **~o** *a* pure

**castor** *m* beaver

**castra|ción** *f* castration. **~r** *vt* castrate

**castrense** *m* military

**casual** *a* chance, accidental. **~idad** *f* chance, coincidence. **~mente** *adv* by chance. **dar la ~idad** happen. **de ~idad, por ~idad** by chance. **¡qué ~idad!** what a coincidence!

**cataclismo** *m* cataclysm

**catador** *m* taster; (*fig*) connoisseur

**catalán** *a* & *m* Catalan

**catalejo** *m* telescope

**catalizador** *m* catalyst

**cat|alogar** [12] *vt* catalogue; (*fig*) classify. **~álogo** *m* catalogue

**Cataluña** *f* Catalonia

**catamarán** *m* catamaran

**cataplúm** *int* crash! bang!

**catapulta** *f* catapult

**catar** *vt* taste, try

**catarata** *f* waterfall, falls; (*med*) cataract

**catarro** *m* cold

**cat|ástrofe** *m* catastrophe. **~astrófico** *a* catastrophic

**catecismo** *m* catechism

**catedral** *f* cathedral

**catedrático** *m* professor; (*de instituto*) teacher, head of department

**categ|oría** *f* category; (*clase*) class. **~órico** *a* categorical. **de ~oría** important. **de primera ~oría** first-class

**catinga** *f* (*LAm*) bad smell

**catita** *f* (*Arg*) parrot

**catoche** *m* (*Mex*) bad mood

**cat|olicismo** *m* catholicism. **~ólico** *a* (Roman) Catholic. ● *m* (Roman) Catholic

**catorce** *a* & *m* fourteen

**cauce** *m* river bed; (*fig, artificial*) channel

**caución** *f* caution; (*jurid*) guarantee

**caucho** *m* rubber

**caudal** *m* (*de río*) flow; (*riqueza*) wealth. **~oso** *a* ⟨*río*⟩ large

**caudillo** *m* leader, caudillo

**causa** *f* cause; (*motivo*) reason; (*jurid*) lawsuit. **~r** *vt* cause. **a ~ de, por ~ de** because of

**cáustico** *a* caustic

**cautel|a** *f* caution. **~arse** *vpr* guard against. **~osamente** *adv* warily, cautiously. **~oso** *a* cautious, wary

**cauterizar** [10] *vt* cauterize; (*fig*) apply drastic measures to

**cautiv|ar** *vt* capture; (*fig, fascinar*) captivate. **~erio** *m*, **~idad** *f* captivity. **~o** *a* & *m* captive

**cauto** *a* cautious

**cavar** *vt/i* dig

**caverna** *f* cave, cavern

**caviar** *m* caviare

**cavidad** *f* cavity

**cavil|ar** *vi* ponder, consider. **~oso** *a* worried

**cayado** *m* (*de pastor*) crook; (*de obispo*) crozier

**caza** *f* hunting; (*una expedición*) hunt; (*animales*) game. ● *m* fighter. **~dor** *m* hunter. **~dora** *f* jacket. **~ mayor** big game hunting. **~ menor** small game hunting. **~r** [10] *vt* hunt; (*fig*) track down; (*obtener*) catch, get. **andar a (la) ~ de** be in search of. **dar ~** chase, go after

**cazo** *m* saucepan; (*cucharón*) ladle. **~leta** *f* (small) saucepan

**cazuela** *f* casserole

**cebada** *f* barley

**ceb|ar** *vt* fatten (up); (*con trampa*) bait; prime ⟨*arma de fuego*⟩. **~o** *m* bait; (*de arma de fuego*) charge

**ceboll|a** *f* onion. **~ana** *f* chive. **~eta** *f* spring onion. **~ino** *m* chive

**cebra** *f* zebra

**cece|ar** *vi* lisp. **~o** *m* lisp

**cedazo** *m* sieve

**ceder** *vt* give up. ● *vi* give in; (*disminuir*) ease off; (*fallar*) give way, collapse. **ceda el paso** give way

**cedilla** *f* cedilla

**cedro** *m* cedar

**cédula** *f* document; (*ficha*) index card

**CE(E)** *abrev* (*Comunidad (Económica) Europea*) E(E)C, European (Economic) Community

**cefalea** *f* severe headache

**ceg|ador** *a* blinding. **~ar** [1 & 12] *vt* blind; (*tapar*) block up. **~arse** *vpr* be blinded (**de** by). **~ato** *a* short-sighted. **~uera** *f* blindness

**ceja** *f* eyebrow

**cejar** *vi* move back; (*fig*) give way

**celada** *f* ambush; (*fig*) trap

**cela|dor** *m* (*de niños*) monitor; (*de cárcel*) prison warder; (*de museo etc*) attendant. **~r** *vt* watch

**celda** f cell

**celebra|ción** f celebration. **~r** vt celebrate; (*alabar*) praise. **~rse** vpr take place

**célebre** a famous; (*fig, gracioso*) funny

**celebridad** f fame; (*persona*) celebrity

**celeridad** f speed

**celest|e** a heavenly. **~ial** a heavenly. **azul ~e** sky-blue

**celibato** m celibacy

**célibe** a celibate

**celo** m zeal. **~s** mpl jealousy. **dar ~s** make jealous. **papel** m **~** adhesive tape, Sellotape (P). **tener ~s** be jealous

**celofán** m cellophane

**celoso** a enthusiastic; (*que tiene celos*) jealous

**celta** a Celtic. ● m & f Celt

**céltico** a Celtic

**célula** f cell

**celular** a cellular

**celuloide** m celluloid

**celulosa** f cellulose

**cellisca** f sleetstorm

**cementerio** m cemetery

**cemento** m cement; (*hormigón*) concrete; (*LAm, cola*) glue

**cena** f dinner; (*comida ligera*) supper. **~duría** f (*Mex*) restaurant

**cenag|al** m marsh, bog; (*fig*) tight spot. **~oso** a muddy

**cenar** vt have for dinner; (*en cena ligera*) have for supper. ● vi have dinner; (*tomar cena ligera*) have supper

**cenicero** m ashtray

**cenit** m zenith

**ceniz|a** f ash. **~o** a ashen. ● m jinx

**censo** m census. **~ electoral** electoral roll

**censura** f censure; (*de prensa etc*) censorship. **~r** vt censure; censor (*prensa etc*)

**centavo** a & m hundredth; (*moneda*) centavo

**centell|a** f flash; (*chispa*) spark. **~ar** vi, **~ear** vi sparkle. **~eo** m sparkle, sparkling

**centena** f hundred. **~r** m hundred. **a ~res** by the hundred

**centenario** a centenary; (*persona*) centenarian. ● m centenary; (*persona*) centenarian

**centeno** m rye

**centésim|a** f hundredth. **~o** a hundredth; (*moneda*) centésimo

**cent|ígrado** a centigrade, Celsius. **~igramo** m centigram. **~ilitro** m centilitre. **~ímetro** m centimetre

**céntimo** a hundredth. ● m cent

**centinela** f sentry

**centolla** f, **centollo** m spider crab

**central** a central. ● f head office. **~ de correos** general post office. **~ eléctrica** power station. **~ nuclear** nuclear power station. **~ telefónica** telephone exchange. **~ismo** m centralism. **~ita** f switchboard

**centraliza|ción** f centralization. **~r** [10] vt centralize

**centrar** vt centre

**céntrico** a central

**centrífugo** a centrifugal

**centro** m centre. **~ comercial** shopping centre

**Centroamérica** f Central America

**centroamericano** a & m Central American

**centuplicar** [7] vt increase a hundredfold

**ceñi|do** a tight. **~r** [5 & 22] vt surround, encircle; (*vestido*) be a tight fit. **~rse** vpr limit o.s. (**a** to)

**ceñ|o** m frown. **~udo** a frowning. **fruncir el ~o** frown

**cepill|ar** vt brush; (*en carpintería*) plane. **~o** m brush; (*en carpintería*) plane. **~o de dientes** toothbrush

**cera** f wax

**cerámic|a** f ceramics; (*materia*) pottery; (*objeto*) piece of pottery. **~o** a ceramic

**cerca** f fence. ● adv near, close. **~s** mpl foreground. **~ de** prep near; (*con números, con tiempo*) nearly. **de ~** from close up, closely

**cercado** m enclosure

**cercan|ía** f nearness, proximity. **~ías** fpl outskirts. **tren** m **de ~ías** local train. **~o** a near, close. **C~o Oriente** m Near East

**cercar** [7] vt fence in, enclose; (*gente*) surround, crowd round; (*asediar*) besiege

**cerciorar** vt convince. **~se** vpr make sure, find out

**cerco** m (*grupo*) circle; (*cercado*) enclosure; (*asedio*) siege

**Cerdeña** f Sardinia

**cerdo** m pig; (*carne*) pork

**cereal** m cereal

**cerebr|al** a cerebral. **~o** m brain; (*fig, inteligencia*) intelligence, brains

**ceremoni|a** f ceremony. **~al** a ceremonial. **~oso** a ceremonious, stiff

**céreo** a wax

**cerez|a** f cherry. **~o** cherry tree

**cerill|a** f match. **~o** m (Mex) match

**cern|er** [1] vt sieve. **~erse** vpr hover; (fig, amenazar) hang over. **~idor** m sieve

**cero** m nought, zero; (fútbol) nil (Brit), zero (Amer); (tenis) love; (persona) nonentity. **partir de ~** start from scratch

**cerquillo** m (LAm, flequillo) fringe

**cerquita** adv very near

**cerra|do** a shut, closed; (espacio) shut in, enclosed; (cielo) overcast; (curva) sharp. **~dura** f lock; (acción de cerrar) shutting, closing. **~jero** m locksmith. **~r** [1] vt shut, close; (con llave) lock; (con cerrojo) bolt; (cercar) enclose; turn off (grifo); block up (agujero etc). ● vi shut, close. **~rse** vpr shut, close; (herida) heal. **~r con llave** lock

**cerro** m hill. **irse por los ~s de Úbeda** ramble on

**cerrojo** m bolt. **echar el ~** bolt

**certamen** m competition, contest

**certero** a accurate

**certeza** f, **certidumbre** f certainty

**certifica|do** a (carta etc) registered. ● m certificate; (carta) registered letter. **~r** [7] vt certify; register (carta etc)

**certitud** f certainty

**cervato** m fawn

**cerve|cería** f beerhouse, bar; (fábrica) brewery. **~za** f beer. **~za de barril** draught beer. **~za de botella** bottled beer

**cesa|ción** f cessation, suspension. **~nte** a out of work. **~r** vt stop. ● vi stop, cease; (dejar un empleo) give up. **sin ~r** incessantly

**cesáreo** a Caesarian. **operación** f **cesárea** Caesarian section

**cese** m cessation; (de un empleo) dismissal

**césped** m grass, lawn

**cest|a** f basket. **~ada** f basketful. **~o** m basket. **~o de los papeles** wastepaper basket

**cetro** m sceptre; (fig) power

**cianuro** m cyanide

**ciática** f sciatica

**cibernética** f cibernetics

**cicatriz** f scar. **~ación** f healing. **~ar** [10] vt/i heal. **~arse** vpr heal

**ciclamino** m cyclamen

**cíclico** a cyclic(al)

**ciclis|mo** m cycling. **~ta** m & f cyclist

**ciclo** m cycle; (LAm, curso) course

**ciclomotor** m moped

**ciclón** m cyclone

**ciclostilo** m cyclostyle, duplicating machine

**ciego** a blind. ● m blind man, blind person. **a ciegas** in the dark

**cielo** m sky; (relig) heaven; (persona) darling. **¡~s!** good heavens!, goodness me!

**ciempiés** m invar centipede

**ciénaga** f bog, swamp

**ciencia** f science; (fig) knowledge. **~s** fpl (univ etc) science. **~s empresariales** business studies. **saber a ~ cierta** know for a fact, know for certain

**cieno** m mud

**científico** a scientific. ● m scientist

**ciento** a & m (delante de nombres, y numerales a los que multiplica **cien**) a hundred, one hundred. **por ~** per cent

**cierne** m blossoming. **en ~** in blossom; (fig) in its infancy

**cierre** m fastener; (acción de cerrar) shutting, closing. **~ de cremallera** zip, zipper (Amer)

**cierro** vb véase **cerrar**

**cierto** a certain; (verdad) true. **estar en lo ~** be right. **lo ~ es que** the fact is that. **no es ~** that's not true. **¿no es ~?** right? **por ~** certainly, by the way. **si bien es ~ que** although

**ciervo** m deer

**cifra** f figure, number; (cantidad) sum. **~do** a coded. **~r** vt code; (resumir) summarize. **en ~** code, in code

**cigala** f (Norway) lobster

**cigarra** f cicada

**cigarr|illo** m cigarette. **~o** m (cigarillo) cigarette; (puro) cigar

**cigüeña** f stork

**cil|índrico** a cylindrical. **~indro** m cylinder; (Mex, organillo) barrel organ

**cima** f top; (fig) summit

**címbalo** m cymbal

**cimbrear** vt shake. **~se** vpr sway

**cimentar** [1] vt lay the foundations of; (fig, reforzar) strengthen

**cimer|a** f crest. **~o** a highest

**cimiento** *m* foundations; (*fig*) source. **desde los ～s** from the very beginning

**cinc** *m* zinc

**cincel** *m* chisel. **～ar** *vt* chisel

**cinco** *a* & *m* five

**cincuent|a** *a* & *m* fifty; (*quincuagésimo*) fiftieth. **～ón** *a* about fifty

**cine** *m* cinema. **～matografiar** [20] *vt* film

**cinético** *a* kinetic

**cínico** *a* cynical; (*desvergonzado*) shameless. ● *m* cynic

**cinismo** *m* cynicism; (*desvergüenza*) shamelessness

**cinta** *f* band; (*adorno de pelo etc*) ribbon; (*película*) film; (*magnética*) tape; (*de máquina de escribir etc*) ribbon. **～ aisladora, ～ aislante** insulating tape. **～ magnetofónica** magnetic tape. **～ métrica** tape measure

**cintur|a** *f* waist. **～ón** *m* belt. **～ón de seguridad** safety belt. **～ón salvavidas** lifebelt

**ciprés** *m* cypress (tree)

**circo** *m* circus

**circuito** *m* circuit; (*viaje*) tour. **～ cerrado** closed circuit. **corto ～** short circuit

**circula|ción** *f* circulation; (*vehículos*) traffic. **～r** *a* circular. ● *vt* circulate. ● *vi* circulate; ⟨*líquidos*⟩ flow; (*conducir*) drive; ⟨*autobús etc*⟩ run

**círculo** *m* circle. **～ vicioso** vicious circle. **en ～** in a circle

**circunci|dar** *vt* circumcise. **～sión** *f* circumcision

**circunda|nte** *a* surrounding. **～r** *vt* surround

**circunferencia** *f* circumference

**circunflejo** *m* circumflex

**circunscri|bir** [*pp* **circunscrito**] *vt* confine. **～pción** *f* (*distrito*) district. **～pción electoral** constituency

**circunspecto** *a* wary, circumspect

**circunstan|cia** *f* circumstance. **～te** *a* surrounding. ● *m* bystander. **los ～tes** those present

**circunvalación** *f*. **carretera** *f* **de ～** bypass, ring road

**cirio** *m* candle

**ciruela** *f* plum. **～ claudia** greengage. **～ damascena** damson

**ciru|gía** *f* surgery. **～jano** *m* surgeon

**cisne** *m* swan

**cisterna** *f* tank, cistern

**cita** *f* appointment; (*entre chico y chica*) date; (*referencia*) quotation. **～ción** *f* quotation; (*jurid*) summons. **～do** *a* aforementioned. **～r** *vt* make an appointment with; (*mencionar*) quote; (*jurid*) summons. **～rse** *vpr* arrange to meet

**cítara** *f* zither

**ciudad** *f* town; (*grande*) city. **～anía** *f* citizenship; (*habitantes*) citizens. **～ano** *a* civic ● *m* citizen, inhabitant; (*habitante de ciudad*) city dweller

**cívico** *a* civic

**civil** *a* civil. ● *m* civil guard. **～idad** *f* politeness

**civiliza|ción** *f* civilization. **～r** [10] *vt* civilize. **～rse** *vpr* become civilized

**civismo** *m* community spirit

**cizaña** *f* (*fig*) discord

**clam|ar** *vi* cry out, clamour. **～or** *m* cry; (*griterío*) noise, clamour; (*protesta*) outcry. **～oroso** *a* noisy

**clandestin|idad** *f* secrecy. **～o** *a* clandestine, secret

**clara** *f* (*de huevo*) egg white

**claraboya** *f* skylight

**clarear** *vi* dawn; (*aclarar*) brighten up. **～se** *vpr* be transparent

**clarete** *m* rosé

**claridad** *f* clarity; (*luz*) light

**clarifica|ción** *f* clarification. **～r** [7] *vt* clarify

**clarín** *m* bugle

**clarinet|e** *m* clarinet; (*músico*) clarinettist. **～ista** *m* & *f* clarinettist

**clarividen|cia** *f* clairvoyance; (*fig*) far-sightedness. **～te** *a* clairvoyant; (*fig*) far-sighted

**claro** *a* (*con mucha luz*) bright; (*transparente, evidente*) clear; (*colores*) light; ⟨*líquido*⟩ thin. ● *m* (*en bosque etc*) clearing; (*espacio*) gap. ● *adv* clearly. ● *int* of course! **～ de luna** moonlight. **¡～ que sí!** yes of course! **¡～ que no!** of course not!

**clase** *f* class; (*aula*) classroom. **～ media** middle class. **～ obrera** working class. **～ social** social class. **dar ～s** teach. **toda ～ de** all sorts of

**clásico** *a* classical; (*fig*) classic. ● *m* classic

**clasifica|ción** *f* classification; (*deportes*) league. **～r** [7] *vt* classify; (*seleccionar*) sort

**claudia** *f* greengage

**claudicar** [7] (*ceder*) give in; (*cojear*) limp

**claustro** *m* cloister; (*univ*) staff
**claustrof|obia** *f* claustrophobia. **~óbico** *a* claustrophobic
**cláusula** *f* clause
**clausura** *f* closure; (*ceremonia*) closing ceremony. **~r** *vt* close
**clava|do** *a* fixed; (*con clavo*) nailed. **~r** *vt* knock in ‹*clavo*›; (*introducir a mano*) stick; (*fijar*) fix; (*juntar*) nail together. **es ~do a su padre** he's the spitting image of his father
**clave** *f* key; (*mus*) clef; (*clavicémbalo*) harpsichord
**clavel** *m* carnation
**clavicémbalo** *m* harpsichord
**clavícula** *f* collar bone, clavicle
**clavija** *f* peg; (*elec*) plug
**clavo** *m* nail; (*culin*) clove
**claxon** *m* (*pl* **claxons**) /'klakson/) horn
**clemen|cia** *f* clemency, mercy. **~te** *a* clement, merciful
**clementina** *f* tangerine
**cleptómano** *m* kleptomaniac
**cler|ecía** *f* priesthood. **~ical** *a* clerical
**clérigo** *m* priest
**clero** *m* clergy
**cliché** *m* cliché; (*foto*) negative
**cliente** *m & f* client, customer; (*de médico*) patient. **~la** *f* clientele, customers; (*de médico*) patients, practice
**clim|a** *m* climate. **~ático** *a* climatic. **~atizado** *a* air-conditioned. **~atológico** *a* climatological
**clínic|a** *f* clinic. **~o** *a* clinical. ● *m* clinician
**clip** *m* (*pl* **clips**) clip
**clo** *m* cluck. **hacer ~ ~** cluck
**cloaca** *f* drain, sewer
**cloque|ar** *vi* cluck. **~o** *m* clucking
**cloro** *m* chlorine
**club** *m* (*pl* **clubs** o **clubes**) club
**coacci|ón** *f* coercion, compulsion. **~onar** *vt* coerce, compel
**coagular** *vt* coagulate; clot ‹*sangre*›; curdle ‹*leche*›. **~se** *vpr* coagulate; ‹*sangre*› clot; ‹*leche*› curdle
**coalición** *f* coalition
**coartada** *f* alibi
**coartar** *vt* hinder; restrict ‹*libertad etc*›
**cobard|e** *a* cowardly. ● *m* coward. **~ía** *f* cowardice
**cobaya** *f*, **cobayo** *m* guinea pig
**cobert|era** *f* (*tapadera*) lid. **~izo** *m* lean-to, shelter. **~or** *m* bedspread; (*manta*) blanket. **~ura** *f* covering

**cobij|a** *f* (*LAm*, *ropa de cama*) bedclothes; (*Mex*, *manta*) blanket. **~ar** *vt* shelter. **~arse** *vpr* shelter, take shelter. **~o** *m* shelter
**cobra** *f* cobra
**cobra|dor** *m* conductor. **~dora** *f* conductress. **~r** *vt* collect; (*ganar*) earn; charge ‹*precio*›; cash ‹*cheque*›; (*recuperar*) recover. ● *vi* be paid. **~rse** *vpr* recover
**cobre** *m* copper; (*mus*) brass (instruments)
**cobro** *m* collection; (*de cheque*) cashing; (*pago*) payment. **ponerse en ~** go into hiding. **presentar al ~** cash
**cocada** *f* (*LAm*) sweet coconut
**cocaína** *f* cocaine
**cocción** *f* cooking; (*tec*) baking, firing
**cocear** *vt/i* kick
**coc|er** [2 & 9] *vt/i* cook; (*hervir*) boil; (*en horno*) bake. **~ido** *a* cooked. ● *m* stew
**cociente** *m* quotient. **~ intelectual** intelligence quotient, IQ
**cocin|a** *f* kitchen; (*arte de cocinar*) cookery, cuisine; (*aparato*) cooker. **~a de gas** gas cooker. **~a eléctrica** electric cooker. **~ar** *vt/i* cook. **~ero** *m* cook
**coco** *m* coconut; (*árbol*) coconut palm; (*cabeza*) head; (*duende*) bogeyman. **comerse el ~** think hard
**cocodrilo** *m* crocodile
**cocotero** *m* coconut palm
**cóctel** *m* (*pl* **cóctels** o **cócteles**) cocktail; (*reunión*) cocktail party
**coche** *m* car (*Brit*), motor car (*Brit*), automobile (*Amer*); (*de tren*) coach, carriage. **~cama** sleeper. **~ fúnebre** hearse. **~ra** *f* garage; (*de autobuses*) depot. **~ restaurante** dining-car. **~s de choque** dodgems
**cochin|ada** *f* dirty thing. **~o** *a* dirty, filthy. ● *m* pig
**cod|azo** *m* nudge (with one's elbow); (*Mex*, *aviso secreto*) tip-off. **~ear** *vt/i* elbow, nudge
**codici|a** *f* greed. **~ado** *a* coveted, sought after. **~ar** *vt* covet. **~oso** *a* greedy (**de** for)
**código** *m* code. **~ de la circulación** Highway Code
**codo** *m* elbow; (*dobladura*) bend. **hablar por los ~s** talk too much. **hasta los ~s** up to one's neck
**codorniz** *m* quail
**coeducación** *f* coeducation

**coerción** f coercion

**coetáneo** a & m contemporary

**coexist|encia** f coexistence. **~ir** vi coexist

**cofradía** f brotherhood

**cofre** m chest

**coger** [14] vt (España) take; catch ⟨tren, autobús, pelota, catarro⟩; (agarrar) take hold of; (del suelo) pick up; pick ⟨frutos etc⟩. ● vi (caber) fit. **~se** vpr trap, catch

**cogollo** m (de lechuga etc) heart; (fig, lo mejor) cream; (fig, núcleo) centre

**cogote** m back of the neck

**cohech|ar** vt bribe. **~o** m bribery

**coherente** a coherent

**cohesión** f cohesion

**cohete** m rocket; (Mex, pistola) pistol

**cohibi|ción** f inhibition. **~r** vt restrict; inhibit ⟨persona⟩. **~rse** vpr feel inhibited; (contenerse) restrain o.s.

**coincid|encia** f coincidence. **~ente** a coincidental. **~ir** vt coincide. **dar la ~encia** happen

**coje|ar** vt limp; ⟨mueble⟩ wobble. **~ra** f lameness

**coj|ín** m cushion. **~inete** m small cushion. **~inete de bolas** ball bearing

**cojo** a lame; ⟨mueble⟩ wobbly. ● m lame person

**col** f cabbage. **~es de Bruselas** Brussel sprouts

**cola** f tail; (fila) queue; (para pegar) glue. **a la ~** at the end. **hacer ~** queue (up). **tener ~, traer ~** have serious consequences

**colabora|ción** f collaboration. **~dor** m collaborator. **~r** vi collaborate

**colada** f washing. **hacer la ~** do the washing

**colador** m strainer

**colapso** m collapse; (fig) stoppage

**colar** [2] vt strain ⟨líquidos⟩; (lavar) wash; pass ⟨moneda falsa etc⟩. ● vi ⟨líquido⟩ seep through; (fig) be believed, wash (fam). **~se** vpr slip; (no hacer caso de la cola) jump the queue; (en fiesta) gatecrash; (meter la pata) put one's foot in it

**colch|a** f bedspread. **~ón** m mattress. **~oneta** f mattress

**colear** vi wag its tail; ⟨asunto⟩ not be resolved. **vivito y coleando** alive and kicking

**colecci|ón** f collection; (fig, gran número de) a lot of. **~onar** vt collect. **~onista** m & f collector

**colecta** f collection

**colectiv|idad** f community. **~o** a collective. ● m (Arg) minibus

**colector** m (en las alcantarillas) main sewer

**colega** m & f colleague

**colegi|al** m schoolboy. **~ala** f schoolgirl. **~o** m private school; (de ciertas profesiones) college. **~o mayor** hall of residence

**colegir** [5 & 14] vt gather

**cólera** f cholera; (ira) anger, fury. **descargar su ~** vent one's anger. **montar en ~** fly into a rage

**colérico** a furious, irate

**colesterol** m cholesterol

**coleta** f pigtail

**colga|nte** a hanging. ● m pendant. **~r** [2 & 12] vt hang; hang out ⟨colada⟩; hang up ⟨abrigo etc⟩. ● vi hang; (teléfono) hang up, ring off. **~rse** vpr hang o.s. **dejar a uno ~do** let s.o. down

**cólico** m colic

**coliflor** m cauliflower

**colilla** f cigarette end

**colina** f hill

**colinda|nte** a adjacent. **~r** vt border (con on)

**colisión** f collision, crash; (fig) clash

**colmar** vt fill to overflowing; (fig) fulfill. **~ a uno de amabilidad** overwhelm s.o. with kindness

**colmena** f beehive, hive

**colmillo** m eye tooth, canine (tooth); (de elefante) tusk; (de otros animales) fang

**colmo** m height. **ser el ~** be the limit, be the last straw

**coloca|ción** f positioning; (empleo) job, position. **~r** [7] vt put, place; (buscar empleo) find work for. **~rse** vpr find a job

**Colombia** f Colombia

**colombiano** a & m Colombian

**colon** m colon

**colón** m (unidad monetaria de Costa Rica y El Salvador) colón

**Colonia** f Cologne

**coloni|a** f colony; (agua de colonia) eau-de-Cologne; (LAm, barrio) suburb. **~a de verano** holiday camp. **~al** a colonial. **~ales** mpl imported foodstuffs; (comestibles en general) groceries. **~alista** m & f colonialist. **~zación** f colonization. **~zar** [10] colonize

**coloqui|al** a colloquial. **~o** m conversation; (congreso) conference

**color** m colour. **~ado** a (rojo) red.
**~ante** m colouring. **~ar** vt colour.
**~ear** vt/i colour. **~ete** m rouge.
**~ido** m colour. **de ~** colour. **en ~**
(fotos, película) colour

**colosal** a colossal; (fig, magnífico,
fam) terrific

**columna** f column; (fig, apoyo)
support

**columpi|ar** vt swing. **~arse** vpr
swing. **~o** m swing

**collar** m necklace; (de perro etc)
collar

**coma** f comma. ● m (med) coma

**comadre** f midwife; (madrina) godmother; (vecina) neighbour. **~ar** vi
gossip

**comadreja** f weasel

**comadrona** f midwife

**comand|ar** vt command. **~ante** m
commander. **~o** m command; (soldado) commando

**comarca** f area, region

**comba** f bend; (juguete) skipping-
rope. **~r** vt bend. **~rse** vpr bend.
**saltar a la ~** skip

**combat|e** m fight; (fig) struggle.
**~iente** m fighter. **~ir** vt/i fight

**combina|ción** f combination;
(bebida) cocktail; (arreglo) plan,
scheme; (prenda) slip. **~r** vt combine; (arreglar) arrange; (armonizar) match, go well with. **~rse** vpr
combine; (ponerse de acuerdo) agree
(para to)

**combustible** m fuel

**comedia** f comedy; (cualquier obra
de teatro) play. **hacer la ~** pretend

**comedi|do** a reserved. **~rse** [5] vpr
be restrained

**comedor** m dining-room; (restaurante) restaurant; (persona)
glutton. **ser buen ~** have a good
appetite

**comensal** m companion at table, fellow diner

**comentar** vt comment on; (anotar)
annotate. **~io** m commentary;
(observación) comment; (fam)
gossip. **~ista** m & f commentator

**comenzar** [1 & 10] vt/i begin, start

**comer** vt eat; (a mediodía) have for
lunch; (corroer) eat away; (en ajedrez) take. ● vi eat; (a mediodía) have
lunch. **~se** vpr eat (up). **dar de ~ a**
feed

**comerci|al** a commercial. **~ante** m
trader; (de tienda) shopkeeper. **~ar**

vt trade (**con, en** in); (con otra persona) do business. **~o** m commerce;
(actividad) trade; (tienda) shop;
(negocio) business

**comestible** a edible. **~s** mpl food.
**tienda de ~s** grocer's (shop) (Brit),
grocery (Amer)

**cometa** m comet. ● f kite

**comet|er** vt commit; make (falta).
**~ido** m task

**comezón** m itch

**comicastro** m poor actor, ham (fam)

**comicios** mpl elections

**cómico** a comic(al). ● m comic actor;
(cualquier actor) actor

**comida** f food; (a mediodía) lunch.
**hacer la ~** prepare the meals

**comidilla** f topic of conversation. **ser
la ~ del pueblo** be the talk of the
town

**comienzo** m beginning, start. **a ~s
de** at the beginning of

**comil|ón** a greedy. **~ona** f feast

**comillas** fpl inverted commas

**comino** m cumin. **(no) me importa
un ~** I couldn't care less

**comisar|ía** f police station. **~io** m
commissioner; (deportes) steward.
**~io de policía** police superintendent

**comisión** f assignment; (comité)
commission, committee; (com)
commission

**comisura** f corner. **~ de los labios**
corner of the mouth

**comité** m committee

**como** adv like, as. ● conj as; (en
cuanto) as soon as. **~ quieras** as you
like. **~ sabes** as you know. **~ si** as if

**cómo** a how? **¿~?** I beg your pardon?
**¿~ está Vd?** how are you? **¡~ no!** (esp
LAm) of course! **¿~ son?** what are
they like? **¿~ te llamas?** what's your
name? **¡y ~!** and how!

**cómoda** f chest of drawers

**comodidad** f comfort. **a su ~** at your
convenience

**cómodo** a comfortable; (útil) handy

**comoquiera** conj. **~ que** since. **~
que sea** however it may be

**compacto** a compact; (denso) dense;
(líneas etc) close

**compadecer** [11] vt feel sorry for.
**~se** vpr. **~se de** feel sorry for

**compadre** m godfather; (amigo)
friend

**compañ|ero** m companion; (de tra-
bajo) colleague; (amigo) friend. **~ía**
f company. **en ~ía de** with

**compara|ble** *a* comparable. **~ción** *f* comparison. **~r** *vt* compare. **~tivo** *a* & *m* comparative. **en ~ción con** in comparison with, compared with

**comparecer** [11] *vi* appear

**comparsa** *f* group; (*en el teatro*) extra

**compartimiento** *m* compartment

**compartir** *vt* share

**compás** *m* (*instrumento*) (pair of) compasses; (*ritmo*) rhythm; (*división*) bar (*Brit*), measure (*Amer*); (*naut*) compass. **a ~** in time

**compasi|ón** *f* compassion, pity. **tener ~ón de** feel sorry for. **~vo** *a* compassionate

**compatib|ilidad** *f* compatibility. **~le** *a* compatible

**compatriota** *m* & *f* compatriot

**compeler** *vt* compel, force

**compendi|ar** *vt* summarize. **~o** *m* summary

**compenetración** *f* mutual understanding

**compensa|ción** *f* compensation. **~ción por despido** redundancy payment. **~r** *vt* compensate

**competen|cia** *f* competition; (*capacidad*) competence; (*terreno*) field, scope. **~te** *a* competent; (*apropiado*) appropriate, suitable

**competi|ción** *f* competition. **~dor** *m* competitor. **~r** [5] *vi* compete

**compilar** *vt* compile

**compinche** *m* accomplice; (*amigo, fam*) friend, mate (*fam*)

**complac|encia** *f* pleasure; (*indulgencia*) indulgence. **~er** [32] *vt* please; (*prestar servicio*) help. **~erse** *vpr* have pleasure, be pleased. **~iente** *a* helpful; ⟨*marido*⟩ complaisant

**complej|idad** *f* complexity. **~o** *a* & *m* complex

**complement|ario** *a* complementary. **~o** *m* complement; (*gram*) object, complement

**complet|ar** *vt* complete. **~o** *a* complete; (*lleno*) full; (*perfecto*) perfect

**complexión** *f* disposition; (*constitución*) constitution

**complica|ción** *f* complication. **~r** [7] *vt* complicate; involve ⟨*persona*⟩. **~rse** *vpr* become complicated

**cómplice** *m* accomplice

**complot** *m* (*pl* **complots**) plot

**compon|ente** *a* component. ● *m* component; (*culin*) ingredient; (*miembro*) member. **~er** [34] *vt*

make up; (*mus, literatura etc*) write, compose; (*reparar*) mend; (*culin*) prepare; (*arreglar*) restore; settle ⟨*estómago*⟩; reconcile ⟨*diferencias*⟩. **~erse** *vpr* be made up; (*arreglarse*) get ready. **~érselas** manage

**comporta|miento** *m* behaviour. **~r** *vt* involve. **~rse** *vpr* behave. **~rse como es debido** behave properly. **~rse mal** misbehave

**composi|ción** *f* composition. **~tor** *m* composer

**compostelano** *a* from Santiago de Compostela. ● *m* native of Santiago de Compostela

**compostura** *f* composition; (*arreglo*) repair; (*culin*) condiment; (*comedimiento*) composure

**compota** *f* stewed fruit

**compra** *f* purchase. **~ a plazos** hire purchase. **~dor** *m* buyer; (*en una tienda*) customer. **~r** *vt* buy. **~venta** *f* dealing. **hacer la ~, ir a la ~, ir de ~s** do the shopping, go shopping. **negocio** *m* **de ~venta** second-hand shop

**compren|der** *vt* understand; (*incluir*) include. **~sible** *a* understandable. **~sión** *f* understanding. **~sivo** *a* understanding; (*que incluye*) comprehensive

**compresa** *f* compress; (*de mujer*) sanitary towel

**compr|esión** *f* compression. **~imido** *a* compressed. ● *m* pill, tablet. **~imir** *vt* compress; keep back ⟨*lágrimas*⟩; (*fig*) restrain

**comproba|nte** *m* (*recibo*) receipt. **~r** *vt* check; (*confirmar*) confirm

**compromet|er** *vt* compromise; (*arriesgar*) endanger. **~erse** *vpr* compromise o.s.; (*obligarse*) agree to. **~ido** *a* ⟨*situación*⟩ awkward, embarrassing

**compromiso** *m* obligation; (*apuro*) predicament; (*cita*) appointment; (*acuerdo*) agreement. **sin ~** without obligation

**compuesto** *a* compound; ⟨*persona*⟩ smart. ● *m* compound

**compungido** *a* sad, sorry

**computador** *m*, **computadora** *f* computer

**computar** *vt* calculate

**cómputo** *m* calculation

**comulgar** [12] *vi* take Communion

**común** *a* common. ● *m* community. **en ~** in common. **por lo ~** generally

**comunal** *a* municipal, communal

**comunica|ción** *f* communication. **~do** *m* communiqué. **~do a la prensa** press release. **~r** [7] *vt/i* communicate; pass on ⟨*enfermedad, información*⟩. **~rse** *vpr* communicate; ⟨*enfermedad*⟩ spread. **~tivo** *a* communicative. **está ~ndo** (*al teléfono*) it's engaged, the line's engaged

**comunidad** *f* community. **~ de vecinos** residents' association. **C~ (Económica) Europea** European (Economic) Community. **en ~ together**

**comunión** *f* communion; (*relig*) (Holy) Communion

**comunis|mo** *m* communism. **~ta** *a & m & f* communist

**comúnmente** *adv* generally, usually

**con** *prep* with; (*a pesar de*) in spite of; (+ *infinitivo*) by. **~ decir la verdad** by telling the truth. **~ que** so. **~ tal que** as long as

**conato** *m* attempt

**concatenación** *f* chain, linking

**cóncavo** *a* concave

**concebir** [5] *vt/i* conceive

**conceder** *vt* concede, grant; award ⟨*premio*⟩; (*admitir*) admit

**concej|al** *m* councillor. **~o** *m* town council

**concentra|ción** *f* concentration. **~do** *m* concentrated. **~r** *vt* concentrate. **~rse** *vpr* concentrate

**concep|ción** *f* conception. **~to** *m* concept; (*opinión*) opinion. **bajo ningún ~to** in no way. **en mi ~to** in my view. **por ningún ~to** in no way

**concerniente** *a* concerning. **en lo ~ a** with regard to

**concertar** [1] *vt* (*mus*) harmonize; (*coordinar*) coordinate; (*poner de acuerdo*) agree. ● *vi* be in tune; (*fig*) agree. **~se** *vpr* agree

**concertina** *f* concertina

**concesión** *f* concession

**conciencia** *f* conscience; (*conocimiento*) consciousness. **~ción** *f* awareness. **~ limpia** clear conscience. **~ sucia** guilty conscience. **a ~ de que** fully aware that. **en ~** honestly. **tener ~ de** be aware of. **tomar ~ de** become aware of

**concienzudo** *a* conscientious

**concierto** *m* concert; (*acuerdo*) agreement; (*mus, composición*) concerto

**concilia|ble** *a* reconcilable. **~ción** *f* reconciliation. **~r** *vt* reconcile. **~r el sueño** get to sleep. **~rse** *vpr* gain

**concilio** *m* council

**conciso** *m* concise

**conciudadano** *m* fellow citizen

**conclu|ir** [17] *vt* finish; (*deducir*) conclude. ● *vi* finish, end. **~irse** *vpr* finish, end. **~sión** *f* conclusion. **~yente** *a* conclusive

**concord|ancia** *f* agreement. **~ar** [2] *vt* reconcile. ● *vi* agree. **~e a** in agreement. **~ia** *f* harmony

**concret|amente** *adv* specifically, to be exact. **~ar** *vt* make specific. **~arse** *vpr* become definite; (*limitarse*) confine o.s. **~o** *a* concrete; (*determinado*) specific, particular. ● *m* (*LAm, hormigón*) concrete. **en ~o** definite; (*concretamente*) to be exact; (*en resumen*) in short

**concurr|encia** *f* coincidence; (*reunión*) crowd, audience. **~ido** *a* crowded, busy. **~ir** *vi* meet; (*asistir*) attend; (*coincidir*) coincide; (*contribuir*) contribute; (*en concurso*) compete

**concurs|ante** *m & f* competitor, contestant. **~ar** *vi* compete, take part. **~o** *m* competition; (*concurrencia*) crowd; (*ayuda*) help

**concha** *f* shell; (*carey*) tortoiseshell

**condado** *m* county

**conde** *m* earl, count

**condena** *f* sentence. **~ción** *f* condemnation. **~do** *m* convict. **~r** *vt* condemn; (*jurid*) convict

**condensa|ción** *f* condensation. **~r** *vt* condense. **~rse** *vpr* condense

**condesa** *f* countess

**condescende|ncia** *f* condescension; (*tolerancia*) indulgence. **~r** [1] *vi* agree; (*dignarse*) condescend

**condici|ón** *f* condition; (*naturaleza*) nature. **~onado** *a*, **~onal** *a* conditional. **~onar** *vt* condition. **a ~ón de (que)** on the condition that

**condiment|ar** *vt* season. **~o** *m* condiment

**condolencia** *f* condolence

**condominio** *m* joint ownership

**condón** *m* condom

**condonar** *vt* (*perdonar*) reprieve; cancel ⟨*deuda*⟩

**conducir** [47] *vt* drive ⟨*vehículo*⟩; carry ⟨*electricidad, gas, agua etc*⟩. ● *vi* drive; (*fig, llevar*) lead. **~se** *vpr* behave. **¿a qué conduce?** what's the point?

**conducta** f behaviour
**conducto** m pipe, tube; (*anat*) duct. **por ~ de** through
**conductor** m driver; (*jefe*) leader; (*elec*) conductor
**conduzco** vb véase **conducir**
**conectar** vt/i connect; (*enchufar*) plug in
**conejo** m rabbit
**conexión** f connection
**confabularse** vpr plot
**confecci|ón** f making; (*prenda*) ready-made garment. **~ones** fpl clothing, clothes. **~onado** a ready-made. **~onar** vt make
**confederación** f confederation
**conferencia** f conference; (*al teléfono*) long-distance call; (*univ etc*) lecture. **~ cumbre**, **~ en la cima**, **~ en la cumbre** summit conference. **~nte** m & f lecturer
**conferir** [4] vt confer; award ⟨*premio*⟩
**confes|ar** [1] vt/i confess. **~arse** vpr confess. **~ión** f confession. **~ional** a confessional. **~ionario** m confessional. **~or** m confessor
**confeti** m confetti
**confia|do** a trusting; (*seguro de sí mismo*) confident. **~nza** f trust; (*en sí mismo*) confidence; (*intimidad*) familiarity. **~r** [20] vt entrust. • vi trust. **~rse** vpr put one's trust in
**confiden|cia** f confidence, secret. **~cial** a confidential. **~te** m & f close friend; (*de policía*) informer
**configuración** f configuration, shape
**conf|ín** m border. **~inar** vt confine; (*desterrar*) banish. • vi border (**con** on). **~ines** mpl outermost parts
**confirma|ción** f confirmation. **~r** vt confirm
**confiscar** [7] vt confiscate
**confit|ería** f sweet-shop (*Brit*), candy store (*Amer*). **~ura** f jam
**conflagración** f conflagration
**conflicto** m conflict
**confluencia** f confluence
**conforma|ción** f conformation, shape. **~r** vt (*acomodar*) adjust. • vi agree. **~rse** vpr conform
**conform|e** a in agreement; (*contento*) happy, satisfied; (*según*) according (**con** to). • conj as. • int OK! **~e a** in accordance with, according to. **~idad** f agreement; (*tolerancia*) resignation. **~ista** m & f conformist

**conforta|ble** a comfortable. **~nte** a comforting. **~r** vt comfort
**confronta|ción** f confrontation; (*comparación*) comparison. **~r** vt confront; (*comparar*) compare
**confu|ndir** vt blur; (*equivocar*) mistake, confuse; (*perder*) lose; (*mezclar*) mix up, confuse. **~ndirse** vpr become confused; (*equivocarse*) make a mistake. **~sión** f confusion; (*vergüenza*) embarrassment. **~so** a confused; (*avergonzado*) embarrassed
**congela|do** a frozen. **~dor** m freezer. **~r** vt freeze
**congeniar** vi get on
**congesti|ón** f congestion. **~onado** a congested. **~onar** vt congest. **~onarse** vpr become congested
**congoja** f distress
**congraciar** vt win over. **~se** vpr ingratiate o.s.
**congratular** vt congratulate
**congrega|ción** f gathering; (*relig*) congregation. **~rse** [12] vpr gather, assemble
**congres|ista** m & f delegate, member of a congress. **~o** m congress, conference. **C~o de los Diputados** House of Commons
**cónico** a conical
**conífer|a** f conifer. **~o** a coniferous
**conjetura** f conjecture, guess. **~r** vt conjecture, guess
**conjunción** f conjunction
**conjunto** a joint. • m collection; (*mus*) band; (*ropa*) suit, outfit. **en ~** altogether
**conjura** f, **conjuración** f conspiracy
**conjurar** vt plot, conspire
**conmemora|ción** f commemoration. **~r** vt commemorate. **~tivo** a commemorative
**conmigo** pron with me
**conminar** vt threaten; (*avisar*) warn
**conmiseración** f commiseration
**conmo|ción** f shock; (*tumulto*) upheaval; (*terremoto*) earthquake. **~cionar** vt shock. **~ cerebral** concussion. **~ver** [2] vt shake; (*emocionar*) move
**conmuta|dor** m switch. **~r** vt exchange
**connivencia** f connivance
**connota|ción** f connotation. **~r** vt connote
**cono** m cone

**conoc|edor** *a & m* expert. **~er** [11] *vt* know; (*por primera vez*) meet; (*reconocer*) recognize, know. **~erse** *vpr* know o.s.; ⟨*dos personas*⟩ know each other; (*notarse*) be obvious. **dar a ~er** make known. **darse a ~er** make o.s. known. **~ido** *a* well-known. ● *m* acquaintance. **~imiento** *m* knowledge; (*sentido*) consciousness; (*conocido*) acquaintance. **perder el ~imiento** faint. **se ~e que** apparently. **tener ~imiento de** know about

**conozco** *vb véase* **conocer**

**conque** *conj* so

**conquense** *a* from Cuenca. ● *m* native of Cuenca

**conquista** *f* conquest. **~dor** *a* conquering. ● *m* conqueror; (*de América*) conquistador; (*fig*) lady-killer. **~r** *vt* conquer, win

**consabido** *a* well-known

**consagra|ción** *f* consecration. **~r** *vt* consecrate; (*fig*) devote. **~rse** *vpr* devote o.s.

**consanguíneo** *m* blood relation

**consciente** *a* conscious

**consecución** *f* acquisition; (*de un deseo*) realization

**consecuen|cia** *f* consequence; (*firmeza*) consistency. **~te** *a* consistent. **a ~cia de** as a result of. **en ~cia, por ~cia** consequently

**consecutivo** *a* consecutive

**conseguir** [5 & 13] *vt* get, obtain; (*lograr*) manage; achieve ⟨*objetivo*⟩

**conseja** *f* story, fable

**consej|ero** *m* adviser; (*miembro de consejo*) member. **~o** *m* advice; (*pol*) council. **~o de ministros** cabinet

**consenso** *m* assent, consent

**consenti|do** *a* ⟨*niño*⟩ spoilt. **~miento** *m* consent. **~r** [4] *vt* allow. ● *vi* consent. **~rse** *vpr* break

**conserje** *m* porter, caretaker. **~ría** *f* porter's office

**conserva** *f* preserves; (*mermelada*) jam, preserve; (*en lata*) tinned food. **~ción** *f* conservation; (*de alimentos*) preservation; (*de edificio*) maintenance. **en ~** preserved

**conservador** *a & m* (*pol*) conservative

**conservar** *vt* keep; preserve ⟨*alimentos*⟩. **~se** *vpr* keep; ⟨*costumbre etc*⟩ survive

**conservatorio** *m* conservatory

**considera|ble** *a* considerable. **~ción** *f* consideration; (*respeto*) respect. **~do** *a* considered; (*amable*) considerate; (*respetado*) respected. **~r** *vt* consider; (*respetar*) respect. **de ~ción** considerable. **de su ~ción** (*en cartas*) yours faithfully. **tomar en ~ción** take into consideration

**consigna** *f* order; (*rail*) left luggage office (*Brit*), baggage room (*Amer*); (*eslogan*) slogan

**consigo** *pron* (*él*) with him; (*ella*) with her; (*Ud, Uds*) with you; (*uno mismo*) with o.s.

**consiguiente** *a* consequent. **por ~** consequently

**consist|encia** *f* consistency. **~ente** *a* consisting (**en** of); (*firme*) solid. **~ir** *vi* consist (**en** of); (*deberse*) be due (**en** to)

**consola|ción** *f* consolation. **~r** [2] *vt* console, comfort

**consolidar** *vt* consolidate. **~se** *vpr* consolidate

**consomé** *m* clear soup, consommé

**consonan|cia** *f* consonance. **~te** *a* consonant. ● *f* consonant

**consorcio** *m* consortium

**consorte** *m & f* consort

**conspicuo** *a* eminent; (*visible*) visible

**conspira|ción** *f* conspiracy. **~dor** *m* conspirator. **~r** *vi* conspire

**constan|cia** *f* constancy. **~te** *a* constant

**constar** *vi* be clear; (*figurar*) appear, figure; (*componerse*) consist. **hacer ~** point out. **me consta que** I'm sure that. **que conste que** believe me

**constatar** *vt* check; (*confirmar*) confirm

**constelación** *f* constellation

**consternación** *f* consternation

**constipa|do** *m* cold. ● *a.* **estar ~do** have a cold. **~rse** *vpr* catch a cold

**constitu|ción** *f* constitution; (*establecimiento*) setting up. **~cional** *a* constitutional. **~ir** [17] *vt* constitute; (*formar*) form; (*crear*) set up, establish. **~irse** *vpr* set o.s. up (**en** as); (*presentarse*) appear. **~tivo** *a*, **~yente** *a* constituent

**constreñir** [5 & 22] *vt* force, oblige; (*restringir*) restrain

**constricción** *f* constriction

**constru|cción** *f* construction. **~ctor** *m* builder. **~ir** [17] *vt* construct; build ⟨*edificio*⟩

**consuelo** *m* consolation, comfort
**consuetudinario** *a* customary
**cónsul** *m* consul
**consula|do** *m* consulate. ~**r** *a* consular
**consult|a** *f* consultation. ~**ar** *vt* consult. ~**orio** *m* surgery. ~**orio sentimental** problem page. **horas** *fpl* de ~**a** surgery hours. **obra** *f* **de** ~**a** reference book
**consumar** *vt* complete; commit ⟨*crimen*⟩; consummate ⟨*matrimonio*⟩
**consum|ición** *f* consumption; (*bebida*) drink; (*comida*) food. ~**ido** *a* ⟨*persona*⟩ skinny, wasted; ⟨*frutas*⟩ shrivelled. ~**idor** *m* consumer. ~**ir** *vt* consume. ~**irse** *vpr* ⟨*persona*⟩ waste away; ⟨*cosa*⟩ wear out; (*quedarse seco*) dry up. ~**ismo** *m* consumerism. ~**o** *m* consumption
**contab|ilidad** *f* book-keeping; (*profesión*) accountancy. ~**le** *m* & *f* accountant
**contacto** *m* contact. **ponerse en** ~ **con** get in touch with
**contado** *a* counted. ~**s** *apl* few. ~**r** *m* meter; (*LAm*, **contable**) accountant. **al** ~ cash
**contagi|ar** *vt* infect ⟨*persona*⟩; pass on ⟨*enfermedd*⟩; (*fig*) contaminate. ~**o** *m* infection. ~**oso** *a* infectious
**contamina|ción** *f* contamination, pollution. ~**r** *vt* contaminate, pollute
**contante** *a*. **dinero** *m* ~ cash
**contar** [2] *vt* count; tell ⟨*relato*⟩. ● *vi* count. ~ **con** rely on, count on. ~**se** *vpr* be included (**entre** among); (*decirse*) be said
**contempla|ción** *f* contemplation. ~**r** *vt* look at; (*fig*) contemplate. **sin** ~**ciones** unceremoniously
**contemporáneo** *a* & *m* contemporary
**contend|er** [1] *vi* compete. ~**iente** *m* & *f* competitor
**conten|er** [40] *vt* contain; (*restringir*) restrain. ~**erse** *vpr* restrain o.s. ~**ido** *a* contained. ● *m* contents
**content|ar** *vt* please. ~**arse** *vpr*. ~**arse de** be satisfied with, be pleased with. ~**o** *a* (*alegre*) happy; (*satisfecho*) pleased
**contesta|ción** *f* answer. ~**dor** *m*. ~ **automático** answering machine. ~**r** *vt/i* answer; (*replicar*) answer back
**contexto** *m* context

**contienda** *f* struggle
**contigo** *pron* with you
**contiguo** *a* adjacent
**continen|cia** *f* continence. ~**tal** *a* continental. ~**te** *m* continent
**contingen|cia** *f* contingency. ~**te** *a* contingent. ● *m* contingent; (*cuota*) quota
**continu|ación** *f* continuation. ~**ar** [21] *vt* continue, resume. ● *vi* continue. ~**ará** (*en revista, TV etc*) to be continued. ~**idad** *f* continuity. ~**o** *a* continuous; (*muy frecuente*) continual. **a** ~**ación** immediately after. **corriente** *f* ~**a** direct current
**contorno** *m* outline; (*geog*) contour. ~**s** *mpl* surrounding area
**contorsión** *f* contortion
**contra** *adv* & *prep* against. ● *m* cons. **en** ~ against
**contraalmirante** *m* rear-admiral
**contraata|car** [7] *vt/i* counterattack. ~**que** *m* counter-attack
**contrabajo** *m* double-bass; (*persona*) double-bass player
**contrabalancear** *vt* counterbalance
**contraband|ista** *m* & *f* smuggler. ~**o** *m* contraband
**contracción** *f* contraction
**contrachapado** *m* plywood
**contrad|ecir** [46] *vt* contradict. ~**icción** *f* contradiction. ~**ictorio** *a* contradictory
**contraer** [41] *vt* contract. ~ **matrimonio** marry. ~**se** *vpr* contract; (*limitarse*) limit o.s.
**contrafuerte** *m* buttress
**contragolpe** *m* backlash
**contrahecho** *a* fake; ⟨*moneda*⟩ counterfeit; ⟨*persona*⟩ hunchbacked
**contraindicación** *f* contraindication
**contralto** *m* alto. ● *f* contralto
**contramano**. **a** ~ in the wrong direction
**contrapartida** *f* compensation
**contrapelo**. **a** ~ the wrong way
**contrapes|ar** *vt* counterbalance. ~**o** *m* counterbalance
**contraponer** [34] oppose; (*comparar*) compare
**contraproducente** *a* counterproductive
**contrari|ar** [20] *vt* oppose; (*molestar*) annoy. ~**edad** *f* obstacle; (*disgusto*) annoyance. ~**o** *a* contrary; ⟨*dirección*⟩ opposite; ⟨*persona*⟩ opposed. **al** ~**o** on the contrary. **al**

~o de contrary to. de lo ~o otherwise. en ~o against. llevar la ~a contradict. por el ~o on the contrary

**contrarrestar** *vt* counteract

**contrasentido** *m* contradiction

**contraseña** *f* secret mark; (*palabra*) password

**contrast|ar** *vt* check, verify. ● *vi* contrast. ~e *m* contrast; (*en oro, plata etc*) hallmark

**contratar** *vt* sign a contract for; engage (*empleados*)

**contratiempo** *m* setback; (*accidente*) accident

**contrat|ista** *m & f* contractor. ~o *m* contract

**contraven|ción** *f* contravention. ~ir [53] *vi*. ~ir a contravene

**contraventana** *f* shutter

**contribu|ción** *f* contribution; (*tributo*) tax. ~ir [17] *vt/i* contribute. ~yente *m & f* contributor; (*que paga impuestos*) taxpayer

**contrincante** *m* rival, opponent

**contrito** *a* contrite

**control** *m* control; (*inspección*) check. ~ar *vt* control; (*examinar*) check

**controversia** *f* controversy

**contundente** *a* (*arma*) blunt; (*argumento etc*) convincing

**conturbar** *vt* perturb

**contusión** *f* bruise

**convalec|encia** *f* convalescence. ~er [11] *vi* convalesce. ~iente *a & m & f* convalescent

**convalidar** *vt* confirm; recognize (*título*)

**convenc|er** [9] *vt* convince. ~imiento *m* conviction

**convenci|ón** *f* convention. ~onal *a* conventional

**conveni|encia** *f* convenience; (*aptitud*) suitability. ~encias (sociales) conventions. ~ente *a* suitable; (*aconsejable*) advisable; (*provechoso*) useful, advantageous. ~o *m* agreement. ~r [53] *vt* agree. ● *vi* agree; (*ser conveniente*) be convenient for, suit; (*ser aconsejable*) be advisable

**convento** *m* (*de monjes*) monastery; (*de monjas*) convent

**convergente** *a* converging

**converger** [14] *vi*, **convergir** [14] *vi* converge

**conversa|ción** *f* conversation. ~r *vi* converse, talk

**conver|sión** *f* conversion. ~so *a* converted. ● *m* convert. ~tible *a* convertible. ~tir [4] *vt* convert. ~tirse *vpr* be converted

**convexo** *a* convex

**convic|ción** *f* conviction. ~to *a* convicted

**convida|do** *m* guest. ~r *vt* invite. te convido a un helado I'll treat you to an ice-cream

**convincente** *a* convincing

**convite** *m* invitation; (*banquete*) banquet

**conviv|encia** *f* coexistence. ~ir *vi* live together

**convocar** [7] *vt* convene (*reunión*); summon (*personas*)

**convoy** *m* convoy; (*rail*) train; (*vinagrera*) cruet

**convulsión** *f* convulsion; (*fig*) upheaval

**conyugal** *a* conjugal; (*vida*) married

**cónyuge** *m* spouse. ~s *mpl* (married) couple

**coñac** *m* (*pl* **coñacs**) brandy

**coopera|ción** *f* co-operation. ~r *vi* co-operate. ~tiva *f* co-operative. ~tivo *a* co-operative

**coord|enada** *f* coordinate. ~inación *f* co-ordination. ~inar *vt* co-ordinate

**copa** *f* glass; (*deportes, fig*) cup. ~s *fpl* (*naipes*) hearts. tomar una ~ have a drink

**copia** *f* copy. ~ en limpio fair copy. ~r *vt* copy. sacar una ~ make a copy

**copioso** *a* copious; (*lluvia, nevada etc*) heavy

**copla** *f* verse; (*canción*) song

**copo** *m* flake. ~ de nieve snowflake. ~s de maíz cornflakes

**coquet|a** *f* flirt; (*mueble*) dressing-table. ~ear *vi* flirt. ~eo *m* flirtation. ~o *a* flirtatious

**coraje** *m* courage; (*rabia*) anger. dar ~ make mad, make furious

**coral** *a* choral. ● *m* (*materia, animal*) coral

**Corán** *m* Koran

**coraza** *f* (*naut*) armour-plating; (*de tortuga*) shell

**coraz|ón** *m* heart; (*persona*) darling. ~onada *f* hunch; (*impulso*) impulse. sin ~ón heartless. tener buen ~ón be good-hearted

**corbata** *f* tie, necktie (*esp Amer*). ~ de lazo bow tie

**corcova** f hump. ∼**do** a hunch-backed

**corchea** f quaver

**corchete** m fastener, hook and eye; (*gancho*) hook; (*paréntesis*) square bracket

**corcho** m cork

**cordel** m cord, thin rope

**cordero** m lamb

**cordial** a cordial, friendly. ● m tonic. ∼**idad** f cordiality, warmth

**cordillera** f mountain range

**córdoba** m (*unidad monetaria de Nicaragua*) córdoba

**Córdoba** f Cordova

**cordón** m string; (*de zapatos*) lace; (*cable*) flex; (*fig*) cordon. ∼ **umbilical** umbilical cord

**corear** vt chant

**coreografía** f choreography

**corista** m & f member of the chorus. ● f (*bailarina*) chorus girl

**cornet|a** f bugle. ∼**in** m cornet

**Cornualles** m Cornwall

**cornucopia** f cornucopia

**cornudo** a horned. ● m cuckold

**coro** m chorus; (*relig*) choir

**corona** f crown; (*de flores*) wreath, garland. ∼**ción** f coronation. ∼**r** vt crown

**coronel** m colonel

**coronilla** f crown. **estar hasta la** ∼ be fed up

**corporación** f corporation

**corporal** a corporal

**corpulento** a stout

**corpúsculo** m corpuscle

**corral** m pen. **aves** fpl **de** ∼ poultry

**correa** f strap; (*de perro*) lead; (*cinturón*) belt

**correc|ción** f correction; (*reprensión*) rebuke; (*cortesía*) good manners. ∼**to** a correct; (*cortés*) polite

**corre|dizo** a running. **nudo** ∼**dizo** slip knot. **puerta** f ∼**diza** sliding door. ∼**dor** m runner; (*pasillo*) corridor; (*agente*) agent, broker. ∼**dor automovilista** racing driver

**corregir** [5 & 14] vt correct; (*reprender*) rebuke

**correlaci|ón** f correlation. ∼**onar** vt correlate

**correo** m courier; (*correos*) post, mail; (*tren*) mail train. ∼**s** mpl post office. **echar al** ∼ post

**correr** vt run; (*viajar*) travel; draw (*cortinas*). ● vi run; (*agua, electricidad etc*) flow; (*tiempo*) pass. ∼**se** vpr (*apartarse*) move along;

(*pasarse*) go too far; (*colores*) run. ∼**se una juerga** have a ball

**correspond|encia** f correspondence. ∼**er** vi correspond; (*ser adecuado*) be fitting; (*contestar*) reply; (*pertenecer*) belong; (*incumbir*) fall to. ∼**erse** vpr (*amarse*) love one another. ∼**iente** a corresponding

**corresponsal** m correspondent

**corrid|a** f run. ∼**a de toros** bullfight. ∼**o** a (*peso*) good; (*continuo*) continuous; (*avergonzado*) embarrassed. **de** ∼**a** from memory

**corriente** a (*agua*) running; (*monedas, publicación, cuenta, año etc*) current; (*ordinario*) ordinary. ● f current; (*de aire*) draught; (*fig*) tendency. ● m current month. **al** ∼ (*al día*) up-to-date; (*enterado*) aware

**corr|illo** m small group, circle. ∼**o** m circle

**corroborar** vt corroborate

**corroer** [24 & 37] vt corrode; (*geol*) erode; (*fig*) eat away. ∼**se** vpr corrode

**corromper** vt rot (*madera*); turn bad (*alimentos*); (*fig*) corrupt. ● vi (*fam*) stink. ∼**se** vpr (*madera*) rot; (*alimentos*) go bad; (*fig*) be corrupted

**corrosi|ón** f corrosion. ∼**vo** a corrosive

**corrupción** f (*de madera etc*) rot; (*soborno*) bribery; (*fig*) corruption

**corsé** m corset

**cortacésped** m lawn-mower

**cortad|o** a cut; (*leche*) sour; (*avergonzado*) embarrassed; (*confuso*) confused. ● m coffee with a little milk. ∼**ura** f cut

**corta|nte** a sharp; (*viento*) biting; (*frío*) bitter. ∼**r** vt cut; (*recortar*) cut out; (*aislar, detener*) cut off; (*interrumpir*) cut in. ● vi cut. ∼**rse** vpr cut o.s.; (*leche etc*) curdle; (*al teléfono*) be cut off; (*fig*) be embarrassed, become tongue-tied. ∼**rse el pelo** have one's hair cut. ∼**rse las uñas** cut one's nails

**cortauñas** m invar nail-clippers

**corte** m cutting; (*de instrumento cortante*) cutting edge; (*de corriente*) cut; (*de prendas de vestir*) cut; (*de tela*) length. ● f court. ∼ **de luz** power cut. ∼ **y confección** dressmaking. **hacer la** ∼ court. **las C**∼**s** the Spanish parliament

**cortej|ar** vt court. **~o** m (de rey etc) entourage. **~o fúnebre** cortège, funeral procession. **~o nupcial** wedding procession

**cortés** a polite

**cortesan|a** f courtesan. **~o** m courtier

**cortesía** f courtesy

**corteza** f bark; (de naranja etc) peel, rind; (de pan) crust

**cortijo** m farm; (casa) farmhouse

**cortina** f curtain

**corto** a short; (escaso) scanty; (apocado) shy. **~circuito** m short circuit. **~ de alcances** dim, thick. **~ de oído** hard of hearing. **~ de vista** short-sighted. **a la corta o a la larga** sooner or later. **quedarse ~** fall short; (miscalcular) under-estimate

**Coruña** f. **La ~** Corunna

**corvo** a bent

**cosa** f thing; (asunto) business; (idea) idea. **~ de** about. **como si tal ~** just like that; (como si no hubiera pasado nada) as if nothing had happened. **decirle a uno cuatro ~s** tell s.o. a thing or two. **lo que son las ~s** much to my surprise

**cosaco** a & m Cossack

**cosech|a** f harvest; (de vino) vintage. **~ar** vt harvest. **~ero** m harvester

**coser** vt sew. **~se** vpr stick to s.o. **eso es ~ y cantar** it's as easy as pie

**cosmético** a & m cosmetic

**cósmico** a cosmic

**cosmonauta** m & f cosmonaut

**cosmopolita** a & m & f cosmopolitan

**cosmos** m cosmos

**cosquillas** fpl ticklishness. **buscar a uno las ~** provoke s.o. **hacer ~** tickle. **tener ~** be ticklish

**costa** f coast. **a ~ de** at the expense of. **a toda ~** at any cost

**costado** m side

**costal** m sack

**costar** [2] vt/i cost. **~ caro** be expensive. **cueste lo que cueste** at any cost

**Costa Rica** f Costa Rica

**costarricense** a & m, **costarriqueño** a & m Costa Rican

**coste** m cost. **~ar** vt pay for; (naut) sail along the coast

**costero** a coastal

**costilla** f rib; (chuleta) chop

**costo** m cost. **~so** a expensive

**costumbre** f custom, habit. **de ~** a usual. ● adv usually

**costur|a** f sewing; (línea) seam; (confección) dressmaking. **~era** f dressmaker. **~ero** m sewing box

**cotejar** vt compare

**cotidiano** a daily

**cotill|ar** vt gossip. **~o** m gossip

**cotiza|ción** f quotation, price. **~r** [10] vt (en la bolsa) quote. ● vi pay one's subscription. **~rse** vpr fetch; (en la bolsa) stand at; (fig) be valued

**coto** m enclosure; (de caza) preserve. **~ de caza** game preserve

**cotorr|a** f parrot; (urraca) magpie; (fig) chatterbox. **~ear** vi chatter

**coyuntura** f joint; (oportunidad) opportunity; (situación) situation; (circunstancia) occasion, juncture

**coz** f kick

**cráneo** m skull

**cráter** m crater

**crea|ción** f creation. **~dor** a creative. ● m creator. **~r** vt create

**crec|er** [11] vi grow; (aumentar) increase. **~ida** f (de río) flood. **~ido** a (persona) grown-up; (número) large, considerable; (plantas) fully-grown. **~iente** a growing; (luna) crescent. **~imiento** m growth

**credencial** a credential. **~es** fpl credentials

**credibilidad** f credibility

**crédito** m credit. **digno de ~** reliable, trustworthy

**credo** m creed. **en un ~** in a flash

**crédulo** a credulous

**cre|encia** f belief. **~er** [18] believe; (pensar) think. **~o que no** I don't think so, I think not. **~o que sí** I think so. ● vi believe. **~erse** vpr consider o.s. **no me lo ~o** I don't believe it. **~íble** a credible. **¡ya lo ~o!** I should think so!

**crema** f cream; (culin) custard. **~ bronceadora** sun-tan cream

**cremación** f cremation; (de basura) incineration

**cremallera** f zip, zipper (Amer)

**crematorio** m crematorium; (de basura) incinerator

**crepitar** vi crackle

**crepúsculo** m twilight

**crescendo** m crescendo

**cresp|o** a frizzy. **~ón** m crêpe

**cresta** f crest; (tupé) toupee; (geog) ridge

**Creta** f Crete

**cretino** m cretin

**creyente** m believer

**cría** *f* breeding; *(animal)* baby animal

**cria|da** *f* maid, servant. **~dero** *m* nursery. **~do** *a* brought up. ● *m* servant. **~dor** *m* breeder. **~nza** *f* breeding. **~r** [20] *vt* suckle; grow *(plantas)*; breed *(animales)*; *(educar)* bring up. **~rse** *vpr* grow up

**criatura** *f* creature; *(niño)* baby

**crim|en** *m* crime. **~inal** *a* & *m* & *f* criminal

**crin** *m* mane; *(relleno)* horsehair

**crinolina** *f* crinoline

**crío** *m* child

**criollo** *a* & *m* Creole

**cripta** *f* crypt

**crisantemo** *m* chrysanthemum

**crisis** *f* crisis

**crisol** *m* melting-pot

**crispar** *vt* twitch; *(irritar, fam)* annoy. **~ los nervios a uno** get on s.o.'s nerves

**cristal** *m* crystal; *(vidrio)* glass; *(de una ventana)* pane of glass. **~ de aumento** magnifying glass. **~ino** *a* crystalline; *(fig)* crystal-clear. **~izar** [10] crystallize. **limpiar los ~es** clean the windows

**cristian|amente** *adv* in a Christian way. **~dad** *f* Christianity. **~ismo** *m* Christianity. **~o** *a* & *m* Christian

**Cristo** *m* Christ

**cristo** *m* crucifix

**criterio** *m* criterion; *(opinión)* opinion

**cr|ítica** *f* criticism; *(reseña)* review. **~iticar** [7] *vt* criticize. **~ítico** *a* critical. ● *m* critic

**croar** *vi* croak

**crom|ado** *a* chromium-plated. **~o** *m* chromium, chrome

**cromosoma** *m* chromosome

**crónic|a** *f* chronicle; *(de periódico)* news. **~o** *a* chronic

**cronista** *m* & *f* reporter

**cronol|ogía** *f* chronology. **~ógico** *a* chronological

**cron|ometraje** *m* timing. **~ometrar** *vt* time. **~ómetro** *m* chronometer; *(en deportes)* stop-watch

**croquet** /'kroket/ *m* croquet

**croqueta** *f* croquette

**cruce** *m* crossing; *(de calles, de carreteras)* crossroads; *(de peatones)* (pedestrian) crossing

**crucial** *a* cross-shaped; *(fig)* crucial

**crucifi|car** [7] *vt* crucify. **~jo** *m* crucifix. **~xión** *f* crucifiction

**crucigrama** *m* crossword (puzzle)

**crudo** *a* raw; *(fig)* crude. **petróleo** *m* **~** crude oil

**cruel** *a* cruel. **~dad** *f* cruelty

**cruji|do** *m* *(de seda, de hojas secas etc)* rustle; *(de muebles etc)* creak. **~r** *vi* *(seda, hojas secas etc)* rustle; *(muebles etc)* creak

**cruz** *f* cross; *(de moneda)* tails. **~ gamada** swastika. **la C~ Roja** the Red Cross

**cruzada** *f* crusade

**cruzar** [10] *vt* cross; *(poner de un lado a otro)* lay across. **~se** *vpr* cross; *(pasar en la calle)* pass

**cuaderno** *m* exercise book; *(para apuntes)* notebook

**cuadra** *f* *(caballeriza)* stable; *(LAm, manzana)* block

**cuadrado** *a* & *m* square

**cuadragésimo** *a* fortieth

**cuadr|ar** *vt* square. ● *vi* suit; *(estar de acuerdo)* agree. **~arse** *vpr* *(mil)* stand to attention; *(fig)* dig one's heels in. **~ilátero** *a* quadrilateral. ● *m* quadrilateral; *(boxeo)* ring

**cuadrilla** *f* group; *(pandilla)* gang

**cuadro** *m* square; *(pintura)* painting; *(de obra de teatro, escena)* scene; *(de jardín)* bed; *(de números)* table; *(de mando etc)* panel; *(conjunto del personal)* staff. **~ de distribución** switchboard. **a ~s, de ~s** check. **en ~** in a square. **¡qué ~!**, **¡vaya un ~!** what a sight!

**cuadrúpedo** *m* quadruped

**cuádruple** *a* & *m* quadruple

**cuajar** *vt* thicken; clot *(sangre)*; curdle *(leche)*; *(llenar)* fill up. ● *vi* *(nieve)* settle; *(fig, fam)* work out. **cuajado de** full of. **~se** *vpr* coagulate; *(sangre)* clot; *(leche)* curdle. **~ón** *m* clot

**cual** *pron* **el ~, la ~** etc *(animales y cosas)* that, which; *(personas, sujeto)* who, that; *(personas, objeto)* whom. ● *adv* as, like. ● *a* such as. **~ si** as if. **~... tal** like... like. **cada ~** everyone. **por lo ~** because of which

**cuál** *pron* which

**cualidad** *f* quality; *(propiedad)* property

**cualquiera** *a* *(delante de nombres* **cualquier,** *pl* **cualesquiera)** any. ● *pron (pl* **cualesquiera)** anyone, anybody; *(cosas)* whatever, whichever. **un ~** a nobody

**cuando** *adv* when. ● *conj* when; *(aunque)* even if. **~ más** at the most.

~ **menos** at the least. ~ **no** if not.
**aun** ~ even if. **de** ~ **en** ~ from time
to time
**cuándo** *adv & conj* when. ¿**de** ~ **acá?**,
¿**desde**~**?**since when?
**cuant|ía** *f* quantity; (*extensión*)
extent. ~**ioso** *a* abundant
**cuanto** *a* as much... as, as many...
as. • *pron* as much as, as many as.
• *adv* as much as. ~ **más, mejor** the
more the merrier. **en** ~ as soon as.
**en** ~ **a** as for. **por** ~ since. **unos** ~**s**
a few, some
**cuánto** *a* (*interrogativo*) how
much?; (*interrogativo en plural*)
how many?; (*exclamativo*) what a
lot of! • *pron* how much?; (*en
plural*) how many? • *adv* how
much. ¿~ **tiempo?** how long? ¡~
**tiempo sin verte!** it's been a long
time! ¿**a** ~? how much? ¿**a** ~**s estamos?** what's the date today? **un Sr.**
**no sé** ~**s** Mr So-and-So
**cuáquero** *m* Quaker
**cuarent|a** *a & m* forty; (*cua-
dragésimo*) fortieth. ~**ena** *f* (about)
forty; (*med*) quarantine. ~**ón** *a*
about forty
**cuaresma** *f* Lent
**cuart|a** *f* (*palmo*) span
**cuartear** *vt* quarter, divide into four;
(*zigzaguear*) zigzag. ~**se** *vpr* crack
**cuartel** *m* (*mil*) barracks. ~ **general**
headquarters. **no dar** ~ show no
mercy
**cuarteto** *m* quartet
**cuarto** *a* fourth. • *m* quarter; (*habitación*) room. ~ **de baño** bathroom.
~ **de estar** living room. ~ **de hora**
quarter of an hour. **estar sin un** ~
be broke. **menos** ~ (a) quarter to. **y**
~ (a) quarter past
**cuarzo** *m* quartz
**cuatro** *a & m* four. ~**cientos** *a & m*
four hundred
**Cuba** *f* Cuba
**cuba:** ~**libre** *m* rum and Coke (P).
~**no** *a & m* Cuban
**cúbico** *a* cubic
**cubículo** *m* cubicle
**cubiert|a** *f* cover, covering; (*de la
cama*) bedspread; (*techo*) roof; (*neumático*) tyre; (*naut*) deck. ~**o** *a*
covered; (*cielo*) overcast. • *m* place
setting, cutlery; (*comida*) meal. **a**
~**o** under cover. **a** ~**o de** safe from
**cubis|mo** *m* cubism. ~**ta** *a & m & f*
cubist

**cubil** *m* den, lair. ~**ete** *m* bowl;
(*molde*) mould; (*para echar los
dados*) cup
**cubo** *m* bucket; (*en geometría y matemáticas*) cube
**cubrecama** *m* bedspread
**cubrir** *vt* [*pp* **cubierto**] cover; (*sonido*) drown; fill (*vacante*). ~**se** *vpr*
cover o.s.; (*ponerse el sombrero*) put
on one's hat; (*el cielo*) cloud over,
become overcast
**cucaracha** *f* cockroach
**cuclillas. en** ~ *adv* squatting
**cuclillo** *m* cuckoo
**cuco** *a* shrewd; (*mono*) pretty, nice.
• *m* cuckoo; (*insecto*) grub
**cucurucho** *m* cornet
**cuchar|a** *f* spoon. ~**ada** *f* spoonful.
~**adita** *f* teaspoonful. ~**illa** *f*, ~**ita** *f*
teaspoon. ~**ón** *m* ladle
**cuchiche|ar** *vi* whisper. ~**o** *m*
whispering
**cuchill|a** *f* large knife; (*de carnicero*)
cleaver; (*hoja de afeitar*) razor
blade. ~**ada** *f* slash; (*herida*) knife
wound. ~**o** *m* knife
**cuchitril** *m* pigsty; (*fig*) hovel
**cuello** *m* neck; (*de camisa*) collar.
**cortar el** ~ **a uno** cut s.o.'s throat
**cuenc|a** *f* hollow; (*del ojo*) (eye)
socket; (*geog*) basin. ~**o** *m* hollow;
(*vasija*) bowl
**cuenta** *f* count; (*acción de contar*)
counting; (*factura*) bill; (*en banco,
relato*) account; (*asunto*) affair; (*de
collar etc*) bead. ~ **corriente** current
account, checking account (*Amer*).
**ajustar las** ~**s** settle accounts. **caer
en la** ~ **de que** realize that. **darse**
~ **de** realize. **en resumidas** ~**s** in
short. **por mi** ~ for myself. **tener en**
~, **tomar en** ~ bear in mind
**cuentakilómetros** *m invar*
milometer
**cuent|ista** *m & f* story-writer; (*de
mentiras*) fibber. ~**o** *m* story; (*mentira*) fib, tall story. • *vb véase* **contar**
**cuerda** *f* rope; (*más fina*) string;
(*mus*) string. ~ **floja** tightrope. **dar**
~ **a** wind up (*un reloj*)
**cuerdo** *a* (*persona*) sane; (*acción*)
sensible
**cuern|a** *f* horns. ~**o** *m* horn
**cuero** *m* leather; (*piel*) skin; (*del
grifo*) washer. ~ **cabelludo** scalp.
**en** ~**s** (*vivos*) stark naked
**cuerpo** *m* body
**cuervo** *m* crow

**cuesta** *f* slope, hill. **∼ abajo** downhill. **∼ arriba** uphill. **a ∼s** on one's back

**cuesti|ón** *f* matter; (*altercado*) quarrel; (*dificultad*) trouble. **∼onario** *m* questionnaire

**cueva** *f* cave; (*sótano*) cellar

**cuida|do** *m* care; (*preocupación*) worry; (*asunto*) affair. **¡∼do!** (be) careful! **∼doso** *a* careful. **∼damente** *adv* carefully. **∼r** *vt* look after. ● *vi*. **∼r de** look after. **∼rse** *vpr* look after o.s. **∼rse de** be careful to. **tener ∼do** be careful

**culata** *f* (*de arma de fuego*) butt; (*auto*) cylinder head. **∼zo** *m* recoil

**culebra** *f* snake

**culebrón** *m* (*LAm*) soap opera

**culinario** *a* culinary

**culmina|ción** *f* culmination. **∼r** *vi* culminate

**culo** *m* (*fam*) bottom. **ir de ∼** go downhill

**culpa** *f* fault; (*jurid*) guilt. **∼bilidad** *f* guilt. **∼ble** *a* guilty. ● *m* culprit. **∼r** *vt* blame (**de** for). **echar la ∼** blame. **por ∼ de** because of. **tener la ∼ de** be to blame for

**cultiv|ar** *vt* farm; grow (*plantas*); (*fig*) cultivate. **∼o** *m* farming; (*de plantas*) growing

**cult|o** *a* (*tierra etc*) cultivated; (*persona*) educated. ● *m* cult; (*homenaje*) worship. **∼ura** *f* culture. **∼ural** *a* cultural

**culturismo** *m* body-building

**cumbre** *f* summit; (*fig*) height

**cumpleaños** *m invar* birthday

**cumplido** *a* perfect; (*grande*) large; (*cortés*) polite. ● *m* compliment. **∼r** *a* reliable. **de ∼** courtesy. **por ∼** out of politeness

**cumplim|entar** *vt* carry out; (*saludar*) pay a courtesy call to; (*felicitar*) congratulate. **∼iento** *m* carrying out, execution

**cumplir** *vt* carry out; observe (*ley*); serve (*condena*); reach (*años*); keep (*promesa*). ● *vi* do one's duty. **∼se** *vpr* expire; (*realizarse*) be fulfilled. **hoy cumple 3 años** he's 3 (years old) today. **por ∼** as a mere formality

**cumulativo** *a* cumulative

**cúmulo** *m* pile, heap

**cuna** *f* cradle; (*fig, nacimiento*) birthplace

**cundir** *vi* spread; (*rendir*) go a long way

**cuneta** *f* gutter

**cuña** *f* wedge

**cuñad|a** *f* sister-in-law. **∼o** *m* brother-in-law

**cuño** *m* stamp. **de nuevo ∼** new

**cuota** *f* quota; (*de sociedad etc*) subscription, fees

**cupe** *vb véase* **caber**

**cupé** *m* coupé

**Cupido** *m* Cupid

**cupo** *m* cuota

**cupón** *m* coupon

**cúpula** *f* dome

**cura** *f* cure; (*tratamiento*) treatment. ● *m* priest. **∼ble** *a* curable. **∼ción** *f* healing. **∼ndero** *m* faith-healer. **∼r** *vt* (*incl culin*) cure; dress (*herida*); (*tratar*) treat; (*fig*) remedy; tan (*pieles*). ● *vi* (*persona*) get better; (*herida*) heal; (*fig*) be cured. **∼rse** *vpr* get better

**curios|ear** *vi* pry; (*mirar*) browse. **∼idad** *f* curiosity; (*limpieza*) cleanliness. **∼o** *a* curious; (*raro*) odd, unusual; (*limpio*) clean

**curriculum vitae** *m* curriculum vitae

**cursar** *vt* send; (*estudiar*) study

**cursi** *a* pretentious, showy. ● *m* affected person

**cursillo** *m* short course

**cursiva** *f* italics

**curso** *m* course; (*univ etc*) year. **en ∼** under way; (*año etc*) current

**curtir** *vt* tan; (*fig*) harden. **∼se** *vpr* become tanned; (*fig*) become hardened

**curv|a** *f* curve; (*de carretera*) bend. **∼o** *a* curved

**cúspide** *f* peak

**custodi|a** *f* care, safe-keeping. **∼ar** *vt* take care of. **∼o** *a & m* guardian

**cutáneo** *a* skin. **enfermedad** *f* **cutánea** skin disease

**cutícula** *f* cuticle

**cutis** *m* skin, complexion

**cuyo** *pron* (*de persona*) whose, of whom; (*de cosa*) whose, of which. **en ∼ caso** in which case

# CH

**chabacano** *a* common; (*chiste etc*) vulgar. ● *m* (*Mex, albaricoque*) apricot

**chabola** *f* shack. **∼s** *fpl* shanty town

**chacal** *m* jackal

**chacota** *f* fun. **echar a ∼** make fun of

**chacra** f (LAm) farm

**cháchara** f chatter

**chacharear** vt (Mex) sell. ● vi chatter

**chafar** vt crush. **quedar chafado** be nonplussed

**chal** m shawl

**chalado** a (fam) crazy

**chalé** m house (with a garden), villa

**chaleco** m waistcoat, vest (Amer). ~ **salvavidas** life-jacket

**chalequear** vt (Arg, Mex) trick

**chalet** m (pl **chalets**) house (with a garden), villa

**chalón** m (LAm) shawl

**chalote** m shallot

**chalupa** f boat

**chamac|a** f (esp Mex) girl. ~**o** m (esp Mex) boy

**chamagoso** a (Mex) filthy

**chamarr|a** f sheepskin jacket. ~**o** m (LAm) coarse blanket

**chamba** f (fam) fluke; (Mex, empleo) job. **por** ~ by fluke

**champán** m, **champaña** m champagne

**champiñón** m mushroom

**champú** m (pl **champúes** o **champús**) shampoo

**chamuscar** [7] vt scorch; (Mex, vender) sell cheaply

**chance** m (esp LAm) chance

**chanclo** m clog; (de caucho) rubber overshoe

**chancho** m (LAm) pig

**chanchullo** m swindle, fiddle (fam)

**chandal** m tracksuit

**chanquete** m whitebait

**chantaj|e** m blackmail. ~**ista** m & f blackmailer

**chanza** f joke

**chapa** f plate, sheet; (de madera) plywood; (de botella) metal top. ~**do** a plated. ~**do a la antigua** old-fashioned. ~**do de oro** gold-plated

**chaparrón** m downpour. **llover a chaparrones** pour (down), rain cats and dogs

**chapotear** vi splash

**chapuce|ar** vt botch; (Mex, engañar) deceive. ~**ro** a (persona) careless; (cosas) shoddy. ● m careless worker

**chapurrar** vt, **chapurrear** vt speak badly, speak a little; mix (licores)

**chapuza** f botched job, mess; (de poca importancia) odd job

**chaqueta** f jacket. **cambiar la ~** change sides

**chaquetero** m turncoat

**charada** f charade

**charc|a** f pond, pool. ~**o** m puddle, pool. **cruzar el ~o** cross the water; (ir a América) cross the Atlantic

**charla** f chat; (conferencia) talk. ~**dor** a talkative. ~**r** vi (fam) chat

**charlatán** a talkative. ● m chatterbox; (curandero) charlatan

**charol** m varnish; (cuero) patent leather

**chárter** a charter

**chascar** [7] vt crack ‹látigo›; click ‹lengua›; snap ‹dedos›. ● vi ‹látigo› crack; (con la lengua) click one's tongue; (los dedos) snap

**chascarrillo** m joke, funny story

**chasco** m disappointment; (broma) joke; (engaño) trick

**chasis** m (auto) chassis

**chasqu|ear** vt crack ‹látigo›; click ‹lengua›; snap ‹dedos›. ● vi ‹látigo› crack; (con la lengua) click one's tongue; (los dedos) snap. ~**ido** m crack; (de la lengua) click; (de los dedos) snap

**chatarra** f scrap iron; (fig) scrap

**chato** a ‹nariz› snub; ‹persona› snub-nosed; ‹objetos› flat. ● m wine glass; (niño, mujer, fam) dear, darling; (hombre, fam) mate (fam)

**chaval** m (fam) boy, lad. ~**a** f girl, lass

**che** int (Arg) listen!, hey!

**checo** a & m Czech. **la república** f **Checa** the Czech Republic

**checoslovaco** a & m (history) Czechoslovak

**Checoslovaquia** f (history) Czechoslovakia

**chelín** m shilling

**chelo** a (Mex, rubio) fair

**cheque** m cheque. ~ **de viaje** traveller's cheque. ~**ra** f cheque-book

**chica** f girl; (criada) maid, servant

**chicano** a & m Chicano, Mexican-American

**chicle** m chewing-gum

**chico** a (fam) small. ● m boy. ~**s** mpl children

**chicoleo** m compliment

**chicoria** f chicory

**chicharra** f cicada; (fig) chatterbox

**chicharrón** m (de cerdo) crackling; (fig) sunburnt person

**chichón** m bump, lump

**chifla|do** a (fam) crazy, daft. ~**r** vt (fam) drive crazy. ~**rse** vpr be mad (**por** about). **le chifla el chocolate**

he's mad about chocolate. **le tiene chiflado esa chica** he's crazy about that girl

**Chile** m Chile

**chile** m chilli

**chileno** a & m Chilean

**chill|ar** vi scream, shriek; ⟨gato⟩ howl; ⟨ratón⟩ squeak; ⟨cerdo⟩ squeal. **~ido** m scream, screech; ⟨de gato etc⟩ howl. **~ón** a noisy; ⟨colores⟩ loud; ⟨sonido⟩ shrill

**chimenea** f chimney; (hogar) fireplace

**chimpancé** m chimpanzee

**China** f China

**chinch|ar** vt (fam) annoy, pester. **~e** m drawing-pin (Brit), thumbtack (Amer); (insecto) bedbug; (fig) nuisance. **~eta** f drawing-pin (Brit), thumbtack (Amer)

**chinela** f slipper

**chino** a & m Chinese

**Chipre** m Cyprus

**chipriota** a & m & f Cypriot

**chiquillo** a childish. ● m child, kid (fam)

**chiquito** a small, tiny. ● m child, kid (fam)

**chiribita** f spark. **estar que echa ~s** be furious

**chirimoya** f custard apple

**chiripa** f fluke. **por ~** by fluke

**chirivía** f parsnip

**chirri|ar** vi creak; ⟨pájaro⟩ chirp. **~do** m creaking; (al freír) sizzling; (de pájaros) chirping

**chis** int sh!, hush!; (para llamar a uno, fam) hey!, psst!

**chism|e** m gadget, thingumajig (fam); (chismorreo) piece of gossip. **~es** mpl things, bits and pieces. **~orreo** m gossip. **~oso** a gossipy. ● m gossip

**chispa** f spark; ⟨gota⟩ drop; ⟨gracia⟩ wit; (fig) sparkle. **estar que echa ~(s)** be furious

**chispea|nte** a sparkling. **~r** vi spark; ⟨lloviznar⟩ drizzle; (fig) sparkle

**chisporrotear** vt throw out sparks; ⟨fuego⟩ crackle; ⟨aceite⟩ sizzle

**chistar** vi speak. **sin ~** without saying a word

**chiste** m joke, funny story. **hacer ~ de** make fun of. **tener ~** be funny

**chistera** f (fam) top hat, topper (fam)

**chistoso** a funny

**chiva|r** vi inform ⟨policía⟩; ⟨niño⟩ tell. **~tazo** m tip-off. **~to** m informer; ⟨niño⟩ telltale

**chivo** m kid, young goat

**choca|nte** a surprising; ⟨persona⟩ odd. **~r** [7] vt clink ⟨vasos⟩; shake ⟨la mano⟩. ● vi collide, hit. **~r con**, **~r contra** crash into. **lo ~nte es que** the surprising thing is that

**chocolate** m chocolate. **tableta f de ~** bar of chocolate

**choch|ear** vi be senile. **~o a** senile; (fig) soft

**chófer** m chauffeur; (conductor) driver

**cholo** a & m (LAm) half-breed

**chopo** m poplar

**choque** m collision; (fig) clash; (eléctrico) shock; (auto, rail etc) crash, accident; (sacudida) jolt

**chorizo** m salami

**chorr|ear** vi gush forth; (fig) be dripping. **~o** m jet, stream; (caudal pequeño) trickle; (fig) stream. **a ~os** (fig) in abundance. **hablar a ~os** jabber

**chovinis|mo** m chauvinism. **~ta** a chauvinistic. ● m & f chauvinist

**choza** f hut

**chubas|co** m squall, heavy shower; (fig) bad patch. **~quero** m raincoat, anorak

**chuchería** f trinket; (culin) sweet

**chufa** f tiger nut

**chuleta** f chop

**chulo** a insolent; (vistoso) showy. ● m ruffian; (rufián) pimp

**chumbo** m prickly pear; (fam) bump. **higo m ~** prickly pear

**chup|ada** f suck; (al cigarro etc) puff. **~ado** a skinny; (fácil, fam) very easy. **~ar** vt suck, lick; puff at ⟨cigarro etc⟩; (absorber) absorb. **~arse** vpr lose weight. **~ete** m dummy (Brit), pacifier (Amer)

**churro** m fritter; (fam) mess. **me salió un ~** I made a mess of it

**chusco** a funny

**chusma** f riff-raff

**chutar** vi shoot. **¡va que chuta!** it's going well!

## D

**dactilógrafo** m typist

**dado** m dice. ● a given; ⟨hora⟩ gone. **~ que** since, given that

**dalia** f dahlia

**daltoniano** a colour-blind

**dama** *f* lady; *(en la corte)* lady-in-waiting. ~s *fpl* draughts *(Brit)*, checkers *(Amer)*

**damasco** *m* damask

**danés** *a* Danish. ● *m* Dane; *(idioma)* Danish

**danza** *f* dance; *(acción)* dancing; *(enredo)* affair. ~r [10] *vt/i* dance

**dañ|ado** *a* damaged. ~ar *vt* damage; harm *(persona)*. ~ino *a* harmful. ~o *m* damage; *(a una persona)* harm. ~oso *a* harmful. ~os y perjuicios damages. hacer ~o a harm; hurt *(persona)*. hacerse ~o hurt o.s.

**dar** [26] *vt* give; *(producir)* yield; strike *(la hora)*. ● *vi* give. **da igual** it doesn't matter. **¡dale!** go on! **da lo mismo** it doesn't matter. ~ **a** *(ventana)* look on to; *(edificio)* face. ~ **a luz** give birth. ~ **con** meet *(persona)*; find *(cosa)*. ~ **de cabeza** fall flat on one's face. ~ **por** assume; ( + *infinitivo*) decide. ~**se** *vpr* give o.s. up; *(suceder)* happen. **dárselas de** make o.s. out to be. ~**se por** consider o.s. **¿qué más da?** it doesn't matter!

**dardo** *m* dart

**dársena** *f* dock

**datar** *vt* date. ● *vi*. ~ **de** date from

**dátil** *m* date

**dato** *m* fact. ~s *mpl* data, information

**de** *prep* of; *(procedencia)* from; *(suposición)* if. ~ **día** by day. ~ **dos en dos** two by two. ~ **haberlo sabido** if I (you, he etc) had known. ~ **niño** as a child. **el libro** ~ **mi amigo** my friend's book. **las 2** ~ **la madrugada** 2 (o'clock) in the morning. **un puente** ~ **hierro** an iron bridge. **soy** ~ **Loughborough** I'm from Loughborough

**deambular** *vi* stroll

**debajo** *adv* underneath. ~ **de** underneath, under. **el de** ~ the one underneath. **por** ~ underneath. **por** ~ **de** below

**debat|e** *m* debate. ~**ir** *vt* debate

**deber** *vt* owe. ● *vi* have to, must. ● *m* duty. ~**es** *mpl* homework. ~**se** *vpr*. ~**se a** be due to. **debo marcharme** I must go, I have to go

**debido** *a* due; *(correcto)* proper. ~ **a** due to. **como es** ~ as is proper. **con el respeto** ~ with due respect

**débil** *a* weak; *(ruido)* faint; *(luz)* dim

**debili|dad** *f* weakness. ~**tar** *vt* weaken. ~**tarse** *vpr* weaken, get weak

**débito** *m* debit; *(deuda)* debt

**debutar** *vi* make one's debut

**década** *f* decade

**deca|dencia** *f* decline. ~**dente** *a* decadent. ~**er** [29] *vi* decline; *(debilitarse)* weaken. ~**ído** *a* depressed. ~**imiento** *m* decline, weakening

**decano** *m* dean; *(miembro más antiguo)* senior member

**decantar** *vt* decant *(vino etc)*

**decapitar** *vt* behead

**decena** *f* ten; *(aproximadamente)* about ten

**decencia** *f* decency, honesty

**decenio** *m* decade

**decente** *a* *(persona)* respectable, honest; *(cosas)* modest; *(limpio)* clean, tidy

**decepci|ón** *f* disappointment. ~**onar** *vt* disappoint

**decibelio** *m* decibel

**decidi|do** *a* decided; *(persona)* determined, resolute. ~**r** *vt* decide; settle *(cuestión etc)*. ● *vi* decide. ~**rse** *vpr* make up one's mind

**decimal** *a & m* decimal

**décimo** *a & m* tenth. ● *m* *(de lotería)* tenth part of a lottery ticket

**decimo**: ~**ctavo** *a & m* eighteenth. ~**cuarto** *a & m* fourteenth. ~**nono** *a & m*, ~**noveno** *a & m* nineteenth. ~**quinto** *a & m* fifteenth. ~**séptimo** *a & m* seventeenth. ~**sexto** *a & m* sixteenth. ~**tercero** *a & m*, ~**tercio** *a & m* thirteenth

**decir** [46] *vt* say; *(contar)* tell. ● *m* saying. ~**se** *vpr* be said. ~ **que no** say no. ~ **que sí** say yes. **dicho de otro modo** in other words. **dicho y hecho** no sooner said than done. **¿dígame?** can I help you? **¡dígame!** *(al teléfono)* hello! **digamos** let's say. **es** ~ that is to say. **mejor dicho** rather. **¡no me digas!** you don't say!, really! **por así** ~, **por** ~**lo así** so to speak, as it were. **querer** ~ mean. **se dice que** it is said that, they say that

**decisi|ón** *f* decision. ~**vo** *a* decisive

**declamar** *vt* declaim

**declara|ción** *f* statement. ~**ción de renta** income tax return. ~**r** *vt/i* declare. ~**rse** *vpr* declare o.s.; *(epidemia etc)* break out

**declina|ción** *f* *(gram)* declension. ~**r** *vt/i* decline; *(salud)* deteriorate

**declive** m slope; (fig) decline. **en ∼** sloping

**decolorar** vt discolour, fade. **∼se** vpr become discoloured, fade

**decora|ción** f decoration. **∼do** m (en el teatro) set. **∼dor** m decorator. **∼r** vt decorate. **∼tivo** a decorative

**decoro** m decorum; (respeto) respect. **∼so** a proper; (modesto) modest; ⟨profesión⟩ honourable

**decrecer** [11] vi decrease, diminish; ⟨aguas⟩ subside

**decrépito** a decrepit

**decret|ar** vt decree. **∼o** m decree

**dedal** m thimble

**dedica|ción** f dedication. **∼r** [7] vt dedicate; devote ⟨tiempo⟩. **∼toria** f dedication, inscription

**ded|il** m finger-stall. **∼illo** m. **al ∼illo** at one's fingertips. **∼o** m finger; (del pie) toe. **∼o anular** ring finger. **∼o corazón** middle finger. **∼o gordo** thumb. **∼o índice** index finger. **∼o meñique** little finger. **∼o pulgar** thumb

**deduc|ción** f deduction. **∼ir** [47] vt deduce; (descontar) deduct

**defect|o** m fault, defect. **∼uoso** a defective

**defen|der** [1] vt defend. **∼sa** f defence. **∼sivo** a defensive. **∼sor** m defender. **abogado** m **∼sor** defence counsel

**deferen|cia** f deference. **∼te** a deferential

**deficien|cia** f deficiency. **∼cia mental** mental handicap. **∼te** a deficient; (imperfecto) defective. **∼te mental** mentally handicapped

**déficit** m invar deficit

**defini|ción** f definition. **∼do** a defined. **∼r** vt define; (aclarar) clarify. **∼tivo** a definitive. **en ∼tiva** (en resumen) in short

**deflación** f deflation

**deform|ación** f deformation; (TV etc) distortion. **∼ar** vt deform; (TV etc) distort. **∼arse** vpr go out of shape. **∼e** a deformed; (feo) ugly

**defraudar** vt cheat; (decepcionar) disappoint; evade ⟨impuestos etc⟩

**defunción** f death

**degenera|ción** f degeneration; (moral) degeneracy. **∼do** a degenerate. **∼r** vi degenerate

**deglutir** vt/i swallow

**degollar** [16] vt cut s.o.'s throat; (fig, arruinar) ruin

**degradar** vt degrade. **∼se** vpr lower o.s.

**degusta|ción** f tasting. **∼r** vt taste

**dehesa** f pasture

**dei|dad** f deity. **∼ficar** [7] vt deify

**deja|ción** f surrender. **∼dez** f abandon; (pereza) laziness. **∼do** a negligent. **∼r** vt leave; (abandonar) abandon; (prestar) lend; (permitir) let. **∼r aparte, ∼r a un lado** leave aside. **∼r de** stop. **no ∼r de** not fail to

**dejo** m aftertaste; (tonillo) accent

**del = de;el**

**delantal** m apron

**delante** adv in front; (enfrente) opposite. **∼ de** in front of. **de ∼** front

**delanter|a** f front; (de teatro etc) front row; (ventaja) advantage. **coger la ∼a** get ahead. **∼o** a front. ● m forward. **llevar la ∼a** be ahead

**delat|ar** vt denounce. **∼or** m informer

**delega|ción** f delegation; (sucursal) branch. **∼do** m delegate; (com) agent, representative. **∼r** [12] vt delegate

**deleit|ar** vt delight. **∼e** m delight

**deletéreo** a deleterious

**deletre|ar** vt spell (out). **∼o** m spelling

**deleznable** a brittle, crumbly; ⟨argumento etc⟩ weak

**delfín** m dolphin

**delgad|ez** f thinness. **∼o** a thin; (esbelto) slim. **∼ucho** a skinny

**delibera|ción** f deliberation. **∼r** vt discuss, decide. ● vi deliberate

**delicad|eza** f delicacy; (fragilidad) frailty; (tacto) tact. **∼o** a delicate; (sensible) sensitive; (discreto) tactful, discreet. **falta de ∼eza** tactlessness

**delici|a** f delight. **∼oso** a delightful; ⟨sabor etc⟩ delicious; (gracioso, fam) funny

**delimitar** vt delimit

**delincuen|cia** f delinquency. **∼te** a & m delinquent

**delinea|nte** m draughtsman. **∼r** vt outline; (dibujar) draw

**delinquir** [8] vi commit an offence

**delir|ante** a delirious. **∼ar** vi be delirious; (fig) talk nonsense. **∼io** m delirium; (fig) frenzy

**delito** m crime, offence

**delta** f delta

**demacrado** a emaciated

**demagogo** *m* demagogue

**demanda** *f.* **en ~ de** asking for; (*en busca de*) in search of. **~nte** *m & f* (*jurid*) plaintiff. **~r** *vt* (*jurid*) bring an action against

**demarca|ción** *f* demarcation. **~r** [7] *vt* demarcate

**demás** *a* rest of the, other. ● *pron* rest, others. **lo ~** the rest. **por ~** useless; (*muy*) very. **por lo ~** otherwise

**demasía** *f* excess; (*abuso*) outrage; (*atrevimiento*) insolence. **en ~** too much

**demasiado** *a* too much; (*en plural*) too many. ● *adv* too much; (*con adjetivo*) too

**demen|cia** *f* madness. **~te** *a* demented, mad

**dem|ocracia** *f* democracy. **~ócrata** *m & f* democrat. **~ocrático** *a* democratic

**demol|er** [2] *vt* demolish. **~ición** *f* demolition

**demonio** *m* devil, demon. **¡~s!** hell! **¿cómo ~s?** how the hell? **¡qué ~s!** what the hell!

**demora** *f* delay. **~r** *vt* delay. ● *vi* stay on. **~rse** *vpr* be a long time

**demostra|ción** *f* demonstration, show. **~r** [2] *vt* demonstrate; (*mostrar*) show; (*probar*) prove. **~tivo** *a* demonstrative

**denegar** [1 & 12] *vt* refuse

**deng|oso** *a* affected, finicky. **~ue** *m* affectation

**denigrar** *vt* denigrate

**denomina|ción** *f* denomination. **~do** *a* called. **~dor** *m* denominator. **~r** *vt* name

**denotar** *vt* denote

**dens|idad** *f* density. **~o** *a* dense, thick

**denta|dura** *f* teeth. **~dura postiza** denture, false teeth. **~l** *a* dental

**dentera** *f.* **dar ~ a uno** set s.o.'s teeth on edge; (*dar envidia*) make s.o. green with envy

**dentífrico** *m* toothpaste

**dentista** *m & f* dentist

**dentro** *adv* inside; (*de un edificio*) indoors. **~ de** in. **~ de poco** soon. **por ~** inside

**denuncia** *f* report; (*acusación*) accusation. **~r** *vt* report (a crime); ⟨*periódico etc*⟩ denounce; (*indicar*) indicate

**departamento** *m* department; (*Arg*, *piso*) flat (*Brit*), apartment (*Amer*)

**dependencia** *f* dependence; (*sección*) section; (*sucursal*) branch

**depender** *vi* depend (**de** on)

**dependient|a** *f* shop assistant. **~e** *a* dependent (**de** on). ● *m* employee; (*de oficina*) clerk; (*de tienda*) shop assistant

**depila|ción** *f* depilation. **~r** *vt* depilate. **~torio** *a* depilatory

**deplora|ble** *a* deplorable. **~r** *vt* deplore, regret

**deponer** [34] *vt* remove from office. ● *vi* give evidence

**deporta|ción** *f* deportation. **~r** *vt* deport

**deport|e** *m* sport. **~ista** *m* sportsman. ● *f* sportswoman. **~ivo** *a* sports. ● *m* sports car. **hacer ~e** take part in sports

**deposición** *f* deposition; (*de un empleo*) removal from office

**dep|ositador** *m* depositor. **~ositante** *m & f* depositor. **~ositar** *vt* deposit; (*poner*) put, place. **~ósito** *m* deposit; (*conjunto de cosas*) store; (*almacén*) warehouse; (*mil*) depot; (*de líquidos*) tank

**deprava|ción** *f* depravity. **~do** *a* depraved. **~r** *vt* deprave. **~rse** *vpr* become depraved

**deprecia|ción** *f* depreciation. **~r** *vt* depreciate. **~rse** *vpr* depreciate

**depresión** *f* depression

**deprim|ente** *a* depressing. **~ido** *a* depressed. **~ir** *vt* depress. **~irse** *vpr* get depressed

**depura|ción** *f* purification; (*pol*) purging. **~r** *vt* purify; (*pol*) purge

**derech|a** *f* (*mano*) right hand; (*lado*) right. **~ista** *a* right-wing. ● *m & f* right-winger. **~o** *a* right; (*vertical*) upright; (*recto*) straight. ● *adv* straight. ● *m* right; (*ley*) law; (*lado*) right side. **~os** *mpl* dues. **~os de autor** royalties. **a la ~a** on the right; (*hacia el lado derecho*) to the right. **todo ~o** straight on

**deriva** *f* drift. **a la ~** drifting, adrift

**deriva|ción** *f* derivation; (*cambio*) diversion. **~do** *a* derived. ● *m* derivative, by-product. **~r** *vt* derive; (*cambiar la dirección de*) divert. ● *vi.* **~r de** derive from, be derived from. **~rse** *vpr* be derived

**derram|amiento** *m* spilling. **~amiento de sangre** bloodshed. **~ar** *vt* spill; (*verter*) pour; shed ⟨*lágrimas*⟩. **~arse** *vpr* spill. **~e** *m* spilling; (*pérdida*) leakage; (*cantidad perdida*) spillage; (*med*) discharge; (*med, de sangre*) haemorrhage

**derretir** [5] *vt* melt. ～**se** *vpr* melt; (*enamorarse*) fall in love (**por** with)

**derriba|do** *a* fallen down. ～**r** *vt* knock down; bring down, overthrow ‹*gobierno etc*›. ～**rse** *vpr* fall down

**derrocar** [7] *vt* bring down, overthrow ‹*gobierno etc*›

**derroch|ar** *vt* squander. ～**e** *m* waste

**derrot|a** *f* defeat; (*rumbo*) course. ～**ar** *vt* defeat. ～**ado** *a* defeated; ‹*vestido*› shabby. ～**ero** *m* course

**derrumba|miento** *m* collapse. ～**r** *vt* (*derribar*) knock down. ～**rse** *vpr* collapse

**desaborido** *a* tasteless; ‹*persona*› dull

**desabotonar** *vt* unbutton, undo. ● *vi* bloom. ～**se** *vpr* come undone

**desabrido** *a* tasteless; ‹*tiempo*› unpleasant; ‹*persona*› surly

**desabrochar** *vt* undo. ～**se** *vpr* come undone

**desacat|ar** *vt* have no respect for. ～**o** *m* disrespect

**desac|ertado** *a* ill-advised; (*erróneo*) wrong. ～**ertar** [1] *vt* be wrong. ～**ierto** *m* mistake

**desaconseja|ble** *a* inadvisable. ～**do** *a* unwise, ill-advised. ～**r** *vt* advise against, dissuade

**desacorde** *a* discordant

**desacostumbra|do** *a* unusual. ～**r** *vt* give up

**desacreditar** *vt* discredit

**desactivar** *vt* defuse

**desacuerdo** *m* disagreement

**desafiar** [20] *vt* challenge; (*afrontar*) defy

**desafilado** *a* blunt

**desafina|do** *a* out of tune. ～**r** *vi* be out of tune. ～**rse** *vpr* go out of tune

**desafío** *m* challenge; (*combate*) duel

**desaforado** *a* ‹*comportamiento*› outrageous; (*desmedido*) excessive; ‹*sonido*› loud; (*enorme*) huge

**desafortunad|amente** *adv* unfortunately. ～**o** *a* unfortunate

**desagrada|ble** *a* unpleasant. ～**r** *vt* displease. ● *vi* be unpleasant. **me** ～ **el sabor** I don't like the taste

**desagradecido** *a* ungrateful

**desagrado** *m* displeasure. **con** ～ unwillingly

**desagravi|ar** *vt* make amends to. ～**o** *m* amends; (*expiación*) atonement

**desagregar** [12] *vt* break up. ～**se** *vpr* disintegrate

**desagüe** *m* drain; (*acción*) drainage. **tubo** *m* **de** ～ drain-pipe

**desaguisado** *a* illegal. ● *m* offence; (*fam*) disaster

**desahog|ado** *a* roomy; (*adinerado*) well-off; (*fig, descarado, fam*) impudent. ～**ar** [12] *vt* relieve; vent ‹*ira*›. ～**arse** *vpr* (*desfogarse*) let off steam. ～**o** *m* comfort; (*alivio*) relief

**desahuci|ar** *vt* deprive of hope; give up hope for ‹*enfermo*›; evict ‹*inquilino*›. ～**o** *m* eviction

**desair|ado** *a* humiliating; ‹*persona*› humiliated, spurned. ～**ar** *vt* snub ‹*persona*›; disregard ‹*cosa*›. ～**e** *m* rebuff

**desajuste** *m* maladjustment; (*avería*) breakdown

**desal|entador** *a* disheartening. ～**entar** [1] *vt* (*fig*) discourage. ～**iento** *m* discouragement

**desaliño** *m* untidiness, scruffiness

**desalmado** *a* wicked

**desalojar** *vt* eject ‹*persona*›; evacuate ‹*sitio*›. ● *vi* move (house)

**desampar|ado** *a* helpless; (*abandonado*) abandoned. ～**ar** *vt* abandon. ～**o** *m* helplessness; (*abandono*) abandonment

**desangelado** *a* insipid, dull

**desangrar** *vt* bleed. ～**se** *vpr* bleed

**desanima|do** *a* down-hearted. ～**r** *vt* discourage. ～**rse** *vpr* lose heart

**desánimo** *m* discouragement

**desanudar** *vt* untie

**desapacible** *a* unpleasant; ‹*sonido*› harsh

**desapar|ecer** [11] *vi* disappear; ‹*efecto*› wear off. ～**ecido** *a* disappeared. ● *m* missing person. ～**ecidos** *mpl* missing. ～**ición** *f* disappearance

**desapasionado** *a* dispassionate

**desapego** *m* indifference

**desapercebido** *a* unnoticed

**desaplicado** *a* lazy

**desaprensi|ón** *f* unscrupulousness. ～**vo** *a* unscrupulous

**desaproba|ción** *f* disapproval. ～**r** [2] *vt* disapprove of; (*rechazar*) reject

**desaprovecha|do** *a* wasted; ‹*alumno*› lazy. ～**r** *vt* waste

**desarm|ar** *vt* disarm; (*desmontar*) take to pieces. ～**e** *m* disarmament

**desarraig|ado** *a* rootless. ～**ar** [12] *vt* uproot; (*fig, erradicar*) wipe out. ～**o** *m* uprooting; (*fig*) eradication

**desarregl|ado** a untidy; (*desordenado*) disorderly. ~**ar** vt mess up; (*deshacer el orden*) make untidy. ~**o** m disorder; (*de persona*) untidiness

**desarroll|ado** a (well-) developed. ~**ar** vt develop; (*desenrollar*) unroll, unfold. ~**arse** vpr (*incl foto*) develop; (*desenrollarse*) unroll; (*suceso*) take place. ~**o** m development

**desarrugar** [12] vt smooth out

**desarticular** vt dislocate (*hueso*); (*fig*) break up

**desaseado** a dirty; (*desordenado*) untidy

**desasirse** [45] vpr let go (**de** of)

**desasos|egar** [1 & 12] vt disturb. ~**egarse** vpr get uneasy. ~**iego** m anxiety; (*intranquilidad*) restlessness

**desastr|ado** a scruffy. ~**e** m disaster. ~**oso** a disastrous

**desata|do** a untied; (*fig*) wild. ~**r** vt untie; (*fig, soltar*) unleash. ~**rse** vpr come undone

**desatascar** [7] vt pull out of the mud; unblock (*tubo etc*)

**desaten|ción** f inattention; (*descortesía*) discourtesy. ~**der** [1] vt not pay attention to; neglect (*deber etc*). ~**to** a inattentive; (*descortés*) discourteous

**desatin|ado** a silly. ~**o** m silliness; (*error*) mistake

**desatornillar** vt unscrew

**desatracar** [7] vt/i cast off

**desautorizar** [10] vt declare unauthorized; (*desmentir*) deny

**desavenencia** f disagreement

**desayun|ar** vt have for breakfast. ● vi have breakfast. ~**o** m breakfast

**desazón** m (*fig*) anxiety

**desbandarse** vpr (*mil*) disband; (*dispersarse*) disperse

**desbarajust|ar** vt throw into confusion. ~**e** m confusion

**desbaratar** vt spoil

**desbloquear** vt unfreeze

**desbocado** a (*vasija etc*) chipped; (*caballo*) runaway; (*persona*) foul-mouthed

**desborda|nte** a overflowing. ~**r** vt go beyond; (*exceder*) exceed. ● vi overflow. ~**rse** vpr overflow

**descabalgar** [12] vi dismount

**descabellado** a crazy

**descabezar** [10] vt behead

**descafeinado** a decaffeinated. ● m decaffeinated coffee

**descalabr|ar** vt injure in the head; (*fig*) damage. ~**o** m disaster

**descalificar** [7] vt disqualify; (*desacreditar*) discredit

**descalz|ar** [10] vt take off (*zapato*). ~**o** a barefoot

**descaminar** vt misdirect; (*fig*) lead astray

**descamisado** a shirtless; (*fig*) shabby

**descampado** a open. ● m open ground

**descans|ado** a rested; (*trabajo*) easy. ~**apiés** m footrest. ~**ar** vt/i rest. ~**illo** m landing. ~**o** m rest; (*descansillo*) landing; (*en deportes*) half-time; (*en el teatro etc*) interval

**descapotable** a convertible

**descarado** a insolent, cheeky; (*sin vergüenza*) shameless

**descarg|a** f unloading; (*mil, elec*) discharge. ~**ar** [12] vt unload; (*mil, elec*) discharge, shock; deal (*golpe etc*). ● vi flow into. ~**o** m unloading; (*recibo*) receipt; (*jurid*) evidence

**descarnado** a scrawny, lean; (*fig*) bare

**descaro** m insolence, cheek; (*cinismo*) nerve, effrontery

**descarriar** [20] vt misdirect; (*fig*) lead astray. ~**se** vpr go the wrong way; (*res*) stray; (*fig*) go astray

**descarrila|miento** m derailment. ~**r** vi be derailed. ~**se** vpr be derailed

**descartar** vt discard; (*rechazar*) reject. ~**se** vpr discard

**descascarar** vt shell

**descen|dencia** f descent; (*personas*) descendants. ~**dente** a descending. ~**der** [1] vt lower, get down; go down (*escalera etc*). ● vi go down; (*provenir*) be descended (**de** from). ~**diente** m & f descendent. ~**so** m descent; (*de temperatura, fiebre etc*) fall, drop

**descentralizar** [10] vt decentralize

**descifrar** vt decipher; decode (*clave*)

**descolgar** [2 & 12] vt take down; pick up (*el teléfono*). ~**se** vpr let o.s. down; (*fig, fam*) turn up

**descolorar** vt discolour, fade

**descolori|do** a discoloured, faded; (*persona*) pale. ~**r** vt discolour, fade

**descomedido** a rude; (*excesivo*) excessive, extreme

**descomp|ás** *m* disproportion. **~asado** *a* disproportionate

**descomp|oner** [34] *vt* break down; decompose ‹*substancia*›; distort ‹*rasgos*›; (*estropear*) break; (*desarreglar*) disturb, spoil. **~onerse** *vpr* decompose; (*persona*) lose one's temper. **~osición** *f* decomposition; (*med*) diarrhoea. **~ostura** *f* breaking; (*de un motor*) breakdown; (*desorden*) disorder. **~uesto** *a* broken; (*podrido*) decomposed; (*encolerizado*) angry. **estar ~uesto** have diarrhoea

**descomunal** *a* (*fam*) enormous

**desconc|ertante** *a* disconcerting. **~ertar** [1] *vt* disconcert; (*dejar perplejo*) puzzle. **~ertarse** *vpr* be put out, be disconcerted; ‹*mecanismo*› break down. **~ierto** *m* confusion

**desconectar** *vt* disconnect

**desconfia|do** *a* distrustful. **~nza** *f* distrust, suspicion. **~r** [20] *vi*. **~r de** not trust; (*no creer*) doubt

**descongelar** *vt* defrost; (*com*) unfreeze

**desconoc|er** [11] *vt* not know, not recognize. **~ido** *a* unknown; (*cambiado*) unrecognizable. ● *m* stranger. **~imiento** *m* ignorance

**desconsidera|ción** *f* lack of consideration. **~do** *a* inconsiderate

**descons|olado** *a* distressed. **~olar** [2] *vt* distress. **~olarse** *vpr* despair. **~uelo** *m* distress; (*tristeza*) sadness

**desconta|do** *a*. **dar por ~do** take for granted. **por ~do** of course. **~r** [2] *vt* discount

**descontent|adizo** *a* hard to please. **~ar** *vt* displease. **~o** *a* unhappy (**de** about), discontented (**de** with). ● *m* discontent

**descontrolado** *a* uncontrolled

**descorazonar** *vt* discourage. **~se** *vpr* lose heart

**descorchar** *vt* uncork

**descorrer** *vt* draw ‹*cortina*›. **~ el cerrojo** unbolt the door

**descort|és** *a* rude, discourteous. **~esía** *f* rudeness

**descos|er** *vt* unpick. **~erse** *vpr* come undone. **~ido** *a* unstitched; (*fig*) disjointed. **como un ~ido** a lot

**descoyuntar** *vt* dislocate

**descrédito** *m* disrepute. **ir en ~ de** damage the reputation of

**descreído** *a* unbelieving

**descremar** *vt* skim

**descri|bir** [*pp* **descrito**] *vt* describe. **~pción** *f* description. **~ptivo** *a* descriptive

**descuartizar** [10] *vt* cut up

**descubierto** *a* discovered; (*no cubierto*) uncovered; (*expuesto*) exposed; ‹*cielo*› clear; (*sin sombrero*) bareheaded. ● *m* overdraft; (*déficit*) deficit. **poner al ~** expose

**descubri|miento** *m* discovery. **~r** [*pp* **descubierto**] *vt* discover; (*quitar lo que cubre*) uncover; (*revelar*) reveal; unveil ‹*estatua*›. **~rse** *vpr* be discovered; ‹*cielo*› clear; (*quitarse el sombrero*) take off one's hat

**descuento** *m* discount

**descuid|ado** *a* careless; ‹*aspecto etc*› untidy; (*desprevenido*) unprepared. **~ar** *vt* neglect. ● *vi* not worry. **~arse** *vpr* be careless; (*no preocuparse*) not worry. ¡**~a!** don't worry! **~o** *m* carelessness; (*negligencia*) negligence. **al ~o** nonchalantly. **estar ~ado** not worry, rest assured

**desde** *prep* (*lugar etc*) from; (*tiempo*) since, from. **~ hace poco** for a short time. **~ hace un mes** for a month. **~ luego** of course. **~ Madrid hasta Barcelona** from Madrid to Barcelona. **~ niño** since childhood

**desdecir** [46, *pero imperativo* **desdice**, *futuro y condicional regulares*] *vi*. **~ de** be unworthy of; (*no armonizar*) not match. **~se** *vpr*. **~ de** take back ‹*palabras etc*›; go back on ‹*promesa*›

**desd|én** *m* scorn. **~eñable** *a* contemptible. **~eñar** *vt* scorn. **~eñoso** *a* scornful

**desdicha** *f* misfortune. **~do** *a* unfortunate. **por ~** unfortunately

**desdoblar** *vt* straighten; (*desplegar*) unfold

**desea|ble** *a* desirable. **~r** *vt* want; wish ‹*algo a uno*›. **de ~r** desirable. **le deseo un buen viaje** I hope you have a good journey. ¿**qué desea Vd?** can I help you?

**desecar** [7] *vt* dry up

**desech|ar** *vt* throw out. **~o** *m* rubbish

**desembalar** *vt* unpack

**desembarazar** [10] *vt* clear. **~se** *vpr* free o.s.

**desembarca|dero** *m* landing stage. **~r** [7] *vt* unload. ● *vi* disembark

**desemboca|dura** *f* (*de río*) mouth; (*de calle*) opening. **~r** [7] *vi*. **~r en**

⟨río⟩ flow into; ⟨calle⟩ join; (fig) lead to, end in

**desembols|ar** vt pay. ~o m payment

**desembragar** [12] vi declutch

**desembrollar** vt unravel

**desembuchar** vi tell, reveal a secret

**desemejan|te** a unlike, dissimilar. ~za f dissimilarity

**desempapelar** vt unwrap

**desempaquetar** vt unpack, unwrap

**desempat|ar** vi break a tie. ~e m tie-breaker

**desempeñ|ar** vt redeem; play ⟨papel⟩; hold ⟨cargo⟩; perform, carry out ⟨deber etc⟩. ~arse vpr get out of debt. ~o m redemption; (de un papel, de un cargo) performance

**desemple|ado** a unemployed. ● m unemployed person. ~o m unemployment. **los ~ados** mpl the unemployed

**desempolvar** vt dust; (fig) unearth

**desencadenar** vt unchain; (fig) unleash. ~se vpr break loose; ⟨guerra etc⟩ break out

**desencajar** vt dislocate; (desconectar) disconnect. ~se vpr become distorted

**desencant|ar** vt disillusion. ~o m disillusionment

**desenchufar** vt unplug

**desenfad|ado** a uninhibited. ~ar vt calm down. ~arse vpr calm down. ~o m openness; (desenvoltura) assurance

**desenfocado** a out of focus

**desenfren|ado** a unrestrained. ~arse vpr rage. ~o m licentiousness

**desenganchar** vt unhook

**desengañ|ar** vt disillusion. ~arse vpr be disillusioned; (darse cuenta) realize. ~o m disillusionment, disappointment

**desengrasar** vt remove the grease from. ● vi lose weight

**desenla|ce** m outcome. ~zar [10] vt undo; solve ⟨problema⟩

**desenmarañar** vt unravel

**desenmascarar** vt unmask

**desenojar** vt calm down. ~se vpr calm down

**desenred|ar** vt unravel. ~arse vpr extricate o.s. ~o m denouement

**desenrollar** vt unroll, unwind

**desenroscar** [7] vt unscrew

**desentenderse** [1] vpr want nothing to do with; (afectar ignorancia)

pretend not to know. **hacerse el desentendido** (fingir no oir) pretend not to hear

**desenterrar** [1] vt exhume; (fig) unearth

**desenton|ar** vi be out of tune; ⟨colores⟩ clash. ~o m rudeness

**desentrañar** vt work out

**desenvoltura** f ease; (falta de timidez) confidence; (descaro) insolence

**desenvolver** [2, pp desenvuelto] vt unwrap; expound ⟨idea etc⟩. ~se vpr act with confidence

**deseo** m wish, desire. ~so a desirous. **arder en ~s de** long for. **buen ~** good intentions. **estar ~so de** be eager to

**desequilibr|ado** a unbalanced. ~io m imbalance

**des|erción** f desertion; (pol) defection. ~ertar vt desert. ~értico a desert-like. ~ertor m deserter

**desespera|ción** f despair. ~do a desperate. ~nte a infuriating. ~r vt drive to despair. ● vi despair (de of). ~rse vpr despair

**desestimar** vt (rechazar) reject

**desfachat|ado** a brazen, impudent. ~ez f impudence

**desfalc|ar** [7] vt embezzle. ~o m embezzlement

**desfallec|er** [11] vt weaken. ● vi get weak; (desmayarse) faint. ~imiento m weakness

**desfas|ado** a ⟨persona⟩ out of place, out of step; ⟨máquina etc⟩ out of phase. ~e m jet-lag. **estar ~ado** have jet-lag

**desfavor|able** a unfavourable. ~ecer [11] vt ⟨ropa⟩ not suit

**desfigurar** vt disfigure; (desdibujar) blur; (fig) distort

**desfiladero** m pass

**desfil|ar** vi march (past). ~e m procession, parade. ~e de modelos fashion show

**desfogar** [12] vt vent (en, con on). ~se vpr let off steam

**desgajar** vt tear off; (fig) uproot ⟨persona⟩. ~se vpr come off

**desgana** f (falta de apetito) lack of appetite; (med) weakness, faintness; (fig) unwillingness

**desgarr|ador** a heart-rending. ~ar vt tear; (fig) break ⟨corazón⟩. ~o m tear, rip; (descaro) insolence. ~ón m tear

**desgast|ar** *vt* wear away; wear out ⟨*ropa*⟩. **~arse** *vpr* wear away; ⟨*ropa*⟩ be worn out; ⟨*persona*⟩ wear o.s. out. **~e** *m* wear

**desgracia** *f* misfortune; (*accidente*) accident; (*mala suerte*) bad luck. **~damente** *adv* unfortunately. **~do** *a* unlucky; (*pobre*) poor; (*desagradable*) unpleasant. ● *m* unfortunate person, poor devil (*fam*). **~r** *vt* spoil. **caer en ~** fall from favour. **estar en ~** be unfortunate. **por ~** unfortunately. **¡qué ~!** what a shame!

**desgranar** *vt* shell ⟨*guisantes etc*⟩

**desgreñado** *a* ruffled, dishevelled

**desgua|ce** *m* scrapyard. **~zar** [10] *vt* scrap

**deshabitado** *a* uninhabited

**deshabituarse** [21] *vpr* get out of the habit

**deshacer** [31] *vt* undo; strip ⟨*cama*⟩; unpack ⟨*maleta*⟩; (*desmontar*) take to pieces; break ⟨*trato*⟩; (*derretir*) melt; (*en agua*) dissolve; (*destruir*) destroy; (*estropear*) spoil; (*derrotar*) defeat. **~se** *vpr* come undone; (*descomponerse*) fall to pieces; (*derretirse*) melt. **~se de algo** get rid of sth. **~se en lágrimas** burst into tears. **~se por hacer algo** go out of one's way to do sth

**deshelar** [1] *vt* thaw. **~se** *vpr* thaw

**desheredar** *vt* disinherit

**deshidratar** *vt* dehydrate. **~se** *vpr* become dehydrated

**deshielo** *m* thaw

**deshilachado** *a* frayed

**deshincha|do** *a* ⟨*neumático*⟩ flat. **~r** *vt* deflate. **~rse** *vpr* go down

**deshollina|dor** *m* (chimney-)sweep. **~r** *vt* sweep ⟨*chimenea*⟩

**deshon|esto** *a* dishonest; (*obsceno*) indecent. **~or** *m*, **~ra** *f* disgrace. **~rar** *vt* dishonour

**deshora** *f*. **a ~** (*a hora desacostumbrada*) at an unusual time; (*a hora inoportuna*) at an inconvenient time; (*a hora avanzada*) very late

**deshuesar** *vt* bone ⟨*carne*⟩; stone ⟨*fruta*⟩

**desidia** *f* laziness

**desierto** *a* deserted. ● *m* desert

**designa|ción** *f* designation. **~r** *vt* designate; (*fijar*) fix

**desigual** *a* unequal; ⟨*terreno*⟩ uneven; (*distinto*) different. **~dad** *f* inequality

**desilusi|ón** *f* disappointment; (*pérdida de ilusiones*) disillusionment. **~onar** *vt* disappoint; (*quitar las ilusiones*) disillusion. **~onarse** *vpr* become disillusioned

**desinfecta|nte** *m* disinfectant. **~r** *vt* disinfect

**desinfestar** *vt* decontaminate

**desinflar** *vt* deflate. **~se** *vpr* go down

**desinhibido** *a* uninhibited

**desintegra|ción** *f* disintegration. **~r** *vt* disintegrate. **~rse** *vpr* disintegrate

**desinter|és** *m* impartiality; (*generosidad*) generosity. **~esado** *a* impartial; (*liberal*) generous

**desistir** *vi*. **~ de** give up

**desleal** *a* disloyal. **~tad** *f* disloyalty

**desleír** [51] *vt* thin down, dilute

**deslenguado** *a* foul-mouthed

**desligar** [12] *vt* untie; (*separar*) separate; (*fig, librar*) free. **~se** *vpr* break away; (*de un compromiso*) free o.s.

**deslizar** [10] *vt* slide, slip. **~se** *vpr* slide, slip; ⟨*tiempo*⟩ slide by, pass; (*fluir*) flow

**deslucido** *a* tarnished; (*gastado*) worn out; (*fig*) undistinguished

**deslumbrar** *vt* dazzle

**deslustrar** *vt* tarnish

**desmadr|ado** *a* unruly. **~arse** *vpr* get out of control. **~e** *m* excess

**desmán** *m* outrage

**desmandarse** *vpr* get out of control

**desmantelar** *vt* dismantle; (*despojar*) strip

**desmañado** *a* clumsy

**desmaquillador** *m* make-up remover

**desmay|ado** *a* unconscious. **~ar** *vi* lose heart. **~arse** *vpr* faint. **~o** *m* faint; (*estado*) unconsciousness; (*fig*) depression

**desmedido** *a* excessive

**desmedrarse** *vpr* waste away

**desmejorarse** *vpr* deteriorate

**desmelenado** *a* dishevelled

**desmembrar** *vt* (*fig*) divide up

**desmemoriado** *a* forgetful

**desmentir** [4] *vt* deny. **~se** *vpr* contradict o.s.; (*desdecirse*) go back on one's word

**desmenuzar** [10] *vt* crumble; chop ⟨*carne etc*⟩

**desmerecer** [11] *vt* be unworthy of. ● *vi* deteriorate

**desmesurado** *a* excessive; (*enorme*) enormous

**desmigajar** *vt*, **desmigar** [12] *vt* crumble

**desmonta|ble** *a* collapsible. **~r** *vt* (*quitar*) remove; (*desarmar*) take to pieces; (*derribar*) knock down; (*allanar*) level. ● *vi* dismount

**desmoralizar** [10] *vt* demoralize

**desmoronar** *vt* wear away; (*fig*) make inroads into. **~se** *vpr* crumble

**desmovilizar** [10] *vt/i* demobilize

**desnatar** *vt* skim

**desnivel** *m* unevenness; (*fig*) difference, inequality

**desnud|ar** *vt* strip; undress, strip (*persona*). **~arse** *vpr* get undressed. **~ez** *f* nudity. **~o** *a* naked; (*fig*) bare. ● *m* nude

**desnutri|ción** *f* malnutrition. **~do** *a* undernourished

**desobed|ecer** [11] *vt* disobey. **~iencia** *f* disobedience. **~iente** *a* disobedient

**desocupa|do** *a* (*asiento etc*) vacant, free; (*sin trabajo*) unemployed; (*ocioso*) idle. **~r** *vt* vacate

**desodorante** *m* deodorant

**desoír** [50] *vt* take no notice of

**desola|ción** *f* desolation; (*fig*) distress. **~do** *a* desolate; (*persona*) sorry, sad. **~r** *vt* ruin; (*desconsolar*) distress

**desollar** *vt* skin; (*fig, criticar*) criticize; (*fig, hacer pagar demasiado*, *fam*) fleece

**desorbitante** *a* excessive

**desorden** *m* disorder, untidiness; (*confusión*) confusion. **~ado** *a* untidy. **~ar** *vt* disarrange, make a mess of

**desorganizar** [10] *vt* disorganize; (*trastornar*) disturb

**desorienta|do** *a* confused. **~r** *vt* disorientate. **~rse** *vpr* lose one's bearings

**desovar** *vi* (*pez*) spawn; (*insecto*) lay eggs

**despabila|do** *a* wide awake; (*listo*) quick. **~r** *vt* (*despertar*) wake up; (*avivar*) brighten up. **~rse** *vpr* wake up; (*avivarse*) brighten up. **¡despabílate!** get a move on!

**despaci|o** *adv* slowly. ● *int* easy does it! **~to** *adv* slowly

**despach|ar** *vt* finish; (*tratar con*) deal with; (*vender*) sell; (*enviar*) send; (*despedir*) send away; issue (*billete*). ● *vi* hurry up. **~arse** *vpr* get rid; (*terminar*) finish. **~o** *m* dispatch; (*oficina*) office; (*venta*) sale; (*del teatro*) box office

**despampanante** *a* stunning

**desparejado** *a* odd

**desparpajo** *m* confidence; (*descaro*) impudence

**desparramar** *vt* scatter; spill (*líquidos*); squander (*fortuna*)

**despavorido** *a* terrified

**despectivo** *a* disparaging; (*sentido etc*) pejorative

**despecho** *m* spite. **a ~ de** in spite of. **por ~** out of spite

**despedazar** [10] *vt* tear to pieces

**despedi|da** *f* goodbye, farewell. **~da de soltero** stag-party. **~r** [5] *vt* say goodbye, see off; dismiss (*empleado*); evict (*inquilino*); (*arrojar*) throw; give off (*olor etc*). **~rse** *vpr*. **~rse de** say goodbye to

**despeg|ado** *a* cold, indifferent. **~ar** [12] *vt* unstick. ● *vi* (*avión*) take off. **~o** *m* indifference. **~ue** *m* take-off

**despeinar** *vt* ruffle the hair of

**despeja|do** *a* clear; (*persona*) wide awake. **~r** *vt* clear; (*aclarar*) clarify. ● *vi* clear. **~rse** *vpr* (*aclararse*) become clear; (*cielo*) clear; (*tiempo*) clear up; (*persona*) liven up

**despellejar** *vt* skin

**despensa** *f* pantry, larder

**despeñadero** *m* cliff

**desperdici|ar** *vt* waste. **~o** *m* waste. **~os** *mpl* rubbish. **no tener ~o** be good all the way through

**desperezarse** [10] *vpr* stretch

**desperfecto** *m* flaw

**desperta|dor** *m* alarm clock. **~r** [1] *vt* wake up; (*fig*) awaken. **~rse** *vpr* wake up

**despiadado** *a* merciless

**despido** *m* dismissal

**despierto** *a* awake; (*listo*) bright

**despilfarr|ar** *vt* waste. **~o** *m* squandering; (*gasto innecesario*) extravagance

**despista|do** *a* (*con estar*) confused; (*con ser*) absent-minded. **~r** *vt* throw off the scent; (*fig*) mislead. **~rse** *vpr* go wrong; (*fig*) get confused

**despiste** *m* swerve; (*error*) mistake; (*confusión*) muddle

**desplaza|do** *a* out of place. **~miento** *m* displacement; (*de opinión etc*) swing, shift. **~r** [10] *vt* displace. **~rse** *vpr* travel

**despl|egar** [1 & 12] *vt* open out; spread ⟨*alas*⟩; (*fig*) show. **~iegue** *m* opening; (*fig*) show

**desplomarse** *vpr* lean; (*caerse*) collapse (

**desplumar** *vt* pluck; (*fig, fam*) fleece

**despobla|do** *m* deserted area. **~r** [2] *vt* depopulate

**despoj|ar** *vt* deprive ⟨*persona*⟩; strip ⟨*cosa*⟩. **~o** *m* plundering; (*botín*) booty. **~os** *mpl* left-overs; (*de res*) offal; (*de ave*) giblets

**desposado** *a & m* newly-wed

**déspota** *m & f* despot

**despreci|able** *a* despicable; ⟨*cantidad*⟩ negligible. **~ar** *vt* despise; (*rechazar*) scorn. **~o** *m* contempt

**desprend|er** *vt* remove; give off ⟨*olor*⟩. **~erse** *vpr* fall off; (*fig*) part with; (*deducirse*) follow. **~imiento** *m* loosening; (*generosidad*) generosity

**despreocupa|ción** *f* carelessness. **~do** *a* unconcerned; (*descuidado*) careless. **~rse** *vpr* not worry

**desprestigiar** *vt* discredit

**desprevenido** *a* unprepared. **coger a uno ~** catch s.o. unawares

**desproporci|ón** *f* disproportion. **~onado** *a* disproportionate

**despropósito** *m* irrelevant remark

**desprovisto** *a.* **~ de** lacking, without

**después** *adv* after, afterwards; (*más tarde*) later; (*a continuación*) then. **~ de** after. **~ de comer** after eating. **~ de todo** after all. **~ que** after. **poco ~** soon after. **una semana ~** a week later

**desquiciar** *vt* (*fig*) disturb

**desquit|ar** *vt* compensate. **~arse** *vpr* make up for; (*vengarse*) take revenge. **~e** *m* compensation; (*venganza*) revenge

**destaca|do** *a* outstanding. **~r** [7] *vt* emphasize. ● *vi* stand out. **~rse** *vpr* stand out

**destajo** *m* piece-work. **hablar a ~** talk nineteen to the dozen

**destap|ar** *vt* uncover; open ⟨*botella*⟩. **~arse** *vpr* reveal one's true self. **~e** *m* (*fig*) permissiveness

**destartalado** *a* ⟨*habitación*⟩ untidy; ⟨*casa*⟩ rambling

**destell|ar** *vi* sparkle. **~o** *m* sparkle; (*de estrella*) twinkle; (*fig*) glimmer

**destemplado** *a* out of tune; (*agrio*) harsh; ⟨*tiempo*⟩ unsettled; ⟨*persona*⟩ out of sorts

**desteñir** [5 & 22] *vt* fade; (*manchar*) discolour. ● *vi* fade. **~se** *vpr* fade; ⟨*color*⟩ run

**desterra|do** *m* exile. **~r** [1] *vt* banish

**destetar** *vt* wean

**destiempo** *m.* **a ~** at the wrong moment

**destierro** *m* exile

**destil|ación** *f* distillation. **~ar** *vt* distil. **~ería** *f* distillery

**destin|ar** *vt* destine; (*nombrar*) appoint. **~atario** *m* addressee. **~o** *m* (*uso*) use, function; (*lugar*) destination; (*empleo*) position; (*suerte*) destiny. **con ~o a** going to, bound for. **dar ~o a** find a use for

**destitu|ción** *f* dismissal. **~ir** [17] *vt* dismiss

**destornilla|dor** *m* screwdriver. **~r** *vt* unscrew

**destreza** *f* skill

**destripar** *vt* rip open

**destroz|ar** [10] *vt* ruin; (*fig*) shatter. **~o** *m* destruction. **causar ~os, hacer ~os** ruin

**destru|cción** *f* destruction. **~ctivo** *a* destructive. **~ir** [17] *vt* destroy; demolish ⟨*edificio*⟩

**desunir** *vt* separate

**desus|ado** *a* old-fashioned; (*insólito*) unusual. **~o** *m* disuse. **caer en ~o** become obsolete

**desvaído** *a* pale; (*borroso*) blurred; ⟨*persona*⟩ dull

**desvalido** *a* needy, destitute

**desvalijar** *vt* rob; burgle ⟨*casa*⟩

**desvalorizar** [10] *vt* devalue

**desván** *m* loft

**desvanec|er** [11] *vt* make disappear; tone down ⟨*colores*⟩; (*borrar*) blur; (*fig*) dispel. **~erse** *vpr* disappear; (*desmayarse*) faint. **~imiento** *m* (*med*) fainting fit

**desvariar** [20] *vi* be delirious; (*fig*) talk nonsense

**desvel|ar** *vt* keep awake. **~arse** *vpr* stay awake, have a sleepless night. **~o** *m* insomnia, sleeplessness

**desvencijar** *vt* break; (*agotar*) exhaust

**desventaja** *f* disadvantage

**desventura** *f* misfortune. **~do** *a* unfortunate

**desverg|onzado** *a* impudent, cheeky. **~üenza** *f* impudence, cheek

**desvestirse** [5] *vpr* undress

**desv|iación** *f* deviation; (*auto*) diversion. **~iar** [20] *vt* deflect, turn aside.

~**iarse** *vpr* be deflected; (*del camino*) make a detour; (*del tema*) stray. ~**ío** *m* diversion; (*frialdad*) *f* indifference

**desvivirse** *vpr* long (**por** for); (*afanarse*) strive, do one's utmost

**detall|ar** *vt* relate in detail. ~**e** *m* detail; (*fig*) gesture. ~**ista** *m & f* retailer. **al** ~**e** in detail; (*al por menor*) retail. **con todo** ~**e** in great detail. **en** ~**es** in detail. **¡qué** ~**e!** how thoughtful!

**detect|ar** *vt* detect. ~**ive** *m* detective

**deten|ción** *f* stopping; (*jurid*) arrest; (*en la cárcel*) detention. ~**er** [40] *vt* stop; (*jurid*) arrest; (*encarcelar*) detain; (*retrasar*) delay. ~**erse** *vpr* stop; (*entretenerse*) spend a lot of time. ~**idamente** *adv* carefully. ~**ido** *a* (*jurid*) under arrest; (*minucioso*) detailed. ● *m* prisoner

**detergente** *a & m* detergent

**deterior|ar** *vt* damage, spoil. ~**arse** *vpr* deteriorate. ~**o** *m* damage

**determina|ción** *f* determination; (*decisión*) decison. ~**nte** *a* decisive. ~**r** *vt* determine; (*decidir*) decide; (*fijar*) fix. **tomar una** ~**ción** make a decision

**detestar** *vt* detest

**detonar** *vi* explode

**detrás** *adv* behind; (*en la parte posterior*) on the back. ~ **de** behind. **por** ~ on the back; (*detrás de*) behind

**detrimento** *m* detriment. **en** ~ **de** to the detriment of

**detrito** *m* debris

**deud|a** *f* debt. ~**or** *m* debtor

**devalua|ción** *f* devaluation. ~**r** [21] *vt* devalue

**devanar** *vt* wind

**devasta|dor** *a* devastating. ~**r** *vt* devastate

**devoción** *f* devotion

**devol|ución** *f* return; (*com*) repayment, refund. ~**ver** [5] (*pp* **devuelto**) *vt* return; (*com*) repay, refund; restore (*edificio etc*). ● *vi* be sick

**devorar** *vt* devour

**devoto** *a* devout; (*amigo etc*) devoted. ● *m* enthusiast

**di** *vb véase* **dar**

**día** *m* day. ~ **de fiesta** (public) holiday. ~ **del santo** saint's day. ~ **festivo** (public) holiday. ~ **hábil,** ~ **laborable** working day. **al** ~ up to

date. **al** ~ **siguiente** (on) the following day. **¡buenos** ~**s!** good morning! **dar los buenos** ~**s** say good morning. **de** ~ by day. **el** ~ **de hoy** today. **el** ~ **de mañana** tomorrow. **en pleno** ~ in broad daylight. **en su** ~ in due course. **todo el santo** ~ all day long. **un** ~ **de estos** one of these days. **un** ~ **sí y otro no** every other day. **vivir al** ~ live from hand to mouth

**diab|etes** *f* diabetes. ~**ético** *a* diabetic

**diab|lo** *m* devil. ~**lura** *f* mischief. ~**ólico** *a* diabolical

**diácono** *m* deacon

**diadema** *f* diadem

**diáfano** *a* diaphanous

**diafragma** *m* diaphragm

**diagn|osis** *f* diagnosis. ~**osticar** [7] *vt* diagnose. ~**óstico** *a* diagnostic

**diagonal** *a & f* diagonal

**diagrama** *m* diagram

**dialecto** *m* dialect

**diálisis** *f* dialysis

**di|alogar** [12] *vi* talk. ~**álogo** *m* dialogue

**diamante** *m* diamond

**diámetro** *m* diameter

**diana** *f* reveille; (*blanco*) bull's-eye

**diapasón** *m* (*para afinar*) tuning fork

**diapositiva** *f* slide, transparency

**diari|amente** *adv* every day. ~**o** *a* daily. ● *m* newspaper; (*libro*) diary. **a** ~**o** daily. ~**o hablado** (*en la radio*) news bulletin. **de** ~**o** everyday, ordinary

**diarrea** *f* diarrhoea

**diatriba** *f* diatribe

**dibuj|ar** *vt* draw. ~**o** *m* drawing. ~**os animados** cartoon (film)

**diccionario** *m* dictionary

**diciembre** *m* December

**dictado** *m* dictation

**dictad|or** *m* dictator. ~**ura** *f* dictatorship

**dictamen** *m* opinion; (*informe*) report

**dictar** *vt* dictate; pronounce (*sentencia etc*)

**dich|a** *f* happiness. ~**o** *a* said; (*susodicho*) aforementioned. ● *m* saying. ~**oso** *a* happy; (*afortunado*) fortunate. ~**o y hecho** no sooner said than done. **mejor** ~**o** rather. **por** ~**a** fortunately

**didáctico** *a* didactic

**dieci|nueve** *a & m* nineteen. **~ocho** *a & m* eighteen. **~séis** *a & m* sixteen. **~siete** *a & m* seventeen

**diente** *m* tooth; (*de tenedor*) prong; (*de ajo*) clove. **~ de león** dandelion. **hablar entre ~s** mumble

**diesel** /'disel/ *a* diesel

**diestr|a** *f* right hand. **~o** *a* (*derecho*) right; (*hábil*) skillful

**dieta** *f* diet

**diez** *a & m* ten

**diezmar** *vt* decimate

**difama|ción** *f* (*con palabras*) slander; (*por escrito*) libel. **~r** *vt* (*hablando*) slander; (*por escrito*) libel

**diferen|cia** *f* difference; (*desacuerdo*) disagreement. **~ciar** *vt* differentiate between. ● *vi* differ. **~ciarse** *vpr* differ. **~te** *a* different

**difer|ido** *a* (*TV etc*) recorded. **~ir** [4] *vt* postpone, defer. ● *vi* differ

**dif|ícil** *a* difficult. **~icultad** *f* difficulty; (*problema*) problem. **~icultar** *vt* make difficult

**difteria** *f* diphtheria

**difundir** *vt* spread; (*TV etc*) broadcast. **~se** *vpr* spread

**difunto** *a* late, deceased. ● *m* deceased

**difusión** *f* spreading

**dige|rir** [4] *vt* digest. **~stión** *f* digestion. **~stivo** *a* digestive

**digital** *a* digital; (*de los dedos*) finger

**dignarse** *vpr* deign. **dígnese Vd** be so kind as

**dign|atario** *m* dignitary. **~idad** *f* dignity; (*empleo*) office. **~o** *a* worthy; (*apropiado*) appropriate

**digo** *vb véase* **decir**

**digresión** *f* digression

**dije** *vb véase* **decir**

**dila|ción** *f* delay. **~tación** *f* dilation, expansion. **~tado** *a* extensive; (*tiempo*) long. **~tar** *vt* expand; (*med*) dilate; (*prolongar*) prolong. **~tarse** *vpr* expand; (*med*) dilate; (*extenderse*) extend. **sin ~ción** immediately

**dilema** *m* dilemma

**diligen|cia** *f* diligence; (*gestión*) job; (*historia*) stagecoach. **~te** *a* diligent

**dilucidar** *vt* explain; solve (*misterio*)

**diluir** [17] *vt* dilute

**diluvio** *m* flood

**dimensión** *f* dimension; (*tamaño*) size

**diminut|ivo** *a & m* diminutive. **~o** *a* minute

**dimi|sión** *f* resignation. **~tir** *vt/i* resign

**Dinamarca** *f* Denmark

**dinamarqués** *a* Danish. ● *m* Dane

**din|ámica** *f* dynamics. **~ámico** *a* dynamic. **~amismo** *m* dynamism

**dinamita** *f* dynamite

**dínamo** *m*, **dinamo** *m* dynamo

**dinastía** *f* dynasty

**dineral** *m* fortune

**dinero** *m* money. **~ efectivo** cash. **~ suelto** change

**dinosaurio** *m* dinosaur

**diócesis** *f* diocese

**dios** *m* god. **~a** *f* goddess. **¡D~ mío!** good heavens! **¡gracias a D~!** thank God! **¡válgame D~!** bless my soul!

**diploma** *m* diploma

**diplomacia** *f* diplomacy

**diplomado** *a* qualified

**diplomático** *a* diplomatic. ● *m* diplomat

**diptongo** *m* diphthong

**diputa|ción** *f* delegation. **~ción provincial** county council. **~do** *m* delegate; (*pol, en España*) member of the Cortes; (*pol, en Inglaterra*) Member of Parliament; (*pol, en Estados Unidos*) congressman

**dique** *m* dike

**direc|ción** *f* direction; (*señas*) address; (*los que dirigen*) management; (*pol*) leadership. **~ción prohibida** no entry. **~ción única** one-way. **~ta** *f* (*auto*) top gear. **~tiva** *f* directive, guideline. **~tivo** *m* executive. **~to** *a* direct; (*línea*) straight; (*tren*) through. **~tor** *m* director; (*mus*) conductor; (*de escuela etc*) headmaster; (*de periódico*) editor; (*gerente*) manager. **~tora** *f* (*de escuela etc*) headmistress. **en ~to** (*TV etc*) live. **llevar la ~ción de** direct

**dirig|ente** *a* ruling. ● *m & f* leader; (*de empresa*) manager. **~ible** *a & m* dirigible. **~ir** [14] *vt* direct; (*mus*) conduct; run (*empresa etc*); address (*carta etc*). **~irse** *vpr* make one's way; (*hablar*) address

**discernir** [1] *vt* distinguish

**disciplina** *f* discipline. **~r** *vt* discipline. **~rio** *a* disciplinary

**discípulo** *m* disciple; (*alumno*) pupil

**disco** *m* disc; (*mus*) record; (*deportes*) discus; (*de teléfono*) dial; (*auto*) lights; (*rail*) signal

**disconforme** *a* not in agreement

**discontinuo** *a* discontinuous

**discord|ante** *a* discordant. **~e** *a* discordant. **~ia** *f* discord

**discoteca** *f* discothèque, disco (*fam*); (*colección de discos*) record library

**discreción** *f* discretion

**discrepa|ncia** *f* discrepancy; (*desacuerdo*) disagreement. **~r** *vi* differ

**discreto** *a* discreet; (*moderado*) moderate; ‹*color*› subdued

**discrimina|ción** *f* discrimination. **~r** *vt* (*distinguir*) discriminate between; (*tratar injustamente*) discriminate against

**disculpa** *f* apology; (*excusa*) excuse. **~r** *vt* excuse, forgive. **~rse** *vpr* apologize. **dar ~s** make excuses. **pedir ~s** apologize

**discurrir** *vt* think up. ● *vi* think (**en** about); ‹*tiempo*› pass

**discurs|ante** *m* speaker. **~ar** *vi* speak (**sobre** about). **~o** *m* speech

**discusión** *f* discussion; (*riña*) argument. **eso no admite ~** there can be no argument about that

**discuti|ble** *a* debatable. **~r** *vt* discuss; (*argumentar*) argue about; (*contradecir*) contradict. ● *vi* discuss; (*argumentar*) argue

**disec|ar** [7] *vt* dissect; stuff ‹*animal muerto*›. **~ción** *f* dissection

**disemina|ción** *f* dissemination. **~r** *vt* disseminate, spread

**disentería** *f* dysentery

**disenti|miento** *m* dissent, disagreement. **~r** [4] *vi* disagree (**de** with) (**en** on)

**diseñ|ador** *m* designer. **~ar** *vt* design. **~o** *m* design; (*fig*) sketch

**disertación** *f* dissertation

**disfraz** *m* disguise; (*vestido*) fancy dress. **~ar** [10] *vt* disguise. **~arse** *vpr*. **~arse de** disguise o.s. as

**disfrutar** *vt* enjoy. ● *vi* enjoy o.s. **~ de** enjoy

**disgregar** [12] *vt* disintegrate

**disgust|ar** *vt* displease; (*molestar*) annoy. **~arse** *vpr* get annoyed, get upset; ‹*dos personas*› fall out. **~o** *m* annoyance; (*problema*) trouble; (*repugnancia*) disgust; (*riña*) quarrel; (*dolor*) sorrow, grief

**disiden|cia** *f* disagreement, dissent. **~te** *a & m & f* dissident

**disímil** *a* (*LAm*) dissimilar

**disimular** *vt* conceal. ● *vi* pretend

**disipa|ción** *f* dissipation; (*de dinero*) squandering. **~r** *vt* dissipate; (*derrochar*) squander

**diskette** *m* floppy disk

**dislocarse** [7] *vpr* dislocate

**disminu|ción** *f* decrease. **~ir** [17] *vi* diminish

**disociar** *vt* dissociate

**disolver** [2, *pp* **disuelto**] *vt* dissolve. **~se** *vpr* dissolve

**disonante** *a* dissonant

**dispar** *a* different

**disparar** *vt* fire. ● *vi* shoot (**contra** at)

**disparat|ado** *a* absurd. **~ar** *vi* talk nonsense. **~e** *m* silly thing; (*error*) mistake. **decir ~es** talk nonsense. **¡qué ~e!** how ridiculous! **un ~e** (*mucho, fam*) a lot, an awful lot (*fam*)

**disparidad** *f* disparity

**disparo** *m* (*acción*) firing; (*tiro*) shot

**dispensar** *vt* distribute; (*disculpar*) excuse. **¡Vd dispense!** forgive me

**dispers|ar** *vt* scatter, disperse. **~arse** *vpr* scatter, disperse. **~ión** *f* dispersion. **~o** *a* scattered

**dispon|er** [34] *vt* arrange; (*preparar*) prepare. ● *vi*. **~er de** have; (*vender etc*) dispose of. **~erse** *vpr* get ready. **~ibilidad** *f* availability. **~ible** *a* available

**disposición** *f* arrangement; (*aptitud*) talent; (*disponibilidad*) disposal; (*jurid*) order, decree. **~ de ánimo** frame of mind. **a la ~ de** at the disposal of. **a su ~** at your service

**dispositivo** *m* device

**dispuesto** *a* ready; (*hábil*) clever; (*inclinado*) disposed; (*servicial*) helpful

**disputa** *f* dispute. **~r** *vt* dispute. ● *vi*. **~r por** argue about; (*competir para*) compete for. **sin ~** undoubtedly

**distan|cia** *f* distance. **~ciar** *vt* space out; (*en deportes*) outdistance. **~ciarse** *vpr* ‹*dos personas*› fall out. **~te** *a* distant. **a ~cia** from a distance. **guardar las ~cias** keep one's distance

**distar** *vi* be away; (*fig*) be far. **dista 5 kilómetros** it's 5 kilometres away

**distin|ción** *f* distinction. **~guido** *a* distinguished; (*en cartas*) Honoured. **~guir** [13] *vt/i* distinguish. **~guirse** *vpr* distinguish o.s.; (*diferenciarse*) differ; (*verse*) be visible. **~tivo** *a* distinctive. ● *m* badge. **~to** *a* different; (*claro*) distinct

**distorsión** *f* distortion; (*med*) sprain

**distra|cción** *f* amusement; (*descuido*) absent-mindedness, inattention. **~er** [41] *vt* distract; (*divertir*) amuse; embezzle ⟨*fondos*⟩. ● *vi* be entertaining. ~**erse** *vpr* amuse o.s.; (*descuidarse*) not pay attention. ~**ído** *a* amusing; (*desatento*) absent-minded

**distribu|ción** *f* distribution. ~**idor** *m* distributor, agent. ~**idor automático** vending machine. ~**ir** [17] *vt* distribute

**distrito** *m* district

**disturbio** *m* disturbance

**disuadir** *vt* dissuade

**diurético** *a* & *m* diuretic

**diurno** *a* daytime

**divagar** [12] *vi* (*al hablar*) digress

**diván** *m* settee, sofa

**diverg|encia** *f* divergence. ~**ente** *a* divergent. ~**ir** [14] *vi* diverge

**diversidad** *f* diversity

**diversificar** [7] *vt* diversify

**diversión** *f* amusement, entertainment; (*pasatiempo*) pastime

**diverso** *a* different

**diverti|do** *a* amusing; (*que tiene gracia*) funny; (*agradable*) enjoyable. ~**r** [4] *vt* amuse, entertain. ~**rse** *vpr* enjoy o.s.

**dividir** *vt* divide; (*repartir*) share out

**divin|idad** *f* divinity. ~**o** *a* divine

**divisa** *f* emblem. ~**s** *fpl* foreign exchange

**divisar** *vt* make out

**divis|ión** *f* division. ~**or** *m* divisor. ~**orio** *a* dividing

**divorci|ado** *a* divorced. ● *m* divorcee. ~**ar** *vt* divorce. ~**arse** *vpr* get divorced. ~**o** *m* divorce

**divulgar** [12] *vt* divulge; (*propagar*) spread. ~**se** *vpr* become known

**do** *m* C; (*solfa*) doh

**dobl|adillo** *m* hem; (*de pantalón*) turn-up (*Brit*), cuff (*Amer*). ~**ado** *a* double; (*plegado*) folded; ⟨*película*⟩ dubbed. ~**ar** *vt* double; (*plegar*) fold; (*torcer*) bend; turn ⟨*esquina*⟩; dub ⟨*película*⟩. ● *vi* turn; ⟨*campana*⟩ toll. ~**arse** *vpr* double; (*encorvarse*) bend; (*ceder*) give in. ~**e** *a* double. ● *m* double; (*pliegue*) fold. ~**egar** [12] *vt* (*fig*) force to give in. ~**egarse** *vpr* give in. **el** ~**e** twice as much

**doce** *a* & *m* twelve. ~**na** *f* dozen. ~**no** *a* twelfth

**docente** *a* teaching. ● *m* & *f* teacher

**dócil** *a* obedient

**doct|o** *a* learned. ~**or** *m* doctor. ~**orado** *m* doctorate. ~**rina** *f* doctrine

**document|ación** *f* documentation, papers. ~**al** *a* & *m* documentary.

~**ar** *vt* document. ~**arse** *vpr* gather information. ~**o** *m* document. **D**~**o Nacional de Identidad** national identity card

**dogm|a** *m* dogma. ~**ático** *a* dogmatic

**dólar** *m* dollar

**dol|er** [2] *vi* hurt, ache; (*fig*) grieve. **me duele la cabeza** my head hurts. **le duele el estómago** he has a pain in his stomach. ~**erse** *vpr* regret; (*quejarse*) complain. ~**or** *m* pain; (*sordo*) ache; (*fig*) sorrow. ~**oroso** *a* painful. ~**or de cabeza** headache. ~**or de muelas** toothache

**domar** *vt* tame; break in ⟨*caballo*⟩

**dom|esticar** [7] *vt* domesticate. ~**éstico** *a* domestic. ● *m* servant

**domicilio** *m* home. **a** ~ at home. **servicio a** ~ home delivery service

**domina|ción** *f* domination. ~**nte** *a* dominant; ⟨*persona*⟩ domineering. ~**r** *vt* dominate; (*contener*) control; (*conocer*) have a good knowledge of. ● *vi* dominate; (*destacarse*) stand out. ~**rse** *vpr* control o.s.

**domin|go** *m* Sunday. ~**guero** *a* Sunday. ~**ical** *a* Sunday

**dominio** *m* authority; (*territorio*) domain; (*fig*) good knowledge

**dominó** *m* (*juego*) dominoes

**don** *m* talent, gift; (*en un sobre*) Mr. ~ **Pedro** Pedro. **tener** ~ **de lenguas** have a gift for languages. **tener** ~ **de gentes** have a way with people

**donación** *f* donation

**donaire** *m* grace, charm

**dona|nte** *m* (*de sangre*) donor. ~**r** *vt* donate

**doncella** *f* (*criada*) maid

**donde** *adv* where

**dónde** *adv* where? **¿hasta** ~**?** how far? **¿por** ~**?** whereabouts?; (*¿por qué camino?*) which way? **¿a** ~ **vas?** where are you going? **¿de** ~ **eres?** where are you from?

**dondequiera** *adv* anywhere; (*en todas partes*) everywhere. ~ **que** wherever. **por** ~ everywhere

**doña** *f* (*en un sobre*) Mrs. ~ **María** María

**dora|do** *a* golden; (*cubierto de oro*) gilt. ~**dura** *f* gilding. ~**r** *vt* gilt; (*culin*) brown

**dormi|lón** *m* sleepyhead. ● *a* lazy. ~**r** [6] *vt* send to sleep. ● *vi* sleep. ~**rse** *vpr* go to sleep. ~**tar** *vi* doze. ~**torio** *m* bedroom. ~**r la siesta**

have an afternoon nap, have a siesta. **echarse a dormir** go to bed

**dors|al** a back. ● m (en deportes) number. ~o m back

**dos** a & m two. ~**cientos** a & m two hundred. **cada** ~ **por tres** every five minutes. **de** ~ **en** ~ in twos, in pairs. **en un** ~ **por tres** in no time. **los dos, las dos** both (of them)

**dosi|ficar** [7] vt dose; (fig) measure out. ~**s** f dose

**dot|ado** a gifted. ~**ar** vt give a dowry; (proveer) endow (**de** with). ~**e** m dowry

**doy** vb véase **dar**

**dragar** [12] vt dredge

**drago** m dragon tree

**dragón** m dragon

**dram|a** m drama; (obra de teatro) play. ~**ático** a dramatic. ~**atizar** [10] vt dramatize. ~**aturgo** m playwright

**drástico** a drastic

**droga** f drug. ~**dicto** m drug addict. ~**do** a drugged. ● m drug addict. ~**r** [12] vt drug. ~**rse** vpr take drugs. ~**ta** m & f (fam) drug addict

**droguería** f hardware shop (Brit), hardware store (Amer)

**dromedario** m dromedary

**ducha** f shower. ~**rse** vpr have a shower

**dud|a** f doubt. ~**ar** vt/i doubt. ~**oso** a doubtful; (sospechoso) dubious. **poner en** ~**a** question. **sin** ~**a (alguna)** without a doubt

**duelo** m duel; (luto) mourning

**duende** m imp

**dueñ|a** f owner, proprietress; (de una pensión) landlady. ~**o** m owner, proprietor; (de una pensión) landlord

**duermo** vb véase **dormir**

**dul|ce** a sweet; (agua) fresh; (suave) soft, gentle. ● m sweet. ~**zura** f sweetness; (fig) gentleness

**duna** f dune

**dúo** m duet, duo

**duodécimo** a & m twelfth

**duplica|do** a in duplicate. ● m duplicate. ~**r** [7] vt duplicate. ~**rse** vpr double

**duque** m duke. ~**sa** f duchess

**dura|ción** f duration, length. ~**dero** a lasting

**durante** prep during, in; (medida de tiempo) for. ~ **todo el año** all year round

**durar** vi last

**durazno** m (LAm, fruta) peach

**dureza** f hardness, toughness; (med) hard patch

**durmiente** a sleeping

**duro** a hard; (culin) tough; (fig) harsh. ● adv hard. ● m five-peseta coin. **ser** ~ **de oído** be hard of hearing

# E

**e** conj and

**ebanista** m & f cabinet-maker

**ébano** m ebony

**ebri|edad** f drunkenness. ~**o** a drunk

**ebullición** f boiling

**eccema** m eczema

**eclesiástico** a ecclesiastical. ● m clergyman

**eclipse** m eclipse

**eco** m echo. **hacer(se)** ~ echo

**ecolog|ía** f ecology. ~**ista** m & f ecologist

**economato** m cooperative store

**econ|omía** f economy; (ciencia) economics. ~**ómicamente** adv economically. ~**ómico** a economic(al); (no caro) inexpensive. ~**omista** m & f economist. ~**omizar** [10] vt/i economize

**ecuación** f equation

**ecuador** m equator. **el E**~ Ecuador

**ecuánime** a level-headed; (imparcial) impartial

**ecuanimidad** f equanimity

**ecuatoriano** a & m Ecuadorian

**ecuestre** a equestrian

**echar** vt throw; post (carta); give off (olor); pour (líquido); sprout (hojas etc); (despedir) throw out; dismiss (empleado); (poner) put on; put out (raices); show (película). ~**se** vpr throw o.s.; (tumbarse) lie down. ~ **a** start. ~ **a perder** spoil. ~ **de menos** miss. ~**se atrás** (fig) back down. **echárselas de** feign

**edad** f age. ~ **avanzada** old age. **E**~ **de Piedra** Stone Age. **E**~ **Media** Middle Ages. **¿qué** ~ **tiene?** how old is he?

**edición** f edition; (publicación) publication

**edicto** m edict

**edific|ación** f building. ~**ante** a edifying. ~**ar** [7] vt build; (fig) edify. ~**io** m building; (fig) structure

**Edimburgo** m Edinburgh

**edit|ar** vt publish. **~or** a publishing. ● m publisher. **~orial** a editorial. ● m leading article. ● f publishing house

**edredón** m eiderdown

**educa|ción** f upbringing; (modales) (good) manners; (enseñanza) education. **~do** a polite. **~dor** m teacher. **~r** [7] vt bring up; (enseñar) educate. **~tivo** a educational. **bien ~do** polite. **falta de ~ción** rudeness, bad manners. **mal ~do** rude

**edulcorante** m sweetener

**EE.UU.** abrev (Estados Unidos) USA, United States (of America)

**efect|ivamente** adv really; (por supuesto) indeed. **~ivo** a effective; (auténtico) real; (empleo) permanent. ● m cash. **~o** m effect; (impresión) impression. **~os** mpl belongings; (com) goods. **~uar** [21] vt carry out, effect; make (viaje, compras etc). **en ~o** in fact; (por supuesto) indeed

**efervescente** a effervescent; (bebidas) fizzy

**efica|cia** f effectiveness; (de persona) efficiency. **~z** a effective; (persona) efficient

**eficien|cia** f efficiency. **~te** a efficient

**efigie** f effigy

**efímero** a ephemeral

**efluvio** m outflow

**efusi|ón** n effusion. **~vo** a effusive; (gracias) warm

**Egeo** m. **mar ~** Aegean Sea

**égida** f aegis

**egipcio** a & m Egyptian

**Egipto** m Egypt

**ego|céntrico** a egocentric. ● m egocentric person. **~ísmo** m selfishness. **~ísta** a selfish. ● m selfish person

**egregio** a eminent

**egresar** vi (LAm) leave; (univ) graduate

**eje** m axis; (tec) axle

**ejecu|ción** f execution; (mus etc) performance. **~tante** m & f executor; (mus etc) performer. **~tar** vt carry out; (mus etc) perform; (matar) execute

**ejecutivo** m director, manager

**ejempl|ar** a exemplary. ● m (ejemplo) example, specimen; (libro) copy; (revista) issue, number. **~ificar** [7] vt exemplify. **~o** m example.

**dar ~o** set an example. **por ~o** for example. **sin ~** unprecedented

**ejerc|er** [9] vt exercise; practise (profesión); exert (influencia). ● vi practise. **~icio** m exercise; (de una profesión) practice. **~itar** vt exercise. **~itarse** vpr exercise. **hacer ~icios** take exercise

**ejército** m army

**el** art def m (pl los) the. ● pron (pl los) the one. **~ de Antonio** Antonio's. **~ que** whoever, the one

**él** pron (persona) he; (persona con prep) him; (cosa) it. **el libro de ~** his book

**elabora|ción** f processing; (fabricación) manufacture. **~r** vt process; manufacture (producto); (producir) produce

**el|asticidad** f elasticity. **~ástico** a & m elastic

**elec|ción** f choice; (de político etc) election. **~ciones** fpl (pol) election. **~tor** m voter. **~torado** m electorate. **~toral** a electoral

**electrici|dad** f electricity. **~sta** m & f electrician

**eléctrico** a electric; (de la electricidad) electrical

**electrificar** [7] vt, **electrizar** [10] vt electrify

**electrocutar** vt electrocute

**electrodo** m electrode

**electrodoméstico** a electrical household. **~s** mpl electrical household appliances

**electrólisis** f electrolysis

**electrón** m electron

**electrónic|a** f electronics. **~o** a electronic

**elefante** m elephant

**elegan|cia** f elegance. **~te** a elegant

**elegía** f elegy

**elegi|ble** a eligible. **~do** a chosen. **~r** [5 & 14] vt choose; (por votación) elect

**element|al** a elementary. **~o** m element; (persona) person, bloke (fam). **~os** mpl (nociones) basic principles

**elenco** m (en el teatro) cast

**eleva|ción** f elevation; (de precios) rise, increase; (acción) raising. **~dor** m (LAm) lift. **~r** vt raise; (promover) promote

**elimina|ción** f elimination. **~r** vt eliminate. **~toria** f preliminary heat

**el|ipse** f ellipse. **~íptico** a elliptical

**élite** /e'lit, e'lite/ *f* elite

**elixir** *m* elixir

**elocución** *f* elocution

**elocuen|cia** *f* eloquence. **~te** *a* eloquent

**elogi|ar** *vt* praise. **~o** *m* praise

**elote** *m* (*Mex*) corn on the cob

**eludir** *vt* avoid, elude

**ella** *pron* (*persona*) she; (*persona con prep*) her; (*cosa*) it. **~s** *pron pl* they; (*con prep*) them. **el libro de ~** her book. **el libro de ~s** their book

**ello** *pron* it

**ellos** *pron pl* they; (*con prep*) them. **el libro de ~** their book

**emaciado** *a* emaciated

**emana|ción** *f* emanation. **~r** *vi* emanate (**de** from); (*originarse*) originate (**de** from, in)

**emancipa|ción** *f* emancipation. **~do** *a* emancipated. **~r** *vt* emancipate. **~rse** *vpr* become emancipated

**embadurnar** *vt* smear

**embajad|a** *f* embassy. **~or** *m* ambassador

**embalar** *vt* pack

**embaldosar** *vt* tile

**embalsamar** *vt* embalm

**embalse** *m* dam; (*pantano*) reservoir

**embaraz|ada** *a* pregnant. ● *f* pregnant woman. **~ar** [10] *vt* hinder. **~o** *m* hindrance; (*de mujer*) pregnancy. **~oso** *a* awkward, embarrassing

**embar|cación** *f* boat. **~cadero** *m* jetty, pier. **~car** [7] *vt* embark (*personas*); ship (*mercancías*). **~carse** *vpr* embark. **~carse en** (*fig*) embark upon

**embargo** *m* embargo; (*jurid*) seizure. **sin ~** however

**embarque** *m* loading

**embarullar** *vt* muddle

**embaucar** [7] *vt* deceive

**embeber** *vt* absorb; (*empapar*) soak. ● *vi* shrink. **~se** *vpr* be absorbed

**embelesar** *vt* delight. **~se** *vpr* be delighted

**embellecer** [11] *vt* embellish

**embesti|da** *f* attack. **~r** [5] *vt/i* attack

**emblema** *m* emblem

**embobar** *vt* amaze

**embobecer** [11] *vt* make silly. **~se** *vpr* get silly

**embocadura** *f* (*de un río*) mouth

**emboquillado** *a* tipped

**embolsar** *vt* pocket

**emborrachar** *vt* get drunk. **~se** *vpr* get drunk

**emborrascarse** [7] *vpr* get stormy

**emborronar** *vt* blot

**embosca|da** *f* ambush. **~rse** [7] *vpr* lie in wait

**embotar** *vt* blunt; (*fig*) dull

**embotella|miento** *m* (*de vehículos*) traffic jam. **~r** *vt* bottle

**embrague** *m* clutch

**embriag|ar** [12] *vt* get drunk; (*fig*) intoxicate; (*fig, enajenar*) enrapture. **~arse** *vpr* get drunk. **~uez** *f* drunkenness; (*fig*) intoxication

**embrión** *m* embryo

**embroll|ar** *vt* mix up; involve (*personas*). **~arse** *vpr* get into a muddle; **en un asunto**) get involved. **~o** *m* tangle; (*fig*) muddle. **~ón** *m* troublemaker

**embromar** *vt* make fun of; (*engañar*) fool

**embruja|do** *a* bewitched; (*casa etc*) haunted. **~r** *vt* bewitch

**embrutecer** [11] *vt* brutalize

**embuchar** *vt* wolf (*comida*)

**embudo** *m* funnel

**embuste** *m* lie. **~ro** *a* deceitful. ● *m* liar

**embuti|do** *m* (*culin*) sausage. **~r** *vt* stuff

**emergencia** *f* emergency; (*acción de emerger*) emergence. **en caso de ~** in case of emergency

**emerger** [14] *vi* appear, emerge; (*submarino*) surface

**emigra|ción** *f* emigration. **~nte** *m* & *f* emigrant. **~r** *vi* emigrate

**eminen|cia** *f* eminence. **~te** *a* eminent

**emisario** *m* emissary

**emis|ión** *f* emission; (*de dinero*) issue; (*TV etc*) broadcast. **~ora** *a* issuing; (*TV etc*) broadcasting. **~ora** *f* radio station

**emitir** *vt* emit; let out (*grito*); (*TV etc*) broadcast; (*expresar*) express; (*poner en circulación*) issue

**emoci|ón** *f* emotion; (*excitación*) excitement. **~onado** *a* moved. **~onante** *a* exciting; (*conmovedor*) moving. **~onar** *vt* excite; (*conmover*) move. **~onarse** *vpr* get excited; (*conmoverse*) be moved. **¡qué ~ón!** how exciting!

**emotivo** *a* emotional; (*conmovedor*) moving

**empacar** [7] *vt* (*LAm*) pack

**empacho** *m* indigestion; *(vergüenza)* embarrassment

**empadronar** *vt* register. **~se** *vpr* register

**empalagoso** *a* sickly; *(demasiado amable)* ingratiating; *(demasiado sentimental)* mawkish

**empalizada** *f* fence

**empalm|ar** *vt* connect, join. ● *vi* meet. **~e** *m* junction; *(de trenes)* connection

**empanad|a** *f* (savoury) pie. **~illa** *f* (small) pie. **~o** *a* fried in breadcrumbs

**empanizado** *a* (*Mex*) fried in breadcrumbs

**empantanar** *vt* flood. **~se** *vpr* become flooded; *(fig)* get bogged down

**empañar** *vt* mist; dull *(metales etc)*; *(fig)* tarnish. **~se** *vpr* *(cristales)* steam up

**empapar** *vt* soak; *(absorber)* soak up. **~se** *vpr* be soaked

**empapela|do** *m* wallpaper. **~r** *vt* paper; *(envolver)* wrap (in paper)

**empaquetar** *vt* package; pack together *(personas)*

**emparedado** *m* sandwich

**emparejar** *vt* match; *(nivelar)* make level. **~se** *vpr* pair off

**empast|ar** *vt* fill *(muela)*. **~e** *m* filling

**empat|ar** *vi* draw. **~e** *m* draw

**empedernido** *a* inveterate; *(insensible)* hard

**empedrar** [1] *vt* pave

**empeine** *m* instep

**empeñ|ado** *a* in debt; *(decidido)* determined; *(acalorado)* heated. **~ar** *vt* pawn; pledge *(palabras)*; *(principiar)* start. **~arse** *vpr* *(endeudarse)* get into debt; *(meterse)* get involved; *(estar decidido a)* insist *(en* on). **~o** *m* pledge; *(resolución)* determination. **casa de ~s** pawnshop

**empeorar** *vt* make worse. ● *vi* get worse. **~se** *vpr* get worse

**empequeñecer** [11] *vt* dwarf; *(fig)* belittle

**empera|dor** *m* emperor. **~triz** *f* empress

**empezar** [1 & 10] *vt/i* start, begin. **para ~** to begin with

**empina|do** *a* upright; *(cuesta)* steep. **~r** *vt* raise. **~rse** *vpr* *(persona)* stand on tiptoe; *(animal)* rear

**empírico** *a* empirical

**emplasto** *m* plaster

**emplaza|miento** *m* *(jurid)* summons; *(lugar)* site. **~r** [10] *vt* summon; *(situar)* site

**emple|ado** *m* employee. **~ar** *vt* use; employ *(persona)*; spend *(tiempo)*. **~arse** *vpr* be used; *(persona)* be employed. **~o** *m* use; *(trabajo)* employment; *(puesto)* job

**empobrecer** [11] *vt* impoverish. **~se** *vpr* become poor

**empolvar** *vt* powder

**empoll|ar** *vt* incubate *(huevos)*; *(estudiar, fam)* swot up (*Brit*), grind away at (*Amer*). ● *vi* *(ave)* sit; *(estudiante)* swot (*Brit*), grind away (*Amer*). **~ón** *m* swot

**emponzoñar** *vt* poison

**emporio** *m* emporium; *(LAm, almacén)* department store

**empotra|do** *a* built-in, fitted. **~r** *vt* fit

**emprendedor** *a* enterprising

**emprender** *vt* undertake; set out on *(viaje etc)*. **~la con uno** pick a fight with s.o.

**empresa** *f* undertaking; *(com)* company, firm. **~rio** *m* impresario; *(com)* contractor

**empréstito** *m* loan

**empuj|ar** *vt* push; press *(botón)*. **~e** *m* push, shove; *(fig)* drive. **~ón** *m* push, shove

**empuñar** *vt* grasp; take up *(pluma, espada)*

**emular** *vt* emulate

**emulsión** *f* emulsion

**en** *prep* in; *(sobre)* on; *(dentro)* inside, in; *(con dirección)* into; *(medio de transporte)* by. **~ casa** at home. **~ coche** by car. **~ 10 días** in 10 days. **de pueblo ~ pueblo** from town to town

**enagua** *f* petticoat

**enajena|ción** *f* alienation; *(éxtasis)* rapture. **~r** *vt* alienate; *(volver loco)* drive mad; *(fig, extasiar)* enrapture. **~ción mental** insanity

**enamora|do** *a* in love. ● *m* lover. **~r** *vt* win the love of. **~rse** *vpr* fall in love **(de** with)

**enan|ito** *m* dwarf. **~o** *a & m* dwarf

**enardecer** [11] *vt* inflame. **~se** *vpr* get excited **(por** about)

**encabeza|miento** *m* heading; *(de periódico)* headline. **~r** [10] *vt* introduce *(escrito)*; *(poner título a)* entitle; head *(una lista)*; lead *(revolución etc)*; *(empadronar)* register

**encadenar** vt chain; (fig) tie down

**encaj|ar** vt fit; fit together ⟨varias piezas⟩. ● vi fit; (estar de acuerdo) tally. ~**arse** vpr squeeze into. ~**e** m lace; (acción de encajar) fitting

**encajonar** vt box; (en sitio estrecho) squeeze in

**encalar** vt whitewash

**encallar** vt run aground; (fig) get bogged down

**encaminar** vt direct. ~**se** vpr make one's way

**encandilar** vt (pasmar) bewilder; (estimular) stimulate

**encanecer** [11] vi go grey

**encant|ado** a enchanted; (hechizado) bewitched; ⟨casa etc⟩ haunted. ~**ador** a charming. ● m magician. ~**amiento** m magic. ~**ar** vt bewitch; (fig) charm, delight. ~**o** m magic; (fig) delight. ¡~**ado!** pleased to meet you! **me** ~**a la leche** I love milk

**encapotado** a ⟨cielo⟩ overcast

**encapricharse** vpr. ~ **con** take a fancy to

**encarar** vt face. ~**se** vpr. ~**se con** face

**encarcelar** vt imprison

**encarecer** [11] vt put up the price of; (alabar) praise. ● vi go up

**encarg|ado** a in charge. ● m manager, attendant, person in charge. ~**ar** [12] vt entrust; (pedir) order. ~**arse** vpr take charge (de of). ~**o** m job; (com) order; (recado) errand. **hecho de** ~**o** made to measure

**encariñarse** vpr. ~ **con** take to, become fond of

**encarna|ción** f incarnation. ~**do** a incarnate; (rojo) red. ● m red

**encarnizado** a bitter

**encarpetar** vt file; (LAm, dar carpetazo) shelve

**encarrilar** vt put back on the rails; (fig) direct, put on the right road

**encasillar** vt pigeonhole

**encastillarse** vpr. ~ **en** (fig) stick to

**encauzar** [10] vt channel

**encend|edor** m lighter. ~**er** [1] vt light; (pegar fuego a) set fire to; switch on, turn on ⟨aparato eléctrico⟩; (fig) arouse. ~**erse** vpr light; (prender fuego) catch fire; (excitarse) get excited; (ruborizarse) blush. ~**ido** a lit; ⟨aparato eléctrico⟩ on; (rojo) bright red. ● m (auto) ignition

**encera|do** a waxed. ● m (pizarra) blackboard. ~**r** vt wax

**encerr|ar** [1] vt shut in; (con llave) lock up; (fig, contener) contain. ~**ona** f trap

**encía** f gum

**encíclica** f encyclical

**enciclop|edia** f encyclopaedia. ~**édico** a encyclopaedic

**encierro** m confinement; (cárcel) prison

**encima** adv on top; (arriba) above. ~ **de** on, on top of; (sobre) over; (además de) besides, as well as. **por** ~ on top; (a la ligera) superficially. **por** ~ **de todo** above all

**encina** f holm oak

**encinta** a pregnant

**enclave** m enclave

**enclenque** a weak; (enfermizo) sickly

**encog|er** [14] vt shrink; (contraer) contract. ~**erse** vpr shrink. ~**erse de hombros** shrug one's shoulders. ~**ido** a shrunk; (fig, tímido) timid

**encolar** vt glue; (pegar) stick

**encolerizar** [10] vt make angry. ~**se** vpr get angry, lose one's temper

**encomendar** [1] vt entrust

**encomi|ar** vt praise. ~**o** m praise

**encono** m bitterness, ill will

**encontra|do** a contrary, conflicting. ~**r** [2] vt find; (tropezar con) meet. ~**rse** vpr meet; (hallarse) be. **no** ~**rse** feel uncomfortable

**encorvar** vt bend, curve. ~**se** vpr stoop

**encrespado** a ⟨pelo⟩ curly; ⟨mar⟩ rough

**encrucijada** f crossroads

**encuaderna|ción** f binding. ~**dor** m bookbinder. ~**r** vt bind

**encuadrar** vt frame

**encub|ierto** a hidden. ~**rir** [pp **encubierto**] vt hide, conceal; shelter ⟨delincuente⟩

**encuentro** m meeting; (colisión) crash; (en deportes) match; (mil) skirmish

**encuesta** f survey; (investigación) inquiry

**encumbra|do** a eminent. ~**r** vt (fig, elevar) exalt. ~**rse** vpr rise

**encurtidos** mpl pickles

**encharcar** [7] vt flood. ~**se** vpr be flooded

**enchuf|ado** a switched on. ~**ar** vt plug in; fit together ⟨tubos etc⟩. ~**e** m socket; (clavija) plug; (de tubos *etc*) joint; (*fig, empleo, fam*) cushy job; (*influencia, fam*) influence. **tener** ∼**e** have friends in the right places

**endeble** *a* weak

**endemoniado** *a* possessed; (*malo*) wicked

**enderezar** [10] *vt* straighten out; (*poner vertical*) put upright (again); (*fig, arreglar*) put right, sort out; (*dirigir*) direct. ∼**se** *vpr* straighten out

**endeudarse** *vpr* get into debt

**endiablado** *a* possessed; (*malo*) wicked

**endomingarse** [12] *vpr* dress up

**endosar** *vt* endorse ⟨*cheque etc*⟩; (*fig, fam*) lumber

**endrogarse** [12] *vpr* (*Mex*) get into debt

**endulzar** [10] *vt* sweeten; (*fig*) soften

**endurecer** [11] *vt* harden. ∼**se** *vpr* harden; (*fig*) become hardened

**enema** *m* enema

**enemi**|**go** *a* hostile. ● *m* enemy. ∼**stad** *f* enmity. ∼**star** *vt* make an enemy of. ∼**starse** *vpr* fall out (**con** with)

**en**|**ergía** *f* energy. ∼**érgico** *a* ⟨*persona*⟩ lively; ⟨*decisión*⟩ forceful

**energúmeno** *m* madman

**enero** *m* January

**enervar** *vt* enervate

**enésimo** *a* nth, umpteenth (*fam*)

**enfad**|**adizo** *a* irritable. ∼**ado** *a* cross, angry. ∼**ar** *vt* make cross, anger; (*molestar*) annoy. ∼**arse** *vpr* get cross. ∼**o** *m* anger; (*molestia*) annoyance

**énfasis** *m invar* emphasis, stress. **poner** ∼ stress, emphasize

**enfático** *a* emphatic

**enferm**|**ar** *vi* fall ill. ∼**edad** *f* illness. ∼**era** *f* nurse. ∼**ería** *f* sick bay. ∼**ero** *m* (male) nurse. ∼**izo** *a* sickly. ∼**o** *a* ill. ● *m* patient

**enflaquecer** [11] *vt* make thin. ● *vi* lose weight

**enfo**|**car** [7] *vt* shine on; focus ⟨*lente etc*⟩; (*fig*) consider. ∼**que** *m* focus; (*fig*) point of view

**enfrascarse** [7] *vpr* (*fig*) be absorbed

**enfrentar** *vt* face, confront; (*poner frente a frente*) bring face to face. ∼**se** *vpr*. ∼**se con** confront; (*en deportes*) meet

**enfrente** *adv* opposite. ∼ **de** opposite. **de** ∼ opposite

**enfria**|**miento** *m* cooling; (*catarro*) cold. ∼**r** [20] *vt* cool (down); (*fig*) cool down. ∼**rse** *vpr* go cold; (*fig*) cool off

**enfurecer** [11] *vt* infuriate. ∼**se** *vpr* lose one's temper; ⟨*mar*⟩ get rough

**enfurruñarse** *vpr* sulk

**engalanar** *vt* adorn. ∼**se** *vpr* dress up

**enganchar** *vt* hook; hang up ⟨*ropa*⟩. ∼**se** *vpr* get caught; (*mil*) enlist

**engañ**|**ar** *vt* deceive, trick; (*ser infiel*) be unfaithful. ∼**arse** *vpr* be wrong, be mistaken; (*no admitir la verdad*) deceive o.s. ∼**o** *m* deceit, trickery; (*error*) mistake. ∼**oso** *a* deceptive; ⟨*persona*⟩ deceitful

**engarzar** [10] *vt* string ⟨*cuentas*⟩; set ⟨*joyas*⟩; (*fig*) link

**engatusar** *vt* (*fam*) coax

**engendr**|**ar** *vt* breed; (*fig*) produce. ∼**o** *m* (*monstruo*) monster; (*fig*) brainchild

**englobar** *vt* include

**engomar** *vt* glue

**engordar** *vt* fatten. ● *vi* get fatter, put on weight

**engorro** *m* nuisance

**engranaje** *m* (*auto*) gear

**engrandecer** [11] *vt* (*enaltecer*) exalt, raise

**engrasar** *vt* grease; (*con aceite*) oil; (*ensuciar*) make greasy

**engreído** *a* arrogant

**engrosar** [2] *vt* swell. ● *vi* ⟨*persona*⟩ get fatter; ⟨*río*⟩ swell

**engullir** [22] *vt* gulp down

**enharinar** *vt* sprinkle with flour

**enhebrar** *vt* thread

**enhorabuena** *f* congratulations. **dar la** ∼ congratulate

**enigm**|**a** *m* enigma. ∼**ático** *a* enigmatic

**enjabonar** *vt* soap; (*fig, fam*) butter up

**enjalbegar** [12] *vt* whitewash

**enjambre** *m* swarm

**enjaular** *vt* put in a cage

**enjuag**|**ar** [12] *vt* rinse (out). ∼**atorio** *m* mouthwash. ∼**ue** *m* rinsing; (*para la boca*) mouthwash

**enjugar** [12] *vt* dry; (*limpiar*) wipe; cancel ⟨*deuda*⟩

**enjuiciar** *vt* pass judgement on

**enjuto** *a* ⟨*persona*⟩ skinny

**enlace** *m* connection; (*matrimonial*) wedding

**enlatar** *vt* tin, can

**enlazar** [10] *vt* tie together; (*fig*) relate, connect

**enlodar** *vt*, **enlodazar** [10] *vt* cover in mud

**enloquecer** [11] *vt* drive mad. ● *vi* go mad. **~se** *vpr* go mad

**enlosar** *vt* (*con losas*) pave; (*con baldosas*) tile

**enlucir** [11] *vt* plaster

**enluta|do** *a* in mourning. **~r** *vt* dress in mourning; (*fig*) sadden

**enmarañar** *vt* tangle (up), entangle; (*confundir*) confuse. **~se** *vpr* get into a tangle; (*confundirse*) get confused

**enmarcar** [7] *vt* frame

**enmascarar** *vt* mask. **~se de** masquerade as

**enm|endar** *vt* correct. **~endarse** *vpr* mend one's way. **~ienda** *f* correction; (*de ley etc*) amendment

**enmohecerse** [11] *vpr* (*con óxido*) go rusty; (*con hongos*) go mouldy

**enmudecer** [11] *vi* be dumbstruck; (*callar*) say nothing

**ennegrecer** [11] *vt* blacken

**ennoblecer** [11] *vt* ennoble; (*fig*) add style to

**enoj|adizo** *a* irritable. **~ado** *a* angry, cross. **~ar** *vt* make cross, anger; (*molestar*) annoy. **~arse** *vpr* get cross. **~o** *m* anger; (*molestia*) annoyance. **~oso** *a* annoying

**enorgullecerse** [11] *vpr* be proud

**enorm|e** *a* enormous; (*malo*) wicked. **~emente** *adv* enormously. **~idad** *f* immensity; (*atrocidad*) enormity. **me gusta una ~idad** I like it enormously

**enrabiar** *vt* infuriate

**enraizar** [10 & 20] *vi* take root

**enrarecido** *a* rarefied

**enrasar** *vt* make level

**enred|adera** *f* creeper. **~adero** *a* climbing. **~ar** *vt* tangle (up), entangle; (*confundir*) confuse; (*comprometer a uno*) involve, implicate; (*sembrar la discordia*) cause trouble between. ● *vi* get up to mischief. **~ar con** fiddle with, play with. **~arse** *vpr* get into a tangle; (*confundirse*) get confused; (*persona*) get involved. **~o** *m* tangle; (*fig*) muddle, mess

**enrejado** *m* bars

**enrevesado** *a* complicated

**enriquecer** [11] *vt* make rich; (*fig*) enrich. **~se** *vpr* get rich

**enrojecer** [11] *vt* turn red, redden. **~se** *vpr* (*persona*) go red, blush

**enrolar** *vt* enlist

**enrollar** *vt* roll (up); wind (*hilo etc*)

**enroscar** [7] *vt* coil; (*atornillar*) screw in

**ensalad|a** *f* salad. **~era** *f* salad bowl. **~illa** *f* Russian salad. **armar una ~a** make a mess

**ensalzar** [10] *vt* praise; (*enaltecer*) exalt

**ensambladura** *f*, **ensamblaje** *m* (*acción*) assembling; (*efecto*) joint

**ensamblar** *vt* join

**ensanch|ar** *vt* widen; (*agrandar*) enlarge. **~arse** *vpr* get wider. **~e** *m* widening; (*de ciudad*) new district

**ensangrentar** [1] *vt* stain with blood

**ensañarse** *vpr*. **~ con** treat cruelly

**ensartar** *vt* string (*cuentas etc*)

**ensay|ar** *vt* test; rehearse (*obra de teatro etc*). **~arse** *vpr* rehearse. **~o** *m* test, trial; (*composición literaria*) essay

**ensenada** *f* inlet, cove

**enseña|nza** *f* education; (*acción de enseñar*) teaching. **~nza media** secondary education. **~r** *vt* teach; (*mostrar*) show

**enseñorearse** *vpr* take over

**enseres** *mpl* equipment

**ensillar** *vt* saddle

**ensimismarse** *vpr* be lost in thought

**ensoberbecerse** [11] *vpr* become conceited

**ensombrecer** [11] *vt* darken

**ensordecer** [11] *vt* deafen. ● *vi* go deaf

**ensortijar** *vt* curl (*pelo etc*)

**ensuciar** *vt* dirty. **~se** *vpr* get dirty

**ensueño** *m* dream

**entablar** *vt* (*empezar*) start

**entablillar** *vt* put in a splint

**entalegar** [12] *vt* put into a bag; (*fig*) hoard

**entallar** *vt* fit (*un vestido*). ● *vi* fit

**entarimado** *m* parquet

**ente** *m* entity, being; (*persona rara*, *fam*) odd person; (*com*) firm, company

**entend|er** [1] *vt* understand; (*opinar*) believe, think; (*querer decir*) mean. ● *vi* understand. **~erse** *vpr* make o.s. understood; (*dos personas*) (*comprenderse*) be understood. **~er de** know all about. **~erse con** get on with. **~ido** *a* understood; (*enterado*) well-informed. ● *interj* agreed!, OK! (*fam*). **~imiento** *m* understanding.

**a mi ～er** in my opinion. **dar a ～er** hint. **no darse por ～ido** pretend not to understand, turn a deaf ear

**entenebrecer** [11] vt darken. **～se** vpr get dark

**enterado** a well-informed; (que sabe) aware. **no darse por ～** pretend not to understand, turn a deaf ear

**enteramente** adv entirely, completely

**enterar** vt inform. **～se** vpr. **～se de** find out about, hear of. **¡entérate!** listen! **¿te enteras?** do you understand?

**entereza** f (carácter) strength of character

**enternecer** [11] vt (fig) move, touch. **～se** vpr be moved, be touched

**entero** a entire, whole; (firme) firm. **por ～** entirely, completely

**enterra|dor** m gravedigger. **～r** [1] vt bury

**entibiar** vt cool. **～se** vpr cool down; (fig) cool off

**entidad** f entity; (organización) organization; (com) company

**entierro** m burial; (ceremonia) funeral

**entona|ción** f intonation; (fig) arrogance. **～r** vt intone. ● vi (mus) be in tune; (colores) match. **～rse** vpr (fortalecerse) tone o.s. up; (engreírse) be arrogant

**entonces** adv then. **en aquel ～, por aquel ～** at that time, then

**entontecer** [11] vt make silly. **～se** vpr get silly

**entornar** vt half close; leave ajar (puerta)

**entorpecer** [11] vt (frío etc) numb; (dificultar) hinder

**entra|da** f entrance; (acceso) admission, entry; (billete) ticket; (de datos, tec) input. **～do** a. **～do en años** elderly. **ya ～da la noche** late at night. **～nte** a next, coming. **dar ～da a** (admitir) admit. **de ～da** right away.

**entraña** f (fig) heart. **～s** fpl entrails; (fig) heart. **～ble** a (cariño etc) deep; (amigo) close. **～r** vt involve

**entrar** vt put; (traer) bring. ● vi go in, enter; (venir) come in, enter; (empezar) start, begin. **no ～ ni salir en** have nothing to do with

**entre** prep (de dos personas o cosas) between; (más de dos) among(st)

**entreab|ierto** a half-open. **～rir** [pp entreabierto] vt half open

**entreacto** m interval

**entrecano** a (pelo) greying; (persona) who is going grey

**entrecejo** m forehead. **arrugar el ～, fruncir el ～** frown

**entrecerrar** [1] vt (Amer) half close

**entrecortado** a (voz) faltering; (respiración) laboured

**entrecruzar** [10] vt intertwine

**entrega** f handing over; (de mercancías etc) delivery; (de novela etc) instalment; (dedicación) commitment. **～r** [12] vt hand over, deliver, give. **～rse** vpr surrender, give o.s. up; (dedicarse) devote o.s. (a to)

**entrelazar** [10] vt intertwine

**entremés** m hors-d'oeuvre; (en el teatro) short comedy

**entremet|er** vt insert. **～erse** vpr interfere. **～ido** a interfering

**entremezclar** vt mix

**entrena|dor** m trainer. **～miento** m training. **～r** vt train. **～rse** vpr train

**entrepierna** f crotch

**entresacar** [7] vt pick out

**entresuelo** m mezzanine

**entretanto** adv meanwhile

**entretejer** vt interweave

**entreten|er** [40] vt entertain, amuse; (detener) delay, keep; (mantener) keep alive, keep going. **～erse** vpr amuse o.s.; (tardar) delay, linger. **～ido** a entertaining. **～imiento** m entertainment; (mantenimiento) upkeep

**entrever** [43] vt make out, glimpse

**entrevista** f interview; (reunión) meeting. **～rse** vpr have an interview

**entristecer** [11] vt sadden, make sad. **～se** vpr be sad

**entromet|erse** vpr interfere. **～ido** a interfering

**entroncar** [7] vi be related

**entruchada** f, **entruchado** m (fam) plot

**entumec|erse** [11] vpr go numb. **～ido** a numb

**enturbiar** vt cloud

**entusi|asmar** vt fill with enthusiasm; (gustar mucho) delight. **～asmarse** vpr. **～asmarse con** get enthusiastic about; (ser aficionado a) be mad about, love. **～asmo** m enthusiasm. **～asta** a enthusiastic.

● *m* & *f* enthusiast. ~**ástico** *a* enthusiastic

**enumera|ción** *f* count, reckoning. ~**r** *vt* enumerate

**enuncia|ción** *f* enunciation. ~**r** *vt* enunciate

**envainar** *vt* sheathe

**envalentonar** *vt* encourage. ~**se** *vpr* be brave, pluck up courage

**envanecer** [11] *vt* make conceited. ~**se** *vpr* be conceited

**envas|ado** *a* tinned. ● *m* packaging. ~**ar** *vt* package; (*en latas*) tin, can; (*en botellas*) bottle. ~**e** *m* packing; (*lata*) tin, can; (*botella*) bottle

**envejec|er** [11] *vt* make old. ● *vi* get old, grow old. ~**erse** *vpr* get old, grow old. ~**ido** *a* aged, old

**envenenar** *vt* poison

**envergadura** *f* (*alcance*) scope

**envés** *m* wrong side

**envia|do** *a* sent. ● *m* representative; (*de la prensa*) correspondent. ~**r** *vt* send

**enviciar** *vt* corrupt

**envidi|a** *f* envy; (*celos*) jealousy. ~**able** *a* enviable. ~**ar** *vt* envy, be envious of. ~**oso** *a* envious. **tener** ~**a a** envy

**envilecer** [11] *vt* degrade

**envío** *m* sending, dispatch; (*de mercancías*) consignment; (*de dinero*) remittance. ~ **contra reembolso** cash on delivery. **gastos** *mpl* **de envío** postage and packing (costs)

**enviudar** *vi* ⟨*mujer*⟩ become a widow, be widowed; ⟨*hombre*⟩ become a widower, be widowed

**env|oltura** *f* wrapping. ~**olver** [2, *pp* **envuelto**] *vt* wrap; (*cubrir*) cover; (*fig, acorralar*) corner; (*fig, enredar*) involve; (*mil*) surround. ~**olvimiento** *m* involvement. ~**uelto** *a* wrapped (up)

**enyesar** *vt* plaster; (*med*) put in plaster

**enzima** *f* enzyme

**épica** *f* epic

**epicentro** *m* epicentre

**épico** *a* epic

**epid|emia** *f* epidemic. ~**émico** *a* epidemic

**epil|epsia** *f* epilepsy. ~**éptico** *a* epileptic

**epílogo** *m* epilogue

**episodio** *m* episode

**epístola** *f* epistle

**epitafio** *m* epitaph

**epíteto** *m* epithet

**epítome** *m* epitome

**época** *f* age; (*período*) period. **hacer** ~ make history, be epoch-making

**equidad** *f* equity

**equilátero** *a* equilateral

**equilibr|ar** *vt* balance. ~**io** *m* balance; (*de balanza*) equilibrium. ~**ista** *m* & *f* tightrope walker

**equino** *a* horse, equine

**equinoccio** *m* equinox

**equipaje** *m* luggage (*esp Brit*), baggage (*esp Amer*); (*de barco*) crew

**equipar** *vt* equip; (*de ropa*) fit out

**equiparar** *vt* make equal; (*comparar*) compare

**equipo** *m* equipment; (*en deportes*) team

**equitación** *f* riding

**equivale|ncia** *f* equivalence. ~**nte** *a* equivalent. ~**r** [42] *vi* be equivalent; (*significar*) mean

**equivoca|ción** *f* mistake, error. ~**do** *a* wrong. ~**r** [7] *vt* mistake. ~**rse** *vpr* be mistaken, be wrong, make a mistake. ~**rse de** be wrong about. ~**rse de número** dial the wrong number. **si no me equivoco** if I'm not mistaken

**equívoco** *a* equivocal; (*sospechoso*) suspicious. ● *m* ambiguity; (*juego de palabras*) pun; (*doble sentido*) double meaning

**era** *f* era. ● *vb véase* **ser**

**erario** *m* treasury

**erección** *f* erection; (*fig*) establishment

**eremita** *m* hermit

**eres** *vb véase* **ser**

**erguir** [48] *vt* raise. ~ **la cabeza** hold one's head high. ~**se** *vpr* straighten up

**erigir** [14] *vt* erect. ~**se** *vpr* set o.s. up (**en** as)

**eriza|do** *a* prickly. ~**rse** [10] *vpr* stand on end

**erizo** *m* hedgehog; (*de mar*) sea urchin. ~ **de mar,** ~ **marino** sea urchin

**ermita** *f* hermitage. ~**ño** *m* hermit

**erosi|ón** *f* erosion. ~**onar** *vt* erode

**er|ótico** *a* erotic. ~**otismo** *m* eroticism

**errar** [1, *la* **i** *inicial se escribe* **y**] *vt* miss. ● *vi* wander; (*equivocarse*) make a mistake, be wrong

**errata** *f* misprint

**erróneo** *a* erroneous, wrong

**error** *m* error, mistake. **estar en un** ~ be wrong, be mistaken

**eructar** *vi* belch

**erudi|ción** *f* learning, erudition. ~**to** *a* learned

**erupción** *f* eruption; (*med*) rash

**es** *vb véase* **ser**

**esa** *a véase* **ese**

**ésa** *pron véase* **ése**

**esbelto** *a* slender, slim

**esboz|ar** [10] *vt* sketch, outline. ~**o** *m* sketch, outline

**escabeche** *m* pickle. **en** ~ pickled

**escabroso** *a* ⟨*terreno*⟩ rough; ⟨*asunto*⟩ difficult; (*atrevido*) crude

**escabullirse** [22] *vpr* slip away

**escafandra** *f*, **escafandro** *m* diving-suit

**escala** *f* scale; (*escalera de mano*) ladder; (*de avión*) stopover. ~**da** *f* climbing; (*pol*) escalation. ~**r** *vt* scale; break into ⟨*una casa*⟩. ● *vi* (*pol*) escalate. **hacer** ~ **en** stop at. **vuelo sin** ~**s** non-stop flight

**escaldar** *vt* scald

**escalera** *f* staircase, stairs; (*de mano*) ladder. ~ **de caracol** spiral staircase. ~ **de incendios** fire escape. ~ **mecánica** escalator. ~ **plegable** step-ladder

**escalfa|do** *a* poached. ~**r** *vt* poach

**escalinata** *f* flight of steps

**escalofrío** *m* shiver

**escal|ón** *m* step; (*de escalera interior*) stair; (*de escala*) rung. ~**onar** *vt* spread out

**escalope** *m* escalope

**escam|a** *f* scale; (*de jabón*) flake; (*fig*) suspicion. ~**oso** *a* scaly

**escamotear** *vt* make disappear; (*robar*) steal, pinch (*fam*); disregard ⟨*dificultad*⟩

**escampar** *vi* stop raining

**esc|andalizar** [10] *vt* scandalize, shock. ~**andalizarse** *vpr* be shocked. ~**ándalo** *m* scandal; (*alboroto*) uproar. ~**andaloso** *a* scandalous; (*alborotador*) noisy

**Escandinavia** *f* Scandinavia

**escandinavo** *a* & *m* Scandinavian

**escaño** *m* bench; (*pol*) seat

**escapa|da** *f* escape; (*visita*) flying visit. ~**do** *a* in a hurry. ~**r** *vi* escape. ~**rse** *vpr* escape; ⟨*líquido, gas*⟩ leak. **dejar** ~**r** let out

**escaparate** *m* (*shop*) window. **ir de** ~**s** go window-shopping

**escapatoria** *f* (*fig, fam*) way out

**escape** *m* (*de gas, de líquido*) leak; (*fuga*) escape; (*auto*) exhaust

**escarabajo** *m* beetle

**escaramuza** *f* skirmish

**escarbar** *vt* scratch; pick ⟨*dientes, herida etc*⟩; (*fig, escudriñar*) delve (**en** into)

**escarcha** *f* frost. ~**do** *a* ⟨*fruta*⟩ crystallized

**escarlat|a** *a invar* scarlet. ~**ina** *f* scarlet fever

**escarm|entar** [1] *vt* punish severely. ● *vi* learn one's lesson. ~**iento** *m* punishment; (*lección*) lesson

**escarn|ecer** [11] *vt* mock. ~**io** *m* ridicule

**escarola** *f* endive

**escarpa** *f* slope. ~**do** *a* steep

**escas|ear** *vi* be scarce. ~**ez** *f* scarcity, shortage; (*pobreza*) poverty. ~**o** *a* scarce; (*poco*) little; (*insuficiente*) short; (*muy justo*) barely

**escatimar** *vt* be sparing with

**escayola** *f* plaster. ~**r** *vt* put in plaster

**escena** *f* scene; (*escenario*) stage. ~**rio** *m* stage; (*en el cine*) scenario; (*fig*) scene

**escénico** *a* scenic

**escenografía** *f* scenery

**esc|epticismo** *m* scepticism. ~**éptico** *a* sceptical. ● *m* sceptic

**esclarecer** [11] *vt* (*fig*) throw light on, clarify

**esclavina** *f* cape

**esclav|itud** *f* slavery. ~**izar** [10] *vt* enslave. ~**o** *m* slave

**esclerosis** *f* sclerosis

**esclusa** *f* lock

**escoba** *f* broom

**escocer** [2 & 9] *vt* hurt. ● *vi* sting

**escocés** *a* Scottish. ● *m* Scotsman

**Escocia** *f* Scotland

**escog|er** [14] *vt* choose, select. ~**ido** *a* chosen; (*de buena calidad*) choice

**escolar** *a* school. ● *m* schoolboy. ● *f* schoolgirl. ~**idad** *f* schooling

**escolta** *f* escort

**escombros** *mpl* rubble

**escond|er** *vt* hide. ~**erse** *vpr* hide. ~**idas. a** ~**idas** secretly. ~**ite** *m* hiding place; (*juego*) hide-and-seek. ~**rijo** *m* hiding place

**escopeta** *f* shotgun. ~**zo** *m* shot

**escoplo** *m* chisel

**escoria** *f* slag; (*fig*) dregs

**Escorpión** *m* Scorpio

**escorpión** *m* scorpion

**escot|ado** *a* low-cut. ~**adura** *f* low neckline. ~**ar** *vt* cut out. ● *vi* pay one's share. **~e** *m* low neckline. **ir a ~e, pagar a ~e** share the expenses

**escozor** *m* pain

**escri|bano** *m* clerk. **~biente** *m* clerk. **~bir** [*pp* **escrito**] *vt/i* write. **~bir a máquina** type. **~birse** *vpr* write to each other; (*deletrearse*) be spelt. **~to** *a* written. ● *m* writing; (*documento*) document. **~tor** *m* writer. **~torio** *m* desk; (*oficina*) office. **~tura** *f* (hand)writing; (*documento*) document; (*jurid*) deed. **¿cómo se escribe...?** how do you spell...? **poner por ~to** put into writing

**escr|úpulo** *m* scruple; (*escrupulosidad*) care, scrupulousness. **~uloso** *a* scrupulous

**escrut|ar** *vt* scrutinize; count (*votos*). **~inio** *m* count. **hacer el ~inio** count the votes

**escuadr|a** *f* (*instrumento*) square; (*mil*) squad; (*naut*) fleet. **~ón** *m* squadron

**escuálido** *a* skinny; (*sucio*) squalid

**escuchar** *vt* listen to. ● *vi* listen

**escudilla** *f* bowl

**escudo** *m* shield. **~ de armas** coat of arms

**escudriñar** *vt* examine

**escuela** *f* school. **~ normal** teachers' training college

**escueto** *a* simple

**escuincle** *m* (*Mex, perro*) stray dog; (*Mex, muchacho, fam*) child, kid (*fam*)

**escul|pir** *vt* sculpture. **~tor** *m* sculptor. **~tora** *f* sculptress. **~tura** *f* sculpture; (*en madera*) carving

**escupir** *vt/i* spit

**escurr|eplatos** *m invar* plate-rack. **~idizo** *a* slippery. **~ir** *vt* drain; wring out (*ropa*). ● *vi* drip; (*ser resbaladizo*) be slippery. **~irse** *vpr* slip

**ese** *a* (*f* **esa,** *mpl* **esos,** *fpl* **esas**) that; (*en plural*) those

**ése** *pron* (*f* **ésa,** *mpl* **ésos,** *fpl* **ésas**) that one; (*en plural*) those; (*primero de dos*) the former. **ni por ésas** on no account

**esencia** *f* essence. **~l** *a* essential. **lo ~l** the main thing

**esf|era** *f* sphere; (*de reloj*) face. **~érico** *a* spherical

**esfinge** *f* sphinx

**esf|orzarse** [2 & 10] *vpr* make an effort. **~uerzo** *m* effort

**esfumarse** *vpr* fade away; (*persona*) vanish

**esgrim|a** *f* fencing. **~ir** *vt* brandish; (*fig*) use

**esguince** *m* swerve; (*med*) sprain

**eslab|ón** *m* link. **~onar** *vt* link (together)

**eslavo** *a* Slav, Slavonic

**eslogan** *m* slogan

**esmalt|ar** *vt* enamel; varnish (*uñas*); (*fig*) adorn. **~e** *m* enamel. **~ de uñas, ~e para las uñas** nail varnish (*Brit*), nail polish (*Amer*)

**esmerado** *a* careful

**esmeralda** *f* emerald

**esmerarse** *vpr* take care (**en** over)

**esmeril** *m* emery

**esmero** *m* care

**esmoquin** *m* dinner jacket, tuxedo (*Amer*)

**esnob** *a invar* snobbish. ● *m* & *f* (*pl* **esnobs**) snob. **~ismo** *m* snobbery

**esnórkel** *m* snorkel

**eso** *pron* that. **¡~ es!** that's it! **~ mismo** exactly. **¡~ no!** certainly not! **¡~ sí!** of course. **a ~ de** about. **en ~** at that moment. **¿no es ~?** isn't that right? **por ~** therefore. **y ~ que** although

**esos** *a pl véase* **ese**

**ésos** *pron pl véase* **ése**

**espabila|do** *a* bright. **~r** *vt* snuff (*vela*); (*avivar*) brighten up; (*despertar*) wake up. **~rse** *vpr* wake up; (*apresurarse*) hurry up

**espaci|al** *a* space. **~ar** *vt* space out. **~o** *m* space. **~oso** *a* spacious

**espada** *f* sword. **~s** *fpl* (*en naipes*) spades

**espagueti** *m* spaghetti

**espald|a** *f* back. **~illa** *f* shoulder-blade. **a ~as de uno** behind s.o.'s back. **a las ~as** on one's back. **tener las ~as anchas** be broad-shouldered. **volver la ~a a uno, volver las ~as a uno** give s.o. the cold shoulder

**espant|ada** *f* stampede. **~adizo** *a* timid, timorous. **~ajo** *m,* **~apájaros** *m inv* scarecrow. **~ar** *vt* frighten; (*ahuyentar*) frighten away. **~arse** *vpr* be frightened; (*ahuyentarse*) be frightened away. **~o** *m* terror; (*horror*) horror. **~oso** *a* frightening; (*muy grande*) terrible. **¡qué ~ajo!** what a sight!

**España** *f* Spain

**español** *a* Spanish. ● *m* (*persona*) Spaniard; (*lengua*) Spanish. **los**

**~es** the Spanish. **~izado** a Hispanicized

**esparadrapo** m sticking-plaster, plaster (*Brit*)

**esparci|do** a scattered; (*fig*) widespread. **~r** [9] vt scatter; (*difundir*) spread. **~rse** vpr be scattered; (*difundirse*) spread; (*divertirse*) enjoy o.s.

**espárrago** m asparagus

**esparto** m esparto (grass)

**espasm|o** m spasm. **~ódico** a spasmodic

**espátula** f spatula; (*en pintura*) palette knife

**especia** f spice

**especial** a special. **~idad** f speciality (*Brit*), specialty (*Amer*). **~ista** a & m & f specialist. **~ización** f specialization. **~izar** [10] vt specialize. **~izarse** vpr specialize. **~mente** adv especially. **en ~** especially

**especie** f kind, sort; (*en biología*) species; (*noticia*) piece of news. **en ~** in kind

**especifica|ción** f specification. **~r** [7] vt specify

**específico** a specific

**espect|áculo** m sight; (*diversión*) entertainment, show. **~ador** m & f spectator. **~acular** a spectacular

**espectro** m spectre; (*en física*) spectrum

**especula|ción** f speculation. **~dor** m speculator. **~r** vi speculate. **~tivo** a speculative

**espej|ismo** m mirage. **~o** m mirror. **~o retrovisor** (*auto*) rear-view mirror

**espeleólogo** m potholer

**espeluznante** a horrifying

**espera** f wait. **sala f de ~** waiting room

**espera|nza** f hope. **~r** vt hope; (*aguardar*) wait for; (*creer*) expect. ● vi hope; (*aguardar*) wait. **~r en uno** trust in s.o. **en ~ de** awaiting. **espero que no** I hope not. **espero que sí** I hope so

**esperma** f sperm

**esperpento** m fright; (*disparate*) nonsense

**espes|ar** vt thicken. **~arse** vpr thicken. **~o** a thick; (*pasta etc*) stiff. **~or** m, **~ura** f thickness; (*bot*) thicket

**espetón** m spit

**esp|ía** f spy. **~iar** [20] vt spy on. ● vi spy

**espiga** f (*de trigo etc*) ear

**espina** f thorn; (*de pez*) bone; (*dorsal*) spine; (*astilla*) splinter; (*fig, dificultad*) difficulty. **~ dorsal** spine

**espinaca** f spinach

**espinazo** m spine

**espinilla** f shin; (*med*) blackhead

**espino** m hawthorn. **~ artificial** barbed wire. **~so** a thorny; (*pez*) bony; (*fig*) difficult

**espionaje** m espionage

**espiral** a & f spiral

**espirar** vt/i breathe out

**esp|iritismo** m spiritualism. **~iritoso** a spirited. **~iritista** m & f spiritualist. **~iritu** m spirit; (*mente*) mind; (*inteligencia*) intelligence. **~iritual** a spiritual. **~iritualismo** m spiritualism

**espita** f tap, faucet (*Amer*)

**espl|éndido** a splendid; (*persona*) generous. **~endor** m splendour

**espliego** m lavender

**espolear** vt (*fig*) spur on

**espoleta** f fuse

**espolvorear** vt sprinkle

**esponj|a** f sponge; (*tejido*) towelling. **~oso** a spongy. **pasar la ~a** forget about it

**espont|aneidad** f spontaneity. **~áneo** a spontaneous

**esporádico** a sporadic

**espos|a** f wife. **~as** fpl handcuffs. **~ar** vt handcuff. **~o** m husband. **los ~os** the couple

**espuela** f spur; (*fig*) incentive. **dar de ~s** spur on

**espum|a** f foam; (*en bebidas*) froth; (*de jabón*) lather. **~ar** vt skim. ● vi foam; (*bebidas*) froth; (*jabón*) lather. **~oso** a (*vino*) sparkling. **echar ~a** foam, froth

**esqueleto** m skeleton

**esquem|a** m outline. **~ático** a sketchy

**esqu|í** m (pl **esquís**) ski; (*el deporte*) skiing. **~iador** m skier. **~iar** [20] vi ski

**esquilar** vt shear

**esquimal** a & m Eskimo

**esquina** f corner

**esquirol** m blackleg

**esquiv|ar** vt avoid. **~o** a aloof

**esquizofrénico** a & m schizophrenic

**esta** a véase **este**

**ésta** pron véase **éste**

**estab|ilidad** f stability. **~ilizador** m stabilizer. **~ilizar** [10] vt stabilize. **~le** a stable

**establec|er** [11] *vt* establish. **∼erse**
*vpr* settle; (*com*) start a business.
**∼imiento** *m* establishment

**establo** *m* cowshed

**estaca** *f* stake; (*para apalear*) stick.
**∼da** *f* (*cerca*) fence

**estación** *f* station; (*del año*) season;
(*de vacaciones*) resort. **∼ de servicio**
service station

**estaciona|miento** *m* parking. **∼r** *vt*
station; (*auto*) park. **∼rio** *a*
stationary

**estadio** *m* stadium; (*fase*) stage

**estadista** *m* statesman. ● *f*
stateswoman

**estadístic|a** *f* statistics. **∼o** *a*
statistical

**estado** *m* state. **∼ civil** marital
status. **∼ de ánimo** frame of mind.
**∼ de cuenta** bank statement. **∼
mayor** (*mil*) staff. **en buen ∼** in
good condition. **en ∼ (interesante)**
pregnant

**Estados Unidos** *mpl* United States

**estadounidense** *a* American,
United States. ● *m & f* American

**estafa** *f* swindle. **∼r** *vt* swindle

**estafeta** *f* (*oficina de correos*) (sub-)
post office

**estala|ctita** *f* stalactite. **∼gmita** *f*
stalagmite

**estall|ar** *vi* explode; ⟨*olas*⟩ break;
⟨*guerra, epidemia etc*⟩ break out;
(*fig*) burst. **∼ar en llanto** burst into
tears. **∼ar de risa** burst out laughing. **∼ido** *m* explosion; (*de guerra,
epidemia etc*) outbreak; (*de risa etc*)
outburst

**estamp|a** *f* print; (*aspecto*) appear-
ance. **∼ado** *a* printed. ● *m* printing;
(*tela*) cotton print. **∼ar** *vt* stamp;
(*imprimir*) print. **dar a la ∼a** (*imprimir*) print; (*publicar*) publish. **la
viva ∼a** the image

**estampía. de ∼ía** suddenly

**estampido** *m* explosion

**estampilla** *f* stamp; (*Mex*) (postage)
stamp

**estanca|do** *a* stagnant. **∼miento** *m*
stagnation. **∼r** [7] *vt* stem; (*com*)
turn into a monopoly

**estanci|a** *f* stay; (*Arg, finca*) ranch,
farm; (*cuarto*) room. **∼ero** *m* (*Arg*)
farmer

**estanco** *a* watertight. ● *m* tobacconist's (shop)

**estandarte** *m* standard, banner

**estanque** *m* lake; (*depósito de agua*)
reservoir

**estanquero** *m* tobacconist

**estante** *m* shelf. **∼ría** *f* shelves;
(*para libros*) bookcase

**estañ|o** *m* tin. **∼adura** *f* tin-plating

**estar** [27] *vi* be; (*quedarse*) stay;
(*estar en casa*) be in. **¿estamos?**
alright? **estamos a 29 de noviembre**
it's the 29th of November. **∼ para**
be about to. **∼ por** remain to be;
(*con ganas de*) be tempted to; (*ser
partidario de*) be in favour of. **∼se**
*vpr* stay. **¿cómo está Vd?, ¿cómo
estás?** how are you?

**estarcir** [9] *vt* stencil

**estatal** *a* state

**estático** *a* static; (*pasmado*) dumbfounded

**estatua** *f* statue

**estatura** *f* height

**estatut|ario** *a* statutory. **∼o** *m*
statute

**este** *m* east; (*viento*) east wind. ● *a* (*f*
**esta**, *mpl* **estos**, *fpl* **estas**) this; (*en
plural*) these. ● *int* (*LAm*) well, er

**éste** *pron* (*f* **ésta**, *mpl* **éstos**, *fpl*
**éstas**) this one, (*en plural*) these;
(*segundo de dos*) the latter

**estela** *f* wake; (*arquit*) carved stone

**estera** *f* mat; (*tejido*) matting

**est|éreo** *a* stereo. **∼ereofónico** *a*
stereo, stereophonic

**esterilla** *f* mat

**estereotip|ado** *a* stereotyped. **∼o** *m*
stereotype

**est|éril** *a* sterile; ⟨*mujer*⟩ infertile;
⟨*terreno*⟩ barren. **∼erilidad** *f* ster-
ility; (*de mujer*) infertility; (*de
terreno*) barrenness

**esterlina** *a* sterling. **libra** *f* **∼** pound
sterling

**estético** *a* aesthetic

**estevado** *a* bow-legged

**estiércol** *m* dung; (*abono*) manure

**estigma** *m* stigma. **∼s** *mpl* (*relig*)
stigmata

**estilarse** *vpr* be used

**estil|ista** *m & f* stylist. **∼izar** [10] *vt*
stylize. **∼o** *m* style. **por el ∼o** of
that sort

**estilográfica** *f* fountain pen

**estima** *f* esteem. **∼do** *a* esteemed.
**∼do señor** (*en cartas*) Dear Sir. **∼r**
*vt* esteem; have great respect for
⟨*persona*⟩; (*valorar*) value; (*juzgar*)
think

**est|imulante** *a* stimulating. ● *m*
stimulant. **∼imular** *vt* stimulate;
(*incitar*) incite. **∼ímulo** *m* stimulus

**estipular** *vt* stipulate

**estir|ado** a stretched; ⟨persona⟩ haughty. **~ar** vt stretch; (fig) stretch out. **~ón** m pull, tug; (crecimiento) sudden growth

**estirpe** m stock

**estival** a summer

**esto** pron neutro this; (este asunto) this business. **en ~** at this point. **en ~ de** in this business of. **por ~** therefore

**estofa** f class. **de baja ~** ⟨gente⟩ low-class

**estofa|do** a stewed. ● m stew. **~r** vt stew

**estoic|ismo** m stoicism. **~o** a stoical. ● m stoic

**estómago** m stomach. **dolor** m **de ~** stomach-ache

**estorb|ar** vt hinder, obstruct; (molestar) bother, annoy. ● vi be in the way. **~o** m hindrance; (molestia) nuisance

**estornino** m starling

**estornud|ar** vi sneeze. **~o** m sneeze

**estos** a mpl véase **este**

**éstos** pron mpl véase **éste**

**estoy** vb véase **estar**

**estrabismo** m squint

**estrado** m stage; (mus) bandstand

**estrafalario** a outlandish

**estrag|ar** [12] vt devastate. **~o** m devastation. **hacer ~os** devastate

**estragón** m tarragon

**estrambótico** a outlandish

**estrangula|ción** f strangulation. **~dor** m strangler; (auto) choke. **~miento** m blockage; (auto) bottleneck. **~r** vt strangle

**estraperlo** m black market. **comprar algo de ~** buy sth on the black market

**estratagema** f stratagem

**estrateg|a** m & f strategist. **~ia** f strategy

**estratégic|amente** adv strategically. **~o** a strategic

**estrato** m stratum

**estratosfera** f stratosphere

**estrech|ar** vt make narrower; take in ⟨vestido⟩; (apretar) squeeze; hug ⟨persona⟩. **~ar la mano a uno** shake hands with s.o. **~arse** vpr become narrower; (apretarse) squeeze up. **~ez** f narrowness; (apuro) tight spot; (falta de dinero) want. **~o** a narrow; ⟨vestido etc⟩ tight; (fig, íntimo) close. ● m straits. **~o de miras**, **de miras ~as** narrow-minded

**estregar** [1 & 12] vt rub

**estrella** f star. **~ de mar**, **~mar** m starfish

**estrellar** vt smash; fry ⟨huevos⟩. **~se** vpr smash; (fracasar) fail. **~se contra** crash into

**estremec|er** [11] vt shake. **~erse** vpr tremble (**de** with). **~imiento** m shaking

**estren|ar** vt use for the first time; wear for the first time ⟨vestido etc⟩; show for the first time ⟨película⟩. **~arse** vpr make one's début; ⟨película⟩ have its première; ⟨obra de teatro⟩ open. **~o** m first use; (de película) première; (de obra de teatro) first night

**estreñi|do** a constipated. **~miento** m constipation

**estr|épito** m din. **~epitoso** a noisy; (fig) resounding

**estreptomicina** f streptomycin

**estrés** m stress

**estría** f groove

**estribar** vt rest (**en** on); (consistir) lie (**en** in)

**estribillo** m refrain; (muletilla) catchphrase

**estribo** m stirrup; (de vehículo) step; (contrafuerte) buttress. **perder los ~s** lose one's temper

**estribor** m starboard

**estricto** a strict

**estridente** a strident, raucous

**estrofa** f strophe

**estropajo** m scourer. **~so** a ⟨carne etc⟩ tough; ⟨persona⟩ slovenly

**estropear** vt spoil; (romper) break. **~se** vpr be damaged; ⟨fruta etc⟩ go bad; (fracasar) fail

**estructura** f structure. **~l** a structural

**estruendo** m din; (de mucha gente) uproar. **~so** a deafening

**estrujar** vt squeeze; (fig) drain

**estuario** m estuary

**estuco** m stucco

**estuche** m case

**estudi|ante** m & f student. **~antil** a student. **~ar** vt study. **~o** m study; (de artista) studio. **~oso** a studious

**estufa** f heater; (LAm) cooker

**estupefac|ción** f astonishment. **~iente** a astonishing. ● m narcotic. **~to** a astonished

**estupendo** a marvellous; (hermoso) beautiful

**est|upidez** f stupidity; (acto) stupid thing. **~úpido** a stupid

**estupor** *m* amazement

**esturión** *m* sturgeon

**estuve** *vb véase* **estar**

**etapa** *f* stage. **hacer ~ en** break the journey at. **por ~s** in stages

**etc** *abrev* (*etcétera*) etc

**etcétera** *adv* et cetera

**éter** *m* ether

**etéreo** *a* ethereal

**etern|amente** *adv* eternally. **~idad** *f* eternity. **~izar** [10] *vt* drag out. **~izarse** *vpr* be interminable. **~o** *a* eternal

**étic|a** *f* ethics. **~o** *a* ethical

**etimología** *f* etymology

**etiqueta** *f* ticket, tag; (*ceremonial*) etiquette. **de ~** formal

**étnico** *a* ethnic

**eucalipto** *m* eucalyptus

**eufemismo** *m* euphemism

**euforia** *f* euphoria

**Europa** *f* Europe

**europe|o** *a & m* European. **~izar** [10] *vt* Europeanize

**eutanasia** *f* euthanasia

**evacua|ción** *f* evacuation. **~r** [21 *o regular*] *vt* evacuate

**evadir** *vt* avoid. **~se** *vpr* escape

**evaluar** [21] *vt* evaluate

**evang|élico** *a* evangelical. **~elio** *m* gospel. **~elista** *m & f* evangelist

**evapora|ción** *f* evaporation. **~r** *vi* evaporate. **~rse** *vpr* evaporate; (*fig*) disappear

**evasi|ón** *f* evasion; (*fuga*) escape. **~vo** *a* evasive

**evento** *m* event. **a todo ~** at all events

**eventual** *a* possible. **~idad** *f* eventuality

**eviden|cia** *f* evidence. **~ciar** *vt* show. **~ciarse** *vpr* be obvious. **~te** *a* obvious. **~temente** *adv* obviously. **poner en ~cia** show; (*fig*) make a fool of

**evitar** *vt* avoid; (*ahorrar*) spare

**evocar** [7] *vt* evoke

**evoluci|ón** *f* evolution. **~onado** *a* fully-developed. **~onar** *vi* evolve; (*mil*) manoeuvre

**ex** *pref* ex-, former

**exacerbar** *vt* exacerbate

**exact|amente** *adv* exactly. **~itud** *f* exactness. **~o** *a* exact; (*preciso*) accurate; (*puntual*) punctual. **¡~!** exactly!. **con ~itud** exactly

**exagera|ción** *f* exaggeration. **~do** *a* exaggerated. **~r** *vt/i* exaggerate

**exalta|do** *a* exalted; (*fanático*) fanatical. **~r** *vt* exalt. **~rse** *vpr* get excited

**exam|en** *m* examination; (*escol, univ*) exam(ination). **~inador** *m* examiner. **~inar** *vt* examine. **~inarse** *vpr* take an exam

**exánime** *a* lifeless

**exaspera|ción** *f* exasperation. **~r** *vt* exasperate. **~rse** *vpr* get exasperated

**excava|ción** *f* excavation. **~dora** *f* digger. **~r** *vt* excavate

**exce|dencia** *f* leave of absence. **~nte** *a & m* surplus. **~r** *vi* exceed. **~rse** *vpr* go too far. **~rse a sí mismo** excel o.s.

**excelen|cia** *f* excellence; (*tratamiento*) Excellency. **~te** *a* excellent

**exc|entricidad** *f* eccentricity. **~éntrico** *a & m* eccentric

**excepci|ón** *f* exception. **~onal** *a* exceptional. **a ~ón de, con ~ón de** except (for)

**except|o** *prep* except (for). **~uar** [21] *vt* except

**exces|ivo** *a* excessive. **~o** *m* excess. **~o de equipaje** excess luggage (*esp Brit*), excess baggage (*esp Amer*)

**excita|ble** *a* excitable. **~ción** *f* excitement. **~nte** *a* exciting. ● *m* stimulant. **~r** *vt* excite; (*incitar*) incite. **~rse** *vpr* get excited

**exclama|ción** *f* exclamation. **~r** *vi* exclaim

**exclu|ir** [17] *vt* exclude. **~sión** *f* exclusion. **~siva** *f* sole right; (*en la prensa* exclusive (story). **~sive** *adv* exclusive; (*exclusivamente*) exclusively. **~sivo** *a* exclusive

**excomu|lgar** [12] *vt* excommunicate. **~nión** *f* excommunication

**excremento** *m* excrement

**exculpar** *vt* exonerate; (*jurid*) acquit

**excursi|ón** *f* excursion, trip. **~onista** *m & f* day-tripper. **ir de ~ón** go on an excursion

**excusa** *f* excuse; (*disculpa*) apology. **~r** *vt* excuse. **presentar sus ~s** apologize

**execra|ble** *a* loathsome. **~r** *vt* loathe

**exento** *a* exempt; (*libre*) free

**exequias** *fpl* funeral rites

**exhala|ción** *f* shooting star. **~r** *vt* exhale, breath out; give off (*color etc*). **~rse** *vpr* hurry. **como una ~ción** at top speed

**exhaust|ivo** *a* exhaustive. **~o** *a* exhausted

**exhibi|ción** *f* exhibition. **~cionista** *m & f* exhibitionist. **~r** *vt* exhibit

**exhortar** *vt* exhort (**a** to)

**exhumar** *vt* exhume; (*fig*) dig up

**exig|encia** *f* demand. **~ente** *a* demanding. **~ir** [14] *vt* demand. **tener muchas ~encias** be very demanding

**exiguo** *a* meagre

**exil|(i)ado** *a* exiled. ● *m* exile. **~(i)arse** *vpr* go into exile. **~io** *m* exile

**eximio** *a* distinguished

**eximir** *vt* exempt; (*liberar*) free

**existencia** *f* existence. **~s** *fpl* stock

**existencial** *a* existential. **~ismo** *m* existentialism

**exist|ente** *a* existing. **~ir** *vi* exist

**éxito** *m* success. **no tener ~** fail. **tener ~** be successful

**exitoso** *a* successful

**éxodo** *m* exodus

**exonerar** *vt* (*de un empleo*) dismiss; (*de un honor etc*) strip

**exorbitante** *a* exorbitant

**exorci|smo** *m* exorcism. **~zar** [10] *vt* exorcise

**exótico** *a* exotic

**expan|dir** *vt* expand; (*fig*) spread. **~dirse** *vpr* expand. **~sión** *f* expansion. **~sivo** *a* expansive

**expatria|do** *a & m* expatriate. **~r** *vt* banish. **~rse** *vpr* emigrate; (*exiliarse*) go into exile

**expectativa** *f*. **estar a la ~** be on the lookout

**expedición** *f* dispatch; (*cosa expedida*) shipment; (*mil, científico etc*) expedition

**expediente** *m* expedient; (*jurid*) proceedings; (*documentos*) record, file

**expedi|r** [5] *vt* dispatch, send; issue (*documento*). **~to** *a* clear

**expeler** *vt* expel

**expende|dor** *m* dealer. **~dor automático** vending machine. **~duría** *f* shop; (*de billetes*) ticket office. **~r** *vt* sell

**expensas** *fpl*. **a ~ de** at the expense of. **a mis ~** at my expense

**experiencia** *f* experience

**experiment|al** *a* experimental. **~ar** *vt* test, experiment with; (*sentir*) experience. **~o** *m* experiment

**experto** *a & m* expert

**expiar** [20] *vt* atone for

**expirar** *vi* expire; (*morir*) die

**explana|da** *f* levelled area; (*paseo*) esplanade. **~r** *vt* level

**explayar** *vt* extend. **~se** *vpr* spread out, extend; (*hablar*) be long-winded; (*confiarse*) confide (**a** in)

**expletivo** *m* expletive

**explica|ción** *f* explanation. **~r** [7] *vt* explain. **~rse** *vpr* understand; (*hacerse comprender*) explain o.s. **no me lo explico** I can't understand it

**explícito** *a* explicit

**explora|ción** *f* exploration. **~dor** *m* explorer; (*muchacho*) boy scout. **~r** *vt* explore. **~torio** *a* exploratory

**explosi|ón** *f* explosion; (*fig*) outburst. **~onar** *vt* blow up. **~vo** *a & m* explosive

**explota|ción** *f* working; (*abuso*) exploitation. **~r** *vt* work (*mina*); farm (*tierra*); (*abusar*) exploit. ● *vi* explode

**expone|nte** *m* exponent. **~r** [34] *vt* expose; display (*mercancías*); (*explicar*) expound; exhibit (*cuadros etc*); (*arriesgar*) risk. ● *vi* hold an exhibition. **~rse** *vpr* run the risk (**a** of)

**exporta|ción** *f* export. **~dor** *m* exporter. **~r** *vt* export

**exposición** *f* exposure; (*de cuadros etc*) exhibition; (*en escaparate etc*) display; (*explicación*) exposition, explanation

**expresamente** *adv* specifically

**expres|ar** *vt* express. **~arse** *vpr* express o.s. **~ión** *f* expression. **~ivo** *a* expressive; (*cariñoso*) affectionate

**expreso** *a* express. ● *m* express messenger; (*tren*) express

**exprimi|dor** *m* squeezer. **~r** *vt* squeeze; (*explotar*) exploit

**expropiar** *vt* expropriate

**expuesto** *a* on display; (*lugar etc*) exposed; (*peligroso*) dangerous. **estar ~ a** be liable to

**expuls|ar** *vt* expel; throw out (*persona*); send off (*jugador*). **~ión** *f* expulsion

**expurgar** [12] *vt* expurgate

**exquisit|o** *a* exquisite. **~amente** *adv* exquisitely

**extasiar** [20] *vt* enrapture

**éxtasis** *m invar* ecstasy

**extático** *a* ecstatic

**extend|er** [1] *vt* spread (out); draw up (*documento*). **~erse** *vpr* spread;

⟨paisaje etc⟩ extend, stretch; (tenderse) stretch out. **~ido** a spread out; (generalizado) widespread; ⟨brazos⟩ outstretched

**extens|amente** adv widely; (detalladamente) in full. **~ión** f extension; (amplitud) expanse; (mus) range. **~o** a extensive

**extenuar** [21] vt exhaust

**exterior** a external, exterior; (del extranjero) foreign; ⟨aspecto etc⟩ outward. ● m exterior; (países extranjeros) abroad. **~izar** [10] vt show

**extermin|ación** f extermination. **~ar** vt exterminate. **~io** m extermination

**externo** a external; ⟨signo etc⟩ outward. ● m day pupil

**extin|ción** f extinction. **~guir** [13] vt extinguish. **~guirse** vpr die out; ⟨fuego⟩ go out. **~to** a extinguished; ⟨raza etc⟩ extinct. **~tor** m fire extinguisher

**extirpa|r** vt uproot; extract ⟨muela etc⟩; remove ⟨tumor⟩. **~ción** f (fig) eradication

**extorsi|ón** f (fig) inconvenience. **~onar** vt inconvenience

**extra** a invar extra; (de buena calidad) good-quality; ⟨huevos⟩ large. **paga** f **~** bonus

**extrac|ción** f extraction; (de lotería) draw. **~to** m extract

**extradición** f extradition

**extraer** [41] vt extract

**extranjero** a foreign. ● m foreigner; (países) foreign countries. **del ~** from abroad. **en el ~**, **por el ~** abroad

**extrañ|ar** vt surprise; (encontrar extraño) find strange; (LAm, echar de menos) miss; (desterrar) banish. **~arse** vpr be surprised (de at); ⟨2 personas⟩ grow apart. **~eza** f strangeness; (asombro) surprise. **~o** a strange. ● m stranger

**extraoficial** a unofficial

**extraordinario** a extraordinary. ● m (correo) special delivery; (plato) extra dish; (de periódico etc) special edition. **horas** fpl **extraordinarias** overtime

**extrarradio** m suburbs

**extrasensible** a extra-sensory

**extraterrestre** a extraterrestrial. ● m alien

**extravagan|cia** f oddness, eccentricity. **~te** a odd, eccentric

**extravertido** a & m extrovert

**extrav|iado** a lost; ⟨lugar⟩ isolated. **~iar** [20] vt lose. **~iarse** vpr get lost; ⟨objetos⟩ be missing. **~ío** m loss

**extremar** vt overdo. **~se** vpr make every effort

**extremeño** a from Extremadura. ● m person from Extremadura

**extrem|idad** f extremity. **~idades** fpl extremities. **~ista** a & m & f extremist. **~o** a extreme. ● m end; (colmo) extreme. **en ~o** extremely. **en último ~o** as a last resort

**extrovertido** a & m extrovert

**exuberan|cia** f exuberance. **~te** a exuberant

**exulta|ción** f exultation. **~r** vi exult

**eyacular** vt/i ejaculate

# F

**fa** m F; (solfa) fah

**fabada** f Asturian stew

**fábrica** f factory. **marca** f **de ~** trade mark

**fabrica|ción** f manufacture. **~ción en serie** mass production. **~nte** m & f manufacturer. **~r** [7] vt manufacture; (inventar) fabricate

**fábula** f fable; (mentira) story, lie; (chisme) gossip

**fabuloso** a fabulous

**facci|ón** f faction. **~ones** fpl (de la cara) features

**faceta** f facet

**fácil** a easy; (probable) likely; ⟨persona⟩ easygoing

**facili|dad** f ease; (disposición) aptitude. **~dades** fpl facilities. **~tar** vt facilitate; (proporcionar) provide

**fácilmente** adv easily

**facistol** m lectern

**facón** m (Arg) gaucho knife

**facsímil(e)** m facsimile

**factible** a feasible

**factor** m factor

**factoría** f agency; (esp LAm, fábrica) factory

**factura** f bill, invoice; (hechura) manufacture. **~r** vt (hacer la factura) invoice; (cobrar) charge; (en ferrocarril) register (Brit), check (Amer)

**faculta|d** f faculty; (capacidad) ability; (poder) power. **~tivo** a optional

**facha** f (aspecto, fam) look

**fachada** f façade; (*fig, apariencia*) show

**faena** f job. ~**s domésticas** housework

**fagot** *m* bassoon; (*músico*) bassoonist

**faisán** *m* pheasant

**faja** f (*de tierra*) strip; (*corsé*) corset; (*mil etc*) sash

**fajo** *m* bundle; (*de billetes*) wad

**falang|e** f (*política española*) Falange. ~**ista** *m & f* Falangist

**falda** f skirt; (*de montaña*) side

**fálico** *a* phallic

**fals|ear** *vt* falsify, distort. ~**edad** f falseness; (*mentira*) lie, falsehood. ~**ificación** f forgery. ~**ificador** *m* forger. ~**ificar** [7] *vt* forge. ~**o** *a* false; (*equivocado*) wrong; (*falsificado*) fake

**falt|a** f lack; (*ausencia*) absence; (*escasez*) shortage; (*defecto*) fault, defect; (*culpa*) fault; (*error*) mistake; (*en fútbol etc*) foul; (*en tenis*) fault. ~**ar** *vi* be lacking; (*estar ausente*) be absent. ~**o** *a* lacking (**de** in). **a** ~**a de** for lack of. **echar en** ~**a** miss. **hacer** ~**a** be necessary. **me hace** ~**a** I need. **¡no** ~**aba más!** don't mention it! (*naturalmente*) of course! **sacar** ~**as** find fault

**falla** f (*incl geol*) fault. ~**r** *vi* fail; (*romperse*) break, give way; ⟨*motor, tiro etc*⟩ miss. **sin** ~**r** without fail

**fallec|er** [11] *vi* die. ~**ido** *a* late. ● *m* deceased

**fallido** *a* vain; (*fracasado*) unsuccessful

**fallo** *m* failure; (*defecto*) fault; (*jurid*) sentence

**fama** f fame; (*reputación*) reputation. **de mala** ~ of ill repute. **tener** ~ **de** have the reputation of

**famélico** *a* starving

**famili|a** f family. ~ **numerosa** large family. ~**r** *a* familiar; (*de la familia*) family; (*sin ceremonia*) informal. ~**ridad** f familiarity. ~**rizarse** [10] *vpr* become familiar (**con** with)

**famoso** *a* famous

**fanático** *a* fanatical. ● *m* fanatic

**fanfarr|ón** *a* boastful. ● *m* braggart. ~**onada** f boasting; (*dicho*) boast. ~**onear** *vi* show off

**fango** *m* mud. ~**so** *a* muddy

**fantas|ear** *vi* daydream; (*imaginar*) fantasize. ~**ía** f fantasy. **de** ~ fancy

**fantasma** *m* ghost

**fantástico** *a* fantastic

**fantoche** *m* puppet

**faringe** f pharynx

**fardo** *m* bundle

**farfullar** *vi* jabber, gabble

**farmac|éutico** *a* pharmaceutical. ● *m* chemist (*Brit*), pharmacist, druggist (*Amer*). ~**ia** f (*ciencia*) pharmacy; (*tienda*) chemist's (shop) (*Brit*), pharmacy, drugstore (*Amer*)

**faro** *m* lighthouse; (*aviac*) beacon; (*auto*) headlight

**farol** *m* lantern; (*de la calle*) street lamp. ~**a** f street lamp. ~**ita** f small street lamp

**farsa** f farce

**fas** *adv.* **por** ~ **o por nefas** rightly or wrongly

**fascículo** *m* instalment

**fascina|ción** f fascination. ~**r** *vt* fascinate

**fascis|mo** *m* fascism. ~**ta** *a & m & f* fascist

**fase** f phase

**fastidi|ar** *vt* annoy; (*estropear*) spoil. ~**arse** *vpr* put up with it; (*hacerse daño*) hurt o.s. ~**o** *m* nuisance; (*aburrimiento*) boredom. ~**oso** *a* annoying. **¡para que te** ~**es!** so there! **¡qué** ~**o!** what a nuisance!

**fatal** *a* fateful; (*mortal*) fatal; (*pésimo, fam*) terrible. ~**idad** f fate; (*desgracia*) misfortune. ~**ista** *m & f* fatalist

**fatig|a** f fatigue. ~**as** *fpl* troubles. ~**ar** [12] *vt* tire. ~**arse** *vpr* get tired. ~**oso** *a* tiring

**fatuo** *a* fatuous

**fauna** f fauna

**fausto** *a* lucky

**favor** *m* favour. ~**able** *a* favourable. **a** ~ **de, en** ~ **de** in favour of. **haga el** ~ **de** would you be so kind as to, please. **por** ~ please

**favorec|edor** *a* flattering. ~**er** [11] *vt* favour; ⟨*vestido, peinado etc*⟩ suit. ~**ido** *a* favoured

**favorit|ismo** *m* favouritism. ~**o** *a & m* favourite

**faz** f face

**fe** f faith. **dar** ~ **de** certify. **de buena** ~ in good faith

**fealdad** f ugliness

**febrero** *m* February

**febril** *a* feverish

**fecund|ación** f fertilization. ~**ación artificial** artificial insemination. ~**ar** *vt* fertilize. ~**o** *a* fertile; (*fig*) prolific

**fecha** *f* date. **~r** *vt* date. **a estas ~s** now; (*todavía*) still. **hasta la ~** so far. **poner la ~** date

**fechoría** *f* misdeed

**federa|ción** *f* federation. **~l** *a* federal

**feísimo** *a* hideous

**felici|dad** *f* happiness. **~dades** *fpl* best wishes; (*congratulaciones*) congratulations. **~tación** *f* congratulation. **~tar** *vt* congratulate. **~tarse** *vpr* be glad

**feligr|és** *m* parishioner. **~esía** *f* parish

**felino** *a* & *m* feline

**feliz** *a* happy; (*afortunado*) lucky. **¡Felices Pascuas!** Happy Christmas! **¡F~ Año Nuevo!** Happy New Year!

**felpudo** *a* plush. ● *m* doormat

**femeni|l** *a* feminine. **~no** *a* feminine; (*biol, bot*) female. ● *m* feminine. **~nidad** *f* femininity. **~sta** *a* & *m* & *f* feminist

**fen|omenal** *a* phenomenal. **~ómeno** *m* phenomenon; (*monstruo*) freak

**feo** *a* ugly; (*desagradable*) nasty; (*malo*) bad

**féretro** *m* coffin

**feria** *f* fair; (*verbena*) carnival; (*descanso*) holiday; (*Mex, cambio*) change. **~do** *a*. **día ~do** holiday

**ferment|ación** *f* fermentation. **~ar** *vt/i* ferment. **~o** *m* ferment

**fero|cidad** *f* ferocity. **~z** *a* fierce; (*persona*) savage

**férreo** *a* iron. **vía férrea** railway (*Brit*), railroad (*Amer*)

**ferreter|ía** *f* ironmonger's (shop) (*Brit*), hardware store (*Amer*). **~o** *m* ironmonger (*Brit*), hardware dealer (*Amer*)

**ferro|bús** *m* local train. **~carril** *m* railway (*Brit*), railroad (*Amer*). **~viario** *a* rail. ● *m* railwayman (*Brit*), railroad worker (*Amer*)

**fértil** *a* fertile

**fertili|dad** *f* fertility. **~zante** *m* fertilizer. **~zar** [10] *vt* fertilize

**férvido** *a* fervent

**ferv|iente** *a* fervent. **~or** *m* fervour

**festej|ar** *vt* celebrate; entertain (*persona*); court (*novia etc*); (*Mex, golpear*) beat. **~o** *m* entertainment; (*celebración*) celebration

**festiv|al** *m* festival. **~idad** *f* festivity. **~o** *a* festive; (*humorístico*) humorous. **día ~o** feast day, holiday

**festonear** *vt* festoon

**fétido** *a* stinking

**feto** *m* foetus

**feudal** *a* feudal

**fiado** *m*. **al ~** on credit. **~r** *m* fastener; (*jurid*) guarantor

**fiambre** *m* cold meat

**fianza** *f* (*dinero*) deposit; (*objeto*) surety. **bajo ~** on bail. **dar ~** pay a deposit

**fiar** [20] *vt* guarantee; (*vender*) sell on credit; (*confiar*) confide. ● *vi* trust. **~se** *vpr*. **~se de** trust

**fiasco** *m* fiasco

**fibra** *f* fibre; (*fig*) energy. **~ de vidrio** fibreglass

**fic|ción** *f* fiction. **~ticio** *a* fictitious; (*falso*) false

**fich|a** *f* token; (*tarjeta*) index card; (*en los juegos*) counter. **~ar** *vt* file. **~ero** *m* card index. **estar ~ado** have a (police) record

**fidedigno** *a* reliable

**fidelidad** *f* faithfulness. **alta ~** hi-fi (*fam*), high fidelity

**fideos** *mpl* noodles

**fiebre** *f* fever. **~ del heno** hay fever. **tener ~** have a temperature

**fiel** *a* faithful; (*memoria, relato etc*) reliable. ● *m* believer; (*de balanza*) needle. **los ~es** the faithful

**fieltro** *m* felt

**fier|a** *f* wild animal; (*persona*) brute. **~o** *a* fierce; (*cruel*) cruel. **estar hecho una ~a** be furious

**fierro** *m* (*LAm*) iron

**fiesta** *f* party; (*día festivo*) holiday. **~s** *fpl* celebrations. **~ nacional** bank holiday (*Brit*), national holiday

**figura** *f* figure; (*forma*) shape; (*en obra de teatro*) character; (*en naipes*) court-card. **~r** *vt* feign; (*representar*) represent. ● *vi* figure; (*ser importante*) be important. **~rse** *vpr* imagine. **¡figúrate!** just imagine! **~tivo** *a* figurative

**fij|ación** *f* fixing. **~ar** *vt* fix; stick (*sello*); post (*cartel*). **~arse** *vpr* settle; (*fig, poner atención*) notice. **¡fíjate!** just imagine! **~o** *a* fixed; (*firme*) stable; (*persona*) settled. **de ~o** certainly

**fila** *f* line; (*de soldados etc*) file; (*en el teatro, cine etc*) row; (*cola*) queue. **ponerse en ~** line up

**filamento** *m* filament

**fil|antropía** *f* philanthropy. **~antrópico** *a* philanthropic. **~ántropo** *m* philanthropist

**filarmónico** *a* philharmonic

**filat|elia** *f* stamp collecting, philately. **~élico** *a* philatelic. ● *m* stamp collector, philatelist

**filete** *m* fillet

**filfa** *f (fam)* hoax

**filial** *a* filial. ● *f* subsidiary

**filigrana** *f* filigree (work); *(en papel)* watermark

**Filipinas** *fpl.* **las (islas)** **~** the Philippines

**filipino** *a* Philippine, Filipino

**filmar** *vt* film

**filo** *m* edge; *(de hoja)* cutting edge; *(Mex, hambre)* hunger. **al ~ de las doce** at exactly twelve o'clock. **dar ~ a, sacar ~ a** sharpen

**filología** *f* philology

**filón** *m* vein; *(fig)* gold-mine

**fil|osofía** *f* philosophy. **~osófico** *a* philosophical. **~ósofo** *m* philosopher

**filtr|ar** *vt* filter. **~arse** *vpr* filter; *(dinero)* disappear. **~o** *m* filter; *(bebida)* philtre

**fin** *m* end; *(objetivo)* aim. **~ de semana** weekend. **a ~ de** in order to. **a ~ de cuentas** all things considered. **a ~ de que** in order that. **a ~es de** at the end of. **al ~** finally. **al ~ y al cabo** after all. **dar ~ a** end. **en ~** in short. **poner ~ a** end. **por ~** finally. **sin ~** endless

**final** *a* final, last. ● *m* end. ● *f* final. **~idad** *f* aim. **~ista** *m & f* finalist. **~izar** [10] *vt/i* end. **~mente** *adv* finally

**financi|ar** *vt* finance. **~ero** *a* financial. ● *m* financier

**finca** *f* property; *(tierras)* estate; *(LAm, granja)* farm

**finés** *a* Finnish. ● *m* Finn; *(lengua)* Finnish

**fingi|do** *a* false. **~r** [14] *vt* feign; *(simular)* simulate. ● *vi* pretend. **~rse** *vpr* pretend to be

**finito** *a* finite

**finlandés** *a* Finnish. ● *m (persona)* Finn; *(lengua)* Finnish

**Finlandia** *f* Finland

**fin|o** *a* fine; *(delgado)* slender; *(astuto)* shrewd; *(sentido)* keen; *(cortés)* polite; *(jerez)* dry. **~ura** *f* fineness; *(astucia)* shrewdness; *(de sentido)* keenness; *(cortesía)* politeness

**fiordo** *m* fiord

**firma** *f* signature; *(empresa)* firm

**firmamento** *m* firmament

**firmar** *vt* sign

**firme** *a* firm; *(estable)* stable, steady; *(persona)* steadfast. ● *m (pavimento)* (road) surface. ● *adv* hard. **~za** *f* firmness. **de ~** hard. **en ~** firm, definite

**fisc|al** *a* fiscal. ● *m & f* public prosecutor. **~o** *m* treasury

**fisg|ar** [12] *vt* pry into *(asunto)*; spy on *(persona)*. ● *vi* pry. **~ón** *a* prying. ● *m* busybody

**físic|a** *f* physics. **~o** *a* physical. ● *m* physique; *(persona)* physicist

**fisi|ología** *f* physiology. **~ológico** *a* physiological. **~ólogo** *m* physiologist

**fisioterap|euta** *m & f* physiotherapist. **~ia** *f* physiotherapy. **~ista** *m & f (fam)* physiotherapist

**fisonom|ía** *f* physiognomy, face. **~ista** *m & f.* **ser buen ~ista** be good at remembering faces

**fisura** *f (Med)* fracture

**fláccido** *a* flabby

**flaco** *a* thin, skinny; *(débil)* weak

**flagelo** *m* scourge

**flagrante** *a* flagrant. **en ~** red-handed

**flamante** *a* splendid; *(nuevo)* brand-new

**flamenco** *a* flamenco; *(de Flandes)* Flemish. ● *m (música etc)* flamenco

**flan** *m* crème caramel

**flaqueza** *f* thinness; *(debilidad)* weakness

**flash** *m* flash

**flato** *m*, **flatulencia** *f* flatulence

**flaut|a** *f* flute. ● *m & f (músico)* flautist, flutist *(Amer)*. **~ín** *m* piccolo. **~ista** *m & f* flautist, flutist *(Amer)*

**fleco** *m* fringe

**flecha** *f* arrow

**flem|a** *f* phlegm. **~ático** *a* phlegmatic

**flequillo** *m* fringe

**fletar** *vt* charter

**flexib|ilidad** *f* flexibility. **~le** *a* flexible. ● *m* flex, cable

**flirte|ar** *vi* flirt. **~o** *m* flirting

**floj|ear** *vi* ease up. **~o** *a* loose; *(poco fuerte)* weak; *(viento)* light; *(perezoso)* lazy

**flor** *f* flower; *(fig)* cream. **~a** *f* flora. **~al** *a* floral. **~ecer** [11] *vi* flower, bloom; *(fig)* flourish. **~eciente** *a* *(fig)* flourishing. **~ero** *m* flower vase. **~ido** *a* flowery; *(selecto)* select; *(lenguaje)* florid. **~ista** *m & f* florist

**flota** *f* fleet
**flot|ador** *m* float. **~ar** *vi* float. **~e** *m.* **a ~e** afloat
**flotilla** *f* flotilla
**fluctua|ción** *f* fluctuation. **~r** [21] *vi* fluctuate
**flu|idez** *f* fluidity; (*fig*) fluency. **~ido** *a* fluid; (*fig*) fluent. ● *m* fluid. **~ir** [17] *vi* flow. **~jo** *m* flow. **~o y reflujo** ebb and flow
**fluorescente** *a* fluorescent
**fluoruro** *m* fluoride
**fluvial** *a* river
**fobia** *f* phobia
**foca** *f* seal
**foc|al** *a* focal. **~o** *m* focus; (*lámpara*) floodlight; (*LAm, bombilla*) light bulb
**fogón** *m* (*cocina*) cooker
**fogoso** *a* spirited
**folio** *m* leaf
**folkl|ore** *m* folklore. **~órico** *a* folk
**follaje** *m* foliage
**follet|ín** *m* newspaper serial. **~o** *m* pamphlet
**follón** *m* (*lío*) mess; (*alboroto*) row
**fomentar** *vt* foment, stir up
**fonda** *f* (*pensión*) boarding-house
**fondo** *m* bottom; (*parte más lejana*) bottom, end; (*de escenario, pintura etc*) background; (*profundidad*) depth. **~s** *mpl* funds, money. **a ~** thoroughly. **en el ~** deep down
**fonétic|a** *f* phonetics. **~o** *a* phonetic
**fono** *m* (*LAm, del teléfono*) earpiece
**fontaner|ía** plumbing. **~o** *m* plumber
**footing** /'futin/ *m* jogging
**forastero** *a* alien. ● *m* stranger
**forceje|ar** *vi* struggle. **~o** *m* struggle
**fórceps** *m invar* forceps
**forense** *a* forensic
**forjar** *vt* forge
**forma** *f* form, shape; (*horma*) mould; (*modo*) way; (*de zapatero*) last. **~s** *fpl* conventions. **~ción** *f* formation; (*educación*) training. **dar ~ a** shape; (*expresar*) formulate. **de ~ que** so (that). **de todas ~s** anyway. **estar en ~** be in good form. **guardar ~s** keep up appearances
**formal** *a* formal; (*de fiar*) reliable; (*serio*) serious. **~idad** *f* formality; (*fiabilidad*) reliability; (*seriedad*) seriousness
**formar** *vt* form; (*hacer*) make; (*enseñar*) train. **~se** *vpr* form; (*desarrollarse*) develop

**formato** *m* format
**formidable** *a* formidable; (*muy grande*) enormous; (*muy bueno, fam*) marvellous
**fórmula** *f* formula; (*receta*) recipe
**formular** *vt* formulate; make (*queja etc*); (*expresar*) express
**fornido** *a* well-built
**forraje** *m* fodder. **~ar** *vt/i* forage
**forr|ar** *vt* (*en el interior*) line; (*en el exterior*) cover. **~o** *m* lining; (*cubierta*) cover. **~o del freno** brake lining
**fortale|cer** [11] *vt* strengthen. **~za** *f* strength; (*mil*) fortress; (*fuerza moral*) fortitude
**fortificar** [7] *vt* fortify
**fortuito** *a* fortuitous. **encuentro** *m* **~** chance meeting
**fortuna** *f* fortune; (*suerte*) luck. **por ~** fortunately
**forz|ado** *a* hard. **~ar** [2 & 10] *vt* force. **~osamente** *adv* necessarily. **~oso** *a* inevitable; (*necesario*) necessary
**fosa** *f* grave
**fosfato** *m* phosphate
**fósforo** *m* phosphorus; (*cerilla*) match
**fósil** *a & m* fossil
**fosilizarse** [10] *vpr* fossilize
**foso** *m* ditch
**foto** *f* photo, photograph. **sacar ~s** take photographs
**fotocopia** *f* photocopy. **~dora** *f* photocopier. **~r** *vt* photocopy
**fotogénico** *a* photogenic
**fot|ografía** *f* photography; (*foto*) photograph. **~ografiar** [20] *vt* photograph. **~ográfico** *a* photographic. **~ógrafo** *m* photographer. **sacar ~ografías** take photographs
**foyer** *m* foyer
**frac** *m* (*pl* fraques *o* fracs) tails
**fracas|ar** *vi* fail. **~o** *m* failure
**fracción** *f* fraction; (*pol*) faction
**fractura** *f* fracture. **~r** *vt* fracture, break. **~rse** *vpr* fracture, break
**fragan|cia** *f* fragrance. **~te** *a* fragrant
**fragata** *f* frigate
**fr|ágil** *a* fragile; (*débil*) weak. **~agilidad** *f* fragility; (*debilidad*) weakness
**fragment|ario** *a* fragmentary. **~o** *m* fragment
**fragor** *m* din
**fragoso** *a* rough

**fragua** f forge. ∼r [15] vt forge; (fig) concoct. ● vi harden

**fraile** m friar; (monje) monk

**frambuesa** f raspberry

**francés** a French. ● m (persona) Frenchman; (lengua) French

**Francia** f France

**franco** a frank; (com) free. ● m (moneda) franc

**francotirador** m sniper

**franela** f flannel

**franja** f border; (fleco) fringe

**franque|ar** vt clear; stamp ⟨carta⟩; overcome ⟨obstáculo⟩. ∼o m stamping; (cantidad) postage

**franqueza** f frankness; (familiaridad) familiarity

**franquis|mo** m General Franco's regime; (política) Franco's policy. ∼ta a pro-Franco

**frasco** m small bottle

**frase** f phrase; (oración) sentence. ∼ hecha set phrase

**fratern|al** a fraternal. ∼idad f fraternity

**fraud|e** m fraud. ∼ulento a fraudulent

**fray** m brother, friar

**frecuen|cia** f frequency. ∼tar vt frequent. ∼te a frequent. con ∼cia frequently

**frega|dero** m sink. ∼r [1 & 12] vt scrub; wash up ⟨los platos⟩; mop ⟨el suelo⟩; (LAm, fig, molestar, fam) annoy

**freír** [51, pp **frito**] vt fry; (fig, molestar, fam) annoy. ∼se vpr fry; ⟨persona⟩ be very hot, be boiling (fam)

**frenar** vt brake; (fig) check

**fren|esí** m frenzy. ∼ético a frenzied

**freno** m (de caballería) bit; (auto) brake; (fig) check

**frente** m front. ● f forehead. ∼ a opposite; (en contra de) opposed to. ∼ por ∼ opposite; (en un choque) head-on. al ∼ at the head; (hacia delante) forward. **arrugar la** ∼ frown. **de** ∼ forward. **hacer** ∼ **a** face ⟨cosa⟩; stand up to ⟨persona⟩

**fresa** f strawberry

**fresc|a** f fresh air. ∼o a (frío) cool; (nuevo) fresh; (descarado) cheeky. ● m fresh air; (frescor) coolness; (mural) fresco; (persona) impudent person. ∼or m coolness. ∼ura f freshness; (frío) coolness; (descaro) cheek. **al** ∼o in the open air. **hacer**

∼o be cool. **tomar el** ∼o get some fresh air

**fresno** m ash (tree)

**friable** a friable

**frialdad** f coldness; (fig) indifference

**fricci|ón** f rubbing; (fig, tec) friction; (masaje) massage. ∼onar vt rub

**frigidez** f coldness; (fig) frigidity

**frígido** a frigid

**frigorífico** m refrigerator, fridge (fam)

**frijol** m bean. ∼es refritos (Mex) purée of black beans

**frío** a & m cold. **coger** ∼ catch cold. **hacer** ∼ be cold

**frisar** vi. ∼ **en** be getting on for, be about

**frito** a fried; (exasperado) exasperated. **me tiene** ∼ I'm sick of him

**fr|ivolidad** f frivolity. ∼ívolo a frivolous

**fronda** f foliage

**fronter|a** f frontier; (fig) limit. ∼izo a frontier. ∼o a opposite

**frontón** m pelota court

**frotar** vt rub; strike ⟨cerilla⟩

**fructífero** a fruitful

**frugal** a frugal

**fruncir** [9] vt gather ⟨tela⟩; wrinkle ⟨piel⟩

**fruslería** f trifle

**frustra|ción** f frustration. ∼r vt frustrate. ∼rse vpr (fracasar) fail. **quedar** ∼do be disappointed

**frut|a** f fruit. ∼ería f fruit shop. ∼ero a fruit. ● m fruiterer; (recipiente) fruit bowl. ∼icultura f fruit-growing. ∼illa f (LAm) strawberry. ∼o m fruit

**fucsia** f fuchsia

**fuego** m fire. ∼s artificiales fireworks. **a** ∼ **lento** on a low heat. **tener** ∼ have a light

**fuente** f fountain; (manantial) spring; (plato) serving dish; (fig) source

**fuera** adv out; (al exterior) outside; (en otra parte) away; (en el extranjero) abroad. ● vb véase **ir** y **ser**. ∼ **de** outside; (excepto) except for, besides. **por** ∼ on the outside

**fuerte** a strong; ⟨color⟩ bright; ⟨sonido⟩ loud; ⟨dolor⟩ severe; (duro) hard; (grande) large; ⟨lluvia, nevada⟩ heavy. ● m fort; (fig) strong point. ● adv hard; (con hablar etc) loudly; (mucho) a lot

**fuerza** f strength; (poder) power; (en física) force; (mil) forces. ∼ **de**

voluntad will-power. **a ~ de** by dint of, by means of. **a la ~** by necessity. **por ~** by force; (*por necesidad*) by necessity. **tener ~s para** have the strength to

**fuese** vb véase **ir** y **ser**

**fug|a** f flight, escape; (*de gas etc*) leak; (*mus*) fugue. **~arse** [12] *vpr* flee, escape. **~az** a fleeting. **~itivo** a & m fugitive. **ponerse en ~a** take to flight

**fui** vb véase **ir** y **ser**

**fulano** m so-and-so. **~, mengano y zutano** Tom, Dick and Harry

**fulgor** m brilliance; (*fig*) splendour

**fulminar** vt strike by lightning; (*fig, mirar*) look daggers at

**fuma|dor** a smoking. ● m smoker. **~r** vt/i smoke. **~rse** vpr smoke; (*fig, gastar*) squander. **~rada** f puff of smoke. **~r en pipa** smoke a pipe. **prohibido ~r** no smoking

**funámbulo** m tightrope walker

**funci|ón** f function; (*de un cargo etc*) duties; (*de teatro*) show, performance. **~onal** a functional. **~onar** vi work, function. **~onario** m civil servant. **no ~ona** out of order

**funda** f cover. **~ de almohada** pillowcase

**funda|ción** f foundation. **~mental** a fundamental. **~mentar** vt lay the foundations of; (*fig*) base. **~mento** m foundation. **~r** vt found; (*fig*) base. **~rse** vpr be based

**fundi|ción** f melting; (*de metales*) smelting; (*taller*) foundry. **~r** vt melt; smelt ⟨*metales*⟩; cast ⟨*objeto*⟩; blend ⟨*colores*⟩; (*fusionar*) merge. **~rse** vpr melt; (*unirse*) merge

**fúnebre** a funeral; (*sombrío*) gloomy

**funeral** a funeral. ● m funeral. **~es** mpl funeral

**funicular** a & m funicular

**furg|ón** m van. **~oneta** f van

**fur|ia** f fury; (*violencia*) violence. **~ibundo** a furious. **~ioso** a furious. **~or** m fury

**furtivo** a furtive

**furúnculo** m boil

**fuselaje** m fuselage

**fusible** m fuse

**fusil** m gun. **~ar** vt shoot

**fusión** f melting; (*unión*) fusion; (*com*) merger

**fútbol** m football

**futbolista** m footballer

**fútil** a futile

**futur|ista** a futuristic. ● m & f futurist. **~o** a & m future

# G

**gabán** m overcoat

**gabardina** f raincoat; (*tela*) gabardine

**gabinete** m (*pol*) cabinet; (*en museo etc*) room; (*de dentista, médico etc*) consulting room

**gacela** f gazelle

**gaceta** f gazette

**gachas** fpl porridge

**gacho** a drooping

**gaélico** a Gaelic

**gafa** f hook. **~s** fpl glasses, spectacles. **~s de sol** sun-glasses

**gaf|ar** vt hook; (*fam*) bring bad luck to. **~e** m jinx

**gaita** f bagpipes

**gajo** m (*de naranja, nuez etc*) segment

**gala|s** fpl finery, best clothes. **estar de ~** be dressed up. **hacer ~ de** show off

**galán** m (*en el teatro*) male lead; (*enamorado*) lover

**galante** a gallant. **~ar** vt court. **~ría** f gallantry

**galápago** m turtle

**galardón** m reward

**galaxia** f galaxy

**galeón** m galleon

**galera** f galley

**galería** f gallery

**Gales** m Wales. **país de ~** Wales

**gal|és** a Welsh. ● m Welshman; (*lengua*) Welsh. **~esa** f Welshwoman

**galgo** m greyhound

**Galicia** f Galicia

**galimatías** m invar (*fam*) gibberish

**galón** m gallon; (*cinta*) braid; (*mil*) stripe

**galop|ar** vi gallop. **~e** m gallop

**galvanizar** [10] vt galvanize

**gallard|ía** f elegance. **~o** a elegant

**gallego** a & m Galician

**galleta** f biscuit (*Brit*), cookie (*Amer*)

**gall|ina** f hen, chicken; (*fig, fam*) coward. **~o** m cock

**gama** f scale; (*fig*) range

**gamba** f prawn (*Brit*), shrimp (*Amer*)

**gamberro** m hooligan

**gamuza** f (*piel*) chamois leather

**gana** f wish, desire; (*apetito*) appetite. **de buena** ~ willingly. **de mala** ~ reluctantly. **no me da la** ~ I don't feel like it. **tener** ~**s de** (+ *infinitivo*) feel like (+ *gerundio*)

**ganad|ería** f cattle raising; (*ganado*) livestock. ~**o** m livestock. ~**o de cerda** pigs. ~**o lanar** sheep. ~**o vacuno** cattle

**ganar** vt earn; (*en concurso, juego etc*) win; (*alcanzar*) reach; (*aventajar*) beat. ● vi (*vencer*) win; (*mejorar*) improve. ~**se la vida** earn a living. **salir ganando** come out better off

**ganch|illo** m crochet. ~**o** m hook. ~**oso** a, ~**udo** a hooked. **echar el** ~**o a** hook. **hacer** ~**illo** crochet. **tener** ~**o** be very attractive

**gandul** a & m & f good-for-nothing

**ganga** f bargain; (*buena situación*) easy job, cushy job (*fam*)

**gangrena** f gangrene

**gans|ada** f silly thing. ~**o** m goose

**gañi|do** m yelping. ~**r** [22] vi yelp

**garabat|ear** vt/i (*garrapatear*) scribble. ~**o** m (*garrapato*) scribble

**garaj|e** m garage. ~**ista** m & f garage attendant

**garant|e** m & f guarantor. ~**ía** f guarantee. ~**ir** [24] vt (*esp LAm*), ~**izar** [10] vt guarantee

**garapiñado** a. **almendras** fpl **garapiñadas** sugared almonds

**garbanzo** m chick-pea

**garbo** m poise; (*de escrito*) style. ~**so** a elegant

**garfio** m hook

**garganta** f throat; (*desfiladero*) gorge; (*de botella*) neck

**gárgaras** fpl. **hacer** ~ gargle

**gargarismo** m gargle

**gárgola** f gargoyle

**garita** f hut; (*de centinela*) sentry box

**garito** m gambling den

**garra** f (*de animal*) claw; (*de ave*) talon

**garrafa** f carafe

**garrapata** f tick

**garrapat|ear** vi scribble. ~**o** m scribble

**garrote** m club, cudgel; (*tormento*) garrotte

**gárrulo** a garrulous

**garúa** f (*LAm*) drizzle

**garza** f heron

**gas** m gas. **con** ~ fizzy. **sin** ~ still

**gasa** f gauze

**gaseosa** f lemonade

**gasfitero** m (*Arg*) plumber

**gas|óleo** m diesel. ~**olina** f petrol (*Brit*), gasoline (*Amer*), gas (*Amer*). ~**olinera** f petrol station (*Brit*), gas station (*Amer*); (*lancha*) motor boat. ~**ómetro** m gasometer

**gast|ado** a spent; (*vestido etc*) worn out. ~**ador** m spendthrift. ~**ar** vt spend; (*consumir*) use; (*malgastar*) waste; wear (*vestido etc*); crack (*broma*). ● vi spend. ~**arse** vpr wear out. ~**o** m expense; (*acción de gastar*) spending

**gástrico** a gastric

**gastronomía** f gastronomy

**gat|a** f cat. **a** ~**as** on all fours. ~**ear** vi crawl

**gatillo** m trigger; (*de dentista*) (dental) forceps

**gat|ito** m kitten. ~**o** m cat. **dar** ~**o por liebre** take s.o. in

**gaucho** a & m Gaucho

**gaveta** f drawer

**gavilla** f sheaf; (*de personas*) band, gang

**gaviota** f seagull

**gazpacho** m gazpacho, cold soup

**géiser** m geyser

**gelatina** f gelatine; (*jalea*) jelly

**gelignita** f gelignite

**gema** f gem

**gemelo** m twin. ~**s** mpl (*anteojos*) binoculars; (*de camisa*) cuff-links. **G**~**s** Gemini

**gemido** m groan

**Géminis** mpl Gemini

**gemir** [5] vi groan; (*animal*) whine, howl

**gen** m, **gene** m gene

**geneal|ogía** f genealogy. ~**ógico** a genealogical. **árbol** m ~**ógico** family tree

**generación** f generation

**general** a general; (*corriente*) common. ● m general. ~**ísimo** m generalissimo, supreme commander. ~**ización** f generalization. ~**izar** [10] vt/i generalize. ~**mente** adv generally. **en** ~ in general. **por lo** ~ generally

**generar** vt generate

**género** m type, sort; (*biol*) genus; (*gram*) gender; (*producto*) product. ~**s de punto** knitwear. ~ **humano** mankind

**generos|idad** f generosity. ~**o** a generous; (*vino*) full-bodied

**génesis** m genesis

**genétic|a** f genetics. ~**o** a genetic

**genial** _a_ brilliant; _(agradable)_ pleasant

**genio** _m_ temper; _(carácter)_ nature; _(talento, persona)_ genius

**genital** _a_ genital. **~es** _mpl_ genitals

**gente** _f_ people; _(nación)_ nation; _(familia, fam)_ family; _(Mex, persona)_ person

**gentil** _a_ charming; _(pagano)_ pagan. **~eza** _f_ elegance; _(encanto)_ charm; _(amabilidad)_ kindness

**gentío** _m_ crowd

**genuflexión** _f_ genuflection

**genuino** _a_ genuine

**ge|ografía** _f_ geography. **~ográfico** _a_ geographical. **~ógrafo** _m_ geographer

**ge|ología** _f_ geology. **~ólogo** _m_ geologist

**geom|etría** _f_ geometry. **~étrico** _a_ geometrical

**geranio** _m_ geranium

**geren|cia** _f_ management. **~te** _m_ manager

**geriatría** _f_ geriatrics

**germánico** _a_ & _m_ Germanic

**germen** _m_ germ

**germicida** _f_ germicide

**germinar** _vi_ germinate

**gestación** _f_ gestation

**gesticula|ción** _f_ gesticulation. **~r** _vi_ gesticulate; _(hacer muecas)_ grimace

**gesti|ón** _f_ step; _(administración)_ management. **~onar** _vt_ take steps to arrange; _(dirigir)_ manage

**gesto** _m_ expression; _(ademán)_ gesture; _(mueca)_ grimace

**Gibraltar** _m_ Gibraltar

**gibraltareño** _a_ & _m_ Gibraltarian

**gigante** _a_ gigantic. ● _m_ giant. **~sco** _a_ gigantic

**gimn|asia** _f_ gymnastics. **~asio** _m_ gymnasium, gym _(fam)_. **~asta** _m_ & _f_ gymnast. **~ástica** _f_ gymnastics

**gimotear** _vi_ whine

**ginebra** _f_ gin

**Ginebra** _f_ Geneva

**ginec|ología** _f_ gynaecology. **~ólogo** _m_ gynaecologist

**gira** _f_ excursion; _(a varios sitios)_ tour

**girar** _vt_ spin; _(por giro postal)_ transfer. ● _vi_ rotate, go round; ⟨camino etc⟩ turn

**girasol** _m_ sunflower

**gir|atorio** _a_ revolving. **~o** _m_ turn; _(com)_ draft; _(locución)_ expression. **~o postal** postal order

**giroscopio** _m_ gyroscope

**gis** _m_ chalk

**gitano** _a_ & _m_ gypsy

**glacia|l** _a_ icy. **~r** _m_ glacier

**gladiador** _m_ gladiator

**glándula** _f_ gland

**glasear** _vt_ glaze; _(culin)_ ice

**glicerina** _f_ glycerine

**glicina** _f_ wisteria

**glob|al** _a_ global; _(fig)_ overall. **~o** _m_ globe; _(aeróstato, juguete)_ balloon

**glóbulo** _m_ globule; _(med)_ corpuscle

**gloria** _f_ glory. **~rse** _vpr_ boast _(de_ about)

**glorieta** _f_ bower; _(auto)_ roundabout _(Brit)_, (traffic) circle _(Amer)_

**glorificar** [7] _vt_ glorify

**glorioso** _a_ glorious

**glosario** _m_ glossary

**glot|ón** _a_ gluttonous. ● _m_ glutton. **~onería** _f_ gluttony

**glucosa** _f_ glucose

**gnomo** /'nomo/ _m_ gnome

**gob|ernación** _f_ government. **~ernador** _a_ governing. ● _m_ governor. **~ernante** _a_ governing. **~ernar** [1] _vt_ govern; _(dirigir)_ manage, direct. **~ierno** _m_ government; _(dirección)_ management, direction. **~ierno de la casa** housekeeping. **Ministerio** _m_ **de la G~ernación** Home Office _(Brit)_, Department of the Interior _(Amer)_

**goce** _m_ enjoyment

**gol** _m_ goal

**golf** _m_ golf

**golfo** _m_ gulf; _(niño)_ urchin; _(holgazán)_ layabout

**golondrina** _f_ swallow

**golos|ina** _f_ titbit; _(dulce)_ sweet. **~o** _a_ fond of sweets

**golpe** _m_ blow; _(puñetazo)_ punch; _(choque)_ bump; _(de emoción)_ shock; _(acceso)_ fit; _(en fútbol)_ shot; _(en golf, en tenis, de remo)_ stroke. **~ar** _vt_ hit; _(dar varios golpes)_ beat; _(con mucho ruido)_ bang; _(con el puño)_ punch. ● _vi_ knock. **~ de estado** coup d'etat. **~ de fortuna** stroke of luck. **~ de mano** raid. **~ de vista** glance. **~ militar** military coup. **de ~** suddenly. **de un ~** at one go

**gom|a** _f_ rubber; _(para pegar)_ glue; _(anillo)_ rubber band; _(elástico)_ elastic. **~a de borrar** rubber. **~a de pegar** glue. **~a espuma** foam rubber. **~ita** _f_ rubber band

**gongo** _m_ gong

**gord|a** _f_ _(Mex)_ thick tortilla. **~iflón** _m_ _(fam)_, **~inflón** _m_ _(fam)_ fatty. **~o** _a_ ⟨persona⟩ fat; ⟨carne⟩ fatty;

(*grande*) large, big. ● *m* first prize. ∼**ura** *f* fatness; (*grasa*) fat

**gorila** *f* gorilla

**gorje|ar** *vi* chirp. ∼**o** *m* chirping

**gorra** *f* cap

**gorrión** *m* sparrow

**gorro** *m* cap; (*de niño*) bonnet

**got|a** *f* drop; (*med*) gout. ∼**ear** *vi* drip. ∼**eo** *m* dripping. ∼**era** *f* leak. **ni** ∼**a** nothing

**gótico** *a* Gothic

**gozar** [10] *vt* enjoy. ● *vi*. ∼ **de** enjoy. ∼**se** *vpr* enjoy

**gozne** *m* hinge

**gozo** *m* pleasure; (*alegría*) joy. ∼**so** *a* delighted

**graba|ción** *f* recording. ∼**do** *m* engraving, print; (*en libro*) illustration. ∼**r** *vt* engrave; record (*discos etc*)

**gracejo** *m* wit

**graci|a** *f* grace; (*favor*) favour; (*humor*) wit. ∼**as** *fpl* thanks. ¡∼**as!** thank you!, thanks! ∼**oso** *a* funny. ● *m* fool, comic character. **dar las** ∼**as** thank. **hacer** ∼**a** amuse; (*gustar*) please. ¡**muchas** ∼**as!** thank you very much! **tener** ∼**a** be funny

**grad|a** *f* step; (*línea*) row; (*de anfiteatro*) tier. ∼**ación** *f* gradation. ∼**o** *m* degree; (*escol*) year (*Brit*), grade (*Amer*); (*voluntad*) willingness

**gradua|ción** *f* graduation; (*de alcohol*) proof. ∼**do** *m* graduate. ∼**l** *a* gradual. ∼**r** [21] *vt* graduate; (*medir*) measure; (*univ*) confer a degree on. ∼**rse** *vpr* graduate

**gráfic|a** *f* graph. ∼**o** *a* graphic. ● *m* graph

**grajo** *m* rook

**gram|ática** *f* grammar. ∼**atical** *a* grammatical

**gramo** *m* gram, gramme (*Brit*)

**gramófono** *m* record-player, gramophone (*Brit*), phonograph (*Amer*)

**gran** *a véase* **grande**

**grana** *f* (*color*) scarlet

**granada** *f* pomegranate; (*mil*) grenade

**granate** *m* garnet

**Gran Bretaña** *f* Great Britain

**grande** *a* (*delante de nombre en singular* **gran**) big, large; (*alto*) tall; (*fig*) great. ● *m* grandee. ∼**za** *f* greatness

**grandioso** *a* magnificent

**granel** *m*. **a** ∼ in bulk; (*suelto*) loose; (*fig*) in abundance

**granero** *m* barn

**granito** *m* granite; (*grano*) small grain

**graniz|ado** *m* iced drink. ∼**ar** [10] *vi* hail. ∼**o** *m* hail

**granj|a** *f* farm. ∼**ero** *m* farmer

**grano** *m* grain; (*semilla*) seed; (*de café*) bean; (*med*) spot. ∼**s** *mpl* cereals

**granuja** *m* & *f* rogue

**gránulo** *m* granule

**grapa** *f* staple

**gras|a** *f* grease; (*culin*) fat. ∼**iento** *a* greasy

**gratifica|ción** *f* (*propina*) tip; (*de sueldo*) bonus. ∼**r** [7] *vt* (*dar propina*) tip

**gratis** *adv* free

**gratitud** *f* gratitude

**grato** *a* pleasant; (*bienvenido*) welcome

**gratuito** *a* free; (*fig*) uncalled for

**grava** *f* gravel

**grava|men** *m* obligation. ∼**r** *vt* tax; (*cargar*) burden

**grave** *a* serious; (*pesado*) heavy; (*sonido*) low; (*acento*) grave. ∼**dad** *f* gravity

**gravilla** *f* gravel

**gravita|ción** *f* gravitation. ∼**r** *vi* gravitate; (*apoyarse*) rest (**sobre** on); (*fig, pesar*) weigh (**sobre** on)

**gravoso** *a* onerous; (*costoso*) expensive

**graznar** *vi* (*cuervo*) caw; (*pato*) quack

**Grecia** *f* Greece

**gregario** *a* gregarious

**greguería** *f* uproar

**gremio** *m* union

**greñ|a** *f* mop of hair. ∼**udo** *a* unkempt

**gresca** *f* uproar; (*riña*) quarrel

**griego** *a* & *m* Greek

**grieta** *f* crack

**grifo** *m* tap, faucet (*Amer*); (*animal fantástico*) griffin

**grilletes** *mpl* shackles

**grillo** *m* cricket; (*bot*) shoot. ∼**s** *mpl* shackles

**grima** *f*. **dar** ∼ annoy

**gringo** *m* (*LAm*) Yankee (*fam*), American

**gripe** *f* flu (*fam*), influenza

**gris** *a* grey. ● *m* grey; (*policía, fam*) policeman

**grit|ar** *vt* shout (for); (*como protesta*) boo. ● *vi* shout. ∼**ería** *f*, ∼**erío** *m* uproar. **~o** m shout; (de dolor, sorpresa) cry; (chillido) scream. **dar ~s** shout

**grosella** f redcurrant. **~ negra** blackcurrant

**groser|ía** f coarseness; (palabras etc) coarse remark. **~o** a coarse; (descortés) rude

**grosor** m thickness

**grotesco** a grotesque

**grúa** f crane

**grues|a** f gross. **~o** a thick; (persona) fat, stout. ● m thickness; (fig) main body

**grulla** f crane

**grumo** m clot; (de leche) curd

**gruñi|do** m grunt; (fig) grumble. **~r** [22] vi grunt; (perro) growl; (refunfuñar) grumble

**grupa** f hindquarters

**grupo** m group

**gruta** f grotto

**guacamole** m (Mex) avocado purée

**guadaña** f scythe

**guagua** f trifle; (esp LAm, autobús, fam) bus

**guante** m glove

**guapo** a good-looking; (chica) pretty; (elegante) smart

**guarapo** m (LAm) sugar cane liquor

**guarda** m & f guard; (de parque etc) keeper. ● f protection. **~barros** m invar mudguard. **~bosque** m invar gamekeeper. **~costas** m invar coastguard vessel. **~dor** a careful. ● m keeper. **~espaldas** m invar bodyguard. **~meta** m invar goalkeeper. **~r** vt keep; (vigilar) guard; (proteger) protect; (reservar) save, keep. **~rse** vpr be on one's guard. **~rse de** (+ infinitivo) avoid (+ gerundio). **~rropa** m wardrobe; (en local público) cloakroom. **~vallas** m invar (LAm) goalkeeper

**guardería** f nursery

**guardia** f guard; (custodia) care. ● f guard. **G~ Civil** Civil Guard. **~ municipal** policeman. **~ de tráfico** traffic policeman. **estar de ~** be on duty. **estar en ~** be on one's guard. **montar la ~** mount guard

**guardián** m guardian; (de parque etc) keeper; (de edificio) caretaker

**guardilla** f attic

**guar|ecer** [11] (albergar) give shelter to. **~ecerse** vpr take shelter. **~ida** f den, lair; (de personas) hideout

**guarn|ecer** [11] vt provide; (adornar) decorate; (culin) garnish. **~ición** m decoration; (de caballo) harness; (culin) garnish; (mil) garrison; (de piedra preciosa) setting

**guarro** m pig

**guasa** f joke; (ironía) irony

**guaso** a (Arg) coarse

**guasón** a humorous. ● m joker

**Guatemala** f Guatemala

**guatemalteco** a from Guatemala. ● m person from Guatemala

**guateque** m party

**guayaba** f guava; (dulce) guava jelly

**guayabera** f (Mex) shirt

**gubernamental** a, **gubernativo** a governmental

**güero** a (Mex) fair

**guerr|a** f war; (método) warfare. **~a civil** civil war. **~ear** vi wage war. **~ero** a war; (belicoso) fighting. ● m warrior. **~illa** f band of guerillas. **~illero** m guerilla. **dar ~a** annoy

**guía** m & f guide. ● f guidebook; (de teléfonos) directory; (de ferrocarriles) timetable

**guiar** [20] vt guide; (llevar) lead; (auto) drive. **~se** vpr be guided (por by)

**guij|arro** m pebble. **~o** m gravel

**guillotina** f guillotine

**guind|a** f morello cherry. **~illa** f chilli

**guiñapo** m rag; (fig, persona) reprobate

**guiñ|ar** vt/i wink. **~o** m wink. **hacer ~os** wink

**gui|ón** m hyphen, dash; (de película etc) script. **~onista** m & f scriptwriter

**guirnalda** f garland

**güiro** m (LAm) gourd

**guisa** f manner, way. **a ~ de** as. **de tal ~** in such a way

**guisado** m stew

**guisante** m pea. **~ de olor** sweet pea

**guis|ar** vt/i cook. **~o** m dish

**güisqui** m whisky

**guitarr|a** f guitar. **~ista** m & f guitarist

**gula** f gluttony

**gusano** m worm; (larva de mosca) maggot

**gustar** vt taste. ● vi please. **¿te gusta?** do you like it? **me gusta el vino** I like wine

**gusto** m taste; (placer) pleasure. **~so** a tasty; (agradable) pleasant. **a ~** comfortable. **a mi ~** to my liking.

**buen** ~ (good) taste. **con mucho** ~ with pleasure. **dar** ~ please. **mucho** ~ pleased to meet you

**gutural** *a* guttural

# H

**ha** *vb véase* **haber**

**haba** *f* broad bean; (*de café etc*) bean

**Habana** *f*. **la** ~ Havana

**haban|era** *f* habanera, Cuban dance. ~**ero** *a* from Havana. ● *m* person from Havana. ~**o** *m* (*puro*) Havana

**haber** *v aux* [30] have. ● *v impersonal* (*presente s & pl* **hay**, *imperfecto s & pl* **había**, *pretérito s & pl* **hubo**) be. **hay 5 bancos en la plaza** there are 5 banks in the square. **hay que hacerlo** it must be done, you have to do it. **he aquí** here is, here are. **no hay de qué** don't mention it, not at all. **¿qué hay?** (*¿qué pasa?*) what's the matter?; (*¿qué tal?*) how are you?

**habichuela** *f* bean

**hábil** *a* skilful; (*listo*) clever; (*adecuado*) suitable

**habilidad** *f* skill; (*astucia*) cleverness

**habilita|ción** *f* qualification. ~**r** *vt* qualify

**habita|ble** *a* habitable. ~**ción** *f* room; (*casa etc*) dwelling; (*cuarto de dormir*) bedroom; (*en biología*) habitat. ~**ción de matrimonio**, ~**ción doble** double room. ~**ción individual**, ~**ción sencilla** single room. ~**do** *a* inhabited. ~**nte** *m* inhabitant. ~**r** *vt* live in. ● *vi* live

**hábito** *m* habit

**habitual** *a* usual, habitual; (*cliente*) regular. ~**mente** *adv* usually

**habituar** [21] *vt* accustom. ~**se** *vpr*. ~**se a** get used to

**habla** *f* speech; (*idioma*) language; (*dialecto*) dialect. **al** ~ (*al teléfono*) speaking. **ponerse al** ~ **con** get in touch with. ~**dor** *a* talkative. ● *m* chatterbox. ~**duría** *f* rumour. ~**durías** *fpl* gossip. ~**nte** *a* speaking. ● *m & f* speaker. ~**r** *vt* speak. ● *vi* speak, talk (**con** to). ~**rse** *vpr* speak. **¡ni** ~**r!** out of the question! **se** ~ **español** Spanish spoken

**hacedor** *m* creator, maker

**hacendado** *m* landowner; (*LAm*) farmer

**hacendoso** *a* hard-working

**hacer** [31] *vt* do; (*fabricar, producir etc*) make; (*en matemáticas*) make, be. ● *v impersonal* (*con expresiones meteorológicas*) be; (*con determinado periodo de tiempo*) ago. ~**se** *vpr* become; (*acostumbrarse*) get used (**a** to); (*estar hecho*) be made. ~ **de** act as. ~**se a la mar** put to sea. ~**se el sordo** pretend to be deaf. **hace buen tiempo** it's fine weather. **hace calor** it's hot. **hace frío** it's cold. **hace poco** recently. **hace 7 años** 7 years ago. **hace sol** it's sunny. **hace viento** it's windy. **¿qué le vamos a** ~**?** what are we going to do?

**hacia** *prep* towards; (*cerca de*) near; (*con tiempo*) at about. ~ **abajo** down(wards). ~ **arriba** up(wards). ~ **las dos** at about two o'clock

**hacienda** *f* country estate; (*en LAm*) ranch; (*LAm, ganado*) livestock; (*pública*) treasury. **Ministerio** *m* **de H**~ Ministry of Finance; (*en Gran Bretaña*) Exchequer; (*en Estados Unidos*) Treasury. **ministro** *m* **de H**~ Minister of Finance; (*en Gran Bretaña*) Chancellor of the Exchequer; (*en Estados Unidos*) Secretary of the Treasury

**hacinar** *vt* stack

**hacha** *f* axe; (*antorcha*) torch

**hachís** *m* hashish

**hada** *f* fairy. **cuento** *m* **de** ~**s** fairy tale

**hado** *m* fate

**hago** *vb véase* **hacer**

**Haití** *m* Haiti

**halag|ar** [12] *vt* flatter. ~**üeño** *a* flattering

**halcón** *m* falcon

**hálito** *m* breath

**halo** *m* halo

**hall** /xol/ *m* hall

**halla|r** *vt* find; (*descubrir*) discover. ~**rse** *vpr* be. ~**zgo** *m* discovery

**hamaca** *f* hammock; (*asiento*) deck-chair

**hambr|e** *f* hunger; (*de muchos*) famine. ~**iento** *a* starving. **tener** ~**e** be hungry

**Hamburgo** *m* Hamburg

**hamburguesa** *f* hamburger

**hamp|a** *f* underworld. ~**ón** *m* thug

**handicap** /'xandikap/ *m* handicap

**hangar** *m* hangar

**haragán** *a* lazy, idle. ● *m* layabout

**harap|iento** *a* in rags. ~**o** *m* rag

**harina** *f* flour

**harpa** *f* harp

**hart|ar** *vt* satisfy; (*fastidiar*) annoy. ~**arse** *vpr* eat one's fill; (*cansarse*) get fed up (**de** with). ~**azgo** *m* surfeit. ~**o** *a* full; (*cansado*) tired; (*fastidiado*) fed up (**de** with). ● *adv* enough; (*muy*) very. ~**ura** *f* surfeit; (*abundancia*) plenty; (*de deseo*) satisfaction

**hasta** *prep* as far as; (*con tiempo*) until, till; (*Mex*) not until. ● *adv* even. ¡~ **la vista!** goodbye!, see you! (*fam*). ¡~ **luego!** see you later! ¡~ **mañana!** see you tomorrow! ¡~ **pronto!** see you soon!

**hast|iar** [20] *vt* annoy; (*cansar*) weary, tire; (*aburrir*) bore. ~**iarse** *vpr* get fed up (**de** with). ~**ío** *m* weariness; (*aburrimiento*) boredom; (*asco*) disgust

**hat|illo** *m* bundle (of belongings); (*ganado*) small flock. ~**o** *m* belongings; (*ganado*) flock, herd

**haya** *f* beech (tree). ● *vb véase* **haber**

**Haya** *f*. **la** ~ the Hague

**haz** *m* bundle; (*de trigo*) sheaf; (*de rayos*) beam

**hazaña** *f* exploit

**hazmerreír** *m* laughing-stock

**he** *vb véase* **haber**

**hebdomadario** *a* weekly

**hebilla** *f* buckle

**hebra** *f* thread; (*fibra*) fibre

**hebreo** *a* Hebrew; (*actualmente*) Jewish. ● *m* Hebrew; (*actualmente*) Jew; (*lengua*) Hebrew

**hecatombe** *m* (*fig*) disaster

**hechi|cera** *f* witch. ~**cería** *f* witchcraft. ~**cero** *a* magic. ● *m* wizard. ~**zar** [10] *vt* cast a spell on; (*fig*) fascinate. ~**zo** *m* witchcraft; (*un acto de brujería*) spell; (*fig*) fascination

**hech|o** *pp de* **hacer**. ● *a* mature; (*terminado*) finished; (*vestidos etc*) ready-made; (*culin*) done. ● *m* fact; (*acto*) deed; (*cuestión*) matter; (*suceso*) event. ~**ura** *f* making; (*forma*) form; (*del cuerpo*) build; (*calidad de fabricación*) workmanship. **de** ~**o** in fact

**hed|er** [1] *vi* stink. ~**iondez** *f* stench. ~**iondo** *a* stinking, smelly. ~**or** *m* stench

**hela|da** *f* freeze; (*escarcha*) frost. ~**dera** *f* (*LAm*) refrigerator, fridge (*Brit, fam*). ~**dería** *f* ice-cream shop. ~**do** *a* frozen; (*muy frío*) very cold. ● *m* ice-cream. ~**dora** *f* freezer. ~**r** [1] *vt* freeze. ~**rse** *vpr* freeze

**helecho** *m* fern

**hélice** *f* spiral; (*propulsor*) propeller

**heli|cóptero** *m* helicopter. ~**puerto** *m* heliport

**hembra** *f* female; (*mujer*) woman

**hemisferio** *m* hemisphere

**hemorragia** *f* haemorrhage

**hemorroides** *fpl* haemorrhoids, piles

**henchir** [5] *vt* fill. ~**se** *vpr* stuff o.s.

**hend|er** [1] *vt* split. ~**idura** *f* crack, split; (*geol*) fissure

**heno** *m* hay

**heráldica** *f* heraldry

**herb|áceo** *a* herbaceous. ~**olario** *m* herbalist. ~**oso** *a* grassy

**hered|ad** *f* country estate. ~**ar** *vt/i* inherit. ~**era** *f* heiress. ~**ero** *m* heir. ~**itario** *a* hereditary

**here|je** *m* heretic. ~**ía** *f* heresy

**herencia** *f* inheritance; (*fig*) heritage

**heri|da** *f* injury. ~**do** *a* injured, wounded. ● *m* injured person. ~**r** [4] *vt* injure, wound; (*fig*) hurt. ~**rse** *vpr* hurt o.s. **los** ~**dos** the injured; (*cantidad*) the number of injured

**herman|a** *f* sister. ~**a política** sister-in-law. ~**astra** *f* stepsister. ~**astro** *m* stepbrother. ~**dad** *f* brotherhood. ~**o** *m* brother. ~**o político** brother-in-law. ~**os gemelos** twins

**hermético** *a* hermetic; (*fig*) watertight

**hermos|o** *a* beautiful; (*espléndido*) splendid; ⟨*hombre*⟩ handsome. ~**ura** *f* beauty

**hernia** *f* hernia

**héroe** *m* hero

**hero|ico** *a* heroic. ~**ína** *f* heroine; (*droga*) heroin. ~**ísmo** *m* heroism

**herr|adura** *f* horseshoe. ~**amienta** *f* tool. ~**ería** *f* smithy. ~**ero** *m* blacksmith. ~**umbre** *f* rust

**herv|idero** *m* (*manantial*) spring; (*fig*) hotbed; (*multitud*) throng. ~**ir** [4] *vt/i* boil. ~**or** *m* boiling; (*fig*) ardour

**heterogéneo** *a* heterogeneous

**heterosexual** *a* & *m* & *f* heterosexual

**hex|agonal** *a* hexagonal. ~**ágono** *m* hexagon

**hiato** *m* hiatus

**hiberna|ción** f hibernation. **~r** vi hibernate

**hibisco** m hibiscus

**híbrido** a & m hybrid

**hice** vb véase **hacer**

**hidalgo** m nobleman

**hidrata|nte** a moisturizing. **~r** vt hydrate; ‹crema etc› moisturize. **crema** f **~nte** moisturizing cream

**hidráulico** a hydraulic

**hidroavión** m seaplane

**hidroeléctrico** a hydroelectric

**hidrófilo** a absorbent

**hidr|ofobia** f rabies. **~ófobo** a rabid

**hidrógeno** m hydrogen

**hidroplano** m seaplane

**hiedra** f ivy

**hiel** f (fig) bitterness

**hielo** m ice; (escarcha) frost; (fig) coldness

**hiena** f hyena; (fig) brute

**hierba** f grass; (culin, med) herb. **~buena** f mint. **mala ~** weed; (gente) bad people, evil people

**hierro** m iron

**hígado** m liver

**higi|ene** f hygiene. **~énico** a hygienic

**hig|o** m fig. **~uera** f fig tree

**hij|a** f daughter. **~a política** daughter-in-law. **~astra** f stepdaughter. **~astro** m stepson. **~o** m son. **~o político** son-in-law. **~s** mpl sons; (chicos y chicas) children

**hilar** vt spin. **~ delgado** split hairs

**hilaridad** f laughter, hilarity

**hilera** f row; (mil) file

**hilo** m thread; (elec) wire; (de líquido) trickle; (lino) linen

**hilv|án** m tacking. **~anar** vt tack; (fig, bosquejar) outline

**himno** m hymn. **~ nacional** anthem

**hincapié** m. **hacer ~ en** stress, insist on

**hincar** [7] vt drive in. **~se** vpr sink into. **~se de rodillas** kneel down

**hincha** f (fam) grudge; (aficionado, fam) fan

**hincha|do** a inflated; (med) swollen; ‹persona› arrogant. **~r** vt inflate, blow up. **~rse** vpr swell up; (fig, comer mucho, fam) gorge o.s. **~zón** f swelling; (fig) arrogance

**hindi** m Hindi

**hindú** a Hindu

**hiniesta** f (bot) broom

**hinojo** m fennel

**hiper...** pref hyper...

**hiper|mercado** m hypermarket. **~sensible** a hypersensitive. **~tensión** f high blood pressure

**hípico** a horse

**hipn|osis** f hypnosis. **~ótico** a hypnotic. **~otismo** m hypnotism. **~otizador** m hypnotist. **~otizar** [10] vt hypnotize

**hipo** m hiccup. **tener ~** have hiccups

**hipocondríaco** a & m hypochondriac

**hip|ocresía** f hypocrisy. **~ócrita** a hypocritical. **●** m & f hypocrite

**hipodérmico** a hypodermic

**hipódromo** m racecourse

**hipopótamo** m hippopotamus

**hipoteca** f mortgage. **~r** [7] vt mortgage

**hip|ótesis** f invar hypothesis. **~otético** a hypothetical

**hiriente** a offensive, wounding

**hirsuto** a shaggy

**hirviente** a boiling

**hispánico** a Hispanic

**hispano...** pref Spanish

**Hispanoamérica** f Spanish America

**hispano|americano** a Spanish American. **~hablante** a, **~parlante** a Spanish-speaking

**hist|eria** f hysteria. **~érico** a hysterical. **~erismo** m hysteria

**hist|oria** f history; (cuento) story. **~oriador** m historian. **~órico** a historical. **~orieta** f tale; (con dibujos) strip cartoon. **pasar a la ~oria** go down in history

**hito** m milestone

**hizo** vb véase **hacer**

**hocico** m snout; (fig, de enfado) grimace

**hockey** m hockey. **~ sobre hielo** ice hockey

**hogar** m hearth; (fig) home. **~eño** a home; ‹persona› home-loving

**hogaza** f large loaf

**hoguera** f bonfire

**hoja** f leaf; (de papel, metal etc) sheet; (de cuchillo, espada etc) blade. **~ de afeitar** razor blade. **~lata** f tin. **~latería** f tinware. **~latero** m tinsmith

**hojaldre** m puff pastry, flaky pastry

**hojear** vt leaf through; (leer superficialmente) glance through

**hola** int hello!

**Holanda** f Holland

**holand|és** a Dutch. **●** m Dutchman; (lengua) Dutch. **~esa** f Dutchwoman

**holg|ado** *a* loose; (*fig*) comfortable. **~ar** [2 & 12] *vt* (*no trabajar*) not work, have a day off; (*sobrar*) be unnecessary. **~azán** *a* lazy. ● *m* idler. **~ura** *f* looseness; (*fig*) comfort; (*en mecánica*) play. **huelga decir que** needless to say

**holocausto** *m* holocaust

**hollín** *m* soot

**hombre** *m* man; (*especie humana*) man(kind). ● *int* Good Heavens!; (*de duda*) well. **~ de estado** statesman. **~ de negocios** businessman. **~ rana** frogman. **el ~ de la calle** the man in the street

**hombr|era** *f* epaulette; (*almohadilla*) shoulder pad. **~o** *m* shoulder

**hombruno** *a* masculine

**homenaje** *m* homage; (*fig*) tribute. **rendir ~** a pay tribute to

**home|ópata** *m* homoeopath. **~opatía** *f* homoeopathy. **~opático** *a* homoeopathic

**homicid|a** *a* murderous. ● *m & f* murderer. **~io** *m* murder

**homogéneo** *a* homogeneous

**homosexual** *a* & *m* & *f* homosexual. **~idad** *f* homosexuality

**hond|o** *a* deep. **~onada** *f* hollow. **~ura** *f* depth

**Honduras** *fpl* Honduras

**hondureño** *a* & *m* Honduran

**honest|idad** *f* decency. **~o** *a* proper

**hongo** *m* fungus; (*culin*) mushroom; (*venenoso*) toadstool

**hon|or** *m* honour. **~orable** *a* honourable. **~orario** *a* honorary. **~orarios** *mpl* fees. **~ra** *f* honour; (*buena fama*) good name. **~radez** *f* honesty. **~rado** *a* honest. **~rar** *vt* honour. **~rarse** *vpr* be honoured

**hora** *f* hour; (*momento determinado, momento oportuno*) time. **~ avanzada** late hour. **~ punta** rush hour. **~s** *fpl* **de trabajo** working hours. **~s** *fpl* **extraordinarias** overtime. **a estas ~s** now. **¿a qué ~?** at what time? when? **de ~ en ~** hourly. **de última ~** last-minute. **en buena ~** at the right time. **media ~** half an hour. **¿qué ~ es?** what time is it? **¿tiene Vd ~?** can you tell me the time?

**horario** *a* time; (*cada hora*) hourly. ● *m* timetable. **a ~** (*LAm*) on time

**horca** *f* gallows

**horcajadas. a ~** astride

**horchata** *f* tiger-nut milk

**horda** *f* horde

**horizont|al** *a* & *f* horizontal. **~e** *m* horizon

**horma** *f* mould; (*para fabricar calzado*) last; (*para conservar forma del calzado*) shoe-tree

**hormiga** *f* ant

**hormigón** *m* concrete

**hormigue|ar** *vt* tingle; (*bullir*) swarm. **me ~a la mano** I've got pins and needles in my hand. **~o** *m* tingling; (*fig*) anxiety

**hormiguero** *m* anthill; (*de gente*) swarm

**hormona** *f* hormone

**horn|ada** *f* batch. **~ero** *m* baker. **~illo** *m* cooker. **~o** *m* oven; (*para ladrillos, cerámica etc*) kiln; (*tec*) furnace

**horóscopo** *m* horoscope

**horquilla** *f* pitchfork; (*para el pelo*) hairpin

**horr|endo** *a* awful. **~ible** *a* horrible. **~ipilante** *a* terrifying. **~or** *m* horror; (*atrocidad*) atrocity. **~orizar** [10] *vt* horrify. **~orizarse** *vpr* be horrified. **~oroso** *a* horrifying. **¡qué ~or!** how awful!

**hort|aliza** *f* vegetable. **~elano** *m* market gardener. **~icultura** *f* horticulture

**hosco** *a* surly; ⟨*lugar*⟩ gloomy

**hospeda|je** *m* lodging. **~r** *vt* put up. **~rse** *vpr* lodge

**hospital** *m* hospital

**hospital|ario** *m* hospitable. **~idad** *f* hospitality

**hostal** *m* boarding-house

**hostería** *f* inn

**hostia** *f* (*relig*) host; (*golpe, fam*) punch

**hostigar** [12] *vt* whip; (*fig, excitar*) urge; (*fig, molestar*) pester

**hostil** *a* hostile. **~idad** *f* hostility

**hotel** *m* hotel. **~ero** *a* hotel. ● *m* hotelier

**hoy** *adv* today. **~ (en) día** nowadays. **~ mismo** this very day. **~ por ~** for the time being. **de ~ en adelante** from now on

**hoy|a** *f* hole; (*sepultura*) grave. **~o** *m* hole; (*sepultura*) grave. **~uelo** *m* dimple

**hoz** *f* sickle; (*desfiladero*) pass

**hube** *vb véase* **haber**

**hucha** *f* money box

**hueco** *a* hollow; (*vacío*) empty; (*esponjoso*) spongy; (*resonante*) resonant. ● *m* hollow

**huelg|a** *f* strike. **~a de brazos caídos** sit-down strike. **~a de celo** work-to-rule. **~a de hambre** hunger strike. **~uista** *m & f* striker. **declarar la ~a, declararse en ~a** come out on strike

**huelo** *vb véase* **oler**

**huella** *f* footprint; (*de animal, vehículo etc*) track. **~ dactilar, ~ digital** fingerprint

**huérfano** *a* orphaned. ● *m* orphan. **~ de** without

**huero** *a* empty

**huert|a** *f* market garden (*Brit*), truck farm (*Amer*); (*terreno de regadío*) irrigated plain. **~o** *m* vegetable garden; (*de árboles frutales*) orchard

**huesa** *f* grave

**hueso** *m* bone; (*de fruta*) stone. **~so** *a* bony

**huésped** *m* guest; (*que paga*) lodger; (*animal*) host

**huesudo** *a* bony

**huev|a** *f* roe. **~era** *f* eggcup. **~o** *m* egg. **~o duro** hard-boiled egg. **~o escalfado** poached egg. **~o estrellado, ~o frito** fried egg. **~o pasado por agua** boiled egg. **~os revueltos** scrambled eggs

**hui|da** *f* flight, escape. **~dizo** *a* (*tímido*) shy; (*fugaz*) fleeting. **~r** [17] *vt/i* flee, run away; (*evitar*) avoid

**huipil** *m* (*Mex*) embroidered smock

**huitlacoche** *m* (*Mex*) edible black fungus

**hule** *m* oilcloth, oilskin

**human|idad** *f* mankind; (*fig*) humanity. **~idades** *fpl* humanities. **~ismo** *m* humanism. **~ista** *m & f* humanist. **~itario** *a* humanitarian. **~o** *a* human; (*benévolo*) humane. ● *m* human (being)

**hum|areda** *f* cloud of smoke. **~ear** *vi* smoke; (*echar vapor*) steam

**humed|ad** *f* dampness (*en meteorología*) humidity. **~ecer** [11] *vt* moisten. **~ecerse** *vpr* become moist

**húmedo** *a* damp; (*clima*) humid; (*mojado*) wet

**humi|ldad** *f* humility. **~lde** *a* humble. **~llación** *f* humiliation. **~llar** *vt* humiliate. **~llarse** *vpr* humble o.s.

**humo** *m* smoke; (*vapor*) steam; (*gas nocivo*) fumes. **~s** *mpl* conceit

**humor** *m* mood, temper; (*gracia*) humour. **~ismo** *m* humour. **~ista** *m & f* humorist. **~ístico** *a* humorous. **estar de mal ~** be in a bad mood

**hundi|do** *a* sunken. **~miento** *m* sinking. **~r** *vt* sink; destroy (*edificio*). **~rse** *vpr* sink; (*edificio*) collapse

**húngaro** *a & m* Hungarian

**Hungría** *f* Hungary

**huracán** *m* hurricane

**huraño** *a* unsociable

**hurg|ar** [12] *vt* poke; (*fig*) stir up. **~ón** *m* poker

**hurón** *m* ferret. ● *a* unsociable

**hurra** *int* hurray!

**hurraca** *f* magpie

**hurtadillas. a ~** stealthily

**hurt|ar** *vt* steal. **~o** *m* theft; (*cosa robada*) stolen object

**husmear** *vt* sniff out; (*fig*) pry into

**huyo** *vb véase* **huir**

# I

**Iberia** *f* Iberia

**ibérico** *a* Iberian

**ibero** *a & m* Iberian

**íbice** *m* ibex, mountain goat

**Ibiza** *f* Ibiza

**iceberg** /iθ'ber/ *m* iceberg

**icono** *m* icon

**ictericia** *f* jaundice

**ida** *f* outward journey; (*salida*) departure. **de ~ y vuelta** return (*Brit*), round-trip (*Amer*)

**idea** *f* idea; (*opinión*) opinion. **cambiar de ~** change one's mind. **no tener la más remota ~, no tener la menor ~** not have the slightest idea, not have a clue (*fam*)

**ideal** *a* ideal; (*imaginario*) imaginary. ● *m* ideal. **~ista** *m & f* idealist. **~izar** [10] *vt* idealize

**idear** *vt* think up, conceive; (*inventar*) invent

**ídem** *pron & adv* the same

**idéntico** *a* identical

**identi|dad** *f* identity. **~ficación** *f* identification. **~ficar** [7] *vt* identify. **~ficarse** *vpr*. **~ficarse con** identify with

**ideol|ogía** *f* ideology. **~ógico** *a* ideological

**idílico** *a* idyllic

**idilio** *m* idyll

**idiom|a** *m* language. **~ático** *a* idiomatic

**idiosincrasia** f idiosyncrasy
**idiot|a** a idiotic. ● m & f idiot. ~**ez** f
idiocy
**idiotismo** m idiom
**idolatrar** vt worship; (fig) idolize
**ídolo** m idol
**idóneo** a suitable (**para** for)
**iglesia** f church
**iglú** m igloo
**ignición** f ignition
**ignomini|a** f ignominy, disgrace.
~**oso** a ignominious
**ignora|ncia** f ignorance. ~**nte** a
ignorant. ● m ignoramus. ~**r** vt not
know, be unaware of
**igual** a equal; (mismo) the same;
(similar) like; (llano) even; (liso)
smooth. ● adv easily. ● m equal. ~
**que** (the same) as. **al** ~ **que** the
same as. **da** ~, **es** ~ it doesn't
matter
**igual|ar** vt make equal; (ser igual)
equal; (allanar) level. ~**arse** vpr be
equal. ~**dad** f equality. ~**mente**
adv equally; (también) also, likewise; (respuesta de cortesía) the
same to you
**ijada** f flank
**ilegal** a illegal
**ilegible** a illegible
**ilegítimo** a illegitimate
**ileso** a unhurt
**ilícito** a illicit
**ilimitado** a unlimited
**ilógico** a illogical
**ilumina|ción** f illumination; (alum-
brado) lighting; (fig) enlight-
enment. ~**r** vt light (up); (fig)
enlighten. ~**rse** vpr light up
**ilusi|ón** f illusion; (sueño) dream;
(alegría) joy. ~**onado** a excited.
~**onar** vt give false hope. ~**onarse**
vpr have false hopes. **hacerse**
~**ones** build up one's hopes. **me**
**hace** ~**ón** I'm thrilled; I'm looking
forward to ⟨algo en el futuro⟩
**ilusionis|mo** m conjuring. ~**ta** m & f
conjurer
**iluso** a easily deceived. ● m
dreamer. ~**rio** a illusory
**ilustra|ción** f learning; (dibujo) illus-
tration. ~**do** a learned; (con
dibujos) illustrated. ~**r** vt explain;
(instruir) instruct; (añadir dibujos
etc) illustrate. ~**rse** vpr acquire
knowledge. ~**tivo** a illustrative
**ilustre** a illustrious
**imagen** f image; (TV etc) picture

**imagina|ble** a imaginable. ~**ción** f
imagination. ~**r** vt imagine. ~**rse**
vpr imagine. ~**rio** m imaginary.
~**tivo** a imaginative
**imán** m magnet
**imantar** vt magnetize
**imbécil** a stupid. ● m & f imbecile,
idiot
**imborrable** a indelible; ⟨recuerdo
etc⟩ unforgettable
**imbuir** [17] vt imbue (**de** with)
**imita|ción** f imitation. ~**r** vt imitate
**impacien|cia** f impatience. ~**tarse**
vpr lose one's patience. ~**te** a impa-
tient; (intranquilo) anxious
**impacto** m impact
**impar** a odd
**imparcial** a impartial. ~**idad** f
impartiality
**impartir** vt impart
**impasible** a impassive
**impávido** a fearless; (impasible)
impassive
**impecable** a impeccable
**impedi|do** a disabled. ~**menta** f (esp
mil) baggage. ~**mento** m
hindrance. ~**r** [5] vt prevent;
(obstruir) hinder
**impeler** vt drive
**impenetrable** a impenetrable
**impenitente** a unrepentant
**impensa|ble** a unthinkable. ~**do** a
unexpected
**imperar** vi reign
**imperativo** a imperative; ⟨persona⟩
imperious
**imperceptible** a imperceptible
**imperdible** m safety pin
**imperdonable** a unforgivable
**imperfec|ción** f imperfection. ~**to** a
imperfect
**imperial** a imperial. ● f upper deck.
~**ismo** m imperialism
**imperio** m empire; (poder) rule; (fig)
pride. ~**so** a imperious
**impermeable** a waterproof. ● m
raincoat
**impersonal** a impersonal
**impertérrito** a undaunted
**impertinen|cia** f impertinence. ~**te**
a impertinent
**imperturbable** a imperturbable
**ímpetu** m impetus; (impulso)
impulse; (impetuosidad) impetuosity
**impetuos|idad** f impetuosity;
(violencia) violence. ~**o** a impetuous; (violento) violent

**impío** *a* ungodly; ‹acción› irreverent

**implacable** *a* implacable

**implantar** *vt* introduce

**implica|ción** *f* implication. ~**r** [7] *vt* implicate; (*significar*) imply

**implícito** *a* implicit

**implora|ción** *f* entreaty. ~**r** *vt* implore

**imponderable** *a* imponderable; (*inapreciable*) invaluable

**impon|ente** *a* imposing; (*fam*) terrific. ~**er** [34] *vt* impose; (*requerir*) demand; deposit ‹dinero›. ~**erse** *vpr* be imposed; (*hacerse obedecer*) assert o.s.; (*hacerse respetar*) command respect. ~**ible** *a* taxable

**impopular** *a* unpopular. ~**idad** *f* unpopularity

**importa|ción** *f* import; (*artículo*) import. ~**dor** *a* importing. ● *m* importer

**importa|ncia** *f* importance; (*tamaño*) size. ~**nte** *a* important; (*en cantidad*) considerable. ~**r** *vt* import; (*valer*) cost. ● *vi* be important, matter. ¡le importa...? would you mind...? **no** ~ it doesn't matter

**importe** *m* price; (*total*) amount

**importun|ar** *vt* bother. ~**o** *a* troublesome; (*inoportuno*) inopportune

**imposib|ilidad** *f* impossibility. ~**le** *a* impossible. **hacer lo** ~**le** do all one can

**imposición** *f* imposition; (*impuesto*) tax

**impostor** *m* & *f* impostor

**impotable** *a* undrinkable

**impoten|cia** *f* impotence. ~**te** *a* powerless, impotent

**impracticable** *a* impracticable; (*intransitable*) unpassable

**impreca|ción** *f* curse. ~**r** [7] *vt* curse

**imprecis|ión** *f* vagueness. ~**o** *a* imprecise

**impregnar** *vt* impregnate; (*empapar*) soak; (*fig*) cover

**imprenta** *f* printing; (*taller*) printing house, printer's

**imprescindible** *a* indispensable, essential

**impresi|ón** *f* impression; (*acción de imprimir*) printing; (*tirada*) edition; (*huella*) imprint. ~**onable** *a* impressionable. ~**onante** *a* impressive; (*espantoso*) frightening. ~**onar** *vt* impress; (*conmover*) move; (*foto*) expose. ~**onarse**

*vpr* be impressed; (*conmover*) be moved

**impresionis|mo** *m* impressionism. ~**ta** *a* & *m* & *f* impressionist

**impreso** *a* printed. ● *m* printed paper, printed matter. ~**ra** *f* printer

**imprevis|ible** *a* unforseeable. ~**to** *a* unforeseen

**imprimir** [*pp* **impreso**] *vt* impress; print ‹libro etc›

**improbab|ilidad** *f* improbability. ~**le** *a* unlikely, improbable

**improcedente** *a* unsuitable

**improductivo** *a* unproductive

**improperio** *m* insult. ~**s** *mpl* abuse

**impropio** *a* improper

**improvis|ación** *f* improvisation. ~**adamente** *adv* suddenly. ~**ado** *a* improvised. ~**ar** *vt* improvise. ~**o** *a*. **de** ~**o** suddenly

**impruden|cia** *f* imprudence. ~**te** *a* imprudent

**impuden|cia** *f* impudence. ~**te** *a* impudent

**imp|údico** *a* immodest; (*desvergonzado*) shameless. ~**udor** *m* immodesty; (*desvergüenza*) shamelessness

**impuesto** *a* imposed. ● *m* tax. ~ **sobre el valor añadido** VAT, value added tax

**impugnar** *vt* contest; (*refutar*) refute

**impulsar** *vt* impel

**impuls|ividad** *f* impulsiveness. ~**ivo** *a* impulsive. ~**o** *m* impulse

**impun|e** *a* unpunished. ~**idad** *f* impunity

**impur|eza** *f* impurity. ~**o** *a* impure

**imputa|ción** *f* charge. ~**r** *vt* attribute; (*acusar*) charge

**inacabable** *a* interminable

**inaccesible** *a* inaccessible

**inaceptable** *a* unacceptable

**inacostumbrado** *a* unaccustomed

**inactiv|idad** *f* inactivity. ~**o** *a* inactive

**inadaptado** *a* maladjusted

**inadecuado** *a* inadequate; (*inapropiado*) unsuitable

**inadmisible** *a* inadmissible; (*intolerable*) intolerable

**inadvert|ido** *a* unnoticed. ~**encia** *f* inadvertence

**inagotable** *a* inexhaustible

**inaguantable** *a* unbearable; ‹persona› insufferable

**inaltera|ble** *a* unchangeable; ‹color› fast; ‹carácter› calm. ~**do** *a* unchanged

**inanimado** *a* inanimate
**inaplicable** *a* inapplicable
**inapreciable** *a* imperceptible
**inapropiado** *a* inappropriate
**inarticulado** *a* inarticulate
**inasequible** *a* out of reach
**inaudito** *a* unheard-of
**inaugura|ción** *f* inauguration. ∼l *a* inaugural. ∼r *vt* inaugurate
**inca** *a* Incan. ● *m* & *f* Inca. ∼ico *a* Incan
**incalculable** *a* incalculable
**incandescen|cia** *f* incandescence. ∼te *a* incandescent
**incansable** *a* tireless
**incapa|cidad** *f* incapacity. ∼citar *vt* incapacitate. ∼z *a* incapable
**incauto** *a* unwary; (*fácil de engañar*) gullible
**incendi|ar** *vt* set fire to. ∼arse *vpr* catch fire. ∼ario *a* incendiary. ● *m* arsonist. ∼o *m* fire
**incentivo** *m* incentive
**incertidumbre** *f* uncertainty
**incesante** *a* incessant
**incest|o** *m* incest. ∼uoso *a* incestuous
**inciden|cia** *f* incidence; (*incidente*) incident. ∼tal *a* incidental. ∼te *m* incident
**incidir** *vi* fall; (*influir*) influence
**incienso** *m* incense
**incierto** *a* uncertain
**incinera|ción** *f* incineration; (*de cadáveres*) cremation. ∼dor *m* incinerator. ∼r *vt* incinerate; cremate (*cadáver*)
**incipiente** *a* incipient
**incisión** *f* incision
**incisivo** *a* incisive. ● *m* incisor
**incitar** *vt* incite
**incivil** *a* rude
**inclemen|cia** *f* harshness. ∼te *a* harsh
**inclina|ción** *f* slope; (*de la cabeza*) nod; (*fig*) inclination. ∼r *vt* incline. ∼rse *vpr* lean; (*encorvarse*) stoop; (*en saludo*) bow; (*fig*) be inclined. ∼rse a (*parecerse*) resemble
**inclu|ido** *a* included; (*precio*) inclusive; (*en cartas*) enclosed. ∼ir [17] *vt* include; (*en cartas*) enclose. ∼sión *f* inclusion. ∼sive *adv* inclusive. hasta el lunes ∼sive up to and including Monday. ∼so *a* included; (*en cartas*) enclosed. ● *adv* including; (*hasta*) even
**incógnito** *a* unknown. de ∼ incognito

**incoheren|cia** *f* incoherence. ∼te *a* incoherent
**incoloro** *a* colourless
**incólume** *a* unharmed
**incomestible** *a*, **incomible** *a* uneatable, inedible
**incomodar** *vt* inconvenience; (*molestar*) bother. ∼se *vpr* trouble o.s.; (*enfadarse*) get angry
**incómodo** *a* uncomfortable; (*inoportuno*) inconvenient
**incomparable** *a* imcomparable
**incompatib|ilidad** *f* incompatibility. ∼le *a* incompatible
**incompeten|cia** *f* incompetence. ∼te *a* incompetent
**incompleto** *a* incomplete
**incompren|dido** *a* misunderstood. ∼sible *a* incomprehensible. ∼sión *f* incomprehension
**incomunicado** *a* isolated; (*preso*) in solitary confinement
**inconcebible** *a* inconceivable
**inconciliable** *a* irreconcilable
**inconcluso** *a* unfinished
**incondicional** *a* unconditional
**inconfundible** *a* unmistakable
**incongruente** *a* incongruous
**inconmensurable** *a* (*fam*) enormous
**inconscien|cia** *f* unconsciousness; (*irreflexión*) recklessness. ∼te *a* unconscious; (*irreflexivo*) reckless
**inconsecuente** *a* inconsistent
**inconsiderado** *a* inconsiderate
**inconsistente** *a* insubstantial
**inconsolable** *a* unconsolable
**inconstan|cia** *f* inconstancy. ∼te *a* changeable; (*persona*) fickle
**incontable** *a* countless
**incontaminado** *a* uncontaminated
**incontenible** *a* irrepressible
**incontestable** *a* indisputable
**incontinen|cia** *f* incontinence. ∼te *a* incontinent
**inconvenien|cia** *f* disadvantage. ∼te *a* inconvenient; (*inapropiado*) inappropriate; (*incorrecto*) improper. ● *m* difficulty; (*desventaja*) drawback
**incorpora|ción** *f* incorporation. ∼r *vt* incorporate; (*culin*) mix. ∼rse *vpr* sit up; join (*sociedad, regimiento etc*)
**incorrecto** *a* incorrect; (*acción*) improper; (*descortés*) discourteous
**incorregible** *a* incorrigible
**incorruptible** *a* incorruptible
**incrédulo** *a* incredulous

**increíble** *a* incredible

**increment|ar** *vt* increase. **~o** *m* increase

**incriminar** *vt* incriminate

**incrustar** *vt* encrust

**incuba|ción** *f* incubation. **~dora** *f* incubator. **~r** *vt* incubate; *(fig)* hatch

**incuestionable** *a* unquestionable

**inculcar** [7] *vt* inculcate

**inculpar** *vt* accuse; *(culpar)* blame

**inculto** *a* uncultivated; *⟨persona⟩* uneducated

**incumplimiento** *m* non-fulfilment; *(de un contrato)* breach

**incurable** *a* incurable

**incurrir** *vi*. **~ en** incur; fall into *⟨error⟩*; commit *⟨crimen⟩*

**incursión** *f* raid

**indaga|ción** *f* investigation. **~r** [12] *vt* investigate

**indebido** *a* undue

**indecen|cia** *f* indecency. **~te** *a* indecent

**indecible** *a* inexpressible

**indecis|ión** *f* indecision. **~o** *a* undecided

**indefenso** *a* defenceless

**indefini|ble** *a* indefinable. **~do** *a* indefinite

**indeleble** *a* indelible

**indelicad|eza** *f* indelicacy. **~o** *a* indelicate; *(falto de escrúpulo)* unscrupulous

**indemn|e** *a* undamaged; *⟨persona⟩* unhurt. **~idad** *f* indemnity. **~izar** [10] *vt* indemnify, compensate

**independ|encia** *f* independence. **~iente** *a* independent

**independizarse** [10] *vpr* become independent

**indescifrable** *a* indecipherable, incomprehensible

**indescriptible** *a* indescribable

**indeseable** *a* undesirable

**indestructible** *a* indestructible

**indetermina|ble** *a* indeterminable. **~do** *a* indeterminate

**India** *f*. **la ~** India. **las ~s** *fpl* the Indies

**indica|ción** *f* indication; *(sugerencia)* suggestion. **~ciones** *fpl* directions. **~dor** *m* indicator; *(tec)* gauge. **~r** [7] *vt* show, indicate; *(apuntar)* point at; *(hacer saber)* point out; *(aconsejar)* advise. **~tivo** *a* indicative. ● *m* indicative; *(al teléfono)* dialling code

**índice** *m* indication; *(dedo)* index finger; *(de libro)* index; *(catálogo)* catalogue; *(aguja)* pointer

**indicio** *m* indication, sign; *(vestigio)* trace

**indiferen|cia** *f* indifference. **~te** *a* indifferent. **me es ~te** it's all the same to me

**indígena** *a* indigenous. ● *m* & *f* native

**indigen|cia** *f* poverty. **~te** *a* needy

**indigest|ión** *f* indigestion. **~o** *a* undigested; *(difícil de digerir)* indigestible

**indign|ación** *f* indignation. **~ado** *a* indignant. **~ar** *vt* make indignant. **~arse** *vpr* be indignant. **~o** *a* unworthy; *(despreciable)* contemptible

**indio** *a* & *m* Indian

**indirect|a** *f* hint. **~o** *a* indirect

**indisciplina** *f* lack of discipline. **~do** *a* undisciplined

**indiscre|ción** *f* indiscretion. **~to** *a* indiscreet

**indiscutible** *a* unquestionable

**indisoluble** *a* indissoluble

**indispensable** *a* indispensable

**indisp|oner** [34] *vt* *(enemistar)* set against. **~onerse** *vpr* fall out; *(ponerse enfermo)* fall ill. **~osición** *f* indisposition. **~uesto** *a* indisposed

**indistinto** *a* indistinct

**individu|al** *a* individual; *⟨cama⟩* single. **~alidad** *f* individuality. **~alista** *m* & *f* individualist. **~alizar** [10] *vt* individualize. **~o** *a* & *m* individual

**índole** *f* nature; *(clase)* type

**indolen|cia** *f* indolence. **~te** *a* indolent

**indoloro** *a* painless

**indomable** *a* untameable

**indómito** *a* indomitable

**Indonesia** *f* Indonesia

**inducir** [47] *vt* induce; *(deducir)* infer

**indudable** *a* undoubted. **~mente** *adv* undoubtedly

**indulgen|cia** *f* indulgence. **~te** *a* indulgent

**indult|ar** *vt* pardon; exempt *(de un pago etc)*. **~o** *m* pardon

**industria** *f* industry. **~l** *a* industrial. ● *m* industrialist. **~lización** *f* industrialization. **~lizar** [10] *vt* industrialize

**industriarse** *vpr* do one's best

**industrioso** *a* industrious

**inédito** *a* unpublished; (*fig*) unknown

**ineducado** *a* impolite

**inefable** *a* inexpressible

**ineficaz** *a* ineffective

**ineficiente** *a* inefficient

**inelegible** *a* ineligible

**ineludible** *a* inescapable, unavoidable

**inept|itud** *f* ineptitude. **~o** *a* inept

**inequívoco** *a* unequivocal

**iner|cia** *f* inertia

**inerme** *a* unarmed; (*fig*) defenceless

**inerte** *a* inert

**inesperado** *a* unexpected

**inestable** *a* unstable

**inestimable** *a* inestimable

**inevitable** *a* inevitable

**inexacto** *a* inaccurate; (*incorrecto*) incorrect; (*falso*) untrue

**inexistente** *a* non-existent

**inexorable** *a* inexorable

**inexper|iencia** *f* inexperience. **~to** *a* inexperienced

**inexplicable** *a* inexplicable

**infalible** *a* infallible

**infam|ar** *vt* defame. **~atorio** *a* defamatory. **~e** *a* infamous; (*fig, muy malo, fam*) awful. **~ia** *f* infamy

**infancia** *f* infancy

**infant|a** *f* infanta, princess. **~e** *m* infante, prince; (*mil*) infantryman. **~ería** *f* infantry. **~il** *a* (*de niño*) child's; (*como un niño*) infantile

**infarto** *m* coronary (thrombosis)

**infatigable** *a* untiring

**infatua|ción** *f* conceit. **~rse** *vpr* get conceited

**infausto** *a* unlucky

**infec|ción** *f* infection. **~cioso** *a* infectious. **~tar** *vt* infect. **~tarse** *vpr* become infected. **~to** *a* infected; (*fam*) disgusting

**infecundo** *a* infertile

**infeli|cidad** *f* unhappiness. **~z** *a* unhappy

**inferior** *a* inferior. ● *m & f* inferior. **~idad** *f* lower; (*calidad*) inferiority

**inferir** [4] *vt* infer; (*causar*) cause

**infernal** *a* infernal, hellish

**infestar** *vt* infest; (*fig*) inundate

**infi|delidad** *f* unfaithfulness. **~el** *a* unfaithful

**infierno** *m* hell

**infiltra|ción** *f* infiltration. **~rse** *vpr* infiltrate

**ínfimo** *a* lowest

**infini|dad** *f* infinity. **~tivo** *m* infinitive. **~to** *a* infinite. ● *m* infinite;

(*en matemáticas*) infinity. **una ~dad de** countless

**inflación** *f* inflation; (*fig*) conceit

**inflama|ble** *a* (in)flammable. **~ción** *f* inflammation. **~r** *vt* set on fire; (*fig, med*) inflame. **~rse** *vpr* catch fire; (*med*) become inflamed

**inflar** *vt* inflate; (*fig, exagerar*) exaggerate

**inflexi|ble** *a* inflexible. **~ón** *f* inflexion

**infligir** [14] *vt* inflict

**influ|encia** *f* influence. **~enza** *f* flu (*fam*), influenza. **~ir** [17] *vt/i* influence. **~jo** *m* influence. **~yente** *a* influential

**informa|ción** *f* information. **~ciones** *fpl* (*noticias*) news; (*de teléfonos*) directory enquiries. **~dor** *m* informant

**informal** *a* informal; (*incorrecto*) incorrect

**inform|ante** *m & f* informant. **~ar** *vt/i* inform. **~arse** *vpr* find out. **~ática** *f* information technology. **~ativo** *a* informative

**informe** *a* shapeless. ● *m* report; (*información*) information

**infortun|ado** *a* unfortunate. **~io** *m* misfortune

**infracción** *f* infringement

**infraestructura** *f* infrastructure

**infranqueable** *a* impassable; (*fig*) insuperable

**infrarrojo** *a* infrared

**infrecuente** *a* infrequent

**infringir** [14] *vt* infringe

**infructuoso** *a* fruitless

**infundado** *a* unfounded

**infu|ndir** *vt* instil. **~sión** *f* infusion

**ingeniar** *vt* invent

**ingenier|ía** *f* engineering. **~o** *m* engineer

**ingenio** *m* ingenuity; (*agudeza*) wit; (*LAm, de azúcar*) refinery. **~so** *a* ingenious

**ingenu|idad** *f* ingenuousness. **~o** *a* ingenuous

**ingerir** [4] *vt* swallow

**Inglaterra** *f* England

**ingle** *f* groin

**ingl|és** *a* English. ● *m* Englishman; (*lengua*) English. **~esa** *f* Englishwoman

**ingrat|itud** *f* ingratitude. **~o** *a* ungrateful; (*desagradable*) thankless

**ingrediente** *m* ingredient

**ingres|ar** vt deposit. ● vi. ~**ar en** come in, enter; join ⟨sociedad⟩. ~**o** m entry; (en sociedad, hospital etc) admission. ~**os** mpl income

**inh|ábil** a unskillful; (no apto) unfit. ~**abilidad** f unskillfulness

**inhabitable** a uninhabitable

**inhala|ción** f inhalation. ~**dor** m inhaler. ~**r** vt inhale

**inherente** a inherent

**inhibi|ción** f inhibition. ~**r** vt inhibit

**inhospitalario** a, **inhóspito** a inhospitable

**inhumano** a inhuman

**inicia|ción** f beginning. ~**l** a & f initial. ~**r** vt initiate; (comenzar) begin, start. ~**tiva** f initiative

**inicio** m beginning

**inicuo** a iniquitous

**inigualado** a unequalled

**ininterrumpido** a continuous

**injer|encia** f interference. ~**ir** [4] vt insert. ~**irse** vpr interfere

**injert|ar** vt graft. ~**to** m graft

**injuri|a** f insult; (ofensa) offence. ~**ar** vt insult. ~**oso** a offensive

**injust|icia** f injustice. ~**o** a unjust

**inmaculado** a immaculate

**inmaduro** a unripe; ⟨persona⟩ immature

**inmediaciones** fpl neighbourhood

**inmediat|amente** adv immediately. ~**o** a immediate; (contiguo) next

**inmejorable** a excellent

**inmemorable** a immemorial

**inmens|idad** f immensity. ~**o** a immense

**inmerecido** a undeserved

**inmersión** f immersion

**inmigra|ción** f immigration. ~**nte** a & m immigrant. ~**r** vt immigrate

**inminen|cia** f imminence. ~**te** a imminent

**inmiscuirse** [17] vpr interfere

**inmobiliario** a property

**inmoderado** a immoderate

**inmodesto** a immodest

**inmolar** vt sacrifice

**inmoral** a immoral. ~**idad** f immorality

**inmortal** a immortal. ~**izar** [10] vt immortalize

**inmóvil** a immobile

**inmueble** a. **bienes** ~**s** property

**inmund|icia** f filth. ~**icias** fpl rubbish. ~**o** a filthy

**inmun|e** a immune. ~**idad** f immunity. ~**ización** f immunization. ~**izar** [10] vt immunize

**inmuta|ble** a unchangeable. ~**rse** vpr turn pale

**innato** a innate

**innecesario** a unnecessary

**innegable** a undeniable

**innoble** a ignoble

**innova|ción** f innovation. ~**r** vt/i innovate

**innumerable** a innumerable

**inocen|cia** f innocence. ~**tada** f practical joke. ~**te** a innocent. ~**tón** a naïve

**inocuo** a innocuous

**inodoro** a odourless. ● m toilet

**inofensivo** a inoffensive

**inolvidable** a unforgettable

**inoperable** a inoperable

**inopinado** a unexpected

**inoportuno** a untimely; (incómodo) inconvenient

**inorgánico** a inorganic

**inoxidable** a stainless

**inquebrantable** a unbreakable

**inquiet|ar** vt worry. ~**arse** vpr get worried. ~**o** a worried; (agitado) restless. ~**ud** f anxiety

**inquilino** m tenant

**inquirir** [4] vt enquire into, investigate

**insaciable** a insatiable

**insalubre** a unhealthy

**insanable** a incurable

**insatisfecho** a unsatisfied; (descontento) dissatisfied

**inscri|bir** [pp inscrito] vt inscribe; (en registro etc) enrol, register. ~**birse** vpr register. ~**pción** f inscription; (registro) registration

**insect|icida** m insecticide. ~**o** m insect

**insegur|idad** f insecurity. ~**o** a insecure; (dudoso) uncertain

**insemina|ción** f insemination. ~**r** vt inseminate

**insensato** a senseless

**insensible** a insensitive; (med) insensible; (imperceptible) imperceptible

**inseparable** a inseparable

**insertar** vt insert

**insidi|a** f trap. ~**oso** a insidious

**insigne** a famous

**insignia** f badge; (bandera) flag

**insignificante** a insignificant

**insincero** a insincere

**insinua|ción** f insinuation. ~**nte** a insinuating. ~**r** [21] vt insinuate. ~**rse** vpr ingratiate o.s. ~**rse en** creep into

**insípido** *a* insipid

**insist|encia** *f* insistence. **~ente** *a* insistent. **~ir** *vi* insist; *(hacer hincapié)* stress

**insolación** *f* sunstroke

**insolen|cia** *f* rudeness, insolence. **~te** *a* rude, insolent

**insólito** *a* unusual

**insoluble** *a* insoluble

**insolven|cia** *f* insolvency. **~te** *a & m & f* insolvent

**insomn|e** *a* sleepless. **~io** *m* insomnia

**insondable** *a* unfathomable

**insoportable** *a* unbearable

**insospechado** *a* unexpected

**insostenible** *a* untenable

**inspec|ción** *f* inspection. **~cionar** *vt* inspect. **~tor** *m* inspector

**inspira|ción** *f* inspiration. **~r** *vt* inspire. **~rse** *vpr* be inspired

**instala|ción** *f* installation. **~r** *vt* install. **~rse** *vpr* settle

**instancia** *f* request

**instant|ánea** *f* snapshot. **~áneo** *a* instantaneous; *(café etc)* instant. **~e** *m* instant. **a cada ~e** constantly. **al ~e** immediately

**instar** *vt* urge

**instaura|ción** *f* establishment. **~r** *vt* establish

**instiga|ción** *f* instigation. **~dor** *m* instigator. **~r** [12] *vt* instigate; *(incitar)* incite

**instint|ivo** *a* instinctive. **~o** *m* instinct

**institu|ción** *f* institution. **~cional** *a* institutional. **~ir** [17] *vt* establish. **~to** *m* institute; *(escol)* (secondary) school. **~triz** *f* governess

**instru|cción** *f* instruction. **~ctivo** *a* instructive. **~ctor** *m* instructor. **~ir** [17] *vt* instruct; *(enseñar)* teach

**instrument|ación** *f* instrumentation. **~al** *a* instrumental. **~o** *m* instrument; *(herramienta)* tool

**insubordina|ción** *f* insubordination. **~r** *vt* stir up. **~rse** *vpr* rebel

**insuficien|cia** *f* insufficiency; *(inadecuación)* inadequacy. **~te** *a* insufficient

**insufrible** *a* insufferable

**insular** *a* insular

**insulina** *f* insulin

**insulso** *a* tasteless; *(fig)* insipid

**insult|ar** *vt* insult. **~o** *m* insult

**insuperable** *a* insuperable; *(excelente)* excellent

**insurgente** *a* insurgent

**insurrec|ción** *f* insurrection. **~to** *a* insurgent

**intacto** *a* intact

**intachable** *a* irreproachable

**intangible** *a* intangible

**integra|ción** *f* integration. **~l** *a* integral; *(completo)* complete; *(pan)* wholemeal *(Brit)*, wholewheat *(Amer)*. **~r** *vt* make up

**integridad** *f* integrity; *(entereza)* wholeness

**íntegro** *a* complete; *(fig)* upright

**intelect|o** *m* intellect. **~ual** *a & m & f* intellectual

**inteligen|cia** *f* intelligence. **~te** *a* intelligent

**inteligible** *a* intelligible

**intemperancia** *f* intemperance

**intemperie** *f* bad weather. **a la ~** in the open

**intempestivo** *a* untimely

**intenci|ón** *f* intention. **~onado** *a* deliberate. **~onal** *a* intentional. **bien ~onado** well-meaning. **mal ~onado** malicious. **segunda ~ón** duplicity

**intens|idad** *f* intensity. **~ificar** [7] *vt* intensify. **~ivo** *a* intensive. **~o** *a* intense

**intent|ar** *vt* try. **~o** *m* intent; *(tentativa)* attempt. **de ~o** intentionally

**intercalar** *vt* insert

**intercambio** *m* exchange

**interceder** *vt* intercede

**interceptar** *vt* intercept

**intercesión** *f* intercession

**interdicto** *m* ban

**inter|és** *m* interest; *(egoísmo)* self-interest. **~esado** *a* interested; *(parcial)* biassed; *(egoísta)* selfish. **~esante** *a* interesting. **~esar** *vt* interest; *(afectar)* concern. ● *vi* be of interest. **~esarse** *vpr* take an interest *(por* in)

**interfer|encia** *f* interference. **~ir** [4] *vi* interfere

**interino** *a* temporary; *(persona)* acting. ● *m* stand-in; *(médico)* locum

**interior** *a* interior. ● *m* inside. **Ministerio** *m* **del I~** Home Office *(Brit)*, Department of the Interior *(Amer)*

**interjección** *f* interjection

**interlocutor** *m* speaker

**interludio** *m* interlude

**intermediario** *a & m* intermediary

**intermedio** *a* intermediate. ● *m* interval

**interminable** *a* interminable
**intermitente** *a* intermittent. ● *m* indicator
**internacional** *a* international
**intern|ado** *m* (*escol*) boarding-school. ~**ar** *vt* intern; (*en manicomio*) commit. ~**arse** *vpr* penetrate. ~**o** *a* internal; (*escol*) boarding. ● *m* (*escol*) boarder
**interpelar** *vt* appeal
**interponer** [34] *vt* interpose. ~**se** *vpr* intervene
**int|erpretación** *f* interpretation. ~**erpretar** *vt* interpret. ~**érprete** *m* interpreter; (*mus*) performer
**interroga|ción** *f* question; (*acción*) interrogation; (*signo*) question mark. ~**r** [12] *vt* question. ~**tivo** *a* interrogative
**interru|mpir** *vt* interrupt; (*suspender*) stop. ~**pción** *f* interruption. ~**ptor** *m* switch
**intersección** *f* intersection
**interurbano** *a* inter-city; (*conferencia*) long-distance
**intervalo** *m* interval; (*espacio*) space. **a** ~**s** at intervals
**interven|ir** [53] *vt* control; (*med*) operate on. ● *vi* intervene; (*participar*) take part. ~**tor** *m* inspector; (*com*) auditor
**intestino** *m* intestine
**intim|ar** *vi* become friendly. ~**idad** *f* intimacy
**intimidar** *vt* intimidate
**íntimo** *a* intimate. ● *m* close friend
**intitular** *vt* entitle
**intolera|ble** *a* intolerable. ~**nte** *a* intolerant
**intoxicar** [7] *vt* poison
**intranquil|izar** [10] *vt* worry. ~**o** *a* worried
**intransigente** *a* intransigent
**intransitable** *a* impassable
**intransitivo** *a* intransitive
**intratable** *a* intractable
**intrépido** *a* intrepid
**intriga** *f* intrigue. ~**nte** *a* intriguing. ~**r** [12] *vt/i* intrigue
**intrincado** *a* intricate
**intrínseco** *a* intrinsic
**introduc|ción** *f* introduction. ~**ir** [47] *vt* introduce; (*meter*) insert. ~**irse** *vpr* get into; (*entrometerse*) interfere
**intromisión** *f* interference
**introvertido** *a* & *m* introvert
**intrus|ión** *f* intrusion. ~**o** *a* intrusive. ● *m* intruder

**intui|ción** *f* intuition. ~**r** [17] *vt* sense. ~**tivo** *a* intuitive
**inunda|ción** *f* flooding. ~**r** *vt* flood
**inusitado** *a* unusual
**in|útil** *a* useless; (*vano*) futile. ~**utilidad** *f* uselessness
**invadir** *vt* invade
**inv|alidez** *f* invalidity; (*med*) disability. ~**álido** *a* & *m* invalid
**invaria|ble** *a* invariable. ~**do** *a* unchanged
**invas|ión** *f* invasion. ~**or** *a* invading. ● *m* invader
**invectiva** *f* invective
**invencible** *a* invincible
**inven|ción** *f* invention. ~**tar** *vt* invent
**inventario** *m* inventory
**invent|iva** *f* inventiveness. ~**ivo** *a* inventive. ~**or** *m* inventor
**invernadero** *m* greenhouse
**invernal** *a* winter
**inverosímil** *a* improbable
**inversión** *f* inversion; (*com*) investment
**inverso** *a* inverse; (*contrario*) opposite. **a la inversa** the other way round
**invertebrado** *a* & *m* invertebrate
**inverti|do** *a* inverted; (*homosexual*) homosexual. ● *m* homosexual. ~**r** [4] *vt* reverse; (*volcar*) turn upside down; (*com*) invest; spend (*tiempo*)
**investidura** *f* investiture
**investiga|ción** *f* investigation; (*univ*) research. ~**dor** *m* investigator. ~**r** [12] *vt* investigate
**investir** [5] *vt* invest
**inveterado** *a* inveterate
**invicto** *a* unbeaten
**invierno** *m* winter
**inviolable** *a* inviolate
**invisib|ilidad** *f* invisibility. ~**le** *a* invisible
**invita|ción** *f* invitation. ~**do** *m* guest. ~**r** *vt* invite. **te invito a una copa** I'll buy you a drink
**invoca|ción** *f* invocation. ~**r** [7] *vt* invoke
**involuntario** *a* involuntary
**invulnerable** *a* invulnerable
**inyec|ción** *f* injection. ~**tar** *vt* inject
**ion** *m* ion
**ir** [49] *vi* go; (*ropa*) (*convenir*) suit. ● *m* going. ~**se** *vpr* go away. ~ **a hacer** be going to do. ~ **a pie** walk. ~ **de paseo** go for a walk. ~ **en coche** go by car. **no me va ni me viene** it's all the same to me. **no**

**vaya a ser que** in case. **¡qué va!** nonsense! **va mejorando** it's gradually getting better. **¡vamos!**, **¡vámonos!** come on! let's go! **¡vaya!** fancy that! **¡vete a saber!** who knows? **¡ya voy!** I'm coming!

**ira** f anger. **~cundo** a irascible

**Irak** m Iraq

**Irán** m Iran

**iraní** a & m & f Iranian

**iraquí** a & m & f Iraqi

**iris** m (anat) iris; (arco iris) rainbow

**Irlanda** f Ireland

**irland|és** a Irish. ● m Irishman; (lengua) Irish. **~esa** f Irishwoman

**ir|onía** f irony. **~ónico** a ironic

**irracional** a irrational

**irradiar** vt/i radiate

**irrazonable** a unreasonable

**irreal** a unreal. **~idad** f unreality

**irrealizable** a unattainable

**irreconciliable** a irreconcilable

**irreconocible** a unrecognizable

**irrecuperable** a irretrievable

**irreducible** a irreducible

**irreflexión** f impetuosity

**irrefutable** a irrefutable

**irregular** a irregular. **~idad** f irregularity

**irreparable** a irreparable

**irreprimible** a irrepressible

**irreprochable** a irreproachable

**irresistible** a irresistible

**irresoluto** a irresolute

**irrespetuoso** a disrespectful

**irresponsable** a irresponsible

**irrevocable** a irrevocable

**irriga|ción** f irrigation. **~r** [12] vt irrigate

**irrisorio** a derisive; (insignificante) ridiculous

**irrita|ble** a irritable. **~ción** f irritation. **~r** vt irritate. **~rse** vpr get annoyed

**irrumpir** vi burst (**en** in)

**irrupción** f irruption

**isla** f island. **las I~s Británicas** the British Isles

**Islam** m Islam

**islámico** a Islamic

**islandés** a Icelandic. ● m Icelander; (lengua) Icelandic

**Islandia** f Iceland

**isleño** a island. ● m islander

**Israel** m Israel

**israelí** a & m Israeli

**istmo** /'ismo/ m isthmus

**Italia** f Italy

**italiano** a & m Italian

**itinerario** a itinerary

**IVA** abrev (impuesto sobre el valor añadido) VAT, value added tax

**izar** [10] vt hoist

**izquierd|a** f left(-hand); (pol) left (-wing). **~ista** m & f leftist. **~o** a left. **a la ~a** on the left; (con movimiento) to the left

# J

**ja** int ha!

**jabalí** m wild boar

**jabalina** f javelin

**jab|ón** m soap. **~onar** vt soap. **~onoso** a soapy

**jaca** f pony

**jacinto** m hyacinth

**jacta|ncia** f boastfulness; (acción) boasting. **~rse** vpr boast

**jadea|nte** a panting. **~r** vi pant

**jaez** m harness

**jaguar** m jaguar

**jalea** f jelly

**jaleo** m row, uproar. **armar un ~** kick up a fuss

**jalón** m (LAm, tirón) pull; (Mex, trago) drink

**Jamaica** f Jamaica

**jamás** adv never; (en frases afirmativas) ever

**jamelgo** m nag

**jamón** m ham. **~ de York** boiled ham. **~ serrano** cured ham

**Japón** m. **el ~** Japan

**japonés** a & m Japanese

**jaque** m check. **~ mate** checkmate

**jaqueca** f migraine. **dar ~** bother

**jarabe** m syrup

**jardín** m garden. **~ de la infancia** kindergarten, nursery school

**jardiner|ía** f gardening. **~o** m gardener

**jarocho** a (Mex) from Veracruz

**jarr|a** f jug. **~o** m jug. **echar un ~o de agua fría** a throw cold water on. **en ~as** with hands on hips

**jaula** f cage

**jauría** f pack of hounds

**jazmín** m jasmine

**jef|a** f boss. **~atura** f leadership; (sede) headquarters. **~e** m boss; (pol etc) leader. **~e de camareros** head waiter. **~e de estación** stationmaster. **~e de ventas** sales manager

**jengibre** m ginger

**jeque** *m* sheikh

**jer|arquía** *f* hierarchy. **~árquico** *a* hierarchical

**jerez** *m* sherry. **al ~** with sherry

**jerga** *f* coarse cloth; (*argot*) jargon

**jerigonza** *f* jargon; (*galimatías*) gibberish

**jeringa** *f* syringe; (*LAm, molestia*) nuisance. **~r** [12] *vt* (*fig, molestar, fam*) annoy

**jeroglífico** *m* hieroglyph(ic)

**jersey** *m* (*pl* **jerseys**) jersey

**Jerusalén** *m* Jerusalem

**Jesucristo** *m* Jesus Christ. **antes de ~ BC**, before Christ

**jesuita** *a* & *m* & *f* Jesuit

**Jesús** *m* Jesus. ● *int* good heavens!; (*al estornudar*) bless you!

**jícara** *f* small cup

**jilguero** *m* goldfinch

**jinete** *m* rider, horseman

**jipijapa** *f* straw hat

**jirafa** *f* giraffe

**jirón** *m* shred, tatter

**jitomate** *m* (*Mex*) tomato

**jocoso** *a* funny, humorous

**jorna|da** *f* working day; (*viaje*) journey; (*etapa*) stage. **~l** *m* day's wage; (*trabajo*) day's work. **~lero** *m* day labourer

**joroba** *f* hump. **~do** *a* hunchbacked. ● *m* hunchback. **~r** *vt* annoy

**jota** *f* letter J; (*danza*) jota, popular dance; (*fig*) iota. **ni ~** nothing

**joven** (*pl* **jóvenes**) *a* young. ● *m* young man, youth. ● *f* young woman, girl

**jovial** *a* jovial

**joy|a** *f* jewel. **~as** *fpl* jewellery. **~ería** *f* jeweller's (shop). **~ero** *m* jeweller; (*estuche*) jewellery box

**juanete** *m* bunion

**jubil|ación** *f* retirement. **~ado** *a* retired. **~ar** *vt* pension off. **~arse** *vpr* retire. **~eo** *m* jubilee

**júbilo** *m* joy

**jubiloso** *a* jubilant

**judaísmo** *m* Judaism

**judía** *f* Jewish woman; (*alubia*) bean. **~ blanca** haricot bean. **~ escarlata** runner bean. **~ verde** French bean

**judicial** *a* judicial

**judío** *a* Jewish. ● *m* Jewish man

**judo** *m* judo

**juego** *m* game; (*de niños, tec*) play; (*de azar*) gambling; (*conjunto*) set. ● *vb véase* **jugar**. **estar en ~** be at stake. **estar fuera de ~** be offside. **hacer ~** match

**juerga** *f* spree

**jueves** *m* Thursday

**juez** *m* judge. **~ de instrucción** examining magistrate. **~ de línea** linesman

**juga|dor** *m* player; (*en juegos de azar*) gambler. **~r** [3] *vt* play. ● *vi* play; (*a juegos de azar*) gamble; (*apostar*) bet. **~rse** *vpr* risk. **~r al fútbol** play football

**juglar** *m* minstrel

**jugo** *m* juice; (*de carne*) gravy; (*fig*) substance. **~so** *a* juicy; (*fig*) substantial

**juguet|e** *m* toy. **~ear** *vi* play. **~ón** *a* playful

**juicio** *m* judgement; (*opinión*) opinion; (*razón*) reason. **~so** *a* wise. **a mi ~** in my opinion

**juliana** *f* vegetable soup

**julio** *m* July

**junco** *m* rush, reed

**jungla** *f* jungle

**junio** *m* June

**junt|a** *f* meeting; (*consejo*) board, committee; (*pol*) junta; (*tec*) joint. **~ar** *vt* join; (*reunir*) collect. **~arse** *vpr* join; (*gente*) meet. **~o** *a* joined; (*en plural*) together. **~o a** next to. **~ura** *f* joint. **por ~o** all together

**jura|do** *a* sworn. ● *m* jury; (*miembro de jurado*) juror. **~mento** *m* oath. **~r** *vt/i* swear. **~r en falso** commit perjury. **jurárselas a uno** have it in for s.o. **prestar ~mento** take the oath

**jurel** *m* (type of) mackerel

**jurídico** *a* legal

**juris|dicción** *f* jurisdiction. **~prudencia** *f* jurisprudence

**justamente** *a* exactly; (*con justicia*) fairly

**justicia** *f* justice

**justifica|ción** *f* justification. **~r** [7] *vt* justify

**justo** *a* fair, just; (*exacto*) exact; ‹*ropa*› tight. ● *adv* just. **~ a tiempo** just in time

**juven|il** *a* youthful. **~tud** *f* youth; (*gente joven*) young people

**juzga|do** *m* (*tribunal*) court. **~r** [12] *vt* judge. **a ~r por** judging by

# K

**kilo** *m*, **kilogramo** *m* kilo, kilogram
**kil|ometraje** *m* distance in kilometres, mileage. ~**ométrico** *a (fam)* endless. ~**ómetro** *m* kilometre. ~**ómetro cuadrado** square kilometre
**kilovatio** *m* kilowatt
**kiosco** *m* kiosk

# L

**la** *m* A; *(solfa)* lah. ● *art def f* the. ● *pron (ella)* her; *(Vd)* you; *(ello)* it. ~ **de** the one. ~ **de Vd** your one, yours. ~ **que** whoever, the one
**laberinto** *m* labyrinth, maze
**labia** *f* glibness
**labio** *m* lip
**labor** *f* work; *(tarea)* job. ~**able** *a* working. ~**ar** *vi* work. ~**es** *fpl* **de aguja** needlework. ~**es** *fpl* **de ganchillo** crochet. ~**es** *fpl* **de punto** knitting. ~**es** *fpl* **domésticas** housework
**laboratorio** *m* laboratory
**laborioso** *a* laborious
**laborista** *a* Labour. ● *m & f* member of the Labour Party
**labra|do** *a* worked; *‹madera›* carved; *‹metal›* wrought; *‹tierra›* ploughed. ~**dor** *m* farmer; *(obrero)* labourer. ~**nza** *f* farming. ~**r** *vt* work; carve *‹madera›*; cut *‹piedra›*; till *‹la tierra›*; *(fig, causar)* cause
**labriego** *m* peasant
**laca** *f* lacquer
**lacayo** *m* lackey
**lacerar** *vt* lacerate
**lacero** *m* lassoer; *(cazador)* poacher
**lacio** *a* straight; *(flojo)* limp
**lacón** *m* shoulder of pork
**lacónico** *a* laconic
**lacra** *f* scar
**lacr|ar** *vt* seal. ~**e** *m* sealing wax
**lactante** *a* breast-fed
**lácteo** *a* milky. **productos** *mpl* ~**s** dairy products
**ladear** *vt/i* tilt. ~**se** *vpr* lean
**ladera** *f* slope
**ladino** *a* astute
**lado** *m* side. **al** ~ near. **al** ~ **de** at the side of, beside. **los de al** ~ the next

door neighbours. **por otro** ~ on the other hand. **por todos** ~**s** on all sides. **por un** ~ on the one hand
**ladr|ar** *vi* bark. ~**ido** *m* bark
**ladrillo** *m* brick; *(de chocolate)* block
**ladrón** *a* thieving. ● *m* thief
**lagart|ija** *f* (small) lizard. ~**o** *m* lizard
**lago** *m* lake
**lágrima** *f* tear
**lagrimoso** *a* tearful
**laguna** *f* small lake; *(fig, omisión)* gap
**laico** *a* lay
**lamé** *m* lamé
**lamedura** *f* lick
**lament|able** *a* lamentable, pitiful. ~**ar** *vt* be sorry about. ~**arse** *vpr* lament; *(quejarse)* complain. ~**o** *m* moan
**lamer** *vt* lick; *‹olas etc›* lap
**lámina** *f* sheet; *(foto)* plate; *(dibujo)* picture
**lamina|do** *a* laminated. ~**r** *vt* laminate
**lámpara** *f* lamp; *(bombilla)* bulb; *(lamparón)* grease stain. ~ **de pie** standard lamp
**lamparón** *m* grease stain
**lampiño** *a* clean-shaven, beardless
**lana** *f* wool. ~**r** *a*. **ganado** *m* ~**r** sheep. **de** ~ wool(len)
**lanceta** *f* lancet
**lancha** *f* boat. ~ **motora** *f* motor boat. ~ **salvavidas** lifeboat
**lanero** *a* wool(len)
**langost|a** *f* *(crustáceo marino)* lobster; *(insecto)* locust. ~**ino** *m* prawn
**languide|cer** [11] *vi* languish. ~**z** *f* languor
**lánguido** *a* languid; *(decaído)* listless
**lanilla** *f* nap; *(tela fina)* flannel
**lanudo** *a* woolly
**lanza** *f* lance, spear
**lanza|llamas** *m* *invar* flamethrower. ~**miento** *m* throw; *(acción de lanzar)* throwing; *(de proyectil, de producto)* launch. ~**r** [10] *vt* throw; *(de un avión)* drop; launch *‹proyectil, producto›*. ~**rse** *vpr* fling o.s.
**lapicero** *m* (propelling) pencil
**lápida** *f* memorial tablet. ~ **sepulcral** tombstone
**lapidar** *vt* stone
**lápiz** *m* pencil; *(grafito)* lead. ~ **de labios** lipstick
**Laponia** *f* Lapland

**lapso** *m* lapse

**larg|a** *f.* **a la ~a** in the long run. **dar ~as** put off. **~ar** [12] *vt* slacken; (*dar, fam*) give; (*fam*) deal ⟨*bofetada etc*⟩. **~arse** *vpr* (*fam*) go away, clear off (*fam*). **~o** *a* long; (*demasiado*) too long. ● *m* length. **¡~o!** go away! **~ueza** *f* generosity. **a lo ~o** lengthwise. **a lo ~o de** along. **tener 100 metros de ~o** be 100 metres long

**laring|e** *f* larynx. **~itis** *f* laryngitis

**larva** *f* larva

**las** *art def fpl* the. ● *pron* them. **~ de** those, the ones. **~ de Vd** your ones, yours. **~ que** whoever, the ones

**lascivo** *a* lascivious

**láser** *m* laser

**lástima** *f* pity; (*queja*) complaint. **dar ~** be pitiful. **ella me da ~** I feel sorry for her. **¡qué ~!** what a pity!

**lastim|ado** *a* hurt. **~ar** *vt* hurt. **~arse** *vpr* hurt o.s. **~ero** *a* doleful. **~oso** *a* pitiful

**lastre** *m* ballast

**lata** *f* tinplate; (*envase*) tin (*esp Brit*), can; (*molestia, fam*) nuisance. **dar la ~** be a nuisance. **¡qué ~!** what a nuisance!

**latente** *a* latent

**lateral** *a* side, lateral

**latido** *m* beating; (*cada golpe*) beat

**latifundio** *m* large estate

**latigazo** *m* (*golpe*) lash; (*chasquido*) crack

**látigo** *m* whip

**latín** *m* Latin. **saber ~** (*fam*) not be stupid

**latino** *a* Latin. **L~américa** *f* Latin America. **~americano** *a* & *m* Latin American

**latir** *vi* beat; ⟨*herida*⟩ throb

**latitud** *f* latitude

**latón** *m* brass

**latoso** *a* annoying; (*pesado*) boring

**laucha** *f* (*Arg*) mouse

**laúd** *m* lute

**laudable** *a* laudable

**laureado** *a* honoured; (*premiado*) prize-winning

**laurel** *m* laurel; (*culin*) bay

**lava** *f* lava

**lava|ble** *a* washable. **~bo** *m* washbasin; (*retrete*) toilet. **~dero** *m* sink, wash-basin. **~do** *m* washing. **~do de cerebro** brainwashing. **~do en seco** dry-cleaning. **~dora** *f* washing machine. **~ndería** *f* laundry. **~ndería automática** launderette, laundromat (*esp Amer*). **~parabrisas** *m*

*invar* windscreen washer (*Brit*), windshield washer (*Amer*). **~platos** *m* & *f invar* dishwasher; (*Mex, fregadero*) sink. **~r** *vt* wash. **~r en seco** dry-clean. **~rse** *vpr* have a wash. **~rse las manos** (*incl fig*) wash one's hands. **~tiva** *f* enema. **~vajillas** *m* & *f inv* dishwasher

**lax|ante** *a* & *m* laxative. **~o** *a* loose

**laz|ada** *f* bow. **~o** *m* knot; (*lazada*) bow; (*fig, vínculo*) tie; (*cuerda con nudo corredizo*) lasso; (*trampa*) trap

**le** *pron* (*acusativo, él*) him; (*acusativo, Vd*) you; (*dativo, él*) (to) him; (*dativo, ella*) (to) her; (*dativo, ello*) (to) it; (*dativo, Vd*) (to) you

**leal** *a* loyal; (*fiel*) faithful. **~tad** *f* loyalty; (*fidelidad*) faithfulness

**lebrel** *m* greyhound

**lección** *f* lesson; (*univ*) lecture

**lect|or** *m* reader; (*univ*) language assistant. **~ura** *f* reading

**leche** *f* milk; (*golpe*) bash. **~ condensada** condensed milk. **~ desnatada** skimmed milk. **~ en polvo** powdered milk. **~ra** *f* (*vasija*) milk jug. **~ría** *f* dairy. **~ro** *a* milk, dairy. ● *m* milkman. **~ sin desnatar** whole milk. **tener mala ~** be spiteful

**lecho** *m* bed

**lechoso** *a* milky

**lechuga** *f* lettuce

**lechuza** *f* owl

**leer** [18] *vt/i* read

**legación** *f* legation

**legado** *m* legacy; (*enviado*) legate

**legajo** *m* bundle, file

**legal** *a* legal. **~idad** *f* legality. **~izar** [10] *vt* legalize; (*certificar*) authenticate. **~mente** *adv* legally

**legar** [12] *vt* bequeath

**legendario** *a* legendary

**legible** *a* legible

**legi|ón** *f* legion. **~onario** *m* legionary

**legisla|ción** *f* legislation. **~dor** *m* legislator. **~r** *vi* legislate. **~tura** *f* legislature

**leg|itimidad** *f* legitimacy. **~ítimo** *a* legitimate; (*verdadero*) real

**lego** *a* lay; (*ignorante*) ignorant. ● *m* layman

**legua** *f* league

**legumbre** *f* vegetable

**lejan|ía** *f* distance. **~o** *a* distant

**lejía** *f* bleach

**lejos** *adv* far. **~ de** far from. **a lo ~** in the distance. **desde ~** from a distance, from afar

**lelo** a stupid

**lema** m motto

**lencería** f linen; (de mujer) lingerie

**lengua** f tongue; (idioma) language. **irse de la ~** talk too much. **morderse la ~** hold one's tongue. **tener mala ~** have a vicious tongue

**lenguado** m sole

**lenguaje** m language

**lengüeta** f (de zapato) tongue

**lengüetada** f, **lengüetazo** m lick

**lente** f lens. **~s** mpl glasses. **~s de contacto** contact lenses

**lenteja** f lentil. **~uela** f sequin

**lentilla** f contact lens

**lent|itud** f slowness. **~o** a slow

**leña** f firewood. **~ador** m woodcutter. **~o** m log

**Leo** m Leo

**le|ón** m lion. **León** Leo. **~ona** f lioness

**leopardo** m leopard

**leotardo** m thick tights

**lepr|a** f leprosy. **~oso** m leper

**lerdo** a dim; (torpe) clumsy

**les** pron (acusativo) them; (acusativo, Vds) you; (dativo) (to) them; (dativo, Vds) (to) you

**lesbia(na)** f lesbian

**lesbiano** a, **lesbio** a lesbian

**lesi|ón** f wound. **~onado** a injured. **~onar** vt injure; (dañar) damage

**letal** a lethal

**letanía** f litany

**let|árgico** a lethargic. **~argo** m lethargy

**letr|a** f letter; (escritura) handwriting; (de una canción) words, lyrics. **~a de cambio** bill of exchange. **~a de imprenta** print. **~ado** a learned. **~ero** m notice; (cartel) poster

**letrina** f latrine

**leucemia** f leukaemia

**levadizo** a. **puente** m **~** drawbridge

**levadura** f yeast. **~ en polvo** baking powder

**levanta|miento** m lifting; (sublevación) uprising. **~r** vt raise, lift; (construir) build; (recoger) pick up; (separar) take off. **~rse** vpr get up; (ponerse de pie) stand up; (erguirse, sublevarse) rise up

**levante** m east; (viento) east wind. **L~** Levant

**levar** vt weigh (ancla). ● vi set sail

**leve** a light; (enfermedad etc) slight; (de poca importancia) trivial. **~dad** f lightness; (fig) slightness

**léxico** m vocabulary

**lexicografía** f lexicography

**ley** f law; (parlamentaria) act. **plata** f **de ~** sterling silver

**leyenda** f legend

**liar** [20] vt tie; (envolver) wrap up; roll (cigarillo); (fig, confundir) confuse; (fig, enredar) involve. **~se** vpr get involved

**libanés** a & m Lebanese

**Líbano** m. **el ~** Lebanon

**libel|ista** m & f satirist. **~o** m satire

**libélula** f dragonfly

**libera|ción** f liberation. **~dor** a liberating. ● m liberator

**liberal** a & m & f liberal. **~idad** f liberality. **~mente** adv liberally

**liber|ar** vt free. **~tad** f freedom. **~tad de cultos** freedom of worship. **~tad de imprenta** freedom of the press. **~tad provisional** bail. **~tar** vt free. **en ~tad** free

**libertino** m libertine

**Libia** f Libya

**libido** m libido

**libio** a & m Libyan

**libra** f pound. **~ esterlina** pound sterling

**Libra** f Libra

**libra|dor** m (com) drawer. **~r** vt free; (de un peligro) rescue. **~rse** vpr free o.s. **~rse de** get rid of

**libre** a free; (aire) open; (en natación) freestyle. **~ de impuestos** tax-free. ● m (Mex) taxi

**librea** f livery

**libr|ería** f bookshop (Brit), bookstore (Amer); (mueble) bookcase. **~ero** m bookseller. **~eta** f notebook. **~o** m book. **~o de bordo** logbook. **~o de bolsillo** paperback. **~o de ejercicios** exercise book. **~o de reclamaciones** complaints book

**licencia** f permission; (documento) licence. **~do** m graduate. **~ para manejar** (LAm) driving licence. **~r** vt (mil) discharge; (echar) dismiss. **~tura** f degree

**licencioso** a licentious

**liceo** m (esp LAm) (secondary) school

**licita|dor** m bidder. **~r** vt bid for

**lícito** a legal; (permisible) permissible

**licor** m liquid; (alcohólico) liqueur

**licua|dora** f liquidizer. **~r** [21] liquefy

**lid** f fight. **en buena ~** by fair means

**líder** *m* leader

**liderato** *m*, **liderazgo** *m* leadership

**lidia** *f* bullfighting; (*lucha*) fight; (*LAm*, *molestia*) nuisance. **~r** *vt/i* fight

**liebre** *f* hare

**lienzo** *m* linen; (*del pintor*) canvas; (*muro*, *pared*) wall

**liga** *f* garter; (*alianza*) league; (*mezcla*) mixture. **~dura** *f* bond; (*mus*) slur; (*med*) ligature. **~mento** *m* ligament. **~r** [12] *vt* tie; (*fig*) join; (*mus*) slur. • *vi* mix. **~r con** (*fig*) pick up. **~rse** *vpr* (*fig*) commit o.s.

**liger|eza** *f* lightness; (*agilidad*) agility; (*rapidez*) swiftness; (*de carácter*) fickleness. **~o** *a* light; (*rápido*) quick; (*ágil*) agile; (*superficial*) superficial; (*de poca importancia*) slight. • *adv* quickly. **a la ~a** lightly, superficially

**liguero** *m* suspender belt

**lija** *f* dogfish; (*papel de lija*) sandpaper. **~r** *vt* sand

**lila** *f* lilac

**Lima** *f* Lima

**lima** *f* file; (*fruta*) lime. **~duras** *fpl* filings. **~r** *vt* file (down)

**limbo** *m* limbo

**limita|ción** *f* limitation. **~do** *a* limited. **~r** *vt* limit. **~r con** border on. **~tivo** *a* limiting

**límite** *m* limit. **~ de velocidad** speed limit

**limítrofe** *a* bordering

**limo** *m* mud

**lim|ón** *m* lemon. **~onada** *f* lemonade

**limosn|a** *f* alms. **~ear** *vi* beg. **pedir ~a** beg

**limpia** *f* cleaning. **~botas** *m invar* bootblack. **~parabrisas** *m inv* windscreen wiper (*Brit*), windshield wiper (*Amer*). **~pipas** *m invar* pipe-cleaner. **~r** *vt* clean; (*enjugar*) wipe

**limpi|eza** *f* cleanliness; (*acción de limpiar*) cleaning. **~eza en seco** dry-cleaning. **~o** *a* clean; (*cielo*) clear; (*fig*, *honrado*) honest. • *adv* fairly. **en ~o** (*com*) net. **jugar ~o** play fair

**linaje** *m* lineage; (*fig*, *clase*) kind

**lince** *m* lynx

**linchar** *vt* lynch

**lind|ante** *a* bordering (**con** on). **~ar** *vi* border (**con** on). **~e** *f* boundary. **~ero** *m* border

**lindo** *a* pretty, lovely. **de lo ~** (*fam*) a lot

**línea** *f* line. **en ~s generales** in broad outline. **guardar la ~** watch one's figure

**lingote** *m* ingot

**lingü|ista** *m & f* linguist. **~ística** *f* linguistics. **~ístico** *a* linguistic

**lino** *m* flax; (*tela*) linen

**linóleo** *m*, **linóleum** *m* lino, linoleum

**linterna** *f* lantern; (*de bolsillo*) torch, flashlight (*Amer*)

**lío** *m* bundle; (*jaleo*) fuss; (*embrollo*) muddle; (*amorío*) affair

**liquen** *m* lichen

**liquida|ción** *f* liquidation; (*venta especial*) (clearance) sale. **~r** *vt* liquify; (*com*) liquidate; settle ⟨*cuenta*⟩

**líquido** *a* liquid; (*com*) net. • *m* liquid

**lira** *f* lyre; (*moneda italiana*) lira

**líric|a** *f* lyric poetry. **~o** *a* lyric(al)

**lirio** *m* iris. **~ de los valles** lily of the valley

**lirón** *m* dormouse; (*fig*) sleepyhead. **dormir como un ~** sleep like a log

**Lisboa** *f* Lisbon

**lisia|do** *a* disabled. **~r** *vt* disable; (*herir*) injure

**liso** *a* smooth; ⟨*pelo*⟩ straight; ⟨*tierra*⟩ flat; (*sencillo*) plain

**lisonj|a** *f* flattery. **~eador** *a* flattering. • *m* flatterer. **~ear** *vt* flatter. **~ero** *a* flattering

**lista** *f* stripe; (*enumeración*) list; (*de platos*) menu. **~ de correos** poste restante. **~do** *a* striped. **a ~s** striped

**listo** *a* clever; (*preparado*) ready

**listón** *m* ribbon; (*de madera*) strip

**lisura** *f* smoothness

**litera** *f* (*en barco*) berth; (*en tren*) sleeper; (*en habitación*) bunk bed

**literal** *a* literal

**litera|rio** *a* literary. **~tura** *f* literature

**litig|ar** [12] *vi* dispute; (*jurid*) litigate. **~io** *m* dispute; (*jurid*) litigation

**litografía** *f* (*arte*) lithography; (*cuadro*) lithograph

**litoral** *a* coastal. • *m* coast

**litro** *m* litre

**lituano** *a & m* Lithuanian

**liturgia** *f* liturgy

**liviano** *a* fickle, inconstant

**lívido** *a* livid

**lizo** *m* warp thread

**lo** *art def neutro*. ~ **importante** what is important, the important thing. ● *pron* (*él*) him; (*ello*) it. ~ **que** what(ever), that which

**loa** *f* praise. ~**ble** *a* praiseworthy. ~**r** *vt* praise

**lobo** *m* wolf

**lóbrego** *a* gloomy

**lóbulo** *m* lobe

**local** *a* local. ● *m* premises; (*lugar*) place. ~**idad** *f* locality; (*de un espectáculo*) seat; (*entrada*) ticket. ~**izar** [10] *vt* localize; (*encontrar*) find, locate

**loción** *f* lotion

**loco** *a* mad; (*fig*) foolish. ● *m* lunatic. ~ **de alegría** mad with joy. **estar** ~ **por** be crazy about. **volverse** ~ go mad

**locomo|ción** *f* locomotion. ~**tora** *f* locomotive

**locuaz** *a* talkative

**locución** *f* expression

**locura** *f* madness; (*acto*) crazy thing. **con** ~ madly

**locutor** *m* announcer

**locutorio** *m* (*de teléfono*) telephone booth

**lod|azal** *m* quagmire. ~**o** *m* mud

**logaritmo** *m* logarithm, log

**lógic|a** *f* logic. ~**o** *a* logical

**logística** *f* logistics

**logr|ar** *vt* get; win (*premio*). ~ **hacer** manage to do. ~**o** *m* achievement; (*de premio*) winning; (*éxito*) success

**loma** *f* small hill

**lombriz** *f* worm

**lomo** *m* back; (*de libro*) spine; (*doblez*) fold. ~ **de cerdo** loin of pork

**lona** *f* canvas

**loncha** *f* slice; (*de tocino*) rasher

**londinense** *a* from London. ● *m* Londoner

**Londres** *m* London

**loneta** *f* thin canvas

**longánimo** *a* magnanimous

**longaniza** *f* sausage

**longev|idad** *f* longevity. ~**o** *a* long-lived

**longitud** *f* length; (*geog*) longitude

**lonja** *f* slice; (*de tocino*) rasher; (*com*) market

**lord** *m* (*pl* **lores**) lord

**loro** *m* parrot

**los** *art def mpl* the. ● *pron* them. ~ **de Antonio** Antonio's. ~ **que** who-ever, the ones

**losa** *f* slab; (*baldosa*) flagstone. ~ **sepulcral** tombstone

**lote** *m* share

**lotería** *f* lottery

**loto** *m* lotus

**loza** *f* crockery

**lozano** *a* fresh; (*vegetación*) lush; (*persona*) lively

**lubri(fi)ca|nte** *a* lubricating. ● *m* lubricant. ~**r** [7] *vt* lubricate

**lucero** *m* (*estrella*) bright star; (*planeta*) Venus

**lucid|ez** *f* lucidity. ~**o** *a* splendid

**lúcido** *a* lucid

**luciérnaga** *f* glow-worm

**lucimiento** *m* brilliance

**lucir** [11] *vt* (*fig*) show off. ● *vi* shine; (*lámpara*) give off light; (*joya*) sparkle. ~**se** *vpr* (*fig*) shine, excel

**lucr|ativo** *a* lucrative. ~**o** *m* gain

**lucha** *f* fight. ~**dor** *m* fighter. ~**r** *vi* fight

**luego** *adv* then; (*más tarde*) later. ● *conj* therefore. ~ **que** as soon as. **desde** ~ of course

**lugar** *m* place. ~ **común** cliché. ~**eño** *a* village. **dar** ~ **a** give rise to. **en** ~ **de** instead of. **en primer** ~ in the first place. **hacer** ~ make room. **tener** ~ take place

**lugarteniente** *m* deputy

**lúgubre** *a* gloomy

**lujo** *m* luxury. ~**so** *a* luxurious. **de** ~ de luxe

**lujuria** *f* lust

**lumbago** *m* lumbago

**lumbre** *f* fire; (*luz*) light. ¿**tienes** ~? have you got a light?

**luminoso** *a* luminous; (*fig*) brilliant

**luna** *f* moon; (*de escaparate*) window; (*espejo*) mirror. ~ **de miel** honeymoon. ~**r** *a* lunar. ● *m* mole. **claro de** ~ moonlight. **estar en la** ~ be miles away

**lunes** *m* Monday. **cada** ~ **y cada martes** day in, day out

**lupa** *f* magnifying glass

**lúpulo** *m* hop

**lustr|abotas** *m inv* (*LAm*) bootblack. ~**ar** *vt* shine, polish. ~**e** *m* shine; (*fig*, *esplendor*) splendour. ~**oso** *a* shining. **dar** ~**e a**, **sacar** ~**e** a polish

**luto** *m* mourning. **estar de** ~ be in mourning

**luxación** *f* dislocation

**Luxemburgo** *m* Luxemburg

**luz** *f* light; (*electricidad*) electricity. **luces** *fpl* intelligence. ~ **antiniebla**

(*auto*) fog light. **a la ~ de** in the light of. **a todas luces** obviously. **dar a ~** give birth. **hacer la ~ sobre** shed light on. **sacar a la ~** bring to light

# LL

**llaga** *f* wound; (*úlcera*) ulcer

**llama** *f* flame; (*animal*) llama

**llamada** *f* call; (*golpe*) knock; (*señal*) sign

**llama|do** *a* known as. **~miento** *m* call. **~r** *vt* call; (*por teléfono*) ring (up). ● *vi* call; (*golpear en la puerta*) knock; (*tocar el timbre*) ring. **~rse** *vpr* be called. **~r por teléfono** ring (up), telephone. **¿cómo te ~s?** what's your name?

**llamarada** *f* blaze; (*fig*) blush; (*fig, de pasión etc*) outburst

**llamativo** *a* loud, gaudy

**llamear** *vi* blaze

**llan|eza** *f* simplicity. **~o** *a* flat, level; (*persona*) natural; (*sencillo*) plain. ● *m* plain

**llanta** *f* (*auto*) (wheel) rim; (*LAm, neumático*) tyre

**llanto** *m* weeping

**llanura** *f* plain

**llave** *f* key; (*para tuercas*) spanner; (*grifo*) tap (*Brit*), faucet (*Amer*); (*elec*) switch. **~ inglesa** monkey wrench. **~ro** *m* key-ring. **cerrar con ~** lock. **echar la ~** lock up

**llega|da** *f* arrival. **~r** [12] *vi* arrive, come; (*alcanzar*) reach; (*bastar*) be enough. **~rse** *vpr* come near; (*ir*) go (round). **~r a** (*conseguir*) manage to. **~r a saber** find out. **~r a ser** become

**llen|ar** *vt* fill (up); (*rellenar*) fill in. **~o** *a* full. ● *m* (*en el teatro etc*) full house. **de ~** completely

**lleva|dero** *a* tolerable. **~r** *vt* carry; (*inducir, conducir*) lead; (*acompañar*) take; wear (*ropa*); (*traer*) bring. **~rse** *vpr* run off with (*cosa*). **~rse bien** get on well together. **¿cuánto tiempo ~s aquí?** how long have you been here? **llevo 3 años estudiando inglés** I've been studying English for 3 years

**llor|ar** *vi* cry; (*ojos*) water. **~iquear** *vi* whine. **~iqueo** *m* whining. **~o** *m* crying. **~ón** *a* whining. ● *m* crybaby. **~oso** *a* tearful

**llov|er** [2] *vi* rain. **~izna** *f* drizzle. **~iznar** *vi* drizzle

**llueve** *vb* *véase* **llover**

**lluvi|a** *f* rain; (*fig*) shower. **~oso** *a* rainy; (*clima*) wet

# M

**maca** *f* defect; (*en fruta*) bruise

**macabro** *a* macabre

**macaco** *a* (*LAm*) ugly. ● *m* macaque (monkey)

**macadam** *m*, **macadán** *m* Tarmac (*P*)

**macanudo** *a* (*fam*) great

**macarrón** *m* macaroon. **~es** *mpl* macaroni

**macerar** *vt* macerate

**maceta** *f* mallet; (*tiesto*) flowerpot

**macilento** *a* wan

**macizo** *a* solid. ● *m* mass; (*de plantas*) bed

**macrobiótico** *a* macrobiotic

**mácula** *f* stain

**macuto** *m* knapsack

**mach** /mak/ *m.* **(número de) ~** Mach (number)

**machac|ar** [7] *vt* crush. ● *vi* go on (en about). **~ón** *a* boring. ● *m* bore

**machamartillo. a ~** *adv* firmly

**machaqueo** *m* crushing

**machet|azo** *m* blow with a machete; (*herida*) wound from a machete. **~e** *m* machete

**mach|ista** *m* male chauvinist. **~o** *a* male; (*varonil*) macho

**machón** *m* buttress

**machucar** [7] *vt* crush; (*estropear*) damage

**madeja** *f* skein

**madera** *m* (*vino*) Madeira. ● *f* wood; (*naturaleza*) nature. **~ble** *a* yielding timber. **~je** *m*, **~men** *m* woodwork

**madero** *m* log; (*de construcción*) timber

**madona** *f* Madonna

**madr|astra** *f* stepmother. **~e** *f* mother. **~eperla** *f* mother-of-pearl. **~eselva** *f* honeysuckle

**madrigal** *m* madrigal

**madriguera** *f* den; (*de liebre*) burrow

**madrileño** *a* of Madrid. ● *m* person from Madrid

**madrina** *f* godmother; (*en una boda*) chief bridesmaid

**madroño** *m* strawberry-tree

**madrug|ada** f dawn. **~ador** a who gets up early. ● m early riser. **~ar** [12] vi get up early. **~ón** m. **darse un ~ón** get up very early

**madur|ación** f maturing; (de fruta) ripening. **~ar** vt/i mature; (fruta) ripen. **~ez** f maturity; (de fruta) ripeness. **~o** a mature; (fruta) ripe

**maestr|a** f teacher. **~ía** f skill. **~o** m master. **~a, ~o (de escuela)** schoolteacher

**mafia** f Mafia

**magdalena** f madeleine, small sponge cake

**magia** f magic

**mágico** a magic; (maravilloso) magical

**magín** m (fam) imagination

**magisterio** m teaching (profession); (conjunto de maestros) teachers

**magistrado** m magistrate; (juez) judge

**magistral** a teaching; (bien hecho) masterly; (lenguaje) pedantic

**magistratura** f magistracy

**magn|animidad** f magnanimity. **~ánimo** a magnanimous

**magnate** m magnate

**magnesia** f magnesia. **~ efervescente** milk of magnesia

**magnético** a magnetic

**magneti|smo** m magnetism. **~zar** [10] vt magnetize

**magnetofón** m, **magnetófono** m tape recorder

**magnificencia** f magnificence

**magnífico** a magnificent

**magnitud** f magnitude

**magnolia** f magnolia

**mago** m magician. **los (tres) reyes ~s** the Magi

**magr|a** f slice of ham. **~o** a lean; (tierra) poor; (persona) thin

**magulla|dura** f bruise. **~r** vt bruise

**mahometano** a & m Muhammadan

**maíz** m maize, corn (Amer)

**majada** f sheepfold; (estiércol) manure; (LAm) flock of sheep

**majader|ía** f silly thing. **~o** m idiot; (mano del mortero) pestle. ● a stupid

**majador** m crusher

**majagranzas** m idiot

**majar** vt crush; (molestar) bother

**majest|ad** f majesty. **~uoso** a majestic

**majo** a nice

**mal** adv badly; (poco) poorly; (difícilmente) hardly; (equivocadamente) wrongly. ● a see

**malo.** ● m evil; (daño) harm; (enfermedad) illness. **~ que bien** somehow (or other). **de ~ en peor** worse and worse. **hacer ~ en** be wrong to. **¡menos ~!** thank goodness!

**malabar** a. **juegos ~es** juggling. **~ismo** m juggling. **~ista** m & f juggler

**malaconsejado** a ill-advised

**malacostumbrado** a with bad habits

**malagueño** a of Málaga. ● m person from Málaga

**malamente** adv badly; (fam) hardly enough

**malandanza** f misfortune

**malapata** m & f nuisance

**malaria** f malaria

**Malasia** f Malaysia

**malasombra** m & f clumsy person

**malavenido** a incompatible

**malaventura** f misfortune. **~do** a unfortunate

**malayo** a Malay(an)

**malbaratar** vt sell off cheap; (malgastar) squander

**malcarado** a ugly

**malcasado** a unhappily married; (infiel) unfaithful

**malcomer** vi eat poorly

**malcriad|eza** f (LAm) bad manners. **~o** a (niño) spoilt

**maldad** f evil; (acción) wicked thing

**maldecir** [46 pero imperativo **maldice**, futuro y condicional regulares, pp **maldecido** o **maldito**] vt curse. ● vi speak ill (de of); (quejarse) complain (de about)

**maldici|ente** a backbiting; (que blasfema) foul-mouthed. **~ón** f curse

**maldit|a** f tongue. **¡~a sea!** damn it! **~o** a damned. ● m (en el teatro) extra

**maleab|ilidad** f malleability. **~le** a malleable

**malea|nte** a wicked. ● m vagrant. **~r** vt damage; (pervertir) corrupt. **~rse** vpr be spoilt; (pervertirse) be corrupted

**malecón** m breakwater; (rail) embankment; (para atracar) jetty

**maledicencia** f slander

**maleficio** m curse

**maléfico** a evil

**malestar** m indisposition; (fig) uneasiness

**malet|a** f (suit)case; (auto) boot, trunk (Amer); (LAm, lío de ropa) bundle; (*LAm, de bicicleta*) saddle-bag. **hacer la ~a** pack one's bags. ● *m* & *f* (*fam*) bungler. **~ero** *m* porter; (*auto*) boot, trunk (*Amer*). **~ín** *m* small case

**malevolencia** *f* malevolence

**malévolo** *a* malevolent

**maleza** *f* weeds; (*matorral*) undergrowth

**malgasta|dor** *a* wasteful. ● *m* spendthrift. **~r** *vt* waste

**malgeniado** *a* (*LAm*) bad-tempered

**malhablado** *a* foul-mouthed

**malhadado** *a* unfortunate

**malhechor** *m* criminal

**malhumorado** *a* bad-tempered

**malici|a** *f* malice. **~ar** *vpr* suspect. **~as** *fpl* (*fam*) suspicions. **~oso** *a* malicious

**malign|idad** *f* malice; (*med*) malignancy. **~o** *a* malignant; ⟨*persona*⟩ malicious

**malintencionado** *a* malicious

**malmandado** *a* disobedient

**malmirado** *a* (*con estar*) disliked; (*con ser*) inconsiderate

**malo** *a* (*delante de nombre masculino en singular* **mal**) bad; (*enfermo*) ill. **~ de** difficult. **estar de malas** be out of luck; (*malhumorado*) be in a bad mood. **lo ~ es que** the trouble is that. **ponerse a malas con uno** fall out with s.o. **por las malas** by force

**malogr|ar** *vt* waste; (*estropear*) spoil. **~arse** *vpr* fall through. **~o** *m* failure

**maloliente** *a* smelly

**malparto** *m* miscarriage

**malpensado** *a* nasty, malicious

**malquerencia** *f* dislike

**malquist|ar** *vt* set against. **~arse** *vpr* fall out. **~o** *a* disliked

**malsano** *a* unhealthy; (*enfermizo*) sickly

**malsonante** *a* ill-sounding; (*grosero*) offensive

**malta** *f* malt; (*cerveza*) beer

**maltés** *a* & *m* Maltese

**maltratar** *vt* ill-treat

**maltrecho** *a* battered

**malucho** *a* (*fam*) poorly

**malva** *f* mallow. **(color de) ~** *a invar* mauve

**malvado** *a* wicked

**malvavisco** *m* marshmallow

**malvender** *vt* sell off cheap

**malversa|ción** *f* embezzlement. **~dor** *a* embezzling. ● *m* embezzler. **~r** *vt* embezzle

**Malvinas** *fpl*. **las islas ~** .the Falkland Islands

**malla** *f* mesh. **cota de ~** coat of mail

**mallo** *m* mallet

**Mallor|ca** *f* Majorca. **~quín** *a* & *m* Majorcan

**mama** *f* teat; (*de mujer*) breast

**mamá** *f* mum(my)

**mama|da** *f* sucking. **~r** *vt* suck; (*fig*) grow up with; (*engullir*) gobble

**mamario** *a* mammary

**mamarrach|adas** *fpl* nonsense. **~o** *m* clown; (*cosa ridícula*) (ridiculous) sight

**mameluco** *a* Brazilian half-breed; (*necio*) idiot

**mamífero** *a* mammalian. ● *m* mammal

**mamola** *f*. **hacer la ~** chuck (under the chin); (*fig*) make fun of

**mamotreto** *m* notebook; (*libro voluminoso*) big book

**mampara** *f* screen

**mamporro** *m* blow

**mampostería** *f* masonry

**mamut** *m* mammoth

**maná** *f* manna

**manada** *f* herd; (*de lobos*) pack. **en ~** in crowds

**manager** /'manaʒer/ *m* manager

**mana|ntial** *m* spring; (*fig*) source. **~r** *vi* flow; (*fig*) abound. ● *vt* run with

**manaza** *f* big hand; (*sucia*) dirty hand. **ser un ~s** be clumsy

**manceb|a** *f* concubine. **~ía** *f* brothel. **~o** *m* youth; (*soltero*) bachelor

**mancera** *f* plough handle

**mancilla** *f* stain. **~r** *vt* stain

**manco** *a* (*de una mano*) one-handed; (*de las dos manos*) handless; (*de un brazo*) one-armed; (*de los dos brazos*) armless

**mancomún** *adv*. **de ~** jointly

**mancomun|adamente** *adv* jointly. **~ar** *vt* unite; (*jurid*) make jointly liable. **~arse** *vpr* unite. **~idad** *f* union

**mancha** *f* stain

**Mancha** *f*. **la ~** la Mancha (region of Spain). **el canal de la ~** the English Channel

**mancha|do** *a* dirty; ⟨*animal*⟩ spotted. **~r** *vt* stain. **~rse** *vpr* get dirty

**manchego** *a* of la Mancha. ● *m* person from la Mancha

**manchón** *m* large stain

**manda** f legacy

**manda|dero** m messenger. ~**miento** m order; (relig) commandment. ~**r** vt order; (enviar) send; (gobernar) rule. ● vi be in command. ¿**mande**? (esp LAm) pardon?

**mandarín** m mandarin

**mandarin|a** f (naranja) mandarin; (lengua) Mandarin. ~**o** m mandarin tree

**mandat|ario** m attorney. ~**o** m order; (jurid) power of attorney

**mandíbula** f jaw

**mandil** m apron

**mandioca** f cassava

**mando** m command; (pol) term of office. ~ **a distancia** remote control. **los** ~**s** the leaders

**mandolina** f mandolin

**mandón** a bossy

**manducar** [7] vt (fam) stuff oneself with

**manecilla** f needle; (de reloj) hand

**manej|able** a manageable. ~**ar** vt handle; (fig) manage; (LAm, conducir) drive. ~**arse** vpr behave. ~**o** m handling; (intriga) intrigue

**manera** f way. ~**s** fpl manners. **de** ~ **que** so (that). **de ninguna** ~ not at all. **de otra** ~ otherwise. **de todas** ~**s** anyway

**manga** f sleeve; (tubo de goma) hose(pipe); (red) net; (para colar) filter

**mangante** m beggar; (fam) scrounger

**mangle** m mangrove

**mango** m handle; (fruta) mango

**mangonear** vt boss about. ● vi (entrometerse) interfere

**manguera** f hose(pipe)

**manguito** m muff

**manía** f mania; (antipatía) dislike

**maniaco** a, **maníaco** a maniac(al). ● m maniac

**maniatar** vt tie s.o.'s hands

**maniático** a maniac(al); (fig) crazy

**manicomio** m lunatic asylum

**manicura** f manicure; (mujer) manicurist

**manido** a stale; (carne) high

**manifesta|ción** f manifestation; (pol) demonstration. ~**nte** m demonstrator. ~**r** [1] vi manifest; (pol) state. ~**rse** vpr show; (pol) demonstrate

**manifiesto** a clear; (error) obvious; (verdad) manifest. ● m manifesto

**manilargo** a light-fingered

**manilla** f bracelet; (de hierro) handcuffs

**manillar** m handlebar(s)

**maniobra** f manoeuvring; (rail) shunting; (fig) manoeuvre. ~**r** vt operate; (rail) shunt. ● vi manoeuvre. ~**s** fpl (mil) manoeuvres

**manipula|ción** f manipulation. ~**r** vt manipulate

**maniquí** m dummy. ● f model

**manirroto** a extravagant. ● m spendthrift

**manita** f little hand

**manivela** f crank

**manjar** m (special) dish

**mano** f hand; (de animales) front foot; (de perros, gatos) front paw. ~ **de obra** work force. ¡~**s arriba!** hands up! **a** ~ by hand; (próximo) handy. **de segunda** ~ second hand. **echar una** ~ lend a hand. **tener buena** ~ **para** be good at

**manojo** m bunch

**manose|ar** vt handle; (fig) overwork. ~**o** m handling

**manotada** f, **manotazo** m slap

**manote|ar** vi gesticulate. ~**o** m gesticulation

**mansalva. a** ~ adv without risk

**mansarda** f attic

**mansedumbre** f gentleness; (de animal) tameness

**mansión** f stately home

**manso** a gentle; (animal) tame

**manta** f blanket. ~ **eléctrica** electric blanket. **a** ~ (de Dios) a lot

**mantec|a** f fat; (LAm) butter. ~**ado** m bun; (helado) ice-cream. ~**oso** a greasy

**mantel** m tablecloth; (del altar) altar cloth. ~**ería** f table linen

**manten|er** [40] vt support; (conservar) keep; (sostener) maintain. ~**erse** vpr remain. ~ **de/con** live off. ~**imiento** m maintenance

**mantequ|era** f butter churn. ~**ería** f dairy. ~**illa** f butter

**mantilla** f mantilla

**manto** m cloak

**mantón** m shawl

**manual** a & m manual

**manubrio** m crank

**manufactura** f manufacture; (fábrica) factory

**manuscrito** a handwritten. ● m manuscript

**manutención** f maintenance

**manzana** *f* apple. ~**r** *m* (*apple*) orchard

**manzanilla** *f* camomile tea; (*vino*) manzanilla, pale dry sherry

**manzano** *m* apple tree

**maña** *f* skill. ~**s** *fpl* cunning

**mañan|a** *f* morning; (*el día siguiente*) tomorrow. ● *m* future. ● *adv* tomorrow. ~**ero** *a* who gets up early. ● *m* early riser. ~**a por la** ~**a** tomorrow morning. **pasado** ~**a** the day after tomorrow. **por la** ~**a** in the morning

**mañoso** *a* clever; (*astuto*) crafty

**mapa** *m* map. ~**mundi** *m* map of the world

**mapache** *m* racoon

**mapurite** *m* skunk

**maqueta** *f* scale model

**maquiavélico** *a* machiavellian

**maquilla|je** *m* make-up. ~**r** *vt* make up. ~**rse** *vpr* make up

**máquina** *f* machine; (*rail*) engine. ~ **de escribir** typewriter. ~ **fotográfica** camera

**maquin|ación** *f* machination. ~**al** *a* mechanical. ~**aria** *f* machinery. ~**ista** *m* & *f* operator; (*rail*) engine driver

**mar** *m* & *f* sea. **alta** ~ high seas. **la** ~ **de** (*fam*) lots of

**maraña** *f* thicket; (*enredo*) tangle; (*embrollo*) muddle

**maravedí** *m* (*pl* **maravedís, maravedises**) maravedi, old Spanish coin

**maravill|a** *f* wonder. ~**ar** *vt* astonish. ~**arse** *vpr* be astonished (**con** at). ~**oso** *a* marvellous, wonderful. **a** ~**a, a las mil** ~**as** marvellously. **contar/decir** ~**as de** speak wonderfully of. **hacer** ~**as** work wonders

**marbete** *m* label

**marca** *f* mark; (*de fábrica*) trademark; (*deportes*) record. ~**do** *a* marked. ~**dor** *m* marker; (*deportes*) scoreboard. ~**r** [7] *vt* mark; (*señalar*) show; (*anotar*) note down; score ‹*un gol*›; dial ‹*número de teléfono*›. ● *vi* score. **de** ~ brand name; (*fig*) excellent. **de** ~ **mayor** (*fam*) first-class

**marcial** *a* martial

**marciano** *a* & *m* Martian

**marco** *m* frame; (*moneda alemana*) mark; (*deportes*) goal-posts

**marcha** *f* (*incl mus*) march; (*auto*) gear; (*curso*) course. **a toda** ~ at full speed. **dar/hacer** ~ **atrás** put into

reverse. **poner en** ~ start; (*fig*) set in motion

**marchante** *m* (*f* **marchanta**) dealer; (*LAm, parroquiano*) client

**marchar** *vi* go; (*funcionar*) work, go. ~**se** *vpr* go away, leave

**marchit|ar** *vt* wither. ~**arse** *vpr* wither. ~**o** *a* withered

**marea** *f* tide. ~**do** *a* sick; (*en el mar*) seasick; (*aturdido*) dizzy; (*borracho*) drunk. ~**r** *vt* sail, navigate; (*baquetear*) annoy. ~**rse** *vpr* feel sick; (*en un barco*) be seasick; (*estar aturdido*) feel dizzy; (*irse la cabeza*) feel faint; (*emborracharse*) get slightly drunk

**marejada** *f* swell; (*fig*) wave

**maremagno** *m* (*de cosas*) sea; (*de gente*) (noisy) crowd

**mareo** *m* sickness; (*en el mar*) seasickness; (*aturdimiento*) dizziness; (*fig, molestia*) nuisance

**marfil** *m* ivory. ~**eño** *a* ivory. **torre** *f* **de** ~ ivory tower

**margarina** *f* margarine

**margarita** *f* pearl; (*bot*) daisy

**marg|en** *m* margin; (*borde*) edge, border; (*de un río*) bank; (*de un camino*) side; (*nota marginal*) marginal note. ~**inado** *a* on the edge. ● *m* outcast. ~**inal** *a* marginal. ~**inar** *vt* (*excluir*) exclude; (*dejar márgenes*) leave margins; (*poner notas*) write notes in the margin. **al** ~**en** (*fig*) outside

**mariachi** (*Mex*) *m* (*música popular de Jalisco*) Mariachi; (*conjunto popular*) Mariachi band

**mariano** *a* Marian

**marica** *f* (*hombre afeminado*) sissy; (*urraca*) magpie

**maricón** *m* homosexual, queer (*sl*)

**marid|aje** *m* married life; (*fig*) harmony. ~**o** *m* husband

**mariguana** *f*, **marihuana** *f* marijuana

**marimacho** *m* mannish woman

**marimandona** *f* bossy woman

**marimba** *f* (type of) drum; (*LAm, especie de xilofón*) marimba

**marimorena** *f* (*fam*) row

**marin|a** *f* coast; (*cuadro*) seascape; (*conjunto de barcos*) navy; (*arte de navegar*) seamanship. ~**era** *f* seamanship; (*conjunto de marineros*) crew. ~**ero** *a* marine; ‹*barco*› seaworthy. ● *m* sailor. ~**o** *a* marine. ~**a de guerra** navy. ~**a mercante** merchant navy. **a la** ~**era** in tomato and garlic sauce. **azul** ~o navy blue

**marioneta** f puppet. ~s fpl puppet show

**maripos|a** f butterfly. ~ear vi be fickle; (galantear) flirt. ~n m flirt. ~a nocturna moth

**mariquita** f ladybird, ladybug (Amer)

**marisabidilla** f know-all

**mariscador** m shell-fisher

**mariscal** m marshal

**maris|co** m seafood, shellfish. ~quero m (persona que pesca mariscos) seafood fisherman; (persona que vende mariscos) seafood seller

**marital** a marital

**marítimo** a maritime; ‹ciudad etc› coastal, seaside

**maritornes** f uncouth servant

**marmit|a** f pot. ~ón m kitchen boy

**mármol** m marble

**marmol|era** f marblework, marbles. ~ista m & f marble worker

**marmóreo** a marble

**marmota** f marmot

**maroma** f rope; (LAm, función de volatines) tightrope walking

**marqu|és** m marquess. ~esa f marchioness. ~esina f glass canopy

**marquetería** f marquetry

**marrajo** a ‹toro› vicious; ‹persona› cunning. ● m shark

**marran|a** f sow. ~ada f filthy thing; (cochinada) dirty trick. ~o a filthy. ● m hog

**marrar** vt (errar) miss; (fallar) fail

**marrón** a & m brown

**marroquí** a & m & f Moroccan. ● m (tafilete) morocco

**marrubio** m (bot) horehound

**Marruecos** m Morocco

**marruller|ía** f cajolery. ~o a cajoling. ● m cajoler

**marsopa** f porpoise

**marsupial** a & m marsupial

**marta** f marten

**martajar** vt (Mex) grind ‹maíz›

**Marte** m Mars

**martes** m Tuesday

**martill|ada** f blow with a hammer. ~ar vt hammer. ~azo m blow with a hammer. ~ear vt hammer. ~eo m hammering. ~o m hammer

**martín** m pescador kingfisher

**martinete** m (macillo del piano) hammer; (mazo) drop hammer

**martingala** f (ardid) trick

**mártir** m & f martyr

**martir|io** m martyrdom. ~izar [10] vt martyr; (fig) torment, torture. ~ologio m martyrology

**marxis|mo** m Marxism. ~ta a & m & f Marxist

**marzo** m March

**más** adv & a (comparativo) more; (superlativo) most. ~ caro dearer. ~ curioso more curious. el ~ caro the dearest; (de dos) the dearer. el ~ curioso the most curious; (de dos) the more curious. ● conj and, plus. ● m plus (sign). ~ bien rather. ~ de (cantidad indeterminada) more than. ~ o menos more or less. ~ que more than. ~ y ~ more and more. a lo ~ at (the) most. de ~ too many. es ~ moreover. no ~ no more

**masa** f dough; (cantidad) mass; (física) mass. en ~ en masse

**masacre** f massacre

**masaj|e** m massage. ~ista m masseur. ● f masseuse

**masca|da** f (LAm) plug of tobacco. ~dura f chewing. ~r [7] vt chew

**máscara** f mask; (persona) masked figure/person

**mascar|ada** f masquerade. ~illa f mask. ~ón m (large) mask

**mascota** f mascot

**masculin|idad** f masculinity. ~o a masculine; ‹sexo› male. ● m masculine

**mascullar** [3] vt mumble

**masilla** f putty

**masivo** a massive, large-scale

**mas|ón** m (free)mason. ~onería f (free)masonry. ~ónico a masonic

**masoquis|mo** m masochism. ~ta a masochistic. ● m & f masochist

**mastate** m (Mex) loincloth

**mastelero** m topmast

**mastica|ción** f chewing. ~r [7] vt chew; (fig) chew over

**mástil** m mast; (palo) pole; (en instrumentos de cuerda) neck

**mastín** m mastiff

**mastitis** f mastitis

**mastodonte** m mastodon

**mastoides** a & f mastoid

**mastuerzo** m cress

**masturba|ción** f masturbation. ~rse vpr masturbate

**mata** f grove; (arbusto) bush

**matad|ero** m slaughterhouse. ~or a killing. ● m killer; (torero) matador

**matadura** f sore

**matamoscas** *m invar* fly swatter

**mata|nza** *f* killing. **~r** *vt* kill ⟨*personas*⟩; slaughter ⟨*reses*⟩. **~rife** *m* butcher. **~rse** *vpr* commit suicide; (*en un acidente*) be killed. **estar a ~r con uno** be deadly enemies with s.o.

**matarratas** *m invar* cheap liquor

**matasanos** *m invar* quack

**matasellos** *m invar* postmark

**match** *m* match

**mate** *a* matt, dull; ⟨*sonido*⟩ dull. **●** *m* (*ajedrez*) (check)mate; (*LAm*, *bebida*) maté

**matemátic|as** *fpl* mathematics, maths (*fam*), math (*Amer*, *fam*). **~o** *a* mathematical. **●** *m* mathematician

**materia** *f* matter; (*material*) material. **~ prima** raw material. **en ~ de** on the question of

**material** *a* & *m* material. **~idad** *f* material nature. **~ismo** *m* materialism. **~ista** *a* materialistic. **●** *m* & *f* materialist. **~izar** [10] *vt* materialize. **~izarse** *vpr* materialize. **~mente** *adv* materially; (*absolutamente*) absolutely

**matern|al** *a* maternal; (*como de madre*) motherly. **~idad** *f* motherhood; (*casa de maternidad*) maternity home. **~o** *a* motherly; ⟨*lengua*⟩ mother

**matin|al** *a* morning. **~ée** *m* matinée

**matiz** *m* shade. **~ación** *f* combination of colours. **~ar** [10] *vt* blend ⟨*colores*⟩; (*introducir variedad*) vary; (*teñir*) tinge (**de** with)

**matojo** *m* bush

**mat|ón** *m* bully. **~onismo** *m* bullying

**matorral** *m* scrub; (*conjunto de matas*) thicket

**matra|ca** *f* rattle. **~quear** *vt* rattle; (*dar matraca*) pester. **dar ~ca** pester. **ser un(a) ~ca** be a nuisance

**matraz** *m* flask

**matriarca|do** *m* matriarchy. **~l** *a* matriarchal

**matr|ícula** *f* (*lista*) register, list; (*acto de matricularse*) registration; (*auto*) registration number. **~icular** *vt* register. **~icularse** *vpr* enrol, register

**matrimoni|al** *a* matrimonial. **~o** *m* marriage; (*pareja*) married couple

**matritense** *a* from Madrid

**matriz** *f* matrix; (*anat*) womb, uterus

**matrona** *f* matron; (*partera*) midwife

**Matusalén** *m* Methuselah. **más viejo que ~** as old as Methuselah

**matute** *m* smuggling. **~ro** *m* smuggler

**matutino** *a* morning

**maula** *f* piece of junk

**maull|ar** *vi* miaow. **~ido** *m* miaow

**mauritano** *a* & *m* Mauritanian

**mausoleo** *m* mausoleum

**maxilar** *a* maxillary. **hueso ~** jaw(bone)

**máxima** *f* maxim

**máxime** *adv* especially

**máximo** *a* maximum; (*más alto*) highest. **●** *m* maximum

**maya** *f* daisy; (*persona*) Maya Indian

**mayestático** *a* majestic

**mayo** *m* May; (*palo*) maypole

**mayólica** *f* majolica

**mayonesa** *f* mayonnaise

**mayor** *a* (*más grande, comparativo*) bigger; (*más grande, superlativo*) biggest; (*de edad, comparativo*) older; (*de edad, superlativo*) oldest; (*adulto*) grown-up; (*principal*) main, major; (*mus*) major. **●** *m* & *f* boss; (*adulto*) adult. **~al** *m* foreman; (*pastor*) head shepherd. **~azgo** *m* entailed estate. **al por ~** wholesale

**mayordomo** *m* butler

**mayor|ía** *f* majority. **~ista** *m* & *f* wholesaler. **~mente** *adv* especially

**mayúscul|a** *f* capital (letter). **~o** *a* capital; (*fig, grande*) big

**maza** *f* mace

**mazacote** *m* hard mass

**mazapán** *m* marzipan

**mazmorra** *f* dungeon

**mazo** *m* mallet; (*manojo*) bunch

**mazorca** *f*. **~ de maíz** corn on the cob

**me** *pron* (*acusativo*) me; (*dativo*) (to) me; (*reflexivo*) (to) myself

**meandro** *m* meander

**mecánic|a** *f* mechanics. **~o** *a* mechanical. **●** *m* mechanic

**mecani|smo** *m* mechanism. **~zación** *f* mechanization. **~zar** [10] *vt* mechanize

**mecanograf|ía** *f* typing. **~iado** *a* typed, typewritten. **~iar** [20] *vt* type

**mecanógrafo** *m* typist

**mecate** *m* (*LAm*) (*pita*) rope

**mecedora** *f* rocking chair

**mecenazgo** *m* patronage

**mecer** [9] *vt* rock; swing ‹*columpio*›. ~**se** *vpr* rock; (*en un columpio*) swing

**mecha** *f* (*de vela*) wick; (*de mina*) fuse

**mechar** *vt* stuff, lard

**mechero** *m* (cigarette) lighter

**mechón** *m* (*de pelo*) lock

**medall|a** *f* medal. ~**ón** *m* medallion; (*relicario*) locket

**media** *f* stocking; (*promedio*) average

**mediación** *f* mediation

**mediado** *a* half full; ‹*trabajo etc*› halfway through. **a** ~**s de marzo** in the middle of March

**mediador** *m* mediator

**medialuna** *f* croissant

**median|amente** *adv* fairly. ~**era** *f* party wall. ~**ero** *a* ‹*muro*› party. ~**a** *f* average circumstances. ~**o** *a* average, medium; (*mediocre*) mediocre

**medianoche** *f* midnight; (*culin*) small sandwich

**mediante** *prep* through, by means of

**mediar** *vi* mediate; (*llegar a la mitad*) be halfway (**en** through)

**mediatizar** [10] *vt* annex

**medic|ación** *f* medication. ~**amento** *m* medicine. ~**ina** *f* medicine. ~**inal** *a* medicinal. ~**inar** *vt* administer medicine

**medición** *f* measurement

**médico** *a* medical. ● *m* doctor. ~ **de cabecera** GP, general practitioner

**medid|a** *f* measurement; (*unidad*) measure; (*disposición*) measure, step; (*prudencia*) moderation. ~**or** *m* (*LAm*) meter. **a la** ~**a** made to measure. **a** ~**a que** as. **en cierta** ~**a** to a certain point

**mediero** *m* share-cropper

**medieval** *a* medieval. ~**ista** *m & f* medievalist

**medio** *a* half (a); (*mediano*) average. ~ **litro** half a litre. ● *m* middle; (*manera*) means; (*en deportes*) half(-back). **en** ~ in the middle (**de** of). **por** ~ **de** through

**mediocr|e** *a* (*mediano*) average; (*de escaso mérito*) mediocre. ~**idad** *f* mediocrity

**mediodía** *m* midday, noon; (*sur*) south

**medioevo** *m* Middle Ages

**Medio Oriente** *m* Middle East

**medir** [5] *vt* medir; weigh up ‹*palabras etc*›. ● *vi* measure, be. ~**se** *vpr* (*moderarse*) be moderate

**medita|bundo** *a* thoughtful. ~**ción** *f* meditation. ~**r** *vt* think about. ● *vi* meditate

**Mediterráneo** *m* Mediterranean

**mediterráneo** *a* Mediterranean

**médium** *m & f* medium

**medrar** *vi* thrive

**medroso** *a* (*con estar*) frightened; (*con ser*) fearful

**médula** *f* marrow

**medusa** *f* jellyfish

**mefítico** *a* noxious

**mega...** *pref* mega...

**megáfono** *m* megaphone

**megal|ítico** *a* megalithic. ~**ito** *m* megalith

**megal|omanía** *f* megalomania. ~**ómano** *m* megalomaniac

**mejicano** *a & m* Mexican

**Méjico** *m* Mexico

**mejido** *a* ‹*huevo*› beaten

**mejilla** *f* cheek

**mejillón** *m* mussel

**mejor** *a & adv* (*comparativo*) better; (*superlativo*) best. ~**a** *f* improvement. ~**able** *a* improvable. ~**amiento** *m* improvement. ~ **dicho** rather. **a lo** ~ perhaps. **tanto** ~ so much the better

**mejorana** *f* marjoram

**mejorar** *vt* improve, better. ● *vi* get better

**mejunje** *m* mixture

**melanc|olía** *f* melancholy. ~**ólico** *a* melancholic

**melaza** *f* molasses, treacle (*Amer*)

**melen|a** *f* long hair; (*de león*) mane. ~**udo** *a* long-haired

**melifluo** *a* mellifluous

**melillense** *a* of/from Melilla. ● *m* person from Melilla

**melindr|e** *m* (*mazapán*) sugared marzipan cake; (*masa frita con miel*) honey fritter. ~**oso** *a* affected

**melocot|ón** *m* peach. ~**onero** *m* peach tree

**mel|odía** *f* melody. ~**ódico** *a* melodic. ~**odioso** *a* melodious

**melodram|a** *m* melodrama. ~**áticamente** *adv* melodramatically. ~**ático** *a* melodramatic

**melómano** *m* music lover

**mel|ón** *m* melon; (*bobo*) fool. ~**onada** *f* something stupid

**meloncillo** *m* (*animal*) mongoose

**melos|idad** *f* sweetness. ~**o** *a* sweet

**mella** f notch. ~**do** a jagged. ~**r** vt notch

**mellizo** a & m twin

**membran|a** f membrane. ~**oso** a membranous

**membrete** m letterhead

**membrill|ero** m quince tree. ~**o** m quince

**membrudo** a burly

**memez** f something silly

**memo** a stupid. ● m idiot

**memorable** a memorable

**memorando** m, **memorándum** m notebook; (nota) memorandum

**memoria** f memory; (informe) report; (tesis) thesis. ~**s** fpl (recuerdos personales) memoirs. **de ~** from memory

**memorial** m memorial. ~**ista** m amanuensis

**memor|ión** m good memory. ~**ista** a having a good memory. ~**ístico** a memory

**mena** f ore

**menaje** m furnishings

**menci|ón** f mention. ~**onado** a aforementioned. ~**onar** vt mention

**menda|cidad** f mendacity. ~**z** a lying

**mendi|cante** a & m mendicant. ~**cidad** f begging. ~**gar** [12] vt beg (for). ● vi beg. ~**go** m beggar

**mendrugo** m (pan) hard crust; (zoquete) blockhead

**mene|ar** vt move, shake. ~**arse** upr move, shake. ~**o** m movement, shake

**menester** m need. ~**oso** a needy. **ser ~** be necessary

**menestra** f stew

**menestral** m artesan

**mengano** m so-and-so

**mengua** f decrease; (falta) lack; (descrédito) discredit. ~**do** a miserable; (falto de carácter) spineless. ~**nte** a decreasing; (luna) waning; (marea) ebb. ● f (del mar) ebb tide; (de un río) low water. ~**r** [15] vt/i decrease, diminish

**meningitis** f meningitis

**menisco** m meniscus

**menjurje** m mixture

**menopausia** f menopause

**menor** a (más pequeño, comparativo) smaller; (más pequeño, superlativo) smallest; (más joven, comparativo) younger; (más joven) youngest; (mus) minor. ● m & f (menor de edad) minor. **al por ~** retail

**Menorca** f Minorca

**menorquín** a & m Minorcan

**menos** a (comparativo) less; (comparativo, con plural) fewer; (superlativo) least; (superlativo, con plural) fewest. ● adv (comparativo) less; (superlativo) least. ● prep except. ~**cabar** vt lessen; (fig, estropear) damage. ~**cabo** m lessening. ~**preciable** a contemptible. ~**preciar** vt despise. ~**precio** m contempt. **a ~ que** unless. **al ~** at least. **ni mucho ~** far from it. **por lo ~** at least

**mensaje** m message. ~**ro** m messenger

**menso** a (Mex) stupid

**menstru|ación** f menstruation. ~**al** a menstrual. ~**ar** [21] vi menstruate. ~**o** m menstruation

**mensual** a monthly. ~**idad** f monthly pay

**ménsula** f bracket

**mensurable** a measurable

**menta** f mint

**mental** a mental. ~**idad** f mentality. ~**mente** adv mentally

**mentar** [1] vt mention, name

**mente** f mind

**mentecato** a stupid. ● m idiot

**mentir** [4] vi lie. ~**a** f lie. ~**oso** a lying. ● m liar. **de ~ijillas** for a joke

**mentís** m invar denial

**mentol** m menthol

**mentor** m mentor

**menú** m menu

**menudear** vi happen frequently

**menudencia** f trifle

**menudeo** m retail trade

**menudillos** mpl giblets

**menudo** a tiny; (lluvia) fine; (insignificante) insignificant. ~**s** mpl giblets. **a ~** often

**meñique** a (dedo) little. ● m little finger

**meollo** m brain; (médula) marrow; (parte blanda) soft part; (fig, inteligencia) brains

**meramente** adv merely

**mercachifle** m hawker; (fig) profiteer

**mercader** m (LAm) merchant

**mercado** m market. **M~ Común** Common Market. ~ **negro** black market

**mercan|cía** f article. ~**cías** fpl goods, merchandise. ~**te** a & m

merchant. **~til** *a* mercantile, commercial. **~tilismo** *m* mercantilism
**mercar** [7] *vt* buy
**merced** *f* favour. **su/vuestra ~** your honour
**mercenario** *a & m* mercenary
**mercer|ía** *f* haberdashery, notions (*Amer*). **~o** *m* haberdasher
**mercurial** *a* mercurial
**Mercurio** *m* Mercury
**mercurio** *m* mercury
**merec|edor** *a* deserving. **~er** [11] *vt* deserve. **●** *vi* be deserving. **~idamente** *adv* deservedly. **~ido** *a* well deserved. **~imiento** *m* (*mérito*) merit
**merend|ar** [1] *vt* have as an afternoon snack. **●** *vi* have an afternoon snack. **~ero** *m* snack bar; (*lugar*) picnic area
**merengue** *m* meringue
**meretriz** *f* prostitute
**mergo** *m* cormorant
**meridian|a** *f* (*diván*) couch. **~o** *a* midday; (*fig*) dazzling. **●** *m* meridian
**meridional** *a* southern. **●** *m* southerner
**merienda** *f* afternoon snack
**merino** *a* merino
**mérito** *m* merit; (*valor*) worth
**meritorio** *a* meritorious. **●** *m* unpaid trainee
**merlo** *m* black wrasse
**merluza** *f* hake
**merma** *f* decrease. **~r** *vt/i* decrease, reduce
**mermelada** *f* jam
**mero** *a* mere; (*Mex, verdadero*) real. **●** *adv* (*Mex, precisamente*) exactly; (*Mex, verdaderamente*) really. **●** *m* grouper
**merode|ador** *a* marauding. **●** *m* marauder. **~ar** *vi* maraud. **~o** *m* marauding
**merovingio** *a & m* Merovingian
**mes** *m* month; (*mensualidad*) monthly pay
**mesa** *f* table; (*para escribir o estudiar*) desk. **poner la ~** lay the table
**mesana** *f* (*palo*) mizen-mast
**mesarse** *vpr* tear at one's hair
**mesenterio** *m* mesentery
**meseta** *f* plateau; (*descansillo*) landing
**mesiánico** *a* Messianic
**Mesías** *m* Messiah
**mesilla** *f* small table. **~ de noche** bedside table

**mesón** *m* inn
**mesoner|a** *f* landlady. **~o** *m* landlord
**mestiz|aje** *m* crossbreeding. **~o** *a* (*persona*) half-caste; (*animal*) cross-bred. **●** *m* (*persona*) half-caste; (*animal*) cross-breed
**mesura** *f* moderation. **~do** *a* moderate
**meta** *f* goal; (*de una carrera*) finish
**metabolismo** *m* metabolism
**metacarpiano** *m* metacarpal
**metafísic|a** *f* metaphysics. **~o** *a* metaphysical
**met|áfora** *f* metaphor. **~afórico** *a* metaphorical
**met|al** *m* metal; (*instrumentos de latón*) brass; (*de la voz*) timbre. **~álico** *a* (*objeto*) metal; (*sonido*) metallic. **~alizarse** [10] *vpr* (*fig*) become mercenary
**metal|urgia** *f* metallurgy. **~úrgico** *a* metallurgical
**metam|órfico** *a* metamorphic. **~orfosear** *vt* transform. **~orfosis** *f* metamorphosis
**metano** *m* methane
**metatarsiano** *m* metatarsal
**metátesis** *f invar* metathesis
**metedura** *f*. **~ de pata** blunder
**mete|órico** *a* meteoric. **~orito** *m* meteorite. **~oro** *m* meteor. **~orología** *f* meteorology. **~orológico** meteorological. **~orólogo** *m* meteorologist
**meter** *vt* put, place; (*ingresar*) deposit; score (*un gol*); (*enredar*) involve; (*causar*) make. **~se** *vpr* get; (*entrometerse*) meddle. **~se con uno** pick a quarrel with s.o.
**meticulos|idad** *f* meticulousness. **~o** *a* meticulous
**metido** *m* reprimand. **●** *a*. **~ en años** getting on. **estar muy ~ con uno** be well in with s.o.
**metilo** *m* methyl
**metódico** *a* methodical
**metodis|mo** *m* Methodism. **~ta** *a & m & f* Methodist
**método** *m* method
**metodología** *f* methodology
**metomentodo** *m* busybody
**metraje** *m* length. **de largo ~** (*película*) feature
**metrall|a** *f* shrapnel. **~eta** *f* submachine gun
**métric|a** *f* metrics. **~o** *a* metric; (*verso*) metrical

**metro** *m* metre; (*tren*) underground, subway (*Amer*). ~ **cuadrado** cubic metre

**metrónomo** *m* metronome

**metr|ópoli** *f* metropolis. ~**opolitano** *a* metropolitan. ● *m* metropolitan; (*tren*) underground, subway (*Amer*)

**mexicano** *a* & *m* (*LAm*) Mexican

**México** *m* (*LAm*) Mexico. ~ **D. F.** Mexico City

**mezcal** *m* (*Mex*) (type of) brandy

**mezc|la** *f* (*acción*) mixing; (*substancia*) mixture; (*argamasa*) mortar. ~**lador** *m* mixer. ~**lar** *vt* mix; shuffle (*los naipes*). ~**larse** *vpr* mix; (*intervenir*) interfere. ~**olanza** *f* mixture

**mezquin|dad** *f* meanness. ~**o** *a* mean; (*escaso*) meagre. ● *m* mean person

**mezquita** *f* mosque

**mi** *a* my. ● *m* (*mus*) E; (*solfa*) mi

**mí** *pron* me

**miaja** *f* crumb

**miasma** *m* miasma

**miau** *m* miaow

**mica** *f* (*silicato*) mica; (*Mex, embriaguez*) drunkenness

**mico** *m* (long-tailed) monkey

**micro...** *pref* micro...

**microbio** *m* microbe

**micro:** ~**biología** *f* microbiology. ~**cosmo** *m* microcosm. ~**film(e)** *m* microfilm

**micrófono** *m* microphone

**micrómetro** *m* micrometer

**microonda** *f* microwave. **horno** *m* de ~**s** microwave oven

**microordenador** *m* microcomputer

**microsc|ópico** *a* microscopic. ~**opio** *m* microscope

**micro:** ~**surco** *m* long-playing record. ~**taxi** *m* minicab

**miedo** *m* fear. ~**so** *a* fearful. **dar** ~ frighten. **morirse de** ~ be scared to death. **tener** ~ be frightened

**miel** *f* honey

**mielga** *f* lucerne, alfalfa (*Amer*)

**miembro** *m* limb; (*persona*) member

**mientras** *conj* while. ● *adv* meanwhile. ~ **que** whereas. ~ **tanto** in the meantime

**miércoles** *m* Wednesday. ~ **de ceniza** Ash Wednesday

**mierda** *f* (*vulgar*) shit

**mies** *f* corn, grain (*Amer*)

**miga** *f* crumb; (*fig, meollo*) essence. ~**jas** *fpl* crumbs. ~**r** [12] *vt* crumble

**migra|ción** *f* migration. ~**torio** *a* migratory

**mijo** *m* millet

**mil** *a* & *m* a/one thousand. ~**es de** thousands of. ~ **novecientos noventa y dos** nineteen ninety-two. ~ **pesetas** a thousand pesetas

**milagro** *m* miracle. ~**so** *a* miraculous

**milano** *m* kite

**mildeu** *m*, **mildiu** *m* mildew

**milen|ario** *a* millenial. ~**io** *m* millennium

**milenrama** *f* milfoil

**milésimo** *a* & *m* thousandth

**mili** *f* (*fam*) military service

**milicia** *f* soldiering; (*gente armada*) militia

**mili|gramo** *m* milligram. ~**litro** *m* millilitre

**milímetro** *m* millimetre

**militante** *a* militant

**militar** *a* military. ● *m* soldier. ~**ismo** *m* militarism. ~**ista** *a* militaristic. ● *m* & *f* militarist. ~**izar** [10] *vt* militarize

**milonga** *f* (*Arg, canción*) popular song; (*Arg, baile*) popular dance

**milord** *m*. **vivir como un** ~ live like a lord

**milpies** *m invar* woodlouse

**milla** *f* mile

**millar** *m* thousand. **a** ~**es** by the thousand

**mill|ón** *m* million. ~**onada** *f* fortune. ~**onario** *m* millionaire. ~**onésimo** *a* & *m* millionth. **un** ~**n de libros** a million books

**mimar** *vt* spoil

**mimbre** *m* & *f* wicker. ~**arse** *vpr* sway. ~**ra** *f* osier. ~**ral** *m* osier-bed

**mimetismo** *m* mimicry

**mímic|a** *f* mime. ~**o** *a* mimic

**mimo** *m* mime; (*a un niño*) spoiling; (*caricia*) caress

**mimosa** *f* mimosa

**mina** *f* mine. ~**r** *vt* mine; (*fig*) undermine

**minarete** *m* minaret

**mineral** *m* mineral; (*mena*) ore. ~**ogía** *f* mineralogy. ~**ogista** *m* & *f* mineralogist

**miner|ía** *f* mining. ~**o** *a* mining. ● *m* miner

**mini...** *pref* mini...

**miniar** *vt* paint in miniature

**miniatura** *f* miniature

**minifundio** *m* smallholding

**minimizar** [10] *vt* minimize

**mínim|o** *a & m* minimum. **~um** *m* minimum

**minino** *m* (*fam*) cat, puss (*fam*)

**minio** *m* red lead

**minist|erial** *a* ministerial. **~erio** *m* ministry. **~ro** *m* minister

**minor|ación** *f* diminution. **~a** *f* minority. **~idad** *f* minority. **~ista** *m & f* retailer

**minuci|a** *f* trifle. **~osidad** *f* thoroughness. **~oso** *a* thorough; (*con muchos detalles*) detailed

**minué** *m* minuet

**minúscul|a** *f* small letter, lower case letter. **~o** *a* tiny

**minuta** *f* draft; (*menú*) menu

**minut|ero** *m* minute hand. **~o** *m* minute

**mío** *a & pron* mine. **un amigo ~** a friend of mine

**miop|e** *a* short-sighted. ● *m & f* short-sighted person. **~ía** *f* short-sightedness

**mira** *f* sight; (*fig, intención*) aim. **~da** *f* look. **~do** *a* thought of; (*comedido*) considerate; (*cirunspecto*) circumspect. **~dor** *m* windowed balcony; (*lugar*) viewpoint. **~miento** *m* consideration. **~r** *vt* look at; (*observar*) watch; (*considerar*) consider. **~r fijamente** a stare at. ● *vi* look; (*edificio etc*) face. **~rse** *vpr* (*personas*) look at each other. **a la ~** on the lookout. **con ~s a** with a view to. **echar una ~da a** a glance at

**mirilla** *f* peephole

**miriñaque** *m* crinoline

**mirlo** *m* blackbird

**mirón** *a* nosey. ● *m* nosey-parker; (*espectador*) onlooker

**mirra** *f* myrrh

**mirto** *m* myrtle

**misa** *f* mass

**misal** *m* missal

**mis|antropía** *f* misanthropy. **~antrópico** *a* misanthropic. **~ántropo** *m* misanthropist

**miscelánea** *f* miscellany; (*Mex, tienda*) corner shop

**miser|able** *a* very poor; (*lastimoso*) miserable; (*tacaño*) mean. **~ia** *f* extreme poverty; (*suciedad*) squalor

**misericordi|a** *f* pity; (*piedad*) mercy. **~oso** *a* merciful

**mísero** *a* very poor; (*lastimoso*) miserable; (*tacaño*) mean

**misil** *m* missile

**misi|ón** *f* mission. **~onal** *a* missionary. **~onero** *m* missionary

**misiva** *f* missive

**mism|amente** *adv* just. **~ísimo** *a* very same. **~o** *a* same; (*después de pronombre personal*) myself, yourself, himself, herself, itself, ourselves, yourselves, themselves; (*enfático*) very. ● *adv* right. **ahora ~** right now. **aquí ~** right here

**mis|oginia** *f* misogyny. **~ógino** *m* misogynist

**misterio** *m* mystery. **~so** *a* mysterious

**míst|ica** *f* mysticism. **~o** *a* mystical

**mistifica|ción** *f* falsification; (*engaño*) trick. **~r** [7] *vt* falsify; (*engañar*) deceive

**mitad** *f* half; (*centro*) middle

**mítico** *a* mythical

**mitiga|ción** *f* mitigation. **~r** [12] *vt* mitigate; quench ⟨*sed*⟩; relieve ⟨*dolor etc*⟩

**mitin** *m* meeting

**mito** *m* myth. **~logía** *f* mythology. **~lógico** *a* mythological

**mitón** *m* mitten

**mitote** *m* (*LAm*) Indian dance

**mitra** *f* mitre. **~do** *m* prelate

**mixteca** *f* (*Mex*) southern Mexico

**mixt|o** *a* mixed. ● *m* passenger and goods train; (*cerilla*) match. **~ura** *f* mixture

**mnemotécnic|a** *f* mnemonics. **~o** *a* mnemonic

**moaré** *m* moiré

**mobiliario** *m* furniture

**moblaje** *m* furniture

**moca** *m* mocha

**moce|dad** *f* youth. **~ro** *m* young people. **~tón** *m* strapping lad

**moción** *f* motion

**moco** *m* mucus

**mochales** *a invar.* **estar ~** be round the bend

**mochila** *f* rucksack

**mocho** *a* blunt. ● *m* butt end

**mochuelo** *m* little owl

**moda** *f* fashion. **~l** *a* modal. **~les** *mpl* manners. **~lidad** *f* kind. **de ~** in fashion

**model|ado** *m* modelling. **~ador** *m* modeller. **~ar** *vt* model; (*fig, configurar*) form. **~o** *m* model

**modera|ción** *f* moderation. **~do** *a* moderate. **~r** *vt* moderate; reduce ⟨*velocidad*⟩. **~rse** *vpr* control oneself

**modern|amente** *adv* recently. **~idad** *f* modernity. **~ismo** *m* modernism. **~ista** *m & f* modernist. **~izar** [10] *vt* modernize. **~o** *a* modern

**modest|ia** *f* modesty. **~o** *a* modest

**modicidad** *f* reasonableness

**módico** *a* moderate

**modifica|ción** *f* modification. **~r** [7] *vt* modify

**modismo** *m* idiom

**modist|a** *f* dressmaker. **~o** *m & f* designer

**modo** *m* manner, way; (*gram*) mood; (*mus*) mode. **~ de ser** character. **de ~ que** so that. **de ningún ~** certainly not. **de todos ~s** anyhow

**modorr|a** *f* drowsiness. **~o** *a* drowsy

**modoso** *a* well-behaved

**modula|ción** *f* modulation. **~dor** *m* modulator. **~r** *vt* modulate

**módulo** *m* module

**mofa** *f* mockery. **~rse** *vpr*. **~rse de** make fun of

**mofeta** *f* skunk

**moflet|e** *m* chubby cheek. **~udo** *a* with chubby cheeks

**mogol** *m* Mongol. **el Gran M~** the Great Mogul

**moh|ín** *m* grimace. **~ino** *a* sulky. **hacer un ~ín** pull a face

**moho** *m* mould; (*óxido*) rust. **~so** *a* mouldy; ‹*metales*› rusty

**moisés** *m* Moses basket

**mojado** *a* damp, wet

**mojama** *f* salted tuna

**mojar** *vt* wet; (*empapar*) soak; (*humedecer*) moisten, dampen. ● *vi*. **~ en** get involved in

**mojicón** *m* blow in the face; (*bizcocho*) sponge cake

**mojiganga** *f* masked ball; (*en el teatro*) farce

**mojigat|ería** *f* hypocrisy. **~o** *m* hypocrite

**mojón** *m* boundary post; (*señal*) signpost

**molar** *m* molar

**mold|e** *m* mould; (*aguja*) knitting needle. **~ear** *vt* mould, shape; (*fig*) form. **~ura** *f* moulding

**mole** *f* mass, bulk. ● *m* (*Mex, guisado*) (Mexican) stew with chili sauce

**mol|écula** *f* molecule. **~ecular** *a* molecular

**mole|dor** *a* grinding. ● *m* grinder; (*persona*) bore. **~r** [2] grind; (*hacer polvo*) pulverize

**molest|ar** *vt* annoy; (*incomodar*) bother. **¿le ~a que fume?** do you mind if I smoke? **no ~ar** do not disturb. ● *vi* be a nuisance. **~arse** *vpr* bother; (*ofenderse*) take offence. **~ia** *f* bother, nuisance; (*inconveniente*) inconvenience; (*incomodidad*) discomfort. **~o** *a* annoying; (*inconveniente*) inconvenient; (*ofendido*) offended

**molicie** *f* softness; (*excesiva comodidad*) easy life

**molido** *a* ground; (*fig, muy cansado*) worn out

**molienda** *f* grinding

**molin|ero** *m* miller. **~ete** *m* toy windmill. **~illo** *m* mill; (*juguete*) toy windmill. **~o** *m* (water) mill. **~o de viento** windmill

**molusco** *m* mollusc

**mollar** *a* soft

**molleja** *f* gizzard

**mollera** *f* (*de la cabeza*) crown; (*fig, sesera*) brains

**moment|áneamente** *adv* momentarily; (*por el momento*) right now. **~áneo** *a* momentary. **~o** *m* moment; (*mecánica*) momentum

**momi|a** *f* mummy. **~ficación** *f* mummification. **~ficar** [7] *vt* mummify. **~ficarse** *vpr* become mummified

**momio** *a* lean. ● *m* bargain; (*trabajo*) cushy job

**monaca|l** *a* monastic. **~to** *m* monasticism

**monada** *f* beautiful thing; (*de un niño*) charming way; (*acción tonta*) silliness

**monaguillo** *m* altar boy

**mon|arca** *m & f* monarch. **~arquía** *f* monarchy. **~árquico** *a* monarchic(al). **~arquismo** *m* monarchism

**mon|asterio** *m* monastery. **~ástico** *a* monastic

**monda** *f* pruning; (*peladura*) peel

**mond|adientes** *m invar* toothpick. **~adura** *f* pruning; (*peladura*) peel. **~ar** *vt* peel ‹*fruta etc*›; dredge ‹*un río*›. **~o** *a* (*sin pelo*) bald; (*sin dinero*) broke; (*sencillo*) plain

**mondongo** *m* innards

**moned|a** *f* coin; (*de un país*) currency. **~ero** *m* minter; (*portamonedas*) purse

**monetario** *a* monetary

**mongol** *a* & *m* Mongolian

**mongolismo** *m* Down's syndrome

**monigote** *m* weak character; *(muñeca)* rag doll; *(dibujo)* doodle

**monises** *mpl* money, dough *(fam)*

**monitor** *m* monitor

**monj|a** *f* nun. ~**e** *m* monk. ~**il** *a* nun's; *(como de monja)* like a nun

**mono** *m* monkey; *(sobretodo)* overalls. ● *a* pretty

**mono...** *pref* mono...

**monocromo** *a* & *m* monochrome

**monóculo** *m* monocle

**mon|ogamia** *f* monogamy. ~**ógamo** *a* monogamous

**monografía** *f* monograph

**monograma** *m* monogram

**monol|ítico** *a* monolithic. ~**ito** *m* monolith

**mon|ologar** [12] *vi* soliloquize. ~**ólogo** *m* monologue

**monoman|ía** *f* monomania. ~**iaco** *m* monomaniac

**monoplano** *m* monoplane

**monopoli|o** *m* monopoly. ~**zar** [10] *vt* monopolize

**monos|ilábico** *a* monosyllabic. ~**ílabo** *m* monosyllable

**monoteís|mo** *m* monotheism. ~**ta** *a* monotheistic. ● *m* & *f* monotheist

**mon|otonía** *f* monotony. ~**ótono** *a* monotonous

**monseñor** *m* monsignor

**monserga** *f* boring talk

**monstruo** *m* monster. ~**sidad** *f* monstrosity. ~**so** *a* monstrous

**monta** *f* mounting; *(valor)* value

**montacargas** *m invar* service lift

**monta|do** *a* mounted. ~**dor** *m* fitter. ~**je** *m* assembly; *(cine)* montage; *(teatro)* staging, production

**montañ|a** *f* mountain. ~**ero** *a* mountaineer. ~**és** *a* mountain. ● *m* highlander. ~**ismo** *m* mountaineering. ~**oso** *a* mountainous. ~**a rusa** big dipper

**montaplatos** *m invar* service lift

**montar** *vt* ride; *(subirse)* get on; *(ensamblar)* assemble; cock *‹arma›*; set up *‹una casa, un negocio›*. ● *vi* ride; *(subirse a)* mount. ~ **a caballo** ride a horse

**montaraz** *a* *‹animales›* wild; *‹personas›* mountain

**monte** *m* *(montaña)* mountain; *(terreno inculto)* scrub; *(bosque)* forest. ~ **de piedad** pawn-shop. **ingeniero** *m* **de** ~**s** forestry expert

**montepío** *m* charitable fund for dependents

**monter|a** *f* cloth cap. ~**o** *m* hunter

**montés** *a* wild

**Montevideo** *m* Montevideo

**montevideano** *a* & *m* Montevidean

**montículo** *m* hillock

**montón** *m* heap, pile. **a montones** in abundance, lots of

**montuoso** *a* hilly

**montura** *f* mount; *(silla)* saddle

**monument|al** *a* monumental; *(fig, muy grande)* enormous. ~**o** *m* monument

**monzón** *m* & *f* monsoon

**moñ|a** *f* hair ribbon. ~**o** *m* bun

**moque|o** *m* runny nose. ~**ro** *m* handkerchief

**moqueta** *f* fitted carpet

**moquillo** *m* distemper

**mora** *f* mulberry; *(zarzamora)* blackberry

**morada** *f* dwelling

**morado** *a* purple

**morador** *m* inhabitant

**moral** *m* mulberry tree. ● *f* morals. ● *a* moral. ~**eja** *f* moral. ~**idad** *f* morality. ~**ista** *m* & *f* moralist. ~**izador** *a* moralizing. ● *m* moralist. ~**izar** [10] *vt* moralize

**morapio** *m* *(fam)* cheap red wine

**morar** *vi* live

**moratoria** *f* moratorium

**morbidez** *f* softness

**mórbido** *a* soft; *(malsano)* morbid

**morbo** *m* illness. ~**sidad** *f* morbidity. ~**so** *a* unhealthy

**morcilla** *f* black pudding

**morda|cidad** *f* bite. ~**z** *a* biting

**mordaza** *f* gag

**mordazmente** *adv* bitingly

**morde|dura** *f* bite. ~**r** [2] *vt* bite; *(fig, quitar porciones a)* eat into; *(denigrar)* gossip about. ● *vi* bite

**mordis|car** [7] *vt* nibble (at). ● *vi* nibble. ~**co** *m* bite. ~**quear** *vt* nibble (at)

**morelense** *a* *(Mex)* from Morelos. ● *m* & *f* person from Morelos

**morena** *f* *(geol)* moraine

**moreno** *a* dark; *(de pelo obscuro)* dark-haired; *(de raza negra)* negro

**morera** *f* mulberry tree

**morería** *f* Moorish lands; *(barrio)* Moorish quarter

**moretón** *m* bruise

**morfema** *m* morpheme

**morfin|a** *f* morphine. ~**ómano** *a* morphine. ● *m* morphine addict

**morfol|ogía** *f* morphology. **~ógico**
*a* morphological
**moribundo** *a* moribund
**morillo** *m* andiron
**morir** [6] (*pp* **muerto**) *vi* die; (*fig*,
*extinguirse*) die away; (*fig*, *terminar*) end. **~se** *vpr* die. **~se de
hambre** starve to death; (*fig*) be
starving. **se muere por una flauta**
she's dying to have a flute
**moris|co** *a* Moorish. ● *m* Moor.
**~ma** *f* Moors
**morm|ón** *m* & *f* Mormon. **~ónico** *a*
Mormon. **~onismo** *m* Mormonism
**moro** *a* Moorish. ● *m* Moor
**moros|idad** *f* dilatoriness. **~o** *a*
dilatory
**morrada** *f* butt; (*puñetazo*) punch
**morral** *m* (*mochila*) rucksack; (*del
cazador*) gamebag; (*para caballos*)
nosebag
**morralla** *f* rubbish
**morrillo** *m* nape of the neck
**morriña** *f* homesickness
**morro** *m* snout
**morrocotudo** *a* (*esp Mex*) (*fam*) terrific (*fam*)
**morsa** *f* walrus
**mortaja** *f* shroud
**mortal** *a* & *m* & *f* mortal. **~idad** *f*
mortality. **~mente** *adv* mortally
**mortandad** *f* death toll
**mortecino** *a* failing; (*color*) faded
**mortero** *m* mortar
**mortífero** *a* deadly
**mortifica|ción** *f* mortification. **~r**
[7] *vt* (*med*) damage; (*atormentar*)
plague; (*humillar*) humiliate. **~rse**
*vpr* (*Mex*) feel embarrassed
**mortuorio** *a* death
**morueco** *m* ram
**moruno** *a* Moorish
**mosaico** *a* of Moses, Mosaic. ● *m*
mosaic
**mosca** *f* fly. **~rda** *f* blowfly. **~rdón**
*m* botfly; (*mosca de cuerpo azul*)
bluebottle
**moscatel** *a* muscatel
**moscón** *m* botfly; (*mosca de cuerpo
azul*) bluebottle
**moscovita** *a* & *m* & *f* Muscovite
**Moscú** *m* Moscow
**mosque|arse** *vpr* get cross. **~o** *m*
resentment
**mosquete** *m* musket. **~ro** *m*
musketeer
**mosquit|ero** *m* mosquito net. **~o** *m*
mosquito; (*mosca pequeña*) fly, gnat
**mostacho** *m* moustache

**mostachón** *m* macaroon
**mostaza** *f* mustard
**mosto** *m* must
**mostrador** *m* counter
**mostrar** [2] *vt* show. **~se** *vpr* (show
oneself to) be. **se mostró muy
amable** he was very kind
**mostrenco** *a* ownerless; (*animal*)
stray; (*torpe*) thick; (*gordo*) fat
**mota** *f* spot, speck
**mote** *m* nickname; (*lema*) motto
**motea|do** *a* speckled. **~r** *vt* speckle
**motejar** *vt* call
**motel** *m* motel
**motete** *m* motet
**motín** *m* riot; (*rebelión*) uprising; (*de
tropas*) mutiny
**motiv|ación** *f* motivation. **~ar** *vt*
motivate; (*explicar*) explain. **~o** *m*
reason. **con ~o de** because of
**motocicl|eta** *f* motor cycle, motor
bike (*fam*). **~ista** *m* & *f* motorcyclist
**motón** *m* pulley
**motonave** *f* motor boat
**motor** *a* motor. ● *m* motor, engine.
**~a** *f* motor boat. **~ de arranque**
starter motor
**motoris|mo** *m* motorcycling. **~ta**
*m* & *f* motorist; (*de una moto*)
motorcyclist
**motorizar** [10] *vt* motorize
**motriz** *af* motive, driving
**move|dizo** *a* movable; (*poco firme*)
unstable; (*persona*) fickle. **~r** [2] *vt*
move; shake (*la cabeza*); (*provocar*)
cause. **~rse** *vpr* move; (*darse prisa*)
hurry up. **arenas** *fpl* **~dizas**
quicksand
**movi|ble** *a* movable. **~do** *a* moved;
(*foto*) blurred; (*inquieto*) fidgety
**móvil** *a* movable. ● *m* motive
**movili|dad** *f* mobility. **~zación** *f*
mobilization. **~zar** [10] *vt* mobilize
**movimiento** *m* movement, motion;
(*agitación*) bustle
**moza** *f* girl; (*sirvienta*) servant,
maid. **~lbete** *m* young lad
**mozárabe** *a* Mozarabic. ● *m* & *f*
Mozarab
**moz|o** *m* boy, lad. **~uela** *f* young
girl. **~uelo** *m* young boy/lad
**muaré** *m* moiré
**mucam|a** *f* (*Arg*) servant. **~o** *m*
(*Arg*) servant
**mucos|idad** *f* mucus. **~o** *a* mucous
**muchach|a** *f* girl; (*sirvienta*)
servant, maid. **~o** *m* boy, lad; (*criado*) servant

**muchedumbre** f crowd

**muchísimo** a very much. ● adv a lot

**mucho** a much (pl many), a lot of. ● pron a lot; (personas) many (people). ● adv a lot, very much; (de tiempo) long, a long time. **ni ~ menos** by no means. **por ~ que** however much

**muda** f change of clothing; (de animales) moult. **~ble** a changeable; (personas) fickle. **~nza** f change; (de casa) removal. **~r** vt/i change. **~rse** (de ropa) change one's clothes; (de casa) move (house)

**mudéjar** a & m & f Mudéjar

**mud|ez** f dumbness. **~o** a dumb; (callado) silent

**mueble** a movable. ● m piece of furniture

**mueca** f grimace, face. **hacer una ~** pull a face

**muela** f (diente) tooth; (diente molar) molar; (piedra de afilar) grindstone; (piedra de molino) millstone

**muelle** a soft. ● m spring; (naut) wharf; (malecón) jetty

**muérdago** m mistletoe

**muero** vb véase **morir**

**muert|e** f death; (homicidio) murder. **~o** a dead; (matado, fam) killed; (colores) pale. ● m dead person; (cadáver) body, corpse

**muesca** f nick; (ranura) slot

**muestra** f sample; (prueba) proof; (modelo) model; (seal) sign. **~rio** m collection of samples

**muestro** vb véase **mostrar**

**muevo** vb véase **mover**

**mugi|do** m moo. **~r** [14] vi moo; (fig) roar

**mugr|e** m dirt. **~iento** a dirty, filthy

**mugrón** m sucker

**muguete** m lily of the valley

**mujer** f woman; (esposa) wife. ● int my dear! **~iego** a (hombre) fond of the women. **~il** a womanly. **~ío** m (crowd of) women. **~zuela** f prostitute

**mújol** m mullet

**mula** f mule; (Mex) unsaleable goods. **~da** f drove of mules

**mulato** a & m mulatto

**mulero** m muleteer

**mulet|a** f crutch; (fig) support; (toreo) stick with a red flag

**mulo** m mule

**multa** f fine. **~r** vt fine

**multi...** pref multi...

**multicolor** a multicolour(ed)

**multicopista** m copying machine

**multiforme** a multiform

**multilateral** a multilateral

**multilingüe** a multilingual

**multimillonario** m multimillionaire

**múltiple** a multiple

**multiplic|ación** f multiplication. **~ar** [7] vt multiply. **~arse** vpr multiply; (fig) go out of one's way. **~idad** f multiplicity

**múltiplo** a & m multiple

**multitud** f multitude, crowd. **~inario** a multitudinous

**mulli|do** a soft. ● m stuffing. **~r** [22] vt soften

**mund|ano** a wordly; (de la sociedad elegante) society. ● m socialite. **~ial** a world-wide. **la segunda guerra ~ial** the Second World War. **~illo** m world, circles. **~o** m world. **~ología** f worldly wisdom. **todo el ~o** everybody

**munición** f ammunition; (provisiones) supplies

**municip|al** a municipal. **~alidad** f municipality. **~io** m municipality; (ayuntamiento) town council

**mun|ificencia** f munificence. **~ífico** a munificent

**muñe|ca** f (anat) wrist; (juguete) doll; (maniquí) dummy. **~co** m boy doll. **~quera** f wristband

**muñón** m stump

**mura|l** a mural, wall. ● m mural. **~lla** f (city) wall. **~r** vt wall

**murciélago** m bat

**murga** f street band; (lata) bore, nuisance. **dar la ~** bother, be a pain (fam)

**murmullo** m (de personas) whisper(ing), murmur(ing); (del agua) rippling; (del viento) sighing, rustle

**murmura|ción** f gossip. **~dor** a gossiping. ● m gossip. **~r** vi murmur; (hablar en voz baja) whisper; (quejarse en voz baja) mutter; (criticar) gossip

**muro** m wall

**murri|a** f depression. **~o** a depressed

**mus** m card game

**musa** f muse

**musaraña** f shrew

**muscula|r** a muscular. **~tura** f muscles

**músculo** m muscle

**musculoso** a muscular

**muselina** f muslin

**museo** *m* museum. ~ **de arte** art gallery

**musgaño** *m* shrew

**musgo** *m* moss. ~**so** *a* mossy

**música** *f* music

**musical** *a* & *m* musical

**músico** *a* musical. ● *m* musician

**music|ología** *f* musicology. ~**ólogo** *m* musicologist

**musitar** *vt/i* mumble

**muslímico** *a* Muslim

**muslo** *m* thigh

**mustela** *a* weasel

**musti|arse** *vpr* wither, wilt. ~**o** *a* ⟨*plantas*⟩ withered; ⟨*cosas*⟩ faded; ⟨*personas*⟩ gloomy; (*Mex, hipócrita*) hypocritical

**musulmán** *a* & *m* Muslim

**muta|bilidad** *f* mutability. ~**ción** *f* change; (*en biología*) mutation

**mutila|ción** *f* mutilation. ~**do** *a* crippled. ● *m* cripple. ~**r** *vt* mutilate; cripple, maim ⟨*persona*⟩

**mutis** *m* (*en el teatro*) exit. ~**mo** *m* silence

**mutu|alidad** *f* mutuality; (*asociación*) friendly society. ~**amente** *adv* mutually. ~**o** *a* mutual

**muy** *adv* very; (*demasiado*) too

# N

**nab|a** *f* swede. ~**o** *m* turnip

**nácar** *m* mother-of-pearl

**nac|er** [11] *vi* be born; ⟨*huevo*⟩ hatch; ⟨*planta*⟩ sprout. ~**ido** *a* born. ~**iente** *a* ⟨*sol*⟩ rising. ~**imiento** *m* birth; (*de río*) source; (*belén*) crib. **dar** ~**imiento a** give rise to. **lugar m de** ~**imiento** place of birth. **recien** ~**ido** newborn. **volver a** ~**er** have a narrow escape

**naci|ón** *f* nation. ~**onal** *a* national. ~**onalidad** *f* nationality. ~**onalismo** *m* nationalism. ~**onalista** *m* & *f* nationalist. ~**onalizar** [10] *vt* nationalize. ~**onalizarse** *vpr* become naturalized

**nada** *pron* nothing, not anything. ● *adv* not at all. **¡~ de eso!** nothing of the sort! **antes de** ~ first of all. **¡de** ~**!** (*después de 'gracias'*) don't mention it! **para** ~ (not) at all. **por** ~ **del mundo** not for anything in the world

**nada|dor** *m* swimmer. ~**r** *vi* swim

**nadería** *f* trifle

**nadie** *pron* no one, nobody

**nado** *adv.* **a** ~ swimming

**nafta** *f* (*LAm, gasolina*) petrol, (*Brit*), gas (*Amer*)

**nailon** *m* nylon

**naipe** *m* (playing) card. **juegos** *mpl* **de** ~**s** card games

**nalga** *f* buttock. ~**s** *fpl* bottom

**nana** *f* lullaby

**Nápoles** *m* Naples

**naranj|a** *f* orange. ~**ada** *f* orangeade. ~**al** *m* orange grove. ~**o** *m* orange tree

**narcótico** *a* & *m* narcotic

**nariz** *f* nose; (*orificio de la nariz*) nostril. **¡narices!** rubbish!

**narra|ción** *f* narration. ~**dor** *m* narrator. ~**r** *vt* tell. ~**tivo** *a* narrative

**nasal** *a* nasal

**nata** *f* cream

**natación** *f* swimming

**natal** *a* birth; ⟨*pueblo etc*⟩ home. ~**idad** *f* birth rate

**natillas** *fpl* custard

**natividad** *f* nativity

**nativo** *a* & *m* native

**nato** *a* born

**natural** *a* natural. ● *m* native. ~**eza** *f* nature; (*nacionalidad*) nationality; (*ciudadanía*) naturalization. ~**eza muerta** still life. ~**idad** *f* naturalness. ~**ista** *m* & *f* naturalist. ~**izar** [10] *vt* naturalize. ~**izarse** *vpr* become naturalized. ~**mente** *adv* naturally. ● *int* of course!

**naufrag|ar** [12] *vi* ⟨*barco*⟩ sink; ⟨*persona*⟩ be shipwrecked; (*fig*) fail. ~**io** *m* shipwreck

**náufrago** *a* shipwrecked. ● *m* shipwrecked person

**náusea** *f* nausea. **dar** ~**s a uno** make s.o. feel sick. **sentir** ~**s** feel sick

**nauseabundo** *a* sickening

**náutico** *a* nautical

**navaja** *f* penknife; (*de afeitar*) razor. ~**zo** *m* slash

**naval** *a* naval

**Navarra** *f* Navarre

**nave** *f* ship; (*de iglesia*) nave. ~ **espacial** spaceship. **quemar las** ~**s** burn one's boats

**navega|ble** *a* navigable; ⟨*barco*⟩ seaworthy. ~**ción** *f* navigation. ~**nte** *m* & *f* navigator. ~**r** [12] *vi* sail; ⟨*avión*⟩ fly

**Navid|ad** *f* Christmas. ~**eño** *a* Christmas. **en** ~**ades** at Christmas. **¡feliz** ~**ad!** Happy Christmas! **por** ~**ad** at Christmas

**navío** m ship

**nazi** a & m & f Nazi

**neblina** f mist

**nebuloso** a misty; (*fig*) vague

**necedad** f foolishness. **decir** ~es talk nonsense. **hacer una** ~ do sth stupid

**necesari|amente** adv necessarily. ~o a necessary

**necesi|dad** f necessity; (*pobreza*) poverty. ~**dades** fpl hardships. **por** ~**dad** (out) of necessity. ~**tado** a in need (**de** of); (*pobre*) needy. ~**tar** vt need. ● vi. ~**tar de** need

**necio** a silly. ● m idiot

**necrología** f obituary column

**néctar** m nectar

**nectarina** f nectarine

**nefasto** a unfortunate, ominous

**nega|ción** f negation; (*desmentimiento*) denial; (*gram*) negative. ~**do** a incompetent. ~**r** [1 & 12] vt deny; (*rehusar*) refuse. ~**rse** vpr. ~**rse a** refuse. ~**tiva** f negative; (*acción*) denial; (*acción de rehusar*) refusal. ~**tivo** a & m negative

**negligen|cia** f negligence. ~**te** a negligent

**negoci|able** a negotiable. ~**ación** f negotiation. ~**ante** m & f dealer. ~**ar** vt/i negotiate. ~**ar en** trade in. ~**o** m business; (*com, trato*) deal. ~**os** mpl business. **hombre** m **de** ~**os** businessman

**negr|a** f Negress; (*mus*) crotchet. ~**o** a black; ⟨*persona*⟩ Negro. ● m (*color*) black; (*persona*) Negro. ~**ura** f blackness. ~**uzco** a blackish

**nene** m & f baby, child

**nenúfar** m water lily

**neo...** pref neo...

**neocelandés** a from New Zealand. ● m New Zealander

**neolítico** a Neolithic

**neón** m neon

**nepotismo** m nepotism

**nervio** m nerve; (*tendón*) sinew; (*bot*) vein. ~**sidad** f, ~**sismo** m nervousness; (*impaciencia*) impatience. ~**so** a nervous; (*de temperamento*) highly-strung. **crispar los** ~**s a uno** (*fam*) get on s.o.'s nerves. **ponerse** ~**so** get excited

**neto** a clear; ⟨*verdad*⟩ simple; (*com*) net

**neumático** a pneumatic. ● m tyre

**neumonía** f pneumonia

**neuralgia** f neuralgia

**neur|ología** f neurolgy. ~**ólogo** m neurologist

**neur|osis** f neurosis. ~**ótico** a neurotic

**neutr|al** a neutral. ~**alidad** f neutrality. ~**alizar** [10] vt neutralize. ~**o** a neutral; (*gram*) neuter

**neutrón** m neutron

**neva|da** f snowfall. ~**r** [1] vi snow. ~**sca** f blizzard

**nevera** f fridge (*Brit*, *fam*), refrigerator

**nevisca** f light snowfall. ~**r** [7] vi snow lightly

**nexo** m link

**ni** conj nor, neither; (*ni siquiera*) not even. ~**...** ~ neither... nor. ~ **que** as if. ~ **siquiera** not even

**Nicaragua** f Nicaragua

**nicaragüense** a & m & f Nicaraguan

**nicotina** f nicotine

**nicho** m niche

**nido** m nest; (*de ladrones*) den; (*escondrijo*) hiding-place

**niebla** f fog; (*neblina*) mist. **hay** ~ it's foggy

**niet|a** f granddaughter. ~**o** m grandson. ~**os** mpl grandchildren

**nieve** f snow; (*LAm, helado*) ice-cream

**Nigeria** f Nigeria. ~**no** a Nigerian

**niki** m T-shirt

**nilón** m nylon

**nimbo** m halo

**nimi|edad** f triviality. ~**o** a insignificant

**ninfa** f nymph

**ninfea** f water lily

**ningún** véase **ninguno**

**ninguno** a (*delante de nombre masculino en singular* **ningún**) no, not any. ● pron none; (*persona*) no-one, nobody; (*de dos*) neither. **de ninguna manera, de ningún modo** by no means. **en ninguna parte** nowhere

**niñ|a** f (little) girl. ~**ada** f childish thing. ~**era** f nanny. ~**ería** f childish thing. ~**ez** f childhood. ~**o** a childish. ● m (little) boy. **de** ~**o** as a child. **desde** ~**o** from childhood

**níquel** m nickel

**níspero** m medlar

**nitidez** f clearness

**nítido** a clear; (*foto*) sharp

**nitrato** m nitrate

**nítrico** a nitric

**nitrógeno** m nitrogen

**nivel** *m* level; (*fig*) standard. ~**ar** *vt* level. ~**arse** *vpr* become level. ~ **de vida** standard of living

**no** *adv* not; (*como respuesta*) no. ¿~? isn't it? ~ **más** only. ¡a que ~! I bet you don't! ¡**cómo** ~! of course! **Felipe** ~ **tiene hijos** Felipe has no children. ¡**que** ~! certainly not!

**nob|iliario** *a* noble. ~**le** *a & m & f* noble. ~**leza** *f* nobility

**noción** *f* notion. **nociones** *fpl* rudiments

**nocivo** *a* harmful

**nocturno** *a* nocturnal; (*clase*) evening; (*tren etc*) night. ● *m* nocturne

**noche** *f* night. ~ **vieja** New Year's Eve. **de** ~ at night. **hacer** ~ spend the night. **media** ~ midnight. **por la** ~ at night

**Nochebuena** *f* Christmas Eve

**nodo** *m* (*Esp, película*) newsreel

**nodriza** *f* nanny

**nódulo** *m* nodule

**nogal** *m* walnut(-tree)

**nómada** *a* nomadic. ● *m & f* nomad

**nombr|adía** *f* fame. ~**ado** *a* famous; (*susodicho*) aforementioned. ~**amiento** *m* appointment. ~**ar** *vt* appoint; (*citar*) mention. ~**e** *m* name; (*gram*) noun; (*fama*) renown. ~**e de pila** Christian name. **en** ~**e de** in the name of. **no tener** ~**e** be unspeakable. **poner de** ~**e** call

**nomeolvides** *m invar* forget-me-not

**nómina** *f* payroll

**nominal|l** *a* nominal. ~**tivo** *a & m* nominative. ~**tivo** *a* (*cheque etc*) made out to

**non** *a* odd. ● *m* odd number

**nonada** *f* trifle

**nono** *a* ninth

**nordeste** *a* (*región*) north-eastern; (*viento*) north-easterly. ● *m* north-east

**nórdico** *a* northern. ● *m* northerner

**noria** *f* water-wheel; (*en una feria*) ferris wheel

**norma** *f* rule

**normal** *a* normal. ●*f* teachers' training college. ~**idad** normality (*Brit*), normalcy (*Amer*). ~**izar** [10] *vt* normalize. ~**mente** *adv* normally, usually

**Normandía** *f* Normandy

**noroeste** *a* (*región*) north-western; (*viento*) north-westerly. ● *m* north-west

**norte** *m* north; (*viento*) north wind; (*fig, meta*) aim

**Norteamérica** *f* (North) America

**norteamericano** *a & m* (North) American

**norteño** *a* northern. ● *m* northerner

**Noruega** *f* Norway

**noruego** *a & m* Norwegian

**nos** *pron* (*acusativo*) us; (*dativo*) (to) us; (*reflexivo*) (to) ourselves; (*recíproco*) (to) each other

**nosotros** *pron* we; (*con prep*) us

**nost|algia** *f* nostalgia; (*de casa, de patria*) homesickness. ~**álgico** *a* nostalgic

**nota** *f* note; (*de examen etc*) mark. ~**ble** *a* notable. ~**ción** *f* notation. ~**r** *vt* notice; (*apuntar*) note down. **de mala** ~ notorious. **de** ~ famous. **digno de** ~ notable. **es de** ~**r** it should be noted. **hacerse** ~**r** stand out

**notario** *m* notary

**notici|a** *f* (piece of) news. ~**as** *fpl* news. ~**ario** *m* news. ~**ero** *a* news. **atrasado de** ~**as** behind the times. **tener** ~**as de** hear from

**notifica|ción** *f* notification. ~**r** [7] *vt* notify

**notori|edad** *f* notoriety. ~**o** *a* well-known; (*evidente*) obvious

**novato** *m* novice

**novecientos** *a & m* nine hundred

**noved|ad** *f* newness; (*noticia*) news; (*cambio*) change; (*moda*) latest fashion. ~**oso** *a* (*LAm*) novel. **sin** ~**ad** no news

**novel|a** *f* novel. ~**ista** *m & f* novelist

**noveno** *a* ninth

**novent|a** *a & m* ninety; (*nonagésimo*) ninetieth. ~**ón** *a & m* ninety-year-old

**novia** *f* girlfriend; (*prometida*) fiancée; (*en boda*) bride. ~**zgo** *m* engagement

**novicio** *m* novice

**noviembre** *m* November

**novilunio** *m* new moon

**novill|a** *f* heifer. ~**o** *m* bullock. **hacer** ~**os** play truant

**novio** *m* boyfriend; (*prometido*) fiancé; (*en boda*) bridegroom. **los** ~**s** the bride and groom

**novísimo** *a* very new

**nub|arrón** *m* large dark cloud. ~**e** *f* cloud; (*de insectos etc*) swarm. ~**lado** *a* cloudy, overcast. ● *m* cloud. ~**lar** vt cloud. ~**larse** vpr become cloudy. ~**loso** a cloudy

**nuca** f back of the neck

**nuclear** a nuclear

**núcleo** m nucleus

**nudillo** m knuckle

**nudis|mo** m nudism. ~**ta** m & f nudist

**nudo** m knot; (de asunto etc) crux. ~**so** a knotty. **tener un ~ en la garganta** have a lump in one's throat

**nuera** f daughter-in-law

**nuestro** a our; (pospuesto al sustantivo) of ours. ● pron ours. ~ **coche** our car. **un coche ~** a car of ours

**nueva** f (piece of) news. ~**s** fpl news. ~**mente** adv newly; (de nuevo) again

**Nueva** York f New York

**Nueva** Zelanda f, **Nueva Zelandia** f (LAm) New Zealand

**nueve** a & m nine

**nuevo** a new. **de ~** again

**nuez** f nut; (del nogal) walnut; (anat) Adam's apple. ~ **de Adán** Adam's apple. ~ **moscada** nutmeg

**nul|idad** f incompetence; (persona, fam) nonentity. ~**o** a useless; (jurid) null and void

**num|eración** f numbering. ~**eral** a & m numeral. ~**erar** vt number. ~**érico** a numerical

**número** m number; (arábigo, romano) numeral; (de zapatos etc) size. **sin ~** countless

**numeroso** a numerous

**nunca** adv never, not ever. ~ (**ja)más** never again. **casi ~** hardly ever. **más que ~** more than ever

**nupcia|l** a nuptial. ~**s** fpl wedding. **banquete ~l** wedding breakfast

**nutria** f otter

**nutri|ción** f nutrition. ~**do** a nourished, fed; (fig) large; (aplausos) loud; (fuego) heavy. ~**r** vt nourish, feed; (fig) feed. ~**tivo** a nutritious. **valor** m ~**tivo** nutritional value

**nylon** m nylon

# Ñ

**ña** f (LAm, fam) Mrs

**ñacanina** f (Arg) poisonous snake

**ñame** m yam

**ñapindá** m (Arg) mimosa

**ñato** (LAm) snub-nosed

**ño** m (LAm, fam) Mr

**ñoñ|ería** f, ~**ez** f insipidity. ~**o** a insipid; (tímido) bashful; (quisquilloso) prudish

**ñu** m gnu

# O

**o** conj or. ~ **bien** rather. ~**... ~** either... or. ~ **sea** in other words

**oasis** m invar oasis

**obcecar** [7] vt blind

**obed|ecer** [11] vt/i obey. ~**iencia** f obedience. ~**iente** a obedient

**obelisco** m obelisk

**obertura** f overture

**obes|idad** f obesity. ~**o** a obese

**obispo** m bishop

**obje|ción** f objection. ~**tar** vt/i object

**objetiv|idad** f objectivity. ~**o** a objective. ● m objective; (foto etc) lens

**objeto** m object

**objetor** m objector. ~ **de conciencia** conscientious objector

**oblicuo** a oblique; (mirada) sidelong

**obliga|ción** f obligation; (com) bond. ~**do** a obliged; (forzoso) obligatory; ~**r** [12] vt force, oblige. ~**rse** vpr. ~**rse a** undertake to. ~**torio** a obligatory

**oboe** m oboe; (músico) oboist

**obra** f work; (de teatro) play; (construcción) building. ~ **maestra** masterpiece. **en ~s** under construction. **por ~ de** thanks to. ~**r** vt do; (construir) build

**obrero** a labour; (clase) working. ● m workman; (en fábrica) worker

**obscen|idad** f obscenity. ~**o** a obscene

**obscu... véase oscu...**

**obsequi|ar** vt lavish attention on. ~**ar con** give, present with. ~**o** m gift, present; (agasajo) attention. ~**oso** a obliging. **en ~o de** in honour of

**observa|ción** f observation; (objeción) objection. ~**dor** m observer. ~**ncia** f observance. ~**nte** a observant. ~**r** vt observe; (notar) notice. ~**rse** vpr be noted. ~**torio** m observatory. **hacer una ~ción** make a remark

**obses|ión** f obsession. ∼**ionar** vt obsess. ∼**ivo** a obsessive. ∼**o** a obsessed

**obst|aculizar** [10] vt hinder. ∼**áculo** m obstacle

**obstante. no** ∼ adv however, nevertheless. ● prep in spite of

**obstar** vi. ∼ **para** prevent

**obstétrico** a obstetric

**obstina|ción** f obstinacy. ∼**do** a obstinate. ∼**rse** vpr be obstinate. ∼**rse en** (+ infinitivo) persist in (+ gerundio)

**obstru|cción** f obstruction. ∼**ir** [17] vt obstruct

**obtener** [40] vt get, obtain

**obtura|dor** m (foto) shutter. ∼**r** vt plug; fill ⟨muela etc⟩

**obtuso** a obtuse

**obviar** vt remove

**obvio** a obvious

**oca** f goose

**ocasi|ón** f occasion; (oportunidad) opportunity; (motivo) cause. ∼**onal** a chance. ∼**onar** vt cause. **aprovechar la** ∼**ón** take the opportunity. **con** ∼**ón de** on the occasion of. **de** ∼**ón** bargain; (usado) second-hand. **en** ∼**ones** sometimes. **perder una** ∼**ón** miss a chance

**ocaso** m sunset; (fig) decline

**occident|al** a western. ● m & f westerner. ∼**e** m west

**océano** m ocean

**ocio** m idleness; (tiempo libre) leisure time. ∼**sidad** f idleness. ∼**so** a idle; (inútil) pointless

**oclusión** f occlusion

**octano** m octane. **índice** m **de** ∼ octane number, octane rating

**octav|a** f octave. ∼**o** a & m eighth

**octogenario** a & m octogenarian, eighty-year-old

**oct|ogonal** a octagonal. ∼**ógono** m octagon

**octubre** m October

**oculista** m & f oculist, optician

**ocular** a eye

**ocult|ar** vt hide. ∼**arse** vpr hide. ∼**o** a hidden; (secreto) secret

**ocupa|ción** f occupation. ∼**do** a occupied; ⟨persona⟩ busy. ∼**nte** m occupant. ∼**r** vt occupy. ∼**rse** vpr look after

**ocurr|encia** f occurrence, event; (idea) idea; (que tiene gracia) witty remark. ∼**ir** vi happen. ∼**irse** vpr occur. **¿qué** ∼**e?** what's the matter? **se me** ∼**e que** it occurs to me that

**ochent|a** a & m eighty. ∼**ón** a & m eighty-year-old

**ocho** a & m eight. ∼**cientos** a & m eight hundred

**oda** f ode

**odi|ar** vt hate. ∼**o** m hatred. ∼**oso** a hateful

**odisea** f odyssey

**oeste** m west; (viento) west wind

**ofen|der** vt offend; (insultar) insult. ∼**derse** vpr take offence. ∼**sa** f offence. ∼**siva** f offensive. ∼**sivo** a offensive

**oferta** f offer; (en subasta) bid; (regalo) gift. ∼**s de empleo** situations vacant. **en** ∼ on (special) offer

**oficial** a official. ● m skilled worker; (funcionario) civil servant; (mil) officer. ∼**a** f skilled (woman) worker

**oficin|a** f office. ∼**a de colocación** employment office. ∼**a de Estado** government office. ∼**a de turismo** tourist office. ∼**ista** m & f office worker. **horas** fpl **de** ∼**a** business hours

**oficio** m job; (profesión) profession; (puesto) post. ∼**so** a (no oficial) unofficial

**ofrec|er** [11] vt offer; give ⟨fiesta, banquete etc⟩; (prometer) promise. ∼**erse** vpr ⟨persona⟩ volunteer; ⟨cosa⟩ occur. ∼**imiento** m offer

**ofrenda** f offering. ∼**r** vt offer

**ofusca|ción** f blindness; (confusión) confusion. ∼**r** [7] vt blind; (confundir) confuse. ∼**rse** vpr be dazzled

**ogro** m ogre

**oí|ble** a audible. ∼**da** f hearing. ∼**do** m hearing; (anat) ear. **al** ∼**do** in one's ear. **de** ∼**das** by hearsay. **de** ∼**do** by ear. **duro de** ∼**do** hard of hearing

**oigo** vb véase **oír**

**oír** [50] vt hear. ∼ **misa** go to mass. **¡oiga!** listen!; (al teléfono) hello!

**ojal** m buttonhole

**ojalá** int I hope so! ● conj if only

**ojea|da** f glance. ∼**r** vt eye; (para inspeccionar) see; (ahuyentar) scare away. **dar una** ∼**da a, echar una** ∼**da a** glance at

**ojeras** fpl (del ojo) bags

**ojeriza** f ill will. **tener** ∼ **a** have a grudge against

**ojete** m eyelet

**ojo** *m* eye; (*de cerradura*) keyhole; (*de un puente*) span. ¡~! careful!

**ola** *f* wave

**olé** *int* bravo!

**olea|da** *f* wave. **~je** *m* swell

**óleo** *m* oil; (*cuadro*) oil painting

**oleoducto** *m* oil pipeline

**oler** [2, *las formas que empezarían por* **ue** *se escriben* **hue**] *vt* smell; (*curiosear*) pry into; (*descubrir*) discover. ● *vi* smell (**a** of)

**olfat|ear** *vt* smell, sniff; (*fig*) sniff out. **~o** *m* (sense of) smell; (*fig*) intuition

**olimpiada** *f*, **olimpíada** *f* Olympic games, Olympics

**olímpico** *a* (*juegos*) Olympic

**oliv|a** *f* olive; (*olivo*) olive tree. **~ar** *m* olive grove. **~o** *m* olive tree

**olmo** *m* elm (tree)

**olor** *m* smell. **~oso** *a* sweet-smelling

**olvid|adizo** *a* forgetful. **~ar** *vt* forget. **~arse** *vpr* forget; (*estar olvidado*) be forgotten. **~o** *m* oblivion; (*acción de olvidar*) forgetfulness. **se me ~ó** I forgot

**olla** *f* pot, casserole; (*guisado*) stew. **~ a/de presión**, **~ exprés** pressure cooker. **~ podrida** Spanish stew

**ombligo** *m* navel

**ominoso** *a* awful, abominable

**omi|sión** *f* omission; (*olvido*) forgetfulness. **~tir** *vt* omit

**ómnibus** *a* omnibus

**omnipotente** *a* omnipotent

**omóplato** *m*, **omoplato** *m* shoulder blade

**once** *a & m* eleven

**ond|a** *f* wave. **~a corta** short wave. **~a larga** long wave. **~ear** *vi* wave; (*agua*) ripple. **~ulación** *f* undulation; (*del pelo*) wave. **~ular** *vi* wave. **longitud** *f* **de ~a** wavelength

**oneroso** *a* onerous

**ónice** *m* onyx

**onomástico** *a*. **día ~**, **fiesta onomástica** name-day

**ONU** *abrev* (*Organización de las Naciones Unidas*) UN, United Nations

**onza** *f* ounce

**opa** *a* (*LAm*) stupid

**opaco** *a* opaque; (*fig*) dull

**ópalo** *m* opal

**opción** *f* option

**ópera** *f* opera

**opera|ción** *f* operation; (*com*) transaction. **~dor** *m* operator; (*cirujano*) surgeon; (*TV*) cameraman. **~r** *vt* operate on; work (*milagro etc*). ● *vi* operate; (*com*) deal. **~rse** *vpr* occur; (*med*) have an operation. **~torio** *a* operative

**opereta** *f* operetta

**opin|ar** *vi* think. **~ión** *f* opinion. **la ~ión pública** public opinion

**opio** *m* opium

**opone|nte** *a* opposing. ● *m & f* opponent. **~r** *vt* oppose; offer (*resistencia*); raise (*objeción*). **~rse** *vpr* be opposed; (*dos personas*) oppose each other

**oporto** *m* port (wine)

**oportun|idad** *f* opportunity; (*cualidad de oportuno*) timeliness. **~ista** *m & f* opportunist. **~o** *a* opportune; (*apropiado*) suitable

**oposi|ción** *f* opposition. **~ciones** *fpl* competition, public examination. **~tor** *m* candidate

**opres|ión** *f* oppression; (*ahogo*) difficulty in breathing. **~ivo** *a* oppressive. **~o** *a* oppressed. **~or** *m* oppressor

**oprimir** *vt* squeeze; press (*botón etc*); (*ropa*) be too tight for; (*fig*) oppress

**oprobio** *m* disgrace

**optar** *vi* choose. **~ por** opt for

**óptic|a** *f* optics; (*tienda*) optician's (shop). **~o** *a* optic(al). ● *m* optician

**optimis|mo** *m* optimism. **~ta** *a* optimisitic. ● *m & f* optimist

**opuesto** *a* opposite; (*enemigo*) opposed

**opulen|cia** *f* opulence. **~to** *a* opulent

**oración** *f* prayer; (*discurso*) speech; (*gram*) sentence

**oráculo** *m* oracle

**orador** *m* speaker

**oral** *a* oral

**orar** *vi* pray

**oratori|a** *f* oratory. **~o** *a* oratorical. ● *m* (*mus*) oratorio

**orbe** *m* orb

**órbita** *f* orbit

**orden** *m & f* order; (*Mex, porción*) portion. **~ado** *a* tidy. **~ del día** agenda. **órdenes** *fpl* **sagradas** Holy Orders. **a sus órdenes** (*esp Mex*) can I help you? **en ~** in order. **por ~** in turn

**ordenador** *m* computer

**ordena|nza** *f* order. ● *m* (*mil*) orderly. **~r** *vt* put in order; (*mandar*) order; (*relig*) ordain

**ordeñar** *vt* milk

**ordinal** *a & m* ordinal

**ordinario** *a* ordinary; *(grosero)* common

**orear** *vt* air

**orégano** *m* oregano

**oreja** *f* ear

**orfanato** *m* orphanage

**orfebre** *m* goldsmith, silversmith

**orfeón** *m* choral society

**orgánico** *a* organic

**organigrama** *m* flow chart

**organillo** *m* barrel-organ

**organismo** *m* organism

**organista** *m & f* organist

**organiza|ción** *f* organization. **~dor** *m* organizer. **~r** [10] *vt* organize. **~rse** *vpr* get organized

**órgano** *m* organ

**orgasmo** *m* orgasm

**orgía** *f* orgy

**orgullo** *m* pride. **~so** *a* proud

**orientación** *f* direction

**oriental** *a & m & f* oriental

**orientar** *vt* position. **~se** *vpr* point; ⟨*persona*⟩ find one's bearings

**oriente** *m* east. **O~ Medio** Middle East

**orificio** *m* hole

**orig|en** *m* origin. **~inal** *a* original; *(excéntrico)* odd. **~inalidad** *f* originality. **~inar** *vt* give rise to. **~inario** *a* original; *(nativo)* native. **dar ~en a** give rise to. **ser ~inario de** come from

**orilla** *f* ⟨*del mar*⟩ shore; ⟨*de río*⟩ bank; *(borde)* edge

**orín** *m* rust

**orina** *f* urine. **~l** *m* chamber-pot. **~r** *vi* urinate

**oriundo** *a.* **~ de** ⟨*persona*⟩ (originating) from; ⟨*animal etc*⟩ native to

**orla** *f* border

**ornamental** *a* ornamental

**ornitología** *f* ornithology

**oro** *m* gold. **~s** *mpl* Spanish card suit. **~ de ley** 9 carat gold. **hacerse de ~** make a fortune. **prometer el ~ y el moro** promise the moon

**oropel** *m* tinsel

**orquesta** *f* orchestra. **~l** *a* orchestral. **~r** *vt* orchestrate

**orquídea** *f* orchid

**ortiga** *f* nettle

**ortodox|ia** *f* orthodoxy. **~o** *a* orthodox

**ortografía** *f* spelling

**ortop|edia** *f* orthopaedics. **~édico** *a* orthopaedic

**oruga** *f* caterpillar

**orzuelo** *m* sty

**os** *pron (acusativo)* you; *(dativo)* (to) you; *(reflexivo)* (to) yourselves; *(recíproco)* (to) each other

**osad|ía** *f* boldness. **~o** *a* bold

**oscila|ción** *f* swinging; *(de precios)* fluctuation; *(tec)* oscillation. **~r** *vi* swing; ⟨*precio*⟩ fluctuate; *(tec)* oscillate; *(fig, vacilar)* hesitate

**oscur|ecer** [11] *vi* darken; *(fig)* obscure. **~ecerse** *vpr* grow dark; *(nublarse)* cloud over. **~idad** *f* darkness; *(fig)* obscurity. **~o** *a* dark; *(fig)* obscure. **a ~as** in the dark

**óseo** *a* bony

**oso** *m* bear. **~ de felpa, ~ de peluche** teddy bear

**ostensible** *a* obvious

**ostent|ación** *f* ostentation. **~ar** *vt* show off; *(mostrar)* show. **~oso** *a* ostentatious

**osteoartritis** *f* osteoarthritis

**oste|ópata** *m & f* osteopath. **~opatía** *f* osteopathy

**ostión** *m (esp Mex)* oyster

**ostra** *f* oyster

**ostracismo** *m* ostracism

**Otan** *abrev (Organización del Tratado del Atlántico Norte)* NATO, North Atlantic Treaty Organization

**otear** *vt* observe; *(escudriñar)* scan, survey

**otitis** *f* inflammation of the ear

**otoño** *m* autumn *(Brit)*, fall *(Amer)*

**otorga|miento** *m* granting; *(documento)* authorization. **~r** [12] *vt* give; *(jurid)* draw up

**otorrinolaringólogo** *m* ear, nose and throat specialist

**otro** *a* other; *(uno más)* another. ● *pron* another (one); *(en plural)* others; *(otra persona)* someone else. **el ~** the other. **el uno al ~** one another, each other

**ovación** *f* ovation

**oval** *a* oval

**óvalo** *m* oval

**ovario** *m* ovary

**oveja** *f* sheep; *(hembra)* ewe

**overol** *m (LAm)* overalls

**ovino** *a* sheep

**ovillo** *m* ball. **hacerse un ~** curl up

**OVNI** *abrev (objeto volante no identificado)* UFO, unidentified flying object

**ovulación** *f* ovulation

**oxida|ción** f rusting. ~r vi rust.
~rse vpr go rusty
**óxido** m oxide
**oxígeno** m oxygen
**oye** vb véase **oír**
**oyente** a listening. ● m & f listener
**ozono** m ozone

# P

**pabellón** m bell tent; (edificio) building; (de instrumento) bell; (bandera) flag
**pabilo** m wick
**paceño** a from La Paz. ● m person from La Paz
**pacer** [11] vi graze
**pacien|cia** f patience. ~te a & m & f patient
**pacificar** [7] vt pacify; reconcile ⟨dos personas⟩. ~se vpr calm down
**pacífico** a peaceful. **el (Océano** m **) P**~ the Pacific (Ocean)
**pacifis|mo** m pacifism. ~ta a & m & f pacifist
**pact|ar** vi agree, make a pact. ~o m pact, agreement
**pachucho** a ⟨fruta⟩ overripe; ⟨persona⟩ poorly
**padec|er** [11] vt/i suffer (de from); (soportar) bear. ~imiento m suffering; (enfermedad) ailment
**padrastro** m stepfather
**padre** a (fam) great. ● m father. ~s mpl parents
**padrino** m godfather; (en boda) best man
**padrón** m census
**paella** f paella
**paga** f pay, wages. ~ble a, ~dero a payable
**pagano** a & m pagan
**pagar** [12] vt pay; pay for ⟨compras⟩. ● vi pay. ~é m IOU
**página** f page
**pago** m payment
**pagoda** f pagoda
**país** m country; (región) region. ~ **natal** native land. **el P**~ **Vasco** the Basque Country. **los P**~**es Bajos** the Low Countries
**paisa|je** m countryside. ~no a of the same country. ● m compatriot
**paja** f straw; (fig) nonsense
**pajarera** f aviary
**pájaro** m bird. ~ **carpintero** woodpecker

**paje** m page
**Pakistán** m. **el** ~ Pakistan
**pala** f shovel; (laya) spade; (en deportes) bat; (de tenis) racquet
**palabr|a** f word; (habla) speech. ~ota f swear-word. **decir** ~otas swear. **pedir la** ~a ask to speak. **sol-tar** ~otas swear. **tomar la** ~a (begin to) speak
**palacio** m palace; (casa grande) mansion
**paladar** m palate
**paladino** a clear; (público) public
**palanca** f lever; (fig) influence. ~ **de cambio (de velocidades)** gear lever (Brit), gear shift (Amer)
**palangana** f wash-basin
**palco** m (en el teatro) box
**Palestina** f Palestine
**palestino** a & m Palestinian
**palestra** f (fig) arena
**paleta** f (de pintor) palette; (de albañil) trowel
**paleto** m yokel
**paliativo** a & m palliative
**palide|cer** [11] vi turn pale. ~z f paleness
**pálido** a pale
**palillo** m small stick; (de dientes) toothpick
**palique** m. **estar de** ~ be chatting
**paliza** f beating
**palizada** f fence; (recinto) enclosure
**palma** f (de la mano) palm; (árbol) palm (tree); (de dátiles) date palm. ~s fpl applause. ~da f slap. ~das fpl applause. **dar** ~(da)s clap. **tocar las** ~s clap
**palmera** f date palm
**palmo** m span; (fig, pequeña cantidad) small amount. ~ **a** ~ inch by inch
**palmote|ar** vi clap, applaud. ~o m clapping, applause
**palo** m stick; (del teléfono etc) pole; (mango) handle; (de golf) club; (golpe) blow; (de naipes) suit; (mástil) mast
**paloma** f pigeon, dove
**palomitas** fpl popcorn
**palpa|ble** a palpable. ~r vt feel
**palpita|ción** f palpitation. ~nte a throbbing. ~r vi throb; (latir) beat
**palta** f (LAm) avocado pear
**pal|údico** a marshy; (de paludismo) malarial. ~udismo m malaria
**pamp|a** f pampas. ~ear vi (LAm) travel across the pampas. ~ero a of the pampas

**pan** *m* bread; (*barra*) loaf. ~ **integral** wholemeal bread (*Brit*), wholewheat bread (*Amer*). ~ **tostado** toast. ~ **rallado** breadcrumbs. **ganarse el** ~ earn one's living

**pana** *f* corduroy

**panacea** *f* panacea

**panader|ía** *f* bakery; (*tienda*) baker's (shop). ~**o** *m* baker

**panal** *m* honeycomb

**Panamá** *f* Panama

**panameño** *a* & *m* Panamanian

**pancarta** *f* placard

**panda** *m* panda; (*pandilla*) gang

**pander|eta** *f* (small) tambourine. ~**o** *m* tambourine

**pandilla** *f* gang

**panecillo** *m* (bread) roll

**panel** *m* panel

**panfleto** *m* pamphlet

**pánico** *m* panic

**panor|ama** *m* panorama. ~**ámico** *a* panoramic

**panqué** *m* (*LAm*) pancake

**pantaletas** *fpl* (*LAm*) underpants, knickers

**pantal|ón** *m* trousers. ~**ones** *mpl* trousers. ~**ón corto** shorts. ~**ón tejano**, ~**ón vaquero** jeans

**pantalla** *f* screen; (*de lámpara*) (lamp)shade

**pantano** *m* marsh; (*embalse*) reservoir. ~**so** *a* boggy

**pantera** *f* panther

**pantomima** *f* pantomime

**pantorrilla** *f* calf

**pantufla** *f* slipper

**panucho** *m* (*Mex*) stuffed tortilla

**panz|a** *f* belly. ~**ada** *f* (*hartazgo, fam*) bellyful; (*golpe, fam*) blow in the belly. ~**udo** *a* fat, pot-bellied

**pañal** *m* nappy (*Brit*), diaper (*Amer*)

**pañ|ería** *f* draper's (shop). ~**o** *m* material; (*de lana*) woollen cloth; (*trapo*) cloth. ~**o de cocina** dishcloth; (*para secar*) tea towel. ~**o higiénico** sanitary towel. **en** ~**os menores** in one's underclothes

**pañuelo** *m* handkerchief; (*de cabeza*) scarf

**papa** *m* pope. ● *f* (*esp LAm*) potato. ~**s francesas** (*LAm*) chips

**papá** *m* dad(dy). ~**s** *mpl* parents. **P~ Noel** Father Christmas

**papada** *f* (*de persona*) double chin

**papado** *m* papacy

**papagayo** *m* parrot

**papal** *a* papal

**papanatas** *m inv* simpleton

**paparrucha** *f* (*tontería*) silly thing

**papaya** *f* pawpaw

**papel** *m* paper; (*en el teatro etc*) role. ~ **carbón** carbon paper. ~ **celofán** celophane paper. ~ **de calcar** carbon paper. ~ **de embalar**, ~ **de envolver** wrapping paper. ~ **de plata** silver paper. ~ **de seda** tissue paper. ~**era** *f* waste-paper basket. ~**ería** *f* stationer's (shop). ~**eta** *f* ticket; (*para votar*) paper. ~ **higiénico** toilet paper. ~ **pintado** wallpaper. ~ **secante** blotting paper. **blanco como el** ~ as white as a sheet. **desempeñar un** ~, **hacer un** ~ play a role

**paperas** *fpl* mumps

**paquebote** *m* packet (boat)

**paquete** *m* packet; (*paquebote*) packet (boat); (*Mex, asunto difícil*) difficult job. ~ **postal** parcel

**paquistaní** *a* & *m* Pakistani

**par** *a* equal; (*número*) even. ● *m* couple; (*dos cosas iguales*) pair; (*igual*) equal; (*título*) peer. **a la** ~ at the same time; (*monedas*) at par. **al** ~ **que** at the same time. **a** ~**es** two by two. **de** ~ **en** ~ wide open. **sin** ~ without equal

**para** *prep* for; (*hacia*) towards; (*antes del infinitivo*) (in order) to. ~ **con** to(wards). **¿** ~ **qué?** why? ~ **que** so that

**parabienes** *mpl* congratulations

**parábola** *f* (*narración*) parable

**parabrisas** *m inv* windscreen (*Brit*), windshield (*Amer*)

**paraca** *f* (*LAm*) strong wind (from the Pacific)

**paraca|idas** *m inv* parachute. ~**idista** *m* & *f* parachutist; (*mil*) paratrooper

**parachoques** *m inv* bumper (*Brit*), fender (*Amer*); (*rail*) buffer

**parad|a** *f* (*acción*) stopping; (*sitio*) stop; (*de taxis*) rank; (*mil*) parade. ~**ero** *m* whereabouts; (*alojamiento*) lodging. ~**o** *a* stationary; (*obrero*) unemployed; (*lento*) slow. **dejar** ~**o** confuse. **tener mal** ~**ero** come to a sticky end

**paradoja** *f* paradox

**parador** *m* state-owned hotel

**parafina** *f* paraffin

**par|afrasear** *vt* paraphrase. ~**áfrasis** *f inv* paraphrase

**paraguas** *m inv* umbrella

**Paraguay** *m* Paraguay

**paraguayo** *a* & *m* Paraguayan

**paraíso** *m* paradise; (*en el teatro*) gallery

**paralel|a** *f* parallel (line). **~as** *fpl* parallel bars. **~o** *a* & *m* parallel

**par|álisis** *f inv* paralysis. **~alítico** *a* paralytic. **~alizar** [10] *vt* paralyse

**paramilitar** *a* paramilitary

**páramo** *m* barren plain

**parang|ón** *m* comparison. **~onar** *vt* compare

**paraninfo** *m* hall

**paranoi|a** *f* paranoia. **~co** *a* paranoiac

**parapeto** *m* parapet; (*fig*) barricade

**parapléjico** *a* & *m* paraplegic

**parar** *vt/i* stop. **~se** *vpr* stop. **sin ~** continuously

**pararrayos** *m inv* lightning conductor

**parásito** *a* parasitic. **●** *m* parasite

**parasol** *m* parasol

**parcela** *f* plot. **~r** *vt* divide into plots

**parcial** *a* partial. **~idad** *f* prejudice; (*pol*) faction. **a tiempo ~** part-time

**parco** *a* sparing, frugal

**parche** *m* patch

**pardo** *a* brown

**parear** *vt* pair off

**parec|er** *m* opinion; (*aspecto*) appearance. **●** *vi* [11] seem; (*asemejarse*) look like; (*aparecer*) appear. **~erse** *vpr* resemble, look like. **~ido** *a* similar. **●** *m* similarity. **al ~er** apparently. **a mi ~er** in my opinion. **bien ~ido** good-looking. **me ~e** I think. **¿qué te parece?** what do you think? **según ~e** apparently

**pared** *f* wall. **~ón** *m* thick wall; (*de ruinas*) standing wall. **~ por medio** next door. **llevar al ~ón** shoot

**parej|a** *f* pair; (*hombre y mujer*) couple; (*la otra persona*) partner. **~o** *a* alike, the same; (*liso*) smooth

**parente|la** *f* relations. **~sco** *m* relationship

**paréntesis** *m inv* parenthesis; (*signo ortográfico*) bracket. **entre ~** (*fig*) by the way

**paria** *m* & *f* outcast

**paridad** *f* equality

**pariente** *m* & *f* relation, relative

**parihuela** *f*, **parihuelas** *fpl* stretcher

**parir** *vt* give birth to. **●** *vi* have a baby, give birth

**París** *m* Paris

**parisiense** *a* & *m* & *f*, **parisino** *a* & *m* Parisian

**parking** /'parkin/ *m* car park (*Brit*), parking lot (*Amer*)

**parlament|ar** *vi* discuss. **~ario** *a* parliamentary. **●** *m* member of parliament (*Brit*), congressman (*Amer*). **~o** *m* parliament

**parlanchín** *a* talkative. **●** *m* chatterbox

**parmesano** *a* Parmesan

**paro** *m* stoppage; (*desempleo*) unemployment; (*pájaro*) tit

**parodia** *f* parody. **~r** *vt* parody

**parpadear** *vi* blink; ⟨*luz*⟩ flicker; ⟨*estrella*⟩ twinkle

**párpado** *m* eyelid

**parque** *m* park. **~ de atracciones** funfair. **~ infantil** children's playground. **~ zoológico** zoo, zoological gardens

**parqué** *m* parquet

**parquedad** *f* frugality; (*moderación*) moderation

**parra** *f* grapevine

**párrafo** *m* paragraph

**parrilla** *f* grill; (*LAm, auto*) radiator grill. **~da** *f* grill. **a la ~** grilled

**párroco** *m* parish priest

**parroquia** *f* parish; (*iglesia*) parish church. **~no** *m* parishioner; (*cliente*) customer

**parsimoni|a** *f* thrift. **~oso** *a* thrifty

**parte** *m* message; (*informe*) report. **●** *f* part; (*porción*) share; (*lado*) side; (*jurid*) party. **dar ~** report. **de mi ~** for me. **de ~ de** from. **¿de ~ de quién?** (*al teléfono*) who's speaking? **en cualquier ~** anywhere. **en gran ~** largely. **en ~** partly. **en todas ~s** everywhere. **la mayor ~** the majority. **ninguna ~** nowhere. **por otra ~** on the other hand. **por todas ~s** everywhere

**partera** *f* midwife

**partición** *f* sharing out

**participa|ción** *f* participation; (*noticia*) notice; (*de lotería*) lottery ticket. **~nte** *a* participating. **●** *m* & *f* participant. **~r** *vt* notify. **●** *vi* take part

**participio** *m* participle

**partícula** *f* particle

**particular** *a* particular; ⟨*clase*⟩ private. **●** *m* matter. **~idad** *f* peculiarity. **~izar** [10] *vt* distinguish; (*detallar*) give details about. **en ~** in particular. **nada de ~** nothing special

**partida** *f* departure; (*en registro*) entry; (*documento*) certificate; (*juego*) game; (*de gente*) group. **mala ~** dirty trick

**partidario** *a & m* partisan. ~ **de** keen on

**parti|do** *a* divided. ● *m* (*pol*) party; (*encuentro*) match, game; (*equipo*) team. ~**r** *vt* divide; (*romper*) break; (*repartir*) share; crack ⟨*nueces*⟩. ● *vi* leave; (*empezar*) start. ~**rse** *vpr* (*romperse*) break; (*dividirse*) split. **a** ~**r de** (starting) from

**partitura** *f* (*mus*) score

**parto** *m* birth; (*fig*) creation. **estar de** ~ be in labour

**párvulo** *m*. **colegio de** ~**s** nursery school

**pasa** *f* raisin. ~ **de Corinto** currant. ~ **de Esmirna** sultana

**pasa|ble** *a* passable. ~**da** *f* passing; (*de puntos*) row. ~**dero** *a* passable. ~**dizo** *m* passage. ~**do** *a* past; ⟨*día, mes etc*⟩ last; (*anticuado*) old-fashioned; ⟨*comida*⟩ bad, off. ~**do mañana** the day after tomorrow. ~**dor** *m* bolt; (*de pelo*) hair-slide; (*culin*) strainer. **de** ~**da** in passing. **el lunes** ~**do** last Monday

**pasaje** *m* passage; (*naut*) crossing; (*viajeros*) passengers. ~**ro** *a* passing. ● *m* passenger

**pasamano(s)** *m* handrail; (*barandilla de escalera*) banister(s)

**pasamontañas** *m inv* Balaclava (helmet)

**pasaporte** *m* passport

**pasar** *vt* pass; (*poner*) put; (*filtrar*) strain; spend ⟨*tiempo*⟩; (*tragar*) swallow; show ⟨*película*⟩; (*tolerar*) tolerate, overlook; give ⟨*mensaje, enfermedad*⟩. ● *vi* pass; (*suceder*) happen; (*ir*) go; (*venir*) come; ⟨*tiempo*⟩ go by. ~ **de** have no interest in. ~**se** *vpr* pass; (*terminarse*) be over; ⟨*flores*⟩ wither; ⟨*comida*⟩ go bad; spend ⟨*tiempo*⟩; (*excederse*) go too far. ~**lo bien** have a good time. **como si no hubiese pasado nada** as if nothing had happened. **lo que pasa es que** the fact is that. **pase lo que pase** whatever happens. **¡pase Vd!** come in!, go in! **¡que lo pases bien!** have a good time! **¿qué pasa?** what's the matter?, what's happening?

**pasarela** *f* footbridge; (*naut*) gangway

**pasatiempo** *m* hobby, pastime

**pascua** *f* (*fiesta de los hebreos*) Passover; (*de Resurrección*) Easter; (*Navidad*) Christmas. ~**s** *fpl* Christmas. **hacer la** ~ **a uno** mess things up for s.o. **¡y santas** ~**s!** and that's that!

**pase** *m* pass

**pase|ante** *m & f* passer-by. ~**ar** *vt* take for a walk; (*exhibir*) show off. ● *vi* go for a walk; (*en coche etc*) go for a ride. ~**arse** *vpr* go for a walk; (*en coche etc*) go for a ride. ~**o** *m* walk; (*en coche etc*) ride; (*calle*) avenue. ~**o marítimo** promenade. **dar un** ~**o** go for a walk. **¡vete a** ~**o!** (*fam*) go away!, get lost! (*fam*)

**pasillo** *m* passage

**pasión** *f* passion

**pasiv|idad** *f* passiveness. ~**o** *a* passive

**pasm|ar** *vt* astonish. ~**arse** *vpr* be astonished. ~**o** *m* astonishment. ~**oso** *a* astonishing

**paso** *a* ⟨*fruta*⟩ dried ● *m* step; (*acción de pasar*) passing; (*huella*) footprint; (*manera de andar*) walk; (*camino*) way through; (*entre montañas*) pass; (*estrecho*) strait(s). ~ **a nivel** level crossing (*Brit*), grade crossing (*Amer*). ~ **de cebra** Zebra crossing. ~ **de peatones** pedestrian crossing. ~ **elevado** flyover. **a cada** ~ at every turn. **a dos** ~**s** very near. **al** ~ **que** at the same time as. **a** ~ **lento** slowly. **ceda el** ~ give way. **de** ~ in passing. **de** ~ **por** on the way through. **prohibido el** ~ no entry

**pasodoble** *m* (*baile*) pasodoble

**pasota** *m & f* drop-out

**pasta** *f* paste; (*masa*) dough; (*dinero, fam*) money. ~**s** *fpl* pasta; (*pasteles*) pastries. ~ **de dientes**, ~ **dentífrica** toothpaste

**pastar** *vt/i* graze

**pastel** *m* cake; (*empanada*) pie; (*lápiz*) pastel. ~**ería** *f* cakes; (*tienda*) cake shop, confectioner's

**paste(u)rizar** [10] *vt* pasteurize

**pastiche** *m* pastiche

**pastilla** *f* pastille; (*de jabón*) bar; (*de chocolate*) piece

**pastinaca** *f* parsnip

**pasto** *m* pasture; (*hierba*) grass; (*Mex, césped*) lawn. ~**r** *m* shepherd; (*relig*) minister. ~**ral** *a* pastoral

**pata** *f* leg; (*pie*) paw, foot. ~**s arriba** upside down. **a cuatro** ~**s** on all fours. **meter la** ~ put one's foot in it. **tener mala** ~ have bad luck

**pataca** *f* Jerusalem artichoke

**pata|da** *f* kick. ~**lear** *vt* stamp; ⟨*niño pequeño*⟩ kick

**pataplum** *int* crash!

**patata** *f* potato. **~s fritas** chips (*Brit*), French fries (*Amer*). **~s fritas (a la inglesa)** (potato) crisps (*Brit*), potato chips (*Amer*)

**patent|ar** *vt* patent. **~e** *a* obvious. ● *f* licence. **~e de invención** patent

**patern|al** *a* paternal; ⟨cariño etc⟩ fatherly. **~idad** *f* paternity. **~o** *a* paternal; ⟨cariño etc⟩ fatherly

**patético** *a* moving

**patillas** *fpl* sideburns

**patín** *m* skate; (*juguete*) scooter

**pátina** *f* patina

**patina|dero** *m* skating rink. **~dor** *m* skater. **~je** *m* skating. **~r** *vi* skate; (*deslizarse*) slide. **~zo** *m* skid; (*fig, fam*) blunder

**patio** *m* patio. **~ de butacas** stalls (*Brit*), orchestra (*Amer*)

**pato** *m* duck

**patol|ogía** *f* pathology. **~ógico** *a* pathological

**patoso** *a* clumsy

**patraña** *f* hoax

**patria** *f* native land

**patriarca** *m* patriarch

**patrimonio** *m* inheritance; (*fig*) heritage

**patri|ota** *a* patriotic. ● *m & f* patriot. **~ótico** *a* patriotic. **~otismo** *m* patriotism

**patrocin|ar** *vt* sponsor. **~io** *m* sponsorship

**patr|ón** *m* patron; (*jefe*) boss; (*de pensión etc*) landlord; (*modelo*) pattern. **~onato** *m* patronage; (*fundación*) trust, foundation

**patrulla** *f* patrol; (*fig, cuadrilla*) group. **~r** *vt/i* patrol

**paulatinamente** *adv* slowly

**pausa** *f* pause. **~do** *a* slow

**pauta** *f* guideline

**paviment|ar** *vt* pave. **~o** *m* pavement

**pavo** *m* turkey. **~ real** peacock

**pavor** *m* terror. **~oso** *a* terrifying

**payas|ada** *f* buffoonery. **~o** *m* clown

**paz** *f* peace. **La P~** La Paz

**peaje** *m* toll

**peatón** *m* pedestrian

**pebet|a** *f* (*LAm*) little girl. **~e** *m* little boy

**peca** *f* freckle

**peca|do** *m* sin; (*defecto*) fault. **~dor** *m* sinner. **~minoso** *a* sinful. **~r** [7] *vi* sin

**pecoso** *a* freckled

**pectoral** *a* pectoral; (*para la tos*) cough

**peculiar** *a* peculiar, particular. **~idad** *f* peculiarity

**pech|era** *f* front. **~ero** *m* bib. **~o** *m* chest; (*de mujer*) breast; (*fig, corazón*) heart. **~uga** *f* breast. **dar el ~o** breast-feed ⟨a un niño⟩; (*afrontar*) confront. **tomar a ~o** take to heart

**pedagogo** *m* teacher

**pedal** *m* pedal. **~ear** *vi* pedal

**pedante** *a* pedantic

**pedazo** *m* piece, bit. **a ~s** in pieces. **hacer ~s** break to pieces. **hacerse ~s** fall to pieces

**pedernal** *m* flint

**pedestal** *m* pedestal

**pedestre** *a* pedestrian

**pediatra** *m & f* paediatrician

**pedicuro** *m* chiropodist

**pedi|do** *m* order. **~r** [5] *vt* ask (for); (*com, en restaurante*) order. ● *vi* ask. **~r prestado** borrow

**pegadizo** *a* sticky; (*mus*) catchy

**pegajoso** *a* sticky

**pega|r** [12] *vt* stick (on); (*coser*) sew on; give ⟨enfermedad etc⟩; (*juntar*) join; (*golpear*) hit; (*dar*) give. ● *vi* stick. **~rse** *vpr* stick; (*pelearse*) hit each other. **~r fuego** a set fire to. **~tina** *f* sticker

**pein|ado** *m* hairstyle. **~ar** *vt* comb. **~arse** *vpr* comb one's hair. **~e** *m* comb. **~eta** *f* ornamental comb

**p.ej.** *abrev* (*por ejemplo*) e.g., for example

**pela|do** *a* ⟨fruta⟩ peeled; ⟨cabeza⟩ bald; ⟨número⟩ exactly; ⟨terreno⟩ barren. ● *m* bare patch. **~dura** *f* (*acción*) peeling; (*mondadura*) peelings

**pela|je** *m* (*de animal*) fur; (*fig, aspecto*) appearance. **~mbre** *m* (*de animal*) fur; (*de persona*) thick hair

**pelar** *vt* cut the hair; (*mondar*) peel; (*quitar el pellejo*) skin

**peldaño** *m* step; (*de escalera de mano*) rung

**pelea** *f* fight; (*discusión*) quarrel. **~r** *vi* fight. **~rse** *vpr* fight

**peletería** *f* fur shop

**peliagudo** *a* difficult, tricky

**pelícano** *m*, **pelicano** *m* pelican

**película** *f* film (*esp Brit*), movie (*Amer*). **~ de dibujos (animados)** cartoon (film). **~ en colores** colour film

**peligro** *m* danger; (*riesgo*) risk. **~so** *a* dangerous. **poner en ~** endanger

**pelirrojo** *a* red-haired

**pelma** *m & f*, **pelmazo** *m* bore, nuisance

**pel|o** *m* hair; (*de barba o bigote*) whisker. **~ón** *a* bald; (*rapado*) with very short hair. **no tener ~os en la lengua** be outspoken. **tomar el ~o a uno** pull s.o.'s leg

**pelota** *f* ball; (*juego vasco*) pelota. **~ vasca** pelota. **en ~(s)** naked

**pelotera** *f* squabble

**pelotilla** *f*. **hacer la ~ a** ingratiate o.s. with

**peluca** *f* wig

**peludo** *a* hairy

**peluquer|ía** *f* (*de mujer*) hairdresser's; (*de hombre*) barber's. **~o** *m* (*de mujer*) hairdresser; (*de hombre*) barber

**pelusa** *f* down; (*celos, fam*) jealousy

**pelvis** *f* pelvis

**pella** *f* lump

**pelleja** *f*, **pellejo** *m* skin

**pellizc|ar** [7] *vt* pinch. **~o** *m* pinch

**pena** *f* sadness; (*dificultad*) difficulty. **~ de muerte** death penalty. **a duras ~s** with difficulty. **da ~ que** it's a pity that. **me da ~ que** I'm sorry that. **merecer la ~** be worthwhile. **¡qué ~!** what a pity! **valer la ~** be worthwhile

**penacho** *m* tuft; (*fig*) plume

**penal** *a* penal; (*criminal*) criminal. ● *m* prison. **~idad** *f* suffering; (*jurid*) penalty. **~izar** [10] *vt* penalize

**penalty** *m* penalty

**penar** *vt* punish. ● *vi* suffer. **~ por** long for

**pend|er** *vi* hang. **~iente** *a* hanging; ⟨*terreno*⟩ sloping; ⟨*cuenta*⟩ outstanding; (*fig*) ⟨*asunto etc*⟩ pending. ● *m* earring. ● *f* slope

**pendón** *m* banner

**péndulo** *a* hanging. ● *m* pendulum

**pene** *m* penis

**penetra|nte** *a* penetrating; ⟨*sonido*⟩ piercing; ⟨*herida*⟩ deep. **~r** *vt* penetrate; (*fig*) pierce; (*entender*) understand. ● *vi* penetrate; (*entrar*) go into

**penicilina** *f* penicillin

**pen|ínsula** *f* peninsula. **península Ibérica** Iberian Peninsula. **~insular** *a* peninsular

**penique** *m* penny

**peniten|cia** *f* penitence; (*castigo*) penance. **~te** *a & m & f* penitent

**penoso** *a* painful; (*difícil*) difficult

**pensa|do** *a* thought. **~dor** *m* thinker. **~miento** *m* thought. **~r** [1] *vt* think; (*considerar*) consider. ● *vi* think. **~r en** think about. **~tivo** *a* thoughtful. **bien ~do** all things considered. **cuando menos se piensa** when least expected. **menos ~do** least expected. **¡ni ~rlo!** certainly not! **pienso que sí** I think so

**pensi|ón** *f* pension; (*casa de huéspedes*) guest-house. **~ón completa** full board. **~onista** *m & f* pensioner; (*huésped*) lodger; (*escol*) boarder

**pentágono** *m* pentagon

**pentagrama** *m* stave

**Pentecostés** *m* Whitsun; (*fiesta judía*) Pentecost

**penúltimo** *a & m* penultimate, last but one

**penumbra** *f* half-light

**penuria** *f* shortage

**peñ|a** *f* rock; (*de amigos*) group; (*club*) club. **~ón** *m* rock. **el peñón de Gibraltar** The Rock (of Gibraltar)

**peón** *m* labourer; (*en ajedrez*) pawn; (*en damas*) piece; (*juguete*) (spinning) top

**peonía** *f* peony

**peonza** *f* (spinning) top

**peor** *a* (*comparativo*) worse; (*superlativo*) worst. ● *adv* worse. **~ que ~** worse and worse. **lo ~** the worst thing. **tanto ~** so much the worse

**pepin|illo** *m* gherkin. **~o** *m* cucumber. **(no) me importa un ~o** I couldn't care less

**pepita** *f* pip

**pepitoria** *f* fricassee

**pequeñ|ez** *f* smallness; (*minucia*) trifle. **~ito** *a* very small, tiny. **~o** *a* small, little. **de ~o** as a child. **en ~o** in miniature

**pequinés** *m* (*perro*) Pekingese

**pera** *f* (*fruta*) pear. **~l** *m* pear (tree)

**percance** *m* setback

**percatarse** *vpr*. **~ de** notice

**perc|epción** *f* perception. **~eptible** *a* perceptible. **~eptivo** *a* perceptive. **~ibir** *vt* perceive; earn ⟨*dinero*⟩

**percusión** *f* percussion

**percutir** *vt* tap

**percha** *f* hanger; (*de aves*) perch. **de ~** off the peg

**perde|dor** *a* losing. ● *m* loser. **~r** [1] *vt* lose; (*malgastar*) waste; miss ⟨*tren etc*⟩. ● *vi* lose; ⟨*tela*⟩ fade. **~rse** *vpr* get lost; (*desaparecer*) disappear;

(*desperdiciarse*) be wasted; (*estropearse*) be spoilt. **echar(se) a** ~**r** spoil

**pérdida** *f* loss; (*de líquido*) leak; (*de tiempo*) waste

**perdido** *a* lost

**perdiz** *f* partridge

**perd|ón** *m* pardon, forgiveness. ● *int* sorry! ~**onar** *vt* excuse, forgive; (*jurid*) pardon. **¡~one (Vd)!** sorry! **pedir** ~**ón** apologize

**perdura|ble** *a* lasting. ~**r** *vi* last

**perece|dero** *a* perishable. ~**r** [11] *vi* perish

**peregrin|ación** *f* pilgrimage. ~**ar** *vi* go on a pilgrimage; (*fig, fam*) travel. ~**o** *a* strange. ● *m* pilgrim

**perejil** *m* parsley

**perengano** *m* so-and-so

**perenne** *a* everlasting; (*bot*) perennial

**perentorio** *a* peremptory

**perez|a** *f* laziness. ~**oso** *a* lazy

**perfec|ción** *f* perfection. ~**cionamiento** *m* perfection; (*mejora*) improvement. ~**cionar** *vt* perfect; (*mejorar*) improve. ~**cionista** *m & f* perfectionist. ~**tamente** *adv* perfectly. ● *int* of course! ~**to** *a* perfect; (*completo*) complete. **a la** ~**ción** perfectly, to perfection

**perfidia** *f* treachery

**pérfido** *a* treacherous

**perfil** *m* profile; (*contorno*) outline; ~**es** *mpl* (*fig, rasgos*) features. ~**ado** *a* (*bien terminado*) well-finished. ~**ar** *vt* draw in profile; (*fig*) put the finishing touches to

**perfora|ción** *f* perforation. ~**do** *m* perforation. ~**dora** *f* punch. ~**r** *vt* pierce, perforate; punch (*papel, tarjeta etc*)

**perfum|ar** *vt* perfume. ~**arse** *vpr* put perfume on. ~**e** *m* perfume, scent. ~**ería** *f* perfumery

**pergamino** *m* parchment

**pericia** *f* expertise

**pericón** *m* popular Argentinian dance

**perif|eria** *f* (*de población*) outskirts. ~**érico** *a* peripheral

**perilla** *f* (*barba*) goatee

**perímetro** *m* perimeter

**periódico** *a* periodic(al). ● *m* newspaper

**periodis|mo** *m* journalism. ~**ta** *m & f* journalist

**período** *m*, **periodo** *m* period

**periquito** *m* budgerigar

**periscopio** *m* periscope

**perito** *a & m* expert

**perju|dicar** [7] *vt* harm; (*desfavorecer*) not suit. ~**dicial** *a* harmful. ~**icio** *m* harm. **en** ~**icio de** to the detriment of

**perjur|ar** *vi* perjure o.s. ~**io** *m* perjury

**perla** *f* pearl. **de** ~**s** *adv* very well. ● *a* excellent

**permane|cer** [11] *vi* remain. ~**ncia** *f* permanence; (*estancia*) stay. ~**nte** *a* permanent. ● *f* perm

**permeable** *a* permeable

**permi|sible** *a* permissible. ~**sivo** *a* permissive. ~**so** *m* permission; (*documento*) licence; (*mil etc*) leave. ~**so de conducción**, ~**so de conducir** driving licence (*Brit*), driver's license (*Amer*). ~**tir** *vt* allow, permit. ~**tirse** *vpr* be allowed. **con** ~**so** excuse me. **¿me** ~**te?** may I?

**permutación** *f* exchange; (*math*) permutation

**pernicioso** *a* pernicious; (*persona*) wicked

**pernio** *m* hinge

**perno** *m* bolt

**pero** *conj* but. ● *m* fault; (*objeción*) objection

**perogrullada** *f* platitude

**perol** *m* pan

**peronista** *m & f* follower of Juan Perón

**perorar** *vi* make a speech

**perpendicular** *a & f* perpendicular

**perpetrar** *vt* perpetrate

**perpetu|ar** [21] *vt* perpetuate. ~**o** *a* perpetual

**perplej|idad** *f* perplexity. ~**o** *a* perplexed

**perr|a** *f* (*animal*) bitch; (*moneda*) coin, penny (*Brit*), cent (*Amer*); (*rabieta*) tantrum. ~**era** *f* kennel. ~**ería** *f* (*mala jugada*) dirty trick; (*palabra*) harsh word. ~**o** *a* awful. ● *m* dog. ~**o corredor** hound. ~**o de aguas** spaniel. ~**o del hortelano** dog in the manger. ~**o galgo** greyhound. **de** ~**os** awful. **estar sin una** ~**a** be broke

**persa** *a & m & f* Persian

**perse|cución** *f* pursuit; (*tormento*) persecution. ~**guir** [5 & 13] *vt* pursue; (*atormentar*) persecute

**persevera|ncia** *f* perseverance. ~**nte** *a* persevering. ~**r** *vi* persevere

**persiana** *f* (Venetian) blind

**persist|encia** f persistence. **~ente** a persistent. **~ir** vi persist

**person|a** f person. **~as** fpl people. **~aje** m (persona importante) important person; (de obra literaria) character. **~al** a personal; (para una persona) single. • m staff. **~alidad** f personality. **~arse** vpr appear in person. **~ificar** [7] vt personify. **~ificación** f personification

**perspectiva** f perspective

**perspica|cia** f shrewdness; (de vista) keen eye-sight. **~z** a shrewd; (vista) keen

**persua|dir** vt persuade. **~sión** f persuasion. **~sivo** a persuasive

**pertenecer** [11] vi belong

**pertinaz** a persistent

**pertinente** a relevant

**perturba|ción** f disturbance. **~r** vt perturb

**Perú** m. **el ~** Peru

**peruano** a & m Peruvian

**perver|sión** f perversion. **~so** a perverse. • m pervert. **~tir** [4] vt pervert

**pervivir** vi live on

**pesa** f weight. **~dez** f weight; (de cabeza etc) heaviness; (lentitud) sluggishness; (cualidad de fastidioso) tediousness; (cosa fastidiosa) bore, nuisance

**pesadilla** f nightmare

**pesad|o** a heavy; (lento) slow; (duro) hard; (aburrido) boring, tedious. **~umbre** f (pena) sorrow

**pésame** m sympathy, condolences

**pesar** vt/i weigh. • m sorrow; (remordimiento) regret. **a ~ de (que)** in spite of. **me pesa que** I'm sorry that. **pese a (que)** in spite of

**pesario** m pessary

**pesca** f fishing; (peces) fish; (pescado) catch. **~da** f hake. **~dería** f fish shop. **~dilla** f whiting. **~do** m fish. **~dor** a fishing. • m fisherman. **~r** [7] vt catch. • vi fish. **ir de ~** go fishing

**pescuezo** m neck

**pesebre** m manger

**pesero** m (Mex) minibus taxi

**peseta** f peseta; (Mex) twenty-five centavos

**pesimis|mo** m pessimism. **~ta** a pessimistic. • m & f pessimist

**pésimo** a very bad, awful

**peso** m weight; (moneda) peso. **~ bruto** gross weight. **~ neto** net weight. **a ~** by weight. **de ~** influential

**pesquero** a fishing

**pesquisa** f inquiry

**pestañ|a** f eyelash. **~ear** vi blink. **sin ~ear** without batting an eyelid

**pest|e** f plague; (hedor) stench. **~icida** m pesticide. **~ilencia** f pestilence; (hedor) stench

**pestillo** m bolt

**pestiño** m pancake with honey

**petaca** f tobacco case; (LAm, maleta) suitcase

**pétalo** m petal

**petardo** m firework

**petición** f request; (escrito) petition. **a ~ de** at the request of

**petirrojo** m robin

**petrificar** [7] vt petrify

**petr|óleo** m oil. **~olero** a oil. • m oil tanker. **~olífero** a oil-bearing

**petulante** a arrogant

**peyorativo** a pejorative

**pez** f fish; (substancia negruzca) pitch. **~ espada** swordfish

**pezón** m nipple; (bot) stalk

**pezuña** f hoof

**piada** f chirp

**piadoso** a compassionate; (devoto) devout

**pian|ista** m & f pianist. **~o** m piano. **~o de cola** grand piano

**piar** [20] vi chirp

**pib|a** f (LAm) little girl. **~e** m (LAm) little boy

**picad|illo** m mince; (guiso) stew. **~o** a perforated; (carne) minced; (ofendido) offended; (mar) choppy; (diente) bad. **~ura** f bite, sting; (de polilla) moth hole

**picante** a hot; (palabras etc) cutting

**picaporte** m door-handle; (aldaba) knocker

**picar** [7] vt prick, pierce; (ave) peck; (insecto, pez) bite; (avispa) sting; (comer poco) pick at; mince (carne). • vi prick; (ave) peck; (insecto, pez) bite; (sol) scorch; (sabor fuerte) be hot. **~ alto** aim high

**picard|ear** vt corrupt. **~ía** f wickedness; (travesura) naughty thing

**picaresco** a roguish; (literatura) picaresque

**pícaro** a villainous; (niño) mischievous. • m rogue

**picatoste** m toast; (frito) fried bread

**picazón** f itch

**pico** m beak; (punta) corner; (herramienta) pickaxe; (cima) peak.

~**tear** *vt* peck; (*comer, fam*) pick at. **y** ~ (*con tiempo*) a little after; (*con cantidad*) a little more than

**picudo** *a* pointed

**pich|ona** *f* (*fig*) darling; ~**ón** *m* pigeon

**pido** *vb véase* **pedir**

**pie** *m* foot; (*bot, de vaso*) stem. ~ **cuadrado** square foot. **a cuatro** ~**s** on all fours. **al** ~ **de la letra** literally. **a** ~ **on** foot. **a** ~**(s) juntillas** (*fig*) firmly. **buscarle tres** ~**s al gato** split hairs. **de** ~ standing (up). **de** ~**s a cabeza** from head to foot. **en** ~ standing (up). **ponerse de/en** ~ stand up

**piedad** *f* pity; (*relig*) piety

**piedra** *f* stone; (*de mechero*) flint; (*granizo*) hailstone

**piel** *f* skin; (*cuero*) leather. **artículos de** ~ leather goods

**pienso** *vb véase* **pensar**

**pierdo** *vb véase* **perder**

**pierna** *f* leg. **estirar las** ~**s** stretch one's legs

**pieza** *f* piece; (*parte*) part; (*obra teatral*) play; (*moneda*) coin; (*habitación*) room. ~ **de recambio** spare part

**pífano** *m* fife

**pigment|ación** *f* pigmentation. ~**o** *m* pigment

**pigmeo** *a & m* pygmy

**pijama** *m* pyjamas

**pila** *f* (*montón*) pile; (*recipiente*) basin; (*eléctrica*) battery. ~ **bautismal** font

**píldora** *f* pill

**pilot|ar** *vt* pilot. ~**o** *m* pilot

**pilla|je** *m* pillage. ~**r** *vt* pillage; (*alcanzar, agarrar*) catch; (*atropellar*) run over

**pillo** *a* wicked. ● *m* rogue

**pim|entero** *m* (*vasija*) pepper-pot. ~**entón** *m* paprika, cayenne pepper. ~**ienta** *f* pepper. ~**iento** *m* pepper. **grano** *m* **de** ~**ienta** peppercorn

**pináculo** *m* pinnacle

**pinar** *m* pine forest

**pincel** *m* paintbrush. ~**ada** *f* brush-stroke. **la última** ~**ada** (*fig*) the finishing touch

**pinch|ar** *vt* pierce, prick; puncture ⟨*neumático*⟩; (*fig, incitar*) push; (*med, fam*) give an injection to. ~**azo** *m* prick; (*en neumático*) puncture. ~**itos** *mpl* kebab(s); (*tapas*) savoury snacks. ~**o** *m* point

**ping|ajo** *m* rag. ~**o** *m* rag

**ping-pong** *m* table tennis, ping-pong

**pingüino** *m* penguin

**pino** *m* pine (tree)

**pint|a** *f* spot; (*fig, aspecto*) appearance. ~**ada** *f* graffiti. ~**ar** *vt* paint. ~**arse** *vpr* put on make-up. ~**or** *m* painter. ~**or de brocha gorda** painter and decorator. ~**oresco** *a* picturesque. ~**ura** *f* painting. **no** ~**a nada** (*fig*) it doesn't count. **tener** ~**a de** look like

**pinza** *f* (clothes-)peg (*Brit*), (clothes-) pin (*Amer*); (*de cangrejo etc*) claw. ~**s** *fpl* tweezers

**pinzón** *m* chaffinch

**piñ|a** *f* pine cone; (*ananás*) pineapple; (*fig, grupo*) group. ~**ón** *m* (*semilla*) pine nut

**pío** *a* pious; ⟨*caballo*⟩ piebald. ● *m* chirp. **no decir (ni)** ~ not say a word

**piocha** *f* pickaxe

**piojo** *m* louse

**pionero** *m* pioneer

**pipa** *f* pipe; (*semilla*) seed; (*de girasol*) sunflower seed

**pipián** *m* (*LAm*) stew

**pique** *m* resentment; (*rivalidad*) rivalry. **irse a** ~ sink

**piqueta** *f* pickaxe

**piquete** *m* picket

**piragua** *f* canoe

**pirámide** *f* pyramid

**pirata** *m & f* pirate

**Pirineos** *mpl* Pyrenees

**piropo** *m* (*fam*) compliment

**piruet|a** *f* pirouette. ~**ear** *vi* pirouette

**pirulí** *m* lollipop

**pisa|da** *f* footstep; (*huella*) footprint. ~**papeles** *m invar* paperweight. ~**r** *vt* tread on; (*apretar*) press; (*fig*) walk over. ● *vi* tread. **no** ~**r el césped** keep off the grass

**piscina** *f* swimming pool; (*para peces*) fish-pond

**Piscis** *m* Pisces

**piso** *m* floor; (*vivienda*) flat (*Brit*), apartment (*Amer*); (*de zapato*) sole

**pisotear** *vt* trample (on)

**pista** *f* track; (*fig, indicio*) clue. ~ **de aterrizaje** runway. ~ **de baile** dance floor. ~ **de hielo** skating-rink. ~ **de tenis** tennis court

**pistacho** *m* pistachio (nut)

**pisto** *m* fried vegetables

**pistol|a** *f* pistol. ~**era** *f* holster. ~**ero** *m* gunman

**pistón** m piston

**pit|ar** vt whistle at. ● vi blow a whistle; (auto) sound one's horn. ~**ido** m whistle

**pitill|era** f cigarette case. ~**o** m cigarette

**pito** m whistle; (auto) horn

**pitón** m python

**pitorre|arse** vpr. ~**arse de** make fun of. ~**o** m teasing

**pitorro** m spout

**pivote** m pivot

**pizarr|a** f slate; (encerrado) blackboard. ~**ón** m (LAm) blackboard

**pizca** f (fam) tiny piece; (de sal) pinch. **ni** ~ not at all

**pizz|a** f pizza. ~**ería** f pizzeria

**placa** f plate; (conmemorativa) plaque; (distintivo) badge

**pláceme** m congratulations

**place|ntero** a pleasant. ~**r** [32] vt please. **me** ~ I like. ● m pleasure

**plácido** a placid

**plaga** f plague; (fig, calamidad) disaster; (fig, abundancia) glut. ~**r** [12] vt fill

**plagi|ar** vt plagiarize. ~**o** m plagiarism

**plan** m plan; (med) course of treatment. **a todo** ~ on a grand scale. **en** ~ **de** as

**plana** f (llanura) plain; (página) page. **en primera** ~ on the front page

**plancha** f iron; (lámina) sheet. ~**do** m ironing. ~**r** vt/i iron. **a la** ~ grilled. **tirarse una** ~ put one's foot in it

**planeador** m glider

**planear** vt plan. ● vi glide

**planeta** m planet. ~**rio** a planetary. ● m planetarium

**planicie** f plain

**planifica|ción** f planning. ~**r** [7] vt plan

**planilla** f (LAm) list

**plano** a flat. ● m plane; (de ciudad) plan. **primer** ~ foreground; (foto) close-up

**planta** f (anat) sole; (bot, fábrica) plant; (plano) ground plan; (piso) floor. ~ **baja** ground floor (Brit), first floor (Amer)

**planta|ción** f plantation. ~**do** a planted. ~**r** vt plant; deal (golpe). ~**r en la calle** throw out. ~**rse** vpr stand; (fig) stand firm. **bien** ~**do** good-looking

**plantear** vt (exponer) expound; (causar) create; raise (cuestión)

**plantilla** f insole; (modelo) pattern; (personal) personnel

**plaqué** m plate

**plasma** m plasma

**plástico** a & m plastic

**plata** f silver; (fig, dinero, fam) money. ~ **de ley** sterling silver. ~ **alemana** nickel silver

**plataforma** f platform

**plátano** m plane (tree); (fruta) banana; (platanero) banana tree

**platea** f stalls (Brit), orchestra (Amer)

**plateado** a silver-plated; (color de plata) silver

**pl|ática** f chat, talk. ~**aticar** [7] vi chat, talk

**platija** f plaice

**platillo** m saucer; (mus) cymbal. ~ **volante** flying saucer

**platino** m platinum. ~**s** mpl (auto) points

**plato** m plate; (comida) dish; (parte de una comida) course

**platónico** a platonic

**plausible** a plausible; (loable) praiseworthy

**playa** f beach; (fig) seaside

**plaza** f square; (mercado) market; (sitio) place; (empleo) job. ~ **de toros** bullring

**plazco** vb véase **placer**

**plazo** m period; (pago) instalment; (fecha) date. **comprar a** ~**s** buy on hire purchase (Brit), buy on the installment plan (Amer)

**plazuela** f little square

**pleamar** f high tide

**plebe** f common people. ~**yo** a & m plebeian

**plebiscito** m plebiscite

**plectro** m plectrum

**plega|ble** a pliable; (silla etc) folding. ~**r** [1 & 12] vt fold. ~**rse** vpr bend; (fig) give way

**pleito** m (court) case; (fig) dispute

**plenilunio** m full moon

**plen|itud** f fullness; (fig) height. ~**o** a full. **en** ~**o día** in broad daylight. **en** ~**o verano** at the height of the summer

**pleuresía** f pleurisy

**plieg|o** m sheet. ~**ue** m fold; (en ropa) pleat

**plinto** m plinth

**plisar** vt pleat

**plom|ero** *m* (*esp LAm*) plumber. ~o *m* lead; (*elec*) fuse. **de** ~o lead

**pluma** *f* feather; (*para escribir*) pen. ~ **estilográfica** fountain pen. ~**je** *m* plumage

**plúmbeo** *a* leaden

**plum|ero** *m* feather duster; (*para plumas, lapices etc*) pencil-case. ~**ón** *m* down

**plural** *a & m* plural. ~**idad** *f* plurality; (*mayoría*) majority. **en** ~ in the plural

**pluriempleo** *m* having more than one job

**plus** *m* bonus

**pluscuamperfecto** *m* pluperfect

**plusvalía** *f* appreciation

**plut|ocracia** *f* plutocracy. ~**ócrata** *m & f* plutocrat. ~**ocrático** *a* plutocratic

**plutonio** *m* plutonium

**pluvial** *a* rain

**pobla|ción** *f* population; (*ciudad*) city, town; (*pueblo*) village. ~**do** *a* populated. ● *m* village. ~**r** [2] *vt* populate; (*habitar*) inhabit. ~**rse** *vpr* get crowded

**pobre** *a* poor. ● *m & f* poor person; (*fig*) poor thing. **¡**~**cito!** poor (little) thing! **¡**~ **de mí!** poor (old) me! ~**za** *f* poverty

**pocilga** *f* pigsty

**poción** *f* potion

**poco** *a* not much, little; (*en plural*) few; (*unos*) a few. ● *m* (a) little. ● *adv* little, not much; (*con adjetivo*) not very; (*poco tiempo*) not long. ~ **a** ~ little by little, gradually. **a** ~ **de** soon after. **dentro de** ~ soon. **hace** ~ not long ago. **poca cosa** nothing much. **por** ~ (*fam*) nearly

**podar** *vt* prune

**poder** [33] *vi* be able. **no pudo venir** he couldn't come. **¿puedo hacer algo?** can I do anything? **¿puedo pasar?** may I come in? ● *m* power. ~**es** *mpl* **públicos** authorities. ~**oso** *a* powerful. **en el** ~ in power. **no** ~ **con** not be able to cope with; (*no aguantar*) not be able to stand. **no** ~ **más** be exhausted; (*estar harto de algo*) not be able to manage any more. **no** ~ **menos que** not be able to help. **puede que** it is possible that. **puede ser** it is possible. **¿se puede ...?** may I ...?

**podrido** *a* rotten

**po|ema** *m* poem. ~**esía** *f* poetry; (*poema*) poem. ~**eta** *m* poet. ~**ético** *a* poetic

**polaco** *a* Polish. ● *m* Pole; (*lengua*) Polish

**polar** *a* polar. **estrella** ~ polestar

**polarizar** [10] *vt* polarize

**polca** *f* polka

**polea** *f* pulley

**pol|émica** *f* controversy. ~**émico** *a* polemic(al). ~**emizar** [10] *vi* argue

**polen** *m* pollen

**policía** *f* police (force); (*persona*) policewoman. ● *m* policeman. ~**co** *a* police; (*novela etc*) detective

**policlínica** *f* clinic, hospital

**policromo, polícromo** *a* polychrome

**polideportivo** *m* sports centre

**poliéster** *m* polyester

**poliestireno** *m* polystyrene

**polietileno** *m* polythene

**pol|igamia** *f* polygamy. ~**ígamo** *a* polygamous

**polígloto** *m & f* polyglot

**polígono** *m* polygon

**polilla** *f* moth

**polio(mielitis)** *f* polio(myelitis)

**pólipo** *m* polyp

**politécnic|a** *f* polytechnic. ~**o** *a* polytechnic

**polític|a** *f* politics. ~**o** *a* political; ⟨*pariente*⟩ -in-law. ● *m* politician. **padre** *m* ~**o** father-in-law

**póliza** *f* document; (*de seguros*) policy

**polo** *m* pole; (*helado*) ice lolly (*Brit*); (*juego*) polo. ~ **helado** ice lolly (*Brit*). ~ **norte** North Pole

**Polonia** *f* Poland

**poltrona** *f* armchair

**polución** *f* (*contaminación*) pollution

**polv|areda** *f* cloud of dust; (*fig, escándalo*) scandal. ~**era** *f* compact. ~**o** *m* powder; (*suciedad*) dust. ~**os** *mpl* powder. **en** ~**o** powdered. **estar hecho** ~**o** be exhausted. **quitar el** ~**o** dust

**pólvora** *f* gunpowder; (*fuegos artificiales*) fireworks

**polvor|iento** *a* dusty. ~**ón** *m* Spanish Christmas shortcake

**poll|ada** *f* brood. ~**era** *f* (*para niños*) baby-walker; (*LAm, falda*) skirt. ~**ería** *f* poultry shop. ~**o** *m* chicken; (*gallo joven*) chick

**pomada** *f* ointment

**pomelo** *m* grapefruit

**pómez** *a*. **piedra** *f* ~ pumice stone

**pomp|a** *f* bubble; (*esplendor*) pomp. ~**as fúnebres** funeral. ~**oso** *a* pompous; (*espléndido*) splendid

**pómulo** m cheek; (*hueso*) cheekbone

**poncha|do** a (*Mex*) punctured, flat. **~r** vt (*Mex*) puncture

**ponche** m punch

**poncho** m poncho

**ponderar** vt (*alabar*) speak highly of

**poner** [34] vt put; put on ⟨*ropa, obra de teatro, TV etc*⟩; (*suponer*) suppose; lay ⟨*la mesa, un huevo*⟩; (*hacer*) make; (*contribuir*) contribute; give ⟨*nombre*⟩; show ⟨*película, interés*⟩; open ⟨*una tienda*⟩; equip ⟨*una casa*⟩. ● vi lay. **~se** vpr put o.s.; (*volverse*) get; put on ⟨*ropa*⟩; ⟨*sol*⟩ set. **~ con** (*al teléfono*) put through to. **~ en claro** clarify. **~ por escrito** put into writing. **~ una multa** fine. **~se a** start to. **~se a mal con uno** fall out with s.o. **pongamos** let's suppose

**pongo** vb véase **poner**

**poniente** m west; (*viento*) west wind

**pont|ificado** m pontificate. **~ifical** a pontifical. **~ificar** [7] vi pontificate. **~ifice** m pontiff

**pontón** m pontoon

**popa** f stern

**popelín** m poplin

**popul|acho** m masses. **~ar** a popular; ⟨*lenguaje*⟩ colloquial. **~aridad** f popularity. **~arizar** [10] vt popularize. **~oso** a populous

**póquer** m poker

**poquito** m a little bit. ● adv a little

**por** prep for; (*para*) (in order) to; (*a través de*) through; (*a causa de*) because of; (*como agente*) by; (*en matemática*) times; (*como función*) as; (*en lugar de*) instead of. **~ la calle** along the street. **~ mí** as for me, for my part. **~ si** in case. **~ todo el país** throughout the country. **50 kilómetros ~ hora** 50 kilometres per hour

**porcelana** f china

**porcentaje** m percentage

**porcino** a pig. ● m small pig

**porción** f portion; (*de chocolate*) piece

**pordiosero** m beggar

**porf|ía** f persistence; (*disputa*) dispute. **~iado** a persistent. **~iar** [20] vi insist. **a ~ía** in competition

**pormenor** m detail

**pornogr|afía** f pornography. **~áfico** a pornographic

**poro** m pore. **~so** a porous

**poroto** m (*LAm, judía*) bean

**porque** conj because; (*para que*) so that

**porqué** m reason

**porquería** f filth; (*basura*) rubbish; (*grosería*) dirty trick

**porra** f club; (*culin*) fritter

**porrón** m wine jug (with a long spout)

**portaaviones** m invar aircraft-carrier

**portada** f façade; (*de libro*) title page

**portador** m bearer

**porta|equipaje(s)** m invar boot (*Brit*), trunk (*Amer*); (*encima del coche*) roof-rack. **~estandarte** m standard-bearer

**portal** m hall; (*puerta principal*) main entrance; (*soportal*) porch

**porta|lámparas** m invar socket. **~ligas** m invar suspender belt. **~monedas** m invar purse

**portarse** vpr behave

**portátil** a portable

**portavoz** m megaphone; (*fig, persona*) spokesman

**portazgo** m toll

**portazo** m bang. **dar un ~** slam the door

**porte** m transport; (*precio*) carriage. **~ador** m carrier

**portento** m marvel

**porteño** a (*de Buenos Aires*) from Buenos Aires. ● m person from Buenos Aires

**porter|ía** f caretaker's lodge, porter's lodge; (*en deportes*) goal. **~o** m caretaker, porter; (*en deportes*) goalkeeper. **~o automático** intercom (*fam*)

**portezuela** f small door; (*auto*) door

**pórtico** m portico

**portill|a** f gate; (*en barco*) porthole. **~o** m opening

**portorriqueño** a Puerto Rican

**Portugal** m Portugal

**portugués** a & m Portuguese

**porvenir** m future

**posada** f guest house; (*mesón*) inn

**posaderas** fpl (*fam*) bottom

**posar** vt put. ● vi ⟨*pájaro*⟩ perch; ⟨*modelo*⟩ sit. **~se** vpr settle

**posdata** f postscript

**pose|edor** m owner. **~er** [18] vt have, own; (*saber*) know well. **~ído** a possessed. **~sión** f possession. **~sionar** vt. **~sionar de** hand over. **~sionarse** vpr. **~sionarse de** take possession of. **~sivo** a possessive

**posfechar** vt postdate

**posguerra** *f* post-war years
**posib|ilidad** *f* possibility. ~**le** *a* possible. **de ser** ~**le** if possible. **en lo** ~**le** as far as possible. **hacer todo lo** ~**le para** do everything possible to. **si es** ~**le** if possible
**posición** *f* position
**positivo** *a* positive
**poso** *m* sediment
**posponer** [34] *vt* put after; (*diferir*) postpone
**posta** *f*. **a** ~ on purpose
**postal** *a* postal. ● *f* postcard
**poste** *m* pole
**postergar** [12] *vt* pass over; (*diferir*) postpone
**posteri|dad** *f* posterity. ~**or** *a* back; (*ulterior*) later. ~**ormente** *adv* later
**postigo** *m* door; (*contraventana*) shutter
**postizo** *a* false, artificial. ● *m* hairpiece
**postra|do** *a* prostrate. ~**r** *vt* prostrate. ~**rse** *vpr* prostrate o.s.
**postre** *m* dessert, sweet (*Brit*). **de** ~ for dessert
**postular** *vt* postulate; collect ⟨*dinero*⟩
**póstumo** *a* posthumous
**postura** *f* position, stance
**potable** *a* drinkable; ⟨*agua*⟩ drinking
**potaje** *m* vegetable stew
**potasio** *m* potassium
**pote** *m* jar
**poten|cia** *f* power. ~**cial** *a* & *m* potential. ~**te** *a* powerful. **en** ~**cia** potential
**potingue** *m* (*fam*) concoction
**potr|a** *f* filly. ~**o** *m* colt; (*en gimnasia*) horse. **tener** ~**a** be lucky
**pozo** *m* well; (*hoyo seco*) pit; (*de mina*) shaft
**pozole** *m* (*Mex*) stew
**práctica** *f* practice; (*destreza*) skill. **en la** ~ in practice. **poner en** ~ put into practice
**practica|ble** *a* practicable. ~**nte** *m* & *f* nurse. ~**r** [7] *vt* practise; play ⟨*deportes*⟩; (*ejecutar*) carry out
**práctico** *a* practical; (*diestro*) skilled. ● *m* practitioner
**prad|era** *f* meadow; (*terreno grande*) prairie. ~**o** *m* meadow
**pragmático** *a* pragmatic
**preámbulo** *m* preamble
**precario** *a* precarious
**precaución** *f* precaution; (*cautela*) caution. **con** ~ cautiously

**precaver** *vt* guard against
**prece|ncia** *f* precedence; (*prioridad*) priority. ~**nte** *a* preceding. ● *m* precedent. ~**r** *vt/i* precede
**precepto** *m* precept. ~**r** *m* tutor
**precia|do** *a* valuable; (*estimado*) esteemed. ~**rse** *vpr* boast
**precinto** *m* seal
**precio** *m* price. ~ **de venta al público** retail price. **al** ~ **de** at the cost of. **no tener** ~ be priceless. **¿qué** ~ **tiene?** how much is it?
**precios|idad** *f* value; (*cosa preciosa*) beautiful thing. ~**o** *a* precious; (*bonito*) beautiful. **¡es una** ~**idad!** it's beautiful!
**precipicio** *m* precipice
**precipita|ción** *f* precipitation. ~**damente** *adv* hastily. ~**do** *a* hasty. ~**r** *vt* hurl; (*acelerar*) accelerate; (*apresurar*) hasten. ~**rse** *vpr* throw o.s.; (*correr*) rush; (*actuar sin reflexionar*) act rashly
**precis|amente** *a* exactly. ~**ar** *vt* require; (*determinar*) determine. ~**ión** *f* precision; (*necesidad*) need. ~**o** *a* precise; (*necesario*) necessary
**preconcebido** *a* preconceived
**precoz** *a* early; ⟨*niño*⟩ precocious
**precursor** *m* forerunner
**predecesor** *m* predecessor
**predecir** [46]; *o* [46, *pero imperativo* **predice**, *futuro y condicional regulares*] *vt* foretell
**predestina|ción** *f* predestination. ~**r** *vt* predestine
**prédica** *f* sermon
**predicamento** *m* influence
**predicar** [7] *vt/i* preach
**predicción** *f* prediction; (*del tiempo*) forecast
**predilec|ción** *f* predilection. ~**to** *a* favourite
**predisponer** [34] *vt* predispose
**predomin|ante** *a* predominant. ~**ar** *vt* dominate. ● *vi* predominate. ~**io** *m* predominance
**preeminente** *a* pre-eminent
**prefabricado** *a* prefabricated
**prefacio** *m* preface
**prefect|o** *m* prefect. ~**ura** *f* prefecture
**prefer|encia** *f* preference. ~**ente** *a* preferential. ~**ible** *a* preferable. ~**ido** *a* favourite. ~**ir** [4] *vt* prefer. **de** ~**encia** preferably
**prefigurar** *vt* foreshadow
**prefij|ar** *vt* fix beforehand; (*gram*) prefix. ~**o** *m* prefix; (*telefónico*) dialling code

**preg|ón** *m* announcement. **~onar** *vt* announce

**pregunta** *f* question. **~r** *vt/i* ask. **~rse** *vpr* wonder. **hacer ~s** ask questions

**prehistórico** *a* prehistoric

**preju|icio** *m* prejudice. **~zgar** [12] *vt* prejudge

**prelado** *m* prelate

**preliminar** *a* & *m* preliminary

**preludio** *m* prelude

**premarital** *a*, **prematrimonial** *a* premarital

**prematuro** *a* premature

**premedita|ción** *f* premeditation. **~r** *vt* premeditate

**premi|ar** *vt* give a prize to; (*recompensar*) reward. **~o** *m* prize; (*recompensa*) reward; (*com*) premium. **~o gordo** first prize

**premonición** *f* premonition

**premura** *f* urgency; (*falta*) lack

**prenatal** *a* antenatal

**prenda** *f* pledge; (*de vestir*) article of clothing, garment; (*de cama etc*) linen. **~s** *fpl* (*cualidades*) talents; (*juego*) forfeits. **~r** *vt* captivate. **~rse** *vpr* be captivated (**de** by); (*enamorarse*) fall in love (**de** with)

**prender** *vt* capture; (*sujetar*) fasten. ● *vi* catch; (*arraigar*) take root. **~se** *vpr* (*encenderse*) catch fire

**prensa** *f* press. **~r** *vt* press

**preñado** *a* pregnant; (*fig*) full

**preocupa|ción** *f* worry. **~do** *a* worried. **~r** *vt* worry. **~rse** *vpr* worry. **~rse** de look after. **¡no te preocupes!** don't worry!

**prepara|ción** *f* preparation. **~do** *a* prepared. ● *m* preparation. **~r** *vt* prepare. **~rse** *vpr* get ready. **~tivo** *a* preparatory. ● *m* preparation. **~torio** *a* preparatory

**preponderancia** *f* preponderance

**preposición** *f* preposition

**prepotente** *a* powerful; (*fig*) presumptuous

**prerrogativa** *f* prerogative

**presa** *f* (*acción*) capture; (*cosa*) catch; (*embalse*) dam

**presagi|ar** *vt* presage. **~o** *m* omen; (*premonición*) premonition

**présbita** *a* long-sighted

**presb|iteriano** *a* & *m* Presbyterian. **~iterio** *m* presbytery. **~ítero** *m* priest

**prescindir** *vi*. **~ de** do without; (*deshacerse de*) dispense with

**prescri|bir** (*pp* **prescrito**) *vt* prescribe. **~pción** *f* prescription

**presencia** *f* presence; (*aspecto*) appearance. **~r** *vt* be present at; (*ver*) witness. **en ~ de** in the presence of

**presenta|ble** *a* presentable. **~ción** *f* presentation; (*aspecto*) appearance; (*de una persona a otra*) introduction. **~dor** *m* presenter. **~r** *vt* present; (*ofrecer*) offer; (*hacer conocer*) introduce; show (*película*). **~rse** *vpr* present o.s.; (*hacerse conocer*) introduce o.s.; (*aparecer*) turn up

**presente** *a* present; (*este*) this. ● *m* present. **los ~s** those present. **tener ~** remember

**presenti|miento** *m* presentiment; (*de algo malo*) foreboding. **~r** [4] *vt* have a presentiment of

**preserva|ción** *f* preservation. **~r** *vt* preserve. **~tivo** *m* condom

**presiden|cia** *f* presidency; (*de asamblea*) chairmanship. **~cial** *a* presidential. **~ta** *f* (woman) president. **~te** *m* president; (*de asamblea*) chairman. **~te del gobierno** leader of the government, prime minister

**presidi|ario** *m* convict. **~o** *m* prison

**presidir** *vt* preside over

**presilla** *f* fastener

**presi|ón** *f* pressure. **~onar** *vt* press; (*fig*) put pressure on. **a ~ón** under pressure. **hacer ~ón** press

**preso** *a* under arrest; (*fig*) stricken. ● *m* prisoner

**presta|do** *a* (*a uno*) lent; (*de uno*) borrowed. **~mista** *m* & *f* moneylender. **pedir ~do** borrow

**préstamo** *m* loan; (*acción de pedir prestado*) borrowing

**prestar** *vt* lend; give (*ayuda etc*); pay (*atención*). ● *vi* lend

**prestidigita|ción** *f* conjuring. **~dor** *m* magician

**prestigio** *m* prestige. **~so** *a* prestigious

**presu|mido** *a* presumptuous. **~mir** *vt* presume. ● *vi* be conceited. **~nción** *f* presumption. **~nto** *a* presumed. **~ntuoso** *a* presumptuous

**presup|oner** [34] *vt* presuppose. **~uesto** *m* budget

**presuroso** *a* quick

**preten|cioso** *a* pretentious. **~der** *vt* try to; (*afirmar*) claim; (*solicitar*) apply for; (*cortejar*) court. **~dido** *a* so-called. **~diente** *m* pretender; (*a* *una mujer*) suitor. **~sión** *f* pretension; (*aspiración*) aspiration

**pretérito** *m* preterite, past

**pretexto** *m* pretext. **a ~ de** on the pretext of

**prevalec|er** [11] *vi* prevail. **~iente** *a* prevalent

**prevalerse** [42] *vpr* take advantage

**preven|ción** *f* prevention; (*prejuicio*) prejudice. **~ido** *a* ready; (*precavido*) cautious. **~ir** [53] *vt* prepare; (*proveer*) provide; (*precaver*) prevent; (*advertir*) warn. **~tivo** *a* preventive

**prever** [43] *vt* foresee; (*prepararse*) plan

**previo** *a* previous

**previs|ible** *a* predictable. **~ión** *f* forecast; (*prudencia*) prudence. **~ión de tiempo** weather forecast. **~to** *a* foreseen

**prima** *f* (*pariente*) cousin; (*cantidad*) bonus

**primario** *a* primary

**primate** *m* primate; (*fig, persona*) important person

**primavera** *f* spring. **~l** *a* spring

**primer** *a véase* **primero**

**primer|a** *f* (*auto*) first (gear); (*en tren etc*) first class. **~o** *a* (*delante de nombre masculino en singular* **primer**) first; (*principal*) main; (*anterior*) former; (*mejor*) best. ● *n* (the) first. ● *adv* first. **~a enseñanza** primary education. **a ~os de** at the beginning of. **de ~a** first-class

**primitivo** *a* primitive

**primo** *m* cousin; (*fam*) fool. **hacer el ~** be taken for a ride

**primogénito** *a & m* first-born, eldest

**primor** *m* delicacy; (*cosa*) beautiful thing

**primordial** *a* basic

**princesa** *f* princess

**principado** *m* principality

**principal** *a* principal. ● *m* (*jefe*) head, boss (*fam*)

**príncipe** *m* prince

**principi|ante** *m & f* beginner. **~ar** *vt/i* begin, start. **~o** *m* beginning; (*moral, idea*) principle; (*origen*) origin. **al ~o** at first. **a ~o(s) de** at the beginning of. **dar ~o a** a start. **desde el ~o** from the outset. **en ~o** in principle. **~os** *mpl* (*nociones*) rudiments

**pring|oso** *a* greasy. **~ue** *m* dripping; (*mancha*) grease mark

**prior** *m* prior. **~ato** *m* priory

**prioridad** *f* priority

**prisa** *f* hurry, haste. **a ~** quickly. **a toda ~** (*fam*) as quickly as possible. **correr ~** be urgent. **darse ~** hurry (up). **de ~** quickly. **tener ~** be in a hurry

**prisi|ón** *f* prison; (*encarcelamiento*) imprisonment. **~onero** *m* prisoner

**prism|a** *m* prism. **~áticos** *mpl* binoculars

**priva|ción** *f* deprivation. **~do** *a* (*particular*) private. **~r** *vt* deprive (**de** of); (*prohibir*) prevent (**de** from). ● *vi* be popular. **~tivo** *a* exclusive (**de** to)

**privilegi|ado** *a* privileged; (*muy bueno*) exceptional. **~o** *m* privilege

**pro** *prep* for. ● *m* advantage. ● *pref* pro-. **el ~ y el contra** the pros and cons. **en ~ de** on behalf of. **los ~s y los contras** the pros and cons

**proa** *f* bows

**probab|ilidad** *f* probability. **~le** *a* probable, likely. **~lemente** *adv* probably

**proba|dor** *m* fitting-room. **~r** [2] *vt* try; try on ‹*ropa*›; (*demostrar*) prove. ● *vi* try. **~rse** *vpr* try on

**probeta** *f* test-tube

**problem|a** *m* problem. **~ático** *a* problematic

**procaz** *a* insolent

**proced|encia** *f* origin. **~ente** *a* (*razonable*) reasonable. **~ente de** (coming) from. **~er** *m* conduct. ● *vi* proceed. **~er contra** start legal proceedings against. **~er de** come from. **~imiento** *m* procedure; (*sistema*) process; (*jurid*) proceedings

**procesador** *m.* **~ de textos** word processor

**procesal** *a.* **costas ~es** legal costs

**procesamiento** *m* processing. **~ de textos** word-processing.

**procesar** *vt* prosecute

**procesión** *f* procession

**proceso** *m* process; (*jurid*) trial; (*transcurso*) course

**proclama** *f* proclamation. **~ción** *f* proclamation. **~r** *vt* proclaim

**procrea|ción** *f* procreation. **~r** *vt* procreate

**procura|dor** *m* attorney, solicitor. **~r** *vt* try; (*obtener*) get; (*dar*) give

**prodigar** [12] *vt* lavish. **~se** *vpr* do one's best

**prodigio** *m* prodigy; (*milagro*) miracle. ~**ioso** *a* prodigious

**pródigo** *a* prodigal

**produc|ción** *f* production. ~**ir** [47] *vt* produce; (*causar*) cause. ~**irse** *vpr* (*aparecer*) appear; (*suceder*) happen. ~**tivo** *a* productive. ~**to** *m* product. ~**tor** *m* producer. ~**to derivado** by-product. ~**tos agrícolas** farm produce. ~**tos de belleza** cosmetics. ~**tos de consumo** consumer goods

**proeza** *f* exploit

**profan|ación** *f* desecration. ~**ar** *vt* desecrate. ~**o** *a* profane

**profecía** *f* prophecy

**proferir** [4] *vt* utter; hurl (*insultos etc*)

**profes|ar** *vt* profess; practise (*profesión*). ~**ión** *f* profession. ~**ional** *a* professional. ~**or** *m* teacher; (*en universidad etc*) lecturer. ~**orado** *m* teaching profession; (*conjunto de profesores*) staff

**prof|eta** *m* prophet. ~**ético** *a* prophetic. ~**etizar** [10] *vt/i* prophesize

**prófugo** *a* & *m* fugitive

**profund|idad** *f* depth. ~**o** *a* deep; (*fig*) profound

**profus|ión** *f* profusion. ~**o** *a* profuse. **con** ~**ión** profusely

**progenie** *f* progeny

**programa** *m* programme; (*de ordenador*) program; (*de estudios*) curriculum. ~**ción** *f* programming; (*TV etc*) programmes; (*en periódico*) TV guide. ~**r** *vt* programme; program (*ordenador*). ~**dor** *m* computer programmer

**progres|ar** *vi* (make) progress. ~**ión** *f* progression. ~**ista** *a* progressive. ~**ivo** *a* progressive. ~**o** *m* progress. **hacer** ~**os** make progress

**prohibi|ción** *f* prohibition. ~**do** *a* forbidden. ~**r** *vt* forbid. ~**tivo** *a* prohibitive

**prójimo** *m* fellow man

**prole** *f* offspring

**proletari|ado** *m* proletariat. ~**o** *a* & *m* proletarian

**prol|iferación** *f* proliferation. ~**iferar** *vi* proliferate. ~**ífico** *a* prolific

**prolijo** *a* long-winded, extensive

**prólogo** *m* prologue

**prolongar** [12] *vt* prolong; (*alargar*) lengthen. ~**se** *vpr* go on

**promedio** *m* average

**prome|sa** *f* promise. ~**ter** *vt/i* promise. ~**terse** *vpr* (*novios*) get engaged. ~**térselas muy felices** have high hopes. ~**tida** *f* fiancée. ~**tido** *a* promised; (*novios*) engaged. ● *m* fiancé

**prominen|cia** *f* prominence. ~**te** *a* prominent

**promiscu|idad** *f* promiscuity. ~**o** *a* promiscuous

**promoción** *f* promotion

**promontorio** *m* promontory

**promo|tor** *m* promoter. ~**ver** [2] *vt* promote; (*causar*) cause

**promulgar** [12] *vt* promulgate

**pronombre** *m* pronoun

**pron|osticar** [7] *vt* predict. ~**óstico** *m* prediction; (*del tiempo*) forecast; (*med*) prognosis

**pront|itud** *f* quickness. ~**o** *a* quick; (*preparado*) ready. ● *adv* quickly; (*dentro de poco*) soon; (*temprano*) early. ● *m* urge. **al** ~**o** at first. **de** ~**o** suddenly. **por lo** ~**o** for the time being; (*al menos*) anyway. **tan** ~**o como** as soon as

**pronuncia|ción** *f* pronunciation. ~**miento** *m* revolt. ~**r** *vt* pronounce; deliver (*discurso*). ~**rse** *vpr* be pronounced; (*declararse*) declare o.s.; (*sublevarse*) rise up

**propagación** *f* propagation

**propaganda** *f* propaganda; (*anuncios*) advertising

**propagar** [12] *vt/i* propagate. ~**se** *vpr* spread

**propano** *m* propane

**propasarse** *vpr* go too far

**propens|ión** *f* inclination. ~**o** *a* inclined

**propiamente** *adv* exactly

**propici|ar** *vt* (*provocar*) cause, bring about. ~**o** *a* favourable

**propie|dad** *f* property; (*posesión*) possession. ~**tario** *m* owner

**propina** *f* tip

**propio** *a* own; (*característico*) typical; (*natural*) natural; (*apropiado*) proper. **de** ~ on purpose. **el médico** ~ the doctor himself

**proponer** [34] *vt* propose. ~**se** *vpr* propose

**proporci|ón** *f* proportion. ~**onado** *a* proportioned. ~**onal** *a* proportional. ~**onar** *vt* proportion; (*facilitar*) provide

**proposición** *f* proposition

**propósito** *m* intention. **a** ~ (*adrede*) on purpose; (*de paso*) incidentally.

a ~ de with regard to. de ~ on purpose

**propuesta** *f* proposal

**propuls|ar** *vt* propel; *(fig)* promote. ~ión *f* propulsion. ~ión a chorro jet propulsion

**prórroga** *f* extension

**prorrogar** [12] *vt* extend

**prorrumpir** *vi* burst out

**prosa** *f* prose. ~ico *a* prosaic

**proscri|bir** (*pp* proscrito) *vt* banish; *(prohibido)* ban. ~to *a* banned. ● *m* exile; *(persona)* outlaw

**prosecución** *f* continuation

**proseguir** [5 & 13] *vt/i* continue

**prospección** *f* prospecting

**prospecto** *m* prospectus

**prosper|ar** *vi* prosper. ~idad *f* prosperity; *(éxito)* success

**próspero** *a* prosperous. ¡P~ Año Nuevo! Happy New Year!

**prostit|ución** *f* prostitution. ~uta *f* prostitute

**protagonista** *m* & *f* protagonist

**prote|cción** *f* protection. ~ctor *a* protective. ● *m* protector; *(patrocinador)* patron. ~ger [14] *vt* protect. ~gida *f* protegée. ~gido *a* protected. ● *m* protegé

**proteína** *f* protein

**protesta** *f* protest; *(declaración)* protestation

**protestante** *a* & *m* & *f* *(relig)* Protestant

**protestar** *vt/i* protest

**protocolo** *m* protocol

**protuberan|cia** *f* protuberance. ~te *a* protuberant

**provecho** *m* benefit. ¡buen ~! enjoy your meal! de ~ useful. en ~ de to the benefit of. sacar ~ de benefit from

**proveer** [18] *(pp* proveído *y* provisto) *vt* supply, provide

**provenir** [53] *vi* come (de from)

**proverbi|al** *a* proverbial. ~o *m* proverb

**providencia** *f* providence. ~l *a* providential

**provincia** *f* province. ~l *a*, ~no *a* provincial

**provisi|ón** *f* provision; *(medida)* measure. ~onal *a* provisional

**provisto** *a* provided (de with)

**provoca|ción** *f* provocation. ~r [7] *vt* provoke; *(causar)* cause. ~tivo *a* provocative

**próximamente** *adv* soon

**proximidad** *f* proximity

**próximo** *a* next; *(cerca)* near

**proyec|ción** *f* projection. ~tar *vt* hurl; cast *(luz)*; show *(película)*. ~til *m* missile. ~to *m* plan. ~to de ley bill. ~tor *m* projector. en ~to planned

**pruden|cia** *f* prudence. ~nte *a* prudent, sensible

**prueba** *f* proof; *(examen)* test; *(de ropa)* fitting. a ~ on trial. a ~ de proof against. a ~ de agua waterproof. en ~ de in proof of. poner a ~ test

**pruebo** *vb véase* **probar**

**psicoan|álisis** *f* psychoanalysis. ~alista *m* & *f* psychoanalyst. ~alizar [10] *vt* psychoanalyse

**psicodélico** *a* psychedelic

**psic|ología** *f* psychology. ~ológico *a* psychological. ~ólogo *m* psychologist

**psicópata** *m* & *f* psychopath

**psicosis** *f* psychosis

**psique** *f* psyche

**psiqui|atra** *m* & *f* psychiatrist. ~atría *f* psychiatry. ~átrico *a* psychiatric

**psíquico** *a* psychic

**ptas, pts** *abrev (pesetas)* pesetas

**púa** *f* sharp point; *(bot)* thorn; *(de erizo)* quill; *(de peine)* tooth; *(mus)* plectrum

**pubertad** *f* puberty

**publica|ción** *f* publication. ~r [7] *vt* publish; *(anunciar)* announce

**publici|dad** *f* publicity; *(com)* advertising. ~tario *a* advertising

**público** *a* public. ● *m* public; *(de espectáculo etc)* audience. dar al ~ publish

**puchero** *m* cooking pot; *(guisado)* stew. hacer ~s *(fig, fam)* pout

**pude** *vb véase* **poder**

**púdico** *a* modest

**pudiente** *a* rich

**pudín** *m* pudding

**pudor** *m* modesty. ~oso *a* modest

**pudrir** *(pp* podrido) *vt* rot; *(fig, molestar)* annoy. ~se *vpr* rot

**puebl|ecito** *m* small village. ~o *m* town; *(aldea)* village; *(nación)* nation, people

**puedo** *vb véase* **poder**

**puente** *m* bridge; *(fig, fam)* long weekend. ~ colgante suspension bridge. ~ levadizo drawbridge. hacer ~ *(fam)* have a long weekend

**puerco** *a* filthy; *(grosero)* coarse. ● *m* pig. ~ espín porcupine

**pueril** *a* childish

**puerro** *m* leek

**puerta** *f* door; (*en deportes*) goal; (*de ciudad*) gate. ~ **principal** main entrance. **a** ~ **cerrada** behind closed doors

**puerto** *m* port; (*fig, refugio*) refuge; (*entre montañas*) pass. ~ **franco** free port

**Puerto Rico** *m* Puerto Rico

**puertorriqueño** *a & m* Puerto Rican

**pues** *adv* (*entonces*) then; (*bueno*) well. ● *conj* since

**puest|a** *f* setting; (*en juegos*) bet. ~**a de sol** sunset. ~**a en escena** staging. ~**a en marcha** starting. ~**o** *a* put; (*vestido*) dressed. ● *m* place; (*empleo*) position, job; (*en mercado etc*) stall. ● *conj.* ~**o que** since. ~**o de socorro** first aid post

**pugna** *f* fight. ~**r** *vt* fight

**puja** *f* effort; (*en subasta*) bid. ~**r** *vt* struggle; (*en subasta*) bid

**pulcro** *a* neat

**pulga** *f* flea; (*de juego*) tiddly-wink. **tener malas** ~**s** be bad-tempered

**pulga|da** *f* inch. ~**r** *m* thumb; (*del pie*) big toe

**puli|do** *a* neat. ~**mentar** *vt* polish. ~**mento** *m* polishing; (*substancia*) polish. ~**r** *vt* polish; (*suavizar*) smooth

**pulm|ón** *m* lung. ~**onar** *a* pulmonary. ~**onía** *f* pneumonia

**pulpa** *f* pulp

**pulpería** *f* (*LAm*) grocer's shop (*Brit*), grocery store (*Amer*)

**púlpito** *m* pulpit

**pulpo** *m* octopus

**pulque** *m* (*Mex*) pulque, alcoholic Mexican drink

**pulsa|ción** *f* pulsation. ~**dor** *a* pulsating. ● *m* button. ~**r** *vt* (*mus*) play

**pulsera** *f* bracelet; (*de reloj*) strap

**pulso** *m* pulse; (*muñeca*) wrist; (*firmeza*) steady hand; (*fuerza*) strength; (*fig, tacto*) tact. **tomar el** ~ **a uno** take s.o.'s pulse

**pulular** *vi* teem with

**pulveriza|dor** *m* (*de perfume*) atomizer. ~**r** [10] *vt* pulverize; atomize ‹*líquido*›

**pulla** *f* cutting remark

**pum** *int* bang!

**puma** *m* puma

**puna** *f* puna, high plateau

**punitivo** *a* punitive

**punta** *f* point; (*extremo*) tip; (*clavo*) (small) nail. **estar de** ~ be in a bad

mood. **estar de** ~ **con uno** be at odds with s.o. **ponerse de** ~ **con uno** fall out with s.o.. **sacar** ~ **a** sharpen; (*fig*) find fault with

**puntada** *f* stitch

**puntal** *m* prop, support

**puntapié** *m* kick

**puntear** *vt* mark; (*mus*) pluck

**puntera** *f* toe

**puntería** *f* aim; (*destreza*) markmanship

**puntiagudo** *a* sharp, pointed

**puntilla** *f* (*encaje*) lace. **de** ~**s** on tiptoe

**punto** *m* point; (*señal*) dot; (*de examen*) mark; (*lugar*) spot, place; (*de taxis*) stand; (*momento*) moment; (*punto final*) full stop (*Brit*), period (*Amer*); (*puntada*) stitch; (*de tela*) mesh. ~ **de admiración** exclamation mark. ~ **de arranque** starting point. ~ **de exclamación** exclamation mark. ~ **de interrogación** question mark. ~ **de vista** point of view. ~ **final** full stop. ~ **muerto** (*auto*) neutral (gear). ~ **y aparte** full stop, new paragraph (*Brit*), period, new paragraph (*Amer*). ~ **y coma** semicolon. **a** ~ on time; (*listo*) ready. **a** ~ **de** on the point of. **de** ~ knitted. **dos** ~**s** colon. **en** ~ exactly. **hacer** ~ knit. **hasta cierto** ~ to a certain extent

**puntuación** *f* punctuation; (*en deportes, acción*) scoring; (*en deportes, número de puntos*) score

**puntual** *a* punctual; (*exacto*) accurate. ~**idad** *f* punctuality; (*exactitud*) accuracy

**puntuar** [21] *vt* punctuate. ● *vi* score

**punza|da** *f* prick; (*dolor*) pain; (*fig*) pang. ~**nte** *a* sharp. ~**r** [10] *vt* prick

**puñado** *m* handful. **a** ~**s** by the handful

**puñal** *m* dagger. ~**ada** *f* stab

**puñ|etazo** *m* punch. ~**o** *m* fist; (*de ropa*) cuff; (*mango*) handle. **de su** ~**o (y letra)** in his own handwriting

**pupa** *f* spot; (*en los labios*) cold sore. **hacer** ~ hurt. **hacerse** ~ hurt o.s.

**pupila** *f* pupil

**pupitre** *m* desk

**puquío** *m* (*Arg*) spring

**puré** *m* purée; (*sopa*) thick soup. ~ **de patatas** mashed potato

**pureza** *f* purity

**purga** *f* purge. ~**r** [12] *vt* purge. ~**torio** *m* purgatory

**purifica|ción** f purification. **~r** [7] vt purify

**purista** m & f purist

**puritano** a puritanical. ● m puritan

**puro** a pure; ‹cielo› clear; (fig) simple. ● m cigar. **de ~** so. **de pura casualidad** by sheer chance

**púrpura** f purple

**purpúreo** a purple

**pus** m pus

**puse** vb véase **poner**

**pusilánime** a cowardly

**pústula** f spot

**puta** f whore

**putrefacción** f putrefaction

**pútrido** a rotten, putrid

# Q

**que** pron rel ‹personas, sujeto› who; ‹personas, complemento› whom; ‹cosas› which, that. ● conj that. **¡~ tengan Vds buen viaje!** have a good journey! **¡que venga!** let him come! **~ venga o no venga** whether he comes or not. **a que** I bet. **creo que tiene razón** I think (that) he is right. **de ~** from which. **yo ~ tú** if I were you

**qué** a ‹con sustantivo› what; ‹con a o adv› how. ● pron what. **¡~ bonito!** how nice. **¿en ~ piensas?** what are you thinking about?

**quebra|da** f gorge; ‹paso› pass. **~dizo** a fragile. **~do** a broken; (com) bankrupt. ● m (math) fraction. **~dura** f fracture; ‹hondonada› gorge. **~ntar** vt break; ‹debilitar› weaken. **~nto** m ‹pérdida› loss; ‹daño› damage. **~r** [1] vt break. ● vi break; (com) go bankrupt. **~rse** vpr break

**quechua** a & m & f Quechuan

**queda** f curfew

**quedar** vi stay, remain; ‹estar› be; ‹faltar, sobrar› be left. **~ bien** come off well. **~se** vpr stay. **~ con** arrange to meet. **~ en** agree to. **~ en nada** come to nothing. **~ por** (+ infinitivo) remain to be (+ pp)

**quehacer** m job. **~es domésticos** household chores

**quej|a** f complaint; ‹de dolor› moan. **~arse** vpr complain (**de** about); ‹gemir› moan. **~ido** m moan. **~oso** a complaining

**quema|do** a burnt; (fig, fam) bitter. **~dor** m burner. **~dura** f burn. **~r** vt burn; ‹prender fuego a› set fire to. ● vi burn. **~rse** vpr burn o.s.; ‹consumirse› burn up; ‹con el sol› get sunburnt. **~rropa** adv. **a ~rropa** point-blank

**quena** f Indian flute

**quepo** vb véase **caber**

**queque** m (Mex) cake

**querella** f ‹riña› quarrel, dispute; ‹jurid› charge

**quer|er** [35] vt want; ‹amar› love; ‹necesitar› need. **~er decir** mean. **~ido** a dear; ‹amado› loved. ● m darling; ‹amante› lover. **como quiera que** since; ‹de cualquier modo› however. **cuando quiera que** whenever. **donde quiera** wherever. **¿quieres darme ese libro?** would you pass me that book? **quiere llover** it's trying to rain. **¿quieres un helado?** would you like an ice-cream? **quisiera ir a la playa** I'd like to go to the beach. **sin ~er** without meaning to

**queroseno** m kerosene

**querubín** m cherub

**ques|adilla** f cheesecake; (Mex, empanadilla) pie. **~o** m cheese. **~o de bola** Edam cheese

**quiá** int never!, surely not!

**quicio** m frame. **sacar de ~ a uno** infuriate s.o.

**quiebra** f break; (fig) collapse; (com) bankruptcy

**quiebro** m dodge

**quien** pron rel ‹sujeto› who; ‹complemento› whom

**quién** pron interrogativo ‹sujeto› who; ‹tras preposición› whom. **¿de ~?** whose. **¿de ~ son estos libros?** whose are these books?

**quienquiera** pron whoever

**quiero** vb véase **querer**

**quiet|o** a still; ‹inmóvil› motionless; ‹carácter etc› calm. **~ud** f stillness

**quijada** f jaw

**quilate** m carat

**quilla** f keel

**quimera** f (fig) illusion

**químic|a** f chemistry. **~o** a chemical. ● m chemist

**quincalla** f hardware; ‹de adorno› trinket

**quince** a & m fifteen. **~ días** a fortnight. **~na** f fortnight. **~nal** a fortnightly

**quincuagésimo** a fiftieth

**quiniela** *f* pools coupon. **~s** *fpl* (football) pools
**quinientos** *a & m* five hundred
**quinino** *m* quinine
**quinqué** *m* oil-lamp; (*fig, fam*) shrewdness
**quinquenio** *m* (period of) five years
**quinta** *f* (*casa*) villa
**quintaesencia** *f* quintessence
**quintal** *m* a hundred kilograms
**quinteto** *m* quintet
**quinto** *a & m* fifth
**quiosco** *m* kiosk; (*en jardin*) summerhouse; (*en parque etc*) bandstand
**quirúrgico** *a* surgical
**quise** *vb véase* **querer**
**quisque** *pron.* **cada ~** (*fam*) (absolutely) everybody
**quisquill|a** *f* trifle; (*camarón*) shrimp. **~oso** *a* irritable; (*chinchorrero*) fussy
**quita|manchas** *m invar* stain remover. **~nieves** *m invar* snow plough. **~r** *vt* remove, take away; take off ‹*ropa*›; (*robar*) steal. **~ndo** (*a excepción de, fam*) apart from. **~rse** be removed; take off ‹*ropa*›. **~rse de** (*no hacerlo más*) stop. **~rse de en medio** get out of the way. **~sol** *m invar* sunshade
**Quito** *m* Quito
**quizá(s)** *adv* perhaps
**quórum** *m* quorum

# R

**rábano** *m* radish. **~ picante** horseradish. **me importa un ~** I couldn't care less
**rabi|a** *f* rabies; (*fig*) rage. **~ar** *vi* (*de dolor*) be in great pain; (*estar enfadado*) be furious; (*fig, tener ganas, fam*) long. **~ar por algo** long for sth. **~ar por hacer algo** long to do sth. **~eta** *f* tantrum. **dar ~a** infuriate
**rabino** *m* Rabbi
**rabioso** *a* rabid; (*furioso*) furious; ‹*dolor etc*› violent
**rabo** *m* tail
**racial** *a* racial
**racimo** *m* bunch
**raciocinio** *m* reason; (*razonamiento*) reasoning
**ración** *f* share, ration; (*de comida*) portion

**racional** *a* rational. **~izar** [10] *vt* rationalize
**racionar** *vt* (*limitar*) ration; (*repartir*) ration out
**racis|mo** *m* racism. **~ta** *a* racist
**racha** *f* gust of wind; (*fig*) spate
**radar** *m* radar
**radiación** *f* radiation
**radiactiv|idad** *f* radioactivity. **~o** *a* radioactive
**radiador** *m* radiator
**radial** *a* radial
**radiante** *a* radiant
**radical** *a & m & f* radical
**radicar** [7] *vi* (*estar*) be. **~ en** (*fig*) lie in
**radio** *m* radius; (*de rueda*) spoke; (*elemento metálico*) radium. **●** *f* radio
**radioactiv|idad** *f* radioactivity. **~o** *a* radioactive
**radio|difusión** *f* broadcasting. **~emisora** *f* radio station. **~escucha** *m & f* listener
**radiografía** *f* radiography
**radi|ología** *f* radiology. **~ólogo** *m* radiologist
**radioterapia** *f* radiotherapy
**radioyente** *m & f* listener
**raer** [36] *vt* scrape off
**ráfaga** *f* (*de viento*) gust; (*de luz*) flash; (*de ametralladora*) burst
**rafia** *f* raffia
**raído** *a* threadbare
**raigambre** *f* roots; (*fig*) tradition
**raíz** *f* root. **a ~ de** immediately after. **echar raíces** (*fig*) settle
**raja** *f* split; (*culin*) slice. **~r** *vt* split. **~rse** *vpr* split; (*fig*) back out
**rajatabla. a ~** vigorously
**ralea** *f* sort
**ralo** *a* sparse
**ralla|dor** *m* grater. **~r** *vt* grate
**rama** *f* branch. **~je** *m* branches. **~l** *m* branch. **en ~** raw
**rambla** *f* gully; (*avenida*) avenue
**ramera** *f* prostitute
**ramifica|ción** *f* ramification. **~rse** [7] *vpr* branch out
**ramilla** *f* twig
**ramillete** *m* bunch
**ramo** *m* branch; (*de flores*) bouquet
**rampa** *f* ramp, slope
**ramplón** *a* vulgar
**rana** *f* frog. **ancas** *fpl* **de ~** frogs' legs. **no ser ~** not be stupid
**rancio** *a* rancid; ‹*vino*› old; (*fig*) ancient

**ranch|ero** _m_ cook; (_LAm, jefe de rancho_) farmer. **~o** _m_ (_LAm_) ranch, farm

**rango** _m_ rank

**ranúnculo** _m_ buttercup

**ranura** _f_ groove; (_para moneda_) slot

**rapar** _vt_ shave; crop ‹_pelo_›

**rapaz** _a_ rapacious; ‹_ave_› of prey. ● _m_ bird of prey

**rapidez** _f_ speed

**rápido** _a_ fast, quick. ● _adv_ quickly. ● _m_ (_tren_) express. **~s** _mpl_ rapids

**rapiña** _f_ robbery. **ave** _f_ **de ~** bird of prey

**rapsodia** _f_ rhapsody

**rapt|ar** _vt_ kidnap. **~o** _m_ kidnapping; (_de ira etc_) fit; (_éxtasis_) ecstasy

**raqueta** _f_ racquet

**raramente** _adv_ seldom, rarely

**rarefacción** _f_ rarefaction

**rar|eza** _f_ rarity; (_cosa rara_) oddity. **~o** _a_ rare; (_extraño_) odd. **es ~o que** it is strange that. **¡qué ~o!** how strange!

**ras** _m._ **a ~ de** level with

**rasar** _vt_ level; (_rozar_) graze

**rasca|cielos** _m invar_ skyscraper. **~dura** _f_ scratch. **~r** [7] _vt_ scratch; (_raspar_) scrape

**rasgar** [12] _vt_ tear

**rasgo** _m_ stroke. **~s** _mpl_ (_facciones_) features

**rasguear** _vt_ strum; (_fig, escribir_) write

**rasguñ|ar** _vt_ scratch. **~o** _m_ scratch

**raso** _a_ (_llano_) flat; (_liso_) smooth; ‹_cielo_› clear; ‹_cucharada etc_› level; ‹_vuelo etc_› low. ● _m_ satin. **al ~** in the open air. **soldado** _m_ **~** private

**raspa** _f_ (_de pescado_) backbone

**raspa|dura** _f_ scratch; (_acción_) scratching. **~r** _vt_ scratch; (_rozar_) scrape

**rastr|a|r** _vt_ rake. **a ~as** dragging. **~ear** _vt_ track. **~eo** _m_ dragging. **~ero** _a_ creeping; ‹_vuelo_› low. **~illar** _vt_ rake. **~illo** _m_ rake. **~o** _m_ rake; (_huella_) track; (_señal_) sign. **el R~o** the flea market in Madrid. **ni ~o** not a trace

**rata** _f_ rat

**rate|ar** _vt_ steal. **~ría** _f_ pilfering. **~ro** _m_ petty thief

**ratifica|ción** _f_ ratification. **~r** [7] _vt_ ratify

**rato** _m_ moment, short time. **~s libres** spare time. **a ~s** at times. **hace un ~** a moment ago. **¡hasta otro ~!** (_fam_) see you soon! **pasar mal ~** have a rough time

**rat|ón** _m_ mouse. **~onera** _f_ mouse-trap; (_madriguera_) mouse hole

**raud|al** _m_ torrent; (_fig_) floods. **~o** _a_ swift

**raya** _f_ line; (_lista_) stripe; (_de pelo_) parting. **~r** _vt_ rule. ● _vi_ border (**con** on). **a ~s** striped. **pasar de la ~** go too far

**rayo** _m_ ray; (_descarga eléctrica_) lightning. **~s X** X-rays

**raza** _f_ race; (_de animal_) breed. **de ~** ‹_caballo_› thoroughbred; ‹_perro_› pedigree

**raz|ón** _f_ reason. **a ~ón de** at the rate of. **perder la ~ón** go out of one's mind. **tener ~ón** be right. **~onable** _a_ reasonable. **~onamiento** _m_ reasoning. **~onar** _vt_ reason out. ● _vi_ reason

**re** _m_ D; (_solfa_) re

**reac|ción** _f_ reaction. **~cionario** _a_ & _m_ reactionary. **~ción en cadena** chain reaction. **~tor** _m_ reactor; (_avión_) jet

**real** _a_ real; (_de rey etc_) royal. ● _m_ real, old Spanish coin

**realce** _m_ relief; (_fig_) splendour

**realidad** _f_ reality; (_verdad_) truth. **en ~** in fact

**realis|mo** _m_ realism. **~ta** _a_ realistic. ● _m_ & _f_ realist; (_monárquico_) royalist

**realiza|ción** _f_ fulfilment. **~r** [10] _vt_ carry out; make ‹_viaje_›; achieve ‹_meta_›; (_vender_) sell. **~rse** _vpr_ ‹_plan etc_› be carried out; ‹_sueño, predicción etc_› come true; ‹_persona_› fulfil o.s.

**realzar** [10] _vt_ (_fig_) enhance

**reanima|ción** _f_ revival. **~r** _vt_ revive. **~rse** _vpr_ revive

**reanudar** _vt_ resume; renew ‹_amistad_›

**reaparecer** [11] _vi_ reappear

**rearm|ar** _vt_ rearm. **~e** _m_ rearmament

**reavivar** _vt_ revive

**rebaja** _f_ reduction. **~do** _a_ ‹_precio_› reduced. **~r** _vt_ lower. **en ~s** in the sale

**rebanada** _f_ slice

**rebaño** _m_ herd; (_de ovejas_) flock

**rebasar** _vt_ exceed; (_dejar atrás_) leave behind

**rebatir** _vt_ refute

**rebel|arse** _vpr_ rebel. **~de** _a_ rebellious. ● _m_ rebel. **~día** _f_ rebelliousness. **~ión** _f_ rebellion

**reblandecer** [11] _vt_ soften

**rebosa|nte** *a* overflowing. **~r** *vi* overflow; (*abundar*) abound

**rebot|ar** *vt* bounce; (*rechazar*) repel. ● *vi* bounce; (*bala*) ricochet. **~e** *m* bounce, rebound. **de ~e** on the rebound

**rebozar** [10] *vt* wrap up; (*culin*) coat in batter

**rebullir** [22] *vi* stir

**rebusca|do** *a* affected. **~r** [7] *vt* search thoroughly

**rebuznar** *vi* bray

**recabar** *vt* claim

**recado** *m* errand; (*mensaje*) message. **dejar ~** leave a message

**reca|er** [29] *vi* fall back; (*med*) relapse; (*fig*) fall. **~ída** *f* relapse

**recalcar** [7] *vt* squeeze; (*fig*) stress

**recalcitrante** *a* recalcitrant

**recalentar** [1] *vt* (*de nuevo*) reheat; (*demasiado*) overheat

**recamar** *vt* embroider

**recámara** *f* small room; (*de arma de fuego*) chamber; (*LAm, dormitorio*) bedroom

**recambio** *m* change; (*de pluma etc*) refill. **~s** *mpl* spare parts. **de ~** spare

**recapitula|ción** *f* summing up. **~r** *vt* sum up

**recarg|ar** [12] *vt* overload; (*aumentar*) increase; recharge (*batería*). **~o** *m* increase

**recat|ado** *a* modest. **~ar** *vt* hide. **~arse** *vpr* hide o.s. away; (*actuar discretamente*) act discreetly. **~o** *m* prudence; (*modestia*) modesty. **sin ~arse, sin ~o** openly

**recauda|ción** *f* (*cantidad*) takings. **~dor** *m* tax collector. **~r** *vt* collect

**recel|ar** *vt/i* suspect. **~o** *m* distrust; (*temor*) fear. **~oso** *a* suspicious

**recepci|ón** *f* reception. **~onista** *m* & *f* receptionist

**receptáculo** *m* receptacle

**recept|ivo** *a* receptive. **~or** *m* receiver

**recesión** *f* recession

**receta** *f* recipe; (*med*) prescription

**recib|imiento** *m* (*acogida*) welcome. **~ir** *vt* receive; (*acoger*) welcome. ● *vi* entertain. **~irse** *vpr* graduate. **~o** *m* receipt. **acusar ~o** acknowledge receipt

**reci|én** *adv* recently; (*casado, nacido etc*) newly. **~ente** *a* recent; (*culin*) fresh

**recinto** *m* enclosure

**recio** *a* strong; (*voz*) loud. ● *adv* hard; (*en voz alta*) loudly

**recipiente** *m* (*persona*) recipient; (*cosa*) receptacle

**recíproco** *a* reciprocal. **a la recíproca** vice versa

**recita|l** *m* recital; (*de poesías*) reading. **~r** *vt* recite

**reclama|ción** *f* claim; (*queja*) complaint. **~r** *vt* claim. ● *vi* appeal

**reclinar** *vi* lean. **~se** *vpr* lean

**reclu|ir** [17] *vt* shut away. **~sión** *f* seclusion; (*cárcel*) prison. **~so** *m* prisoner

**recluta** *m* recruit. ● *f* recruitment. **~miento** *m* recruitment; (*conjunto de reclutas*) recruits. **~r** *vt* recruit

**recobrar** *vt* recover. **~se** *vpr* recover

**recodo** *m* bend

**recog|er** [14] *vt* collect; pick up (*cosa caída*); (*cosechar*) harvest; (*dar asilo*) shelter. **~erse** *vpr* withdraw; (*ir a casa*) go home; (*acostarse*) go to bed. **~ida** *f* collection; (*cosecha*) harvest. **~ido** *a* withdrawn; (*pequeño*) small

**recolección** *f* harvest

**recomenda|ción** *f* recommendation. **~r** [1] *vt* recommend; (*encomendar*) entrust

**recomenzar** [1 & 10] *vt/i* start again

**recompensa** *f* reward. **~r** *vt* reward

**recomponer** [34] *vt* mend

**reconcilia|ción** *f* reconciliation. **~r** *vt* reconcile. **~rse** *vpr* be reconciled

**recóndito** *a* hidden

**reconoc|er** [11] *vt* recognize; (*admitir*) acknowledge; (*examinar*) examine. **~imiento** *m* recognition; (*admisión*) acknowledgement; (*agradecimiento*) gratitude; (*examen*) examination

**reconozco** *vb véase* **reconocer**

**reconquista** *f* reconquest. **~r** *vt* reconquer; (*fig*) win back

**reconsiderar** *vt* reconsider

**reconstitu|ir** [17] *vt* reconstitute. **~yente** *m* tonic

**reconstru|cción** *f* reconstruction. **~ir** [17] *vt* reconstruct

**récord** /'rekor/ *m* record. **batir un ~** break a record

**recordar** [2] *vt* remember; (*hacer acordar*) remind; (*Lam, despertar*) wake up. ● *vi* remember. **que yo recuerde** as far as I remember. **si mal no recuerdo** if I remember rightly

**recorr|er** vt tour ‹país›; (pasar por) travel through; cover ‹distancia›; (registrar) look over. **~ido** m journey; (itinerario) route

**recort|ado** a jagged. **~ar** vt cut (out). **~e** m cutting (out); (de periódico etc) cutting

**recoser** vt mend

**recostar** [2] vt lean. **~se** vpr lie back

**recoveco** m bend; (rincón) nook

**recre|ación** f recreation. **~ar** vt recreate; (divertir) entertain. **~arse** vpr amuse o.s. **~ativo** a recreational. **~o** m recreation; (escol) break

**recrimina|ción** f recrimination. **~r** vt reproach

**recrudecer** [11] vi increase, worsen, get worse

**recta** f straight line

**rect|angular** a rectangular; ‹triángulo› right-angled. **~ángulo** a rectangular; ‹triángulo› right-angled. ● m rectangle

**rectifica|ción** f rectification. **~r** [7] vt rectify

**rect|itud** f straightness; (fig) honesty. **~o** a straight; (fig, justo) fair; (fig, honrado) honest. ● m rectum. **todo ~o** straight on

**rector** a governing. ● m rector

**recuadro** m (en periódico) box

**recubrir** [pp recubierto] vt cover

**recuerdo** m memory; (regalo) souvenir. ● vb véase **recordar**. **~s** mpl (saludos) regards

**recupera|ción** f recovery. **~r** vt recover. **~rse** vpr recover. **~r el tiempo perdido** make up for lost time

**recur|rir** vi. **~rir a** resort to ‹cosa›; turn to ‹persona›. **~so** m resort; (medio) resource; (jurid) appeal. **~sos** mpl resources

**recusar** vt refuse

**rechaz|ar** [10] vt repel; reflect ‹luz›; (no aceptar) refuse; (negar) deny. **~o** m. **de ~o** on the rebound; (fig) consequently

**rechifla** f booing; (burla) derision

**rechinar** vi squeak; ‹madera etc› creak; ‹dientes› grind

**rechistar** vt murmur. **sin ~** without saying a word

**rechoncho** a stout

**red** f network; (malla) net; (para equipaje) luggage rack; (fig, engaño) trap

**redac|ción** f editing; (conjunto de redactores) editorial staff; (oficina) editorial office; (escol, univ) essay. **~tar** vt write. **~tor** m writer; (de periódico) editor

**redada** f casting; (de policía) raid

**redecilla** f small net; (para el pelo) hairnet

**rededor** m. **al ~, en ~** around

**reden|ción** f redemption. **~tor** a redeeming

**redil** f sheepfold

**redimir** vt redeem

**rédito** m interest

**redoblar** vt redouble; (doblar) bend back

**redoma** f flask

**redomado** a sly

**redond|a** f (de imprenta) roman (type); (mus) semibreve (Brit), whole note (Amer). **~amente** adv (categóricamente) flatly. **~ear** vt round off. **~el** m circle; (de plaza de toros) arena. **~o** a round; (completo) complete. ● m circle. **a la ~a** around. **en ~o** round; (categóricamente) flatly

**reduc|ción** f reduction. **~ido** a reduced; (limitado) limited; (pequeño) small; (precio) low. **~ir** [47] vt reduce. **~irse** vpr be reduced; (fig) amount

**reduje** vb véase **reducir**

**redundan|cia** f redundancy. **~te** a redundant

**reduplicar** [7] vt (aumentar) redouble

**reduzco** vb véase **reducir**

**reedificar** [7] vt reconstruct

**reembols|ar** vt reimburse. **~o** m repayment. **contra ~o** cash on delivery

**reemplaz|ar** [10] vt replace. **~o** m replacement

**reemprender** vt start again

**reenviar** [20] vt, **reexpedir** [5] vt forward

**referencia** f reference; (información) report. **con ~ a** with reference to. **hacer ~ a** refer to

**referéndum** m (pl referéndums) referendum

**referir** [4] vt tell; (remitir) refer. **~se** vpr refer. **por lo que se refiere a** as regards

**refiero** vb véase **referir**

**refilón. de ~** obliquely

**refin|amiento** m refinement. **~ar** vt refine. **~ería** f refinery

**reflector** m reflector; (*proyector*) searchlight

**reflej|ar** vt reflect. ~**o** a reflected; (*med*) reflex. ● m reflection; (*med*) reflex; (*en el pelo*) highlights

**reflexi|ón** f reflection. ~**onar** vi reflect. ~**vo** a (*persona*) thoughtful; (*gram*) reflexive. **con** ~**ón** on reflection. **sin** ~**ón** without thinking

**reflujo** m ebb

**reforma** f reform. ~**s** fpl (*reparaciones*) repairs. ~**r** vt reform. ~**rse** vpr reform

**reforzar** [2 & 10] vt reinforce

**refrac|ción** f refraction. ~**tar** vt refract. ~**tario** a heat-resistant

**refrán** m saying

**refregar** [1 & 12] vt rub

**refrenar** vt rein in (*caballo*); (*fig*) restrain

**refrendar** vt endorse

**refresc|ar** [7] vt refresh; (*enfriar*) cool. ● vi get cooler. ~**arse** vpr refresh o.s.; (*salir*) go out for a walk. ~**o** m cold drink. ~**os** mpl refreshments

**refrigera|ción** f refrigeration; (*aire acondicionado*) air-conditioning. ~**r** vt refrigerate. ~**dor** m, ~**dora** f refrigerator

**refuerzo** m reinforcement

**refugi|ado** m refugee. ~**arse** vpr take refuge. ~**o** m refuge, shelter

**refulgir** [14] vi shine

**refundir** vt (*fig*) revise, rehash

**refunfuñar** vi grumble

**refutar** vt refute

**regadera** f watering-can; (*Mex, ducha*) shower

**regala|damente** adv very well. ~**do** a as a present, free; (*cómodo*) comfortable. ~**r** vt give; (*agasajar*) treat very well. ~**rse** vpr indulge o.s.

**regaliz** m liquorice

**regalo** m present, gift; (*placer*) joy; (*comodidad*) comfort

**regañ|adientes**. **a** ~**adientes** reluctantly. ~**ar** vt scold. ● vi moan; (*dos personas*) quarrel. ~**o** m (*represión*) scolding

**regar** [1 & 12] vt water

**regata** f regatta

**regate** m dodge; (*en deportes*) dribbling. ~**ar** vt haggle over; (*economizar*) economize on. ● vi haggle; (*en deportes*) dribble. ~**o** m haggling; (*en deportes*) dribbling

**regazo** m lap

**regencia** f regency

**regenerar** vt regenerate

**regente** m & f regent; (*director*) manager

**régimen** m (*pl* **regímenes**) rule; (*pol*) regime; (*med*) diet. ~ **alimenticio** diet

**regimiento** m regiment

**regio** a royal

**regi|ón** f region. ~**onal** a regional

**regir** [5 & 14] vt rule; govern (*país*); run (*colegio, empresa*). ● vi apply, be in force

**registr|ado** a registered. ~**ador** m recorder; (*persona*) registrar. ~**ar** vt register; (*grabar*) record; (*examinar*) search. ~**arse** vpr register; (*darse*) be reported. ~**o** m (*acción de registrar*) registration; (*libro*) register; (*cosa anotada*) entry; (*inspección*) search. ~**o civil** (*oficina*) register office

**regla** f ruler; (*norma*) rule; (*menstruación*) period, menstruation. ~**mentación** f regulation. ~**mentar** vt regulate. ~**mentario** a obligatory. ~**mento** m regulations. **en** ~ in order. **por** ~ **general** as a rule

**regocij|ar** vt delight. ~**arse** vpr be delighted. ~**o** m delight. ~**os** mpl festivities

**regode|arse** vpr be delighted. ~**o** m delight

**regordete** a chubby

**regres|ar** vi return. ~**ión** f regression. ~**ivo** a backward. ~**o** m return

**reguer|a** f irrigation ditch. ~**o** m irrigation ditch; (*señal*) trail

**regula|dor** m control. ~**r** a regular; (*mediano*) average; (*no bueno*) so-so. ● vt regulate; (*controlar*) control. ~**ridad** f regularity. **con** ~**ridad** regularly. **por lo** ~**r** as a rule

**rehabilita|ción** f rehabilitation; (*en un empleo etc*) reinstatement. ~**r** vt rehabilitate; (*al empleo etc*) reinstate

**rehacer** [31] vt redo; (*repetir*) repeat; (*reparar*) repair. ~**se** vpr recover

**rehén** m hostage

**rehogar** [12] vt sauté

**rehuir** [17] vt avoid

**rehusar** vt/i refuse

**reimpr|esión** f reprinting. ~**imir** (*pp* **reimpreso**) vt reprint

**reina** f queen. ~**do** m reign. ~**nte** a ruling; (*fig*) prevailing. ~**r** vi reign; (*fig*) prevail

**reincidir** *vi* relapse, repeat an offence

**reino** *m* kingdom. **R~ Unido** United Kingdom

**reinstaurar** *vt* restore

**reintegr|ar** *vt* reinstate ⟨*persona*⟩; refund ⟨*cantidad*⟩. **~arse** *vpr* return. **~o** *m* refund

**reír** [51] *vi* laugh. **~se** *vpr* laugh. **~se de** laugh at. **echarse a ~** burst out laughing

**reivindica|ción** *f* claim. **~r** [7] *vt* claim; (*restaurar*) restore

**rej|a** *f* grille, grating. **~illa** *f* grille, grating; (*red*) luggage rack; (*de mimbre*) wickerwork. **entre ~as** behind bars

**rejuvenecer** [11] *vt/i* rejuvenate. **~se** *vpr* be rejuvenated

**relaci|ón** *f* relation(ship); (*relato*) tale; (*lista*) list. **~onado** *a* concerning. **~onar** *vt* relate (**con** to). **~onarse** *vpr* be connected. **~onado** well-connected. **con ~ón a, en ~ón a** in relation to. **hacer ~ón a** refer to

**relaja|ción** *f* relaxation; (*aflojamiento*) slackening. **~do** *a* loose. **~r** *vt* relax; (*aflojar*) slacken. **~rse** *vpr* relax

**relamerse** *vpr* lick one's lips

**relamido** *a* overdressed

**rel|ámpago** *m* (flash of) lightning. **~ampaguear** *vi* thunder; (*fig*) sparkle

**relatar** *vt* tell, relate

**relativ|idad** *f* relativity. **~o** *a* relative. **en lo ~o a** in relation to

**relato** *m* tale; (*informe*) report

**relegar** [12] *vt* relegate. **~ al olvido** forget about

**relev|ante** *a* outstanding. **~ar** *vt* relieve; (*substituir*) replace. **~o** *m* relief. **carrera** *f* **de ~os** relay race

**relieve** *m* relief; (*fig*) importance. **de ~** important. **poner de ~** emphasize

**religi|ón** *f* religion. **~osa** *f* nun. **~oso** *a* religious. ● *m* monk

**relinch|ar** *vi* neigh. **~o** *m* neigh

**reliquia** *f* relic

**reloj** *m* clock; (*de bolsillo o pulsera*) watch. **~ de caja** grandfather clock. **~ de pulsera** wrist-watch. **~ de sol** sundial. **~ despertador** alarm clock. **~ería** *f* watchmaker's (shop). **~ero** *m* watchmaker

**reluci|ente** *a* shining. **~r** [11] *vi* shine; (*destellar*) sparkle

**relumbrar** *vi* shine

**rellano** *m* landing

**rellen|ar** *vt* refill; (*culin*) stuff; fill in ⟨*formulario*⟩. **~o** *a* full up; (*culin*) stuffed. ● *m* filling; (*culin*) stuffing

**remach|ar** *vt* rivet; (*fig*) drive home. **~e** *m* rivet

**remangar** [12] *vt* roll up

**remanso** *m* pool; (*fig*) haven

**remar** *vi* row

**remat|ado** *a* (*total*) complete; ⟨*niño*⟩ very naughty. **~ar** *vt* finish off; (*agotar*) use up; (*com*) sell off cheap. **~e** *m* end; (*fig*) finishing touch. **de ~e** completely

**remedar** *vt* imitate

**remedi|ar** *vt* remedy; (*ayudar*) help; (*poner fin a*) put a stop to; (*fig, resolver*) solve. **~o** *m* remedy; (*fig*) solution. **como último ~o** as a last resort. **no hay más ~o** there's no other way. **no tener más ~o** have no choice

**remedo** *m* imitation

**rem|endar** [1] *vt* repair. **~iendo** *m* patch; (*fig, mejora*) improvement

**remilg|ado** *a* fussy; (*afectado*) affected. **~o** *m* fussiness; (*afectación*) affectation

**reminiscencia** *f* reminiscence

**remirar** *vt* look again at

**remisión** *f* sending; (*referencia*) reference; (*perdón*) forgiveness

**remiso** *a* remiss

**remit|e** *m* sender's name and address. **~ente** *m* sender. **~ir** *vt* send; (*referir*) refer. ● *vi* diminish

**remo** *m* oar

**remoj|ar** *vt* soak; (*fig, fam*) celebrate. **~o** *m* soaking. **poner a ~o** soak

**remolacha** *f* beetroot. **~ azucarera** sugar beet

**remolcar** [7] *vt* tow

**remolino** *m* swirl; (*de aire etc*) whirl; (*de gente*) throng

**remolque** *m* towing; (*cabo*) towrope; (*vehículo*) trailer. **a ~** on tow. **dar ~ a** tow

**remontar** *vt* mend. **~se** *vpr* soar; (*con tiempo*) go back to

**rémora** *f* (*fig*) hindrance

**remord|er** [2] (*fig*) worry. **~imiento** *m* remorse. **tener ~imientos** feel remorse

**remoto** *a* remote

**remover** [2] *vt* move; stir ⟨*líquido*⟩; turn over ⟨*tierra*⟩; (*quitar*) remove; (*fig, activar*) revive

**remozar** [10] *vt* rejuvenate ⟨*persona*⟩; renovate ⟨*edificio etc*⟩
**remunera|ción** *f* remuneration. **∼r** *vt* remunerate
**renac|er** [11] *vi* be reborn; (*fig*) revive. **∼imiento** *m* rebirth. **R∼** Renaissance
**renacuajo** *m* tadpole; (*fig*) tiddler
**rencilla** *f* quarrel
**rencor** *m* bitterness. **∼oso** *a* (*estar*) resentful; (*ser*) spiteful. **guardar ∼ a** have a grudge against
**rendi|ción** *f* surrender. **∼do** *a* submissive; (*agotado*) exhausted
**rendija** *f* crack
**rendi|miento** *m* efficiency; (*com*) yield. **∼r** [5] *vt* yield; (*vencer*) defeat; (*agotar*) exhaust; pay ⟨*homenaje*⟩. ● *vi* pay; (*producir*) produce. **∼rse** *vpr* surrender
**renega|do** *a* & *m* renegade. **∼r** [1 & 12] *vt* deny. ● *vi* grumble. **∼r de** renounce ⟨*fe etc*⟩; disown ⟨*personas*⟩
**RENFE** *abrev* (*Red Nacional de los Ferrocarriles Españoles*) Spanish National Railways
**renglón** *m* line; (*com*) item. **a ∼ seguido** straight away
**reno** *m* reindeer
**renombr|ado** *a* renowned. **∼e** *m* renown
**renova|ción** *f* renewal; (*de edificio*) renovation; (*de cuarto*) decorating. **∼r** *vt* renew; renovate ⟨*edificio*⟩; decorate ⟨*cuarto*⟩
**rent|a** *f* income; (*alquiler*) rent; (*deuda*) national debt. **∼able** *a* profitable. **∼ar** *vt* produce, yield; (*LAm, alquilar*) rent, hire. **∼a vitalicia** (life) annuity. **∼ista** *m* & *f* person of independent means
**renuncia** *f* renunciation. **∼r** *vi*. **∼r a** renounce, give up
**reñi|do** *a* hard-fought. **∼r** [5 & 22] *vt* tell off. ● *vi* quarrel. **estar ∼do con** be incompatible with ⟨*cosas*⟩; be on bad terms with ⟨*personas*⟩
**reo** *m* & *f* culprit; (*jurid*) accused. **∼ de Estado** person accused of treason. **∼ de muerte** prisoner sentenced to death
**reojo. mirar de ∼** look out of the corner of one's eye at; (*fig*) look askance at
**reorganizar** [10] *vt* reorganize
**repanchigarse** [12] *vpr*, **repantigarse** [12] *vpr* sprawl out
**repar|ación** *f* repair; (*acción*) repairing; (*fig, compensación*) reparation.

**∼ar** *vt* repair; (*fig*) make amends for; (*notar*) notice. ● *vi*. **∼ar en** notice; (*hacer caso de*) pay attention to. **∼o** *m* fault; (*objeción*) objection.
**poner ∼os** raise objections
**repart|ición** *f* division. **∼idor** *m* delivery man. **∼imiento** *m* distribution. **∼ir** *vt* distribute, share out; deliver ⟨*cartas, leche etc*⟩; hand out ⟨*folleto, premio*⟩. **∼o** *m* distribution; (*de cartas, leche etc*) delivery; (*actores*) cast
**repas|ar** *vt* go over; check ⟨*cuenta*⟩; revise ⟨*texto*⟩; (*leer a la ligera*) glance through; (*coser*) mend. ● *vi* go back. **∼o** *m* revision; (*de ropa*) mending. **dar un ∼o** look through
**repatria|ción** *f* repatriation. **∼r** *vt* repatriate
**repecho** *m* steep slope
**repele|nte** *a* repulsive. **∼r** *vt* repel
**repensar** [1] *vt* reconsider
**repent|e. de ∼** suddenly. **∼ino** *a* sudden
**repercu|sión** *f* repercussion. **∼tir** *vi* reverberate; (*fig*) have repercussions (**en** on)
**repertorio** *m* repertoire; (*lista*) index
**repeti|ción** *f* repetition; (*mus*) repeat. **∼damente** *adv* repeatedly. **∼r** [5] *vt* repeat; (*imitar*) copy; ● *vi*. **∼r de** have a second helping of. **¡que se repita!** encore!
**repi|car** [7] *vt* ring ⟨*campanas*⟩. **∼que** *m* peal
**repisa** *f* shelf. **∼ de chimenea** mantlepiece
**repito** *vb véase* **repetir**
**replegarse** [1 & 12] *vpr* withdraw
**repleto** *a* full up
**réplica** *a* answer; (*copia*) replica
**replicar** [7] *vi* answer
**repliegue** *m* crease; (*mil*) withdrawal
**repollo** *m* cabbage
**reponer** [34] *vt* replace; revive ⟨*obra de teatro*⟩; (*contestar*) reply. **∼se** *vpr* recover
**report|aje** *m* report. **∼ero** *m* reporter
**repos|ado** *a* quiet; (*sin prisa*) unhurried. **∼ar** *vi* rest. **∼arse** *vpr* settle. **∼o** *m* rest
**repost|ar** *vt* replenish; refuel ⟨*avión*⟩; fill up ⟨*coche etc*⟩. **∼ería** *f* cake shop
**repren|der** *vt* reprimand. **∼sible** *a* reprehensible

**represalia** _f_ reprisal. **tomar** ~**s** retaliate

**representa|ción** _f_ representation; (_en el teatro_) performance. **en** ~**ción de** representing. ~**nte** _m_ representative; (_actor_) actor. ● _f_ representative; (_actriz_) actress. ~**r** _vt_ represent; perform ⟨_obra de teatro_⟩; play ⟨_papel_⟩; (_aparentar_) look. ~**rse** _vpr_ imagine. ~**tivo** _a_ representative

**represi|ón** _f_ repression. ~**vo** _a_ repressive

**reprimenda** _f_ reprimand

**reprimir** _vt_ supress. ~**se** _vpr_ stop o.s.

**reprobar** [2] _vt_ condemn; reproach ⟨_persona_⟩

**réprobo** _a_ & _m_ reprobate

**reproch|ar** _vt_ reproach. ~**e** _m_ reproach

**reproduc|ción** _f_ reproduction. ~**ir** [47] _vt_ reproduce. ~**tor** _a_ reproductive

**reptil** _m_ reptile

**rep|ública** _f_ republic. ~**ublicano** _a_ & _m_ republican

**repudiar** _vt_ repudiate

**repuesto** _m_ store; (_auto_) spare (part). **de** ~ in reserve

**repugna|ncia** _f_ disgust. ~**nte** _a_ repugnant. ~**r** _vt_ disgust

**repujar** _vt_ emboss

**repuls|a** _f_ rebuff. ~**ión** _f_ repulsion. ~**ivo** _a_ repulsive

**reputa|ción** _f_ reputation. ~**do** _a_ reputable. ~**r** _vt_ consider

**requebrar** [1] _vt_ flatter

**requemar** _vt_ scorch; (_culin_) burn; tan ⟨_piel_⟩

**requeri|miento** _m_ request; (_jurid_) summons. ~**r** [4] _vt_ need; (_pedir_) ask

**requesón** _m_ cottage cheese

**requete...** _pref_ extremely

**requiebro** _m_ compliment

**réquiem** _m_ (_pl_ **réquiems**) _m_ requiem

**requis|a** _f_ inspection; (_mil_) requisition. ~**ar** _vt_ requisition. ~**ito** _m_ requirement

**res** _f_ animal. ~ **lanar** sheep. ~ **vacuna** (_vaca_) cow; (_toro_) bull; (_buey_) ox. **carne de** ~ (_Mex_) beef

**resabido** _a_ well-known; ⟨_persona_⟩ pedantic

**resabio** _m_ (unpleasant) after-taste; (_vicio_) bad habit

**resaca** _f_ undercurrent; (_después de beber alcohol_) hangover

**resaltar** _vi_ stand out. **hacer** ~ emphasize

**resarcir** [9] _vt_ repay; (_compensar_) compensate. ~**se** _vpr_ make up for

**resbal|adizo** _a_ slippery. ~**ar** _vi_ slip; (_auto_) skid; ⟨_líquido_⟩ trickle. ~**arse** _vpr_ slip; (_auto_) skid; ⟨_líquido_⟩ trickle. ~**ón** _m_ slip; (_de vehículo_) skid

**rescat|ar** _vt_ ransom; (_recuperar_) recapture; (_fig_) recover. ~**e** _m_ ransom; (_recuperación_) recapture; (_salvamento_) rescue

**rescindir** _vt_ cancel

**rescoldo** _m_ embers

**resecar** [7] _vt_ dry up; (_med_) remove. ~**se** _vpr_ dry up

**resenti|do** _a_ resentful. ~**miento** _m_ resentment. ~**rse** _vpr_ feel the effects; (_debilitarse_) be weakened; (_ofenderse_) take offence (**de** at)

**reseña** _f_ account; (_en periódico_) report, review. ~**r** _vt_ describe; (_en periódico_) report on, review

**resero** _m_ (_Arg_) herdsman

**reserva** _f_ reservation; (_provisión_) reserve(s). ~**ción** _f_ reservation. ~**do** _a_ reserved. ~**r** _vt_ reserve; (_guardar_) keep, save. ~**rse** _vpr_ save o.s. **a** ~ **de** except for. **a** ~ **de que** unless. **de** ~ in reserve

**resfria|do** _m_ cold; (_enfriamiento_) chill. ~**r** _vt_. ~**r a uno** give s.o. a cold. ~**rse** _vpr_ catch a cold; (_fig_) cool off

**resguard|ar** _vt_ protect. ~**arse** _vpr_ protect o.s.; (_fig_) take care. ~**o** _m_ protection; (_garantía_) guarantee; (_recibo_) receipt

**resid|encia** _f_ residence; (_univ_) hall of residence, dormitory (_Amer_); (_de ancianos etc_) home. ~**encial** _a_ residential. ~**ente** _a_ & _m_ & _f_ resident. ~**ir** _vi_ reside; (_fig_) lie

**residu|al** _a_ residual. ~**o** _m_ remainder. ~**os** _mpl_ waste

**resigna|ción** _f_ resignation. ~**damente** _adv_ with resignation. ~**r** _vt_ resign. ~**rse** _vpr_ resign o.s. (**a**, **con** to)

**resina** _f_ resin

**resist|encia** _f_ resistence. ~**ente** _a_ resistent. ~**ir** _vt_ resist; (_soportar_) bear. ● _vi_ resist. **oponer** ~**encia a** resist

**resma** _f_ ream

**resobado** _a_ trite

**resol|ución** _f_ resolution; (_solución_) solution; (_decisión_) decision. ~**ver**

[2] (*pp* **resuelto**) resolve; solve (*problema etc*). **~verse** *vpr* be solved; (*resultar bien*) work out; (*decidirse*) make up one's mind

**resollar** [2] *vi* breathe heavily. **sin ~** without saying a word

**resona|ncia** *f* resonance. **~nte** *a* resonant; (*fig*) resounding. **~r** [2] *vi* resound. **tener ~ncia** cause a stir

**resopl|ar** *vi* puff; (*por enfado*) snort; (*por cansancio*) pant. **~ido** *m* heavy breathing; (*de enfado*) snort; (*de cansancio*) panting

**resorte** *m* spring. **tocar (todos los) ~s** (*fig*) pull strings

**respald|ar** *vt* back; (*escribir*) endorse. **~arse** *vpr* lean back. **~o** *m* back

**respect|ar** *vi* concern. **~ivo** *a* respective. **~o** *m* respect. **al ~o** on the matter. (**con**) **~o a** as regards. **en/por lo que ~ a** as regards

**respet|able** *a* respectable. **● m** audience. **~ar** *vt* respect. **~o** *m* respect. **~uoso** *a* respectful. **de ~o** best. **faltar al ~o a** be disrespectful to. **hacerse ~ar** command respect

**respingo** *m* start

**respir|ación** *f* breathing; (*med*) respiration; (*ventilación*) ventilation. **~ador** *a* respiratory. **~ar** *vi* breathe; (*fig*) breathe a sigh of relief. **no ~ar** (*no hablar*) not say a word. **~o** *m* breathing; (*fig*) rest

**respland|ecer** [11] *vi* shine. **~eciente** *a* shining. **~or** *m* brilliance; (*de llamas*) glow

**responder** *vi* answer; (*replicar*) answer back; (*fig*) reply, respond. **~ de** answer for

**responsab|ilidad** *f* responsibility. **~le** *a* responsible. **hacerse ~le de** assume responsibilty for

**respuesta** *f* reply, answer

**resquebra|dura** *f* crack. **~jar** *vt* crack. **~jarse** *vpr* crack

**resquemor** *m* (*fig*) uneasiness

**resquicio** *m* crack; (*fig*) possibility

**resta** *f* subtraction

**restablecer** [11] *vt* restore. **~se** *vpr* recover

**restallar** *vi* crack

**restante** *a* remaining. **lo ~** the rest

**restar** *vt* take away; (*substraer*) subtract. **● vi** be left

**restaura|ción** *f* restoration. **~nte** *m* restaurant. **~r** *vt* restore

**restitu|ción** *f* restitution. **~ir** [17] *vt* return; (*restaurar*) restore

**resto** *m* rest, remainder;. (*en matemática*) remainder. **~s** *mpl* remains; (*de comida*) leftovers

**restorán** *m* restaurant

**restregar** [1 & 12] *vt* rub

**restri|cción** *f* restriction. **~ngir** [14] *vt* restrict, limit

**resucitar** *vt* resuscitate; (*fig*) revive. **● vi** return to life

**resuelto** *a* resolute

**resuello** *m* breath; (*respiración*) breathing

**resulta|do** *m* result. **~r** *vi* result; (*salir*) turn out; (*ser*) be; (*ocurrir*) happen; (*costar*) come to

**resum|en** *m* summary. **~ir** *vt* summarize; (*recapitular*) sum up; (*abreviar*) abridge. **en ~en** in short

**resur|gir** [14] *vi* reappear; (*fig*) revive. **~gimiento** *m* resurgence. **~rección** *f* resurrection

**retaguardia** *f* (*mil*) rearguard

**retahíla** *f* string

**retal** *m* remnant

**retama** *f*, **retamo** *m* (*LAm*) broom

**retar** *vt* challenge

**retardar** *vt* slow down; (*demorar*) delay

**retazo** *m* remnant; (*fig*) piece, bit

**retemblar** [1] *vi* shake

**rete...** *pref* extremely

**reten|ción** *f* retention. **~er** [40] *vt* keep; (*en la memoria*) retain; (*no dar*) withhold

**reticencia** *f* insinuation; (*reserva*) reticence, reluctance

**retina** *f* retina

**retintín** *m* ringing. **con ~** (*fig*) sarcastically

**retir|ada** *f* withdrawal. **~ado** *a* secluded; (*jubilado*) retired. **~ar** *vt* move away; (*quitar*) remove; withdraw (*dinero*); (*jubilar*) pension off. **~arse** *vpr* draw back; (*mil*) withdraw; (*jubilarse*) retire; (*acostarse*) go to bed. **~o** *m* retirement; (*pensión*) pension; (*lugar apartado*) retreat

**reto** *m* challenge

**retocar** [7] *vt* retouch

**retoño** *m* shoot

**retoque** *m* (*acción*) retouching; (*efecto*) finishing touch

**retorc|er** [2 & 9] *vt* twist; wring (*ropa*). **~erse** *vpr* get twisted up; (*de dolor*) writhe. **~imiento** *m* twisting; (*de ropa*) wringing

**retóric|a** *f* rhetoric; (*grandilocuencia*) grandiloquence. **~o** *m* rhetorical

**retorn|ar** *vt/i* return. **~o** *m* return

**retortijón** *m* twist; (*de tripas*) stomach cramp

**retoz|ar** [10] *vi* romp, frolic. **~ón** *a* playful

**retractar** *vt* retract. **~se** *vpr* retract

**retra|er** [41] *vt* retract. **~erse** *vpr* withdraw. **~ído** *a* retiring

**retransmitir** *vt* relay

**retras|ado** *a* behind; (*reloj*) slow; (*poco desarrollado*) backward; (*anticuado*) old-fashioned; (*med*) mentally retarded. **~ar** *vt* delay; put back (*reloj*); (*retardar*) slow down. ● *vi* fall behind; (*reloj*) be slow. **~arse** *vpr* be behind; (*reloj*) be slow. **~o** *m* delay; (*poco desarrollo*) backwardness; (*de reloj*) slowness. **~os** *mpl* arrears. **con 5 minutos de ~o** 5 minutes late. **traer ~o** be late

**retrat|ar** *vt* paint a portrait of; (*foto*) photograph; (*fig*) protray. **~ista** *m* & *f* portrait painter. **~o** *m* portrait; (*fig*, *descripción*) description. **ser el vivo ~o de** be the living image of

**retreparse** *vpr* lean back

**retreta** *f* retreat

**retrete** *m* toilet

**retribu|ción** *f* payment. **~ir** [17] *vt* pay

**retroce|der** *vi* move back; (*fig*) back down. **~so** *m* backward movement; (*de arma de fuego*) recoil; (*med*) relapse

**retrógrado** *a* & *m* (*pol*) reactionary

**retropropulsión** *f* jet propulsion

**retrospectivo** *a* retrospective

**retrovisor** *m* rear-view mirror

**retumbar** *vt* echo; (*trueno etc*) boom

**reuma** *m*, **reúma** *m* rheumatism

**reum|ático** *a* rheumatic. **~atismo** *m* rheumatism

**reuni|ón** *f* meeting; (*entre amigos*) reunion. **~r** [23] *vt* join together; (*recoger*) gather (together). **~rse** *vpr* join together; (*personas*) meet

**rev|álida** *f* final exam. **~alidar** *vt* confirm; (*escol*) take an exam in

**revancha** *f* revenge. **tomar la ~** get one's own back

**revela|ción** *f* revelation. **~do** *m* developing. **~dor** *a* revealing. **~r** *vt* reveal; (*foto*) develop

**revent|ar** [1] *vi* burst; (*tener ganas*) be dying to. **~arse** *vpr* burst. **~ón** *m* burst; (*auto*) puncture

**reverbera|ción** *f* (*de luz*) reflection; (*de sonido*) reverberation. **~r** *vi*

(*luz*) be reflected; · (*sonido*) reverberate

**reveren|cia** *f* reverence; (*muestra de respeto*) bow; (*muestra de respeto de mujer*) curtsy. **~ciar** *vt* revere. **~do** *a* respected; (*relig*) reverend. **~te** *a* reverent

**revers|ible** *a* reversible. **~o** *m* reverse

**revertir** [4] *vi* revert

**revés** *m* wrong side; (*desgracia*) misfortune; (*en deportes*) backhand. **al ~** the other way round; (*con lo de arriba abajo*) upside down; (*con lo de dentro fuera*) inside out

**revesti|miento** *m* coating. **~r** [5] *vt* cover; put on (*ropa*); (*fig*) take on

**revis|ar** *vt* check; overhaul (*mecanismo*); service (*coche etc*). **~ión** *f* check(ing); (*inspección*) inspection; (*de coche etc*) service. **~or** *m* inspector

**revist|a** *f* magazine; (*inspección*) inspection; (*artículo*) review; (*espectáculo*) revue. **~ero** *m* critic; (*mueble*) magazine rack. **pasar ~a a** inspect

**revivir** *vi* come to life again

**revocar** [7] *vt* revoke; whitewash (*pared*)

**revolcar** [2 & 7] *vt* knock over. **~se** *vpr* roll

**revolotear** *vi* flutter

**revoltijo** *m*, **revoltillo** *m* mess. **~ de huevos** scrambled eggs

**revoltoso** *a* rebellious; (*niño*) naughty

**revoluci|ón** *f* revolution. **~onar** *vt* revolutionize. **~onario** *a* & *m* revolutionary

**revolver** [2, *pp* **revuelto**] *vt* mix; stir (*líquido*); (*desordenar*) mess up; (*pol*) stir up. **~se** *vpr* turn round. **~se contra** turn on

**revólver** *m* revolver

**revoque** *m* (*con cal*) whitewashing

**revuelo** *m* fluttering; (*fig*) stir

**revuelt|a** *f* turn; (*de calle etc*) bend; (*motín*) revolt; (*conmoción*) disturbance. **~o** *a* mixed up; (*líquido*) cloudy; (*mar*) rough; (*tiempo*) unsettled; (*huevos*) scrambled

**rey** *m* king. **~es** *mpl* king and queen

**reyerta** *f* quarrel

**rezagarse** [12] *vpr* fall behind

**rez|ar** [10] *vt* say. ● *vi* pray; (*decir*) say. **~o** *m* praying; (*oración*) prayer

**rezongar** [12] *vi* grumble

**rezumar** *vt/i* ooze
**ría** *f* estuary
**riachuelo** *m* stream
**riada** *f* flood
**ribera** *f* bank
**ribete** *m* border; (*fig*) embellishment
**ricino** *m*. **aceite de** ~ castor oil
**rico** *a* rich; (*culin*, *fam*) delicious. ● *m* rich person
**rid|ículo** *a* ridiculous. ~**iculizar** [10] *vt* ridicule
**riego** *m* watering; (*irrigación*) irrigation
**riel** *m* rail
**rienda** *f* rein
**riesgo** *m* risk. **a** ~ **de** at the risk of. **correr (el)** ~ **de** run the risk of
**rifa** *f* raffle. ~**r** *vt* raffle. ~**rse** *vpr* (*fam*) quarrel over
**rifle** *m* rifle
**rigidez** *f* rigidity; (*fig*) inflexibility
**rígido** *a* rigid; (*fig*) inflexible
**rig|or** *m* strictness; (*exactitud*) exactness; (*de clima*) severity. ~**uroso** *a* rigorous. **de** ~**or** compulsory. **en** ~**or** strictly speaking
**rima** *f* rhyme. ~**r** *vt/i* rhyme
**rimbombante** *a* resounding; (*lenguaje*) pompous; (*fig*, *ostentoso*) showy
**rimel** *m* mascara
**rincón** *m* corner
**rinoceronte** *m* rhinoceros
**riña** *f* quarrel; (*pelea*) fight
**riñ|ón** *m* kidney. ~**onada** *f* loin; (*guiso*) kidney stew
**río** *m* river; (*fig*) stream. ● *vb véase* **reír**. ~ **abajo** downstream. ~ **arriba** upstream
**rioja** *m* Rioja wine
**riqueza** *f* wealth; (*fig*) richness. ~**s** *fpl* riches
**riquísimo** *a* delicious
**risa** *f* laugh. **desternillarse de** ~ split one's sides laughing. **la** ~ laughter
**risco** *m* cliff
**ris|ible** *a* laughable. ~**otada** *f* guffaw
**ristra** *f* string
**risueño** *a* smiling; (*fig*) happy
**rítmico** *a* rhythmic(al)
**ritmo** *m* rhythm; (*fig*) rate
**rit|o** *m* rite; (*fig*) ritual. ~**ual** *a* & *m* ritual. **de** ~**ual** customary
**rival** *a* & *m* & *f* rival. ~**idad** *f* rivalry. ~**izar** [10] *vi* rival
**riz|ado** *a* curly. ~**ar** [10] *vt* curl; ripple (*agua*). ~**o** *m* curl; (*en agua*) ripple. ~**oso** *a* curly

**róbalo** *m* bass
**robar** *vt* steal (*cosa*); rob (*persona*); (*raptar*) kidnap
**roble** *m* oak (tree)
**roblón** *m* rivet
**robo** *m* theft; (*fig*, *estafa*) robbery
**robot** (*pl* **robots**) *m* robot
**robust|ez** *f* strength. ~**o** *a* strong
**roca** *f* rock
**roce** *m* rubbing; (*toque ligero*) touch; (*señal*) mark; (*fig*, *entre personas*) contact
**rociar** [20] *vt* spray
**rocín** *m* nag
**rocío** *m* dew
**rodaballo** *m* turbot
**rodado** *m* (*Arg*, *vehículo*) vehicle
**rodaja** *f* disc; (*culin*) slice
**roda|je** *m* (*de película*) shooting; (*de coche*) running in. ~**r** [2] *vt* shoot (*película*); run in (*coche*); (*recorrer*) travel. ● *vi* roll; (*coche*) run; (*hacer una película*) shoot
**rode|ar** *vt* surround. ~**arse** *vpr* surround o.s. (**de** with). ~**o** *m* long way round; (*de ganado*) round-up. **andar con** ~**os** beat about the bush. **sin** ~**os** plainly
**rodill|a** *f* knee. ~**era** *f* knee-pad. **de** ~**as** kneeling
**rodillo** *m* roller; (*culin*) rolling-pin
**rododendro** *m* rhododendron
**rodrigón** *m* stake
**roe|dor** *m* rodent. ~**r** [37] *vt* gnaw
**rogar** [2 & 12] *vt/i* ask; (*relig*) pray. **se ruega a los Sres pasajeros...** passengers are requested.... **se ruega no fumar** please do not smoke
**roj|ete** *m* rouge. ~**ez** *f* redness. ~**izo** *a* reddish. ~**o** *a* & *m* red. **ponerse** ~**o** blush
**roll|izo** *a* round; (*persona*) plump. ~**o** *m* roll; (*de cuerda*) coil; (*culin*, *rodillo*) rolling-pin; (*fig*, *pesadez*, *fam*) bore
**romance** *a* Romance. ● *m* Romance language; (*poema*) romance. **hablar en** ~ speak plainly
**rom|ánico** *a* Romanesque; (*lengua*) Romance. ~**ano** *a* & *m* Roman. **a la** ~**ana** (*culin*) (deep-)fried in batter
**rom|anticismo** *m* romanticism. ~**ántico** *a* romantic
**romería** *f* pilgrimage
**romero** *m* rosemary
**romo** *a* blunt; (*nariz*) snub; (*fig*, *torpe*) dull
**rompe|cabezas** *m invar* puzzle; (*con tacos de madera*) jigsaw (puzzle).

⁓**nueces** *m invar* nutcrackers.
⁓**olas** *m invar* breakwater

**romp|er** (*pp* **roto**) *vt* break; break off ⟨*relaciones etc*⟩. ● *vi* break; ⟨*sol*⟩ break through. ⁓**erse** *vpr* break. ⁓**er** a burst out. ⁓**imiento** *m* (*de relaciones etc*) breaking off

**ron** *m* rum

**ronc|ar** [7] *vi* snore. ⁓**o** *a* hoarse

**roncha** *f* lump; (*culin*) slice

**ronda** *f* round; (*patrulla*) patrol; (*carretera*) ring road. ⁓**lla** *f* group of serenaders; (*invención*) story. ⁓**r** *vt/i* patrol

**rondón. de** ⁓ unannounced

**ronquedad** *f*, **ronquera** *f* hoarseness

**ronquido** *m* snore

**ronronear** *vi* purr

**ronzal** *m* halter

**roñ|a** *f* (*suciedad*) grime. ⁓**oso** *a* dirty; (*oxidado*) rusty; (*tacaño*) mean

**rop|a** *f* clothes, clothing. ⁓**a blanca** linen; (*ropa interior*) underwear. ⁓**a de cama** bedclothes. ⁓**a hecha** ready-made clothes. ⁓**a interior** underwear. ⁓**aje** *m* robes; (*excesivo*) heavy clothing. ⁓**ero** *m* wardrobe

**ros|a** *a invar* pink. ● *f* rose; (*color*) pink. ⁓**áceo** *a* pink. ⁓**ado** *a* rosy. ● *m* (*vino*) rosé. ⁓**al** *m* rose-bush

**rosario** *m* rosary; (*fig*) series

**rosbif** *m* roast beef

**rosc|a** *f* coil; (*de tornillo*) thread; (*de pan*) roll. ⁓**o** *m* roll

**rosetón** *m* rosette

**rosquilla** *f* doughnut; (*oruga*) grub

**rostro** *m* face

**rota|ción** *f* rotation. ⁓**tivo** *a* rotary

**roto** *a* broken

**rótula** *f* kneecap

**rotulador** *m* felt-tip pen

**rótulo** *m* sign; (*etiqueta*) label

**rotundo** *a* emphatic

**rotura** *f* break

**roturar** *vt* plough

**roza** *f* groove. ⁓**dura** *f* scratch

**rozagante** *a* showy

**rozar** [10] *vt* rub against; (*ligeramente*) brush against; (*ensuciar*) dirty; (*fig*) touch on. ⁓**se** *vpr* rub; (*con otras personas*) mix

**Rte.** *abrev* (*Remite(nte)*) sender

**rúa** *f* (small) street

**rubéola** *f* German measles

**rubí** *m* ruby

**rubicundo** *a* ruddy

**rubio** *a* ⟨*pelo*⟩ fair; ⟨*persona*⟩ fair-haired; ⟨*tabaco*⟩ Virginian

**rubor** *m* blush; (*fig*) shame. ⁓**izado** *a* blushing; (*fig*) ashamed. ⁓**izar** [10] *vt* make blush. ⁓**izarse** *vpr* blush

**rúbrica** *f* red mark; (*de firma*) flourish; (*título*) heading

**rudeza** *f* roughness

**rudiment|al** *a* rudimentary. ⁓**os** *mpl* rudiments

**rudo** *a* rough; (*sencillo*) simple

**rueda** *f* wheel; (*de mueble*) castor; (*de personas*) ring; (*culin*) slice. ⁓ **de prensa** press conference

**ruedo** *m* edge; (*redondel*) arena

**ruego** *m* request; (*súplica*) entreaty. ● *vb véase* **rogar**

**rufi|án** *m* pimp; (*granuja*) villain. ⁓**anesco** *a* roguish

**rugby** *m* Rugby

**rugi|do** *m* roar. ⁓**r** [14] *vi* roar

**ruibarbo** *m* rhubarb

**ruido** *m* noise; (*alboroto*) din; (*escándalo*) commotion. ⁓**so** *a* noisy; (*fig*) sensational

**ruin** *a* despicable; (*tacaño*) mean

**ruina** *f* ruin; (*colapso*) collapse

**ruindad** *f* meanness

**ruinoso** *a* ruinous

**ruiseñor** *m* nightingale

**ruleta** *f* roulette

**rulo** *m* (*culin*) rolling-pin; (*del pelo*) curler

**Rumania** *f* Romania

**rumano** *a & m* Romanian

**rumba** *f* rumba

**rumbo** *m* direction; (*fig*) course; (*fig, generosidad*) lavishness. ⁓**so** *a* lavish. **con** ⁓ **a** in the direction of. **hacer** ⁓ **a** head for

**rumia|nte** *a & m* ruminant. ⁓**r** *vt* chew; (*fig*) chew over. ● *vi* ruminate

**rumor** *m* rumour; (*ruido*) murmur. ⁓**earse** *vpr* be rumoured. ⁓**oso** *a* murmuring

**runr|ún** *m* rumour; (*ruido*) murmur. ⁓**unearse** *vpr* be rumoured

**ruptura** *f* break; (*de relaciones etc*) breaking off

**rural** *a* rural

**Rusia** *f* Russia

**ruso** *a & m* Russian

**rústico** *a* rural; (*de carácter*) coarse. **en rústica** paperback

**ruta** *f* route; (*camino*) road; (*fig*) course

**rutilante** *a* shining

**rutina** *f* routine. ⁓**rio** *a* routine

# S

**S.A.** *abrev* (*Sociedad Anónima*) Ltd, Limited, plc, Public Limited Company

**sábado** *m* Saturday

**sabana** *f* (*esp LAm*) savannah

**sábana** *f* sheet

**sabandija** *f* bug

**sabañón** *m* chilblain

**sabático** *a* sabbatical

**sab|elotodo** *m & f invar* know-all (*fam*). **~er** [38] *vt* know; (*ser capaz de*) be able to, know how to; (*enterarse de*) learn. ● *vi*. **~er a** taste of. **~er** *m* knowledge. **~ido** *a* well-known. **~iduría** *f* wisdom; (*conocimientos*) knowledge. **a ~er si** I wonder if. **¡haberlo ~ido!** if only I'd known! **hacer ~er** let know. **no sé cuántos** what's-his-name. **para que lo sepas** let me tell you. **¡qué sé yo!** how should I know? **que yo sepa** as far as I know. **¿~es nadar?** can you swim? **un no sé qué** a certain sth. **¡yo qué sé!** how should I know?

**sabiendas. a ~** knowingly; (*a propósito*) on purpose

**sabio** *a* learned; (*prudente*) wise

**sabor** *m* taste, flavour; (*fig*) flavour. **~ear** *vt* taste; (*fig*) savour

**sabot|aje** *m* sabotage. **~eador** *m* saboteur. **~ear** *vt* sabotage

**sabroso** *a* tasty; (*fig, substancioso*) meaty

**sabueso** *m* (*perro*) bloodhound; (*fig, detective*) detective

**saca|corchos** *m invar* corkscrew. **~puntas** *m invar* pencil-sharpener

**sacar** [7] *vt* take out; put out (*parte del cuerpo*); (*quitar*) remove; take (*foto*); win (*premio*); get (*billete, entrada etc*); withdraw (*dinero*); reach (*solución*); draw (*conclusión*); make (*copia*). **~ adelante** bring up (*niño*); carry on (*negocio*)

**sacarina** *f* saccharin

**sacerdo|cio** *m* priesthood. **~tal** *a* priestly. **~te** *m* priest

**saciar** *vt* satisfy

**saco** *m* bag; (*anat*) sac; (*LAm, chaqueta*) jacket; (*de mentiras*) pack. **~ de dormir** sleeping-bag

**sacramento** *m* sacrament

**sacrific|ar** [7] *vt* sacrifice. **~arse** *vpr* sacrifice o.s. **~io** *m* sacrifice

**sacr|ilegio** *m* sacrilege. **~ílego** *a* sacrilegious

**sacro** *a* sacred, holy. **~santo** *a* sacrosanct

**sacudi|da** *f* shake; (*movimiento brusco*) jolt, jerk; (*fig*) shock. **~da eléctrica** electric shock. **~r** *vt* shake; (*golpear*) beat; (*ahuyentar*) chase away. **~rse** *vpr* shake off; (*fig*) get rid of

**sádico** *a* sadistic. ● *m* sadist

**sadismo** *m* sadism

**saeta** *f* arrow; (*de reloj*) hand

**safari** *m* safari

**sagaz** *a* shrewd

**Sagitario** *m* Sagittarius

**sagrado** *a* sacred, holy. ● *m* sanctuary

**Sahara** *m*, **Sáhara** /'saxara/ *m* Sahara

**sainete** *m* short comedy

**sal** *f* salt

**sala** *f* room; (*en teatro*) house. **~ de espectáculos** concert hall, auditorium. **~ de espera** waiting-room. **~ de estar** living-room. **~ de fiestas** nightclub

**sala|do** *a* salty; (*agua del mar*) salt; (*vivo*) lively; (*encantador*) cute; (*fig*) witty. **~r** *vt* salt

**salario** *m* wages

**salazón** *f* (*carne*) salted meat; (*pescado*) salted fish

**salchich|a** *f* (pork) sausage. **~ón** *m* salami

**sald|ar** *vt* pay (*cuenta*); (*vender*) sell off; (*fig*) settle. **~o** *m* balance; (*venta*) sale; (*lo que queda*) remnant

**salero** *m* salt-cellar

**salgo** *vb véase* **salir**

**sali|da** *f* departure; (*puerta*) exit, way out; (*de gas, de líquido*) leak; (*de astro*) rising; (*com, posibilidad de venta*) opening; (*chiste*) witty remark; (*fig*) way out. **~da de emergencia** emergency exit. **~ente** *a* projecting; (*fig*) outstanding. **~r** [52] *vi* leave; (*de casa etc*) go out; (*revista etc*) be published; (*resultar*) turn out; (*astro*) rise; (*aparecer*) appear. **~rse** *vpr* leave; (*recipiente, líquido etc*) leak. **~r adelante** get by. **~rse con la suya** get one's own way

**saliva** *f* saliva

**salmo** *m* psalm

**salm|ón** *m* salmon. **~onete** *m* red mullet

**salmuera** *f* brine

**salón** *m* lounge, sitting-room. **~ de actos** assembly hall. **~ de fiestas** dancehall

**salpica|dero** m (auto) dashboard. **~dura** f splash; (acción) splashing. **~r** [7] vt splash; (fig) sprinkle

**sals|a** f sauce; (para carne asada) gravy; (fig) spice. **~a verde** parsley sauce. **~era** f sauce-boat

**salt|amontes** m invar grasshopper. **~ar** vt jump (over); (fig) miss out. ● vi jump; (romperse) break; (líquido) spurt out; (desprenderse) come off; ⟨pelota⟩ bounce; (estallar) explode. **~eador** m highwayman. **~ear** vt rob; (culin) sauté. ● vi skip through

**saltimbanqui** m acrobat

**salt|o** m jump; (al agua) dive. **~o de agua** waterfall. **~ón** a ⟨ojos⟩ bulging. ● m grasshopper. **a ~os** by jumping; (fig) by leaps and bounds. **de un ~o** with one jump

**salud** f health; (fig) welfare. ● int cheers! **~able** a healthy

**salud|ar** vt greet, say hello to; (mil) salute. **~o** m greeting; (mil) salute. **~os** mpl best wishes. **le ~a atentamente** (en cartas) yours faithfully

**salva** f salvo; (de aplausos) thunders

**salvación** f salvation

**salvado** m bran

**Salvador** m. **El ~** El Salvador

**salvaguardia** f safeguard

**salvaje** a ⟨planta, animal⟩ wild; (primitivo) savage. ● m & f savage

**salvamanteles** m invar table-mat

**salva|mento** m rescue. **~r** vt save, rescue; (atravesar) cross; (recorrer) travel; (fig) overcome. **~rse** vpr save o.s. **~vidas** m invar lifebelt. **chaleco** m **~vidas** life-jacket

**salvia** f sage

**salvo** a safe. ● adv & prep except (for). **~ que** unless. **~conducto** m safe-conduct. **a ~** out of danger. **poner a ~** put in a safe place

**samba** f samba

**San** a Saint, St. **~ Miguel** St Michael

**sana|r** vt cure. ● vi recover. **~torio** m sanatorium

**sanci|ón** f sanction. **~onar** vt sanction

**sancocho** m (LAm) stew

**sandalia** f sandal

**sándalo** m sandalwood

**sandía** f water melon

**sandwich** /'sambitʃ/ m (pl **sandwichs, sandwiches**) sandwich

**sanear** vt drain

**sangr|ante** a bleeding; (fig) flagrant. **~ar** vt/i bleed. **~e** f blood. **a ~e fría** in cold blood

**sangría** f (bebida) sangria

**sangriento** a bloody

**sangu|ijuela** f leech. **~íneo** a blood

**san|idad** f health. **~itario** a sanitary. **~o** a healthy; (seguro) sound. **~o y salvo** safe and sound. **cortar por lo ~o** settle things once and for all

**santiamén** m. **en un ~** in an instant

**sant|idad** f sanctity. **~ificar** [7] vt sanctify. **~iguar** [15] vt make the sign of the cross over. **~iguarse** vpr cross o.s. **~o** a holy; (delante de nombre) Saint, St. ● m saint; (día) saint's day, name day. **~uario** m sanctuary. **~urrón** a sanctimonious, hypocritical

**sañ|a** f fury; (crueldad) cruelty. **~oso** a, **~udo** a furious

**sapo** m toad; (bicho, fam) small animal, creature

**saque** m (en tenis) service; (en fútbol) throw-in; (inicial en fútbol) kick-off

**saque|ar** vt loot. **~o** m looting

**sarampión** m measles

**sarape** m (Mex) blanket

**sarc|asmo** m sarcasm. **~ástico** a sarcastic

**sardana** f Catalonian dance

**sardina** f sardine

**sardo** a & m Sardinian

**sardónico** a sardonic

**sargento** m sergeant

**sarmiento** m vine shoot

**sarpullido** m rash

**sarta** f string

**sartén** f frying-pan (Brit), fry-pan (Amer)

**sastre** m tailor. **~ría** f tailoring; (tienda) tailor's (shop)

**Satanás** m Satan

**satánico** a satanic

**satélite** m satellite

**satinado** a shiny

**sátira** f satire

**satírico** a satirical. ● m satirist

**satisf|acción** f satisfaction. **~acer** [31] vt satisfy; (pagar) pay; (gustar) please; meet ⟨gastos, requisitos⟩. **~acerse** vpr satisfy o.s.; (vengarse) take revenge. **~actorio** a satisfactory. **~echo** a satisfied. **~echo de sí mismo** smug

**satura|ción** f saturation. **~r** vt saturate

**Saturno** m Saturn

**sauce** m willow. **~ llorón** weeping willow

**saúco** *m* elder

**savia** *f* sap

**sauna** *f* sauna

**saxofón** *m*, **saxófono** *m* saxophone

**saz|ón** *f* ripeness; (*culin*) seasoning. **~onado** *a* ripe; (*culin*) seasoned. **~onar** *vt* ripen; (*culin*) season. **en ~ón** in season

**se** *pron* (*él*) him; (*ella*) her; (*Vd*) you; (*reflexivo, él*) himself; (*reflexivo, ella*) herself; (*reflexivo, ello*) itself; (*reflexivo, uno*) oneself; (*reflexivo, Vd*) yourself; (*reflexivo, ellos, ellas*) themselves; (*reflexivo, Vds*) yourselves; (*recíproco*) (to) each other. **~ dice** people say, they say, it is said (**que** that). **~ habla español** Spanish spoken

**sé** *vb véase* **saber** *y* **ser**

**sea** *vb véase* **ser**

**sebo** *m* tallow; (*culin*) suet

**seca|dor** *m* drier; (*de pelo*) hairdrier. **~nte** *a* drying. ● *m* blotting-paper. **~r** [7] *vt* dry. **~rse** *vpr* dry; ⟨*río etc*⟩ dry up; ⟨*persona*⟩ dry o.s.

**sección** *f* section

**seco** *a* dry; ⟨*frutos, flores*⟩ dried; (*flaco*) thin; ⟨*respuesta*⟩ curt; (*escueto*) plain. **a secas** just. **en ~** (*bruscamente*) suddenly. **lavar en ~** dry-clean

**secre|ción** *f* secretion. **~tar** *vt* secrete

**secretar|ía** *f* secretariat. **~io** *m* secretary

**secreto** *a & m* secret

**secta** *f* sect. **~rio** *a* sectarian

**sector** *m* sector

**secuela** *f* consequence

**secuencia** *f* sequence

**secuestr|ar** *vt* confiscate; kidnap ⟨*persona*⟩; hijack ⟨*avión*⟩. **~o** *m* seizure; (*de persona*) kidnapping; (*de avión*) hijack(ing)

**secular** *a* secular

**secundar** *vt* second, help. **~io** *a* secondary

**sed** *f* thirst. ● *vb véase* **ser**. **tener ~** be thirsty. **tener ~ de** (*fig*) be hungry for

**seda** *f* silk

**sedante** *a & m*, **sedativo** *a & m* sedative

**sede** *f* seat; (*relig*) see

**sedentario** *a* sedentary

**sedici|ón** *f* sedition. **~oso** *a* seditious

**sediento** *a* thirsty

**sediment|ar** *vi* deposit. **~arse** *vpr* settle. **~o** *m* sediment

**seduc|ción** *f* seduction. **~ir** [47] *vt* seduce; (*atraer*) attract. **~tor** *a* seductive. ● *m* seducer

**sega|dor** *m* harvester. **~dora** *f* harvester, mower. **~r** [1 & 12] *vt* reap

**seglar** *a* secular. ● *m* layman

**segmento** *m* segment

**segoviano** *m* person from Segovia

**segrega|ción** *f* segregation. **~r** [12] *vt* segregate

**segui|da** *f*. **en ~da** immediately. **~do** *a* continuous; (*en plural*) consecutive. ● *adv* straight; (*después*) after. **todo ~do** straight ahead. **~dor** *a* following. ● *m* follower. **~r** [5 & 13] *vt* follow (*continuar*) continue

**según** *prep* according to. ● *adv* it depends; (*a medida que*) as

**segundo** *a* second. ● *m* second; (*culin*) second course

**segur|amente** *adv* certainly; (*muy probablemente*) surely. **~idad** *f* safety; (*certeza*) certainty; (*aplomo*) confidence. **~idad en sí mismo** self-confidence. **~idad social** social security. **~o** *a* safe; (*cierto*) certain, sure; (*firme*) secure; (*de fiar*) reliable. ● *adv* for certain. ● *m* insurance; (*dispositivo de seguridad*) safety device. **~o de sí mismo** self-confident. **~o de terceros** third-party insurance

**seis** *a & m* six. **~cientos** *a & m* six hundred

**seísmo** *m* earthquake

**selec|ción** *f* selection. **~cionar** *vt* select, choose. **~tivo** *a* selective. **~to** *a* selected; (*fig*) choice

**selva** *f* forest; (*jungla*) jungle

**sell|ar** *vt* stamp; (*cerrar*) seal. **~o** *m* stamp; (*en documento oficial*) seal; (*fig, distintivo*) hallmark

**semáforo** *m* semaphore; (*auto*) traffic lights; (*rail*) signal

**semana** *f* week. **~l** *a* weekly. **~rio** *a & m* weekly. **S~** Santa Holy Week

**semántic|a** *f* semantics. **~o** *a* semantic

**semblante** *m* face; (*fig*) look

**sembrar** [1] *vt* sow; (*fig*) scatter

**semeja|nte** *a* similar; (*tal*) such. ● *m* fellow man; (*cosa*) equal. **~nza** *f* similarity. **~r** *vi* seem. **~rse** *vpr* look alike. **a ~nza de** like. **tener ~nza con** resemble

**semen** *m* semen. ~**tal** *a* stud. ● *m* stud animal

**semestr|al** *a* half-yearly. ~**e** *m* six months

**semibreve** *m* semibreve (*Brit*), whole note (*Amer*)

**semic|ircular** *a* semicircular. ~**írculo** *m* semicircle

**semicorchea** *f* semiquaver (*Brit*), sixteenth note (*Amer*)

**semifinal** *f* semifinal

**semill|a** *f* seed. ~**ero** *m* nursery; (*fig*) hotbed

**seminario** *m* (*univ*) seminar; (*relig*) seminary

**sem|ita** *a* Semitic. ● *m* Semite. ~**ítico** *a* Semitic

**sémola** *f* semolina

**senado** *m* senate; (*fig*) assembly. ~**r** *m* senator

**sencill|ez** *f* simplicity. ~**o** *a* simple; (*uno solo*) single

**senda** *f*, **sendero** *m* path

**sendos** *apl* each

**seno** *m* bosom. ~ **materno** womb

**sensaci|ón** *f* sensation. ~**onal** *a* sensational

**sensat|ez** *f* good sense. ~**o** *a* sensible

**sensi|bilidad** *f* sensibility. ~**ble** *a* sensitive; (*notable*) notable; (*lamentable*) lamentable. ~**tivo** *a* ⟨*órgano*⟩ sense

**sensual** *a* sensual. ~**idad** *f* sensuality

**senta|do** *a* sitting (down). **dar algo por** ~**do** take something for granted. ~**r** [1] *vt* place; (*establecer*) establish. ● *vi* suit; (*de medidas*) fit; ⟨*comida*⟩ agree with. ~**rse** *vpr* sit (down); ⟨*sedimento*⟩ settle

**sentencia** *f* saying; (*jurid*) sentence. ~**r** *vt* sentence

**sentido** *a* deeply felt; (*sincero*) sincere; (*sensible*) sensitive. ● *m* sense; (*dirección*) direction. ~ **común** common sense. ~ **del humor** sense of humour. ~ **único** one-way. **doble** ~ double meaning. **no tener** ~ not make sense. **perder el** ~ faint. **sin** ~ unconscious; ⟨*cosa*⟩ senseless

**sentim|ental** *a* sentimental. ~**iento** *m* feeling; (*sentido*) sense; (*pesar*) regret

**sentir** [4] *vt* feel; (*oír*) hear; (*lamentar*) be sorry for. ● *vi* feel; (*lamentarse*) be sorry. ● *m* (*opinión*) opinion. ~**se** *vpr* feel. **lo siento** I'm sorry

**seña** *f* sign. ~**s** *fpl* (*dirección*) address; (*descripción*) description

**señal** *f* sign; (*rail etc*) signal; (*telefónico*) tone; (*com*) deposit. ~**ado** *a* notable. ~**ar** *vt* signal; (*poner señales en*) mark; (*apuntar*) point out; ⟨*manecilla, aguja*⟩ point to; (*determinar*) fix. ~**arse** *vpr* stand out. **dar** ~**es de** show signs of. **en** ~ **de** as a token of

**señero** *a* alone; (*sin par*) unique

**señor** *m* man; (*caballero*) gentleman; (*delante de nombre propio*) Mr; (*tratamiento directo*) sir. ~**a** *f* lady, woman; (*delante de nombre propio*) Mrs; (*esposa*) wife; (*tratamiento directo*) madam. ~**ial** *a* ⟨*casa*⟩ stately. ~**ita** *f* young lady; (*delante de nombre propio*) Miss; (*tratamiento directo*) miss. ~**ito** *m* young gentleman. **el** ~ **alcalde** the mayor. **el** ~ **Mr.** **muy** ~ **mío** Dear Sir. **¡no** ~**!** certainly not! **ser** ~ **de** be master of, control

**señuelo** *m* lure

**sepa** *vb véase* **saber**

**separa|ción** *f* separation. ~**do** *a* separate. ~**r** *vt* separate; (*apartar*) move away; (*de empleo*) dismiss. ~**rse** *vpr* separate; ⟨*amigos*⟩ part. ~**tista** *a* & *m* & *f* separatist. **por** ~**do** separately

**septentrional** *a* north(ern)

**séptico** *a* septic

**septiembre** *m* September

**séptimo** *a* seventh

**sepulcro** *m* sepulchre

**sepult|ar** *vt* bury. ~**ura** *f* burial; (*tumba*) grave. ~**urero** *m* gravedigger

**sequ|edad** *f* dryness. ~**ía** *f* drought

**séquito** *m* entourage; (*fig*) aftermath

**ser** [39] *vi* be. ● *m* being. ~ **de** be made of; (*provenir de*) come from; (*pertenecer a*) belong to. ~ **humano** human being. **a no** ~ **que** unless. **¡así sea!** so be it! **es más** what is more. **lo que sea** anything. **no sea que, no vaya a** ~ **que** in case. **o sea** in other words. **sea lo que fuere** be that as it may. **sea... sea** either... or. **siendo así que** since. **soy yo** it's me

**seren|ar** *vt* calm down. ~**arse** *vpr* calm down; ⟨*tiempo*⟩ clear up. ~**ata** *f* serenade. ~**idad** *f* serenity. ~**o** *a* ⟨*cielo*⟩ clear; ⟨*tiempo*⟩ fine; (*fig*) calm. ● *m* night watchman. **al** ~**o** in the open

seri|al *m* serial. ~e *f* series. fuera de ~e (*fig*, *extraordinario*) special. producción *f* en ~ mass production
seri|edad *f* seriousness. ~o *a* serious; (*confiable*) reliable. en ~o seriously. poco ~o frivolous
sermón *m* sermon
serp|enteante *a* winding. ~entear *vi* wind. ~iente *f* snake. ~iente de cascabel rattlesnake
serrano *a* mountain; ⟨*jamón*⟩ cured
serr|ar [1] *vt* saw. ~ín *m* sawdust. ~ucho *m* (hand)saw
servi|cial *a* helpful. ~cio *m* service; (*conjunto*) set; (*aseo*) toilet. ~cio a domicilio delivery service. ~dor *m* servant. ~dumbre *f* servitude; (*criados*) servants, staff. ~l *a* servile. su (seguro) ~dor (*en cartas*) yours faithfully
servilleta *f* serviette, (table) napkin
servir [5] *vt* serve; (*ayudar*) help; (*en restaurante*) wait on. ● *vi* serve; (*ser útil*) be of use. ~se *vpr* help o.s. ~se de use. no ~ de nada be useless. para ~le at your service. sírvase sentarse please sit down
sesear *vi* pronounce the Spanish *c* as an *s*
sesent|a *a* & *m* sixty. ~ón *a* & *m* sixty-year-old
seseo *m* pronunciation of the Spanish *c* as an *s*
sesg|ado *a* slanting. ~o *m* slant; (*fig*, *rumbo*) turn
sesión *f* session; (*en el cine*) showing; (*en el teatro*) performance
ses|o *m* brain; (*fig*) brains. ~udo *a* inteligent; (*sensato*) sensible
seta *f* mushroom
sete|cientos *a* & *m* seven hundred. ~nta *a* & *m* seventy. ~ntón *a* & *m* seventy-year-old
setiembre *m* September
seto *m* fence; (*de plantas*) hedge. ~ vivo hedge
seudo... *pref* pseudo...
seudónimo *m* pseudonym
sever|idad *f* severity. ~o *a* severe; ⟨*disciplina*, *profesor etc*⟩ strict
Sevilla *f* Seville
sevillan|as *fpl* popular dance from Seville. ~o *m* person from Seville
sexo *m* sex
sext|eto *m* sextet. ~o *a* sixth
sexual *a* sexual. ~idad *f* sexuality
si *m* (*mus*) B; (*solfa*) te. ● *conj* if; (*dubitativo*) whether. ~ no or else. por ~ (*acaso*) in case

sí *pron reflexivo* (*él*) himself; (*ella*) herself; (*ello*) itself; (*uno*) oneself; (*Vd*) yourself; (*ellos*, *ellas*) themselves; (*Vds*) yourselves; (*recíproco*) each other
sí *adv* yes. ● *m* consent
Siamés *a* & *m* Siamese
Sicilia *f* Sicily
sida *m* Aids
siderurgia *f* iron and steel industry
sidra *f* cider
siega *f* harvesting; (*época*) harvest time
siembra *f* sowing; (*época*) sowing time
siempre *adv* always. ~ que if. como ~ as usual. de ~ (*acostumbrado*) usual. lo de ~ the same old story. para ~ for ever
sien *f* temple
siento *vb véase* sentar *y* sentir
sierra *f* saw; (*cordillera*) mountain range
siervo *m* slave
siesta *f* siesta
siete *a* & *m* seven
sífilis *f* syphilis
sifón *m* U-bend; (*de soda*) syphon
sigilo *m* secrecy
sigla *f* initials, abbreviation
siglo *m* century; (*época*) time, age; (*fig*, *mucho tiempo*, *fam*) ages; (*fig*, *mundo*) world
significa|ción *f* meaning; (*importancia*) significance. ~do *a* (*conocido*) well-known. ● *m* meaning. ~r [7] *vt* mean; (*expresar*) express. ~rse *vpr* stand out. ~tivo *a* significant
signo *m* sign. ~ de admiración exclamation mark. ~ de interrogación question mark
sigo *vb véase* seguir
siguiente *a* following, next. lo ~ the following
sílaba *f* syllable
silb|ar *vt/i* whistle. ~ato *m*, ~ido *m* whistle
silenci|ador *m* silencer. ~ar *vt* hush up. ~o *m* silence. ~oso *a* silent
sílfide *f* sylph
silicio *m* silicon
silo *m* silo
silueta *f* silhouette; (*dibujo*) outline
silvestre *a* wild
sill|a *f* chair; (*de montar*) saddle; (*relig*) see. ~a de ruedas wheelchair. ~ín *m* saddle. ~ón *m* armchair

**simb|ólico** *a* symbolic(al). ~**olismo** *m* symbolism. ~**olizar** [10] *vt* symbolize

**símbolo** *m* symbol

**sim|etría** *f* symmetry. ~**étrico** *a* symmetric(al)

**simiente** *f* seed

**similar** *a* similar

**simp|atía** *f* liking; *(cariño)* affection; *(fig, amigo)* friend. ~**ático** *a* nice, likeable; *(amable)* kind. ~**atizante** *m & f* sympathizer. ~**atizar** [10] *vi* get on (well together). **me es** ~**ático** I like

**simpl|e** *a* simple; *(mero)* mere. ~**eza** *f* simplicity; *(tontería)* stupid thing; *(insignificancia)* trifle. ~**icidad** *f* simplicity. ~**ificar** [7] *vt* simplify. ~**ón** *m* simpleton

**simposio** *m* symposium

**simula|ción** *f* simulation. ~**r** *vt* feign

**simultáneo** *a* simultaneous

**sin** *prep* without. ~ **que** without

**sinagoga** *f* synagogue

**sincer|idad** *f* sincerity. ~**o** *a* sincere

**síncopa** *f (mus)* syncopation

**sincopar** *vt* syncopate

**sincronizar** [10] *vt* synchronize

**sindica|l** *a* (trade-)union. ~**lista** *m & f* trade-unionist. ~**to** *m* trade union

**síndrome** *m* syndrome

**sinfín** *m* endless number

**sinf|onía** *f* symphony. ~**ónico** *a* symphonic

**singular** *a* singular; *(excepcional)* exceptional. ~**izar** [10] *vt* single out. ~**izarse** *vpr* stand out

**siniestro** *a* sinister; *(desgraciado)* unlucky. ● *m* disaster

**sinnúmero** *m* endless number

**sino** *m* fate. ● *conj* but; *(salvo)* except

**sínodo** *m* synod

**sinónimo** *a* synonymous. ● *m* synonym

**sinrazón** *f* wrong

**sintaxis** *f* syntax

**síntesis** *f invar* synthesis

**sint|ético** *a* synthetic. ~**etizar** [10] *vt* synthesize; *(resumir)* summarize

**síntoma** *f* symptom

**sintomático** *a* symptomatic

**sinton|ía** *f (en la radio)* signature tune. ~**izar** [10] *vt* (con la radio) tune (in)

**sinuoso** *a* winding

**sinvergüenza** *m & f* scoundrel

**sionis|mo** *m* Zionism. ~**ta** *m & f* Zionist

**siquiera** *conj* even if. ● *adv* at least. **ni** ~ not even

**sirena** *f* siren

**Siria** *f* Syria

**sirio** *a & m* Syrian

**siroco** *m* sirocco

**sirvienta** *f*, **sirviente** *m* servant

**sirvo** *vb véase* **servir**

**sise|ar** *vt/i* hiss. ~**o** *m* hissing

**sísmico** *a* seismic

**sismo** *m* earthquake

**sistem|a** *m* system. ~**ático** *a* systematic. **por** ~**a** as a rule

**sitiar** *vt* besiege; *(fig)* surround

**sitio** *m* place; *(espacio)* space; *(mil)* siege. **en cualquier** ~ anywhere

**situa|ción** *f* position. ~**r** [21] *vt* situate; *(poner)* put; *(depositar)* deposit. ~**rse** *vpr* be successful, establish o.s.

**slip** /es'lip/ *m* (*pl* **slips** /es'lip/) underpants, briefs

**slogan** /es'logan/ *m* (*pl* **slogans** /es'logan/) slogan

**smoking** /es'mokin/ *m* (*pl* **smokings** /es'mokin/) dinner jacket *(Brit)*, tuxedo *(Amer)*

**sobaco** *m* armpit

**sobar** *vt* handle; knead ⟨masa⟩

**soberan|ía** *f* sovereignty. ~**o** *a* sovereign; *(fig)* supreme. ● *m* sovereign

**soberbi|a** *f* pride; *(altanería)* arrogance. ~**o** *a* proud; *(altivo)* arrogant

**soborn|ar** *vt* bribe. ~**o** *m* bribe

**sobra** *f* surplus. ~**s** *fpl* leftovers. ~**do** *a* more than enough. ~**nte** *a* surplus. ~**r** *vi* be left over; *(estorbar)* be in the way. **de** ~ more than enough

**sobrasada** *f* Majorcan sausage

**sobre** *prep* on; *(encima de)* on top of; *(más o menos)* about; *(por encima de)* above; *(sin tocar)* over; *(además de)* on top of. ● *m* envelope. ~**cargar** [12] *vt* overload. ~**coger** [14] *vt* startle. ~**cogerse** *vpr* be startled. ~**cubierta** *f* dust cover. ~**dicho** *a* aforementioned. ~**entender** [1] *vt* understand, infer. ~**entendido** *a* implicit. ~**humano** *a* superhuman. ~**llevar** *vt* bear. ~**mesa** *f*. **de** ~**mesa** after-dinner. ~**natural** *a* supernatural. ~**nombre** *m* nickname. ~**pasar** *vt* exceed. ~**poner** [34] *vt* superimpose; *(fig, anteponer)* put before. ~**ponerse** *vpr* overcome. ~**pujar** *vt* surpass. ~**saliente** *a (fig)* outstanding. ● *m* excellent mark. ~**salir** [52] *vi* stick out;

(*fig*) stand out. ~**saltar** *vt* startle. ~**salto** *m* fright. ~**sueldo** *m* bonus. ~**todo** *m* overall; (*abrigo*) overcoat. ~ **todo** above all, especially. ~**venir** [53] *vi* happen. ~**viviente** *a* surviving. • *m* & *f* survivor. ~**vivir** *vi* survive. ~**volar** *vt* fly over

**sobriedad** *f* restraint
**sobrin|a** *f* niece. ~**o** *m* nephew
**sobrio** *a* moderate, sober
**socarr|ón** *a* sarcastic; (*taimado*) sly. ~**onería** *f* sarcasm
**socavar** *vt* undermine
**soci|able** *a* sociable. ~**al** *a* social. ~**aldemocracia** *f* social democracy. ~**aldemócrata** *m* & *f* social democrat. ~**alismo** *m* socialsim. ~**alista** *a* & *m* & *f* socialist. ~**alizar** [10] *vt* nationalize. ~**edad** *f* society; (*com*) company. ~**edad anónima** limited company. ~**o** *m* member; (*com*) partner. ~**ología** *f* sociology. ~**ólogo** *m* sociologist
**socorr|er** *vt* help. ~**o** *m* help
**soda** *f* (*bebida*) soda (water)
**sodio** *m* sodium
**sofá** *m* sofa, settee
**sofistica|ción** *f* sophistication. ~**do** *a* sophisticated. ~**r** [7] *vt* adulterate
**sofoca|ción** *f* suffocation. ~**nte** *a* (*fig*) stifling. ~**r** [7] *vt* suffocate; (*fig*) stifle. ~**rse** *vpr* suffocate; (*ruborizarse*) blush
**soga** *f* rope
**soja** *f* soya (bean)
**sojuzgar** [12] *vt* subdue
**sol** *m* sun; (*luz solar*) sunlight; (*mus*) G; (*solfa*) soh. **al** ~ in the sun. **día** *m* **de** ~ sunny day. **hace** ~, **hay** ~ it is sunny. **tomar el** ~ sunbathe
**solamente** *adv* only
**solapa** *f* lapel; (*de bolsillo etc*) flap. ~**do** *a* sly. ~**r** *vt/i* overlap
**solar** *a* solar. • *m* plot
**solariego** *a* (*casa*) ancestral
**solaz** *m* relaxation
**soldado** *m* soldier. ~ **raso** private
**solda|dor** *m* welder; (*utensilio*) soldering iron. ~**r** [2] *vt* weld, solder
**solea|do** *a* sunny. ~**r** *vt* put in the sun
**soledad** *f* solitude; (*aislamiento*) loneliness
**solemn|e** *a* solemn. ~**idad** *f* solemnity; (*ceremonia*) ceremony
**soler** [2] *vi* be in the habit of. **suele despertarse a las 6** he usually wakes up at 6 o'clock

**sol|icitar** *vt* request; apply for (*empleo*); attract (*atención*). ~**icito** *a* solicitous. ~**icitud** *f* (*atención*) concern; (*petición*) request; (*para un puesto*) application
**solidaridad** *f* solidarity
**solid|ez** *f* solidity; (*de color*) fastness. ~**ificar** [7] *vt* solidify. ~**ificarse** *vpr* solidify
**sólido** *a* solid; (*color*) fast; (*robusto*) strong. • *m* solid
**soliloquio** *m* soliloquy
**solista** *m* & *f* soloist
**solitario** *a* solitary; (*aislado*) lonely. • *m* recluse; (*juego, diamante*) solitaire
**solo** *a* (*sin compañía*) alone; (*aislado*) lonely; (*único*) only; (*mus*) solo; (*café*) black. • *m* solo; (*juego*) solitaire. **a solas** alone
**sólo** *adv* only. ~ **que** only. **aunque** ~ **sea** even if it is only. **con** ~ **que** if; (*con tal que*) as long as. **no** ~... **sino también** not only... but also. ~... **tan** ~ only
**solomillo** *m* sirloin
**solsticio** *m* solstice
**soltar** [2] *vt* let go of; (*dejar caer*) drop; (*dejar salir, decir*) let out; give (*golpe etc*). ~**se** *vpr* come undone; (*librarse*) break loose
**solter|a** *f* single woman. ~**o** *a* single. • *m* bachelor. **apellido** *m* **de** ~**a** maiden name
**soltura** *f* looseness; (*agilidad*) agility; (*en hablar*) ease, fluency
**solu|ble** *a* soluble. ~**ción** *f* solution. ~**cionar** *vt* solve; settle (*huelga, asunto*)
**solvent|ar** *vt* resolve; settle (*deuda*). ~**e** *a* & *m* solvent
**sollo** *m* sturgeon
**solloz|ar** [10] *vi* sob. ~**o** *m* sob
**sombr|a** *f* shade; (*imagen oscura*) shadow. ~**eado** *a* shady. **a la** ~**a** in the shade
**sombrero** *m* hat. ~ **hongo** bowler hat
**sombrío** *a* sombre
**somero** *a* shallow
**someter** *vt* subdue; subject (*persona*); (*presentar*) submit. ~**se** *vpr* give in
**somn|oliento** *a* sleepy. ~**ífero** *m* sleeping-pill
**somos** *vb véase* **ser**
**son** *m* sound. • *vb véase* **ser**
**sonámbulo** *m* sleepwalker

**sonar** [2] *vt* blow; ring ⟨*timbre*⟩. ● *vi* sound; ⟨*timbre, teléfono etc*⟩ ring; ⟨*reloj*⟩ strike; ⟨*pronunciarse*⟩ be pronounced; (*mus*) play; (*fig, ser conocido*) be familiar. ~se *vpr* blow one's nose. ~ a sound like

**sonata** *f* sonata

**sonde|ar** *vt* sound; (*fig*) sound out. ~o *m* sounding; (*fig*) poll

**soneto** *m* sonnet

**sónico** *a* sonic

**sonido** *m* sound

**sonoro** *a* sonorous; ⟨*ruidoso*⟩ loud

**sonr|eír** [51] *vi* smile. ~eírse *vpr* smile. ~iente *a* smiling. ~isa *f* smile

**sonroj|ar** *vt* make blush. ~arse *vpr* blush. ~o *m* blush

**sonrosado** *a* rosy, pink

**sonsacar** [7] *vt* wheedle out

**soñ|ado** *a* dream. ~ador *m* dreamer. ~ar [2] *vi* dream (**con** of). ¡**ni** ~**arlo!** not likely! **(que) ni** ~**ado** marvellous

**sopa** *f* soup

**sopesar** *vt* (*fig*) weigh up

**sopl|ar** *vt* blow; blow out ⟨*vela*⟩; blow off ⟨*polvo*⟩; (*inflar*) blow up. ● *vi* blow. ~ete *m* blowlamp. ~o *m* puff; (*fig, momento*) moment

**soporífero** *a* soporific. ● *m* sleeping-pill

**soport|al** *m* porch. ~ales *mpl* arcade. ~ar *vt* support; (*fig*) bear. ~e *m* support

**soprano** *f* soprano

**sor** *f* sister

**sorb|er** *vt* suck; sip ⟨*bebida*⟩; (*absorber*) absorb. ~ete *m* sorbet, water-ice. ~o *m* swallow; (*pequeña cantidad*) sip

**sord|amente** *adv* silently, dully. ~era *f* deafness

**sórdido** *a* squalid; (*tacaño*) mean

**sordo** *a* deaf; (*silencioso*) quiet. ● *m* deaf person. ~**mudo** *a* deaf and dumb. **a la sorda, a sordas** on the quiet. **hacerse el** ~ turn a deaf ear

**sorna** *f* sarcasm. **con** ~ sarcastically

**soroche** *m* (*LAm*) mountain sickness

**sorpre|ndente** *a* surprising. ~**nder** *vt* surprise; (*coger desprevenido*) catch. ~**sa** *f* surprise

**sorte|ar** *vt* draw lots for; (*rifar*) raffle; (*fig*) avoid. ● *vi* draw lots; (*con moneda*) toss up. ~o *m* draw; (*rifa*) raffle; (*fig*) avoidance

**sortija** *f* ring; (*de pelo*) ringlet

**sortilegio** *m* witchcraft; (*fig*) spell

**sos|egado** *a* calm. ~**egar** [1 & 12] *vt* calm. ● *vi* rest. ~**iego** *m* calmness. **con** ~**iego** calmly

**soslayo. al** ~, **de** ~ sideways

**soso** *a* tasteless; (*fig*) dull

**sospech|a** *f* suspicion. ~**ar** *vt/i* suspect. ~**oso** *a* suspicious. ● *m* suspect

**sost|én** *m* support; (*prenda femenina*) bra (*fam*), brassière. ~**ener** [40] *vt* support; (*sujetar*) hold; (*mantener*) maintain; (*alimentar*) sustain. ~**enerse** *vpr* support o.s.; (*continuar*) remain. ~**enido** *a* sustained; (*mus*) sharp. ● *m* (*mus*) sharp

**sota** *f* (*de naipes*) jack

**sótano** *m* basement

**sotavento** *m* lee

**soto** *m* grove; (*matorral*) thicket

**soviético** *a* (*historia*) Soviet

**soy** *vb véase* **ser**

**Sr** *abrev* (*Señor*) Mr. ~**a** *abrev* (*Señora*) Mrs. ~**ta** *abrev* (*Señorita*) Miss

**su** *a* (*de él*) his; (*de ella*) her; (*de ello*) its; (*de uno*) one's; (*de Vd*) your; (*de ellos, de ellas*) their; (*de Vds*) your

**suav|e** *a* smooth; (*fig*) gentle; ⟨*color, sonido*⟩ soft. ~**idad** *f* smoothness, softness. ~**izar** [10] *vt* smooth, soften

**subalimentado** *a* underfed

**subalterno** *a* secondary; ⟨*persona*⟩ auxiliary

**subarrendar** [1] *vt* sublet

**subasta** *f* auction; (*oferta*) tender. ~**r** *vt* auction

**sub|campeón** *m* runner-up. ~**consciencia** *f* subconscious. ~**consciente** *a* & *m* subconscious. ~**continente** *m* subcontinent. ~**desarrollado** *a* under-developed. ~**director** *m* assistant manager

**súbdito** *m* subject

**sub|dividir** *vt* subdivide. ~**estimar** *vt* underestimate. ~**gerente** *m* & *f* assistant manager

**subi|da** *f* ascent; (*aumento*) rise; (*pendiente*) slope. ~**do** *a* ⟨*precio*⟩ high; ⟨*color*⟩ bright; ⟨*olor*⟩ strong. ~**r** *vt* go up; (*poner*) put; (*llevar*) take up; (*aumentar*) increase. ● *vi* go up. ~**r a** get into ⟨*coche*⟩; get on ⟨*autobús, avión, barco, tren*⟩; (*aumentar*) increase. ~**rse** *vpr* climb up. ~**rse a** get on ⟨*tren etc*⟩

**súbito** *a* sudden. ● *adv* suddenly. **de** ~ suddenly

**subjetivo** *a* subjective

**subjuntivo** *a & m* subjunctive

**subleva|ción** *f* uprising. **~r** *vt* incite to rebellion. **~rse** *vpr* rebel

**sublim|ar** *vt* sublimate. **~e** *a* sublime

**submarino** *a* underwater. ● *m* submarine

**subordinado** *a & m* subordinate

**subrayar** *vt* underline

**subrepticio** *a* surreptitious

**subsanar** *vt* remedy; overcome ⟨*dificultad*⟩

**subscri|bir** *vt* (*pp* **subscrito**) sign. **~birse** *vpr* subscribe. **~pción** *f* subscription

**subsidi|ario** *a* subsidiary. **~o** *m* subsidy. **~o de paro** unemployment benefit

**subsiguiente** *a* subsequent

**subsist|encia** *f* subsistence. **~ir** *vi* subsist; (*perdurar*) survive

**substanci|a** *f* substance. **~al** *a* important. **~oso** *a* substantial

**substantivo** *m* noun

**substitu|ción** *f* substitution. **~ir** [17] *vt/i* substitute. **~to** *a & m* substitute

**substraer** [41] *vt* take away

**subterfugio** *m* subterfuge

**subterráneo** *a* underground. ● *m* (*bodega*) cellar; (*conducto*) underground passage

**subtítulo** *m* subtitle

**suburb|ano** *a* suburban. ● *m* suburban train. **~io** *m* suburb; (*en barrio pobre*) slum

**subvenci|ón** *f* grant. **~onar** *vt* subsidize

**subver|sión** *f* subversion. **~sivo** *a* subversive. **~tir** [4] *vt* subvert

**subyugar** [12] *vt* subjugate; (*fig*) subdue

**succión** *f* suction

**suce|der** *vi* happen; (*seguir*) follow; (*substituir*) succeed. **~dido** *m* event. **lo ~dido** what happened. **~sión** *f* succession. **~sivo** *a* successive; (*consecutivo*) consecutive. **~so** *m* event; (*incidente*) incident. **~sor** *m* successor. **en lo ~sivo** in future. **lo que ~de es que** the trouble is that. **¿qué ~de?** what's the matter?

**suciedad** *f* dirt; (*estado*) dirtiness

**sucinto** *a* concise; (*prenda*) scanty

**sucio** *a* dirty; (*vil*) mean; ⟨*conciencia*⟩ guilty. **en ~** in rough

**sucre** *m* (*unidad monetaria del Ecuador*) sucre

**suculento** *a* succulent

**sucumbir** *vi* succumb

**sucursal** *f* branch (office)

**Sudáfrica** *m & f* South Africa

**sudafricano** *a & m* South African

**Sudamérica** *f* South America

**sudamericano** *a & m* South American

**sudar** *vt* work hard for. ● *vi* sweat

**sud|este** *m* south-east; (*viento*) south-east wind. **~oeste** *m* south-west; (*viento*) south-west wind

**sudor** *m* sweat

**Suecia** *f* Sweden

**sueco** *a* Swedish. ● *m* (*persona*) Swede; (*lengua*) Swedish. **hacerse el ~** pretend not to hear

**suegr|a** *f* mother-in-law. **~o** *m* father-in-law. **mis ~os** my in-laws

**suela** *f* sole

**sueldo** *m* salary

**suelo** *m* ground; (*dentro de edificio*) floor; (*tierra*) land. ● *vb véase* **soler**

**suelto** *a* loose; (*libre*) free; (*sin pareja*) odd; ⟨*lenguaje*⟩ fluent. ● *m* (*en periódico*) item; (*dinero*) change

**sueño** *m* sleep; (*ilusión*) dream. **tener ~** be sleepy

**suero** *m* serum; (*de leche*) whey

**suerte** *f* luck; (*destino*) fate; (*azar*) chance. **de otra ~** otherwise. **de ~ que** so. **echar ~s** draw lots. **por ~** fortunately. **tener ~** be lucky

**suéter** *m* jersey

**suficien|cia** *f* sufficiency; (*presunción*) smugness; (*aptitud*) suitability. **~te** *a* sufficient; (*presumido*) smug. **~temente** *adv* enough

**sufijo** *m* suffix

**sufragio** *m* (*voto*) vote

**sufri|do** *a* ⟨*persona*⟩ long-suffering; ⟨*tela*⟩ hard-wearing. **~miento** *m* suffering. **~r** *vt* suffer; (*experimentar*) undergo; (*soportar*) bear. ● *vi* suffer

**suge|rencia** *f* suggestion. **~rir** [4] *vt* suggest. **~stión** *f* suggestion. **~stionable** *a* impressionable. **~stionar** *vt* influence. **~stivo** *a* (*estimulante*) stimulating; (*atractivo*) attractive

**suicid|a** *a* suicidal. ● *m & f* suicide; (*fig*) maniac. **~arse** *vpr* commit suicide. **~io** *m* suicide

**Suiza** *f* Switzerland

**suizo** *a* Swiss. ● *m* Swiss; (*bollo*) bun

**suje|ción** f subjection. **~tador** m fastener; (*de pelo, papeles etc*) clip; (*prenda femenina*) bra (*fam*), brassière. **~tapapeles** m *invar* paperclip. **~tar** vt fasten; (*agarrar*) hold; (*fig*) restrain. **~tarse** vr subject o.s.; (*ajustarse*) conform. **~to** a fastened; (*susceptible*) subject. ● m individual

**sulfamida** f sulpha (drug)

**sulfúrico** a sulphuric

**sult|án** m sultan. **~ana** f sultana

**suma** f sum; (*total*) total. **en ~** in short. **~mente** adv extremely. **~r** vt add (up); (*fig*) gather. ● vi add up. **~rse** vpr. **~rse a** join in

**sumario** a brief. ● m summary; (*jurid*) indictment

**sumergi|ble** m submarine. ● a submersible. **~r** [14] vt submerge

**sumidero** m drain

**suministr|ar** vt supply. **~o** m supply; (*acción*) supplying

**sumir** vt sink; (*fig*) plunge

**sumis|ión** f submission. **~o** a submissive

**sumo** a greatest; (*supremo*) supreme. **a lo ~** at the most

**suntuoso** a sumptuous

**supe** vb véase **saber**

**superar** vt surpass; (*vencer*) overcome; (*dejar atrás*) get past. **~se** vpr excel o.s.

**superchería** f swindle

**superestructura** f superstructure

**superfici|al** a superficial. **~e** f surface; (*extensión*) area. **de ~e** surface

**superfluo** a superfluous

**superhombre** m superman

**superintendente** m superintendent

**superior** a superior; (*más alto*) higher; (*mejor*) better; (*piso*) upper. ● m superior. **~idad** f superiority

**superlativo** a & m superlative

**supermercado** m supermarket

**supersónico** a supersonic

**superstici|ón** f superstition. **~oso** a superstitious

**supervis|ión** f supervision. **~or** m supervisor

**superviviente** a surviving. ● m & f survivor

**suplantar** vt supplant

**suplement|ario** a supplementary. **~o** m supplement

**suplente** a & m & f substitute

**súplica** f entreaty; (*petición*) request

**suplicar** [7] vt beg

**suplicio** m torture

**suplir** vt make up for; (*reemplazar*) replace

**supo|ner** [34] vt suppose; (*significar*) mean; (*costar*) cost. **~sición** f supposition

**supositorio** m suppository

**suprem|acía** f supremacy. **~o** a supreme; (*momento etc*) critical

**supr|esión** f suppression. **~imir** vt suppress; (*omitir*) omit

**supuesto** a supposed. ● m assumption. **~ que** if. **¡por ~!** of course!

**sur** m south; (*viento*) south wind

**surc|ar** [7] vt plough. **~o** m furrow; (*de rueda*) rut; (*en la piel*) wrinkle

**surgir** [14] vi spring up; (*elevarse*) loom up; (*aparecer*) appear; (*dificultad, oportunidad*) arise, crop up

**surrealis|mo** m surrealism. **~ta** a & m & f surrealist

**surti|do** a well-stocked; (*variado*) assorted. ● m assortment, selection. **~dor** m (*de gasolina*) petrol pump (*Brit*), gas pump (*Amer*). **~r** vt supply; have (*efecto*). **~rse** vpr provide o.s. (**de** with)

**susceptib|ilidad** f susceptibility; (*sensibilidad*) sensitivity. **~le** a susceptible; (*sensible*) sensitive

**suscitar** vt provoke; arouse (*curiosidad, interés, sospechas*)

**suscr...** véase **subscr...**

**susodicho** a aforementioned

**suspen|der** vt hang (up); (*interrumpir*) suspend; (*univ etc*) fail. **~derse** vpr stop. **~sión** f suspension. **~so** a hanging; (*pasmado*) amazed; (*univ etc*) failed. ● m fail. **en ~so** pending

**suspicaz** a suspicious

**suspir|ar** vi sigh. **~o** m sigh

**sust...** véase **subst...**

**sustent|ación** f support. **~ar** vt support; (*alimentar*) sustain; (*mantener*) maintain. **~o** m support; (*alimento*) sustenance

**susto** m fright. **caerse del ~** be frightened to death

**susurr|ar** vi (*persona*) whisper; (*agua*) murmur; (*hojas*) rustle. **~o** m (*de persona*) whisper; (*de agua*) murmur; (*de hojas*) rustle

**sutil** a fine; (*fig*) subtle. **~eza** f fineness; (*fig*) subtlety

**suyo** a & pron (*de él*) his; (*de ella*) hers; (*de ello*) its; (*de uno*) one's; (*de Vd*) yours; (*de ellos, de ellas*) theirs;

*(de Vds)* yours. **un amigo** ~ a friend of his, a friend of theirs, etc

# T

**taba** *f (anat)* ankle-bone; *(juego)* jacks

**tabac|alera** *f* (state) tobacconist. ~**alero** *a* tobacco. ~**o** *m* tobacco; *(cigarillos)* cigarettes; *(rapé)* snuff

**tabalear** *vi* drum (with one's fingers)

**Tabasco** *m* Tabasco (**P**)

**tabern|a** *f* bar. ~**ero** *m* barman; *(dueño)* landlord

**tabernáculo** *m* tabernacle

**tabique** *m* (thin) wall

**tabl|a** *f* plank; *(de piedra etc)* slab; *(estante)* shelf; *(de vestido)* pleat; *(lista)* list; *(índice)* index; *(en matemática etc)* table. ~**ado** *m* platform; *(en el teatro)* stage. ~**ao** *m* place where flamenco shows are held. ~**as reales** backgammon. ~**ero** *m* board. ~**ero de mandos** dashboard. **hacer** ~**a rasa de** disregard

**tableta** *f* tablet; *(de chocolate)* bar

**tabl|illa** *f* small board. ~**ón** *m* plank. ~**ón de anuncios** notice board *(esp Brit)*, bulletin board *(Amer)*

**tabú** *m* taboo

**tabular** *vt* tabulate

**taburete** *m* stool

**tacaño** *a* mean

**tacita** *f* small cup

**tácito** *a* tacit

**taciturno** *a* taciturn; *(triste)* miserable

**taco** *m* plug; *(LAm, tacón)* heel; *(de billar)* cue; *(de billetes)* book; *(fig, lío, fam)* mess; *(Mex, culin)* filled tortilla

**tacógrafo** *m* tachograph

**tacón** *m* heel

**táctic|a** *f* tactics. ~**o** *a* tactical

**táctil** *a* tactile

**tacto** *m* touch; *(fig)* tact

**tacuara** *f (Arg)* bamboo

**tacurú** *m* (small) ant

**tacha** *f* fault; *(clavo)* tack. **poner** ~**s a** find fault with. **sin** ~ flawless

**tachar** *vt (borrar)* rub out; *(con raya)* cross out. ~ **de** accuse of

**tafia** *f (LAm)* rum

**tafilete** *m* morocco

**tahúr** *m* card-sharp

**Tailandia** *f* Thailand

**tailandés** *a & m* Thai

**taimado** *a* sly

**taj|ada** *f* slice. ~**ante** *a* sharp. ~**o** *m* slash; *(fig, trabajo, fam)* job; *(culin)* chopping block. **sacar** ~**ada** profit

**Tajo** *m* Tagus

**tal** *a* such; *(ante sustantivo en singular)* such a. ● *pron (persona)* someone; *(cosa)* such a thing. ● *adv* so; *(de tal manera)* in such a way. ~ **como** the way. ~ **cual** *(tal como)* way; *(regular)* fair. ~ **para cual** *(fam)* two of a kind. **con** ~ **que** as long as. **¿qué** ~**?** how are you? **un** ~ a certain

**taladr|ar** *vt* drill. ~**o** *m* drill; *(agujero)* drill hole

**talante** *m* mood. **de buen** ~ willingly

**talar** *vt* fell; *(fig)* destroy

**talco** *m* talcum powder

**talcualillo** *a (fam)* so so

**talega** *f*, **talego** *m* sack

**talento** *m* talent

**TALGO** *m* high-speed train

**talismán** *m* talisman

**tal|ón** *m* heel; *(recibo)* counterfoil; *(cheque)* cheque. ~**onario** *m* receipt book; *(de cheques)* cheque book

**tall|a** *f* carving; *(grabado)* engraving; *(de piedra preciosa)* cutting; *(estatura)* height; *(medida)* size; *(palo)* measuring stick; *(Arg, charla)* gossip. ~**do** *a* carved. ● *m* carving. ~**dor** *m* engraver

**tallarín** *m* noodle

**talle** *m* waist; *(figura)* figure; *(medida)* size

**taller** *m* workshop; *(de pintor etc)* studio

**tallo** *m* stem, stalk

**tamal** *m (LAm)* tamale

**tamaño** *a (tan grande)* so big a; *(tan pequeño)* so small a. ● *m* size. **de** ~ **natural** life-size

**tambalearse** *vpr (persona)* stagger; *(cosa)* wobble

**también** *adv* also, too

**tambor** *m* drum. ~ **del freno** brake drum. ~**ilear** *vi* drum

**Támesis** *m* Thames

**tamiz** *m* sieve. ~**ar** [10] *vt* sieve

**tampoco** *adv* nor, neither, not either

**tampón** *m* tampon; *(para entintar)* ink-pad

**tan** *adv* so. **tan...** ~ as... as

**tanda** *f* group; (*capa*) layer; (*de obreros*) shift

**tangente** *a* & *f* tangent

**Tánger** *m* Tangier

**tangible** *a* tangible

**tango** *m* tango

**tanque** *m* tank; (*camión, barco*) tanker

**tante|ar** *vt* estimate; (*ensayar*) test; (*fig*) weigh up. ● *vi* score. ~o *m* estimate; (*prueba*) test; (*en deportes*) score

**tanto** *a* (*en singular*) so much; (*en plural*) so many; (*comparación en singular*) as much; (*comparación en plural*) as many. ● *pron* so much; (*en plural*) so many. ● *adv* so much; (*tiempo*) so long. ● *m* certain amount; (*punto*) point; (*gol*) goal. ~ **como** as well as; (*cantidad*) as much as. ~ **más... cuanto que** all the more... because. ~ **si... como si** whether... or. **a** ~**s de** sometime in. **en** ~, **entre** ~ meanwhile. **en** ~ **que** while. **entre** ~ meanwhile. **estar al** ~ **de** be up to date with. **hasta** ~ **que** until. **no es para** ~ it's not as bad as all that. **otro** ~ the same; (*el doble*) as much again. **por (lo)** ~ so. **un** ~ *adv* somewhat

**tañer** [22] *vt* play

**tapa** *f* lid; (*de botella*) top; (*de libro*) cover. ~**s** *fpl* savoury snacks

**tapacubos** *m invar* hub-cap

**tapa|dera** *f* cover, lid; (*fig*) cover. ~**r** *vt* cover; (*abrigar*) wrap up; (*obturar*) plug; put the top on ‹*botella*›

**taparrabo(s)** *m invar* loincloth; (*bañador*) swimming-trunks

**tapete** *m* (*de mesa*) table cover; (*alfombra*) rug

**tapia** *f* wall. ~**r** *vt* enclose

**tapicería** *f* tapestry; (*de muebles*) upholstery

**tapioca** *f* tapioca

**tapiz** *m* tapestry. ~**ar** [10] *vt* hang with tapestries; upholster ‹*muebles*›

**tap|ón** *m* stopper; (*corcho*) cork; (*med*) tampon; (*tec*) plug. ~**onazo** *m* pop

**taqui|grafía** *f* shorthand. ~**ígrafo** *m* shorthand writer

**taquill|a** *f* ticket office; (*archivador*) filing cabinet; (*fig, dinero*) takings. ~**ero** *m* clerk, ticket seller. ● *a* box-office

**tara** *f* (*peso*) tare; (*defecto*) defect

**taracea** *f* marquetry

**tarántula** *f* tarantula

**tararear** *vt/i* hum

**tarda|nza** *f* delay. ~**r** *vi* take; (*mucho tiempo*) take a long time. **a más** ~**r** at the latest. **sin** ~**r** without delay

**tard|e** *adv* late. ● *f* (*antes del atardecer*) afternoon; (*después del atardecer*) evening. ~**e o temprano** sooner or later. ~**ío** *a* late. **de** ~**e en** ~**e** from time to time. **por la** ~**e** in the afternoon

**tardo** *a* (*torpe*) slow

**tarea** *f* task, job

**tarifa** *f* rate, tariff

**tarima** *f* platform

**tarjeta** *f* card. ~ **de crédito** credit card. ~ **postal** postcard

**tarro** *m* jar

**tarta** *f* cake; (*torta*) tart. ~ **helada** ice-cream gateau

**tartamud|ear** *vi* stammer. ~**o** *a* stammering. ● *m* stammerer. **es** ~**o** he stammers

**tártaro** *m* tartar

**tarugo** *m* chunk

**tasa** *f* valuation; (*precio*) fixed price; (*índice*) rate. ~**r** *vt* fix a price for; (*limitar*) ration; (*evaluar*) value

**tasca** *f* bar

**tatarabuel|a** *f* great-great-grandmother. ~**o** *m* great-great-grandfather

**tatua|je** *m* (*acción*) tattooing; (*dibujo*) tattoo. ~**r** [21] *vt* tattoo

**taurino** *a* bullfighting

**Tauro** *m* Taurus

**tauromaquia** *f* bullfighting

**tax|i** *m* taxi. ~**ímetro** *m* taxi meter. ~**ista** *m* & *f* taxi-driver

**tayuyá** *m* (*Arg*) water melon

**taz|a** *f* cup. ~**ón** *m* bowl

**te** *pron* (*acusativo*) you; (*dativo*) (to) you; (*reflexivo*) (to) yourself

**té** *m* tea. **dar el** ~ bore

**tea** *f* torch

**teatr|al** *a* theatre; (*exagerado*) theatrical. ~**alizar** [10] *vt* dramatize. ~**o** *m* theatre; (*literatura*) drama. **obra** *f* ~**al** play

**tebeo** *m* comic

**teca** *f* teak

**tecla** *f* key. ~**do** *m* keyboard. **tocar la** ~, **tocar una** ~ pull strings

**técnica** *f* technique

**tecn|icismo** *m* technicality

**técnico** *a* technical. ● *m* technician

**tecnol|ogía** *f* technology. ~**ógico** *a* technological

**tecolote** *m* (*Mex*) owl

**tecomate** *m* (*Mex*) earthenware cup

**tech|ado** *m* roof. **~ar** *vt* roof. **~o** *m* (*interior*) ceiling; (*exterior*) roof. **~umbre** *f* roofing. **bajo ~ado** indoors

**teja** *f* tile. **~do** *m* roof. **a toca ~** cash

**teje|dor** *m* weaver. **~r** *vt* weave; (*hacer punto*) knit

**tejemaneje** *m* (*fam*) fuss; (*intriga*) scheming

**tejido** *m* material; (*anat, fig*) tissue. **~s** *mpl* textiles

**tejón** *m* badger

**tela** *f* material; (*de araña*) web; (*en líquido*) skin

**telar** *m* loom. **~es** *mpl* textile mill

**telaraña** *f* spider's web, cobweb

**tele** *f* (*fam*) television

**tele|comunicación** *f* telecommunication. **~diario** *m* television news. **~dirigido** *a* remote-controlled. **~férico** *m* cable-car; (*tren*) cable-railway

**tel|efonear** *vt/i* telephone. **~efónico** *a* telephone. **~efonista** *m* & *f* telephonist. **~éfono** *m* telephone. **al ~éfono** on the phone

**tel|egrafía** *f* telegraphy. **~egrafiar** [20] *vt* telegraph. **~egráfico** *a* telegraphic. **~égrafo** *m* telegraph

**telegrama** *m* telegram

**telenovela** *f* television soap opera

**teleobjetivo** *m* telephoto lens

**telep|atía** *f* telepathy. **~ático** *a* telepathic

**telesc|ópico** *a* telescopic. **~opio** *m* telescope

**telesilla** *m* ski-lift, chair-lift

**telespectador** *m* viewer

**telesquí** *m* ski-lift

**televi|dente** *m* & *f* viewer. **~sar** *vt* televise. **~sión** *f* television. **~sor** *m* television (set)

**télex** *m* telex

**telón** *m* curtain. **~ de acero** (*historia*) Iron Curtain

**tema** *m* subject; (*mus*) theme

**templ|ar** [1] *vi* shake; (*de miedo*) tremble; (*de frío*) shiver; (*fig*) shudder. **~or** *m* shaking; (*de miedo*) trembling; (*de frío*) shivering. **~or de tierra** earthquake. **~oroso** *a* trembling

**temer** *vt* be afraid (of). ● *vi* be afraid. **~se** *vpr* be afraid

**temerario** *a* reckless

**tem|eroso** *a* frightened. **~ible** *a* fearsome. **~or** *m* fear

**témpano** *m* floe

**temperamento** *m* temperament

**temperatura** *f* temperature

**temperie** *f* weather

**tempest|ad** *f* storm. **~uoso** *a* stormy. **levantar ~ades** (*fig*) cause a storm

**templ|ado** *a* moderate; (*tibio*) warm; (*clima, tiempo*) mild; (*valiente*) courageous; (*listo*) bright. **~anza** *f* moderation; (*de clima o tiempo*) mildness. **~ar** *vt* temper; (*calentar*) warm; (*mus*) tune. **~e** *m* tempering; (*temperatura*) temperature; (*humor*) mood

**templ|ete** *m* niche; (*pabellón*) pavilion. **~o** *m* temple

**tempora|da** *f* time; (*época*) season. **~l** *a* temporary. ● *m* (*tempestad*) storm; (*período de lluvia*) rainy spell

**tempran|ero** *a* (*frutos*) early. **~o** *a* & *adv* early. **ser ~ero** be an early riser

**tena|cidad** *f* tenacity

**tenacillas** *fpl* tongs

**tenaz** *a* tenacious

**tenaza** *f*, **tenazas** *fpl* pliers; (*para arrancar clavos*) pincers; (*para el fuego, culin*) tongs

**tende|ncia** *f* tendency. **~nte** *a*. **~nte a** aimed at. **~r** [1] *vt* spread (out); hang out (*ropa a secar*); (*colocar*) lay. ● *vi* have a tendency (**a** to). **~rse** *vpr* stretch out

**tender|ete** *m* stall. **~o** *m* shopkeeper

**tendido** *a* spread out; (*ropa*) hung out; (*persona*) stretched out. ● *m* (*en plaza de toros*) front rows. **~s** *mpl* (*ropa lavada*) washing

**tendón** *m* tendon

**tenebroso** *a* gloomy; (*turbio*) shady

**tenedor** *m* fork; (*poseedor*) holder

**tener** [40] *vt* have (of); (*agarrar*) hold; be (*años, calor, celos, cuidado, frío, ganas, hambre, miedo, razón, sed etc*). **¡ten cuidado!** be careful! **tengo calor** I'm hot. **tiene 3 años** he's 3 (years old). **~se** *vpr* stand up; (*considerarse*) consider o.s., think o.s. **~ al corriente**, **~ al día** keep up to date. **~ 2 cm de largo** be 2 cms long. **~ a uno por** consider s.o. **~ que** have (got) to. **tenemos que comprar pan** we've got to buy some bread. **¡ahí tienes!** there you are! **no ~ nada que ver con** have nothing to do with. **¿qué tienes?** what's the matter (with you)? **¡tenga!** here you are!

**tengo** *vb véase* **tener**

**teniente** *m* lieutenant. **~ de alcalde** deputy mayor

**tenis** *m* tennis. **~ta** *m & f* tennis player

**tenor** *m* sense; (*mus*) tenor. **a este ~** in this fashion

**tens|ión** *f* tension; (*presión*) pressure; (*arterial*) blood pressure; (*elec*) voltage; (*de persona*) tenseness. **~o** *a* tense

**tentación** *f* temptation

**tentáculo** *m* tentacle

**tenta|dor** *a* tempting. **~r** [1] *vt* feel; (*seducir*) tempt

**tentativa** *f* attempt

**tenue** *a* thin; (*luz, voz*) faint

**teñi|do** *m* dye. **~r** [5 & 22] *vt* dye; (*fig*) tinge (**de** with). **~rse** *vpr* dye one's hair

**te|ología** *f* theology. **~ológico** *a* theological. **~ólogo** *m* theologian

**teorema** *m* theorem

**te|oría** *f* theory. **~órico** *a* theoretical

**tepache** *m* (*Mex*) (alcoholic) drink

**tequila** *f* tequila

**TER** *m* high-speed train

**terap|éutico** *a* therapeutic. **~ia** *f* therapy

**tercer** *a véase* **tercero**. **~a** *f* (*auto*) third (gear). **~o** *a* (*delante de nombre masculino en singular* **tercer**) third. ● *m* third party

**terceto** *m* trio

**terciar** *vi* mediate. **~ en** join in. **~se** *vpr* occur

**tercio** *m* third

**terciopelo** *m* velvet

**terco** *a* obstinate

**tergiversar** *vt* distort

**terma|l** *a* thermal. **~s** *fpl* thermal baths

**termes** *m invar* termite

**térmico** *a* thermal

**termina|ción** *f* ending; (*conclusión*) conclusion. **~l** *a & m* terminal. **~nte** *a* categorical. **~r** *vt* finish, end. **~rse** *vpr* come to an end. **~r por** end up

**término** *m* end; (*palabra*) term; (*plazo*) period. **~ medio** average. **~ municipal** municipal district. **dar ~ a** finish off. **en último ~** as a last resort. **estar en buenos ~s con** be on good terms with. **llevar a ~** carry

out. **poner ~ a** put an end to. **primer ~** foreground

**terminología** *f* terminology

**termita** *f* termite

**termo** *m* Thermos flask (P), flask

**termómetro** *m* thermometer

**termo|nuclear** *a* thermonuclear. **~sifón** *m* boiler. **~stato** *m* thermostat

**terner|a** *f* (*carne*) veal. **~o** *m* calf

**ternura** *f* tenderness

**terquedad** *f* stubbornness

**terracota** *f* terracotta

**terrado** *m* flat roof

**terraplén** *m* embankment

**terrateniente** *m & f* landowner

**terraza** *f* terrace; (*terrado*) flat roof

**terremoto** *m* earthquake

**terre|no** *a* earthly. ● *m* land; (*solar*) plot; (*fig*) field. **~stre** *a* earthly; (*mil*) ground

**terr|ible** *a* terrible. **~iblemente** *adv* awfully. **~ífico** *a* terrifying

**territori|al** *a* territorial. **~o** *m* territory

**terrón** *m* (*de tierra*) clod; (*culin*) lump

**terror** *m* terror. **~ífico** *a* terrifying. **~ismo** *m* terrorism. **~ista** *m & f* terrorist

**terr|oso** *a* earthy; (*color*) brown. **~uño** *m* land; (*patria*) native land

**terso** *a* polished; (*piel*) smooth

**tertulia** *f* social gathering, get-together (*fam*). **~r** *vi* (*LAm*) get together. **estar de ~** chat. **hacer ~** get together

**tesi|na** *f* dissertation. **~s** *f inv* thesis; (*opinión*) theory

**tesón** *m* perseverance

**tesor|ería** *f* treasury. **~ero** *m* treasurer. **~o** *m* treasure; (*tesorería*) treasury; (*libro*) thesaurus

**testa** *f* (*fam*) head. **~ferro** *m* figurehead

**testa|mento** *m* will. **T~mento** (*relig*) Testament. **~r** *vi* make a will

**testarudo** *a* stubborn

**testículo** *m* testicle

**testi|ficar** [7] *vt/i* testify. **~go** *m* witness. **~go de vista**, **~go ocular**, **~go presencial** eyewitness. **~monio** *m* testimony

**teta** *f* nipple; (*de biberón*) teat

**tétanos** *m* tetanus

**tetera** *f* (*para el té*) teapot; (*Mex, biberón*) feeding-bottle

**tetilla** *f* nipple; (*de biberón*) teat

**tétrico** *a* gloomy

**textil** *a & m* textile

**text|o** *m* text. **~ual** *a* textual

**textura** *f* texture

**teyú** *m* (*Arg*) iguana

**tez** *f* complexion

**ti** *pron* you

**tía** *f* aunt; (*fam*) woman

**tiara** *f* tiara

**tibio** *a* lukewarm. **ponerle ~ a uno** insult s.o.

**tiburón** *m* shark

**tic** *m* tic

**tiempo** *m* time; (*atmosférico*) weather; (*mus*) tempo; (*gram*) tense; (*en deportes*) half. **a su ~** in due course. **a ~** in time. **¿cuánto ~?** how long? **hace buen ~** the weather is fine. **hace ~** some time ago. **mucho ~** a long time. **perder el ~** waste time. **¿qué ~ hace?** what is the weather like?

**tienda** *f* shop; (*de campaña*) tent. **~ de comestibles, ~ de ultramarinos** grocer's (shop) (*Brit*), grocery store (*Amer*)

**tiene** *vb véase* **tener**

**tienta. a ~s** gropingly. **andar a ~s** grope one's way

**tiento** *m* touch; (*de ciego*) blind person's stick; (*fig*) tact

**tierno** *a* tender; (*joven*) young

**tierra** *f* land; (*planeta, elec*) earth; (*suelo*) ground; (*geol*) soil, earth. **caer por ~** (*fig*) crumble. **por ~** overland, by land

**tieso** *a* stiff; (*firme*) firm; (*engreído*) conceited; (*orgulloso*) proud

**tiesto** *m* flowerpot

**tifoideo** *a* typhoid

**tifón** *m* typhoon

**tifus** *m* typhus; (*fiebre tifoidea*) typhoid (fever); (*en el teatro*) people with complimentary tickets

**tigre** *m* tiger

**tijera** *f*, **tijeras** *fpl* scissors; (*de jardín*) shears

**tijeret|a** *f* (*insecto*) earwig; (*bot*) tendril. **~ear** *vt* snip

**tila** *f* lime(-tree); (*infusión*) lime tea

**tild|ar** *vt.* **~ar de** (*fig*) call. **~e** *m* tilde

**tilín** *m* tinkle. **hacer ~** appeal

**tilingo** *a* (*Arg, Mex*) silly

**tilma** *f* (*Mex*) poncho

**tilo** *m* lime(-tree)

**timar** *vt* swindle

**timbal** *m* drum; (*culin*) timbale, meat pie

**timbiriche** *m* (*Mex*) (alcoholic) drink

**timbr|ar** *vt* stamp. **~e** *m* (*sello*) stamp; (*elec*) bell; (*sonido*) timbre. **tocar el ~e** ring the bell

**timidez** *f* shyness

**tímido** *a* shy

**timo** *m* swindle

**timón** *m* rudder; (*fig*) helm

**tímpano** *m* kettledrum; (*anat*) eardrum. **~s** *mpl* (*mus*) timpani

**tina** *f* tub. **~ja** *f* large earthenware jar

**tinglado** *m* (*fig*) intrigue

**tinieblas** *fpl* darkness; (*fig*) confusion

**tino** *f* (*habilidad*) skill; (*moderación*) moderation; (*tacto*) tact

**tint|a** *f* ink. **~e** *m* dyeing; (*color*) dye; (*fig*) tinge. **~ero** *m* ink-well. **de buena ~a** on good authority

**tint|ín** *m* tinkle; (*de vasos*) chink, clink. **~inear** *vi* tinkle; ⟨*vasos*⟩ chink, clink

**tinto** *a* ⟨*vino*⟩ red

**tintorería** *f* dyeing; (*tienda*) dry cleaner's

**tintura** *f* dyeing; (*color*) dye; (*noción superficial*) smattering

**tío** *m* uncle; (*fam*) man. **~s** *mpl* uncle and aunt

**tiovivo** *m* merry-go-round

**típico** *a* typical

**tipo** *m* type; (*persona, fam*) person; (*figura de mujer*) figure; (*figura de hombre*) build; (*com*) rate

**tip|ografía** *f* typography. **~ográfico** *a* typographic(al). **~ógrafo** *m* printer

**típula** *f* crane-fly, daddy-long-legs

**tique** *m*, **tíquet** *m* ticket

**tiquete** *m* (*LAm*) ticket

**tira** *f* strip. **la ~ de** lots of

**tirabuzón** *m* corkscrew; (*de pelo*) ringlet

**tirad|a** *f* distance; (*serie*) series; (*de libros etc*) edition. **~o** *a* (*barato*) very cheap; (*fácil, fam*) very easy. **~or** *m* (*asa*) handle; (*juguete*) catapult (*Brit*), slingshot (*Amer*). **de una ~a** at one go

**tiran|ía** *f* tyranny. **~izar** [10] *vt* tyrannize. **~o** *a* tyrannical. **●** *m* tyrant

**tirante** *a* tight; (*fig*) tense; ⟨*relaciones*⟩ strained. **●** *m* shoulder strap. **~s** *mpl* braces (*esp Brit*), suspenders (*Amer*)

**tirar** *vt* throw; (*desechar*) throw away; (*derribar*) knock over; give ⟨*golpe, coz etc*⟩; (*imprimir*) print. **●** *vi* (*disparar*) shoot. **~se** *vpr* throw o.s.; (*tumbarse*) lie down. ～ **a** tend to (be); (*parecerse a*) resemble. ～ **de** pull; (*atraer*) attract. **a todo** ～ at the most. **ir tirando** get by

**tirita** *f* sticking-plaster, plaster (*Brit*)

**tirit|ar** *vi* shiver. ～**ón** *m* shiver

**tiro** *m* throw; (*disparo*) shot; (*alcance*) range. ～ **a gol** shot at goal. **a** ～ within range. **errar el** ～ miss. **pegarse un** ～ shoot o.s.

**tiroides** *m* thyroid (gland)

**tirón** *m* tug. **de un** ～ in one go

**tirote|ar** *vt* shoot at. ～**o** *m* shooting

**tisana** *f* herb tea

**tisis** *f* tuberculosis

**tisú** *m* (*pl* tisus) tissue

**títere** *m* puppet. ～ **de guante** glove puppet. ～**s** *mpl* puppet show

**titilar** *vi* quiver; (*estrella*) twinkle

**titiritero** *m* puppeteer; (*acróbata*) acrobat; (*malabarista*) juggler

**titube|ante** *a* shaky; (*fig*) hesitant. ～**ar** *vi* stagger; (*cosa*) be unstable; (*fig*) hesitate. ～**o** *m* hesitation

**titula|do** *a* (*libro*) entitled; (*persona*) qualified. ～**r** *m* headline; (*persona*) holder. ● *vt* call. ～**rse** *vpr* be called

**título** *m* title; (*persona*) titled person; (*académico*) qualification; (*univ*) degree; (*de periódico etc*) headline; (*derecho*) right. **a** ～ **de** as, by way of

**tiza** *f* chalk

**tiz|nar** *vt* dirty. ～**ne** *m* soot. ～**ón** *m* half-burnt stick; (*fig*) stain

**toall|a** *f* towel. ～**ero** *m* towel-rail

**tobillo** *m* ankle

**tobogán** *m* slide; (*para la nieve*) toboggan

**tocadiscos** *m invar* record-player

**toca|do** *a* (*con sombrero*) wearing. ● *m* hat. ～**dor** *m* dressing-table. ～**dor de señoras** ladies' room. ～**nte** *a* touching. ～**r** [7] *vt* touch; (*mus*) play; ring (*timbre*); (*mencionar*) touch on; (*barco*) stop at. ● *vi* knock; (*corresponder a uno*) be one's turn. ～**rse** *vpr* touch each other; (*cubrir la cabeza*) cover one's head. **en lo que** ～ **a, en lo** ～**nte a** as for. **estar** ～**do** (**de la cabeza**) be mad. **te** ～ **a ti** it's your turn

**tocateja. a** ～ cash

**tocayo** *m* namesake

**tocino** *m* bacon

**tocólogo** *m* obstetrician

**todavía** *adv* still, yet. ～ **no** not yet

**todo** *a* all; (*entero*) the whole; (*cada*) every. ● *adv* completely, all. ● *m* whole. ● *pron* everything, all; (*en plural*) everyone. ～ **el día** all day. ～ **el mundo** everyone. ～ **el que** anyone who. ～ **incluido** all in. ～ **lo contrario** quite the opposite. ～ **lo que** anything which. ～**s los días** every day. ～**s los dos** both (of them). ～**s los tres** all three. **ante** ～ above all. **a** ～ **esto** meanwhile. **con** ～ still, however. **del** ～ completely. **en** ～ **el mundo** anywhere. **estar en** ～ be on the ball. **es** ～ **uno** it's all the same. **nosotros** ～**s** all of us. **sobre** ～ above all

**toldo** *m* sunshade

**tolera|ncia** *f* tolerance. ～**nte** *a* tolerant. ～**r** *vt* tolerate

**tolondro** *m* (*chichón*) lump

**toma** *f* taking; (*med*) dose; (*de agua*) outlet; (*elec*) socket; (*elec, clavija*) plug. ● *int* well!, fancy that! ～ **de corriente** power point. ～**dura** *f*. ～**dura de pelo** hoax. ～**r** *vt* take; catch (*autobús, tren etc*); (*beber*) drink, have; (*comer*) eat, have. ● *vi* take; (*dirigirse*) go. ～**rse** *vpr* take; (*beber*) drink, have; (*comer*) eat, have. ～**r a bien** take well. ～**r a mal** take badly. ～**r en serio** take seriously. ～**rla con uno** pick on s.o. ～**r nota** take note. ～**r por** take for. ～ **y daca** give and take. ¿**qué va a** ～**r?** what would you like?

**tomate** *m* tomato

**tomavistas** *m invar* cine-camera

**tómbola** *f* tombola

**tomillo** *m* thyme

**tomo** *m* volume

**ton. sin** ～ **ni son** without rhyme or reason

**tonada** *f*, **tonadilla** *f* tune

**tonel** *m* barrel. ～**ada** *f* ton. ～**aje** *m* tonnage

**tónic|a** *f* tonic water; (*mus*) tonic. ～**o** *a* tonic; (*sílaba*) stressed. ● *m* tonic

**tonificar** [7] *vt* invigorate

**tono** *m* tone; (*mus, modo*) key; (*color*) shade

**tont|ería** *f* silliness; (*cosa*) silly thing; (*dicho*) silly remark. ～**o** *a* silly. ● *m* fool, idiot; (*payaso*) clown. **dejarse de** ～**erías** stop wasting time. **hacer el** ～**o** act the fool. **hacerse el** ～**o** feign ignorance

**topacio** *m* topaz

**topar** vt ⟨animal⟩ butt; ⟨persona⟩ bump into; (fig) run into. ● vi. ~ **con** run into

**tope** a maximum. ● m end; (de tren) buffer. **hasta los** ~**s** crammed full. **ir a** ~ go flat out

**tópico** a topical. ● m cliché

**topo** m mole

**topogr|afía** f topography. ~**áfico** a topographical

**toque** m touch; (sonido) sound; (de campana) peal; (de reloj) stroke; (fig) crux. ~ **de queda** curfew. ~**tear** vt keep fingering, fiddle with. **dar el último** ~ put the finishing touches

**toquilla** f shawl

**tórax** m thorax

**torbellino** m whirlwind; (de polvo) cloud of dust; (fig) whirl

**torcer** [2 & 9] vt twist; (doblar) bend; wring out ⟨ropa⟩. ● vi turn. ~**se** vpr twist; (fig, desviarse) go astray; (fig, frustrarse) go wrong

**tordo** a dapple grey. ● m thrush

**tore|ar** vt fight; (evitar) dodge; (entretener) put off. ● vi fight (bulls). ~**o** m bullfighting. ~**ro** m bullfighter

**torment|a** f storm. ~**o** m torture. ~**oso** a stormy

**tornado** m tornado

**tornar** vt return

**tornasolado** a irridescent

**torneo** m tournament

**tornillo** m screw

**torniquete** m (entrada) turnstile

**torno** m lathe; (de alfarero) wheel. **en** ~ a around

**toro** m bull. ~**s** mpl bullfighting. **ir a los** ~**s** go to a bullfight

**toronja** f grapefruit

**torpe** a clumsy; (estúpido) stupid

**torped|ero** m torpedo-boat. ~**o** m torpedo

**torpeza** f clumsiness; (de inteligencia) slowness

**torpor** m torpor

**torrado** m toasted chick-pea

**torre** f tower; (en ajedrez) castle, rook

**torrefac|ción** f roasting. ~**to** a roasted

**torren|cial** a torrential. ~**te** m torrent; (circulatorio) bloodstream; (fig) flood

**tórrido** a torrid

**torrija** f French toast

**torsión** f twisting

**torso** m torso

**torta** f tart; (bollo, fam) cake; (golpe) slap, punch; (Mex, bocadillo) sandwich. ~**zo** m slap, punch. **no entender ni** ~ not understand a word of it. **pegarse un** ~**zo** have a bad accident

**tortícolis** f stiff neck

**tortilla** f omelette; (Mex, de maíz) tortilla, maize cake. ~ **francesa** plain omelette

**tórtola** f turtle-dove

**tortuga** f tortoise; (de mar) turtle

**tortuoso** a winding; (fig) devious

**tortura** f torture. ~**r** vt torture

**torvo** a grim

**tos** f cough. ~ **ferina** whooping cough

**tosco** a crude; ⟨persona⟩ coarse

**toser** vi cough

**tósigo** m poison

**tosquedad** f crudeness; (de persona) coarseness

**tost|ada** f toast. ~**ado** a ⟨pan⟩ toasted; ⟨café⟩ roasted; ⟨persona⟩ tanned; (marrón) brown. ~**ar** vt toast ⟨pan⟩; roast ⟨café⟩; tan ⟨piel⟩. ~**ón** m (pan) crouton; (lata) bore

**total** a total. ● adv after all. ● m total; (totalidad) whole. ~**idad** f whole. ~**itario** a totalitarian. ~**izar** [10] vt total. ~ **que** so, to cut a long story short

**tóxico** a toxic

**toxicómano** m drug addict

**toxina** f toxin

**tozudo** a stubborn

**traba** f bond; (fig, obstáculo) obstacle. **poner** ~**s a** hinder

**trabaj|ador** a hard-working. ● m worker. ~**ar** vt work (de as); knead ⟨masa⟩; (estudiar) work at; ⟨actor⟩ act. ● vi work. ~**o** m work. ~**os** mpl hardships. ~**os forzados** hard labour. ~**oso** a hard. **costar** ~**o** be difficult. **¿en qué** ~**as?** what work do you do?

**trabalenguas** m invar tongue-twister

**traba|r** vt (sujetar) fasten; (unir) join; (empezar) start; (culin) thicken. ~**rse** vpr get tangled up. **trabársele la lengua** get tongue-tied. ~**zón** f joining; (fig) connection

**trabucar** [7] vt mix up

**trácala** f (Mex) trick

**tracción** f traction

**tractor** m tractor

**tradici|ón** f tradition. **~onal** a traditional. **~onalista** m & f traditionalist

**traduc|ción** f translation. **~ir** [47] vt translate (**al** into). **~tor** m translator

**traer** [41] vt bring; (llevar) carry; (atraer) attract. **traérselas** be difficult

**trafica|nte** m & f dealer. **~r** [7] vi deal

**tráfico** m traffic; (com) trade

**traga|deras** fpl (fam) throat. **tener buenas ~deras** (ser crédulo) swallow anything; (ser tolerante) be easygoing. **~luz** m skylight. **~perras** f invar slot-machine. **~r** [12] vt swallow; (comer mucho) devour; (absorber) absorb; (fig) swallow up. **no (poder) ~r** not be able to stand. **~rse** vpr swallow; (fig) swallow up

**tragedia** f tragedy

**trágico** a tragic. ● m tragedian

**trag|o** m swallow, gulp; (pequeña porción) sip; (fig, disgusto) blow. **~ón** a greedy. ● m glutton. **ech-ar(se) un ~o** have a drink

**trai|ción** f treachery; (pol) treason. **~cionar** vt betray. **~cionero** a treacherous. **~dor** a treacherous. ● m traitor

**traigo** vb véase **traer**

**traje** m dress; (de hombre) suit. ● vb véase **traer**. **~ de baño** swimming-costume. **~ de ceremonia**, **~ de etiqueta**, **~ de noche** evening dress

**traj|ín** m (transporte) haulage; (jaleo, fam) bustle. **~inar** vt transport. ● vi bustle about

**trama** f weft; (fig) link; (fig, argumento) plot. **~r** vt weave; (fig) plot

**tramitar** vt negotiate

**trámite** m step. **~s** mpl procedure. **en ~** in hand

**tramo** m (parte) section; (de escalera) flight

**tramp|a** f trap; (puerta) trapdoor; (fig) trick. **~illa** f trapdoor. **hacer ~a** cheat

**trampolín** m trampoline; (fig, de piscina) springboard

**tramposo** a cheating. ● m cheat

**tranca** f stick; (de puerta) bar

**trance** m moment; (hipnótico etc) trance. **a todo ~** at all costs

**tranco** m stride

**tranquil|idad** f (peace and) quiet; (de espíritu) peace of mind. **~izar** [10] vt reassure. **~o** a quiet; (conciencia)

clear; (mar) calm; (despreocupado) thoughtless. **estáte ~o** don't worry

**trans...** pref (véase también **tras...**) trans...

**transacción** f transaction; (acuerdo) compromise

**transatlántico** a transatlantic. ● m (ocean) liner

**transbord|ador** m ferry. **~ar** vt transfer. **~arse** vpr change. **~o** m transfer. **hacer ~o** change (**en** at)

**transcri|bir** (pp **transcrito**) vt transcribe. **~pción** f transcription

**transcur|rir** vi pass. **~so** m course

**transeúnte** a temporary. ● m & f passer-by

**transfer|encia** f transfer. **~ir** [4] vt transfer

**transfigurar** vt transfigure

**transforma|ción** f transformation. **~dor** m transformer. **~r** vt transform

**transfusión** f transfusion. **hacer una ~** give a blood transfusion

**transgre|dir** vt transgress. **~sión** f transgression

**transición** f transition

**transido** a overcome

**transigir** [14] vi give in, compromise

**transistor** m transistor; (radio) radio

**transita|ble** a passable. **~r** vi go

**transitivo** a transitive

**tránsito** m transit; (tráfico) traffic

**transitorio** a transitory

**translúcido** a translucent

**transmi|sión** f transmission; (radio, TV) broadcast. **~sor** m transmitter. **~sora** f broadcasting station. **~tir** vt transmit; (radio, TV) broadcast; (fig) pass on

**transparen|cia** f transparency. **~tar** vt show. **~te** a transparent

**transpira|ción** f perspiration. **~r** vi transpire; (sudar) sweat

**transponer** [34] vt move. ● vi disappear round (esquina etc); disappear behind (montaña etc). **~se** vpr disappear

**transport|ar** vt transport. **~e** m transport. **empresa** f **de ~es** removals company

**transversal** a transverse; (calle) side

**tranvía** m tram

**trapacería** f swindle

**trapear** vt (LAm) mop

**trapecio** m trapeze; (math) trapezium

**trapiche** m (*para azúcar*) mill; (*para aceitunas*) press

**trapicheo** m fiddle

**trapisonda** f (*jaleo, fam*) row; (*enredo, fam*) plot

**trapo** m rag; (*para limpiar*) cloth. ~**s** mpl (*fam*) clothes. **a todo** ~ out of control

**tráquea** f windpipe, trachea

**traquete|ar** vt bang, rattle. ~**o** m banging, rattle

**tras** prep after; (*detrás*) behind; (*encima de*) as well as

**tras...** pref (*véase también* **trans...**) trans...

**trascende|ncia** f importance. ~**ntal** a transcendental; (*importante*) important. ~**r** [1] vi (*oler*) smell (**a** of); (*saberse*) become known; (*extenderse*) spread

**trasegar** [1 & 12] vt move around

**trasero** a back, rear. • m (*anat*) bottom

**trasgo** m goblin

**traslad|ar** vt move; (*aplazar*) postpone; (*traducir*) translate; (*copiar*) copy. ~**o** m transfer; (*copia*) copy; (*mudanza*) removal. **dar** ~**o** send a copy

**trasl|úcido** a translucent. ~**ucirse** [11] vpr be translucent; (*dejarse ver*) show through; (*fig, revelarse*) be revealed. ~**uz** m. **al** ~**uz** against the light

**trasmano** m. **a** ~ out of reach; (*fig*) out of the way

**trasnochar** vt (*acostarse tarde*) go to bed late; (*no acostarse*) stay up all night; (*no dormir*) be unable to sleep; (*pernoctar*) spend the night

**traspas|ar** vt pierce; (*transferir*) transfer; (*pasar el límite*) go beyond. ~**o** m transfer. **se** ~**a** for sale

**traspié** m trip; (*fig*) slip. **dar un** ~ stumble; (*fig*) slip up

**trasplant|ar** vt transplant. ~**e** m transplanting; (*med*) transplant

**trastada** f stupid thing; (*jugada*) dirty trick, practical joke

**traste** m fret. **dar al** ~ **con** ruin. **ir al** ~ fall through

**trastero** m storeroom

**trastienda** f back room; (*fig*) shrewdness

**trasto** m piece of furniture; (*cosa inútil*) piece of junk; (*persona*) useless person, dead loss (*fam*)

**trastorn|ado** a mad. ~**ar** vt upset; (*volver loco*) drive mad; (*fig, gustar*

mucho, fam) delight. ~**arse** vpr get upset; (*volverse loco*) go mad. ~**o** m (*incl med*) upset; (*pol*) disturbance; (*fig*) confusion

**trastrocar** [2 & 7] vt change round

**trat|able** a friendly. ~**ado** m treatise; (*acuerdo*) treaty. ~**amiento** m treatment; (*título*) title. ~**ante** m & f dealer. ~**ar** vt (*incl med*) treat; deal with ⟨*asunto etc*⟩; (*com*) deal; (*manejar*) handle; (*de tú, de Vd*) address (**de** as); (*llamar*) call. • vi deal (with). ~**ar con** have to do with; know ⟨*persona*⟩; (*com*) deal in. ~**ar de** be about; (*intentar*) try. ~**o** m treatment; (*acuerdo*) agreement; (*título*) title; (*relación*) relationship. **¡~o hecho!** agreed! ~**os** mpl dealings. **¿de qué se** ~**a?** what's it about?

**traum|a** m trauma. ~**ático** a traumatic

**través** m (*inclinación*) slant. **a** ~ **de** through; (*de un lado a otro*) across. **de** ~ across; (*de lado*) sideways. **mirar de** ~ look askance at

**travesaño** m crosspiece

**travesía** f crossing; (*calle*) side-street

**trav|esura** f prank. ~**ieso** a ⟨*niño*⟩ mischievous, naughty

**trayecto** m road; (*tramo*) stretch; (*ruta*) route; (*viaje*) journey. ~**ria** f trajectory; (*fig*) course

**traz|a** f plan; (*aspecto*) look, appearance; (*habilidad*) skill. ~**ado** a. **bien** ~**ado** good-looking. **mal** ~**ado** unattractive. • m plan. ~**ar** [10] vt draw; (*bosquejar*) sketch. ~**o** m line

**trébol** m clover. ~**es** mpl (*en naipes*) clubs

**trece** a & m thirteen

**trecho** m stretch; (*distancia*) distance; (*tiempo*) while. **a** ~**s** in places. **de** ~ **en** ~ at intervals

**tregua** f truce; (*fig*) respite

**treinta** a & m thirty

**tremendo** a terrible; (*extraordinario*) terrific

**trementina** f turpentine

**tren** m train; (*equipaje*) luggage. ~ **de aterrizaje** landing gear. ~ **de vida** lifestyle

**tren|cilla** f braid. ~**za** f braid; (*de pelo*) plait. ~**zar** [10] vt plait

**trepa|dor** a climbing. ~**r** vt/i climb

**tres** a & m three. ~**cientos** a & m three hundred. ~**illo** m three-piece suite; (*mus*) triplet

**treta** f trick

**tri|angular** *a* triangular. **~ángulo** *m* triangle

**trib|al** *a* tribal. **~u** *f* tribe

**tribulación** *f* tribulation

**tribuna** *f* platform; (*de espectadores*) stand

**tribunal** *m* court; (*de examen etc*) board; (*fig*) tribunal

**tribut|ar** *vt* pay. **~o** *m* tribute; (*impuesto*) tax

**triciclo** *m* tricycle

**tricolor** *a* three-coloured

**tricornio** *a* three-cornered. **●** *m* three-cornered hat

**tricotar** *vt/i* knit

**tridimensional** *a* three-dimensional

**tridente** *m* trident

**trigésimo** *a* thirtieth

**trig|al** *m* wheat field. **~o** *m* wheat

**trigonometría** *f* trigonometry

**trigueño** *a* olive-skinned; (*pelo*) dark blonde

**trilogía** *f* trilogy

**trilla|do** *a* (*fig, manoseado*) trite; (*fig, conocido*) well-known. **~r** *vt* thresh

**trimestr|al** *a* quarterly. **~e** *m* quarter; (*escol, univ*) term

**trin|ar** *vi* warble. **estar que trina** be furious

**trinchar** *vt* carve

**trinchera** *f* ditch; (*mil*) trench; (*rail*) cutting; (*abrigo*) trench coat

**trineo** *m* sledge

**trinidad** *f* trinity

**Trinidad** *f* Trinidad

**trino** *m* warble

**trío** *m* trio

**tripa** *f* intestine; (*culin*) tripe; (*fig, vientre*) tummy, belly. **~s** *fpl* (*de máquina etc*) parts, workings. **me duele la ~** I've got tummy-ache. **revolver las ~s** turn one's stomach

**tripicallos** *mpl* tripe

**tripl|e** *a* triple. **●** *m*. **el ~e (de)** three times as much (as). **~icado** *a*. **por ~icado** in triplicate. **~icar** [7] *vt* treble

**trípode** *m* tripod

**tríptico** *m* triptych

**tripula|ción** *f* crew. **~nte** *m* & *f* member of the crew. **~r** *vt* man

**triquitraque** *m* (*ruido*) clatter

**tris** *m* crack; (*de papel etc*) ripping noise. **estar en un ~** be on the point of

**triste** *a* sad; (*paisaje, tiempo etc*) gloomy; (*fig, insignificante*) miserable. **~za** *f* sadness

**tritón** *m* newt

**triturar** *vt* crush

**triunf|al** *a* triumphal. **~ante** *a* triumphant. **~ar** *vi* triumph (**de**, **sobre** over). **~o** *m* triumph

**triunvirato** *m* triumvirate

**trivial** *a* trivial

**triza** *f* piece. **hacer algo ~s** smash sth to pieces

**trocar** [2 & 7] *vt* (ex)change

**trocear** *vt* cut up, chop

**trocito** *m* small piece

**trocha** *f* narrow path; (*atajo*) short cut

**trofeo** *m* trophy

**tromba** *f* waterspout. **~ de agua** heavy downpour

**trombón** *m* trombone; (*músico*) trombonist

**trombosis** *f invar* thrombosis

**trompa** *f* horn; (*de orquesta*) French horn; (*de elefante*) trunk; (*hocico*) snout; (*juguete*) (spinning) top; (*anat*) tube. **●** *m* horn player. **coger una ~** (*fam*) get drunk

**trompada** *f*, **trompazo** *m* bump

**trompet|a** *f* trumpet; (*músico*) trumpeter, trumpet player; (*clarín*) bugle. **~illa** *f* ear-trumpet

**trompicar** [7] *vi* trip

**trompo** *m* (*juguete*) (spinning) top

**trona|da** *f* thunder storm. **~r** *vt* (*Mex*) shoot. **●** *vi* thunder

**tronco** *m* trunk. **dormir como un ~** sleep like a log

**tronchar** *vt* bring down; (*fig*) cut short. **~se de risa** laugh a lot

**trono** *m* throne

**trop|a** *f* troops. **~el** *m* mob. **ser de ~a** be in the army

**tropero** *m* (*Arg, vaquero*) cowboy

**tropez|ar** [1 & 10] *vi* trip; (*fig*) slip up. **~ar con** run into. **~ón** *m* stumble; (*fig*) slip

**tropical** *a* tropical

**trópico** *a* tropical. **●** *m* tropic

**tropiezo** *m* slip; (*desgracia*) mishap

**trot|ar** *vi* trot. **~e** *m* trot; (*fig*) toing and froing. **al ~e** trotting; (*de prisa*) in a rush. **de mucho ~e** hard-wearing

**trozo** *m* piece, bit. **a ~s** in bits

**truco** *m* knack; (*ardid*) trick. **coger el ~** get the knack

**trucha** *f* trout

**trueno** *m* thunder; (*estampido*) bang

**trueque** *m* exchange. **aun a ~ de** even at the expense of

**trufa** *f* truffle. **~r** *vt* stuff with truffles

**truhán** *m* rogue; (*gracioso*) jester

**truncar** [7] *vt* truncate; (*fig*) cut short

**tu** *a* your

**tú** *pron* you

**tuba** *f* tuba

**tubérculo** *m* tuber

**tuberculosis** *f* tuberculosis

**tub|ería** *f* pipes; (*oleoducto etc*) pipeline. **~o** *m* tube. **~o de ensayo** test tube. **~o de escape** (*auto*) exhaust (pipe). **~ular** *a* tubular

**tuerca** *f* nut

**tuerto** *a* one-eyed, blind in one eye. ● *m* one-eyed person

**tuétano** *m* marrow; (*fig*) heart. **hasta los ~s** completely

**tufo** *m* fumes; (*olor*) bad smell

**tugurio** *m* hovel, slum

**tul** *m* tulle

**tulipán** *m* tulip

**tulli|do** *a* paralysed. **~r** [22] *vt* cripple

**tumba** *f* grave, tomb

**tumb|ar** *vt* knock down, knock over; (*fig, en examen, fam*) fail; (*pasmar, fam*) overwhelm. **~arse** *vpr* lie down. **~o** *m* jolt. **dar un ~o** tumble. **~ona** *f* settee; (*sillón*) armchair; (*de lona*) deckchair

**tumefacción** *f* swelling

**tumido** *a* swollen

**tumor** *m* tumour

**tumulto** *m* turmoil; (*pol*) riot

**tuna** *f* prickly pear; (*de estudiantes*) student band

**tunante** *m* & *f* rogue

**túnel** *m* tunnel

**Túnez** *m* (*ciudad*) Tunis; (*país*) Tunisia

**túnica** *f* tunic

**Tunicia** *f* Tunisia

**tupé** *m* toupee; (*fig*) nerve

**tupido** *a* thick

**turba** *f* peat; (*muchedumbre*) mob

**turba|ción** *f* disturbance, upset; (*confusión*) confusion. **~do** *a* upset

**turbante** *m* turban

**turbar** *vt* upset; (*molestar*) disturb. **~se** *vpr* be upset

**turbina** *f* turbine

**turbi|o** *a* cloudy; (*vista*) blurred; (*asunto etc*) unclear. **~ón** *m* squall

**turbulen|cia** *f* turbulence; (*disturbio*) disturbance. **~te** *a* turbulent; (*persona*) restless

**turco** *a* Turkish. ● *m* Turk; (*lengua*) Turkish

**tur|ismo** *m* tourism; (*coche*) car. **~ista** *m* & *f* tourist. **~ístico** *a* tourist. **oficina** *f* **de ~ismo** tourist office

**turn|arse** *vpr* take turns (**para** to). **~o** *m* turn; (*de trabajo*) shift. **por ~o** in turn

**turquesa** *f* turquoise

**Turquía** *f* Turkey

**turrón** *m* nougat

**turulato** *a* (*fam*) stunned

**tutear** *vt* address as *tú*. **~se** *vpr* be on familiar terms

**tutela** *f* (*jurid*) guardianship; (*fig*) protection

**tuteo** *m* use of the familiar *tú*

**tutor** *m* guardian; (*escol*) form master

**tuve** *vb véase* **tener**

**tuyo** *a* & *pron* yours. **un amigo ~** a friend of yours

# U

**u** *conj* or

**ubicuidad** *f* ubiquity

**ubre** *f* udder

**ucraniano** *a* & *m* Ukranian

**Ud** *abrev* (*Usted*) you

**uf** *int* phew!; (*de repugnancia*) ugh!

**ufan|arse** *vpr* be proud (**con, de** of); (*jactarse*) boast (**con, de** about). **~o** *a* proud

**ujier** *m* usher

**úlcera** *f* ulcer

**ulterior** *a* later; ‹*lugar*› further. **~mente** *adv* later, subsequently

**últimamente** *adv* (*recientemente*) recently; (*al final*) finally; (*en último caso*) as a last resort

**ultim|ar** *vt* complete. **~átum** *m* ultimatum

**último** *a* last; (*más reciente*) latest; (*más lejano*) furthest; (*más alto*) top; (*más bajo*) bottom; (*fig, extremo*) extreme. **estar en las últimas** be on one's last legs; (*sin dinero*) be down to one's last penny. **por ~** finally. **ser lo ~** (*muy bueno*) be marvellous; (*muy malo*) be awful. **vestido a la última** dressed in the latest fashion

**ultra** *a* ultra, extreme

**ultraj|ante** *a* outrageous. **~e** *m* outrage

**ultramar** *m* overseas countries. **de ~, en ~** overseas

**ultramarino** *a* overseas. **~s** *mpl* groceries. **tienda de ~s** grocer's (shop) (*Brit*), grocery store (*Amer*)

**ultranza a ~** (*con decisión*) decisively; (*extremo*) extreme

**ultra|sónico** *a* ultrasonic. **~violeta** *a invar* ultraviolet

**ulular** *vi* howl; ‹*búho*› hoot

**umbilical** *a* umbilical

**umbral** *m* threshold

**umbrío** *a*, **umbroso** *a* shady

**un** *art indef m* (*pl* **unos**) a. ● *a* one. **~os** *a pl* some

**una** *art indef* f a. **la ~** one o'clock

**un|ánime** *a* unanimous. **~animidad** *f* unanimity

**undécimo** *a* eleventh

**ung|ir** [14] *vt* anoint. **~üento** *m* ointment

**únic|amente** *adv* only. **~o** *a* only; (*fig, incomparable*) unique

**unicornio** *m* unicorn

**unid|ad** *f* unit; (*cualidad*) unity. **~o** *a* united

**unifica|ción** *f* unification. **~r** [7] *vt* unite, unify

**uniform|ar** *vt* standardize; (*poner uniforme a*) put into uniform. **~e** *a* & *m* uniform. **~idad** *f* uniformity

**uni|génito** *a* only. **~lateral** *a* unilateral

**uni|ón** *f* union; (*cualidad*) unity; (*tec*) joint. **~r** *vt* join; mix ‹*líquidos*›. **~rse** *vpr* join together

**unísono** *m* unison. **al ~** in unison

**unitario** *a* unitary

**universal** *a* universal

**universi|dad** *f* university. **U~dad a Distancia** Open University. **~tario** *a* university

**universo** *m* universe

**uno** *a* one; (*en plural*) some. ● *pron* one; (*alguien*) someone, somebody. ● *m* one. **~ a otro** each other. **~ y otro** both. **(los) ~s... (los) otros** some... others

**untar** *vt* grease; (*med*) rub; (*fig, sobornar, fam*) bribe

**uña** *f* nail; (*de animal*) claw; (*casco*) hoof

**upa** *int* up!

**uranio** *m* uranium

**Urano** *m* Uranus

**urban|idad** *f* politeness. **~ismo** *m* town planning. **~ístico** *a* urban. **~ización** *f* development. **~izar** [10] *vt* civilize; develop ‹*terreno*›. **~o** *a* urban

**urbe** *f* big city

**urdimbre** *f* warp

**urdir** *vt* (*fig*) plot

**urg|encia** *f* urgency; · (*emergencia*) emergency; (*necesidad*) urgent need. **~ente** *a* urgent. **~ir** [14] *vi* be urgent. **carta** *f* **~ente** express letter

**urinario** *m* urinal

**urna** *f* urn; (*pol*) ballot box

**urraca** *f* magpie

**URSS** *abrev* (*historia*) (*Unión de Repúblicas Socialistas Soviéticas*) USSR, Union of Soviet Socialist Republics

**Uruguay** *m*. **el ~** Uruguay

**uruguayo** *a* & *m* Uruguayan

**us|ado** *a* used; (*ropa etc*) worn. **~anza** *f* usage, custom. **~ar** *vt* use; (*llevar*) wear. **~o** *m* use; (*costumbre*) usage, custom. **al ~o** (*de moda*) in fashion; (*a la manera de*) in the style of. **de ~o externo** for external use

**usted** *pron* you

**usual** *a* usual

**usuario** *a* user

**usur|a** *f* usury. **~ero** *m* usurer

**usurpar** *vt* usurp

**usuta** *f* (*Arg*) sandal

**utensilio** *m* tool; (*de cocina*) utensil. **~s** *mpl* equipment

**útero** *m* womb

**útil** *a* useful. **~es** *mpl* implements

**utili|dad** *f* usefulness. **~tario** *a* utilitarian; ‹*coche*› utility. **~zación** *f* use, utilization. **~zar** [10] *vt* use, utilize

**uva** *f* grape. **~ pasa** raisin. **mala ~** bad mood

# V

**vaca** *f* cow; (*carne*) beef

**vacaciones** *fpl* holiday(s). **estar de ~** be on holiday. **ir de ~** go on holiday

**vaca|nte** *a* vacant. ● *f* vacancy. **~r** [7] *vi* fall vacant

**vaci|ar** [20] *vt* empty; (*ahuecar*) hollow out; (*en molde*) cast; (*afilar*) sharpen. **~edad** *f* emptiness; (*tontería*) silly thing, frivolity

**vacila|ción** *f* hesitation. **~nte** *a* unsteady; (*fig*) hesitant. **~r** *vi* sway; (*dudar*) hesitate; (*fam*) tease

**vacío** *a* empty; (*vanidoso*) vain. ● *m* empty space; (*estado*) emptiness; (*en física*) vacuum; (*fig*) void

**vacuidad** *f* emptiness; *(tontería)* silly thing, frivolity

**vacuna** *f* vaccine. **~ción** *f* vaccination. **~r** *vt* vaccinate

**vacuno** *a* bovine

**vacuo** *a* empty

**vade** *m* folder

**vad|ear** *vt* ford. **~o** *m* ford

**vaga|bundear** *vi* wander. **~bundo** *a* vagrant; *(perro)* stray. ● *m* tramp. **~r** [12] *vi* wander (about)

**vagina** *f* vagina

**vago** *a* vague; *(holgazán)* idle; *(foto)* blurred. ● *m* idler

**vag|ón** *m* carriage; *(de mercancías)* truck, wagon. **~ón restaurante** dining-car. **~oneta** *f* truck

**vahído** *m* dizzy spell

**vaho** *m* breath; *(vapor)* steam. **~s** *mpl* inhalation

**vaina** *f* sheath; *(bot)* pod

**vainilla** *f* vanilla

**vaivén** *m* swaying; *(de tráfico)* coming and going; *(fig, de suerte)* change. **vaivenes** *mpl* *(fig)* ups and downs

**vajilla** *f* dishes, crockery. **lavar la ~** wash up

**vale** *m* voucher; *(pagaré)* IOU. **~dero** *a* valid

**valenciano** *a* from Valencia

**valent|ía** *f* courage; *(acción)* brave deed. **~ón** *m* braggart

**valer** [42] *vt* be worth; *(costar)* cost; *(fig, significar)* mean. ● *vi* be worth; *(costar)* cost; *(servir)* be of use; *(ser valedero)* be valid; *(estar permitido)* be allowed. ● *m* worth. **~ la pena** be worthwhile, be worth it. **¿cuánto vale?** how much is it? **no ~ para nada** be useless. **¡vale!** all right!, OK! *(fam).* **¿vale?** all right?, OK? *(fam)*

**valeroso** *a* courageous

**valgo** *vb véase* **valer**

**valía** *f* worth

**validez** *f* validity. **dar ~ a** validate

**válido** *a* valid

**valiente** *a* brave; *(valentón)* boastful; *(en sentido irónico)* fine. ● *m* brave person; *(valentón)* braggart

**valija** *f* case; *(de correos)* mailbag. **~ diplomática** diplomatic bag

**val|ioso** *a* valuable. **~or** *m* value, worth; *(descaro, fam)* nerve. **~ores** *mpl* securities. **~oración** *f* valuation. **~orar** *vt* value. **conceder ~or a** attach importance to. **objetos**

*mpl* **de ~or** valuables. **sin ~or** worthless

**vals** *m invar* waltz

**válvula** *f* valve

**valla** *f* fence; *(fig)* barrier

**valle** *m* valley

**vampiro** *m* vampire

**vanagloriarse** [20 *o regular*] *vpr* boast

**vanamente** *adv* uselessly, in vain

**vandalismo** *m* vandalism

**vándalo** *m* vandal

**vanguardia** *f* vanguard. **de ~** *(en arte, música etc)* avant-garde

**vanid|ad** *f* vanity. **~oso** *a* vain

**vano** *a* vain; *(inútil)* useless. **en ~** in vain

**vapor** *m* steam; *(gas)* vapour; *(naut)* steamer. **~izador** *m* spray. **~izar** [10] vaporize. **al ~** *(culin)* steamed

**vaquer|ía** *f* dairy. **~o** *m* cow-herd, cowboy. **~os** *mpl* jeans

**vara** *f* stick; *(de autoridad)* staff; *(medida)* yard

**varar** *vi* run aground

**varia|ble** *a & f* variable. **~ción** *f* variation. **~nte** *f* version. **~ntes** *fpl* hors d'oeuvres. **~r** [20] *vt* change; *(dar variedad a)* vary. ● *vi* vary; *(cambiar)* change

**varice** *f* varicose vein

**varicela** *f* chickenpox

**varicoso** *a* having varicose veins

**variedad** *f* variety

**varilla** *f* stick; *(de metal)* rod

**vario** *a* varied; *(en plural)* several

**variz** *f* varicose vein

**var|ón** *a* male. ● *m* man; *(niño)* boy. **~onil** *a* manly

**vasc|o** *a & m* Basque. **~ongado** *a* Basque. **~uence** *a & m* Basque. **las V~ongadas** the Basque provinces

**vasectomía** *f* vasectomy

**vaselina** *f* Vaseline (P), petroleum jelly

**vasija** *f* pot, container

**vaso** *m* glass; *(anat)* vessel

**vástago** *m* shoot; *(descendiente)* descendant; *(varilla)* rod

**vasto** *a* vast

**Vaticano** *m* Vatican

**vaticin|ar** *vt* prophesy. **~io** *m* prophesy

**vatio** *m* watt

**vaya** *vb véase* **ir**

**Vd** *abrev (Usted)* you

**vecin|dad** *f* neighbourhood, vicinity; *(vecinos)* neighbours. **~dario** *m* inhabitants, neighbourhood. ~o *a* neighbouring; (*de al lado*) next-door. ● *m* neighbour

**veda|do** *m* preserve. ~**do de caza** game preserve. ~**r** *vt* prohibit

**vega** *f* fertile plain

**vegeta|ción** *f* vegetation. ~**l** *a* vegetable. ● *m* plant, vegetable. ~**r** *vi* grow; (*persona*) vegetate. ~**riano** *a & m* vegetarian

**vehemente** *a* vehement

**vehículo** *m* vehicle

**veinte** *a & m* twenty. ~**na** *f* score

**veinti|cinco** *a & m* twenty-five. ~**cuatro** *a & m* twenty-four. ~**dós** *a & m* twenty-two. ~**nueve** *a & m* twenty-nine. ~**ocho** *a & m* twenty-eight. ~**séis** *a & m* twenty-six. ~**siete** *a & m* twenty-seven. ~**trés** *a & m* twenty-three. ~**ún** *a* twenty-one. ~**uno** *a & m* (*delante de nombre masculino* **veintiún**) twenty-one

**vejar** *vt* humiliate; (*molestar*) vex

**vejez** *f* old age

**vejiga** *f* bladder; (*med*) blister

**vela** *f* (*naut*) sail; (*de cera*) candle; (*falta de sueño*) sleeplessness; (*vigilia*) vigil. **pasar la noche en ~** have a sleepless night

**velada** *f* evening party

**vela|do** *a* veiled; (*foto*) blurred. ~**r** *vt* watch over; (*encubrir*) veil; (*foto*) blur. ● *vi* stay awake, not sleep. ~**r por** look after. ~**rse** *vpr* (*foto*) blur

**velero** *m* sailing-ship

**veleta** *f* weather vane

**velo** *m* veil

**veloc|idad** *f* speed; (*auto etc*) gear. ~**ímetro** *m* speedometer. ~**ista** *m & f* sprinter. **a toda ~idad** at full speed

**velódromo** *m* cycle-track

**veloz** *a* fast, quick

**vell|o** *m* down. ~**ón** *m* fleece. ~**udo** *a* hairy

**vena** *f* vein; (*en madera*) grain. **estar de/en ~** be in the mood

**venado** *m* deer; (*culin*) venison

**vencedor** *a* winning. ● *m* winner

**vencejo** *m* (*pájaro*) swift

**venc|er** [9] *vt* beat; (*superar*) overcome. ● *vi* win; (*plazo*) expire. ~**erse** *vpr* collapse; (*persona*) control o.s. ~**ido** *a* beaten; (*com, atrasado*) in arrears. **darse por ~ido** give up. **los ~idos** *mpl* (*en deportes etc*) the losers

**venda** *f* bandage. ~**je** *m* dressing. ~**r** *vt* bandage

**vendaval** *m* gale

**vende|dor** *a* selling. ● *m* seller, salesman. ~**dor ambulante** pedlar. ~**r** *vt* sell. ~**rse** *vpr* sell. ~**rse caro** play hard to get. **se ~** for sale

**vendimia** *f* grape harvest; (*de vino*) vintage, year

**Venecia** *f* Venice

**veneciano** *a* Venetian

**veneno** *m* poison; (*fig, malevolencia*) spite. ~**so** *a* poisonous

**venera** *f* scallop shell

**venera|ble** *a* venerable. ~**ción** *f* reverence. ~**r** *vt* revere

**venéreo** *a* venereal

**venero** *m* (*yacimiento*) seam; (*de agua*) spring; (*fig*) source

**venezolano** *a & m* Venezuelan

**Venezuela** *f* Venezuela

**venga|nza** *f* revenge. ~**r** [12] *vt* avenge. ~**rse** *vpr* take revenge (**de, por** for) (**de, en** on). ~**tivo** *a* vindictive

**vengo** *vb* *véase* **venir**

**venia** *f* (*permiso*) permission

**venial** *a* venial

**veni|da** *f* arrival; (*vuelta*) return. ~**dero** *a* coming. ~**r** [53] *vi* come; (*estar, ser*) be. ~**r a para** come to. ~**r bien** suit. **la semana que viene** next week. **¡venga!** come on!

**venta** *f* sale; (*posada*) inn. **en ~** for sale

**ventaj|a** *f* advantage. ~**oso** *a* advantageous

**ventan|a** *f* window; (*de la nariz*) nostril. ~**illa** *f* window

**ventarrón** *m* (*fam*) strong wind

**ventear** *vt* (*olfatear*) sniff

**ventero** *m* innkeeper

**ventila|ción** *f* ventilation. ~**dor** *m* fan. ~**r** *vt* air

**vent|isca** *f* blizzard. ~**olera** *f* gust of wind. ~**osa** *f* sucker. ~**osidad** *f* wind, flatulence. ~**oso** *a* windy

**ventrílocuo** *m* ventriloquist

**ventrudo** *a* pot-bellied

**ventur|a** *f* happiness; (*suerte*) luck. ~**oso** *a* happy, lucky. **a la ~a** at random. **echar la buena ~a a uno** tell s.o.'s fortune. **por ~a** by chance; (*afortunadamente*) fortunately

**Venus** *f* Venus

**ver** [43] *vt* see; watch (*televisión*). ● *vi* see. ~**se** *vpr* see o.s.; (*encontrarse*) find o.s.; (*dos personas*) meet. **a mi (modo de) ~** in my view. **a ~** let's see. **de buen ~** good-looking. **dejarse ~** show. **¡habráse**

**visto!** did you ever! **no poder** ~ not be able to stand. **no tener nada que** ~ **con** have nothing to do with. **¡para que veas!** so there! **vamos a** ~ let's see. **ya lo veo** that's obvious. **ya** ~**ás** you'll see. **ya** ~**emos** we'll see

**vera** f edge; (*de río*) bank

**veracruzano** a from Veracruz

**veran|eante** m & f tourist, holiday-maker. ~**ear** vi spend one's holiday. ~**eo** m (summer) holiday. ~**iego** a summer. ~**o** m summer. **casa** f **de** ~**eo** summer-holiday home. **ir de** ~**eo** go on holiday. **lugar** m **de** ~**eo** holiday resort

**veras** fpl. **de** ~ really

**veraz** a truthful

**verbal** a verbal

**verbena** f (*bot*) verbena; (*fiesta*) fair; (*baile*) dance

**verbo** m verb. ~**so** a verbose

**verdad** f truth. **¿**~**?** isn't it?, aren't they?, won't it? etc. ~**eramente** adv really. ~**ero** a true; (*fig*) real. **a decir** ~ to tell the truth. **de** ~ really. **la pura** ~ the plain truth. **si bien es** ~ **que** although

**verd|e** a green; (*fruta etc*) unripe; (*chiste etc*) dirty, blue. ● m green; (*hierba*) grass. ~**or** m greenness

**verdugo** m executioner; (*fig*) tyrant

**verdu|lería** f greengrocer's (shop). ~**lero** m greengrocer. ~**ra** f (green) vegetable(s)

**vereda** f path; (*LAm*, *acera*) pavement (*Brit*), sidewalk (*Amer*)

**veredicto** m verdict

**vergel** m large garden; (*huerto*) orchard

**verg|onzoso** a shameful; (*tímido*) shy. ~**üenza** f shame; (*timidez*) shyness. **¡es una** ~**üenza!** it's a disgrace! **me da** ~**üenza** I'm ashamed; (*tímido*) I'm shy about. **tener** ~**üenza** be ashamed; (*tímido*) be shy

**verídico** a true

**verifica|ción** f verification. ~**r** [7] vt check. ~**rse** vpr take place; (*resultar verdad*) come true

**verja** f grating; (*cerca*) railings; (*puerta*) iron gate

**vermú** m, **vermut** m vermouth

**vernáculo** a vernacular

**verosímil** a likely; (*relato etc*) credible

**verraco** m boar

**verruga** f wart

**versado** a versed

**versar** vi turn. ~ **sobre** be about

**versátil** a versatile; (*fig*) fickle

**versión** f version; (*traducción*) translation

**verso** m verse; (*línea*) line

**vértebra** f vertebra

**verte|dero** m rubbish tip; (*desaguadero*) drain. ~**dor** m drain. ~**r** [1] vt pour; (*derramar*) spill. ● vi flow

**vertical** a & f vertical

**vértice** f vertex

**vertiente** f slope

**vertiginoso** a dizzy

**vértigo** m dizziness; (*med*) vertigo. **de** ~ (*fam*) amazing

**vesania** f rage; (*med*) insanity

**vesícula** f blister. ~ **biliar** gall-bladder

**vespertino** a evening

**vestíbulo** m hall; (*de hotel, teatro etc*) foyer

**vestido** m (*de mujer*) dress; (*ropa*) clothes

**vestigio** m trace. ~**s** mpl remains

**vest|imenta** f clothing. ~**ir** [5] vt (*ponerse*) put on; (*llevar*) wear; dress (*niño etc*). ● vi dress; (*llevar*) wear. ~**irse** vpr get dressed; (*llevar*) wear. ~**uario** m wardrobe; (*cuarto*) dressing-room

**Vesuvio** m Vesuvius

**vetar** vt veto

**veterano** a veteran

**veterinari|a** f veterinary science. ~**o** a veterinary. ● m vet (*fam*), veterinary surgeon (*Brit*), veterinarian (*Amer*)

**veto** m veto. **poner el** ~ a veto

**vetusto** a ancient

**vez** f time; (*turno*) turn. **a la** ~ at the same time; (*de una vez*) in one go. **alguna que otra** ~ from time to time. **alguna** ~ sometimes; (*en preguntas*) ever. **algunas veces** sometimes. **a su** ~ in (his) turn. **a veces** sometimes. **cada** ~ **más** more and more. **de una** ~ in one go. **de una** ~ **para siempre** once and for all. **de** ~ **en cuando** from time to time. **dos veces** twice. **2 veces 4** 2 times 4. **en** ~ **de** instead of. **érase una** ~, **había una** ~ once upon a time. **muchas veces** often. **otra** ~ again. **pocas veces**, **rara** ~ rarely. **repetidas veces** again and again. **tal** ~ perhaps. **una** ~ **(que)** once

**vía** f road; (*rail*) line; (*anat*) tract; (*fig*) way. ● prep via. ~ **aérea** by air.

~ **de comunicación** f means of communication. ~ **férrea** railway (Brit), railroad (Amer). ~ **rápida** fast lane. **estar en** ~**s de** be in the process of

**viab|ilidad** f viability. ~**le** a viable

**viaducto** m viaduct

**viaj|ante** m & f commercial traveller. ~**ar** vi travel. ~**e** m journey; (corto) trip. ~**e de novios** honeymoon. ~**ero** m traveller; (pasajero) passenger. **¡buen** ~**e!** have a good journey!

**víbora** f viper

**vibra|ción** f vibration. ~**nte** a vibrant. ~**r** vt/i vibrate

**vicario** m vicar

**vice...** pref vice-...

**viceversa** adv vice versa

**vici|ado** a corrupt; (aire) stale. ~**ar** vt corrupt; (estropear) spoil. ~**o** m vice; (mala costumbre) bad habit. ~**oso** a dissolute; (círculo) vicious

**vicisitud** f vicissitude

**víctima** f victim; (de un accidente) casualty

**victori|a** f victory. ~**oso** a victorious

**vid** f vine

**vida** f life; (duración) lifetime. **¡**~ **mía!** my darling! **de por** ~ for life. **en mi** ~ never (in my life). **en** ~ **de** during the lifetime of. **estar en** ~ be alive

**vídeo** m video recorder

**video|cinta** f videotape. ~**juego** m video game

**vidriar** vt glaze

**vidri|era** f stained glass window; (puerta) glass door; (LAm, escaparate) shop window. ~**ería** f glass works. ~**ero** m glazier. ~**o** m glass. ~**oso** a glassy

**vieira** f scallop

**viejo** a old. ● m old person

**Viena** f Vienna

**viene** vb véase **venir**

**viento** m wind. **hacer** ~ be windy

**vientre** m belly; (matriz) womb; (intestino) bowels. **llevar un niño en el** ~ be pregnant

**viernes** m Friday. **V**~ **Santo** Good Friday

**viga** f beam; (de metal) girder

**vigen|cia** f validity. ~**te** a valid; (ley) in force. **entrar en** ~**cia** come into force

**vigésimo** a twentieth

**vigía** f (torre) watch-tower; (persona) lookout

**vigil|ancia** f vigilance. ~**ante** a vigilant. ● m watchman, supervisor. ~**ar** vt keep an eye on. ● vi be vigilant; (vigía etc) keep watch. ~**ia** f vigil; (relig) fasting

**vigor** m vigour; (vigencia) force. ~**oso** a vigorous. **entrar en** ~ come into force

**vil** a vile. ~**eza** f vileness; (acción) vile deed

**vilipendiar** vt abuse

**vilo. en** ~ in the air

**villa** f town; (casa) villa. **la V**~ Madrid

**villancico** m (Christmas) carol

**villano** a rustic; (grosero) coarse

**vinagre** m vinegar. ~**ra** f vinegar bottle. ~**ras** fpl cruet. ~**ta** f vinaigrette (sauce)

**vincular** vt bind

**vínculo** m bond

**vindicar** [7] vt avenge; (justificar) vindicate

**vine** vb véase **venir**

**vinicult|or** m wine-grower. ~**ura** f wine growing

**vino** m wine. ~ **de Jerez** sherry. ~ **de la casa** house wine. ~ **de mesa** table wine

**viña** f, **viñedo** m vineyard

**viola** f viola; (músico) viola player

**violación** f violation; (de una mujer) rape

**violado** a & m violet

**violar** vt violate; break (ley); rape (mujer)

**violen|cia** f violence; (fuerza) force; (embarazo) embarrassment. ~**tar** vt force; break into (casa etc). ~**tarse** vpr force o.s. ~**to** a violent; (fig) awkward. **hacer** ~**cia** a force

**violeta** a invar & f violet

**viol|ín** m violin; (músico) violinist. ~**inista** m & f violinist. ~**ón** m double bass; (músico) double-bass player. ~**onc(h)elista** m & f cellist. ~**onc(h)elo** m cello

**vira|je** m turn. ~**r** vt turn. ● vi turn; (fig) change direction

**virg|en** a & f virgin. ~**inal** a virginal. ~**inidad** f virginity

**Virgo** m Virgo

**viril** a virile. ~**idad** f virility

**virtual** a virtual

**virtud** f virtue; (capacidad) ability. **en** ~ **de** by virtue of

**virtuoso** a virtuous. ● m virtuoso

**viruela** f smallpox. **picado de ~s** pock-marked

**virulé. a la ~** (fam) crooked; (estropeado) damaged

**virulento** a virulent

**virus** m invar virus

**visa|do** m visa. **~r** vt endorse

**vísceras** fpl entrails

**viscos|a** f viscose. **~o** a viscous

**visera** f visor; (de gorra) peak

**visib|ilidad** f visibility. **~le** a visible

**visig|odo** a Visigodo; (fig) Visigoth. **~ótico** a Visigothic

**visillo** m (cortina) net curtain

**visi|ón** f vision; (vista) sight. **~onario** a & m visionary

**visita** f visit; (persona) visitor. **~ de cumplido** courtesy call. **~nte** m & f visitor. **~r** vt visit. **tener ~** have visitors

**vislumbr|ar** vt glimpse. **~e** f glimpse; (resplandor, fig) glimmer

**viso** m sheen; (aspecto) appearance

**visón** m mink

**visor** m viewfinder

**víspera** f day before, eve

**vista** f sight, vision; (aspecto, mirada) look; (panorama) view. **apartar la ~** look away; (fig) turn a blind eye. **a primera ~, a simple ~** at first sight. **clavar la ~ en** stare at. **con ~s a** with a view to. **en ~ de** in view of, considering. **estar a la ~** be obvious. **hacer la ~ gorda** turn a blind eye. **perder de ~** lose sight of. **tener a la ~** have in front of one. **volver la ~ atrás** look back

**vistazo** m glance. **dar/echar un ~ a** glance at

**visto** a seen; (corriente) common; (considerado) considered. ● vb véase **vestir**. **~ bueno** passed. **~ que** since. **bien ~** acceptable. **está ~ que** it's obvious that. **lo nunca ~** an unheard-of thing. **mal ~** unacceptable. **por lo ~** apparently

**vistoso** a colourful, bright

**visual** a visual. ● f glance. **echar una ~ a** have a look at

**vital** a vital. **~icio** a life. ● m (life) annuity. **~idad** f vitality

**vitamina** f vitamin

**viticult|or** m wine-grower. **~ura** f wine growing

**vitorear** vt cheer

**vítreo** a vitreous

**vitrina** f showcase

**vituper|ar** vt censure. **~io** m censure. **~ios** mpl abuse

**viud|a** f widow. **~ez** f widowhood. **~o** a widowed. ● m widower

**viva** m cheer

**vivacidad** f liveliness

**vivamente** adv vividly; (sinceramente) sincerely

**vivaz** a (bot) perennial; (vivo) lively

**víveres** mpl supplies

**vivero** m nursery; (fig) hotbed

**viveza** f vividness; (de inteligencia) sharpness; (de carácter) liveliness

**vívido** a true

**vívido** a vivid

**vivienda** f housing; (casa) house; (piso) flat

**viviente** a living

**vivificar** [7] vt (animar) enliven

**vivir** vt live through. ● vi live. ● m life. **~ de** live on. **de mal ~** dissolute. ¡**viva**! hurray! ¡**viva el rey**! long live the king!

**vivisección** f vivisection

**vivo** a alive; (viviente) living; ‹color› bright; (listo) clever; (fig) lively. **a lo ~, al ~** vividly

**Vizcaya** f Biscay

**vizconde** m viscount. **~sa** f viscountess

**vocab|lo** m word. **~ulario** m vocabulary

**vocación** f vocation

**vocal** a vocal. ● f vowel. ● m & f member. **~ista** m & f vocalist

**voce|ar** vt call ‹mercancías›; (fig) proclaim. ● vi shout. **~río** m shouting

**vociferar** vi shout

**vodka** m & f vodka

**vola|da** f flight. **~dor** a flying. ● m rocket. **~ndas. en ~ndas** in the air; (fig, rápidamente) very quickly. **~nte** a flying. ● m (auto) steering-wheel; (nota) note; (rehilete) shuttlecock; (tec) flywheel. **~r** [2] vt blow up. ● vi fly; (desaparecer, fam) disappear

**volátil** a volatile

**volcán** m volcano. **~ico** a volcanic

**vol|car** [2 & 7] vt knock over; (adrede) empty out. ● vi overturn. **~carse** vpr fall over; (vehículo) overturn; (fig) do one's utmost. **~carse en** throw o.s. into

**vol(e)ibol** m volleyball

**volquete** m tipper, dump truck

**voltaje** m voltage

**volte|ar** vt turn over; (en el aire) toss; ring ‹campanas›. **~reta** f somersault

**voltio** *m* volt

**voluble** *a* (*fig*) fickle

**volum|en** *m* volume; (*importancia*) importance. **~inoso** *a* voluminous

**voluntad** *f* will; (*fuerza de voluntad*) will-power; (*deseo*) wish; (*intención*) intention. **buena ~** goodwill. **mala ~** ill will

**voluntario** *a* voluntary. ● *m* volunteer. **~so** *a* willing; (*obstinado*) wilful

**voluptuoso** *a* voluptuous

**volver** [2, *pp* **vuelto**] *vt* turn; (*de arriba a abajo*) turn over; (*devolver*) restore. ● *vi* return; (*fig*) revert. **~se** *vpr* turn round; (*regresar*) return; (*hacerse*) become. **~ a hacer algo** do sth again. **~ en sí** come round

**vomit|ar** *vt* bring up. ● *vi* be sick, vomit. **~ivo** *m* emetic. ● *a* disgusting

**vómito** *m* vomit; (*acción*) vomiting

**vorágine** *f* maelstrom

**voraz** *a* voracious

**vos** *pron* (*LAm*) you

**vosotros** *pron* you; (*reflexivo*) yourselves. **el libro de ~** your book

**vot|ación** *f* voting; (*voto*) vote. **~ante** *m* & *f* voter. **~ar** *vt* vote for. ● *vi* vote. **~o** *m* vote; (*relig*) vow; (*maldición*) curse. **hacer ~os por** hope for

**voy** *vb véase* **ir**

**voz** *f* voice; (*grito*) shout; (*rumor*) rumour; (*palabra*) word. **~ pública** public opinion. **aclarar la ~** clear one's throat. **a media ~** softly. **a una ~** unanimously. **dar voces** shout. **en ~ alta** loudly

**vuelco** *m* upset. **el corazón me dio un ~** my heart missed a beat

**vuelo** *m* flight; (*acción*) flying; (*de ropa*) flare. **al ~** in flight; (*fig*) in passing

**vuelta** *f* turn; (*curva*) bend; (*paseo*) walk; (*revolución*) revolution; (*regreso*) return; (*dinero*) change. **a la ~** on one's return; (*de página*) over the page. **a la ~ de la esquina** round the corner. **dar la ~ al mundo** go round the world. **dar una ~** go for a walk. **estar de ~** be back. **¡hasta la ~!** see you soon!

**vuelvo** *vb véase* **volver**

**vuestro** *a* your. ● *pron* yours. **un amigo ~** a friend of yours

**vulg|ar** *a* vulgar; ⟨*persona*⟩ common. **~aridad** *f* ordinariness;

(*trivialidad*) triviality; (*grosería*) vulgarity. **~arizar** [10] *vt* popularize. **~o** *m* common people

**vulnerab|ilidad** *f* vulnerability. **~le** *a* vulnerable

# W

**wáter** *m* toilet

**whisky** /'wiski/ *m* whisky

# X

**xenofobia** *f* xenophobia

**xilófono** *m* xylophone

# Y

**y** *conj* and

**ya** *adv* already; (*ahora*) now; (*luego*) later; (*en seguida*) immediately; (*pronto*) soon. ● *int* of course! **~ no** no longer. **~ que** since. **¡~, ~!** oh yes!, all right!

**yacaré** *m* (*LAm*) alligator

**yac|er** [44] *vi* lie. **~imiento** *m* deposit; (*de petróleo*) oilfield

**yanqui** *m* & *f* American, Yank(ee)

**yate** *m* yacht

**yegua** *f* mare

**yeísmo** *m* pronunciation of the Spanish *ll* like the Spanish *y*

**yelmo** *m* helmet

**yema** *f* (*bot*) bud; (*de huevo*) yolk; (*golosina*) sweet. **~ del dedo** fingertip

**yergo** *vb véase* **erguir**

**yermo** *a* uninhabited; (*no cultivable*) barren. ● *m* wasteland

**yerno** *m* son-in-law

**yerro** *m* mistake. ● *vb véase* **errar**

**yerto** *a* stiff

**yeso** *m* gypsum; (*arquit*) plaster. **~ mate** plaster of Paris

**yo** *pron* I. ● *m* ego. **~ mismo** I myself. **soy ~** it's me

**yodo** *m* iodine

**yoga** *m* yoga

**yogur** *m* yog(h)urt

**York. de ~** ⟨*jamón*⟩ cooked

**yuca** *f* yucca

**Yucatán** *m* Yucatán

**yugo** *m* yoke

**Yugoslavia** f Yugoslavia
**yugoslavo** a & m Yugoslav
**yunque** m anvil
**yunta** f yoke
**yuxtaponer** [34] vt juxtapose
**yuyo** m (*Arg*) weed

# Z

**zafarse** vpr escape; get out of ⟨obligación etc⟩
**zafarrancho** m (*confusión*) mess; (*riña*) quarrel
**zafio** a coarse
**zafiro** m sapphire
**zaga** f rear. **no ir en ~** not be inferior
**zaguán** m hall
**zaherir** [4] vt hurt one's feelings
**zahorí** m clairvoyant; (*de agua*) water diviner
**zaino** a ⟨caballo⟩ chestnut; ⟨vaca⟩ black
**zalamer|ía** f flattery. **~o** a flattering. ● m flatterer
**zamarra** f (*piel*) sheepskin; (*prenda*) sheepskin jacket
**zamarrear** vt shake
**zamba** f (*esp LAm*) South American dance; (*samba*) samba
**zambulli|da** f dive. **~r** [22] vt plunge. **~rse** vpr dive
**zamparse** vpr fall; (*comer*) gobble up
**zanahoria** f carrot
**zancad|a** f stride. **~illa** f trip. **echar la ~illa a uno, poner la ~illa a uno** trip s.o. up
**zanc|o** m stilt. **~udo** a long-legged. ● m (*LAm*) mosquito
**zanganear** vi idle
**zángano** m drone; (*persona*) idler
**zangolotear** vt fiddle with. ● vi rattle; ⟨persona⟩ fidget
**zanja** f ditch. **~r** vt (*fig*) settle
**zapapico** m pickaxe

**zapat|ear** vt/i tap with one's feet. **~ería** f shoe shop; (*arte*) shoemaking. **~ero** m shoemaker; (*el que remienda zapatos*) cobbler. **~illa** f slipper. **~illas deportivas** trainers. **~o** m shoe
**zaragata** f turmoil
**Zaragoza** f Saragossa
**zarand|a** f sieve. **~ear** vt sieve; (*sacudir*) shake
**zarcillo** m earring
**zarpa** f claw, paw
**zarpar** vi weigh anchor
**zarza** f bramble. **~mora** f blackberry
**zarzuela** f musical, operetta
**zascandil** m scatterbrain
**zenit** m zenith
**zigzag** m zigzag. **~uear** vi zigzag
**zinc** m zinc
**zipizape** m (*fam*) row
**zócalo** m skirting-board; (*pedestal*) plinth
**zodiaco** m, **zodíaco** m zodiac
**zona** f zone; (*área*) area
**zoo** m zoo. **~logía** f zoology. **~lógico** a zoological
**zoólogo** m zoologist
**zopenco** a stupid. ● m idiot
**zoquete** m (*de madera*) block; (*persona*) blockhead
**zorr|a** f fox; (*hembra*) vixen. **~o** m fox
**zozobra** f (*fig*) anxiety. **~r** vi be shipwrecked; (*fig*) be ruined
**zueco** m clog
**zulú** a & m Zulu
**zumb|ar** vt (*fam*) give ⟨golpe etc⟩. ● vi buzz. **~ido** m buzzing
**zumo** m juice
**zurci|do** m darning. **~r** [9] vt darn
**zurdo** a left-handed; ⟨mano⟩ left
**zurrar** vt (*fig*, dar golpes, *fam*) beat up
**zurriago** m whip
**zutano** m so-and-so

# A

**a** /ə, eɪ/ *indef art* (*before vowel* **an**) un *m*; una *f*

**aback** /ə'bæk/ *adv.* **be taken** ~ quedar desconcertado

**abacus** /'æbəkəs/ *n* ábaco *m*

**abandon** /ə'bændən/ *vt* abandonar. ● *n* abandono *m*, desenfado *m*. ~**ed** *a* abandonado; ⟨*behaviour*⟩ perdido. ~**ment** *n* abandono *m*

**abase** /ə'beɪs/ *vt* degradar. ~**ment** *n* degradación *f*

**abashed** /ə'bæʃt/ *a* confuso

**abate** /ə'beɪt/ *vt* disminuir. ● *vi* disminuir; ⟨*storm etc*⟩ calmarse. ~**ment** *n* disminución *f*

**abattoir** /'æbətwɑː(r)/ *n* matadero *m*

**abbess** /'æbɪs/ *n* abadesa *f*

**abbey** /'æbɪ/ *n* abadía *f*

**abbot** /'æbət/ *n* abad *m*

**abbreviat|e** /ə'briːvɪeɪt/ *vt* abreviar. ~**ion** /-'eɪʃn/ *n* abreviatura *f*; (*act*) abreviación *f*

**ABC** /'eɪbiː'siː/ *n* abecé *m*, abecedario *m*

**abdicat|e** /'æbdɪkeɪt/ *vt/i* abdicar. ~**ion** /-'eɪʃn/ *n* abdicación *f*

**abdom|en** /'æbdəmən/ *n* abdomen *m*. ~**inal** /-'dɒmɪnl/ *a* abdominal

**abduct** /æb'dʌkt/ *vt* secuestrar. ~**ion** /-ʃn/ *n* secuestro *m*. ~**or** *n* secuestrador *m*

**aberration** /æbə'reɪʃn/ *n* aberración *f*

**abet** /ə'bet/ *vt* (*pt* **abetted**) (*jurid*) ser cómplice de

**abeyance** /ə'beɪəns/ *n*. **in** ~ en suspenso

**abhor** /əb'hɔː(r)/ *vt* (*pt* **abhorred**) aborrecer. ~**rence** /-'hɒrəns/ *n* aborrecimiento *m*; (*thing*) abominación *f*. ~**rent** /-'hɒrənt/ *a* aborrecible

**abide** /ə'baɪd/ *vt* (*pt* **abided**) soportar. ● *vi* (*old use, pt* **abode**) morar. ~ **by** atenerse a; cumplir ⟨*promise*⟩

**abiding** /ə'baɪdɪŋ/ *a* duradero, permanente

**ability** /ə'bɪlətɪ/ *n* capacidad *f*; (*cleverness*) habilidad *f*

**abject** /'æbdʒekt/ *a* (*wretched*) miserable; (*vile*) abyecto

**ablaze** /ə'bleɪz/ *a* en llamas

**able** /'eɪbl/ *a* (**-er, -est**) capaz. **be** ~ poder; (*know how to*) saber

**ablutions** /ə'bluːʃnz/ *npl* ablución *f*

**ably** /'eɪblɪ/ *adv* hábilmente

**abnormal** /æb'nɔːml/ *a* anormal. ~**ity** /-'mælətɪ/ *n* anormalidad *f*

**aboard** /ə'bɔːd/ *adv* a bordo. ● *prep* a bordo de

**abode** /ə'bəʊd/ *see* **abide**. ● *n* (*old use*) domicilio *m*

**abolish** /ə'bɒlɪʃ/ *vt* suprimir, abolir

**abolition** /æbə'lɪʃn/ *n* supresión *f*, abolición *f*

**abominable** /ə'bɒmɪnəbl/ *a* abominable

**abominat|e** /ə'bɒmɪneɪt/ *vt* abominar. ~**ion** /-'neɪʃn/ *n* abominación *f*

**aborigin|al** /æbə'rɪdʒənl/ *a & n* aborigen (*m & f*), indígena (*m & f*). ~**es** /-iːz/ *npl* aborígenes *mpl*

**abort** /ə'bɔːt/ *vt* hacer abortar. ● *vi* abortar. ~**ion** /-ʃn/ *n* aborto *m* provocado; (*fig*) aborto *m*. ~**ionist** *n* abortista *m & f*. ~**ive** *a* abortivo; (*fig*) fracasado

**abound** /ə'baʊnd/ *vi* abundar (**in** de, en)

**about** /ə'baʊt/ *adv* (*approximately*) alrededor de; (*here and there*) por todas partes; (*in existence*) por aquí. ~ **here** por aquí. **be** ~ **to** estar a punto de. **be up and** ~ estar levantado. ● *prep* sobre; (*around*) alrededor de; (*somewhere in*) en. **talk** ~ hablar de. ~**face** *n* (*fig*) cambio *m* rotundo. ~**turn** *n* (*fig*) cambio *m* rotundo

**above** /ə'bʌv/ *adv* arriba. ● *prep* encima de; (*more than*) más de. ~ **all** sobre todo. ~**board** *a* honrado.

● *adv* abiertamente. **~mentioned** *a* susodicho

**abrasi|on** /ə'breɪʒn/ *n* abrasión *f*. **~ve** /ə'breɪsɪv/ *a* & *n* abrasivo (*m*); (*fig*) agresivo, brusco

**abreast** /ə'brest/ *adv* de frente. **keep ~ of** mantenerse al corriente de

**abridge** /ə'brɪdʒ/ *vt* abreviar. **~ment** *n* abreviación *f*; (*abstract*) resumen *m*

**abroad** /ə'brɔːd/ *adv* (*be*) en el extranjero; (*go*) al extranjero; (*far and wide*) por todas partes

**abrupt** /ə'brʌpt/ *a* brusco. **~ly** *adv* (*suddenly*) repentinamente; (*curtly*) bruscamente. **~ness** *n* brusquedad *f*

**abscess** /'æbsɪs/ *n* absceso *m*

**abscond** /əb'skɒnd/ *vi* fugarse

**absen|ce** /'æbsəns/ *n* ausencia *f*; (*lack*) falta *f*. **~t** /'æbsənt/ *a* ausente. /æb'sent/ *vr*. **~ o.s.** ausentarse. **~tly** *adv* distraídamente. **~t-minded** *a* distraído. **~t-mindedness** *n* distracción *f*, despiste *m*

**absentee** /æbsən'tiː/ *n* ausente *m* & *f*. **~ism** *n* absentismo *m*

**absinthe** /'æbsɪnθ/ *n* ajenjo *m*

**absolute** /'æbsəluːt/ *a* absoluto. **~ly** *adv* absolutamente

**absolution** /æbsə'luːʃn/ *n* absolución *f*

**absolve** /əb'zɒlv/ *vt* (*from sin*) absolver; (*from obligation*) liberar

**absor|b** /əb'zɔːb/ *vt* absorber. **~bent** *a* absorbente. **~ption** *n* absorción *f*

**abstain** /əb'steɪn/ *vi* abstenerse (**from** de)

**abstemious** /əb'stiːmɪəs/ *a* abstemio

**abstention** /əb'stenʃn/ *n* abstención *f*

**abstinen|ce** /'æbstɪnəns/ *n* abstinencia *f*. **~t** *a* abstinente

**abstract** /'æbstrækt/ *a* abstracto. ● *n* (*quality*) abstracto *m*; (*summary*) resumen *m*. /əb'strækt/ *vt* extraer; (*summarize*) resumir. **~ion** /-ʃn/ *n* abstracción *f*

**abstruse** /əb'struːs/ *a* abstruso

**absurd** /əb'sɜːd/ *a* absurdo. **~ity** *n* absurdo *m*, disparate *m*

**abundan|ce** /ə'bʌndəns/ *n* abundancia *f*. **~t** *a* abundante

**abuse** /ə'bjuːz/ *vt* (*misuse*) abusar de; (*ill-treat*) maltratar; (*insult*) insultar. /ə'bjuːs/ *n* abuso *m*; (*insults*) insultos *mpl*

**abusive** /ə'bjuːsɪv/ *a* injurioso

**abut** /ə'bʌt/ *vi* (*pt* **abutted**) confinar (**on** con)

**abysmal** /ə'bɪzməl/ *a* abismal; (*bad*, *fam*) pésimo; (*fig*) profundo

**abyss** /ə'bɪs/ *n* abismo *m*

**acacia** /ə'keɪʃə/ *n* acacia *f*

**academic** /ækə'demɪk/ *a* académico; (*pej*) teórico. ● *n* universitario *m*, catedrático *m*. **~ian** /-də'mɪʃn/ *n* académico *m*

**academy** /ə'kædəmɪ/ *n* academia *f*. **~ of music** conservatorio *m*

**accede** /ək'siːd/ *vi*. **~ to** acceder a (*request*); tomar posesión de (*office*). **~ to the throne** subir al trono

**accelerat|e** /ək'seləreɪt/ *vt* acelerar. **~ion** /-'reɪʃn/ *n* aceleración *f*. **~or** *n* acelerador *m*

**accent** /'æksənt/ *n* acento *m*. /æk'sent/ *vt* acentuar

**accentuate** /ək'sentʃʊeɪt/ *vt* acentuar

**accept** /ək'sept/ *vt* aceptar. **~able** *a* aceptable. **~ance** *n* aceptación *f*; (*approval*) aprobación *f*

**access** /'ækses/ *n* acceso *m*. **~ibility** /-ɪ'bɪlətɪ/ *n* accesibilidad *f*. **~ible** /ək'sesəbl/ *a* accesible; (*person*) tratable

**accession** /æk'seʃn/ *n* (*to power*, *throne etc*) ascenso *m*; (*thing added*) adquisición *f*

**accessory** /ək'sesərɪ/ *a* accesorio. ● *n* accesorio *m*, complemento *m*; (*jurid*) cómplice *m* & *f*

**accident** /'æksɪdənt/ *n* accidente *m*; (*chance*) casualidad *f*. **by ~** por accidente, por descuido, sin querer; (*by chance*) por casualidad. **~al** /-'dentl/ *a* accidental, fortuito. **~ally** /-'dentəlɪ/ *adv* por accidente, por descuido, sin querer; (*by chance*) por casualidad

**acclaim** /ə'kleɪm/ *vt* aclamar. ● *n* aclamación *f*

**acclimatiz|ation** /əklaɪmətaɪ'zeɪʃn/ *n* aclimatación *f*. **~e** /ə'klaɪmətaɪz/ *vt* aclimatar. ● *vi* aclimatarse

**accolade** /'ækəleɪd/ *n* (*of knight*) acolada *f*; (*praise*) encomio *m*

**accommodat|e** /ə'kɒmədeɪt/ *vt* (*give hospitality to*) alojar; (*adapt*) acomodar; (*supply*) proveer; (*oblige*) complacer. **~ing** *a* complaciente. **~ion** /-ʃn/ *n* alojamiento *m*; (*rooms*) habitaciones *fpl*

**accompan|iment** /ə'kʌmpənɪmənt/ *n* acompañamiento *m*. **~ist** *n* acompañante *m* & *f*. **~y** /ə'kʌmpənɪ/ *vt* acompañar

**accomplice** /ə'kʌmplɪs/ n cómplice m & f

**accomplish** /ə'kʌmplɪʃ/ vt (complete) acabar; (achieve) realizar; (carry out) llevar a cabo. ∼ed a consumado. ∼ment n realización f; (ability) talento m; (thing achieved) triunfo m, logro m

**accord** /ə'kɔ:d/ vi concordar. ● vt conceder. ● n acuerdo m; (harmony) armonía f. of one's own ∼ espontáneamente. ∼ance n. in ∼ance with de acuerdo con

**according** /ə'kɔ:dɪŋ/ adv. ∼ to según. ∼ly adv en conformidad; (therefore) por consiguiente

**accordion** /ə'kɔ:dɪən/ n acordeón m

**accost** /ə'kɒst/ vt abordar

**account** /ə'kaʊnt/ n cuenta f; (description) relato m; (importance) importancia f. on ∼ of a causa de. on no ∼ de ninguna manera. on this ∼ por eso. take into ∼ tener en cuenta. ● vt considerar. ∼ for dar cuenta de, explicar

**accountab|ility** /əkaʊntə'bɪləti/ n responsabilidad f. ∼le a responsable (for de)

**accountan|cy** /ə'kaʊntənsɪ/ n contabilidad f. ∼t n contable m & f

**accoutrements** /ə'ku:trəmənts/ npl equipo m

**accredited** /ə'kredɪtɪd/ a acreditado; (authorized) autorizado

**accrue** /ə'kru:/ vi acumularse

**accumulat|e** /ə'kju:mjʊleɪt/ vt acumular. ● vi acumularse. ∼ion /-'leɪʃn/ n acumulación f. ∼or n (elec) acumulador m

**accura|cy** /'ækjərəsɪ/ n exactitud f, precisión f. ∼te a exacto, preciso

**accus|ation** /ækju:'zeɪʃn/ n acusación f. ∼e vt acusar

**accustom** /ə'kʌstəm/ vt acostumbrar. ∼ed a acostumbrado. get ∼ed (to) acostumbrarse (a)

**ace** /eɪs/ n as m

**acetate** /'æsɪteɪt/ n acetato m

**ache** /eɪk/ n dolor m. ● vi doler. my leg ∼s me duele la pierna

**achieve** /ə'tʃi:v/ vt realizar; lograr (success). ∼ment n realización f; (feat) éxito m; (thing achieved) proeza f, logro m

**acid** /'æsɪd/ a & n ácido (m). ∼ity /ə'sɪdəti/ n acidez f

**acknowledge** /ək'nɒlɪdʒ/ vt reconocer. ∼ receipt of acusar recibo de.

∼ment n reconocimiento m; (com) acuse m de recibo

**acme** /'ækmɪ/ n cima f

**acne** /'æknɪ/ n acné m

**acorn** /'eɪkɔ:n/ n bellota f

**acoustic** /ə'ku:stɪk/ a acústico. ∼s npl acústica f

**acquaint** /ə'kweɪnt/ vt. ∼ s.o. with poner a uno al corriente de. be ∼ed with conocer (person); saber (fact). ∼ance n conocimiento m; (person) conocido m

**acquiesce** /ækwɪ'es/ vi consentir (in en). ∼nce n aquiescencia f, consentimiento m

**acqui|re** /ə'kwaɪə(r)/ vt adquirir; aprender (language). ∼re a taste for tomar gusto a. ∼sition /ækwɪ'zɪʃn/ n adquisición f. ∼sitive /-'kwɪzətɪv/ a codicioso

**acquit** /ə'kwɪt/ vt (pt acquitted) absolver; ∼ o.s. well defenderse bien, tener éxito. ∼tal n absolución f

**acre** /'eɪkə(r)/ n acre m. ∼age n superficie f (en acres)

**acrid** /'ækrɪd/ a acre

**acrimon|ious** /ækrɪ'məʊnɪəs/ a cáustico, mordaz. ∼y /'ækrɪmənɪ/ n acrimonia f, acritud f

**acrobat** /'ækrəbæt/ n acróbata m & f. ∼ic /-'bætɪk/ a acrobático. ∼ics /-'bætɪks/ npl acrobacia f

**acronym** /'ækrənɪm/ n acrónimo m, siglas fpl

**across** /ə'krɒs/ adv & prep (side to side) de un lado al otro; (on other side) del otro lado de; (crosswise) a través. go or walk ∼ atravesar

**act** /ækt/ n acto m; (action) acción f; (in variety show) número m; (decree) decreto m. ● vt hacer (part, role). ● vi actuar; (pretend) fingir; (function) funcionar. ∼ as actuar de. ∼ for representar. ∼ing a interino. ● n (of play) representación f; (by actor) interpretación f; (profession) profesión f de actor

**action** /'ækʃn/ n acción f; (jurid) demanda f; (plot) argumento m. out of ∼ (on sign) no funciona. put out of ∼ inutilizar. take ∼ tomar medidas

**activate** /'æktɪveɪt/ vt activar

**activ|e** /'æktɪv/ a activo; (energetic) enérgico; (volcano) en actividad. ∼ity /-'tɪvətɪ/ n actividad f

**act|or** /'æktə(r)/ n actor m. ∼ress n actriz f

**actual** /'æktʃʊəl/ *a* verdadero. ~**ity** /-'ælətɪ/ *n* realidad *f*. ~**ly** *adv* en realidad, efectivamente; (*even*) incluso

**actuary** /'æktʃʊərɪ/ *n* actuario *m*

**actuate** /'æktʃʊeɪt/ *vt* accionar, impulsar

**acumen** /'ækjʊmen/ *n* perspicacia *f*

**acupunctur|e** /'ækjʊpʌŋktʃə(r)/ *n* acupuntura *f*. ~**ist** *n* acupunturista *m & f*

**acute** /ə'kju:t/ *a* agudo. ~**ly** *adv* agudamente. ~**ness** *n* agudeza *f*

**ad** /æd/ *n* (*fam*) anuncio *m*

**AD** /eɪ'di:/ *abbr* (*Anno Domini*) d.J.C.

**adamant** /'ædəmənt/ *a* inflexible

**Adam's apple** /'ædəmz'æpl/ *n* nuez *f* (de Adán)

**adapt** /ə'dæpt/ *vt* adaptar. ● *vi* adaptarse

**adaptab|ility** /ədæptə'bɪlətɪ/ *n* adaptabilidad *f*. ~**le** /ə'dæptəbl/ *a* adaptable

**adaptation** /ædæp'teɪʃn/ *n* adaptación *f*; (*of book etc*) versión *f*

**adaptor** /ə'dæptə(r)/ *n* (*elec*) adaptador *m*

**add** /æd/ *vt* añadir. ● *vi* sumar. ~ **up** sumar; (*fig*) tener sentido. ~ **up to** equivaler a

**adder** /'ædə(r)/ *n* víbora *f*

**addict** /'ædɪkt/ *n* adicto *m*; (*fig*) entusiasta *m & f*. ~**ed** /ə'dɪktɪd/ *a*. ~**ed to** adicto a; (*fig*) fanático de. ~**ion** /-ʃn/ *n* (*med*) dependencia *f*; (*fig*) afición *f*. ~**ive** *a* que crea dependencia

**adding machine** /'ædɪŋməʃi:n/ *n* máquina *f* de sumar, sumadora *f*

**addition** /ə'dɪʃn/ *n* suma *f*. in ~ además. ~**al** /-ʃənl/ *a* suplementario

**additive** /'ædɪtɪv/ *a & n* aditivo (*m*)

**address** /ə'dres/ *n* señas *fpl*, dirección *f*; (*speech*) discurso *m*. ● *vt* poner la dirección; (*speak to*) dirigirse a. ~**ee** /ædre'si:/ *n* destinatario *m*

**adenoids** /'ædɪnɔɪdz/ *npl* vegetaciones *fpl* adenoideas

**adept** /'ædept/ *a & n* experto (*m*)

**adequa|cy** /'ædɪkwəsɪ/ *n* suficiencia *f*. ~**te** *a* suficiente, adecuado. ~**tely** *adv* suficientemente, adecuadamente

**adhere** /əd'hɪə(r)/ *vi* adherirse (**to** a); observar (*rule*). ~**nce** /-rəns/ *n* adhesión *f*; (*to rules*) observancia *f*

**adhesion** /əd'hi:ʒn/ *n* adherencia *f*

**adhesive** /əd'hi:sɪv/ *a & n* adhesivo (*m*)

**ad infinitum** /ædɪnfɪ'naɪtəm/ *adv* hasta el infinito

**adjacent** /ə'dʒeɪsnt/ *a* contiguo

**adjective** /'ædʒɪktɪv/ *n* adjetivo *m*

**adjoin** /ə'dʒɔɪn/ *vt* lindar con. ~**ing** *a* contiguo

**adjourn** /ə'dʒɜ:n/ *vt* aplazar; suspender (*meeting etc*). ● *vi* suspenderse. ~ **to** trasladarse a

**adjudicate** /ə'dʒu:dɪkeɪt/ *vt* juzgar. ● *vi* actuar como juez

**adjust** /ə'dʒʌst/ *vt* ajustar (*machine*); (*arrange*) arreglar. ● *vi*. ~ (**to**) adaptarse (a). ~**able** *a* ajustable. ~**ment** *n* adaptación *f*; (*tec*) ajuste *m*

**ad lib** /æd'lɪb/ *a* improvisado. ● *vi* (*pt* -**libbed**) (*fam*) improvisar

**administer** /əd'mɪnɪstə(r)/ *vt* administrar, dar, proporcionar

**administrat|ion** /ədmɪnɪ'streɪʃn/ *n* administración *f*. ~**or** *n* administrador *m*

**admirable** /'ædmərəbl/ *a* admirable

**admiral** /'ædmərəl/ *n* almirante *m*

**admiration** /ædmə'reɪʃn/ *n* admiración *f*

**admire** /əd'maɪə(r)/ *vt* admirar. ~**r** /-'maɪərə(r)/ *n* admirador *m*; (*suitor*) enamorado *m*

**admissible** /əd'mɪsəbl/ *a* admisible

**admission** /əd'mɪʃn/ *n* admisión *f*; (*entry*) entrada *f*

**admit** /əd'mɪt/ *vt* (*pt* **admitted**) dejar entrar; (*acknowledge*) admitir, reconocer. ~ **to** confesar. be ~**ted** (*to hospital etc*) ingresar. ~**tance** *n* entrada *f*. ~**tedly** *adv* es verdad que

**admoni|sh** /əd'mɒnɪʃ/ *vt* reprender; (*advise*) aconsejar. ~**tion** /-'nɪʃn/ *n* represión *f*

**ado** /ə'du:/ *n* alboroto *m*; (*trouble*) dificultad *f*. **without more** ~ en seguida, sin más

**adolescen|ce** /ædə'lesns/ *n* adolescencia *f*. ~**t** *a & n* adolescente (*m & f*)

**adopt** /ə'dɒpt/ *vt* adoptar. ~**ed** *a* (*child*) adoptivo. ~**ion** /-ʃn/ *n* adopción *f*. ~**ive** *a* adoptivo

**ador|able** /ə'dɔ:rəbl/ *a* adorable. ~**ation** /ædə'reɪʃn/ *n* adoración *f*. ~**e** /ə'dɔ:(r)/ *vt* adorar

**adorn** /ə'dɔ:n/ *vt* adornar. ~**ment** *n* adorno *m*

**adrenalin** /ə'drenəlɪn/ *n* adrenalina *f*

**adrift** /ə'drɪft/ *a* & *adv* a la deriva

**adroit** /ə'drɔɪt/ *a* diestro

**adulation** /ædjʊ'leɪʃn/ *n* adulación *f*

**adult** /'ædʌlt/ *a* & *n* adulto (*m*)

**adulterat|ion** /ədʌltə'reɪʃn/ *n* adulteración *f*. **~e** /ə'dʌltəreɪt/ *vt* adulterar

**adulter|er** /ə'dʌltərə(r)/ *n* adúltero *m*. **~ess** *n* adúltera *f*. **~ous** *a* adúltero. **~y** *n* adulterio *m*

**advance** /əd'vɑːns/ *vt* adelantar. ● *vi* adelantarse. ● *n* adelanto *m*. **in ~** con anticipación, por adelantado. **~d** *a* avanzado; ‹*studies*› superior. **~ment** *n* adelanto *m*; (*in job*) promoción *f*

**advantage** /əd'vɑːntɪdʒ/ *n* ventaja *f*. **take ~ of** aprovecharse de; abusar de ‹*person*›. **~ous** /ædvən'teɪdʒəs/ *a* ventajoso

**advent** /'ædvənt/ *n* venida *f*. **A~** *n* adviento *m*

**adventur|e** /əd'ventʃə(r)/ *n* aventura *f*. **~er** *n* aventurero *m*. **~ous** *a* ‹*persona*› aventurero; ‹*cosa*› arriesgado; (*fig, bold*) llamativo

**adverb** /'ædvɜːb/ *n* adverbio *m*

**adversary** /'ædvəsərɪ/ *n* adversario *m*

**advers|e** /'ædvɜːs/ *a* adverso, contrario, desfavorable. **~ity** /əd'vɜːsətɪ/ *n* infortunio *m*

**advert** /'ædvɜːt/ *n* (*fam*) anuncio *m*. **~ise** /'ædvətaɪz/ *vt* anunciar. ● *vi* hacer publicidad; (*seek, sell*) poner un anuncio. **~isement** /əd'vɜːtɪsmənt/ *n* anuncio *m*. **~iser** /-ə(r)/ *n* anunciante *m* & *f*

**advice** /əd'vaɪs/ *n* consejo *m*; (*report*) informe *m*

**advis|able** /əd'vaɪzəbl/ *a* aconsejable. **~e** *vt* aconsejar; (*inform*) avisar. **~e against** aconsejar en contra de. **~er** *n* consejero *m*; (*consultant*) asesor *m*. **~ory** *a* consultivo

**advocate** /'ædvəkət/ *n* defensor *m*; (*jurid*) abogado *m*. /'ædvəkeɪt/ *vt* recomendar

**aegis** /'iːdʒɪs/ *n* égida *f*. **under the ~ of** bajo la tutela de, patrocinado por

**aeon** /'iːən/ *n* eternidad *f*

**aerial** /'eərɪəl/ *a* aéreo. ● *n* antena *f*

**aerobatics** /eərə'bætɪks/ *npl* acrobacia *f* aérea

**aerobics** /eə'rɒbɪks/ *npl* aeróbica *f*

**aerodrome** /'eərədrəʊm/ *n* aeródromo *m*

**aerodynamic** /eərəʊdaɪ'næmɪk/ *a* aerodinámico

**aeroplane** /'eərəpleɪn/ *n* avión *m*

**aerosol** /'eərəsɒl/ *n* aerosol *m*

**aesthetic** /iːs'θetɪk/ *a* estético

**afar** /ə'fɑː(r)/ *adv* lejos

**affable** /'æfəbl/ *a* afable

**affair** /ə'feə(r)/ *n* asunto *m*. (**love**) **~** aventura *f*, amorío *m*. **~s** *npl* (*business*) negocios *mpl*

**affect** /ə'fekt/ *vt* afectar; (*pretend*) fingir

**affect|ation** /æfek'teɪʃn/ *n* afectación *f*. **~ed** *a* afectado, amanerado

**affection** /ə'fekʃn/ *n* cariño *m*; (*disease*) afección *f*. **~ate** /-ʃənət/ *a* cariñoso

**affiliat|e** /ə'fɪlɪeɪt/ *vt* afiliar. **~ion** /-'eɪʃn/ *n* afiliación *f*

**affinity** /ə'fɪnətɪ/ *n* afinidad *f*

**affirm** /ə'fɜːm/ *vt* afirmar. **~ation** /æfə'meɪʃn/ *n* afirmación *f*

**affirmative** /ə'fɜːmətɪv/ *a* afirmativo. ● *n* respuesta *f* afirmativa

**affix** /ə'fɪks/ *vt* sujetar; añadir ‹*signature*›; pegar ‹*stamp*›

**afflict** /ə'flɪkt/ *vt* afligir. **~ion** /-ʃn/ *n* aflicción *f*, pena *f*

**affluen|ce** /'æflʊəns/ *n* riqueza *f*. **~t** *a* rico. ● *n* (*geog*) afluente *m*

**afford** /ə'fɔːd/ *vt* permitirse; (*provide*) dar

**affray** /ə'freɪ/ *n* reyerta *f*

**affront** /ə'frʌnt/ *n* afrenta *f*, ofensa *f*. ● *vt* afrentar, ofender

**afield** /ə'fiːld/ *adv*. **far ~** muy lejos

**aflame** /ə'fleɪm/ *adv* & *a* en llamas

**afloat** /ə'fləʊt/ *adv* a flote

**afoot** /ə'fʊt/ *adv*. **sth is ~** se está tramando algo

**aforesaid** /ə'fɔːsed/ *a* susodicho

**afraid** /ə'freɪd/ *a*. **be ~** tener miedo (**of** a); (*be sorry*) sentir, lamentar

**afresh** /ə'freʃ/ *adv* de nuevo

**Africa** /'æfrɪkə/ *n* África *f*. **~n** *a* & *n* africano (*m*)

**after** /'ɑːftə(r)/ *adv* después; (*behind*) detrás. ● *prep* después de; (*behind*) detrás de. **be ~** (*seek*) buscar, andar en busca de. ● *conj* después de que. ● *a* posterior

**afterbirth** /'ɑːftəbɜːθ/ *n* placenta *f*

**after-effect** /'ɑːftərɪfekt/ *n* consecuencia *f*, efecto *m* secundario

**aftermath** /'ɑːftəmæθ/ *n* secuelas *fpl*

**afternoon** /ɑːftə'nuːn/ *n* tarde *f*

**aftershave** /'ɑːftəʃeɪv/ *n* loción *f* para después del afeitado

**afterthought** /'ɑ:ftəθɔ:t/ *n* ocurrencia *f* tardía

**afterwards** /'ɑ:ftəwədz/ *adv* después

**again** /ə'gen/ *adv* otra vez; (*besides*) además. ~ **and** ~ una y otra vez

**against** /ə'genst/ *prep* contra, en contra de

**age** /eɪdʒ/ *n* edad *f*. **of** ~ mayor de edad. **under** ~ menor de edad. ● *vt/i* (*pres p* **ageing**) envejecer. ~**d** /'eɪdʒd/ *a* de ... años. ~**d 10** de 10 años, que tiene 10 años. ~**d** /'eɪdʒɪd/ *a* viejo, anciano. ~**less** *a* siempre joven; (*eternal*) eterno, inmemorial. ~**s** (*fam*) siglos *mpl*

**agency** /'eɪdʒənsɪ/ *n* agencia *f*, organismo *m*, oficina *f*; (*means*) mediación *f*

**agenda** /ə'dʒendə/ *npl* orden *m* del día

**agent** /'eɪdʒənt/ *n* agente *m & f*; (*representative*) representante *m & f*

**agglomeration** /əglɒmə'reɪʃn/ *n* aglomeración *f*

**aggravat|e** /'ægrəveɪt/ *vt* agravar; (*irritate*, *fam*) irritar. ~**ion** /-'veɪʃn/ *n* agravación *f*, (*irritation*, *fam*) irritación *f*

**aggregate** /'ægrɪgət/ *a* total. ● *n* conjunto *m*. /'ægrɪgeɪt/ *vt* agregar. ● *vi* ascender a

**aggress|ion** /ə'greʃn/ *n* agresión *f*. ~**ive** *a* agresivo. ~**iveness** *n* agresividad *f*. ~**or** *n* agresor *m*

**aggrieved** /ə'gri:vd/ *a* apenado, ofendido

**aghast** /ə'gɑ:st/ *a* horrorizado

**agil|e** /'ædʒaɪl/ *a* ágil. ~**ity** /ə'dʒɪlətɪ/ *n* agilidad *f*

**agitat|e** /'ædʒɪteɪt/ *vt* agitar. ~**ion** /-'teɪʃn/ *n* agitación *f*, excitación *f*. ~**or** *n* agitador *m*

**agnostic** /æg'nɒstɪk/ *a & n* agnóstico (*m*). ~**ism** /-sɪzəm/ *n* agnosticismo *m*

**ago** /ə'gəʊ/ *adv* hace. **a long time** ~ hace mucho tiempo. **3 days** ~ hace 3 días

**agog** /ə'gɒg/ *a* ansioso

**agon|ize** /'ægənaɪz/ *vi* atormentarse. ~**izing** *a* atroz, angustioso, doloroso. ~**y** *n* dolor *m* (agudo); (*mental*) angustia *f*

**agree** /ə'gri:/ *vt* acordar. ● *vi* estar de acuerdo; (*of figures*) concordar; (*get on*) entenderse. ~ **with** (*of food etc*) sentar bien a. ~**able** /ə'gri:əbl/ *a* agradable. **be** ~**able** (*willing*) estar

de acuerdo. ~**d** *a* (*time*, *place*) convenido. ~**ment** /ə'gri:mənt/ *n* acuerdo *m*. **in** ~**ment** de acuerdo

**agricultur|al** /ægrɪ'kʌltʃərəl/ *a* agrícola. ~**e** /'ægrɪkʌltʃə(r)/ *n* agricultura *f*

**aground** /ə'graʊnd/ *adv.* **run** ~ (*of ship*) varar, encallar

**ahead** /ə'hed/ *adv* delante; (*of time*) antes de. **be** ~ ir delante

**aid** /eɪd/ *vt* ayudar. ● *n* ayuda *f*. **in** ~ **of** a beneficio de

**aide** /eɪd/ *n* (*Amer*) ayudante *m & f*

**AIDS** /eɪdz/ *n* (*med*) SIDA *m*

**ail** /eɪl/ *vt* afligir. ~**ing** *a* enfermo. ~**ment** *n* enfermedad *f*

**aim** /eɪm/ *vt* apuntar; (*fig*) dirigir. ● *vi* apuntar; (*fig*) pretender. ● *n* puntería *f*, (*fig*) propósito *m*. ~**less** *a*, ~**lessly** *adv* sin objeto, sin rumbo

**air** /eə(r)/ *n* aire *m*. **be on the** ~ estar en el aire. **put on** ~**s** darse aires. ● *vt* airear. ● *a* (*base etc*) aéreo. ~**borne** *a* en el aire; (*mil*) aerotransportado. ~**conditioned** *a* climatizado, con aire acondicionado. ~**craft** /'eəkrɑ:ft/ *n* (*pl invar*) avión *m*. ~**field** /'eəfi:ld/ *n* aeródromo *m*. **A~ Force** fuerzas *fpl* aéreas. ~**gun** /'eəgʌn/ *n* escopeta *f* de aire comprimido. ~**lift** /'eəlɪft/ *n* puente *m* aéreo. ~**line** /'eəlaɪn/ *n* línea *f* aérea. ~**lock** /'eəlɒk/ *n* (*in pipe*) burbuja *f* de aire; (*chamber*) esclusa *f* de aire. ~ **mail** *n* correo *m* aéreo. ~**man** /'eəmən/ *n* (*pl* -**men**) *n* aviador *m*. ~**port** /'eəpɔ:t/ *n* aeropuerto *m*. ~**tight** /'eətaɪt/ *a* hermético. ~**worthy** /'eəwɜ:ðɪ/ *a* en condiciones de vuelo. ~**y** /'eərɪ/ *a* (-**ier**, -**iest**) aireado; (*manner*) ligero

**aisle** /aɪl/ *n* nave *f* lateral; (*gangway*) pasillo *m*

**ajar** /ə'dʒɑ:(r)/ *adv & a* entreabierto

**akin** /ə'kɪn/ *a* semejante (**a** to)

**alabaster** /'æləbɑ:stə(r)/ *n* alabastro *m*

**alacrity** /ə'lækrətɪ/ *n* prontitud *f*

**alarm** /ə'lɑ:m/ *n* alarma *f*; (*clock*) despertador *m*. ● *vt* asustar. ~**ist** *n* alarmista *m & f*

**alas** /ə'læs/ *int* ¡ay!, ¡ay de mí!

**albatross** /'ælbətrɒs/ *n* albatros *m*

**albino** /æl'bi:nəʊ/ *a & n* albino (*m*)

**album** /'ælbəm/ *n* álbum *m*

**alchem|ist** /'ælkəmɪst/ *n* alquimista *m & f*. ~**y** *n* alquimia *f*

**alcohol** /'ælkəhɒl/ *n* alcohol *m*. ~**ic** /-'hɒlɪk/ *a & n* alcohólico (*m*). ~**ism** *n* alcoholismo *m*

**alcove** /'ælkəʊv/ n nicho m

**ale** /eɪl/ n cerveza f

**alert** /ə'lɜːt/ a vivo; (watchful) vigilante. ● n alerta f. **on the** ~ alerta. ● vt avisar. ~ness n vigilancia f

**algebra** /'ældʒɪbrə/ n álgebra f

**Algeria** /æl'dʒɪərɪə/ n Argelia f. ~n a & n argelino (m)

**alias** /'eɪlɪəs/ n (pl -ases) alias m invar. ● adv alias

**alibi** /'ælɪbaɪ/ (pl -is) coartada f

**alien** /'eɪlɪən/ n extranjero m. ● a ajeno

**alienat|e** /'eɪlɪəneɪt/ vt enajenar. ~ion /-'neɪʃn/ n enajenación f

**alight**[1] /ə'laɪt/ vi bajar; (bird) posarse

**alight**[2] /ə'laɪt/ a ardiendo; (light) encendido

**align** /ə'laɪn/ vt alinear. ~ment n alineación f

**alike** /ə'laɪk/ a parecido, semejante. **look** or **be** ~ parecerse. ● adv de la misma manera

**alimony** /'ælɪmənɪ/ n pensión f alimenticia

**alive** /ə'laɪv/ a vivo. ~ **to** sensible a. ~ **with** lleno de

**alkali** /'ælkəlaɪ/ n (pl -is) álcali m. ~ne a alcalino

**all** /ɔːl/ a & pron todo. ~ **but one** todos excepto uno. ~ **of it** todo. ● adv completamente. ~ **but** casi. ~ **in** (fam) rendido. ~ **of a sudden** de pronto. ~ **over** (finished) acabado; (everywhere) por todas partes. ~ **right!** ¡vale! **be** ~ **for** estar a favor de. **not at** ~ de ninguna manera; (after thanks!) ¡no hay de qué!

**allay** /ə'leɪ/ vt aliviar (pain); aquietar (fears etc)

**all-clear** /ɔːl'klɪə(r)/ n fin m de (la) alarma

**allegation** /ælɪ'geɪʃn/ n alegato m

**allege** /ə'ledʒ/ vt alegar. ~dly /-ɪdlɪ/ adv según se dice, supuestamente

**allegiance** /ə'liːdʒəns/ n lealtad f

**allegor|ical** /ælɪ'gɒrɪkl/ a alegórico. ~y /'ælɪgərɪ/ n alegoría f

**allerg|ic** /ə'lɜːdʒɪk/ a alérgico. ~y /'ælədʒɪ/ n alergia f

**alleviat|e** /ə'liːvɪeɪt/ vt aliviar. ~ion /-'eɪʃn/ n alivio m

**alley** /'ælɪ/ (pl -eys) n callejuela f; (for bowling) bolera f

**alliance** /ə'laɪəns/ n alianza f

**allied** /'ælaɪd/ a aliado

**alligator** /'ælɪgeɪtə(r)/ n caimán m

**allocat|e** /'æləkeɪt/ vt asignar; (share out) repartir. ~ion /-'keɪʃn/ n asignación f; (share) ración f; (distribution) reparto m

**allot** /ə'lɒt/ vt (pt allotted) asignar. ~ment n asignación f; (share) ración f; (land) parcela f

**all-out** /ɔːl'aʊt/ a máximo

**allow** /ə'laʊ/ vt permitir; (grant) conceder; (reckon on) prever; (agree) admitir. ~ **for** tener en cuenta. ~ance /ə'laʊəns/ n concesión f; (pension) pensión f; (com) rebaja f. **make** ~ances **for** ser indulgente con; (take into account) tener en cuenta

**alloy** /'ælɔɪ/ n aleación f. /ə'lɔɪ/ vt alear

**all-round** /ɔːl'raʊnd/ a completo

**allude** /ə'luːd/ vi aludir

**allure** /ə'lʊə(r)/ vt atraer. ● n atractivo m

**allusion** /ə'luːʒn/ n alusión f

**ally** /'ælaɪ/ n aliado m. /ə'laɪ/ vt aliarse

**almanac** /'ɔːlmənæk/ n almanaque m

**almighty** /ɔːl'maɪtɪ/ a todopoderoso; (big, fam) enorme. ● n. **the A**~ el Todopoderoso m

**almond** /'ɑːmənd/ n almendra f; (tree) almendro (m)

**almost** /'ɔːlməʊst/ adv casi

**alms** /ɑːmz/ n limosna f

**alone** /ə'ləʊn/ a solo. ● adv sólo, solamente

**along** /ə'lɒŋ/ prep por, a lo largo de. ● adv. ~ **with** junto con. **all** ~ todo el tiempo. **come** ~ venga

**alongside** /əlɒŋ'saɪd/ adv (naut) al costado. ● prep al lado de

**aloof** /ə'luːf/ adv apartado. ● a reservado. ~ness n reserva f

**aloud** /ə'laʊd/ adv en voz alta

**alphabet** /'ælfəbet/ n alfabeto m. ~ical /-'betɪkl/ a alfabético

**alpine** /'ælpaɪn/ a alpino

**Alps** /ælps/ npl. **the** ~ los Alpes mpl

**already** /ɔːl'redɪ/ adv ya

**Alsatian** /æl'seɪʃn/ n (geog) alsaciano m; (dog) pastor m alemán

**also** /'ɔːlsəʊ/ adv también; (moreover) además

**altar** /'ɔːltə(r)/ n altar m

**alter** /'ɔːltə(r)/ vt cambiar. ● vi cambiarse. ~ation /-'reɪʃn/ n modificación f; (to garment) arreglo m

**alternate** /ɔːl'tɜːnət/ a alterno. /'ɔːltəneɪt/ vt/i alternar. ~ly adv alternativamente

**alternative** /ɔːlˈtɜːnətɪv/ *a* alternativo. ● *n* alternativa *f.* ~**ly** *adv* en cambio, por otra parte
**although** /ɔːlˈðəʊ/ *conj* aunque
**altitude** /ˈæltɪtjuːd/ *n* altitud *f*
**altogether** /ɔːltəˈɡeðə(r)/ *adv* completamente; (*on the whole*) en total
**altruis|m** /ˈæltruːɪzəm/ *n* altruismo *m.* ~**t** /ˈæltruːɪst/ *n* altruista *m* & *f.* ~**tic** /-ˈɪstɪk/ *a* altruista
**aluminium** /æljʊˈmɪnɪəm/ *n* aluminio *m*
**always** /ˈɔːlweɪz/ *adv* siempre
**am** /æm/ *see* **be**
**a.m.** /ˈeɪem/ *abbr* (*ante meridiem*) de la mañana
**amalgamate** /əˈmælɡəmeɪt/ *vt* amalgamar. ● *vi* amalgamarse
**amass** /əˈmæs/ *vt* amontonar
**amateur** /ˈæmətə(r)/ *n* aficionado *m.* ● *a* no profesional; (*in sports*) amateur. ~**ish** *a* (*pej*) torpe, chapucero
**amaz|e** /əˈmeɪz/ *vt* asombrar. ~**ed** *a* asombrado, estupefacto. **be** ~**ed at** quedarse asombrado de, asombrarse de. ~**ement** *n* asombro *m.* ~**ingly** *adv* extraordinariamente
**ambassador** /æmˈbæsədə(r)/ *n* embajador *m*
**amber** /ˈæmbə(r)/ *n* ámbar *m*; (*auto*) luz *f* amarilla
**ambidextrous** /æmbɪˈdekstrəs/ *a* ambidextro
**ambience** /ˈæmbɪəns/ *n* ambiente *m*
**ambigu|ity** /æmbɪˈɡjuːətɪ/ *n* ambigüedad *f.* ~**ous** /æmˈbɪɡjʊəs/ *a* ambiguo
**ambit** /ˈæmbɪt/ *n* ámbito *m*
**ambiti|on** /æmˈbɪʃn/ *n* ambición *f.* ~**ous** *a* ambicioso
**ambivalen|ce** /æmˈbɪvələns/ *n* ambivalencia *f.* ~**t** *a* ambivalente
**amble** /ˈæmbl/ *vi* andar despacio, andar sin prisa
**ambulance** /ˈæmbjʊləns/ *n* ambulancia *f*
**ambush** /ˈæmbʊʃ/ *n* emboscada *f.* ● *vt* tender una emboscada a
**amen** /ɑːˈmen/ *int* amén
**amenable** /əˈmiːnəbl/ *a.* ~ **to** (*responsive*) sensible a, flexible a
**amend** /əˈmend/ *vt* enmendar. ~**ment** *n* enmienda *f.* ~**s** *npl.* **make** ~**s** reparar
**amenities** /əˈmiːnətɪz/ *npl* atractivos *mpl*, comodidades *fpl*, instalaciones *fpl*
**America** /əˈmerɪkə/ *n* América; (*North America*) Estados *mpl*

Unidos. ~**n** *a* & *n* americano (*m*); (*North American*) estadounidense (*m* & *f*). ~**nism** *n* americanismo *m.* ~**nize** *vt* americanizar
**amethyst** /ˈæmɪθɪst/ *n* amatista *f*
**amiable** /ˈeɪmɪəbl/ *a* simpático
**amicabl|e** /ˈæmɪkəbl/ *a* amistoso. ~**y** *adv* amistosamente
**amid(st)** /əˈmɪd(st)/ *prep* entre, en medio de
**amiss** /əˈmɪs/ *a* malo. ● *adv* mal. **sth** ~ algo que no va bien. **take sth** ~ llevar algo a mal
**ammonia** /əˈməʊnɪə/ *n* amoníaco *m*, amoniaco *m*
**ammunition** /æmjʊˈnɪʃn/ *n* municiones *fpl*
**amnesia** /æmˈniːzɪə/ *n* amnesia *f*
**amnesty** /ˈæmnəstɪ/ *n* amnistía *f*
**amok** /əˈmɒk/ *adv.* **run** ~ volverse loco
**among(st)** /əˈmʌŋ(st)/ *prep* entre
**amoral** /eɪˈmɒrəl/ *a* amoral
**amorous** /ˈæmərəs/ *a* amoroso
**amorphous** /əˈmɔːfəs/ *a* amorfo
**amount** /əˈmaʊnt/ *n* cantidad *f*; (*total*) total *m*, suma *f.* ● *vi.* ~ **to** sumar; (*fig*) equivaler a, significar
**amp(ere)** /ˈæmp(eə(r))/ *n* amperio *m*
**amphibi|an** /æmˈfɪbɪən/ *n* anfibio *m.* ~**ous** *a* anfibio
**amphitheatre** /ˈæmfɪθɪətə(r)/ *n* anfiteatro *m*
**ampl|e** /ˈæmpl/ *a* (**-er, -est**) amplio; (*enough*) suficiente; (*plentiful*) abundante. ~**y** *adv* ampliamente, bastante
**amplif|ier** /ˈæmplɪfaɪə(r)/ *n* amplificador *m.* ~**y** *vt* amplificar
**amputat|e** /ˈæmpjʊteɪt/ *vt* amputar. ~**ion** /-ˈteɪʃn/ *n* amputación *f*
**amus|e** /əˈmjuːz/ *vt* divertir. ~**ement** *n* diversión *f.* ~**ing** *a* divertido
**an** /ən, æn/ *see* **a**
**anachronism** /əˈnækrənɪzəm/ *n* anacronismo *m*
**anaemi|a** /əˈniːmɪə/ *n* anemia *f.* ~**c** *a* anémico
**anaesthe|sia** /ænɪsˈθiːzɪə/ *n* anestesia *f.* ~**tic** /ænɪsˈθetɪk/ *n* anestésico *m.* ~**tist** /əˈniːsθɪtɪst/ *n* anestesista *m* & *f*
**anagram** /ˈænəɡræm/ *n* anagrama *m*
**analogy** /əˈnælədʒɪ/ *n* analogía *f*
**analys|e** /ˈænəlaɪz/ *vt* analizar. ~**is** /əˈnæləsɪs/ *n* (*pl* **-yses** /-siːz/) *n* análisis *m.* ~**t** /ˈænəlɪst/ *n* analista *m* & *f*

**analytic(al)** /ænə'lɪtɪk(əl)/ *a* analítico

**anarch|ist** /'ænəkɪst/ *n* anarquista *m & f*. **~y** *n* anarquía *f*

**anathema** /ə'næθəmə/ *n* anatema *m*

**anatom|ical** /ænə'tomɪkl/ *a* anatómico. **~y** /ə'nætəmɪ/ *n* anatomía *f*

**ancest|or** /'ænsestə(r)/ *n* antepasado *m*. **~ral** /-'sestrəl/ *a* ancestral. **~ry** /'ænsestrɪ/ *n* ascendencia *f*

**anchor** /'æŋkə(r)/ *n* ancla *f*. ● *vt* anclar; *(fig)* sujetar. ● *vi* anclar

**anchovy** /'æntʃəvɪ/ *n* *(fresh)* boquerón *m*; *(tinned)* anchoa *f*

**ancient** /'eɪnʃənt/ *a* antiguo, viejo

**ancillary** /æn'sɪlərɪ/ *a* auxiliar

**and** /ənd, ænd/ *conj* y; *(before i- and hi-)* e. **go ~ see him** vete a verle. **more ~ more** siempre más, cada vez más. **try ~ come** ven si puedes, trata de venir

**Andalusia** /ændə'lu:zjə/ *f* Andalucía *f*

**anecdote** /'ænɪkdəʊt/ *n* anécdota *f*

**anew** /ə'nju:/ *adv* de nuevo

**angel** /'eɪndʒl/ *n* ángel *m*. **~ic** /æn'dʒelɪk/ *a* angélico

**anger** /'æŋgə(r)/ *n* ira *f*. ● *vt* enojar

**angle**[1] /'æŋgl/ *n* ángulo *m*; *(fig)* punto *m* de vista

**angle**[2] /'æŋgl/ *vi* pescar con caña. **~ for** *(fig)* buscar. **~r** /-ə(r)/ *n* pescador *m*

**Anglican** /'æŋglɪkən/ *a & n* anglicano *(m)*

**Anglo-...** /'æŋgləʊ/ *pref* anglo...

**Anglo-Saxon** /'æŋgləʊ'sæksn/ *a & n* anglosajón *(m)*

**angr|ily** /'æŋgrɪlɪ/ *adv* con enojo. **~y** /'æŋgrɪ/ *a* (**-ier, -iest**) enojado. **get ~y** enfadarse

**anguish** /'æŋgwɪʃ/ *n* angustia *f*

**angular** /'æŋgjʊlə(r)/ *a* angular; *(face)* anguloso

**animal** /'ænɪml/ *a & n* animal *(m)*

**animat|e** /'ænɪmət/ *a* vivo. /'ænɪmeɪt/ *vt* animar. **~ion** /-'meɪʃn/ *n* animación *f*

**animosity** /ænɪ'mɒsətɪ/ *n* animosidad *f*

**aniseed** /'ænɪsi:d/ *n* anís *m*

**ankle** /'æŋkl/ *n* tobillo *m*. **~ sock** escarpín *m*, calcetín *m*

**annals** /'ænlz/ *npl* anales *mpl*

**annex** /ə'neks/ *vt* anexionar. **~ation** /ænek'seɪʃn/ *n* anexión *f*

**annexe** /'æneks/ *n* anexo *m*, dependencia *f*

**annihilat|e** /ə'naɪəleɪt/ *vt* aniquilar. **~ion** /-'leɪʃn/ *n* aniquilación *f*

**anniversary** /ænɪ'vɜːsərɪ/ *n* aniversario *m*

**annotat|e** /'ænəteɪt/ *vt* anotar. **~ion** /-'teɪʃn/ *n* anotación *f*

**announce** /ə'naʊns/ *vt* anunciar, comunicar. **~ment** *n* anuncio *m*, aviso *m*, declaración *f*. **~r** /-ə(r)/ *n* *(radio, TV)* locutor *m*

**annoy** /ə'nɔɪ/ *vt* molestar. **~ance** *n* disgusto *m*. **~ed** *a* enfadado. **~ing** *a* molesto

**annual** /'ænjʊəl/ *a* anual. ● *n* anuario *m*. **~ly** *adv* cada año

**annuity** /ə'nju:ətɪ/ *n* anualidad *f*. **life ~** renta *f* vitalicia

**annul** /ə'nʌl/ *vt* (*pt* **annulled**) anular. **~ment** *n* anulación *f*

**anoint** /ə'nɔɪnt/ *vt* ungir

**anomal|ous** /ə'nɒmələs/ *a* anómalo. **~y** *n* anomalía *f*

**anon** /ə'nɒn/ *adv* *(old use)* dentro de poco

**anonymous** /ə'nɒnɪməs/ *a* anónimo

**anorak** /'ænəræk/ *n* anorac *m*

**another** /ə'nʌðə(r)/ *a & pron* otro *(m)*. **~ 10 minutes** 10 minutos más. **in ~ way** de otra manera. **one ~** unos a otros

**answer** /'ɑːnsə(r)/ *n* respuesta *f*; *(solution)* solución *f*. ● *vt* contestar a; escuchar, oír *(prayer)*. **~ the door** abrir la puerta. ● *vi* contestar. **~ back** replicar. **~ for** ser responsable de. **~able** *a* responsable. **~ing-machine** *n* contestador *m* automático

**ant** /ænt/ *n* hormiga *f*

**antagoni|sm** /æn'tægənɪzəm/ *n* antagonismo *m*. **~stic** /-'nɪstɪk/ *a* antagónico, opuesto. **~ze** /æn'tægənaɪz/ *vt* provocar la enemistad de

**Antarctic** /æn'tɑːktɪk/ *a* antártico. ● *n* Antártico *m*

**ante-...** /'æntɪ/ *pref* ante...

**antecedent** /æntɪ'si:dnt/ *n* antecedente *m*

**antelope** /'æntɪləʊp/ *n* antílope *m*

**antenatal** /'æntɪneɪtl/ *a* prenatal

**antenna** /æn'tenə/ *n* antena *f*

**anthem** /'ænθəm/ *n* himno *m*

**anthill** /'ænthɪl/ *n* hormiguero *m*

**anthology** /æn'θɒlədʒɪ/ *n* antología *f*

**anthropolog|ist** /ænθrə'pɒlədʒɪst/ *n* antropólogo *m*. **~y** *n* antropología *f*

**anti-...** /'æntɪ/ *pref* anti... **~aircraft** *a* antiaéreo

**antibiotic** /æntɪbaɪˈɒtɪk/ a & n antibiótico (m)

**antibody** /ˈæntɪbɒdɪ/ n anticuerpo m

**antic** /ˈæntɪk/ n payasada f, travesura f

**anticipat|e** /ænˈtɪsɪpeɪt/ vt anticiparse a; (foresee) prever; (forestall) prevenir. ~ion /-ˈpeɪʃn/ n anticipación f; (expectation) esperanza f

**anticlimax** /æntɪˈklaɪmæks/ n decepción f

**anticlockwise** /æntɪˈklɒkwaɪz/ adv & a en sentido contrario al de las agujas del reloj, hacia la izquierda

**anticyclone** /æntɪˈsaɪkləʊn/ n anticiclón m

**antidote** /ˈæntɪdəʊt/ m antídoto m

**antifreeze** /ˈæntɪfriːz/ n anticongelante m

**antipathy** /ænˈtɪpəθɪ/ n antipatía f

**antiquarian** /æntɪˈkweərɪən/ a & n anticuario (m)

**antiquated** /ˈæntɪkweɪtɪd/ a anticuado

**antique** /ænˈtiːk/ a antiguo. ● n antigüedad f. ~ **dealer** anticuario m. ~ **shop** tienda f de antigüedades

**antiquity** /ænˈtɪkwətɪ/ n antigüedad f

**anti-Semitic** /æntɪsɪˈmɪtɪk/ a antisemítico

**antiseptic** /æntɪˈseptɪk/ a & n antiséptico (m)

**antisocial** /æntɪˈsəʊʃl/ a antisocial

**antithesis** /ænˈtɪθəsɪs/ n (pl -eses /-siːz/) antítesis f

**antler** /ˈæntlər/ n cornamenta f

**anus** /ˈeɪnəs/ n ano m

**anvil** /ˈænvɪl/ n yunque m

**anxiety** /æŋˈzaɪətɪ/ n ansiedad f; (worry) inquietud f; (eagerness) anhelo m

**anxious** /ˈæŋkʃəs/ a inquieto; (eager) deseoso. ~ly adv con inquietud; (eagerly) con impaciencia

**any** /ˈenɪ/ a algún m; (negative) ningún m; (whatever) cualquier; (every) todo. at ~ **moment** en cualquier momento. **have you** ~ **wine?** ¿tienes vino? ● pron alguno; (negative) ninguno. **have we** ~? ¿tenemos algunos? **not** ~ **ninguno**. ● adv (a little) un poco, algo. **is it** ~ **better?** ¿está algo mejor? **it isn't** ~ **good** no sirve para nada

**anybody** /ˈenɪbɒdɪ/ pron alguien; (after negative) nadie. ~ **can do it**

cualquiera sabe hacerlo, cualquiera puede hacerlo

**anyhow** /ˈenɪhaʊ/ adv de todas formas; (in spite of all) a pesar de todo; (badly) de cualquier modo

**anyone** /ˈenɪwʌn/ pron alguien; (after negative) nadie

**anything** /ˈenɪθɪŋ/ pron algo; (whatever) cualquier cosa; (after negative) nada. ~ **but** todo menos

**anyway** /ˈenɪweɪ/ adv de todas formas

**anywhere** /ˈenɪweə(r)/ adv en cualquier parte; (after negative) en ningún sitio; (everywhere) en todas partes. ~ **else** en cualquier otro lugar. ~ **you go** dondequiera que vayas

**apace** /əˈpeɪs/ adv rápidamente

**apart** /əˈpɑːt/ adv aparte; (separated) apartado, separado. ~ **from** aparte de. **come** ~ romperse. **take** ~ desmontar

**apartheid** /əˈpɑːtheɪt/ n segregación f racial, apartheid m

**apartment** /əˈpɑːtmənt/ n (Amer) apartamento m

**apath|etic** /æpəˈθetɪk/ a apático, indiferente. ~y /ˈæpəθɪ/ n apatía f

**ape** /eɪp/ n mono m. ● vt imitar

**aperient** /əˈpɪərɪənt/ a & n laxante (m)

**aperitif** /əˈperɪtɪf/ n aperitivo m

**aperture** /ˈæpətʃʊə(r)/ n abertura f

**apex** /ˈeɪpeks/ n ápice m

**aphorism** /ˈæfərɪzəm/ n aforismo m

**aphrodisiac** /æfrəˈdɪzɪæk/ a & n afrodisíaco (m), afrodisiaco (m)

**apiece** /əˈpiːs/ adv cada uno

**aplomb** /əˈplɒm/ n aplomo m

**apolog|etic** /əpɒləˈdʒetɪk/ a lleno de disculpas. **be** ~**etic** disculparse. ~**ize** /əˈpɒlədʒaɪz/ vi disculparse (for de). ~y /əˈpɒlədʒɪ/ n disculpa f; (poor specimen) birria f

**apople|ctic** /æpəˈplektɪk/ a apoléptico. ~**xy** /ˈæpəpleksɪ/ n apoplejía f

**apostle** /əˈpɒsl/ n apóstol m

**apostrophe** /əˈpɒstrəfɪ/ n (punctuation mark) apóstrofo m

**appal** /əˈpɔːl/ vt (pt appalled) horrorizar. ~**ling** a espantoso

**apparatus** /æpəˈreɪtəs/ n aparato m

**apparel** /əˈpærəl/ n ropa f, indumentaria f

**apparent** /əˈpærənt/ a aparente; (clear) evidente. ~**ly** adv por lo visto

**apparition** /æpəˈrɪʃn/ n aparición f

**appeal** /ə'pi:l/ *vi* apelar; (*attract*) atraer. ● *n* llamamiento *m*; (*attraction*) atractivo *m*; (*jurid*) apelación *f*. ~**ing** *a* atrayente

**appear** /ə'pɪə(r)/ *vi* aparecer; (*arrive*) llegar; (*seem*) parecer; (*on stage*) actuar. ~**ance** *n* aparición *f*; (*aspect*) aspecto *m*

**appease** /ə'pi:z/ *vt* aplacar; (*pacify*) apaciguar

**append** /ə'pend/ *vt* adjuntar. ~**age** /ə'pendɪdʒ/ *n* añadidura *f*

**appendicitis** /əpendɪ'saɪtɪs/ *n* apendicitis *f*

**appendix** /ə'pendɪks/ *n* (*pl* -**ices** /-si:z/) (*of book*) apéndice *m*. (*pl* -**ixes**) (*anat*) apéndice *m*

**appertain** /æpə'teɪn/ *vi* relacionarse (**to** con)

**appetite** /'æpɪtaɪt/ *n* apetito *m*

**appetiz|er** /'æpɪtaɪzə(r)/ *n* aperitivo *m*. ~**ing** *a* apetitoso

**applaud** /ə'plɔ:d/ *vt/i* aplaudir. ~**se** *n* aplausos *mpl*

**apple** /'æpl/ *n* manzana *f*. ~**tree** *n* manzano *m*

**appliance** /ə'plaɪəns/ *n* aparato *m*. **electrical** ~ electrodoméstico *m*

**applicable** /'æplɪkəbl/ *a* aplicable; (*relevant*) pertinente

**applicant** /'æplɪkənt/ *n* candidato *m*, solicitante *m & f*

**application** /æplɪ'keɪʃn/ *n* aplicación *f*; (*request*) solicitud *f*. ~ **form** formulario *m* (de solicitud)

**appl|ied** /ə'plaɪd/ *a* aplicado. ~**y** /ə'plaɪ/ *vt* aplicar. ● *vi* aplicarse; (*ask*) dirigirse. ~**y for** solicitar ‹*job etc*›

**appoint** /ə'pɔɪnt/ *vt* nombrar; (*fix*) señalar. ~**ment** *n* cita *f*; (*job*) empleo *m*

**apportion** /ə'pɔ:ʃn/ *vt* repartir

**apposite** /'æpəzɪt/ *a* apropiado

**apprais|al** /ə'preɪzl/ *n* evaluación *f*. ~**e** *vt* evaluar

**appreciable** /ə'pri:ʃəbl/ *a* sensible; (*considerable*) considerable

**appreciat|e** /ə'pri:ʃɪeɪt/ *vt* apreciar; (*understand*) comprender; (*be grateful for*) agradecer. ● *vi* (*increase value*) aumentar en valor. ~**ion** /-'eɪʃn/ *n* aprecio *m*; (*gratitude*) agradecimiento *m*. ~**ive** /ə'pri:ʃɪətɪv/ *a* (*grateful*) agradecido

**apprehen|d** /æprɪ'hend/ *vt* detener; (*understand*) comprender. ~**sion** /-ʃn/ *n* detención *f*; (*fear*) recelo *m*

**apprehensive** /æprɪ'hensɪv/ *a* aprensivo

**apprentice** /ə'prentɪs/ *n* aprendiz *m*. ● *vt* poner de aprendiz. ~**ship** *n* aprendizaje *m*

**approach** /ə'prəʊtʃ/ *vt* acercarse a. ● *vi* acercarse. ● *n* acercamiento *m*; (*to problem*) enfoque *m*; (*access*) acceso *m*. **make** ~**es to** dirigirse a. ~**able** *a* accesible

**approbation** /æprə'beɪʃn/ *n* aprobación *f*

**appropriate** /ə'prəʊprɪət/ *a* apropiado. /ə'prəʊprɪeɪt/ *vt* apropiarse de. ~**ly** *adv* apropiadamente

**approval** /ə'pru:vl/ *n* aprobación *f*. **on** ~ a prueba

**approv|e** /ə'pru:v/ *vt/i* aprobar. ~**ingly** *adv* con aprobación

**approximat|e** /ə'prɒksɪmət/ *a* aproximado. /ə'prɒksɪmeɪt/ *vt* aproximarse a. ~**ely** *adv* aproximadamente. ~**ion** /-'meɪʃn/ *n* aproximación *f*

**apricot** /'eɪprɪkɒt/ *n* albaricoque *m*, chabacano *m* (*Mex*). ~**tree** *n* albaricoquero *m*, chabacano *m* (*Mex*)

**April** /'eɪprəl/ *n* abril *m*. ~ **fool!** ¡inocentón!

**apron** /'eɪprən/ *n* delantal *m*

**apropos** /'æprəpəʊ/ *adv* a propósito

**apse** /æps/ *n* ábside *m*

**apt** /æpt/ *a* apropiado; (*pupil*) listo. **be** ~ **to** tener tendencia a

**aptitude** /'æptɪtju:d/ *n* aptitud *f*

**aptly** /'æptlɪ/ *adv* acertadamente

**aqualung** /'ækwəlʌŋ/ *n* pulmón *m* acuático

**aquarium** /ə'kweərɪəm/ *n* (*pl* -**ums**) acuario *m*

**Aquarius** /ə'kweərɪəs/ *n* Acuario *m*

**aquatic** /ə'kwætɪk/ *a* acuático

**aqueduct** /'ækwɪdʌkt/ *n* acueducto *m*

**aquiline** /'ækwɪlaɪn/ *a* aquilino

**Arab** /'ærəb/ *a & n* árabe *m*. ~**ian** /ə'reɪbɪən/ *a* árabe. ~**ic** /'ærəbɪk/ *a & n* árabe (*m*). ~**ic numerals** números *mpl* arábigos

**arable** /'ærəbl/ *a* cultivable

**arbiter** /'ɑ:bɪtə(r)/ *n* árbitro *m*

**arbitrary** /'ɑ:bɪtrərɪ/ *a* arbitrario

**arbitrat|e** /'ɑ:bɪtreɪt/ *vi* arbitrar. ~**ion** /-'treɪʃn/ *n* arbitraje *m*. ~**or** *n* árbitro *m*

**arc** /ɑ:k/ *n* arco *m*

**arcade** /ɑ:'keɪd/ *n* arcada *f*; (*around square*) soportales *mpl*; (*shops*)

galería f. **amusement** ~ galería f de
atracciones

**arcane** /ɑ:ˈkeɪn/ a misterioso

**arch**¹ /ɑ:tʃ/ n arco m. ● vt arquear.
● vi arquearse

**arch**² /ɑ:tʃ/ a malicioso

**archaeolog|ical** /ɑ:kɪəˈlɒdʒɪkl/ a
arqueológico. **~ist** /ɑ:kɪˈɒlədʒɪst/ n
arqueólogo m. **~y** /ɑ:kɪˈɒlədʒɪ/ n
arqueología f

**archaic** /ɑ:ˈkeɪk/ a arcaico

**archbishop** /ɑ:tʃˈbɪʃəp/ n arzobispo m

**arch-enemy** /ɑ:tʃˈenəmɪ/ n enemigo
m jurado

**archer** /ˈɑ:tʃə(r)/ n arquero m. **~y** n
tiro m al arco

**archetype** /ˈɑ:kɪtaɪp/ n arquetipo m

**archipelago** /ɑ:kɪˈpeləgəʊ/ n (pl -os)
archipiélago m

**architect** /ˈɑ:kɪtekt/ n arquitecto m.
**~ure** /ˈɑ:kɪtektʃə(r)/ n arquitectura f.
**~ural** /-ˈtektʃərəl/ a arquitectónico

**archiv|es** /ˈɑ:kaɪvz/ npl archivo m.
**~ist** /-ɪvɪst/ n archivero m

**archway** /ˈɑ:tʃweɪ/ n arco m

**Arctic** /ˈɑ:ktɪk/ a ártico. ● n Ártico m

**arctic** /ˈɑ:ktɪk/ a glacial

**ardent** /ˈɑ:dənt/ a ardiente, fervoroso, apasionado. **~ly** adv
ardientemente

**ardour** /ˈɑ:də(r)/ n ardor m, fervor m,
pasión f

**arduous** /ˈɑ:djʊəs/ a arduo

**are** /ɑ:(r)/ see **be**

**area** /ˈeərɪə/ n (surface) superficie f,
(region) zona f, (fig) campo m

**arena** /əˈri:nə/ n arena f, (in circus)
pista f, (in bullring) ruedo m

**aren't** /ɑ:nt/ = **are not**

**Argentin|a** /ɑ:dʒənˈti:nə/ n Argentina
f. **~ian** /-ˈtɪnɪən/ a & n argentino (m)

**arguable** /ˈɑ:gjʊəbl/ a discutible

**argue** /ˈɑ:gju:/ vi discutir; (reason)
razonar

**argument** /ˈɑ:gjʊmənt/ n disputa f,
(reasoning) argumento m. **~ative**
/-ˈmentətɪv/ a discutidor

**arid** /ˈærɪd/ a árido

**Aries** /ˈeərɪːz/ n Aries m

**arise** /əˈraɪz/ vi (pt arose, pp arisen)
levantarse; (fig) surgir. ~ from resultar de

**aristocra|cy** /ærɪˈstɒkrəsɪ/ n aristocracia f. **~t** /ˈærɪstəkræt/ n aristócrata m & f. **~tic** /-ˈkrætɪk/ a
aristocrático

**arithmetic** /əˈrɪθmətɪk/ n aritmética
f

**ark** /ɑ:k/ n (relig) arca f

**arm**¹ /ɑ:m/ n brazo m. ~ **in** ~ cogidos
del brazo

**arm**² /ɑ:m/ n. **~s** npl armas fpl. ● vt
armar

**armada** /ɑ:ˈmɑ:də/ n armada f

**armament** /ˈɑ:məmənt/ n armamento
m

**armchair** /ˈɑ:mtʃeə(r)/ n sillón m

**armed robbery** /ɑ:md'rɒbərɪ/ n robo
m a mano armada

**armful** /ˈɑ:mfʊl/ n brazada f

**armistice** /ˈɑ:mɪstɪs/ n armisticio m

**armlet** /ˈɑ:mlɪt/ n brazalete m

**armour** /ˈɑ:mə(r)/ n armadura f. **~ed**
a blindado

**armoury** /ˈɑ:mərɪ/ n arsenal m

**armpit** /ˈɑ:mpɪt/ n sobaco m, axila f

**army** /ˈɑ:mɪ/ n ejército m

**aroma** /əˈrəʊmə/ n aroma m. **~tic**
/ærəˈmætɪk/ a aromático

**arose** /əˈrəʊz/ see **arise**

**around** /əˈraʊnd/ adv alrededor;
(near) cerca. **all** ~ por todas partes.
● prep alrededor de; (with time) a
eso de

**arouse** /əˈraʊz/ vt despertar

**arpeggio** /ɑ:ˈpedʒɪəʊ/ n arpegio m

**arrange** /əˈreɪndʒ/ vt arreglar; (fix)
fijar. **~ment** n arreglo m; (agreement) acuerdo m; (pl, plans) preparativos mpl

**array** /əˈreɪ/ vt (dress) ataviar; (mil)
formar. ● n atavío m; (mil) orden m;
(fig) colección f, conjunto m

**arrears** /əˈrɪəz/ npl atrasos mpl. **in** ~
atrasado en pagos

**arrest** /əˈrest/ vt detener; llamar ‹attention›. ● n detención f. **under** ~
detenido

**arriv|al** /əˈraɪvl/ n llegada f. **new** ~**al**
recien llegado m. **~e** /əˈraɪv/ vi
llegar

**arrogan|ce** /ˈærəgəns/ n arrogancia
f. **~t** a arrogante. **~tly** adv con
arrogancia

**arrow** /ˈærəʊ/ n flecha f

**arsenal** /ˈɑ:sənl/ n arsenal m

**arsenic** /ˈɑ:snɪk/ n arsénico m

**arson** /ˈɑ:sn/ n incendio m provocado.
**~ist** n incendiario m

**art**¹ /ɑ:t/ n arte m. **A~s** npl (Univ)
Filosofía y Letras fpl. **fine** ~**s** bellas
artes fpl

**art**² /ɑ:t/ (old use, with thou) = **are**

**artefact** /ˈɑ:tɪfækt/ n artefacto m

**arterial** /ɑ:ˈtɪərɪəl/ a arterial. ~ **road**
n carretera f nacional

**artery** /ˈɑ:tərɪ/ n arteria f

**artesian** /ɑːˈtiːzjən/ a. ~ **well** pozo m artesiano

**artful** /ˈɑːtfʊl/ a astuto. ~**ness** n astucia f

**art gallery** /ˈɑːtgælərɪ/ n museo m de pinturas, pinacoteca f, galería f de arte

**arthriti|c** /ɑːˈθrɪtɪk/ a artrítico. ~**s** /ɑːˈθraɪtɪs/ n artritis f

**artichoke** /ˈɑːtɪtʃəʊk/ n alcachofa f. **Jerusalem** ~ pataca f

**article** /ˈɑːtɪkl/ n artículo m. ~ **of clothing** prenda f de vestir. **leading** ~ artículo de fondo

**articulat|e** /ɑːˈtɪkjʊlət/ a articulado; ‹person› elocuente. /ɑːˈtɪkjʊleɪt/ vt/i articular. ~**ed lorry** n camión m con remolque. ~**ion** /-ˈleɪʃn/ n articulación f

**artifice** /ˈɑːtɪfɪs/ n artificio m

**artificial** /ɑːtɪˈfɪʃl/ a artificial; ‹hair etc› postizo

**artillery** /ɑːˈtɪlərɪ/ n artillería f

**artisan** /ɑːtɪˈzæn/ n artesano m

**artist** /ˈɑːtɪst/ n artista m & f

**artiste** /ɑːˈtiːst/ n (in theatre) artista m & f

**artist|ic** /ɑːˈtɪstɪk/ a artístico. ~**ry** n arte m, habilidad f

**artless** /ˈɑːtlɪs/ a ingenuo

**arty** /ˈɑːtɪ/ a (fam) que se las da de artista

**as** /æz, əz/ adv & conj como; (since) ya que; (while) mientras. ~ **big** ~ tan grande como. ~ **far** ~ (distance) hasta; (qualitative) en cuanto a. ~ **far** ~ **I know** que yo sepa. ~ **if** como si. ~ **long** ~ mientras. ~ **much** ~ tanto como. ~ **soon** ~ tan pronto como. ~ **well** también

**asbestos** /æzˈbestɒs/ n amianto m, asbesto m

**ascen|d** /əˈsend/ vt/i subir. ~**t** /əˈsent/ n subida f

**ascertain** /æsəˈteɪn/ vt averiguar

**ascetic** /əˈsetɪk/ a ascético. ● n asceta m & f

**ascribe** /əˈskraɪb/ vt atribuir

**ash**[1] /æʃ/ n ceniza f

**ash**[2] /æʃ/ n. ~**(-tree)** fresno m

**ashamed** /əˈʃeɪmd/ a avergonzado. **be** ~ avergonzarse

**ashen** /ˈæʃn/ a ceniciento

**ashore** /əˈʃɔː(r)/ adv a tierra. **go** ~ desembarcar

**ash:** ~**tray** /ˈæʃtreɪ/ n cenicero m. **A~ Wednesday** n Miércoles m de Ceniza

**Asia** /ˈeɪʃə/ n Asia f. ~**n** a & n asiático (m). ~**tic** /-ˈætɪk/ a asiático

**aside** /əˈsaɪd/ adv a un lado. ● n (in theatre) aparte m

**asinine** /ˈæsɪnaɪn/ a estúpido

**ask** /ɑːsk/ vt pedir; preguntar ‹question›; (invite) invitar. ~ **about** enterarse de. ~ **after** pedir noticias de. ~ **for help** pedir ayuda. ~ **for trouble** buscarse problemas. ~ **s.o. in** invitar a uno a pasar

**askance** /əˈskæns/ adv. **look** ~ **at** mirar de soslayo

**askew** /əˈskjuː/ adv & a ladeado

**asleep** /əˈsliːp/ adv & a dormido. **fall** ~ dormirse, quedar dormido

**asparagus** /əˈspærəgəs/ n espárrago m

**aspect** /ˈæspekt/ n aspecto m; (of house etc) orientación f

**aspersions** /əˈspɜːʃnz/ npl. **cast** ~ **on** difamar

**asphalt** /ˈæsfælt/ n asfalto m. ● vt asfaltar

**asphyxia** /æsˈfɪksɪə/ n asfixia f. ~**te** /əsˈfɪksɪeɪt/ vt asfixiar. ~**tion** /-ˈeɪʃn/ n asfixia f

**aspic** /ˈæspɪk/ n gelatina f

**aspir|ation** /æspɪˈreɪʃn/ n aspiración f. ~**e** /əsˈpaɪə(r)/ vi aspirar

**aspirin** /ˈæsprɪn/ n aspirina f

**ass** /æs/ n asno m; (fig, fam) imbécil m

**assail** /əˈseɪl/ vt asaltar. ~**ant** n asaltador m

**assassin** /əˈsæsɪn/ n asesino m. ~**ate** /əˈsæsɪneɪt/ vt asesinar. ~**ation** /-ˈeɪʃn/ n asesinato m

**assault** /əˈsɔːlt/ n (mil) ataque m; (jurid) atentado m. ● vt asaltar

**assemblage** /əˈsemblɪdʒ/ n (of things) colección f; (of people) reunión f; (mec) montaje m

**assemble** /əˈsembl/ vt reunir; (mec) montar. ● vi reunirse

**assembly** /əˈsemblɪ/ n reunión f; (pol etc) asamblea f. ~ **line** n línea f de montaje

**assent** /əˈsent/ n asentimiento m. ● vi asentir

**assert** /əˈsɜːt/ vt afirmar; hacer valer ‹one's rights›. ~**ion** /-ʃn/ n afirmación f. ~**ive** a positivo, firme

**assess** /əˈses/ vt valorar; (determine) determinar; fijar ‹tax etc›. ~**ment** n valoración f

**asset** /ˈæset/ n (advantage) ventaja f; (pl, com) bienes mpl

**assiduous** /əˈsɪdjʊəs/ a asiduo

**assign** /ə'saɪn/ vt asignar; (appoint) nombrar

**assignation** /æsɪg'neɪʃn/ n asignación f; (meeting) cita f

**assignment** /ə'saɪnmənt/ n asignación f, misión f; (task) tarea f

**assimilat|e** /ə'sɪmɪleɪt/ vt asimilar. ● vi asimilarse. ∼ion /-'eɪʃn/ n asimilación f

**assist** /ə'sɪst/ vt/i ayudar. ∼ance n ayuda f. ∼ant /ə'sɪstənt/ n ayudante m & f; (shop) dependienta f, dependiente m. ● a auxiliar, adjunto

**associat|e** /ə'səʊʃɪeɪt/ vt asociar. ● vi asociarse. /ə'səʊʃɪət/ a asociado. ● n colega m & f; (com) socio m. ∼ion /-'eɪʃn/ n asociación f. A∼ion football n fútbol m

**assort|ed** /ə'sɔːtɪd/ a surtido. ∼ment n surtido m

**assume** /ə'sjuːm/ vt suponer; tomar ⟨power, attitude⟩; asumir ⟨role, burden⟩

**assumption** /ə'sʌmpʃn/ n suposición f. the A∼ la Asunción f

**assur|ance** /ə'ʃʊərəns/ n seguridad f; (insurance) seguro m. ∼e /ə'ʃʊə(r)/ vt asegurar. ∼ed a seguro. ∼edly /-rɪdlɪ/ adv seguramente

**asterisk** /'æstərɪsk/ n asterisco m

**astern** /ə'stɜːn/ adv a popa

**asthma** /'æsmə/ n asma f. ∼tic /-'mætɪk/ a & n asmático (m)

**astonish** /ə'stɒnɪʃ/ vt asombrar. ∼ing a asombroso. ∼ment n asombro m

**astound** /ə'staʊnd/ vt asombrar

**astray** /ə'streɪ/ adv & a. go ∼ extraviarse. lead ∼ llevar por mal camino

**astride** /ə'straɪd/ adv a horcajadas. ● prep a horcajadas sobre

**astringent** /ə'strɪndʒənt/ a astringente; (fig) austero. ● n astringente m

**astrolog|er** /ə'strɒlədʒə(r)/ n astrólogo m. ∼y n astrología f

**astronaut** /'æstrənɔːt/ n astronauta m & f

**astronom|er** /ə'strɒnəmə(r)/ n astrónomo m. ∼ical /æstrə'nɒmɪkl/ a astronómico. ∼y /ə'strɒnəmɪ/ n astronomía f

**astute** /ə'stjuːt/ a astuto. ∼ness n astucia f

**asunder** /ə'sʌndə(r)/ adv en pedazos; (in two) en dos

**asylum** /ə'saɪləm/ n asilo m. lunatic ∼ manicomio m

**at** /ət, æt/ prep a. ∼ home en casa. ∼ night por la noche. ∼ Robert's en casa de Roberto. ∼ once en seguida; (simultaneously) a la vez. ∼ sea en el mar. ∼ the station en la estación. ∼ times a veces. not ∼ all nada; (after thanks) ¡de nada!

**ate** /et/ see eat

**atheis|m** /'eɪθɪɪzəm/ n ateísmo m. ∼t /'eɪθɪɪst/ n ateo m

**athlet|e** /'æθliːt/ n atleta m & f. ∼ic /-'letɪk/ a atlético. ∼ics /-'letɪks/ npl atletismo m

**Atlantic** /ət'læntɪk/ a & n atlántico (m). ● n. ∼ (Ocean) (Océano m) Atlántico m

**atlas** /'ætləs/ n atlas m

**atmospher|e** /'ætməsfɪə(r)/ n atmósfera f; (fig) ambiente m. ∼ic /-'ferɪk/ a atmosférico. ∼ics /-'ferɪks/ npl parásitos mpl

**atom** /'ætəm/ n átomo m. ∼ic /ə'tɒmɪk/ a atómico

**atomize** /'ætəmaɪz/ vt atomizar. ∼r /'ætəmaɪzə(r)/ n atomizador m

**atone** /ə'təʊn/ vi. ∼ for expiar. ∼ment n expiación f

**atroci|ous** /ə'trəʊʃəs/ a atroz. ∼ty /ə'trɒsətɪ/ n atrocidad f

**atrophy** /'ætrəfɪ/ n atrofia f

**attach** /ə'tætʃ/ vt sujetar; adjuntar ⟨document etc⟩. be ∼ed to (be fond of) tener cariño a

**attaché** /ə'tæʃeɪ/ n agregado m. ∼ case maletín m

**attachment** /ə'tætʃmənt/ n (affection) cariño m; (tool) accesorio m

**attack** /ə'tæk/ n ataque m. ● vt/i atacar. ∼er n agresor m

**attain** /ə'teɪn/ vt conseguir. ∼able a alcanzable. ∼ment n logro m. ∼ments npl conocimientos mpl, talento m

**attempt** /ə'tempt/ vt intentar. ● n tentativa f; (attack) atentado m

**attend** /ə'tend/ vt asistir a; (escort) acompañar. ● vi prestar atención. ∼ to (look after) ocuparse de. ∼ance n asistencia f; (people present) concurrencia f. ∼ant /ə'tendənt/ a concomitante. ● n encargado m; (servant) sirviente m

**attention** /ə'tenʃn/ n atención f. ∼! (mil) ¡firmes! pay ∼ prestar atención

**attentive** /ə'tentɪv/ a atento. ∼ness n atención f

**attenuate** /ə'tenjʊeɪt/ vt atenuar

**attest** /əˈtest/ vt atestiguar. ● vi dar testimonio. **∼ation** /æteˈsteɪʃn/ n testimonio m

**attic** /ˈætɪk/ n desván m

**attire** /əˈtaɪə(r)/ n atavío m. ● vt vestir

**attitude** /ˈætɪtjuːd/ n postura f

**attorney** /əˈtɜːnɪ/ n (pl -eys) apoderado m; (Amer) abogado m

**attract** /əˈtrækt/ vt atraer. **∼ion** /-ʃn/ n atracción f; (charm) atractivo m

**attractive** /əˈtræktɪv/ a atractivo; (interesting) atrayente. **∼ness** n atractivo m

**attribute** /əˈtrɪbjuːt/ vt atribuir. /ˈætrɪbjuːt/ n atributo m

**attrition** /əˈtrɪʃn/ n desgaste m

**aubergine** /ˈəʊbəʒiːn/ n berenjena f

**auburn** /ˈɔːbən/ a castaño

**auction** /ˈɔːkʃn/ n subasta f. ● vt subastar. **∼eer** /-əˈnɪə(r)/ n subastador m

**audaci|ous** /ɔːˈdeɪʃəs/ a audaz. **∼ty** /-æsətɪ/ n audacia f

**audible** /ˈɔːdəbl/ a audible

**audience** /ˈɔːdɪəns/ n (interview) audiencia f; (teatro, radio) público m

**audio-visual** /ɔːdɪəʊˈvɪʒʊəl/ a audio-visual

**audit** /ˈɔːdɪt/ n revisión f de cuentas. ● vt revisar

**audition** /ɔːˈdɪʃn/ n audición f. ● vt dar audición a

**auditor** /ˈɔːdɪtə(r)/ n interventor m de cuentas

**auditorium** /ɔːdɪˈtɔːrɪəm/ n sala f, auditorio m

**augment** /ɔːgˈment/ vt aumentar

**augur** /ˈɔːgə(r)/ vt augurar. **it ∼s well** es de buen agüero

**august** /ɔːˈgʌst/ a augusto

**August** /ˈɔːgəst/ n agosto m

**aunt** /ɑːnt/ n tía f

**au pair** /əʊˈpeə(r)/ n chica f au pair

**aura** /ˈɔːrə/ n atmósfera f, halo m

**auspices** /ˈɔːspɪsɪz/ npl auspicios mpl

**auspicious** /ɔːˈspɪʃəs/ a propicio

**auster|e** /ɔːˈstɪə(r)/ a austero. **∼ity** /-erətɪ/ n austeridad f

**Australia** /ɒˈstreɪlɪə/ n Australia f. **∼n** a & n australiano (m)

**Austria** /ˈɒstrɪə/ n Austria f. **∼n** a & n austríaco (m)

**authentic** /ɔːˈθentɪk/ a auténtico. **∼ate** /ɔːˈθentɪkeɪt/ vt autenticar. **∼ity** /-ənˈtɪsətɪ/ n autenticidad f

**author** /ˈɔːθə(r)/ n autor m. **∼ess** n autora f

**authoritarian** /ɔːθɒrɪˈteərɪən/ a autoritario

**authoritative** /ɔːˈθɒrɪtətɪv/ a autorizado; (manner) autoritario

**authority** /ɔːˈθɒrətɪ/ n autoridad f; (permission) autorización f

**authoriz|ation** /ɔːθəraɪˈzeɪʃn/ n autorización f. **∼e** /ˈɔːθəraɪz/ vt autorizar

**authorship** /ˈɔːθəʃɪp/ n profesión f de autor; (origin) paternidad f literaria

**autistic** /ɔːˈtɪstɪk/ a autista

**autobiography** /ɔːtəʊbaɪˈɒgrəfɪ/ n autobiografía f

**autocra|cy** /ɔːˈtɒkrəsɪ/ n autocracia f. **∼t** /ˈɔːtəkræt/ n autócrata m & f. **∼tic** /-ˈkrætɪk/ a autocrático

**autograph** /ˈɔːtəgrɑːf/ n autógrafo m. ● vt firmar

**automat|e** /ˈɔːtəmeɪt/ vt automatizar. **∼ic** /ɔːtəˈmætɪk/ a automático. **∼ion** /-ˈmeɪʃn/ n automatización f. **∼on** /ɔːˈtɒmətən/ n autómata m

**automobile** /ˈɔːtəməbiːl/ n (Amer) coche m, automóvil m

**autonom|ous** /ɔːˈtɒnəməs/ a autónomo. **∼y** n autonomía f

**autopsy** /ˈɔːtɒpsɪ/ n autopsia f

**autumn** /ˈɔːtəm/ n otoño m. **∼al** /-ˈtʌmnəl/ a de otoño, otoñal

**auxiliary** /ɔːgˈzɪlɪərɪ/ a auxiliar. ● n asistente m; (verb) verbo m auxiliar; (pl, troops) tropas fpl auxiliares

**avail** /əˈveɪl/ vt/i servir. **∼ o.s. of** aprovecharse de. ● n ventaja f. **to no ∼** inútil

**availab|ility** /əveɪləˈbɪlətɪ/ n disponibilidad f. **∼le** /əˈveɪləbl/ a disponible

**avalanche** /ˈævəlɑːnʃ/ n avalancha f

**avaric|e** /ˈævərɪs/ n avaricia f. **∼ious** /-ˈrɪʃəs/ a avaro

**avenge** /əˈvendʒ/ vt vengar

**avenue** /ˈævənjuː/ n avenida f; (fig) vía f

**average** /ˈævərɪdʒ/ n promedio m. **on ∼** por término medio. ● a medio. ● vt calcular el promedio de. ● vi alcanzar un promedio de

**avers|e** /əˈvɜːs/ a enemigo (to de). **be ∼e to** sentir repugnancia por, no gustarle. **∼ion** /-ʃn/ n repugnancia f

**avert** /ə'vɜːt/ vt (*turn away*) apartar; (*ward off*) desviar

**aviary** /'eɪvɪərɪ/ n pajarera f

**aviation** /eɪvɪ'eɪʃn/ n aviación f

**aviator** /'eɪvɪeɪtə(r)/ n (*old use*) aviador m

**avid** /'ævɪd/ a ávido. **∼ity** /-'vɪdətɪ/ n avidez f

**avocado** /ævə'kɑːdəʊ/ n (pl -os) aguacate m

**avoid** /ə'vɔɪd/ vt evitar. **∼able** a evitable. **∼ance** n el evitar m

**avuncular** /ə'vʌŋkjʊlə(r)/ a de tío

**await** /ə'weɪt/ vt esperar

**awake** /ə'weɪk/ vt/i (pt awoke, pp awoken) despertar. ● a despierto. **wide ∼** completamente despierto; (*fig*) despabilado. **∼n** /ə'weɪkən/ vt/i despertar. **∼ning** n el despertar m

**award** /ə'wɔːd/ vt otorgar; (*jurid*) adjudicar. ● n premio m; (*jurid*) adjudicación f; (*scholarship*) beca f

**aware** /ə'weə(r)/ a consciente. **are you ∼ that?** ¿te das cuenta de que? **∼ness** n conciencia f

**awash** /ə'wɒʃ/ a inundado

**away** /ə'weɪ/ adv (*absent*) fuera; (*far*) lejos; (*persistently*) sin parar. ● a & n. **∼ (match)** partido m fuera de casa

**awe** /ɔː/ n temor m. **∼some** a imponente. **∼struck** a atemorizado

**awful** /'ɔːfʊl/ a terrible, malísimo. **∼ly** adv terriblemente

**awhile** /ə'waɪl/ adv un rato

**awkward** /'ɔːkwəd/ a difícil; (*inconvenient*) inoportuno; (*clumsy*) desmañado; (*embarrassed*) incómodo. **∼ly** adv con dificultad; (*clumsily*) de manera torpe. **∼ness** n dificultad f; (*discomfort*) molestia f; (*clumsiness*) torpeza f

**awning** /'ɔːnɪŋ/ n toldo m

**awoke, awoken** /ə'wəʊk, ə'wəʊkən/ see **awake**

**awry** /ə'raɪ/ adv & a ladeado. **go ∼** salir mal

**axe** /æks/ n hacha f. ● vt (*pres p* axing) cortar con hacha; (*fig*) recortar

**axiom** /'æksɪəm/ n axioma m

**axis** /'æksɪs/ n (pl axes /-iːz/) eje m

**axle** /'æksl/ n eje m

**ay(e)** /aɪ/ adv & n sí (m)

# B

**BA** *abbr see* **bachelor**

**babble** /'bæbl/ vi balbucir; (*chatter*) parlotear; (*of stream*) murmullar. ● n balbuceo m; (*chatter*) parloteo m; (*of stream*) murmullo m

**baboon** /bə'buːn/ n mandril m

**baby** /'beɪbɪ/ n niño m, bebé m; (*Amer, sl*) chica f. **∼ish** /'beɪbɪʃ/ a infantil. **∼sit** vi cuidar a los niños, hacer de canguro. **∼sitter** n persona f que cuida a los niños, canguro m

**bachelor** /'bætʃələ(r)/ n soltero m. **B∼ of Arts (BA)** licenciado m en filosofía y letras. **B∼ of Science (BSc)** licenciado m en ciencias

**back** /bæk/ n espalda f; (*of car*) parte f trasera; (*of chair*) respaldo m; (*of cloth*) revés m; (*of house*) parte f de atrás; (*of animal, book*) lomo m; (*of hand, document*) dorso m; (*football*) defensa m & f. **∼ of beyond** en el quinto pino. ● a trasero; (*taxes*) atrasado. ● adv atrás; (*returned*) de vuelta. ● vt apoyar; (*betting*) apostar a; dar marcha atrás a ⟨car⟩. ● vi retroceder; ⟨car⟩ dar marcha atrás. **∼ down** vi volverse atrás. **∼ out** vi retirarse. **∼ up** vi (*auto*) retroceder. **∼ache** /'bækeɪk/ n dolor m de espalda. **∼bencher** n (*pol*) diputado m sin poder ministerial. **∼biting** /'bækbaɪtɪŋ/ n maledicencia f. **∼bone** /'bækbəʊn/ n columna f vertebral; (*fig*) pilar m. **∼chat** /'bæktʃæt/ n impertinencias fpl. **∼date** /bæk'deɪt/ vt antedatar. **∼er** /'bækə(r)/ n partidario m; (*com*) financiador m. **∼fire** /bæk'faɪə(r)/ vi (*auto*) petardear; (*fig*) fallar, salir el tiro por la culata. **∼gammon** /bæk'gæmən/ n backgammon m. **∼ground** /'bækgraʊnd/ n fondo m; (*environment*) antecedentes mpl. **∼hand** /'bækhænd/ n (*sport*) revés m. **∼handed** a dado con el dorso de la mano; (*fig*) equívoco, ambiguo. **∼hander** n (*sport*) revés m; (*fig*) ataque m indirecto; (*bribe, sl*) soborno m. **∼ing** /'bækɪŋ/ n apoyo m. **∼lash** /'bæklæʃ/ n reacción f. **∼log** /'bæklɒg/ n atrasos mpl. **∼side** /bæk'saɪd/ n (*fam*) trasero m. **∼stage** /bæk'steɪdʒ/ a de bastidores. ● adv entre bastidores. **∼stroke** /'bækstrəʊk/ n (*tennis etc*) revés m; (*swimming*) braza f de espaldas. **∼up** n apoyo m. **∼ward** /'bækwəd/ a ⟨step, etc⟩ hacia atrás;

(*retarded*) atrasado. ~**wards** /'bækwədz/ *adv* hacia atrás; (*fall*) de espaldas; (*back to front*) al revés. **go** ~**wards and forwards** ir de acá para allá. ~**water** /'bækwɔːtə(r)/ *n* agua *f* estancada; (*fig*) lugar *m* apartado

**bacon** /'beɪkən/ *n* tocino *m*

**bacteria** /bæk'tɪərɪə/ *npl* bacterias *fpl*. ~**l** *a* bacteriano

**bad** /bæd/ *a* (**worse, worst**) malo; (*serious*) grave; (*harmful*) nocivo; (*language*) indecente. **feel** ~ sentirse mal

**bade** /beɪd/ *see* **bid**

**badge** /bædʒ/ *n* distintivo *m*, chapa *f*

**badger** /'bædʒə(r)/ *n* tejón *m*. ● *vt* acosar

**bad**: ~**ly** *adv* mal. **want** ~**ly** desear muchísimo. ~**ly off** mal de dinero. ~**-mannered** *a* mal educado

**badminton** /'bædmɪntən/ *n* bádminton *m*

**bad-tempered** /bæd'tempəd/ *a* (*always*) de mal genio; (*temporarily*) de mal humor

**baffle** /'bæfl/ *vt* desconcertar

**bag** /bæg/ *n* bolsa *f*; (*handbag*) bolso *m*. ● *vt* (*pt* **bagged**) ensacar; (*take*) coger (*not LAm*), agarrar (*LAm*). ~**s** *npl* (*luggage*) equipaje *m*. ~**s of** (*fam*) montones de

**baggage** /'bægɪdʒ/ *n* equipaje *m*

**baggy** /'bægɪ/ *a* (*clothes*) holgado

**bagpipes** /'bægpaɪps/ *npl* gaita *f*

**Bahamas** /bə'hɑːməz/ *npl*. **the** ~ las Bahamas *fpl*

**bail**[1] /beɪl/ *n* caución *f*, fianza *f*. ● *vt* poner en libertad bajo fianza. ~**s.o. out** obtener la libertad de uno bajo fianza

**bail**[2] /beɪl/ *n* (*cricket*) travesaño *m*

**bail**[3] /beɪl/ *vt* (*naut*) achicar

**bailiff** /'beɪlɪf/ *n* alguacil *m*; (*estate*) administrador *m*

**bait** /beɪt/ *n* cebo *m*. ● *vt* cebar; (*torment*) atormentar

**bak**\e /beɪk/ *vt* cocer al horno. ● *vi* cocerse. ~**er** *n* panadero *m*. ~**ery** /'beɪkərɪ/ *n* panadería *f*. ~**ing** *n* cocción *f*; (*batch*) hornada *f*. ~**ing-powder** *n* levadura *f* en polvo

**balance** /'bæləns/ *n* equilibrio *m*; (*com*) balance *m*; (*sum*) saldo *m*; (*scales*) balanza *f*; (*remainder*) resto *m*. ● *vt* equilibrar; (*com*) saldar; nivelar (*budget*). ● *vi* equilibrarse; (*com*) saldarse. ~**d** *a* equilibrado

**balcony** /'bælkənɪ/ *n* balcón *m*

**bald** /bɔːld/ *a* (**-er, -est**) calvo; (*tyre*) desgastado

**balderdash** /'bɔːldədæʃ/ *n* tonterías *fpl*

**bald**: ~**ly** *adv* escuetamente. ~**ness** *n* calvicie *f*

**bale** /beɪl/ *n* bala *f*, fardo *m*. ● *vi*. ~ **out** lanzarse en paracaídas

**Balearic** /bælɪ'ærɪk/ *a*. ~ **Islands** Islas *fpl* Baleares

**baleful** /'beɪlfʊl/ *a* funesto

**balk** /bɔːk/ *vt* frustrar. ● *vi*. ~ (**at**) resistirse (a)

**ball**[1] /bɔːl/ *n* bola *f*; (*tennis etc*) pelota *f*; (*football etc*) balón *m*; (*of yarn*) ovillo *m*

**ball**[2] /bɔːl/ (*dance*) baile *m*

**ballad** /'bæləd/ *n* balada *f*

**ballast** /'bæləst/ *n* lastre *m*

**ball**: ~**bearing** *n* cojinete *m* de bolas. ~**cock** *n* llave *f* de bola

**ballerina** /bælə'riːnə/ *f* bailarina *f*

**ballet** /'bæleɪ/ *n* ballet *m*

**ballistic** /bə'lɪstɪk/ *a* balístico. ~**s** *n* balística *f*

**balloon** /bə'luːn/ *n* globo *m*

**balloonist** /bə'luːnɪst/ *n* aeronauta *m & f*

**ballot** /'bælət/ *n* votación *f*. ~ (**-paper**) *n* papeleta *f*. ~**-box** *n* urna *f*

**ball-point** /'bɔːlpɔɪnt/ *n*. ~ (**pen**) bolígrafo *m*

**ballroom** /'bɔːlruːm/ *n* salón *m* de baile

**ballyhoo** /bælɪ'huː/ *n* (*publicity*) publicidad *f* sensacionalista; (*uproar*) jaleo *m*

**balm** /bɑːm/ *n* bálsamo *m*. ~**y** *a* (*mild*) suave; (*sl*) chiflado

**baloney** /bə'ləʊnɪ/ *n* (*sl*) tonterías *fpl*

**balsam** /'bɔːlsəm/ *n* bálsamo *m*

**balustrade** /bælə'streɪd/ *n* barandilla *f*

**bamboo** /bæm'buː/ *n* bambú *m*

**bamboozle** /bæm'buːzl/ *vt* engatusar

**ban** /bæn/ *vt* (*pt* **banned**) prohibir. ~ **from** excluir de. ● *n* prohibición *f*

**banal** /bə'nɑːl/ *a* banal. ~**ity** /-ælətɪ/ *n* banalidad *f*

**banana** /bə'nɑːnə/ *n* plátano *m*, banana *f* (*LAm*). ~**-tree** plátano *m*, banano *m*

**band**[1] /bænd/ *n* banda *f*

**band**[2] /bænd/ *n* (*mus*) orquesta *f*; (*military, brass*) banda *f*. ● *vi*. ~ **together** juntarse

**bandage** /'bændɪdʒ/ n venda f. ● vt vendar

**b & b** abbr (bed and breakfast) cama f y desayuno

**bandit** /'bændɪt/ n bandido m

**bandstand** /'bændstænd/ n quiosco m de música

**bandwagon** /'bændwægən/ n. **jump on the ~** (fig) subirse al carro

**bandy**[1] /'bændɪ/ a (-ier, -iest) patizambo

**bandy**[2] /'bændɪ/ vt. **~ about** repetir. **be bandied about** estar en boca de todos

**bandy-legged** /'bændɪlegd/ a patizambo

**bane** /beɪn/ n (fig) perdición f. **~ful** a funesto

**bang** /bæŋ/ n (noise) ruido m; (blow) golpe m; (of gun) estampido m; (of door) golpe m. ● vt/i golpear. ● adv exactamente. ● int ¡pum!

**banger** /'bæŋə(r)/ n petardo m; (culin, sl) salchicha f

**bangle** /'bæŋgl/ n brazalete m

**banish** /'bænɪʃ/ vt desterrar

**banisters** /'bænɪstəz/ npl barandilla f

**banjo** /'bændʒəʊ/ n (pl -os) banjo m

**bank**[1] /bæŋk/ n (of river) orilla f. ● vt cubrir (fire). ● vi (aviat) ladearse

**bank**[2] /bæŋk/ n banco m. ● vt depositar. **~ on** vt contar con. **~ with** tener una cuenta con. **~er** n banquero m. **~ holiday** n día m festivo, fiesta f. **~ing** n (com) banca f. **~note** /'bæŋknəʊt/ n billete m de banco

**bankrupt** /'bæŋkrʌpt/ a & n quebrado (m). ● vt hacer quebrar. **~cy** n bancarrota f, quiebra f

**banner** /'bænə(r)/ n bandera f; (in demonstration) pancarta f

**banns** /bænz/ npl amonestaciones fpl

**banquet** /'bæŋkwɪt/ n banquete m

**bantamweight** /'bæntəmweɪt/ n peso m gallo

**banter** /'bæntə(r)/ n chanza f. ● vi chancearse

**bap** /bæp/ n panecillo m blando

**baptism** /'bæptɪzəm/ n bautismo m; (act) bautizo m

**Baptist** /'bæptɪst/ n bautista m & f

**baptize** /bæp'taɪz/ vt bautizar

**bar** /bɑː(r)/ n barra f; (on window) reja f; (of chocolate) tableta f; (of soap) pastilla f; (pub) bar m; (mus) compás m; (jurid) abogacía f; (fig)

obstáculo m. ● vt (pt barred) atrancar (door); (exclude) excluir; (prohibit) prohibir. ● prep excepto

**barbar|ian** /bɑː'beərɪən/ a & n bárbaro (m). **~ic** /bɑː'bærɪk/ a bárbaro. **~ity** /-ətɪ/ n barbaridad f. **~ous** a /'bɑːbərəs/ a bárbaro

**barbecue** /'bɑːbɪkjuː/ n barbacoa f. ● vt asar a la parilla

**barbed** /bɑːbd/ a. **~ wire** alambre m de espinas

**barber** /'bɑːbə(r)/ n peluquero m, barbero m

**barbiturate** /bɑː'bɪtjʊrət/ n barbitúrico m

**bare** /beə(r)/ a (-er, est) desnudo; (room) con pocos muebles; (mere) simple; (empty) vacío. ● vt desnudar; (uncover) descubrir. **~ one's teeth** mostrar los dientes. **~back** /'beəbæk/ adv a pelo. **~faced** /'beəfeɪst/ a descarado. **~foot** a descalzo. **~headed** /'beəhedɪd/ a descubierto. **~ly** adv apenas. **~ness** n desnudez f

**bargain** /'bɑːgɪn/ n (agreement) pacto m; (good buy) ganga f. ● vi negociar; (haggle) regatear. **~ for** esperar, contar con

**barge** /bɑːdʒ/ n barcaza f. ● vi. **~ in** irrumpir

**baritone** /'bærɪtəʊn/ n barítono m

**barium** /'beərɪəm/ n bario m

**bark**[1] /bɑːk/ n (of dog) ladrido m. ● vi ladrar

**bark**[2] /bɑːk/ (of tree) corteza f

**barley** /'bɑːlɪ/ n cebada f. **~water** n hordiate m

**bar: ~maid** /'bɑːmeɪd/ n camarera f. **~man** /'bɑːmən/ n (pl -men) camarero m

**barmy** /'bɑːmɪ/ a (sl) chiflado

**barn** /bɑːn/ n granero m

**barometer** /bə'rɒmɪtə(r)/ n barómetro m

**baron** /'bærən/ n barón m. **~ess** n baronesa f

**baroque** /bə'rɒk/ a & n barroco (m)

**barracks** /'bærəks/ npl cuartel m

**barrage** /'bærɑːʒ/ n (mil) barrera f; (dam) presa f; (of questions) bombardeo m

**barrel** /'bærəl/ n tonel m; (of gun) cañón m. **~organ** n organillo m

**barren** /'bærən/ a estéril. **~ness** n esterilidad f, aridez f

**barricade** /bærɪ'keɪd/ n barricada f. ● vt cerrar con barricadas

**barrier** /'bærɪə(r)/ n barrera f

**barring** /'bɑːrɪŋ/ *prep* salvo

**barrister** /'bærɪstə(r)/ *n* abogado *m*

**barrow** /'bærəʊ/ *n* carro *m*; (*wheel-barrow*) carretilla *f*

**barter** /'bɑːtə(r)/ *n* trueque *m*. ● *vt* trocar

**base** /beɪs/ *n* base *f*. ● *vt* basar. ● *a* vil

**baseball** /'beɪsbɔːl/ *n* béisbol *m*

**baseless** /'beɪslɪs/ *a* infundado

**basement** /'beɪsmənt/ *n* sótano *m*

**bash** /bæʃ/ *vt* golpear. ● *n* golpe *m*. **have a ~** (*sl*) probar

**bashful** /'bæʃfl/ *a* tímido

**basic** /'beɪsɪk/ *a* básico, fundamental. **~ally** *adv* fundamentalmente

**basil** /'bæzl/ *n* albahaca *f*

**basilica** /bə'zɪlɪkə/ *n* basílica *f*

**basin** /'beɪsn/ *n* (*for washing*) palangana *f*; (*for food*) cuenco *m*; (*geog*) cuenca *f*

**basis** /'beɪsɪs/ *n* (*pl* **bases** /-siːz/) base *f*

**bask** /bɑːsk/ *vi* asolearse; (*fig*) gozar (in de)

**basket** /'bɑːskɪt/ *n* cesta *f*; (*big*) cesto *m*. **~ball** /'bɑːskɪtbɔːl/ *n* baloncesto *m*

**Basque** /bɑːsk/ *a* & *n* vasco (*m*). **~ Country** *n* País *m* Vasco. **~ Provinces** *npl* Vascongadas *fpl*

**bass**[1] /beɪs/ *a* bajo. ● *n* (*mus*) bajo *m*

**bass**[2] /bæs/ *n* (*marine fish*) róbalo *m*; (*freshwater fish*) perca *f*

**bassoon** /bə'suːn/ *n* fagot *m*

**bastard** /'bɑːstəd/ *a* & *n* bastardo (*m*). **you ~!** (*fam*) ¡cabrón!

**baste** /beɪst/ *vt* (*sew*) hilvanar; (*culin*) lard(e)ar

**bastion** /'bæstɪən/ *n* baluarte *m*

**bat**[1] /bæt/ *n* bate *m*; (*for table tennis*) raqueta *f*. **off one's own ~** por sí solo. ● *vt* (*pt* **batted**) golpear. ● *vi* batear

**bat**[2] /bæt/ *n* (*mammal*) murciélago *m*

**bat**[3] /bæt/ *vt*. **without ~ting an eyelid** sin pestañear

**batch** /bætʃ/ *n* (*of people*) grupo *m*; (*of papers*) lío *m*; (*of goods*) remesa *f*; (*of bread*) hornada *f*

**bated** /'beɪtɪd/ *a*. **with ~ breath** con aliento entrecortado

**bath** /bɑːθ/ *n* (*pl* **-s** /bɑːðz/) baño *m*; (*tub*) bañera *f*; (*pl, swimming pool*) piscina *f*. ● *vt* bañar. ● *vi* bañarse

**bathe** /beɪð/ *vt* bañar. ● *vi* bañarse. ● *n* baño *m*. **~r** /-ə(r)/ *n* bañista *m* & *f*

**bathing** /'beɪðɪŋ/ *n* baños *mpl*. **~costume** *n* traje *m* de baño

**bathroom** /'bɑːθrʊm/ *n* cuarto *m* de baño

**batman** /'bætmən/ *n* (*pl* **-men**) (*mil*) ordenanza *f*

**baton** /'bætən/ *n* (*mil*) bastón *m*; (*mus*) batuta *f*

**batsman** /'bætsmən/ *n* (*pl* **-men**) bateador *m*

**battalion** /bə'tælɪən/ *n* batallón *m*

**batter**[1] /'bætə(r)/ *vt* apalear

**batter**[2] /'bætə(r)/ *n* batido *m* para rebozar, albardilla *f*

**batter**: **~ed** *a* (*car etc*) estropeado; (*wife etc*) golpeado. **~ing** *n* (*fam*) bombardeo *m*

**battery** /'bætərɪ/ *n* (*mil, auto*) batería *f*; (*of torch, radio*) pila *f*

**battle** /'bætl/ *n* batalla *f*; (*fig*) lucha *f*. ● *vi* luchar. **~axe** /'bætlæks/ *n* (*woman, fam*) arpía *f*. **~field** /'bætlfiːld/ *n* campo *m* de batalla. **~ments** /'bætlmənts/ *npl* almenas *fpl*. **~ship** /'bætlʃɪp/ *n* acorazado *m*

**batty** /'bætɪ/ *a* (*sl*) chiflado

**baulk** /bɔːlk/ *vt* frustrar. ● *vi*. **~ (at)** resistirse (a)

**bawd||iness** /'bɔːdɪnəs/ *n* obscenidad *f*. **~y** /'bɔːdɪ/ *a* (**-ier, -iest**) obsceno, verde

**bawl** /bɔːl/ *vt/i* gritar

**bay**[1] /beɪ/ *n* (*geog*) bahía *f*

**bay**[2] /beɪ/ *n* (*bot*) laurel *m*

**bay**[3] /beɪ/ *n* (*of dog*) ladrido *m*. **keep at ~** mantener a raya. ● *vi* ladrar

**bayonet** /'beɪənet/ *n* bayoneta *f*

**bay window** /beɪ'wɪndəʊ/ *n* ventana *f* salediza

**bazaar** /bə'zɑː(r)/ *n* bazar *m*

**BC** /biː'siː/ *abbr* (*before Christ*) a. de C., antes de Cristo

**be** /biː/ *vi* (*pres am*, **are**, **is**; *pt* **was**, **were**; *pp* **been**) (*position or temporary*) estar; (*permanent*) ser. **~ cold/hot, etc** tener frío/calor, etc. **~ reading/singing, etc** (*aux*) leer/cantar, etc. **~ that as it may** sea como fuere. **he is 30** (*age*) tiene 30 años. **he is to come** (*must*) tiene que venir. **how are you?** ¿cómo estás? **how much is it?** ¿cuánto vale?, ¿cuánto es? **have been to** haber estado en. **it is cold/hot, etc** (*weather*) hace frío/calor, etc

**beach** /biːtʃ/ *n* playa *f*

**beachcomber** /'biːtʃkəʊmə(r)/ *n* raquero *m*

**beacon** /'biːkən/ *n* faro *m*

**bead** /biːd/ *n* cuenta *f*; (*of glass*) abalorio *m*

**beak** /biːk/ *n* pico *m*

**beaker** /'biːkə(r)/ *n* jarra *f*, vaso *m*

**beam** /biːm/ *n* viga *f*; (*of light*) rayo *m*; (*naut*) bao *m*. ● *vt* emitir. ● *vi* irradiar; (*smile*) sonreír. **~ends** *npl*. **be on one's ~ends** no tener más dinero. **~ing** *a* radiante

**bean** /biːn/ *n* judía; (*broad bean*) haba *f*; (*of coffee*) grano *m*

**beano** /'biːnəʊ/ *n* (*pl* **-os**) (*fam*) juerga *f*

**bear**[1] /beə(r)/ *vt* (*pt* **bore**, *pp* **borne**) llevar; parir (*niño*); (*endure*) soportar. **~ right** torcer a la derecha. **~ in mind** tener en cuenta. **~ with** tener paciencia con

**bear**[2] /beə(r)/ *n* oso *m*

**bearable** /'beərəbl/ *a* soportable

**beard** /biəd/ *n* barba *f*. **~ed** *a* barbudo

**bearer** /'beərə(r)/ *n* portador *m*; (*of passport*) poseedor *m*

**bearing** /'beərɪŋ/ *n* comportamiento *m*; (*relevance*) relación *f*; (*mec*) cojinete *m*. **get one's ~s** orientarse

**beast** /biːst/ *n* bestia *f*; (*person*) bruto *m*. **~ly** /'biːstlɪ/ *a* (**-ier**, **-iest**) bestial; (*fam*) horrible

**beat** /biːt/ *vt* (*pt* **beat**, *pp* **beaten**) golpear; (*culin*) batir; (*defeat*) derrotar; (*better*) sobrepasar; (*baffle*) dejar perplejo. **~ a retreat** (*mil*) batirse en retirada. **~ it** (*sl*) largarse. ● *vi* (*heart*) latir. ● *n* latido *m*; (*mus*) ritmo *m*; (*of policeman*) ronda *f*. **~ up** dar una paliza a; (*culin*) batir. **~er** *n* batidor *m*. **~ing** *n* paliza *f*

**beautician** /bjuː'tɪʃn/ *n* esteticista *m* & *f*

**beautiful** /'bjuːtɪfl/ *a* hermoso. **~ly** *adv* maravillosamente

**beautify** /'bjuːtɪfaɪ/ *vt* embellecer

**beauty** /'bjuːtɪ/ *n* belleza *f*. **~ parlour** *n* salón *m* de belleza. **~ spot** (*on face*) lunar *m*; (*site*) lugar *m* pintoresco

**beaver** /'biːvə(r)/ *n* castor *m*

**became** /bɪ'keɪm/ *see* **become**

**because** /bɪ'kɒz/ *conj* porque. ● *adv*. **~ of** a causa de

**beck** /bek/ *n*. **be at the ~ and call of** estar a disposición de

**beckon** /'bekən/ *vt/i*. **~ (to)** hacer señas (a)

**become** /bɪ'kʌm/ *vt* (*pt* **became**, *pp* **become**) (*clothes*) sentar bien. ● *vi*

hacerse, llegar a ser, volverse, convertirse en. **what has ~ of her?** ¿qué es de ella?

**becoming** /bɪ'kʌmɪŋ/ *a* (*clothes*) favorecedor

**bed** /bed/ *n* cama *f*; (*layer*) estrato *m*; (*of sea, river*) fondo *m*; (*of flowers*) macizo *m*. ● *vi* (*pt* **bedded**). **~ down** acostarse. **~ and breakfast (b & b)** cama y desayuno. **~bug** /'bedbʌg/ *n* chinche *f*. **~clothes** /'bedkləʊðz/ *npl*, **~ding** *n* ropa *f* de cama

**bedevil** /bɪ'devl/ *vt* (*pt* **bedevilled**) (*torment*) atormentar

**bedlam** /'bedləm/ *n* confusión *f*, manicomio *m*

**bed**: **~pan** /'bedpæn/ *n* orinal *m* de cama. **~post** /'bedpəʊst/ *n* columna *f* de la cama

**bedraggled** /bɪ'drægld/ *a* sucio

**bed**: **~ridden** /'bedrɪdn/ *a* encamado. **~room** /'bedrʊm/ *n* dormitorio *m*, habitación *f*. **~side** /'bedsaɪd/ *n* cabecera *f*. **~sitting-room** /bed'sɪtɪŋruːm/ *n* salón *m* con cama, estudio *m*. **~spread** /'bedspred/ *n* colcha *f*. **~time** /'bedtaɪm/ *n* hora *f* de acostarse

**bee** /biː/ *n* abeja *f*. **make a ~-line for** ir en línea recta hacia

**beech** /biːtʃ/ *n* haya *f*

**beef** /biːf/ *n* carne *f* de vaca, carne *f* de res (*LAm*). ● *vi* (*sl*) quejarse. **~burger** /'biːfbɜːgə(r)/ *n* hamburguesa *f*

**beefeater** /'biːfiːtə(r)/ *n* alabardero *m* de la torre de Londres

**beefsteak** /biː'fsteɪk/ *n* filete *m*, bistec *m*, bife *m* (*Arg*)

**beefy** /'biːfɪ/ *a* (**-ier**, **-iest**) musculoso

**beehive** /'biːhaɪv/ *n* colmena *f*

**been** /biːn/ *see* **be**

**beer** /bɪə(r)/ *n* cerveza *f*

**beet** /biːt/ *n* remolacha *f*

**beetle** /'biːtl/ *n* escarabajo *m*

**beetroot** /'biːtruːt/ *n* invar remolacha *f*

**befall** /bɪ'fɔːl/ *vt* (*pt* **befell**, *pp* **befallen**) acontecer a. ● *vi* acontecer

**befit** /bɪ'fɪt/ *vt* (*pt* **befitted**) convenir a

**before** /bɪ'fɔː(r)/ *prep* (*time*) antes de; (*place*) delante de. **~ leaving** antes de marcharse. ● *adv* (*place*) delante; (*time*) antes. **a week ~** una semana antes. **the week ~** la semana anterior. ● *conj* (*time*) antes de que. **~ he leaves** antes de que se vaya. **~hand** /bɪˈfɔːhænd/ adv de antemano

**befriend** /bɪˈfrend/ vt ofrecer amistad a

**beg** /beg/ vt/i (pt **begged**) mendigar; (entreat) suplicar; (ask) pedir. **~ s.o.'s pardon** pedir perdón a uno. **I ~ your pardon!** ¡perdone Vd! **I ~ your pardon?** ¿cómo? **it's going ~ging** no lo quiere nadie

**began** /bɪˈgæn/ see **begin**

**beget** /bɪˈget/ vt (pt **begot**, pp **begotten**, pres p **begetting**) engendrar

**beggar** /ˈbegə(r)/ n mendigo m; (sl) individuo m, tío m (fam)

**begin** /bɪˈgɪn/ vt/i (pt **began**, pp **begun**, pres p **beginning**) comenzar, empezar. **~ner** n principiante m & f. **~ning** n principio m

**begot, begotten** /bɪˈgɒt, bɪˈgɒtn/ see **beget**

**begrudge** /bɪˈgrʌdʒ/ vt envidiar; (give) dar de mala gana

**beguile** /bɪˈgaɪl/ vt engañar, seducir; (entertain) entretener

**begun** /bɪˈgʌn/ see **begin**

**behalf** /bɪˈhɑːf/ n. **on ~ of** de parte de, en nombre de

**behav|e** /bɪˈheɪv/ vi comportarse, portarse. **~ (o.s.)** portarse bien. **~iour** /bɪˈheɪvjə(r)/ n comportamiento m

**behead** /bɪˈhed/ vt decapitar

**beheld** /bɪˈheld/ see **behold**

**behind** /bɪˈhaɪnd/ prep detrás de. ● adv detrás; (late) atrasado. ● n (fam) trasero m

**behold** /bɪˈhəʊld/ vt (pt **beheld**) (old use) mirar, contemplar

**beholden** /bɪˈhəʊldən/ a agradecido

**being** /ˈbiːɪŋ/ n ser m. **come into ~** nacer

**belated** /bɪˈleɪtɪd/ a tardío

**belch** /beltʃ/ vi eructar. ● vt. **~ out** arrojar (smoke)

**belfry** /ˈbelfrɪ/ n campanario m

**Belgi|an** /ˈbeldʒən/ a & n belga (m & f). **~um** /ˈbeldʒəm/ n Bélgica f

**belie** /bɪˈlaɪ/ vt desmentir

**belie|f** /bɪˈliːf/ n (trust) fe f; (opinion) creencia f. **~ve** /bɪˈliːv/ vt/i creer. **make ~ve** fingir. **~ver** /-ə(r)/ n creyente m & f; (supporter) partidario m

**belittle** /bɪˈlɪtl/ vt empequeñecer; (fig) despreciar

**bell** /bel/ n campana f; (on door) timbre m

**belligerent** /bɪˈlɪdʒərənt/ a & n beligerante (m & f)

**bellow** /ˈbeləʊ/ vt gritar. ● vi bramar

**bellows** /ˈbeləʊz/ npl fuelle m

**belly** /ˈbelɪ/ n vientre m. **~ful** /ˈbelɪfʊl/ n panzada f. **have a ~ful of** (sl) estar harto de

**belong** /bɪˈlɒŋ/ vi pertenecer; (club) ser socio (**to** de)

**belongings** /bɪˈlɒŋɪŋz/ npl pertenencias fpl. **personal ~** efectos mpl personales

**beloved** /bɪˈlʌvɪd/ a & n querido (m)

**below** /bɪˈləʊ/ prep debajo de; (fig) inferior a. ● adv abajo

**belt** /belt/ n cinturón m; (area) zona f. ● vt (fig) rodear; (sl) pegar

**bemused** /bɪˈmjuːzd/ a perplejo

**bench** /bentʃ/ n banco m. **the B~** (jurid) la magistratura f

**bend** /bend/ vt (pt & pp **bent**) doblar; torcer (arm, leg). ● vi doblarse; (road) torcerse. ● n curva f. **~ down/over** inclinarse

**beneath** /bɪˈniːθ/ prep debajo de; (fig) inferior a. ● adv abajo

**benediction** /benɪˈdɪkʃn/ n bendición f

**benefactor** /ˈbenɪfæktə(r)/ n bienhechor m, benefactor m

**beneficial** /benɪˈfɪʃl/ a provechoso

**beneficiary** /benɪˈfɪʃərɪ/ a & n beneficiario (m)

**benefit** /ˈbenɪfɪt/ n provecho m, ventaja f; (allowance) subsidio m; (financial gain) beneficio m. ● vt (pt **benefited**, pres p **benefiting**) aprovechar. ● vi aprovecharse

**benevolen|ce** /bɪˈnevələns/ n benevolencia f. **~t** a benévolo

**benign** /bɪˈnaɪn/ a benigno

**bent** /bent/ see **bend**. ● n inclinación f. ● a encorvado; (sl) corrompido

**bequeath** /bɪˈkwiːð/ vt legar

**bequest** /bɪˈkwest/ n legado m

**bereave|d** /bɪˈriːvd/ n. **the ~d** la familia f del difunto. **~ment** n pérdida f; (mourning) luto m

**bereft** /bɪˈreft/ a. **~ of** privado de

**beret** /ˈbereɪ/ n boina f

**Bermuda** /bəˈmjuːdə/ n Islas fpl Bermudas

**berry** /ˈberɪ/ n baya f

**berserk** /bəˈsɜːk/ a. **go ~** volverse loco, perder los estribos

**berth** /bɜːθ/ n litera f; (anchorage) amarradero m. **give a wide ~ to** evitar. ● vi atracar

**beseech** /bɪ'siːtʃ/ *vt* (*pt* **besought**) suplicar

**beset** /bɪ'set/ *vt* (*pt* **beset, pres p besetting**) acosar

**beside** /bɪ'saɪd/ *prep* al lado de. **be ~ o.s.** estar fuera de sí

**besides** /bɪ'saɪdz/ *prep* además de; (*except*) excepto. ● *adv* además

**besiege** /bɪ'siːdʒ/ *vt* asediar; (*fig*) acosar

**besought** /bɪ'sɔːt/ *see* **beseech**

**bespoke** /bɪ'spəʊk/ *a* ⟨*tailor*⟩ que confecciona a la medida

**best** /best/ *a* (el) mejor. **the ~ thing is to...** lo mejor es... ● *adv* (lo) mejor. **like ~** preferir. ● *n* lo mejor. **at ~** a lo más. **do one's ~** hacer todo lo posible. **make the ~ of** contentarse con. **~ man** *n* padrino *m* (de boda)

**bestow** /bɪ'stəʊ/ *vt* conceder

**bestseller** /best'selə(r)/ *n* éxito *m* de librería, bestseller *m*

**bet** /bet/ *n* apuesta *f*. ● *vt/i* (*pt* **bet** or **betted**) apostar

**betray** /bɪ'treɪ/ *vt* traicionar. **~al** *n* traición *f*

**betroth|al** /bɪ'trəʊðəl/ *n* esponsales *mpl*. **~ed** *a* prometido

**better** /'betə(r)/ *a* & *adv* mejor. **~ off** en mejores condiciones; (*richer*) más rico. **get ~** mejorar. **all the ~** tanto mejor. **I'd ~** más vale que. **the ~ part of** la mayor parte de. **the sooner the ~** cuanto antes mejor. ● *vt* mejorar; (*beat*) sobrepasar. ● *n* superior *m*. **get the ~ of** vencer a. **one's ~s** sus superiores *mpl*

**between** /bɪ'twiːn/ *prep* entre. ● *adv* en medio

**beverage** /'bevərɪdʒ/ *n* bebida *f*

**bevy** /'bevɪ/ *n* grupo *m*

**beware** /bɪ'weə(r)/ *vi* tener cuidado. ● *int* ¡cuidado!

**bewilder** /bɪ'wɪldə(r)/ *vt* desconcertar. **~ment** *n* aturdimiento *m*

**bewitch** /bɪ'wɪtʃ/ *vt* hechizar

**beyond** /bɪ'jɒnd/ *prep* más allá de; (*fig*) fuera de. **~ doubt** sin lugar a duda. **~ reason** irrazonable. ● *adv* más allá

**bias** /'baɪəs/ *n* predisposición *f*; (*prejudice*) prejuicio *m*; (*sewing*) sesgo *m*. ● *vt* (*pt* **biased**) influir en. **~ed** *a* parcial

**bib** /bɪb/ *n* babero *m*

**Bible** /'baɪbl/ *n* Biblia *f*

**biblical** /'bɪblɪkl/ *a* bíblico

**bibliography** /bɪblɪ'ɒgrəfɪ/ *n* bibliografía *f*

**biceps** /'baɪseps/ *n* bíceps *m*

**bicker** /'bɪkə(r)/ *vi* altercar

**bicycle** /'baɪsɪkl/ *n* bicicleta *f*. ● *vi* ir en bicicleta

**bid** /bɪd/ *n* (*offer*) oferta *f*; (*attempt*) tentativa *f*. ● *vi* hacer una oferta. ● *vt* (*pt* **bid**, *pres p* **bidding**) ofrecer; (*pt* **bid**, *pp* **bidden**, *pres p* **bidding**) mandar; dar ⟨*welcome, good-day etc*⟩. **~der** *n* postor *m*. **~ding** *n* (*at auction*) ofertas *fpl*; (*order*) mandato *m*

**bide** /baɪd/ *vt*. **~ one's time** esperar el momento oportuno

**biennial** /baɪ'enɪəl/ *a* bienal. ● *n* (*event*) bienal *f*; (*bot*) planta *f* bienal

**bifocals** /baɪ'fəʊklz/ *npl* gafas *fpl* bifocales, anteojos *mpl* bifocales (*LAm*)

**big** /bɪg/ *a* (**bigger, biggest**) grande; (*generous, sl*) generoso. ● *adv*. **talk ~** fanfarronear

**bigam|ist** /'bɪgəmɪst/ *n* bígamo *m*. **~ous** *a* bígamo. **~y** *n* bigamia *f*

**big-headed** /bɪg'hedɪd/ *a* engreído

**bigot** /'bɪgət/ *n* fanático *m*. **~ed** *a* fanático. **~ry** *n* fanatismo *m*

**bigwig** /'bɪgwɪg/ *n* (*fam*) pez *m* gordo

**bike** /baɪk/ *n* (*fam*) bicicleta *f*, bici *f* (*fam*)

**bikini** /bɪ'kiːnɪ/ *n* (*pl* **-is**) biquini *m*, bikini *m*

**bilberry** /'bɪlbərɪ/ *n* arándano *m*

**bile** /baɪl/ *n* bilis *f*

**bilingual** /baɪ'lɪŋgwəl/ *a* bilingüe

**bilious** /'bɪlɪəs/ *a* (*med*) bilioso

**bill**[1] /bɪl/ *n* cuenta *f*; (*invoice*) factura *f*; (*notice*) cartel *m*; (*Amer, banknote*) billete *m*; (*pol*) proyecto *m* de ley. ● *vt* pasar la factura; (*in theatre*) anunciar

**bill**[2] /bɪl/ *n* (*of bird*) pico *m*

**billet** /'bɪlɪt/ *n* (*mil*) alojamiento *m*. ● *vt* alojar

**billiards** /'bɪlɪədz/ *n* billar *m*

**billion** /'bɪlɪən/ *n* billón *m*; (*Amer*) mil millones *mpl*

**billy-goat** /'bɪlɪgəʊt/ *n* macho *m* cabrío

**bin** /bɪn/ *n* recipiente *m*; (*for rubbish*) cubo *m*; (*for waste paper*) papelera *f*

**bind** /baɪnd/ *vt* (*pt* **bound**) atar; encuadernar ⟨*book*⟩; (*jurid*) obligar. ● *n* (*sl*) lata *f*. **~ing**

/'baɪndɪŋ/ n (of books) encuadernación f; (braid) ribete m

**binge** /bɪndʒ/ n (sl) (of food) comilona f; (of drink) borrachera f. **go on a** ~ ir de juerga

**bingo** /'bɪŋgəʊ/ n bingo m

**binoculars** /bɪ'nɒkjʊləz/ npl prismáticos mpl

**biochemistry** /baɪəʊ'kemɪstrɪ/ n bioquímica f

**biograph|er** /baɪ'ɒgrəfə(r)/ n biógrafo m. ~y n biografía f

**biolog|ical** /baɪə'lɒdʒɪkl/ a biológico. ~ist n biólogo m. ~ /baɪ'ɒlədʒɪ/ n biología f

**biped** /'baɪped/ n bípedo m

**birch** /bɜːtʃ/ n (tree) abedul m; (whip) férula f

**bird** /bɜːd/ n ave f; (small) pájaro m; (fam) tipo m; (girl, sl) chica f

**Biro** /'baɪərəʊ/ n (pl -os) (P) bolígrafo m, biromen m (Arg)

**birth** /bɜːθ/ n nacimiento m. ~certificate n partida f de nacimiento. ~control n control m de la natalidad. ~day /'bɜːθdeɪ/ n cumpleaños m invar. ~mark /'bɜːθmɑːk/ n marca f de nacimiento. ~rate n natalidad f. ~right /'bɜːθraɪt/ n derechos mpl de nacimiento

**biscuit** /'bɪskɪt/ n galleta f

**bisect** /baɪ'sekt/ vt bisecar

**bishop** /'bɪʃəp/ n obispo m

**bit**[1] /bɪt/ n trozo m; (quantity) poco m

**bit**[2] /bɪt/ see **bite**

**bit**[3] /bɪt/ n (of horse) bocado m; (mec) broca f

**bitch** /bɪtʃ/ n perra f; (woman, fam) mujer f maligna, bruja f (fam). • vi (fam) quejarse (**about** de). ~y a malintencionado

**bit|e** /baɪt/ vt/i (pt bit, pp bitten) morder. ~e one's nails morderse las uñas. • n mordisco m; (mouthful) bocado m; (of insect etc) picadura f. ~ing /'baɪtɪŋ/ a mordaz

**bitter** /'bɪtə(r)/ a amargo; (of weather) glacial. **to the** ~ **end** hasta el final. • n cerveza f amarga. ~ly adv amargamente. **it's** ~ly **cold** hace un frío glacial. ~ness n amargor m; (resentment) amargura f

**bizarre** /bɪ'zɑː(r)/ a extraño

**blab** /blæb/ vi (pt blabbed) chismear

**black** /blæk/ a (-er, -est) negro. ~ **and blue** amoratado. • n negro m. • vt ennegrecer; limpiar ‹shoes›. ~

**out** desmayarse; (make dark) apagar las luces de

**blackball** /'blækbɔːl/ vt votar en contra de

**blackberry** /'blækbərɪ/ n zarzamora f

**blackbird** /'blækbɜːd/ n mirlo m

**blackboard** /'blækbɔːd/ n pizarra f

**blackcurrant** /blæk'kʌrənt/ n casis f

**blacken** /'blækən/ vt ennegrecer. • vi ennegrecerse

**blackguard** /'blægɑːd/ n canalla m

**blackleg** /'blækleg/ n esquirol m

**blacklist** /'blæklɪst/ vt poner en la lista negra

**blackmail** /'blækmeɪl/ n chantaje m. • vt chantajear. ~er n chantajista m & f

**black-out** /'blækaʊt/ n apagón m; (med) desmayo m; (of news) censura f

**blacksmith** /'blæksmɪθ/ n herrero m

**bladder** /'blædə(r)/ n vejiga f

**blade** /bleɪd/ n hoja f; (razor-blade) cuchilla f. ~ **of grass** brizna f de hierba

**blame** /bleɪm/ vt echar la culpa a. **be to** ~ tener la culpa. • n culpa f. ~less a inocente

**bland** /blænd/ a (-er, -est) suave

**blandishments** /'blændɪʃmənts/ npl halagos mpl

**blank** /blæŋk/ a en blanco; ‹cartridge› sin bala; (fig) vacío. ~ **verse** n verso m suelto. • n blanco m

**blanket** /'blæŋkɪt/ n manta f; (fig) capa f. • vt (pt blanketed) (fig) cubrir (**in, with** de)

**blare** /bleə(r)/ vi sonar muy fuerte. • n estrépito m

**blarney** /'blɑːnɪ/ n coba f. • vt dar coba

**blasé** /'blɑːzeɪ/ a hastiado

**blasphem|e** /blæs'fiːm/ vt/i blasfemar. ~er n blasfemador m. ~ous /'blæsfəməs/ a blasfemo. ~y /'blæsfəmɪ/ n blasfemia f

**blast** /blɑːst/ n explosión f; (gust) ráfaga f; (sound) toque m. • vt volar. ~ed a maldito. ~furnace n alto horno m. ~off n (of missile) despegue m

**blatant** /'bleɪtnt/ a patente; (shameless) descarado

**blaze** /bleɪz/ n llamarada f; (of light) resplandor m; (fig) arranque m. • vi arder en llamas; (fig) brillar. ~ **a trail** abrir un camino

**blazer** /'bleɪzə(r)/ n chaqueta f

**bleach** /bliːtʃ/ n lejía f; (for hair) decolorante m. ● vt blanquear; decolorar ⟨hair⟩. ● vi blanquearse

**bleak** /bliːk/ a (-er, -est) desolado; (fig) sombrío

**bleary** /ˈblɪərɪ/ a ⟨eyes⟩ nublado; (indistinct) indistinto

**bleat** /bliːt/ n balido m. ● vi balar

**bleed** /bliːd/ vt/i (pt bled) sangrar

**bleep** /bliːp/ n pitido m. ~er n busca m, buscapersonas m

**blemish** /ˈblemɪʃ/ n tacha f

**blend** /blend/ n mezcla f. ● vt mezclar. ● vi combinarse

**bless** /bles/ vt bendecir. ~ you! (on sneezing) ¡Jesús! ~ed a bendito. be ~ed with estar dotado de. ~ing n bendición f; (advantage) ventaja f

**blew** /bluː/ see **blow**[1]

**blight** /blaɪt/ n añublo m, tizón m; (fig) plaga f. ● vt añublar, atizonar; (fig) destrozar

**blighter** /ˈblaɪtə(r)/ n (sl) tío m (fam), sinvergüenza m

**blind** /blaɪnd/ a ciego. ~ alley n callejón m sin salida. ● n persiana f; (fig) pretexto m. ● vt cegar. ~fold /ˈblaɪndfəʊld/ a & adv con los ojos vendados. ● n venda f. ● vt vendar los ojos. ~ly adv a ciegas. ~ness n ceguera f

**blink** /blɪŋk/ vi parpadear; (of light) centellear

**blinkers** /ˈblɪŋkəz/ npl anteojeras fpl; (auto) intermitente m

**bliss** /blɪs/ n felicidad f. ~fully adv felizmente; (completely) completamente

**blister** /ˈblɪstə(r)/ n ampolla f. ● vi formarse ampollas

**blithe** /blaɪð/ a alegre

**blitz** /blɪts/ n bombardeo m aéreo. ● vt bombardear

**blizzard** /ˈblɪzəd/ n ventisca f

**bloated** /ˈbləʊtɪd/ a hinchado (with de)

**bloater** /ˈbləʊtə(r)/ n arenque m ahumado

**blob** /blɒb/ n gota f; (stain) mancha f

**bloc** /blɒk/ n (pol) bloque m

**block** /blɒk/ n bloque m; (of wood) zoquete m; (of buildings) manzana f, cuadra f (LAm); (in pipe) obstrucción f. in ~ letters en letra de imprenta. traffic ~ embotellamiento m. ● vt obstruir. ~ade /blɒˈkeɪd/ n bloqueo m. ● vt bloquear. ~age n obstrucción f

**blockhead** /ˈblɒkhed/ n (fam) zopenco m

**bloke** /bləʊk/ n (fam) tío m (fam), tipo m

**blond** /blɒnd/ a & n rubio (m). ~e a & n rubia (f)

**blood** /blʌd/ n sangre f. ~ count n recuento m sanguíneo. ~-curdling a horripilante

**bloodhound** /ˈblʌdhaʊnd/ n sabueso m

**blood**: ~ pressure n tensión f arterial. high ~ pressure hipertensión f. ~shed /ˈblʌdʃed/ n efusión f de sangre, derramamiento m de sangre, matanza f. ~shot /ˈblʌdʃɒt/ a sanguinolento; ⟨eye⟩ inyectado de sangre. ~stream /ˈblʌdstriːm/ n sangre f

**bloodthirsty** /ˈblʌdθɜːstɪ/ a sanguinario

**bloody** /ˈblʌdɪ/ a (-ier, -iest) sangriento; (stained) ensangrentado; (sl) maldito. ~y-minded a (fam) terco

**bloom** /bluːm/ n flor f. ● vi florecer

**bloomer** /ˈbluːmə(r)/ n (sl) metedura f de pata

**blooming** a floreciente; (fam) maldito

**blossom** /ˈblɒsəm/ n flor f. ● vi florecer. ~ out (into) (fig) llegar a ser

**blot** /blɒt/ n borrón m. ● vt (pt blotted) manchar; (dry) secar. ~ out oscurecer

**blotch** /blɒtʃ/ n mancha f. ~y a lleno de manchas

**blotter** /ˈblɒtə(r)/ n, **blotting-paper** /ˈblɒtɪŋpeɪpə(r)/ n papel m secante

**blouse** /blaʊz/ n blusa f

**blow**[1] /bləʊ/ vt (pt blew, pp blown) soplar; fundir ⟨fuse⟩; tocar ⟨trumpet⟩. ● vi soplar; ⟨fuse⟩ fundirse; (sound) sonar. ● n (puff) soplo m. ~ down vt derribar. ~ out apagar ⟨candle⟩. ~ over pasar. ~ up vt inflar; ⟨explode⟩ volar; (photo) ampliar. ● vi (explode) estallar; (burst) reventar

**blow**[2] /bləʊ/ n (incl fig) golpe m

**blow-dry** /ˈbləʊdraɪ/ vt secar con secador

**blowlamp** /ˈbləʊlæmp/ n soplete m

**blow**: ~out n (of tyre) reventón m. ~up n (photo) ampliación f

**blowzy** /ˈblaʊzɪ/ a desaliñado

**blubber** /ˈblʌbə(r)/ n grasa f de ballena

**bludgeon** /'blʌdʒən/ n cachiporra f.
● vt aporrear

**blue** /blu:/ a (-er, -est) azul; ⟨joke⟩
verde. ● n azul m. **out of the ~**
totalmente inesperado. **~s** npl.
**have the ~s** tener tristeza

**bluebell** /'blu:bel/ n campanilla f

**bluebottle** /'blu:bɒtl/ n moscarda f

**blueprint** /'blu:prɪnt/ n ferro-
prusiato m; ⟨fig, plan⟩ anteproyecto
m

**bluff** /blʌf/ a ⟨person⟩ brusco. ● n
⟨poker⟩ farol m. ● vt engañar. ● vi
⟨poker⟩ tirarse un farol

**blunder** /'blʌndə(r)/ vi cometer un
error. ● n metedura f de pata

**blunt** /blʌnt/ a desafilado; ⟨person⟩
directo, abrupto. ● vt desafilar. **~ly**
adv francamente. **~ness** n embot-
adura f; ⟨fig⟩ franqueza f, brusquedad f

**blur** /blɜ:(r)/ n impresión f indis-
tinta. ● vt (pt **blurred**) hacer
borroso

**blurb** /blɜ:b/ n resumen m
publicitario

**blurt** /blɜ:t/ vt. **~ out** dejar escapar

**blush** /blʌʃ/ vi ruborizarse. ● n
sonrojo m

**bluster** /'blʌstə(r)/ vi ⟨weather⟩ bramar; ⟨person⟩ fanfarronear. **~y** a
tempestuoso

**boar** /bɔ:(r)/ n verraco m

**board** /bɔ:d/ n tabla f, tablero m; ⟨for
notices⟩ tablón m; ⟨food⟩ pensión f;
⟨admin⟩ junta f. **~ and lodging** casa
y comida. **above ~** correcto. **full ~**
pensión f completa. **go by the ~** ser
abandonado. ● vt alojar; ⟨naut⟩
embarcar en. ● vi alojarse ⟨with en
casa de⟩; ⟨at school⟩ ser interno. **~er**
n huésped m; ⟨schol⟩ interno m.
**~ing-house** n casa f de huéspedes,
pensión f. **~ing-school** n internado
m

**boast** /bəʊst/ vt enorgullecerse de.
● vi jactarse. ● n jactancia f. **~er** n
jactancioso m. **~ful** a jactancioso

**boat** /bəʊt/ n barco m; ⟨large⟩ navío
m; ⟨small⟩ barca f

**boater** /'bəʊtə(r)/ n ⟨hat⟩ canotié m

**boatswain** /'bəʊsn/ n con-
tramaestre m

**bob**¹ /bɒb/ vi (pt **bobbed**) menearse,
subir y bajar. **~ up** presentarse
súbitamente

**bob**² /bɒb/ n invar ⟨sl⟩ chelín m

**bobbin** /'bɒbɪn/ n carrete m; ⟨in sewing machine⟩ canilla f

**bobby** /'bɒbɪ/ n ⟨fam⟩ policía m, poli
m ⟨fam⟩

**bobsleigh** /'bɒbsleɪ/ n bob(sleigh) m

**bode** /bəʊd/ vi presagiar. **~ well/ill**
ser de buen/mal agüero

**bodice** /'bɒdɪs/ n corpiño m

**bodily** /'bɒdɪlɪ/ a físico, corporal.
● adv físicamente; ⟨in person⟩ en
persona

**body** /'bɒdɪ/ n cuerpo m. **~guard**
/'bɒdɪgɑ:d/ n guardaespaldas m
invar. **~work** n carrocería f

**boffin** /'bɒfɪn/ n ⟨sl⟩ científico m

**bog** /bɒg/ n ciénaga f. ● vt (pt
**bogged**). **get ~ged down**
empantanarse

**bogey** /'bəʊgɪ/ n duende m; ⟨nuis-
ance⟩ pesadilla f

**boggle** /'bɒgl/ vi sobresaltarse. **the
mind ~s** ¡no es posible!

**bogus** /'bəʊgəs/ a falso

**bogy** /'bəʊgɪ/ n duende m; ⟨nuis-
ance⟩ pesadilla f

**boil**¹ /bɔɪl/ vt/i hervir. **be ~ing hot**
estar ardiendo; ⟨weather⟩ hacer
mucho calor. **~ away** evaporarse.
**~ down to** reducirse a. **~ over**
rebosar

**boil**² /bɔɪl/ n furúnculo m

**boiled** /'bɔɪld/ a hervido; ⟨egg⟩ pasado por agua

**boiler** /'bɔɪlə(r)/ n caldera f. **~ suit** n
mono m

**boisterous** /'bɔɪstərəs/ a ruidoso,
bullicioso

**bold** /bəʊld/ a (-er, -est) audaz.
**~ness** n audacia f

**Bolivia** /bə'lɪvɪə/ n Bolivia f. **~n** a &
n boliviano (m)

**bollard** /'bɒləd/ n ⟨naut⟩ noray m;
⟨Brit, auto⟩ poste m

**bolster** /'bəʊlstə(r)/ n cabezal m.
● vt. **~ up** sostener

**bolt** /bəʊlt/ n cerrojo m; ⟨for nut⟩
perno m; ⟨lightning⟩ rayo m; ⟨leap⟩
fuga f. ● vt echar el cerrojo a ⟨door⟩;
engullir ⟨food⟩. ● vi fugarse. ● adv.
**~ upright** rígido

**bomb** /bɒm/ n bomba f. ● vt bombardear. **~ard** /bɒm'bɑ:d/ vt
bombardear

**bombastic** /bɒm'bæstɪk/ a ampuloso

**bomb**: **~er** /'bɒmə(r)/ n bom-
bardero m. **~ing** n bombardeo m.
**~shell** n bomba f

**bonanza** /bə'nænzə/ n bonanza f

**bond** /bɒnd/ n ⟨agreement⟩ obli-
gación f; ⟨link⟩ lazo m; ⟨com⟩ bono m

**bondage** /'bɒndɪdʒ/ n esclavitud f
**bone** /bəʊn/ n hueso m; (of fish) espina f. ● vt deshuesar. **~-dry** a completamente seco. **~ idle** a holgazán
**bonfire** /'bɒnfaɪə(r)/ n hoguera f
**bonnet** /'bɒnɪt/ n gorra f; (auto) capó m, tapa f del motor (Mex)
**bonny** /'bɒnɪ/ a (-ier, -iest) bonito
**bonus** /'bəʊnəs/ n prima f; (fig) plus m
**bony** /'bəʊnɪ/ a (-ier, -iest) huesudo; (fish) lleno de espinas
**boo** /buː/ int ¡bu! ● vt/i abuchear
**boob** /buːb/ n (mistake, sl) metedura f de pata. ● vi (sl) meter la pata
**booby** /'buːbɪ/ n bobo m. **~ trap** trampa f; (mil) trampa f explosiva
**book** /bʊk/ n libro m; (of cheques etc) talonario m; (notebook) libreta f, (exercise book) cuaderno m; (pl, com) cuentas fpl. ● vt (enter) registrar; (reserve) reservar. ● vi reservar. **~able** a que se puede reservar. **~case** /'bʊkkeɪs/ n estantería f, librería f. **~ing-office** (in theatre) taquilla f; (rail) despacho m de billetes. **~let** /'bʊklɪt/ n folleto m
**bookkeeping** /'bʊkiːpɪŋ/ n contabilidad f
**bookmaker** /'bʊkmeɪkə(r)/ . n corredor m de apuestas
**book: ~mark** /'bʊkmɑː(r)k/ n señal f. **~seller** /'bʊksələ(r)/ n librero m. **~shop** /'bʊkʃɒp/ n librería f. **~stall** /'bʊkstɔːl/ n quiosco m de libros. **~worm** /'bʊkwɜːm/ n (fig) ratón m de biblioteca
**boom** /buːm/ vi retumbar; (fig) prosperar. ● n estampido m; (com) auge m
**boon** /buːn/ n beneficio m
**boor** /bʊə(r)/ n patán m. **~ish** a grosero
**boost** /buːst/ vt estimular; reforzar (morale); aumentar (price); (publicize) hacer publicidad por. ● n empuje m. **~er** n (med) revacunación f
**boot** /buːt/ n bota f; (auto) maletero m, baúl m (LAm). **get the ~** (sl) ser despedido
**booth** /buːð/ n cabina f; (at fair) puesto m
**booty** /'buːtɪ/ n botín m
**booze** /buːz/ vi (fam) beber mucho. ● n (fam) alcohol m; (spree) borrachera f

**border** /'bɔːdə(r)/ n borde m; (frontier) frontera f; (in garden) arriate m. ● vi. **~ on** lindar con
**borderline** /'bɔːdəlaɪn/ n línea f divisoria. **~ case** n caso m dudoso
**bore**¹ /bɔː(r)/ vt (tec) taladrar. ● vi taladrar
**bore**² /bɔː(r)/ vt (annoy) aburrir. ● n (person) pelmazo m; (thing) lata f
**bore**³ /bɔː(r)/ see **bear**¹
**boredom** /'bɔːdəm/ n aburrimiento m
**boring** /'bɔːrɪŋ/ a aburrido, pesado
**born** /bɔːn/ a nato. **be ~** nacer
**borne** /bɔːn/ see **bear**¹
**borough** /'bʌrə/ n municipio m
**borrow** /'bɒrəʊ/ vt pedir prestado
**Borstal** /'bɔːstl/ n reformatorio m
**bosh** /bɒʃ/ int & n (sl) tonterías (fpl)
**bosom** /'bʊzəm/ n seno m. **~ friend** n amigo m íntimo
**boss** /bɒs/ n (fam) jefe m. ● vt. **~ (about)** (fam) dar órdenes a. **~y** /'bɒsɪ/ a mandón
**botan|ical** /bə'tænɪkl/ a botánico. **~ist** /'bɒtənɪst/ n botánico m. **~y** /'bɒtənɪ/ n botánica f
**botch** /bɒtʃ/ vt chapucear. ● n chapuza f
**both** /bəʊθ/ a & pron ambos (mpl), los dos (mpl). ● adv al mismo tiempo, a la vez
**bother** /'bɒðə(r)/ vt molestar; (worry) preocupar. **~ it!** int ¡caramba! ● vi molestarse. **~ about** preocuparse de. **~ doing** tenerse la molestia de hacer. ● n molestia f
**bottle** /'bɒtl/ n botella f; (for baby) biberón m. ● vt embotellar. **~ up** (fig) reprimir. **~neck** /'bɒtlnek/ n (traffic jam) embotellamiento m. **~-opener** n destapador m, abrebotellas m invar; (corkscrew) sacacorchos m invar
**bottom** /'bɒtəm/ n fondo m; (of hill) pie m; (buttocks) trasero m. ● a último, inferior. **~less** a sin fondo
**bough** /baʊ/ n rama f
**bought** /bɔːt/ see **buy**
**boulder** /'bəʊldə(r)/ n canto m
**boulevard** /'buːləvɑːd/ n bulevar m
**bounc|e** /baʊns/ vt hacer rebotar. ● vi rebotar; (person) saltar; (cheque, sl) ser rechazado. ● n rebote m. **~ing** /'baʊnsɪŋ/ a robusto
**bound**¹ /baʊnd/ vi saltar. ● n salto m
**bound**² /baʊnd/ n. **out of ~s** zona f prohibida

**bound**³ /baʊnd/ a. be ~ for dirigirse a

**bound**⁴ /baʊnd/ see bind. ~ to obligado a; (certain) seguro de

**boundary** /'baʊndərɪ/ n límite m

**boundless** /'baʊndləs/ a ilimitado

**bountiful** /'baʊntɪfl/ a abundante

**bouquet** /bʊ'keɪ/ n ramo m; (perfume) aroma m; (of wine) buqué m, nariz f

**bout** /baʊt/ n período m; (med) ataque m; (sport) encuentro m

**bow**¹ /bəʊ/ n (weapon, mus) arco m; (knot) lazo m

**bow**² /baʊ/ n reverencia f. ● vi inclinarse. ● vt inclinar

**bow**³ /baʊ/ n (naut) proa f

**bowels** /'baʊəlz/ npl intestinos mpl; (fig) entrañas fpl

**bowl**¹ /bəʊl/ n cuenco m; (for washing) palangana f; (of pipe) cazoleta f

**bowl**² /bəʊl/ n (ball) bola f. ● vt (cricket) arrojar. ● vi (cricket) arrojar la pelota. ~ over derribar

**bow-legged** /bəʊ'legɪd/ a estevado

**bowler**¹ /'bəʊlə(r)/ n (cricket) lanzador m

**bowler**² /'bəʊlə(r)/ n. ~ (hat) hongo m, bombín m

**bowling** /'bəʊlɪŋ/ n bolos mpl

**bow-tie** /bəʊ'taɪ/ n corbata f de lazo, pajarita f

**box**¹ /bɒks/ n caja f; (for jewels etc) estuche m; (in theatre) palco m

**box**² /bɒks/ vt boxear contra. ~ s.o.'s ears dar una manotada a uno. ● vi boxear. ~er n boxeador m. ~ing n boxeo m

**box**: B~ing Day n el 26 de diciembre. ~-office n taquilla f. ~-room n trastero m

**boy** /bɔɪ/ n chico m, muchacho m; (young) niño m

**boycott** /'bɔɪkɒt/ vt boicotear. ● n boicoteo m

**boy**: ~friend n novio m. ~hood n niñez f. ~ish a de muchacho; (childish) infantil

**bra** /brɑː/ n sostén m, sujetador m

**brace** /breɪs/ n abrazadera f; (dental) aparato m. ● vt asegurar. ~ o.s. prepararse. ~s npl tirantes mpl

**bracelet** /'breɪslɪt/ n pulsera f

**bracing** /'breɪsɪŋ/ a vigorizante

**bracken** /'brækən/ n helecho m

**bracket** /'brækɪt/ n soporte m; (group) categoría f; (typ) paréntesis m invar. square ~s corchetes mpl.

● vt poner entre paréntesis; (join together) agrupar

**brag** /bræg/ vi (pt bragged) jactarse (about de)

**braid** /breɪd/ n galón m; (of hair) trenza f

**brain** /breɪn/ n cerebro m. ● vt romper la cabeza

**brain-child** /'breɪntʃaɪld/ n invento m

**brain**: ~ drain (fam) fuga f de cerebros. ~less a estúpido. ~s npl (fig) inteligencia f

**brainstorm** /'breɪnstɔːm/ n ataque m de locura; (Amer, brainwave) idea f genial

**brainwash** /'breɪnwɒʃ/ vt lavar el cerebro

**brainwave** /'breɪnweɪv/ n idea f genial

**brainy** /'breɪnɪ/ a (-ier, -iest) inteligente

**braise** /breɪz/ vt cocer a fuego lento

**brake** /breɪk/ n freno m. disc ~ freno de disco. hand ~ freno de mano. ● vt/i frenar. ~ fluid n líquido m de freno. ~ lining n forro m del freno. ~ shoe n zapata f del freno

**bramble** /bræmbl/ n zarza f

**bran** /bræn/ n salvado m

**branch** /brɑːntʃ/ n rama f; (of road) bifurcación f; (com) sucursal m; (fig) ramo m. ● vi. ~ off bifurcarse. ~ out ramificarse

**brand** /brænd/ n marca f; (iron) hierro m. ● vt marcar; (reputation) tildar de

**brandish** /'brændɪʃ/ vt blandir

**brand-new** /brænd'njuː/ a flamante

**brandy** /'brændɪ/ n coñac m

**brash** /bræʃ/ a descarado

**brass** /brɑːs/ n latón m. get down to ~ tacks (fig) ir al grano. top ~ (sl) peces mpl gordos. ~y a (-ier, -iest) descarado

**brassière** /'bræsjeə(r)/ n sostén m, sujetador m

**brat** /bræt/ n (pej) mocoso m

**bravado** /brə'vɑːdəʊ/ n bravata f

**brave** /breɪv/ a (-er, -est) valiente. ● n (Red Indian) guerrero m indio. ● vt afrontar. ~ry /-ərɪ/ n valentía f, valor m

**brawl** /brɔːl/ n alboroto m. ● vi pelearse

**brawn** /brɔːn/ n músculo m; (strength) fuerza f muscular. ~y a musculoso

**bray** /breɪ/ n rebuzno m. ● vi rebuznar

**brazen** /'breɪzn/ a descarado

**brazier** /'breɪzɪə(r)/ n brasero m

**Brazil** /brə'zɪl/ n el Brasil m. ~ian a & n brasileño (m)

**breach** /bri:tʃ/ n violación f; (of contract) incumplimiento m; (gap) brecha f. ● vt abrir una brecha en

**bread** /bred/ n pan m. loaf of ~ pan. ~crumbs /'bredkrʌmz/ npl migajas fpl; (culin) pan rallado. ~line n. on the ~line en la miseria

**breadth** /bredθ/ n anchura f

**bread-winner** /'bredwɪnə(r)/ n sostén m de la familia, cabeza f de familia

**break** /breɪk/ vt (pt broke, pp broken) romper; quebrantar ⟨law⟩; batir ⟨record⟩; comunicar ⟨news⟩; interrumpir ⟨journey⟩. ● vi romperse; ⟨news⟩ divulgarse. ● n ruptura f; ⟨interval⟩ intervalo m; ⟨chance, fam⟩ oportunidad f; ⟨in weather⟩ cambio m. ~ away escapar. ~ down vt derribar; analizar ⟨figures⟩. ● vi estropearse; ⟨auto⟩ averiarse; ⟨med⟩ sufrir un colapso; ⟨cry⟩ deshacerse en lágrimas. ~ into forzar ⟨house etc⟩; ⟨start doing⟩ ponerse a. ~ off interrumpirse. ~ out ⟨war, disease⟩ estallar; ⟨run away⟩ escaparse. ~ up romperse; ⟨schools⟩ terminar. ~able a frágil. ~age n rotura f

**breakdown** /'breɪkdaʊn/ n (tec) falla f; (med) colapso m, crisis f nerviosa; (of figures) análisis f

**breaker** /'breɪkə(r)/ n ⟨wave⟩ cachón m

**breakfast** /'brekfəst/ n desayuno m

**breakthrough** /'breɪkθru:/ n adelanto m

**breakwater** /'breɪkwɔ:tə(r)/ n rompeolas m invar

**breast** /brest/ n pecho m; (of chicken etc) pechuga f. ~stroke n braza f de pecho

**breath** /breθ/ n aliento m, respiración f. out of ~ sin aliento. under one's ~ a media voz. ~alyser /'breθəlaɪzə(r)/ n alcoholímetro m

**breathe** /bri:ð/ vt/i respirar. ~er /'bri:ðə(r)/ n descanso m, pausa f. ~ing n respiración f

**breathtaking** /'breθteɪkɪŋ/ a impresionante

**bred** /bred/ see **breed**

**breeches** /'brɪtʃɪz/ npl calzones mpl

**breed** /bri:d/ vt/i (pt bred) reproducirse; (fig) engendrar. ● n raza f. ~er n criador m. ~ing n cría f; (manners) educación f

**breeze** /bri:z/ n brisa f. ~y a de mucho viento; ⟨person⟩ despreocupado. it is ~y hace viento

**Breton** /'bretən/ a & n bretón (m)

**brew** /bru:/ vt hacer. ● vi fermentar; ⟨tea⟩ reposar; (fig) prepararse. ● n infusión f. ~er n cervecero m. ~ery n fábrica f de cerveza, cervecería f

**bribe** /braɪb/ n soborno m. ● vt sobornar. ~ry /-ərɪ/ n soborno m

**brick** /brɪk/ n ladrillo m. ● vt. ~ up tapar con ladrillos. ~layer /'brɪkleɪə(r)/ n albañil m

**bridal** /'braɪdl/ a nupcial

**bride** /braɪd/ n novia f. ~groom /'braɪdgrʊm/ n novio m. ~smaid /'braɪdzmeɪd/ n dama f de honor

**bridge¹** /brɪdʒ/ n puente m; (of nose) caballete m. ● vt tender un puente sobre. ~ a gap llenar un vacío

**bridge²** /brɪdʒ/ n (cards) bridge m

**bridle** /'braɪdl/ n brida f. ● vt embridar. ~path n camino m de herradura

**brief** /bri:f/ a (-er, -est) breve. ● n (jurid) escrito m. ● vt dar instrucciones a. ~case /'bri:fkeɪs/ n maletín m. ~ly adv brevemente. ~s npl (man's) calzoncillos mpl; (woman's) bragas fpl

**brigade** /brɪ'geɪd/ n brigada f. ~ier /-ə'dɪə(r)/ n general m de brigada

**bright** /braɪt/ a (-er, -est) brillante, claro; (clever) listo; (cheerful) alegre. ~en /'braɪtn/ vt aclarar; hacer más alegre ⟨house etc⟩. ● vi ⟨weather⟩ aclararse; ⟨face⟩ animarse. ~ly adv brillantemente. ~ness n claridad f

**brilliance** /'brɪljəns/ n brillantez f, brillo m. ~t a brillante

**brim** /brɪm/ n borde m; (of hat) ala f. ● vi (pt brimmed). ~ over desbordarse

**brine** /braɪn/ n salmuera f

**bring** /brɪŋ/ vt (pt brought) traer ⟨thing⟩; conducir ⟨person, vehicle⟩. ~ about causar. ~ back devolver. ~ down derribar; rebajar ⟨price⟩. ~ off lograr. ~ on causar. ~ out sacar; lanzar ⟨product⟩; publicar ⟨book⟩. ~ round/to hacer volver en sí ⟨unconscious person⟩. ~ up (med) vomitar; educar ⟨children⟩; plantear ⟨question⟩

**brink** /brɪŋk/ n borde m

**brisk** /brɪsk/ a (-er, -est) enérgico, vivo. ~**ness** n energía f

**bristl|e** /ˈbrɪsl/ n cerda f. ● vi erizarse. ~**ing with** erizado de

**Brit|ain** /ˈbrɪtən/ n Gran Bretaña f. ~**ish** /ˈbrɪtɪʃ/ a británico. **the** ~**ish** los británicos. ~**on** /ˈbrɪtən/ n británico m

**Brittany** /ˈbrɪtənɪ/ n Bretaña f

**brittle** /ˈbrɪtl/ a frágil, quebradizo

**broach** /brəʊtʃ/ vt abordar ⟨subject⟩; espitar ⟨cask⟩

**broad** /brɔːd/ a (-er, -est) ancho. **in** ~ **daylight** en pleno día. ~ **bean** n haba f

**broadcast** /ˈbrɔːdkɑːst/ n emisión f. ● vt (pt broadcast) emitir. ● vi hablar por la radio. ~**ing** a de radio-difusión f n radio-difusión f

**broad:** ~**en** /ˈbrɔːdn/ vt ensanchar. ● vi ensancharse. ~**ly** adv en general. ~**-minded** a de . miras amplias, tolerante, liberal

**brocade** /brəˈkeɪd/ n brocado m

**broccoli** /ˈbrɒkəlɪ/ n invar brécol m

**brochure** /ˈbrəʊʃə(r)/ n folleto m

**brogue** /brəʊg/ n abarca f; ⟨accent⟩ acento m regional

**broke** /brəʊk/ see **break**. ● a (sl) sin blanca

**broken** /ˈbrəʊkən/ see **break**. ● a. ~ **English** inglés m chapurreado. ~**hearted** a con el corazón destrozado

**broker** /ˈbrəʊkə(r)/ n corredor m

**brolly** /ˈbrɒlɪ/ n (fam) paraguas m invar

**bronchitis** /brɒŋˈkaɪtɪs/ n bronquitis f

**bronze** /brɒnz/ n bronce m. ● vt broncear. ● vi broncearse

**brooch** /brəʊtʃ/ n broche m

**brood** /bruːd/ n cría f; (joc) prole m. ● vi empollar; (fig) meditar. ~**y** a contemplativo

**brook**[1] /brʊk/ n arroyo m

**brook**[2] /brʊk/ vt soportar

**broom** /bruːm/ n hiniesta f; (brush) escoba f. ~**stick** /ˈbruːmstɪk/ n palo m de escoba

**broth** /brɒθ/ n caldo m

**brothel** /ˈbrɒθl/ n burdel m

**brother** /ˈbrʌðə(r)/ n hermano m. ~**hood** n fraternidad f, (relig) hermandad f. ~**in-law** n cuñado m. ~**ly** a fraternal

**brought** /brɔːt/ see **bring**

**brow** /braʊ/ n frente f; (of hill) cima f

**browbeat** /ˈbraʊbiːt/ vt (pt -beat, pp -beaten) intimidar

**brown** /braʊn/ a (-er, -est) marrón; ⟨skin⟩ moreno; ⟨hair⟩ castaño. ● n marrón m. ● vt poner moreno; (culin) dorar. ● vi ponerse moreno; (culin) dorarse. **be** ~**ed off** (sl) estar hasta la coronilla

**Brownie** /ˈbraʊnɪ/ n niña f exploradora

**browse** /braʊz/ vi (in a shop) curiosear; ⟨animal⟩ pacer

**bruise** /bruːz/ n magulladura f. ● vt magullar; machucar ⟨fruit⟩. ● vi magullarse; ⟨fruit⟩ machacarse

**brunch** /brʌntʃ/ n (fam) desayuno m tardío

**brunette** /bruːˈnet/ n morena f

**brunt** /brʌnt/ n. **the** ~ **of** lo más fuerte de

**brush** /brʌʃ/ n cepillo m; (large) escoba; (for decorating) brocha f; (artist's) pincel; (skirmish) escaramuza f. ● vt cepillar. ~ **against** rozar. ~ **aside** rechazar. ~ **off** (rebuff) desairar. ~ **up (on)** refrescar

**brusque** /bruːsk/ a brusco. ~**ly** adv bruscamente

**Brussels** /ˈbrʌslz/ n Bruselas f. ~ **sprout** col m de Bruselas

**brutal** /ˈbruːtl/ a brutal. ~**ity** /-ˈtælətɪ/ n brutalidad f

**brute** /bruːt/ n bestia f. ~ **force** fuerza f bruta

**BSc** abbr see **bachelor**

**bubble** /ˈbʌbl/ n burbuja f. ● vi burbujear. ~ **over** desbordarse

**bubbly** /ˈbʌblɪ/ a burbujeante. ● n (fam) champaña m, champán m (fam)

**buck**[1] /bʌk/ a macho. ● n (deer) ciervo m. ● vi (of horse) corcovear. ~ **up** (hurry, sl) darse prisa; (cheer up, sl) animarse

**buck**[2] /bʌk/ (Amer, sl) dólar m

**buck**[3] /bʌk/ n. **pass the** ~ **to s.o.** echarle a uno el muerto

**bucket** /ˈbʌkɪt/ n cubo m

**buckle** /ˈbʌkl/ n hebilla f. ● vt abrochar. ● vi torcerse. ~ **down to** dedicarse con empeño a

**bud** /bʌd/ n brote m. ● vi (pt budded) brotar.

**Buddhis|m** /ˈbʊdɪzəm/ n budismo m. ~**t** /ˈbʊdɪst/ a & n budista (m & f)

**budding** /ˈbʌdɪŋ/ a (fig) en ciernes

**buddy** /'bʌdɪ/ n (fam) compañero m, amigote m (fam)

**budge** /bʌdʒ/ vt mover. ● vi moverse

**budgerigar** /'bʌdʒərɪgɑ:(r)/ n periquito m

**budget** /'bʌdʒɪt/ n presupuesto m. ● vi (pt budgeted) presupuestar

**buff** /bʌf/ n (colour) color m de ante; (fam) aficionado m. ● vt pulir

**buffalo** /'bʌfələʊ/ n (pl -oes or -o) búfalo m

**buffer** /'bʌfə(r)/ n parachoques m invar. ~ state n estado m tapón

**buffet** /'bʊfeɪ/ n (meal, counter) bufé m. /'bʌfɪt/ n golpe m; (slap) bofetada f. ● vt (pt buffeted) golpear

**buffoon** /bə'fu:n/ n payaso m, bufón m

**bug** /bʌg/ n bicho m; (germ, sl) microbio m; (device, sl) micrófono m oculto. ● vt (pt bugged) ocultar un micrófono en; intervenir ⟨telephone⟩; (Amer, sl) molestar

**bugbear** /'bʌgbeə(r)/ n pesadilla f

**buggy** /'bʌgɪ/ n. **baby** ~ (esp Amer) cochecito m de niño

**bugle** /'bju:gl/ n corneta f

**build** /bɪld/ vt/i (pt built) construir. ~ **up** vt urbanizar; (increase) aumentar. ● n (of person) figura f, tipo m. ~**er** n constructor m. ~**up** n aumento m; (of gas etc) acumulación f; (fig) propaganda f

**built** /bɪlt/ see **build**. ~**in** a empotrado. ~**up area** n zona f urbanizada

**bulb** /bʌlb/ n bulbo m; (elec) bombilla f. ~**ous** a bulboso

**Bulgaria** /bʌl'geərɪə/ n Bulgaria f. ~**n** a & n búlgaro (m)

**bulge** /bʌldʒ/ n protuberancia f. ● vi pandearse; (jut out) sobresalir. ~**ing** a abultado; ⟨eyes⟩ saltón

**bulk** /bʌlk/ n bulto m, volumen m. **in** ~ a granel; (loose) suelto. **the** ~ **of** la mayor parte de. ~**y** a voluminoso

**bull** /bʊl/ n toro m

**bulldog** /'bʊldɒg/ n buldog m

**bulldozer** /'bʊldəʊzə(r)/ n oruga f aplanadora, bulldozer m

**bullet** /'bʊlɪt/ n bala f

**bulletin** /'bʊlɪtɪn/ n anuncio m; (journal) boletín m

**bullet-proof** /'bʊlɪtpru:f/ a a prueba de balas

**bullfight** /'bʊlfaɪt/ n corrida f (de toros). ~**er** n torero m

**bullion** /'bʊljən/ n (gold) oro m en barras; (silver) plata f en barras

**bull:** ~**ring** /'bʊlrɪŋ/ n plaza f de toros. ~'**s-eye** n centro m del blanco, diana f

**bully** /'bʊlɪ/ n matón m. ● vt intimidar. ~**ing** n intimidación f

**bum**[1] /bʌm/ n (bottom, sl) trasero m

**bum**[2] /bʌm/ n (Amer, sl) holgazán m

**bumble-bee** /'bʌmblbi:/ n abejorro m

**bump** /bʌmp/ vt chocar contra. ● vi dar sacudidas. ● n choque m; (swelling) chichón m. ~ **into** chocar contra; (meet) encontrar

**bumper** /'bʌmpə(r)/ n parachoques m invar. ● a abundante. ~ **edition** n edición f especial

**bumpkin** /'bʌmpkɪn/ n patán m, paleto m (fam)

**bumptious** /'bʌmpʃəs/ a presuntuoso

**bun** /bʌn/ n bollo m; (hair) moño m

**bunch** /bʌntʃ/ n manojo m; (of people) grupo m; (of bananas, grapes) racimo m, (of flowers) ramo m

**bundle** /'bʌndl/ n bulto m; (of papers) legajo m; (of nerves) manojo m. ● vt. ~ **up** atar

**bung** /bʌŋ/ n tapón m. ● vt tapar; (sl) tirar

**bungalow** /'bʌŋgələʊ/ n casa f de un solo piso, chalé m, bungalow m

**bungle** /'bʌŋgl/ vt chapucear

**bunion** /'bʌnjən/ n juanete m

**bunk** /bʌŋk/ n litera f

**bunker** /'bʌŋkə(r)/ n carbonera f; (golf) obstáculo m; (mil) refugio m, búnker m

**bunkum** /'bʌŋkəm/ n tonterías fpl

**bunny** /'bʌnɪ/ n conejito m

**buoy** /bɔɪ/ n boya f. ● vt. ~ **up** hacer flotar; (fig) animar

**buoyan|cy** /'bɔɪənsɪ/ n flotabilidad f; (fig) optimismo m. ~**t** /'bɔɪənt/ a boyante; (fig) alegre

**burden** /'bɜːdn/ n carga f. ● vt cargar (**with** de). ~**some** a pesado

**bureau** /'bjʊərəʊ/ n (pl -**eaux** /-əʊz/) escritorio m; (office) oficina f

**bureaucra|cy** /bjʊə'rɒkrəsɪ/ n burocracia f. ~**t** /'bjʊərəkræt/ n burócrata m & f. ~**tic** /-'krætɪk/ a burocrático

**burgeon** /'bɜːdʒən/ vi brotar; (fig) crecer

**burgl|ar** /'bɜːglə(r)/ n ladrón m. ~**ary** n robo m con allanamiento de

morada. **~e** /'bɜːgl/ vt robar con
allanamiento

**Burgundy** /'bɜːgəndɪ/ n Borgoña f;
(wine) vino m de Borgoña

**burial** /'berɪəl/ n entierro m

**burlesque** /bɜːˈlesk/ n burlesco m

**burly** /'bɜːlɪ/ a (-ier, -iest) corpulento

**Burm|a** /'bɜːmə/ Birmania f. **~ese**
/-ˈmiːz/ a & n birmano (m)

**burn** /bɜːn/ vt (pt **burned** or **burnt**)
quemar. ● vi quemarse. **~ down** vt
destruir con fuego. ● n quemadura
f. **~er** n quemador m. **~ing** a ardiente; (food) que quema; (question)
candente

**burnish** /'bɜːnɪʃ/ vt lustrar, pulir

**burnt** /bɜːnt/ see **burn**

**burp** /bɜːp/ n (fam) eructo m. ● vi
(fam) eructar

**burr** /bɜː(r)/ n (bot) erizo m

**burrow** /'bʌrəʊ/ n madriguera f. ● vt
excavar

**bursar** /'bɜːsə(r)/ n tesorero m. **~y**
/'bɜːsərɪ/ n beca f

**burst** /bɜːst/ vt (pt **burst**) reventar.
● vi reventarse; (tyre) pincharse.
● n reventón m; (mil) ráfaga f; (fig)
explosión f. **~ of laughter** carcajada f

**bury** /'berɪ/ vt enterrar; (hide)
ocultar

**bus** /bʌs/ n (pl **buses**) autobús m,
camión m (Mex). ● vi (pt **bussed**) ir
en autobús

**bush** /bʊʃ/ n arbusto m; (land)
monte m. **~y** a espeso

**busily** /'bɪzɪlɪ/ adv afanosamente

**business** /'bɪznɪs/ n negocio m;
(com) negocios mpl; (profession)
ocupación f; (fig) asunto m. **mind
one's own** **~** ocuparse de sus pro-
pios asuntos. **~like** a práctico,
serio. **~man** n hombre m de
negocios

**busker** /'bʌskə(r)/ n músico m
ambulante

**bus-stop** /'bʌsstɒp/ n parada f de
autobús

**bust**[1] /bʌst/ n busto m; (chest) pecho
m

**bust**[2] /bʌst/ vt (pt **busted** or **bust**) (sl)
romper. ● vi romperse. ● a roto. **go
~** (sl) quebrar

**bustle** /'bʌsl/ vi apresurarse. ● n
bullicio m

**bust-up** /'bʌstʌp/ n (sl) riña f

**busy** /'bɪzɪ/ a (-ier, -iest) ocupado;
(street) concurrido. ● vt. **~ o.s. with**
ocuparse de

**busybody** /'bɪzɪbɒdɪ/ n entrometido
m

**but** /bʌt/ conj pero; (after negative)
sino. ● prep menos. **~ for** si no
fuera por. **last ~ one** penúltimo.
● adv solamente

**butane** /'bjuːteɪn/ n butano m

**butcher** /'bʊtʃə(r)/ n carnicero m.
● vt matar; (fig) hacer una carnicería con. **~y** n carnicería f, matanza f

**butler** /'bʌtlə(r)/ n mayordomo m

**butt** /bʌt/ n (of gun) culata f; (of
cigarette) colilla f; (target) blanco m.
● vi topar. **~ in** interrumpir

**butter** /'bʌtə(r)/ n mantequilla f. ● vt
untar con mantequilla. **~ up** vt
(fam) lisonjear, dar jabón a. **~bean**
n judía f

**buttercup** /'bʌtəkʌp/ n ranúnculo m

**butter-fingers** /'bʌtəfɪŋgəz/ n man-
azas m invar, torpe m

**butterfly** /'bʌtəflaɪ/ n mariposa f

**buttock** /'bʌtək/ n nalga f

**button** /'bʌtn/ n botón m. ● vt
abotonar. ● vi abotonarse. **~hole**
/'bʌtnhəʊl/ n ojal m. ● vt (fig)
detener

**buttress** /'bʌtrɪs/ n contrafuerte m.
● vt apoyar

**buxom** /'bʌksəm/ a (woman) rollizo

**buy** /baɪ/ vt (pt **bought**) comprar.
● n compra f. **~er** n comprador m

**buzz** /bʌz/ n zumbido m; (phone call,
fam) llamada f. ● vi zumbar. **~ off**
(sl) largarse. **~er** n timbre m

**by** /baɪ/ prep por; (near) cerca de;
(before) antes de; (according to)
según. **~ and large** en conjunto, en
general. **~ car** en coche. **~ oneself**
por sí solo

**bye-bye** /'baɪbaɪ/ int (fam) ¡adiós!

**by-election** /'baɪɪlekʃn/ n elección f
parcial

**bygone** /'baɪgɒn/ a pasado

**by-law** /'baɪlɔː/ n reglamento m
(local)

**bypass** /'baɪpɑːs/ n carretera f de circunvalación. ● vt evitar

**by-product** /'baɪprɒdʌkt/ n subproducto m

**bystander** /'baɪstændə(r)/ n espectador m

**byword** /'baɪwɜːd/ n sinónimo m. **be
a ~ for** ser conocido por

# C

**cab** /kæb/ n taxi m; (of lorry, train) cabina f

**cabaret** /'kæbəreɪ/ n espectáculo m

**cabbage** /'kæbɪdʒ/ n col m, repollo m

**cabin** /'kæbɪn/ n cabaña f; (in ship) camarote m; (in plane) cabina f

**cabinet** /'kæbɪnɪt/ n (cupboard) armario m; (for display) vitrina f. **C~** (pol) gabinete m. **~-maker** n ebanista m & f

**cable** /'keɪbl/ n cable m. ● vt cablegrafiar. **~ railway** n funicular m

**cache** /kæʃ/ n (place) escondrijo m; (things) reservas fpl escondidas. ● vt ocultar

**cackle** /'kækl/ n (of hen) cacareo m; (laugh) risotada f. ● vi cacarear; (laugh) reírse a carcajadas

**cacophon|ous** /kə'kɒfənəs/ a cacofónico. **~y** n cacofonía f

**cactus** /'kæktəs/ n (pl **-ti** /-taɪ/) cacto m

**cad** /kæd/ n sinvergüenza m. **~dish** a desvergonzado

**caddie** /'kædɪ/ n (golf) portador m de palos

**caddy** /'kædɪ/ n cajita f

**cadence** /'keɪdəns/ n cadencia f

**cadet** /kə'det/ n cadete m

**cadge** /kædʒ/ vt/i gorronear. **~r** /-ə(r)/ n gorrón m

**Caesarean** /sɪ'zeərɪən/ a cesáreo. **~ section** n cesárea f

**café** /'kæfeɪ/ n cafetería f

**cafeteria** /kæfɪ'tɪərɪə/ n autoservicio m

**caffeine** /'kæfiːn/ n cafeína f

**cage** /keɪdʒ/ n jaula f. ● vt enjaular

**cagey** /'keɪdʒɪ/ a (fam) evasivo

**Cairo** /'kaɪərəʊ/ n el Cairo m

**cajole** /kə'dʒəʊl/ vt engatusar. **~ry** n engatusamiento m

**cake** /keɪk/ n pastel m, tarta f; (sponge) bizcocho m. **~ of soap** pastilla f de jabón. **~d** a incrustado

**calamit|ous** /kə'læmɪtəs/ a desastroso. **~y** /kə'læmətɪ/ n calamidad f

**calcium** /'kælsɪəm/ n calcio m

**calculat|e** /'kælkjʊleɪt/ vt/i calcular; (Amer) suponer. **~ing** a calculador. **~ion** /-'leɪʃn/ n cálculo m. **~or** n calculadora f

**calculus** /'kælkjʊləs/ n (pl **-li**) cálculo m

**calendar** /'kælɪndə(r)/ n calendario m

**calf**[1] /kɑːf/ n (pl **calves**) ternero m

**calf**[2] /kɑːf/ n (pl **calves**) (of leg) pantorrilla f

**calibre** /'kælɪbə(r)/ n calibre m

**calico** /'kælɪkəʊ/ n calicó m

**call** /kɔːl/ vt/i llamar. ● n llamada f; (shout) grito m; (visit) visita f. **be on ~** estar de guardia. **long distance ~** conferencia f. **~ back** vt hacer volver; (on phone) volver a llamar. ● vi volver; (on phone) volver a llamar. **~ for** pedir; (fetch) ir a buscar. **~ off** cancelar. **~ on** visitar. **~ out** dar voces. **~ together** convocar. **~ up** (mil) llamar al servicio militar; (phone) llamar. **~-box** n cabina f telefónica. **~er** n visita f; (phone) el que llama m. **~ing** n vocación f

**callous** /'kæləs/ a insensible, cruel. **~ness** n crueldad f

**callow** /'kæləʊ/ a (**-er**, **-est**) inexperto

**calm** /kɑːm/ a (**-er**, **-est**) tranquilo; (weather) calmoso. ● n tranquilidad f, calma f. ● vt calmar. ● vi calmarse. **~ness** n tranquilidad f, calma f

**calorie** /'kælərɪ/ n caloría f

**camber** /'kæmbə(r)/ n curvatura f

**came** /keɪm/ see **come**

**camel** /'kæml/ n camello m

**camellia** /kə'miːljə/ n camelia f

**cameo** /'kæmɪəʊ/ n (pl **-os**) camafeo m

**camera** /'kæmərə/ n máquina f (fotográfica); (TV) cámara f. **~man** n (pl **-men**) operador m, cámara m

**camouflage** /'kæməflɑːʒ/ n camuflaje m. ● vt encubrir; (mil) camuflar

**camp**[1] /kæmp/ n campamento m. ● vi acamparse

**camp**[2] /kæmp/ a (affected) amanerado

**campaign** /kæm'peɪn/ n campaña f. ● vi hacer campaña

**camp: ~bed** n catre m de tijera. **~er** n campista m & f; (vehicle) caravana f. **~ing** n camping m. **go ~ing** hacer camping. **~site** /'kæmpsaɪt/ n camping m

**campus** /'kæmpəs/ n (pl **-puses**) ciudad f universitaria

**can**[1] /kæn/ v aux (pt **could**) (be able to) poder; (know how to) saber. **~not** (neg), **~'t** (neg, fam). **I ~not/ ~'t go** no puedo ir

**can**[2] /kæn/ *n* lata *f*. ● *vt* (*pt* **canned**) enlatar. **~ned music** música *f* grabada

**Canad|a** /'kænədə/ *n* el Canadá *m*. **~ian** /kə'neɪdɪən/ *a* & *n* canadiense (*m* & *f*)

**canal** /kə'næl/ *n* canal *m*

**canary** /kə'neərɪ/ *n* canario *m*

**cancel** /'kænsl/ *vt/i* (*pt* **cancelled**) anular; cancelar ⟨*contract etc*⟩; suspender ⟨*appointment etc*⟩; (*delete*) tachar. **~lation** /-'leɪʃn/ *n* cancelación *f*

**cancer** /'kænsə(r)/ *n* cáncer *m*. **C~** *n* (*Astr*) Cáncer *m*. **~ous** *a* canceroso

**candid** /'kændɪd/ *a* franco

**candida|cy** /'cændɪdəsɪ/ *n* candidatura *f*. **~te** /'kændɪdeɪt/ *n* candidato *m*

**candle** /'kændl/ *n* vela *f*. **~stick** /'kændlstɪk/ *n* candelero *m*

**candour** /'kændə(r)/ *n* franqueza *f*

**candy** /'kændɪ/ *n* (*Amer*) caramelo *m*. **~floss** *n* algodón *m* de azúcar

**cane** /keɪn/ *n* caña *f*; (*for baskets*) mimbre *m*; (*stick*) bastón *m*. ● *vt* (*strike*) castigar con palmeta

**canine** /'keɪnaɪn/ *a* canino

**canister** /'kænɪstə(r)/ *n* bote *m*

**cannabis** /'kænəbɪs/ *n* cáñamo *m* índico, hachís *m*, mariguana *f*

**cannibal** /'kænɪbl/ *n* caníbal *m*. **~ism** *n* canibalismo *m*

**cannon** /'kænən/ *n invar* cañón *m*. **~ shot** cañonazo *m*

**cannot** /'kænət/ *see* **can**[1]

**canny** /'kænɪ/ *a* astuto

**canoe** /kə'nu:/ *n* canoa *f*, piragua *f*. ● *vi* ir en canoa. **~ist** *n* piragüista *m* & *f*

**canon** /'kænən/ *n* canon *m*; (*person*) canónigo *m*. **~ize** /'kænənaɪz/ *vt* canonizar

**can-opener** /'kænəʊpnə(r)/ *n* abrelatas *m invar*

**canopy** /'kænəpɪ/ *n* dosel *m*; (*of parachute*) casquete *m*

**cant** /kænt/ *n* jerga *f*

**can't** /kɑ:nt/ *see* **can**[1]

**cantankerous** /kæn'tæŋkərəs/ *a* malhumorado

**canteen** /kæn'ti:n/ *n* cantina *f*; (*of cutlery*) juego *m*; (*flask*) cantimplora *f*

**canter** /'kæntə(r)/ *n* medio galope *m*. ● *vi* ir a medio galope

**canvas** /'kænvəs/ *n* lona *f*; (*artist's*) lienzo *m*

**canvass** /'kænvəs/ *vi* hacer campaña, solicitar votos. **~ing** *n* solicitación *f* (de votos)

**canyon** /'kænjən/ *n* cañón *m*

**cap** /kæp/ *n* gorra *f*; (*lid*) tapa *f*; (*of cartridge*) cápsula *f*; (*academic*) birrete *m*; (*of pen*) capuchón *m*; (*mec*) casquete *m*. ● *vt* (*pt* **capped**) tapar, poner cápsula a; (*outdo*) superar

**capab|ility** /keɪpə'bɪlətɪ/ *n* capacidad *f*. **~le** /'keɪpəbl/ *a* capaz. **~ly** *adv* competentemente

**capacity** /kə'pæsətɪ/ *n* capacidad *f*; (*function*) calidad *f*

**cape**[1] /keɪp/ *n* (*cloak*) capa *f*

**cape**[2] /keɪp/ *n* (*geog*) cabo *m*

**caper**[1] /'keɪpə(r)/ *vi* brincar. ● *n* salto *m*; (*fig*) travesura *f*

**caper**[2] /'keɪpə(r)/ *n* (*culin*) alcaparra *f*

**capital** /'kæpɪtl/ *a* capital. **~ letter** *n* mayúscula *f*. ● *n* (*town*) capital *f*; (*money*) capital *m*

**capitalis|m** /'kæpɪtəlɪzəm/ *n* capitalismo *m*. **~t** *a* & *n* capitalista (*m* & *f*)

**capitalize** /'kæpɪtəlaɪz/ *vt* capitalizar; (*typ*) escribir con mayúsculas. **~ on** aprovechar

**capitulat|e** /kə'pɪtʃʊleɪt/ *vi* capitular. **~ion** /-'leɪʃn/ *n* capitulación *f*

**capon** /'keɪpən/ *n* capón *m*

**capricious** /kə'prɪʃəs/ *a* caprichoso

**Capricorn** /'kæprɪkɔ:n/ *n* Capricornio *m*

**capsicum** /'kæpsɪkəm/ *n* pimiento *m*

**capsize** /kæp'saɪz/ *vt* hacer zozobrar. ● *vi* zozobrar

**capsule** /'kæpsju:l/ *n* cápsula *f*

**captain** /'kæptɪn/ *n* capitán *m*. ● *vt* capitanear

**caption** /'kæpʃn/ *n* (*heading*) título *m*; (*of cartoon etc*) leyenda *f*

**captivate** /'kæptɪveɪt/ *vt* encantar

**captiv|e** /'kæptɪv/ *a* & *n* cautivo (*m*). **~ity** /-'tɪvətɪ/ *n* cautiverio *m*, cautividad *f*

**capture** /'kæptʃə(r)/ *vt* prender; llamar ⟨*attention*⟩; (*mil*) tomar. ● *n* apresamiento *m*; (*mil*) toma *f*

**car** /kɑ:(r)/ *n* coche *m*, carro *m* (*LAm*)

**carafe** /kə'ræf/ *n* jarro *m*, garrafa *f*

**caramel** /'kærəmel/ *n* azúcar *m* quemado; (*sweet*) caramelo *m*

**carat** /'kærət/ *n* quilate *m*

**caravan** /'kærəvæn/ *n* caravana *f*

**carbohydrate** /kɑ:bəʊ'haɪdreɪt/ *n* hidrato *m* de carbono

**carbon** /'kɑːbən/ n carbono m; (*paper*) carbón m. ~ **copy** copia f al carbón

**carburettor** /kɑːbjʊ'retə(r)/ n carburador m

**carcass** /'kɑːkəs/ n cadáver m, esqueleto m

**card** /kɑːd/ n tarjeta f; (*for games*) carta f; (*membership*) carnet m; (*records*) ficha f

**cardboard** /'kɑːdbɔːd/ n cartón m

**cardiac** /'kɑːdɪæk/ a cardíaco

**cardigan** /'kɑːdɪgən/ n chaqueta f de punto, rebeca f

**cardinal** /'kɑːdɪnəl/ a cardinal. ● n cardenal m

**card-index** /'kɑːdɪndeks/ n fichero m

**care** /keə(r)/ n cuidado m; (*worry*) preocupación f; (*protection*) cargo m. ~ **of** a cuidado de, en casa de. **take** ~ **of** cuidar de ⟨*person*⟩; ocuparse de ⟨*matter*⟩. ● vi interesarse. **I don't** ~ me es igual. ~ **about** interesarse por. ~ **for** cuidar de; (*like*) querer

**career** /kə'rɪə(r)/ n carrera f. ● vi correr a toda velocidad

**carefree** /'keəfriː/ a despreocupado

**careful** /'keəfʊl/ a cuidadoso; (*cautious*) prudente. ~**ly** adv con cuidado

**careless** /'keəlɪs/ a negligente; (*not worried*) indiferente. ~**ly** adv descuidadamente. ~**ness** n descuido m

**caress** /kə'res/ n caricia f. ● vt acariciar

**caretaker** /'keəteɪkə(r)/ n vigilante m; (*of flats etc*) portero m

**car-ferry** /'kɑːferɪ/ n transbordador m de coches

**cargo** /'kɑːgəʊ/ n (*pl* -**oes**) carga f

**Caribbean** /kærɪ'biːən/ a caribe. ~ **Sea** n mar m Caribe

**caricature** /'kærɪkətʃʊə(r)/ n caricatura f. ● vt caricaturizar

**carnage** /'kɑːnɪdʒ/ n carnicería f, matanza f

**carnal** /'kɑːnl/ a carnal

**carnation** /kɑː'neɪʃn/ n clavel m

**carnival** /'kɑːnɪvl/ n carnaval m

**carol** /'kærəl/ n villancico m

**carouse** /kə'raʊz/ vi correrse una juerga

**carousel** /kærə'sel/ n tiovivo m

**carp**[1] /kɑːp/ n invar carpa f

**carp**[2] /kɑːp/ vi. ~ **at** quejarse de

**car park** /'kɑːpɑːk/ n aparcamiento m

**carpent|er** /'kɑːpɪntə(r)/ n carpintero m. ~**ry** n carpintería f

**carpet** /'kɑːpɪt/ n alfombra f. **be on the** ~ (*fam*) recibir un rapapolvo; (*under consideration*) estar sobre el tapete. ● vt alfombrar. ~**sweeper** n escoba f mecánica

**carriage** /'kærɪdʒ/ n coche m; (*mec*) carro m; (*transport*) transporte m; (*cost, bearing*) porte m

**carriageway** /'kærɪdʒweɪ/ n calzada f, carretera f

**carrier** /'kærɪə(r)/ n transportista m & f; (*company*) empresa f de transportes; (*med*) portador m. ~**bag** bolsa f

**carrot** /'kærət/ n zanahoria f

**carry** /'kærɪ/ vt llevar; transportar ⟨*goods*⟩; (*involve*) llevar consigo, implicar. ● vi ⟨*sounds*⟩ llegar, oírse. ~ **off** llevarse. ~ **on** continuar; (*complain, fam*) quejarse. ~ **out** realizar; cumplir ⟨*promise, threat*⟩. ~**cot** n capazo m

**cart** /kɑːt/ n carro m. ● vt acarrear; (*carry, fam*) llevar

**cartilage** /'kɑːtɪlɪdʒ/ n cartílago m

**carton** /'kɑːtən/ n caja f (de cartón)

**cartoon** /kɑː'tuːn/ n caricatura f, chiste m; (*strip*) historieta f; (*film*) dibujos mpl animados. ~**ist** n caricaturista m & f

**cartridge** /'kɑːtrɪdʒ/ n cartucho m

**carve** /kɑːv/ vt tallar; trinchar ⟨*meat*⟩

**cascade** /kæs'keɪd/ n cascada f. ● vi caer en cascadas

**case** /keɪs/ n caso m; (*jurid*) proceso m; (*crate*) cajón m; (*box*) caja f; (*suitcase*) maleta f. **in any** ~ en todo caso. **in** ~ **he comes** por si viene. **in** ~ **of** en caso de. **lower** ~ caja f baja, minúscula f. **upper** ~ caja f alta, mayúscula f

**cash** /kæʃ/ n dinero m efectivo. **pay (in)** ~ pagar al contado. ● vt cobrar. ~ **in (on)** aprovecharse de. ~ **desk** n caja f

**cashew** /'kæʃuː/ n anacardo m

**cashier** /kæ'ʃɪə(r)/ n cajero m

**cashmere** /kæʃ'mɪə(r)/ n casimir m, cachemir m

**casino** /kə'siːnəʊ/ n (*pl* -**os**) casino m

**cask** /kɑːsk/ n barril m

**casket** /'kɑːskɪt/ n cajita f

**casserole** /'kæsərəʊl/ n cacerola f; (*stew*) cazuela f

**cassette** /kə'set/ n casete m

**cast** /kɑːst/ vt (*pt* cast) arrojar; fundir ⟨*metal*⟩; dar ⟨*vote*⟩; (*in theatre*) repartir. ● *n* lanzamiento *m*; (*in play*) reparto *m*; (*mould*) molde *m*

**castanets** /ˌkæstəˈnets/ *npl* castañuelas *fpl*

**castaway** /ˈkɑːstəweɪ/ *n* náufrago *m*

**caste** /kɑːst/ *n* casta *f*

**cast:** ~ **iron** *n* hierro *m* fundido. ~**iron** *a* de hierro fundido; (*fig*) sólido

**castle** /ˈkɑːsl/ *n* castillo *m*; (*chess*) torre *f*

**cast-offs** /ˈkɑːstɒfs/ *npl* desechos *mpl*

**castor** /ˈkɑːstə(r)/ *n* ruedecilla *f*

**castor** oil /ˌkɑːstərˈɔɪl/ *n* aceite *m* de ricino

**castor** sugar /ˈkɑːstəˌʃʊgə(r)/ *n* azúcar *m* extrafino

**castrat|e** /kæˈstreɪt/ *vt* castrar. ~**ion** /-ʃn/ *n* castración *f*

**casual** /ˈkæʒʊəl/ *a* casual; (*meeting*) fortuito; (*work*) ocasional; (*attitude*) despreocupado; (*clothes*) informal, de sport. ~**ly** *adv* de paso

**casualt|y** /ˈkæʒʊəltɪ/ *n* accidente *m*; (*injured*) víctima *f*, herido *m*; (*dead*) víctima *f*, muerto *m*. ~**ies** *npl* (*mil*) bajas *fpl*

**cat** /kæt/ *n* gato *m*

**cataclysm** /ˈkætəklɪzəm/ *n* cataclismo *m*

**catacomb** /ˈkætəkuːm/ *n* catacumba *f*

**catalogue** /ˈkætəlɒg/ *n* catálogo *m*. ● *vt* catalogar

**catalyst** /ˈkætəlɪst/ *n* catalizador *m*

**catamaran** /ˌkætəməˈræn/ *n* catamarán *m*

**catapult** /ˈkætəpʌlt/ *n* catapulta *f*; (*child's*) tirador *m*, tirachinos *m invar*

**cataract** /ˈkætərækt/ *n* catarata *f*

**catarrh** /kəˈtɑː(r)/ *n* catarro *m*

**catastroph|e** /kəˈtæstrəfi/ *n* catástrofe *m*. ~**ic** /ˌkætəˈstrɒfɪk/ *a* catastrófico

**catch** /kætʃ/ *vt* (*pt* **caught**) coger (*not LAm*), agarrar; (*grab*) asir; tomar (*train, bus*); (*unawares*) sorprender; (*understand*) comprender; contraer (*disease*). ~ **a cold** resfriarse. ~ **sight of** avistar. ● *vi* (*get stuck*) engancharse; (*fire*) prenderse. ● *n* cogida *f*; (*of fish*) pesca *f*; (*on door*) pestillo *m*; (*on window*) cerradura *f*. ~ **on** (*fam*) hacerse popular. ~ **up** poner al día. ~ **up with** alcanzar; ponerse al corriente de (*news etc*)

**catching** /ˈkætʃɪŋ/ *a* contagioso

**catchment** /ˈkætʃmənt/ *n*. ~ **area** *n* zona *f* de captación

**catch-phrase** /ˈkætʃfreɪz/ *n* eslogan *m*

**catchword** /ˈkætʃwɜːd/ *n* eslogan *m*, consigna *f*

**catchy** /ˈkætʃɪ/ *a* pegadizo

**catechism** /ˈkætɪkɪzəm/ *n* catecismo *m*

**categorical** /ˌkætɪˈgɒrɪkl/ *a* categórico

**category** /ˈkætɪgərɪ/ *n* categoría *f*

**cater** /ˈkeɪtə(r)/ *vi* proveer comida a. ~ **for** proveer a (*needs*). ~**er** *n* proveedor *m*

**caterpillar** /ˈkætəpɪlə(r)/ *n* oruga *f*

**cathedral** /kəˈθiːdrəl/ *n* catedral *f*

**catholic** /ˈkæθəlɪk/ *a* universal. **C~** *a* & *n* católico (*m*). **C~ism** /kəˈθɒlɪsɪzəm/ *n* catolicismo *m*

**catnap** /ˈkætnæp/ *n* sueñecito *m*

**cat's eyes** /ˈkætsaɪz/ *npl* catafotos *mpl*

**cattle** /ˈkætl/ *npl* ganado *m* (vacuno)

**cat|ty** /ˈkætɪ/ *a* malicioso. ~**walk** /ˈkætwɔːk/ *n* pasarela *f*

**caucus** /ˈkɔːkəs/ *n* comité *m* electoral

**caught** /kɔːt/ *see* **catch**

**cauldron** /ˈkɔːldrən/ *n* caldera *f*

**cauliflower** /ˈkɒlɪflaʊə(r)/ *n* coliflor *f*

**cause** /kɔːz/ *n* causa *f*, motivo *m*. ● *vt* causar

**causeway** /ˈkɔːzweɪ/ *n* calzada *f* elevada, carretera *f* elevada

**caustic** /ˈkɔːstɪk/ *a* & *n* cáustico (*m*)

**cauterize** /ˈkɔːtəraɪz/ *vt* cauterizar

**caution** /ˈkɔːʃn/ *n* cautela *f*; (*warning*) advertencia *f*. ● *vt* advertir; (*jurid*) amonestar

**cautious** /ˈkɔːʃəs/ *a* cauteloso, prudente. ~**ly** *adv* con precaución, cautelosamente

**cavalcade** /ˌkævəlˈkeɪd/ *n* cabalgata *f*

**cavalier** /ˌkævəˈlɪə(r)/ *a* arrogante

**cavalry** /ˈkævəlrɪ/ *n* caballería *f*

**cave** /keɪv/ *n* cueva *f*. ● *vi*. ~ **in** hundirse. ~**man** *n* (*pl* -**men**) troglodita *m*

**cavern** /ˈkævən/ *n* caverna *f*, cueva *f*

**caviare** /ˈkævɪɑː(r)/ *n* caviar *m*

**caving** /ˈkeɪvɪŋ/ *n* espeleología *f*

**cavity** /ˈkævɪtɪ/ *n* cavidad *f*; (*in tooth*) caries *f*

**cavort** /kəˈvɔːt/ *vi* brincar

**cease** /siːs/ *vt/i* cesar. ● *n*. **without** ~ sin cesar. ~**fire** *n* tregua *f*, alto *m* el fuego. ~**less** *a* incesante

**cedar** /ˈsiːdə(r)/ *n* cedro *m*

**cede** /si:d/ vt ceder

**cedilla** /sɪ'dɪlə/ n cedilla f

**ceiling** /'si:lɪŋ/ n techo m

**celebrat|e** /'selɪbreɪt/ vt celebrar.
● vi divertirse. ~ed /'selɪbreɪtɪd/ a
célebre. ~ion /-'breɪʃn/ n cele-
bración f; (party) fiesta f

**celebrity** /sɪ'lebrətɪ/ n celebridad f

**celery** /'selərɪ/ n apio m

**celestial** /sɪ'lestjəl/ a celestial

**celiba|cy** /'selɪbəsɪ/ n celibato m.
~te /'selɪbət/ a & n célibe (m & f)

**cell** /sel/ n celda f; (biol) célula f;
(elec) pila f

**cellar** /'selə(r)/ n sótano m; (for wine)
bodega f

**cell|ist** /'tʃelɪst/ n violonc(h)elo m &
f, violonc(h)elista m & f. ~o
/'tʃeləʊ/ n (pl -os) violonc(h)elo m

**Cellophane** /'seləfeɪn/ n (P) celofán
m (P)

**cellular** /'seljʊlə(r)/ a celular

**celluloid** /'seljʊlɔɪd/ n celuloide m

**cellulose** /'seljʊləʊs/ n celulosa f

**Celt** /kelt/ n celta m & f. ~ic a céltico

**cement** /sɪ'ment/ n cemento m. ● vt
cementar; (fig) consolidar

**cemetery** /'semətrɪ/ n cementerio m

**cenotaph** /'senəta:f/ n cenotafio m

**censor** /'sensə(r)/ n censor m. ● vt
censurar. ~ship n censura f

**censure** /'senʃə(r)/ n censura f. ● vt
censurar

**census** /'sensəs/ n censo m

**cent** /sent/ n centavo m

**centenary** /sen'ti:nərɪ/ n centenario
m

**centigrade** /'sentɪgreɪd/ a centí-
grado

**centilitre** /'sentɪli:tə(r)/ n centilitro
m

**centimetre** /'sentɪmi:tə(r)/ n centí-
metro m

**centipede** /'sentɪpi:d/ n ciempiés m
invar

**central** /'sentrəl/ a central; (of town)
céntrico. ~ heating n calefacción f
central. ~ize vt centralizar. ~ly
adv (situated) en el centro

**centre** /'sentə(r)/ n centro m. ● vt (pt
centred) vi concentrarse

**centrifugal** /sen'trɪfjʊgəl/ a
centrífugo

**century** /'sentʃərɪ/ n siglo m

**ceramic** /sɪ'ræmɪk/ a cerámico. ~s
npl cerámica f

**cereal** /'sɪərɪəl/ n cereal m

**cerebral** /'serɪbrəl/ a cerebral

**ceremon|ial** /serɪ'məʊnɪəl/ a & n
ceremonial (m). ~ious /-'məʊnɪəs/
a ceremonioso. ~y /'serɪmənɪ/ n
ceremonia f

**certain** /'sɜ:tn/ a cierto. for ~
seguro. make ~ of asegurarse de.
~ly adv desde luego. ~ty n certeza
f

**certificate** /sə'tɪfɪkət/ n certificado
m; (of birth, death etc) partida f

**certify** /'sɜ:tɪfaɪ/ vt certificar

**cessation** /se'seɪʃən/ n cesación f

**cesspit** /'sespɪt/ n, **cesspool** /'sespu:l/
n pozo m negro; (fam) sentina f

**chafe** /tʃeɪf/ vt rozar. ● vi rozarse;
(fig) irritarse

**chaff** /tʃæf/ vt zumbarse de

**chaffinch** /'tʃæfɪntʃ/ n pinzón m

**chagrin** /'ʃægrɪn/ n disgusto m

**chain** /tʃeɪn/ n cadena f. ● vt encadenar. ~ reaction n reacción f en
cadena. ~smoker n fumador m que
siempre tiene un cigarillo encendido. ~ store n sucursal m

**chair** /tʃeə(r)/ n silla f; (univ) cátedra
f. ● vt presidir. ~lift n telesilla m

**chairman** /'tʃeəmən/ n (pl -men) pre-
sidente m

**chalet** /'ʃæleɪ/ n chalé m

**chalice** /'tʃælɪs/ n cáliz m

**chalk** /tʃɔ:k/ n creta f; (stick) tiza f.
~y a cretáceo

**challeng|e** /'tʃælɪndʒ/ n desafío m;
(fig) reto m. ● vt desafiar; (question)
poner en duda. ~ing a estimulante

**chamber** /'tʃeɪmbə(r)/ n (old use)
cámara f. ~maid /'tʃeɪmbəmeɪd/ n
camarera f. ~pot n orinal m. ~s
npl despacho m, bufete m

**chameleon** /kə'mi:ljən/ n camaleón
m

**chamois** /'ʃæmɪ/ n gamuza f

**champagne** /ʃæm'peɪn/ n champaña m, champán m (fam)

**champion** /'tʃæmpɪən/ n campeón
m. ● vt defender. ~ship n campeonato m

**chance** /tʃɑ:ns/ n casualidad f; (likelihood) probabilidad f; (opportunity) oportunidad f; (risk) riesgo
m. by ~ por casualidad. ● a fortuito. ● vt arriesgar. ● vi suceder. ~
upon tropezar con

**chancellor** /'tʃɑ:nsələ(r)/ n canciller
m; (univ) rector m. C~ of the
Exchequer Ministro m de Hacienda

**chancy** /'tʃɑ:nsɪ/ a arriesgado; (uncertain) incierto

**chandelier** /ˌʃændəˈlɪə(r)/ n araña f
(de luces)

**change** /tʃeɪndʒ/ vt cambiar; (substitute) reemplazar. ~ one's mind
cambiar de idea. ● vi cambiarse.
● n cambio m; (small coins) suelto
m. ~ of life menopausia f. ~able a
cambiable; (weather) variable.
~over n cambio m

**channel** /ˈtʃænl/ n canal m; (fig)
medio m. the C~ Islands npl las
islas fpl Anglonormandas. the
(English) C~ el canal de la Mancha.
● vt (pt channelled) acanalar; (fig)
encauzar

**chant** /tʃɑːnt/ n canto m. ● vt/i cantar; (fig) salmodiar

**chao|s** /ˈkeɪɒs/ n caos m, desorden
m. ~tic /-ˈɒtɪk/ a caótico,
desordenado

**chap**[1] /tʃæp/ n (crack) grieta f. ● vt
(pt chapped) agrietar. ● vi
agrietarse

**chap**[2] /tʃæp/ n (fam) hombre m, tío m
(fam)

**chapel** /ˈtʃæpl/ n capilla f

**chaperon** /ˈʃæpərəʊn/ n acom-
pañanta f. ● vt acompañar

**chaplain** /ˈtʃæplɪn/ n capellán m

**chapter** /ˈtʃæptə(r)/ n capítulo m

**char**[1] /tʃɑː(r)/ vt (pt charred)
carbonizar

**char**[2] /tʃɑː(r)/ n asistenta f

**character** /ˈkærəktə(r)/ n carácter m;
(in play) personaje m. in ~
característico

**characteristic** /kærəktəˈrɪstɪk/ a característico. ~ally adv típicamente

**characterize** /ˈkærəktəraɪz/ vt
caracterizar

**charade** /ʃəˈrɑːd/ n charada f, farsa f

**charcoal** /ˈtʃɑːkəʊl/ n carbón m
vegetal; (for drawing) carboncillo
m

**charge** /tʃɑːdʒ/ n precio m; (elec, mil)
carga f; (jurid) acusación f; (task,
custody) encargo m; (responsibility)
responsabilidad f. in ~ of responsable de, encargado de. take ~ of
encargarse de. ● vt pedir; (elec, mil)
cargar; (jurid) acusar; (entrust)
encargar. ● vi cargar; (money)
cobrar. ~able a a cargo (de)

**chariot** /ˈtʃærɪət/ n carro m

**charisma** /kəˈrɪzmə/ n carisma m.
~tic /-ˈmætɪk/ a carismático

**charitable** /ˈtʃærɪtəbl/ a caritativo

**charity** /ˈtʃærɪtɪ/ n caridad f; (society)
institución f benéfica

**charlatan** /ˈʃɑːlətən/ n charlatán m

**charm** /tʃɑːm/ n encanto m; (spell)
hechizo m; (on bracelet) dije m,
amuleto m. ● vt encantar. ~ing a
encantador

**chart** /tʃɑːt/ n (naut) carta f de
marear; (table) tabla f. ● vt poner en
una carta de marear

**charter** /ˈtʃɑːtə(r)/ n carta f. ● vt conceder carta a, estatuir; alquilar
(bus, train); fletar (plane, ship).
~ed accountant n contador m titu-
lado. ~ flight n vuelo m charter

**charwoman** /ˈtʃɑːwʊmən/ n (pl
-women) asistenta f

**chary** /ˈtʃeərɪ/ a cauteloso

**chase** /tʃeɪs/ vt perseguir. ● vi
correr. ● n persecución f. ~ away,
~ off ahuyentar

**chasm** /ˈkæzəm/ n abismo m

**chassis** /ˈʃæsɪ/ n chasis m

**chaste** /tʃeɪst/ a casto

**chastise** /tʃæsˈtaɪz/ vt castigar

**chastity** /ˈtʃæstətɪ/ n castidad f

**chat** /tʃæt/ n charla f. have a ~ charlar. ● vi (pt chatted) charlar

**chattels** /ˈtʃætlz/ n bienes mpl
muebles

**chatter** /ˈtʃætə(r)/ n charla f. ● vi
charlar. his teeth are ~ing le cas-
tañetean los dientes. ~box
/ˈtʃætəbɒks/ n parlanchín m

**chatty** a hablador; (style) familiar

**chauffeur** /ˈʃəʊfə(r)/ n chófer m

**chauvinis|m** /ˈʃəʊvɪnɪzəm/ n patri-
otería f; (male) machismo m. ~t
/ˈʃəʊvɪnɪst/ n patriotero m; (male)
machista m & f

**cheap** /tʃiːp/ a (-er, -est) barato;
(poor quality) de baja calidad; (rate)
económico. ~en /ˈtʃiːpən/ vt abar-
atar. ~(ly) adv barato, a bajo
precio. ~ness n baratura f

**cheat** /tʃiːt/ vt defraudar; (deceive)
engañar. ● vi (at cards) hacer
trampas. ● n trampa f; (person)
tramposo m

**check**[1] /tʃek/ vt comprobar; (examine) inspeccionar; (curb) detener;
(chess) dar jaque a. ● vi comprobar.
● n comprobación f; (of tickets) control m; (curb) freno m; (chess) jaque
m; (bill, Amer) cuenta f. ~ in regis-
trarse; (at airport) facturar el
equipaje. ~ out pagar la cuenta y
marcharse. ~ up comprobar. ~ up
on investigar

**check**[2] /tʃek/ n (pattern) cuadro m.
~ed a a cuadros

**checkmate** /ˈtʃekmeɪt/ n jaque m mate. ● vt dar mate a

**check-up** /ˈtʃekʌp/ n examen m

**cheek** /tʃiːk/ n mejilla f; (fig) descaro m. **~bone** n pómulo m. **~y** a descarado

**cheep** /tʃiːp/ vi piar

**cheer** /tʃɪə(r)/ n alegría f; (applause) viva m. ● vt alegrar; (applaud) aplaudir. ● vi alegrarse; (applaud) aplaudir. **~ up!** ¡anímate! **~ful** a alegre. **~fulness** n alegría f

**cheerio** /tʃɪərɪˈəʊ/ int (fam) ¡adiós!, ¡hasta luego!

**cheer: ~less** /ˈtʃɪəlɪs/ a triste. **~s!** ¡salud!

**cheese** /tʃiːz/ n queso m

**cheetah** /ˈtʃiːtə/ n guepardo m

**chef** /ʃef/ n cocinero m

**chemical** /ˈkemɪkl/ a químico. ● n producto m químico

**chemist** /ˈkemɪst/ n farmacéutico m; (scientist) químico m. **~ry** n química f. **~'s (shop)** n farmacia f

**cheque** /tʃek/ n cheque m, talón m. **~book** n talonario m

**chequered** /ˈtʃekəd/ a a cuadros; (fig) con altibajos

**cherish** /ˈtʃerɪʃ/ vt cuidar; (love) querer; abrigar (hope)

**cherry** /ˈtʃerɪ/ n cereza f. **~tree** n cerezo m

**cherub** /ˈtʃerəb/ n (pl -im) (angel) querubín m

**chess** /tʃes/ n ajedrez m. **~board** n tablero m de ajedrez

**chest** /tʃest/ n pecho m; (box) cofre m, cajón m. **~ of drawers** n cómoda f

**chestnut** /ˈtʃesnʌt/ n castaña f. **~tree** n castaño m

**chew** /tʃuː/ vt masticar; (fig) rumiar. **~ing-gum** n chicle m

**chic** /ʃiːk/ a elegante. ● n elegancia f

**chick** /tʃɪk/ n polluelo m. **~en** /ˈtʃɪkɪn/ n pollo m. ● a (sl) cobarde. ● vi. **~en out** (sl) retirarse. **~en-pox** n varicela f

**chicory** /ˈtʃɪkərɪ/ n (in coffee) achicoria f; (in salad) escarola f

**chide** /tʃaɪd/ vt (pt **chided**) reprender

**chief** /tʃiːf/ n jefe m. ● a principal. **~ly** adv principalmente

**chilblain** /ˈtʃɪlbleɪn/ n sabañón m

**child** /tʃaɪld/ n (pl **children** /ˈtʃɪldrən/) niño m; (offspring) hijo m. **~birth** /ˈtʃaɪldbɜːθ/ n parto m. **~hood** n niñez f. **~ish** a infantil.

**~less** a sin hijos. **~like** a inocente, infantil

**Chile** /ˈtʃɪlɪ/ n Chile m. **~an** a & n chileno (m)

**chill** /tʃɪl/ n frío m; (illness) resfriado m. ● a frío. ● vt enfriar; refrigerar (food)

**chilli** /ˈtʃɪlɪ/ n (pl **-ies**) chile m

**chilly** /ˈtʃɪlɪ/ a frío

**chime** /tʃaɪm/ n carillón m. ● vt tocar (bells); dar (hours). ● vi repicar

**chimney** /ˈtʃɪmnɪ/ n (pl **-eys**) chimenea f. **~pot** n cañón m de chimenea. **~sweep** n deshollinador m

**chimpanzee** /tʃɪmpænˈziː/ n chimpancé m

**chin** /tʃɪn/ n barbilla f

**china** /ˈtʃaɪnə/ n porcelana f

**Chin|a** /ˈtʃaɪnə/ n China f. **~ese** /-ˈniːz/ a & n chino (m)

**chink**[1] /tʃɪŋk/ n (crack) grieta f

**chink**[2] /tʃɪŋk/ n (sound) tintín m. ● vt hacer tintinear. ● vi tintinear

**chip** /tʃɪp/ n pedacito m; (splinter) astilla f; (culin) patata f frita; (gambling) ficha f. **have a ~ on one's shoulder** guardar rencor. ● vt (pt **chipped**) desportillar. ● vi desportillarse. **~ in** (fam) interrumpir; (with money) contribuir

**chiropodist** /kɪˈrɒpədɪst/ n callista m & f

**chirp** /tʃɜːp/ n pío m. ● vi piar

**chirpy** /ˈtʃɜːpɪ/ a alegre

**chisel** /ˈtʃɪzl/ n formón m. ● vt (pt **chiselled**) cincelar

**chit** /tʃɪt/ n vale m, nota f

**chit-chat** /ˈtʃɪttʃæt/ n cháchara f

**chivalr|ous** a /ˈʃɪvəlrəs/ a caballeroso. **~y** /ˈʃɪvəlrɪ/ n caballerosidad f

**chive** /tʃaɪv/ n cebollino m

**chlorine** /ˈklɔːriːn/ n cloro m

**chock** /tʃɒk/ n calzo m. **~-a-block** a, **~-full** a atestado

**chocolate** /ˈtʃɒklɪt/ n chocolate m; (individual sweet) bombón m

**choice** /tʃɔɪs/ n elección f; (preference) preferencia f. ● a escogido

**choir** /ˈkwaɪə(r)/ n coro m. **~boy** /ˈkwaɪbɔɪ/ n niño m de coro

**choke** /tʃəʊk/ vt sofocar. ● vi sofocarse. ● n (auto) estrangulador m, estárter m

**cholera** /ˈkɒlərə/ n cólera m

**cholesterol** /kəˈlestərɒl/ n colesterol m

**choose** /tʃuːz/ vt/i (pt **chose,** pp **chosen**) elegir. ~**y** /'tʃuːzɪ/ a (fam) exigente

**chop** /tʃɒp/ vt (pt **chopped**) cortar. ● n (culin) chuleta f. ~ **down** talar. ~ **off** cortar. ~**per** n hacha f; (butcher's) cuchilla f; (sl) helicóptero m

**choppy** /'tʃɒpɪ/ a picado

**chopstick** /'tʃɒpstɪk/ n palillo m (chino)

**choral** /'kɔːrəl/ a coral

**chord** /kɔːd/ n cuerda f; (mus) acorde m

**chore** /tʃɔː(r)/ n tarea f, faena f. **household** ~**s** npl faenas fpl domésticas

**choreographer** /kɒrɪ'ɒgrəfə(r)/ n coreógrafo m

**chorister** /'kɒrɪstə(r)/ n (singer) corista m & f

**chortle** /'tʃɔːtl/ n risita f alegre. ● vi reírse alegremente

**chorus** /'kɔːrəs/ n coro m; (of song) estribillo m

**chose, chosen** /tʃəʊz, 'tʃəʊzn/ see **choose**

**Christ** /kraɪst/ n Cristo m

**christen** /'krɪsn/ vt bautizar. ~**ing** n bautizo m

**Christian** /'krɪstjən/ a & n cristiano (m). ~ **name** n nombre m de pila

**Christmas** /'krɪsməs/ n Navidad f; (period) Navidades fpl. ● a de Navidad, navideño. ~**box** n aguinaldo m. ~ **day** n día m de Navidad. ~ **Eve** n Nochebuena f. **Father** ~ n Papá m Noel. **Happy** ~! ¡Felices Pascuas!

**chrom|e** /krəʊm/ n cromo m. ~**ium** /'krəʊmɪəm/ n cromo m. ~**ium plating** n cromado m

**chromosome** /'krəʊməsəʊm/ n cromosoma m

**chronic** /'krɒnɪk/ a crónico; (bad, fam) terrible

**chronicle** /'krɒnɪkl/ n crónica f. ● vt historiar

**chronolog|ical** /krɒnə'lɒdʒɪkl/ a cronológico. ~**y** /krə'nɒlədʒɪ/ n cronología f

**chrysanthemum** /krɪ'sænθəməm/ n crisantemo m

**chubby** /'tʃʌbɪ/ a (-**ier**, -**iest**) regordete; (face) mofletudo

**chuck** /tʃʌk/ vt (fam) arrojar. ~ **out** tirar

**chuckle** /'tʃʌkl/ n risa f ahogada. ● vi reírse entre dientes

**chuffed** /tʃʌft/ a (sl) contento

**chug** /tʃʌg/ vi (pt **chugged**) (of motor) traquetear

**chum** /tʃʌm/ n amigo m, compinche m. ~**my** a. be ~**my** ser muy amigos. be ~**my with** ser muy amigo de

**chump** /tʃʌmp/ n (sl) tonto m. ~ **chop** n chuleta f

**chunk** /tʃʌŋk/ n trozo m grueso. ~**y** /tʃʌŋkɪ/ a macizo

**church** /tʃɜːtʃ/ n iglesia f. ~**yard** /'tʃɜːtʃjɑːd/ n cementerio m

**churlish** /'tʃɜːlɪʃ/ a grosero

**churn** /tʃɜːn/ n (for milk) lechera f, cántara f; (for butter) mantequera f. ● vt agitar. ~ **out** producir en profusión

**chute** /ʃuːt/ n tobogán m

**chutney** /'tʃʌtnɪ/ n (pl -**eys**) condimento m agridulce

**cider** /'saɪdə(r)/ n sidra f

**cigar** /sɪ'gɑː(r)/ n puro m

**cigarette** /sɪgə'ret/ n cigarillo m. ~**holder** n boquilla f

**cine-camera** /'sɪnɪkæmərə/ n cámara f, tomavistas m invar

**cinema** /'sɪnəmə/ n cine m

**cinnamon** /'sɪnəmən/ n canela f

**cipher** /'saɪfə(r)/ n (math, fig) cero m; (secret system) cifra f

**circle** /'sɜːkl/ n círculo m; (in theatre) anfiteatro m. ● vt girar alrededor de. ● vi dar vueltas

**circuit** /'sɜːkɪt/ n circuito m; (chain) cadena f

**circuitous** /sɜː'kjuːɪtəs/ a indirecto

**circular** /'sɜːkjʊlə(r)/ a & n circular (f)

**circularize** /'sɜːkjʊləraɪz/ vt enviar circulares a

**circulat|e** /'sɜːkjʊleɪt/ vt hacer circular. ● vi circular. ~**ion** /-'leɪʃn/ n circulación f; (of journals) tirada f

**circumcis|e** /'sɜːkəmsaɪz/ vt circuncidar. ~**ion** /-'sɪʒn/ n circuncisión f

**circumference** /sə'kʌmfərəns/ n circunferencia f

**circumflex** /'sɜːkəmfleks/ a & n circunflejo (m)

**circumspect** /'sɜːkəmspekt/ a circunspecto

**circumstance** /'sɜːkəmstəns/ n circunstancia f. ~**s** (means) npl situación f económica

**circus** /'sɜːkəs/ n circo m

**cistern** /'sɪstən/ n depósito m; (of WC) cisterna f

**citadel** /'sɪtədl/ n ciudadela f

**citation** /saɪˈteɪʃn/ n citación f
**cite** /saɪt/ vt citar
**citizen** /ˈsɪtɪzn/ n ciudadano m;
(inhabitant) habitante m & f. **~ship**
n ciudadanía f
**citrus** /ˈsɪtrəs/ n. **~ fruits** cítricos
mpl
**city** /ˈsɪtɪ/ n ciudad f; **the C~** el centro m financiero de Londres
**civic** /ˈsɪvɪk/ a cívico. **~s** npl cívica f
**civil** /ˈsɪvl/ a civil, cortés
**civilian** /sɪˈvɪlɪən/ a & n civil (m & f).
**~ clothes** npl traje m de paisano
**civility** /sɪˈvɪlətɪ/ n cortesía f
**civiliz|ation** /sɪvɪlaɪˈzeɪʃn/ n civil-
ización f. **~e** /ˈsɪvəlaɪz/ vt civilizar.
**civil: ~ servant** n funcionario m. **~**
**service** n administración f pública
**civvies** /ˈsɪvɪz/ npl. **in ~** (sl) en traje
m de paisano
**clad** /klæd/ see **clothe**
**claim** /kleɪm/ vt reclamar; (assert)
pretender. **●** n reclamación f;
(right) derecho m; (jurid) demanda
f. **~ant** n demandante m & f; (to
throne) pretendiente m
**clairvoyant** /kleəˈvɔɪənt/ n clarividente m & f
**clam** /klæm/ n almeja f
**clamber** /ˈklæmbə(r)/ vi trepar a
gatas
**clammy** /ˈklæmɪ/ a (-ier, -iest)
húmedo
**clamour** /ˈklæmə(r)/ n clamor m.
**●** vi. **~ for** pedir a voces
**clamp** /klæmp/ n abrazadera f;
(auto) cepo m. **●** vt sujetar con abrazadera. **~ down on** reprimir
**clan** /klæn/ n clan m
**clandestine** /klænˈdestɪn/ a clandestino
**clang** /klæŋ/ n sonido m metálico
**clanger** /ˈklæŋə(r)/ n (sl) metedura f
de pata
**clap** /klæp/ vt (pt clapped) aplaudir;
batir (hands). **●** vi aplaudir. **●** n palmada f; (of thunder) trueno m
**claptrap** /ˈklæptræp/ n charlatanería
f, tonterías fpl
**claret** /ˈklærət/ n clarete m
**clarif|ication** /klærɪfɪˈkeɪʃn/ n acla-
ración f. **~y** /ˈklærɪfaɪ/ vt aclarar.
**●** vi aclararse
**clarinet** /klærɪˈnet/ n clarinete m
**clarity** /ˈklærətɪ/ n claridad f
**clash** /klæʃ/ n choque m; (noise)
estruendo m; (contrast) contraste
m; (fig) conflicto m. **●** vt golpear.
**●** vi encontrarse; (dates) coincidir;

(opinions) estar en desacuerdo; (colours) desentonar
**clasp** /klɑːsp/ n cierre m. **●** vt agarrar;
apretar (hand); (fasten) abrochar
**class** /klɑːs/ n clase f. **evening ~** n
clase nocturna. **●** vt clasificar
**classic** /ˈklæsɪk/ a & n clásico (m).
**~al** a clásico. **~s** npl estudios mpl
clásicos
**classif|ication** /klæsɪfɪˈkeɪʃn/ n
clasificación f. **~y** /ˈklæsɪfaɪ/ vt
clasificar
**classroom** /ˈklɑːsruːm/ n aula f
**classy** /ˈklɑːsɪ/ a (sl) elegante
**clatter** /ˈklætə(r)/ n estrépito m. **●** vi
hacer ruido
**clause** /klɔːz/ n cláusula f; (gram)
oración f
**claustrophobia** /klɔːstrəˈfəʊbɪə/ n
claustrofobia f
**claw** /klɔː/ n garra f; (of cat) uña f; (of
crab) pinza f; (device) garfio m. **●** vt
arañar
**clay** /kleɪ/ n arcilla f
**clean** /kliːn/ a (-er, -est) limpio;
(stroke) neto. **●** adv completamente.
**●** vt limpiar. **●** vi hacer la limpieza.
**~ up** hacer la limpieza. **~-cut** a bien
definido. **~er** n mujer f de la limpieza. **~liness** /ˈklenlɪnɪs/ n limpieza f
**cleans|e** /klenz/ vt limpiar; (fig) pur-
ificar. **~ing cream** n crema f
desmaquilladora
**clear** /klɪə(r)/ a (-er, -est) claro;
(transparent) transparente; (without obstacles) libre; (profit) neto;
(sky) despejado. **keep ~ of** evitar.
**●** adv claramente. **●** vt despejar;
liquidar (goods); (jurid) absolver;
(jump over) saltar por encima de;
quitar (table). **●** vi (weather) despejarse; (fog) disolverse. **~ off** vi (sl),
**~ out** vi (sl) largarse. **~ up** vt (tidy)
poner en orden; aclarar (mystery).
**●** vi (weather) despejarse
**clearance** /ˈklɪərəns/ n espacio m
libre; (removal of obstructions)
despeje m; (authorization) permiso
m; (by customs) despacho m; (by
security) acreditación f. **~ sale** n
liquidación f
**clearing** /ˈklɪərɪŋ/ n claro m
**clearly** /ˈklɪəlɪ/ adv evidentemente
**clearway** /ˈklɪəweɪ/ n carretera f en
la que no se permite parar
**cleavage** /ˈkliːvɪdʒ/ n escote m; (fig)
división f
**cleave** /kliːv/ vt (pt cleaved, clove or
cleft; pp cloven or cleft) hender. **●** vi
henderse

**clef** /klef/ n (mus) clave f

**cleft** /kleft/ see **cleave**

**clemen|cy** /'klemənsı/ n clemencia f. ~t a clemente

**clench** /klentʃ/ vt apretar

**clergy** /'klɜːdʒı/ n clero m. ~man n (pl -men) clérigo m

**cleric** /'klerık/ n clérigo m. ~al a clerical; (of clerks) de oficina

**clerk** /klɑːk/ n empleado m; (jurid) escribano m

**clever** /'klevə(r)/ a (-er, -est) listo; (skilful) hábil. ~ly adv inteligentemente; (with skill) hábilmente. ~ness n inteligencia f

**cliché** /'kliːʃeı/ n tópico m, frase f hecha

**click** /klık/ n golpecito m. ● vi chascar; (sl) llevarse bien

**client** /'klaıənt/ n cliente m & f

**clientele** /kliːən'tel/ n clientela f

**cliff** /klıf/ n acantilado m

**climat|e** /'klaımıt/ n clima m. ~ic /-'mætık/ a climático

**climax** /'klaımæks/ n punto m culminante

**climb** /klaım/ vt subir (stairs); trepar (tree); escalar (mountain). ● vi subir. ● n subida f. ~ down bajar; (fig) volverse atrás, rajarse. ~er n (sport) alpinista m & f; (plant) trepadora f

**clinch** /klıntʃ/ vt cerrar (deal)

**cling** /klıŋ/ vi (pt clung) agarrarse; (stick) pegarse

**clinic** /'klınık/ n clínica f. ~al /'klınıkl/ a clínico

**clink** /klıŋk/ n sonido m metálico. ● vt hacer tintinear. ● vi tintinear

**clinker** /'klıŋkə(r)/ n escoria f

**clip**[1] /klıp/ n (for paper) sujetapapeles m invar; (for hair) horquilla f. ● vt (pt clipped) (join) sujetar

**clip**[2] /klıp/ n (with scissors) tijeretada f; (blow, fam) golpe m. ● vt (pt clipped) (cut) cortar; (fam) golpear. ~pers /'klıpəz/ npl (for hair) maquinilla f para cortar el pelo; (for nails) cortauñas m invar. ~ping n recorte m

**clique** /kliːk/ n pandilla f

**cloak** /kləuk/ n capa f. ~room /'kləukruːm/ n guardarropa m; (toilet) servicios mpl

**clobber** /'klɒbə(r)/ n (sl) trastos mpl. ● vt (sl) dar una paliza a

**clock** /klɒk/ n reloj m. **grandfather** ~ reloj de caja. ● vi. ~ **in** fichar, registrar la llegada. ~**wise** /'klɒkwaız/ a & adv en el sentido de las agujas del reloj, a la derecha. ~**work** /'klɒkwɜːk/ n mecanismo m de relojería. **like** ~**work** con precisión

**clod** /klɒd/ n terrón m

**clog** /klɒg/ n zueco m. ● vt (pt clogged) atascar. ● vi atascarse

**cloister** /'klɒıstə(r)/ n claustro m

**close**[1] /kləus/ a (-er, -est) cercano; (together) apretado; (friend) íntimo; (weather) bochornoso; (link etc) estrecho; (game, battle) reñido. **have a** ~ **shave** (fig) escaparse de milagro. ● adv cerca. ● n recinto m

**close**[2] /kləuz/ vt cerrar. ● vi cerrarse; (end) terminar. ● n fin m. ~**d shop** n empresa f que emplea solamente a miembros del sindicato

**close:** ~**ly** adv de cerca; (with attention) atentamente; (exactly) exactamente. ~**ness** n proximidad f; (togetherness) intimidad f

**closet** /'klɒzıt/ n (Amer) armario m

**close-up** /'kləusʌp/ n (cinema etc) primer plano m

**closure** /'kləuʒə(r)/ n cierre m

**clot** /klɒt/ n (culin) grumo m; (med) coágulo m; (sl) tonto m. ● vi (pt clotted) cuajarse

**cloth** /klɒθ/ n tela f; (duster) trapo m; (table-cloth) mantel m

**cloth|e** /kləuð/ vt (pt **clothed** or **clad**) vestir. ~**es** /kləuðz/ npl, ~**ing** n ropa f

**cloud** /klaud/ n nube f. ● vi nublarse. ~**burst** /'klaudbɜːst/ n chaparrón m. ~**y** a (-ier, -iest) nublado; (liquid) turbio

**clout** /klaut/ n bofetada f. ● vt abofetear

**clove**[1] /kləuv/ n clavo m

**clove**[2] /kləuv/ n. ~ **of garlic** n diente m de ajo

**clove**[3] /kləuv/ see **cleave**

**clover** /'kləuvə(r)/ n trébol m

**clown** /klaun/ n payaso m. ● vi hacer el payaso

**cloy** /klɒı/ vt empalagar

**club** /klʌb/ n club m; (weapon) porra f; (at cards) trébol m. ● vt (pt clubbed) aporrear. ● vi. ~ **together** reunirse, pagar a escote

**cluck** /klʌk/ vi cloquear

**clue** /kluː/ n pista f; (in crosswords) indicación f. **not to have a** ~ no tener la menor idea

**clump** /klʌmp/ n grupo m. ● vt agrupar. ● vi pisar fuertemente

**clums|iness** /'klʌmzınıs/ n torpeza f. ~y /'klʌmzı/ a (-ier, -iest) torpe

**clung** /klʌŋ/ see **cling**

**cluster** /'klʌstə(r)/ n grupo m. ● vi agruparse

**clutch** /klʌtʃ/ vt agarrar. ● n (auto) embrague m

**clutter** /'klʌtə(r)/ n desorden m. ● vt llenar desordenadamente

**coach** /kəʊtʃ/ n autocar m; (of train) vagón m; (horse-drawn) coche m; (sport) entrenador m. ● vt dar clases particulares; (sport) entrenar

**coagulate** /kəʊ'ægjʊleıt/ vt coagular. ● vi coagularse

**coal** /kəʊl/ n carbón m. ~field /'kəʊlfi:ld/ n yacimiento m de carbón

**coalition** /kəʊə'lıʃn/ n coalición f

**coarse** /kɔ:s/ a (-er, -est) grosero; (material) basto. ~ness n grosería f; (texture) basteza f

**coast** /kəʊst/ n costa f. ● vi (with cycle) deslizarse cuesta abajo; (with car) ir en punto muerto. ~al a costero. ~er /'kəʊstə(r)/ n (ship) barco m de cabotaje; (for glass) posavasos m invar. ~guard /'kəʊstgɑ:d/ n guardacostas m invar. ~line /'kəʊstlaın/ n litoral m

**coat** /kəʊt/ n abrigo m; (jacket) chaqueta f; (of animal) pelo m; (of paint) mano f. ● vt cubrir, revestir. ~ing n capa f. ~ of arms n escudo m de armas

**coax** /kəʊks/ vt engatusar

**cob** /kɒb/ n (of corn) mazorca f

**cobble**[1] /'kɒbl/ n guijarro m, adoquín m. ● vt empedrar con guijarros, adoquinar

**cobble**[2] /'kɒbl/ vt (mend) remendar. ~r /'kɒblə(r)/ n (old use) remendón m

**cobweb** /'kɒbweb/ n telaraña f

**cocaine** /kə'keın/ n cocaína f

**cock** /kɒk/ n gallo m; (mec) grifo m; (of gun) martillo m. ● vt amartillar (gun); aguzar (ears). ~-and-bull story n patraña f. ~erel /'kɒkərəl/ n gallo m. ~-eyed a (sl) torcido

**cockle** /'kɒkl/ n berberecho m

**cockney** /'kɒknı/ a & n (pl -eys) londinense (m & f) (del este de Londres)

**cockpit** /'kɒkpıt/ n (in aircraft) cabina f del piloto

**cockroach** /'kɒkrəʊtʃ/ n cucaracha f

**cocksure** /kɒk'ʃʊə(r)/ a presuntuoso

**cocktail** /'kɒkteıl/ n cóctel m. **fruit** ~ macedonia f de frutas

**cock-up** /'kɒkʌp/ n (sl) lío m

**cocky** /'kɒkı/ a (-ier, -iest) engreído

**cocoa** /'kəʊkəʊ/ n cacao m; (drink) chocolate m

**coconut** /'kəʊkənʌt/ n coco m

**cocoon** /kə'ku:n/ n capullo m

**cod** /kɒd/ n (pl cod) bacalao m, abadejo m

**coddle** /'kɒdl/ vt mimar; (culin) cocer a fuego lento

**code** /kəʊd/ n código m; (secret) cifra f

**codify** /'kəʊdıfaı/ vt codificar

**cod-liver oil** /'kɒdlıvə(r)ɔıl/ n aceite m de hígado de bacalao

**coeducational** /kəʊedʒʊ'keıʃənl/ a mixto

**coerc|e** /kəʊ'ɜ:s/ vt obligar. ~ion /-ʃn/ n coacción f

**coexist** /kəʊıg'zıst/ vi coexistir. ~ence n coexistencia f

**coffee** /'kɒfı/ n café m. ~-mill n molinillo m de café. ~-pot n cafetera f

**coffer** /'kɒfə(r)/ n cofre m

**coffin** /'kɒfın/ n ataúd m

**cog** /kɒg/ n diente m; (fig) pieza f

**cogent** /'kəʊdʒənt/ a convincente

**cohabit** /kəʊ'hæbıt/ vi cohabitar

**coherent** /kəʊ'hıərənt/ a coherente

**coil** /kɔıl/ vt enrollar. ● n rollo m; (one ring) vuelta f

**coin** /kɔın/ n moneda f. ● vt acuñar. ~age n sistema m monetario

**coincide** /kəʊın'saıd/ vi coincidir

**coinciden|ce** /kəʊ'ınsıdəns/ n casualidad f. ~tal /-'dentl/ a casual; (coinciding) coincidente

**coke** /kəʊk/ n (coal) coque m

**colander** /'kʌləndə(r)/ n colador m

**cold** /kəʊld/ a (-er, -est) frío. **be** ~ tener frío. **it is** ~ hace frío. ● n frío m; (med) resfriado m. **have a** ~ estar constipado. ~-blooded a insensible. ~ **cream** n crema f. ~ **feet** (fig) mieditis f. ~ness n frialdad f. ~-shoulder vt tratar con frialdad. ~ **sore** n herpes m labial. ~ **storage** n conservación f en frigorífico

**coleslaw** /'kəʊlslɔ:/ n ensalada f de col

**colic** /'kɒlık/ n cólico m

**collaborat|e** /kə'læbəreıt/ vi colaborar. ~ion /-'reıʃn/ n colaboración f. ~or n colaborador m

**collage** /'kɒlɑːʒ/ n collage m

**collaps|e** /kə'læps/ vi derrumbarse; (med) sufrir un colapso. ● n derrumbamiento m; (med) colapso m. **~ible** /kə'læpsəbl/ a plegable

**collar** /'kɒlə(r)/ n cuello m; (for animals) collar m. ● vt (fam) hurtar. **~bone** n clavícula f

**colleague** /'kɒliːg/ n colega m & f

**collect** /kə'lekt/ vt reunir; (hobby) coleccionar; (pick up) recoger; recaudar (rent). ● vi (people) reunirse; (things) acumularse. **~ed** /kə'lektɪd/ a reunido; (person) tranquilo. **~ion** /-ʃn/ n colección f; (in church) colecta f; (of post) recogida f. **~ive** /kə'lektɪv/ a colectivo. **~or** n coleccionista m & f; (of taxes) recaudador m

**college** /'kɒlɪdʒ/ n colegio m; (of art, music etc) escuela f; (univ) colegio m mayor

**collide** /kə'laɪd/ vi chocar

**colliery** /'kɒlɪərɪ/ n mina f de carbón

**collision** /kə'lɪʒn/ n choque m

**colloquial** /kə'ləʊkwɪəl/ a familiar. **~ism** n expresión f familiar

**collusion** /kə'luːʒn/ n connivencia f

**colon** /'kəʊlən/ n (gram) dos puntos mpl; (med) colon m

**colonel** /'kɜːnl/ n coronel m

**colon|ial** /kə'ləʊnɪəl/ a colonial. **~ize** /'kɒlənaɪz/ vt colonizar. **~y** /'kɒlənɪ/ n colonia f

**colossal** /kə'lɒsl/ a colosal

**colour** /'kʌlə(r)/ n color m. **off** ~ (fig) indispuesto. de color(es), en color(es). ● vt colorar; (dye) teñir. ● vi (blush) sonrojarse. **~ bar** n barrera f racial. **~-blind** a daltoniano. **~ed** /'kʌləd/ a de color. **~ful** a lleno de color; (fig) pintoresco. **~less** a incoloro. **~s** npl (flag) bandera f

**colt** /kəʊlt/ n potro m

**column** /'kɒləm/ n columna f. **~ist** /'kɒləmnɪst/ n columnista m & f

**coma** /'kəʊmə/ n coma m

**comb** /kəʊm/ n peine m. ● vt peinar; (search) registrar

**combat** /'kɒmbæt/ n combate m. ● vt (pt **combated**) combatir. **~ant** /-ətənt/ n combatiente m & f

**combination** /kɒmbɪ'neɪʃn/ n combinación f

**combine** /kəm'baɪn/ vt combinar. ● vi combinarse. /'kɒmbaɪn/ n asociación f. **~harvester** n cosechadora f

**combustion** /kəm'bʌstʃən/ n combustión f

**come** /kʌm/ vi (pt **came**, pp **come**) venir; (occur) pasar. ~ **about** ocurrir. ~ **across** encontrarse con (person); encontrar (object). ~ **apart** deshacerse. ~ **away** marcharse. ~ **back** volver. ~ **by** obtener; (pass) pasar. ~ **down** bajar. ~ **in** entrar. ~ **in for** recibir. ~ **into** heredar (money). ~ **off** desprenderse; (succeed) tener éxito. ~ **off it!** (fam) ¡no me vengas con eso! ~ **out** salir; (result) resultar. ~ **round** (after fainting) volver en sí; (be converted) cambiar de idea. ~ **to** llegar a (decision etc). ~ **up** subir; (fig) salir. ~ **up with** proponer (idea)

**comeback** /'kʌmbæk/ n retorno m; (retort) réplica f

**comedian** /kə'miːdɪən/ n cómico m

**comedown** /'kʌmdaʊn/ n revés m

**comedy** /'kɒmədɪ/ n comedia f

**comely** /'kʌmlɪ/ a (**-ier**, **-iest**) (old use) bonito

**comet** /'kɒmɪt/ n cometa m

**comeuppance** /kʌm'ʌpəns/ n (Amer) merecido m

**comf|ort** /'kʌmfət/ n bienestar m; (consolation) consuelo m. ● vt consolar. **~ortable** a cómodo; (wealthy) holgado. **~y** /'kʌmfɪ/ a (fam) cómodo

**comic** /'kɒmɪk/ a cómico. ● n cómico m; (periodical) tebeo m. **~al** a cómico. ~ **strip** n historieta f

**coming** /'kʌmɪŋ/ n llegada f. ● a próximo; (week, month etc) que viene. ~ **and going** ir y venir

**comma** /'kɒmə/ n coma f

**command** /kə'mɑːnd/ n orden f; (mastery) dominio m. ● vt mandar; (deserve) merecer

**commandeer** /kɒmən'dɪə(r)/ vt requisar

**commander** /kə'mɑːndə(r)/ n comandante m

**commanding** /kə'mɑːndɪŋ/. a imponente

**commandment** /kə'mɑːndmənt/ n mandamiento m

**commando** /kə'mɑːndəʊ/ n (pl **-os**) comando m

**commemorat|e** /kə'meməreɪt/ vt conmemorar. **~ion** /-'reɪʃn/ n conmemoración f. **~ive** /-ətɪv/ a conmemorativo

**commence** /kə'mens/ vt/i empezar. **~ment** n principio m

**commend** /kə'mend/ vt alabar; (*entrust*) encomendar. **~able** a loable. **~ation** /kɒmen'deɪʃn/ n elogio m

**commensurate** /kə'menʃərət/ a proporcionado

**comment** /'kɒment/ n observación f. ● vi hacer observaciones

**commentary** /'kɒməntrɪ/ n comentario m; (*radio, TV*) reportaje m

**commentat|e** /'kɒmənteɪt/ vi narrar. **~or** n (*radio, TV*) locutor m

**commerc|e** /'kɒmɜːs/ n comercio m. **~ial** /kə'mɜːʃl/ a comercial. ● n anuncio m. **~ialize** vt comercializar

**commiserat|e** /kə'mɪzəreɪt/ vt compadecer. ● vi compadecerse (**with** de). **~ion** /-'reɪʃn/ n conmiseración f

**commission** /kə'mɪʃn/ n comisión f. **out of ~** fuera de servicio. ● vt encargar; (*mil*) nombrar

**commissionaire** /kəmɪʃə'neə(r)/ n portero m

**commissioner** /kə'mɪʃənə(r)/ n comisario m; (*of police*) jefe m

**commit** /kə'mɪt/ vt (pt **committed**) cometer; (*entrust*) confiar. **~ o.s.** comprometerse. **~ to memory** aprender de memoria. **~ment** n compromiso m

**committee** /kə'mɪtɪ/ n comité m

**commodity** /kə'mɒdətɪ/ n producto m, artículo m

**common** /'kɒmən/ a (**-er, -est**) común; (*usual*) corriente; (*vulgar*) ordinario. ● n ejido m

**commoner** /'kɒmənə(r)/ n plebeyo m

**common: ~ law** n derecho m consuetudinario. **~ly** adv comúnmente. **C~ Market** n Mercado m Común

**commonplace** /'kɒmənpleɪs/ a banal. ● n banalidad f

**common: ~room** n sala f común, salón m común. **~ sense** n sentido m común

**Commonwealth** /'kɒmənwelθ/ n. **the ~** la Mancomunidad f Británica

**commotion** /kə'məʊʃn/ n confusión f

**communal** /'kɒmjʊnl/ a comunal

**commune**[1] /'kɒmjuːn/ n comuna f

**commune**[2] /kə'mjuːn/ vi comunicarse

**communicat|e** /kə'mjuːnɪkeɪt/ vt comunicar. ● vi comunicarse. **~ion**

/-'keɪʃn/ n comunicación f. **~ive** /-ətɪv/ a comunicativo

**communion** /kə'mjuːnɪən/ n comunión f

**communiqué** /kə'mjuːnɪkeɪ/ n comunicado m

**communis|m** /'kɒmjʊnɪsəm/ n comunismo m. **~t** /'kɒmjʊnɪst/ n comunista m & f

**community** /kə'mjuːnətɪ/ n comunidad f. **~ centre** n centro m social

**commute** /kə'mjuːt/ vi viajar diariamente. ● vt (*jurid*) conmutar. **~r** /-ə(r)/ n viajero m diario

**compact** /kəm'pækt/ a compacto. /'kɒmpækt/ n (*for powder*) polvera f. **~ disc** /'kɒm-/ n disco m compacto

**companion** /kəm'pænɪən/ n compañero m. **~ship** n compañerismo m

**company** /'kʌmpənɪ/ n compañía f; (*guests, fam*) visita f; (*com*) sociedad f

**compar|able** /'kɒmpərəbl/ a comparable. **~ative** /kəm'pærətɪv/ a comparativo; (*fig*) relativo. ● n (*gram*) comparativo m. **~e** /kəm'peə(r)/ vt comparar. ● vi poderse comparar. **~ison** /kəm'pærɪsn/ n comparación f

**compartment** /kəm'pɑːtmənt/ n compartimiento m; (*on train*) departamento m

**compass** /'kʌmpəs/ n brújula f. **~es** npl compás m

**compassion** /kəm'pæʃn/ n compasión f. **~ate** a compasivo

**compatib|ility** /kəmpætə'bɪlətɪ/ n compatibilidad f. **~le** /kəm'pætəbl/ a compatible

**compatriot** /kəm'pætrɪət/ n compatriota m & f

**compel** /kəm'pel/ vt (pt **compelled**) obligar. **~ling** a irresistible

**compendium** /kəm'pendɪəm/ n compendio m

**compensat|e** /'kɒmpənseɪt/ vt compensar; (*for loss*) indemnizar. ● vi compensar. **~ion** /-'seɪʃn/ n compensación f; (*financial*) indemnización f

**compère** /'kɒmpeə(r)/ n presentador m. ● vt presentar

**compete** /kəm'piːt/ vi competir

**competen|ce** /'kɒmpətəns/ n competencia f, aptitud f. **~t** /'kɒmpɪtənt/ a competente, capaz

**competit|ion** /kɒmpə'tɪʃn/ n (*contest*) concurso m; (*com*) competencia f. **~ive** /kəm'petətɪv/ a

competidor; ⟨price⟩ competitivo.
**~or** /kəm'petɪtə(r)/ n competidor
m; (in contest) concursante m & f

**compile** /kəm'paɪl/ vt compilar. **~r**
/-ə(r)/ n recopilador m, compilador
m

**complacen|cy** /kəm'pleɪsənsɪ/ n
satisfacción f de sí mismo. **~t**
/kəm'pleɪsnt/ a satisfecho de sí
mismo

**complain** /kəm'pleɪn/ vi. **~ (about)**
quejarse (de). **~ of** (med) sufrir de.
**~t** /kəm'pleɪnt/ n queja f; (med)
enfermedad f

**complement** /'kɒmplɪmənt/ n complemento m. ● vt complementar.
**~ary** /-'mentrɪ/ a complementario

**complet|e** /kəm'pli:t/ a completo;
(finished) acabado; (downright)
total. ● vt acabar; llenar ⟨a form⟩.
**~ely** adv completamente. **~ion**
/-ʃn/ n conclusión f

**complex** /'kɒmpleks/ a complejo.
● n complejo m

**complexion** /kəm'plekʃn/ n tez f;
(fig) aspecto m

**complexity** /kəm'pleksətɪ/ n com-
plejidad f

**complian|ce** /kəm'plaɪəns/ n sumi-
sión f. in **~ce with** de acuerdo con.
**~t** a sumiso

**complicat|e** /'kɒmplɪkeɪt/ vt com-
plicar. **~ed** a complicado. **~ion**
/-'keɪʃn/ n complicación f

**complicity** /kəm'plɪsətɪ/ n com-
plicidad f

**compliment** /'kɒmplɪmənt/ n cumplido m; (amorous) piropo m. ● vt
felicitar. **~ary** /-'mentrɪ/ a hal-
agador; (given free) de favor. **~s** npl
saludos mpl

**comply** /kəm'plaɪ/ vi. **~ with** conformarse con

**component** /kəm'pəʊnənt/ a & n
componente (m)

**compose** /kəm'pəʊz/ vt componer.
**~ o.s.** tranquilizarse. **~d** a sereno

**compos|er** /kəm'pəʊzə(r)/ n com-
positor m. **~ition** /kɒmpə'zɪʃn/ n
composición f

**compost** /'kɒmpɒst/ n abono m

**composure** /kəm'pəʊʒə(r)/ n ser-
enidad f

**compound**[1] /'kɒmpaʊnd/ n compuesto m. ● a compuesto; ⟨fracture⟩
complicado. /kəm'paʊnd/ vt componer; agravar ⟨problem etc⟩. ● vi
(settle) arreglarse

**compound**[2] /'kɒmpaʊnd/ n (enclosure) recinto m

**comprehen|d** /kɒmprɪ'hend/ vt
comprender. **~sion** /kɒmprɪ'henʃn/
n comprensión f

**comprehensive** /kɒmprɪ'hensɪv/ a
extenso; ⟨insurance⟩ a todo riesgo.
**~ school** n instituto m

**compress** /'kɒmpres/ n (med) compresa f. /kəm'pres/ vt comprimir;
(fig) condensar. **~ion** /-ʃn/ n com-
presión f

**comprise** /kəm'praɪz/ vt comprender

**compromise** /'kɒmprəmaɪz/ n
acuerdo m, acomodo m, arreglo m.
● vt comprometer. ● vi llegar a un
acuerdo

**compuls|ion** /kəm'pʌlʃn/ n obli-
gación f, impulso m. **~ive**
/kəm'pʌlsɪv/ a compulsivo. **~ory**
/kəm'pʌlsərɪ/ a obligatorio

**compunction** /kəm'pʌŋkʃn/ n
remordimiento m

**computer** /kəm'pju:tə(r)/ n ordenador m. **~ize** vt instalar ord-
enadores en. **be ~ized** tener
ordenador

**comrade** /'kɒmreɪd/ n camarada m
& f. **~ship** n camaradería f

**con**[1] /kɒn/ vt (pt **conned**) (fam)
estafar. ● n (fam) estafa f

**con**[2] /kɒn/ see **pro and con**

**concave** /'kɒŋkeɪv/ a cóncavo

**conceal** /kən'si:l/ vt ocultar. **~ment**
n encubrimiento m

**concede** /kən'si:d/ vt conceder

**conceit** /kən'si:t/ n vanidad f. **~ed** a
engreído

**conceiv|able** /kən'si:vəbl/ a con-
cebible. **~ably** adv. may **~ably** es
concebible que. **~e** /kən'si:v/ vt/i
concebir

**concentrat|e** /'kɒnsəntreɪt/ vt con-
centrar. ● vi concentrarse. **~ion**
/-'treɪʃn/ n concentración f. **~ion
camp** n campo m de concentración

**concept** /'kɒnsept/ n concepto m

**conception** /kən'sepʃn/ n con-
cepción f

**conceptual** /kən'septʃʊəl/ a conceptual

**concern** /kən'sɜ:n/ n asunto m;
(worry) preocupación f; (com)
empresa f. ● vt tener que ver con;
(deal with) tratar de. **as far as I'm
~ed** en cuanto a mí. **be ~ed about**
preocuparse por. **~ing** prep acerca
de

**concert** /'kɒnsət/ n concierto m. **in ~ de** común acuerdo. **~ed** /kən'sɜ:tɪd/ a concertado

**concertina** /kɒnsə'ti:nə/ n concertina f

**concerto** /kən'tʃɜ:təʊ/ n (pl **-os**) concierto m

**concession** /kən'seʃn/ n concesión f

**conciliat|e** /kən'sɪlɪeɪt/ vt conciliar. **~ion** /-'eɪʃn/ n conciliación f

**concise** /kən'saɪs/ a conciso. **~ly** adv concisamente. **~ness** n concisión f

**conclu|de** /kən'klu:d/ vt concluir. ● vi concluirse. **~ding** a final. **~sion** n conclusión f

**conclusive** /kən'klu:sɪv/ a decisivo. **~ly** adv concluyentemente

**concoct** /kən'kɒkt/ vt confeccionar; (fig) inventar. **~ion** /-ʃn/ n mezcla f; (drink) brebaje m

**concourse** /'kɒŋkɔ:s/ n (rail) vestíbulo m

**concrete** /'kɒŋkri:t/ n hormigón m. ● a concreto. ● vt cubrir con hormigón

**concur** /kən'kɜ:(r)/ vi (pt **concurred**) estar de acuerdo)

**concussion** /kən'kʌʃn/ n conmoción f cerebral

**condemn** /kən'dem/ vt condenar. **~ation** /kɒndem'neɪʃn/ n condenación f, condena f; (censure) censura f

**condens|ation** /kɒnden'seɪʃn/ n condensación f. **~e** /kən'dens/ vt condensar. ● vi condensarse

**condescend** /kɒndɪ'send/ vi dignarse (**to** a). **~ing** a superior

**condiment** /'kɒndɪmənt/ n condimento m

**condition** /kən'dɪʃn/ n condición f. **on ~ that** a condición de que. ● vt condicionar. **~al** a condicional. **~er** n acondicionador m; (for hair) suavizante m

**condolences** /kən'dəʊlənsɪz/ npl pésame m

**condom** /'kɒndɒm/ n condón m

**condone** /kən'dəʊn/ vt condonar

**conducive** /kən'dju:sɪv/ a. **be ~ to** ser favorable a

**conduct** /kən'dʌkt/ vt conducir; dirigir ⟨orchestra⟩. /'kɒndʌkt/ n conducta f. **~or** /kən'dʌktə(r)/ n director m; (of bus) cobrador m. **~ress** n cobradora f

**cone** /kəʊn/ n cono m; (for ice-cream) cucurucho m

**confectioner** /kən'fekʃənə(r)/ n pastelero m. **~y** n dulces mpl, golosinas fpl

**confederation** /kənfedə'reɪʃn/ n confederación f

**confer** /kən'fɜ:(r)/ vt (pt **conferred**) conferir. ● vi consultar

**conference** /'kɒnfərəns/ n congreso m

**confess** /kən'fes/ vt confesar. ● vi confesarse. **~ion** /-ʃn/ n confesión f. **~ional** n confes(i)onario m. **~or** n confesor m

**confetti** /kən'fetɪ/ n confeti m, confetis mpl

**confide** /kən'faɪd/ vt/i confiar

**confiden|ce** /'kɒnfɪdəns/ n confianza f; (secret) confidencia f. **~ce trick** n estafa f, timo m. **~t** /'kɒnfɪdənt/ a seguro

**confidential** /kɒnfɪ'denʃl/ a confidencial

**confine** /kən'faɪn/ vt confinar; (limit) limitar. **~ment** n (imprisonment) prisión f; (med) parto m

**confines** /'kɒnfaɪnz/ npl confines mpl

**confirm** /kən'fɜ:m/ vt confirmar. **~ation** /kɒnfə'meɪʃn/ n confirmación f. **~ed** a inveterado

**confiscat|e** /'kɒnfɪskeɪt/ vt confiscar. **~ion** /-'keɪʃn/ n confiscación f

**conflagration** /kɒnflə'greɪʃn/ n conflagración f

**conflict** /'kɒnflɪkt/ n conflicto m. /kən'flɪkt/ vi chocar. **~ing** /kən-/ a contradictorio

**conform** /kən'fɔ:m/ vt conformar. ● vi conformarse. **~ist** n conformista m & f

**confound** /kən'faʊnd/ vt confundir. **~ed** a (fam) maldito

**confront** /kən'frʌnt/ vt hacer frente a; (face) enfrentarse con. **~ation** /kɒnfrʌn'teɪʃn/ n confrontación f

**confus|e** /kən'fju:z/ vt confundir. **~ing** a desconcertante. **~ion** /-ʒn/ n confusión f

**congeal** /kən'dʒi:l/ vt coagular. ● vi coagularse

**congenial** /kən'dʒi:nɪəl/ a simpático

**congenital** /kən'dʒenɪtl/ a congénito

**congest|ed** /kən'dʒestɪd/ a congestionado. **~ion** /-tʃən/ n congestión f

**congratulat|e** /kən'grætjʊleɪt/ vt felicitar. **~ions** /-'leɪʃnz/ npl felicitaciones fpl

**congregat|e** /'kɒŋgrɪgeɪt/ vi congregarse. **~ion** /-'geɪʃn/ n asamblea f; (relig) fieles mpl, feligreses mpl

**congress** /'kɒŋgres/ n congreso m. **C~** (Amer) el Congreso

**conic(al)** /'kɒnɪk(l)/ a cónico

**conifer** /'kɒnɪfə(r)/ n conífera f

**conjecture** /kən'dʒektʃə(r)/ n conjetura f. ● vt conjeturar. ● vi hacer conjeturas

**conjugal** /'kɒndʒʊgl/ a conyugal

**conjugat|e** /'kɒndʒʊgeɪt/ vt conjugar. **~ion** /-'geɪʃn/ n conjugación f

**conjunction** /kən'dʒʌŋkʃn/ n conjunción f

**conjur|e** /'kʌndʒə(r)/ vi hacer juegos de manos. ● vt. **~ up** evocar. **~or** n prestidigitador m

**conk** /kɒŋk/ vi. **~ out** (sl) fallar; (person) desmayarse

**conker** /'kɒŋkə(r)/ n (fam) castaña f de Indias

**conman** /'kɒnmæn/ n (fam) estafador m, timador m

**connect** /kə'nekt/ vt juntar; (elec) conectar. ● vi unirse; (elec) conectarse. **~ with** (train) enlazar con. **~ed** a unido; (related) relacionado. **be ~ed with** tener que ver con, estar emparentado con

**connection** /kə'nekʃn/ n unión f; (rail) enlace m; (elec, mec) conexión f; (fig) relación f en **~ with** a propósito de, con respecto a. **~s** npl relaciones fpl

**conniv|ance** /kə'naɪvəns/ n connivencia f. **~e** /kə'naɪv/ vi. **~e at** hacer la vista gorda a

**connoisseur** /kɒnə'sɜ:(r)/ n experto m

**connot|ation** /kɒnə'teɪʃn/ n connotación f. **~e** /kə'nəʊt/ vt connotar; (imply) implicar

**conquer** /'kɒŋkə(r)/ vt conquistar; (fig) vencer. **~or** n conquistador m

**conquest** /'kɒŋkwest/ n conquista f

**conscience** /'kɒnʃəns/ n conciencia f

**conscientious** /kɒnʃɪ'enʃəs/ a concienzudo

**conscious** /'kɒnʃəs/ a consciente; (deliberate) intencional. **~ly** adv a sabiendas. **~ness** n consciencia f; (med) conocimiento m

**conscript** /'kɒnskrɪpt/ n recluta m. /kən'skrɪpt/ vt reclutar. **~ion** /kən'skrɪpʃn/ n reclutamiento m

**consecrat|e** /'kɒnsɪkreɪt/ vt consagrar. **~ion** /-'kreɪʃn/ n consagración f

**consecutive** /kən'sekjʊtɪv/ a sucesivo

**consensus** /kən'sensəs/ n consenso m

**consent** /kən'sent/ vi consentir. ● n consentimiento m

**consequen|ce** /'kɒnsɪkwəns/ n consecuencia f. **~t** /'kɒnsɪkwənt/ a consiguiente. **~tly** adv por consiguiente

**conservation** /kɒnsə'veɪʃn/ n conservación f, preservación f. **~ist** /kɒnsə'veɪʃənɪst/ n conservacionista m & f

**conservative** /kən'sɜ:vətɪv/ a conservador; (modest) prudente, moderado. **C~** a & n conservador (m)

**conservatory** /kən'sɜ:vətrɪ/ n (greenhouse) invernadero m

**conserve** /kən'sɜ:v/ vt conservar

**consider** /kən'sɪdə(r)/ vt considerar; (take into account) tomar en cuenta. **~able** /kən'sɪdərəbl/ a considerable. **~ably** adv considerablemente

**considerat|e** /kən'sɪdərət/ a considerado. **~ion** /-'reɪʃn/ n consideración f

**considering** /kən'sɪdərɪŋ/ prep en vista de

**consign** /kən'saɪn/ vt consignar; (send) enviar. **~ment** n envío m

**consist** /kən'sɪst/ vi. **~ of** consistir en

**consistency** /kən'sɪstənsɪ/ n consistencia f; (fig) coherencia f

**consistent** /kən'sɪstənt/ a coherente; (unchanging) constante. **~ with** compatible con. **~ly** adv constantemente

**consolation** /kɒnsə'leɪʃn/ n consuelo m

**console** /kən'səʊl/ vt consolar

**consolidat|e** /kən'sɒlɪdeɪt/ vt consolidar. ● vi consolidarse. **~ion** /-'deɪʃn/ n consolidación f

**consonant** /'kɒnsənənt/ n consonante f

**consort** /'kɒnsɔ:t/ n consorte m & f. /kən'sɔ:t/ vi. **~ with** asociarse con

**consortium** /kən'sɔ:tɪəm/ n (pl -tia) consorcio m

**conspicuous** /kən'spɪkjʊəs/ a (easily seen) visible; (showy) llamativo; (noteworthy) notable

**conspir|acy** /kən'spɪrəsɪ/ n complot m, conspiración f. **~e** /kən'spaɪə(r)/ vi conspirar

**constab|le** /'kʌnstəbl/ n policía m,
guardia m. **~ulary** /kən'stæbjʊlərɪ/
n policía f
**constant** /'kɒnstənt/ a constante.
**~ly** adv constantemente
**constellation** /kɒnstə'leɪʃn/ n constelación f
**consternation** /kɒnstə'neɪʃn/ n consternación f
**constipat|ed** /'kɒnstɪpeɪtɪd/ a
estreñido. **~ion** /-'peɪʃn/ n estreñ-
imiento m
**constituen|cy** /kən'stɪtjʊənsɪ/ n dis-
trito m electoral. **~t** /kən'stɪtjʊənt/
n componente m; (pol) elector m
**constitut|e** /'kɒnstɪtjuːt/ vt consti-
tuir. **~ion** /-'tjuːʃn/ n constitución f.
**~ional** /-'tjuːʃənl/ a constitucional.
● n paseo m
**constrain** /kən'streɪn/ vt forzar,
obligar, constreñir. **~t**
/kən'streɪnt/ n fuerza f
**constrict** /kən'strɪkt/ vt apretar.
**~ion** /-ʃn/ n constricción f
**construct** /kən'strʌkt/ vt construir.
**~ion** /-ʃn/ n construcción f. **~ive**
/kən'strʌktɪv/ a constructivo
**construe** /kən'struː/ vt interpretar;
(gram) construir
**consul** /'kɒnsl/ n cónsul m. **~ar**
/-jʊlə(r)/ a consular. **~ate** /-ət/ n
consulado m
**consult** /kən'sʌlt/ vt/i consultar.
**~ant** /kən'sʌltənt/ n asesor m;
(med) especialista m & f; (tec) consejero m técnico. **~ation**
/kɒnsəl'teɪʃn/ n consulta f
**consume** /kən'sjuːm/ vt consumir;
(eat) comer; (drink) beber. **~r** /-ə(r)/
n consumidor m. ● a de consumo.
**~rism** /kən'sjuːmərɪzəm/ n protección f del consumidor, con-
sumismo m
**consummat|e** /'kɒnsəmeɪt/ vt con-
sumar. **~ion** /-'meɪʃn/ n con-
sumación f
**consumption** /kən'sʌmpʃn/ n consumo m; (med) tisis f
**contact** /'kɒntækt/ n contacto m.
● vt ponerse en contacto con
**contagious** /kən'teɪdʒəs/ a contagioso
**contain** /kən'teɪn/ vt contener. **~**
o.s. contenerse. **~er** n recipiente m;
(com) contenedor m
**contaminat|e** /kən'tæmɪneɪt/ vt con-
taminar. **~ion** /-'neɪʃn/ n contaminación f

**contemplat|e** /'kɒntəmpleɪt/ vt
contemplar; (consider) considerar.
**~ion** /-'pleɪʃn/ n contemplación f
**contemporary** /kən'tempərərɪ/ a &
n contemporáneo (m)
**contempt** /kən'tempt/ n desprecio
m. **~ible** a despreciable. **~uous**
/-tjʊəs/ a desdeñoso
**contend** /kən'tend/ vt sostener. ● vi
contender. **~er** n contendiente m &
f
**content¹** /kən'tent/ a satisfecho. ● vt
contentar
**content²** /'kɒntent/ n contenido m
**contented** /kən'tentɪd/ a satisfecho
**contention** /kən'tenʃn/ n contienda
f; (opinion) opinión f, argumento m
**contentment** /kən'tentmənt/ n contento m
**contest** /'kɒntest/ n (competition)
concurso m; (fight) contienda f.
/kən'test/ vt disputar. **~ant** n contendiente m & f, concursante m & f
**context** /'kɒntekst/ n contexto m
**continent** /'kɒntɪnənt/ n continente
m. the C~ Europa f. **~al** /-'nentl/ a
continental
**contingency** /kən'tɪndʒənsɪ/ n con-
tingencia f
**contingent** /kən'tɪndʒənt/ a & n con-
tingente (m)
**continu|al** /kən'tɪnjʊəl/ a continuo.
**~ance** /kən'tɪnjʊəns/ n continuación f. **~ation** /-ʊ'eɪʃn/ n continuación f. **~e** /kən'tɪnjuː/ vt/i
continuar; (resume) seguir. **~ed** a
continuo. **~ity** /kɒntɪ'njuːɪtɪ/ n con-
tinuidad f. **~ity girl** (cinema, TV)
secretaria f de rodaje. **~ous**
/kən'tɪnjʊəs/ a continuo. **~ously**
adv continuamente
**contort** /kən'tɔːt/ vt retorcer. **~ion**
/-ʃn/ n contorsión f. **~ionist**
/-ʃənɪst/ n contorsionista m & f
**contour** /'kɒntʊə(r)/ n contorno m.
**~ line** n curva f de nivel
**contraband** /'kɒntrəbænd/ n contrabando m
**contracepti|on** /kɒntrə'sepʃn/ n
contracepción f. **~ve** /kɒntrə-
'septɪv/ a & n anticonceptivo (m)
**contract** /'kɒntrækt/ n contrato m.
/kən'trækt/ vt contraer. ● vi con-
traerse. **~ion** /kən'trækʃn/ n contracción f. **~or** /kən'træktə(r)/ n
contratista m & f
**contradict** /kɒntrə'dɪkt/ vt con-
tradecir. **~ion** /-ʃn/ n contradicción
f. **~ory** a contradictorio

**contraption** /kən'træpʃn/ n (fam) artilugio m

**contrary** /'kɒntrərɪ/ a & n contrario (m). on the ~ al contrario. ● adv. ~ to contrariamente a. /kən'treərɪ/ a terco

**contrast** /'kɒntrɑːst/ n contraste m. /kən'trɑːst/ vt poner en contraste. ● vi contrastar. ~ing a contrastante

**contraven|e** /kɒntrə'viːn/ vt contravenir. ~tion /-'venʃn/ n contravención f

**contribut|e** /kən'trɪbjuːt/ vt/i contribuir. ~e to escribir para (newspaper). ~ion /kɒntrɪ'bjuːʃn/ n contribución f; (from salary) cotización f. ~or n contribuyente m & f; (to newspaper) colaborador m

**contrite** /'kɒntraɪt/ a arrepentido, pesaroso

**contriv|ance** /kən'traɪvəns/ n invención f. ~e /kən'traɪv/ vt idear. ~e to conseguir

**control** /kən'trəʊl/ vt (pt controlled) controlar. ● n control m. ~s npl (mec) mandos mpl

**controvers|ial** /kɒntrə'vɜːʃl/ a polémico, discutible. ~y /'kɒntrəvɜːsɪ/ n controversia f

**conundrum** /kə'nʌndrəm/ n adivinanza f; (problem) enigma m

**conurbation** /kɒnɜː'beɪʃn/ n conurbación f

**convalesce** /kɒnvə'les/ vi convalecer. ~nce n convalecencia f. ~nt a & n convaleciente (m & f). ~nt home n casa f de convalecencia

**convector** /kən'vektə(r)/ n estufa f de convección

**convene** /kən'viːn/ vt convocar. ● vi reunirse

**convenien|ce** /kən'viːnɪəns/ n conveniencia f, comodidad f. all modern ~ces todas las comodidades. at your ~ce según le convenga. ~ces npl servicios mpl. ~t /kən'viːnɪənt/ a cómodo; (place) bien situado; (time) oportuno. be ~t convenir. ~tly adv convenientemente

**convent** /'kɒnvənt/ n convento m

**convention** /kən'venʃn/ n convención f; (meeting) congreso m. ~al a convencional

**converge** /kən'vɜːdʒ/ vi convergir

**conversant** /kən'vɜːsənt/ a. ~ with versado en

**conversation** /kɒnvə'seɪʃn/ n conversación f. ~al a de la conversación. ~alist n hábil conversador m

**converse**[1] /kən'vɜːs/ vi conversar

**converse**[2] /'kɒnvɜːs/ a inverso. ● n lo contrario. ~ly adv a la inversa

**conver|sion** /kən'vɜːʃn/ n conversión f. ~t /kən'vɜːt/ vt convertir. /'kɒnvɜːt/ n converso m. ~tible /kən'vɜːtɪbl/ a convertible. ● n (auto) descapotable m

**convex** /'kɒnveks/ a convexo

**convey** /kən'veɪ/ vt llevar; transportar (goods); comunicar (idea, feeling). ~ance n transporte m. ~or belt n cinta f transportadora

**convict** /kən'vɪkt/ vt condenar. /'kɒnvɪkt/ n presidiario m. ~ion /kən'vɪkʃn/ n condena f; (belief) creencia f

**convinc|e** /kən'vɪns/ vt convencer. ~ing a convincente

**convivial** /kən'vɪvɪəl/ a alegre

**convoke** /kən'vəʊk/ vt convocar

**convoluted** /'kɒnvəluːtɪd/ a enrollado; (argument) complicado

**convoy** /'kɒnvɔɪ/ n convoy m

**convuls|e** /kən'vʌls/ vt convulsionar. be ~ed with laughter desternillarse de risa. ~ion /-ʃn/ n convulsión f

**coo** /kuː/ vi arrullar

**cook** /kʊk/ vt cocinar; (alter, fam) falsificar. ~ up (fam) inventar. ● n cocinero m

**cooker** /'kʊkə(r)/ n cocina f

**cookery** /'kʊkərɪ/ n cocina f

**cookie** /'kʊkɪ/ n (Amer) galleta f

**cool** /kuːl/ a (-er, -est) fresco; (calm) tranquilo; (unfriendly) frío. ● n fresco m; (sl) calma f. ● vt enfriar. ● vi enfriarse. ~ down (person) calmarse. ~ly adv tranquilamente. ~ness n frescura f

**coop** /kuːp/ n gallinero m. ● vt. ~ up encerrar

**co-operat|e** /kəʊ'ɒpəreɪt/ vi cooperar. ~ion /-'reɪʃn/ n cooperación f

**cooperative** /kəʊ'ɒpərətɪv/ a cooperativo. ● n cooperativa f

**co-opt** /kəʊ'ɒpt/ vt cooptar

**co-ordinat|e** /kəʊ'ɔːdɪneɪt/ vt coordinar. ~ion /-'neɪʃn/ n coordinación f

**cop** /kɒp/ vt (pt copped) (sl) prender. ● n (sl) policía m

**cope** /kəʊp/ vi (fam) arreglárselas. ~ **with** enfrentarse con

**copious** /'kəʊpɪəs/ a abundante

**copper**¹ /'kɒpə(r)/ n cobre m; (coin) perra f. ● a de cobre

**copper**² /'kɒpə(r)/ n (sl) policía m

**coppice** /'kɒpɪs/ n, **copse** /kɒps/ n bosquecillo m

**Coptic** /'kɒptɪk/ a copto

**copulat|e** /'kɒpjʊleɪt/ vi copular. ~**ion** /-'leɪʃn/ n cópula f

**copy** /'kɒpɪ/ n copia f; (typ) material m. ● vt copiar

**copyright** /'kɒpɪraɪt/ n derechos mpl de autor

**copy-writer** /'kɒpɪraɪtə(r)/ n redactor m de textos publicitarios

**coral** /'kɒrəl/ n coral m

**cord** /kɔːd/ n cuerda f; (fabric) pana f. ~**s** npl pantalones mpl de pana

**cordial** /'kɔːdɪəl/ a & n cordial (m)

**cordon** /'kɔːdn/ n cordón m. ● vt. ~ **off** acordonar

**corduroy** /'kɔːdərɔɪ/ n pana f

**core** /kɔː(r)/ n (of apple) corazón m; (fig) meollo m

**cork** /kɔːk/ n corcho m. ● vt taponar. ~**screw** /'kɔːkskruː/ n sacacorchos m invar

**corn**¹ /kɔːn/ n (wheat) trigo m; (Amer) maíz m; (seed) grano m

**corn**² /kɔːn/ n (hard skin) callo m

**corned** /'kɔːnd/ a. ~ **beef** n carne f de vaca en lata

**corner** /'kɔːnə(r)/ n ángulo m; (inside) rincón m; (outside) esquina f; (football) saque m de esquina. ● vt arrinconar; (com) acaparar. ~**stone** n piedra f angular

**cornet** /'kɔːnɪt/ n (mus) corneta f; (for ice-cream) cucurucho m

**cornflakes** /'kɔːnfleɪks/ npl copos mpl de maíz

**cornflour** /'kɔːnflaʊə(r)/ n harina f de maíz

**cornice** /'kɔːnɪs/ n cornisa f

**cornucopia** /kɔːnjʊ'kəʊpɪə/ n cuerno m de la abundancia

**Corn|ish** /'kɔːnɪʃ/ a de Cornualles. ~**wall** /'kɔːnwəl/ n Cornualles f

**corny** /'kɔːnɪ/ a (trite, fam) gastado; (mawkish) sentimental, sensiblero

**corollary** /kə'rɒlərɪ/ n corolario m

**coronary** /'kɒrənərɪ/ n trombosis f coronaria

**coronation** /kɒrə'neɪʃn/ n coronación f

**coroner** /'kɒrənə(r)/ n juez m de primera instancia

**corporal**¹ /'kɔːpərəl/ n cabo m

**corporal**² /'kɔːpərəl/ a corporal

**corporate** /'kɔːpərət/ a corporativo

**corporation** /kɔːpə'reɪʃn/ n corporación f; (of town) ayuntamiento m

**corps** /kɔː(r)/ n (pl **corps** /kɔːz/) cuerpo m

**corpse** /kɔːps/ n cadáver m

**corpulent** /'kɔːpjʊlənt/ a gordo, corpulento

**corpuscle** /'kɔːpʌsl/ n glóbulo m

**corral** /kə'rɑːl/ n (Amer) corral m

**correct** /kə'rekt/ a correcto; (time) exacto. ● vt corregir. ~**ion** /-ʃn/ n corrección f

**correlat|e** /'kɒrəleɪt/ vt poner en correlación. ~**ion** /-'leɪʃn/ n correlación f

**correspond** /kɒrɪ'spɒnd/ vi corresponder; (write) escribirse. ~**ence** n correspondencia f. ~**ent** n corresponsal m & f

**corridor** /'kɒrɪdɔː(r)/ n pasillo m

**corroborate** /kə'rɒbəreɪt/ vt corroborar

**corro|de** /kə'rəʊd/ vt corroer. ● vi corroerse. ~**sion** n corrosión f

**corrugated** /'kɒrəgeɪtɪd/ a ondulado. ~ **iron** n hierro m ondulado

**corrupt** /kə'rʌpt/ a corrompido. ● vt corromper. ~**ion** /-ʃn/ n corrupción f

**corset** /'kɔːsɪt/ n corsé m

**Corsica** /'kɔːsɪkə/ n Córcega f. ~**n** a & n corso (m)

**cortège** /kɔːteɪʒ/ n cortejo m

**cos** /kɒs/ n lechuga f romana

**cosh** /kɒʃ/ n cachiporra f. ● vt aporrear

**cosiness** /'kəʊzɪnɪs/ n comodidad f

**cosmetic** /kɒz'metɪk/ a & n cosmético (m)

**cosmic** /'kɒzmɪk/ a cósmico

**cosmonaut** /'kɒzmənɔːt/ n cosmonauta m & f

**cosmopolitan** /kɒzmə'pɒlɪtən/ a & n cosmopolita (m & f)

**cosmos** /'kɒzmɒs/ n cosmos m

**Cossack** /'kɒsæk/ a & n cosaco (m)

**cosset** /'kɒsɪt/ vt (pt **cosseted**) mimar

**cost** /kɒst/ vi (pt cost) costar, valer. ● vt (pt costed) calcular el coste de. ● n precio m. **at all** ~**s** cueste lo que cueste. **to one's** ~ a sus expensas. ~**s** npl (jurid) costas fpl

**Costa Rica** /kɒstə'riːkə/ n Costa f Rica. ~**n** a & n costarricense (m & f), costarriqueño (m)

**costly** /'kɒstlɪ/ *a* (**-ier, -iest**) caro, costoso

**costume** /'kɒstjuːm/ *n* traje *m*

**cosy** /'kəʊzɪ/ *a* (**-ier, -iest**) cómodo; ⟨*place*⟩ acogedor. ● *n* cubierta *f* (de tetera)

**cot** /kɒt/ *n* cuna *f*

**cottage** /'kɒtɪdʒ/ *n* casita *f* de campo. ~ **cheese** *n* requesón *m*. ~ **industry** *n* industria *f* casera. ~ **pie** *n* carne *f* picada con puré de patatas

**cotton** /'kɒtn/ *n* algodón *m*. ● *vi.* ~ **on** (*sl*) comprender. ~ **wool** *n* algodón hidrófilo

**couch** /kaʊtʃ/ *n* sofá *m*. ● *vt* expresar

**couchette** /kuː'ʃet/ *n* litera *f*

**cough** /kɒf/ *vi* toser. ● *n* tos *f*. ~ **up** (*sl*) pagar. ~ **mixture** *n* jarabe *m* para la tos

**could** /kʊd, kəd/ *pt of* **can**

**couldn't** /'kʊdnt/ = **could not**

**council** /'kaʊnsl/ *n* consejo *m*; (*of town*) ayuntamiento *m*. ~ **house** *n* vivienda *f* protegida. ~**lor** /'kaʊnsələ(r)/ *n* concejal *m*

**counsel** /'kaʊnsl/ *n* consejo *m*; (*pl invar*) (*jurid*) abogado *m*. ~**lor** *n* consejero *m*

**count**[1] /kaʊnt/ *n* recuento *m*. ● *vt/i* contar

**count**[2] /kaʊnt/ *n* (*nobleman*) conde *m*

**countdown** /'kaʊntdaʊn/ *n* cuenta *f* atrás

**countenance** /'kaʊntɪnəns/ *n* semblante *m*. ● *vt* aprobar

**counter** /'kaʊntə(r)/ *n* (*in shop etc*) mostrador *m*; (*token*) ficha *f*. ● *adv*. ~ **to** en contra de. ● *a* opuesto. ● *vt* oponerse a; parar ⟨*blow*⟩. ● *vi* contraatacar

**counter...** /'kaʊntə(r)/ *pref* contra...

**counteract** /kaʊntər'ækt/ *vt* contrarrestar

**counter-attack** /'kaʊntərətæk/ *n* contraataque *m*. ● *vt/i* contraatacar

**counterbalance** /'kaʊntəbæləns/ *n* contrapeso *m*. ● *vt/i* contrapesar

**counterfeit** /'kaʊntəfɪt/ *a* falsificado. ● *n* falsificación *f*. ● *vt* falsificar

**counterfoil** /'kaʊntəfɔɪl/ *n* talón *m*

**counterpart** /'kaʊntəpɑːt/ *n* equivalente *m*; (*person*) homólogo *m*

**counter-productive** /'kaʊntəprə'dʌktɪv/ *a* contraproducente

**countersign** /'kaʊntəsaɪn/ *vt* refrendar

**countess** /'kaʊntɪs/ *n* condesa *f*

**countless** /'kaʊntlɪs/ *a* innumerable

**countrified** /'kʌntrɪfaɪd/ *a* rústico

**country** /'kʌntrɪ/ *n* (*native land*) país *m*; (*countryside*) campo *m*. ~ **folk** *n* gente *f* del campo. **go to the** ~ ir al campo; (*pol*) convocar elecciones generales

**countryman** /'kʌntrɪmən/ *n* (*pl -men*) campesino *m*; (*of one's own country*) compatriota *m*

**countryside** /'kʌntrɪsaɪd/ *n* campo *m*

**county** /'kaʊntɪ/ *n* condado *m*, provincia *f*

**coup** /kuː/ *n* golpe *m*

**coupé** /'kuːpeɪ/ *n* cupé *m*

**couple** /'kʌpl/ *n* (*of things*) par *m*; (*of people*) pareja *f*; (*married*) matrimonio *m*. **a** ~ **of** un par de. ● *vt* unir; (*tec*) acoplar. ● *vi* copularse

**coupon** /'kuːpɒn/ *n* cupón *m*

**courage** /'kʌrɪdʒ/ *n* valor *m*. ~**ous** /kə'reɪdʒəs/ *a* valiente. ~**ously** *adv* valientemente

**courgette** /kʊə'ʒet/ *n* calabacín *m*

**courier** /'kʊrɪə(r)/ *n* mensajero *m*; (*for tourists*) guía *m* & *f*

**course** /kɔːs/ *n* curso *m*; (*behaviour*) conducta *f*; (*aviat, naut*) rumbo *m*; (*culin*) plato *m*; (*for golf*) campo *m*. **in due** ~ a su debido tiempo. **in the** ~ **of** en el transcurso de, durante. **of** ~ desde luego, por supuesto

**court** /kɔːt/ *n* corte *f*; (*tennis*) pista *f*; (*jurid*) tribunal *m*. ● *vt* cortejar; buscar ⟨*danger*⟩

**courteous** /'kɜːtɪəs/ *a* cortés

**courtesan** /kɔːtɪ'zæn/ *n* (*old use*) cortesana *f*

**courtesy** /'kɜːtəsɪ/ *n* cortesía *f*

**court:** ~**ier** /'kɔːtɪə(r)/ *n* (*old use*) cortesano *m*. ~ **martial** *n* (*pl courts martial*) consejo *m* de guerra. ~**martial** *vt* (*pt* ~**martialled**) juzgar en consejo de guerra. ~**ship** /'kɔːtʃɪp/ *n* cortejo *m*

**courtyard** /'kɔːtjɑːd/ *n* patio *m*

**cousin** /'kʌzn/ *n* primo *m*. **first** ~ primo carnal. **second** ~ primo segundo

**cove** /kəʊv/ *n* cala *f*

**covenant** /'kʌvənənt/ *n* acuerdo *m*

**Coventry** /'kɒvntrɪ/ *n*. **send to** ~ hacer el vacío

**cover** /'kʌvə(r)/ *vt* cubrir; (*journalism*) hacer un reportaje sobre. ~

**up** cubrir; (*fig*) ocultar. ● *n* cubierta *f*; (*shelter*) abrigo *m*; (*lid*) tapa *f*; (*for furniture*) funda *f*; (*pretext*) pretexto *m*; (*of magazine*) portada *f*. ~**age** /'kʌvərɪdʒ/ *n* reportaje *m*. ~ **charge** *n* precio *m* del cubierto. ~**ing** *n* cubierta *f*. ~**ing letter** *n* carta *f* explicatoria, carta *f* adjunta

**covet** /'kʌvɪt/ *vt* codiciar

**cow** /kaʊ/ *n* vaca *f*

**coward** /'kaʊəd/ *n* cobarde *m*. ~**ly** *a* cobarde. ~**ice** /'kaʊədɪs/ *n* cobardía *f*

**cowboy** /'kaʊbɔɪ/ *n* vaquero *m*

**cower** /'kaʊə(r)/ *vi* encogerse, acobardarse

**cowl** /kaʊl/ *n* capucha *f*; (*of chimney*) sombrerete *m*

**cowshed** /'kaʊʃed/ *n* establo *m*

**coxswain** /'kɒksn/ *n* timonel *m*

**coy** /kɔɪ/ *a* (**-er, -est**) (falsamente) tímido, remilgado

**crab**[1] /kræb/ *n* cangrejo *m*

**crab**[2] /kræb/ *vi* (*pt* **crabbed**) quejarse

**crab-apple** /'kræbæpl/ *n* manzana *f* silvestre

**crack** /kræk/ *n* grieta *f*; (*noise*) crujido *m*; (*of whip*) chasquido *m*; (*joke, sl*) chiste *m*. ● *a* (*fam*) de primera. ● *vt* agrietar; chasquear ⟨whip, fingers⟩; cascar ⟨nut⟩; gastar ⟨joke⟩; resolver ⟨problem⟩. ● *vi* agrietarse. **get** ~**ing** (*fam*) darse prisa. ~ **down on** (*fam*) tomar medidas enérgicas contra. ~ **up** *vi* fallar; ⟨person⟩ volverse loco. ~**ed** /krækt/ *a* (*sl*) chiflado

**cracker** /'krækə(r)/ *n* petardo *m*; (*culin*) galleta *f* (soso); (*culin, Amer*) galleta *f*

**crackers** /'krækəz/ *a* (*sl*) chiflado

**crackl|e** /'krækl/ *vi* crepitar. ● *n* crepitación *f*, crujido *m*. ~**ing** /'kræklɪŋ/ *n* crepitación *f*, crujido *m*; (*of pork*) chicharrón *m*

**crackpot** /'krækpɒt/ *n* (*sl*) chiflado *m*

**cradle** /'kreɪdl/ *n* cuna *f*. ● *vt* acunar

**craft** /krɑːft/ *n* destreza *f*; (*technique*) arte *f*; (*cunning*) astucia *f*. ● *n invar* (*boat*) barco *m*

**craftsman** /'krɑːftsmən/ *n* (*pl* **-men**) artesano *m*. ~**ship** *n* artesanía *f*

**crafty** /'krɑːftɪ/ *a* (**-ier, -iest**) astuto

**crag** /kræg/ *n* despeñadero *m*. ~**gy** *a* peñascoso

**cram** /kræm/ *vt* (*pt* **crammed**) rellenar. ~ **with** llenar de. ● *vi* (*for exams*) empollar. ~**-full** *a* atestado

**cramp** /kræmp/ *n* calambre *m*

**cramped** /kræmpt/ *a* apretado

**cranberry** /'krænbərɪ/ *n* arándano *m*

**crane** /kreɪn/ *n* grúa *f*; (*bird*) grulla *f*. ● *vt* estirar ⟨neck⟩

**crank**[1] /kræŋk/ *n* manivela *f*

**crank**[2] /kræŋk/ *n* (*person*) excéntrico *m*. ~**y** *a* excéntrico

**cranny** /'krænɪ/ *n* grieta *f*

**crash** /kræʃ/ *n* accidente *m*; (*noise*) estruendo *m*; (*collision*) choque *m*; (*com*) quiebra *f*. ● *vt* estrellar. ● *vi* quebrar con estrépito; (*have accident*) tener un accidente; ⟨car etc⟩ chocar; (*fail*) fracasar. ~ **course** *n* curso *m* intensivo. ~**-helmet** *n* casco *m* protector. ~**land** *vi* hacer un aterrizaje de emergencia, hacer un aterrizaje forzoso

**crass** /kræs/ *a* craso, burdo

**crate** /kreɪt/ *n* cajón *m*. ● *vt* embalar

**crater** /'kreɪtə(r)/ *n* cráter *m*

**cravat** /krə'væt/ *n* corbata *f*, fular *m*

**crav|e** /kreɪv/ *vi*. ~**e for** anhelar. ~**ing** *n* ansia *f*

**crawl** /krɔːl/ *vi* andar a gatas; (*move slowly*) avanzar lentamente; (*drag o.s.*) arrastrarse. ● *n* (*swimming*) crol *m*. **at a** ~ a paso lento. ~ **to** humillarse ante. ~ **with** hervir de

**crayon** /'kreɪən/ *n* lápiz *m* de color

**craze** /kreɪz/ *n* manía *f*

**craz|iness** /'kreɪzɪnɪs/ *n* locura *f*. ~**y** /'kreɪzɪ/ *a* (**-ier, -iest**) loco. **be** ~**y about** andar loco por. ~**y paving** *n* enlosado *m* irregular

**creak** /kriːk/ *n* crujido *m*; (*of hinge*) chirrido *m*. ● *vi* crujir; ⟨hinge⟩ chirriar

**cream** /kriːm/ *n* crema *f*; (*fresh*) nata *f*. ● *a* (*colour*) color de crema. ● *vt* (*remove*) desnatar; (*beat*) batir. ~ **cheese** *n* queso *m* de nata. ~**y** *a* cremoso

**crease** /kriːs/ *n* pliegue *m*; (*crumple*) arruga *f*. ● *vt* plegar; (*wrinkle*) arrugar. ● *vi* arrugarse

**creat|e** /kriː'eɪt/ *vt* crear. ~**ion** /-ʃn/ *n* creación *f*. ~**ive** *a* creativo. ~**or** *n* creador *m*

**creature** /'kriːtʃə(r)/ *n* criatura *f*, bicho *m*, animal *m*

**crèche** /kreɪʃ/ *n* guardería *f* infantil

**credence** /'kriːdns/ *n* creencia *f*, fe *f*

**credentials** /krɪ'denʃlz/ *npl* credenciales *mpl*

**credib|ility** /kredə'bɪlətɪ/ *n* credibilidad *f*. ~**le** /'kredəbl/ *a* creíble

**credit** /'kredɪt/ *n* crédito *m*; (*honour*) honor *m*. **take the** ~ **for** atribuirse el mérito de. ● *vt* (*pt* **credited**) acreditar; (*believe*) creer. ~ **s.o. with** atribuir a uno. ~**able** *a* loable. ~ **card** *n* tarjeta *f* de crédito. ~**or** *n* acreedor *m*

**credulous** /'krədjʊləs/ *a* crédulo

**creed** /kri:d/ *n* credo *m*

**creek** /kri:k/ *n* ensenada *f*. **up the** ~ (*sl*) en apuros

**creep** /kri:p/ *vi* (*pt* **crept**) arrastrarse; (*plant*) trepar. ● *n* (*sl*) persona *f* desagradable. ~**er** *n* enredadera *f*. ~**s** /kri:ps/ *npl*. **give s.o. the** ~**s** dar repugnancia a uno

**cremat|e** /krɪ'meɪt/ *vt* incinerar. ~**ion** /-ʃn/ *n* cremación *f*. ~**orium** /kremə'tɔ:rɪəm/ *n* (*pl* **-ia**) crematorio *m*

**Creole** /'kri:əʊl/ *a* & *n* criollo (*m*)

**crêpe** /kreɪp/ *n* crespón *m*

**crept** /krept/ *see* **creep**

**crescendo** /krɪ'ʃendəʊ/ *n* (*pl* **-os**) crescendo *m*

**crescent** /'kresnt/ *n* media luna *f*; (*street*) calle *f* en forma de media luna

**cress** /kres/ *n* berro *m*

**crest** /krest/ *n* cresta *f*; (*coat of arms*) blasón *m*

**Crete** /kri:t/ *n* Creta *f*

**cretin** /'kretɪn/ *n* cretino *m*

**crevasse** /krɪ'væs/ *n* grieta *f*

**crevice** /'krevɪs/ *n* grieta *f*

**crew**[1] /kru:/ *n* tripulación *f*; (*gang*) pandilla *f*

**crew**[2] /kru:/ *see* **crow**[2]

**crew:** ~ **cut** *n* corte *m* al rape. ~ **neck** *n* cuello *m* redondo

**crib** /krɪb/ *n* cuna *f*; (*relig*) belén *m*; (*plagiarism*) plagio *m*. ● *vt/i* (*pt* **cribbed**) plagiar

**crick** /krɪk/ *n* calambre *m*; (*in neck*) tortícolis *f*

**cricket**[1] /'krɪkɪt/ *n* criquet *m*

**cricket**[2] /'krɪkɪt/ *n* (*insect*) grillo *m*

**cricketer** /'krɪkɪtə(r)/ *n* jugador *m* de criquet

**crim|e** /kraɪm/ *n* crimen *m*; (*acts*) criminalidad *f*. ~**inal** /'krɪmɪnl/ *a* & *n* criminal (*m*)

**crimp** /krɪmp/ *vt* rizar

**crimson** /'krɪmzn/ *a* & *n* carmesí (*m*)

**cringe** /krɪndʒ/ *vi* encogerse; (*fig*) humillarse

**crinkle** /'krɪŋkl/ *vt* arrugar. ● *vi* arrugarse. ● *n* arruga *f*

**crinoline** /'krɪnəlɪn/ *n* miriñaque *m*

**cripple** /'krɪpl/ *n* lisiado *m*, mutilado *m*. ● *vt* lisiar; (*fig*) paralizar

**crisis** /'kraɪsɪs/ *n* (*pl* **crises** /'kraɪsi:z/) crisis *f*

**crisp** /krɪsp/ *a* (**-er, -est**) (*culin*) crujiente; (*air*) vigorizador. ~**s** *npl* patatas *fpl* fritas a la inglesa

**criss-cross** /'krɪskrɒs/ *a* entrecruzado. ● *vt* entrecruzar. ● *vi* entrecruzarse

**criterion** /kraɪ'tɪərɪən/ *n* (*pl* **-ia**) criterio *m*

**critic** /'krɪtɪk/ *n* crítico *m*

**critical** /'krɪtɪkl/ *a* crítico. ~**ly** *adv* críticamente; (*ill*) gravemente

**critici|sm** /'krɪtɪsɪzəm/ *n* crítica *f*. ~**ze** /'krɪtɪsaɪz/ *vt/i* criticar

**croak** /krəʊk/ *n* (*of person*) gruñido *m*; (*of frog*) canto *m*. ● *vi* gruñir; (*frog*) croar

**crochet** /'krəʊʃeɪ/ *n* croché *m*, ganchillo *m*. ● *vt* hacer ganchillo

**crock**[1] /krɒk/ *n* (*person*, *fam*) vejancón *m*; (*old car*) cacharro *m*

**crock**[2] /krɒk/ *n* vasija *f* de loza

**crockery** /'krɒkərɪ/ *n* loza *f*

**crocodile** /'krɒkədaɪl/ *n* cocodrilo *m*. ~ **tears** *npl* lágrimas *fpl* de cocodrilo

**crocus** /'krəʊkəs/ *n* (*pl* **-es**) azafrán *m*

**crony** /'krəʊnɪ/ *n* amigote *m*

**crook** /krʊk/ *n* (*fam*) maleante *m* & *f*, estafador *m*, criminal *m*; (*stick*) cayado *m*; (*of arm*) pliegue *m*

**crooked** /'krʊkɪd/ *a* torcido; (*winding*) tortuoso; (*dishonest*) poco honrado

**croon** /kru:n/ *vt/i* canturrear

**crop** /krɒp/ *n* cosecha *f*; (*fig*) montón *m*. ● *vt* (*pt* **cropped**) *vi* cortar. ~ **up** surgir

**cropper** /'krɒpə(r)/ *n*. **come a** ~ (*fall*, *fam*) caer; (*fail*, *fam*) fracasar

**croquet** /'krəʊkeɪ/ *n* croquet *m*

**croquette** /krə'ket/ *n* croqueta *f*

**cross** /krɒs/ *n* cruz *f*; (*of animals*) cruce *m*. ● *vt/i* cruzar; (*oppose*) contrariar. ~ **off** tachar. ~ **o.s.** santiguarse. ~ **out** tachar. ~ **s.o.'s mind** ocurrírsele a uno. ● *a* enfadado. **talk at** ~ **purposes** hablar sin entenderse

**crossbar** /'krɒsbɑ:(r)/ *n* travesaño *m*

**cross-examine** /krɒsɪg'zæmɪn/ *vt* interrogar

**cross-eyed** /'krɒsaɪd/ *a* bizco

**crossfire** /'krɒsfaɪə(r)/ *n* fuego *m* cruzado

**crossing** /'krɒsɪŋ/ *n* (*by boat*) travesía *f*; (*on road*) paso *m* para peatones

**crossly** /'krɒslɪ/ *adv* con enfado

**cross-reference** /krɒs'refrəns/ *n* referencia *f*

**crossroads** /'krɒsrəʊdz/ *n* cruce *m* (de carreteras)

**cross-section** /krɒs'sekʃn/ *n* sección *f* transversal; (*fig*) muestra *f* representativa

**crosswise** /'krɒswaɪz/ *adv* al través

**crossword** /'krɒswɜːd/ *n* crucigrama *m*

**crotch** /krɒtʃ/ *n* entrepiernas *fpl*

**crotchety** /'krɒtʃɪtɪ/ *a* de mal genio

**crouch** /kraʊtʃ/ *vi* agacharse

**crow**[1] /krəʊ/ *n* cuervo *m*. **as the ~ flies** en línea recta

**crow**[2] /krəʊ/ *vi* (*pt* **crew**) cacarear

**crowbar** /'krəʊbɑː(r)/ *n* palanca *f*

**crowd** /kraʊd/ *n* muchedumbre *f*. ● *vt* amontonar; (*fill*) llenar. ● *vi* amontonarse; (*gather*) reunirse. **~ed** *a* atestado

**crown** /kraʊn/ *n* corona *f*; (*of hill*) cumbre *f*; (*of head*) coronilla *f*. ● *vt* coronar; poner una corona a (*tooth*). **C~ Court** *n* tribunal *m* regional. **C~ prince** *n* príncipe *m* heredero

**crucial** /'kruːʃl/ *a* crucial

**crucifix** /'kruːsɪfɪks/ *n* crucifijo *m*. **~ion** /-'fɪkʃn/ *n* crucifixión *f*

**crucify** /'kruːsɪfaɪ/ *vt* crucificar

**crude** /kruːd/ *a* (**-er, -est**) (*raw*) crudo; (*rough*) tosco; (*vulgar*) ordinario

**cruel** /krʊəl/ *a* (**crueller, cruellest**) cruel. **~ty** *n* crueldad *f*

**cruet** /'kruːɪt/ *n* vinagreras *fpl*

**cruise** /kruːz/ *n* crucero *m*. ● *vi* hacer un crucero; (*of car*) circular lentamente. **~r** *n* crucero *m*

**crumb** /krʌm/ *n* migaja *f*

**crumble** /'krʌmbl/ *vt* desmenuzar. ● *vi* desmenuzarse; (*collapse*) derrumbarse

**crummy** /'krʌmɪ/ *a* (**-ier, -iest**) (*sl*) miserable

**crumpet** /'krʌmpɪt/ *n* bollo *m* blando

**crumple** /'krʌmpl/ *vt* arrugar; estrujar (*paper*). ● *vi* arrugarse

**crunch** /krʌntʃ/ *vt* hacer crujir; (*bite*) ronzar, morder, masticar. ● *n* crujido *m*; (*fig*) momento *m* decisivo

**crusade** /kruː'seɪd/ *n* cruzada *f*. **~r** /-ə(r)/ *n* cruzado *m*

**crush** /krʌʃ/ *vt* aplastar; arrugar (*clothes*); estrujar (*paper*). ● *n* (*crowd*) aglomeración *f*. **have a ~**

**on** (*sl*) estar perdido por. **orange ~** *n* naranjada *f*

**crust** /krʌst/ *n* corteza *f*. **~y** *a* (*bread*) de corteza dura; (*person*) malhumorado

**crutch** /krʌtʃ/ *n* muleta *f*; (*anat*) entrepiernas *fpl*

**crux** /krʌks/ *n* (*pl* **cruxes**) punto *m* más importante, quid *m*, busilis *m*

**cry** /kraɪ/ *n* grito *m*. **be a far ~ from** (*fig*) distar mucho de. ● *vi* llorar; (*call out*) gritar. **~ off** rajarse. **~-baby** *n* llorón *m*

**crypt** /krɪpt/ *n* cripta *f*

**cryptic** /'krɪptɪk/ *a* enigmático

**crystal** /'krɪstl/ *n* cristal *m*. **~lize** *vt* cristalizar. ● *vi* cristalizarse

**cub** /kʌb/ *n* cachorro *m*. **C~ (Scout)** *n* niño *m* explorador

**Cuba** /'kjuːbə/ *n* Cuba *f*. **~n** *a* & *n* cubano (*m*)

**cubby-hole** /'kʌbɪhəʊl/ *n* casilla *f*; (*room*) chiribitil *m*, cuchitril *m*

**cub|e** /kjuːb/ *n* cubo *m*. **~ic** *a* cúbico

**cubicle** /'kjuːbɪkl/ *n* cubículo *m*; (*changing room*) caseta *f*

**cubis|m** /'kjuːbɪzm/ *n* cubismo *m*. **~t** *a* & *n* cubista (*m* & *f*)

**cuckold** /'kʌkəʊld/ *n* cornudo *m*

**cuckoo** /'kʊkuː/ *n* cuco *m*, cuclillo *m*

**cucumber** /'kjuːkʌmbə(r)/ *n* pepino *m*

**cuddl|e** /'kʌdl/ *vt* abrazar. ● *vi* abrazarse. ● *n* abrazo *m*. **~y** *a* mimoso

**cudgel** /'kʌdʒl/ *n* porra *f*. ● *vt* (*pt* **cudgelled**) aporrear

**cue**[1] /kjuː/ *n* indicación *f*; (*in theatre*) pie *m*

**cue**[2] /kjuː/ *n* (*in billiards*) taco *m*

**cuff** /kʌf/ *n* puño *m*; (*blow*) bofetada *f*. **speak off the ~** hablar de improviso. ● *vt* abofetear. **~-link** *n* gemelo *m*

**cul-de-sac** /'kʌldəsæk/ *n* callejón *m* sin salida

**culinary** /'kʌlɪnərɪ/ *a* culinario

**cull** /kʌl/ *vt* coger (*flowers*); entresacar (*animals*)

**culminat|e** /'kʌlmɪneɪt/ *vi* culminar. **~ion** /-'neɪʃn/ *n* culminación *f*

**culottes** /kʊ'lɒts/ *npl* falda *f* pantalón

**culprit** /'kʌlprɪt/ *n* culpable *m*

**cult** /kʌlt/ *n* culto *m*

**cultivat|e** /'kʌltɪveɪt/ *vt* cultivar. **~ion** /-'veɪʃn/ *n* cultivo *m*; (*fig*) cultura *f*

**cultur|al** /'kʌltʃərəl/ a cultural. ~e /'kʌltʃə(r)/ n cultura f; (bot etc) cultivo m. ~ed a cultivado; ⟨person⟩ culto

**cumbersome** /'kʌmbəsəm/ a incómodo; (heavy) pesado

**cumulative** /'kju:mjʊlətɪv/ a cumulativo

**cunning** /'kʌnɪŋ/ a astuto. ● n astucia f

**cup** /kʌp/ n taza f; (prize) copa f

**cupboard** /'kʌbəd/ n armario m

**Cup Final** /kʌp'faɪnl/ n final f del campeonato

**cupful** /'kʌpfʊl/ n taza f

**cupidity** /kju:'pɪdɪtɪ/ n codicia f

**curable** /'kjʊərəbl/ a curable

**curate** /'kjʊərət/ n coadjutor m

**curator** /kjʊə'reɪtə(r)/ n (of museum) conservador m

**curb** /kɜ:b/ n freno m. ● vt refrenar

**curdle** /'kɜ:dl/ vt cuajar. ● vi cuajarse; ⟨milk⟩ cortarse

**curds** /kɜ:dz/ npl cuajada f, requesón m

**cure** /kjʊə(r)/ vt curar. ● n cura f

**curfew** /'kɜ:fju:/ n queda f; (signal) toque m de queda

**curio** /'kjʊərɪəʊ/ n (pl -os) curiosidad f

**curio|us** /'kjʊərɪəs/ a curioso. ~sity /-'ɒsɪtɪ/ n curiosidad f

**curl** /kɜ:l/ vt rizar ⟨hair⟩. ~ o.s. up acurrucarse. ● vi ⟨hair⟩ rizarse; ⟨paper⟩ arrollarse. ● n rizo m. ~er /'kɜ:lə(r)/ n bigudí m, rulo m. ~y /'kɜ:lɪ/ a (-ier, -iest) rizado

**currant** /'kʌrənt/ n pasa f de Corinto

**currency** /'kʌrənsɪ/ n moneda f; (acceptance) uso m (corriente)

**current** /'kʌrənt/ a & n corriente (f). ~ events asuntos mpl de actualidad. ~ly adv actualmente

**curriculum** /kə'rɪkjʊləm/ n (pl -la) programa m de estudios. ~ vitae n curriculum m vitae

**curry¹** /'kʌrɪ/ n curry m

**curry²** /'kʌrɪ/ vt. ~ favour with congraciarse con

**curse** /kɜ:s/ n maldición f; (oath) palabrota f. ● vt maldecir. ● vi decir palabrotas

**cursory** /'kɜ:sərɪ/ a superficial

**curt** /kɜ:t/ a brusco

**curtail** /kɜ:'teɪl/ vt abreviar; reducir ⟨expenses⟩

**curtain** /'kɜ:tn/ n cortina f; (in theatre) telón m

**curtsy** /'kɜ:tsɪ/ n reverencia f. ● vi hacer una reverencia

**curve** /kɜ:v/ n curva f. ● vt encurvar. ● vi encorvarse; ⟨road⟩ torcerse

**cushion** /'kʊʃn/ n cojín m. ● vt amortiguar ⟨a blow⟩; (fig) proteger

**cushy** /'kʊʃɪ/ a (-ier, -iest) (fam) fácil

**custard** /'kʌstəd/ n natillas fpl

**custodian** /kʌ'stəʊdɪən/ n custodio m

**custody** /'kʌstədɪ/ n custodia f. be in ~ (jurid) estar detenido

**custom** /'kʌstəm/ n costumbre f; (com) clientela f

**customary** /'kʌstəmərɪ/ a acostumbrado

**customer** /'kʌstəmə(r)/ n cliente m

**customs** /'kʌstəmz/ npl aduana f. ~ officer n aduanero m

**cut** /kʌt/ vt/i (pt cut, pres p cutting) cortar; reducir ⟨prices⟩. ● n corte m; (reduction) reducción f. ~ across atravesar. ~ back, ~ down reducir. ~ in interrumpir. ~ off cortar; (phone) desconectar; (fig) aislar. ~ out recortar; (omit) suprimir. ~ through atravesar. ~ up cortar en pedazos. be ~ up about (fig) afligirse por

**cute** /kju:t/ a (-er, -est) (fam) listo; (Amer) mono

**cuticle** /'kju:tɪkl/ n cutícula f

**cutlery** /'kʌtlərɪ/ n cubiertos mpl

**cutlet** /'kʌtlɪt/ n chuleta f

**cut-price** /'kʌtpraɪs/ a a precio reducido

**cut-throat** /'kʌtθrəʊt/ a despiadado

**cutting** /'kʌtɪŋ/ a cortante; ⟨remark⟩ mordaz. ● n (from newspaper) recorte m; (of plant) esqueje m

**cyanide** /'saɪənaɪd/ n cianuro m

**cybernetics** /saɪbə'netɪks/ n cibernética f

**cyclamen** /'sɪkləmən/ n ciclamen m

**cycle** /'saɪkl/ n ciclo m; (bicycle) bicicleta f. ● vi ir en bicicleta

**cyclic(al)** /'saɪklɪk(l)/ a cíclico

**cycli|ng** /'saɪklɪŋ/ n ciclismo m. ~st n ciclista m & f

**cyclone** /'saɪkləʊn/ n ciclón m

**cylind|er** /'sɪlɪndə(r)/ n cilindro m. ~er head (auto) n culata f. ~rical /-'lɪndrɪkl/ a cilíndrico

**cymbal** /'sɪmbl/ n címbalo m

**cynic** /'sɪnɪk/ n cínico m. ~al a cínico. ~ism /-sɪzəm/ n cinismo m

**cypress** /'saɪprəs/ n ciprés m

**Cypr|iot** /'sɪprɪət/ a & n chipriota (m & f). **~us** /'saɪprəs/ n Chipre f

**cyst** /sɪst/ n quiste m

**czar** /zɑ:(r)/ n zar m

**Czech** /tʃek/ a & n checo (m). **the ~ Republic** n la república f Checa

**Czechoslovak** /tʃekəʊ'sləʊvæk/ a & n (history) checoslovaco (m). **~ia** /-ə'vækɪə/ n (history) Checoslovaquia f

# D

**dab** /dæb/ vt (pt **dabbed**) tocar ligeramente. ● n toque m suave. **a ~ of** un poquito de

**dabble** /'dæbl/ vi. **~ in** meterse (superficialmente) en. **~r** /ə(r)/ n aficionado m

**dad** /dæd/ n (fam) papá m. **~dy** n (children's use) papá m. **~dy-long-legs** n típula f

**daffodil** /'dæfədɪl/ n narciso m

**daft** /dɑ:ft/ a (**-er, -est**) tonto

**dagger** /'dægə(r)/ n puñal m

**dahlia** /'deɪlɪə/ n dalia f

**daily** /'deɪlɪ/ a diario. ● adv diariamente, cada día. ● n diario m; (cleaner, fam) asistenta f

**dainty** /'deɪntɪ/ a (**-ier, -iest**) delicado

**dairy** /'deərɪ/ n vaquería f; (shop) lechería f. ● a lechero

**dais** /deɪs/ n estrado m

**daisy** /'deɪzɪ/ n margarita f

**dale** /deɪl/ n valle m

**dally** /'dælɪ/ vi tardar; (waste time) perder el tiempo

**dam** /dæm/ n presa f. ● vt (pt **dammed**) embalsar

**damag|e** /'dæmɪdʒ/ n daño m; (pl, jurid) daños mpl y perjuicios mpl. ● vt (fig) dañar, estropear. **~ing** a perjudicial

**damask** /'dæməsk/ n damasco m

**dame** /deɪm/ n (old use) dama f; (Amer, sl) chica f

**damn** /dæm/ vt condenar; (curse) maldecir. ● int ¡córcholis! ● a maldito. ● n. **I don't care a ~** (no) me importa un comino. **~ation** /-'neɪʃn/ n condenación f, perdición f

**damp** /dæmp/ n humedad f. ● a (**-er, -est**) húmedo. ● vt mojar; (fig) ahogar. **~er** /'dæmpə(r)/ n apagador m, sordina f; (fig) aguafiestas m invar. **~ness** n humedad f

**damsel** /'dæmzl/ n (old use) doncella f

**dance** /dɑ:ns/ vt/i bailar. ● n baile m. **~-hall** n salón m de baile. **~r** /-ə(r)/ n bailador m; (professional) bailarín m

**dandelion** /'dændɪlaɪən/ n diente m de león

**dandruff** /'dændrʌf/ n caspa f

**dandy** /'dændɪ/ n petimetre m

**Dane** /deɪn/ n danés m

**danger** /'deɪndʒə(r)/ n peligro m; (risk) riesgo m. **~ous** a peligroso

**dangle** /'dæŋgl/ vt balancear. ● vi suspender, colgar

**Danish** /'deɪnɪʃ/ a danés. ● m (lang) danés m

**dank** /dæŋk/ a (**-er, -est**) húmedo, malsano

**dare** /deə(r)/ vt desafiar. ● vi atreverse a. **I ~ say** probablemente. ● n desafío m

**daredevil** /'deədevl/ n atrevido m

**daring** /'deərɪŋ/ a atrevido

**dark** /dɑ:k/ a (**-er, -est**) oscuro; (gloomy) sombrío; ‹skin, hair› moreno. ● n oscuridad f; (nightfall) atardecer. **in the ~** a oscuras. **~en** /'dɑ:kən/ vt oscurecer. ● vi oscurecerse. **~ horse** n persona f de talentos desconocidos. **~ness** n oscuridad f. **~room** n cámara f oscura

**darling** /'dɑ:lɪŋ/ a querido. ● n querido m

**darn** /dɑ:n/ vt zurcir

**dart** /dɑ:t/ n dardo m. ● vi lanzarse; (run) precipitarse. **~board** /'dɑ:tbɔ:d/ n blanco m. **~s** npl los dardos mpl

**dash** /dæʃ/ vi precipitarse. **~ off** marcharse apresuradamente. **~ out** salir corriendo. ● vt lanzar; (break) romper; defraudar ‹hopes›. ● n carrera f; (small amount) poquito m; (stroke) raya f. **cut a ~** causar sensación

**dashboard** /'dæʃbɔ:d/ n tablero m de mandos

**dashing** /'dæʃɪŋ/ a vivo; (showy) vistoso

**data** /'deɪtə/ npl datos mpl. **~ processing** n proceso m de datos

**date**[1] /deɪt/ n fecha f; (fam) cita f. **to ~** hasta la fecha. ● vt fechar; (go out with, fam) salir con. ● vi datar; (be old-fashioned) quedar anticuado

**date**[2] /deɪt/ n (fruit) dátil m

**dated** /'deɪtɪd/ a pasado de moda

**daub** /dɔːb/ vt embadurnar

**daughter** /'dɔːtə(r)/ n hija f. **~-in-law** n nuera f

**daunt** /dɔːnt/ vt intimidar

**dauntless** /'dɔːntlɪs/ a intrépido

**dawdle** /'dɔːdl/ vi andar despacio; (waste time) perder el tiempo. **~r** /-ə(r)/ n rezagado m

**dawn** /dɔːn/ n amanecer m. ● vi amanecer; (fig) nacer. **it ~ed on me that** caí en la cuenta de que, comprendí que

**day** /deɪ/ n día m; (whole day) jornada f; (period) época f. **~break** n amanecer m. **~dream** n ensueño m. ● vi soñar despierto. **~light** /'deɪlaɪt/ n luz f del día. **~time** /'deɪtaɪm/ n día m

**daze** /deɪz/ vt aturdir. ● n aturdimiento m. **in a ~** aturdido

**dazzle** /'dæzl/ vt deslumbrar

**deacon** /'diːkən/ n diácono m

**dead** /ded/ a muerto; (numb) entumecido. **~ centre** justo en medio. ● adv completamente. **~ beat** rendido. **~ on time** justo a tiempo. **~ slow** muy lento. **stop ~** parar en seco. ● n muertos mpl. **in the ~ of night** en plena noche. **the ~** los muertos mpl. **~en** /'dedn/ vt amortiguar (sound, blow); calmar (pain). **~ end** n callejón m sin salida. **~ heat** n empate m

**deadline** /'dedlaɪn/ n fecha f tope, fin m de plazo

**deadlock** /'dedlɒk/ n punto m muerto

**deadly** /'dedlɪ/ a (-ier, -iest) mortal; (harmful) nocivo; (dreary) aburrido

**deadpan** /'dedpæn/ a impasible

**deaf** /def/ a (-er, -est) sordo. **~-aid** n audífono m. **~en** /'defn/ vt ensordecer. **~ening** a ensordecedor. **~mute** n sordomudo m. **~ness** n sordera f

**deal** /diːl/ n (transaction) negocio m; (agreement) pacto m; (of cards) reparto m; (treatment) trato m; (amount) cantidad f. **a great ~** muchísimo. ● vt (pt dealt) distribuir; dar (a blow, cards). ● vi. **~ in** comerciar en. **~ with** tratar con (person); tratar de (subject etc); ocuparse de (problem etc). **~er** n comerciante m. **~ings** /'diːlɪŋz/ npl trato m

**dean** /diːn/ n deán m; (univ) decano m

**dear** /dɪə(r)/ a (-er, -est) querido; (expensive) caro. ● n querido m; (child) pequeño m. ● adv caro. ● int ¡Dios mío! **~ me!** ¡Dios mío! **~ly** adv tiernamente; (pay) caro; (very much) muchísimo

**dearth** /dɜːθ/ n escasez f

**death** /deθ/ n muerte f. **~ duty** n derechos mpl reales. **~ly** a mortal; (silence) profundo. ● adv como la muerte. **~'s head** n calavera f. **~trap** n lugar m peligroso.

**débâcle** /deɪ'bɑːkl/ n fracaso m, desastre m

**debar** /dɪ'bɑː(r)/ vt (pt debarred) excluir

**debase** /dɪ'beɪs/ vt degradar

**debat|able** /dɪ'beɪtəbl/ a discutible. **~e** /dɪ'beɪt/ n debate m. ● vt debatir, discutir. ● vi discutir; (consider) considerar

**debauch** /dɪ'bɔːtʃ/ vt corromper. **~ery** n libertinaje m

**debilit|ate** /dɪ'bɪlɪteɪt/ vt debilitar. **~y** /dɪ'bɪlətɪ/ n debilidad f

**debit** /'debɪt/ n debe m. ● vt. **~ s.o.'s account** cargar en cuenta a uno

**debonair** /debə'neə(r)/ a alegre

**debris** /'debriː/ n escombros mpl

**debt** /det/ n deuda f. **be in ~** tener deudas. **~or** n deudor m

**debutante** /'debjuːtɑːnt/ n (old use) debutante f

**decade** /'dekeɪd/ n década f

**decaden|ce** /'dekədəns/ n decadencia f. **~t** /'dekədənt/ a decadente

**decant** /dɪ'kænt/ vt decantar. **~er** /ə(r)/ n garrafa f

**decapitate** /dɪ'kæpɪteɪt/ vt decapitar

**decay** /dɪ'keɪ/ vi decaer; (tooth) cariarse. ● n decadencia f; (of tooth) caries f

**deceased** /dɪ'siːst/ a difunto

**deceit** /dɪ'siːt/ n engaño m. **~ful** a falso. **~fully** adv falsamente

**deceive** /dɪ'siːv/ vt engañar

**December** /dɪ'sembə(r)/ n diciembre m

**decen|cy** /'diːsənsɪ/ n decencia f. **~t** /'diːsnt/ a decente; (good, fam) bueno; (kind, fam) amable. **~tly** adv decentemente

**decentralize** /diː'sentrəlaɪz/ vt descentralizar

**decepti|on** /dɪ'sepʃn/ n engaño m. **~ve** /dɪ'septɪv/ a engañoso

**decibel** /'desɪbel/ n decibel(io) m

**decide** /dɪˈsaɪd/ vt/i decidir. **~d**
/-ɪd/ a resuelto; (*unquestionable*)
indudable. **~dly** /-ɪdlɪ/ adv deci-
didamente; (*unquestionably*) indudablemente
**decimal** /ˈdesɪml/ a & n decimal (f).
**~ point** n coma f (decimal)
**decimate** /ˈdesɪmeɪt/ vt diezmar
**decipher** /dɪˈsaɪfə(r)/ vt descifrar
**decision** /dɪˈsɪʒn/ n decisión f
**decisive** /dɪˈsaɪsɪv/ a decisivo; (*manner*) decidido. **~ly** adv de manera
decisiva
**deck** /dek/ n cubierta f; (*of cards,
Amer*) baraja f. **top ~** (*of bus*)
imperial m. ● vt adornar. **~chair** n
tumbona f
**declaim** /dɪˈkleɪm/ vt declamar
**declar|ation** /dekləˈreɪʃn/ n decla-
ración f. **~e** /dɪˈkleə(r)/ vt declarar
**decline** /dɪˈklaɪn/ vt rehusar; (*gram*)
declinar. ● vi disminuir; (*deteriorate*) deteriorarse; (*fall*) bajar. ● n
decadencia f; (*decrease*) disminución f; (*fall*) baja f
**decode** /diːˈkəʊd/ vt descifrar
**decompos|e** /diːkəmˈpəʊz/ vt
descomponer. ● vi descomponerse.
**~ition** /-ɒmpəˈzɪʃn/ n descom-
posición f
**décor** /ˈdeɪkɔː(r)/ n decoración f
**decorat|e** /ˈdekəreɪt/ vt decorar;
empapelar y pintar ⟨room⟩. **~ion**
/-ˈreɪʃn/ n (*act*) decoración f; (*ornament*) adorno m. **~ive** /-ətɪv/ a
decorativo. **~or** /ˈdekəreɪtə(r)/ n
pintor m decorador. **interior ~or**
decorador m de interiores
**decorum** /dɪˈkɔːrəm/ n decoro m
**decoy** /ˈdiːkɔɪ/ n señuelo m. /dɪˈkɔɪ/
vt atraer con señuelo
**decrease** /dɪˈkriːs/ vt disminuir. ● vi
disminuirse. /ˈdiːkriːs/ n disminución f
**decree** /dɪˈkriː/ n decreto m; (*jurid*)
sentencia f. ● vt (*pt* **decreed**)
decretar
**decrepit** /dɪˈkrepɪt/ a decrépito
**decry** /dɪˈkraɪ/ vt denigrar
**dedicat|e** /ˈdedɪkeɪt/ vt dedicar.
**~ion** /-ˈkeɪʃn/ n dedicación f; (*in
book*) dedicatoria f
**deduce** /dɪˈdjuːs/ vt deducir
**deduct** /dɪˈdʌkt/ vt deducir. **~ion**
/-ʃn/ n deducción f
**deed** /diːd/ n hecho m; (*jurid*) escritura f
**deem** /diːm/ vt juzgar, considerar

**deep** /diːp/ a (**-er, est**) adv profundo.
**get into ~ waters** meterse en honduras. **go off the ~ end** enfadarse.
● adv profundamente. **be ~ in
thought** estar absorto en sus pen-
samientos. **~en** /ˈdiːpən/ vt pro-
fundizar. ● vi hacerse más
profundo. **~freeze** n congelador
m. **~ly** adv profundamente
**deer** /dɪə(r)/ n invar ciervo m
**deface** /dɪˈfeɪs/ vt desfigurar
**defamation** /defəˈmeɪʃn/ n difa-
mación f
**default** /dɪˈfɔːlt/ vi faltar. ● n. **by ~**
en rebeldía. **in ~ of** en ausencia de
**defeat** /dɪˈfiːt/ vt vencer; (*frustrate*)
frustrar. ● n derrota f; (*of plan etc*)
fracaso m. **~ism** /dɪˈfiːtɪzm/ n
derrotismo m. **~ist** /dɪˈfiːtɪst/ n
derrotista m & f
**defect** /ˈdiːfekt/ n defecto m.
/dɪˈfekt/ vi desertar. **~ to** pasar a.
**~ion** /dɪˈfekʃn/ n deserción f. **~ive**
/dɪˈfektɪv/ a defectuoso
**defence** /dɪˈfens/ n defensa f. **~less**
a indefenso
**defend** /dɪˈfend/ vt defender. **~ant**
n (*jurid*) acusado m
**defensive** /dɪˈfensɪv/ a defensivo.
● n defensiva f
**defer** /dɪˈfɜː(r)/ vt (*pt* **deferred**)
aplazar
**deferen|ce** /ˈdefərəns/ n deferencia
f. **~tial** /-ˈrenʃl/ a deferente
**defian|ce** /dɪˈfaɪəns/ n desafío m. **in
~ce of** a despecho de. **~t** a desafi-
ante. **~tly** adv con tono retador
**deficien|cy** /dɪˈfɪʃənsɪ/ n falta f. **~t**
/dɪˈfɪʃnt/ a deficiente. **be ~t in** carecer de
**deficit** /ˈdefɪsɪt/ n déficit m
**defile** /dɪˈfaɪl/ vt ensuciar; (*fig*)
deshonrar
**define** /dɪˈfaɪn/ vt definir
**definite** /ˈdefɪnɪt/ a determinado;
(*clear*) claro; (*firm*) categórico. **~ly**
adv claramente; (*certainly*)
seguramente
**definition** /defɪˈnɪʃn/ n definición f
**definitive** /dɪˈfɪnətɪv/ a definitivo
**deflat|e** /dɪˈfleɪt/ vt desinflar. ● vi
desinflarse. **~ion** /-ʃn/ n (*com*)
deflación f
**deflect** /dɪˈflekt/ vt desviar. ● vi
desviarse
**deform** /dɪˈfɔːm/ vt deformar. **~ed**
a deforme. **~ity** n deformidad f
**defraud** /dɪˈfrɔːd/ vt defraudar
**defray** /dɪˈfreɪ/ vt pagar

**defrost** /diːˈfrɒst/ vt descongelar

**deft** /deft/ a (**-er, -est**) hábil. ∼**ness** n destreza f

**defunct** /dɪˈfʌŋkt/ a difunto

**defuse** /diːˈfjuːz/ vt desactivar ⟨bomb⟩; (fig) calmar

**defy** /dɪˈfaɪ/ vt desafiar; (resist) resistir

**degenerate** /dɪˈdʒenəreɪt/ vi degenerar. /dɪˈdʒenərət/ a & n degenerado (m)

**degrad|ation** /degrəˈdeɪʃn/ n degradación f. ∼**e** /dɪˈgreɪd/ vt degradar

**degree** /dɪˈgriː/ n grado m; (univ) licenciatura f; (rank) rango m. **to a certain** ∼ hasta cierto punto. **to a** ∼ (fam) sumamente

**dehydrate** /diːˈhaɪdreɪt/ vt deshidratar

**de-ice** /diːˈaɪs/ vt descongelar

**deign** /deɪn/ vi. ∼ **to** dignarse

**deity** /ˈdiːɪtɪ/ n deidad f

**deject|ed** /dɪˈdʒektɪd/ a desanimado. ∼**ion** /-ʃn/ n abatimiento m

**delay** /dɪˈleɪ/ vt retardar; (postpone) aplazar. ● vi demorarse. ● n demora f

**delectable** /dɪˈlektəbl/ a deleitable

**delegat|e** /ˈdelɪgeɪt/ vt delegar. /ˈdelɪgət/ n delegado m. ∼**ion** /-ˈgeɪʃn/ n delegación f

**delet|e** /dɪˈliːt/ vt tachar. ∼**ion** /-ʃn/ n tachadura f

**deliberat|e** /dɪˈlɪbəreɪt/ vt/i deliberar. /dɪˈlɪbərət/ a intencionado; ⟨steps etc⟩ pausado. ∼**ely** adv a propósito. ∼**ion** /-ˈreɪʃn/ n deliberación f

**delica|cy** /ˈdelɪkəsɪ/ n delicadeza f; (food) manjar m; (sweet food) golosina f. ∼**te** /ˈdelɪkət/ a delicado

**delicatessen** /delɪkəˈtesn/ n charcutería f fina

**delicious** /dɪˈlɪʃəs/ a delicioso

**delight** /dɪˈlaɪt/ n placer m. ● vt encantar. ● vi deleitarse. ∼**ed** a encantado. ∼**ful** a delicioso

**delineat|e** /dɪˈlɪnɪeɪt/ vt delinear. ∼**ion** /-ˈeɪʃn/ n delineación f

**delinquen|cy** /dɪˈlɪŋkwənsɪ/ n delincuencia f. ∼**t** /dɪˈlɪŋkwənt/ a & n delincuente (m & f)

**deliri|ous** /dɪˈlɪrɪəs/ a delirante. ∼**um** n delirio m

**deliver** /dɪˈlɪvə(r)/ vt entregar; (utter) pronunciar; (aim) lanzar; (set free) librar; (med) asistir al parto de. ∼**ance** n liberación f. ∼**y** n

entrega f; (of post) reparto m; (med) parto m

**delta** /ˈdeltə/ n (geog) delta m

**delude** /dɪˈluːd/ vt engañar. ∼ **o.s.** engañarse

**deluge** /ˈdeljuːdʒ/ n diluvio m

**delusion** /dɪˈluːʒn/ n ilusión f

**de luxe** /dɪˈlʌks/ a de lujo

**delve** /delv/ vi cavar. ∼ **into** (investigate) investigar

**demagogue** /ˈdeməgɒg/ n demagogo m

**demand** /dɪˈmɑːnd/ vt exigir. ● n petición f; (claim) reclamación f; (com) demanda f. **in** ∼ muy popular, muy solicitado. **on** ∼ a solicitud. ∼**ing** a exigente. ∼**s** npl exigencias fpl

**demarcation** /diːmɑːˈkeɪʃn/ n demarcación f

**demean** /dɪˈmiːn/ vt. ∼ **o.s.** degradarse. ∼**our** /dɪˈmiːnə(r)/ n conducta f

**demented** /dɪˈmentɪd/ a demente

**demerara** /deməˈreərə/ n. ∼ (**sugar**) n azúcar m moreno

**demise** /dɪˈmaɪz/ n fallecimiento m

**demo** /ˈdeməʊ/ n (pl **-os**) (fam) manifestación f

**demobilize** /diːˈməʊbəlaɪz/ vt desmovilizar

**democra|cy** /dɪˈmɒkrəsɪ/ n democracia f. ∼**t** /ˈdeməkræt/ n demócrata m & f. ∼**tic** /-ˈkrætɪk/ a democrático

**demoli|sh** /dɪˈmɒlɪʃ/ vt derribar. ∼**tion** /deməˈlɪʃn/ n demolición f

**demon** /ˈdiːmən/ n demonio m

**demonstrat|e** /ˈdemənstreɪt/ vt demostrar. ● vi manifestarse, hacer una manifestación. ∼**ion** /-ˈstreɪʃn/ n demostración f; (pol etc) manifestación f

**demonstrative** /dɪˈmɒnstrətɪv/ a demostrativo

**demonstrator** /ˈdemənstreɪtə(r)/ n demostrador m; (pol etc) manifestante m & f

**demoralize** /dɪˈmɒrəlaɪz/ vt desmoralizar

**demote** /dɪˈməʊt/ vt degradar

**demure** /dɪˈmjʊə(r)/ a recatado

**den** /den/ n (of animal) guarida f, madriguera f

**denial** /dɪˈnaɪəl/ n denegación f; (statement) desmentimiento m

**denigrate** /ˈdenɪgreɪt/ vt denigrar

**denim** /ˈdenɪm/ n dril m (de algodón azul grueso). ∼**s** npl pantalón m vaquero

**Denmark** /'denmɑ:k/ n Dinamarca f
**denomination** /dɪnɒmɪ'neɪʃn/ n denominación f; (relig) secta f
**denote** /dɪ'nəʊt/ vt denotar
**denounce** /dɪ'naʊns/ vt denunciar
**dens|e** /dens/ a (-er, -est) espeso; (person) torpe. ~ely adv densamente. ~ity n densidad f
**dent** /dent/ n abolladura f. ● vt abollar
**dental** /'dentl/ a dental. ~ surgeon n dentista m & f
**dentist** /'dentɪst/ n dentista m & f. ~ry n odontología f
**denture** /'dentʃə(r)/ n dentadura f postiza
**denude** /dɪ'nju:d/ vt desnudar; (fig) despojar
**denunciation** /dɪnʌnsɪ'eɪʃn/ n denuncia f
**deny** /dɪ'naɪ/ vt negar; desmentir (rumour); (disown) renegar
**deodorant** /dɪ'əʊdərənt/ a & n desodorante (m)
**depart** /dɪ'pɑ:t/ vi marcharse; (train etc) salir. ~ from apartarse de
**department** /dɪ'pɑ:tmənt/ n departamento m; (com) sección f. ~ store n grandes almacenes mpl
**departure** /dɪ'pɑ:tʃə(r)/ n partida f; (of train etc) salida f. ~ from (fig) desviación f
**depend** /dɪ'pend/ vi depender. ~ on depender de; (rely) contar con. ~able a seguro. ~ant /dɪ'pendənt/ n familiar m & f dependiente. ~ence n dependencia f. ~ent a dependiente. be ~ent on depender de
**depict** /dɪ'pɪkt/ vt pintar; (in words) describir
**deplete** /dɪ'pli:t/ vt agotar
**deplor|able** /dɪ'plɔ:rəbl/ a lamentable. ~e /dɪ'plɔ:(r)/ vt lamentar
**deploy** /dɪ'plɔɪ/ vt desplegar. ● vi desplegarse
**depopulate** /di:'pɒpjʊleɪt/ vt despoblar
**deport** /dɪ'pɔ:t/ vt deportar. ~ation /di:pɔ:'teɪʃn/ n deportación f
**depose** /dɪ'pəʊz/ vt deponer
**deposit** /dɪ'pɒzɪt/ vt (pt deposited) depositar. ● n depósito m. ~or n depositante m & f
**depot** /'depəʊ/ n depósito m; (Amer) estación f
**deprav|e** /dɪ'preɪv/ vt depravar. ~ity /-'prævətɪ/ n depravación f

**deprecate** /'deprɪkeɪt/ vt desaprobar
**depreciat|e** /dɪ'pri:ʃɪeɪt/ vt depreciar. ● vi depreciarse. ~ion /-'eɪʃn/ n depreciación f
**depress** /dɪ'pres/ vt deprimir; (press down) apretar. ~ion /-ʃn/ n depresión f
**depriv|ation** /deprɪ'veɪʃn/ n privación f. ~e /dɪ'praɪv/ vt. ~ of privar de
**depth** /depθ/ n profundidad f. be out of one's ~ perder pie; (fig) meterse en honduras. in the ~s of en lo más hondo de
**deputation** /depjʊ'teɪʃn/ n diputación f
**deputize** /'depjʊtaɪz/ vi. ~ for sustituir a
**deputy** /'depjʊtɪ/ n sustituto m. ~ chairman n vicepresidente m
**derail** /dɪ'reɪl/ vt hacer descarrilar. ~ment n descarrilamiento m
**deranged** /dɪ'reɪndʒd/ a (mind) trastornado
**derelict** /'derəlɪkt/ a abandonado
**deri|de** /dɪ'raɪd/ vt mofarse de. ~sion /-'rɪʒn/ n mofa f. ~sive a burlón. ~sory /dɪ'raɪsərɪ/ a mofador; (offer etc) irrisorio
**deriv|ation** /derɪ'veɪʃn/ n derivación f. ~ative /dɪ'rɪvətɪv/ a & n derivado (m). ~e /dɪ'raɪv/ vt/i derivar
**derogatory** /dɪ'rɒgətrɪ/ a despectivo
**derv** /dɜ:v/ n gasóleo m
**descen|d** /dɪ'send/ vt/i descender, bajar. ~dant n descendiente m & f. ~t /dɪ'sent/ n descenso m; (lineage) descendencia f
**descri|be** /dɪs'kraɪb/ vt describir. ~ption /-'krɪpʃn/ n descripción f. ~ptive /-'krɪptɪv/ a descriptivo
**desecrat|e** /'desɪkreɪt/ vt profanar. ~ion /-'kreɪʃn/ n profanación f
**desert**[1] /dɪ'zɜ:t/ vt abandonar. ● vi (mil) desertar
**desert**[2] /'dezət/ a & n desierto (m)
**deserter** /dɪ'zɜ:tə(r)/ n desertor m
**deserts** /dɪ'zɜ:ts/ npl lo merecido. get one's ~ llevarse su merecido
**deserv|e** /dɪ'zɜ:v/ vt merecer. ~edly adv merecidamente. ~ing a (person) digno de; (action) meritorio
**design** /dɪ'zaɪn/ n diseño m; (plan) proyecto m; (pattern) modelo m; (aim) propósito m. have ~s on

poner la mira en. ● *vt* diseñar; (*plan*) proyectar

**designat|e** /'dezɪgneɪt/ *vt* designar; (*appoint*) nombrar. **∼ion** /-'neɪʃn/ *n* denominación *f*; (*appointment*) nombramiento *m*

**designer** /dɪ'zaɪnə(r)/ *n* diseñador *m*; (*of clothing*) modisto *m*; (*in theatre*) escenógrafo *m*

**desirab|ility** /dɪzaɪərə'bɪlətɪ/ *n* conveniencia *f*. **∼le** /dɪ'zaɪrəbl/ *a* deseable

**desire** /dɪ'zaɪə(r)/ *n* deseo *m*. ● *vt* desear

**desist** /dɪ'zɪst/ *vi* desistir

**desk** /desk/ *n* escritorio *m*; (*at school*) pupitre *m*; (*in hotel*) recepción *f*; (*com*) caja *f*

**desolat|e** /'desələt/ *a* desolado; (*uninhabited*) deshabitado. **∼ion** /-'leɪʃn/ *n* desolación *f*

**despair** /dɪ'speə(r)/ *n* desesperación *f*. ● *vi*. **∼ of** desesperarse de

**desperat|e** /'despərət/ *a* desesperado; (*dangerous*) peligroso. **∼ely** *adv* desesperadamente. **∼ion** /-'reɪʃn/ *n* desesperación *f*

**despicable** /dɪ'spɪkəbl/ *a* despreciable

**despise** /dɪ'spaɪz/ *vt* despreciar

**despite** /dɪ'spaɪt/ *prep* a pesar de

**desponden|cy** /dɪ'spɒndənsɪ/ *n* abatimiento *m*. **∼t** /dɪ'spɒndənt/ *a* desanimado

**despot** /'despɒt/ *n* déspota *m*

**dessert** /dɪ'zɜːt/ *n* postre *m*. **∼spoon** *n* cuchara *f* de postre

**destination** /destɪ'neɪʃn/ *n* destino *m*

**destine** /'destɪn/ *vt* destinar

**destiny** /'destɪnɪ/ *n* destino *m*

**destitute** /'destɪtjuːt/ *a* indigente. **∼ of** desprovisto de

**destroy** /dɪ'strɔɪ/ *vt* destruir

**destroyer** /dɪ'strɔɪə(r)/ *n* (*naut*) destructor *m*

**destructi|on** /dɪ'strʌkʃn/ *n* destrucción *f*. **∼ve** *a* destructivo

**desultory** /'desəltrɪ/ *a* irregular

**detach** /dɪ'tætʃ/ *vt* separar. **∼able** *a* separable. **∼ed** *a* separado. **∼ed house** *n* chalet *m*. **∼ment** /dɪ'tætʃmənt/ *n* separación *f*; (*mil*) destacamento *m*; (*fig*) indiferencia *f*

**detail** /'diːteɪl/ *n* detalle *m*. ● *vt* detallar; (*mil*) destacar. **∼ed** *a* detallado

**detain** /dɪ'teɪn/ *vt* detener; (*delay*) retener. **∼ee** /diːteɪ'niː/ *n* detenido *m*

**detect** /dɪ'tekt/ *vt* percibir; (*discover*) descubrir. **∼ion** /-ʃn/ *n* descubrimiento *m*, detección *f*. **∼or** *n* detector *m*

**detective** /dɪ'tektɪv/ *n* detective *m*. **∼ story** *n* novela *f* policíaca

**detention** /dɪ'tenʃn/ *n* detención *f*

**deter** /dɪ'tɜː(r)/ *vt* (*pt* **deterred**) disuadir; (*prevent*) impedir

**detergent** /dɪ'tɜːdʒənt/ *a & n* detergente (*m*)

**deteriorat|e** /dɪ'tɪərɪəreɪt/ *vi* deteriorarse. **∼ion** /-'reɪʃn/ *n* deterioro *m*

**determination** /dɪtɜːmɪ'neɪʃn/ *n* determinación *f*

**determine** /dɪ'tɜːmɪn/ *vt* determinar; (*decide*) decidir. **∼d** *a* determinado; (*resolute*) resuelto

**deterrent** /dɪ'terənt/ *n* fuerza *f* de disuasión

**detest** /dɪ'test/ *vt* aborrecer. **∼able** *a* odioso

**detonat|e** /'detəneɪt/ *vt* hacer detonar. ● *vi* detonar. **∼ion** /-'neɪʃn/ *n* detonación *f*. **∼or** *n* detonador *m*

**detour** /'diːtʊə(r)/ *n* desviación *f*

**detract** /dɪ'trækt/ *vi*. **∼ from** (*lessen*) disminuir

**detriment** /'detrɪmənt/ *n* perjuicio *m*. **∼al** /-'mentl/ *a* perjudicial

**devalu|ation** /diːvæljuː'eɪʃn/ *n* desvalorización *f*. **∼e** /diː'væljuː/ *vt* desvalorizar

**devastat|e** /'devəsteɪt/ *vt* devastar. **∼ing** *a* devastador; (*fig*) arrollador

**develop** /dɪ'veləp/ *vt* desarrollar; contraer ⟨*illness*⟩; urbanizar ⟨*land*⟩. ● *vi* desarrollarse; (*show*) aparecerse. **∼er** *n* (*foto*) revelador *m*. **∼ing country** *n* país *m* en vías de desarrollo. **∼ment** *n* desarrollo *m*. (**new**) **∼ment** novedad *f*

**deviant** /'diːvɪənt/ *a* desviado

**deviat|e** /'diːvɪeɪt/ *vi* desviarse. **∼ion** /-'eɪʃn/ *n* desviación *f*

**device** /dɪ'vaɪs/ *n* dispositivo *m*; (*scheme*) estratagema *f*

**devil** /'devl/ *n* diablo *m*. **∼ish** *a* diabólico

**devious** /'diːvɪəs/ *a* tortuoso

**devise** /dɪ'vaɪz/ *vt* idear

**devoid** /dɪ'vɔɪd/ *a*. **∼ of** desprovisto de

**devolution** /diːvə'luːʃn/ *n* descentralización *f*; (*of power*) delegación *f*

**devot|e** /dɪ'vəʊt/ *vt* dedicar. **∼ed** *a* leal. **∼edly** *adv* con devoción *f*. **∼ee**

/devəˈti:/ *n* partidario *m*. ~ion /-ʃn/ *n* dedicación *f*. ~ions *npl* (*relig*) oraciones *fpl*

**devour** /dɪˈvaʊə(r)/ *vt* devorar

**devout** /dɪˈvaʊt/ *a* devoto

**dew** /dju:/ *n* rocío *m*

**dext|erity** /dekˈsterətɪ/ *n* destreza *f*. ~(e)rous /ˈdekstrəs/ *a* diestro

**diabet|es** /daɪəˈbi:ti:z/ *n* diabetes *f*. ~ic /-ˈbetɪk/ *a & n* diabético (*m*)

**diabolical** /daɪəˈbɒlɪkl/ *a* diabólico

**diadem** /ˈdaɪədem/ *n* diadema *f*

**diagnos|e** /ˈdaɪəgnəʊz/ *vt* diagnosticar. ~is /daɪəgˈnəʊsɪs/ *n* (*pl* -oses /-si:z/) diagnóstico *m*

**diagonal** /daɪˈægənl/ *a & n* diagonal (*f*)

**diagram** /ˈdaɪəgræm/ *n* diagrama *m*

**dial** /ˈdaɪəl/ *n* cuadrante *m*; (*on phone*) disco *m*. ● *vt* (*pt* dialled) marcar

**dialect** /ˈdaɪəlekt/ *n* dialecto *m*

**dial:** ~ling code *n* prefijo *m*. ~ling tone *n* señal *f* para marcar

**dialogue** /ˈdaɪəlɒg/ *n* diálogo *m*

**diameter** /daɪˈæmɪtə(r)/ *n* diámetro *m*

**diamond** /ˈdaɪəmənd/ *n* diamante *m*; (*shape*) rombo *m*. ~s *npl* (*cards*) diamantes *mpl*

**diaper** /ˈdaɪəpə(r)/ *n* (*Amer*) pañal *m*

**diaphanous** /daɪˈæfənəs/ *a* diáfano

**diaphragm** /ˈdaɪəfræm/ *n* diafragma *m*

**diarrhoea** /daɪəˈrɪə/ *n* diarrea *f*

**diary** /ˈdaɪərɪ/ *n* diario *m*; (*book*) agenda *f*

**diatribe** /ˈdaɪətraɪb/ *n* diatriba *f*

**dice** /daɪs/ *n invar* dado *m*. ● *vt* (*culin*) cortar en cubitos

**dicey** /ˈdaɪsɪ/ *a* (*sl*) arriesgado

**dictat|e** /dɪkˈteɪt/ *vt/i* dictar. ~es /ˈdɪkteɪts/ *npl* dictados *mpl*. ~ion /dɪkˈteɪʃn/ *n* dictado *m*

**dictator** /dɪkˈteɪtə(r)/ *n* dictador *m*. ~ship *n* dictadura *f*

**diction** /ˈdɪkʃn/ *n* dicción *f*

**dictionary** /ˈdɪkʃənərɪ/ *n* diccionario *m*

**did** /dɪd/ *see* do

**didactic** /daɪˈdæktɪk/ *a* didáctico

**diddle** /ˈdɪdl/ *vt* (*sl*) estafar

**didn't** /ˈdɪdnt/ = did not

**die**[1] /daɪ/ *vi* (*pres p* dying) morir. be dying to morirse por. ~ down disminuir. ~ out extinguirse

**die**[2] /daɪ/ *n* (*tec*) cuño *m*

**die-hard** /ˈdaɪhɑ:d/ *n* intransigente *m & f*

**diesel** /ˈdi:zl/ *n* (*fuel*) gasóleo *m*. ~ engine *n* motor *m* diesel

**diet** /ˈdaɪət/ *n* alimentación *f*; (*restricted*) régimen *m*. ● *vi* estar a régimen. ~etic /daɪəˈtetɪk/ *a* dietético. ~itian *n* dietético *m*

**differ** /ˈdɪfə(r)/ *vi* ser distinto; (*disagree*) no estar de acuerdo. ~ence /ˈdɪfrəns/ *n* diferencia *f*; (*disagreement*) desacuerdo *m*. ~ent /ˈdɪfrənt/ *a* distinto, diferente

**differentia|l** /dɪfəˈrenʃl/ *a & n* diferencial (*f*). ~te /dɪfəˈrenʃɪeɪt/ *vt* diferenciar. ● *vi* diferenciarse

**differently** /ˈdɪfrəntlɪ/ *adv* de otra manera

**difficult** /ˈdɪfɪkəlt/ *a* difícil. ~y *n* dificultad *f*

**diffiden|ce** /ˈdɪfɪdəns/ *n* falta *f* de confianza. ~t /ˈdɪfɪdənt/ *a* que falta confianza

**diffus|e** /dɪˈfju:s/ *a* difuso. /dɪˈfju:z/ *vt* difundir. ● *vi* difundirse. ~ion /-ʒn/ *n* difusión *f*

**dig** /dɪg/ *n* (*poke*) empujón *m*; (*poke with elbow*) codazo *m*; (*remark*) indirecta *f*; (*archaeol*) excavación *f*. ● *vt* (*pt* dug, *pres p* digging) cavar; (*thrust*) empujar. ● *vi* cavar. ~ out extraer. ~ up desenterrar. ~s *npl* (*fam*) alojamiento *m*

**digest** /ˈdaɪdʒest/ *n* resumen *m*. ● *vt* digerir. ~ible *a* digerible. ~ion /-ʃn/ *n* digestión *f*. ~ive *a* digestivo

**digger** /ˈdɪgə(r)/ *n* (*mec*) excavadora *f*

**digit** /ˈdɪdʒɪt/ *n* cifra *f*; (*finger*) dedo *m*. ~al /ˈdɪdʒɪtl/ *a* digital

**dignif|ied** /ˈdɪgnɪfaɪd/ *a* solemne. ~y /ˈdɪgnɪfaɪ/ *vt* dignificar

**dignitary** /ˈdɪgnɪtərɪ/ *n* dignatario *m*

**dignity** /ˈdɪgnətɪ/ *n* dignidad *f*

**digress** /daɪˈgres/ *vi* divagar. ~ from apartarse de. ~ion /-ʃn/ *n* digresión *f*

**dike** /daɪk/ *n* dique *m*

**dilapidated** /dɪˈlæpɪdeɪtɪd/ *a* ruinoso

**dilat|e** /daɪˈleɪt/ *vt* dilatar. ● *vi* dilatarse. ~ion /-ʃn/ *n* dilatación *f*

**dilatory** /ˈdɪlətərɪ/ *a* dilatorio, lento

**dilemma** /daɪˈlemə/ *n* dilema *m*

**diligen|ce** /ˈdɪlɪdʒəns/ *n* diligencia *f*. ~t /ˈdɪlɪdʒənt/ *a* diligente

**dilly-dally** /ˈdɪlɪdælɪ/ *vi* (*fam*) perder el tiempo

**dilute** /daɪˈlju:t/ *vt* diluir

**dim** /dɪm/ *a* (**dimmer, dimmest**) (*weak*) débil; (*dark*) oscuro; (*stupid*, *fam)* torpe. ● *vt* (*pt* **dimmed**) amortiguar. ● *vi* apagarse. ~ **the headlights** bajar los faros

**dime** /daɪm/ *n* (*Amer*) moneda *f* de diez centavos

**dimension** /daɪˈmenʃn/ *n* dimensión *f*

**diminish** /dɪˈmɪnɪʃ/ *vt/i* disminuir

**diminutive** /dɪˈmɪnjʊtɪv/ *a* diminuto. ● *n* diminutivo *m*

**dimness** /ˈdɪmnɪs/ *n* debilidad *f*; (*of room etc*) oscuridad *f*

**dimple** /ˈdɪmpl/ *n* hoyuelo *m*

**din** /dɪn/ *n* jaleo *m*

**dine** /daɪn/ *vi* cenar. ~**r** /-ə(r)/ *n* comensal *m* & *f*; (*rail*) coche *m* restaurante

**dinghy** /ˈdɪŋɪ/ *n* (*inflatable*) bote *m* neumático

**ding|iness** /ˈdɪndʒɪnɪs/ *n* suciedad *f*. ~**y** /ˈdɪndʒɪ/ *a* (**-ier, -iest**) miserable, sucio

**dining-room** /ˈdaɪnɪŋruːm/ *n* comedor *m*

**dinner** /ˈdɪnə(r)/ *n* cena *f*. ~**jacket** *n* esmoquin *m*. ~ **party** *n* cena *f*

**dinosaur** /ˈdaɪnəsɔː(r)/ *n* dinosaurio *m*

**dint** /dɪnt/ *n*. **by ~ of** a fuerza de

**diocese** /ˈdaɪəsɪs/ *n* diócesis *f*

**dip** /dɪp/ *vt* (*pt* **dipped**) sumergir. ● *vi* bajar. ~ **into** hojear (*book*). ● *n* (*slope*) inclinación *f*; (*in sea*) baño *m*

**diphtheria** /dɪfˈθɪərɪə/ *n* difteria *f*

**diphthong** /ˈdɪfθɒŋ/ *n* diptongo *m*

**diploma** /dɪˈpləʊmə/ *n* diploma *m*

**diplomacy** /dɪˈpləʊməsɪ/ *n* diplomacia *f*

**diplomat** /ˈdɪpləmæt/ *n* diplomático *m*. ~**ic** /-ˈmætɪk/ *a* diplomático

**dipstick** /ˈdɪpstɪk/ *n* (*auto*) varilla *f* del nivel de aceite

**dire** /daɪə(r)/ *a* (**-er, -est**) terrible; (*need, poverty*) extremo

**direct** /dɪˈrekt/ *a* directo. ● *adv* directamente. ● *vt* dirigir; (*show the way*) indicar

**direction** /dɪˈrekʃn/ *n* dirección *f*. ~**s** *npl* instrucciones *fpl*

**directly** /dɪˈrektlɪ/ *adv* directamente; (*at once*) en seguida. ● *conj* (*fam*) en cuanto

**director** /dɪˈrektə(r)/ *n* director *m*

**directory** /dɪˈrektərɪ/ *n* guía *f*

**dirge** /dɜːdʒ/ *n* canto *m* fúnebre

**dirt** /dɜːt/ *n* suciedad *f*. ~**track** *n* (*sport*) pista *f* de ceniza. ~**y** /ˈdɜːtɪ/ *a* (**-ier, -iest**) sucio. ~**y trick** *n* mala jugada *f*. ~**y word** *n* palabrota *f*. ● *vt* ensuciar

**disability** /dɪsəˈbɪlətɪ/ *n* invalidez *f*

**disable** /dɪsˈeɪbl/ *vt* incapacitar. ~**d** *a* minusválido

**disabuse** /dɪsəˈbjuːz/ *vt* desengañar

**disadvantage** /dɪsədˈvɑːntɪdʒ/ *n* desventaja *f*. ~**d** *a* desventajado

**disagree** /dɪsəˈgriː/ *vi* no estar de acuerdo; (*food, climate*) sentar mal a. ~**able** /dɪsəˈgriːəbl/ *a* desagradable. ~**ment** *n* desacuerdo *m*; (*quarrel*) riña *f*

**disappear** /dɪsəˈpɪə(r)/ *vi* desaparecer. ~**ance** *n* desaparición *f*

**disappoint** /dɪsəˈpɔɪnt/ *vt* desilusionar, decepcionar. ~**ment** *n* desilusión *f*, decepción *f*

**disapprov|al** /dɪsəˈpruːvl/ *n* desaprobación *f*. ~**e** /dɪsəˈpruːv/ *vi*. ~ **of** desaprobar

**disarm** /dɪsˈɑːm/ *vt/i* desarmar. ~**ament** *n* desarme *m*

**disarray** /dɪsəˈreɪ/ *n* desorden *m*

**disast|er** /dɪˈzɑːstə(r)/ *n* desastre *m*. ~**rous** *a* catastrófico

**disband** /dɪsˈbænd/ *vt* disolver. ● *vi* disolverse

**disbelief** /dɪsbɪˈliːf/ *n* incredulidad *f*

**disc** /dɪsk/ *n* disco *m*

**discard** /dɪsˈkɑːd/ *vt* descartar; abandonar (*beliefs etc*)

**discern** /dɪˈsɜːn/ *vt* percibir. ~**ible** *a* perceptible. ~**ing** *a* perspicaz

**discharge** /dɪsˈtʃɑːdʒ/ *vt* descargar; cumplir (*duty*); (*dismiss*) despedir; poner en libertad (*prisoner*); (*mil*) licenciar. /ˈdɪstʃɑːdʒ/ *n* descarga *f*; (*med*) secreción *f*; (*mil*) licenciamiento *m*; (*dismissal*) despedida *f*

**disciple** /dɪˈsaɪpl/ *n* discípulo *m*

**disciplin|arian** /dɪsɪplɪˈneərɪən/ *n* ordenancista *m* & *f*. ~**ary** *a* disciplinario. ~**e** /ˈdɪsɪplɪn/ *n* disciplina *f*. ● *vt* disciplinar; (*punish*) castigar

**disc jockey** /ˈdɪskdʒɒkɪ/ *n* (*on radio*) pinchadiscos *m* & *f invar*

**disclaim** /dɪsˈkleɪm/ *vt* desconocer. ~**er** *n* renuncia *f*

**disclos|e** /dɪsˈkləʊz/ *vt* revelar. ~**ure** /-ʒə(r)/ *n* revelación *f*

**disco** /ˈdɪskəʊ/ *n* (*pl* **-os**) (*fam*) discoteca *f*

**discolo|ur** /dɪsˈkʌlə(r)/ *vt* decolorar. ● *vi* decolorarse. ~**ration** /-ˈreɪʃn/ *n* decoloración *f*

**discomfort** /dɪs'kʌmfət/ n malestar m; (lack of comfort) incomodidad f

**disconcert** /dɪskən'sɜːt/ vt desconcertar

**disconnect** /dɪskə'nekt/ vt separar; (elec) desconectar

**disconsolate** /dɪs'kɒnsələt/ a desconsolado

**discontent** /dɪskən'tent/ n descontento m. **~ed** a descontento

**discontinue** /dɪskən'tɪnjuː/ vt interrumpir

**discord** /'dɪskɔːd/ n discordia f; (mus) disonancia f. **~ant** /-'skɔːdənt/ a discorde; (mus) disonante

**discothèque** /'dɪskətek/ n discoteca f

**discount** /'dɪskaʊnt/ n descuento m. /dɪs'kaʊnt/ vt hacer caso omiso de; (com) descontar

**discourage** /dɪs'kʌrɪdʒ/ vt desanimar; (dissuade) disuadir

**discourse** /'dɪskɔːs/ n discurso m

**discourteous** /dɪs'kɜːtɪəs/ a descortés

**discover** /dɪs'kʌvə(r)/ vt descubrir. **~y** n descubrimiento m

**discredit** /dɪs'kredɪt/ vt (pt discredited) desacreditar. ● n descrédito m

**discreet** /dɪs'kriːt/ a discreto. **~ly** adv discretamente

**discrepancy** /dɪ'skrepənsɪ/ n discrepancia f

**discretion** /dɪ'skreʃn/ n discreción f

**discriminat|e** /dɪs'krɪmɪneɪt/ vt/i discriminar. **~e between** distinguir entre. **~ing** a perspicaz. **~ion** /-'neɪʃn/ n discernimiento m; (bias) discriminación f

**discus** /'dɪskəs/ n disco m

**discuss** /dɪ'skʌs/ vt discutir. **~ion** /-ʃn/ n discusión f

**disdain** /dɪs'deɪn/ n desdén m. ● vt desdeñar. **~ful** a desdeñoso

**disease** /dɪ'ziːz/ n enfermedad f. **~d** a enfermo

**disembark** /dɪsɪm'bɑːk/ vt/i desembarcar

**disembodied** /dɪsɪm'bɒdɪd/ a incorpóreo

**disenchant** /dɪsɪn'tʃɑːnt/ vt desencantar. **~ment** n desencanto m

**disengage** /dɪsɪn'geɪdʒ/ vt soltar. **~ the clutch** desembragar. **~ment** n soltura f

**disentangle** /dɪsɪn'tæŋgl/ vt desenredar

**disfavour** /dɪs'feɪvə(r)/ . n desaprobación f. **fall into ~** ⟨person⟩ caer en desgracia; ⟨custom, word⟩ caer en desuso

**disfigure** /dɪs'fɪgə(r)/ vt desfigurar

**disgorge** /dɪs'gɔːdʒ/ vt arrojar; ⟨river⟩ descargar; (fig) restituir

**disgrace** /dɪs'greɪs/ n deshonra f; (disfavour) desgracia f. ● vt deshonrar. **~ful** a vergonzoso

**disgruntled** /dɪs'grʌntld/ a descontento

**disguise** /dɪs'gaɪz/ vt disfrazar. ● n disfraz m. **in ~** disfrazado

**disgust** /dɪs'gʌst/ n repugnancia f, asco m. ● vt repugnar, dar asco. **~ing** a repugnante, asqueroso

**dish** /dɪʃ/ n plato m. ● vt. **~ out** (fam) distribuir. **~ up** servir. **~cloth** /'dɪʃklɒθ/ n bayeta f

**dishearten** /dɪs'hɑːtn/ vt desanimar

**dishevelled** /dɪ'ʃevld/ a desaliñado; ⟨hair⟩ despeinado

**dishonest** /dɪs'ɒnɪst/ a ⟨person⟩ poco honrado; ⟨means⟩ fraudulento. **~y** n falta f de honradez

**dishonour** /dɪs'ɒnə(r)/ n deshonra f. ● vt deshonrar. **~able** a deshonroso. **~ably** adv deshonrosamente

**dishwasher** /'dɪʃwɒʃə(r)/ n lavaplatos m & f

**disillusion** /dɪsɪ'luːʒn/ vt desilusionar. **~ment** n desilusión

**disincentive** /dɪsɪn'sentɪv/ n freno m

**disinclined** /dɪsɪn'klaɪnd/ a poco dispuesto

**disinfect** /dɪsɪn'fekt/ vt desinfectar. **~ant** n desinfectante m

**disinherit** /dɪsɪn'herɪt/ vt desheredar

**disintegrate** /dɪs'ɪntɪgreɪt/ vt desintegrar. ● vi desintegrarse

**disinterested** /dɪs'ɪntrəstɪd/ a desinteresado

**disjointed** /dɪs'dʒɔɪntɪd/ a inconexo

**disk** /dɪsk/ n disco m

**dislike** /dɪs'laɪk/ n aversión f. ● vt tener aversión a

**dislocat|e** /'dɪsləkeɪt/ vt dislocar(se) ⟨limb⟩. **~ion** /-'keɪʃn/ n dislocación f

**dislodge** /dɪs'lɒdʒ/ vt sacar; (oust) desalojar

**disloyal** /dɪs'lɔɪəl/ a desleal. **~ty** n deslealtad f

**dismal** /'dɪzməl/ a triste; (bad) fatal

**dismantle** /dɪs'mæntl/ vt desarmar

**dismay** /dɪs'meɪ/ n consternación f. ● vt consternar

**dismiss** /dɪs'mɪs/ vt despedir; (reject) rechazar. ~al n despedida f; (of idea) abandono m

**dismount** /dɪs'maʊnt/ vi apearse

**disobedien|ce** /dɪsə'biːdɪəns/ n desobediencia f. ~t /dɪsə'biːdɪənt/ a desobediente

**disobey** /dɪsə'beɪ/ vt/i desobedecer

**disorder** /dɪs'ɔːdə(r)/ n desorden m; (ailment) trastorno m. ~ly a desordenado

**disorganize** /dɪs'ɔːgənaɪz/ vt desorganizar

**disorientate** /dɪs'ɔːrɪənteɪt/ vt desorientar

**disown** /dɪs'əʊn/ vt repudiar

**disparaging** /dɪs'pærɪdʒɪŋ/ a despreciativo. ~ly adv con desprecio

**disparity** /dɪs'pærətɪ/ n disparidad f

**dispassionate** /dɪs'pæʃənət/ a desapasionado

**dispatch** /dɪs'pætʃ/ vt enviar. ● n envío m; (report) despacho m. ~-rider n correo m

**dispel** /dɪs'pel/ vt (pt dispelled) disipar

**dispensable** /dɪs'pensəbl/ a prescindible

**dispensary** /dɪs'pensərɪ/ n farmacia f

**dispensation** /dɪspen'seɪʃn/ n distribución f; (relig) dispensa f

**dispense** /dɪs'pens/ vt distribuir; (med) preparar; (relig) dispensar; administrar ⟨justice⟩. ~ with prescindir de. ~r /-ə(r)/ n (mec) distribuidor m automático; (med) farmacéutico m

**dispers|al** /dɪs'pɜːsl/ n dispersión f. ~e /dɪs'pɜːs/ vt dispersar. ● vi dispersarse

**dispirited** /dɪs'pɪrɪtɪd/ a desanimado

**displace** /dɪs'pleɪs/ vt desplazar

**display** /dɪs'pleɪ/ vt mostrar; exhibir ⟨goods⟩; manifestar ⟨feelings⟩. ● n exposición f; (of feelings) manifestación f; (pej) ostentación f

**displeas|e** /dɪs'pliːz/ vt desagradar. be ~ed with estar disgustado con. ~ure /-'pleʒə(r)/ n desagrado m

**dispos|able** /dɪs'pəʊzəbl/ a desechable. ~al n (of waste) eliminación f. at s.o.'s ~al a la disposición de uno. ~e /dɪs'pəʊz/ vt disponer. be

**well ~ed towards** estar bien dispuesto hacia. ● vi. ~e of deshacerse de

**disposition** /dɪspə'zɪʃn/ n disposición f

**disproportionate** /dɪsprə'pɔːʃənət/ a desproporcionado

**disprove** /dɪs'pruːv/ vt refutar

**dispute** /dɪs'pjuːt/ vt disputar. ● n disputa f. in ~ disputado

**disqualif|ication** /dɪskwɒlɪfɪ'keɪʃn/ n descalificación f. ~y /dɪs'kwɒlɪfaɪ/ vt incapacitar; (sport) descalificar

**disquiet** /dɪs'kwaɪət/ n inquietud f

**disregard** /dɪsrɪ'gɑːd/ vt no hacer caso de. ● n indiferencia f (for a)

**disrepair** /dɪsrɪ'peə(r)/ n mal estado m

**disreputable** /dɪs'repjʊtəbl/ a de mala fama

**disrepute** /dɪsrɪ'pjuːt/ n descrédito m

**disrespect** /dɪsrɪs'pekt/ n falta f de respeto

**disrobe** /dɪs'rəʊb/ vt desvestir. ● vi desvestirse

**disrupt** /dɪs'rʌpt/ vt interrumpir; trastornar ⟨plans⟩. ~ion /-ʃn/ n interrupción f; (disorder) desorganización f. ~ive a desbaratador

**dissatisfaction** /dɪsætɪs'fækʃn/ n descontento m

**dissatisfied** /dɪ'sætɪsfaɪd/ a descontento

**dissect** /dɪ'sekt/ vt disecar. ~ion /-ʃn/ n disección f

**disseminat|e** /dɪ'semɪneɪt/ vt diseminar. ~ion /-'neɪʃn/ n diseminación f

**dissent** /dɪ'sent/ vi disentir. ● n disentimiento m

**dissertation** /dɪsə'teɪʃn/ n disertación f; (univ) tesis f

**disservice** /dɪs'sɜːvɪs/ n mal servicio m

**dissident** /'dɪsɪdənt/ a & n disidente (m & f)

**dissimilar** /dɪ'sɪmɪlə(r)/ a distinto

**dissipate** /'dɪsɪpeɪt/ vt disipar; (fig) desvanecer. ~d a disoluto

**dissociate** /dɪ'səʊʃɪeɪt/ vt disociar

**dissolut|e** /'dɪsəluːt/ a disoluto. ~ion /dɪsə'luːʃn/ n disolución f

**dissolve** /dɪ'zɒlv/ vt disolver. ● vi disolverse

**dissuade** /dɪ'sweɪd/ vt disuadir

**distan|ce** /'dɪstəns/ n distancia f. from a ~ce desde lejos. in the ~ce a lo lejos. **~t** /'dɪstənt/ *a* lejano; (*aloof*) frío

**distaste** /dɪs'teɪst/ *n* aversión *f.* **~ful** *a* desagradable

**distemper**[1] /dɪ'stempə(r)/ *n* (*paint*) temple *m.* ● *vt* pintar al temple

**distemper**[2] /dɪ'stempə(r)/ *n* (*of dogs*) moquillo *m*

**distend** /dɪs'tend/ *vt* dilatar. ● *vi* dilatarse

**distil** /dɪs'tɪl/ *vt* (*pt* distilled) destilar. **~lation** /-'leɪʃn/ *n* destilación *f.* **~lery** /dɪs'tɪlərɪ/ *n* destilería *f*

**distinct** /dɪs'tɪŋkt/ *a* distinto; (*clear*) claro; (*marked*) marcado. **~ion** /-ʃn/ *n* distinción *f*; (*in exam*) sobresaliente *m.* **~ive** *a* distintivo. **~ly** *adv* claramente

**distinguish** /dɪs'tɪŋgwɪʃ/ *vt/i* distinguir. **~ed** *a* distinguido

**distort** /dɪs'tɔːt/ *vt* torcer. **~ion** /-ʃn/ *n* deformación *f*

**distract** /dɪs'trækt/ *vt* distraer. **~ed** *a* aturdido. **~ing** *a* molesto. **~ion** /-ʃn/ *n* distracción *f*; (*confusion*) aturdimiento *m*

**distraught** /dɪs'trɔːt/ *a* aturdido

**distress** /dɪs'tres/ *n* angustia *f*; (*poverty*) miseria *f*; (*danger*) peligro *m.* ● *vt* afligir. **~ing** *a* penoso

**distribute** /dɪs'trɪbjuːt/ *vt* distribuir. **~ion** /-'bjuːʃn/ *n* distribución *f*. **~or** *n* distribuidor *m*; (*auto*) distribuidor *m* de encendido

**district** /'dɪstrɪkt/ *n* distrito *m*; (*of town*) barrio *m*

**distrust** /dɪs'trʌst/ *n* desconfianza *f.* ● *vt* desconfiar de

**disturb** /dɪs'tɜːb/ *vt* molestar; (*perturb*) inquietar; (*move*) desordenar; (*interrupt*) interrumpir. **~ance** *n* disturbio *m*; (*tumult*) alboroto *m.* **~ed** *a* trastornado. **~ing** *a* inquietante

**disused** /dɪs'juːzd/ *a* fuera de uso

**ditch** /dɪtʃ/ *n* zanja *f*; (*for irrigation*) acequia *f.* ● *vt* (*sl*) abandonar

**dither** /'dɪðə(r)/ *vi* vacilar

**ditto** /'dɪtəʊ/ *adv* ídem

**divan** /dɪ'væn/ *n* diván *m*

**dive** /daɪv/ *vi* tirarse de cabeza; (*rush*) meterse (precipitadamente); (*underwater*) bucear. ● *n* salto *m*; (*of plane*) picado *m*; (*place, fam*) taberna *f.* **~r** *n* saltador *m*; (*underwater*) buzo *m*

**diverge** /daɪ'vɜːdʒ/ *vi* divergir. **~nt** /daɪ'vɜːdʒənt/ *a* divergente

**divers|e** /daɪ'vɜːs/ *a* diverso. **~ify** /daɪ'vɜːsɪfaɪ/ *vt* diversificar. **~ity** /daɪ'vɜːsətɪ/ *n* diversidad *f*

**diver|sion** /daɪ'vɜːʃn/ *n* desvío *m*; (*distraction*) diversión *f.* **~t** /daɪ'vɜːt/ *vt* desviar; (*entertain*) divertir

**divest** /daɪ'vest/ *vt.* **~ of** despojar de

**divide** /dɪ'vaɪd/ *vt* dividir. ● *vi* dividirse

**dividend** /'dɪvɪdend/ *n* dividendo *m*

**divine** /dɪ'vaɪn/ *a* divino

**diving-board** /'daɪvɪŋbɔːd/ *n* trampolín *m*

**diving-suit** /'daɪvɪŋsuːt/ *n* escafandra *f*

**divinity** /dɪ'vɪnɪtɪ/ *n* divinidad *f*

**division** /dɪ'vɪʒn/ *n* división *f*

**divorce** /dɪ'vɔːs/ *n* divorcio *m.* ● *vt* divorciarse de; (*judge*) divorciar. ● *vi* divorciarse. **~e** /dɪvɔː'siː/ *n* divorciado *m*

**divulge** /daɪ'vʌldʒ/ *vt* divulgar

**DIY** *abbr see* **do-it-yourself**

**dizz|iness** /'dɪzɪnɪs/ *n* vértigo *m.* **~y** /'dɪzɪ/ *a* (-ier, -iest) mareado; (*speed*) vertiginoso. **be** *or* **feel ~y** marearse

**do** /duː/ *vt* (3 *sing pres* does, *pt* did, *pp* done) hacer; (*swindle, sl*) engañar. ● *vi* hacer; (*fare*) ir; (*be suitable*) convenir; (*be enough*) bastar. ● *n* (*pl* dos *or* do's) (*fam*) fiesta *f.* ● *v aux.* **~ you speak Spanish? Yes I ~** ¿habla Vd español? Sí. **doesn't he?, don't you?** ¿verdad? **~ come in!** (*emphatic*) ¡pase Vd! **~ away with** abolir. **~ in** (*exhaust, fam*) agotar; (*kill, sl*) matar. **~ out** (*clean*) limpiar. **~ up** abotonar (*coat etc*); renovar (*house*). **~ with** tener que ver con; (*need*) necesitar. **~ without** prescindir de. **~ne for** (*fam*) arruinado. **~ne in** (*fam*) agotado. **well ~ne** (*culin*) bien hecho. **well ~ne!** ¡muy bien!

**docile** /'dəʊsaɪl/ *a* dócil

**dock**[1] /dɒk/ *n* dique *m.* ● *vt* poner en dique. ● *vi* atracar al muelle

**dock**[2] /dɒk/ *n* (*jurid*) banquillo *m* de los acusados

**dock: ~er** *n* estibador *m.* **~yard** /'dɒkjɑːd/ *n* astillero *m*

**doctor** /'dɒktə(r)/ *n* médico *m*, doctor *m*; (*univ*) doctor *m.* ● *vt* castrar (*cat*); (*fig*) adulterar

**doctorate** /'dɒktərət/ *n* doctorado *m*

**doctrine** /'dɒktrɪn/ *n* doctrina *f*

**document** /'dɒkjʊmənt/ *n* documento *m.* **~ary** /-'mentrɪ/ *a* & *n* documental (*m*)

**doddering** /'dɒdərɪŋ/ a chocho

**dodge** /dɒdʒ/ vt esquivar. ● vi esquivarse. ● n regate m; (fam) truco m

**dodgems** /'dɒdʒəmz/ npl autos mpl de choque

**dodgy** /'dɒdʒɪ/ a (-ier, -iest) (awkward) difícil

**does** /dʌz/ see **do**

**doesn't** /'dʌznt/ = **does not**

**dog** /dɒg/ n perro m. ● vt (pt dogged) perseguir. ~collar n (relig, fam) alzacuello m. ~eared a ⟨book⟩ sobado

**dogged** /'dɒgɪd/ a obstinado

**doghouse** /'dɒghaʊs/ n (Amer) perrera f. **in the ~** (sl) en desgracia

**dogma** /'dɒgmə/ n dogma m. ~tic /-'mætɪk/ a dogmático

**dogsbody** /'dɒgzbɒdɪ/ n (fam) burro m de carga

**doh** /dəʊ/ n (mus, first note of any musical scale) do m

**doily** /'dɔɪlɪ/ n tapete m

**doings** /'duːɪŋz/ npl (fam) actividades fpl

**do-it-yourself** /duːɪtjɔː'self/ (abbr **DIY**) n bricolaje m. ~ **enthusiast** n manitas m

**doldrums** /'dɒldrəmz/ npl. **be in the ~** estar abatido

**dole** /dəʊl/ vt. ~ **out** distribuir. ● n (fam) subsidio m de paro. **on the ~** (fam) parado

**doleful** /'dəʊlfl/ a triste

**doll** /dɒl/ n muñeca f. ● vt. ~ **up** (fam) emperejilar

**dollar** /'dɒlə(r)/ n dólar m

**dollop** /'dɒləp/ n (fam) masa f

**dolphin** /'dɒlfɪn/ n delfín m

**domain** /dəʊ'meɪn/ n dominio m; (fig) campo m

**dome** /dəʊm/ n cúpula f. ~d a abovedado

**domestic** /də'mestɪk/ a doméstico; ⟨trade, flights, etc⟩ nacional

**domesticated** a ⟨animal⟩ domesticado

**domesticity** /dɒme'stɪsətɪ/ n domesticidad f

**domestic: ~ science** n economía f doméstica. ~ **servant** n doméstico m

**dominant** /'dɒmɪnənt/ a dominante

**dominate** /'dɒmɪneɪt/ vt/i dominar. ~ion /-'neɪʃn/ n dominación f

**domineer** /dɒmɪ'nɪə(r)/ vi tiranizar

**Dominican Republic** /dəmɪnɪkən rɪ'pʌblɪk/ n República f Dominicana

**dominion** /də'mɪnjən/ n dominio m

**domino** /'dɒmɪnəʊ/ n (pl ~es) ficha f de dominó. ~es npl (game) dominó m

**don¹** /dɒn/ n profesor m

**don²** /dɒn/ vt (pt donned) ponerse

**donate** /dəʊ'neɪt/ vt donar. ~ion /-ʃn/ n donativo m

**done** /dʌn/ see **do**

**donkey** /'dɒŋkɪ/ n burro m. ~work n trabajo m penoso

**donor** /'dəʊnə(r)/ n donante m & f

**don't** /dəʊnt/ = **do not**

**doodle** /'duːdl/ vi garrapatear

**doom** /duːm/ n destino m; (death) muerte f. ● vt. **be ~ed to** ser condenado a

**doomsday** /'duːmzdeɪ/ n día m del juicio final

**door** /dɔː(r)/ n puerta f. ~man /'dɔːmən/ n (pl -men) portero m. ~mat /'dɔːmæt/ n felpudo m. ~step /'dɔːstep/ n peldaño m. ~way /'dɔːweɪ/ n entrada f

**dope** /dəʊp/ n (fam) droga f; (idiot, sl) imbécil m. ● vt (fam) drogar. ~y a (sl) torpe

**dormant** /'dɔːmənt/ a inactivo

**dormer** /'dɔːmə(r)/ n. ~ **(window)** buhardilla f

**dormitory** /'dɔːmɪtrɪ/ n dormitorio m

**dormouse** /'dɔːmaʊs/ n (pl -mice) lirón m

**dos|age** /'dəʊsɪdʒ/ n dosis f. ~e /dəʊs/ n dosis f

**doss** /dɒs/ vi (sl) dormir. ~house n refugio m

**dot** /dɒt/ n punto m. **on the ~** en punto. ● vt (pt dotted) salpicar. **be ~ted with** estar salpicado de

**dote** /dəʊt/ vi. ~ **on** adorar

**dotted line** /dɒtɪd'laɪn/ n línea f de puntos

**dotty** /'dɒtɪ/ a (-ier, -iest) (fam) chiflado

**double** /'dʌbl/ a doble. ● adv doble, dos veces. ● n doble m; (person) doble m & f. **at the ~** corriendo. ● vt doblar; redoblar ⟨efforts etc⟩. ● vi doblarse. ~bass n contrabajo m. ~bed n cama f de matrimonio. ~breasted a cruzado. ~chin n papada f. ~cross vt traicionar. ~dealing n doblez m & f. ~decker n autobús m de dos pisos. ~ **Dutch** n galimatías *m.* **~-jointed** *a* con articulaciones dobles. **~s** *npl* (*tennis*) doble *m*

**doubt** /daʊt/ *n* duda *f*. ● *vt* dudar; (*distrust*) dudar de, desconfiar de. **~ful** *a* dudoso. **~less** *adv* sin duda

**doubly** /'dʌblɪ/ *adv* doblemente

**dough** /dəʊ/ *n* masa *f*; (*money, sl*) dinero *m*, pasta *f* (*sl*)

**doughnut** /'dəʊnʌt/ *n* buñuelo *m*

**douse** /daʊs/ *vt* mojar; apagar (*fire*)

**dove** /dʌv/ *n* paloma *f*

**dowager** /'daʊədʒə(r)/ *n* viuda *f* (con bienes o título del marido)

**dowdy** /'daʊdɪ/ *a* (**-ier, -iest**) poco atractivo

**down**¹ /daʊn/ *adv* abajo. **~ with** abajo. **come ~** bajar. **go ~** bajar; (*sun*) ponerse. **● prep** abajo. **● a** (*sad*) triste. **● vt** derribar; (*drink, fam*) beber

**down**² /daʊn/ *n* (*feathers*) plumón *m*

**down-and-out** /'daʊnənd'aʊt/ *n* vagabundo *m*

**downcast** /'daʊnkɑːst/ *a* abatido

**downfall** /'daʊnfɔːl/ *n* caída *f*; (*fig*) perdición *f*

**downgrade** /daʊn'greɪd/ *vt* degradar

**down-hearted** /daʊn'hɑːtɪd/ *a* abatido

**downhill** /daʊn'hɪl/ *adv* cuesta abajo

**down payment** /'daʊnpeɪmənt/ *n* depósito *m*

**downpour** /'daʊnpɔː(r)/ *n* aguacero *m*

**downright** /'daʊnraɪt/ *a* completo; (*honest*) franco. ● *adv* completamente

**downs** /daʊnz/ *npl* colinas *fpl*

**downstairs** /daʊn'steəz/ *adv* abajo. /'daʊnsteəz/ *a* de abajo

**downstream** /'daʊnstriːm/ *adv* río abajo

**down-to-earth** /daʊntʊ'ɜːθ/ *a* práctico

**downtrodden** /'daʊntrɒdn/ *a* oprimido

**down: ~ under** en las antípodas; (*in Australia*) en Australia. **~ward** /'daʊnwəd/ *a* & *adv*, **~wards** *adv* hacia abajo

**dowry** /'daʊərɪ/ *n* dote *f*

**doze** /dəʊz/ *vi* dormitar. **~ off** dormirse, dar una cabezada. ● *n* sueño *m* ligero

**dozen** /'dʌzn/ *n* docena *f*. **~s of** (*fam*) miles de, muchos

**Dr** *abbr* (*Doctor*) Dr, Doctor *m*. **~ Broadley** (el) Doctor Broadley

**drab** /dræb/ *a* monótono

**draft** /drɑːft/ *n* borrador *m*; (*outline*) bosquejo *m*; (*com*) letra *f* de cambio; (*Amer, mil*) reclutamiento *m*; (*Amer, of air*) corriente *f* de aire. ● *vt* bosquejar; (*mil*) destacar; (*Amer, conscript*) reclutar

**drag** /dræg/ *vt* (*pt* **dragged**) arrastrar; rastrear (*river*). ● *vi* arrastrarse por el suelo. ● *n* (*fam*) lata *f*. **in ~** (*man, sl*) vestido de mujer

**dragon** /'drægən/ *n* dragón *m*

**dragon-fly** /'drægənflaɪ/ *n* libélula *f*

**drain** /dreɪn/ *vt* desaguar; apurar (*tank, glass*); (*fig*) agotar. ● *vi* escurrirse. ● *n* desaguadero *m*. **be a ~ on** agotar. **~ing-board** *n* escurridero *m*

**drama** /'drɑːmə/ *n* drama *m*; (*art*) arte *m* teatral. **~tic** /drə'mætɪk/ *a* dramático. **~tist** /'dræmətɪst/ *n* dramaturgo *m*. **~tize** /'dræmətaɪz/ *vt* adaptar al teatro; (*fig*) dramatizar

**drank** /dræŋk/ *see* **drink**

**drape** /dreɪp/ *vt* cubrir; (*hang*) colgar. **~s** *npl* (*Amer*) cortinas *fpl*

**drastic** /'dræstɪk/ *a* drástico

**draught** /drɑːft/ *n* corriente *f* de aire. **~ beer** *n* cerveza *f* de barril. **~s** *n pl* (*game*) juego *m* de damas

**draughtsman** /'drɑːftsmən/ *n* (*pl* **-men**) diseñador *m*

**draughty** /'drɑːftɪ/ *a* lleno de corrientes de aire

**draw** /drɔː/ *vt* (*pt* **drew**, *pp* **drawn**) tirar; (*attract*) atraer; dibujar (*picture*); trazar (*line*); retirar (*money*). **~ the line at** trazar el límite. ● *vi* (*sport*) empatar; dibujar (*pictures*); (*in lottery*) sortear. ● *n* (*sport*) empate *m*; (*in lottery*) sorteo *m*. **~ out** sacar (*money*). **~ up** pararse; redactar (*document*); acercar (*chair*)

**drawback** /'drɔːbæk/ *n* desventaja *f*

**drawbridge** /'drɔːbrɪdʒ/ *n* puente *m* levadizo

**drawer** /drɔː(r)/ *n* cajón *m*. **~s** /drɔːz/ *npl* calzoncillos *mpl*; (*women's*) bragas *fpl*

**drawing** /'drɔːɪŋ/ *n* dibujo *m*. **~-pin** *n* chinche *m*, chincheta *f*

**drawing-room** /'drɔːɪŋruːm/ *n* salón *m*

**drawl** /drɔːl/ *n* habla *f* lenta

**drawn** /drɔːn/ *see* **draw**. ● *a* (*face*) ojeroso

**dread** /dred/ n terror m. ● vt temer. ~**ful** /'dredfl/ a terrible. ~**fully** adv terriblemente

**dream** /dri:m/ n sueño m. ● vt/i (pt **dreamed** or **dreamt**) soñar. ● a ideal. ~ **up** idear. ~**er** n soñador m. ~**y** a soñador

**drear|iness** /'drɪərɪnɪs/ n tristeza f; (monotony) monotonía f. ~**y** /'drɪərɪ/ a (-ier, -iest) triste; (boring) monótono

**dredge**[1] /dredʒ/ n draga f. ● vt dragar

**dredge**[2] /dredʒ/ n (culin) espolvorear

**dredger**[1] /'dredʒə(r)/ n draga f

**dredger**[2] /'dredʒə(r)/ n (for sugar) espolvoreador m

**dregs** /dregz/ npl heces fpl; (fig) hez f

**drench** /drentʃ/ vt empapar

**dress** /dres/ n vestido m; (clothing) ropa f. ● vt vestir; (decorate) adornar; (med) vendar; (culin) aderezar, aliñar. ● vi vestirse. ~ **circle** n primer palco m

**dresser**[1] /'dresə(r)/ n (furniture) aparador m

**dresser**[2] /'dresə(r)/ n (in theatre) camarero m

**dressing** /'dresɪŋ/ n (sauce) aliño m; (bandage) vendaje m. ~**case** n neceser m. ~**down** n rapapolvo m, reprensión f. ~**gown** n bata f. ~**room** n tocador m; (in theatre) camarín m. ~**table** n tocador m

**dressmak|er** /'dresmeɪkə(r)/ n modista m & f. ~**ing** n costura f

**dress** rehearsal /'dresrɪhɜ:sl/ n ensayo m general

**dressy** /'dresɪ/ a (-ier, -iest) elegante

**drew** /dru:/ see **draw**

**dribble** /'drɪbl/ vi gotear; (baby) babear; (in football) regatear

**dribs and drabs** /drɪbzn'dræbz/ npl. **in** ~ poco a poco, en cantidades pequeñas

**drie|d** /draɪd/ a (food) seco; (fruit) paso. ~**r** /'draɪə(r)/ n secador m

**drift** /drɪft/ vi ir a la deriva; (snow) amontonarse. ● n (movement) dirección f; (of snow) montón m; (meaning) significado m. ~**er** n persona f sin rumbo. ~**wood** /'drɪftwʊd/ n madera f flotante

**drill** /drɪl/ n (tool) taladro m; (training) ejercicio m; (fig) lo normal. ● vt taladrar, perforar; (train) entrenar. ● vi entrenarse

**drily** /'draɪlɪ/ adv secamente

**drink** /drɪŋk/ vt/i (pt **drank**, pp **drunk**) beber. ● n bebida f. ~**able** a bebible; (water) potable. ~**er** n bebedor m. ~**ing-water** n agua f potable

**drip** /drɪp/ vi (pt **dripped**) gotear. ● n gota f; (med) goteo m intravenoso; (person, sl) mentecato m. ~**dry** a que no necesita plancharse

**dripping** /'drɪpɪŋ/ n (culin) pringue m

**drive** /draɪv/ vt (pt **drove**, pp **driven**) empujar; conducir, manejar (LAm) (car etc). ~ **in** clavar (nail). ~ **s.o. mad** volver loco a uno. ● vi conducir. ~ **in** (in car) entrar en coche. ● n paseo m; (road) camino m de entrada; (private road) camino m de entrada; (fig) energía f; (pol) campaña f. ~ **at** querer decir. ~**r** /'draɪvə(r)/ n conductor m, chófer m (LAm)

**drivel** /'drɪvl/ n tonterías fpl

**driving** /'draɪvɪŋ/ n conducción f. ~**licence** n carné m de conducir. ~ **school** n autoescuela f

**drizzl|e** /'drɪzl/ n llovizna f. ● vi lloviznar. ~**y** a lloviznoso

**dromedary** /'drɒmədərɪ/ n dromedario m

**drone** /drəʊn/ n (noise) zumbido m; (bee) zángano m. ● vi zumbar; (fig) hablar en voz monótona; (idle, fam) holgazanear

**drool** /dru:l/ vi babear

**droop** /dru:p/ vt inclinar. ● vi inclinarse; (flowers) marchitarse

**drop** /drɒp/ n gota f; (fall) caída f; (decrease) baja f; (of cliff) precipicio m. ● vt (pt **dropped**) dejar caer; (lower) bajar. ● vi caer. ~ **in on** pasar por casa de. ~ **off** (sleep) dormirse. ~ **out** retirarse; (student) abandonar los estudios. ~**out** n marginado m

**droppings** /'drɒpɪŋz/ npl excremento m

**dross** /drɒs/ n escoria f

**drought** /draʊt/ n sequía f

**drove**[1] /drəʊv/ see **drive**

**drove**[2] /drəʊv/ n manada f

**drown** /draʊn/ vt ahogar. ● vi ahogarse

**drowsy** /'draʊzɪ/ a soñoliento

**drudge** /drʌdʒ/ n esclavo m del trabajo. ~**ry** /-ərɪ/ n trabajo m pesado

**drug** /drʌg/ n droga f; (med) medicamento m. ● vt (pt **drugged**) drogar. ~ **addict** n toxicómano m

**drugstore** /'drʌgstɔː(r)/ n (Amer) farmacia f (que vende otros artículos también)

**drum** /drʌm/ n tambor m; (for oil) bidón m. ● vi (pt drummed) tocar el tambor. ● vt. ~ into s.o. inculcar en la mente de uno. ~mer n tambor m; (in group) batería f. ~s npl batería f. ~stick /'drʌmstɪk/ n baqueta f, (culin) pierna f (de pollo)

**drunk** /drʌŋk/ see drink. ● a borracho. get ~ emborracharse. ~ard n borracho m. ~en a borracho. ~enness n embriaguez f

**dry** /draɪ/ a (drier, driest) seco. ● vt secar. ● vi secarse. ~ up (fam) secar los platos. ~clean vt limpiar en seco. ~cleaner n tintorero m. ~cleaner's (shop) tintorería f. ~ness n sequedad f

**dual** /'djuːəl/ a doble. ~ carriageway n autovía f, carretera f de doble calzada. ~purpose a de doble uso

**dub** /dʌb/ vt (pt dubbed) doblar ⟨film⟩; (nickname) apodar

**dubious** /'djuːbɪəs/ a dudoso; ⟨person⟩ sospechoso

**duchess** /'dʌtʃɪs/ n duquesa f

**duck**[1] /dʌk/ n pato m

**duck**[2] /dʌk/ vt sumergir; bajar ⟨head etc⟩. ● vi agacharse

**duckling** /'dʌklɪŋ/ n patito m

**duct** /dʌkt/ n conducto m

**dud** /dʌd/ a inútil; ⟨cheque⟩ sin fondos; ⟨coin⟩ falso

**due** /djuː/ a debido; (expected) esperado. ~ to debido a. ● adv. ~ north n derecho hacia el norte. ~s npl derechos mpl

**duel** /'djuːəl/ n duelo m

**duet** /djuː'et/ n dúo m

**duffle** /'dʌfl/ a. ~ bag n bolsa f de lona. ~coat n trenca f

**dug** /dʌg/ see dig

**duke** /djuːk/ n duque m

**dull** /dʌl/ a (-er, -est) ⟨weather⟩ gris; ⟨colour⟩ apagado; ⟨person, play, etc⟩ pesado; ⟨sound⟩ sordo; (stupid) torpe. ● vt aliviar ⟨pain⟩; entorpecer ⟨mind⟩

**duly** /'djuːlɪ/ adv debidamente

**dumb** /dʌm/ a (-er, -est) mudo; (fam) estúpido

**dumbfound** /dʌm'faʊnd/ vt pasmar

**dummy** /'dʌmɪ/ n muñeco m; (of tailor) maniquí m; (of baby) chupete m. ● a falso. ~ run n prueba f

**dump** /dʌmp/ vt descargar; (fam) deshacerse de. ● n vertedero m;

(mil) depósito m; (fam) lugar m desagradable. be down in the ~s estar deprimido

**dumpling** /'dʌmplɪŋ/ n bola f de masa hervida

**dumpy** /'dʌmpɪ/ a (-ier, -iest) regordete

**dunce** /dʌns/ n burro m

**dung** /dʌŋ/ n excremento m; (manure) estiércol m

**dungarees** /dʌŋgə'riːz/ npl mono m, peto m

**dungeon** /'dʌndʒən/ n calabozo m

**dunk** /dʌŋk/ vt remojar

**duo** /'djuːəʊ/ n dúo m

**dupe** /djuːp/ vt engañar. ● n inocentón m

**duplicat|e** /'djuːplɪkət/ a & n duplicado (m). /'djuːplɪkeɪt/ vt duplicar; (on machine) reproducir. ~or n multicopista f

**duplicity** /djuː'plɪsətɪ/ n doblez f

**durable** /'djʊərəbl/ a resistente; (enduring) duradero

**duration** /djʊ'reɪʃn/ n duración f

**duress** /djʊ'res/ n coacción f

**during** /'djʊərɪŋ/ prep durante

**dusk** /dʌsk/ n crepúsculo m

**dusky** /'dʌskɪ/ a (-ier, -iest) oscuro

**dust** /dʌst/ n polvo m. ● vt quitar el polvo a; (sprinkle) espolvorear

**dustbin** /'dʌstbɪn/ n cubo m de la basura

**dust-cover** /'dʌstkʌvə(r)/ n sobrecubierta f

**duster** /'dʌstə(r)/ n trapo m

**dust-jacket** /'dʌstdʒækɪt/ n sobrecubierta f

**dustman** /'dʌstmən/ n (pl -men) basurero m

**dustpan** /'dʌstpæn/ n recogedor m

**dusty** /'dʌstɪ/ a (-ier, -iest) polvoriento

**Dutch** /dʌtʃ/ a & n holandés (m). go ~ pagar a escote. ~man m holandés m. ~woman n holandesa f

**dutiful** /'djuːtɪfl/ a obediente

**duty** /'djuːtɪ/ n deber m; (tax) derechos mpl de aduana. on ~ de servicio. ~free a libre de impuestos

**duvet** /'djuːveɪ/ n edredón m

**dwarf** /dwɔːf/ n (pl -s) enano m. ● vt empequeñecer

**dwell** /dwel/ vi (pt dwelt) morar. ~ on dilatarse. ~er n habitante m & f. ~ing n morada f

**dwindle** /'dwɪndl/ vi disminuir

**dye** /daɪ/ vt (pres p **dyeing**) teñir. ● n tinte m

**dying** /'daɪɪŋ/ see **die**

**dynamic** /daɪ'næmɪk/ a dinámico. ~s npl dinámica f

**dynamite** /'daɪnəmaɪt/ n dinamita f. ● vt dinamitar

**dynamo** /'daɪnəməʊ/ n dinamo f, dínamo f

**dynasty** /'dɪnəstɪ/ n dinastía f

**dysentery** /'dɪsəntrɪ/ n disentería f

**dyslexia** /dɪs'leksɪə/ n dislexia f

# E

**each** /iːtʃ/ a cada. ● pron cada uno. ~ **one** cada uno. ~ **other** uno a otro, el uno al otro. **they love** ~ **other** se aman

**eager** /'iːgə(r)/ a impaciente; (enthusiastic) ávido. ~**ly** adv con impaciencia. ~**ness** n impaciencia f, ansia f

**eagle** /'iːgl/ n águila f

**ear**¹ /ɪə(r)/ n oído m; (outer) oreja f

**ear**² /ɪə(r)/ n (of corn) espiga f

**ear**: ~**ache** /'ɪəreɪk/ n dolor m de oído. ~**drum** n tímpano m

**earl** /ɜːl/ n conde m

**early** /'ɜːlɪ/ a (-ier, -iest) temprano; (before expected time) prematuro. **in the** ~ **spring** a principios de la primavera. ● adv temprano; (ahead of time) con anticipación

**earmark** /'ɪəmɑːk/ vt. ~ **for** destinar a

**earn** /ɜːn/ vt ganar; (deserve) merecer

**earnest** /'ɜːnɪst/ a serio. **in** ~ en serio

**earnings** /'ɜːnɪŋz/ npl ingresos mpl; (com) ganacias fpl

**ear**: ~**phones** /'ɪəfəʊnz/ npl auricular m. ~**ring** n pendiente m

**earshot** /'ɪəʃɒt/ n. **within** ~ al alcance del oído

**earth** /ɜːθ/ n tierra f. ● vt (elec) conectar a tierra. ~**ly** a terrenal

**earthenware** /'ɜːθnweə(r)/ n loza f de barro

**earthquake** /'ɜːθkweɪk/ n terremoto m

**earthy** /'ɜːθɪ/ a terroso; (coarse) grosero

**earwig** /'ɪəwɪg/ n tijereta f

**ease** /iːz/ n facilidad f; (comfort) tranquilidad f. **at** ~ a gusto; (mil) en posición de descanso. **ill at** ~ molesto. **with** ~ fácilmente. ● vt calmar; aliviar ⟨pain⟩; tranquilizar ⟨mind⟩; (loosen) aflojar. ● vi calmarse; (lessen) disminuir

**easel** /'iːzl/ n caballete m

**east** /iːst/ n este m, oriente m. ● a del este, oriental. ● adv hacia el este.

**Easter** /'iːstə(r)/ n Semana f Santa; (relig) Pascua f de Resurrección. ~ **egg** n huevo m de Pascua

**east**: ~**erly** a este; ⟨wind⟩ del este. ~**ern** a del este, oriental. ~**ward** adv, ~**wards** adv hacia el este

**easy** /'iːzɪ/ a (-ier, -iest) fácil; (relaxed) tranquilo. **go** ~ **on** (fam) tener cuidado con. **take it** ~ no preocuparse. ● int ¡despacio! ~ **chair** n sillón m. ~**going** a acomodadizo

**eat** /iːt/ vt/i (pt **ate**, pp **eaten**) comer. ~ **into** corroer. ~**able** a comestible. ~**er** n comedor m

**eau-de-Cologne** /əʊdəkə'ləʊn/ n agua f de colonia

**eaves** /iːvz/ npl alero m

**eavesdrop** /'iːvzdrɒp/ vi (pt -**dropped**) escuchar a escondidas

**ebb** /eb/ n reflujo m. ● vi bajar; (fig) decaer

**ebony** /'ebənɪ/ n ébano m

**ebullient** /ɪ'bʌlɪənt/ a exuberante

**EC** /iː'siː/ abbr (European Community) CE (Comunidad f Europea)

**eccentric** /ɪk'sentrɪk/ a & n excéntrico (m). ~**ity** /eksen'trɪsətɪ/ n excentricidad f

**ecclesiastical** /ɪkliːzɪ'æstɪkl/ a eclesiástico

**echelon** /'eʃəlɒn/ n escalón m

**echo** /'ekəʊ/ n (pl -**oes**) eco m. ● vt (pt **echoed**, pres p **echoing**) repetir; (imitate) imitar. ● vi hacer eco

**eclectic** /ɪk'lektɪk/ a & n ecléctico (m)

**eclipse** /ɪ'klɪps/ n eclipse m. ● vt eclipsar

**ecology** /ɪ'kɒlədʒɪ/ n ecología f

**econom|ic** /iːkə'nɒmɪk/ a económico. ~**ical** a económico. ~**ics** n economía f. ~**ist** /ɪ'kɒnəmɪst/ n economista m & f. ~**ize** /ɪ'kɒnəmaɪz/ vi economizar. ~**y** /ɪ'kɒnəmɪ/ n economía f

**ecsta|sy** /'ekstəsɪ/ n éxtasis f. ~**tic** /ɪk'stætɪk/ a extático. ~**tically** adv con éxtasis

**Ecuador** /'ekwədɔː(r)/ n el Ecuador m

**ecumenical** /iːkjuːˈmenɪkl/ a ecuménico

**eddy** /ˈedɪ/ n remolino m

**edge** /edʒ/ n borde m, margen m; (of knife) filo m; (of town) afueras fpl. **have the ~ on** (fam) llevar la ventaja a. **on ~** nervioso. ● vt ribetear; (move) mover poco a poco. ● vi avanzar cautelosamente. **~ways** adv de lado

**edging** /ˈedʒɪŋ/ n borde m; (sewing) ribete m

**edgy** /ˈedʒɪ/ a nervioso

**edible** /ˈedɪbl/ a comestible

**edict** /ˈiːdɪkt/ n edicto m

**edifice** /ˈedɪfɪs/ n edificio m

**edify** /ˈedɪfaɪ/ vt edificar

**edit** /ˈedɪt/ vt dirigir ⟨newspaper⟩; preparar una edición de ⟨text⟩; (write) redactar; montar ⟨film⟩. **~ed by** a cargo de. **~ion** /ɪˈdɪʃn/ n edición f. **~or** /ˈedɪtə(r)/ n (of newspaper) director m; (of text) redactor m. **~orial** /edɪˈtɔːrɪəl/ a editorial. ● n artículo m de fondo. **~or in chief** n jefe m de redacción

**educat|e** /ˈedʒʊkeɪt/ vt instruir, educar. **~ed** a culto. **~ion** /-ˈkeɪʃn/ n enseñanza f; (culture) cultura f; (upbringing) educación f. **~ional** /-ˈkeɪʃənl/ a instructivo

**EEC** /iːiːˈsiː/ abbr (European Economic Community) CEE (Comunidad f Económica Europea)

**eel** /iːl/ n anguila f

**eerie** /ˈɪərɪ/ a (-ier, -iest) misterioso

**efface** /ɪˈfeɪs/ vt borrar

**effect** /ɪˈfekt/ n efecto m. **in ~** efectivamente. **take ~** entrar en vigor. ● vt efectuar

**effective** /ɪˈfektɪv/ a eficaz; (striking) impresionante; (mil) efectivo. **~ly** adv eficazmente. **~ness** n eficacia f

**effeminate** /ɪˈfemɪnət/ a afeminado

**effervescent** /efəˈvesnt/ a efervescente

**effete** /ɪˈfiːt/ a agotado

**efficien|cy** /ɪˈfɪʃənsɪ/ n eficiencia f; (mec) rendimiento m. **~t** /ɪˈfɪʃnt/ a eficiente. **~tly** adv eficientemente

**effigy** /ˈefɪdʒɪ/ n efigie f

**effort** /ˈefət/ n esfuerzo m. **~less** a fácil

**effrontery** /ɪˈfrʌntərɪ/ n descaro m

**effusive** /ɪˈfjuːsɪv/ a efusivo

**e.g.** /iːˈdʒiː/ abbr (exempli gratia) p.ej., por ejemplo

**egalitarian** /ɪgælɪˈteərɪən/ a & n igualitario (m)

**egg**[1] /eg/ n huevo m

**egg**[2] /eg/ vt. **~ on** (fam) incitar

**egg-cup** /ˈegkʌp/ n huevera f

**egg-plant** /ˈegplɑːnt/ n berenjena f

**eggshell** /ˈegʃel/ n cáscara f de huevo

**ego** /ˈiːgəʊ/ n (pl -os) yo m. **~ism** n egoísmo m. **~ist** n egoísta m & f. **~centric** /iːgəʊˈsentrɪk/ a egocéntrico. **~tism** n egotismo m. **~tist** n egotista m & f

**Egypt** /ˈiːdʒɪpt/ n Egipto m. **~ian** /ɪˈdʒɪpʃn/ a & n egipcio (m)

**eh** /eɪ/ int (fam) ¡eh!

**eiderdown** /ˈaɪdədaʊn/ n edredón m

**eight** /eɪt/ a & n ocho (m)

**eighteen** /eɪˈtiːn/ a & n dieciocho (m). **~th** a & n decimoctavo (m)

**eighth** /eɪtθ/ a & n octavo (m)

**eight|ieth** /ˈeɪtɪəθ/ a & n ochenta (m), octogésimo (m). **~y** /ˈeɪtɪ/ a & n ochenta (m)

**either** /ˈaɪðə(r)/ a cualquiera de los dos; (negative) ninguno de los dos; (each) cada. ● pron uno u otro; (with negative) ni uno ni otro. ● adv (after negative) tampoco. ● conj o. **~ he** or o él o; (with negative) ni él ni

**ejaculate** /ɪˈdʒækjʊleɪt/ vt/i (exclaim) exclamar

**eject** /ɪˈdʒekt/ vt expulsar, echar

**eke** /iːk/ vt. **~ out** hacer bastar; (increase) complementar

**elaborate** /ɪˈlæbərət/ a complicado. /ɪˈlæbəreɪt/ vt elaborar. ● vi explicarse

**elapse** /ɪˈlæps/ vi (of time) transcurrir

**elastic** /ɪˈlæstɪk/ a & n elástico (m). **~ band** n goma f (elástica)

**elasticity** /ɪlæˈstɪsətɪ/ n elasticidad f

**elat|ed** /ɪˈleɪtɪd/ a regocijado. **~ion** /-ʃn/ n regocijo m

**elbow** /ˈelbəʊ/ n codo m

**elder**[1] /ˈeldə(r)/ a & n mayor (m)

**elder**[2] /ˈeldə(r)/ n (tree) saúco m

**elderly** /ˈeldəlɪ/ a mayor, anciano

**eldest** /ˈeldɪst/ a & n el mayor (m)

**elect** /ɪˈlekt/ vt elegir. **~ to do** decidir hacer. ● a electo. **~ion** /-ʃn/ n elección f

**elector** /ɪˈlektə(r)/ n elector m. **~al** a electoral. **~ate** n electorado m

**electric** /ɪˈlektrɪk/ a eléctrico. **~al** a eléctrico. **~ blanket** n manta f eléctrica. **~ian** /ɪlekˈtrɪʃn/ n electricista *m & f.* **~ity** /ɪlek'trɪsətɪ/ *n* electricidad *f*

**electrify** /ɪ'lektrɪfaɪ/ *vt* electrificar; (*fig*) electrizar

**electrocute** /ɪ'lektrəkjuːt/ *vt* electrocutar

**electrolysis** /ɪlek'trɒlɪsɪs/ *n* electrólisis *f*

**electron** /ɪ'lektrɒn/ *n* electrón *m*

**electronic** /ɪlek'trɒnɪk/ *a* electrónico. **~s** *n* electrónica *f*

**elegan|ce** /'elɪgəns/ *n* elegancia *f*. **~t** /'elɪgənt/ *a* elegante. **~tly** *adv* elegantemente

**element** /'elɪmənt/ *n* elemento *m*. **~ary** /-'mentrɪ/ *a* elemental

**elephant** /'elɪfənt/ *n* elefante *m*

**elevat|e** /'elɪveɪt/ *vt* elevar. **~ion** /-'veɪʃn/ *n* elevación *f*. **~or** /'elɪveɪtə(r)/ *n* (*Amer*) ascensor *m*

**eleven** /ɪ'levn/ *a & n* once (*m*). **~th** *a & n* undécimo (*m*)

**elf** /elf/ *n* (*pl* **elves**) duende *m*

**elicit** /ɪ'lɪsɪt/ *vt* sacar

**eligible** /'elɪdʒəbl/ *a* elegible. **be ~ for** tener derecho a

**eliminat|e** /ɪ'lɪmɪneɪt/ *vt* eliminar. **~ion** /-'neɪʃn/ *n* eliminación *f*

**élite** /eɪ'liːt/ *n* elite *f*, élite *m*

**elixir** /ɪ'lɪksɪə(r)/ *n* elixir *m*

**ellip|se** /ɪ'lɪps/ *n* elipse *f*. **~tical** *a* elíptico

**elm** /elm/ *n* olmo *m*

**elocution** /elə'kjuːʃn/ *n* elocución *f*

**elongate** /'iːlɒŋgeɪt/ *vt* alargar

**elope** /ɪ'ləʊp/ *vi* fugarse con el amante. **~ment** *n* fuga *f*

**eloquen|ce** /'eləkwəns/ *n* elocuencia *f*. **~t** /'eləkwənt/ *a* elocuente. **~tly** *adv* con elocuencia

**El Salvador** /el'sælvədɔː(r)/ *n* El Salvador *m*

**else** /els/ *adv* más. **everybody ~** todos los demás. **nobody ~** ningún otro, nadie más. **nothing ~** nada más. **or ~** o bien. **somewhere ~** en otra parte

**elsewhere** /els'weə(r)/ *adv* en otra parte

**elucidate** /ɪ'luːsɪdeɪt/ *vt* aclarar

**elude** /ɪ'luːd/ *vt* eludir

**elusive** /ɪ'luːsɪv/ *a* esquivo

**emaciated** /ɪ'meɪʃɪeɪtɪd/ *a* esquelético

**emanate** /'eməneɪt/ *vi* emanar

**emancipat|e** /ɪ'mænsɪpeɪt/ *vt* emancipar. **~ion** /-'peɪʃn/ *n* emancipación *f*

**embalm** /ɪm'bɑːm/ *vt* embalsamar

**embankment** /ɪm'bæŋkmənt/ *n* terraplén *m*; (*of river*) dique *m*

**embargo** /ɪm'bɑːgəʊ/ *n* (*pl* -oes) prohibición *f*

**embark** /ɪm'bɑːk/ *vt* embarcar. ● *vi* embarcarse. **~ on** (*fig*) emprender. **~ation** /embɑː'keɪʃn/ *n* (*of people*) embarco *m*; (*of goods*) embarque *m*

**embarrass** /ɪm'bærəs/ *vt* desconcertar; (*shame*) dar vergüenza. **~ment** *n* desconcierto *m*; (*shame*) vergüenza *f*

**embassy** /'embəsɪ/ *n* embajada *f*

**embed** /ɪm'bed/ *vt* (*pt* **embedded**) embutir; (*fig*) fijar

**embellish** /ɪm'belɪʃ/ *vt* embellecer. **~ment** *n* embellecimiento *m*

**embers** /'embəz/ *npl* ascua *f*

**embezzle** /ɪm'bezl/ *vt* desfalcar. **~ment** *n* desfalco *m*

**embitter** /ɪm'bɪtə(r)/ *vt* amargar

**emblem** /'embləm/ *n* emblema *m*

**embod|iment** /ɪm'bɒdɪmənt/ *n* encarnación *f*. **~y** /ɪm'bɒdɪ/ *vt* encarnar; (*include*) incluir

**emboss** /ɪm'bɒs/ *vt* grabar en relieve, repujar. **~ed** *a* en relieve, repujado

**embrace** /ɪm'breɪs/ *vt* abrazar; (*fig*) abarcar. ● *vi* abrazarse. ● *n* abrazo *m*

**embroider** /ɪm'brɔɪdə(r)/ *vt* bordar. **~y** *n* bordado *m*

**embroil** /ɪm'brɔɪl/ *vt* enredar

**embryo** /'embrɪəʊ/ *n* (*pl* -os) embrión *m*. **~nic** /-'ɒnɪk/ *a* embrionario

**emend** /ɪ'mend/ *vt* enmendar

**emerald** /'emərəld/ *n* esmeralda *f*

**emerge** /ɪ'mɜːdʒ/ *vi* salir. **~nce** /-əns/ *n* aparición *f*

**emergency** /ɪ'mɜːdʒənsɪ/ *n* emergencia *f*. **in an ~** en caso de emergencia. **~ exit** *n* salida *f* de emergencia

**emery** /'emərɪ/ *n* esmeril *m*. **~board** *n* lima *f* de uñas

**emigrant** /'emɪgrənt/ *n* emigrante *m & f*

**emigrat|e** /'emɪgreɪt/ *vi* emigrar. **~ion** /-'greɪʃn/ *n* emigración *f*

**eminen|ce** /'emɪnəns/ *n* eminencia *f*. **~t** /'emɪnənt/ *a* eminente. **~tly** *adv* eminentemente

**emissary** /'emɪsərɪ/ *n* emisario *m*

**emission** /ɪ'mɪʃn/ *n* emisión *f*

**emit** /ɪ'mɪt/ *vt* (*pt* **emitted**) emitir

**emollient** /ɪ'mɒlɪənt/ *a & n* emoliente (*m*)

**emoti|on** /ɪ'məʊʃn/ n emoción f. **∼onal** a emocional; ⟨person⟩ emotivo; ⟨moving⟩ conmovedor. **∼ve** /ɪ'məʊtɪv/ a emotivo

**empathy** /'empəθɪ/ n empatía f

**emperor** /'empərə(r)/ n emperador m

**emphasi|s** /'emfəsɪs/ n (pl ∼ses /-siːz/) énfasis m. **∼ze** /'emfəsaɪz/ vt subrayar; ⟨single out⟩ destacar

**emphatic** /ɪm'fætɪk/ a categórico; ⟨resolute⟩ decidido

**empire** /'empaɪə(r)/ n imperio m

**empirical** /ɪm'pɪrɪkl/ a empírico

**employ** /ɪm'plɔɪ/ vt emplear. **∼ee** /emplɔɪ'iː/ n empleado m. **∼er** n patrón m. **∼ment** n empleo m. **∼ment agency** n agencia f de colocaciones

**empower** /ɪm'paʊə(r)/ vt autorizar (**to do** a hacer)

**empress** /'emprɪs/ n emperatriz f

**empt|ies** /'emptɪz/ npl envases mpl. **∼iness** n vacío m. **∼y** /'emptɪ/ a vacío; ⟨promise⟩ vano. **on an ∼y stomach** con el estómago vacío. ● vt vaciar. ● vi vaciarse

**emulate** /'emjʊleɪt/ vt emular

**emulsion** /ɪ'mʌlʃn/ n emulsión f

**enable** /ɪ'neɪbl/ vt. **∼ s.o. to** permitir a uno

**enact** /ɪ'nækt/ vt ⟨jurid⟩ decretar; ⟨in theatre⟩ representar

**enamel** /ɪ'næml/ n esmalte m. ● vt (pt **enamelled**) esmaltar

**enamoured** /ɪ'næməd/ a. **be ∼ of** estar enamorado de

**encampment** /ɪn'kæmpmənt/ n campamento m

**encase** /ɪn'keɪs/ vt encerrar

**enchant** /ɪn'tʃɑːnt/ vt encantar. **∼ing** a encantador. **∼ment** n encanto m

**encircle** /ɪn'sɜːkl/ vt rodear

**enclave** /'enkleɪv/ n enclave m

**enclos|e** /ɪn'kləʊz/ vt cercar ⟨land⟩; (with letter) adjuntar; (in receptacle) encerrar. **∼ed** a ⟨space⟩ encerrado; ⟨com⟩ adjunto. **∼ure** /ɪn'kləʊʒə(r)/ n cercamiento m; ⟨area⟩ recinto m; ⟨com⟩ documento m adjunto

**encompass** /ɪn'kʌmpəs/ vt cercar; (include) incluir, abarcar

**encore** /'ɒŋkɔː(r)/ int ¡bis! ● n bis m, repetición f

**encounter** /ɪn'kaʊntə(r)/ vt encontrar. ● n encuentro m

**encourage** /ɪn'kʌrɪdʒ/ vt animar; (stimulate) estimular. **∼ment** n estímulo m

**encroach** /ɪn'krəʊtʃ/ vi. **∼ on** invadir ⟨land⟩; quitar ⟨time⟩. **∼ment** n usurpación f

**encumb|er** /ɪn'kʌmbə(r)/ vt (hamper) estorbar; ⟨burden⟩ cargar. **be ∼ered with** estar cargado de. **∼rance** n estorbo m; ⟨burden⟩ carga f

**encyclical** /ɪn'sɪklɪkl/ n encíclica f

**encyclopaedi|a** /ɪnsaɪklə'piːdɪə/ n enciclopedia f. **∼c** a enciclopédico

**end** /end/ n fin m; (furthest point) extremo m. **in the ∼** por fin. **make ∼s meet** poder llegar a fin de mes. **no ∼** (fam) muy. **no ∼ of** muchísimos. **on ∼** de pie; (consecutive) seguido. ● vt/i terminar, acabar

**endanger** /ɪn'deɪndʒə(r)/ vt arriesgar

**endear|ing** /ɪn'dɪərɪŋ/ a simpático. **∼ment** n palabra f cariñosa

**endeavour** /ɪn'devə(r)/ n tentativa f. ● vi. **∼ to** esforzarse por

**ending** /'endɪŋ/ n fin m

**endive** /'endɪv/ n escarola f, endibia f

**endless** /'endlɪs/ a interminable; ⟨patience⟩ infinito

**endorse** /ɪn'dɔːs/ vt endosar; (fig) aprobar. **∼ment** n endoso m; (fig) aprobación f; ⟨auto⟩ nota f de inhabilitación

**endow** /ɪn'daʊ/ vt dotar

**endur|able** /ɪn'djʊərəbl/ a aguantable. **∼ance** n resistencia f. **∼e** /ɪn'djʊə(r)/ vt aguantar. ● vi durar. **∼ing** a perdurable

**enemy** /'enəmɪ/ n & a enemigo (m)

**energ|etic** /enə'dʒetɪk/ a enérgico. **∼y** /'enədʒɪ/ n energía f

**enervat|e** /'enɜːveɪt/ vt debilitar. **∼ing** a debilitante

**enfold** /ɪn'fəʊld/ vt envolver; (in arms) abrazar

**enforce** /ɪn'fɔːs/ vt aplicar; (impose) imponer; hacer cumplir ⟨law⟩. **∼d** a forzado

**engage** /ɪn'geɪdʒ/ vt emplear ⟨staff⟩; (reserve) reservar; ocupar ⟨attention⟩; ⟨mec⟩ hacer engranar. ● vi ⟨mec⟩ engranar. **∼d** a prometido; (busy) ocupado. **get ∼d** prometerse. **∼ment** n compromiso m; (undertaking) obligación f

**engaging** /ɪn'geɪdʒɪŋ/ a atractivo

**engender** /ɪn'dʒendə(r)/ vt engendrar

**engine** /'endʒɪn/ n motor m; (of train) locomotora f. **∼-driver** n maquinista m

**engineer** /endʒɪ'nɪə(r)/ n ingeniero m; (mechanic) mecánico m. ● vt (contrive, fam) lograr. ~ing n ingeniería f

**England** /'ɪŋglənd/ n Inglaterra f

**English** /'ɪŋglɪʃ/ a inglés. ● n (lang) inglés m; (people) ingleses mpl. ~man n inglés m. ~woman n inglesa f. the ~ Channel n el canal m de la Mancha

**engrave** /ɪn'greɪv/ vt grabar. ~ing n grabado m

**engrossed** /ɪn'grəʊst/ a absorto

**engulf** /ɪn'gʌlf/ vt tragar(se)

**enhance** /ɪn'hɑːns/ vt aumentar

**enigma** /ɪ'nɪgmə/ n enigma m. ~tic /enɪg'mætɪk/ a enigmático

**enjoy** /ɪn'dʒɔɪ/ vt gozar de. ~ o.s. divertirse. I ~ reading me gusta la lectura. ~able a agradable. ~ment n placer m

**enlarge** /ɪn'lɑːdʒ/ vt agrandar; (foto) ampliar. ● vi agrandarse. ~ upon extenderse sobre. ~ment n (foto) ampliación f

**enlighten** /ɪn'laɪtn/ vt aclarar; (inform) informar. ~ment n aclaración f. the E~ment el siglo m de la luces

**enlist** /ɪn'lɪst/ vt alistar; (fig) conseguir. ● vi alistarse

**enliven** /ɪn'laɪvn/ vt animar

**enmity** /'enmətɪ/ n enemistad f

**ennoble** /ɪ'nəʊbl/ vt ennoblecer

**enormity** /ɪ'nɔːmətɪ/ n enormidad f. ~ous /ɪ'nɔːməs/ a enorme

**enough** /ɪ'nʌf/ a & adv bastante. ● n bastante m, suficiente m. ● int ¡basta!

**enquire** /ɪn'kwaɪə(r)/ vt/i preguntar. ~e about informarse de. ~y n pregunta f; (investigation) investigación f

**enrage** /ɪn'reɪdʒ/ vt enfurecer

**enrapture** /ɪn'ræptʃə(r)/ vt extasiar

**enrich** /ɪn'rɪtʃ/ vt enriquecer

**enrol** /ɪn'rəʊl/ vt (pt enrolled) inscribir; matricular (student). ● vi inscribirse; (student) matricularse. ~ment n inscripción f; (of student) matrícula f

**ensconce** /ɪn'skɒns/ vt. ~ o.s. arrellanarse

**ensemble** /ɒn'sɒmbl/ n conjunto m

**enshrine** /ɪn'ʃraɪn/ vt encerrar

**ensign** /'ensaɪn/ n enseña f

**enslave** /ɪn'sleɪv/ vt esclavizar

**ensue** /ɪn'sjuː/ vi resultar, seguirse

**ensure** /ɪn'ʃʊə(r)/ vt asegurar

**entail** /ɪn'teɪl/ vt suponer;. acarrear (trouble etc)

**entangle** /ɪn'tæŋgl/ vt enredar. ~ment n enredo m; (mil) alambrada f

**enter** /'entə(r)/ vt entrar en; (write) escribir; matricular (school etc); hacerse socio de (club). ● vi entrar

**enterprise** /'entəpraɪz/ n empresa f; (fig) iniciativa f

**enterprising** /'entəpraɪzɪŋ/ a emprendedor

**entertain** /entə'teɪn/ vt divertir; recibir (guests); abrigar (ideas, hopes); (consider) considerar. ~ment n diversión f; (performance) espectáculo m; (reception) recepción f

**enthral** /ɪn'θrɔːl/ vt (pt enthralled) cautivar

**enthuse** /ɪn'θjuːz/ vi. ~ over entusiasmarse por

**enthusiasm** /ɪn'θjuːzɪæzəm/ n entusiasmo m. ~tic /-'æstɪk/ a entusiasta; (thing) entusiástico. ~tically /-'æstɪklɪ/ adv con entusiasmo. ~t /ɪn'θjuːzɪæst/ n entusiasta m & f

**entice** /ɪn'taɪs/ vt atraer. ~ment n atracción f

**entire** /ɪn'taɪə(r)/ a entero. ~ly adv completamente. ~ty /ɪn'taɪərətɪ/ n. in its ~ty en su totalidad

**entitle** /ɪn'taɪtl/ vt titular; (give a right) dar derecho a. be ~d to tener derecho a. ~ment n derecho m

**entity** /'entətɪ/ n entidad f

**entomb** /ɪn'tuːm/ vt sepultar

**entrails** /'entreɪlz/ npl entrañas fpl

**entrance**[1] /'entrəns/ n entrada f; (right to enter) admisión f

**entrance**[2] /ɪn'trɑːns/ vt encantar

**entrant** /'entrənt/ n participante m & f; (in exam) candidato m

**entreat** /ɪn'triːt/ vt suplicar. ~y n súplica f

**entrench** /ɪn'trentʃ/ vt atrincherar

**entrust** /ɪn'trʌst/ vt confiar

**entry** /'entrɪ/ n entrada f; (of street) bocacalle f; (note) apunte m

**entwine** /ɪn'twaɪn/ vt entrelazar

**enumerate** /ɪ'njuːməreɪt/ vt enumerar

**enunciate** /ɪ'nʌnsɪeɪt/ vt pronunciar; (state) enunciar

**envelop** /ɪn'veləp/ vt (pt enveloped) envolver

**envelope** /'envələʊp/ n sobre m

**enviable** /'envɪəbl/ a envidiable

**envious** /'envɪəs/ a envidioso. ~**ly** adv con envidia

**environment** /ɪn'vaɪərənmənt/ n medio m ambiente. ~**al** /-'mentl/ a ambiental

**envisage** /ɪn'vɪzɪdʒ/ vt prever; (imagine) imaginar

**envoy** /'envoɪ/ n enviado m

**envy** /'envɪ/ n envidia f. ● vt envidiar

**enzyme** /'enzaɪm/ n enzima f

**epaulette** /'epəʊlet/ n charretera f

**ephemeral** /ɪ'femərəl/ a efímero

**epic** /'epɪk/ n épica f. ● a épico

**epicentre** /'epɪsentə(r)/ n epicentro m

**epicure** /'epɪkjʊə(r)/ n sibarita m & f; (gourmet) gastrónomo m

**epidemic** /epɪ'demɪk/ n epidemia f. ● a epidémico

**epilep|sy** /'epɪlepsɪ/ n epilepsia f. ~**tic** /-'leptɪk/ a & n epiléptico (m)

**epilogue** /'epɪlɒg/ n epílogo m

**episode** /'epɪsəʊd/ n episodio m

**epistle** /ɪ'pɪsl/ n epístola f

**epitaph** /'epɪtɑ:f/ n epitafio m

**epithet** /'epɪθet/ n epíteto m

**epitom|e** /ɪ'pɪtəmɪ/ n epítome m, personificación f. ~**ize** vt epitomar, personificar, ser la personificación de

**epoch** /'i:pɒk/ n época f. ~**-making** a que hace época

**equal** /'i:kwəl/ a & n igual (m & f). ~ **to** (a task) a la altura de. ● vt (pt **equalled**) ser igual a; (math) ser. ~**ity** /ɪ'kwɒlətɪ/ n igualdad f. ~**ize** /'i:kwəlaɪz/ vt/i igualar. ~**izer** /-ə(r)/ n (sport) tanto m de empate. ~**ly** adv igualmente

**equanimity** /ekwə'nɪmətɪ/ n ecuanimidad f

**equate** /ɪ'kweɪt/ vt igualar

**equation** /ɪ'kweɪʒn/ n ecuación f

**equator** /ɪ'kweɪtə(r)/ n ecuador m. ~**ial** /ekwə'tɔ:rɪəl/ a ecuatorial

**equestrian** /ɪ'kwestrɪən/ a ecuestre

**equilateral** /i:kwɪ'lætərl/ a equilátero

**equilibrium** /i:kwɪ'lɪbrɪəm/ n equilibrio m

**equinox** /'i:kwɪnɒks/ n equinoccio m

**equip** /ɪ'kwɪp/ vt (pt **equipped**) equipar. ~**ment** n equipo m

**equitable** /'ekwɪtəbl/ a equitativo

**equity** /'ekwətɪ/ n equidad f; (pl, com) acciones fpl ordinarias

**equivalen|ce** /ɪ'kwɪvələns/ n equivalencia f. ~**t** /ɪ'kwɪvələnt/ a & n equivalente (m)

**equivocal** /ɪ'kwɪvəkl/ a equívoco

**era** /'ɪərə/ n era f

**eradicate** /ɪ'rædɪkeɪt/ vt extirpar

**erase** /ɪ'reɪz/ vt borrar. ~**r** /-ə(r)/ n borrador m

**erect** /ɪ'rekt/ a erguido. ● vt levantar. ~**ion** /-ʃn/ n erección f, montaje m

**ermine** /'ɜ:mɪn/ n armiño m

**ero|de** /ɪ'rəʊd/ vt desgastar. ~**sion** /-ʒn/ n desgaste m

**erotic** /ɪ'rɒtɪk/ a erótico. ~**ism** /-sɪzəm/ n erotismo m

**err** /ɜ:(r)/ vi errar; (sin) pecar

**errand** /'erənd/ n recado m

**erratic** /ɪ'rætɪk/ a irregular; (person) voluble

**erroneous** /ɪ'rəʊnɪəs/ a erróneo

**error** /'erə(r)/ n error m

**erudit|e** /'eru:daɪt/ a erudito. ~**ion** /-'dɪʃn/ n erudición f

**erupt** /ɪ'rʌpt/ vi estar en erupción; (fig) estallar. ~**ion** /-ʃn/ n erupción f

**escalat|e** /'eskəleɪt/ vt intensificar. ● vi intensificarse. ~**ion** /-'leɪʃn/ n intensificación f

**escalator** /'eskəleɪtə(r)/ n escalera f mecánica

**escapade** /eskə'peɪd/ n aventura f

**escap|e** /ɪ'skeɪp/ vi escaparse. ● vt evitar. ● n fuga f; (avoidance) evasión f. **have a narrow** ~**e** escapar por un pelo. ~**ism** /ɪ'skeɪpɪzəm/ n escapismo m

**escarpment** /ɪs'kɑ:pmənt/ n escarpa f

**escort** /'eskɔ:t/ n acompañante m; (mil) escolta f. /ɪ'skɔ:t/ vt acompañar; (mil) escoltar

**Eskimo** /'eskɪməʊ/ n (pl -**os**, -**o**) esquimal (m & f)

**especial** /ɪ'speʃl/ a especial. ~**ly** adv especialmente

**espionage** /'espɪənɑ:ʒ/ n espionaje m

**esplanade** /esplə'neɪd/ n paseo m marítimo

**Esq.** /ɪ'skwaɪə(r)/ abbr (Esquire) (in address). **E. Ashton,** ~ Sr. D. E. Ashton

**essay** /'eseɪ/ n ensayo m; (at school) composición f

**essence** /'esns/ n esencia f. **in** ~ esencialmente

**essential** /ɪ'senʃl/ a esencial. ● n lo esencial. ~**ly** adv esencialmente

**establish** /ɪ'stæblɪʃ/ vt establecer; (*prove*) probar. **~ment** n establecimiento m. **the E~ment** los que mandan, el sistema m

**estate** /ɪ'steɪt/ n finca f; (*possessions*) bienes mpl. **~ agent** n agente m inmobiliario. **~ car** n furgoneta f

**esteem** /ɪ'stiːm/ vt estimar. ● n estimación f, estima f

**estimat|e** /'estɪmət/ n cálculo m; (*com*) presupuesto m. /'estɪmeɪt/ vt calcular. **~ion** /-'meɪʃn/ n estima f, estimación f; (*opinion*) opinión f

**estranged** /ɪs'treɪndʒd/ a alejado

**estuary** /'estʃʊərɪ/ n estuario m

**etc.** /et'setrə/ abbr (*et cetera*) etc., etcétera

**etching** /'etʃɪŋ/ n aguafuerte m

**eternal** /ɪ'tɜːnl/ a eterno

**eternity** /ɪ'tɜːnətɪ/ n eternidad f

**ether** /'iːθə(r)/ n éter m

**ethereal** /ɪ'θɪərɪəl/ a etéreo

**ethic** /'eθɪk/ n ética f. **~s** npl ética f. **~al** a ético

**ethnic** /'eθnɪk/ a étnico

**ethos** /'iːθɒs/ n carácter m distintivo

**etiquette** /'etɪket/ n etiqueta f

**etymology** /etɪ'mɒlədʒɪ/ n etimología f

**eucalyptus** /juːkə'lɪptəs/ n (*pl* **-tuses**) eucalipto m

**eulogy** /'juːlədʒɪ/ n encomio m

**euphemism** /'juːfəmɪzəm/ n eufemismo m

**euphoria** /juː'fɔːrɪə/ n euforia f

**Europe** /'jʊərəp/ n Europa f. **~an** /-'pɪən/ a & n europeo (m)

**euthanasia** /juːθə'neɪzɪə/ n eutanasia f

**evacuat|e** /ɪ'vækjʊeɪt/ vt evacuar; desocupar (*building*). **~ion** /-'eɪʃn/ n evacuación f

**evade** /ɪ'veɪd/ vt evadir

**evaluate** /ɪ'væljʊeɪt/ vt evaluar

**evangeli|cal** /iːvæn'dʒelɪkl/ a evangélico. **~st** /ɪ'vændʒəlɪst/ n evangelista m & f

**evaporat|e** /ɪ'væpəreɪt/ vi evaporarse. **~ion** /-'reɪʃn/ n evaporación f

**evasion** /ɪ'veɪʒn/ n evasión f

**evasive** /ɪ'veɪsɪv/ a evasivo

**eve** /iːv/ n víspera f

**even** /'iːvn/ a regular; (*flat*) llano; ⟨*surface*⟩ liso; ⟨*amount*⟩ igual; ⟨*number*⟩ par. **get ~ with** desquitarse con. ● vt nivelar. **~ up** igualar. ● adv aun, hasta, incluso. **~ if**

aunque. **~ so** aun así. **not ~** ni siquiera

**evening** /'iːvnɪŋ/ n tarde f; (*after dark*) noche f. **~ class** n clase f nocturna. **~ dress** n (*man's*) traje m de etiqueta; (*woman's*) traje m de noche

**evensong** /'iːvənsɒŋ/ n vísperas fpl

**event** /ɪ'vent/ n acontecimiento m; (*sport*) prueba f. **in the ~ of** en caso de. **~ful** a lleno de acontecimientos

**eventual** /ɪ'ventʃʊəl/ a final, definitivo. **~ity** /-'ælətɪ/ n eventualidad f. **~ly** adv finalmente

**ever** /'evə(r)/ adv jamás, nunca; (*at all times*) siempre. **~ after** desde entonces. **~ since** desde entonces. ● conj después de que. **~ so** (*fam*) muy. **for ~** para siempre. **hardly ~** casi nunca

**evergreen** /'evəgriːn/ a de hoja perenne. ● n árbol m de hoja perenne

**everlasting** /'evəlɑːstɪŋ/ a eterno

**every** /'evrɪ/ a cada, todo. **~ child** todos los niños. **~ one** cada uno. **~ other day** cada dos días

**everybody** /'evrɪbɒdɪ/ pron todo el mundo

**everyday** /'evrɪdeɪ/ a todos los días

**everyone** /'evrɪwʌn/ pron todo el mundo. **~ else** todos los demás

**everything** /'evrɪθɪŋ/ pron todo

**everywhere** /'evrɪweə(r)/ adv en todas partes

**evict** /ɪ'vɪkt/ vt desahuciar. **~ion** /-ʃn/ n desahucio m

**eviden|ce** /'evɪdəns/ n evidencia f; (*proof*) pruebas fpl; (*jurid*) testimonio m. **~ce of** señales de. **in ~ce** visible. **~t** /'evɪdənt/ a evidente. **~tly** adv evidentemente

**evil** /'iːvl/ a malo. ● n mal m, maldad f

**evocative** /ɪ'vɒkətɪv/ a evocador

**evoke** /ɪ'vəʊk/ vt evocar

**evolution** /iːvə'luːʃn/ n evolución f

**evolve** /ɪ'vɒlv/ vt desarrollar. ● vi desarrollarse, evolucionar

**ewe** /juː/ n oveja f

**ex...** /eks/ pref ex...

**exacerbate** /ɪg'zæsəbeɪt/ vt exacerbar

**exact** /ɪg'zækt/ a exacto. ● vt exigir (from a). **~ing** a exigente. **~itude** n exactitud f. **~ly** adv exactamente

**exaggerat|e** /ɪg'zædʒəreɪt/ vt exagerar. **~ion** /-'reɪʃn/ n exageración f

**exalt** /ɪg'zɔːlt/ vt exaltar

**exam** /ɪg'zæm/ n (fam) examen m.
~ination /ɪgzæmɪ'neɪʃn/ n examen
m. ~ine /ɪg'zæmɪn/ vt examinar;
interrogar ⟨witness⟩. ~iner /-ə(r)/ n
examinador m

**example** /ɪg'zɑːmpl/ n ejemplo m.
**make an** ~ **of** infligir castigo ejemplar a

**exasperat|e** /ɪg'zæspəreɪt/ vt
exasperar. ~ion /-'reɪʃn/ n
exasperación f

**excavat|e** /'ekskəveɪt/ vt excavar.
~ion /-'veɪʃn/ n excavación f

**exceed** /ɪk'siːd/ vt exceder. ~ingly
adv extremadamente

**excel** /ɪk'sel/ vi (pt **excelled**) sobresalir. ● vt superar

**excellen|ce** /'eksələns/ n excelencia
f. ~t /'eksələnt/ a excelente. ~tly
adv excelentemente

**except** /ɪk'sept/ prep excepto, con
excepción de. ~ **for** con excepción
de. ● vt exceptuar. ~ing prep con
excepción de

**exception** /ɪk'sepʃən/ n excepción f.
**take** ~ **to** ofenderse por. ~al
/ɪk'sepʃənl/ a excepcional. ~ally
adv excepcionalmente

**excerpt** /'eksɜːpt/ n extracto m

**excess** /ɪk'ses/ n exceso m. /'ekses/ a
excedente. ~ **fare** n suplemento m.
~ **luggage** n exceso m de equipaje

**excessive** /ɪk'sesɪv/ a excesivo. ~ly
adv excesivamente

**exchange** /ɪk'stʃeɪndʒ/ vt cambiar.
● n cambio m. (**telephone**) ~ central f telefónica

**exchequer** /ɪks'tʃekə(r)/ n (pol) erario m, hacienda f

**excise¹** /'eksaɪz/ n impuestos mpl
indirectos

**excise²** /ek'saɪz/ vt quitar

**excit|able** /ɪk'saɪtəbl/ a excitable.
~e /ɪk'saɪt/ vt emocionar; (stimulate) excitar. ~ed a entus-
iasmado. ~ement n emoción f;
(enthusiasm) entusiasmo m. ~ing a
emocionante

**excla|im** /ɪk'skleɪm/ vi exclamar.
~mation /eksklə'meɪʃn/ n exclamación f. ~mation mark n signo m
de admiración f, punto m de
exclamación

**exclu|de** /ɪk'skluːd/ vt excluir.
~sion /-ʒən/ n exclusión f

**exclusive** /ɪk'skluːsɪv/ a exclusivo;
⟨club⟩ selecto. ~ **of** excluyendo.
~ly adv exclusivamente

**excomunicate** /ekskə'mjuːnɪkeɪt/ vt
excomulgar

**excrement** /'ekskrɪmənt/ n excremento m

**excruciating** /ɪk'skruːʃıeɪtɪŋ/ a
atroz, insoportable

**excursion** /ɪk'skɜːʃn/ n excursión f

**excus|able** /ɪk'skjuːzəbl/ a per-
donable. ~e /ɪk'skjuːz/ vt perdonar.
~e **from** dispensar de. ~e **me!** ¡perdón! /ɪk'skjuːs/ n excusa f

**ex-directory** /eksdɪ'rektərɪ/ a que
no está en la guía telefónica

**execrable** /'eksɪkrəbl/ a execrable

**execut|e** /'eksɪkjuːt/ vt ejecutar.
~ion /eksɪ'kjuːʃn/ n ejecución f.
~ioner n verdugo m

**executive** /ɪg'zekjutɪv/ a & n ejecutivo (m)

**executor** /ɪg'zekjʊtə(r)/ n (jurid)
testamentario m

**exemplary** /ɪg'zemplərɪ/ a ejemplar

**exemplify** /ɪg'zemplɪfaɪ/ vt ilustrar

**exempt** /ɪg'zempt/ a exento. ● vt dispensar. ~ion /-ʃn/ n exención f

**exercise** /'eksəsaɪz/ n ejercicio m.
● vt ejercer. ● vi hacer ejercicios. ~
**book** n cuaderno m

**exert** /ɪg'zɜːt/ vt ejercer. ~ **o.s.** esforzarse. ~ion /-ʃn/ n esfuerzo m

**exhal|ation** /ekshə'leɪʃn/ n exhala-
ción f. ~e /eks'heɪl/ vt/i exhalar

**exhaust** /ɪg'zɔːst/ vt agotar. ● n
(auto) tubo m de escape. ~ed a agotado. ~ion /-stʃən/ n agotamiento
m. ~ive /ɪg'zɔːstɪv/ a exhaustivo

**exhibit** /ɪg'zɪbɪt/ vt exponer; (jurid)
exhibir; (fig) mostrar. ● n objeto m
expuesto; (jurid) documento m

**exhibition** /eksɪ'bɪʃn/ n exposición
f; (act of showing) demostración f;
(univ) beca f. ~ist n exhibicionista
m & f

**exhibitor** /ɪg'zɪbɪtə(r)/ n expositor m

**exhilarat|e** /ɪg'zɪləreɪt/ vt alegrar.
~ion /-'reɪʃn/ n regocijo m

**exhort** /ɪg'zɔːt/ vt exhortar

**exile** /'eksaɪl/ n exilio m; (person)
exiliado m. ● vt desterrar

**exist** /ɪg'zɪst/ vi existir. ~ence n
existencia f. **in** ~ence existente

**existentialism** /egzɪs'tenʃəlɪzəm/ n
existencialismo m

**exit** /'eksɪt/ n salida f

**exodus** /'eksədəs/ n éxodo m

**exonerate** /ɪg'zɒnəreɪt/ vt disculpar

**exorbitant** /ɪg'zɔːbɪtənt/ a exorbitante

**exorcis|e** /'eksɔːsaɪz/ *vt* exorcizar. **~m** /-sɪzəm/ *n* exorcismo *m*

**exotic** /ɪgˈzɒtɪk/ *a* exótico

**expand** /ɪkˈspænd/ *vt* extender; dilatar ⟨*metal*⟩; (*develop*) desarrollar. ● *vi* extenderse; (*develop*) desarrollarse; ⟨*metal*⟩ dilatarse

**expanse** /ɪkˈspæns/ *n* extensión *f*

**expansion** /ɪkˈspænʃn/ *n* extensión *f*; (*of metal*) dilatación *f*

**expansive** /ɪkˈspænsɪv/ *a* expansivo

**expatriate** /eksˈpætrɪət/ *a* & *n* expatriado (*m*)

**expect** /ɪkˈspekt/ *vt* esperar; (*suppose*) suponer; (*demand*) contar con. **I ~ so** supongo que sí

**expectan|cy** /ɪkˈspektənsɪ/ *n* esperanza *f*. **life ~cy** esperanza *f* de vida. **~t** /ɪkˈspektənt/ *a* expectante. **~t mother** *n* futura madre *f*

**expectation** /ekspek'teɪʃn/ *n* esperanza *f*

**expedien|cy** /ɪkˈspiːdɪənsɪ/ *n* conveniencia *f*. **~t** /ɪkˈspiːdɪənt/ *a* conveniente

**expedite** /'ekspɪdaɪt/ *vt* acelerar

**expedition** /ekspɪˈdɪʃn/ *n* expedición *f*. **~ary** *a* expedicionario

**expel** /ɪkˈspel/ *vt* (*pt* **expelled**) expulsar

**expend** /ɪkˈspend/ *vt* gastar. **~able** *a* prescindible

**expenditure** /ɪkˈspendɪtʃə(r)/ *n* gastos *mpl*

**expens|e** /ɪkˈspens/ *n* gasto *m*; (*fig*) costa *f*. **at s.o.'s ~e** a costa de uno. **~ive** /ɪkˈspensɪv/ *a* caro. **~ively** *adv* costosamente

**experience** /ɪkˈspɪərɪəns/ *n* experiencia. ● *vt* experimentar. **~d** *a* experto

**experiment** /ɪkˈsperɪmənt/ *n* experimento *m*. ● *vi* experimentar. **~al** /-'mentl/ *a* experimental

**expert** /'ekspɜːt/ *a* & *n* experto (*m*). **~ise** /ekspɜːˈtiːz/ *n* pericia *f*. **~ly** *adv* hábilmente

**expir|e** /ɪkˈspaɪə(r)/ *vi* expirar. **~y** *n* expiración *f*

**expla|in** /ɪkˈspleɪn/ *vt* explicar. **~nation** /eksplə'neɪʃn/ *n* explicación *f*. **~natory** /ɪksˈplænətərɪ/ *a* explicativo

**expletive** /ɪkˈspliːtɪv/ *n* palabrota *f*

**explicit** /ɪkˈsplɪsɪt/ *a* explícito

**explode** /ɪkˈspləʊd/ *vt* hacer explotar; (*tec*) explosionar. ● *vi* estallar

**exploit** /'eksplɔɪt/ *n* hazaña *f*. /ɪkˈsplɔɪt/ *vt* explotar. **~ation** /eksplɔɪˈteɪʃn/ *n* explotación *f*

**explor|ation** /eksplə'reɪʃn/ *n* exploración *f*. **~atory** /ɪkˈsplɒrətrɪ/ *a* exploratorio. **~e** /ɪkˈsplɔː(r)/ *vt* explorar. **~er** *n* explorador *m*

**explosi|on** /ɪkˈspləʊʒn/ *n* explosión *f*. **~ve** *a* & *n* explosivo (*m*)

**exponent** /ɪkˈspəʊnənt/ *n* exponente *m*

**export** /ɪkˈspɔːt/ *vt* exportar. /'ekspɔːt/ *n* exportación *f*. **~er** /ɪksˈpɔːtə(r)/ *n* exportador *m*

**expos|e** /ɪkˈspəʊz/ *vt* exponer; (*reveal*) descubrir. **~ure** /-ʒə(r)/ *n* exposición *f*. **die of ~ure** morir de frío

**expound** /ɪkˈspaʊnd/ *vt* exponer

**express**[1] /ɪkˈspres/ *vt* expresar

**express**[2] /ɪkˈspres/ *a* expreso; ⟨*letter*⟩ urgente. ● *adv* (*by express post*) por correo urgente. ● *n* (*train*) rápido *m*, expreso *m*

**expression** /ɪkˈspreʃn/ *n* expresión *f*

**expressive** /ɪkˈspresɪv/ *a* expresivo

**expressly** /ɪkˈspreslɪ/ *adv* expresamente

**expulsion** /ɪkˈspʌlʃn/ *n* expulsión *f*

**expurgate** /'ekspəgeɪt/ *vt* expurgar

**exquisite** /'ekskwɪzɪt/ *a* exquisito. **~ly** *adv* primorosamente

**ex-serviceman** /eks'sɜːvɪsmən/ *n* (*pl* **-men**) excombatiente *m*

**extant** /ek'stænt/ *a* existente

**extempore** /ek'stempərɪ/ *a* improvisado. ● *adv* de improviso

**exten|d** /ɪkˈstend/ *vt* extender; (*prolong*) prolongar; ensanchar ⟨*house*⟩. ● *vi* extenderse. **~sion** *n* extensión *f*; (*of road, time*) prolongación *f*; (*building*) anejo *m*; (*com*) prórroga *f*

**extensive** /ɪkˈstensɪv/ *a* extenso. **~ly** *adv* extensamente

**extent** /ɪkˈstent/ *n* extensión *f*; (*fig*) alcance *m*. **to a certain ~** hasta cierto punto

**extenuate** /ɪkˈstenjʊeɪt/ *vt* atenuar

**exterior** /ɪkˈstɪərɪə(r)/ *a* & *n* exterior (*m*)

**exterminat|e** /ɪkˈstɜːmɪneɪt/ *vt* exterminar. **~ion** /-'neɪʃn/ *n* exterminio *m*

**external** /ɪkˈstɜːnl/ *a* externo. **~ly** *adv* externamente

**extinct** /ɪkˈstɪŋkt/ *a* extinto. **~ion** /-ʃn/ *n* extinción *f*

**extinguish** /ɪkˈstɪŋgwɪʃ/ *vt* extinguir. **~er** *n* extintor *m*

**extol** /ɪkˈstəʊl/ *vt* (*pt* **extolled**) alabar

**extort** /ɪk'stɔ:t/ vt sacar por la fuerza. **~ion** /-ʃn/ n exacción f. **~ionate** /ɪk'stɔ:ʃənət/ a exorbitante

**extra** /'ekstrə/ a suplementario. ● adv extraordinariamente. ● n suplemento m; (cinema) extra m & f

**extract** /'ekstrækt/ n extracto m. /ɪk'strækt/ vt extraer; (fig) arrancar. **~ion** /-ʃn/ n extracción f; (lineage) origen m

**extradit|e** /'ekstrədaɪt/ vt extraditar. **~ion** /-'dɪʃn/ n extradición f

**extramarital** /ekstrə'mærɪtl/ a fuera del matrimonio

**extramural** /ekstrə'mjʊərəl/ a fuera del recinto universitario; (for external students) para estudiantes externos

**extraordinary** /ɪk'strɔ:dnrɪ/ a extraordinario

**extra-sensory** /ekstrə'sensərɪ/ a extrasensorial

**extravagan|ce** /ɪk'strævəgəns/ n prodigalidad f, extravagancia f. **~t** /ɪk'strævəgənt/ a pródigo, extravagante

**extrem|e** /ɪk'stri:m/ a & n extremo (m). **~ely** adv extremadamente. **~ist** n extremista m & f. **~ity** /ɪk'stremətɪ/ n extremidad f

**extricate** /'ekstrɪkeɪt/ vt desenredar, librar

**extrovert** /'ekstrəvɜ:t/ n extrovertido m

**exuberan|ce** /ɪg'zju:bərəns/ n exuberancia f. **~t** /ɪg'zju:bərənt/ a exuberante

**exude** /ɪg'zju:d/ vt rezumar

**exult** /ɪg'zʌlt/ vi exultar

**eye** /aɪ/ n ojo m. **keep an ~ on** no perder de vista. **see ~ to ~** estar de acuerdo con. ● vt (pt eyed, pres p eyeing) mirar. **~ball** /'aɪbɔ:l/ n globo m del ojo. **~brow** /'aɪbraʊ/ n ceja f. **~ful** /'aɪfʊl/ n (fam) espectáculo m sorprendente. **~lash** /'aɪlæʃ/ n pestaña f. **~let** /'aɪlɪt/ n ojete m. **~lid** /'aɪlɪd/ n párpado m. **~opener** n (fam) revelación f. **~shadow** n sombra f de ojos, sombreador m. **~sight** /'aɪsaɪt/ n vista f. **~sore** /'aɪsɔ:(r)/ n (fig, fam) monstruosidad f, horror m. **~witness** /'aɪwɪtnɪs/ n testigo m ocular

# F

**fable** /'feɪbl/ n fábula f

**fabric** /'fæbrɪk/ n tejido m, tela f

**fabrication** /fæbrɪ'keɪʃn/ n invención f

**fabulous** /'fæbjʊləs/ a fabuloso

**façade** /fə'sɑ:d/ n fachada f

**face** /feɪs/ n cara f, rostro m; (of watch) esfera f; (aspect) aspecto m. **~ down(wards)** boca abajo. **~ up(wards)** boca arriba. **in the ~ of** frente a. **lose ~** quedar mal. **pull ~s** hacer muecas. ● vt mirar hacia; ⟨house⟩ dar a; (confront) enfrentarse con. ● vi volverse. **~ up to** enfrentarse con. **~ flannel** n paño m (para lavarse la cara). **~less** a anónimo. **~lift** n cirugía f estética en la cara

**facet** /'fæsɪt/ n faceta f

**facetious** /fə'si:ʃəs/ a chistoso, gracioso

**facial** /'feɪʃl/ a facial. ● n masaje m facial

**facile** /'fæsaɪl/ a fácil

**facilitate** /fə'sɪlɪteɪt/ vt facilitar

**facility** /fə'sɪlɪtɪ/ n facilidad f

**facing** /'feɪsɪŋ/ n revestimiento m. **~s** npl (on clothes) vueltas fpl

**facsimile** /fæk'sɪmɪlɪ/ n facsímile m

**fact** /fækt/ n hecho m. **as a matter of ~, in ~** en realidad, a decir verdad

**faction** /'fækʃn/ n facción f

**factor** /'fæktə(r)/ n factor m

**factory** /'fæktərɪ/ n fábrica f

**factual** /'fæktʃʊəl/ a basado en hechos, factual

**faculty** /'fækəltɪ/ n facultad f

**fad** /fæd/ n manía f, capricho m

**fade** /feɪd/ vi ⟨colour⟩ descolorarse; ⟨flowers⟩ marchitarse; ⟨light⟩ apagarse; ⟨memory, sound⟩ desvanecerse

**faeces** /'fi:si:z/ npl excrementos mpl

**fag**[1] /fæg/ n (chore, fam) faena f; (cigarette, sl) cigarrillo m, pitillo m

**fag**[2] /fæg/ n (homosexual, Amer, sl) marica m

**fagged** /fægd/ a. **~ (out)** rendido

**fah** /fɑ/ n (mus, fourth note of any musical scale) fa m

**fail** /feɪl/ vi fallar; (run short) acabarse. **he ~ed to arrive** no llegó. ● vt no aprobar ⟨exam⟩; suspender ⟨candidate⟩; (disappoint) fallar. **~ s.o.** faltarle a uno. ● n. **without ~** sin falta

**failing** /'feɪlɪŋ/ n defecto m. ● prep a falta de

**failure** /'feɪljə(r)/ n fracaso m; (person) fracasado m; (med) ataque m; (mec) fallo m. ~ **to do** dejar m de hacer

**faint** /feɪnt/ a (-er, -est) (weak) débil; (indistinct) indistinto. **feel** ~ estar mareado. **the** ~**est idea** la más remota idea. ● vi desmayarse. ● n desmayo m. ~**-hearted** a pusilánime, cobarde. ~**ly** adv (weakly) débilmente; (indistinctly) indistintamente. ~**ness** n debilidad f

**fair**[1] /feə(r)/ a (-er, -est) (just) justo; ⟨weather⟩ bueno; ⟨amount⟩ razonable; ⟨hair⟩ rubio; ⟨skin⟩ blanco. ~ **play** n juego m limpio. ● adv limpio

**fair**[2] /feə(r)/ n feria f

**fair**: ~**ly** adv (justly) justamente; (rather) bastante. ~**ness** n justicia f

**fairy** /'feərɪ/ n hada f. ~**land** n país m de las hadas. ~ **story**, ~**tale** cuento m de hadas

**fait accompli** /feɪtə'kɒmpliː/ n hecho m consumado

**faith** /feɪθ/ n (trust) confianza f; (relig) fe f. ~**ful** a fiel. ~**fully** adv fielmente. ~**fulness** n fidelidad f. ~**healing** n curación f por la fe

**fake** /feɪk/ n falsificación f; (person) impostor m. ● a falso. ● vt falsificar; (pretend) fingir

**fakir** /'feɪkɪə(r)/ n faquir m

**falcon** /'fɔːlkən/ n halcón m

**Falkland** /'fɔːlkland/ n. **the** ~ **Islands** npl las islas fpl Malvinas

**fall** /fɔːl/ vi (pt **fell**, pp **fallen**) caer. ● n caída f; (autumn, Amer) otoño m; (in price) baja f. ~ **back on** recurrir a. ~ **down** (fall) caer; (be unsuccessful) fracasar. ~ **for** (fam) enamorarse de ⟨person⟩; (fam) dejarse engañar por ⟨trick⟩. ~ **in** (mil) formar filas. ~ **off** (diminish) disminuir. ~ **out** (quarrel) reñir (with con); (drop out) caer. ~ **over** caer(se). ~ **over sth** tropezar con algo. ~ **short** ser insuficiente. ~ **through** fracasar

**fallacy** /'fæləsɪ/ n error m

**fallible** /'fælɪbl/ a falible

**fallout** /'fɔːlaʊt/ n lluvia f radiactiva

**fallow** /'fæləʊ/ a en barbecho

**false** /fɔːls/ a falso. ~**hood** n mentira f. ~**ly** adv falsamente. ~**ness** n falsedad f

**falsetto** /fɔːl'setəʊ/ n (pl **-os**) falsete m

**falsify** /'fɔːlsɪfaɪ/ vt falsificar

**falter** /'fɔːltə(r)/ vi vacilar

**fame** /feɪm/ n fama f. ~**d** a famoso

**familiar** /fə'mɪlɪə(r)/ a familiar. **be** ~ **with** conocer. ~**ity** /-'ærətɪ/ n familiaridad f. ~**ize** vt familiarizar

**family** /'fæməlɪ/ n familia f. ● a de (la) familia, familiar

**famine** /'fæmɪn/ n hambre f, hambruna f (Amer)

**famished** /'fæmɪʃt/ a hambriento

**famous** /'feɪməs/ a famoso. ~**ly** adv (fam) a las mil maravillas

**fan**[1] /fæn/ n abanico m; (mec) ventilador m. ● vt (pt **fanned**) abanicar; soplar ⟨fire⟩. ● vi. ~ **out** desparramarse en forma de abanico

**fan**[2] /fæn/ n (of person) admirador m; (enthusiast) aficionado m, entusiasta m & f

**fanatic** /fə'nætɪk/ n fanático m. ~**al** a fanático. ~**ism** /-sɪzəm/ n fanatismo m

**fan belt** /'fænbelt/ n correa f de ventilador

**fancier** /'fænsɪə(r)/ n aficionado m

**fanciful** /'fænsɪfl/ a (imaginative) imaginativo; (unreal) imaginario

**fancy** /'fænsɪ/ n fantasía f; (liking) gusto m. **take a** ~ **to** tomar cariño a ⟨person⟩; aficionarse a ⟨thing⟩. ● a de lujo; (extravagant) excesivo. ● vt (imagine) imaginar; (believe) creer; (want, fam) apetecer a. ~ **dress** n disfraz m

**fanfare** /'fænfeə(r)/ n fanfarria f

**fang** /fæŋ/ n (of animal) colmillo m; (of snake) diente m

**fanlight** /'fænlaɪt/ n montante m

**fantasize** /'fæntəsaɪz/ vi fantasear

**fantastic** /fæn'tæstɪk/ a fantástico

**fantasy** /'fæntəsɪ/ n fantasía f

**far** /fɑː(r)/ adv lejos; (much) mucho. **as** ~ **as** hasta. **as** ~ **as I know** que yo sepa. **by** ~ con mucho. ● a (further, furthest or farther, farthest) lejano

**far-away** /'fɑːrəweɪ/ a lejano

**farc|e** /fɑːs/ n farsa f. ~**ical** a ridículo

**fare** /feə(r)/ n (for transport) tarifa f; (food) comida f. ● vi irle. **how did you** ~? ¿qué tal te fue?

**Far East** /fɑː(r)'iːst/ n Extremo/Lejano Oriente m

**farewell** /feə'wel/ int & n adiós (m)

**far-fetched** /fɑː'fetʃt/ a improbable

**farm** /fɑːm/ n granja f. ● vt cultivar. ~ **out** arrendar. ● vi ser agricultor. ~**er** n agricultor m. ~**house** n granja f. ~**ing** n agricultura f. ~**yard** n corral m

**far:** ~**off** *a* lejano. ~**reaching** *a* trascendental. ~**seeing** *a* clarividente. ~**sighted** *a* hipermétrope; (*fig*) clarividente

**farther, farthest** /'fɑːðə(r), 'fɑːðəst/ *see* **far**

**fascinat|e** /'fæsɪneɪt/ *vt* fascinar. ~**ion** /-'neɪʃn/ *n* fascinación *f*

**fascis|m** /'fæʃɪzəm/ *n* fascismo *m*. ~**t** /'fæʃɪst/ *a & n* fascista (*m & f*)

**fashion** /'fæʃn/ *n* (*manner*) manera *f*; (*vogue*) moda *f*. ~**able** *a* de moda

**fast**[1] /fɑːst/ *a* (-**er, -est**) rápido; ⟨*clock*⟩ adelantado; (*secure*) fijo; ⟨*colours*⟩ sólido. ● *adv* rápidamente; (*securely*) firmemente. ~ **asleep** profundamente dormido

**fast**[2] /fɑːst/ *vi* ayunar. ● *n* ayuno *m*

**fasten** /'fɑːsn/ *vt/i* sujetar; cerrar ⟨*windows, doors*⟩; abrochar ⟨*belt etc*⟩. ~**er** *n*, ~**ing** *n* (*on box, window*) cierre *m*; (*on door*) cerrojo *m*

**fastidious** /fə'stɪdɪəs/ *a* exigente, minucioso

**fat** /fæt/ *n* grasa *f*. ● *a* (**fatter, fattest**) gordo; ⟨*meat*⟩ que tiene mucha grasa; (*thick*) grueso. **a ~ lot of** (*sl*) muy poco

**fatal** /'feɪtl/ *a* mortal; (*fateful*) fatídico

**fatalis|m** /'feɪtəlɪzəm/ *n* fatalismo *m*. ~**t** *n* fatalista *m & f*

**fatality** /fə'tælətɪ/ *n* calamidad *f*; (*death*) muerte *f*

**fatally** /'feɪtlɪ/ *adv* mortalmente; (*by fate*) fatalmente

**fate** /feɪt/ *n* destino *m*; (*one's lot*) suerte *f*. ~**d** *a* predestinado. ~**ful** *a* fatídico

**fat-head** /'fæthed/ *n* imbécil *m*

**father** /'fɑːðə(r)/ *n* padre *m*. ~**hood** *m* paternidad *f*. ~**in-law** *m* (*pl* **fathers-in-law**) *m* suegro *m*. ~**ly** *a* paternal

**fathom** /'fæðəm/ *n* braza *f*. ● *vt*. ~ (**out**) comprender

**fatigue** /fə'tiːg/ *n* fatiga *f*. ● *vt* fatigar

**fat:** ~**ness** *n* gordura *f*. ~**ten** *vt/i* engordar. ~**tening** *a* que engorda. ~**ty** *a* graso. ● *n* (*fam*) gordinflón *m*

**fatuous** /'fætjʊəs/ *a* fatuo

**faucet** /'fɔːsɪt/ *n* (*Amer*) grifo *m*

**fault** /fɔːlt/ *n* defecto *m*; (*blame*) culpa *f*; (*tennis*) falta *f*; (*geol*) falla *f*. **at ~** culpable. ● *vt* criticar. ~**less** *a* impecable. ~**y** *a* defectuoso

**fauna** /'fɔːnə/ *n* fauna *f*

**faux pas** /fəʊ'pɑː/ (*pl* **faux pas** /fəʊ'pɑː/) *n* metedura *f* de pata, paso *m* en falso

**favour** /'feɪvə(r)/ *n* favor *m*. ● *vt* favorecer; (*support*) estar a favor de; (*prefer*) preferir. ~**able** *a* favorable. ~**ably** *adv* favorablemente

**favourit|e** /'feɪvərɪt/ *a & n* preferido (*m*). ~**ism** *n* favoritismo *m*

**fawn**[1] /fɔːn/ *n* cervato *m*. ● *a* color de cervato, beige, beis

**fawn**[2] /fɔːn/ *vi*. ~ **on** adular

**fax** /fæks/ *n* telefacsímil *m*, fax *m*

**fear** /fɪə(r)/ *n* miedo *m*. ● *vt* temer. ~**ful** *a* (*frightening*) espantoso; (*frightened*) temeroso. ~**less** *a* intrépido. ~**lessness** *n* intrepidez *f*. ~**some** *a* espantoso

**feasib|ility** /fiːzə'bɪlətɪ/ *n* viabilidad *f*. ~**le** /'fiːzəbl/ *a* factible; (*likely*) posible

**feast** /fiːst/ *n* (*relig*) fiesta *f*; (*meal*) banquete *m*, comilona *f*. ● *vt* banquetear, festejar. ~ **on** regalarse con

**feat** /fiːt/ *n* hazaña *f*

**feather** /'feðə(r)/ *n* pluma *f*. ● *vt*. ~ **one's nest** hacer su agosto. ~**brained** *a* tonto. ~**weight** *n* peso *m* pluma

**feature** /'fiːtʃə(r)/ *n* (*on face*) facción *f*; (*characteristic*) característica *f*; (*in newspaper*) artículo *m*; ~ (**film**) película *f* principal, largometraje *m*. ● *vt* presentar; (*give prominence to*) destacar. ● *vi* figurar

**February** /'februərɪ/ *n* febrero *m*

**feckless** /'feklɪs/ *a* inepto; (*irresponsible*) irreflexivo

**fed** /fed/ *see* **feed**. ● *a*. ~ **up** (*sl*) harto (**with** de)

**federal** /'fedərəl/ *a* federal

**federation** /fedə'reɪʃn/ *n* federación *f*

**fee** /fiː/ *n* (*professional*) honorarios *mpl*; (*enrolment*) derechos *mpl*; (*club*) cuota *f*

**feeble** /'fiːbl/ *a* (-**er, -est**) débil. ~**minded** *a* imbécil

**feed** /fiːd/ *vt* (*pt* **fed**) dar de comer a; (*supply*) alimentar. ● *vi* comer. ● *n* (*for animals*) pienso *m*; (*for babies*) comida *f*. ~**back** *n* reacciones *fpl*, comentarios *mpl*

**feel** /fiːl/ *vt* (*pt* **felt**) sentir; (*touch*) tocar; (*think*) parecerle. **do you ~ it's a good idea?** te parece buena idea? **I ~ it is necessary** me parece necesario. ~ **as if** tener la impresión de que. ~ **hot/hungry** tener calor/hambre. ~ **like** (*want, fam*) tener ganas de. ~ **up to** sentirse capaz de

**feeler** /'fiːlə(r)/ n (*of insects*) antena f. **put out a** ~ (*fig*) hacer un sondeo

**feeling** /'fiːlɪŋ/ n sentimiento m; (*physical*) sensación f

**feet** /fiːt/ *see* **foot**

**feign** /feɪn/ vt fingir

**feint** /feɪnt/ n finta f

**felicitous** /fə'lɪsɪtəs/ a feliz, oportuno

**feline** /'fiːlaɪn/ a felino

**fell**[1] /fel/ *see* **fall**

**fell**[2] /fel/ vt derribar

**fellow** /'feləʊ/ n (*fam*) tipo m; (*comrade*) compañero m; (*society*) socio m. ~**countryman** n compatriota m & f. ~ **passenger/traveller** n compañero m de viaje. ~**ship** n compañerismo m; (*group*) asociación f

**felony** /'feləni/ n crimen m

**felt**[1] /felt/ n fieltro m

**felt**[2] /felt/ *see* **feel**

**female** /'fiːmeɪl/ a hembra; (*voice, sex etc*) femenino. ● n mujer f; (*animal*) hembra f

**femini|ne** /'femənɪn/ a & n femenino (m). ~**nity** /-'nɪnəti/ n feminidad f. ~**st** n feminista m & f

**fenc|e** /fens/ n cerca f; (*person, sl*) perista m & f (*fam*). ● vt. ~**e (in)** encerrar, cercar. ● vi (*sport*) practicar la esgrima. ~**er** n esgrimidor m. ~**ing** n (*sport*) esgrima f

**fend** /fend/ vi. ~ **for o.s.** valerse por sí mismo. ● vt. ~ **off** defenderse de

**fender** /'fendə(r)/ n guardafuego m; (*mudguard, Amer*) guardabarros m invar; (*naut*) defensa f

**fennel** /'fenl/ n hinojo m

**ferment** /'fɜːment/ n fermento m; (*fig*) agitación f. /fə'ment/ vt/i fermentar. ~**ation** /-'teɪʃn/ n fermentación f

**fern** /fɜːn/ n helecho m

**feroci|ous** /fə'rəʊʃəs/ a feroz. ~**ty** /fə'rɒsəti/ n ferocidad f

**ferret** /'ferɪt/ n hurón m. ● vi (*pt ferreted*) huronear. ● vt. ~ **out** descubrir

**ferry** /'feri/ n ferry m. ● vt transportar

**fertil|e** /'fɜːtaɪl/ a fértil; (*biol*) fecundo. ~**ity** /-'tɪləti/ n fertilidad f; (*biol*) fecundidad f

**fertilize** /'fɜːtəlaɪz/ vt abonar; (*biol*) fecundar. ~**r** n abono m

**fervent** /'fɜːvənt/ a ferviente

**fervour** /'fɜːvə(r)/ n fervor m

**fester** /'festə(r)/ vi enconarse

**festival** /'festəvl/ n fiesta f; (*of arts*) festival m

**festive** /'festɪv/ a festivo. ~ **season** n temporada f de fiestas

**festivity** /fe'stɪvəti/ n festividad f

**festoon** /fe'stuːn/ vi. ~ **with** adornar de

**fetch** /fetʃ/ vt (*go for*) ir a buscar; (*bring*) traer; (*be sold for*) venderse por

**fetching** /'fetʃɪŋ/ a atractivo

**fête** /feɪt/ n fiesta f. ● vt festejar

**fetid** /'fetɪd/ a fétido

**fetish** /'fetɪʃ/ n fetiche m; (*psych*) obsesión f

**fetter** /'fetə(r)/ vt encadenar. ~**s** npl grilletes mpl

**fettle** /'fetl/ n condición f

**feud** /fjuːd/ n enemistad f (inveterada)

**feudal** /fjuːdl/ a feudal. ~**ism** n feudalismo m

**fever** /'fiːvə(r)/ n fiebre f. ~**ish** a febril

**few** /fjuː/ a pocos. ● n pocos mpl. a ~ unos (pocos). **a good** ~, **quite a** ~ (*fam*) muchos. ~**er** a & n menos. ~**est** a & n el menor número de

**fiancé** /fɪ'ɒnseɪ/ n novio m. ~**e** /fɪ'ɒnseɪ/ n novia f

**fiasco** /fɪ'æskəʊ/ n (*pl* -**os**) fiasco m

**fib** /fɪb/ n mentirijilla f. ~**ber** n mentiroso m

**fibre** /'faɪbə(r)/ n fibra f. ~**glass** n fibra f de vidrio

**fickle** /'fɪkl/ a inconstante

**fiction** /'fɪkʃn/ n ficción f. (**works of**) ~ novelas fpl. ~**al** a novelesco

**fictitious** /fɪk'tɪʃəs/ a ficticio

**fiddle** /'fɪdl/ n (*fam*) violín m; (*swindle, sl*) trampa f. ● vt (*sl*) falsificar. ~ **with** juguetear con, toquetear, manosear. ~**r** n (*fam*) violinista m & f; (*cheat, sl*) tramposo m

**fidelity** /fɪ'deləti/ n fidelidad f

**fidget** /'fɪdʒɪt/ vi (*pt fidgeted*) moverse, ponerse nervioso. ~ **with** juguetear con. ● n azogado m. ~**y** a azogado

**field** /fiːld/ n campo m. ~ **day** n gran ocasión f. ~ **glasses** npl gemelos mpl. **F**~ **Marshal** n mariscal m de campo, capitán m general. ~**work** n investigaciones fpl en el terreno

**fiend** /fiːnd/ n demonio m. ~**ish** a diabólico

**fierce** /fɪəs/ a (**-er, -est**) feroz; ⟨attack⟩ violento. **~ness** n ferocidad f, violencia f

**fiery** /'faɪərɪ/ a (**-ier, -iest**) ardiente

**fifteen** /fɪf'ti:n/ a & n quince (m). **~th** a & n quince (m), decimoquinto (m). ● n (fraction) quinzavo m

**fifth** /fɪfθ/ a & n quinto (m). ~ **column** n quinta columna f

**fift|ieth** /'fɪftɪəθ/ a & n cincuenta (m). **~y** a & n cincuenta (m). **~y-~y** mitad y mitad, a medias. a **~y-~y chance** una posibilidad f de cada dos

**fig** /fɪg/ n higo m

**fight** /faɪt/ vt/i (pt **fought**) luchar; (quarrel) disputar. ~ **shy of** evitar. ● n lucha f; (quarrel) disputa f; (mil) combate m. ~ **back** defenderse. ~ **off** rechazar ⟨attack⟩; luchar contra ⟨illness⟩. **~er** n luchador m; (mil) combatiente m & f; (aircraft) avión m de caza. **~ing** n luchas fpl

**figment** /'fɪgmənt/ n invención f

**figurative** /'fɪgjʊrətɪv/ a figurado

**figure** /'fɪgə(r)/ n (number) cifra f; (diagram) figura f; (shape) forma f; (of woman) tipo m. ● vt imaginar. ● vi figurar. **that ~s** (Amer, fam) es lógico. ~ **out** explicarse. **~head** n testaferro m, mascarón m de proa. ~ **of speech** n tropo m, figura f. **~s** npl (arithmetic) aritmética f

**filament** /'fɪləmənt/ n filamento m

**filch** /fɪltʃ/ vt hurtar

**file**[1] /faɪl/ n carpeta f; (set of papers) expediente m. ● vt archivar ⟨papers⟩

**file**[2] /faɪl/ n (row) fila f. ● vi. ~ **in** entrar en fila. ~ **past** desfilar ante

**file**[3] /faɪl/ n (tool) lima f. ● vt limar

**filings** /'faɪlɪŋz/ npl limaduras fpl

**fill** /fɪl/ vt llenar. ● vi llenarse. ~ **in** rellenar ⟨form⟩. ~ **out** (get fatter) engordar. ~ **up** (auto) llenar, repostar. ● n. **eat one's ~** hartarse de comer. **have had one's ~ of** estar harto de

**fillet** /'fɪlɪt/ n filete m. ● vt (pt **filleted**) cortar en filetes

**filling** /'fɪlɪŋ/ n (in tooth) empaste m. ~ **station** n estación f de servicio

**film** /fɪlm/ n película f. ● vt filmar. ~ **star** n estrella f de cine. **~strip** n tira f de película

**filter** /'fɪltə(r)/ n filtro m. ● vt filtrar. ● vi filtrarse. **~tipped** a con filtro

**filth** /fɪlθ/ n inmundicia f. **~iness** n inmundicia f. **~y** a inmundo

**fin** /fɪn/ n aleta f

**final** /'faɪnl/ a último; (conclusive) decisivo. ● n (sport) final f. **~s** npl (schol) exámenes mpl de fin de curso

**finale** /fɪ'nɑ:lɪ/ n final m

**final: ~ist** n finalista m & f. **~ize** vt concluir. **~ly** adv (lastly) finalmente, por fin; (once and for all) definitivamente

**financ|e** /'faɪnæns/ n finanzas fpl. ● vt financiar. **~ial** /faɪ'nænʃl/ a financiero. **~ially** adv económicamente. **~ier** /faɪ'nænsɪə(r)/ n financiero m

**finch** /fɪntʃ/ n pinzón m

**find** /faɪnd/ vt (pt **found**) encontrar. ~ **out** enterarse de. **~er** n el m que encuentra, descubridor m. **~ings** npl resultados mpl

**fine**[1] /faɪn/ a (**-er, -est**) fino; (excellent) excelente. ● n muy bien; (small) en trozos pequeños

**fine**[2] /faɪn/ n multa f. ● vt multar

**fine: ~ arts** npl bellas artes fpl. **~ly** adv (admirably) espléndidamente; (cut) en trozos pequeños. **~ry** /'faɪnərɪ/ n galas fpl

**finesse** /fɪ'nes/ n tino m

**finger** /'fɪŋgə(r)/ n dedo m. ● vt tocar. **~nail** n uña f. **~print** n huella f dactilar. **~stall** n dedil m. **~tip** n punta f del dedo

**finicking** /'fɪnɪkɪŋ/ a, **finicky** /'fɪnɪkɪ/ a melindroso

**finish** /'fɪnɪʃ/ vt/i terminar. ~ **doing** terminar de hacer. ~ **up doing** terminar por hacer. ● n fin m; (of race) llegada f, meta f; (appearance) acabado m

**finite** /'faɪnaɪt/ a finito

**Fin|land** /'fɪnlənd/ n Finlandia f. **~n** n finlandés m. **~nish** a & n finlandés (m)

**fiord** /fjɔ:d/ n fiordo m

**fir** /fɜ:(r)/ n abeto m

**fire** /faɪə(r)/ n fuego m; (conflagration) incendio m. ● vt disparar ⟨bullet etc⟩; (dismiss) despedir; (fig) excitar, enardecer, inflamar. ● vi tirar. **~arm** n arma f de fuego. ~ **brigade** n cuerpo m de bomberos. **~cracker** n (Amer) petardo m. ~ **department** n (Amer) cuerpo m de bomberos. **~engine** n coche m de bomberos. **~escape** n escalera f de incendios. **~light** n

lumbre *f*. ～**man** *n* bombero *m*.
～**place** *n* chimenea *f*. ～**side** *n* hogar
*m*. ～ **station** *n* parque *m* de bomberos. ～**wood** *n* leña *f*. ～**work** *n*
fuego *m* artificial
**firing-squad** /'faɪərɪŋskwɒd/ *n* pelotón *m* de ejecución
**firm**[1] /fɜːm/ *n* empresa *f*
**firm**[2] /fɜːm/ *a* (**-er, -est**) firme. ～**ly**
*adv* firmemente. ～**ness** *n* firmeza *f*
**first** /fɜːst/ *a* primero. *at* ～ **hand** directamente. **at** ～ **sight** a primera
vista. ● *n* primero *m*. ● *adv* primero; (*first time*) por primera vez.
～ **of all** ante todo. ～ **aid** *n* primeros
auxilios *mpl*. ～**-born** *a* primogénito. ～**-class** *a* de primera clase.
～ **floor** *n* primer piso *m*; (*Amer*)
planta *f* baja. **F**～ **Lady** *n* (*Amer*)
Primera Dama *f*. ～**ly** *adv* en primer
lugar. ～ **name** *n* nombre *m* de pila.
～**rate** *a* excelente
**fiscal** /'fɪskl/ *a* fiscal
**fish** /fɪʃ/ *n* (*usually invar*) (*alive in
water*) pez *m*; (*food*) pescado *m*. ● *vi*
pescar. ～ **for** pescar. ～ **out** (*take
out, fam*) sacar. **go** ～**ing** ir de pesca.
～**erman** /'fɪʃəmən/ *n* pescador *m*.
～**ing** *n* pesca *f*. ～**ing-rod** *n* caña *f*
de pesca. ～**monger** *n* pescadero *m*.
～**shop** *n* pescadería *f*. ～**y** *a* (*smell*)
a pescado; (*questionable, fam*)
sospechoso
**fission** /'fɪʃn/ *n* fisión *f*
**fist** /fɪst/ *n* puño *m*
**fit**[1] /fɪt/ *a* (**fitter, fittest**) con-
veniente; (*healthy*) sano; (*good
enough*) adecuado; (*able*) capaz. ● *n*
(*of clothes*) corte *m*. ● *vt* (*pt* **fitted**)
(*adapt*) adaptar; (*be the right size
for*) sentar bien a; (*install*) colocar.
● *vi* encajar; (*in certain space*)
caber; (*clothes*) sentar. ～ **out**
equipar. ～ **up** equipar
**fit**[2] /fɪt/ *n* ataque *m*
**fitful** /'fɪtfl/ *a* irregular
**fitment** /'fɪtmənt/ *n* mueble *m*
**fitness** /'fɪtnɪs/ *n* (*buena*) salud *f*; (*of
remark*) conveniencia *f*
**fitting** /'fɪtɪŋ/ *a* apropiado. ● *n* (*of
clothes*) prueba *f*. ～**s** /'fɪtɪŋz/ *npl* (*in
house*) accesorios *mpl*
**five** /faɪv/ *a & n* cinco (*m*). ～**r**
/'faɪvə(r)/ *n* (*fam*) billete *m* de cinco
libras
**fix** /fɪks/ *vt* (*make firm, attach,
decide*) fijar; (*mend, deal with*) arreglar. ● *n*. **in a** ～ en un aprieto.

～**ation** /-eɪʃn/ *n* fijación *f*. ～**ed** *a*
fijo
**fixture** /'fɪkstʃə(r) *n* (*sport*) partido *m*.
～**s** (*in house*) accesorios *mpl*
**fizz** /fɪz/ *vi* burbujear. ● *n* efer-
vescencia *f*. ～**le** /fɪzl/ *vi* burbujear.
～**le out** fracasar. ～**y** *a* efervescente; (*water*) con gas
**flab** /flæb/ *n* (*fam*) flaccidez *f*
**flabbergast** /'flæbəgɑːst/ *vt* pasmar
**flabby** /'flæbɪ/ *a* flojo
**flag** /flæg/ *n* bandera *f*. ● *vt* (*pt*
**flagged**). ～ **down** hacer señales de
parada a. ● *vi* (*pt* **flagged**) (*weaken*)
flaquear; (*interest*) decaer; (*conversation*) languidecer
**flagon** /'flægən/ *n* botella *f* grande,
jarro *m*
**flag-pole** /'flægpəʊl/ *n* asta *f* de
bandera
**flagrant** /'fleɪgrənt/ *a* (*glaring*)
flagrante; (*scandalous*) escandaloso
**flagstone** /'flægstəʊn/ *n* losa *f*
**flair** /fleə(r)/ *n* don *m* (**for** de)
**flak|e** /fleɪk/ *n* copo *m*; (*of paint,
metal*) escama *f*. ● *vi* desconcharse.
～**e out** (*fam*) caer rendido. ～**y** *a*
escamoso
**flamboyant** /flæm'bɔɪənt/ *a* (*clothes*) vistoso; (*manner*) extravagante
**flame** /fleɪm/ *n* llama *f*. ● *vi* llamear
**flamingo** /flə'mɪŋgəʊ/ *n* (*pl* **-o(e)s**)
flamenco *m*
**flammable** /'flæməbl/ *a* inflamable
**flan** /flæn/ *n* tartaleta *f*, tarteleta *f*
**flank** /flæŋk/ *n* (*of animal*) ijada *f*,
flanco *m*; (*of person*) costado *m*; (*of
mountain*) falda *f*; (*mil*) flanco *m*
**flannel** /'flænl/ *n* franela *f* (de lana);
(*for face*) paño *m* (para lavarse la
cara). ～**ette** *n* franela *f* (de
algodón), muletón *m*
**flap** /flæp/ *vi* (*pt* **flapped**) ondear;
(*wings*) aletear; (*become agitated,
fam*) ponerse nervioso. ● *vt* sacudir; batir (*wings*). ● *n* (*of pocket*)
cartera *f*; (*of table*) ala *f*. **get into a**
～ ponerse nervioso
**flare** /fleə(r)/ *n* llamarada *f*; (*mil*)
bengala *f*; (*in skirt*) vuelo *m*. ● *vi*. ～
**up** llamear; (*fighting*) estallar; (*person*) encolerizarse. ～**d** *a* (*skirt*)
acampanado
**flash** /flæʃ/ ● *vi* brillar; (*on and off*)
destellar. ● *vt* despedir; (*aim torch*)
dirigir; (*flaunt*) hacer ostentación
de. ～ **past** pasar como un rayo. ● *n*
relámpago *m*; (*of news, camera*)

flash *m*. ∼**back** *n* escena *f* retrospectiva. ∼**light** *n* (*torch*) linterna *f*

**flashy** /'flæʃɪ/ *a* ostentoso

**flask** /flɑːsk/ *n* frasco *m*; (*vacuum flask*) termo *m*

**flat**[1] /flæt/ *a* (**flatter, flattest**) llano; ⟨*tyre*⟩ desinflado; (*refusal*) categórico; ⟨*fare, rate*⟩ fijo; (*mus*) desafinado. ● *adv*. ∼ **out** (*at top speed*) a toda velocidad

**flat**[2] /flæt/ *n* (*rooms*) piso *m*, apartamento *m*; ⟨*tyre*⟩ (*fam*) pinchazo *m*; (*mus*) bemol *m*

**flat**: ∼**ly** *adv* categóricamente. ∼**ness** *n* llanura *f*. ∼**ten** /'flætn/ *vt* allanar, aplanar. ● *vi* allanarse, aplanarse

**flatter** /'flætə(r)/ *vt* adular. ∼**er** *n* adulador *m*. ∼**ing** *a* ⟨*person*⟩ lisonjero; ⟨*clothes*⟩ favorecedor. ∼**y** *n* adulación *f*

**flatulence** /'flætjʊləns/ *n* flatulencia *f*

**flaunt** /flɔːnt/ *vt* hacer ostentación de

**flautist** /'flɔːtɪst/ *n* flautista *m* & *f*

**flavour** /'fleɪvə(r)/ *n* sabor *m*. ● *vt* condimentar. ∼**ing** *n* condimento *m*

**flaw** /flɔː/ *n* defecto *m*. ∼**less** *a* perfecto

**flax** /flæks/ *n* lino *m*. ∼**en** *a* de lino; ⟨*hair*⟩ rubio

**flea** /fliː/ *n* pulga *f*

**fleck** /flek/ *n* mancha *f*, pinta *f*

**fled** /fled/ *see* **flee**

**fledged** /fledʒd/ *a*. **fully** ∼ ⟨*doctor etc*⟩ hecho y derecho; ⟨*member*⟩ de pleno derecho

**fledg(e)ling** /'fledʒlɪŋ/ *n* pájaro *m* volantón

**flee** /fliː/ *vi* (*pt* **fled**) huir. ● *vt* huir de

**fleece** /fliːs/ *n* vellón *m*. ● *vt* (*rob*) desplumar

**fleet** /fliːt/ *n* (*naut, aviat*) flota *f*; (*of cars*) parque *m*

**fleeting** /'fliːtɪŋ/ *a* fugaz

**Flemish** /'flemɪʃ/ *a* & *n* flamenco (*m*)

**flesh** /fleʃ/ *n* carne *f*. **in the** ∼ en persona. **one's own** ∼ **and blood** los de su sangre. ∼**y** *a* ⟨*fruit*⟩ carnoso

**flew** /fluː/ *see* **fly**[1]

**flex** /fleks/ *vt* doblar; flexionar ⟨*muscle*⟩. ● *n* (*elec*) cable *m*, flexible *m*

**flexib|ility** /fleksə'bɪlətɪ/ *n* flexibilidad *f*. ∼**le** /'fleksəbl/ *a* flexible

**flexitime** /'fleksɪ'taɪm/ *n* horario *m* flexible

**flick** /flɪk/ *n* golpecito *m*. ● *vt* dar un golpecito a. ∼ **through** hojear

**flicker** /'flɪkə(r)/ *vi* temblar; (*light*) parpadear. ● *n* temblor *m*; (*of hope*) resquicio *m*; (*of light*) parpadeo *m*

**flick**: ∼**knife** *n* navaja *f* de muelle. ∼**s** *npl* cine *m*

**flier** /'flaɪə(r)/ *n* aviador *m*; (*circular, Amer*) prospecto *m*, folleto *m*

**flies** /flaɪz/ *npl* (*on trousers, fam*) bragueta *f*

**flight** /flaɪt/ *n* vuelo *m*; (*fleeing*) huida *f*, fuga *f*. ∼ **of stairs** tramo *m* de escalera *f*. **put to** ∼ poner en fuga. **take (to)** ∼ darse a la fuga. ∼**deck** *n* cubierta *f* de vuelo

**flighty** /'flaɪtɪ/ *a* (**-ier, -iest**) frívolo

**flimsy** /'flɪmzɪ/ *a* (**-ier, -iest**) flojo, débil, poco substancioso

**flinch** /flɪntʃ/ *vi* (*draw back*) retroceder (**from** ante). **without** ∼**ing** (*without wincing*) sin pestañear

**fling** /flɪŋ/ *vt* (*pt* **flung**) arrojar. ● *n*. **have a** ∼ echar una cana al aire

**flint** /flɪnt/ *n* pedernal *m*; (*for lighter*) piedra *f*

**flip** /flɪp/ *vt* (*pt* **flipped**) dar un golpecito a. ∼ **through** hojear. ● *n* golpecito *m*. ∼ **side** *n* otra cara *f*

**flippant** /'flɪpənt/ *a* poco serio; (*disrespectful*) irrespetuoso

**flipper** /'flɪpə(r)/ *n* aleta *f*

**flirt** /flɜːt/ *vi* coquetear. ● *n* (*woman*) coqueta *f*; (*man*) mariposón *m*, coqueto *m*. ∼**ation** /-'teɪʃn/ *n* coqueteo *m*

**flit** /flɪt/ *vi* (*pt* **flitted**) revolotear

**float** /fləʊt/ *vi* flotar. ● *vt* hacer flotar. ● *n* flotador *m*; (*on fishing line*) corcho *m*; (*cart*) carroza *f*

**flock** /flɒk/ *n* (*of birds*) bandada *f*; (*of sheep*) rebaño *m*; (*of people*) muchedumbre *f*, multitud *f*. ● *vi* congregarse

**flog** /flɒg/ *vt* (*pt* **flogged**) (*beat*) azotar; (*sell, sl*) vender

**flood** /flʌd/ *n* inundación *f*; (*fig*) torrente *m*. ● *vt* inundar. ● *vi* ⟨*building etc*⟩ inundarse; ⟨*river*⟩ desbordar

**floodlight** /'flʌdlaɪt/ *n* foco *m*. ● *vt* (*pt* **floodlit**) iluminar (con focos)

**floor** /flɔː(r)/ *n* suelo *m*; (*storey*) piso *m*; (*for dancing*) pista *f*. ● *vt* (*knock down*) derribar; (*baffle*) confundir

**flop** /flɒp/ *vi* (*pt* **flopped**) dejarse caer pesadamente; (*fail, sl*) fracasar. ● *n* (*sl*) fracaso *m*. ~**py** *a* flojo

**flora** /'flɔːrə/ *n* flora *f*

**floral** /'flɔːrəl/ *a* floral

**florid** /'florɪd/ *a* florido

**florist** /'florɪst/ *n* florista *m & f*

**flounce** /flaʊns/ *n* volante *m*

**flounder**[1] /'flaʊndə(r)/ *vi* avanzar con dificultad, no saber qué hacer

**flounder**[2] /'flaʊndə(r)/ *n* (*fish*) platija *f*

**flour** /flaʊə(r)/ *n* harina *f*

**flourish** /'flʌrɪʃ/ *vi* prosperar. ● *vt* blandir. ● *n* ademán *m* elegante; (*in handwriting*) rasgo *m*. ~**ing** *a* próspero

**floury** /'flaʊərɪ/ *a* harinoso

**flout** /flaʊt/ *vt* burlarse de

**flow** /fləʊ/ *vi* correr; (*hang loosely*) caer. ~ **into** (*river*) desembocar en. ● *n* flujo *m*; (*jet*) chorro *m*; (*stream*) corriente *f*; (*of words, tears*) torrente *m*. ~ **chart** *n* organigrama *m*

**flower** /'flaʊə(r)/ *n* flor *f*. ~**bed** *n* macizo *m* de flores. ~**ed** *a* floreado, de flores. ~**y** *a* florido

**flown** /fləʊn/ *see* **fly**[1]

**flu** /fluː/ *n* (*fam*) gripe *f*

**fluctuat|e** /'flʌktjʊeɪt/ *vi* fluctuar. ~**ion** /-eɪʃn/ *n* fluctuación *f*

**flue** /fluː/ *n* humero *m*

**fluen|cy** /'fluːənsɪ/ *n* facilidad *f*. ~**t** *a* (*style*) fluido; (*speaker*) elocuente. be ~**t** (**in a language**) hablar (un idioma) con soltura. ~**tly** *adv* con fluidez; (*lang*) con soltura

**fluff** /flʌf/ *n* pelusa *f*. ~**y** *a* (**-ier, -iest**) velloso

**fluid** /'fluːɪd/ *a & n* fluido (*m*)

**fluke** /fluːk/ *n* (*stroke of luck*) chiripa *f*

**flung** /flʌŋ/ *see* **fling**

**flunk** /flʌŋk/ *vt* (*Amer, fam*) ser suspendido en (*exam*); suspender (*person*). ● *vi* (*fam*) ser suspendido

**fluorescent** /flʊə'resnt/ *a* fluorescente

**fluoride** /flʊəraɪd/ *n* fluoruro *m*

**flurry** /'flʌrɪ/ *n* (*squall*) ráfaga *f*; (*fig*) agitación *f*

**flush**[1] /flʌʃ/ *vi* ruborizarse. ● *vt* limpiar con agua. ~ **the toilet** tirar de la cadena. ● *n* (*blush*) rubor *m*; (*fig*) emoción *f*

**flush**[2] /flʌʃ/ *a*. ~ (**with**) a nivel (con)

**flush**[3] /flʌʃ/ *vt/i*. ~ **out** (*drive out*) echar fuera

**fluster** /'flʌstə(r)/ *vt* poner nervioso

**flute** /fluːt/ *n* flauta *f*

**flutter** /'flʌtə(r)/ *vi* ondear; (*bird*) revolotear. ● *n* (*of wings*) revoloteo *m*; (*fig*) agitación *f*

**flux** /flʌks/ *n* flujo *m*. be in a state of ~ estar siempre cambiando

**fly**[1] /flaɪ/ *vi* (*pt* **flew**, *pp* **flown**) volar; (*passenger*) ir en avión; (*flag*) flotar; (*rush*) correr. ● *vt* pilotar (*aircraft*); transportar en avión (*passengers, goods*); izar (*flag*). ● *n* (*of trousers*) bragueta *f*

**fly**[2] /flaɪ/ *n* mosca *f*

**flyer** /'flaɪə(r)/ *n* aviador *m*; (*circular, Amer*) prospecto *m*, folleto *m*

**flying** /'flaɪɪŋ/ *a* volante; (*hasty*) relámpago *invar*. ● *n* (*activity*) aviación *f*. ~ **visit** *n* visita *f* relámpago

**fly:** ~**leaf** *n* guarda *f*. ~**over** *n* paso *m* elevado. ~**weight** *n* peso *m* mosca

**foal** /fəʊl/ *n* potro *m*

**foam** /fəʊm/ *n* espuma *f*. ~(**rubber**) *n* goma *f* espuma. ● *vi* espumar

**fob** /fob/ *vt* (*pt* **fobbed**). ~ **off on s.o.** (*palm off*) encajar a uno

**focal** /'fəʊkl/ *a* focal

**focus** /'fəʊkəs/ *n* (*pl* -**cuses** *or* -**ci** /-saɪ/) foco *m*; (*fig*) centro *m*. in ~ enfocado. out of ~ desenfocado. ● *vt/i* (*pt* **focused**) enfocar(se); (*fig*) concentrar

**fodder** /'fodə(r)/ *n* forraje *m*

**foe** /fəʊ/ *n* enemigo *m*

**foetus** /'fiːtəs/ *n* (*pl* -**tuses**) feto *m*

**fog** /fog/ *n* niebla *f*. ● *vt* (*pt* **fogged**) envolver en niebla; (*photo*) velar. ● *vi*. ~ (**up**) empañarse; (*photo*) velarse

**fog(e)y** /fəʊgɪ/ *n*. be an old ~ estar chapado a la antigua

**foggy** /'fogɪ/ *a* (-**ier, -iest**) nebuloso. it is ~ hay niebla

**foghorn** /'foghɔːn/ *n* sirena *f* de niebla

**foible** /'fɔɪbl/ *n* punto *m* débil

**foil**[1] /fɔɪl/ *vt* (*thwart*) frustrar

**foil**[2] /fɔɪl/ *n* papel *m* de plata; (*fig*) contraste *m*

**foist** /fɔɪst/ *vt* encajar (on a)

**fold**[1] /fəʊld/ *vt* doblar; cruzar (*arms*). ● *vi* doblarse; (*fail*) fracasar. ● *n* pliegue *m*

**fold**[2] /fəʊld/ *n* (*for sheep*) redil *m*

**folder** /'fəʊldə(r)/ *n* (*file*) carpeta *f*; (*leaflet*) folleto *m*

**folding** /'fəʊldɪŋ/ *a* plegable

**foliage** /'fəʊlɪɪdʒ/ *n* follaje *m*

**folk** /fəʊk/ n gente f. ● a popular. ~lore n folklore m. ~s npl (one's relatives) familia f

**follow** /'fɒləʊ/ vt/i seguir. ~ up seguir; (investigate further) investigar. ~er n seguidor m. ~ing n partidarios mpl. ● a siguiente. ● prep después de

**folly** /'fɒlɪ/ n locura f

**foment** /fə'ment/ vt fomentar

**fond** /fɒnd/ a (-er, -est) (loving) cariñoso; ⟨hope⟩ vivo. be ~ of s.o. tener(le) cariño a uno. be ~ of sth ser aficionado a algo

**fondle** /'fɒndl/ vt acariciar

**fondness** /'fɒndnɪs/ n cariño m; (for things) afición f

**font** /fɒnt/ n pila f bautismal

**food** /fu:d/ n alimento m, comida f. ~ processor n robot m de cocina, batidora f

**fool** /fu:l/ n tonto m. ● vt engañar. ● vi hacer el tonto

**foolhardy** /'fu:lhɑ:dɪ/ a temerario

**foolish** /'fu:lɪʃ/ a tonto. ~ly adv tontamente. ~ness n tontería f

**foolproof** /'fu:lpru:f/ a infalible, a toda prueba, a prueba de tontos

**foot** /fʊt/ n (pl feet) pie m; (measure) pie m (= 30,48 cm); (of animal, furniture) pata f. get under s.o.'s feet estorbar a uno. on ~ a pie. on/to one's feet de pie. put one's ~ in it meter la pata. ● vt pagar ⟨bill⟩. ~ it ir andando

**footage** /'fʊtɪdʒ/ n (of film) secuencia f

**football** /'fʊtbɔ:l/ n (ball) balón m; (game) fútbol m. ~er n futbolista m & f

**footbridge** /'fʊtbrɪdʒ/ n puente m para peatones

**foothills** /'fʊthɪlz/ npl estribaciones fpl

**foothold** /'fʊthəʊld/ n punto m de apoyo m

**footing** /'fʊtɪŋ/ n pie m

**footlights** /'fʊtlaɪts/ npl candilejas fpl

**footloose** /'fʊtlu:s/ a libre

**footman** /'fʊtmən/ n lacayo m

**footnote** /'fʊtnəʊt/ n nota f (al pie de la página)

**foot:** ~path n (in country) senda f; (in town) acera f, vereda f (Arg), banqueta f (Mex), ~print n huella f. ~sore a. be ~sore tener los pies doloridos. ~step n paso m. ~stool n escabel m. ~wear n calzado m

**for** /fɔ:(r)/, unstressed /fə(r)/ prep (expressing purpose) para; (on behalf of) por; (in spite of) a pesar de; (during) durante; (in favour of) a favor de. he has been in Madrid ~ two months hace dos meses que está en Madrid. ● conj ya que

**forage** /'fɒrɪdʒ/ vi forrajear. ● n forraje m

**foray** /'fɒreɪ/ n incursión f

**forbade** /fə'bæd/ see forbid

**forbear** /fɔ:'beə(r)/ vt/i (pt forbore, pp forborne) contenerse. ~ance n paciencia f

**forbid** /fə'bɪd/ vt (pt forbade, pp forbidden) prohibir (s.o. to do a uno hacer). ~ s.o. sth prohibir algo a uno

**forbidding** /fə'bɪdɪŋ/ a imponente

**force** /fɔ:s/ n fuerza f. come into ~ entrar en vigor. the ~s las fuerzas fpl armadas. ● vt forzar. ~ on imponer a. ~d a forzado. ~feed vt alimentar a la fuerza. ~ful /'fɔ:sfʊl/ a enérgico

**forceps** /'fɔ:seps/ n invar tenazas fpl; (for obstetric use) fórceps m invar; (for dental use) gatillo m

**forcibl|e** /'fɔ:səbl/ a a la fuerza. ~y adv a la fuerza

**ford** /fɔ:d/ n vado m, botadero m (Mex). ● vt vadear

**fore** /fɔ:(r)/ a anterior. ● n. come to the ~ hacerse evidente

**forearm** /'fɔ:rɑ:m/ n antebrazo m

**foreboding** /fɔ:'bəʊdɪŋ/ n presentimiento m

**forecast** /'fɔ:kɑ:st/ vt (pt forecast) pronosticar. ● n pronóstico m

**forecourt** /'fɔ:kɔ:t/ n patio m

**forefathers** /'fɔ:fɑ:ðəz/ npl antepasados mpl

**forefinger** /'fɔ:fɪŋɡə(r)/ n (dedo m) índice m

**forefront** /'fɔ:frʌnt/ n vanguardia f. in the ~ a/en vanguardia, en primer plano

**foregone** /'fɔ:gɒn/ a. ~ conclusion resultado m previsto

**foreground** /'fɔ:graʊnd/ n primer plano m

**forehead** /'fɒrɪd/ n frente f

**foreign** /'fɒrən/ a extranjero; ⟨trade⟩ exterior; ⟨travel⟩ al extranjero, en el extranjero. ~er n extranjero m. F~ Secretary n ministro m de Asuntos Exteriores

**foreman** /'fɔ:mən/ n capataz m, caporal m

**foremost** /'fɔːməʊst/ a primero.
● *adv.* **first and ~** ante todo
**forensic** /fə'rensɪk/ a forense
**forerunner** /'fɔːrʌnə(r)/ n precursor
m
**foresee** /fɔː'siː/ vt (*pt* **-saw,** *pp* **-seen**)
prever. **~able** a previsible
**foreshadow** /fɔː'ʃædəʊ/ vt presagiar
**foresight** /'fɔːsaɪt/ n previsión f
**forest** /'fɒrɪst/ n bosque m
**forestall** /fɔː'stɔːl/ vt anticiparse a
**forestry** /'fɒrɪstrɪ/ n silvicultura f
**foretaste** /'fɔːteɪst/ n anticipación f
**foretell** /fɔː'tel/ vt (*pt* **foretold**)
predecir
**forever** /fə'revə(r)/ adv para
siempre
**forewarn** /fɔː'wɔːn/ vt prevenir
**foreword** /'fɔːwɜːd/ n prefacio m
**forfeit** /'fɔːfɪt/ n (*penalty*) pena f; (*in
game*) prenda f; (*fine*) multa f. ● vt
perder
**forgave** /fə'geɪv/ *see* **forgive**
**forge**[1] /fɔːdʒ/ n fragua f. ● vt fra-
guar; (*copy*) falsificar
**forge**[2] /fɔːdʒ/ vi avanzar. **~ahead**
adelantarse rápidamente
**forge: ~r** /'fɔːdʒə(r)/ n falsificador
m. **~ry** n falsificación f
**forget** /fə'get/ vt (*pt* **forgot,** *pp* **forgotten**) olvidar. **~ o.s.** propasarse,
extralimitarse. ● vi olvidar(se). **I
forgot** se me olvidó. **~ful** a olvi-
dadizo. **~ful of** olvidando. **~me-
not** n nomeolvides f *invar*
**forgive** /fə'gɪv/ vt (*pt* **forgave,** *pp*
**forgiven**) perdonar. **~ness** n perdón m
**forgo** /fɔː'gəʊ/ vt (*pt* **forwent,** *pp* **for-
gone**) renunciar a
**fork** /fɔːk/ n tenedor m; (*for digging*)
horca f; (*in road*) bifurcación f. ● vi
(*road*) bifurcarse. **~ out** (*sl*) aflojar
la bolsa (*fam*), pagar. **~ed** a ahor-
quillado; (*road*) bifurcado. **~lift
truck** n carretilla f elevadora
**forlorn** /fə'lɔːn/ a (*hopeless*) desesperado; (*abandoned*) abandonado.
**~ hope** n empresa f desesperada
**form** /fɔːm/ n forma f; (*document*)
impreso m, formulario m; (*schol*)
clase f. ● vt formar. ● vi formarse
**formal** /'fɔːml/ a formal; (*person*)
formalista; (*dress*) de etiqueta. **~ity**
/-'mælətɪ/ n formalidad f. **~ly** adv
oficialmente
**format** /'fɔːmæt/ n formato m
**formation** /fɔː'meɪʃn/ n formación f
**formative** /'fɔːmətɪv/ a formativo

**former** /'fɔːmə(r)/ a anterior; (*first of
two*) primero. **~ly** adv antes
**formidable** /'fɔːmɪdəbl/ a formidable
**formless** /'fɔːmlɪs/ a informe
**formula** /'fɔːmjʊlə/ n (*pl* **-ae** /-iː/ or
**-as**) fórmula f
**formulate** /'fɔːmjʊleɪt/ vt formular
**fornicate** /'fɔːnɪkeɪt/ vi fornicar.
**~ion** /-'keɪʃn/ n fornicación f
**forsake** /fə'seɪk/ vt (*pt* **forsook,** *pp*
**forsaken**) abandonar
**fort** /fɔːt/ n (*mil*) fuerte m
**forte** /'fɔːteɪ/ n (*talent*) fuerte m
**forth** /fɔːθ/ adv en adelante. **and so
~** y así sucesivamente. **go back and
~** ir y venir
**forthcoming** /fɔːθ'kʌmɪŋ/ a próximo, venidero; (*sociable, fam*)
comunicativo
**forthright** /'fɔːθraɪt/ a directo
**forthwith** /fɔːθ'wɪθ/ adv inmediatamente
**fortieth** /'fɔːtɪɪθ/ a cuarenta, cuadragésimo. ● n cuadragésima parte
f
**fortif|ication** /fɔːtɪfɪ'keɪʃn/ n for-
tificación f. **~y** /'fɔːtɪfaɪ/ vt
fortificar
**fortitude** /'fɔːtɪtjuːd/ n valor m
**fortnight** /'fɔːtnaɪt/ n quince días
*mpl*, quincena f. **~ly** a bimensual.
● adv cada quince días
**fortress** /'fɔːtrɪs/ n fortaleza f
**fortuitous** /fɔː'tjuːɪtəs/ a fortuito
**fortunate** /'fɔːtʃənət/ a afortunado.
**be ~** tener suerte. **~ly** adv
afortunadamente
**fortune** /'fɔːtʃuːn/ n fortuna f. **have
the good ~ to** tener la suerte de.
**~teller** n adivino m
**forty** /'fɔːtɪ/ a & n cuarenta (m). **~
winks** un sueñecito m
**forum** /'fɔːrəm/ n foro m
**forward** /'fɔːwəd/ a delantero;
(*advanced*) precoz; (*pert*) impertinente. ● n (*sport*) delantero m.
● adv adelante. **come ~** presentarse. **go ~** avanzar. ● vt hacer seguir (*letter*); enviar (*goods*); (*fig*)
favorecer. **~ness** n precocidad f
**forwards** /'fɔːwədz/ adv adelante
**fossil** /'fɒsl/ a & n fósil (m)
**foster** /'fɒstə(r)/ vt (*promote*)
fomentar; criar (*child*). **~child** n
hijo m adoptivo. **~mother** n madre
f adoptiva
**fought** /fɔːt/ *see* **fight**

**foul** /faʊl/ a (-er, -est) ⟨smell, weather⟩ asqueroso; (dirty) sucio; ⟨language⟩ obsceno; ⟨air⟩ viciado. ~ **play** n jugada f sucia; (crime) delito m. ● n (sport) falta f. ● vt ensuciar; manchar ⟨reputation⟩. ~**mouthed** a obsceno

**found¹** /faʊnd/ see **find**

**found²** /faʊnd/ vt fundar

**found³** /faʊnd/ vt (tec) fundir

**foundation** /faʊn'deɪʃn/ n fundación f; (basis) fundamento. ~**s** npl (archit) cimientos mpl

**founder¹** /'faʊndə(r)/ n fundador m

**founder²** /'faʊndə(r)/ vi ⟨ship⟩ hundirse

**foundry** /'faʊndrɪ/ n fundición f

**fountain** /'faʊntɪn/ n fuente f. ~**pen** n estilográfica f

**four** /fɔː(r)/ a & n cuatro (m). ~**fold** a cuádruple. ● adv cuatro veces. ~**poster** n cama f con cuatro columnas

**foursome** /'fɔːsəm/ n grupo m de cuatro personas

**fourteen** /'fɔːtiːn/ a & n catorce (m). ~**th** a & n catorce (m), decimocuarto (m). ● n (fraction) catorceavo m

**fourth** /fɔːθ/ a & n cuarto (m)

**fowl** /faʊl/ n ave f

**fox** /fɒks/ n zorro m, zorra f. ● vt (baffle) dejar perplejo; (deceive) engañar

**foyer** /'fɔɪeɪ/ n (hall) vestíbulo m

**fraction** /'frækʃn/ n fracción f

**fractious** /'frækʃəs/ a díscolo

**fracture** /'fræktʃə(r)/ n fractura f. ● vt fracturar. ● vi fracturarse

**fragile** /'frædʒaɪl/ a frágil

**fragment** /'frægmənt/ n fragmento m. ~**ary** a fragmentario

**fragran|ce** /'freɪgrəns/ n fragancia f. ~**t** a fragante

**frail** /freɪl/ a (-er, -est) frágil

**frame** /freɪm/ n (of picture, door, window) marco m; (of spectacles) montura f; (fig, structure) estructura f; (temporary state) estado m. ~ **of mind** estado m de ánimo. ● vt enmarcar; (fig) formular; (jurid, sl) incriminar falsamente. ~**up** n (sl) complot m

**framework** /'freɪmwɜːk/ n estructura f; (context) marco m

**France** /frɑːns/ n Francia f

**franchise** /'fræntʃaɪz/ n (pol) derecho m a votar; (com) concesión f

**Franco...** /'fræŋkəʊ/ pref franco...

**frank** /fræŋk/ a sincero. ● vt franquear. ~**ly** adv sinceramente. ~**ness** n sinceridad f

**frantic** /'fræntɪk/ a frenético. ~ **with** loco de

**fraternal** /frə'tɜːnl/ a fraternal

**fraternity** /frə'tɜːnɪtɪ/ n fraternidad f; (club) asociación f

**fraternize** /'frætənaɪz/ vi fraternizar

**fraud** /frɔːd/ n (deception) fraude m; (person) impostor m. ~**ulent** a fraudulento

**fraught** /frɔːt/ a (tense) tenso. ~ **with** cargado de

**fray¹** /freɪ/ vt desgastar. ● vi deshilacharse

**fray²** /freɪ/ n riña f

**freak** /friːk/ n (caprice) capricho m; (monster) monstruo m; (person) chalado m. ● a anormal. ~**ish** a anormal

**freckle** /'frekl/ n peca f. ~**d** a pecoso

**free** /friː/ a (freer /'friːə(r)/, freest /'friːɪst/) libre; (gratis) gratis; (lavish) generoso. ~ **kick** n golpe m franco. ~ **of charge** gratis. ~ **speech** n libertad f de expresión. **give a** ~ **hand** dar carta blanca. ● vt (pt **freed**) (set at liberty) poner en libertad; (relieve from) liberar (**from/of** de); (untangle) desenredar; (loosen) soltar

**freedom** /'friːdəm/ n libertad f

**freehold** /'friːhəʊld/ n propiedad f absoluta

**freelance** /'friːlɑːns/ a independiente

**freely** /'friːlɪ/ adv libremente

**Freemason** /'friːmeɪsn/ n masón m. ~**ry** n masonería f

**free-range** /'friːreɪndʒ/ a ⟨eggs⟩ de granja

**freesia** /'friːzjə/ n fresia f

**freeway** /'friːweɪ/ n (Amer) autopista f

**freez|e** /'friːz/ vt (pt **froze**, pp **frozen**) helar; congelar ⟨food, wages⟩. ● vi helarse, congelarse; (become motionless) quedarse inmóvil. ● n helada f; (of wages, prices) congelación f. ~**er** n congelador m. ~**ing** a glacial. ● n congelación f. **below** ~**ing** bajo cero

**freight** /freɪt/ n (goods) mercancías fpl; (hire of ship etc) flete m. ~**er** n (ship) buque m de carga

**French** /frentʃ/ a francés. ● n (lang) francés m. ~**man** n francés m. ~**speaking** a francófono. ~ **window** n puertaventana f. ~**woman** f francesa f

**frenz|ied** /'frenzɪd/ a frenético. ~y n frenesí m

**frequency** /'fri:kwənsɪ/ n frecuencia f

**frequent** /frɪ'kwent/ vt frecuentar. /'fri:kwənt/ a frecuente. ~ly adv frecuentemente

**fresco** /'freskəʊ/ n (pl -o(e)s) fresco m

**fresh** /freʃ/ a (-er, -est) fresco; (different, additional) nuevo; (cheeky) fresco, descarado; ⟨water⟩ dulce. ~en vi refrescar. ~en up ⟨person⟩ refrescarse. ~ly adv recientemente. ~man n estudiante m de primer año. ~ness n frescura f

**fret** /fret/ vi (pt fretted) inquietarse. ~ful a (discontented) quejoso; (irritable) irritable

**Freudian** /'frɔɪdjən/ a freudiano

**friar** /fraɪə(r)/ n fraile m

**friction** /'frɪkʃn/ n fricción f

**Friday** /'fraɪdeɪ/ n viernes m. **Good ~** Viernes Santo

**fridge** /frɪdʒ/ n (fam) nevera f, refrigerador m, refrigeradora f

**fried** /fraɪd/ see **fry**. ● a frito

**friend** /frend/ n amigo m. ~liness /'frendlɪnɪs/ n simpatía f. ~ly a (-ier, -iest) simpático. **F~ly Society** n mutualidad f. ~ship /'frendʃɪp/ n amistad f

**frieze** /fri:z/ n friso m

**frigate** /'frɪgət/ n fragata f

**fright** /fraɪt/ n susto m; (person) espantajo m; (thing) horror m

**frighten** /'fraɪtn/ vt asustar. ~ off ahuyentar. ~ed a asustado. **be ~ed** tener miedo (**of** de)

**frightful** /'fraɪtfl/ a espantoso, horrible. ~ly adv terriblemente

**frigid** /'frɪdʒɪd/ a frío; (psych) frígido. ~ity /-'dʒɪdətɪ/ n frigidez f

**frill** /frɪl/ n volante m. ~s npl (fig) adornos mpl. **with no ~s** sencillo

**fringe** /frɪndʒ/ n (sewing) fleco m; (ornamental border) franja f; (of hair) flequillo m; (of area) periferia f; (of society) margen m. ~ **benefits** npl beneficios mpl suplementarios. ~ **theatre** n teatro m de vanguardia

**frisk** /frɪsk/ vt (search) cachear

**frisky** /'frɪskɪ/ a (-ier, -iest) retozón; ⟨horse⟩ fogoso

**fritter**[1] /'frɪtə(r)/ vt. ~ **away** desperdiciar

**fritter**[2] /'frɪtə(r)/ n buñuelo m

**frivol|ity** /frɪ'vɒlətɪ/ n frivolidad f. ~ous /'frɪvələs/ a frívolo

**frizzy** /'frɪzɪ/ a crespo

**fro** /frəʊ/ see **to and fro**

**frock** /frɒk/ n vestido m; (of monk) hábito m

**frog** /frɒg/ n rana f. **have a ~ in one's throat** tener carraspera

**frogman** /'frɒgmən/ n hombre m rana

**frolic** /'frɒlɪk/ vi (pt frolicked) retozar. ● n broma f

**from** /frɒm/, unstressed /frəm/ prep de; (with time, prices, etc) a partir de; (habit, conviction) por; (according to) según. **take ~ (away from)** quitar a

**front** /frʌnt/ n parte f delantera; (of building) fachada f; (of clothes) delantera f; (mil, pol) frente f; (of book) principio m; (fig, appearance) apariencia f; (sea front) paseo m marítimo. **in ~ of** delante de. **put a bold ~ on** hacer de tripas corazón, mostrar firmeza. ● a delantero; (first) primero. ~**age** n fachada f. ~**al** a frontal; ⟨attack⟩ de frente. ~ **door** n puerta f principal. ~ **page** n (of newspaper) primera plana f

**frontier** /'frʌntɪə(r)/ n frontera f

**frost** /frɒst/ n (freezing) helada f; (frozen dew) escarcha f. ~**bite** n congelación f. ~**bitten** a congelado. ~**ed** a ⟨glass⟩ esmerilado

**frosting** /'frɒstɪŋ/ n (icing, Amer) azúcar m glaseado

**frosty** a ⟨weather⟩ de helada; ⟨window⟩ escarchado; (fig) glacial

**froth** /frɒθ/ n espuma f. ● vi espumar. ~y a espumoso

**frown** /fraʊn/ vi fruncir el entrecejo. ~ **on** desaprobar. ● n ceño m

**froze** /frəʊz/, **frozen** /'frəʊzn/ see **freeze**

**frugal** /'fru:gl/ a frugal. ~ly adv frugalmente

**fruit** /fru:t/ n (bot, on tree, fig) fruto m; (as food) fruta f. ~**erer** n frutero m. ~**ful** /'fru:tfl/ a fértil; (fig) fructífero. ~**less** a infructuoso. ~ **machine** n (máquina f) tragaperras m. ~ **salad** n macedonia f de frutas. ~y /'fru:tɪ/ a ⟨taste⟩ que sabe a fruta

**fruition** /fru:'ɪʃn/ n. **come to ~** realizarse

**frump** /frʌmp/ n espantajo m

**frustrat|e** /frʌ'streɪt/ vt frustrar. ~**ion** /-ʃn/ n frustración f; (disappointment) decepción f

**fry**[1] /fraɪ/ vt (pt fried) freír. ● vi freírse

**fry²** /fraɪ/ n (pl **fry**). **small** ~ gente f de poca monta

**frying-pan** /'fraɪɪŋpæn/ n sartén f

**fuchsia** /'fjuːʃə/ n fucsia f

**fuddy-duddy** /'fʌdɪdʌdɪ/ n. **be a** ~ (sl) estar chapado a la antigua

**fudge** /fʌdʒ/ n dulce m de azúcar

**fuel** /'fjuːəl/ n combustible m; (for car engine) carburante m; (fig) pábulo m. ● vt (pt **fuelled**) alimentar de combustible

**fugitive** /'fjuːdʒɪtɪv/ a & n fugitivo (m)

**fugue** /fjuːg/ n (mus) fuga f

**fulfil** /fʊl'fɪl/ vt (pt **fulfilled**) cumplir (con) ⟨promise, obligation⟩; satisfacer ⟨condition⟩; realizar ⟨hopes, plans⟩; llevar a cabo ⟨task⟩. ~**ment** n (of promise, obligation) cumplimiento m; (of conditions) satisfacción f; (of hopes, plans) realización f; (of task) ejecución f

**full** /fʊl/ a (-er, -est) lleno; ⟨bus, hotel⟩ completo; ⟨skirt⟩ amplio; ⟨account⟩ detallado. **at** ~ **speed** a máxima velocidad. **be** ~ (**up**) (with food) no poder más. **in** ~ **swing** en plena marcha. ● n. **in** ~ sin quitar nada. **to the** ~ completamente. **write in** ~ escribir con todas las letras. ~ **back** n (sport) defensa m & f. ~-**blooded** a vigoroso. ~ **moon** n plenilunio m. ~-**scale** a ⟨drawing⟩ de tamaño natural; (fig) amplio. ~ **stop** n punto m; (at end of paragraph, fig) punto m final. ~ **time** a de jornada completa. ~**y** adv completamente

**fulsome** /'fʊlsəm/ a excesivo

**fumble** /'fʌmbl/ vi buscar (torpemente)

**fume** /fjuːm/ vi humear; (fig, be furious) estar furioso. ~**s** npl humo m

**fumigate** /'fjuːmɪgeɪt/ vt fumigar

**fun** /fʌn/ n (amusement) diversión f; (merriment) alegría f. **for** ~ en broma. **have** ~ divertirse. **make** ~ **of** burlarse de

**function** /'fʌŋkʃn/ n (purpose, duty) función f; (reception) recepción f. ● vi funcionar. ~**al** a funcional

**fund** /fʌnd/ n fondo m. ● vt proveer fondos para

**fundamental** /fʌndə'mentl/ a fundamental

**funeral** /'fjuːnərəl/ n funeral m, funerales mpl. ● a fúnebre

**fun-fair** /'fʌnfeə(r)/ n parque m de atracciones

**fungus** /'fʌŋgəs/ n (pl -**gi** /-gaɪ/) hongo m

**funicular** /fjuː'nɪkjʊlə(r)/ n funicular m

**funk** /fʌŋk/ m (fear, sl) miedo m; (state of depression, Amer, sl) depresión f. **be in a** (**blue**) ~ tener (mucho) miedo; (Amer) estar (muy) deprimido. ● vi rajarse

**funnel** /'fʌnl/ n (for pouring) embudo m; (of ship) chimenea f

**funn|ily** /'fʌnɪlɪ/ adv graciosamente; (oddly) curiosamente. ~**y** a (-**ier**, -**iest**) divertido, gracioso; (odd) curioso, raro. ~**y-bone** n cóndilo m del húmero. ~**y business** n engaño m

**fur** /fɜː(r)/ n pelo m; (pelt) piel f; (in kettle) sarro m

**furbish** /'fɜːbɪʃ/ vt pulir; (renovate) renovar

**furious** /'fjʊərɪəs/ a furioso. ~**ly** adv furiosamente

**furnace** /'fɜːnɪs/ n horno m

**furnish** /'fɜːnɪʃ/ vt (with furniture) amueblar; (supply) proveer. ~**ings** npl muebles mpl, mobiliario m

**furniture** /'fɜːnɪtʃə(r)/ n muebles mpl, mobiliario m

**furrier** /'fʌrɪə(r)/ n peletero m

**furrow** /'fʌrəʊ/ n surco m

**furry** /'fɜːrɪ/ a peludo

**furthe|r** /'fɜːðə(r)/ a más lejano; (additional) nuevo. ● adv más lejos; (more) además. ● vt fomentar. ~**rmore** adv además. ~**rmost** a más lejano. ~**st** a más lejano. ● adv más lejos

**furtive** /'fɜːtɪv/ a furtivo

**fury** /'fjʊərɪ/ n furia f

**fuse¹** /fjuːz/ vt (melt) fundir; (fig, unite) fusionar. ~ **the lights** fundir los plomos. ● vi fundirse; (fig) fusionarse. ● n fusible m, plomo m

**fuse²** /fjuːz/ n (of bomb) mecha f

**fuse-box** /'fjuːzbɒks/ n caja f de fusibles

**fuselage** /'fjuːzəlɑːʒ/ n fuselaje m

**fusion** /'fjuːʒn/ n fusión f

**fuss** /fʌs/ n (commotion) jaleo m. **kick up a** ~ armar un lío, armar una bronca, protestar. **make a** ~ **of** tratar con mucha atención. ~**y** a (-**ier**, -**iest**) (finicky) remilgado; (demanding) exigente; (ornate) recargado

**fusty** /'fʌstɪ/ a (-**ier**, -**iest**) que huele a cerrado

**futile** /'fju:taɪl/ *a* inútil, vano

**future** /'fju:tʃə(r)/ *a* futuro. ● *n* futuro *m*, porvenir *m*; (*gram*) futuro *m*. **in ~** en lo sucesivo, de ahora en adelante

**futuristic** /fju:tʃə'rɪstɪk/ *a* futurista

**fuzz** /fʌz/ *n* (*fluff*) pelusa *f*; (*police, sl*) policía *f*, poli *f* (*fam*)

**fuzzy** /'fʌzɪ/ *a* ⟨*hair*⟩ crespo; ⟨*photograph*⟩ borroso

# G

**gab** /gæb/ *n* charla *f*. **have the gift of the ~** tener un pico de oro

**gabardine** /gæbə'di:n/ *n* gabardina *f*

**gabble** /'gæbl/ *vt* decir atropelladamente. ● *vi* hablar atropelladamente. ● *n* torrente *m* de palabras

**gable** /'geɪbl/ *n* aguilón *m*

**gad** /gæd/ *vi* (*pt* gadded). **~ about** callejear

**gadget** /'gædʒɪt/ *n* chisme *m*

**Gaelic** /'geɪlɪk/ *a & n* gaélico (*m*)

**gaffe** /gæf/ *n* plancha *f*, metedura *f* de pata

**gag** /gæg/ *n* mordaza *f*; (*joke*) chiste *m*. ● *vt* (*pt* gagged) amordazar

**gaga** /'gɑ:gɑ:/ *a* (*sl*) chocho

**gaiety** /'geɪətɪ/ *n* alegría *f*

**gaily** /'geɪlɪ/ *adv* alegremente

**gain** /geɪn/ *vt* ganar; (*acquire*) adquirir; (*obtain*) conseguir. ● *vi* ⟨*clock*⟩ adelantar. ● *n* ganancia *f*; (*increase*) aumento *m*. **~ful** *a* lucrativo

**gainsay** /geɪn'seɪ/ *vt* (*pt* gainsaid) (*formal*) negar

**gait** /geɪt/ *n* modo *m* de andar

**gala** /'gɑ:lə/ *n* fiesta *f*; (*sport*) competición *f*

**galaxy** /'gæləksɪ/ *n* galaxia *f*

**gale** /geɪl/ *n* vendaval *m*; (*storm*) tempestad *f*

**gall** /gɔ:l/ *n* bilis *f*; (*fig*) hiel *f*; (*impudence*) descaro *m*

**gallant** /'gælənt/ *a* (*brave*) valiente; (*chivalrous*) galante. **~ry** *n* valor *m*

**gall-bladder** /'gɔ:lblædə(r)/ *n* vesícula *f* biliar

**galleon** /'gælɪən/ *n* galeón *m*

**gallery** /'gælərɪ/ *n* galería *f*

**galley** /'gælɪ/ *n* (*ship*) galera *f*; (*ship's kitchen*) cocina *f*. **~ (proof)** *n* (*typ*) galerada *f*

**Gallic** /'gælɪk/ *a* gálico. **~ism** *n* galicismo *m*

**gallivant** /'gælɪvænt/ *vi* (*fam*) callejear

**gallon** /'gælən/ *n* galón *m* (*imperial* = 4,546*l*; *Amer* = 3,785*l*)

**gallop** /'gæləp/ *n* galope *m*. ● *vi* (*pt* galloped) galopar

**gallows** /'gæləʊz/ *n* horca *f*

**galore** /gə'lɔ:(r)/ *adv* en abundancia

**galosh** /gə'lɒʃ/ *n* chanclo *m*

**galvanize** /'gælvənaɪz/ *vt* galvanizar

**gambit** /'gæmbɪt/ *n* (*in chess*) gambito *m*; (*fig*) táctica *f*

**gamble** /'gæmbl/ *vt/i* jugar. **~e on** contar con. ● *n* (*venture*) empresa *f* arriesgada; (*bet*) jugada *f*; (*risk*) riesgo *m*. **~er** *n* jugador *m*. **~ing** *n* juego *m*

**game**[1] /geɪm/ *n* juego *m*; (*match*) partido *m*; (*animals, birds*) caza *f*. ● *a* valiente. **~ for** listo para

**game**[2] /geɪm/ *a* (*lame*) cojo

**gamekeeper** /'geɪmki:pə(r)/ *n* guardabosque *m*

**gammon** /'gæmən/ *n* jamón *m* ahumado

**gamut** /'gæmət/ *n* gama *f*

**gamy** /'geɪmɪ/ *a* manido

**gander** /'gændə(r)/ *n* ganso *m*

**gang** /gæŋ/ *n* pandilla *f*; (*of workmen*) equipo *m*. ● *vi.* **~ up** unirse (on contra)

**gangling** /'gæŋglɪŋ/ *a* larguirucho

**gangrene** /'gæŋgri:n/ *n* gangrena *f*

**gangster** /'gæŋstə(r)/ *n* bandido *m*, gangster *m*

**gangway** /'gæŋweɪ/ *n* pasillo *m*; (*of ship*) pasarela *f*

**gaol** /dʒeɪl/ *n* cárcel *f*. **~bird** *n* criminal *m* empedernido. **~er** *n* carcelero *m*

**gap** /gæp/ *n* vacío *m*; (*breach*) brecha *f*; (*in time*) intervalo *m*; (*deficiency*) laguna *f*; (*difference*) diferencia *f*

**gape** /geɪp/ *vi* quedarse boquiabierto; (*be wide open*) estar muy abierto. **~ing** *a* abierto; (*person*) boquiabierto

**garage** /'gærɑ:ʒ/ *n* garaje *m*; (*petrol station*) gasolinera *f*; (*for repairs*) taller *m*. ● *vt* dejar en (el) garaje

**garb** /gɑ:b/ *n* vestido *m*

**garbage** /'gɑ:bɪdʒ/ *n* basura *f*

**garble** /'gɑ:bl/ *vt* mutilar

**garden** /'gɑ:dn/ *n* (*of flowers*) jardín *m*; (*of vegetables/fruit*) huerto *m*. ● *vi* trabajar en el jardín/huerto. **~er** *n* jardinero/hortelano *m*. **~ing** *n* jardinería/horticultura *f*

**gargantuan** /gɑːˈɡæntjʊən/ a gigantesco

**gargle** /ˈɡɑːɡl/ vi hacer gárgaras. n gargarismo m

**gargoyle** /ˈɡɑːɡɔɪl/ n gárgola f

**garish** /ˈɡeərɪʃ/ a chillón

**garland** /ˈɡɑːlənd/ n guirnalda f

**garlic** /ˈɡɑːlɪk/ n ajo m

**garment** /ˈɡɑːmənt/ n prenda f (de vestir)

**garnet** /ˈɡɑːnɪt/ n granate m

**garnish** /ˈɡɑːnɪʃ/ vt aderezar. • n aderezo m

**garret** /ˈɡærət/ n guardilla f, buhardilla f

**garrison** /ˈɡærɪsn/ n guarnición f

**garrulous** /ˈɡærələs/ a hablador

**garter** /ˈɡɑːtə(r)/ n liga f

**gas** /ɡæs/ n (pl gases) gas m; (med) anestésico m; (petrol, Amer, fam) gasolina f. • vt (pt gassed) asfixiar con gas. • vi (fam) charlar. ~ fire n estufa f de gas

**gash** /ɡæʃ/ n cuchillada f. • vt acuchillar

**gasket** /ˈɡæskɪt/ n junta f

**gas:** ~ mask n careta f antigás a invar. ~ meter n contador m de gas

**gasoline** /ˈɡæsəliːn/ n (petrol, Amer) gasolina f

**gasometer** /ɡæˈsɒmɪtə(r)/ n gasómetro m

**gasp** /ɡɑːsp/ vi jadear; (with surprise) quedarse boquiabierto. • n jadeo m

**gas:** ~ ring n hornillo m de gas. ~ station n (Amer) gasolinera f

**gastric** /ˈɡæstrɪk/ a gástrico

**gastronomy** /ɡæˈstrɒnəmɪ/ n gastronomía f

**gate** /ɡeɪt/ n puerta f; (of metal) verja f; (barrier) barrera f

**gateau** /ˈɡætəʊ/ n (pl gateaux) tarta f

**gate:** ~crasher n intruso m (que ha entrado sin ser invitado o sin pagar). ~way n puerta f

**gather** /ˈɡæðə(r)/ vt reunir ⟨people, things⟩; (accumulate) acumular; (pick up) recoger; recoger ⟨flowers⟩; (fig, infer) deducir; (sewing) fruncir. ~ speed acelerar. • vi ⟨people⟩ reunirse; ⟨things⟩ acumularse. ~ing n reunión f

**gauche** /ɡəʊʃ/ a torpe

**gaudy** /ˈɡɔːdɪ/ a (-ier, -iest) chillón

**gauge** /ɡeɪdʒ/ n (measurement) medida f; (rail) entrevía f; (instrument) indicador m. • vt medir; (fig) estimar

**gaunt** /ɡɔːnt/ a macilento; (grim) lúgubre

**gauntlet** /ˈɡɔːntlɪt/ n. run the ~ of estar sometido a

**gauze** /ɡɔːz/ n gasa f

**gave** /ɡeɪv/ see give

**gawk** /ɡɔːk/ vi. ~ at mirar como un tonto

**gawky** /ˈɡɔːkɪ/ a (-ier, -iest) torpe

**gawp** /ɡɔːp/ vi. ~ at mirar como un tonto

**gay** /ɡeɪ/ a (-er, -est) (joyful) alegre; (homosexual, fam) homosexual, gay (fam)

**gaze** /ɡeɪz/ vi. ~ (at) mirar (fijamente). • n mirada f (fija)

**gazelle** /ɡəˈzel/ n gacela f

**gazette** /ɡəˈzet/ n boletín m oficial, gaceta f

**gazump** /ɡəˈzʌmp/ vt aceptar un precio más elevado de otro comprador

**GB** abbr see **Great Britain**

**gear** /ɡɪə(r)/ n equipo m; (tec) engranaje m; (auto) marcha f. in ~ engranado. out of ~ desengranado. • vt adaptar. ~box n (auto) caja f de cambios

**geese** /ɡiːs/ see goose

**geezer** /ˈɡiːzə(r)/ n (sl) tipo m

**gelatine** /ˈdʒelətiːn/ n gelatina f

**gelignite** /ˈdʒelɪɡnaɪt/ n gelignita f

**gem** /dʒem/ n piedra f preciosa

**Gemini** /ˈdʒemɪnaɪ/ n (astr) Gemelos mpl, Géminis mpl

**gen** /dʒen/ n (sl) información f

**gender** /ˈdʒendə(r)/ n género m

**gene** /dʒiːn/ n gene m

**genealogy** /dʒiːnɪˈælədʒɪ/ n genealogía f

**general** /ˈdʒenərəl/ a general. • n general m. in ~ generalmente. ~ election n elecciones fpl generales

**generaliz|ation** /dʒenərəlaɪˈzeɪʃn/ n generalización f. ~e vt/i generalizar

**generally** /ˈdʒenərəlɪ/ adv generalmente

**general practitioner** /ˈdʒenərəl prækˈtɪʃənə(r)/ n médico m de cabecera

**generate** /ˈdʒenəreɪt/ vt producir; (elec) generar

**generation** /dʒenəˈreɪʃn/ n generación f

**generator** /ˈdʒenəreɪtə(r)/ n (elec) generador m

**genero|sity** /dʒenəˈrɒsətɪ/ n generosidad f. ~us /ˈdʒenərəs/ a generoso; (plentiful) abundante

**genetic** /dʒɪ'netɪk/ a genético. ~s n
genética f

**Geneva** /dʒɪ'niːvə/ n Ginebra f

**genial** /'dʒiːnɪəl/ a simpático, afable;
⟨climate⟩ suave, templado

**genital** /'dʒenɪtl/ a genital. ~s npl
genitales mpl

**genitive** /'dʒenɪtɪv/ a & n genitivo
(m)

**genius** /'dʒiːnɪəs/ n (pl -uses) genio
m

**genocide** /'dʒenəsaɪd/ n genocidio m

**genre** /ʒɑːŋr/ n género m

**gent** /dʒent/ n (sl) señor m. ~s n
aseo m de caballeros

**genteel** /dʒen'tiːl/ a distinguido;
(excessively refined) cursi

**gentle** /'dʒentl/ a (-er, -est) (mild,
kind) amable, dulce; (slight) ligero;
⟨hint⟩ discreto

**gentlefolk** /'dʒentlfəʊk/ npl gente f
de buena familia

**gentleman** /'dʒentlmən/ n señor m;
(well-bred) caballero m

**gentleness** /'dʒentlnɪs/ n amabilidad f

**gentlewoman** /'dʒentlwʊmən/ n
señora f (de buena familia)

**gently** /'dʒentlɪ/ adv amablemente;
(slowly) despacio

**gentry** /'dʒentrɪ/ npl pequeña aris-
tocracia f

**genuflect** /'dʒenjuːflekt/ vi doblar la
rodilla

**genuine** /'dʒenjʊɪn/ a verdadero;
⟨person⟩ sincero

**geograph|er** /dʒɪ'ɒgrəfə(r)/ n geó-
grafo m. ~ical /dʒɪə'græfɪkl/ a geo-
gráfico. ~y /dʒɪ'ɒgrəfɪ/ n geografía f

**geolog|ical** /dʒɪə'lɒdʒɪkl/ a geoló-
gico. ~ist n geólogo m. ~y
/dʒɪ'ɒlədʒɪ/ n geología f

**geometr|ic(al)** /dʒɪə'metrɪk(l)/ a
geométrico. ~y /dʒɪ'ɒmətrɪ/ n geometría f

**geranium** /dʒə'reɪnɪəm/ n geranio m

**geriatrics** /dʒerɪ'ætrɪks/ n geriatría f

**germ** /dʒɜːm/ n (rudiment, seed) germen m; (med) microbio m

**German** /'dʒɜːmən/ a & n alemán
(m). ~ic /dʒɜ'mænɪk/ a germánico.
~ measles n rubéola f. ~ shepherd
(dog) n (perro m) pastor m alemán.
~y n Alemania f

**germicide** /'dʒɜːmɪsaɪd/ n germicida
m

**germinate** /'dʒɜːmɪneɪt/ vi germinar. ● vt hacer germinar

**gerrymander** /'dʒerɪmændə(r)/ n
falsificación f electoral

**gestation** /dʒe'steɪʃn/ n gestación f

**gesticulate** /dʒe'stɪkjʊleɪt/ vi hacer
ademanes, gesticular

**gesture** /'dʒestʃə(r)/ n ademán m;
(fig) gesto m

**get** /get/ vt (pt & pp got, pp Amer
gotten, pres p getting) obtener,
tener; (catch) coger (not LAm),
agarrar (esp LAm); (buy) comprar;
(find) encontrar; (fetch) buscar,
traer; (understand, sl) comprender,
caer (fam). ~ s.o. to do sth conseguir que uno haga algo. ● vi (go)
ir; (become) hacerse; (start to) empezar a; (manage) conseguir. ~ married casarse. ~ ready prepararse.
~ about (person) salir mucho;
(after illness) levantarse. ~ along
(manage) ir tirando; (progress)
hacer progresos. ~ along with llevarse bien con. ~ at (reach) llegar
a; (imply) querer decir. ~ away
salir; (escape) escaparse. ~ back vi
volver. ● vt (recover) recobrar. ~ by
(manage) ir tirando; (pass) pasar. ~
down bajar; (depress) deprimir. ~
in entrar; subir ⟨vehicle⟩; (arrive)
llegar. ~ off bajar de ⟨train, car
etc⟩; (leave) irse; (jurid) salir
absuelto. ~ on (progress) hacer
progresos; (succeed) tener éxito. ~
on with (be on good terms with) llevarse bien con; (continue) seguir. ~
out (person) salir; (take out) sacar.
~ out of (fig) librarse de. ~ over
reponerse de ⟨illness⟩. ~ round sos-
layar ⟨difficulty etc⟩; engatusar ⟨per-
son⟩. ~ through (pass) pasar;
(finish) terminar; (on phone) comunicar con. ~ up levantarse;
(climb) subir; (organize) preparar.
~away n huida f. ~up n traje m

**geyser** /'giːzə(r)/ n calentador m de
agua; (geog) géiser m

**Ghana** /'gɑːnə/ n Ghana f

**ghastly** /'gɑːstlɪ/ a (-ier, -iest) horrible; (pale) pálido

**gherkin** /'gɜːkɪn/ n pepinillo m

**ghetto** /'getəʊ/ n (pl -os) (Jewish
quarter) judería f; (ethnic settlement) barrio m pobre habitado
por un grupo étnico

**ghost** /gəʊst/ n fantasma m. ~ly a
espectral

**ghoulish** /'guːlɪʃ/ a macabro

**giant** /'dʒaɪənt/ n gigante m. ● a
gigantesco

**gibberish** /'dʒibəriʃ/ n jerigonza f

**gibe** /dʒaib/ n mofa f

**giblets** /'dʒiblɪts/ npl menudillos mpl

**Gibraltar** /dʒɪ'brɔːltə(r)/ n Gibraltar m

**gidd|iness** /'gɪdɪnɪs/ n vértigo m. ∼y a (-ier, -iest) mareado; ⟨speed⟩ vertiginoso. **be/feel** ∼y estar/sentirse mareado

**gift** /gɪft/ n regalo m; ⟨ability⟩ don m. ∼ed a dotado de talento. ∼wrap vt envolver para regalo

**gig** /gɪg/ n (fam) concierto m

**gigantic** /dʒaɪ'gæntɪk/ a gigantesco

**giggle** /'gɪgl/ vi reírse tontamente. ● n risita f. **the** ∼s la risa f tonta

**gild** /gɪld/ vt dorar

**gills** /gɪlz/ npl agallas fpl

**gilt** /gɪlt/ a dorado. ∼-edged a ⟨com⟩ de máxima garantía

**gimmick** /'gɪmɪk/ n truco m

**gin** /dʒɪn/ n ginebra f

**ginger** /'dʒɪndʒə(r)/ n jengibre m. ● a rojizo. ● vt. ∼ up animar. ∼ ale n, ∼ beer n cerveza f de jengibre. ∼bread n pan m de jengibre

**gingerly** /'dʒɪndʒəlɪ/ adv cautelosamente

**gingham** /'gɪŋəm/ n guinga f

**gipsy** /'dʒɪpsɪ/ n gitano m

**giraffe** /dʒɪ'rɑːf/ n jirafa f

**girder** /'gɜːdə(r)/ n viga f

**girdle** /'gɜːdl/ n ⟨belt⟩ cinturón m; ⟨corset⟩ corsé m

**girl** /gɜːl/ n chica f, muchacha f; ⟨child⟩ niña f. ∼friend n amiga f; ⟨of boy⟩ novia f. ∼hood n ⟨up to adolescence⟩ niñez f; ⟨adolescence⟩ juventud f. ∼ish a de niña; ⟨boy⟩ afeminado

**giro** /'dʒaɪrəʊ/ n (pl -os) giro m ⟨bancario⟩

**girth** /gɜːθ/ n circunferencia f

**gist** /dʒɪst/ n lo esencial invar

**give** /gɪv/ vt (pt gave, pp given) dar; ⟨deliver⟩ entregar; regalar ⟨present⟩; prestar ⟨aid, attention⟩; ⟨grant⟩ conceder; ⟨yield⟩ ceder; ⟨devote⟩ dedicar. ∼ o.s. to darse a. ● vi dar; ⟨yield⟩ ceder; ⟨stretch⟩ estirarse. ● n elasticidad f. ∼ away regalar; descubrir ⟨secret⟩. ∼ back devolver. ∼ in ⟨yield⟩ rendirse. ∼ off emitir. ∼ o.s. up entregarse (a). ∼ out distribuir; ⟨announce⟩ anunciar; ⟨become used up⟩ agotarse. ∼ over ⟨devote⟩ dedicar; ⟨stop, fam⟩ dejar (de). ∼ up ⟨renounce⟩ renunciar a; ⟨yield⟩ ceder

**given** /'gɪvn/ see **give**. ● a dado. ∼ name n nombre m de pila

**glacier** /'glæsɪə(r)/ n glaciar m

**glad** /glæd/ a contento. ∼den vt alegrar

**glade** /gleɪd/ n claro m

**gladiator** /'glædɪeɪtə(r)/ n gladiador m

**gladiolus** /glædɪ'əʊləs/ n (pl -li /-laɪ/) estoque m, gladiolo m, gladíolo m

**gladly** /'glædlɪ/ adv alegremente; ⟨willingly⟩ con mucho gusto

**glamo|rize** /'glæməraɪz/ vt embellecer. ∼rous a atractivo. ∼ur n encanto m

**glance** /glɑːns/ n ojeada f. ● vi. ∼ at dar un vistazo a

**gland** /glænd/ n glándula f

**glar|e** /gleə(r)/ vi deslumbrar; ⟨stare angrily⟩ mirar airadamente. ● n deslumbramiento m; ⟨stare, fig⟩ mirada f airada. ∼ing a deslumbrador; ⟨obvious⟩ manifiesto

**glass** /glɑːs/ n ⟨material⟩ vidrio m; ⟨without stem or for wine⟩ vaso m; ⟨with stem⟩ copa f; ⟨for beer⟩ caña f; ⟨mirror⟩ espejo m. ∼es npl ⟨spectacles⟩ gafas fpl, anteojos (LAm) mpl. ∼y a vítreo

**glaze** /gleɪz/ vt poner cristales a ⟨windows, doors⟩; vidriar ⟨pottery⟩. ● n barniz m; ⟨for pottery⟩ esmalte m. ∼d a ⟨object⟩ vidriado; ⟨eye⟩ vidrioso

**gleam** /gliːm/ n destello m. ● vi destellar

**glean** /gliːn/ vt espigar

**glee** /gliː/ n regocijo m. ∼ club n orfeón m. ∼ful a regocijado

**glen** /glen/ n cañada f

**glib** /glɪb/ a de mucha labia; ⟨reply⟩ fácil. ∼ly adv con poca sinceridad

**glid|e** /glaɪd/ vi deslizarse; ⟨plane⟩ planear. ∼er n planeador m. ∼ing n planeo m

**glimmer** /'glɪmə(r)/ n destello m. ● vi destellar

**glimpse** /glɪmps/ n vislumbre f. **catch a** ∼ **of** vislumbrar. ● vt vislumbrar

**glint** /glɪnt/ n destello m. ● vi destellar

**glisten** /'glɪsn/ vi brillar

**glitter** /'glɪtə(r)/ vi brillar. ● n brillo m

**gloat** /gləʊt/ vi. ∼ **on/over** regodearse

**global** /ˈgləʊbl/ a (*world-wide*) mundial; (*all-embracing*) global

**globe** /gləʊb/ n globo m

**globule** /ˈglɒbjuːl/ n glóbulo m

**gloom** /gluːm/ n oscuridad f; (*sadness, fig*) tristeza f. **~y** a (**-ier, -iest**) triste; (*pessimistic*) pesimista

**glorify** /ˈglɔːrɪfaɪ/ vt glorificar

**glorious** /ˈglɔːrɪəs/ a espléndido; (*deed, hero etc*) glorioso

**glory** /ˈglɔːrɪ/ n gloria f; (*beauty*) esplendor m. ● vi. **~ in** enorgullecerse de. **~hole** n (*untidy room*) leonera f

**gloss** /glɒs/ n lustre m. ● a brillante. ● vi. **~ over** (*make light of*) minimizar; (*cover up*) encubrir

**glossary** /ˈglɒsərɪ/ n glosario m

**glossy** /ˈglɒsɪ/ a brillante

**glove** /glʌv/ n guante m. **~ compartment** n (*auto*) guantera f, gaveta f. **~d** a enguantado

**glow** /gləʊ/ vi brillar; (*with health*) rebosar de; (*with passion*) enardecerse. ● n incandescencia f; (*of cheeks*) rubor m

**glower** /ˈglaʊə(r)/ vi. **~ (at)** mirar airadamente

**glowing** /ˈgləʊɪŋ/ a incandescente; (*account*) entusiasta; (*complexion*) rojo; (*with health*) rebosante de

**glucose** /ˈgluːkəʊs/ n glucosa f

**glue** /gluː/ n cola f. ● vt (*pres p gluing*) pegar

**glum** /glʌm/ a (**glummer, glummest**) triste

**glut** /glʌt/ n superabundancia f

**glutton** /ˈglʌtn/ n glotón m. **~ous** a glotón. **~y** n glotonería f

**glycerine** /ˈglɪsəriːn/ n glicerina f

**gnarled** /nɑːld/ a nudoso

**gnash** /næʃ/ vt. **~ one's teeth** rechinar los dientes

**gnat** /næt/ n mosquito m

**gnaw** /nɔː/ vt/i roer

**gnome** /nəʊm/ n gnomo m

**go** /gəʊ/ vi (*pt* **went**, *pp* **gone**) ir; (*leave*) irse; (*work*) funcionar; (*become*) hacerse; (*be sold*) venderse; (*vanish*) desaparecer. **~ ahead!** ¡adelante! **~ bad** pasarse. **~ riding** montar a caballo. **~ shopping** ir de compras. **be ~ing to do** ir a hacer. ● n (*pl* **goes**) (*energy*) energía f. **be on the ~** trabajar sin cesar. **have a ~** intentar. **it's your ~** te toca a ti. **make a ~ of** tener éxito en. **~ across** cruzar. **~ away** irse. **~ back** volver. **~ back on** faltar a

(*promise etc*). **~ by** pasar. **~ down** bajar; (*sun*) ponerse. **~ for** buscar, traer; (*like*) gustar; (*attack, sl*) atacar. **~ in** entrar. **~ in for** presentarse para (*exam*). **~ off** (*leave*) irse; (*go bad*) pasarse; (*explode*) estallar. **~ on** seguir; (*happen*) pasar. **~ out** salir; (*light, fire*) apagarse. **~ over** (*check*) examinar. **~ round** (*be enough*) ser bastante. **~ through** (*suffer*) sufrir; (*check*) examinar. **~ under** hundirse. **~ up** subir. **~ without** pasarse sin

**goad** /gəʊd/ vt aguijonear

**go-ahead** /ˈgəʊəhed/ n luz f verde. ● a dinámico

**goal** /gəʊl/ n fin m, objeto m; (*sport*) gol m. **~ie** n (*fam*) portero m. **~keeper** n portero m. **~post** n poste m (de la portería)

**goat** /gəʊt/ n cabra f

**goatee** /gəʊˈtiː/ n perilla f, barbas fpl de chivo

**gobble** /ˈgɒbl/ vt engullir

**go-between** /ˈgəʊbɪtwiːn/ n intermediario m

**goblet** /ˈgɒblɪt/ n copa f

**goblin** /ˈgɒblɪn/ n duende m

**God** /gɒd/ n Dios m. **~forsaken** a olvidado de Dios

**god** /gɒd/ n dios m. **~child** n ahijado m. **~daughter** n ahijada f. **~dess** /ˈgɒdɪs/ n diosa f. **~father** n padrino m. **~ly** a devoto. **~mother** n madrina f. **~send** n beneficio m inesperado. **~son** n ahijado m

**go-getter** /gəʊˈgetə(r)/ n persona f ambiciosa

**goggle** /ˈgɒgl/ vi. **~ (at)** mirar con los ojos desmesuradamente abiertos

**goggles** /ˈgɒglz/ npl gafas fpl protectoras

**going** /ˈgəʊɪŋ/ n camino m; (*racing*) (estado m del) terreno m. **it is slow/hard ~** es lento/difícil. ● a (*price*) actual; (*concern*) en funcionamiento. **~s-on** npl actividades fpl anormales, tejemaneje m

**gold** /gəʊld/ n oro m. ● a de oro. **~en** /ˈgəʊldən/ a de oro; (*in colour*) dorado; (*opportunity*) único. **~en wedding** n bodas fpl de oro. **~fish** n invar pez m de colores, carpa f dorada. **~mine** n mina f de oro; (*fig*) fuente f de gran riqueza. **~plated** a chapado en oro. **~smith** n orfebre m

**golf** /gɒlf/ *n* golf *m*. **~course** *n* campo *m* de golf. **~er** *n* jugador *m* de golf

**golly** /'gɒli/ *int* ¡caramba!

**golosh** /gə'lɒʃ/ *n* chanclo *m*

**gondol|a** /'gɒndələ/ *n* góndola *f*. **~ier** /gɒndə'liə(r)/ *n* gondolero *m*

**gone** /gɒn/ *see* **go**. ● *a* pasado. **~ six o'clock** después de las seis

**gong** /gɒŋ/ *n* gong(o) *m*

**good** /gʊd/ *a* (**better, best**) bueno, (*before masculine singular noun*) buen. **~ afternoon!** ¡buenas tardes! **~ evening!** (*before dark*) ¡buenas tardes!; (*after dark*) ¡buenas noches! **G~ Friday** *n* Viernes *m* Santo. **~ morning!** ¡buenos días! **~ name** *n* (buena) reputación *f*. **~ night!** ¡buenas noches! **a ~ deal** bastante. **as ~ as** (*almost*) casi. **be ~ with** entender. **do ~** hacer bien. **feel ~** sentirse bien. **have a ~ time** divertirse. **it is ~ for you** le sentará bien. ● *n* bien *m*. **for ~** para siempre. **it is no ~ shouting/etc** es inútil gritar/etc.

**goodbye** /gʊd'baɪ/ *int* ¡adiós! ● *n* adiós *m*. **say ~ to** despedirse de

**good:** **~for-nothing** *a & n* inútil (*m*). **~looking** *a* guapo

**goodness** /'gʊdnɪs/ *n* bondad *f*. **~!**, **~ gracious!**, **~ me!**, **my ~!** ¡Dios mío!

**goods** /gʊdz/ *npl* (*merchandise*) mercancías *fpl*

**goodwill** /gʊd'wɪl/ *n* buena voluntad *f*

**goody** /'gʊdi/ *n* (*culin, fam*) golosina *f*; (*in film*) bueno *m*. **~goody** *n* mojigato *m*

**gooey** /'guːɪ/ *a* (**gooier, gooiest**) (*sl*) pegajoso; (*fig*) sentimental

**goof** /guːf/ *vi* (*Amer, blunder*) cometer una pifia. **~y** *a* (*sl*) necio

**goose** /guːs/ *n* (*pl* **geese**) oca *f*

**gooseberry** /'gʊzbərɪ/ *n* uva *f* espina, grosella *f*

**goose-flesh** /'guːsfleʃ/ *n*, **goosepimples** /'guːspɪmplz/ *n* carne *f* de gallina

**gore** /gɔː(r)/ *n* sangre *f*. ● *vt* cornear

**gorge** /gɔːdʒ/ *n* (*geog*) garganta *f*. ● *vt*. **~ o.s.** hartarse (**on** de)

**gorgeous** /'gɔːdʒəs/ *a* magnífico

**gorilla** /gə'rɪlə/ *n* gorila *m*

**gormless** /'gɔːmlɪs/ *a* (*sl*) idiota

**gorse** /gɔːs/ *n* aulaga *f*

**gory** /'gɔːrɪ/ *a* (**-ier, -iest**) (*covered in blood*) ensangrentado; (*horrific, fig*) horrible

**gosh** /gɒʃ/ *int* ¡caramba!

**go-slow** /gəʊ'sləʊ/ *n* huelga *f* de celo

**gospel** /'gɒspl/ *n* evangelio *m*

**gossip** /'gɒsɪp/ *n* (*idle chatter*) charla *f*; (*tittle-tattle*) comadreo *m*; (*person*) chismoso *m*. ● *vi* (*pt* **gossiped**) (*chatter*) charlar; (*repeat scandal*) comadrear. **~y** *a* chismoso

**got** /gɒt/ *see* **get**. **have ~** tener. **have ~ to do** tener que hacer

**Gothic** /'gɒθɪk/ *a* (*archit*) gótico; (*people*) godo

**gouge** /gaʊdʒ/ *vt*. **~ out** arrancar

**gourmet** /'gʊəmeɪ/ *n* gastrónomo *m*

**gout** /gaʊt/ *n* (*med*) gota *f*

**govern** /'gʌvn/ *vt/i* gobernar

**governess** /'gʌvənɪs/ *n* institutriz *f*

**government** /'gʌvənmənt/ *n* gobierno *m*. **~al** /gʌvən'mentl/ *a* gubernamental

**governor** /'gʌvənə(r)/ *n* gobernador *m*

**gown** /gaʊn/ *n* vestido *m*; (*of judge, teacher*) toga *f*

**GP** *abbr see* **general practitioner**

**grab** /græb/ *vt* (*pt* **grabbed**) agarrar

**grace** /greɪs/ *n* gracia *f*. **~ful** *a* elegante

**gracious** /'greɪʃəs/ *a* (*kind*) amable; (*elegant*) elegante

**gradation** /grə'deɪʃn/ *n* gradación *f*

**grade** /greɪd/ *n* clase *f*, categoría *f*; (*of goods*) clase *f*, calidad *f*; (*on scale*) grado *m*; (*school mark*) nota *f*; (*class, Amer*) curso *m*. **~ school** *n* (*Amer*) escuela *f* primaria. ● *vt* clasificar; (*schol*) calificar

**gradient** /'greɪdɪənt/ *n* (*slope*) pendiente *f*

**gradual** /'grædʒʊəl/ *a* gradual. **~ly** *adv* gradualmente

**graduat|e** /'grædjʊət/ *n* (*univ*) licenciado. ● *vi* /'grædjʊeɪt/ licenciarse. ● *vt* graduar. **~ion** /-'eɪʃn/ *n* entrega *f* de títulos

**graffiti** /grə'fiːtɪ/ *npl* pintada *f*

**graft**[1] /grɑːft/ *n* (*med, bot*) injerto *m*. ● *vt* injertar

**graft**[2] /grɑːft/ *n* (*bribery, fam*) corrupción *f*

**grain** /greɪn/ *n* grano *m*

**gram** /græm/ *n* gramo *m*

**gramma|r** /'græmə(r)/ *n* gramática *f*. **~tical** /grə'mætɪkl/ *a* gramatical

**gramophone** /'græməfəʊn/ *n* tocadiscos *m invar*

**grand** /grænd/ *a* (**-er, -est**) magnífico; (*excellent, fam*) estupendo. **~child** *n* nieto *m*. **~daughter** *n* nieta *f*

**grandeur** /'grændʒə(r)/ n grandiosidad f

**grandfather** /'grændfɑːðə(r)/ n abuelo m

**grandiose** /'grændɪəʊs/ a grandioso

**grand:** ~**mother** n abuela f. ~**parents** npl abuelos mpl. ~ **piano** n piano m de cola. ~**son** n nieto m

**grandstand** /'grænstænd/ n tribuna f

**granite** /'grænɪt/ n granito m

**granny** /'grænɪ/ n (fam) abuela f, nana f (fam)

**grant** /grɑːnt/ vt conceder; (give) donar; (admit) admitir (**that** que). **take for** ~**ed** dar por sentado. ● n concesión f; (univ) beca f

**granulated** /'grænjʊleɪtɪd/ a. ~ **sugar** n azúcar m granulado

**granule** /'grænuːl/ n gránulo m

**grape** /greɪp/ n uva f

**grapefruit** /'greɪpfruːt/ n invar toronja f, pomelo m

**graph** /grɑːf/ n gráfica f

**graphic** /'græfɪk/ a gráfico

**grapple** /'græpl/ vi. ~ **with** intentar vencer

**grasp** /grɑːsp/ vt agarrar. ● n (hold) agarro m; (strength of hand) apretón m; (reach) alcance m; (fig) comprensión f

**grasping** /'grɑːspɪŋ/ a avaro

**grass** /grɑːs/ n hierba f. ~**hopper** n saltamontes m invar. ~**land** n pradera f. ~ **roots** npl base f popular. ● a popular. ~**y** a cubierto de hierba

**grate** /greɪt/ n (fireplace) parrilla f. ● vt rallar. ~ **one's teeth** hacer rechinar los dientes. ● vi rechinar

**grateful** /'greɪtfl/ a agradecido. ~**ly** adv con gratitud

**grater** /'greɪtə(r)/ n rallador m

**gratif|ied** /'grætɪfaɪd/ a contento. ~**y** vt satisfacer; (please) agradar a. ~**ying** a agradable

**grating** /'greɪtɪŋ/ n reja f

**gratis** /'grɑːtɪs/ a & adv gratis (a invar)

**gratitude** /'grætɪtjuːd/ n gratitud f

**gratuitous** /grə'tjuːɪtəs/ a gratuito

**gratuity** /grə'tjuːətɪ/ n (tip) propina f; (gift of money) gratificación f

**grave**[1] /greɪv/ n sepultura f

**grave**[2] /greɪv/ a (-er, -est) (serious) serio. /grɑːv/ a. ~ **accent** n acento m grave

**grave-digger** /'greɪvdɪgə(r)/ n sepulturero m

**gravel** /'grævl/ n grava f

**gravely** /'greɪvlɪ/ a (seriously) seriamente

**grave:** ~**stone** n lápida f. ~**yard** n cementerio m

**gravitat|e** /'grævɪteɪt/ vi gravitar. ~**ion** / -'teɪʃn/ n gravitación f

**gravity** /'grævətɪ/ n gravedad f

**gravy** /'greɪvɪ/ n salsa f

**graze**[1] /greɪz/ vt/i (eat) pacer

**graze**[2] /greɪz/ vt (touch) rozar; (scrape) raspar. ● n rozadura f

**greas|e** /griːs/ n grasa f. ● vt engrasar. ~**e-paint** n maquillaje m. ~**e-proof paper** n papel m a prueba de grasa, apergaminado m. ~**y** a grasiento

**great** /greɪt/ a (-er, -est) grande, (before singular noun) gran; (very good, fam) estupendo. **G**~ **Britain** n Gran Bretaña f. ~**grandfather** n bisabuelo m. ~**grandmother** n bisabuela f. ~**ly** /'greɪtlɪ/ adv (very) muy; (much) mucho. ~**ness** n grandeza f

**Greece** /griːs/ n Grecia f

**greed** /griːd/ n avaricia f; (for food) glotonería f. ~**y** a avaro; (for food) glotón

**Greek** /griːk/ a & n griego (m)

**green** /griːn/ a (-er, -est) verde; (fig) crédulo. ● n verde m; (grass) césped m. ~ **belt** n zona f verde. ~**ery** n verdor m. ~ **fingers** npl habilidad f con las plantas

**greengage** /'griːngeɪdʒ/ n (plum) claudia f

**greengrocer** /'griːngrəʊsə(r)/ n verdulero m

**greenhouse** /'griːnhaʊs/ n invernadero m

**green:** ~ **light** n luz f verde. ~**s** npl verduras fpl

**Greenwich Mean Time** /grenɪtʃ'miːntaɪm/ n hora f media de Greenwich

**greet** /griːt/ vt saludar; (receive) recibir. ~**ing** n saludo m. ~**ings** npl (in letter) recuerdos mpl

**gregarious** /grɪ'geərɪəs/ a gregario

**grenade** /grɪ'neɪd/ n granada f

**grew** /gruː/ see **grow**

**grey** /greɪ/ a & n (-er, -est) gris (m). ● vi ⟨hair⟩ encanecer

**greyhound** /'greɪhaʊnd/ n galgo m

**grid** /grɪd/ n reja f; (network, elec) red f; (culin) parrilla f; (on map) cuadrícula f

**grief** /griːf/ n dolor m. **come to ~** ⟨person⟩ sufrir un accidente; ⟨fail⟩ fracasar

**grievance** /'griːvns/ n queja f

**grieve** /griːv/ vt afligir. ●vi afligirse. **~ for** llorar

**grievous** /'griːvəs/ a doloroso; ⟨serious⟩ grave

**grill** /grɪl/ n ⟨cooking device⟩ parrilla f; ⟨food⟩ parrillada f, asado m, asada f. ●vt asar a la parrilla; ⟨interrogate⟩ interrogar

**grille** /grɪl/ n rejilla f

**grim** /grɪm/ a (**grimmer, grimmest**) severo

**grimace** /'grɪməs/ n mueca f. ●vi hacer muecas

**grim|e** /graɪm/ n mugre f. **~y** a mugriento

**grin** /grɪn/ vt (pt **grinned**) sonreír. ●n sonrisa f (abierta)

**grind** /graɪnd/ vt (pt **ground**) moler ⟨coffee, corn etc⟩; ⟨pulverize⟩ pulverizar; ⟨sharpen⟩ afilar. **~ one's teeth** hacer rechinar los dientes. ●n faena f

**grip** /grɪp/ vt (pt **gripped**) agarrar; ⟨interest⟩ captar la atención de. ●n ⟨hold⟩ agarro m; ⟨strength of hand⟩ apretón m. **come to ~s** encararse ⟨with a/con⟩

**gripe** /graɪp/ n. **~s** npl (med) cólico m

**grisly** /'grɪzlɪ/ a (**-ier, -iest**) horrible

**gristle** /'grɪsl/ n cartílago m

**grit** /grɪt/ n arena f; (fig) valor m, aguante m. ●vt (pt **gritted**) echar arena en ⟨road⟩. **~ one's teeth** (fig) acorazarse

**grizzle** /'grɪzl/ vi lloriquear

**groan** /grəʊn/ vi gemir. ●n gemido m

**grocer** /'grəʊsə(r)/ n tendero m. **~ies** npl comestibles mpl. **~y** n tienda f de comestibles

**grog** /grɒg/ n grog m

**groggy** /'grɒgɪ/ a (**weak**) débil; ⟨unsteady⟩ inseguro; ⟨ill⟩ malucho

**groin** /grɔɪn/ n ingle f

**groom** /gruːm/ n mozo m de caballos; ⟨bridegroom⟩ novio m. ●vt almohazar ⟨horses⟩; (fig) preparar. **well-~ed** a bien arreglado

**groove** /gruːv/ n ranura f; ⟨in record⟩ surco m

**grope** /grəʊp/ vi ⟨find one's way⟩ moverse a tientas. **~ for** buscar a tientas

**gross** /grəʊs/ a (**-er, -est**) ⟨coarse⟩ grosero; ⟨com⟩ bruto; ⟨fat⟩ grueso; ⟨flagrant⟩ grave. ●n invar gruesa f. **~ly** adv groseramente; ⟨very⟩ enormemente

**grotesque** /grəʊ'tesk/ a grotesco

**grotto** /'grɒtəʊ/ n (pl **-oes**) gruta f

**grotty** /'grɒtɪ/ a (sl) desagradable; ⟨dirty⟩ sucio

**grouch** /graʊtʃ/ vi ⟨grumble, fam⟩ rezongar

**ground**¹ /graʊnd/ n suelo m; ⟨area⟩ terreno m; ⟨reason⟩ razón f; ⟨elec, Amer⟩ toma f de tierra. ●vt varar ⟨ship⟩; prohibir despegar ⟨aircraft⟩. **~s** npl jardines mpl; ⟨sediment⟩ poso m

**ground**² /graʊnd/ see **grind**

**ground: ~ floor** n planta f baja. **~ rent** n alquiler m del terreno

**grounding** /'graʊndɪŋ/ n base f, conocimientos mpl ⟨in de⟩

**groundless** /'graʊndlɪs/ a infundado

**ground: ~sheet** n tela f impermeable. **~swell** n mar m de fondo. **~work** n trabajo m preparatorio

**group** /gruːp/ n grupo m. ●vt agrupar. ●vi agruparse

**grouse**¹ /graʊs/ n invar ⟨bird⟩ urogallo m. **red ~** lagópodo m escocés

**grouse**² /graʊs/ vi ⟨grumble, fam⟩ rezongar

**grove** /grəʊv/ n arboleda f. **lemon ~** n limonar m. **olive ~** n olivar m. **orange ~** n naranjal m. **pine ~** n pinar m

**grovel** /'grɒvl/ vi (pt **grovelled**) arrastrarse, humillarse. **~ling** a servil

**grow** /grəʊ/ vi (pt **grew**, pp **grown**) crecer; ⟨cultivated plant⟩ cultivarse; ⟨become⟩ volverse, ponerse. ●vt cultivar. **~ up** hacerse mayor. **~er** n cultivador m

**growl** /graʊl/ vi gruñir. ●n gruñido m

**grown** /grəʊn/ see **grow**. ●a adulto. **~-up** a & n adulto (m)

**growth** /grəʊθ/ n crecimiento m; ⟨increase⟩ aumento m; ⟨development⟩ desarrollo m; ⟨med⟩ tumor m

**grub** /grʌb/ n ⟨larva⟩ larva f; ⟨food, sl⟩ comida f

**grubby** /'grʌbɪ/ a (**-ier, -iest**) mugriento

**grudg|e** /grʌdʒ/ vt dar de mala gana; ⟨envy⟩ envidiar. **~e doing** molestarle hacer. **he ~ed paying** le molestó pagar. ● *n* rencor *m*. **bear/ have a ~e against s.o.** guardar rencor a alguien. **~ingly** *adv* de mala gana

**gruelling** /'gru:əlɪŋ/ *a* agotador
**gruesome** /'gru:səm/ *a* horrible
**gruff** /grʌf/ *a* (**-er, -est**) ⟨*manners*⟩ brusco; ⟨*voice*⟩ ronco
**grumble** /'grʌmbl/ *vi* rezongar
**grumpy** /'grʌmpɪ/ *a* (**-ier, -iest**) malhumorado
**grunt** /grʌnt/ *vi* gruñir. ● *n* gruñido *m*
**guarant|ee** /gærən'ti:/ *n* garantía *f*. ● *vt* garantizar. **~or** *n* garante *m* & *f*
**guard** /ga:d/ *vt* proteger; (*watch*) vigilar. ● *vi*. **~ against** guardar de. ● *n* (*vigilance, mil group*) guardia *f*; (*person*) guardia *m*; (*on train*) jefe *m* de tren
**guarded** /'ga:dɪd/ *a* cauteloso
**guardian** /'ga:dɪən/ *n* guardián *m*; (*of orphan*) tutor *m*
**guer(r)illa** /gə'rɪlə/ *n* guerrillero *m*. **~ warfare** *n* guerra *f* de guerrillas
**guess** /ges/ *vt/i* adivinar; (*suppose, Amer*) creer. ● *n* conjetura *f*. **~work** *n* conjetura(s) *f(pl)*
**guest** /gest/ *n* invitado *m*; (*in hotel*) huésped *m*. **~house** *n* casa *f* de huéspedes
**guffaw** /gʌ'fɔ:/ *n* carcajada *f*. ● *vi* reírse a carcajadas
**guidance** /'gaɪdəns/ *n* (*advice*) consejos *mpl*; (*information*) información *f*
**guide** /gaɪd/ *n* (*person*) guía *m* & *f*; (*book*) guía *f*. **Girl G~** exploradora *f*, guía *f* (*fam*). ● *vt* guiar. **~book** *n* guía *f*. **~d missile** *n* proyectil *m* teledirigido. **~lines** *npl* pauta *f*
**guild** /gɪld/ *n* gremio *m*
**guile** /gaɪl/ *n* astucia *f*
**guillotine** /'gɪləti:n/ *n* guillotina *f*
**guilt** /gɪlt/ *n* culpabilidad *f*. **~y** *a* culpable
**guinea-pig** /'gɪnɪpɪg/ *n* (*including fig*) cobaya *f*
**guise** /gaɪz/ *n* (*external appearance*) apariencia *f*; (*style*) manera *f*
**guitar** /gɪ'ta:(r)/ *n* guitarra *f*. **~ist** *n* guitarrista *m* & *f*
**gulf** /gʌlf/ *n* (*part of sea*) golfo *m*; (*hollow*) abismo *m*
**gull** /gʌl/ *n* gaviota *f*
**gullet** /'gʌlɪt/ *n* esófago *m*
**gullible** /'gʌləbl/ *a* crédulo
**gully** /'gʌlɪ/ *n* (*ravine*) barranco *m*

**gulp** /gʌlp/ *vt*. **~ down** tragarse de prisa. ● *vi* tragar; (*from fear etc*) sentir dificultad para tragar. ● *n* trago *m*
**gum¹** /gʌm/ *n* goma *f*; (*for chewing*) chicle *m*. ● *vt* (*pt* **gummed**) engomar
**gum²** /gʌm/ *n* (*anat*) encía *f*. **~boil** /'gʌmbɔɪl/ *n* flemón *m*
**gumboot** /'gʌmbu:t/ *n* bota *f* de agua
**gumption** /'gʌmpʃn/ *n* (*fam*) iniciativa *f*; (*common sense*) sentido *m* común
**gun** /gʌn/ *n* (*pistol*) pistola *f*; (*rifle*) fusil *m*; (*large*) cañón *m*. ● *vt* (*pt* **gunned**). **~ down** abatir a tiros. **~fire** *n* tiros *mpl*
**gun:** **~man** /'gʌnmən/ *n* pistolero *m*. **~ner** /'gʌnə(r)/ *n* artillero *m*. **~powder** *n* pólvora *f*. **~shot** *n* disparo *m*
**gurgle** /'gɜ:gl/ *n* (*of liquid*) gorgoteo *m*; (*of baby*) gorjeo *m*. ● *vi* ⟨*liquid*⟩ gorgotear; ⟨*baby*⟩ gorjear
**guru** /'guru:/ *n* (*pl* **-us**) mentor *m*
**gush** /gʌʃ/ *vi*. **~ (out)** salir a borbotones. ● *n* (*of liquid*) chorro *m*; (*fig*) torrente *m*. **~ing** *a* efusivo
**gusset** /'gʌsɪt/ *n* escudete *m*
**gust** /gʌst/ *n* ráfaga *f*; (*of smoke*) bocanada *f*
**gusto** /'gʌstəʊ/ *n* entusiasmo *m*
**gusty** /'gʌstɪ/ *a* borrascoso
**gut** /gʌt/ *n* tripa *f*, intestino *m*. ● *vt* (*pt* **gutted**) destripar; ⟨*fire*⟩ destruir. **~s** *npl* tripas *fpl*; (*courage, fam*) valor *m*
**gutter** /'gʌtə(r)/ *n* (*on roof*) canalón *m*; (*in street*) cuneta *f*; (*slum, fig*) arroyo *m*. **~snipe** *n* golfillo *m*
**guttural** /'gʌtərəl/ *a* gutural
**guy** /gaɪ/ *n* (*man, fam*) hombre *m*, tío *m* (*fam*)
**guzzle** /'gʌzl/ *vt/i* soplarse, tragarse
**gym** /dʒɪm/ *n* (*gymnasium, fam*) gimnasio *m*; (*gymnastics, fam*) gimnasia *f*
**gymkhana** /dʒɪmka:nə/ *n* gincana *f*, gymkhana *f*
**gymnasium** /dʒɪm'neɪzɪəm/ *n* gimnasio *m*
**gymnast** /'dʒɪmnæst/ *n* gimnasta *m* & *f*. **~ics** *npl* gimnasia *f*
**gym-slip** /'dʒɪmslɪp/ *n* túnica *f* (de gimnasia)
**gynaecolog|ist** /gaɪnɪ'kɒlədʒɪst/ *n* ginecólogo *m*. **~y** *n* ginecología *f*
**gypsy** /'dʒɪpsɪ/ *n* gitano *m*

**gyrate** /dʒaɪə'reɪt/ *vi* girar
**gyroscope** /'dʒaɪərəskəʊp/ *n* giroscopio *m*

# H

**haberdashery** /hæbə'dæʃərɪ/ *n* mercería *f*
**habit** /'hæbɪt/ *n* costumbre *f*; (*costume, relig*) hábito *m*. **be in the ~ of** (+ *gerund*) tener la costumbre de (+ *infinitive*), soler (+ *infinitive*). **get into the ~ of** (+ *gerund*) acostumbrarse a (+ *infinitive*)
**habitable** /'hæbɪtəbl/ *a* habitable
**habitat** /'hæbɪtæt/ *n* hábitat *m*
**habitation** /hæbɪ'teɪʃn/ *n* habitación *f*
**habitual** /hə'bɪtjʊəl/ *a* habitual; ‹*smoker, liar*› inveterado. **~ly** *adv* de costumbre
**hack** /hæk/ *n* (*old horse*) jamelgo *m*; (*writer*) escritorzuelo *m*. ● *vt* cortar. **~ to pieces** cortar en pedazos
**hackney** /'hæknɪ/ *a*. **~ carriage** *n* coche *m* de alquiler, taxi *m*
**hackneyed** /'hæknɪd/ *a* manido
**had** /hæd/ *see* **have**
**haddock** /'hædək/ *n invar* eglefino *m*. **smoked ~** *n* eglefino *m* ahumado
**haemorrhage** /'hemərɪdʒ/ *n* hemorragia *f*
**haemorrhoids** /'hemərɔɪdz/ *npl* hemorroides *fpl*, almorranas *fpl*
**hag** /hæg/ *n* bruja *f*
**haggard** /'hægəd/ *a* ojeroso
**haggle** /'hægl/ *vi* regatear
**Hague** /heɪg/ *n*. **The ~** La Haya *f*
**hail**[1] /heɪl/ *n* granizo *m*. ● *vi* granizar
**hail**[2] /heɪl/ *vt* (*greet*) saludar; llamar ‹*taxi*›. ● *vi*. **~ from** venir de
**hailstone** /'heɪlstəʊn/ *n* grano *m* de granizo
**hair** /heə(r)/ *n* pelo *m*. **~brush** *n* cepillo *m* para el pelo. **~cut** *n* corte *m* de pelo. **have a ~cut** cortarse el pelo. **~do** *n* (*fam*) peinado *m*. **~dresser** *n* peluquero *m*. **~dresser's (shop)** *n* peluquería *f*. **~dryer** *n* secador *m*. **~pin** *n* horquilla *f*. **~pin bend** *n* curva *f* cerrada. **~raising** *a* espeluznante. **~style** *n* peinado *m*

**hairy** /'heərɪ/ *a* (**-ier, -iest**) peludo; (*terrifying, sl*) espeluznante
**hake** /heɪk/ *n invar* merluza *f*
**halcyon** /'hælsɪən/ *a* sereno. **~ days** *npl* época *f* feliz
**hale** /heɪl/ *a* robusto
**half** /hɑːf/ *n* (*pl* **halves**) mitad *f*. ● *a* medio. **~ a dozen** media docena *f*. **~ an hour** media hora *f*. ● *adv* medio, a medias. **~back** *n* (*sport*) medio *m*. **~caste** *a & n* mestizo (*m*). **~hearted** *a* poco entusiasta. **~term** *n* vacaciones *fpl* de medio trimestre. **~time** *n* (*sport*) descanso *m*. **~way** *a* medio. ● *adv* a medio camino. **~wit** *n* imbécil *m & f*. **at ~mast** a media asta
**halibut** /'hælɪbət/ *n invar* hipogloso *m*, halibut *m*
**hall** /hɔːl/ *n* (*room*) sala *f*; (*mansion*) casa *f* solariega; (*entrance*) vestíbulo *m*. **~ of residence** *n* colegio *m* mayor
**hallelujah** /hælɪ'luːjə/ *int & n* aleluya (*f*)
**hallmark** /'hɔːlmɑːk/ *n* (*on gold etc*) contraste *m*; (*fig*) sello *m* (*distintivo*)
**hallo** /hə'ləʊ/ *int* = **hello**
**hallow** /'hæləʊ/ *vt* santificar. **H~e'en** *n* víspera *f* de Todos los Santos
**hallucination** /həluːsɪ'neɪʃn/ *n* alucinación *f*
**halo** /'heɪləʊ/ *n* (*pl* **-oes**) aureola *f*
**halt** /hɔːlt/ *n* alto *m*. ● *vt* parar. ● *vi* pararse
**halve** /hɑːv/ *vt* dividir por mitad
**ham** /hæm/ *n* jamón *m*; (*theatre, sl*) racionista *m & f*
**hamburger** /'hæmbɜːgə(r)/ *n* hamburguesa *f*
**hamlet** /'hæmlɪt/ *n* aldea *f*, caserío *m*
**hammer** /'hæmə(r)/ *n* martillo *m*. ● *vt* martill(e)ar; (*defeat, fam*) machacar
**hammock** /'hæmək/ *n* hamaca *f*
**hamper**[1] /'hæmpə(r)/ *n* cesta *f*
**hamper**[2] /'hæmpə(r)/ *vt* estorbar, poner trabas
**hamster** /'hæmstə(r)/ *n* hámster *m*
**hand** /hænd/ *n* (*including cards*) mano *f*; (*of clock*) manecilla *f*; (*writing*) escritura *f*, letra *f*; (*worker*) obrero *m*. **at ~** a mano. **by ~** a mano. **lend a ~** echar una mano. **on ~** a mano. **on one's ~s** (*fig*) en (las) manos de uno. **on the one ~... on the other ~** por un lado... por otro.

**out of** ~ fuera de control. **to** ~ a mano. • *vt* dar. ~ **down** pasar. ~ **in** entregar. ~ **over** entregar. ~ **out** distribuir. ~**bag** *n* bolso *m*, cartera *f* (*LAm*). ~**book** *n* (*manual*) manual *m*; (*guidebook*) guía *f*. ~**cuffs** *npl* esposas *fpl*. ~**ful** /ˈhændfʊl/ *n* puñado *m*; (*person, fam*) persona *f* difícil. ~**luggage** *n* equipaje *m* de mano. ~**out** *n* folleto *m*; (*money*) limosna *f*

**handicap** /ˈhændɪkæp/ *n* desventaja *f*; (*sport*) handicap *m*. • *vt* (*pt* **handicapped**) imponer impedimentos a

**handicraft** /ˈhændɪkrɑːft/ *n* artesanía *f*

**handiwork** /ˈhændɪwɜːk/ *n* obra *f*, trabajo *m* manual

**handkerchief** /ˈhæŋkətʃɪf/ *n* (*pl* **-fs**) pañuelo *m*

**handle** /ˈhændl/ *n* (*of door etc*) tirador *m*; (*of implement*) mango *m*; (*of cup, bag, basket etc*) asa *f*. • *vt* manejar; (*touch*) tocar; (*control*) controlar

**handlebar** /ˈhændlbɑː(r)/ *n* (*on bicycle*) manillar *m*

**handshake** /ˈhændʃeɪk/ *n* apretón *m* de manos

**handsome** /ˈhænsəm/ *a* (*good-looking*) guapo; (*generous*) generoso; (*large*) considerable

**handwriting** /ˈhændraɪtɪŋ/ *n* escritura *f*, letra *f*

**handy** /ˈhændɪ/ *a* (**-ier, -iest**) (*useful*) cómodo; (*person*) diestro; (*near*) a mano. ~**man** *n* hombre *m* habilidoso

**hang** /hæŋ/ *vt* (*pt* **hung**) colgar; (*pt* **hanged**) (*capital punishment*) ahorcar. • *vi* colgar; (*hair*) caer. ~ **in. get the** ~ **of sth** coger el truco de algo. ~ **about** holgazanear. ~ **on** (*hold out*) resistir; (*wait, sl*) esperar. ~ **out** *vi* tender; (*live, sl*) vivir. ~ **up** (*telephone*) colgar

**hangar** /ˈhæŋə(r)/ *n* hangar *m*

**hanger** /ˈhæŋə(r)/ *n* (*for clothes*) percha *f*. ~**on** *n* parásito *m*, pegote *m*

**hang-gliding** /ˈhæŋglaɪdɪŋ/ *n* vuelo *m* libre

**hangman** /ˈhæŋmən/ *n* verdugo *m*

**hangover** /ˈhæŋəʊvə(r)/ *n* (*after drinking*) resaca *f*

**hang-up** /ˈhæŋʌp/ *n* (*sl*) complejo *m*

**hanker** /ˈhæŋkə(r)/ *vi*. ~ **after** anhelar. ~**ing** *n* anhelo *m*

**hanky-panky** /ˈhæŋkɪpæŋkɪ/ *n* (*trickery, sl*) trucos *mpl*

**haphazard** /hæpˈhæzəd/ *a* fortuito. ~**ly** *adv* al azar

**hapless** /ˈhæplɪs/ *a* desafortunado

**happen** /ˈhæpən/ *vi* pasar, suceder, ocurrir. **if he** ~**s to come** si acaso viene. ~**ing** *n* acontecimiento *m*

**happ|ily** /ˈhæpɪlɪ/ *adv* felizmente; (*fortunately*) afortunadamente. ~**iness** *n* felicidad *f*. ~**y** *a* (**-ier, -iest**) feliz. ~**y-go-lucky** *a* despreocupado. ~**y medium** *n* término *m* medio

**harangue** /həˈræŋ/ *n* arenga *f*. • *vt* arengar

**harass** /ˈhærəs/ *vt* acosar. ~**ment** *n* tormento *m*

**harbour** /ˈhɑːbə(r)/ *n* puerto *m*. • *vt* encubrir (*criminal*); abrigar (*feelings*)

**hard** /hɑːd/ *a* (**-er, -est**) duro; (*difficult*) difícil. ~ **of hearing** duro de oído. • *adv* mucho; (*pull*) fuerte. ~ **by** (muy) cerca. ~ **done by** tratado injustamente. ~ **up** (*fam*) sin un cuarto. ~**board** *n* chapa *f* de madera, tabla *f*. ~**boiled egg** *n* huevo *m* duro. ~**en** /ˈhɑːdn/ *vt* endurecer. • *vi* endurecerse. ~**headed** *a* realista

**hardly** /ˈhɑːdlɪ/ *adv* apenas. ~ **ever** casi nunca

**hardness** /ˈhɑːdnɪs/ *n* dureza *f*

**hardship** /ˈhɑːdʃɪp/ *n* apuro *m*

**hard:** ~ **shoulder** *n* arcén *m*. ~**ware** *n* ferretería *f*; (*computer*) hardware *m*. ~**working** *a* trabajador

**hardy** /ˈhɑːdɪ/ *a* (**-ier, -iest**) (*bold*) audaz; (*robust*) robusto; (*bot*) resistente

**hare** /heə(r)/ *n* liebre *f*. ~**brained** *a* aturdido

**harem** /ˈhɑːriːm/ *n* harén *m*

**haricot** /ˈhærɪkəʊ/ *n*. ~ **bean** alubia *f*, judía *f*

**hark** /hɑːk/ *vi* escuchar. ~ **back to** volver a

**harlot** /ˈhɑːlət/ *n* prostituta *f*

**harm** /hɑːm/ *n* daño *m*. **there is no** ~ **in** (+ *gerund*) no hay ningún mal en (+ *infinitive*). • *vt* hacer daño a (*person*); dañar (*thing*); perjudicar (*interests*). ~**ful** *a* perjudicial. ~**less** *a* inofensivo

**harmonica** /hɑːˈmɒnɪkə/ *n* armónica *f*

**harmon|ious** /hɑːˈməʊnɪəs/ *a* armonioso. ~**ize** *vt/i* armonizar. ~**y** *n* armonía *f*

**harness** /'hɑːnɪs/ n (for horses) guarniciones fpl; (for children) andadores mpl. ● vt poner guarniciones a ⟨horse⟩; (fig) aprovechar

**harp** /hɑːp/ n arpa f. ● vi. ~ **on** (about) machacar. ~**ist** /'hɑːpɪst/ n arpista m & f

**harpoon** /hɑːˈpuːn/ n arpón m

**harpsichord** /'hɑːpsɪkɔːd/ n clavicémbalo m, clave m

**harrowing** / 'hærəʊɪŋ/ a desgarrador

**harsh** /hɑːʃ/ a (-er, -est) duro, severo; ⟨taste, sound⟩ áspero. ~**ly** adv severamente. ~**ness** n severidad f

**harvest** /'hɑːvɪst/ n cosecha f. ● vt cosechar. ~**er** n (person) segador; (machine) cosechadora f

**has** /hæz/ see **have**

**hash** /hæʃ/ n picadillo m. **make a ~ of sth** hacer algo con los pies, estropear algo

**hashish** /'hæʃiːʃ/ n hachís m

**hassle** /'hæsl/ n (quarrel) pelea f; (difficulty) problema m, dificultad f; (bother, fam) pena f, follón m, lío m. ● vt (harass) acosar, dar la lata

**haste** /heɪst/ n prisa f. **in ~** de prisa. **make ~** darse prisa

**hasten** /'heɪsn/ vt apresurar. ● vi apresurarse, darse prisa

**hast|ily** /'heɪstɪlɪ/ adv de prisa. ~**y** a (-ier, -iest) precipitado; (rash) irreflexivo

**hat** /hæt/ n sombrero m. **a ~ trick** n tres victorias fpl consecutivas

**hatch**[1] /hætʃ/ n (for food) ventanilla f; (naut) escotilla f

**hatch**[2] /hætʃ/ vt empollar ⟨eggs⟩; tramar ⟨plot⟩. ● vi salir del cascarón

**hatchback** /'hætʃbæk/ n (coche m) cincopuertas m invar, coche m con puerta trasera

**hatchet** /'hætʃɪt/ n hacha f

**hate** /heɪt/ n odio m. ● vt odiar. ~**ful** a odioso

**hatred** /'heɪtrɪd/ n odio m

**haughty** /'hɔːtɪ/ a (-ier, -iest) altivo

**haul** /hɔːl/ vt arrastrar; transportar ⟨goods⟩. ● n (catch) redada f; (stolen goods) botín m; (journey) recorrido m. ~**age** n transporte m. ~**ier** n transportista m & f

**haunch** /hɔːntʃ/ n anca f

**haunt** /hɔːnt/ vt frecuentar. ● n sitio m preferido. ~**ed house** n casa f frecuentada por fantasmas

**Havana** /həˈvænə/ n La Habana f

**have** /hæv/ vt (3 sing pres tense **has**, pt **had**) tener; (eat, drink) tomar. ~ **it out with** resolver el asunto. ~ **sth done** hacer hacer algo. ~ **to do** tener que hacer. ● v aux haber. ~ **just done** acabar de hacer. ● n. **the ~s and ~nots** los ricos mpl y los pobres mpl

**haven** /'heɪvn/ n puerto m; (refuge) refugio m

**haversack** /'hævəsæk/ n mochila f

**havoc** /'hævək/ n estragos mpl

**haw** /hɔː/ see **hum**

**hawk**[1] /hɔːk/ n halcón m

**hawk**[2] /hɔːk/ vt vender por las calles. ~**er** n vendedor m ambulante

**hawthorn** /'hɔːθɔːn/ n espino m (blanco)

**hay** /heɪ/ n heno m. ~ **fever** n fiebre f del heno. ~**stack** n almiar m

**haywire** /'heɪwaɪə(r)/ a. **go ~** ⟨plans⟩ desorganizarse; ⟨machine⟩ estropearse

**hazard** /'hæzəd/ n riesgo m. ● vt arriesgar; aventurar ⟨guess⟩. ~**ous** a arriesgado

**haze** /heɪz/ n neblina f

**hazel** /'heɪzl/ n avellano m. ~**nut** n avellana f

**hazy** /'heɪzɪ/ a (-ier, -iest) nebuloso

**he** /hiː/ pron él. ● n (animal) macho m; (man) varón m

**head** /hed/ n cabeza f; (leader) jefe m; (of beer) espuma f. ~**s or tails** cara o cruz. ● a principal. ~ **waiter** n jefe m de comedor. ● vt encabezar. ~ **the ball** dar un cabezazo. ~ **for** dirigirse a. ~**ache** n dolor m de cabeza. ~**dress** n tocado m. ~**er** n (football) cabezazo m. ~ **first** adv de cabeza. ~**gear** n tocado m

**heading** /'hedɪŋ/ n título m, encabezamiento m

**headlamp** /'hedlæmp/ n faro m

**headland** /'hedlənd/ n promontorio m

**headlight** /'hedlaɪt/ n faro m

**headline** /'hedlaɪn/ n titular m

**headlong** /'hedlɒŋ/ adv de cabeza; (precipitately) precipitadamente

**head: ~master** n director m. ~**mistress** n directora f. ~**on** a & adv de frente. ~**phone** n auricular m, audífono m (LAm)

**headquarters** /hed'kwɔːtəz/ n (of organization) sede f; (of business) oficina f central; (mil) cuartel m general

**headstrong** /'hedstrɒŋ/ a testarudo

**headway** /'hedweɪ/ n progreso m. **make ~** hacer progresos

**heady** /'hedɪ/ a (**-ier, -iest**) (*impetuous*) impetuoso; (*intoxicating*) embriagador

**heal** /hiːl/ vt curar. ● vi ‹wound› cicatrizarse; (*fig*) curarse

**health** /helθ/ n salud f. **~y** a sano

**heap** /hiːp/ n montón m. ● vt amontonar. **~s of** (*fam*) montones de, muchísimos

**hear** /hɪə(r)/ vt/i (pt **heard** /hɜːd/) oír. **~, ~!** ¡bravo! **not ~ of** (*refuse to allow*) no querer oír. **~ about** oir hablar de. **~ from** recibir noticias de. **~ of** oir hablar de

**hearing** /'hɪərɪŋ/ n oído m; (*of witness*) audición f. **~-aid** n audífono m

**hearsay** /'hɪəseɪ/ n rumores mpl. **from ~** según los rumores

**hearse** /hɜːs/ n coche m fúnebre

**heart** /hɑːt/ n corazón m. **at ~** en el fondo. **by ~** de memoria. **lose ~** descorozonarse. **~ache** n pena f. **~ attack** n ataque m al corazón. **~break** n pena f. **~breaking** a desgarrador. **~broken** a. **be ~broken** partírsele el corazón

**heartburn** /'hɑːtbɜːn/ n acedía f

**hearten** /'hɑːtn/ vt animar

**heartfelt** /'hɑːtfelt/ a sincero

**hearth** /hɑːθ/ n hogar m

**heartily** /'hɑːtɪlɪ/ adv de buena gana; (*sincerely*) sinceramente

**heart: ~less** a cruel. **~searching** n examen m de conciencia. **~to-~** a abierto

**hearty** /'hɑːtɪ/ a (*sincere*) sincero; ‹meal› abundante

**heat** /hiːt/ n calor m; (*contest*) eliminatoria f. ● vt calentar. ● vi calentarse. **~ed** a (*fig*) acalorado. **~er** /'hiːtə(r)/ n calentador m

**heath** /hiːθ/ n brezal m, descampado m, terreno m baldío

**heathen** /'hiːðn/ n & a pagano (m)

**heather** /'heðə(r)/ n brezo m

**heat: ~ing** n calefacción f. **~stroke** n insolación f. **~wave** n ola f de calor

**heave** /hiːv/ vt (*lift*) levantar; exhalar ‹sigh›; (*throw, fam*) lanzar. ● vi (*retch*) sentir náuseas

**heaven** /'hevn/ n cielo m. **~ly** a celestial; (*astronomy*) celeste; (*excellent, fam*) divino

**heavily** /'hevɪlɪ/ adv pesadamente; (*smoke, drink*) mucho. **~y** a (**-ier, -iest**) pesado; ‹sea› grueso; ‹traffic› denso; ‹work› duro. **~yweight** n peso m pesado

**Hebrew** /'hiːbruː/ a & n hebreo (m)

**heckle** /'hekl/ vt interrumpir ‹speaker›

**hectic** /'hektɪk/ a febril

**hedge** /hedʒ/ n seto m vivo. ● vt rodear con seto vivo. ● vi escaparse por la tangente

**hedgehog** /'hedʒhɒg/ n erizo m

**heed** /hiːd/ vt hacer caso de. ● n atención f. **pay ~ to** hacer caso de. **~less** a desatento

**heel** /hiːl/ n talón m; (*of shoe*) tacón m. **down at ~, down at the ~s** (*Amer*) desharrapado

**hefty** /'heftɪ/ a (**-ier, -iest**) (*sturdy*) fuerte; (*heavy*) pesado

**heifer** /'hefə(r)/ n novilla f

**height** /haɪt/ n altura f; (*of person*) estatura f; (*of fame, glory*) cumbre f; (*of joy, folly, pain*) colmo m

**heighten** /'haɪtn/ vt (*raise*) elevar; (*fig*) aumentar

**heinous** /'heɪnəs/ a atroz

**heir** /eə(r)/ n heredero m. **~ess** n heredera f. **~loom** /'eəluːm/ n reliquia f heredada

**held** /held/ see **hold**[1]

**helicopter** /'helɪkɒptə(r)/ n helicóptero m

**heliport** /'helɪpɔːt/ n helipuerto m

**hell** /hel/ n infierno m. **~-bent** a resuelto. **~ish** a infernal

**hello** /hə'ləʊ/ int ¡hola!; (*telephone, caller*) ¡oiga!, ¡bueno! (*Mex*), ¡hola! (*Arg*); (*telephone, person answering*) ¡diga!, ¡bueno! (*Mex*), ¡hola! (*Arg*); (*surprise*) ¡vaya! **say ~ to** saludar

**helm** /helm/ n (*of ship*) timón m

**helmet** /'helmɪt/ n casco m

**help** /help/ vt/i ayudar. **he cannot ~ laughing** no puede menos de reír. **~ o.s. to** servirse. **it cannot be ~ed** no hay más remedio. ● n ayuda f; (*charwoman*) asistenta f. **~er** n ayudante m. **~ful** a útil; ‹person› amable

**helping** /'helpɪŋ/ n porción f

**helpless** /'helplɪs/ a (*unable to manage*) incapaz; (*powerless*) impotente

**helter-skelter** /heltə'skeltə(r)/ n tobogán m. ● adv atropelladamente

**hem** /hem/ n dobladillo m. ● vt (pt **hemmed**) hacer un dobladillo. **~ in** encerrar

**hemisphere** /'hemisfiə(r)/ *n* hemisferio *m*

**hemp** /hemp/ *n* (*plant*) cáñamo *m*; (*hashish*) hachís *m*

**hen** /hen/ *n* gallina *f*

**hence** /hens/ *adv* de aquí. **~forth** *adv* de ahora en adelante

**henchman** /'hentʃmən/ *n* secuaz *m*

**henna** /'henə/ *n* alheña *f*

**hen-party** /'henpɑːtɪ/ *n* (*fam*) reunión *f* de mujeres

**henpecked** /'henpekt/ *a* dominado por su mujer

**her** /hɜː(r)/ *pron* (*accusative*) la; (*dative*) le; (*after prep*) ella. **I know ~** la conozco. ● *a* su, sus *pl*

**herald** /'herəld/ *vt* anunciar

**heraldry** /'herəldrɪ/ *n* heráldica *f*

**herb** /hɜːb/ *n* hierba *f*. **~s** *npl* hierbas *fpl* finas

**herbaceous** /hɜːˈbeɪʃəs/ *a* herbáceo

**herbalist** /'hɜːbəlɪst/ *n* herbolario *m*

**herculean** /hɜːkjʊˈliːən/ *a* hercúleo

**herd** /hɜːd/ *n* rebaño *m*. ● *vt.* ~ **together** reunir

**here** /hɪə(r)/ *adv* aquí. ~**!** (*take this*) ¡tenga! **~abouts** *adv* por aquí. **~after** *adv* en el futuro. **~by** *adv* por este medio; (*in letter*) por la presente

**heredit|ary** /hɪˈredɪtərɪ/ *a* hereditario. **~y** /hɪˈredɪtɪ/ *n* herencia *f*

**here|sy** /'herəsɪ/ *n* herejía *f*. **~tic** *n* hereje *m* & *f*

**herewith** /hɪəˈwɪð/ *adv* adjunto

**heritage** /'herɪtɪdʒ/ *n* herencia *f*; (*fig*) patrimonio *m*

**hermetic** /hɜːˈmetɪk/ *a* hermético

**hermit** /'hɜːmɪt/ *n* ermitaño *m*

**hernia** /'hɜːnɪə/ *n* hernia *f*

**hero** /'hɪərəʊ/ *n* (*pl* -**oes**) héroe *m*. **~ic** *a* heroico

**heroin** /'herəʊɪn/ *n* heroína *f*

**hero: ~ine** /'herəʊɪn/ *n* heroína *f*. **~ism** /'herəʊɪzm/ *n* heroismo *m*

**heron** /'herən/ *n* garza *f* real

**herring** /'herɪŋ/ *n* arenque *m*

**hers** /hɜːz/ *poss pron* suyo *m*, suya *f*, suyos *mpl*, suyas *fpl*, de ella

**herself** /hɜːˈself/ *pron* ella misma; (*reflexive*) se; (*after prep*) sí

**hesitant** /'hezɪtənt/ *a* vacilante

**hesitat|e** /'hezɪteɪt/ *vi* vacilar. **~ion** /-'teɪʃn/ *n* vacilación *f*

**hessian** /'hesɪən/ *n* arpillera *f*

**het** /het/ *a.* ~ **up** (*sl*) nervioso

**heterogeneous** /hetərəʊˈdʒiːnɪəs/ *a* heterogéneo

**heterosexual** /hetərəʊˈseksjʊəl/ *a* heterosexual

**hew** /hjuː/ *vt* (*pp* **hewn**) cortar; (*cut into shape*) tallar

**hexagon** /'heksəgən/ *n* hexágono *m*. **~al** /-'ægənl/ *a* hexagonal

**hey** /heɪ/ *int* ¡eh!

**heyday** /'heɪdeɪ/ *n* apogeo *m*

**hi** /haɪ/ *int* (*fam*) ¡hola!

**hiatus** /haɪˈeɪtəs/ *n* (*pl* -**tuses**) hiato *m*

**hibernat|e** /'haɪbəneɪt/ *vi* hibernar. **~ion** *n* hibernación *f*

**hibiscus** /hɪˈbɪskəs/ *n* hibisco *m*

**hiccup** /'hɪkʌp/ *n* hipo *m*. **have (the) ~s** tener hipo. ● *vi* tener hipo

**hide**¹ /haɪd/ *vt* (*pt* **hid**, *pp* **hidden**) esconder. ● *vi* esconderse

**hide**² /haɪd/ *n* piel *f*, cuero *m*

**hideous** /'hɪdɪəs/ *a* (*dreadful*) horrible; (*ugly*) feo

**hide-out** /'haɪdaʊt/ *n* escondrijo *m*

**hiding**¹ /'haɪdɪŋ/ *n* (*thrashing*) paliza *f*

**hiding**² /'haɪdɪŋ/ *n*. **go into ~** esconderse

**hierarchy** /'haɪərɑːkɪ/ *n* jerarquía *f*

**hieroglyph** /'haɪərəglɪf/ *n* jeroglífico *m*

**hi-fi** /'haɪfaɪ/ *a* de alta fidelidad. ● *n* (equipo *m* de) alta fidelidad (*f*)

**higgledy-piggledy** /hɪgldɪˈpɪgldɪ/ *adv* en desorden

**high** /haɪ/ *a* (-**er**, -**est**) alto; ⟨*price*⟩ elevado; ⟨*number, speed*⟩ grande; ⟨*wind*⟩ fuerte; (*intoxicated, fam*) ebrio; ⟨*voice*⟩ agudo; ⟨*meat*⟩ manido. **in the ~ season** en plena temporada. ● *n* alto nivel *m*. **a (new) ~** un récord *m*. ● *adv* alto

**highbrow** /'haɪbraʊ/ *a* & *n* intelectual (*m* & *f*)

**higher education** /haɪər edʒʊˈkeɪʃn/ *n* enseñanza *f* superior

**high-falutin** /haɪfəˈluːtɪn/ *a* pomposo

**high-handed** /haɪˈhændɪd/ *a* despótico

**high jump** /'haɪdʒʌmp/ *n* salto *m* de altura

**highlight** /'haɪlaɪt/ *n* punto *m* culminante. ● *vt* destacar

**highly** /'haɪlɪ/ *adv* muy; ⟨*paid*⟩ muy bien. **~ strung** *a* nervioso

**highness** /'haɪnɪs/ *n* (*title*) alteza *f*

**high: ~rise building** *n* rascacielos *m*. **~ school** *n* instituto *m*. **~speed** *a* de gran velocidad. **~ spot** *n* (*fam*) punto *m* culminante. **~ street** *n* calle f mayor. **~strung** a (*Amer*) nervioso. **~ tea** n merienda f substanciosa

**highway** /'haɪweɪ/ n carretera f. **~man** n salteador m de caminos

**hijack** /'haɪdʒæk/ vt secuestrar. ● n secuestro m. **~er** n secuestrador

**hike** /haɪk/ n caminata f. ● vi darse la caminata. **~r** n excursionista m & f

**hilarious** /hɪ'leərɪəs/ a (*funny*) muy divertido

**hill** /hɪl/ n colina f; (*slope*) cuesta f. **~billy** n rústico m. **~side** n ladera f. **~y** a montuoso

**hilt** /hɪlt/ n (*of sword*) puño m. **to the ~** totalmente

**him** /hɪm/ pron le, lo; (*after prep*) él. **I know ~** le/lo conozco

**himself** /hɪm'self/ pron él mismo; (*reflexive*) se

**hind** /haɪnd/ a trasero

**hinder** /'hɪndə(r)/ vt estorbar; (*prevent*) impedir

**hindrance** /'hɪndrəns/ n obstáculo m

**hindsight** /'haɪnsaɪt/ n. **with ~** retrospectivamente

**Hindu** /hɪn'duː/ n & a hindú (m & f). **~ism** n hinduismo m

**hinge** /hɪndʒ/ n bisagra f. ● vi. **~ on** (*depend on*) depender de

**hint** /hɪnt/ n indirecta f; (*advice*) consejo m. ● vt dar a entender. ● vi soltar una indirecta. **~ at** hacer alusión a

**hinterland** /'hɪntəlænd/ n interior m

**hip** /hɪp/ n cadera f

**hippie** /'hɪpɪ/ n hippie m & f

**hippopotamus** /hɪpə'pɒtəməs/ n (pl **-muses** or **-mi**) hipopótamo m

**hire** /haɪə(r)/ vt alquilar ⟨*thing*⟩; contratar ⟨*person*⟩. ● n alquiler m. **~purchase** n compra f a plazos

**hirsute** /'hɜːsjuːt/ a hirsuto

**his** /hɪz/ a su, sus pl. ● poss pron el suyo m, la suya f, los suyos mpl, las suyas fpl

**Hispan|ic** /hɪ'spænɪk/ a hispánico. **~ist** /'hɪspənɪst/ n hispanista m & f. **~o...** pref hispano...

**hiss** /hɪs/ n silbido. ● vt/i silbar

**histor|ian** /hɪ'stɔːrɪən/ n historiador m. **~ic(al)** /hɪ'stɒrɪkl/ a histórico. **~y** /'hɪstərɪ/ n historia f. **make ~y** pasar a la historia

**histrionic** /hɪstrɪ'ɒnɪk/ a histriónico

**hit** /hɪt/ vt (pt hit, pres p hitting) golpear; (*collide with*) chocar con;

(*find*) dar con; (*affect*) afectar. **~ it off with** hacer buenas migas con. ● n (*blow*) golpe m; (*fig*) éxito m. **~ on** vi encontrar, dar con

**hitch** /hɪtʃ/ vt (*fasten*) atar. ● n (*snag*) problema m. **~ a lift, ~hike** vi hacer autostop, hacer dedo (*Arg*), pedir aventón (*Mex*). **~hiker** n autostopista m & f

**hither** /'hɪðə(r)/ adv acá. **~ and thither** acá y allá

**hitherto** /'hɪðətuː/ adv hasta ahora

**hit-or-miss** /'hɪtɔː'mɪs/ a (*fam*) a la buena de Dios, a ojo

**hive** /haɪv/ n colmena f. ● vt. **~off** separar; (*industry*) desnacionalizar

**hoard** /hɔːd/ vt acumular. ● n provisión f; (*of money*) tesoro m

**hoarding** /'hɔːdɪŋ/ n cartelera f, valla f publicitaria

**hoar-frost** /'hɔːfrɒst/ n escarcha f

**hoarse** /hɔːs/ a (-er, -est) ronco. **~ness** n (*of voice*) ronquera f; (*of sound*) ronquedad f

**hoax** /həʊks/ n engaño m. ● vt engañar

**hob** /hɒb/ n repisa f; (*of cooker*) fogón m

**hobble** /'hɒbl/ vi cojear

**hobby** /'hɒbɪ/ n pasatiempo m

**hobby-horse** /'hɒbɪhɔːs/ n (*toy*) caballito m (de niño); (*fixation*) caballo m de batalla

**hobnail** /'hɒbneɪl/ n clavo m

**hob-nob** /'hɒbnɒb/ vi (pt **hob-nobbed**). **~ with** codearse con

**hock**[1] /hɒk/ n vino m del Rin

**hock**[2] /hɒk/ vt (*pawn, sl*) empeñar

**hockey** /'hɒkɪ/ n hockey m

**hodgepodge** /'hɒdʒpɒdʒ/ n mezcolanza f

**hoe** /həʊ/ n azada f. ● vt (pres p **hoeing**) azadonar

**hog** / hɒg/ n cerdo m. ● vt (pt **hogged**) (*fam*) acaparar

**hoist** /hɔɪst/ vt levantar; izar ⟨*flag*⟩. ● n montacargas m invar

**hold**[1] /həʊld/ vt (pt **held**) tener; (*grasp*) coger (not *LAm*); (*contain*) contener; mantener ⟨*interest*⟩; (*believe*) creer; contener ⟨*breath*⟩. **~ one's tongue** callarse. ● vi mantenerse. ● n asidero m; (*influence*) influencia f. **get ~ of** agarrar; (*fig, acquire*) adquirir. **~ back** (*contain*) contener; (*conceal*) ocultar. **~ on** (*stand firm*) resistir; (*wait*) esperar. **~ on to** (*keep*) guardar; (*cling to*) agarrarse a. **~**

**out** vt (offer) ofrecer. ● vi (resist) resistir. ~ **over** aplazar. ~ **up** (support) sostener; (delay) retrasar; (rob) atracar. ~ **with** aprobar

**hold²** /həʊld/ n (of ship) bodega f

**holdall** /'həʊldɔ:l/ n bolsa f (de viaje)

**holder** /'həʊldə(r)/ n tenedor m; (of post) titular m; (for object) soporte m

**holding** /'həʊldɪŋ/ n (land) propiedad f

**hold-up** /'həʊldʌp/ n atraco m

**hole** /həʊl/ n agujero m; (in ground) hoyo m; (in road) bache m. ● vt agujerear

**holiday** /'hɒlɪdeɪ/ n vacaciones fpl; (public) fiesta f. ● vi pasar las vacaciones. ~-**maker** n veraneante m

**holiness** /'həʊlɪnɪs/ n santidad f

**Holland** /'hɒlənd/ n Holanda f

**hollow** /'hɒləʊ/ a & n hueco (m). ● vt ahuecar

**holly** /'hɒlɪ/ n acebo m. ~**hock** n malva f real

**holocaust** /'hɒləkɔ:st/ n holocausto m

**holster** /'həʊlstə(r)/ n pistolera f

**holy** /'həʊlɪ/ a (-ier, -iest) santo, sagrado. H~ **Ghost** n, H~ **Spirit** n Espíritu m Santo. ~ **water** n agua f bendita

**homage** /'hɒmɪdʒ/ n homenaje m

**home** /həʊm/ n casa f; (institution) asilo m; (for soldiers) hogar m; (native land) patria f. **feel at** ~ **with** sentirse como en su casa. ● a casera, de casa; (of family) de familia; (pol) interior; (match) de casa. ● adv. (at) ~ en casa. H~ **Counties** npl región f alrededor de Londres. ~**land** n patria f. ~**less** a sin hogar. ~**ly** /'həʊmlɪ/ a (-ier, -iest) casero; (ugly) feo. H~ **Office** n Ministerio m del Interior. H~ **Secretary** n Ministro m del Interior. ~**sick** a. **be** ~**sick** tener morriña. ~ **town** n ciudad f natal. ~ **truths** npl las verdades fpl del Interior, las cuatro verdades fpl. ~**ward** /'həʊmwəd/ a (journey) de vuelta. ● adv hacia casa. ~**work** n deberes mpl

**homicide** /'hɒmɪsaɪd/ n homicidio m

**homoeopath|ic** /həʊmɪəʊ'pæθɪk/ a homeopático. ~**y** /-'ɒpəθɪ/ n homeopatía f

**homogeneous** /həʊməʊ'dʒi:nɪəs/ a homogéneo

**homosexual** /həʊməʊ'seksjʊəl/ a & n homosexual (m)

**hone** /həʊn/ vt afilar

**honest** /'ɒnɪst/ a honrado; (frank) sincero. ~**ly** adv honradamente. ~**y** n honradez f

**honey** /'hʌnɪ/ n miel f; (person, fam) cielo m, cariño m. ~**comb** /'hʌnɪkəʊm/ n panal m

**honeymoon** /'hʌnɪmu:n/ n luna f de miel

**honeysuckle** /'hʌnɪsʌkl/ n madreselva f

**honk** /hɒŋk/ vi tocar la bocina

**honorary** /'ɒnərərɪ/ a honorario

**honour** /'ɒnə(r)/ n honor m. ● vt honrar. ~**able** a honorable

**hood** /hʊd/ n capucha f; (car roof) capota f; (car bonnet) capó m

**hoodlum** /'hu:dləm/ n gamberro m, matón m

**hoodwink** /'hʊdwɪŋk/ vt engañar

**hoof** /hu:f/ n (pl hoofs or hooves) casco m

**hook** /hʊk/ n gancho m; (on garment) corchete m; (for fishing) anzuelo m. **by** ~ **or by crook** por fas o por nefas, por las buenas o por las malas. **get s.o. off the** ~ sacar a uno de un apuro. **off the** ~ (telephone) descolgado. ● vt enganchar. ● vi engancharse

**hooked** /hʊkt/ a ganchudo. ~ **on** (sl) adicto a

**hooker** /'hʊkə(r)/ n (rugby) talonador m; (Amer, sl) prostituta f

**hookey** /'hʊkɪ/ n. **play** ~ (Amer, sl) hacer novillos

**hooligan** /'hu:lɪgən/ n gamberro m

**hoop** /hu:p/ n aro m

**hooray** /hʊ'reɪ/ int & n ¡viva! (m)

**hoot** /hu:t/ n (of horn) bocinazo m; (of owl) ululato m. ● vi tocar la bocina; (owl) ulular

**hooter** /'hu:tə(r)/ n (of car) bocina f; (of factory) sirena f

**Hoover** /'hu:və(r)/ n (P) aspiradora f. ● vt pasar la aspiradora

**hop¹** /hɒp/ vi (pt hopped) saltar a la pata coja. ~ **in** (fam) subir. ~ **it** (sl) largarse. ~ **out** (fam) bajar. ● n salto m; (flight) etapa f

**hop²** /hɒp/ n. ~(**s**) lúpulo m

**hope** /həʊp/ n esperanza f. ● vt/i esperar. ~ **for** esperar. ~**ful** a esperanzador. ~**fully** adv con optimismo; (it is hoped) se espera. ~**less** a desesperado. ~**lessly** adv sin esperanza

**hopscotch** /'hɒpskɒtʃ/ n tejo m

**horde** /hɔ:d/ n horda f

**horizon** /hə'raɪzn/ *n* horizonte *m*

**horizontal** /hɒrɪ'zɒntl/ *a* horizontal. **∼ly** *adv* horizontalmente

**hormone** /'hɔːməʊn/ *n* hormona *f*

**horn** /hɔːn/ *n* cuerno *m*; (*of car*) bocina *f*; (*mus*) trompa *f*. ● *vt*. **∼ in** (*sl*) entrometerse. **∼ed** *a* con cuernos

**hornet** /'hɔːnɪt/ *n* avispón *m*

**horny** /'hɔːnɪ/ *a* ⟨hands⟩ calloso

**horoscope** /'hɒrəskəʊp/ *n* horóscopo *m*

**horri|ble** /'hɒrəbl/ *a* horrible. **∼d** /'hɒrɪd/ *a* horrible

**horrif|ic** /hə'rɪfɪk/ *a* horroroso. **∼y** /'hɒrɪfaɪ/ *vt* horrorizar

**horror** /'hɒrə(r)/ *n* horror *m*. **∼ film** *n* película *f* de miedo

**hors-d'oevre** /ɔː'dɜːvr/ *n* entremés *m*

**horse** /hɔːs/ *n* caballo *m*. **∼back** *n*. **on ∼back** a caballo

**horse chestnut** /hɔːs'tʃesnʌt/ *n* castaña *f* de Indias

**horse:** **∼man** *n* jinete *m*. **∼play** *n* payasadas *fpl*. **∼power** *n* (*unit*) caballo *m* (de fuerza). **∼-racing** *n* carreras *fpl* de caballos

**horseradish** /'hɔːsrædɪʃ/ *n* rábano *m* picante

**horse:** **∼ sense** *n* (*fam*) sentido *m* común. **∼shoe** /'hɔːsʃuː/ *n* herradura *f*

**horsy** /'hɔːsɪ/ *a* ⟨face etc⟩ caballuno

**horticultur|al** /hɔːtɪ'kʌltʃərəl/ *a* hortícola. **∼e** /'hɔːtɪkʌltʃə(r)/ *n* horticultura *f*

**hose** /həʊz/ *n* (*tube*) manga *f*. ● *vt* (*water*) regar con una manga; (*clean*) limpiar con una manga. **∼pipe** *n* manga *f*

**hosiery** /'həʊzɪərɪ/ *n* calcetería *f*

**hospice** /'hɒspɪs/ *n* hospicio *m*

**hospitabl|e** /hɒ'spɪtəbl/ *a* hospitalario. **∼y** *adv* con hospitalidad

**hospital** /'hɒspɪtl/ *n* hospital *m*

**hospitality** /hɒspɪ'tælətɪ/ *n* hospitalidad *f*

**host**[1] /həʊst/ *n*. **a ∼ of** un montón de

**host**[2] /həʊst/ *n* (*master of house*) huésped *m*, anfitrión *m*

**host**[3] /həʊst/ *n* (*relig*) hostia *f*

**hostage** /'hɒstɪdʒ/ *n* rehén *m*

**hostel** /'hɒstl/ *n* (*for students*) residencia *f*. **youth ∼** albergue *m* juvenil

**hostess** /'həʊstɪs/ *n* huéspeda *f*, anfitriona *f*

**hostil|e** /'hɒstaɪl/ *a* hostil. **∼ity** *n* hostilidad *f*

**hot** /hɒt/ *a* (**hotter, hottest**) caliente; (*culin*) picante; ⟨news⟩ de última hora. **be/feel ∼** tener calor. **in ∼ water** (*fam*) en un apuro. **it is ∼** hace calor. ● *vt/i.* **∼ up** (*fam*) calentarse

**hotbed** /'hɒtbed/ *n* (*fig*) semillero *m*

**hotchpotch** /'hɒtʃpɒtʃ/ *n* mezcolanza *f*

**hot dog** /hɒt'dɒg/ *n* perrito *m* caliente

**hotel** /həʊ'tel/ *n* hotel *m*. **∼ier** *n* hotelero *m*

**hot:** **∼head** *n* impetuoso *m*. **∼-headed** *a* impetuoso. **∼house** *n* invernadero *m*. **∼line** *n* teléfono *m* rojo. **∼plate** *n* calentador *m*. **∼water bottle** *n* bolsa *f* de agua caliente

**hound** /haʊnd/ *n* perro *m* de caza. ● *vt* perseguir

**hour** /aʊə(r)/ *n* hora *f*. **∼ly** *a & adv* cada hora. **∼ly pay** *n* sueldo *m* por hora. **paid ∼ly** pagado por hora

**house** /haʊs/ *n* (*pl* **-s** /'haʊzɪz/) casa *f*; (*theatre building*) sala *f*; (*theatre audience*) público *m*; (*pol*) cámara *f*. /haʊz/ *vt* alojar; (*keep*) guardar. **∼boat** *n* casa *f* flotante. **∼breaking** *n* robo *m* de casa. **∼hold** /'haʊshəʊld/ *n* casa *f*, familia *f*. **∼holder** *n* dueño *m* de una casa; (*head of household*) cabeza *f* de familia. **∼keeper** *n* ama *f* de llaves. **∼keeping** *n* gobierno *m* de la casa. **∼maid** *n* criada *f*, mucama *f* (*LAm*). **H∼ of Commons** *n* Cámara *f* de los Comunes. **∼proud** *a* meticuloso. **∼warming** *n* inauguración *f* de una casa. **∼wife** /'haʊswaɪf/ *n* ama *f* de casa. **∼work** *n* quehaceres *mpl* domésticos

**housing** /'haʊzɪŋ/ *n* alojamiento *m*. **∼ estate** *n* urbanización *f*

**hovel** /'hɒvl/ *n* casucha *f*

**hover** /'hɒvə(r)/ *vi* ⟨bird, threat etc⟩ cernerse; (*loiter*) rondar. **∼craft** *n* aerodeslizador *m*

**how** /haʊ/ *adv* cómo. **∼ about a walk?** ¿qué le parece si damos un paseo? **∼ are you?** ¿cómo está Vd? **∼ do you do?** (*in introduction*) mucho gusto. **∼ long?** ¿cuánto tiempo? **∼ many?** ¿cuántos? **∼ much?** ¿cuánto? **∼ often?** ¿cuántas veces? **and ∼!** ¡y cómo!

**however** /haʊ'evə(r)/ *adv* (*with verb*) de cualquier manera que (+ *subjunctive*); (*with adjective or adverb*) por... que (+ *subjunctive*);

(*nevertheless*) no obstante, sin embargo. ~ **much it rains** por mucho que llueva

**howl** /haʊl/ n aullido. ● vi aullar

**howler** /'haʊlə(r)/ n (*fam*) plancha f

**HP** *abbr see* **hire-purchase**

**hp** *abbr see* **horsepower**

**hub** /hʌb/ n (*of wheel*) cubo m; (*fig*) centro m

**hubbub** /'hʌbʌb/ n barahúnda f

**hub-cap** /'hʌbkæp/ n tapacubos m *invar*

**huddle** /'hʌdl/ vi apiñarse

**hue**[1] /hju:/ n (*colour*) color m

**hue**[2] /hju:/ n. ~ **and cry** clamor m

**huff** /hʌf/ n. **in a** ~ enojado

**hug** /hʌg/ vt (*pt* **hugged**) abrazar; (*keep close to*) no apartarse de. ● n abrazo m

**huge** /hju:dʒ/ a enorme. ~**ly** adv enormemente

**hulk** /hʌlk/ n (*of ship*) barco m viejo; (*person*) armatoste m

**hull** /hʌl/ n (*of ship*) casco m

**hullabaloo** /hʌləbə'lu:/ n tumulto m

**hullo** /hə'ləʊ/ int = **hello**

**hum** /hʌm/ vt/i (*pt* **hummed**) (*person*) canturrear; (*insect, engine*) zumbar. ● n zumbido m. ~ **(or hem) and haw (or ha)** vacilar

**human** /'hju:mən/ a & n humano (m). ~ **being** n ser m humano

**humane** /hju:'meɪn/ a humano

**humanism** /'hju:mənɪzəm/ n humanismo m

**humanitarian** /hju:mænɪ'teərɪən/ a humanitario

**humanity** /hju:'mænətɪ/ n humanidad f

**humble** /'hʌmbl/ a (**-er, -est**) humilde. ● vt humillar. ~**y** adv humildemente

**humbug** /'hʌmbʌg/ n (*false talk*) charlatanería f; (*person*) charlatán m; (*sweet*) caramelo m de menta

**humdrum** /'hʌmdrʌm/ a monótono

**humid** /'hju:mɪd/ a húmedo. ~**ifier** n humedecedor m. ~**ity** /hju:'mɪdətɪ/ n humedad f

**humiliate** /hju:'mɪlɪeɪt/ vt humillar. ~**ion** /-'eɪʃn/ n humillación f

**humility** /hju:'mɪlətɪ/ n humildad f

**humorist** /'hju:mərɪst/ n humorista m & f

**humorous** /'hju:mərəs/ a divertido. ~**ously** adv con gracia. ~**ur** /'hju:mə(r)/ n humorismo m; (*mood*) humor m. **sense of** ~**ur** n sentido m del humor

**hump** /hʌmp/ n montecillo m; (*of the spine*) joroba f. **the** ~ (*sl*) malhumor m. ● vt encorvarse; (*hoist up*) llevar al hombro

**hunch** /hʌntʃ/ vt encorvar. ~**ed up** encorvado. ● n presentimiento m; (*lump*) joroba f. ~**back** /'hʌntʃbæk/ n jorobado m

**hundred** /'hʌndrəd/ a ciento, (*before noun*) cien. ● n ciento m. ~**fold** a céntuplo. ● adv cien veces. ~**s of** centenares de. ~**th** a centésimo. ● n centésimo m, centésima parte f

**hundredweight** /'hʌndrədweɪt/ n 50,8kg; (*Amer*) 45,36kg

**hung** /hʌŋ/ *see* **hang**

**Hungar|ian** /hʌŋ'geərɪən/ a & n húngaro (m). ~**y** /'hʌŋgərɪ/ n Hungría f

**hunger** /'hʌŋgə(r)/ n hambre f. ● vi. ~ **for** tener hambre de. ~**strike** n huelga f de hambre

**hungr|ily** /'hʌŋgrəlɪ/ adv ávidamente. ~**y** a (**-ier, -iest**) hambriento. **be** ~**y** tener hambre

**hunk** /hʌŋk/ n (buen) pedazo m

**hunt** /hʌnt/ vt/i cazar. ~ **for** buscar. ● n caza f. ~**er** n cazador m. ~**ing** n caza f

**hurdle** /'hɜ:dl/ n (*sport*) valla f; (*fig*) obstáculo m

**hurdy-gurdy** /'hɜ:dɪgɜ:dɪ/ n organillo m

**hurl** /hɜ:l/ vt lanzar

**hurly-burly** /'hɜ:lɪbɜ:lɪ/ n tumulto m

**hurrah** /hʊ'rɑ:/, **hurray** /hʊ'reɪ/ int & n ¡viva! (m)

**hurricane** /'hʌrɪkən/ n huracán m

**hurried** /'hʌrɪd/ a apresurado. ~**ly** adv apresuradamente

**hurry** /'hʌrɪ/ vi apresurarse, darse prisa. ● vt apresurar, dar prisa a. ● n prisa f. **be in a** ~ tener prisa

**hurt** /hɜ:t/ vt/i (*pt* **hurt**) herir. ● n (*injury*) herida f; (*harm*) daño m. ~**ful** a hiriente; (*harmful*) dañoso

**hurtle** /'hɜ:tl/ vt lanzar. ● vi. ~ **along** mover rápidamente

**husband** /'hʌzbənd/ n marido m

**hush** /hʌʃ/ vt acallar. n silencio m. ~ **up** ocultar (*affair*). ~~ a (*fam*) muy secreto

**husk** /hʌsk/ n cáscara f

**husky** /'hʌskɪ/ a (**-ier, -iest**) (*hoarse*) ronco; (*burly*) fornido

**hussy** /'hʌsɪ/ n desvergonzada f

**hustle** /'hʌsl/ vt (*jostle*) empujar. ● vi (*hurry*) darse prisa. ● n empuje m. ~ **and bustle** n bullicio m

**hut** /hʌt/ n cabaña f

**hutch** /hʌtʃ/ n conejera f

**hyacinth** /'haɪəsɪnθ/ n jacinto m

**hybrid** /'haɪbrɪd/ a & n híbrido (m)

**hydrangea** /haɪ'dreɪndʒə/ n hortensia f

**hydrant** /'haɪdrənt/ n. (fire) ~ n boca f de riego

**hydraulic** /haɪ'drɔːlɪk/ a hidráulico

**hydroelectric** /haɪdrəʊ'lektrɪk/ a hidroeléctrico

**hydrofoil** /'haɪdrəfɔɪl/ n aerodeslizador m

**hydrogen** /'haɪdrədʒən/ n hidrógeno m. ~ **bomb** n bomba f de hidrógeno. ~ **peroxide** n peróxido m de hidrógeno

**hyena** /haɪ'iːnə/ n hiena f

**hygien|e** /'haɪdʒiːn/ n higiene f. ~**ic** a higiénico

**hymn** /hɪm/ n himno m

**hyper...** /'haɪpə(r)/ pref hiper...

**hypermarket** /'haɪpəmɑːkɪt/ n hipermercado m

**hyphen** /'haɪfn/ n guión m. ~**ate** vt escribir con guión

**hypno|sis** /hɪp'nəʊsɪs/ n hipnosis f. ~**tic** /-'nɒtɪk/ a hipnótico. ~**tism** /hɪpnə'tɪzəm/ n hipnotismo m. ~**tist** n hipnotista m & f. ~**tize** vt hipnotizar

**hypochondriac** /haɪpə'kɒndriæk/ n hipocondríaco m

**hypocrisy** /hɪ'pɒkrəsɪ/ n hipocresía f

**hypocrit|e** /'hɪpəkrɪt/ n hipócrita m & f. ~**ical** a hipócrita

**hypodermic** /haɪpə'dɜːmɪk/ a hipodérmico. ● n jeringa f hipodérmica

**hypothe|sis** /haɪ'pɒθəsɪs/ n (pl -theses /-siːz/) hipótesis f. ~**tical** /-ə'θetɪkl/ a hipotético

**hysteri|a** /hɪ'stɪərɪə/ n histerismo m. ~**cal** /-'terɪkl/ a histérico. ~**cs** /hɪ'sterɪks/ npl histerismo m. have ~**cs** ponerse histérico; (laugh) morir de risa

# I

**I** /aɪ/ pron yo

**ice** /aɪs/ n hielo m. ● vt helar; glasear ⟨cake⟩. ● vi. ~ (**up**) helarse. ~**berg** n iceberg m, témpano m. ~**cream** n helado m. ~**cube** n cubito m de hielo. ~ **hockey** n hockey m sobre hielo

**Iceland** /'aɪslənd/ n Islandia f. ~**er** n islandés m. ~**ic** /-'lændɪk/ a islandés

**ice lolly** /aɪs'lɒlɪ/ polo m, paleta f (LAm)

**icicle** /'aɪsɪkl/ n carámbano m

**icing** /'aɪsɪŋ/ n (sugar) azúcar m glaseado

**icon** /'aɪkɒn/ n icono m

**icy** /'aɪsɪ/ a (-ier, -iest) glacial

**idea** /aɪ'dɪə/ n idea f

**ideal** /aɪ'dɪəl/ a ideal. ● n ideal m. ~**ism** n idealismo m. ~**ist** n idealista m & f. ~**istic** /-'lɪstɪk/ a idealista. ~**ize** vt idealizar. ~**ly** adv idealmente

**identical** /aɪ'dentɪkl/ a idéntico

**identif|ication** /aɪdentɪfɪ'keɪʃn/ n identificación f. ~**y** /aɪ'dentɪfaɪ/ vt identificar. ● vi. ~**y with** identificarse con

**identikit** /aɪ'dentɪkɪt/ n retrato-robot m

**identity** /aɪ'dentɪtɪ/ n identidad f

**ideolog|ical** /aɪdɪə'lɒdʒɪkl/ a ideológico. ~**y** /aɪdɪ'ɒlədʒɪ/ n ideología f

**idiocy** /'ɪdɪəsɪ/ n idiotez f

**idiom** /'ɪdɪəm/ n locución f. ~**atic** /-'mætɪk/ a idiomático

**idiosyncrasy** /ɪdɪəʊ'sɪŋkrəsɪ/ n idiosincrasia f

**idiot** /'ɪdɪət/ n idiota m & f. ~**ic** /-'ɒtɪk/ a idiota

**idle** /'aɪdl/ a (-er, -est) ocioso; (lazy) holgazán; (out of work) desocupado; ⟨machine⟩ parado. ● vt ⟨engine⟩ marchar en vacío. ● vt. ~ **away** perder. ~**ness** n ociosidad f. ~**r** /-ə(r)/ n ocioso m

**idol** /'aɪdl/ n ídolo m. ~**ize** vt idolatrar

**idyllic** /ɪ'dɪlɪk/ a idílico

**i.e.** /aɪ'iː/ abbr (id est) es decir

**if** /ɪf/ conj si

**igloo** /'ɪgluː/ n iglú m

**ignite** /ɪg'naɪt/ vt encender. ● vi encenderse

**ignition** /ɪg'nɪʃn/ n ignición f; (auto) encendido m. ~ (**switch**) n contacto m

**ignoramus** /ɪgnə'reɪməs/ n (pl -muses) ignorante

**ignoran|ce** /'ɪgnərəns/ n ignorancia f. ~**t** a ignorante. ~**tly** adv por ignorancia

**ignore** /ɪg'nɔː(r)/ vt no hacer caso de

**ilk** /ɪlk/ n ralea f

**ill** /ɪl/ a enfermo; (bad) malo. ~ **will** n mala voluntad f. ● adv mal. ~ **at**

**ease** inquieto. ● *n* mal *m*. **~advised** *a* imprudente. **~bred** *a* mal educado

**illegal** /ɪˈliːɡl/ *a* ilegal

**illegible** /ɪˈledʒəbl/ *a* ilegible

**illegitima|cy** /ɪlɪˈdʒɪtɪməsɪ/ *n* ilegitimidad *f*. **~te** *a* ilegítimo

**ill: ~fated** *a* malogrado. **~gotten** *a* mal adquirido

**illitera|cy** /ɪˈlɪtərəsɪ/ *n* analfabetismo *m*. **~te** *a* & *n* analfabeto (*m*)

**ill: ~natured** *a* poco afable. **~ness** *n* enfermedad *f*

**illogical** /ɪˈlɒdʒɪkl/ *a* ilógico

**ill: ~starred** *a* malogrado. **~treat** *vt* maltratar

**illuminat|e** /ɪˈluːmɪneɪt/ *vt* iluminar. **~ion** /-ˈneɪʃn/ *n* iluminación *f*

**illus|ion** /ɪˈluːʒn/ *n* ilusión *f*. **~sory** *a* ilusorio

**illustrat|e** /ˈɪləstreɪt/ *vt* ilustrar. **~ion** *n* (*example*) ejemplo *m*; (*picture in book*) grabado *m*, lámina *f*. **~ive** *a* ilustrativo

**illustrious** /ɪˈlʌstrɪəs/ *a* ilustre

**image** /ˈɪmɪdʒ/ *n* imagen *f*. **~ry** *n* imágenes *fpl*

**imagin|able** /ɪˈmædʒɪnəbl/ *a* imaginable. **~ary** *a* imaginario. **~ation** /-ˈneɪʃn/ *n* imaginación *f*. **~ative** *a* imaginativo. **~e** *vt* imaginar(se)

**imbalance** /ɪmˈbæləns/ *n* desequilibrio *m*

**imbecil|e** /ˈɪmbəsiːl/ *a* & *n* imbécil (*m* & *f*). **~ity** /-ˈsɪlətɪ/ *n* imbecilidad *f*

**imbibe** /ɪmˈbaɪb/ *vt* embeber; (*drink*) beber

**imbue** /ɪmˈbjuː/ *vt* empapar (**with** de)

**imitat|e** /ˈɪmɪteɪt/ *vt* imitar. **~ion** /-ˈteɪʃn/ *n* imitación *f*. **~or** *n* imitador *m*

**immaculate** /ɪˈmækjʊlət/ *a* inmaculado

**immaterial** /ɪməˈtɪərɪəl/ *a* inmaterial; (*unimportant*) insignificante

**immature** /ɪməˈtjʊə(r)/ *a* inmaduro

**immediate** /ɪˈmiːdɪət/ *a* inmediato. **~ly** *adv* inmediatamente. **~ly you hear me** en cuanto me oigas. ● *conj* en cuanto (+ *subj*)

**immens|e** /ɪˈmens/ *a* inmenso. **~ely** *adv* inmensamente; (*very much*, *fam*) muchísimo. **~ity** *n* inmensidad *f*

**immers|e** /ɪˈmɜːs/ *vt* sumergir. **~ion** /ɪˈmɜːʃn/ *n* inmersión *f*. **~ion heater** *n* calentador *m* de inmersión

**immigra|nt** /ˈɪmɪɡrənt/ *a* & *n* inmigrante (*m* & *f*). **~te** *vi* inmigrar. **~tion** /-ˈɡreɪʃn/ *n* inmigración *f*

**imminen|ce** /ˈɪmɪnəns/ *n* inminencia *f*. **~t** *a* inminente

**immobil|e** /ɪˈməʊbaɪl/ *a* inmóvil. **~ize** /-bɪlaɪz/ *vt* inmovilizar

**immoderate** /ɪˈmɒdərət/ *a* inmoderado

**immodest** /ɪˈmɒdɪst/ *a* inmodesto

**immoral** /ɪˈmɒrəl/ *a* inmoral. **~ity** /ɪməˈrælətɪ/ *n* inmoralidad *f*

**immortal** /ɪˈmɔːtl/ *a* inmortal. **~ity** /-ˈtælətɪ/ *n* inmortalidad *f*. **~ize** *vt* inmortalizar

**immun|e** /ɪˈmjuːn/ *a* inmune (**from**, **to** a, contra). **~ity** *n* inmunidad *f*. **~ization** /ɪmjʊnaɪˈzeɪʃn/ *n* inmunización *f*. **~ize** *vt* inmunizar

**imp** /ɪmp/ *n* diablillo *m*

**impact** /ˈɪmpækt/ *n* impacto *m*

**impair** /ɪmˈpeə(r)/ *vt* perjudicar

**impale** /ɪmˈpeɪl/ *vt* empalar

**impart** /ɪmˈpɑːt/ *vt* comunicar

**impartial** /ɪmˈpɑːʃl/ *a* imparcial. **~ity** /-ɪˈælətɪ/ *n* imparcialidad *f*

**impassable** /ɪmˈpɑːsəbl/ *a* ‹*barrier etc*› infranqueable; ‹*road*› impracticable

**impasse** /æmˈpɑːs/ *n* callejón *m* sin salida

**impassioned** /ɪmˈpæʃnd/ *a* apasionado

**impassive** /ɪmˈpæsɪv/ *a* impasible

**impatien|ce** /ɪmˈpeɪʃəns/ *n* impaciencia *f*. **~t** *a* impaciente. **~tly** *adv* con impaciencia

**impeach** /ɪmˈpiːtʃ/ *vt* acusar

**impeccable** /ɪmˈpekəbl/ *a* impecable

**impede** /ɪmˈpiːd/ *vt* estorbar

**impediment** /ɪmˈpedɪmənt/ *n* obstáculo *m*. **(speech) ~** *n* defecto *m* del habla

**impel** /ɪmˈpel/ *vt* (*pt* **impelled**) impeler

**impending** /ɪmˈpendɪŋ/ *a* inminente

**impenetrable** /ɪmˈpenɪtrəbl/ *a* impenetrable

**imperative** /ɪmˈperətɪv/ *a* imprescindible. ● *n* (*gram*) imperativo *m*

**imperceptible** /ɪmpəˈseptəbl/ *a* imperceptible

**imperfect** /ɪmˈpɜːfɪkt/ *a* imperfecto. **~ion** /-əˈfekʃn/ *n* imperfección *f*

**imperial** /ɪmˈpɪərɪəl/ *a* imperial. **~ism** *n* imperialismo *m*

**imperil** /ɪm'perəl/ *vt* (*pt* **imperilled**) poner en peligro

**imperious** /ɪm'pɪərɪəs/ *a* imperioso

**impersonal** /ɪm'pɜːsənl/ *a* impersonal

**impersonat|e** /ɪm'pɜːsəneɪt/ *vt* hacerse pasar por; (*mimic*) imitar. **∼ion** /-'neɪʃn/ *n* imitación *f*. **∼or** *n* imitador *m*

**impertinen|ce** /ɪm'pɜːtɪnəns/ *n* impertinencia *f*. **∼t** *a* impertinente. **∼tly** *adv* impertinentemente

**impervious** /ɪm'pɜːvɪəs/ *a*. **∼ to** impermeable a; (*fig*) insensible a

**impetuous** /ɪm'petjʊəs/ *a* impetuoso

**impetus** /'ɪmpɪtəs/ *n* ímpetu *m*

**impinge** /ɪm'pɪndʒ/ *vi*. **∼ on** afectar a

**impish** /'ɪmpɪʃ/ *a* travieso

**implacable** /ɪm'plækəbl/ *a* implacable

**implant** /ɪm'plɑːnt/ *vt* implantar

**implement** /'ɪmplɪmənt/ *n* herramienta *f*. /'ɪmplɪment/ *vt* realizar

**implicat|e** /'ɪmplɪkeɪt/ *vt* implicar. **∼ion** /-'keɪʃn/ *n* implicación *f*

**implicit** /ɪm'plɪsɪt/ *a* (*implied*) implícito; (*unquestioning*) absoluto

**implied** /ɪm'plaɪd/ *a* implícito

**implore** /ɪm'plɔː(r)/ *vt* implorar

**imply** /ɪm'plaɪ/ *vt* implicar; (*mean*) querer decir; (*insinuate*) dar a entender

**impolite** /ɪmpə'laɪt/ *a* mal educado

**imponderable** /ɪm'pɒndərəbl/ *a* & *n* imponderable (*m*)

**import** /ɪm'pɔːt/ *vt* importar. /'ɪmpɔːt/ *n* (*article*) importación *f*; (*meaning*) significación *f*

**importan|ce** /ɪm'pɔːtəns/ *n* importancia *f*. **∼t** *a* importante

**importation** /ɪmpɔː'teɪʃn/ *n* importación *f*

**importer** /ɪm'pɔːtə(r)/ *n* importador *m*

**impose** /ɪm'pəʊz/ *vt* imponer. ● *vi*. **∼ on** abusar de la amabilidad de

**imposing** /ɪm'pəʊzɪŋ/ *a* imponente

**imposition** /ɪmpə'zɪʃn/ *n* imposición *f*; (*fig*) molestia *f*

**impossib|ility** /ɪmpɒsə'bɪlətɪ/ *n* imposibilidad *f*. **∼le** *a* imposible

**impostor** /ɪm'pɒstə(r)/ *n* impostor *m*

**impoten|ce** /'ɪmpətəns/ *n* impotencia *f*. **∼t** *a* impotente

**impound** /ɪm'paʊnd/ *vt* confiscar

**impoverish** /ɪm'pɒvərɪʃ/ *vt* empobrecer

**impracticable** /ɪm'præktɪkəbl/ *a* impracticable

**impractical** /ɪm'præktɪkl/ *a* poco práctico

**imprecise** /ɪmprɪ'saɪs/ *a* impreciso

**impregnable** /ɪm'pregnəbl/ *a* inexpugnable

**impregnate** /'ɪmpregneɪt/ *vt* impregnar (**with** de)

**impresario** /ɪmprɪ'sɑːrɪəʊ/ *n* (*pl* **-os**) empresario *m*

**impress** /ɪm'pres/ *vt* impresionar; (*imprint*) imprimir. **∼ on s.o.** hacer entender a uno

**impression** /ɪm'preʃn/ *n* impresión *f*. **∼able** *a* impresionable

**impressive** /ɪm'presɪv/ *a* impresionante

**imprint** /'ɪmprɪnt/ *n* impresión *f*. /ɪm'prɪnt/ *vt* imprimir

**imprison** /ɪm'prɪzn/ *vt* encarcelar. **∼ment** *n* encarcelamiento *m*

**improbab|ility** /ɪmprɒbə'bɪlətɪ/ *n* improbabilidad *f*. **∼le** *a* improbable

**impromptu** /ɪm'prɒmptjuː/ *a* improvisado. ● *adv* de improviso

**improper** /ɪm'prɒpə(r)/ *a* impropio; (*incorrect*) incorrecto

**impropriety** /ɪmprə'praɪətɪ/ *n* inconveniencia *f*

**improve** /ɪm'pruːv/ *vt* mejorar. ● *vi* mejorar(se). **∼ment** *n* mejora *f*

**improvis|ation** /ɪmprəvaɪ'zeɪʃn/ *n* improvisación *f*. **∼e** *vt*/*i* improvisar

**imprudent** /ɪm'pruːdənt/ *a* imprudente

**impuden|ce** /'ɪmpjʊdəns/ *n* insolencia *f*. **∼t** *a* insolente

**impulse** /'ɪmpʌls/ *n* impulso *m*. **on ∼** sin reflexionar

**impulsive** /ɪm'pʌlsɪv/ *a* irreflexivo. **∼ly** *adv* sin reflexionar

**impunity** /ɪm'pjuːnətɪ/ *n* impunidad *f*. **with ∼** impunemente

**impur|e** /ɪm'pjʊə(r)/ *a* impuro. **∼ity** *n* impureza *f*

**impute** /ɪm'pjuːt/ *vt* imputar

**in** /ɪn/ *prep* en, dentro de. **∼ a firm manner** de una manera terminante. **∼ an hour('s time)** dentro de una hora. **∼ doing** al hacer. **∼ so far as** en cuanto que. **∼ the evening** por la tarde. **∼ the main** por la mayor parte. **∼ the rain** bajo la lluvia. **∼ the sun** al sol. **one ∼ ten** uno de cada diez. **the best ∼** el mejor de. ● *adv* (*inside*) dentro; (*at home*) en

casa; (*in fashion*) de moda. ● *n*. the
~s **and outs of** los detalles *mpl* de
**inability** /ɪnəˈbɪlətɪ/ *n* incapacidad *f*
**inaccessible** /ɪnækˈsesəbl/ *a*
inaccesible
**inaccura|cy** /ɪnˈækjʊrəsɪ/ *n* inex-
actitud *f*. ~**te** *a* inexacto
**inaction** /ɪnˈækʃn/ *n* inacción *f*
**inactiv|e** /ɪnˈæktɪv/ *a* inactivo. ~**ity**
/-ˈtɪvətɪ/ *n* inactividad *f*
**inadequa|cy** /ɪnˈædɪkwəsɪ/ *a*
insuficiencia *f*. ~**te** *a* insuficiente
**inadmissible** /ɪnədˈmɪsəbl/ *a*
inadmisible
**inadvertently** /ɪnədˈvɜːtəntlɪ/ *adv*
por descuido
**inadvisable** /ɪnədˈvaɪzəbl/ *a* no
aconsejable
**inane** /ɪˈneɪn/ *a* estúpido
**inanimate** /ɪnˈænɪmət/ *a* inanimado
**inappropriate** /ɪnəˈprəʊprɪət/ *a*
inoportuno
**inarticulate** /ɪnɑːˈtɪkjʊlət/ *a* incapaz
de expresarse claramente
**inasmuch as** /ɪnəzˈmʌtʃəz/ *adv* ya
que
**inattentive** /ɪnəˈtentɪv/ *a* desatento
**inaudible** /ɪnˈɔːdəbl/ *a* inaudible
**inaugural** /ɪˈnɔːgjʊrəl/ *a* inaugural
**inaugurat|e** /ɪˈnɔːgjʊreɪt/ *vt* in-
augurar. ~**ion** /-ˈreɪʃn/ *n* inauguración *f*
**inauspicious** /ɪnɔːˈspɪʃəs/ *a* poco
propicio
**inborn** /ˈɪnbɔːn/ *a* innato
**inbred** /ɪnˈbred/ *a* (*inborn*) innato
**incalculable** /ɪnˈkælkjʊləbl/ *a*
incalculable
**incapab|ility** /ɪnkeɪpəˈbɪlətɪ/ *n* inca-
pacidad *f*. ~**le** *a* incapaz
**incapacit|ate** /ɪnkəˈpæsɪteɪt/ *vt* inca-
pacitar. ~**y** *n* incapacidad *f*
**incarcerat|e** /ɪnˈkɑːsəreɪt/ *vt* encar-
celar. ~**ion** /-ˈreɪʃn/ *n* encarcelamiento *m*
**incarnat|e** /ɪnˈkɑːnət/ *a* encarnado.
~**ion** /-ˈneɪʃn/ *n* encarnación *f*
**incautious** /ɪnˈkɔːʃəs/ *a* incauto. ~**ly**
*adv* incautamente
**incendiary** /ɪnˈsendɪərɪ/ *a* incendiario. ● *n* (*person*) incendiario *m*;
(*bomb*) bomba *f* incendiaria
**incense**[1] /ˈɪnsens/ *n* incienso *m*
**incense**[2] /ɪnˈsens/ *vt* enfurecer
**incentive** /ɪnˈsentɪv/ *n* incentivo *m*;
(*payment*) prima *f* de incentivo
**inception** /ɪnˈsepʃn/ *n* principio *m*
**incertitude** /ɪnˈsɜːtɪtjuːd/ *n* incertidumbre *f*

**incessant** /ɪnˈsesnt/ *a* incesante.
~**ly** *adv* sin cesar
**incest** /ˈɪnsest/ *n* incesto *m*. ~**uous**
/-ˈsestjʊəs/ *a* incestuoso
**inch** /ɪntʃ/ *n* pulgada *f* (= *2,54cm*).
● *vi* avanzar palmo a palmo
**incidence** /ˈɪnsɪdəns/ *n* frecuencia *f*
**incident** /ˈɪnsɪdənt/ *n* incidente *m*
**incidental** /ɪnsɪˈdentl/ *a* fortuito.
~**ly** *adv* incidentemente; (*by the
way*) a propósito
**incinerat|e** /ɪnˈsɪnəreɪt/ *vt*
incinerar. ~**or** *n* incinerador *m*
**incipient** /ɪnˈsɪpɪənt/ *a* incipiente
**incision** /ɪnˈsɪʒn/ *n* incisión *f*
**incisive** /ɪnˈsaɪsɪv/ *a* incisivo
**incite** /ɪnˈsaɪt/ *vt* incitar. ~**ment** *n*
incitación *f*
**inclement** /ɪnˈklemənt/ *a* incle-
mente
**inclination** /ɪnklɪˈneɪʃn/ *n* inclinación *f*
**incline**[1] /ɪnˈklaɪn/ *vt* inclinar. ● *vi*
inclinarse. **be** ~**d to** tener tendencia a
**incline**[2] /ˈɪnklaɪn/ *n* cuesta *f*
**inclu|de** /ɪnˈkluːd/ *vt* incluir. ~**ding**
*prep* incluso. ~**sion** /-ʒn/ *n* inclu-
sión *f*
**inclusive** /ɪnˈkluːsɪv/ *a* inclusivo. **be**
~ **of** incluir. ● *adv* inclusive
**incognito** /ɪnkɒgˈniːtəʊ/ *adv* de
incógnito
**incoherent** /ɪnkəʊˈhɪərənt/ *a* in-
coherente
**income** /ˈɪnkʌm/ *n* ingresos *mpl*. ~
**tax** *n* impuesto *m* sobre la renta
**incoming** /ˈɪnkʌmɪŋ/ *a* (*tide*) ascendente; (*tenant etc*) nuevo
**incomparable** /ɪnˈkɒmpərəbl/ *a* incomparable
**incompatible** /ɪnkəmˈpætəbl/ *a* incompatible
**incompeten|ce** /ɪnˈkɒmpɪtəns/ *n*
incompetencia *f*. ~**t** *a* incompetente
**incomplete** /ɪnkəmˈpliːt/ *a* incompleto
**incomprehensible** /ɪnkɒmprɪ-
ˈhensəbl/ *a* incomprensible
**inconceivable** /ɪnkənˈsiːvəbl/ *a* inconcebible
**inconclusive** /ɪnkənˈkluːsɪv/ *a* poco
concluyente
**incongruous** /ɪnˈkɒŋgrʊəs/ *a* incongruente
**inconsequential** /ɪnkɒnsɪˈkwenʃl/ *a*
sin importancia

**inconsiderate** /ɪnkən'sɪdərət/ a desconsiderado

**inconsisten|cy** /ɪnkən'sɪstənsɪ/ n inconsecuencia f. ~t a inconsecuente. be ~t with no concordar con

**inconspicuous** /ɪnkən'spɪkjʊəs/ a que no llama la atención. ~ly adv sin llamar la atención

**incontinen|ce** /ɪn'kɒntɪnəns/ a incontinencia f. ~t a incontinente

**inconvenien|ce** /ɪnkən'viːnɪəns/ a incomodidad f; (drawback) inconveniente m. ~t a incómodo; ⟨time⟩ inoportuno

**incorporat|e** /ɪn'kɔːpəreɪt/ vt incorporar; (include) incluir. ~ion /-'reɪʃn/ n incorporación f

**incorrect** /ɪnkə'rekt/ a incorrecto

**incorrigible** /ɪn'kɒrɪdʒəbl/ a incorregible

**incorruptible** /ɪnkə'rʌptəbl/ a incorruptible

**increase** /'ɪnkriːs/ n aumento m (in, of de). /ɪn'kriːs/ vt/i aumentar

**increasing** /ɪn'kriːsɪŋ/ a creciente. ~ly adv cada vez más

**incredible** /ɪn'kredəbl/ a increíble

**incredulous** /ɪn'kredjʊləs/ a incrédulo

**increment** /'ɪnkrɪmənt/ n aumento m

**incriminat|e** /ɪn'krɪmɪneɪt/ vt acriminar. ~ing a acriminador

**incubat|e** /'ɪŋkjʊbeɪt/ vt incubar. ~ion /-'beɪʃn/ n incubación f. ~or n incubadora f

**inculcate** /'ɪnkʌlkeɪt/ vt inculcar

**incumbent** /ɪn'kʌmbənt/ n titular. ● a. be ~ on incumbir a

**incur** /ɪn'kɜː(r)/ vt (pt incurred) incurrir en; contraer ⟨debts⟩

**incurable** /ɪn'kjʊərəbl/ a incurable

**incursion** /ɪn'kɜːʃn/ n incursión f

**indebted** /ɪn'detɪd/ a. ~ to s.o. estar en deuda con uno

**indecen|cy** /ɪn'diːsnsɪ/ n indecencia f. ~t a indecente

**indecisi|on** /ɪndɪ'sɪʒn/ n indecisión f. ~ve /ɪndɪ'saɪsɪv/ a indeciso

**indeed** /ɪn'diːd/ adv en efecto; (really?) ¿de veras?

**indefatigable** /ɪndɪ'fætɪgəbl/ a incansable

**indefinable** /ɪndɪ'faɪnəbl/ a indefinible

**indefinite** /ɪn'defɪnət/ a indefinido. ~ly adv indefinidamente

**indelible** /ɪn'delɪbl/ a indeleble

**indemni|fy** /ɪn'demnɪfaɪ/ vt indemnizar. ~ty /-ətɪ/ n indemnización f

**indent** /ɪn'dent/ vt endentar ⟨text⟩. ~ation /-'teɪʃn/ n mella f

**independen|ce** /ɪndɪ'pendəns/ n independencia f. ~t a independiente. ~tly adv independientemente. ~tly of independientemente de

**indescribable** /ɪndɪ'skraɪbəbl/ a indescriptible

**indestructible** /ɪndɪ'strʌktəbl/ a indestructible

**indeterminate** /ɪndɪ'tɜːmɪnət/ a indeterminado

**index** /'ɪndeks/ n (pl indexes) índice m. ● vt poner índice a; (enter in the/ an index) poner en el/un índice. ~ finger n (dedo m) índice m. ~linked a indexado

**India** /'ɪndɪə/ n la India f. ~n a & n indio (m). ~n summer n veranillo m de San Martín

**indicat|e** /'ɪndɪkeɪt/ vt indicar. ~ion /-'keɪʃn/ n indicación f. ~ive /ɪn'dɪkətɪv/ a & n indicativo (m). ~or /'ɪndɪkeɪtə(r)/ n indicador m

**indict** /ɪn'daɪt/ vt acusar. ~ment n acusación f

**indifferen|ce** /ɪn'dɪfrəns/ n indiferencia f. ~t a indiferente; (not good) mediocre

**indigenous** /ɪn'dɪdʒɪnəs/ a indígena

**indigesti|ble** /ɪndɪ'dʒestəbl/ a indigesto. ~on /-tʃən/ n indigestión f

**indigna|nt** /ɪn'dɪgnənt/ a indignado. ~tion /-'neɪʃn/ n indignación f

**indignity** /ɪn'dɪgnətɪ/ n indignidad f

**indigo** /'ɪndɪgəʊ/ n añil (m)

**indirect** /ɪndɪ'rekt/ a indirecto. ~ly adv indirectamente

**indiscre|et** /ɪndɪ'skriːt/ a indiscreto. ~tion /-'kreʃn/ n indiscreción f

**indiscriminate** /ɪndɪ'skrɪmɪnət/ a indistinto. ~ly adv indistintamente

**indispensable** /ɪndɪ'spensəbl/ a imprescindible

**indispos|ed** /ɪndɪ'spəʊzd/ a indispuesto. ~ition /-ə'zɪʃn/ n indisposición f

**indisputable** /ɪndɪ'spjuːtəbl/ a indiscutible

**indissoluble** /ɪndɪ'sɒljʊbl/ a indisoluble

**indistinct** /ɪndɪ'stɪŋkt/ a indistinto

**indistinguishable** /ɪndɪ'stɪŋwɪʃəbl/ a indistinguible

**individual** /ɪndɪ'vɪdjʊəl/ a individual. ● n individuo m. ~ist n individualista m & f. ~ity n individualidad *f*. **~ly** *adv* individualmente

**indivisible** /ɪndɪ'vɪzəbl/ *a* indivisible

**Indo-China** /ɪndəʊ'tʃaɪnə/ *n* Indochina *f*

**indoctrinat|e** /ɪn'dɒktrɪneɪt/ *vt* adoctrinar. **~ion** /-'neɪʃn/ *n* adoctrinamiento *m*

**indolen|ce** /'ɪndələns/ *n* indolencia *f*. **~t** *a* indolente

**indomitable** /ɪn'dɒmɪtəbl/ *a* indomable

**Indonesia** /ɪndəʊ'niːzɪə/ *n* Indonesia *f*. **~n** *a & n* indonesio (*m*)

**indoor** /'ɪndɔː(r)/ *a* interior; ⟨*clothes etc*⟩ de casa; (*covered*) cubierto. **~s** *adv* dentro; (*at home*) en casa

**induce** /ɪn'djuːs/ *vt* inducir; (*cause*) provocar. **~ment** *n* incentivo *m*

**induct** /ɪn'dʌkt/ *vt* instalar; (*mil, Amer*) incorporar

**indulge** /ɪn'dʌldʒ/ *vt* satisfacer ⟨*desires*⟩; complacer ⟨*person*⟩. ● *vi*. **~ in** entregarse a. **~nce** /ɪn'dʌldʒəns/ *n* (*of desires*) satisfacción *f*; (*relig*) indulgencia *f*. **~nt** *a* indulgente

**industrial** /ɪn'dʌstrɪəl/ *a* industrial; ⟨*unrest*⟩ laboral. **~ist** *n* industrial *m & f*. **~ized** *a* industrializado

**industrious** /ɪn'dʌstrɪəs/ *a* trabajador

**industry** /'ɪndəstrɪ/ *n* industria *f*; (*zeal*) aplicación *f*

**inebriated** /ɪ'niːbrɪeɪtɪd/ *a* borracho

**inedible** /ɪn'edɪbl/ *a* incomible

**ineffable** /ɪn'efəbl/ *a* inefable

**ineffective** /ɪnɪ'fektɪv/ *a* ineficaz; ⟨*person*⟩ incapaz

**ineffectual** /ɪnɪ'fektjʊəl/ *a* ineficaz

**inefficien|cy** /ɪnɪ'fɪʃnsɪ/ *n* ineficacia *f*; (*of person*) incompetencia *f*. **~t** *a* ineficaz; ⟨*person*⟩ incompetente

**ineligible** /ɪn'elɪdʒəbl/ *a* inelegible. **be ~ for** no tener derecho a

**inept** /ɪ'nept/ *a* inepto

**inequality** /ɪnɪ'kwɒlətɪ/ *n* desigualdad *f*

**inert** /ɪ'nɜːt/ *a* inerte

**inertia** /ɪ'nɜːʃə/ *n* inercia *f*

**inescapable** /ɪnɪ'skeɪpəbl/ *a* ineludible

**inestimable** /ɪn'estɪməbl/ *a* inestimable

**inevitabl|e** /ɪn'evɪtəbl/ *a* inevitable. **~ly** *adv* inevitablemente

**inexact** /ɪnɪg'zækt/ *a* inexacto

**inexcusable** /ɪnɪk'skjuːsəbl/ *a* imperdonable

**inexhaustible** /ɪnɪg'zɔːstəbl/ *a* inagotable

**inexorable** /ɪn'eksərəbl/ *a* inexorable

**inexpensive** /ɪnɪk'spensɪv/ *a* económico, barato

**inexperience** /ɪnɪk'spɪərɪəns/ *n* falta *f* de experiencia. **~d** *a* inexperto

**inexplicable** /ɪnɪk'splɪkəbl/ *a* inexplicable

**inextricable** /ɪnɪk'strɪkəbl/ *a* inextricable

**infallib|ility** /ɪn'fælɪbɪlətɪ/ *n* infalibilidad *f*. **~le** *a* infalible

**infam|ous** /'ɪnfəməs/ *a* infame. **~y** *n* infamia *f*

**infan|cy** /'ɪnfənsɪ/ *n* infancia *f*. **~t** *n* niño *m*. **~tile** /'ɪnfəntaɪl/ *a* infantil

**infantry** /'ɪnfəntrɪ/ *n* infantería *f*

**infatuat|ed** /ɪn'fætjʊeɪtɪd/ *a*. **be ~ed with** encapricharse por. **~ion** /-'eɪʃn/ *n* encaprichamiento *m*

**infect** /ɪn'fekt/ *vt* infectar; (*fig*) contagiar. **~ s.o. with** contagiar a uno. **~ion** /-'fekʃn/ *n* infección *f*; (*fig*) contagio *m*. **~ious** /ɪn'fekʃəs/ *a* contagioso

**infer** /ɪn'fɜː(r)/ *vt* (*pt* **inferred**) deducir. **~ence** /'ɪnfərəns/ *n* deducción *f*

**inferior** /ɪn'fɪərɪə(r)/ *a* inferior. ● *n* inferior *m & f*. **~ity** /-'ɒrətɪ/ *n* inferioridad *f*

**infernal** /ɪn'fɜːnl/ *a* infernal. **~ly** *adv* (*fam*) atrozmente

**inferno** /ɪn'fɜːnəʊ/ *n* (*pl* **-os**) infierno *m*

**infertil|e** /ɪn'fɜːtaɪl/ *a* estéril. **~ity** /-'tɪlətɪ/ *n* esterilidad *f*

**infest** /ɪn'fest/ *vt* infestar. **~ation** /-'steɪʃn/ *n* infestación *f*

**infidelity** /ɪnfɪ'delətɪ/ *n* infidelidad *f*

**infighting** /'ɪnfaɪtɪŋ/ *n* lucha *f* cuerpo a cuerpo; (*fig*) riñas *fpl* (internas)

**infiltrat|e** /ɪnfɪl'treɪt/ *vt* infiltrar. ● *vi* infiltrarse. **~ion** /-'treɪʃn/ *n* infiltración *f*

**infinite** /'ɪnfɪnət/ *a* infinito. **~ly** *adv* infinitamente

**infinitesimal** /ɪnfɪnɪ'tesɪml/ *a* infinitesimal

**infinitive** /ɪn'fɪnətɪv/ *n* infinitivo *m*

**infinity** /ɪn'fɪnətɪ/ *n* (*infinite distance*) infinito *m*; (*infinite quantity*) infinidad *f*

**infirm** /ɪn'fɜːm/ *a* enfermizo

**infirmary** /ɪn'fɜːmərɪ/ *n* hospital *m*; (*sick bay*) enfermería *f*

**infirmity** /ɪn'fɜːmətɪ/ n enfermedad f, (*weakness*) debilidad f

**inflam|e** /ɪn'fleɪm/ vt inflamar. **~mable** /ɪn'flæməbl/ a inflamable. **~mation** /-ə'meɪʃn/ n inflamación f. **~matory** /ɪn'flæmətərɪ/ a inflamatorio

**inflate** /ɪn'fleɪt/ vt inflar

**inflation** /ɪn'fleɪʃn/ n inflación f. **~ary** a inflacionario

**inflection** /ɪn'flekʃn/ n inflexión f

**inflexible** /ɪn'fleksəbl/ a inflexible

**inflict** /ɪn'flɪkt/ vt infligir (**on** a)

**inflow** /'ɪnfləʊ/ n afluencia f

**influence** /'ɪnflʊəns/ n influencia f. **under the ~** (*drunk, fam*) borracho. ● vt influir, influenciar (*esp LAm*)

**influential** /ɪnflʊ'enʃl/ a influyente

**influenza** /ɪnflʊ'enzə/ n gripe f

**influx** /'ɪnflʌks/ n afluencia f

**inform** /ɪn'fɔːm/ vt informar. **keep ~ed** tener al corriente

**informal** /ɪn'fɔːml/ a (*simple*) sencillo, sin ceremonia; (*unofficial*) oficioso. **~ity** /'mælətɪ/ n falta f de ceremonia. **~ly** adv sin ceremonia

**inform|ant** /ɪn'fɔːmənt/ n informador m. **~ation** /ɪnfə'meɪʃn/ n información f. **~ative** /ɪn'fɔːmətɪv/ a informativo. **~er** /ɪn'fɔːmə(r)/ n denunciante m

**infra-red** /ɪnfrə'red/ a infrarrojo

**infrequent** /ɪn'friːkwənt/ a poco frecuente. **~ly** adv raramente

**infringe** /ɪn'frɪndʒ/ vt infringir. **~ on** usurpar. **~ment** n infracción f

**infuriate** /ɪn'fjʊərɪeɪt/ vt enfurecer

**infus|e** /ɪn'fjuːz/ vt infundir. **~ion** /-ʒn/ n infusión f

**ingen|ious** /ɪn'dʒiːnɪəs/ a ingenioso. **~uity** /ɪndʒɪ'njuːətɪ/ n ingeniosidad f

**ingenuous** /ɪn'dʒenjʊəs/ a ingenuo

**ingest** /ɪn'dʒest/ vt ingerir

**ingot** /'ɪŋgət/ n lingote m

**ingrained** /ɪn'greɪnd/ a arraigado

**ingratiate** /ɪn'greɪʃɪeɪt/ vt. **~ o.s. with** congraciarse con

**ingratitude** /ɪn'grætɪtjuːd/ n ingratitud f

**ingredient** /ɪn'griːdɪənt/ n ingrediente m

**ingrowing** /'ɪngrəʊɪŋ/ a. **~ nail** n uñero m, uña f encarnada

**inhabit** /ɪn'hæbɪt/ vt habitar. **~able** a habitable. **~ant** n habitante m

**inhale** /ɪn'heɪl/ vt aspirar. ● vi (*tobacco*) aspirar el humo

**inherent** /ɪn'hɪərənt/ a inherente. **~ly** adv intrínsecamente

**inherit** /ɪn'herɪt/ vt heredar. **~ance** n herencia f

**inhibit** /ɪn'hɪbɪt/ vt inhibir. **be ~ed** tener inhibiciones. **~ion** /-'bɪʃn/ n inhibición f

**inhospitable** /ɪnhə'spɪtəbl/ a (*place*) inhóspito; (*person*) inhospitalario

**inhuman** /ɪn'hjuːmən/ a inhumano. **~e** /ɪnhjuː'meɪn/ a inhumano. **~ity** /ɪnhjuː'mænətɪ/ n inhumanidad f

**inimical** /ɪ'nɪmɪkl/ a hostil

**inimitable** /ɪ'nɪmɪtəbl/ a inimitable

**iniquit|ous** /ɪ'nɪkwɪtəs/ a inicuo. **~y** /-ətɪ/ n iniquidad f

**initial** /ɪ'nɪʃl/ n inicial f. ● vt (*pt initialled*) firmar con iniciales. **he ~led the document** firmó el documento con sus iniciales. ● a inicial. **~ly** adv al principio

**initiat|e** /ɪ'nɪʃɪeɪt/ vt iniciar; promover (*scheme etc*). **~ion** /-'eɪʃn/ n iniciación f

**initiative** /ɪ'nɪʃətɪv/ n iniciativa f

**inject** /ɪn'dʒekt/ vt inyectar; (*fig*) injertar (*new element*). **~ion** /-ʃn/ n inyección f

**injunction** /ɪn'dʒʌŋkʃn/ n (*court order*) entredicho m

**injur|e** /'ɪndʒə(r)/ vt (*wound*) herir; (*fig, damage*) perjudicar. **~y** /'ɪndʒərɪ/ n herida f; (*damage*) perjuicio m

**injustice** /ɪn'dʒʌstɪs/ n injusticia f

**ink** /ɪŋk/ n tinta f

**inkling** /'ɪŋklɪŋ/ n atisbo m

**ink: ~well** n tintero m. **~y** a manchado de tinta

**inland** /'ɪnlənd/ a interior. ● adv tierra adentro. **I~ Revenue** n Hacienda f

**in-laws** /'ɪnlɔːz/ npl parientes mpl políticos

**inlay** /ɪn'leɪ/ vt (*pt inlaid*) taracear, incrustar. /'ɪnleɪ/ n taracea f, incrustación f

**inlet** /'ɪnlet/ n ensenada f; (*tec*) entrada f

**inmate** /'ɪnmeɪt/ n (*of asylum*) internado m; (*of prison*) preso m

**inn** /ɪn/ n posada f

**innards** /'ɪnədz/ npl tripas fpl

**innate** /ɪ'neɪt/ a innato

**inner** /'ɪnə(r)/ a interior; (*fig*) íntimo. **~most** a más íntimo. **~ tube** n cámara f de aire, llanta f (*LAm*)

**innings** /'ɪnɪŋz/ n invar turno m

**innkeeper** /'ɪnkiːpə(r)/ n posadero m

**innocen|ce** /ˈɪnəsns/ n inocencia f.
~t a & n inocente (m & f)

**innocuous** /ɪˈnɒkjʊəs/ a inocuo

**innovat|e** /ˈɪnəveɪt/ vi innovar.
~ion /-ˈveɪʃn/ n innovación f. ~or n
innovador m

**innuendo** /ɪnjuːˈendəʊ/ n (pl -oes)
insinuación f

**innumerable** /ɪˈnjuːmərəbl/ a innumerable

**inoculat|e** /ɪˈnɒkjʊleɪt/ vt inocular.
~ion /-ˈleɪʃn/ n inoculación f

**inoffensive** /ɪnəˈfensɪv/ a inofensivo

**inoperative** /ɪnˈɒpərətɪv/ a inop-
erante

**inopportune** /ɪnˈɒpətjuːn/ a inoportuno

**inordinate** /ɪˈnɔːdɪnət/ a excesivo.
~ly adv excesivamente

**in-patient** /ˈɪnpeɪʃnt/ n paciente m
interno

**input** /ˈɪnpʊt/ n (data) datos mpl;
(comput process) entrada f, input m;
(elec) energía f

**inquest** /ˈɪnkwest/ n investigación f
judicial

**inquir|e** /ɪnˈkwaɪə(r)/ vi preguntar.
~y n (question) pregunta f; (investigation) investigación f

**inquisition** /ɪnkwɪˈzɪʃn/ n inqui-
sición f

**inquisitive** /ɪnˈkwɪzətɪv/ a inquis-
itivo

**inroad** /ˈɪnrəʊd/ n incursión f

**inrush** /ˈɪnrʌʃ/ n irrupción f

**insan|e** /ɪnˈseɪn/ a loco. ~ity
/-ˈsænəti/ n locura f

**insanitary** /ɪnˈsænɪtəri/ a insalubre

**insatiable** /ɪnˈseɪʃəbl/ a insaciable

**inscri|be** /ɪnˈskraɪb/ vt inscribir;
dedicar (book). ~ption /-ɪpʃn/ n
inscripción f; (in book) dedicatoria f

**inscrutable** /ɪnˈskruːtəbl/ a
inescrutable

**insect** /ˈɪnsekt/ n insecto m. ~icide
/ɪnˈsektɪsaɪd/ n insecticida f

**insecur|e** /ɪnsɪˈkjʊə(r)/ a inseguro.
~ity n inseguridad f

**insemination** /ɪnsemɪˈneɪʃn/ n inse-
minación f

**insensible** /ɪnˈsensəbl/ a insensible;
(unconscious) sin conocimiento

**insensitive** /ɪnˈsensətɪv/ a insensible

**inseparable** /ɪnˈsepərəbl/ a inseparable

**insert** /ˈɪnsɜːt/ n materia f insertada.
/ɪnˈsɜːt/ vt insertar. ~ion /-ʃn/ n
inserción f

**inshore** /ɪnˈʃɔː(r)/ a costero

**inside** /ɪnˈsaɪd/ n interior m. ~ out
al revés; (thoroughly) a fondo. ● a
interior. ● adv dentro. ● prep
dentro de. ~s npl tripas fpl

**insidious** /ɪnˈsɪdɪəs/ a insidioso

**insight** /ˈɪnsaɪt/ n (perception) pene-
tración f, revelación f

**insignia** /ɪnˈsɪgnɪə/ npl insignias fpl

**insignificant** /ɪnsɪgˈnɪfɪkənt/ a insignificante

**insincer|e** /ɪnsɪnˈsɪə(r)/ a poco
sincero. ~ity /-ˈserəti/ n falta f de
sinceridad f

**insinuat|e** /ɪnˈsɪnjʊeɪt/ vt insinuar.
~ion /-ˈeɪʃn/ n insinuación f

**insipid** /ɪnˈsɪpɪd/ a insípido

**insist** /ɪnˈsɪst/ vt/i insistir. ~ on
insistir en; (demand) exigir

**insisten|ce** /ɪnˈsɪstəns/ n insistencia
f. ~t a insistente. ~tly adv con
insistencia

**insolen|ce** /ˈɪnsələns/ n insolencia f.
~t a insolente

**insoluble** /ɪnˈsɒljʊbl/ a insoluble

**insolvent** /ɪnˈsɒlvənt/ a insolvente

**insomnia** /ɪnˈsɒmnɪə/ n insomnio m.
~c /-ɪæk/ n insomne m & f

**inspect** /ɪnˈspekt/ vt inspeccionar;
revisar (ticket). ~ion /-ʃn/ n inspección f. ~or n inspector m; (on train,
bus) revisor m

**inspir|ation** /ɪnspəˈreɪʃn/ n inspi-
ración f. ~e /ɪnˈspaɪə(r)/ vt inspirar

**instability** /ɪnstəˈbɪləti/ n ines-
tabilidad f

**install** /ɪnˈstɔːl/ vt instalar. ~ation
/-əˈleɪʃn/ n instalación f

**instalment** /ɪnˈstɔːlmənt/ n (payment) plazo m; (of serial) entrega f

**instance** /ˈɪnstəns/ n ejemplo m;
(case) caso m. for ~ por ejemplo. in
the first ~ en primer lugar

**instant** /ˈɪnstənt/ a inmediato;
(food) instantáneo. ● n instante m.
~aneous /ɪnstənˈteɪnɪəs/ a instantáneo. ~ly /ˈɪnstəntlɪ/ adv inmediatamente

**instead** /ɪnˈsted/ adv en cambio. ~
of doing en vez de hacer. ~ of s.o.
en lugar de uno

**instep** /ˈɪnstep/ n empeine m

**instigat|e** /ˈɪnstɪgeɪt/ vt instigar.
~ion /-ˈgeɪʃn/ n instigación f. ~or n
instigador m

**instil** /ɪnˈstɪl/ vt (pt instilled) in-
fundir

**instinct** /ˈɪnstɪŋkt/ n instinto m.
~ive /ɪnˈstɪŋktɪv/ a instintivo

**institut|e** /'ɪnstɪtjuːt/ *n* instituto *m*.
● *vt* instituir; iniciar ‹*enquiry etc*›.
**~ion** /-'tjuːʃn/ *n* institución *f*

**instruct** /ɪn'strʌkt/ *vt* instruir;
(*order*) mandar. **~ s.o. in sth**
enseñar algo a uno. **~ion** /-ʃn/ *n*
instrucción *f*. **~ions** /-ʃnz/ *npl* (*for
use*) modo *m* de empleo. **~ive** *a*
instructivo

**instrument** /'ɪnstrəmənt/ *n* instrumento *m*. **~al** /ɪnstrə'mentl/ *a*
instrumental. **be ~al in** contribuir
a. **~alist** *n* instrumentalista *m & f*

**insubordinat|e** /ɪnsə'bɔːdɪnət/ *a*
insubordinado. **~ion** /-'neɪʃn/ *n*
insubordinación *f*

**insufferable** /ɪn'sʌfərəbl/ *a* insufrible, insoportable

**insufficient** /ɪnsə'fɪʃnt/ *a* insuficiente. **~ly** *adv* insuficientemente

**insular** /'ɪnsjʊlə(r)/ *a* insular;
(*narrow-minded*) de miras
estrechas

**insulat|e** /'ɪnsjʊleɪt/ *vt* aislar. **~ing
tape** *n* cinta *f* aisladora/aislante.
**~ion** /-'leɪʃn/ *n* aislamiento *m*

**insulin** /'ɪnsjʊlɪn/ *n* insulina *f*

**insult** /ɪn'sʌlt/ *vt* insultar. /'ɪnsʌlt/
*n* insulto *m*

**insuperable** /ɪn'sjuːpərəbl/ *a*
insuperable

**insur|ance** /ɪn'ʃʊərəns/ *n* seguro *m*.
**~e** *vt* asegurar. **~e that** asegurarse
de que

**insurgent** /ɪn'sɜːdʒənt/ *a & n* insur-
recto (*m*)

**insurmountable** /ɪnsə'maʊntəbl/ *a*
insuperable

**insurrection** /ɪnsə'rekʃn/ *n* in-
surrección *f*

**intact** /ɪn'tækt/ *a* intacto

**intake** /'ɪnteɪk/ *n* (*quantity*) número
*m*; (*mec*) admisión *f*; (*of food*) consumo *m*

**intangible** /ɪn'tændʒəbl/ *a*
intangible

**integral** /'ɪntɪɡrəl/ *a* íntegro. **be an
~ part of** ser parte integrante de

**integrat|e** /'ɪntɪɡreɪt/ *vt* integrar.
● *vi* integrarse. **~ion** /-'ɡreɪʃn/ *n*
integración *f*

**integrity** /ɪn'teɡrətɪ/ *n* integridad *f*

**intellect** /'ɪntəlekt/ *n* intelecto *m*.
**~ual** *a & n* intelectual (*m*)

**intelligen|ce** /ɪn'telɪdʒəns/ *n* inte-
ligencia *f*; (*information*) información *f*. **~t** *a* inteligente. **~tly**
*adv* inteligentemente. **~tsia**
/ɪntelɪ'dʒentsɪə/ *n* intelectualidad *f*

**intelligible** /ɪn'telɪdʒəbl/ *a* inteligible

**intemperance** /ɪn'tempərəns/ *n* in-
moderación *f*

**intend** /ɪn'tend/ *vt* destinar. **~ to do**
tener la intención de hacer. **~ed** *a*
intencionado. ● *n* (*future spouse*)
novio *m*

**intense** /ɪn'tens/ *a* intenso; ‹*person*›
apasionado. **~ly** *adv* intensamente;
(*very*) sumamente

**intensif|ication** /ɪntensɪfɪ'keɪʃn/ *n*
intensificación *f*. **~y** /-faɪ/ *vt*
intensificar

**intensity** /ɪn'tensətɪ/ *n* intensidad *f*

**intensive** /ɪn'tensɪv/ *a* intensivo. **~
care** *n* asistencia *f* intensiva, cui-
dados *mpl* intensivos

**intent** /ɪn'tent/ *n* propósito *m*. ● *a*
atento. **~ on** absorto en. **~ on
doing** resuelto a hacer

**intention** /ɪn'tenʃn/ *n* intención *f*.
**~al** *a* intencional

**intently** /ɪn'tentlɪ/ *adv* atentamente

**inter** /ɪn'tɜː(r)/ *vt* (*pt* **interred**)
enterrar

**inter...** /'ɪntə(r)/ *pref* inter..., entre...

**interact** /ɪntər'ækt/ *vi* obrar recí-
procamente. **~ion** /-ʃn/ *n* interacción *f*

**intercede** /ɪntə'siːd/ *vi* interceder

**intercept** /ɪntə'sept/ *vt* interceptar.
**~ion** /-ʃn/ *n* interceptación *f*; (*in
geometry*) intersección *f*

**interchange** /'ɪntətʃeɪndʒ/ *n* (*road
junction*) cruce *m*. **~able**
/-'tʃeɪndʒəbl/ *a* intercambiable

**intercom** /'ɪntəkɒm/ *n* inter-
comunicador *m*

**interconnected** /ɪntəkə'nektɪd/ *a*
relacionado

**intercourse** /'ɪntəkɔːs/ *n* trato *m*;
(*sexual*) trato *m* sexual

**interest** /'ɪntrest/ *n* interés *m*;
(*advantage*) ventaja *f*. ● *vt* inter-
esar. **~ed** *a* interesado. **be ~ed in**
interesarse por. **~ing** *a* interesante

**interfere** /ɪntə'fɪə(r)/ *vi* entrometerse. **~ in** entrometerse en. **~
with** entrometerse en, interferir en;
interferir ‹*radio*›. **~nce** *n* inter-
ferencia *f*

**interim** *a* provisional. ● *n*. **in the ~**
entre tanto

**interior** /ɪn'tɪərɪə(r)/ *a & n* interior
(*m*)

**interjection** /ɪntəˈdʒekʃn/ n interjección f

**interlock** /ɪntəˈlɒk/ vt/i (tec) engranar

**interloper** /ˈɪntələʊpə(r)/ n intruso m

**interlude** /ˈɪntəluːd/ n intervalo m; (theatre, music) interludio m

**intermarr|iage** /ɪntəˈmærɪdʒ/ n matrimonio m entre personas de distintas razas. ~y vi casarse (con personas de distintas razas)

**intermediary** /ɪntəˈmiːdɪərɪ/ a & n intermediario (m)

**intermediate** /ɪntəˈmiːdɪət/ a intermedio

**interminable** /ɪnˈtɜːmɪnəbl/ a interminable

**intermission** /ɪntəˈmɪʃn/ n pausa f; (theatre) descanso m

**intermittent** /ɪntəˈmɪtnt/ a intermitente. ~ly adv con discontinuidad

**intern** /ɪnˈtɜːn/ vt internar. /ˈɪntɜːn/ n (doctor, Amer) interno m

**internal** /ɪnˈtɜːnl/ a interior. ~ly adv interiormente

**international** /ɪntəˈnæʃənl/ a & n internacional (m)

**internee** /ˌɪntɜːˈniː/ n internado m

**internment** /ɪnˈtɜːnmənt/ n internamiento m

**interplay** /ˈɪntəpleɪ/ n interacción f

**interpolate** /ɪnˈtɜːpəleɪt/ vt interpolar

**interpret** /ɪnˈtɜːprɪt/ vt/i interpretar. ~ation /-ˈteɪʃn/ n interpretación f. ~er n intérprete m & f

**interrelated** /ɪntərɪˈleɪtɪd/ a interrelacionado

**interrogat|e** /ɪnˈterəgeɪt/ vt interrogar. ~ion /-ˈgeɪʃn/ n interrogación f; (session of questions) interrogatorio m

**interrogative** /ɪntəˈrɒgətɪv/ a & n interrogativo (m)

**interrupt** /ɪntəˈrʌpt/ vt interrumpir. ~ion /-ʃn/ n interrupción f

**intersect** /ɪntəˈsekt/ vt cruzar. ● vi (roads) cruzarse; (geometry) intersecarse. ~ion /-ʃn/ n (roads) cruce m; (geometry) intersección f

**interspersed** /ɪntəˈspɜːst/ a disperso. ~ with salpicado de

**intertwine** /ɪntəˈtwaɪn/ vt entrelazar. ● vi entrelazarse

**interval** /ˈɪntəvl/ n intervalo m; (theatre) descanso m. at ~s a intervalos

**interven|e** /ɪntəˈviːn/ vi intervenir. ~tion /-ˈvenʃn/ n intervención f

**interview** /ˈɪntəvjuː/ n entrevista f. ● vt entrevistarse con. ~er n entrevistador m

**intestin|al** /ɪnteˈstaɪnl/ a intestinal. ~e /ɪnˈtestɪn/ n intestino m

**intimacy** /ˈɪntɪməsɪ/ n intimidad f

**intimate**[1] /ˈɪntɪmət/ a íntimo

**intimate**[2] /ˈɪntɪmeɪt/ vt (state) anunciar; (imply) dar a entender

**intimately** /ˈɪntɪmətlɪ/ adv íntimamente

**intimidat|e** /ɪnˈtɪmɪdeɪt/ vt intimidar. ~ion /-ˈdeɪʃn/ n intimidación f

**into** /ˈɪntuː/, unstressed /ˈɪntə/ prep en; (translate) a

**intolerable** /ɪnˈtɒlərəbl/ a intolerable

**intoleran|ce** /ɪnˈtɒlərəns/ n intolerancia f. ~t a intolerante

**intonation** /ɪntəˈneɪʃn/ n entonación f

**intoxicat|e** /ɪnˈtɒksɪkeɪt/ vt embriagar; (med) intoxicar. ~ed a ebrio. ~ion /-ˈkeɪʃn/ n embriaguez f; (med) intoxicación f

**intra...** /ˈɪntrə/ pref intra...

**intractable** /ɪnˈtræktəbl/ a (person) intratable; (thing) muy difícil

**intransigent** /ɪnˈtrænsɪdʒənt/ a intransigente

**intransitive** /ɪnˈtrænsɪtɪv/ a intransitivo

**intravenous** /ɪntrəˈviːnəs/ a intravenoso

**intrepid** /ɪnˈtrepɪd/ a intrépido

**intrica|cy** /ˈɪntrɪkəsɪ/ n complejidad f. ~te a complejo

**intrigu|e** /ɪnˈtriːg/ vt/i intrigar. ● n intriga f. ~ing a intrigante

**intrinsic** /ɪnˈtrɪnsɪk/ a intrínseco. ~ally adv intrínsecamente

**introduc|e** /ɪntrəˈdjuːs/ vt introducir; presentar (person). ~tion /ɪntrəˈdʌkʃn/ n introducción f; (to person) presentación f. ~tory /-tərɪ/ a preliminar

**introspective** /ɪntrəˈspektɪv/ a introspectivo

**introvert** /ˈɪntrəvɜːt/ n introvertido m

**intru|de** /ɪnˈtruːd/ vi entrometerse; (disturb) molestar. ~der n intruso m. ~sion n intrusión f

**intuiti|on** /ɪntjuːˈɪʃn/ n intuición f. ~ve /ɪnˈtjuːɪtɪv/ a intuitivo

**inundat|e** /'ɪnʌndeɪt/ *vt* inundar. **~ion** /-'deɪʃn/ *n* inundación *f*

**invade** /ɪn'veɪd/ *vt* invadir. **~r** /-ə(r)/ *n* invasor *m*

**invalid**[1] /'ɪnvəlɪd/ *n* enfermo *m*, inválido *m*

**invalid**[2] /ɪn'vælɪd/ *a* nulo. **~ate** *vt* invalidar

**invaluable** /ɪn'væljʊəbl/ *a* inestimable

**invariabl|e** /ɪn'veərɪəbl/ *a* invariable. **~y** *adv* invariablemente

**invasion** /ɪn'veɪʒn/ *n* invasión *f*

**invective** /ɪn'vektɪv/ *n* invectiva *f*

**inveigh** /ɪn'veɪ/ *vi* dirigir invectivas (**against** contra)

**inveigle** /ɪn'veɪgl/ *vt* engatusar, persuadir

**invent** /ɪn'vent/ *vt* inventar. **~ion** /-'venʃn/ *n* invención *f*. **~ive** *a* inventivo. **~or** *n* inventor *m*

**inventory** /'ɪnvəntərɪ/ *n* inventario *m*

**invers|e** /ɪn'vɜːs/ *a & n* inverso (*m*). **~ely** *adv* inversamente. **~ion** /ɪn'vɜːʃn/ *n* inversión *f*

**invert** /ɪn'vɜːt/ *vt* invertir. **~ed commas** *npl* comillas *fpl*

**invest** /ɪn'vest/ *vt* invertir. ● *vi*. **~ in** hacer una inversión *f*

**investigat|e** /ɪn'vestɪgeɪt/ *vt* investigar. **~ion** /-'geɪʃn/ *n* investigación *f*. **under ~ion** sometido a examen. **~or** *n* investigador *m*

**inveterate** /ɪn'vetərət/ *a* inveterado

**invidious** /ɪn'vɪdɪəs/ *a* (*hateful*) odioso; (*unfair*) injusto

**invigilat|e** /ɪn'vɪdʒɪleɪt/ *vi* vigilar. **~or** *n* celador *m*

**invigorate** /ɪn'vɪgəreɪt/ *vt* vigorizar; (*stimulate*) estimular

**invincible** /ɪn'vɪnsɪbl/ *a* invencible

**invisible** /ɪn'vɪzəbl/ *a* invisible

**invit|ation** /ɪnvɪ'teɪʃn/ *n* invitación *f*. **~e** /ɪn'vaɪt/ *vt* invitar; (*ask for*) pedir. **~ing** *a* atrayente

**invoice** /'ɪnvɔɪs/ *n* factura *f*. ● *vt* facturar

**invoke** /ɪn'vəʊk/ *vt* invocar

**involuntary** /ɪn'vɒləntərɪ/ *a* involuntario

**involve** /ɪn'vɒlv/ *vt* enredar. **~d** *a* (*complex*) complicado. **~d in** embrollado en. **~ment** *n* enredo *m*

**invulnerable** /ɪn'vʌlnərəbl/ *a* invulnerable

**inward** /'ɪnwəd/ *a* interior. ● *adv* interiormente. **~s** *adv* hacia/para dentro

**iodine** /'aɪədiːn/ *n* yodo *m*

**iota** /aɪ'əʊtə/ *n* (*amount*) pizca *f*

**IOU** /aɪəʊ'juː/ *abbr* (*I owe you*) pagaré *m*

**IQ** /aɪ'kjuː/ *abbr* (*intelligence quotient*) cociente *m* intelectual

**Iran** /ɪ'rɑːn/ *n* Irán *m*. **~ian** /ɪ'reɪnɪən/ *a & n* iraní (*m*)

**Iraq** /ɪ'rɑːk/ *n* Irak *m*. **~i** *a & n* iraquí (*m*)

**irascible** /ɪ'ræsəbl/ *a* irascible

**irate** /aɪ'reɪt/ *a* colérico

**ire** /aɪə(r)/ *n* ira *f*

**Ireland** /'aɪələnd/ *n* Irlanda *f*

**iris** /'aɪərɪs/ *n* (*anat*) iris *m*; (*bot*) lirio *m*

**Irish** /'aɪərɪʃ/ *a* irlandés. ● *n* (*lang*) irlandés *m*. **~man** *n* irlandés *m*. **~woman** *n* irlandesa *f*

**irk** /ɜːk/ *vt* fastidiar. **~some** *a* fastidioso

**iron** /'aɪən/ *n* hierro *m*; (*appliance*) plancha *f*. ● *a* de hierro. ● *vt* planchar. **~ out** allanar. **I~ Curtain** *n* telón *m* de acero

**ironic(al)** /aɪ'rɒnɪk(l)/ *a* irónico

**ironing-board** /'aɪənɪŋbɔːd/ *n* tabla *f* de planchar

**ironmonger** /'aɪənmʌŋgə(r)/ *n* ferretero *m*. **~y** *n* ferretería *f*

**ironwork** /'aɪənwɜːk/ *n* herraje *m*

**irony** /'aɪərənɪ/ *n* ironía *f*

**irrational** /ɪ'ræʃənl/ *a* irracional

**irreconcilable** /ɪrekən'saɪləbl/ *a* irreconciliable

**irrefutable** /ɪrɪ'fjuːtəbl/ *a* irrefutable

**irregular** /ɪ'regjʊlə(r)/ *a* irregular. **~ity** /-'lærətɪ/ *n* irregularidad *f*

**irrelevan|ce** /ɪ'reləvəns/ *n* inoportunidad *f*, impertinencia *f*. **~t** *a* no pertinente

**irreparable** /ɪ'repərəbl/ *a* irreparable

**irreplaceable** /ɪrɪ'pleɪsəbl/ *a* irreemplazable

**irrepressible** /ɪrɪ'presəbl/ *a* irreprimible

**irresistible** /ɪrɪ'zɪstəbl/ *a* irresistible

**irresolute** /ɪ'rezəluːt/ *a* irresoluto, indeciso

**irrespective** /ɪrɪ'spektɪv/ *a*. **~ of** sin tomar en cuenta

**irresponsible** /ɪrɪ'spɒnsəbl/ *a* irresponsable

**irretrievable** /ɪrɪ'triːvəbl/ *a* irrecuperable

**irreverent** /ɪ'revərənt/ *a* irreverente

**irreversible** /ɪrɪˈvɜːsəbl/ *a* irreversible; ‹*decision*› irrevocable

**irrevocable** /ɪˈrevəkəbl/ *a* irrevocable

**irrigat|e** /ˈɪrɪgeɪt/ *vt* regar; (*med*) irrigar. **~ion** /-ˈgeɪʃn/ *n* riego *m*; (*med*) irrigación *f*

**irritable** /ˈɪrɪtəbl/ *a* irritable

**irritat|e** /ˈɪrɪteɪt/ *vt* irritar. **~ion** /-ˈteɪʃn/ *n* irritación *f*

**is** /ɪz/ *see* be

**Islam** /ˈɪzlɑːm/ *n* Islam *m*. **~ic** /ɪzˈlæmɪk/ *a* islámico

**island** /ˈaɪlənd/ *n* isla *f*. **traffic ~** *n* refugio *m* (en la calle). **~er** *n* isleño *m*

**isle** /aɪl/ *n* isla *f*

**isolat|e** /ˈaɪsəleɪt/ *vt* aislar. **~ion** /-ˈleɪʃn/ *n* aislamiento *m*

**isotope** /ˈaɪsətəʊp/ *n* isotopo *m*

**Israel** /ˈɪzreɪl/ *n* Israel *m*. **~i** /ɪzˈreɪlɪ/ *a & n* israelí (*m*)

**issue** /ˈɪʃuː/ *n* asunto *m*; (*outcome*) resultado *m*; (*of magazine etc*) número *m*; (*of stamps*) emisión *f*; (*offspring*) descendencia *f*. **at ~** en cuestión. **take ~ with** oponerse a. ● *vt* distribuir; emitir ‹*stamps etc*›; publicar ‹*book*›. ● *vi*. **~ from** salir de

**isthmus** /ˈɪsməs/ *n* istmo *m*

**it** /ɪt/ *pron* (*subject*) el, ella, ello; (*direct object*) lo, la; (*indirect object*) le; (*after preposition*) él, ella, ello. **~ is hot** hace calor. **~ is me** soy yo. **far from ~** ni mucho menos. **that's ~** eso es. **who is ~?** ¿quién es?

**italic** /ɪˈtælɪk/ *a* bastardillo *m*. **~s** *npl* (letra *f*) bastardilla *f*

**ital|ian** /ɪˈtæljən/ *a & n* italiano (*m*). **I~y** /ˈɪtəlɪ/ *n* Italia *f*

**itch** /ɪtʃ/ *n* picazón *f*. ● *vi* picar. **I'm ~ing to** rabio por. **my arm ~es** me pica el brazo. **~y** *a* que pica

**item** /ˈaɪtəm/ *n* artículo *m*; (*on agenda*) asunto *m*. **news ~** *n* noticia *f*. **~ize** *vt* detallar

**itinerant** /aɪˈtɪnərənt/ *a* ambulante

**itinerary** /aɪˈtɪnərərɪ/ *n* itinerario *m*

**its** /ɪts/ *a* su, sus (*pl*). ● *pron* (el) suyo *m*, (la) suya *f*, (los) suyos *mpl*, (las) suyas *fpl*

**it's** /ɪts/ = **it is**, **it has**

**itself** /ɪtˈself/ *pron* él mismo, ella misma, ello mismo; (*reflexive*) se; (*after prep*) sí mismo, sí misma

**ivory** /ˈaɪvərɪ/ *n* marfil *m*. **~ tower** *n* torre *f* de marfil

**ivy** /ˈaɪvɪ/ *n* hiedra *f*

# J

**jab** /dʒæb/ *vt* (*pt* **jabbed**) pinchar; (*thrust*) hurgonear. ● *n* pinchazo *m*

**jabber** /ˈdʒæbə(r)/ *vi* barbullar. ● *n* farfulla *f*

**jack** /dʒæk/ *n* (*mec*) gato *m*; (*cards*) sota *f*. ● *vt*. **~ up** alzar con gato

**jackal** /ˈdʒækl/ *n* chacal *m*

**jackass** /ˈdʒækæs/ *n* burro *m*

**jackdaw** /ˈdʒækdɔː/ *n* grajilla *f*

**jacket** /ˈdʒækɪt/ *n* chaqueta *f*, saco *m* (*LAm*); (*of book*) sobrecubierta *f*, camisa *f*

**jack-knife** /ˈdʒæknaɪf/ *n* navaja *f*

**jackpot** /ˈdʒækpɒt/ *n* premio *m* gordo. **hit the ~** sacar el premio gordo

**jade** /dʒeɪd/ *n* (*stone*) jade *m*

**jaded** /ˈdʒeɪdɪd/ *a* cansado

**jagged** /ˈdʒægɪd/ *a* dentado

**jaguar** /ˈdʒægjʊə(r)/ *n* jaguar *m*

**jail** /dʒeɪl/ *n* cárcel *m*. **~bird** *n* criminal *m* emperdernido. **~er** *n* carcelero *m*

**jalopy** /dʒəˈlɒpɪ/ *n* cacharro *m*

**jam**[1] /dʒæm/ *vt* (*pt* **jammed**) interferir con ‹*radio*›; ‹*traffic*› embotellar; ‹*people*› agolparse en. ● *vi* obstruirse; ‹*mechanism etc*› atascarse. ● *n* (*of people*) agolpamiento *m*; (*of traffic*) embotellamiento *m*; (*situation, fam*) apuro *m*

**jam**[2] /dʒæm/ *n* mermelada *f*

**Jamaica** /dʒəˈmeɪkə/ *n* Jamaica *f*

**jamboree** /dʒæmbəˈriː/ *n* reunión *f*

**jam-packed** /ˈdʒæmˈpækt/ *a* atestado

**jangle** /ˈdʒæŋgl/ *n* sonido *m* metálico (y áspero). ● *vt/i* sonar discordemente

**janitor** /ˈdʒænɪtə(r)/ *n* portero *m*

**January** /ˈdʒænjʊərɪ/ *n* enero *m*

**Japan** /dʒəˈpæn/ *n* el Japón *m*. **~ese** /dʒæpəˈniːz/ *a & n* japonés (*m*)

**jar**[1] /dʒɑː(r)/ *n* tarro *m*, frasco *m*

**jar**[2] /dʒɑː(r)/ *vi* (*pt* **jarred**) ‹*sound*› sonar mal; ‹*colours*› chillar. ● *vt* sacudir

**jar**[3] /dʒɑː(r)/ *n*. **on the ~** (*ajar*) entreabierta

**jargon** /ˈdʒɑːgən/ *n* jerga *f*

**jarring** /ˈdʒɑːrɪŋ/ *a* discorde

**jasmine** /ˈdʒæsmɪn/ *n* jazmín *m*

**jaundice** /ˈdʒɔːndɪs/ *n* ictericia *f*. **~d** *a* (*envious*) envidioso; (*bitter*) amargado

**jaunt** /dʒɔːnt/ *n* excursión *f*

**jaunty** /'dʒɔ:ntɪ/ *a* (**-ier, -iest**) garboso

**javelin** /'dʒævəlɪn/ *n* jabalina *f*

**jaw** /dʒɔ:/ *n* mandíbula *f*. ● *vi* (*talk lengthily, sl*) hablar por los codos

**jay** /dʒeɪ/ *n* arrendajo *m*. ~**walk** *vi* cruzar la calle descuidadamente

**jazz** /dʒæz/ *n* jazz *m*. ● *vt*. ~ **up** animar. ~**y** *a* chillón

**jealous** /'dʒeləs/ *a* celoso. ~**y** *n* celos *mpl*

**jeans** /dʒi:nz/ *npl* (pantalones *mpl*) vaqueros *mpl*

**jeep** /dʒi:p/ *n* jeep *m*

**jeer** /dʒɪə(r)/ *vt/i.* ~ **at** mofarse de, befar; (*boo*) abuchear. ● *n* mofa *f*; (*boo*) abucheo *m*

**jell** /dʒel/ *vi* cuajar. ~**ied** *a* en gelatina

**jelly** /'dʒelɪ/ *n* jalea *f*. ~**fish** *n* medusa *f*

**jeopard|ize** /'dʒepədaɪz/ *vt* arriesgar. ~**y** *n* peligro *m*

**jerk** /dʒɜ:k/ *n* sacudida *f*; (*fool, sl*) idiota *m & f*. ● *vt* sacudir. ~**ily** *adv* a sacudidas. ~**y** *a* espasmódico

**jersey** /'dʒɜ:zɪ/ *n* (*pl* **-eys**) jersey *m*

**jest** /dʒest/ *n* broma *f*. ● *vi* bromear. ~**er** *n* bufón *m*

**Jesus** /'dʒi:zəs/ *n* Jesús *m*

**jet**¹ /dʒet/ *n* (*stream*) chorro *m*; (*plane*) yet *m*, avión *m* de propulsión por reacción

**jet**² /dʒet/ *n* (*mineral*) azabache *m*. ~**black** *a* de azabache, como el azabache

**jet:** ~ **lag** *n* cansancio *m* retardado después de un vuelo largo. **have** ~ **lag** estar desfasado. ~**propelled** *a* (de propulsión) a reacción

**jettison** /'dʒetɪsn/ *vt* echar al mar; (*fig, discard*) deshacerse de

**jetty** /'dʒetɪ/ *n* muelle *m*

**Jew** /dʒu:/ *n* judío *m*

**jewel** /'dʒu:əl/ *n* joya *f*. ~**led** *a* enjoyado. ~**ler** *n* joyero *m*. ~**lery** *n* joyas *fpl*

**Jew:** ~**ess** *n* judía *f*. ~**ish** *a* judío. ~**ry** /'dʒʊərɪ/ *n* los judíos *mpl*

**jib**¹ /dʒɪb/ *n* (*sail*) foque *m*

**jib**² /dʒɪb/ *vi* (*pt* **jibbed**) rehusar. ~ **at** oponerse a.

**jiffy** /'dʒɪfɪ/ *n* momentito *m*. **do sth in a** ~ hacer algo en un santiamén

**jig** /dʒɪg/ *n* (*dance*) giga *f*

**jiggle** /'dʒɪgl/ *vt* zangolotear

**jigsaw** /'dʒɪgsɔ:/ *n* rompecabezas *m invar*

**jilt** /dʒɪlt/ *vt* plantar, dejar plantado

**jingle** /'dʒɪŋgl/ *vt* hacer sonar. ● *vi* tintinear. ● *n* tintineo *m*; (*advert*) anuncio *m* cantado

**jinx** /dʒɪŋks/ *n* (*person*) gafe *m*; (*spell*) maleficio *m*

**jitter|s** /'dʒɪtəz/ *npl*. **have the** ~**s** estar nervioso. ~**y** /-ərɪ/ *a* nervioso. **be** ~**y** estar nervioso

**job** /dʒɒb/ *n* trabajo *m*; (*post*) empleo *m*, puesto *m*. **have a** ~ **doing** costar trabajo hacer. **it is a good** ~ **that** menos mal que. ~**centre** *n* bolsa *f* de trabajo. ~**less** *a* sin trabajo.

**jockey** /'dʒɒkɪ/ *n* jockey *m*. ● *vi* (*manoeuvre*) maniobrar (**for** para)

**jocular** /'dʒɒkjʊlə(r)/ *a* jocoso

**jog** /dʒɒg/ *vt* (*pt* **jogged**) empujar; refrescar ‹*memory*›. ● *vi* hacer footing. ~**ging** *n* jogging *m*

**join** /dʒɔɪn/ *vt* unir, juntar; hacerse socio de ‹*club*›; hacerse miembro de ‹*political group*›; alistarse en ‹*army*›; reunirse con ‹*another person*›. ● *vi* ‹*roads etc*› empalmar; ‹*rivers*› confluir. ~ **in** participar (en). ~ **up** (*mil*) alistarse. ● *n* juntura

**joiner** /'dʒɔɪnə(r)/ *n* carpintero *m*

**joint** /dʒɔɪnt/ *a* común. ~ **author** *n* coautor *m*. ● *n* (*join*) juntura *f*; (*anat*) articulación *f*; (*culin*) asado *m*; (*place, sl*) garito *m*; (*marijuana, sl*) cigarillo de marijuana. **out of** ~ descoyuntado. ~**ly** *adv* conjuntamente

**joist** /dʒɔɪst/ *n* viga *f*

**jok|e** /dʒəʊk/ *n* broma *f*; (*funny story*) chiste *m*. ● *vi* bromear. ~**er** *n* bromista *m & f*; (*cards*) comodín *m*. ~**ingly** *adv* en broma

**joll|ification** /dʒɒlɪfɪ'keɪʃn/ *n* jolgorio *m*. ~**ity** *n* jolgorio *m*. ~**y** *a* (**-ier, -iest**) alegre. ● *adv* (*fam*) muy

**jolt** /dʒɒlt/ *vt* sacudir. ● *vt* ‹*vehicle*› traquetear. ● *n* sacudida *f*

**Jordan** /'dʒɔ:dən/ *n* Jordania *f*. ~**ian** *a & n* /-'deɪnɪən/ jordano (*m*)

**jostle** /'dʒɒsl/ *vt/i* empujar(se)

**jot** /dʒɒt/ *n* pizca *f*. ● *vt* (*pt* **jotted**) apuntar. ~**ter** *n* bloc *m*

**journal** /'dʒɜ:nl/ *n* (*diary*) diario *m*; (*newspaper*) periódico *m*; (*magazine*) revista *f*. ~**ese** /dʒɜ:nə'li:z/ *n* jerga *f* periodística. ~**ism** *n* periodismo *m*. ~**ist** *n* periodista *m & f*

**journey** /'dʒɜ:nɪ/ *n* viaje *m*. ● *vi* viajar

**jovial** /'dʒəʊvɪəl/ *a* jovial

**jowl** /dʒaʊl/ *n* (*jaw*) quijada *f*; (*cheek*) mejilla *f*. **cheek by** ~ muy cerca

**joy** /dʒɔɪ/ n alegría f. ~**ful** a alegre. ~**ride** n paseo m en coche sin permiso del dueño. ~**ous** a alegre

**jubila|nt** /'dʒu:bɪlənt/ a jubiloso. ~**tion** /-'leɪʃn/ n júbilo m

**jubilee** /'dʒu:bɪli:/ n aniversario m especial

**Judaism** /'dʒu:deɪɪzəm/ n judaísmo m

**judder** /dʒʌdə(r)/ vi vibrar. ● n vibración f

**judge** /dʒʌdʒ/ n juez m. ● vt juzgar. ~**ment** n juicio m

**judicia|l** /dʒu:'dɪʃl/ a judicial. ~**ry** n magistratura f

**judicious** /dʒu:'dɪʃəs/ a juicioso

**judo** /'dʒu:dəʊ/ n judo m

**jug** /dʒʌg/ n jarra f

**juggernaut** /'dʒʌgənɔ:t/ n (lorry) camión m grande

**juggle** /'dʒʌgl/ vt/i hacer juegos malabares (con). ~**r** n malabarista m & f

**juic|e** /dʒu:s/ n jugo m, zumo m. ~**y** a jugoso, zumoso; ⟨story etc⟩ (fam) picante

**juke-box** /'dʒu:kbɒks/ n tocadiscos m invar tragaperras

**July** /dʒu:'laɪ/ n julio m

**jumble** /'dʒʌmbl/ vt mezclar. ● n (muddle) revoltijo m. ~ **sale** n venta f de objetos usados, mercadillo m

**jumbo** /'dʒʌmbəʊ/ a. ~ **jet** n jumbo m

**jump** /dʒʌmp/ vt/i saltar. ~ **the gun** obrar prematuramente. ~ **the queue** colarse. ● vi saltar; ⟨start⟩ asustarse; ⟨prices⟩ alzarse. ~ **at** apresurarse a aprovechar. ● n salto m; ⟨start⟩ susto m; ⟨increase⟩ aumento m

**jumper** /'dʒʌmpə(r)/ n jersey m; ⟨dress, Amer⟩ mandil m, falda f con peto

**jumpy** /'dʒʌmpɪ/ a nervioso

**junction** /'dʒʌŋkʃn/ n juntura f; ⟨of roads⟩ cruce m, entronque m (LAm); ⟨rail⟩ empalme m, entronque m (LAm)

**juncture** /'dʒʌŋktʃə(r)/ n momento m; ⟨state of affairs⟩ coyuntura f

**June** /dʒu:n/ n junio m

**jungle** /'dʒʌŋgl/ n selva f

**junior** /'dʒu:nɪə(r)/ a (in age) más joven (**to** que); (in rank) subalterno. ● n menor m. ~ **school** n escuela f

**junk** /dʒʌŋk/ n trastos mpl viejos. ● vt (fam) tirar

**junkie** /'dʒʌŋkɪ/ n (sl) drogadicto m

**junk shop** /'dʒʌŋkʃɒp/ n tienda f de trastos viejos

**junta** /'dʒʌntə/ n junta f

**jurisdiction** /dʒʊərɪs'dɪkʃn/ n jurisdicción f

**jurisprudence** /dʒʊərɪs'pru:dəns/ n jurisprudencia f

**juror** /'dʒʊərə(r)/ n jurado m

**jury** /'dʒʊərɪ/ n jurado m

**just** /dʒʌst/ a (fair) justo. ● adv exactamente; (slightly) apenas; (only) sólo, solamente. ~ **as tall** tan alto (**as** como). ~ **listen!** ¡escucha! **he has** ~ **left** acaba de marcharse

**justice** /'dʒʌstɪs/ n justicia f. **J~ of the Peace** juez m de paz

**justif|iable** /dʒʌstɪ'faɪəbl/ a justificable. ~**iably** adv con razón. ~**ication** /dʒʌstɪfɪ'keɪʃn/ n justificación f. ~**y** /'dʒʌstɪfaɪ/ vt justificar

**justly** /'dʒʌstlɪ/ adv con justicia

**jut** /dʒʌt/ vi (pt jutted). ~ **out** sobresalir

**juvenile** /'dʒu:vənaɪl/ a juvenil; (childish) infantil. ● n joven m & f. ~ **court** n tribunal m de menores

**juxtapose** /dʒʌkstə'pəʊz/ vt yuxtaponer

# K

**kaleidoscope** /kə'laɪdəskəʊp/ n caleidoscopio m

**kangaroo** /kæŋgə'ru:/ n canguro m

**kapok** /'keɪpɒk/ n miraguano m

**karate** /kə'rɑ:tɪ/ n karate m

**kebab** /kɪ'bæb/ n broqueta f

**keel** /ki:l/ n (of ship) quilla f. ● vi. ~ **over** volcarse

**keen** /ki:n/ a (-er, -est) ⟨interest, feeling⟩ vivo; ⟨wind, mind, analysis⟩ penetrante; ⟨edge⟩ afilado; ⟨appetite⟩ bueno; ⟨eyesight⟩ agudo; ⟨eager⟩ entusiasta. **be** ~ **on** gustarle a uno. **he's** ~ **on Shostakovich** le gusta Shostakovich. ~**ly** adv vivamente; (enthusiastically) con entusiasmo. ~**ness** n intensidad f; (enthusiasm) entusiasmo m.

**keep** /ki:p/ vt (pt kept) guardar; cumplir ⟨promise⟩; tener ⟨shop, animals⟩; mantener ⟨family⟩; observar ⟨rule⟩; (celebrate) celebrar; (delay) detener; (prevent) impedir. ● vi ⟨food⟩ conservarse; (remain) quedarse. ● n subsistencia f; (of castle) torreón *m*. **for ~s** (*fam*) para siempre. **~ back** *vt* retener. ● *vi* no acercarse. **~ in** no dejar salir. **~ in with** mantenerse en buenas relaciones con. **~ out** no dejar entrar. **~ up** mantener. **~ up (with)** estar al día (en). **~er** *n* guarda *m*

**keeping** /'ki:pɪŋ/ *n* cuidado *m*. **in ~ with** de acuerdo con

**keepsake** /'ki:pseɪk/ *n* recuerdo *m*

**keg** /keg/ *n* barrilete *m*

**kennel** /'kenl/ *n* perrera *f*

**Kenya** /'kenjə/ *n* Kenia *f*

**kept** /kept/ *see* **keep**

**kerb** /kɜ:b/ *n* bordillo *m*

**kerfuffle** /kə'fʌfl/ *n* (*fuss, fam*) lío *m*

**kernel** /'kɜ:nl/ *n* almendra *f*; (*fig*) meollo *m*

**kerosene** /'kerəsi:n/ *n* queroseno *m*

**ketchup** /'ketʃʌp/ *n* salsa *f* de tomate

**kettle** /'ketl/ *n* hervidor *m*

**key** /ki:/ *n* llave *f*; (*of typewriter, piano etc*) tecla *f*. ● *a* clave. *vt*. **~ up** excitar. **~board** *n* teclado *m*. **~hole** *n* ojo *m* de la cerradura. **~note** *n* (*mus*) tónica *f*; (*speech*) idea *f* fundamental. **~ring** *n* llavero *m*. **~stone** *n* piedra *f* clave

**khaki** /'ka:ki/ *a* caqui

**kibbutz** /kɪ'bʊts/ *n* (*pl* **-im** /-i:m/ *or* **-es**) kibbutz *m*

**kick** /kɪk/ *vt* dar una patada a; ⟨*animals*⟩ tirar una coz a. ● *vi* dar patadas; ⟨*firearm*⟩ dar culatazo. ● *n* patada *f*; (*of animal*) coz *f*; (*of firearm*) culatazo *m*; (*thrill, fam*) placer *m*. **~ out** (*fam*) echar a patadas. **~ up** armar ⟨*fuss etc*⟩. **~back** *n* culatazo *m*; (*payment*) soborno *m*. **~off** *n* (*sport*) saque *m* inicial

**kid** /kɪd/ *n* (*young goat*) cabrito *m*; (*leather*) cabritilla *f*; (*child, sl*) chaval *m*. ● *vt* (*pt* **kidded**) tomar el pelo a. ● *vi* bromear

**kidnap** /'kɪdnæp/ *vt* (*pt* **kidnapped**) secuestrar. **~ping** *n* secuestro *m*

**kidney** /'kɪdnɪ/ *n* riñón *m*. ● *a* renal

**kill** /kɪl/ *vt* matar; (*fig*) acabar con. ● *n* matanza *f*; (*in hunt*) pieza(s) *f*(*pl*). **~er** *n* matador *m*; (*murderer*) asesino *m*. **~ing** *n* matanza *f*; (*murder*) asesinato *m*. ● *a* (*funny, fam*) para morirse de risa; (*tiring, fam*) agotador. **~joy** *n* aguafiestas *m & f invar*

**kiln** /kɪln/ *n* horno *m*

**kilo** /'ki:ləʊ/ *n* (*pl* **-os**) kilo *m*

**kilogram(me)** /'kɪləgræm/ *n* kilogramo *m*

**kilohertz** /'kɪləhɜ:ts/ *n* kilohercio *m*

**kilometre** /'kɪləmi:tə(r)/ *n* kilómetro *m*

**kilowatt** /'kɪləwɒt/ *n* kilovatio *m*

**kilt** /kɪlt/ *n* falda *f* escocesa

**kin** /kɪn/ *n* parientes *mpl*. **next of ~** pariente *m* más próximo, parientes *mpl* más próximos

**kind**[1] /kaɪnd/ *n* clase *f*. **~ of** (*somewhat, fam*) un poco. **in ~** en especie. **be two of a ~** ser tal para cual

**kind**[2] /kaɪnd/ *a* amable

**kindergarten** /'kɪndəga:tn/ *n* escuela *f* de párvulos

**kind-hearted** /kaɪnd'ha:tɪd/ *a* bondadoso

**kindle** /'kɪndl/ *vt/i* encender(se)

**kind: ~liness** *n* bondad *f*. **~ly** *a* (**-ier, -iest**) bondadoso. ● *adv* bondadosamente; (*please*) haga el favor de. **~ness** *n* bondad *f*

**kindred** /'kɪndrɪd/ *a* emparentado. **~ spirits** *npl* almas *fpl* afines

**kinetic** /kɪ'netɪk/ *a* cinético

**king** /kɪŋ/ *n* rey *m*

**kingdom** /'kɪŋdəm/ *n* reino *m*

**kingpin** /'kɪŋpɪn/ *n* (*person*) persona *f* clave; (*thing*) piedra *f* angular

**king-size(d)** /'kɪŋsaɪz(d)/ *a* extraordinariamente grande

**kink** /kɪŋk/ *n* (*in rope*) retorcimiento *m*; (*fig*) manía *f*. **~y** *a* (*fam*) pervertido

**kiosk** /'ki:ɒsk/ *n* quiosco *m*. **telephone ~** cabina *f* telefónica

**kip** /kɪp/ *n* (*sl*) sueño *m*. ● *vi* (*pt* **kipped**) dormir

**kipper** /'kɪpə(r)/ *n* arenque *m* ahumado

**kiss** /kɪs/ *n* beso *m*. ● *vt/i* besar(se)

**kit** /kɪt/ *n* avíos *mpl*; (*tools*) herramientos *mpl*. ● *vt* (*pt* **kitted**). **~ out** equipar de. **~bag** *n* mochila *f*

**kitchen** /'kɪtʃɪn/ *n* cocina *f*. **~ette** /kɪtʃɪ'net/ *n* cocina *f* pequeña. **~ garden** *n* huerto *m*

**kite** /kaɪt/ *n* (*toy*) cometa *f*

**kith** /kɪθ/ *n*. **~ and kin** amigos *mpl* y parientes *mpl*

**kitten** /'kɪtn/ *n* gatito *m*

**kitty** /'kɪtɪ/ *n* (*fund*) fondo *m* común

**kleptomaniac** /kleptəʊ'meɪnɪæk/ *n* cleptómano *m*

**knack** /næk/ *n* truco *m*

**knapsack** /'næpsæk/ *n* mochila *f*

**knave** /neɪv/ *n* (*cards*) sota *f*

**knead** /ni:d/ *vt* amasar

**knee** /ni:/ *n* rodilla *f*. **~cap** *n* rótula *f*

**kneel** /niːl/ *vi* (*pt* **knelt**). ~ **(down)** arrodillarse

**knees-up** /'niːzʌp/ *n* (*fam*) baile *m*

**knell** /nel/ *n* toque *m* de difuntos

**knelt** /nelt/ *see* **kneel**

**knew** /njuː/ *see* **know**

**knickerbockers** /'nɪkəbɒkəz/ *npl* pantalón *m* bombacho

**knickers** /'nɪkəz/ *npl* bragas *fpl*

**knick-knack** /'nɪknæk/ *n* chuchería *f*

**knife** /naɪf/ *n* (*pl* **knives**) cuchillo *m*. ● *vt* acuchillar

**knight** /naɪt/ *n* caballero *m*; (*chess*) caballo *m*. ● *vt* conceder el título de Sir a. ~**hood** *n* título *m* de Sir

**knit** /nɪt/ *vt* (*pt* **knitted** *or* **knit**) tejer. ● *vi* hacer punto. ~ **one's brow** fruncir el ceño. ~**ting** *n* labor *f* de punto. ~**wear** *n* artículos *mpl* de punto

**knob** /nɒb/ *n* botón *m*; (*of door, drawer etc*) tirador *m*. ~**bly** *a* nudoso

**knock** /nɒk/ *vt* golpear; (*criticize*) criticar. ● *vi* golpear; (*at door*) llamar. ● *n* golpe *m*. ~ **about** *vt* maltratar. ● *vi* rodar. ~ **down** derribar; atropellar (*person*); rebajar (*prices*). ~ **off** *vt* hacer caer; (*complete quickly, fam*) despachar; (*steal, sl*) birlar. ● *vi* (*finish work, fam*) terminar, salir del trabajo. ~ **out** (*by blow*) dejar sin conocimiento; (*eliminate*) eliminar; (*tire*) agotar. ~ **over** tirar; atropellar (*person*). ~ **up** preparar de prisa (*meal etc*). ~**down** *a* (*price*) de saldo. ~**er** *n* aldaba *f*. ~**kneed** *a* patizambo. ~**out** *n* (*boxing*) knockout *m*

**knot** /nɒt/ *n* nudo *m*. ● *vt* (*pt* **knotted**) anudar. ~**ty** /'nɒtɪ/ *a* nudoso

**know** /nəʊ/ *vt* (*pt* **knew**) saber; (*be acquainted with*) conocer. ● *vi* saber. ● *n*. **be in the** ~ estar al tanto. ~ **about** entender de (*cars etc*). ~ **of** saber de. ~**all** *n*, ~**it-all** (*Amer*) *n* sabelotodo *m & f*. ~**how** *n* habilidad *f*. ~**ingly** *adv* deliberadamente

**knowledge** /'nɒlɪdʒ/ *n* conocimiento *m*; (*learning*) conocimientos *mpl*. ~**able** *a* informado

**known** /nəʊn/ *see* **know**. ● *a* conocido

**knuckle** /'nʌkl/ *n* nudillo *m*. ● *vi*. ~ **under** someterse

**Koran** /kə'rɑːn/ *n* Corán *m*, Alcorán *m*

**Korea** /kə'rɪə/ *n* Corea *f*

**kosher** /'kəʊʃə(r)/ *a* preparado según la ley judía

**kowtow** /kaʊ'taʊ/ *vi* humillarse (**to** ante)

**kudos** /'kjuːdɒs/ *n* prestigio *m*

# L

**lab** /læb/ *n* (*fam*) laboratorio *m*

**label** /'leɪbl/ *n* etiqueta *f*. ● *vt* (*pt* **labelled**) poner etiqueta a; (*fig, describe as*) describir como

**laboratory** /lə'bɒrətərɪ/ *n* laboratorio *m*

**laborious** /lə'bɔːrɪəs/ *a* penoso

**labour** /'leɪbə(r)/ *n* trabajo *m*; (*workers*) mano *f* de obra. **in** ~ de parto. ● *vi* trabajar. ● *vt* insistir en

**Labour** /'leɪbə(r)/ *n* el partido *m* laborista. ● *a* laborista

**laboured** /'leɪbəd/ *a* penoso

**labourer** /'leɪbərə(r)/ *n* obrero *m*; (*on farm*) labriego *m*

**labyrinth** /'læbərɪnθ/ *n* laberinto *m*

**lace** /leɪs/ *n* encaje *m*; (*of shoe*) cordón *m*, agujeta *f* (*Mex*). ● *vt* (*fasten*) atar. ~ **with** echar a (*a drink*)

**lacerate** /'læsəreɪt/ *vt* lacerar

**lack** /læk/ *n* falta *f*. **for** ~ **of** por falta de. ● *vt* faltarle a uno. **he** ~**s money** carece de dinero. **be** ~**ing** faltar

**lackadaisical** /lækə'deɪzɪkl/ *a* indolente, apático

**lackey** /'lækɪ/ *n* lacayo *m*

**laconic** /lə'kɒnɪk/ *a* lacónico

**lacquer** /'lækə(r)/ *n* laca *f*

**lad** /læd/ *n* muchacho *m*

**ladder** /'lædə(r)/ *n* escalera *f* (de mano); (*in stocking*) carrera *f*. ● *vt* hacer una carrera en. ● *vi* hacerse una carrera

**laden** /'leɪdn/ *a* cargado (**with** de)

**ladle** /'leɪdl/ *n* cucharón *m*

**lady** /'leɪdɪ/ *n* señora *f*. **young** ~ señorita *f*. ~**bird** *n*, ~**bug** *n* (*Amer*) mariquita *f*. ~ **friend** *n* amiga *f*. ~**in-waiting** *n* dama *f* de honor. ~**like** *a* distinguido. ~**ship** *n* Señora *f*

**lag**[1] /læg/ *vi* (*pt* **lagged**). ~ **(behind)** retrasarse. ● *n* (*interval*) intervalo *m*

**lag**[2] /læg/ *vt* (*pt* **lagged**) revestir (*pipes*)

**lager** /'lɑːgə(r)/ *n* cerveza *f* dorada

**laggard** /'lægəd/ *n* holgazán *m*

**lagging** /'lægɪŋ/ n revestimiento m calorífugo

**lagoon** /lə'guːn/ n laguna f

**lah** /lɑː/ n (mus, sixth note of any musical scale) la m

**laid** /leɪd/ see **lay**[1]

**lain** /leɪn/ see **lie**[1]

**lair** /leə(r)/ n guarida f

**laity** /'leɪətɪ/ n laicado m

**lake** /leɪk/ n lago m

**lamb** /læm/ n cordero m. **~swool** lana f de cordero

**lame** /leɪm/ a (-er, -est) cojo; ⟨excuse⟩ poco convincente. **~ly** adv ⟨argue⟩ con poca convicción f

**lament** /lə'ment/ n lamento m. ● vt/i lamentarse (de). **~able** /'læməntəbl/ a lamentable

**laminated** /'læmɪneɪtɪd/ a laminado

**lamp** /læmp/ n lámpara f. **~post** n farol m. **~shade** n pantalla f

**lance** /lɑːns/ n lanza f. ● vt (med) abrir con lanceta. **~corporal** n cabo m interino

**lancet** /'lɑːnsɪt/ n lanceta f

**land** /lænd/ n tierra f; ⟨country⟩ país m; ⟨plot⟩ terreno m. ● a terrestre; ⟨breeze⟩ de tierra; ⟨policy, reform⟩ agrario. ● vt desembarcar; ⟨obtain⟩ conseguir; dar ⟨blow⟩; ⟨put⟩ meter. ● vi ⟨from ship⟩ desembarcar; ⟨aircraft⟩ aterrizar; ⟨fall⟩ caer. **~ up** ir a parar

**landed** /'lændɪd/ a hacendado

**landing** /'lændɪŋ/ n desembarque m; (aviat) aterrizaje m; ⟨top of stairs⟩ descanso m. **~stage** n desembarcadero m

**landlady** /'lændleɪdɪ/ n propietaria f; ⟨of inn⟩ patrona f

**land-locked** /'lændlɒkt/ a rodeado de tierra

**landlord** /'lændlɔːd/ n propietario m; ⟨of inn⟩ patrón m

**land: ~mark** n punto m destacado. **~scape** /'lændskeɪp/ n paisaje. ● vt ajardinar. **~slide** n desprendimiento m de tierras; (pol) victoria f arrolladora

**lane** /leɪn/ n ⟨path, road⟩ camino m; ⟨strip of road⟩ carril m; (aviat) ruta f

**language** /'læŋgwɪdʒ/ n idioma m; ⟨speech, style⟩ lenguaje m

**languid** /'læŋgwɪd/ a lánguido. **~ish** /'læŋgwɪʃ/ vi languidecer. **~or** /'læŋgə(r)/ n languidez f

**lank** /læŋk/ a larguirucho; ⟨hair⟩ lacio. **~y** /'læŋkɪ/ a (-ier, -iest) larguirucho

**lantern** /'læntən/ n linterna f

**lap**[1] /læp/ n regazo m

**lap**[2] /læp/ n (sport) vuelta f. ● vt/i (pt lapped). **~ over** n robo m

**lap**[3] /læp/ vt (pt lapped). **~ up** beber a lengüetazos; (fig) aceptar con entusiasmo. ● vi ⟨waves⟩ chapotear

**lapel** /lə'pel/ n solapa f

**lapse** /læps/ vi ⟨decline⟩ degradarse; ⟨expire⟩ caducar; ⟨time⟩ transcurrir. **~ into** recaer en. ● n error m; ⟨of time⟩ intervalo m

**larceny** /'lɑːsənɪ/ n robo m

**lard** /lɑːd/ n manteca f de cerdo

**larder** /'lɑːdə(r)/ n despensa f

**large** /lɑːdʒ/ a (-er, -est) grande, ⟨before singular noun⟩ gran. ● n. at **~** en libertad. **~ly** adv en gran parte. **~ness** n (gran) tamaño m

**largesse** /lɑː'ʒes/ n generosidad f

**lark**[1] /lɑːk/ n alondra f

**lark**[2] /lɑːk/ n broma f; ⟨bit of fun⟩ travesura f. ● vi andar de juerga

**larva** /'lɑːvə/ n (pl -vae /-viː/) larva f

**laryn|gitis** /lærɪn'dʒaɪtɪs/ n laringitis f. **~x** /'lærɪŋks/ n laringe f

**lascivious** /lə'sɪvɪəs/ a lascivo

**laser** /'leɪzə(r)/ n láser m

**lash** /læʃ/ vt azotar. **~ out** ⟨spend⟩ gastar. **~ out against** atacar. ● n latigazo m; ⟨eyelash⟩ pestaña f

**lashings** /'læʃɪŋz/ npl. **~ of** ⟨cream etc, sl⟩ montones de

**lass** /læs/ n muchacha f

**lassitude** /'læsɪtjuːd/ n lasitud f

**lasso** /læ'suː/ n (pl -os) lazo m

**last**[1] /lɑːst/ a último; ⟨week etc⟩ pasado. **~ Monday** n el lunes pasado. **have the ~ word** decir la última palabra. **the ~ straw** n el colmo m. ● adv por último; ⟨most recently⟩ la última vez. **he came ~** llegó el último. ● n último m; ⟨remainder⟩ lo que queda. **~ but one** penúltimo. **at (long) ~** en fin.

**last**[2] /lɑːst/ vi durar. **~ out** sobrevivir

**last**[3] /lɑːst/ n horma f

**lasting** /'lɑːstɪŋ/ a duradero

**last: ~ly** adv por último. **~ night** n anoche m

**latch** /lætʃ/ n picaporte m

**late** /leɪt/ a (-er, -est) ⟨not on time⟩ tarde; ⟨recent⟩ reciente; ⟨former⟩ antiguo, ex; ⟨fruit⟩ tardío; ⟨hour⟩ avanzado; ⟨deceased⟩ difunto. **in ~ July** a fines de julio. **the ~ Dr Phillips** el difunto Dr. Phillips. ● adv tarde. **of ~** últimamente. **~ly** adv últimamente. **~ness** n ⟨delay⟩ retraso m; ⟨of hour⟩ lo avanzado

**latent** /ˈleɪtnt/ a latente

**lateral** /ˈlætərəl/ a lateral

**latest** /ˈleɪtɪst/ a último. **at the ~** a más tardar

**lathe** /leɪð/ n torno m

**lather** /ˈlɑːðə(r)/ n espuma f. ● vt enjabonar. ● vi hacer espuma

**Latin** /ˈlætɪn/ n (lang) latín m. ● a latino

**latitude** /ˈlætɪtjuːd/ n latitud m

**latrine** /ləˈtriːn/ n letrina f

**latter** /ˈlætə(r)/ a último; (of two) segundo. ● n. **the ~** éste m, ésta f, éstos mpl, éstas fpl. **~-day** a moderno. **~ly** adv últimamente

**lattice** /ˈlætɪs/ n enrejado m

**laudable** /ˈlɔːdəbl/ a laudable

**laugh** /lɑːf/ vi reír(se) (**at** de). ● n risa f. **~able** a ridículo. **~ing-stock** n hazmerreír m invar. **~ter** /ˈlɑːftə(r)/ n (act) risa f; (sound of laughs) risas fpl

**launch**[1] /lɔːntʃ/ vt lanzar. ● n lanzamiento m. **~ (out) into** lanzarse a

**launch**[2] /lɔːntʃ/ n (boat) lancha f

**launching pad** /ˈlɔːntʃɪŋpæd/ n plataforma f de lanzamiento

**laund|er** /ˈlɔːndə(r)/ vt lavar (y planchar). **~erette** n lavandería f automática. **~ress** n lavandera f. **~ry** /ˈlɔːndrɪ/ n (place) lavandería f; (dirty clothes) ropa f sucia; (clean clothes) colada f

**laurel** /ˈlɒrəl/ n laurel m

**lava** /ˈlɑːvə/ n lava f

**lavatory** /ˈlævətərɪ/ n retrete m. **public ~** servicios mpl

**lavender** /ˈlævəndə(r)/ n lavanda f

**lavish** /ˈlævɪʃ/ a (person) pródigo; (plentiful) abundante; (lush) suntuoso. ● vt prodigar. **~ly** adv profusamente

**law** /lɔː/ n ley f; (profession, subject of study) derecho m. **~-abiding** a observante de la ley. **~ and order** n orden m público. **~ court** n tribunal m. **~ful** a (permitted by law) lícito; (recognized by law) legítimo. **~fully** adv legalmente. **~less** a sin leyes

**lawn** /lɔːn/ n césped m. **~-mower** n cortacésped f. **~ tennis** n tenis m (sobre hierba)

**lawsuit** /ˈlɔːsuːt/ n pleito m

**lawyer** /ˈlɔːjə(r)/ n abogado m

**lax** /læks/ a descuidado; (morals etc) laxo

**laxative** /ˈlæksətɪv/ n laxante m

**laxity** /ˈlæksətɪ/ n descuido m

**lay**[1] /leɪ/ vt (pt laid) poner (incl table, eggs); tender (trap); formar (plan). **~ hands on** echar mano a. **~ hold of** agarrar. **~ waste** asolar. **~ aside** dejar a un lado. **~ down** dejar a un lado; imponer (condition). **~ into** (sl) dar una paliza a. **~ off** vt despedir (worker); ● vi (fam) terminar. **~ on** (provide) proveer. **~ out** (design) disponer; (display) exponer; desembolsar (money). **~ up** (store) guardar; obligar a guardar cama (person)

**lay**[2] /leɪ/ a (non-clerical) laico; (opinion etc) profano

**lay**[3] /leɪ/ see **lie**

**layabout** /ˈleɪəbaʊt/ n holgazán m

**lay-by** /ˈleɪbaɪ/ n apartadero m

**layer** /ˈleɪə(r)/ n capa f

**layette** /leɪˈet/ n canastilla f

**layman** /ˈleɪmən/ n lego m

**lay-off** /ˈleɪɒf/ n paro m forzoso

**layout** /ˈleɪaʊt/ n disposición f

**laze** /leɪz/ vi holgazanear; (relax) descansar

**laz|iness** /ˈleɪzɪnɪs/ n pereza f. **~y** a perezoso. **~y-bones** n holgazán m

**lb.** abbr (pound) libra f

**lead**[1] /liːd/ vt (pt led) conducir; dirigir (team); llevar (life); (induce) inducir a. ● vi (go first) ir delante; (road) ir, conducir; (in cards) salir. ● n mando m; (clue) pista f; (leash) correa f; (in theatre) primer papel m; (wire) cable m; (example) ejemplo m. **in the ~** en cabeza. **~ away** llevar. **~ up to** preparar el terreno para

**lead**[2] /led/ n plomo m; (of pencil) mina f. **~en** /ˈledn/ a de plomo

**leader** /ˈliːdə(r)/ n jefe m; (leading article) editorial m. **~ship** n dirección f

**leading** /ˈliːdɪŋ/ a principal; (in front) delantero. **~ article** n editorial m

**leaf** /liːf/ n (pl leaves) hoja f. ● vi. **~ through** hojear

**leaflet** /ˈliːflɪt/ n folleto m

**leafy** /ˈliːfɪ/ a frondoso

**league** /liːg/ n liga f. **be in ~ with** conchabarse con

**leak** /liːk/ n (hole) agujero m; (of gas, liquid) escape m; (of information) filtración f; (in roof) gotera f; (in boat) vía f de agua. ● vi (receptacle, gas, liquid) salirse; (information) filtrarse; (drip) gotear; (boat) hacer agua. ● vt dejar escapar; filtrar (in-

*formation*⟩. **~age** *n* = leak. **~y** *a* ⟨*receptacle*⟩ agujereado; ⟨*roof*⟩ que tiene goteras; ⟨*boat*⟩ que hace agua

**lean**¹ /liːn/ *vt* (*pt* **leaned** *or* **leant** /lent/) apoyar. ● *vi* inclinarse. **~ against** apoyarse en. **~ on** apoyarse en. **~out** asomarse (**of** a). **~ over** inclinarse

**lean**² /liːn/ *a* (**-er**, **-est**) magro. ● *n* carne *f* magra

**leaning** /ˈliːnɪŋ/ *a* inclinado. ● *n* inclinación *f*

**leanness** /ˈliːnnɪs/ *n* (*of meat*) magrez *f*; (*of person*) flaqueza *f*

**lean-to** /ˈliːntuː/ *n* colgadizo *m*

**leap** /liːp/ *vi* (*pt* **leaped** *or* **leapt** /lept/) saltar. ● *n* salto *m*. **~-frog** *n* salto *m*, saltacabrilla *f*. ● *vi* (*pt* **-frogged**) jugar a saltacabrilla. **~ year** *n* año *m* bisiesto

**learn** /lɜːn/ *vt/i* (*pt* **learned** *or* **learnt**) aprender (**to do** a hacer). **~ed** /ˈlɜːnɪd/ *a* culto. **~er** /ˈlɜːnə(r)/ *n* principiante *m*; (*apprentice*) aprendiz *m*; (*student*) estudiante *m* & *f*. **~ing** *n* saber *m*

**lease** /liːs/ *n* arriendo *m*. ● *vt* arrendar

**leash** /liːʃ/ *n* correa *f*

**least** /liːst/ *a*. **the ~** (*smallest amount of*) mínimo; (*slightest*) menor; (*smallest*) más pequeño. ● *n* lo menos. **at ~** a por lo menos. **not in the ~** en absoluto. ● *adv* menos

**leather** /ˈleðə(r)/ *n* piel *f*, cuero *m*

**leave** /liːv/ *vt* (*pt* **left**) dejar; (*depart from*) marcharse de. **~ alone** dejar de tocar ⟨*thing*⟩; dejar en paz ⟨*person*⟩. **be left** (*over*) quedar. ● *vi* marcharse; ⟨*train*⟩ salir. ● *n* permiso *m*. **on ~** (*mil*) de permiso. **take one's ~ of** despedirse de. **~ out** omitir

**leavings** /ˈliːvɪŋz/ *npl* restos *mpl*

**Leban|on** /ˈlebənən/ *n* el Líbano *m*. **~ese** /-ˈniːz/ *a* & *n* libanés (*m*)

**lecher** /ˈletʃə(r)/ *n* libertino *m*. **~ous** *a* lascivo. **~y** *n* lascivia *f*

**lectern** /ˈlektɜːn/ *n* atril *m*; (*in church*) facistol *m*

**lecture** /ˈlektʃə(r)/ *n* conferencia *f*; (*univ*) clase *f*; (*rebuke*) sermón *m*. ● *vt/i* dar una conferencia (a); (*univ*) dar clases (a); (*rebuke*) sermonear. **~r** *n* conferenciante *m*; (*univ*) profesor *m*

**led** /led/ *see* **lead**¹

**ledge** /ledʒ/ *n* repisa *f*, (*of window*) antepecho *m*

**ledger** /ˈledʒə(r)/ *n* libro *m* mayor

**lee** /liː/ *n* sotavento *m*; (*fig*) abrigo *m*

**leech** /liːtʃ/ *n* sanguijuela *f*

**leek** /liːk/ *n* puerro *m*

**leer** /ˈlɪə(r)/ *vi*. **~ (at)** mirar impúdicamente. ● *n* mirada *f* impúdica

**leeway** /ˈliːweɪ/ *n* deriva *f*; (*fig, freedom of action*) libertad *f* de acción. **make up ~** recuperar los atrasos

**left**¹ /left/ *a* izquierdo. ● *adv* a la izquierda. ● *n* izquierda *f*

**left**² /left/ *see* **leave**

**left:** **~-hand** *a* izquierdo. **~-handed** *a* zurdo. **~ist** *n* izquierdista *m* & *f*. **~ luggage** *n* consigna *f*. **~overs** *npl* restos *mpl*

**left-wing** /left'wɪŋ/ *a* izquierdista

**leg** /leg/ *n* pierna *f*; (*of animal, furniture*) pata *f*; (*of pork*) pernil *m*; (*of lamb*) pierna *f*; (*of journey*) etapa *f*. **on its last ~s** en las últimas

**legacy** /ˈlegəsɪ/ *n* herencia *f*

**legal** /ˈliːgl/ *a* (*permitted by law*) lícito; (*recognized by law*) legítimo; ⟨*affairs etc*⟩ jurídico. **~ aid** *n* abogacía *f* de pobres. **~ity** /-ˈgælətɪ/ *n* legalidad *f*. **~ize** *vt* legalizar. **~ly** *adv* legalmente

**legation** /lɪˈgeɪʃn/ *n* legación *f*

**legend** /ˈledʒənd/ *n* leyenda *f*. **~ary** *a* legendario

**leggings** /ˈlegɪŋz/ *npl* polainas *fpl*

**legib|ility** /ˈledʒəbɪlətɪ/ *n* legibilidad *f*. **~le** *a* legible. **~ly** *a* legiblemente

**legion** /ˈliːdʒən/ *n* legión *f*

**legislat|e** /ˈledʒɪsleɪt/ *vi* legislar. **~ion** /-ˈleɪʃn/ *n* legislación *f*. **~ive** *a* legislativo. **~ure** /-eɪtʃə(r)/ *n* cuerpo *m* legislativo

**legitima|cy** /lɪˈdʒɪtɪməsɪ/ *f* legitimidad *f*. **~te** *a* legítimo

**leisure** /ˈleʒə(r)/ *n* ocio *m*. **at one's ~** cuando tenga tiempo. **~ly** *adv* sin prisa

**lemon** /ˈlemən/ *n* limón *m*. **~ade** /lemə'neɪd/ *n* (*fizzy*) gaseosa *f* (de limón); (*still*) limonada *f*

**lend** /lend/ *vt* (*pt* **lent**) prestar. **~ itself to** prestarse a. **~er** *n* prestador *m*; (*moneylender*) prestamista *m* & *f*. **~ing** *n* préstamo *m*. **~ing library** *n* biblioteca *f* de préstamo

**length** /leŋθ/ *n* largo *m*; (*in time*) duración *f*; (*of cloth*) largo *m*; (*of road*) tramo *m*. **at ~** (*at last*) por fin. **at (great) ~** detalladamente. **~en**

/'leŋθən/ vt alargar. ● vi alargarse.
**~ways** adv a lo largo. **~y** a largo

**lenien|cy** /'li:nɪənsɪ/ n indulgencia f.
**~t** a indulgente. **~tly** adv con
indulgencia

**lens** /lenz/ n lente f. **contact ~es** npl
lentillas fpl

**lent** /lent/ see **lend**

**Lent** /lent/ n cuaresma f

**lentil** /'lentl/ a (bean) lenteja f

**Leo** /'li:əʊ/ n (astr) Leo m

**leopard** /'lepəd/ n leopardo m

**leotard** /'li:ətɑ:d/ n leotardo m

**lep|er** /'lepə(r)/ n leproso m. **~rosy**
/'leprəsɪ/ n lepra f

**lesbian** /'lezbɪən/ n lesbiana f. ● a
lesbiano

**lesion** /'li:ʒn/ n lesión f

**less** /les/ a (in quantity) menos; (in
size) menor. ● adv & prep menos. **~
than** menos que; (with numbers)
menos de. ● n menor m. **~ and ~**
cada vez menos. **none the ~** sin
embargo. **~en** /'lesn/ vt/i disminuir. **~er** /'lesə(r)/ a menor

**lesson** /'lesn/ n clase f

**lest** /lest/ conj por miedo de que

**let** /let/ vt (pt let, pres p letting)
dejar; (lease) alquilar. **~ me do it**
déjame hacerlo. ● v aux. **~'s go!**
¡vamos!, ¡vámonos! **~'s see** (vamos)
a ver. **~'s talk/drink** hablemos/
bebamos. ● n alquiler m. **~ down**
bajar; (deflate) desinflar; (fig)
defraudar. **~ go** soltar. **~ in** dejar
entrar. **~ off** disparar (gun); (cause
to explode) hacer explotar; (excuse)
perdonar. **~ off steam** (fig)
desfogarse. **~ on** (sl) revelar. **~ o.s.
in for** meterse en. **~ out** dejar salir.
**~ through** dejar pasar. **~ up** disminuir. **~down** n desilusión f

**lethal** /'li:θl/ a (dose, wound) mortal;
(weapon) mortífero

**letharg|ic** /lɪ'tɑ:dʒɪk/ a letárgico. **~y**
/'leθədʒɪ/ n letargo m

**letter** /'letə(r)/ n (of alphabet) letra f;
(written message) carta f. **~bomb** n
carta f explosiva. **~box** n buzón m.
**~head** n membrete m. **~ing** n
letras fpl

**lettuce** /'letɪs/ n lechuga f

**let-up** /'letʌp/ n (fam) descanso m

**leukaemia** /lu:'ki:mɪə/ n leucemia f

**level** /'levl/ a (flat) llano; (on surface)
horizontal; (in height) a nivel; (in
score) igual; (spoonful) raso. ● n

nivel m. **be on the ~** (fam) ser honrado. ● vt (pt **levelled**) nivelar;
(aim) apuntar. **~ crossing** n paso m
a nivel. **~-headed** a juicioso

**lever** /'li:və(r)/ n palanca f. ● vt apalancar. **~age** /'li:vərɪdʒ/ n apa-
lancamiento m

**levity** /'levətɪ/ n ligereza f

**levy** /'levɪ/ vt exigir (tax). ● n
impuesto m

**lewd** /lu:d/ a (-er, -est) lascivo

**lexicography** /leksɪ'kɒɡrəfɪ/ n lexicografía f

**lexicon** /'leksɪkən/ n léxico m

**liable** /'laɪəbl/ a. **be ~ to do** tener
tendencia a hacer. **~ for** responsable de. **~ to** susceptible de;
expuesto a (fine)

**liability** /laɪə'bɪlətɪ/ n responsabilidad f; (disadvantage, fam)
inconveniente m. **liabilities** npl
(debts) deudas fpl

**liais|e** /lɪ'eɪz/ vi hacer un enlace,
enlazar. **~on** /lɪ'eɪzɒn/ n enlace m;
(love affair) lío m

**liar** /'laɪə(r)/ n mentiroso m

**libel** /'laɪbl/ n libelo m. ● vt (pt
**libelled**) difamar (por escrito)

**Liberal** /'lɪbərəl/ a & n liberal (m & f)

**liberal** /'lɪbərəl/ a liberal; (generous)
generoso; (tolerant) tolerante. **~ly**
adv liberalmente; (generously) gen-
erosamente; (tolerantly) tolerant-
emente

**liberat|e** /'lɪbəreɪt/ vt liberar. **~ion**
/-'reɪʃn/ n liberación f

**libertine** /'lɪbəti:n/ n libertino m

**liberty** /'lɪbətɪ/ n libertad f. **be at ~
to** estar autorizado para. **take lib-
erties** tomarse libertades. **take the
~ of** tomarse la libertad de

**libido** /lɪ'bi:dəʊ/ n (pl -os) libido m

**Libra** /'li:brə/ n (astr) Libra f

**librar|ian** /laɪ'breərɪən/ n biblio-
tecario m. **~y** /'laɪbrərɪ/ n biblioteca f

**libretto** /lɪ'bretəʊ/ n (pl -os) libreto
m

**Libya** /'lɪbɪə/ n Libia f. **~n** a & n libio
(m)

**lice** /laɪs/ see **louse**

**licence** /'laɪsns/ n licencia f, permiso
m; (fig, liberty) libertad f. **~ plate** n
(placa f de) matrícula f. **driving ~**
carné m de conducir

**license** /'laɪsns/ vt autorizar

**licentious** /laɪ'senʃəs/ a licencioso

**lichen** /'laɪkən/ n liquen m

**lick** /lɪk/ *vt* lamer; (*defeat, sl*) dar una paliza a. ~ **one's chops** relamerse. ● *n* lametón *m*

**licorice** /'lɪkərɪs/ *n* (*Amer*) regaliz *m*

**lid** /lɪd/ *n* tapa *f*; (*of pan*) cobertera *f*

**lido** /'liːdəʊ/ *n* (*pl* -os) piscina *f*

**lie**[1] /laɪ/ *vi* (*pt* **lay**, *pp* **lain**, *pres p* **lying**) echarse; (*state*) estar echado; (*remain*) quedarse; (*be*) estar, encontrarse; (*in grave*) yacer. **be lying** estar echado. ~ **down** acostarse. ~ **low** quedarse escondido

**lie**[2] /laɪ/ *n* mentira *f*. ● *vi* (*pt* **lied**, *pres p* **lying**) mentir. **give the** ~ **to** desmentir

**lie-in** /laɪˈɪn/ *n*. **have a** ~**in** quedarse en la cama

**lieu** /ljuː/ *n*. **in** ~ **of** en lugar de

**lieutenant** /lefˈtenənt/ *n* (*mil*) teniente *m*

**life** /laɪf/ *n* (*pl* **lives**) vida *f*. ~**belt** *n* cinturón *m* salvavidas. ~**boat** *n* lancha *f* de salvamento; (*on ship*) bote *m* salvavidas. ~**buoy** *n* boya *f* salvavidas. ~ **cycle** *n* ciclo *m* vital. ~**guard** *n* bañero *m*. ~**jacket** *n* chaleco *m* salvavidas. ~**less** *a* sin vida. ~**like** *a* natural. ~**line** *n* cuerda *f* salvavidas; (*fig*) cordón *m* umbilical. ~**long** *a* de toda la vida. ~**size(d)** *a* de tamaño natural. ~**time** *n* vida *f*

**lift** /lɪft/ *vt* levantar; (*steal, fam*) robar. ● *vi* (*fog*) disiparse. ● *n* ascensor *m*, elevador *m* (*LAm*). **give a** ~ **to s.o.** llevar a uno en su coche, dar aventón a uno (*LAm*). ~**off** *n* (*aviat*) despegue *m*

**ligament** /'lɪgəmənt/ *n* ligamento *m*

**light**[1] /laɪt/ *n* luz *f*; (*lamp*) lámpara *f*, luz *f*; (*flame*) fuego *m*; (*headlight*) faro *m*. **bring to** ~ sacar a luz. **come to** ~ salir a luz. **have you got a** ~? ¿tienes fuego? **the** ~**s** *npl* (*auto, traffic signals*) el semáforo *m*. ● *a* claro. ● *vt* (*pt* **lit** *or* **lighted**) encender; (*illuminate*) alumbrar. ~ **up** *vt/i* iluminar(se)

**light**[2] /laɪt/ *a* (-**er**, -**est**) (*not heavy*) ligero

**lighten**[1] /'laɪtn/ *vt* (*make less heavy*) aligerar

**lighten**[2] /'laɪtn/ *vt* (*give light to*) iluminar; (*make brighter*) aclarar

**lighter** /'laɪtə(r)/ *n* (*for cigarettes*) mechero *m*

**light-fingered** /laɪtˈfɪŋgəd/ *a* largo de uñas

**light-headed** /laɪtˈhedɪd/ *a* (*dizzy*) mareado; (*frivolous*) casquivano

**light-hearted** /laɪtˈhɑːtɪd/ *a* alegre

**lighthouse** /'laɪthaʊs/ *n* faro *m*

**lighting** /'laɪtɪŋ/ *n* (*system*) alumbrado *m*; (*act*) iluminación *f*

**light**: ~**ly** *adv* ligeramente. ~**ness** *n* ligereza *f*

**lightning** /'laɪtnɪŋ/ *n* relámpago *m*. ● *a* relámpago

**lightweight** /'laɪtweɪt/ *a* ligero. ● *n* (*boxing*) peso *m* ligero

**light-year** /'laɪtjɪə(r)/ *n* año *m* luz

**like**[1] /laɪk/ *a* parecido. ● *prep* como. ● *conj* (*fam*) como. ● *n* igual. **the** ~**s of you** la gente como tú

**like**[2] /laɪk/ *vt* gustarle (a uno). **I** ~ **chocolate** me gusta el chocolate. **I should** ~ quisiera. **they** ~ **swimming** (a ellos) les gusta nadar. **would you** ~? ¿quieres? ~**able** *a* simpático. ~**s** *npl* gustos *mpl*

**likelihood** /'laɪklɪhʊd/ *n* probabilidad *f*

**likely** *a* (-**ier**, -**iest**) probable. **he is** ~ **to come** es probable que venga. ● *adv* probablemente. **not** ~! ¡ni hablar!

**like-minded** /laɪkˈmaɪndɪd/ *a*. **be** ~ tener las mismas opiniones

**liken** /'laɪkən/ *vt* comparar

**likeness** /'laɪknɪs/ *n* parecido *m*. **be a good** ~ parecerse mucho

**likewise** /'laɪkwaɪz/ *adv* (*also*) también; (*the same way*) lo mismo

**liking** /'laɪkɪŋ/ *n* (*for thing*) afición *f*; (*for person*) simpatía *f*

**lilac** /'laɪlək/ *n* lila *f*. ● *a* color de lila

**lilt** /lɪlt/ *n* ritmo *m*

**lily** /'lɪlɪ/ *n* lirio *m*. ~ **of the valley** lirio *m* de los valles

**limb** /lɪm/ *n* miembro *m*. **out on a** ~ aislado

**limber** /'lɪmbə(r)/ *vi*. ~ **up** hacer ejercicios preliminares

**limbo** /'lɪmbəʊ/ *n* limbo *m*. **be in** ~ (*forgotten*) estar olvidado

**lime**[1] /laɪm/ *n* (*white substance*) cal *f*

**lime**[2] /laɪm/ *n* (*fruit*) lima *f*

**lime**[3] /laɪm/ *n*. ~**(-tree)** (*linden tree*) tilo *m*

**limelight** /'laɪmlaɪt/ *n*. **be in the** ~ estar muy a la vista

**limerick** /'lɪmərɪk/ *n* quintilla *f* humorística

**limestone** /'laɪmstəʊn/ *n* caliza *f*

**limit** /'lɪmɪt/ *n* límite *m*. ● *vt* limitar. ~**ation** /-'teɪʃn/ *n* limitación *f*. ~**ed**

*a* limitado. **~ed company** *n* sociedad *f* anónima
**limousine** /'lɪməziːn/ *n* limusina *f*
**limp**[1] /lɪmp/ *vi* cojear. ● *n* cojera *f*. **have a ~** cojear
**limp**[2] /lɪmp/ *a* (-er, -est) flojo
**limpid** /'lɪmpɪd/ *a* límpido
**linctus** /'lɪŋktəs/ *n* jarabe *m* (para la tos)
**line**[1] /laɪn/ *n* línea *f*; (*track*) vía *f*; (*wrinkle*) arruga *f*; (*row*) fila *f*; (*of poem*) verso *m*; (*rope*) cuerda *f*; (*of goods*) surtido *m*; (*queue*, *Amer*) cola *f*. **in ~ with** de acuerdo con. ● *vt* (*on paper etc*) rayar; bordear ⟨*streets etc*⟩. **~ up** alinearse; (*in queue*) hacer cola
**line**[2] /laɪn/ *vt* forrar; (*fill*) llenar
**lineage** /'lɪnɪɪdʒ/ *n* linaje *m*
**linear** /'lɪnɪə(r)/ *a* lineal
**linen** /'lɪnɪn/ *n* (*sheets etc*) ropa *f* blanca; (*material*) lino *m*
**liner** /'laɪnə(r)/ *n* transatlántico *m*
**linesman** /'laɪnzmən/ *n* (*football*) juez *m* de línea
**linger** /'lɪŋgə(r)/ *vi* tarder en marcharse; ⟨*smells etc*⟩ persistir. **~ over** dilatarse en
**lingerie** /'lænʒərɪ/ *n* ropa *f* interior, lencería *f*
**lingo** /'lɪŋgəʊ/ *n* (*pl* -os) idioma *m*; (*specialized vocabulary*) jerga *f*
**linguist** /'lɪŋgwɪst/ *n* (*specialist in languages*) políglota *m & f*; (*specialist in linguistics*) lingüista *m & f*. **~ic** /lɪŋ'gwɪstɪk/ *a* lingüístico. **~ics** *n* lingüística *f*
**lining** /'laɪnɪŋ/ *n* forro *m*; (*auto, of brakes*) guarnición *f*
**link** /lɪŋk/ *n* (*of chain*) eslabón *m*; (*fig*) lazo *m*. ● *vt* eslabonar; (*fig*) enlazar. **~ up with** reunirse con. **~age** *n* enlace *m*
**links** /lɪŋks/ *n invar* campo *m* de golf
**lino** /'laɪnəʊ/ *n* (*pl* -os) linóleo *m*. **~leum** /lɪ'nəʊlɪəm/ *n* linóleo *m*
**lint** /lɪnt/ *n* (*med*) hilas *fpl*; (*fluff*) pelusa *f*
**lion** /'laɪən/ *n* león *m*. **the ~'s share** la parte *f* del león. **~ess** *n* leona *f*
**lionize** /'laɪənaɪz/ *vt* tratar como una celebridad
**lip** /lɪp/ *n* labio *m*; (*edge*) borde *m*. **pay ~ service to** aprobar de boquilla. **stiff upper ~** *n* imperturbabilidad *f*. **~-read** *vt/i* leer en los labios. **~salve** *n* crema *f* para los labios. **~stick** *n* lápiz *m* de labios.
**liquefy** /'lɪkwɪfaɪ/ *vt/i* licuar(se)

**liqueur** /lɪ'kjʊə(r)/ *n* licor *m*
**liquid** /'lɪkwɪd/ *a & n* líquido (*m*)
**liquidat|e** /'lɪkwɪdeɪt/ *vt* liquidar. **~ion** /-'deɪʃn/ *n* liquidación *f*
**liquidize** /'lɪkwɪdaɪz/ *vt* licuar. **~r** *n* licuadora *f*
**liquor** /'lɪkə(r)/ *n* bebida *f* alcohólica
**liquorice** /'lɪkərɪs/ *n* regaliz *m*
**lira** /'lɪərə/ *n* (*pl* **lire** /'lɪəreɪ/ *or* **liras**) lira *f*
**lisle** /laɪl/ *n* hilo *m* de Escocia
**lisp** /lɪsp/ *n* ceceo *m*. **speak with a ~** cecear. ● *vi* cecear
**lissom** /'lɪsəm/ *a* flexible, ágil
**list**[1] /lɪst/ *n* lista *f*. ● *vt* hacer una lista de; (*enter in a list*) inscribir
**list**[2] /lɪst/ *vi* ⟨*ship*⟩ escorar
**listen** /'lɪsn/ *vi* escuchar. **~ in (to)** escuchar. **~ to** escuchar. **~er** *n* oyente *m & f*
**listless** /'lɪstlɪs/ *a* apático
**lit** /lɪt/ *see* **light**[1]
**litany** /'lɪtənɪ/ *n* letanía *f*
**literacy** /'lɪtərəsɪ/ *n* capacidad *f* de leer y escribir
**literal** /'lɪtərəl/ *a* literal; (*fig*) prosaico. **~ly** *adv* al pie de la letra, literalmente
**literary** /'lɪtərərɪ/ *a* literario
**literate** /'lɪtərət/ *a* que sabe leer y escribir
**literature** /'lɪtərətʃə(r)/ *n* literatura *f*; (*fig*) impresos *mpl*
**lithe** /laɪð/ *a* ágil
**lithograph** /'lɪθəgrɑːf/ *n* litografía *f*
**litigation** /lɪtɪ'geɪʃn/ *n* litigio *m*
**litre** /'liːtə(r)/ *n* litro *m*
**litter** /'lɪtə(r)/ *n* basura *f*; (*of animals*) camada *f*. ● *vt* ensuciar; (*scatter*) esparcir. **~ed with** lleno de. **~-bin** *n* papelera *f*
**little** /'lɪtl/ *a* pequeño; (*not much*) poco de. ● *n* poco *m*. **a ~** un poco. **a ~ water** un poco de agua. ● *adv* poco. **~ by ~** poco a poco. **~ finger** *n* meñique *m*
**liturgy** /'lɪtədʒɪ/ *n* liturgia *f*
**live**[1] /lɪv/ *vt/i* vivir. **~ down** lograr borrar. **~ it up** echar una cana al aire. **~ on** (*feed o.s. on*) vivir de; (*continue*) perdurar. **~ up to** vivir de acuerdo con; cumplir ⟨*a promise*⟩
**live**[2] /laɪv/ *a* vivo; ⟨*wire*⟩ con corriente; (*broadcast*) en directo. **be a ~ wire** ser una persona enérgica
**livelihood** /'laɪvlɪhʊd/ *n* sustento *m*
**livel|iness** /'laɪvlɪnɪs/ *n* vivacidad *f*. **~y** *a* (-ier, -iest) vivo

**liven** /'laɪvn/ vt/i. ~ **up** animar(se); (*cheer up*) alegrar(se)

**liver** /'lɪvə(r)/ n hígado m

**livery** /'lɪvərɪ/ n librea f

**livestock** /'laɪvstɒk/ n ganado m

**livid** /'lɪvɪd/ a lívido; (*angry, fam*) furioso

**living** /'lɪvɪŋ/ a vivo. ● n vida f. ~**room** n cuarto m de estar, cuarto m de estancia (*LAm*)

**lizard** /'lɪzəd/ n lagartija f; (*big*) lagarto m

**llama** /'lɑ:mə/ n llama f

**load** /ləʊd/ n (*incl elec*) carga f; (*quantity*) cantidad f; (*weight, strain*) peso m. ● vt cargar. ~**ed** a ⟨*incl dice*⟩ cargado; (*wealthy, sl*) muy rico. ~**s of** (*fam*) montones de

**loaf**[1] /ləʊf/ n (*pl* **loaves**) pan m; (*stick of bread*) barra f

**loaf**[2] /ləʊf/ vi. ~ (**about**) holgazanear. ~**er** n holgazán m

**loam** /ləʊm/ n marga f

**loan** /ləʊn/ n préstamo m. **on** ~ prestado. ● vt prestar

**loath** /ləʊθ/ a poco dispuesto (**to** a)

**loath|e** /ləʊð/ vt odiar. ~**ing** n odio m (**of** a). ~**some** a odioso

**lobby** /'lɒbɪ/ n vestíbulo m; (*pol*) grupo m de presión. ● vt hacer presión sobre

**lobe** /ləʊb/ n lóbulo m

**lobster** /'lɒbstə(r)/ n langosta f

**local** /'ləʊkl/ a local. ● n (*pub, fam*) bar m. **the** ~**s** los vecinos mpl

**locale** /ləʊ'kɑ:l/ n escenario m

**local government** /ləʊkl-'gʌvənmənt/ n gobierno m municipal

**locality** /ləʊ'kælətɪ/ n localidad f

**localized** /'ləʊkəlaɪzd/ a localizado

**locally** /'ləʊkəlɪ/ adv localmente; (*nearby*) en la localidad

**locate** /ləʊ'keɪt/ vt (*situate*) situar; (*find*) encontrar

**location** /ləʊ'keɪʃn/ n colocación f; (*place*) situación f. **on** ~ fuera del estudio. **to film on** ~ **in Andalusia** rodar en Andalucía

**lock**[1] /lɒk/ n (*of door etc*) cerradura f; (*on canal*) esclusa f. ● vt/i cerrar(se) con llave. ~ **in** encerrar. ~ **out** cerrar la puerta a. ~ **up** encerrar

**lock**[2] /lɒk/ n (*of hair*) mechón m. ~**s** npl pelo m

**locker** /'lɒkə(r)/ n armario m

**locket** /'lɒkɪt/ n medallón m

**lock-out** /'lɒkaʊt/ n lock-out m

**locksmith** /'lɒksmɪθ/ n cerrajero m

**locomotion** /ləʊkə'məʊʃn/ n locomoción f

**locomotive** /ləʊkə'məʊtɪv/ n locomotora f

**locum** /'ləʊkəm/ n interino m

**locust** /'ləʊkəst/ n langosta f

**lodge** /lɒdʒ/ n (*in park*) casa f del guarda; (*of porter*) portería f. ● vt alojar; presentar ⟨*complaint*⟩; depositar ⟨*money*⟩. ● vi alojarse. ~**r** /-ə(r)/ n huésped m

**lodgings** /'lɒdʒɪŋz/ n alojamiento m; (*room*) habitación f

**loft** /lɒft/ n desván m

**lofty** /'lɒftɪ/ a (-**ier**, -**iest**) elevado; (*haughty*) altanero

**log** /lɒg/ n (*of wood*) leño m; (*naut*) cuaderno m de bitácora. **sleep like a** ~ dormir como un lirón. ● vt (*pt* **logged**) apuntar; (*travel*) recorrer

**logarithm** /'lɒgərɪðəm/ n logaritmo m

**log-book** /'lɒgbʊk/ n cuaderno m de bitácora; (*aviat*) diario m de vuelo

**loggerheads** /'lɒgəhedz/ npl. **be at** ~ **with** estar a matar con

**logic** /'lɒdʒɪk/ a lógica f. ~**al** a lógico. ~**ally** adv lógicamente

**logistics** /lə'dʒɪstɪks/ n logística f

**logo** /'ləʊgəʊ/ n (*pl* -**os**) logotipo m

**loin** /lɔɪn/ n (*culin*) solomillo m. ~**s** npl ijadas fpl

**loiter** /'lɔɪtə(r)/ vi holgazanear

**loll** /lɒl/ vi repantigarse

**loll|ipop** /'lɒlɪpɒp/ n (*boiled sweet*) pirulí m. ~**y** n (*iced*) polo m; (*money, sl*) dinero m

**London** /'lʌndən/ n Londres m. ● a londinense. ~**er** n londinense m & f

**lone** /ləʊn/ a solitario. ~**ly** /'ləʊnlɪ/ a (-**ier**, -**iest**) solitario. **feel** ~**ly** sentirse muy solo. ~**r** /'ləʊnə(r)/ n solitario m. ~**some** a solitario

**long**[1] /lɒŋ/ a (-**er**, -**est**) largo. **a** ~ **time** mucho tiempo. **how** ~ **is it?** ¿cuánto tiene de largo? **in the** ~ **run** a la larga. ● adv largo/mucho tiempo. **as** ~ **as** (*while*) mientras; (*provided that*) con tal que (+ *subjunctive*). **before** ~ dentro de poco. **so** ~! ¡hasta luego! **so** ~ **as** (*provided that*) con tal que (+ *subjunctive*)

**long**[2] /lɒŋ/ vi. ~ **for** anhelar

**long-distance** /lɒŋ'dɪstəns/ a de larga distancia. ~ (**tele)phone call** n conferencia f

**longer** /'lɒŋgə(r)/ adv. **no** ~**er** ya no

**longevity** /lɒn'dʒevətɪ/ n longevidad f

**long:** ~ **face** n cara f triste. ~**hand** n escritura f a mano. ~ **johns** npl (fam) calzoncillos mpl largos. ~ **jump** n salto m de longitud

**longing** /'lɒŋɪŋ/ n anhelo m, ansia f

**longitude** /'lɒŋgɪtjuːd/ n longitud f

**long:** ~**playing record** n elepé m. ~**range** a de gran alcance. ~**sighted** a présbita. ~**standing** a de mucho tiempo. ~**suffering** a sufrido. ~**term** a a largo plazo. ~ **wave** n onda f larga. ~**winded** a ⟨speaker etc⟩ prolijo

**loo** /luː/ n (fam) servicios mpl

**look** /lʊk/ vt mirar; (seem) parecer; representar ⟨age⟩. ● vi mirar; (seem) parecer; (search) buscar. ● n mirada f; (appearance) aspecto m. ~ **after** ocuparse de; cuidar ⟨person⟩. ~ **at** mirar. ~ **down on** despreciar. ~ **for** buscar. ~ **forward to** esperar con ansia. ~ **in on** pasar por casa de. ~ **into** investigar. ~ **like** (resemble) parecerse a. ~ **on to** ⟨room, window⟩ dar a. ~ **out** tener cuidado. ~ **out for** buscar; (watch) tener cuidado con. ~ **round** volver la cabeza. ~ **through** hojear. ~ **up** buscar ⟨word⟩; (visit) ir a ver. ~ **up to** respetar. ~**er-on** n espectador m. ~**ing-glass** n espejo m. ~**out** n (mil) atalaya f; (person) vigía m. ~s npl belleza f. **good** ~s mpl belleza f

**loom**[1] /luːm/ n telar m

**loom**[2] /luːm/ vi aparecerse

**loony** /'luːnɪ/ a & n (sl) chiflado (m) (fam), loco (m). ~ **bin** n (sl) manicomio m

**loop** /luːp/ n lazo m. ● vt hacer presilla con

**loophole** /'luːphəʊl/ n (in rule) escapatoria f

**loose** /luːs/ a (-er, -est) (untied) suelto; (not tight) flojo; (inexact) vago; (immoral) inmoral; (not packed) suelto. **be at a** ~ **end, be at** ~ **ends** (Amer) no tener nada que hacer. ~**ly** adv sueltamente; (roughly) aproximadamente. ~**n** /'luːsn/ vt (slacken) aflojar; (untie) desatar

**loot** /luːt/ n botín m. ● vt saquear. ~**er** n saqueador m. ~**ing** n saqueo m

**lop** /lɒp/ vt (pt lopped). ~ **off** cortar

**lop-sided** /lɒp'saɪdɪd/ a ladeado

**loquacious** /ləʊ'kweɪʃəs/ a locuaz

**lord** /lɔːd/ n señor m; (British title) lord m. **(good)** L~! ¡Dios mío! **the** L~ el Señor m. **the (House of)** L~s la Cámara f de los Lores. ~**ly** señorial; (haughty) altivo. ~**ship** n señoría f

**lore** /lɔː(r)/ n tradiciones fpl

**lorgnette** /lɔː'njet/ n impertinentes mpl

**lorry** /'lɒrɪ/ n camión m

**lose** /luːz/ vt/i (pt lost) perder. ~**r** n perdedor m

**loss** /lɒs/ n pérdida f. **be at a** ~ estar perplejo. **be at a** ~ **for words** no encontrar palabras. **be at a** ~ **to** no saber cómo

**lost** /lɒst/ see **lose**. ● a perdido. ~ **property** n, ~ **and found** (Amer) oficina f de objetos perdidos. **get** ~ perderse

**lot** /lɒt/ n (fate) suerte f; (at auction) lote m; (land) solar m. a ~ **(of)** muchos. **quite a** ~ **of** (fam) bastante. ~**s (of)** (fam) muchos. **the** ~ todos mpl

**lotion** /'ləʊʃn/ n loción f

**lottery** /'lɒtərɪ/ n lotería f

**lotto** /'lɒtəʊ/ n lotería f

**lotus** /'ləʊtəs/ n (pl -uses) loto m

**loud** /laʊd/ a (-er, -est) fuerte; (noisy) ruidoso; (gaudy) chillón. **in** ~ **voz** alta. ~ **hailer** n megáfono m. ~**ly** adv (speak etc) en voz alta; (noisily) ruidosamente. ~**speaker** n altavoz m

**lounge** /laʊndʒ/ vi repantigarse. ● n salón m. ~ **suit** n traje m de calle

**louse** /laʊs/ n (pl lice) piojo m

**lousy** /'laʊzɪ/ a (-ier, -iest) piojoso; (bad, sl) malísimo

**lout** /laʊt/ n patán m

**lovable** /'lʌvəbl/ a adorable

**love** /lʌv/ n amor m; (tennis) cero m. **be in** ~ **with** estar enamorado de. **fall in** ~ **with** enamorarse de. ● vt querer ⟨person⟩; gustarle mucho a uno, encantarle a uno ⟨things⟩. **I** ~ **milk** me encanta la leche. ~ **affair** n amores mpl

**lovely** /'lʌvlɪ/ a (-ier, -iest) hermoso; (delightful, fam) precioso. **have a** ~ **time** divertirse

**lover** /'lʌvə(r)/ n amante m & f

**lovesick** /'lʌvsɪk/ a atortolado

**loving** /'lʌvɪŋ/ a cariñoso

**low**[1] /ləʊ/ a & adv (-er, -est) bajo. ● n (low pressure) área f de baja presión

**low**[2] /ləʊ/ vi mugir

**lowbrow** /'ləʊbraʊ/ *a* poco culto

**low-cut** /'ləʊkʌt/ *a* escotado

**low-down** /'ləʊdaʊn/ *a* bajo. ● *n* (*sl*) informes *mpl*

**lower** /'ləʊə(r)/ *a & adv see* **low**². ● *vt* bajar. ~ **o.s.** envilecerse

**low-key** /'ləʊˈkiː/ *a* moderado

**lowlands** /'ləʊləndz/ *npl* tierra *f* baja

**lowly** /'ləʊlɪ/ *a* (-**ier, -iest**) humilde

**loyal** /'lɔɪəl/ *a* leal. ~**ly** *adv* lealmente. ~**ty** *n* lealtad *f*

**lozenge** /'lɒzɪndʒ/ *n* (*shape*) rombo *m*; (*tablet*) pastilla *f*

**LP** /el'piː/ *abbr* (*long-playing record*) elepé *m*

**Ltd** /'lɪmɪtɪd/ *abbr* (*Limited*) S.A., Sociedad Anónima

**lubrica|nt** /'luːbrɪkənt/ *n* lubricante *m*. ~**te** /-'keɪt/ *vt* lubricar. ~**tion** /-'keɪʃn/ *n* lubricación *f*

**lucid** /'luːsɪd/ *a* lúcido. ~**ity** /-'sɪdətɪ/ *n* lucidez *f*

**luck** /lʌk/ *n* suerte *f*. **bad** ~ *n* mala suerte *f*. ~**ily** /'lʌkɪlɪ/ *adv* afortunadamente. ~**y** *a* (-**ier, -iest**) afortunado

**lucrative** /'luːkrətɪv/ *a* lucrativo

**lucre** /'luːkə(r)/ *n* (*pej*) dinero *m*. **filthy** ~ vil metal *m*

**ludicrous** /'luːdɪkrəs/ *a* ridículo

**lug** /lʌg/ *vt* (*pt* **lugged**) arrastrar

**luggage** /'lʌgɪdʒ/ *n* equipaje *m*. ~**rack** *n* rejilla *f*. ~**van** *n* furgón *m*

**lugubrious** /luːˈguːbrɪəs/ *a* lúgubre

**lukewarm** /'luːkwɔːm/ *a* tibio

**lull** /lʌl/ *vt* (*soothe, send to sleep*) adormecer; (*calm*) calmar. ● *n* periodo *m* de calma

**lullaby** /'lʌləbaɪ/ *n* canción *f* de cuna

**lumbago** /lʌmˈbeɪgəʊ/ *n* lumbago *m*

**lumber** /'lʌmbə(r)/ *n* trastos *mpl* viejos; (*wood*) maderos *mpl*. ● *vt*. ~ **s.o. with** hacer que uno cargue con. ~**jack** *n* leñador *m*

**luminous** /'luːmɪnəs/ *a* luminoso

**lump**¹ /'lʌmp/ *n* protuberancia *f*; (*in liquid*) grumo *m*; (*of sugar*) terrón *m*; (*in throat*) nudo *m*. ● *vt*. ~ **together** agrupar

**lump**² /lʌmp/ *vt*. ~ **it** (*fam*) aguantarlo

**lump:** ~ **sum** *n* suma *f* global. ~**y** *a* ⟨*sauce*⟩ grumoso; (*bumpy*) cubierto de protuberancias

**lunacy** /'luːnəsɪ/ *n* locura *f*

**lunar** /'luːnə(r)/ *a* lunar

**lunatic** /'luːnətɪk/ *n* loco *m*

**lunch** /lʌntʃ/ *n* comida *f*, almuerzo *m*. ● *vi* comer

**luncheon** /'lʌntʃən/ *n* comida *f*, almuerzo *m*. ~ **meat** *n* carne *f* en lata. ~ **voucher** *n* vale *m* de comida

**lung** /lʌŋ/ *n* pulmón *m*

**lunge** /lʌndʒ/ *n* arremetida *f*

**lurch**¹ /lɜːtʃ/ *vi* tambalearse

**lurch**² /lɜːtʃ/ *n*. **leave in the** ~ dejar en la estacada

**lure** /ljʊə(r)/ *vt* atraer. ● *n* (*attraction*) atractivo *m*

**lurid** /'ljʊərɪd/ *a* chillón; (*shocking*) espeluznante

**lurk** /lɜːk/ *vi* esconderse; (*in ambush*) estar al acecho; (*prowl*) rondar

**luscious** /'lʌʃəs/ *a* delicioso

**lush** /lʌʃ/ *a* exuberante. ● *n* (*Amer, sl*) borracho *m*

**lust** /lʌst/ *n* lujuria *f*; (*fig*) ansia *f*. ● *vi*. ~ **after** codiciar. ~**ful** *a* lujurioso

**lustre** /'lʌstə(r)/ *n* lustre *m*

**lusty** /'lʌstɪ/ *a* (-**ier, -iest**) fuerte

**lute** /luːt/ *n* laúd *m*

**Luxemburg** /'lʌksəmbɜːg/ *n* Luxemburgo *m*

**luxuriant** /lʌgˈzjʊərɪənt/ *a* exuberante

**luxur|ious** /lʌgˈzjʊərɪəs/ *a* lujoso. ~**y** /'lʌkʃərɪ/ *n* lujo *m*. ● *a* de lujo

**lye** /laɪ/ *n* lejía *f*

**lying** /'laɪɪŋ/ *see* **lie**¹, **lie**². ● *n* mentiras *fpl*

**lynch** /lɪntʃ/ *vt* linchar

**lynx** /lɪŋks/ *n* lince *m*

**lyre** /'laɪə(r)/ *n* lira *f*

**lyric** /'lɪrɪk/ *a* lírico. ~**al** *a* lírico. ~**ism** /-sɪzəm/ *n* lirismo *m*. ~**s** *npl* letra *f*

# M

**MA** *abbr* (*Master of Arts*) Master *m*, grado *m* universitario entre el de licenciado y doctor

**mac** /mæk/ *n* (*fam*) impermeable *m*

**macabre** /məˈkɑːbrə/ *a* macabro

**macaroni** /mækəˈrəʊnɪ/ *n* macarrones *mpl*

**macaroon** /mækəˈruːn/ *n* mostachón *m*

**mace**¹ /meɪs/ *n* (*staff*) maza *f*

**mace**² /meɪs/ *n* (*spice*) macis *f*

**Mach** /mɑːk/ *n*. ~ (**number**) *n* (número *m* de) Mach (*m*)

**machiavellian** /mækɪəˈvelɪən/ *a* maquiavélico

**machinations** /mækɪ'neɪʃnz/ *npl* maquinaciones *fpl*

**machine** /mə'ʃiːn/ *n* máquina *f*. • *vt* (*sew*) coser a máquina; (*tec*) trabajar a máquina. ~**gun** *n* ametralladora *f*. ~**ry** /mə'ʃiːnərɪ/ *n* maquinaria *f*; (*working parts, fig*) mecanismo *m*. ~ **tool** *n* máquina *f* herramienta

**machinist** /mə'ʃiːnɪst/ *n* maquinista *m & f*

**mach|ismo** /mæ'tʃɪzməʊ/ *n* machismo *m*. ~**o** *a* macho

**mackerel** /'mækrəl/ *n invar* (*fish*) caballa *f*

**mackintosh** /'mækɪntoʃ/ *n* impermeable *m*

**macrobiotic** /mækrəʊbaɪ'ɒtɪk/ *a* macrobiótico

**mad** /mæd/ *a* (**madder, maddest**) loco; (*foolish*) insensato; (*dog*) rabioso; (*angry, fam*) furioso. **be ~ about** estar loco por. **like ~** como un loco; (*a lot*) muchísimo

**Madagascar** /mædə'gæskə(r)/ *n* Madagascar *m*

**madam** /'mædəm/ *n* señora *f*; (*unmarried*) señorita *f*

**madcap** /'mædkæp/ *a* atolondrado. • *n* locuelo *m*

**madden** /'mædn/ *vt* (*make mad*) enloquecer; (*make angry*) enfurecer

**made** /meɪd/ *see* **make**. ~ **to measure** hecho a la medida

**Madeira** /mə'dɪərə/ *n* (*wine*) vino *m* de Madera

**mad: ~house** *n* manicomio *m*. ~**ly** *adv* (*interested, in love etc*) locamente; (*frantically*) como un loco. ~**man** *n* loco *m*. ~**ness** *n* locura *f*

**madonna** /mə'dɒnə/ *n* Virgen *f* María

**madrigal** /'mædrɪgl/ *n* madrigal *m*

**maelstrom** /'meɪlstrəm/ *n* remolino *m*

**maestro** /'maɪstrəʊ/ *n* (*pl* **maestri** /-striː/ *or* **os**) maestro *m*

**Mafia** /'mæfɪə/ *n* mafia *f*

**magazine** /mægə'ziːn/ *n* revista *f*; (*of gun*) recámara *f*

**magenta** /mə'dʒentə/ *a* rojo purpúreo

**maggot** /'mægət/ *n* gusano *m*. ~**y** *a* agusanado

**Magi** /'meɪdʒaɪ/ *npl*. **the ~** los Reyes *mpl* Magos

**magic** /'mædʒɪk/ *n* magia *f*. • *a* mágico. ~**al** *a* mágico. ~**ian** /mə'dʒɪʃn/ *n* mago *m*

**magisterial** /mædʒɪ'stɪərɪəl/ *a* magistral; (*imperious*) autoritario

**magistrate** /'mædʒɪstreɪt/ *n* magistrado *m*, juez *m*

**magnanim|ity** /mægnə'nɪmətɪ/ *n* magnanimidad *f*. ~**ous** /-'nænɪməs/ *a* magnánimo

**magnate** /'mægneɪt/ *n* magnate *m*

**magnesia** /mæg'niːʒə/ *n* magnesia *f*

**magnet** /'mægnɪt/ *n* imán *m*. ~**ic** /-'netɪk/ *a* magnético. ~**ism** *n* magnetismo *m*. ~**ize** *vt* magnetizar

**magnificen|ce** /mæg'nɪfɪsns/ *a* magnificencia *f*. ~**t** *a* magnífico

**magnif|ication** /mægnɪfɪ'keɪʃn/ *n* aumento *m*. ~**ier** /-'faɪə(r)/ *n* lupa *f*, lente *f* de aumento. ~**y** /-'faɪ/ *vt* aumentar. ~**ying-glass** *n* lupa *f*, lente *f* de aumento

**magnitude** /'mægnɪtjuːd/ *n* magnitud *f*

**magnolia** /mæg'nəʊlɪə/ *n* magnolia *f*

**magnum** /'mægnəm/ *n* botella *f* de litro y medio

**magpie** /'mægpaɪ/ *n* urraca *f*

**mahogany** /mə'hɒgənɪ/ *n* caoba *f*

**maid** /meɪd/ *n* (*servant*) criada *f*; (*girl, old use*) doncella *f*. **old ~** solterona *f*

**maiden** /'meɪdn/ *n* doncella *f*. • *a* (*aunt*) soltera; (*voyage*) inaugural. ~**hood** *n* doncellez *f*, virginidad *f*, soltería *f*. ~**ly** *adv* virginal. ~ **name** *n* apellido *m* de soltera

**mail**[1] /meɪl/ *n* correo *m*; (*letters*) cartas *fpl*. • *a* postal, de correos. • *vt* (*post*) echar al correo; (*send*) enviar por correo

**mail**[2] /meɪl/ *n* (*armour*) (cota *f* de) malla *f*

**mail: ~ing list** *n* lista *f* de direcciones. ~**man** *n* (*Amer*) cartero *m*. ~ **order** *n* venta *f* por correo

**maim** /meɪm/ *vt* mutilar

**main** /meɪn/ *n*. (**water~, gas**) ~ cañería *f* principal. **in the ~** en su mayor parte. **the ~s** *npl* (*elec*) la red *f* eléctrica. • *a* principal. **a ~ road** *n* una carretera *f*. ~**land** *n* continente *m*. ~**ly** *adv* principalmente. ~**spring** *n* muelle *m* real; (*fig, motive*) móvil *m* principal. ~**stay** *n* sostén *m*. ~**stream** *n* corriente *f* principal. ~ **street** *n* calle *f* principal.

**maintain** /meɪn'teɪn/ *vt* mantener

**maintenance** /'meɪntənəns/ *n* mantenimiento *m*; (*allowance*) pensión *f* alimenticia

**maisonette** /meɪzə'net/ n (*small house*) casita f; (*part of house*) dúplex m

**maize** /meɪz/ n maíz m

**majestic** /mə'dʒestɪk/ a majestuoso

**majesty** /'mædʒəstɪ/ n majestad f

**major** /'meɪdʒə(r)/ a mayor. **a ~ road** una calle f prioritaria. ● n comandante m. ● vi. **~ in** (*univ, Amer*) especializarse en

**Majorca** /mə'jɔːkə/ n Mallorca f

**majority** /mə'dʒɒrətɪ/ n mayoría f. **the ~ of people** la mayoría f de la gente. ● a mayoritario

**make** /meɪk/ vt/i (*pt* **made**) hacer; (*manufacture*) fabricar; ganar ‹*money*›; tomar ‹*decision*›; llegar a ‹*destination*›. **~ s.o. do sth** obligar a uno a hacer algo. **be made of** estar hecho de. **I cannot ~** anything of it no me lo explico. **I ~ it two o'clock** yo tengo las dos. ● n fabricación f; (*brand*) marca f. **~ as if to** estar a punto de. **~ believe** fingir. **~ do** (*manage*) arreglarse. **~ do with** (*content o.s.*) contentarse con. **~ for** dirigirse a. **~ good** vi tener éxito. ● vt compensar; (*repair*) reparar. **~ it** llegar; (*succeed*) tener éxito. **~ it up** (*become reconciled*) hacer las paces. **~ much of** dar mucha importancia a. **~ off** escaparse (**with** con). **~ out** vt distinguir; (*understand*) entender; (*draw up*) extender; (*assert*) dar a entender. ● vi arreglárselas. **~ over** ceder (**to** a). **~ up** formar; (*prepare*) preparar; inventar ‹*story*›; (*compensate*) compensar. ● vi hacer las paces. **~ up (one's face)** maquillarse. **~ up for** compensar; recuperar ‹*time*›. **~ up to** congraciarse con. **~-believe** a fingido, simulado. ● n ficción f

**maker** /'meɪkə(r)/ n fabricante m & f. **the M~** el Hacedor m, el Creador m

**makeshift** /'meɪkʃɪft/ n expediente m. ● a (*temporary*) provisional; (*improvised*) improvisado

**make-up** /'meɪkʌp/ n maquillaje m

**makeweight** /'meɪkweɪt/ n complemento m

**making** /'meɪkɪŋ/ n. **be the ~ of** ser la causa del éxito de. **he has the ~s of** tiene madera de. **in the ~** en vías de formación

**maladjust|ed** /mælə'dʒʌstɪd/ a inadaptado. **~ment** n inadaptación f

**maladministration** /mæləd mɪnɪ'streɪʃn/ n mala administración f

**malady** /'mælədɪ/ n enfermedad f

**malaise** /mæ'leɪz/ n malestar m

**malaria** /mə'leərɪə/ n paludismo m

**Malay** /mə'leɪ/ a & n malayo (m). **~sia** n Malasia f

**male** /meɪl/ a masculino; (*bot, tec*) macho. ● n macho m; (*man*) varón m

**malefactor** /'mælɪfæktə(r)/ n malhechor m

**malevolen|ce** /mə'levələns/ n malevolencia f. **~t** a malévolo

**malform|ation** /mælfɔː'meɪʃn/ n malformación f. **~ed** a deforme

**malfunction** /mæl'fʌŋkʃn/ n funcionamiento m defectuoso. ● vi funcionar mal

**malic|e** /'mælɪs/ n rencor m. **bear s.o. ~e** guardar rencor a uno. **~ious** /mə'lɪʃəs/ a malévolo. **~iously** adv con malevolencia

**malign** /mə'laɪn/ a maligno. ● vt calumniar

**malignan|cy** /mə'lɪgnənsɪ/ n malignidad f. **~t** a maligno

**malinger** /mə'lɪŋgə(r)/ vi fingirse enfermo. **~er** n enfermo m fingido

**malleable** /'mælɪəbl/ a maleable

**mallet** /'mælɪt/ n mazo m

**malnutrition** /mælnjuː'trɪʃn/ n desnutrición f

**malpractice** /mæl'præktɪs/ n falta f profesional

**malt** /mɔːlt/ n malta f

**Malt|a** /'mɔːltə/ n Malta f. **~ese** /-'tiːz/ a & n maltés (m)

**maltreat** /mæl'triːt/ vt maltratar. **~ment** n maltrato m

**malt whisky** /mɔːlt'wɪskɪ/ n güisqui m de malta

**mammal** /'mæml/ n mamífero m

**mammoth** /'mæməθ/ n mamut m. ● a gigantesco

**man** /mæn/ n (*pl* **men**) hombre m; (*in sports team*) jugador m; (*chess*) pieza f. **~ in the street** hombre m de la calle. **~ to ~** de hombre a hombre. ● vt (*pt* **manned**) guarnecer (de hombres); tripular ‹*ship*›; servir ‹*guns*›

**manacle** /'mænəkl/ n manilla f. ● vt poner esposas a

**manage** /'mænɪdʒ/ vt dirigir; llevar ‹*shop, affairs*›; (*handle*) manejar. ● vi arreglárselas. **~ to do** lograr hacer. **~able** *a* manejable. **~ment** *n* dirección *f*

**manager** /'mænɪdʒ(r)/ *n* director *m*; (*of actor*) empresario *m*. **~ess** /-'res/ *n* directora *f*. **~ial** /-'dʒɪərɪəl/ *a* directivo. **~ial staff** *n* personal *m* dirigente

**managing director** /mænɪdʒɪŋ daɪ'rektə(r)/ *n* director *m* gerente

**mandarin** /'mændərɪn/ *n* mandarín *m*; (*orange*) mandarina *f*

**mandate** /'mændeɪt/ *n* mandato *m*

**mandatory** /'mændətərɪ/ *a* obligatorio

**mane** /meɪn/ *n* (*of horse*) crin *f*; (*of lion*) melena *f*

**manful** /'mænfl/ *a* valiente

**manganese** /'mæŋgəniːz/ *n* manganeso *m*

**manger** /'meɪndʒ(r)/ *n* pesebre *m*

**mangle**[1] /'mæŋgl/ *n* (*for wringing*) exprimidor *m*; (*for smoothing*) máquina *f* de planchar

**mangle**[2] /'mæŋgl/ *vt* destrozar

**mango** /'mæŋgəʊ/ *n* (*pl* **-oes**) mango *m*

**mangy** /'meɪndʒɪ/ *a* sarnoso

**man:** **~handle** *vt* maltratar. **~hole** *n* registro *m*. **~hole cover** *n* tapa *f* de registro. **~hood** *n* edad *f* viril; (*quality*) virilidad *f*. **~hour** *n* hora-hombre *f*. **~hunt** *n* persecución *f*

**mania** /'meɪnɪə/ *n* manía *f*. **~c** /-ɪæk/ *n* maníaco *m*

**manicur|e** /'mænɪkjʊə(r)/ *n* manicura *f*. ● *vt* hacer la manicura a (*person*). **~ist** *n* manicuro *m*

**manifest** /'mænɪfest/ *a* manifiesto. ● *vt* mostrar. **~ation** /-'steɪʃn/ *n* manifestación *f*

**manifesto** /mænɪ'festəʊ/ *n* (*pl* **-os**) manifiesto *m*

**manifold** /'mænɪfəʊld/ *a* múltiple

**manipulat|e** /mə'nɪpjʊleɪt/ *vt* manipular. **~ion** /-'leɪʃn/ *n* manipulación *f*

**mankind** /mæn'kaɪnd/ *n* la humanidad *f*

**man:** **~ly** *adv* viril. **~made** *a* artificial

**mannequin** /'mænɪkɪn/ *n* maniquí *m*

**manner** /'mænə(r)/ *n* manera *f*; (*behaviour*) comportamiento *m*; (*kind*) clase *f*. **~ed** *a* amanerado. **bad-~ed** *a* mal educado. **~s** *npl* (*social behaviour*) educación *f*. **have no ~s** no tener educación

**mannerism** /'mænərɪzəm/ *n* peculiaridad *f*

**mannish** /'mænɪʃ/ *a* (*woman*) hombruna

**manoeuvre** /mə'nuːvə(r)/ *n* maniobra *f*. ● *vt/i* maniobrar

**man-of-war** /mænəv'wɔː(r)/ *n* buque *m* de guerra

**manor** /'mænə(r)/ *n* casa *f* solariega

**manpower** /'mænpaʊə(r)/ *n* mano *f* de obra

**manservant** /'mænsɜːvənt/ *n* criado *m*

**mansion** /'mænʃn/ *n* mansión *f*

**man:** **~size(d)** *a* grande. **~slaughter** *n* homicidio *m* impremeditado

**mantelpiece** /'mæntlpiːs/ *n* repisa *f* de chimenea

**mantilla** /mæn'tɪlə/ *n* mantilla *f*

**mantle** /'mæntl/ *n* manto *m*

**manual** /'mænjʊəl/ *a* manual. ● *n* (*handbook*) manual *m*

**manufacture** /mænjʊ'fæktʃə(r)/ *vt* fabricar. ● *n* fabricación *f*. **~r** /-ə/ *n* fabricante *m*

**manure** /mə'njʊə(r)/ *n* estiércol *m*

**manuscript** /'mænjʊskrɪpt/ *n* manuscrito *m*

**many** /'menɪ/ *a* & *n* muchos (*mpl*). **~ people** mucha gente *f*. **~ a time** muchas veces. **a great/good ~** muchísimos

**map** /mæp/ *n* mapa *m*; (*of streets etc*) plano *m*. ● *vt* (*pt* **mapped**) levantar un mapa de. **~ out** organizar

**maple** /'meɪpl/ *n* arce *m*

**mar** /mɑː/ *vt* (*pt* **marred**) estropear; aguar (*enjoyment*)

**marathon** /'mærəθən/ *n* maratón *m*

**maraud|er** /mə'rɔːdə(r)/ *n* merodeador *m*. **~ing** *a* merodeador

**marble** /'mɑːbl/ *n* mármol *m*; (*for game*) canica *f*

**March** /mɑːtʃ/ *n* marzo *m*

**march** /mɑːtʃ/ *vi* (*mil*) marchar. **~ off** irse. ● *vt*. **~ off** (*lead away*) llevarse. ● *n* marcha *f*

**marchioness** /mɑːʃə'nes/ *n* marquesa *f*

**march-past** /'mɑːtʃpɑːst/ *n* desfile *m*

**mare** /meə(r)/ *n* yegua *f*

**margarine** /mɑːdʒə'riːn/ *n* margarina *f*

**margin** /'mɑːdʒɪn/ *n* margen *f*. **~al** *a* marginal. **~al seat** *n* (*pol*) escaño *m* inseguro. **~ally** *adv* muy poco

**marguerite** /mɑːgə'riːt/ *n* margarita *f*

**marigold** /'mærɪgəʊld/ *n* caléndula *f*

**marijuana** /ˌmærɪ'hwɑːnə/ n marihuana f

**marina** /mə'riːnə/ n puerto m deportivo

**marina|de** /mærɪ'neɪd/ n escabeche m. ~te /'mærɪneɪt/ vt escabechar

**marine** /mə'riːn/ a marino. • n (sailor) soldado m de infantería de marina; (shipping) marina f

**marionette** /ˌmærɪə'net/ n marioneta f

**marital** /'mærɪtl/ a marital, matrimonial. ~ status n estado m civil

**maritime** /'mærɪtaɪm/ a marítimo

**marjoram** /'mɑːdʒərəm/ n mejorana f

**mark**¹ /mɑːk/ n marca f; (trace) huella f; (schol) nota f; (target) blanco m. • vt marcar; poner nota a ⟨exam⟩. ~ time marcar el paso. ~ out trazar; escoger ⟨person⟩

**mark**² /mɑːk/ n (currency) marco m

**marked** /mɑːkt/ a marcado. ~ly /-kɪdlɪ/ adv marcadamente

**marker** /'mɑːkə(r)/ n marcador m; (for book) registro m

**market** /'mɑːkɪt/ n mercado m. **on the** ~ en venta. • vt (sell) vender; (launch) comercializar. ~ **garden** n huerto m. ~**ing** n marketing m

**marking** /'mɑːkɪŋ/ n (marks) marcas fpl

**marksman** /'mɑːksmən/ n tirador m. ~**ship** n puntería f

**marmalade** /'mɑːməleɪd/ n mermelada f de naranja

**marmot** /'mɑːmət/ n marmota f

**maroon** /mə'ruːn/ n granate m. • a de color granate

**marooned** /mə'ruːnd/ a abandonado; (snow-bound etc) aislado

**marquee** /mɑːkiː/ n tienda f de campaña f grande; (awning, Amer) marquesina f

**marquetry** /'mɑːkɪtrɪ/ n marquetería f

**marquis** /'mɑːkwɪs/ n marqués m

**marriage** /'mærɪdʒ/ n matrimonio m; (wedding) boda f. ~**able** a casadero

**married** /'mærɪd/ a casado; ⟨life⟩ conjugal

**marrow** /'mærəʊ/ n (of bone) tuétano m; (vegetable) calabacín m

**marry** /'mærɪ/ vt casarse con; (give or unite in marriage) casar. • vi casarse. **get married** casarse

**marsh** /mɑːʃ/ n pantano m

**marshal** /'mɑːʃl/ n (mil) mariscal m; (master of ceremonies) maestro m de

ceremonias; (at sports events) oficial m. • vt (pt **marshalled**) ordenar; formar ⟨troops⟩

**marsh mallow** /mɑːʃ'mæləʊ/ n (plant) malvavisco m

**marshmallow** /mɑːʃ'mæləʊ/ n (sweet) caramelo m blando

**marshy** /'mɑːʃɪ/ a pantanoso

**martial** /'mɑːʃl/ a marcial. ~ **law** n ley f marcial

**Martian** /'mɑːʃn/ a & n marciano (m)

**martinet** /mɑːtɪ'net/ n ordenancista m & f

**martyr** /'mɑːtə(r)/ n mártir m & f. • vt martirizar. ~**dom** n martirio m

**marvel** /'mɑːvl/ n maravilla f. • vi (pt **marvelled**) maravillarse (**at** con, de). ~**lous** /'mɑːvələs/ a maravilloso

**Marxis|m** /'mɑːksɪzəm/ n marxismo m. ~**t** a & n marxista (m & f)

**marzipan** /'mɑːzɪpæn/ n mazapán m

**mascara** /mæ'skɑːrə/ n rímel m

**mascot** /'mæskɒt/ n mascota f

**masculin|e** /'mæskjʊlɪn/ a & n masculino (m). ~**ity** /-'lɪnətɪ/ n masculinidad f

**mash** /mæʃ/ n mezcla f; (potatoes, fam) puré m de patatas. • vt (crush) machacar; (mix) mezclar. ~**ed potatoes** n puré m de patatas

**mask** /mɑːsk/ n máscara f. • vt enmascarar

**masochis|m** /'mæsəkɪzəm/ n masoquismo m. ~**t** n masoquista m & f

**mason** /'meɪsn/ n (builder) albañil m

**Mason** /'meɪsn/ n. ~ masón m. ~**ic** /mə'sɒnɪk/ a masónico

**masonry** /'meɪsnrɪ/ n albañilería f

**masquerade** /mɑːskə'reɪd/ n mascarada f. • vi. ~ **as** hacerse pasar por

**mass**¹ /mæs/ n masa f; (large quantity) montón m. **the** ~**es** npl las masas fpl. • vt/i agrupar(se)

**mass**² /mæs/ n (relig) misa f. **high** ~ misa f mayor

**massacre** /'mæsəkə(r)/ n masacre f, matanza f. • vt masacrar

**massage** /'mæsɑːʒ/ n masaje m. • vt dar masaje a

**masseu|r** /mæ'sɜː(r)/ n masajista m. ~**se** /mæ'sɜːz/ n masajista f

**massive** /'mæsɪv/ a masivo; (heavy) macizo; (huge) enorme

**mass:** ~ **media** n medios mpl de comunicación. ~**-produce** vt fabricar en serie

**mast** /mɑːst/ n mástil m; (for radio, TV) torre f

**master** /ˈmɑːstə(r)/ n maestro m; (in secondary school) profesor m; (of ship) capitán m. ● vt dominar. **~-key** n llave f maestra. **~ly** a magistral. **~mind** n cerebro m. ● vt dirigir. **M~ of Arts** master m, grado m universitario entre el de licenciado y el de doctor

**masterpiece** /ˈmɑːstəpiːs/ n obra f maestra

**master-stroke** /ˈmɑːstəstrəʊk/ n golpe m maestro

**mastery** /ˈmɑːstərɪ/ n dominio m; (skill) maestría f

**masturbat|e** /ˈmæstəbeɪt/ vi masturbarse. **~ion** /-ˈbeɪʃn/ n masturbación f

**mat** /mæt/ n estera f; (at door) felpudo m

**match**[1] /mætʃ/ n (sport) partido m; (equal) igual m; (marriage) matrimonio m; (s.o. to marry) partido m. ● vt emparejar; (equal) igualar; ‹clothes, colours› hacer juego con. ● vi hacer juego

**match**[2] /mætʃ/ n (of wood) fósforo m; (of wax) cerilla f. **~-box** /ˈmætʃbɒks/ n (for wooden matches) caja f de fósforos; (for wax matches) caja f de cerillas

**matching** /ˈmætʃɪŋ/ a que hace juego

**mate**[1] /meɪt/ n compañero m; (of animals) macho m, hembra f; (assistant) ayudante m. ● vt/i acoplar(se)

**mate**[2] /meɪt/ n (chess) mate m

**material** /məˈtɪərɪəl/ n material m; (cloth) tela f. ● a material; (fig) importante. **~istic** /-ˈlɪstɪk/ a materialista. **~s** npl materiales mpl. **raw ~s** npl materias fpl primas

**materialize** /məˈtɪərɪəlaɪz/ vi materializarse

**maternal** /məˈtɜːnl/ a maternal; ‹relation› materno

**maternity** /məˈtɜːnɪtɪ/ n maternidad f. ● a de maternidad. **~ clothes** npl vestido m pre-mamá. **~ hospital** n maternidad f

**matey** /ˈmeɪtɪ/ a (fam) simpático

**mathematic|ian** /mæθəməˈtɪʃn/ n matemático m. **~al** /-ˈmætɪkl/ a matemático. **~s** /-ˈmætɪks/ n & npl matemáticas fpl

**maths** /mæθs/, **math** (Amer) n & npl matemáticas fpl

**matinée** /ˈmætɪneɪ/ n función f de tarde

**matriculat|e** /məˈtrɪkjʊleɪt/ vt/i matricular(se). **~ion** /-ˈleɪʃn/ n matriculación f

**matrimon|ial** /mætrɪˈməʊnɪəl/ a matrimonial. **~y** /ˈmætrɪmənɪ/ n matrimonio m

**matrix** /ˈmeɪtrɪks/ n (pl matrices /-siːz/) matriz f

**matron** /ˈmeɪtrən/ n (married, elderly) matrona f; (in school) ama f de llaves; (former use, in hospital) enfermera f jefe. **~ly** a matronil

**matt** /mæt/ a mate

**matted** /ˈmætɪd/ a enmarañado

**matter** /ˈmætə(r)/ n (substance) materia f; (affair) asunto m; (pus) pus m. **as a ~ of fact** en realidad. **no ~ no importa. what is the ~?** ¿qué pasa? ● vi importar. **it does not ~** no importa. **~-of-fact** a realista

**matting** /ˈmætɪŋ/ n estera f

**mattress** /ˈmætrɪs/ n colchón m

**matur|e** /məˈtjʊə(r)/ a maduro. ● vt/i madurar. **~ity** n madurez f

**maul** /mɔːl/ vt maltratar

**Mauritius** /məˈrɪʃəs/ n Mauricio m

**mausoleum** /mɔːsəˈlɪəm/ n mausoleo m

**mauve** /məʊv/ a & n color (m) de malva

**mawkish** /ˈmɔːkɪʃ/ a empalagoso

**maxim** /ˈmæksɪm/ n máxima f

**maxim|ize** /ˈmæksɪmaɪz/ vt llevar al máximo. **~um** a & n (pl -ima) máximo (m)

**may** /meɪ/ v aux (pt **might**) poder. **~ I smoke?** ¿se permite fumar? **~ he be happy** ¡que sea feliz! **he ~/might come** puede que venga. **I ~/might as well stay** más vale quedarme. **it ~/might be true** puede ser verdad

**May** /meɪ/ n mayo m. **~ Day** n el primero m de mayo

**maybe** /ˈmeɪbɪ/ adv quizá(s)

**mayhem** /ˈmeɪhem/ n (havoc) alboroto m

**mayonnaise** /meɪəˈneɪz/ n mayonesa f

**mayor** /meə(r)/ n alcalde m, alcaldesa f. **~ess** n alcaldesa f

**maze** /meɪz/ n laberinto m

**me**[1] /miː/ pron me; (after prep) mí. **he knows ~** me conoce. **it's ~** soy yo

**me**[2] /miː/ n (mus, third note of any musical scale) mi m

**meadow** /ˈmedəʊ/ n prado m

**meagre** /ˈmiːgə(r)/ a escaso

**meal**[1] /miːl/ n comida f

**meal**[2] /miːl/ n (grain) harina f

**mealy-mouthed** /miːlɪˈmaʊðd/ a hipócrita

**mean**[1] /miːn/ vt (pt meant) (intend) tener la intención de, querer; (signify) querer decir, significar. ∼ to do tener la intención de hacer. ∼ well tener buenas intenciones. be meant for estar destinado a

**mean**[2] /miːn/ a (-er, -est) (miserly) tacaño; (unkind) malo; (poor) pobre

**mean**[3] /miːn/ a medio. ● n medio m; (average) promedio m

**meander** /mɪˈændə(r)/ vi (river) serpentear; (person) vagar

**meaning** /ˈmiːnɪŋ/ n sentido m. ∼ful a significativo. ∼less a sin sentido

**meanness** /ˈmiːnnɪs/ n (miserliness) tacañería f; (unkindness) maldad f

**means** /miːnz/ n medio m. by all ∼ por supuesto. by no ∼ de ninguna manera. ● npl (wealth) recursos mpl. ∼ test n investigación f financial

**meant** /ment/ see mean[1]

**meantime** /ˈmiːntaɪm/ adv entretanto. in the ∼ entretanto

**meanwhile** /ˈmiːnwaɪl/ adv entretanto

**measles** /ˈmiːzlz/ n sarampión m

**measly** /ˈmiːzlɪ/ a (sl) miserable

**measurable** /ˈmeʒərəbl/ a mensurable

**measure** /ˈmeʒə(r)/ n medida f; (ruler) regla f. ● vt/i medir. ∼ up to estar a la altura de. ∼d a (rhythmical) acompasado; (carefully considered) prudente. ∼ment n medida f

**meat** /miːt/ n carne f. ∼y a carnoso; (fig) sustancioso

**mechanic** /mɪˈkænɪk/ n mecánico m. ∼al /mɪˈkænɪkl/ a mecánico. ∼s n mecánica f

**mechani|sm** /ˈmekənɪzəm/ n mecanismo m. ∼ze vt mecanizar

**medal** /ˈmedl/ n medalla f

**medallion** /mɪˈdælɪən/ n medallón m

**medallist** /ˈmedəlɪst/ n ganador m de una medalla. be a gold ∼ ganar una medalla de oro

**meddle** /ˈmedl/ vi entrometerse (in en); (tinker) tocar. ∼ with (tinker) tocar. ∼some a entrometido

**media** /ˈmiːdɪə/ see medium. ● npl. the ∼ npl los medios mpl de comunicación

**mediat|e** /ˈmiːdɪeɪt/ vi mediar. ∼ion /-eɪʃn/ n mediación f. ∼or n mediador m

**medical** /ˈmedɪkl/ a médico; (student) de medicina. ● n (fam) reconocimiento m médico

**medicat|ed** /ˈmedɪkeɪtɪd/ a medicinal. ∼ion /-ˈkeɪʃn/ n medicación f

**medicin|e** /ˈmedsɪn/ n medicina f. ∼al /mɪˈdɪsɪnl/ a medicinal

**medieval** /medɪˈiːvl/ a medieval

**mediocr|e** /miːdɪˈəʊkə(r)/ a mediocre. ∼ity /-ˈɒkrətɪ/ n mediocridad f

**meditat|e** /ˈmedɪteɪt/ vt/i meditar. ∼ion /-ˈteɪʃn/ n meditación f

**Mediterranean** /medɪtəˈreɪnɪən/ a mediterráneo. ● n. the ∼ el Mediterráneo m

**medium** /ˈmiːdɪəm/ n (pl media) medio m; (pl mediums) (person) médium m. ● a mediano

**medley** /ˈmedlɪ/ n popurrí m

**meek** /miːk/ a (-er, -est) manso

**meet** /miːt/ vt (pt met) encontrar; (bump into s.o.) encontrarse con; (see again) ver; (fetch) ir a buscar; (get to know, be introduced to) conocer. ∼ the bill pagar la cuenta. ● vi encontrarse; (get to know) conocerse; (in session) reunirse. ∼ with tropezar con (obstacles)

**meeting** /ˈmiːtɪŋ/ n reunión f; (accidental between two people) encuentro m; (arranged between two people) cita f

**megalomania** /megələʊˈmeɪnɪə/ n megalomanía f

**megaphone** /ˈmegəfəʊn/ n megáfono m

**melanchol|ic** /melənˈkɒlɪk/ a melancólico. ∼y /ˈmelənkɒlɪ/ n melancolía f. ● a melancólico

**mêlée** /ˈmeleɪ/ n pelea f confusa

**mellow** /ˈmeləʊ/ a (-er, -est) (fruit, person) maduro; (sound, colour) dulce. ● vt/i madurar(se)

**melodi|c** /mɪˈlɒdɪk/ a melódico. ∼ous /mɪˈləʊdɪəs/ a melodioso

**melodrama** /ˈmelədrɑːmə/ n melodrama m. ∼tic /-əˈmætɪk/ a melodramático

**melody** /ˈmelədɪ/ n melodía f

**melon** /ˈmelən/ n melón m

**melt** /melt/ vt (make liquid) derretir; fundir (metals). ● vi (become liquid) derretirse; (metals) fundirse. ∼ing-pot n crisol m

**member** /ˈmembə(r)/ n miembro m. M∼ of Parliament n diputado m.

**~ship** *n* calidad *f* de miembro; (*members*) miembros *mpl*

**membrane** /'membreɪn/ *n* membrana *f*

**memento** /mɪ'mentəʊ/ *n* (*pl* **-oes**) recuerdo *m*

**memo** /'meməʊ/ *n* (*pl* **-os**) (*fam*) nota *f*

**memoir** /'memwɑ:(r)/ *n* memoria *f*

**memorable** /'memərəbl/ *a* memorable

**memorandum** /memə'rændəm/ *n* (*pl* **-ums**) nota *f*

**memorial** /mɪ'mɔ:rɪəl/ *n* monumento *m*. ● *a* conmemorativo

**memorize** /'meməraɪz/ *vt* aprender de memoria

**memory** /'memərɪ/ *n* (*faculty*) memoria *f*; (*thing remembered*) recuerdo *m*. **from ~** de memoria. **in ~ of** en memoria de

**men** /men/ *see* **man**

**menac|e** /'menəs/ *n* amenaza *f*; (*nuisance*) pesado *m*. ● *vt* amenazar. **~ingly** *adv* de manera amenazadora

**menagerie** /mɪ'nædʒərɪ/ *n* casa *f* de fieras

**mend** /mend/ *vt* reparar; (*darn*) zurcir. **~ one's ways** enmendarse. ● *n* remiendo *m*. **be on the ~** ir mejorando

**menfolk** /'menfəʊk/ *n* hombres *mpl*

**menial** /'mi:nɪəl/ *a* servil

**meningitis** /menɪn'dʒaɪtɪs/ *n* meningitis *f*

**menopause** /'menəpɔ:z/ *n* menopausia *f*

**menstruat|e** /'menstrʊeɪt/ *vi* menstruar. **~ion** /-'eɪʃn/ *n* menstruación *f*

**mental** /'mentl/ *a* mental; (*hospital*) psiquiátrico

**mentality** /men'tælətɪ/ *n* mentalidad *f*

**menthol** /'menθɒl/ *n* mentol *m*. **~ated** *a* mentolado

**mention** /'menʃn/ *vt* mencionar. **don't ~ it!** ¡no hay de qué! ● *n* mención *f*

**mentor** /'mentɔ:(r)/ *n* mentor *m*

**menu** /'menju:/ *n* (*set meal*) menú *m*; (*a la carte*) lista *f* (de platos)

**mercantile** /'mɜ:kəntaɪl/ *a* mercantil

**mercenary** /'mɜ:sɪnərɪ/ *a* & *n* mercenario (*m*)

**merchandise** /'mɜ:tʃəndaɪz/ *n* mercancías *fpl*

**merchant** /'mɜ:tʃənt/ *n* comerciante *m*. ● *a* ‹ship, navy› mercante. **~ bank** *n* banco *m* mercantil

**merci|ful** /'mɜ:sɪfl/ *a* misericordioso. **~fully** *adv* (*fortunately, fam*) gracias a Dios. **~less** /'mɜ:sɪlɪs/ *a* despiadado

**mercur|ial** /mɜ:'kjʊərɪəl/ *a* mercurial; (*fig, active*) vivo. **~y** /'mɜ:kjʊrɪ/ *n* mercurio *m*

**mercy** /'mɜ:sɪ/ *n* compasión *f*. **at the ~ of** a merced de

**mere** /mɪə(r)/ *a* simple. **~ly** *adv* simplemente

**merest** /'mɪərɪst/ *a* mínimo

**merge** /mɜ:dʒ/ *vt* unir; fusionar ‹companies›. ● *vi* unirse; ‹companies› fusionarse. **~r** /-ə(r)/ *n* fusión *f*

**meridian** /mə'rɪdɪən/ *n* meridiano *m*

**meringue** /mə'ræŋ/ *n* merengue *m*

**merit** /'merɪt/ *n* mérito *m*. ● *vt* (*pt* **merited**) merecer. **~orious** /-'tɔ:rɪəs/ *a* meritorio

**mermaid** /'mɜ:meɪd/ *n* sirena *f*

**merr|ily** /'merəlɪ/ *adv* alegremente. **~iment** /'merɪmənt/ *n* alegría *f*. **~y** /'merɪ/ *a* (**-ier, -iest**) alegre. **make ~** divertirse. **~y-go-round** *n* tiovivo *m*. **~y-making** *n* holgorio *m*

**mesh** /meʃ/ *n* malla *f*; (*network*) red *f*

**mesmerize** /'mezməraɪz/ *vt* hipnotizar

**mess** /mes/ *n* desorden *m*; (*dirt*) suciedad *f*; (*mil*) rancho *m*. **make a ~ of** chapucear, estropear. ● *vt*. **~ up** desordenar; (*dirty*) ensuciar. ● *vi*. **~ about** entretenerse. **~ with** (*tinker with*) manosear

**message** /'mesɪdʒ/ *n* recado *m*

**messenger** /'mesɪndʒə(r)/ *n* mensajero *m*

**Messiah** /mɪ'saɪə/ *n* Mesías *m*

**Messrs** /'mesəz/ *npl*. **~ Smith** los señores *mpl* o Sres. Smith

**messy** /'mesɪ/ *a* (**-ier, -iest**) en desorden; (*dirty*) sucio

**met** /met/ *see* **meet**

**metabolism** /mɪ'tæbəlɪzəm/ *n* metabolismo *m*

**metal** /'metl/ *n* metal. ● *a* de metal. **~lic** /mɪ'tælɪk/ *a* metálico

**metallurgy** /mɪ'tælədʒɪ/ *n* metalurgia *f*

**metamorphosis** /metə'mɔ:fəsɪs/ *n* (*pl* **-phoses** /-sɪ:z/) metamorfosis *f*

**metaphor** /'metəfə(r)/ *n* metáfora *f*. **~ical** /-'fɒrɪkl/ *a* metafórico

**mete** /miːt/ vt. ~ **out** repartir; dar ⟨punishment⟩

**meteor** /'miːtɪə(r)/ n meteoro m

**meteorite** /'miːtɪəraɪt/ n meteorito m

**meteorolog|ical** /miːtɪərə'lɒdʒɪkl/ a meteorológico. ~y /-'rɒlədʒɪ/ n meteorología f

**meter¹** /'miːtə(r)/ n contador m

**meter²** /'miːtə(r)/ n (Amer) = **metre**

**method** /'meθəd/ n método m

**methodical** /mɪ'θɒdɪkl/ a metódico

**Methodist** /'meθədɪst/ a & n metodista (m & f)

**methylated** /'meθɪleɪtɪd/ a. ~ **spirit** n alcohol m desnaturalizado

**meticulous** /mɪ'tɪkjʊləs/ a meticuloso

**metre** /'miːtə(r)/ n metro m

**metric** /'metrɪk/ a métrico. ~ation /-'keɪʃn/ n cambio m al sistema métrico

**metropolis** /mɪ'trɒpəlɪs/ n metrópoli f

**metropolitan** /metrə'pɒlɪtən/ a metropolitano

**mettle** /'metl/ n valor m

**mew** /mjuː/ n maullido m. ●vi maullar

**mews** /mjuːz/ npl casas fpl pequeñas (que antes eran caballerizas)

**Mexic|an** /'meksɪkən/ a & n mejicano (m); (in Mexico) mexicano (m). ~o /-kəʊ/ n Méjico m; (in Mexico) México m

**mezzanine** /'metsəniːn/ n entresuelo m

**mi** /miː/ n (mus, third note of any musical scale) mi m

**miaow** /miː'aʊ/ n & vi = **mew**

**mice** /maɪs/ see **mouse**

**mickey** /'mɪkɪ/ n. take the ~ out of (sl) tomar el pelo a

**micro...** /'maɪkrəʊ/ pref micro...

**microbe** /'maɪkrəʊb/ n microbio m

**microchip** /'maɪkrəʊtʃɪp/ n pastilla f

**microfilm** /'maɪkrəʊfɪlm/ n microfilme m

**microphone** /'maɪkrəfəʊn/ n micrófono m

**microprocessor** /maɪkrəʊ'prəʊsesə(r)/ n microprocesador m

**microscop|e** /'maɪkrəskəʊp/ n microscopio m. ~ic /-'skɒpɪk/ a microscópico

**microwave** /'maɪkrəʊweɪv/ n microonda f. ~ **oven** n horno m de microondas

**mid** /mɪd/ a. **in** ~ **air** en pleno aire. **in** ~ **March** a mediados de marzo. **in** ~ **ocean** en medio del océano

**midday** /mɪd'deɪ/ n mediodía m

**middle** /'mɪdl/ a de en medio; ⟨quality⟩ mediano. ●n medio m. **in the** ~ of en medio de. ~**-aged** a de mediana edad. **M~ Ages** npl Edad f Media. ~ **class** n clase f media. ~**class** a de la clase media. **M~ East** n Oriente m Medio. ~**man** n intermediario m

**middling** /'mɪdlɪŋ/ a regular

**midge** /mɪdʒ/ n mosquito m

**midget** /'mɪdʒɪt/ n enano m. ●a minúsculo

**Midlands** /'mɪdləndz/ npl región f central de Inglaterra

**midnight** /'mɪdnaɪt/ n medianoche f

**midriff** /'mɪdrɪf/ n diafragma m; (fam) vientre m

**midst** /mɪdst/ n. **in our** ~ entre nosotros. **in the** ~ **of** en medio de

**midsummer** /mɪd'sʌmə(r)/ n pleno verano m; (solstice) solsticio m de verano

**midway** /mɪd'weɪ/ adv a medio camino

**midwife** /'mɪdwaɪf/ n comadrona f

**midwinter** /mɪd'wɪntə(r)/ n pleno invierno m

**might¹** /maɪt/ see **may**

**might²** /maɪt/ n (strength) fuerza f; (power) poder m. ~y a (strong) fuerte; (powerful) poderoso; (very great, fam) enorme. ●adv (fam) muy

**migraine** /'miːgreɪn/ n jaqueca f

**migrant** /'maɪgrənt/ a migratorio. ●n (person) emigrante m & f

**migrat|e** /maɪ'greɪt/ vi emigrar. ~ion /-ʃn/ n migración f

**mike** /maɪk/ n (fam) micrófono m

**mild** /maɪld/ a (-er, -est) ⟨person⟩ apacible; ⟨climate⟩ templado; (slight) ligero; ⟨taste⟩ suave; ⟨illness⟩ benigno

**mild:** ~**ly** adv (slightly) ligeramente. ~**ness** n (of person) apacibilidad f; (of climate, illness) benignidad f; (of taste) suavidad f

**mile** /maɪl/ n milla f. ~**s better** (fam) mucho mejor. ~**s too big** (fam) demasiado grande. ~**age** n (loosely) kilometraje m. ~**stone** n mojón m; (event, stage, fig) hito m

**milieu** /miː'ljɜː/ n ambiente m

**mildew** /'mɪldjuː/ n moho m

**militant** /'mɪlɪtənt/ a & n militante
(m & f)

**military** /'mɪlɪtərɪ/ a militar

**militate** /'mɪlɪteɪt/ vi militar
(**against** contra)

**militia** /mɪ'lɪʃə/ n milicia f

**milk** /mɪlk/ n leche f. • a ‹product›
lácteo; ‹chocolate› con leche. • vt
ordeñar ‹cow›; (exploit) chupar.
~**man** n repartidor m de leche. ~
**shake** n batido m de leche. ~**y** a
lechoso. **M~y Way** n Vía f Láctea

**mill** /mɪl/ n molino m; (for coffee, pepper) molinillo m; (factory) fábrica f.
• vt moler. • vi. ~ **about/around**
apiñarse, circular

**millennium** /mɪ'lenɪəm/ n (pl -ia or
-iums) milenio m

**miller** /'mɪlə(r)/ n molinero m

**millet** /'mɪlɪt/ n mijo m

**milli...** /'mɪlɪ/ pref mili...

**milligram(me)** /'mɪlɪgræm/ n mili-
gramo m

**millimetre** /'mɪlɪmiːtə(r)/ n milímetro m

**milliner** /'mɪlɪnə(r)/ n sombrerero m

**million** /'mɪlɪən/ n millón m. **a ~
pounds** un millón m de libras.
~**aire** n millonario m

**millstone** /'mɪlstəʊn/ n muela f (de
molino); (fig, burden) losa f

**mime** /maɪm/ n pantomima f. • vt
hacer en pantomima. • vi actuar de
mimo

**mimic** /'mɪmɪk/ vt (pt **mimicked**)
imitar. • n imitador m. ~**ry** n imitación f

**mimosa** /mɪ'məʊzə/ n mimosa f

**minaret** /mɪnə'ret/ n alminar m

**mince** /mɪns/ vt desmenuzar; picar
‹meat›. **not to ~ matters/words** no
tener pelos en la lengua. • n carne f
picada. ~**meat** n conserva de fruta
picada. **make ~meat of s.o.** hacer
trizas a uno. ~ **pie** n pastel m con
frutas picadas. ~**r** n máquina f de
picar carne

**mind** /maɪnd/ n mente f; (sanity) juicio m; (opinion) parecer m; (intention) intención f. **be on one's ~**
preocuparle a uno. • vt (look after)
cuidar; (heed) hacer caso de. **I don't
~** me da igual. **I don't ~ the noise**
no me molesta el ruido. **never ~** no
te preocupes, no se preocupe. ~**er**
n cuidador m. ~**ful** a atento (**of** a).
~**less** a estúpido

**mine**[1] /maɪn/ poss pron (el) mío m,
(la) mía f, (los) míos mpl, (las) mías
fpl. **it is ~** es mío

**mine**[2] /maɪn/ n mina f. • vt extraer.
~**field** n campo m de minas. ~**r** n
minero m

**mineral** /'mɪnərəl/ a & n mineral
(m). ~ (**water**) n (fizzy soft drink)
gaseosa f. ~ **water** n (natural) agua
f mineral

**minesweeper** /'maɪnswiːpə(r)/ n
(ship) dragaminas m invar

**mingle** /'mɪŋgl/ vt/i mezclar(se)

**mingy** /'mɪndʒɪ/ a tacaño

**mini...** /'mɪnɪ/ pref mini...

**miniature** /'mɪnɪtʃə(r)/ a & n miniatura (f)

**mini:** ~**bus** n microbús m. ~**cab** n
taxi m

**minim** /'mɪnɪm/ n (mus) blanca f

**minim|al** /'mɪnɪml/ a mínimo. ~**ize**
vt minimizar. ~**um** a & n (pl -**ima**)
mínimo (m)

**mining** /'maɪnɪŋ/ n explotación f.
• a minero

**miniskirt** /'mɪnɪskɜːt/ n minifalda f

**minist|er** /'mɪnɪstə(r)/ n ministro m;
(relig) pastor m. ~**erial** /-'stɪərɪəl/ a
ministerial. ~**ry** n ministerio m

**mink** /mɪŋk/ n visón m

**minor** /'maɪnə(r)/ a (incl mus)
menor; (of little importance) sin
importancia. • n menor m & f de
edad

**minority** /maɪ'nɒrətɪ/ n minoría f.
• a minoritario

**minster** /'mɪnstə(r)/ n catedral f

**minstrel** /'mɪnstrəl/ n juglar m

**mint**[1] /mɪnt/ n (plant) menta f;
(sweet) caramelo m de menta

**mint**[2] /mɪnt/ n. **the M~** n casa f de
la moneda. **a ~** un dineral m. • vt
acuñar. **in ~ condition** como nuevo

**minuet** /mɪnjʊ'et/ n minué m

**minus** /'maɪnəs/ prep menos; (without, fam) sin. • n (sign) menos m. ~
**sign** n menos m

**minuscule** /'mɪnəskjuːl/ a minúsculo

**minute**[1] /'mɪnɪt/ n minuto m. ~**s** npl
(of meeting) actas fpl

**minute**[2] /maɪ'njuːt/ a minúsculo;
(detailed) minucioso

**minx** /mɪŋks/ n chica f descarada

**mirac|le** /'mɪrəkl/ n milagro m. ~**u-
lous** /mɪ'rækjʊləs/ a milagroso

**mirage** /'mɪrɑːʒ/ n espejismo m

**mire** /'maɪə(r)/ n fango m

**mirror** /'mɪrə(r)/ n espejo m. • vt
reflejar

**mirth** /mɜːθ/ n (merriment) alegría f;
(laughter) risas fpl

**misadventure** /mɪsəd'ventʃə(r)/ n desgracia f

**misanthropist** /mɪ'zænθrəpɪst/ n misántropo m

**misapprehension** /mɪsæprɪ'henʃn/ n malentendido m

**misbehav|e** /mɪsbɪ'heɪv/ vi portarse mal. ~**iour** n mala conducta f

**miscalculat|e** /mɪs'kælkjʊleɪt/ vt/i calcular mal. ~**ion** /-'leɪʃn/ n desacierto m

**miscarr|iage** /'mɪskærɪdʒ/ n aborto m. ~**iage of justice** n error m judicial. ~**y** vi abortar

**miscellaneous** /mɪsə'leɪnɪəs/ a vario

**mischief** /'mɪstʃɪf/ n (foolish conduct) travesura f; (harm) daño m. **get into** ~ cometer travesuras. **make** ~ armar un lío

**mischievous** /'mɪstʃɪvəs/ a travieso; (malicious) perjudicial

**misconception** /mɪskən'sepʃn/ n equivocación f

**misconduct** /mɪs'kɒndʌkt/ n mala conducta f

**misconstrue** /mɪskən'struː/ vt interpretar mal

**misdeed** /mɪs'diːd/ n fechoría f

**misdemeanour** /mɪsdɪ'miːnə(r)/ n fechoría f

**misdirect** /mɪsdɪ'rekt/ vt dirigir mal (person)

**miser** /'maɪzə(r)/ n avaro m

**miserable** /'mɪzərəbl/ a (sad) triste; (wretched) miserable; (weather) malo

**miserly** /'maɪzəlɪ/ a avariento

**misery** /'mɪzərɪ/ n (unhappiness) tristeza f; (pain) sufrimiento m; (poverty) pobreza f; (person, fam) aguafiestas m & f

**misfire** /mɪs'faɪə(r)/ vi fallar

**misfit** /'mɪsfɪt/ n (person) inadaptado m; (thing) cosa f mal ajustada

**misfortune** /mɪs'fɔːtʃuːn/ n desgracia f

**misgiving** /mɪs'gɪvɪŋ/ n (doubt) duda f; (apprehension) presentimiento m

**misguided** /mɪs'gaɪdɪd/ a equivocado. **be** ~ equivocarse

**mishap** /'mɪshæp/ n desgracia f

**misinform** /mɪsɪn'fɔːm/ vt informar mal

**misinterpret** /mɪsɪn'tɜːprɪt/ vt interpretar mal

**misjudge** /mɪs'dʒʌdʒ/ vt juzgar mal

**mislay** /mɪs'leɪ/ vt (pt **mislaid**) extraviar

**mislead** /mɪs'liːd/ vt (pt **misled**) engañar. ~**ing** a engañoso

**mismanage** /mɪs'mænɪdʒ/ vt administrar mal. ~**ment** n mala administración f

**misnomer** /mɪs'nəʊmə(r)/ n nombre m equivocado

**misplace** /mɪs'pleɪs/ vt colocar mal; (lose) extraviar

**misprint** /'mɪsprɪnt/ n errata f

**misquote** /mɪs'kwəʊt/ vt citar mal

**misrepresent** /mɪsreprɪ'zent/ vt describir engañosamente

**miss**[1] /mɪs/ vt (fail to hit) errar; (notice absence of) echar de menos; perder (train). ~ **the point** no comprender. ● n fallo m. ~ **out** omitir

**miss**[2] /mɪs/ n (pl **misses**) señorita f

**misshapen** /mɪs'ʃeɪpən/ a deforme

**missile** /'mɪsaɪl/ n proyectil m

**missing** /'mɪsɪŋ/ a (person) (absent) ausente; (person) (after disaster) desaparecido; (lost) perdido. **be** ~ faltar

**mission** /'mɪʃn/ n misión f. ~**ary** /'mɪʃənərɪ/ n misionero m

**missive** /'mɪsɪv/ n misiva f

**misspell** /mɪs'spel/ vt (pt **misspelt** or **misspelled**) escribir mal

**mist** /mɪst/ n neblina f; (at sea) bruma f. ● vt/i empañar(se)

**mistake** /mɪ'steɪk/ n error m. ● vt (pt **mistook**, pp **mistaken**) equivocarse de; (misunderstand) entender mal. ~ **for** tomar por. ~**n** /-ən/ a equivocado. **be** ~**n** equivocarse. ~**nly** adv equivocadamente

**mistletoe** /'mɪsltəʊ/ n muérdago m

**mistreat** /mɪs'triːt/ vt maltratar

**mistress** /'mɪstrɪs/ n (of house) señora f; (primary school teacher) maestra f; (secondary school teacher) profesora f; (lover) amante f

**mistrust** /mɪs'trʌst/ vt desconfiar de. ● n desconfianza f

**misty** /'mɪstɪ/ a (-ier, -iest) nebuloso; (day) de niebla; (glass) empañado. **it is** ~ hay neblina

**misunderstand** /mɪsʌndə'stænd/ vt (pt **-stood**) entender mal. ~**ing** n malentendido m

**misuse** /mɪs'juːz/ vt emplear mal; abusar de (power etc). /mɪs'juːs/ n mal uso m; (unfair use) abuso m

**mite** /maɪt/ n (insect) ácaro m, garrapata f; (child) niño m pequeño

**mitigate** /'mɪtɪgeɪt/ vt mitigar

**mitre** /ˈmaɪtə(r)/ n (head-dress) mitra f

**mitten** /ˈmɪtn/ n manopla f; (leaving fingers exposed) mitón m

**mix** /mɪks/ vt/i mezclar(se). ~ up mezclar; (confuse) confundir. ~ with frecuentar ⟨people⟩. ● n mezcla f

**mixed** /mɪkst/ a ⟨school etc⟩ mixto; (assorted) variado. be ~ up estar confuso

**mixer** /ˈmɪksə(r)/ n (culin) batidora f. be a good ~ tener don de gentes

**mixture** /ˈmɪkstʃə(r)/ n mezcla f

**mix-up** /ˈmɪksʌp/ n lío m

**moan** /məʊn/ n gemido m. ● vi gemir; (complain) quejarse (about de). ~er n refunfuñador m

**moat** /məʊt/ n foso m

**mob** /mɒb/ n (crowd) muchedumbre f; (gang) pandilla f; (masses) populacho m. ● vt (pt mobbed) acosar

**mobil|e** /ˈməʊbaɪl/ a móvil. ~e home n caravana f. ● n móvil m. ~ity /məˈbɪlətɪ/ n movilidad f

**mobiliz|ation** /məʊbɪlaɪˈzeɪʃn/ n movilización f. ~e /ˈməʊbɪlaɪz/ vt/i movilizar

**moccasin** /ˈmɒkəsɪn/ n mocasín m

**mocha** /ˈmɒkə/ n moca m

**mock** /mɒk/ vt burlarse de. ● vi burlarse. ● a fingido

**mockery** /ˈmɒkərɪ/ n burla f. a ~ of una parodia f de

**mock-up** /ˈmɒkʌp/ n maqueta f

**mode** /məʊd/ n (way, method) modo m; (fashion) moda f

**model** /ˈmɒdl/ n modelo m; (mockup) maqueta f; (for fashion) maniquí m. ● a (exemplary) ejemplar; ⟨car etc⟩ en miniatura. ● vt (pt modelled) modelar; presentar ⟨clothes⟩. ● vi ser maniquí; (pose) posar. ~ling n profesión f de maniquí

**moderate** /ˈmɒdərət/ a & n moderado (m). /ˈmɒdəreɪt/ vt/i moderar(se). ~ly /ˈmɒdərətlɪ/ adv (in moderation) moderadamente; (fairly) medianamente

**moderation** /mɒdəˈreɪʃn/ n moderación f. in ~ con moderación

**modern** /ˈmɒdn/ a moderno. ~ize vt modernizar

**modest** /ˈmɒdɪst/ a modesto. ~y n modestia f

**modicum** /ˈmɒdɪkəm/ n. a ~ of un poquito m de

**modif|ication** /mɒdɪfɪˈkeɪʃn/ n modificación f. ~y /-faɪ/ vt/i modificar(se)

**modulat|e** /ˈmɒdjʊleɪt/ vt/i modular. ~ion /-ˈleɪʃn/ n modulación f

**module** /ˈmɒdjuːl/ n módulo m

**mogul** /ˈməʊgəl/ n (fam) magnate m

**mohair** /ˈməʊheə(r)/ n mohair m

**moist** /mɔɪst/ a (-er, -est) húmedo. ~en /ˈmɔɪsn/ vt humedecer

**moistur|e** /ˈmɔɪstʃə(r)/ n humedad f. ~ize /ˈmɔɪstʃəraɪz/ vt humedecer. ~izer n crema f hidratante

**molar** /ˈməʊlə(r)/ n muela f

**molasses** /məˈlæsɪz/ n melaza f

**mold** /məʊld/ (Amer) = **mould**

**mole¹** /məʊl/ n (animal) topo m

**mole²** /məʊl/ n (on skin) lunar m

**mole³** /məʊl/ n (breakwater) malecón m

**molecule** /ˈmɒlɪkjuːl/ n molécula f

**molehill** /ˈməʊlhɪl/ n topera f

**molest** /məˈlest/ vt importunar

**mollify** /ˈmɒlɪfaɪ/ vt apaciguar

**mollusc** /ˈmɒləsk/ n molusco m

**mollycoddle** /ˈmɒlɪkɒdl/ vt mimar

**molten** /ˈməʊltən/ a fundido

**mom** /mɒm/ n (Amer) mamá f

**moment** /ˈməʊmənt/ n momento m. ~arily /ˈməʊməntərɪlɪ/ adv momentáneamente. ~ary a momentáneo

**momentous** /məˈmentəs/ a importante

**momentum** /məˈmentəm/ n momento m; (speed) velocidad f; (fig) ímpetu m

**Monaco** /ˈmɒnəkəʊ/ n Mónaco m

**monarch** /ˈmɒnək/ n monarca m. ~ist n monárquico m. ~y n monarquía f

**monast|ery** /ˈmɒnəstərɪ/ n monasterio m. ~ic /məˈnæstɪk/ a monástico

**Monday** /ˈmʌndeɪ/ n lunes m

**monetar|ist** /ˈmʌnɪtərɪst/ n monetarista m & f. ~y a monetario

**money** /ˈmʌnɪ/ n dinero m. ~box n hucha f. ~ed a adinerado. ~lender n prestamista m & f. ~ order n giro m postal. ~s npl cantidades fpl de dinero. ~spinner n mina f de dinero

**mongol** /ˈmɒŋgl/ n & a (med) mongólico (m)

**mongrel** /ˈmʌŋgrəl/ n perro m mestizo

**monitor** /ˈmɒnɪtə(r)/ n (pupil) monitor m & f; (tec) monitor m. ● vt controlar; escuchar ⟨a broadcast⟩

**monk** /mʌŋk/ n monje m

**monkey** /'mʌŋkɪ/ n mono m. **~-nut** n cacahuete m, maní m (LAm). **~-wrench** n llave f inglesa

**mono** /'mɒnəʊ/ a monofónico

**monocle** /'mɒnəkl/ n monóculo m

**monogram** /'mɒnəgræm/ n monograma m

**monologue** /'mɒnəlɒg/ n monólogo m

**monopol|ize** /mə'nɒpəlaɪz/ vt monopolizar. **~y** n monopolio m

**monosyllab|ic** /mɒnəsɪ'læbɪk/ a monosilábico. **~le** /-'sɪləbl/ n monosílabo m

**monotone** /'mɒnətəʊn/ n monotonía f. **speak in a ~** hablar con una voz monótona

**monoton|ous** /mə'nɒtənəs/ a monótono. **~y** n monotonía f

**monsoon** /mɒn'suːn/ n monzón m

**monster** /'mɒnstə(r)/ n monstruo m

**monstrosity** /mɒn'strɒsətɪ/ n monstruosidad f

**monstrous** /'mɒnstrəs/ a monstruoso

**montage** /mɒn'tɑːʒ/ n montaje m

**month** /mʌnθ/ n mes m. **~ly** /'mʌnθlɪ/ a mensual. ● adv mensualmente. ● n (periodical) revista f mensual

**monument** /'mɒnjʊmənt/ n monumento m. **~al** /-'mentl/ a monumental

**moo** /muː/ n mugido m. ● vi mugir

**mooch** /muːtʃ/ vi (sl) haraganear. ● vt (Amer, sl) birlar

**mood** /muːd/ n humor m. **be in the ~ for** tener ganas de. **in a good/bad ~** de buen/mal humor. **~y** a (-ier, -iest) de humor cambiadizo; (bad-tempered) malhumorado

**moon** /muːn/ n luna f. **~light** n luz f de la luna. **~lighting** n (fam) pluriempleo m. **~lit** a iluminado por la luna; (night) de luna

**moor**[1] /mʊə(r)/ n (open land) páramo m

**moor**[2] /mʊə(r)/ vt amarrar. **~ings** npl (ropes) amarras fpl; (place) amarradero m

**Moor** /mʊə(r)/ n moro m

**moose** /muːs/ n invar alce m

**moot** /muːt/ a discutible. ● vt proponer (question)

**mop** /mɒp/ n fregona f. **~ of hair** pelambrera f. ● vt (pt mopped) fregar. **~ (up)** limpiar

**mope** /məʊp/ vi estar abatido

**moped** /'məʊped/ n ciclomotor m

**moral** /'mɒrəl/ a moral. ● n moraleja f. **~s** npl moralidad f

**morale** /mə'rɑːl/ n moral f

**moral|ist** /'mɒrəlɪst/ n moralista m & f. **~ity** /mə'rælətɪ/ n moralidad f. **~ize** vi moralizar. **~ly** adv moralmente

**morass** /mə'ræs/ n (marsh) pantano m; (fig, entanglement) embrollo m

**morbid** /'mɔːbɪd/ a morboso

**more** /mɔː(r)/ a & n & adv más. **~ and ~** cada vez más. **~ or less** más o menos. **once ~** una vez más. **some ~** más

**moreover** /mɔː'rəʊvə(r)/ adv además

**morgue** /mɔːg/ n depósito m de cadáveres

**moribund** /'mɒrɪbʌnd/ a moribundo

**morning** /'mɔːnɪŋ/ n mañana f; (early hours) madrugada f. **at 11 o'clock in the ~** a las once de la mañana. **in the ~** por la mañana

**Morocc|an** /mə'rɒkən/ a & n marroquí (m & f). **~o** /-kəʊ/ n Marruecos mpl

**moron** /'mɔːrɒn/ n imbécil m & f

**morose** /mə'rəʊs/ a malhumorado

**morphine** /'mɔːfiːn/ n morfina f

**Morse** /mɔːs/ n Morse m. **~ (code)** n alfabeto m Morse

**morsel** /'mɔːsl/ n pedazo m; (mouthful) bocado m

**mortal** /'mɔːtl/ a & n mortal (m). **~ity** /-'tælətɪ/ n mortalidad f

**mortar** /'mɔːtə(r)/ n (all senses) mortero m

**mortgage** /'mɔːgɪdʒ/ n hipoteca f. ● vt hipotecar

**mortify** /'mɔːtɪfaɪ/ vt mortificar

**mortuary** /'mɔːtjʊərɪ/ n depósito m de cadáveres

**mosaic** /məʊ'zeɪk/ n mosaico m

**Moscow** /'mɒskəʊ/ n Moscú m

**Moses** /'məʊzɪz/ a. **~ basket** n moisés m

**mosque** /mɒsk/ n mezquita f

**mosquito** /mɒs'kiːtəʊ/ n (pl -oes) mosquito m

**moss** /mɒs/ n musgo m. **~y** a musgoso

**most** /məʊst/ a más. **for the ~ part** en su mayor parte. **~ of** la mayoría f. **~ of** la mayor parte de. **at ~** a lo más. **make the ~ of** aprovechar al máximo. ● adv más; (very) muy. **~ly** adv principalmente

**MOT** *abbr* (*Ministry of Transport*). ~ (**test**) ITV, inspección *f* técnica de vehículos

**motel** /məʊ'tel/ *n* motel *m*

**moth** /mɒθ/ *n* mariposa *f* (*nocturna*); (*in clothes*) polilla *f*. ~**ball** *n* bola *f* de naftalina. ~**eaten** *a* apolillado

**mother** /mʌðə(r)/ *n* madre *f*. ● *vt* cuidar como a un hijo. ~**hood** *n* maternidad *f*. ~**in-law** *n* (*pl* ~**s-in-law**) suegra *f*. ~**land** *n* patria *f*. ~**ly** *adv* maternalmente. ~**of-pearl** *n* nácar *m*. **M~'s Day** *n* el día *m* de la Madre. ~**to-be** *n* futura madre *f*. ~ **tongue** *n* lengua *f* materna

**motif** /məʊ'tiːf/ *n* motivo *m*

**motion** /'məʊʃn/ *n* movimiento *m*; (*proposal*) moción *f*. ● *vt/i*. ~ (**to**) **s.o. to** hacer señas a uno para que. ~**less** *a* inmóvil

**motivat|e** /'məʊtɪveɪt/ *vt* motivar. ~**ion** /-'veɪʃn/ *n* motivación *f*

**motive** /'məʊtɪv/ *n* motivo *m*

**motley** /'mɒtlɪ/ *a* abigarrado

**motor** /'məʊtə(r)/ *n* motor *m*; (*car*) coche *m*. ● *a* motor; (*fem*) motora, motriz. ● *vi* ir en coche. ~ **bike** *n* (*fam*) motocicleta *f*, moto *f* (*fam*). ~ **boat** *n* lancha *f* motora. ~**cade** /'məʊtəkeɪd/ *n* (*Amer*) desfile *m* de automóviles. ~ **car** *n* coche *m*, automóvil *m*. ~ **cycle** *n* motocicleta *f*. ~**cyclist** *n* motociclista *m & f*. ~**ing** *n* automovilismo *m*. ~**ist** *n* automovilista *m & f*. ~**ize** *vt* motorizar. ~**way** *n* autopista *f*

**mottled** /'mɒtld/ *a* abigarrado

**motto** /'mɒtəʊ/ *n* (*pl* -**oes**) lema *m*

**mould**[1] /məʊld/ *n* molde *m*. ● *vt* moldear

**mould**[2] /məʊld/ *n* (*fungus, rot*) moho *m*

**moulding** /'məʊldɪŋ/ *n* (*on wall etc*) moldura *f*

**mouldy** /'məʊldɪ/ *a* mohoso

**moult** /məʊlt/ *vi* mudar

**mound** /maʊnd/ *n* montículo *m*; (*pile, fig*) montón *m*

**mount**[1] /maʊnt/ *vt/i* subir. ● *n* montura *f*. ~ **up** aumentar

**mount**[2] /maʊnt/ *n* (*hill*) monte *m*

**mountain** /'maʊntɪn/ *n* montaña *f*. ~**eer** /maʊntɪ'nɪə(r)/ *n* alpinista *m & f*. ~**eering** *n* alpinismo *m*. ~**ous** /'maʊntɪnəs/ *a* montañoso

**mourn** /mɔːn/ *vt* llorar. ● *vi* lamentarse. ~ **for** llorar la muerte de. ~**er** *n* persona *f* que acompaña el cortejo fúnebre. ~**ful** *a* triste. ~**ing** *n* luto *m*

**mouse** /maʊs/ *n* (*pl* **mice**) ratón *m*. ~**trap** *n* ratonera *f*

**mousse** /muːs/ *n* (*dish*) crema *f* batida

**moustache** /mə'stɑːʃ/ *n* bigote *m*

**mousy** /'maʊsɪ/ *a* ⟨*hair*⟩ pardusco; (*fig*) tímido

**mouth** /maʊð/ *vt* formar con los labios. /maʊθ/ *n* boca *f*. ~**ful** *n* bocado *m*. ~**organ** *n* armónica *f*. ~**piece** *n* (*mus*) boquilla *f*; (*fig, person*) portavoz *f*, vocero *m* (*LAm*). ~**wash** *n* enjuague *m*

**movable** /'muːvəbl/ *a* móvil, movible

**move** /muːv/ *vt* mover; mudarse de ⟨*house*⟩; (*with emotion*) conmover; (*propose*) proponer. ● *vi* moverse; (*be in motion*) estar en movimiento; (*progress*) hacer progresos; (*take action*) tomar medidas; (*depart*) irse. ~ (**out**) irse. ● *n* movimiento *m*; (*in game*) jugada *f*; (*player's turn*) turno *m*; (*removal*) mudanza *f*. **on the** ~ en movimiento. ~ **along** (hacer) circular. ~ **away** alejarse. ~ **back** (hacer) retroceder. ~ **forward** (hacer) avanzar. ~ **in** instalarse. ~ **on** (hacer) circular. ~ **over** apartarse. ~**ment** /'muːvmənt/ *n* movimiento *m*

**movie** /'muːvɪ/ *n* (*Amer*) película *f*. **the** ~**s** *npl* el cine *m*

**moving** /'muːvɪŋ/ *a* en movimiento; (*touching*) conmovedor

**mow** /məʊ/ *vt* (*pt* **mowed** *or* **mown**) segar. ~ **down** derribar. ~**er** *n* (*for lawn*) cortacésped *m inv*

**MP** *abbr see* **Member of Parliament**

**Mr** /'mɪstə(r)/ *abbr* (*pl* **Messrs**) (*Mister*) señor *m*. ~ **Coldbeck** (el) Sr. Coldbeck

**Mrs** /'mɪsɪz/ *abbr* (*pl* **Mrs**) (*Missis*) señora *f*. ~ **Andrews** (la) Sra. Andrews. **the** ~ **Andrews** (las) Sras. Andrews

**Ms** /mɪz/ *abbr* (*title of married or unmarried woman*) señora *f*, señorita. **Ms Lawton** (la) Sra. Lawton

**much** /mʌtʃ/ *a & n* mucho (*m*). ● *adv* mucho; (*before pp*) muy. ~ **as** por mucho que. ~ **the same** más o menos lo mismo. **so** ~ tanto. **too** ~ demasiado

**muck** /mʌk/ *n* estiércol *m*; (*dirt, fam*) suciedad *f*. ● *vi*. ~ **about** (*sl*) perder el tiempo. ~ **about with** (*sl*)

juguetear con. ● *vt.* ~ **up** (*sl*) echar
a perder. ~ **in** (*sl*) participar. ~**y** *a*
sucio

**mucus** /'mjuːkəs/ *n* moco *m*

**mud** /mʌd/ *n* lodo *m*, barro *m*

**muddle** /'mʌdl/ *vt* embrollar. ● *vi.* ~
**through** salir del paso. ● *n*
desorden *m*; (*mix-up*) lío *m*

**muddy** /'mʌdɪ/ *a* lodoso; ⟨*hands etc*⟩
cubierto de lodo

**mudguard** /'mʌdgaːd/ *n* guardabarros *m invar*

**muff** /mʌf/ *n* manguito *m*

**muffin** /'mʌfɪn/ *n* mollete *m*

**muffle** /'mʌfl/ *vt* tapar; amortiguar
⟨*a sound*⟩. ~ **r** *n* (*scarf*) bufanda *f*

**mug** /mʌg/ *n* tazón *m*; (*for beer*)
jarra *f*; (*face*, *sl*) cara *f*, jeta *f* (*sl*);
(*fool*, *sl*) primo *m*. ● *vt* (*pt* **mugged**)
asaltar. ~**ger** *n* asaltador *m*. ~**ging**
*n* asalto *m*

**muggy** /'mʌgɪ/ *a* bochornoso

**Muhammadan** /mə'hæmɪdən/ *a* & *n*
mahometano (*m*)

**mule**[1] /mjuːl/ *n* mula *f*, mulo *m*

**mule**[2] /mjuːl/ *n* (*slipper*) babucha *f*

**mull**[1] /mʌl/ *vt.* ~ **over** reflexionar
sobre

**mull**[2] /mʌl/ *vt* calentar con especias
⟨*wine*⟩

**multi...** /'mʌltɪ/ *pref* multi...

**multicoloured** /mʌltɪ'kʌləd/ *a*
multicolor

**multifarious** /mʌltɪ'feərɪəs/ *a*
múltiple

**multinational** /mʌltɪ'næʃənl/ *a* & *n*
multinacional (*f*)

**multipl|e** /'mʌltɪpl/ *a* & *n* múltiplo
(*m*). ~**ication** /mʌltɪplɪ'keɪʃn/ *n*
multiplicación *f*. ~**y** /'mʌltɪplaɪ/
*vt/i* multiplicar(se)

**multitude** /'mʌltɪtjuːd/ *n* multitud *f*

**mum**[1] /mʌm/ *n* (*fam*) mamá *f* (*fam*)

**mum**[2] /mʌm/ *a.* **keep** ~ (*fam*)
guardar silencio

**mumble** /'mʌmbl/ *vt* decir entre
dientes. ● *vi* hablar entre dientes

**mummify** /'mʌmɪfaɪ/ *vt/i*
momificar(se)

**mummy**[1] /'mʌmɪ/ *n* (*mother*, *fam*)
mamá *f* (*fam*)

**mummy**[2] /'mʌmɪ/ *n* momia *f*

**mumps** /mʌmps/ *n* paperas *fpl*

**munch** /mʌntʃ/ *vt/i* mascar

**mundane** /mʌn'deɪn/ *a* mundano

**municipal** /mjuː'nɪsɪpl/ *a* municipal.
~**ity** /-'pælətɪ/ *n* municipio *m*

**munificent** /mjuː'nɪfɪsənt/ *a*
munífico

**munitions** /mjuː'nɪʃnz/ *npl* municiones *fpl*

**mural** /'mjʊərəl/ *a* & *n* mural (*f*)

**murder** /'mɜːdə(r)/ *n* asesinato *m*.
● *vt* asesinar. ~**er** *n* asesino *m*.
~**ess** *n* asesina *f*. ~**ous** *a* homicida

**murky** /'mɜːkɪ/ *a* (*-ier*, *-iest*) oscuro

**murmur** /'mɜːmə(r)/ *n* murmullo *m*.
● *vt/i* murmurar

**muscle** /'mʌsl/ *n* músculo *m*. ● *vi.* ~
**in** (*Amer*, *sl*) meterse por fuerza en

**muscular** /'mʌskjʊlə(r)/ *a* muscular;
(*having well-developed muscles*)
musculoso

**muse** /mjuːz/ *vi* meditar

**museum** /mjuː'zɪəm/ *n* museo *m*

**mush** /mʌʃ/ *n* pulpa *f*

**mushroom** /'mʌʃrʊm/ *n* champiñón
*m*; (*bot*) seta *f*. ● *vi* (*appear in large
numbers*) crecer como hongos

**mushy** /'mʌʃɪ/ *a* pulposo

**music** /'mjuːzɪk/ *n* música *f*. ~**al** *a*
musical; ⟨*instrument*⟩ de música;
(*talented*) que tiene don de música.
● *n* comedia *f* musical. ~ **hall** *n*
teatro *m* de variedades. ~**ian**
/mjuː'zɪʃn/ *n* músico *m*

**musk** /mʌsk/ *n* almizcle *m*

**Muslim** /'mʊzlɪm/ *a* & *n* musulmán
(*m*)

**muslin** /'mʌzlɪn/ *n* muselina *f*

**musquash** /'mʌskwɒʃ/ *n* ratón *m*
almizclero

**mussel** /mʌsl/ *n* mejillón *m*

**must** /mʌst/ *v aux* deber, tener que.
**he** ~ **be old** debe ser viejo. **I** ~ **have
done it** debo haberlo hecho. **you** ~
**go** debes marcharte. ● *n.* **be a** ~ ser
imprescindible

**mustard** /'mʌstəd/ *n* mostaza *f*

**muster** /'mʌstə(r)/ *vt/i* reunir(se)

**musty** /'mʌstɪ/ *a* (*-ier*, *-iest*) que
huele a cerrado

**mutation** /mjuː'teɪʃn/ *n* mutación *f*

**mute** /mjuːt/ *a* & *n* mudo (*m*). ~**d** *a*
⟨*sound*⟩ sordo; ⟨*criticism*⟩ callado

**mutilat|e** /'mjuːtɪleɪt/ *vt* mutilar.
~**ion** /-'leɪʃn/ *n* mutilación *f*

**mutin|ous** /'mjuːtɪnəs/ *a* ⟨*sailor etc*⟩
amotinado; (*fig*) rebelde. ~**y** *n*
motín *m*. ● *vi* amotinarse

**mutter** /'mʌtə(r)/ *vt/i* murmurar

**mutton** /'mʌtn/ *n* cordero *m*

**mutual** /'mjuːtʃʊəl/ *a* mutuo; (*common*, *fam*) común. ~**ly** *adv*
mutuamente

**muzzle** /mʌzl/ *n* (*snout*) hocico *m*;
(*device*) bozal *m*; (*of gun*) boca *f*. ● *vt*
poner el bozal a

**my** /maɪ/ *a* mi, mis *pl*

**myopic** /maɪˈɒpɪk/ *a* miope

**myriad** /ˈmɪrɪəd/ *n* miríada *f*

**myself** /maɪˈself/ *pron* yo mismo *m*, yo misma *f*; (*reflexive*) me; (*after prep*) mí (mismo) *m*, mí (misma) *f*

**myster|ious** /mɪˈstɪərɪəs/ *a* misterioso. **~y** /ˈmɪstərɪ/ *n* misterio *m*

**mystic** /ˈmɪstɪk/ *a* & *n* místico (*m*). **~al** *a* místico. **~ism** /-sɪzəm/ *n* misticismo *m*

**mystif|ication** /mɪstɪfɪˈkeɪʃn/ *n* confusión *f*. **~y** /-faɪ/ *vt* dejar perplejo

**mystique** /mɪˈstiːk/ *n* mística *f*

**myth** /mɪθ/ *n* mito *m*. **~ical** *a* mítico. **~ology** /mɪˈθɒlədʒɪ/ *n* mitología *f*

# N

**N** *abbr* (*north*) norte *m*

**nab** /næb/ *vt* (*pt* **nabbed**) (*arrest, sl*) coger (*not LAm*), agarrar (*esp LAm*)

**nag** /næg/ *vt* (*pt* **nagged**) fastidiar; (*scold*) regañar. ● *vi* criticar

**nagging** /ˈnægɪŋ/ *a* persistente, regañón

**nail** /neɪl/ *n* clavo *m*; (*of finger, toe*) uña *f*. **pay on the ~** pagar a tocateja. ● *vt* clavar. **~ polish** *n* esmalte *m* para las uñas

**naïve** /naɪˈiːv/ *a* ingenuo

**naked** /ˈneɪkɪd/ *a* desnudo. **to the ~ eye** a simple vista. **~ly** *adv* desnudamente. **~ness** *n* desnudez *f*

**namby-pamby** /næmbɪˈpæmbɪ/ *a* & *n* ñoño (*m*)

**name** /neɪm/ *n* nombre *m*; (*fig*) fama *f*. ● *vt* nombrar; (*fix*) fijar. **be ~d after** llevar el nombre de. **~less** *a* anónimo. **~ly** /ˈneɪmlɪ/ *adv* a saber. **~sake** /ˈneɪmseɪk/ *n* (*person*) tocayo *m*

**nanny** /ˈnænɪ/ *n* niñera *f*. **~-goat** *n* cabra *f*

**nap**[1] /næp/ *n* (*sleep*) sueñecito *m*; (*after lunch*) siesta *f*. ● *vi* (*pt* **napped**) echarse un sueño. **catch s.o. ~ping** coger a uno desprevenido

**nap**[2] /næp/ *n* (*fibres*) lanilla *f*

**nape** /neɪp/ *n* nuca *f*

**napkin** /ˈnæpkɪn/ *n* (*at meals*) servilleta *f*; (*for baby*) pañal *m*

**nappy** /ˈnæpɪ/ *n* pañal *m*

**narcotic** /nɑːˈkɒtɪk/ *a* & *n* narcótico (*m*)

**narrat|e** /nəˈreɪt/ *vt* contar. **~ion** /-ʃn/ *n* narración *f*. **~ive** /ˈnærətɪv/ *n* relato *m*. **~or** /nəˈreɪtə(r)/ *n* narrador *m*

**narrow** /ˈnærəʊ/ *a* (**-er, -est**) estrecho. **have a ~ escape** escaparse por los pelos. ● *vt* estrechar; (*limit*) limitar. ● *vi* estrecharse. **~ly** *adv* estrechamente; (*just*) por poco. **~-minded** *a* de miras estrechas. **~ness** *n* estrechez *f*

**nasal** /ˈneɪzl/ *a* nasal

**nast|ily** /ˈnɑːstɪlɪ/ *adv* desagradablemente; (*maliciously*) con malevolencia. **~iness** *n* (*malice*) malevolencia *f*. **~y** *a* /ˈnɑːstɪ/ (**-ier, -iest**) desagradable; (*malicious*) malévolo; (*weather*) malo; (*taste, smell*) asqueroso; (*wound*) grave; (*person*) antipático

**natal** /ˈneɪtl/ *a* natal

**nation** /ˈneɪʃn/ *n* nación *f*

**national** /ˈnæʃənl/ *a* nacional. ● *n* súbdito *m*. **~ anthem** *n* himno *m* nacional. **~ism** *n* nacionalismo *m*. **~ity** /næʃəˈnælətɪ/ *n* nacionalidad *f*. **~ize** *vt* nacionalizar. **~ly** *adv* a nivel nacional

**nationwide** /ˈneɪʃnwaɪd/ *a* nacional

**native** /ˈneɪtɪv/ *n* natural *m* & *f*. **be a ~ of** ser natural de. ● *a* nativo; (*country, town*) natal; (*inborn*) innato. **~ speaker of Spanish** hispanohablante *m* & *f*. **~ language** *n* lengua *f* materna

**Nativity** /nəˈtɪvətɪ/ *n*. **the ~** la Natividad *f*

**NATO** /ˈneɪtəʊ/ *abbr* (*North Atlantic Treaty Organization*) OTAN *f*, Organización *f* del Tratado del Atlántico Norte

**natter** /ˈnætə(r)/ *vi* (*fam*) charlar. ● *n* (*fam*) charla *f*

**natural** /ˈnætʃərəl/ *a* natural. **~ history** *n* historia *f* natural. **~ist** *n* naturalista *m* & *f*

**naturaliz|ation** /nætʃərəlaɪˈzeɪʃn/ *n* naturalización *f*. **~e** *vt* naturalizar

**naturally** /ˈnætʃərəlɪ/ *adv* (*of course*) naturalmente; (*by nature*) por naturaleza

**nature** /ˈneɪtʃə(r)/ *n* naturaleza *f*; (*kind*) género *m*; (*of person*) carácter *m*

**naught** /nɔːt/ *n* (*old use*) nada *f*; (*maths*) cero *m*

**naught|ily** /ˈnɔːtɪlɪ/ *adv* mal. **~y** *a* (**-ier, -iest**) malo; (*child*) travieso; (*joke*) verde

**nause|a** /'nɔːzɪə/ n náusea f. **∼ate** vt dar náuseas a. **∼ous** a nauseabundo

**nautical** /'nɔːtɪkl/ a náutico. **∼ mile** n milla f marina

**naval** /'neɪvl/ a naval; ⟨officer⟩ de marina

**Navarre** /nə'vɑː(r)/ n Navarra f. **∼se** a navarro

**nave** /neɪv/ n (of church) nave f

**navel** /'neɪvl/ n ombligo m

**navigable** /'nævɪgəbl/ a navegable

**navigat|e** /'nævɪgeɪt/ vt navegar por ⟨sea etc⟩; gobernar ⟨ship⟩. ● vi navegar. **∼ion** n navegación f. **∼or** n navegante m

**navvy** /'nævɪ/ n peón m caminero

**navy** /'neɪvɪ/ n marina f. **∼ (blue)** azul m marino

**NE** abbr (north-east) noreste m

**near** /nɪə(r)/ adv cerca. **∼ at hand** muy cerca. **∼ by** adv cerca. **draw ∼** acercarse. ● prep. **∼ (to)** cerca de. ● a cercano. ● vt acercarse a. **∼by** a cercano. **N∼ East** n Oriente m Próximo. **∼ly** /'nɪəlɪ/ adv casi. **not ∼ly as pretty as** no es ni con mucho tan guapa como. **∼ness** /'nɪənɪs/ n proximidad f

**neat** /niːt/ a (-er, -est) pulcro; ⟨room etc⟩ bien arreglado; ⟨clever⟩ diestro; ⟨ingenious⟩ hábil; ⟨whisky, brandy etc⟩ solo. **∼ly** adv pulcramente. **∼ness** n pulcritud f

**nebulous** /'nebjʊləs/ a nebuloso

**necessar|ies** /'nesəsərɪz/ npl lo indispensable. **∼ily** /nesə'serɪlɪ/ adv necesariamente. **∼y** a necesario, imprescindible

**necessit|ate** /nə'sesɪteɪt/ vt necesitar. **∼y** /nɪ'sesətɪ/ n necesidad f; ⟨thing⟩ cosa f indispensable

**neck** /nek/ n (of person, bottle, dress) cuello m; (of animal) pescuezo m. **∼ and ∼** parejas. **∼lace** /'nekləs/ n collar m. **∼line** n escote m. **∼tie** n corbata f

**nectar** /'nektə(r)/ n néctar m

**nectarine** /nektə'riːn/ n nectarina f

**née** /neɪ/ a de soltera

**need** /niːd/ n necesidad f. ● vt necesitar; ⟨demand⟩ exigir. **you ∼ not speak** no tienes que hablar

**needle** /'niːdl/ n aguja f. ● vt ⟨annoy, fam⟩ pinchar

**needless** /'niːdlɪs/ a innecesario. **∼ly** adv innecesariamente

**needlework** /'niːdlwɜːk/ n costura f; ⟨embroidery⟩ bordado m

**needy** /'niːdɪ/ a (-ier, -iest) necesitado

**negation** /nɪ'geɪʃn/ n negación f

**negative** /'negətɪv/ a negativo. ● n (of photograph) negativo m; ⟨word, gram⟩ negativa f. **∼ly** adv negativamente

**neglect** /nɪ'glekt/ vt descuidar; no cumplir con ⟨duty⟩. **∼ to do** dejar de hacer. ● n descuido m, negligencia f. **(state of) ∼** abandono m. **∼ful** a descuidado

**négligé** /'neglɪʒeɪ/ n bata f, salto m de cama

**negligen|ce** /'neglɪdʒəns/ n negligencia f, descuido m. **∼t** a descuidado

**negligible** /'neglɪdʒəbl/ a insignificante

**negotiable** /nɪ'gəʊʃəbl/ a negociable

**negotiat|e** /nɪ'gəʊʃɪeɪt/ vt/i negociar. **∼ion** /-'eɪʃn/ n negociación f. **∼or** n negociador m

**Negr|ess** /'niːgrɪs/ n negra f. **∼o** n (pl -oes) negro m. ● a negro

**neigh** /neɪ/ n relincho m. ● vi relinchar

**neighbour** /'neɪbə(r)/ n vecino m. **∼hood** n vecindad f, barrio m. **in the ∼hood of** alrededor de. **∼ing** a vecino. **∼ly** /'neɪbəlɪ/ a amable

**neither** /'naɪðə(r)/ a & pron ninguno m de los dos, ni el uno m ni el otro m. ● adv ni. **∼ big nor small** ni grande ni pequeño. **∼ shall I come** no voy yo tampoco. ● conj tampoco

**neon** /'niːɒn/ n neón m. ● a ⟨lamp etc⟩ de neón

**nephew** /'nevjuː/ n sobrino m

**nepotism** /'nepətɪzəm/ m nepotismo m

**nerve** /nɜːv/ n nervio m; ⟨courage⟩ valor m; ⟨calm⟩ sangre f fría; ⟨impudence, fam⟩ descaro m. **∼-racking** a exasperante. **∼s** npl (before exams etc) nervios mpl

**nervous** /'nɜːvəs/ a nervioso. **be/feel ∼** ⟨afraid⟩ tener miedo (of a). **∼ly** adv ⟨tensely⟩ nerviosamente; ⟨timidly⟩ tímidamente. **∼ness** n nerviosidad f; ⟨fear⟩ miedo m

**nervy** /'nɜːvɪ/ a see **nervous**; ⟨Amer, fam⟩ descarado

**nest** /nest/ n nido m. ● vi anidar. **∼-egg** n ⟨money⟩ ahorros mpl

**nestle** /'nesl/ vi acomodarse. **∼ up to** arrimarse a

**net** /net/ n red f. ● vt (pt **netted**) coger (not LAm), agarrar (esp LAm). ● a (weight etc) neto

**netball** /'netbɔ:l/ n baloncesto m

**Netherlands** /'neðələndz/ npl. **the** ~ los Países mpl Bajos

**netting** /'netɪŋ/ n (nets) redes fpl; (wire) malla f; (fabric) tul m

**nettle** /'netl/ n ortiga f

**network** /'netwɜ:k/ n red f

**neuralgia** /njʊə'rældʒɪə/ n neuralgia f

**neuro|sis** /njʊə'rəʊsɪs/ n (pl **-oses** /-si:z/) neurosis f. ~**tic** a & n neurótico (m)

**neuter** /'nju:tə(r)/ a & n neutro (m). ● vt castrar ⟨animals⟩

**neutral** /'nju:trəl/ a neutral; ⟨colour⟩ neutro; (elec) neutro. ~ (**gear**) (auto) punto m muerto. ~**ity** /-'trælətɪ/ n neutralidad f

**neutron** /'nju:trɒn/ n neutrón m. ~ **bomb** n bomba f de neutrones

**never** /'nevə(r)/ adv nunca, jamás; (not, fam) no. ~ **again** nunca más. ~ **mind** (don't worry) no te preocupes, no se preocupe; (it doesn't matter) no importa. **he** ~ **smiles** no sonríe nunca. **I** ~ **saw him** (fam) no le vi. ~**ending** a interminable

**nevertheless** /nevəðə'les/ adv sin embargo, no obstante

**new** /nju:/ a (-er, -est) (new to owner) nuevo (placed before noun); (brand new) nuevo (placed after noun). ~**born** a recién nacido. ~**comer** n recién llegado m. ~**fangled** a (pej) moderno. ~**laid egg** n huevo m fresco. ~**ly** adv nuevamente; (recently) recién. ~**ly-weds** npl recién casados mpl. ~ **moon** n luna f nueva. ~**ness** n novedad f

**news** /nju:z/ n noticias fpl; (broadcasting, press) informaciones fpl; (on TV) telediario m; (on radio) diario m hablado. ~**agent** n vendedor m de periódicos. ~**caster** n locutor m. ~**letter** n boletín m. ~**paper** n periódico m. ~**reader** n locutor m. ~**reel** n noticiario m, nodo m (in Spain)

**newt** /nju:t/ n tritón m

**new year** /nju:'jɪə(r)/ n año m nuevo. **N**~**'s Day** n día m de Año Nuevo. **N**~**'s Eve** n noche f vieja

**New Zealand** /nju:'zi:lənd/ n Nueva Zelanda f. ~**er** n neozelandés m

**next** /nekst/ a próximo; ⟨week, month etc⟩ que viene, próximo; (adjoining) vecino; (following) siguiente. ● adv la próxima vez; (afterwards) después. ● n siguiente m. ~ **to** junto a. ~ **to nothing** casi nada. ~ **door** al lado (**to** de). ~**door** de al lado. ~**best** mejor alternativa f. ~ **of kin** n pariente m más próximo, parientes mpl más próximos

**nib** /nɪb/ n (of pen) plumilla f

**nibble** /'nɪbl/ vt/i mordisquear. ● n mordisco m

**nice** /naɪs/ a (-er, -est) agradable; (likeable) simpático; (kind) amable; (pretty) bonito; ⟨weather⟩ bueno; (subtle) sutil. ~**ly** adv agradablemente; (kindly) amablemente; (well) bien

**nicety** /'naɪsətɪ/ n (precision) precisión f; (detail) detalle m. **to a** ~ exactamente

**niche** /nɪtʃ, ni:ʃ/ n (recess) nicho m; (fig) buena posición f

**nick** /nɪk/ n corte m pequeño; (prison, sl) cárcel f. **in the** ~ **of time** justo a tiempo. ● vt (steal, arrest, sl) birlar

**nickel** /'nɪkl/ n níquel m; (Amer) moneda f de cinco centavos

**nickname** /'nɪkneɪm/ n apodo m; (short form) diminutivo m. ● vt apodar

**nicotine** /'nɪkəti:n/ n nicotina f

**niece** /ni:s/ n sobrina f

**nifty** /'nɪftɪ/ a (sl) (smart) elegante

**Nigeria** /naɪ'dʒɪərɪə/ n Nigeria f. ~**n** a & n nigeriano (m)

**niggardly** /'nɪgədlɪ/ a ⟨person⟩ tacaño; ⟨thing⟩ miserable

**niggling** /'nɪglɪŋ/ a molesto

**night** /naɪt/ n noche f; (evening) tarde f. ● a nocturno, de noche. ~**cap** n (hat) gorro m de dormir; (drink) bebida f (tomada antes de acostarse). ~**club** n sala f de fiestas, boîte f. ~**dress** n camisón m. ~**fall** n anochecer m. ~**gown** n camisón m

**nightingale** /'naɪtɪŋgeɪl/ n ruiseñor m

**night: ~life** n vida f nocturna. ~**ly** adv todas las noches. ~**mare** n pesadilla f. ~**school** n escuela f nocturna. ~**time** n noche f. ~**watchman** n sereno m

**nil** /nɪl/ n nada f; (sport) cero m

**nimble** /'nɪmbl/ a (-er, -est) ágil

**nine** /naɪn/ a & n nueve (m)

**nineteen** /naɪn'ti:n/ a & n diecinueve (m). ~**th** a & n diecinueve (m), decimonoveno (m)

**ninet|ieth** /'naɪntɪəθ/ a noventa, nonagésimo. **~y** a & n noventa (m)

**ninth** /'naɪnθ/ a & n noveno (m)

**nip**[1] /nɪp/ vt (pt **nipped**) (pinch) pellizcar; (bite) mordisquear. ● vi (rush, sl) correr. ● n (pinch) pellizco m; (cold) frío m

**nip**[2] /nɪp/ n (of drink) trago m

**nipper** /'nɪpə(r)/ n (sl) chaval m

**nipple** /'nɪpl/ n pezón m; (of baby's bottle) tetilla f

**nippy** /'nɪpɪ/ a (**-ier, -iest**) (nimble, fam) ágil; (quick, fam) rápido; (chilly, fam) fresquito

**nitrogen** /'naɪtrədʒən/ n nitrógeno m

**nitwit** /'nɪtwɪt/ n (fam) imbécil m & f

**no** /nəʊ/ a ninguno. **~ entry** prohibido el paso. **~ man's land** n tierra f de nadie. **~ smoking** se prohibe fumar. **~ way!** (Amer, fam) ¡ni hablar! ● adv no. ● n (pl **noes**) no m

**nobility** /nəʊ'bɪlətɪ/ n nobleza f

**noble** /'nəʊbl/ a (**-er, -est**) noble. **~man** n noble m

**nobody** /'nəʊbədɪ/ pron nadie m. ● n nadie m. **~ is there** no hay nadie. **he knows ~** no conoce a nadie

**nocturnal** /nɒk'tɜ:nl/ a nocturno

**nod** /nɒd/ vt (pt **nodded**). **~ one's head** asentir con la cabeza. ● vi (in agreement) asentir con la cabeza; (in greeting) saludar; (be drowsy) dar cabezadas. ● n inclinación f de cabeza

**nodule** /'nɒdjuːl/ n nódulo m

**nois|e** /nɔɪz/ n ruido m. **~eless** a silencioso. **~ily** /'nɔɪzɪlɪ/ adv ruidosamente. **~y** a (**-ier, -iest**) ruidoso

**nomad** /'nəʊmæd/ n nómada m & f. **~ic** /-'mædɪk/ a nómada

**nominal** /'nɒmɪnl/ a nominal

**nominat|e** /'nɒmɪneɪt/ vt nombrar; (put forward) proponer. **~ion** /-'neɪʃn/ n nombramiento m

**non-...** /nɒn/ pref no ...

**nonagenarian** /nəʊnədʒɪ'neərɪən/ a & n nonagenario (m), noventón (m)

**nonchalant** /'nɒnʃələnt/ a imperturbable

**non-commissioned** /nɒnkə'mɪʃnd/ a. **~ officer** n suboficial m

**non-committal** /nɒnkə'mɪtl/ a evasivo

**nondescript** /'nɒndɪskrɪpt/ a inclasificable, anodino

**none** /nʌn/ pron (person) nadie, ninguno; (thing) ninguno, nada. **~ of**

nada de. **~ of us** ninguno de nosotros. **I have ~** no tengo nada. ● adv no, de ninguna manera. **he is ~ the happier** no está más contento

**nonentity** /nɒ'nentətɪ/ n nulidad f

**non-existent** /nɒnɪg'zɪstənt/ a inexistente

**nonplussed** /nɒn'plʌst/ a perplejo

**nonsens|e** /'nɒnsns/ n tonterías fpl, disparates mpl. **~ical** /-'sensɪkl/ a absurdo

**non-smoker** /nɒn'sməʊkə(r)/ n persona f que no fuma; (rail) departamento m de no fumadores

**non-starter** /nɒn'stɑːtə(r)/ n (fam) proyecto m imposible

**non-stop** /nɒn'stɒp/ a ⟨train⟩ directo; ⟨flight⟩ sin escalas. ● adv sin parar; (by train) directamente; (by air) sin escalas

**noodles** /'nuːdlz/ npl fideos mpl

**nook** /nʊk/ n rincón m

**noon** /nuːn/ n mediodía m

**no-one** /'nəʊwʌn/ pron nadie. see nobody

**noose** /nuːs/ n nudo m, corredizo

**nor** /nɔː(r)/ conj ni, tampoco. **neither blue ~ red** ni azul ni rojo. **he doesn't play the piano, ~ do I** no sabe tocar el piano, ni yo tampoco

**Nordic** /'nɔːdɪk/ a nórdico

**norm** /nɔːm/ n norma f; (normal) lo normal

**normal** /'nɔːml/ a normal. **~cy** n (Amer) normalidad f. **~ity** /-'mælətɪ/ n normalidad f. **~ly** adv normalmente

**Norman** /'nɔːmən/ a & n normando (m)

**Normandy** /'nɔːməndɪ/ n Normandía f

**north** /nɔːθ/ n norte m. ● a del norte, norteño. ● adv hacia el norte. **N~ America** n América f del Norte, Norteamérica f. **N~ American** a & n norteamericano (m). **~-east** n nordeste m. **~erly** /'nɔːðəlɪ/ a del norte. **~ern** /'nɔːðən/ a del norte. **~erner** n norteño m. **N~ Sea** n mar m del Norte. **~ward** a hacia el norte. **~wards** adv hacia el norte. **~west** n noroeste m

**Norw|ay** /'nɔːweɪ/ n Noruega f. **~egian** a & n noruego (m)

**nose** /nəʊz/ n nariz f. ● vi. **~ about** curiosear. **~bleed** n hemorragia f nasal. **~dive** n picado m

**nostalgi|a** /nɒ'stældʒə/ n nostalgia f. **~c** a nostálgico

**nostril** /'nɒstrɪl/ n nariz f; (of horse) ollar m

**nosy** /'nəʊzɪ/ a (-ier, -iest) (fam) entrometido

**not** /nɒt/ adv no. ~ **at all** no... nada; (after thank you) de nada. ~ **yet** aún no. **I do** ~ **know** no sé. **I suppose** ~ supongo que no

**notabl|e** /'nəʊtəbl/ a notable. ● n (person) notabilidad f. ~**y** /'nəʊtəblɪ/ adv notablemente

**notary** /'nəʊtərɪ/ n notario m

**notation** /nəʊ'teɪʃn/ n notación f

**notch** /nɒtʃ/ n muesca f. ● vt. ~ **up** apuntar ⟨score etc⟩

**note** /nəʊt/ n nota f; (banknote) billete m. **take** ~**s** tomar apuntes. ● vt notar. ~**book** n libreta f. ~**d** a célebre. ~**paper** n papel m de escribir. ~**worthy** a notable

**nothing** /'nʌθɪŋ/ pron nada. **he eats** ~ no come nada. **for** ~ (free) gratis; (in vain) inútilmente. ● n nada f; (person) nulidad f; (thing of no importance) fruslería f; (zero) cero m. ● adv de ninguna manera. ~ **big** nada grande. ~ **else** nada más. ~ **much** poca cosa

**notice** /'nəʊtɪs/ n (attention) atención f; (advert) anuncio m; (sign) letrero m; (poster) cartel m; (termination of employment) despido m; (warning) aviso m. **(advance)** ~ previo aviso m. ~ **(of dismissal)** despido m. **take** ~ **of** prestar atención a, hacer caso a ⟨person⟩; hacer caso de ⟨thing⟩. ● vt notar. ~**able** a evidente. ~**ably** adv visiblemente. ~**board** n tablón m de anuncios

**notif|ication** /nəʊtɪfɪ'keɪʃn/ n aviso m, notificación f. ~**y** vt avisar

**notion** /'nəʊʃn/ n (concept) concepto m; (idea) idea f. ~**s** npl (sewing goods etc, Amer) artículos mpl de mercería

**notori|ety** /nəʊtə'raɪətɪ/ n notoriedad f; (pej) mala fama f. ~**ous** /nəʊ'tɔːrɪəs/ a notorio. ~**ously** adv notoriamente

**notwithstanding** /nɒtwɪθ'stændɪŋ/ prep a pesar de. ● adv sin embargo

**nougat** /'nuːgɑː/ n turrón m

**nought** /nɔːt/ n cero m

**noun** /naʊn/ n sustantivo m, nombre m

**nourish** /'nʌrɪʃ/ vt alimentar; (incl fig) nutrir. ~**ment** n alimento m

**novel** /'nɒvl/ n novela f. ● a nuevo. ~**ist** n novelista m & f. ~**ty** n novedad f

**November** /nəʊ'vembə(r)/ n noviembre m

**novice** /'nɒvɪs/ n principiante m & f

**now** /naʊ/ adv ahora. ~ **and again**, ~ **and then** de vez en cuando. **just** ~ ahora mismo; (a moment ago) hace poco. ● conj ahora que

**nowadays** /'naʊədeɪz/ adv hoy (en) día

**nowhere** /'nəʊweə(r)/ adv en/por ninguna parte; (after motion towards) a ninguna parte

**noxious** /'nɒkʃəs/ a nocivo

**nozzle** /'nɒzl/ n boquilla f; (tec) tobera f

**nuance** /'njʊɑːns/ n matiz m

**nuclear** /'njuːklɪə(r)/ a nuclear

**nucleus** /'njuːklɪəs/ n (pl -lei /-lɪaɪ/) núcleo m

**nude** /njuːd/ a & n desnudo (m). **in the** ~ desnudo

**nudge** /nʌdʒ/ vt dar un codazo a. ● n codazo m

**nudi|sm** /'njuːdɪzəm/ n desnudismo m. ~**st** n nudista m & f. ~**ty** /'njuːdətɪ/ n desnudez f

**nuisance** /'njuːsns/ n (thing, event) fastidio m; (person) pesado m. **be a** ~ dar la lata

**null** /nʌl/ a nulo. ~**ify** vt anular

**numb** /nʌm/ a entumecido. ● vt entumecer

**number** /'nʌmbə(r)/ n número m. ● vt numerar; (count, include) contar. ~**plate** n matrícula f

**numeracy** /'njuːmərəsɪ/ n conocimientos mpl de matemáticas

**numeral** /'njuːmərəl/ n número m

**numerate** /'njuːmərət/ a que tiene buenos conocimientos de matemáticas

**numerical** /njuː'merɪkl/ a numérico

**numerous** /'njuːmərəs/ a numeroso

**nun** /nʌn/ n monja f

**nurse** /nɜːs/ n enfermera f, enfermero m; (nanny) niñera f. **wet** ~ n nodriza f. ● vt cuidar; abrigar ⟨hope etc⟩. ~**maid** n niñera f

**nursery** /'nɜːsərɪ/ n cuarto m de los niños; (for plants) vivero m. **(day)** ~ n guardería f infantil. ~ **rhyme** n canción f infantil. ~ **school** n escuela f de párvulos

**nursing home** /'nɜːsɪŋhəʊm/ n (for old people) asilo m de ancianos

**nurture** /'nɜːtʃə(r)/ vt alimentar

**nut** /nʌt/ n (walnut, Brazil nut etc) nuez f; (hazlenut) avellana f; (peanut) cacahuete m; (tec) tuerca f;

(*crazy person, sl*) chiflado *m*.
**~crackers** *npl* cascanueces *m invar*
**nutmeg** /'nʌtmeg/ *n* nuez *f* moscada
**nutrient** /'njuːtrɪənt/ *n* alimento *m*
**nutrition** /njuː'trɪʃn/ *n* nutrición *f*.
**~ious** *a* nutritivo
**nuts** /nʌts/ *a* (*crazy, sl*) chiflado
**nutshell** /'nʌtʃel/ *n* cáscara *f* de
nuez. **in a ~** en pocas palabras
**nuzzle** /'nʌzl/ *vt* acariciar con el
hocico
**NW** *abbr* (*north-west*) noroeste *m*
**nylon** /'naɪlɒn/ *n* nailon *m*. **~s** *npl*
medias *fpl* de nailon
**nymph** /nɪmf/ *n* ninfa *f*

# O

**oaf** /əʊf/ *n* (*pl* **oafs**) zoquete *m*
**oak** /əʊk/ *n* roble *m*
**OAP** /əʊeɪ'piː/ *abbr* (*old-age pen-sioner*) *n* pensionista *m* & *f*
**oar** /ɔː(r)/ *n* remo *m*. **~sman** /'ɔːzmən/ *n* (*pl* **-men**) remero *m*
**oasis** /əʊ'eɪsɪs/ *n* (*pl* **oases** /-siːz/)
oasis *m invar*
**oath** /əʊθ/ *n* juramento *m*; (*swear-word*) palabrota *f*
**oatmeal** /'əʊtmiːl/ *n* harina *f* de
avena. **~s** /əʊts/ *npl* avena *f*
**obedience** /əʊ'biːdɪəns/ *n* obedi-encia *f*. **~t** /əʊ'biːdɪənt/ *a* obediente.
**~tly** *adv* obedientemente
**obelisk** /'ɒbəlɪsk/ *n* obelisco *m*
**obese** /əʊ'biːs/ *a* obeso. **~ity** *n* obes-idad *f*
**obey** /əʊ'beɪ/ *vt* obedecer; cumplir
⟨*instructions etc*⟩
**obituary** /ə'bɪtʃʊərɪ/ *n* necrología *f*
**object** /'ɒbdʒɪkt/ *n* objeto *m*.
/əb'dʒekt/ *vi* oponerse
**objection** /əb'dʒekʃn/ *n* objeción *f*.
**~able** /əb'dʒekʃnəbl/ *a* censurable;
(*unpleasant*) desagradable
**objective** /əb'dʒektɪv/ *a* & *n* objetivo
(*m*). **~ively** *adv* objetivamente
**objector** /əb'dʒektə(r)/ *n* objetante
*m* & *f*
**obligation** /ɒblɪ'geɪʃn/ *n* obligación
*f*. **be under an ~ation to** tener obli-gación de. **~atory** /ə'blɪgətrɪ/ *a* obli-gatorio. **~e** /ə'blaɪdʒ/ *vt* obligar; (*do
a small service*) hacer un favor a.
**~ed** *a* agradecido. **much ~ed!** ¡mu-chas gracias! **~ing** *a* atento
**oblique** /ə'bliːk/ *a* oblicuo

**obliterate** /ə'blɪtəreɪt/ *vt* borrar.
**~ion** /-'reɪʃn/ *n* borradura *f*
**oblivion** /ə'blɪvɪən/ *n* olvido *m*. **~us**
/ə'blɪvɪəs/ *a* (*unaware*) inconsciente
(**to, of** de)
**oblong** /'ɒblɒŋ/ *a* & *n* oblongo (*m*)
**obnoxious** /ɒb'nɒkʃəs/ *a* odioso
**oboe** /'əʊbəʊ/ *n* oboe *m*
**obscene** /əb'siːn/ *a* obsceno. **~ity**
/-enətɪ/ *n* obscenidad *f*
**obscure** /əb'skjʊə(r)/ *a* oscuro. ● *vt*
oscurecer; (*conceal*) esconder; (*con-fuse*) confundir. **~ity** *n* oscuridad *f*
**obsequious** /əb'siːkwɪəs/ *a* ob-sequioso
**observance** /əb'zɜːvəns/ *n* obser-vancia *f*. **~t** /əb'zɜːvənt/ *a*
observador
**observation** /ɒbzə'veɪʃn/ *n* ob-servación *f*
**observatory** /əb'zɜːvətrɪ/ *n* ob-servatorio *m*
**observe** /əb'zɜːv/ *vt* observar. **~r** *n*
observador *m*
**obsess** /əb'ses/ *vt* obsesionar. **~ion**
/-ʃn/ *n* obsesión *f*. **~ive** *a* obsesivo
**obsolete** /'ɒbsəliːt/ *a* desusado
**obstacle** /'ɒbstəkl/ *n* obstáculo *m*
**obstetrics** /əb'stetrɪks/ *n* obstetricia
*f*
**obstinacy** /'ɒbstɪnəsɪ/ *n* obsti-nación *f*. **~te** /'ɒbstɪnət/ *a* obsti-nado. **~tely** *adv* obstinadamente
**obstreperous** /ɒb'strepərəs/ *a* tur-bulento, ruidoso, protestón
**obstruct** /əb'strʌkt/ *vt* obstruir.
**~ion** /-ʃn/ *n* obstrucción *f*
**obtain** /əb'teɪn/ *vt* obtener. ● *vi* pre-valecer. **~able** *a* asequible
**obtrusive** /əb'truːsɪv/ *a* importuno
**obtuse** /əb'tjuːs/ *a* obtuso
**obviate** /'ɒbvɪeɪt/ *vt* evitar
**obvious** /'ɒbvɪəs/ *a* obvio. **~ly**
obviamente
**occasion** /ə'keɪʒn/ *n* ocasión *f*, oport-unidad *f*. **on ~** de vez en cuando.
● *vt* ocasionar. **~al** /ə'keɪʒənl/ *a*
poco frecuente. **~ally** *adv* de vez en
cuando
**occult** /ɒ'kʌlt/ *a* oculto
**occupant** /'ɒkjʊpənt/ *n* ocupante *m*
& *f*. **~ation** /ɒkjʊ'peɪʃn/ *n* ocu-pación *f*; (*job*) trabajo *m*, profesión
*f*. **~ational** *a* profesional. **~ier** *n*
ocupante *m* & *f*. **~y** /'ɒkjʊpaɪ/ *vt*
ocupar
**occur** /ə'kɜː(r)/ *vi* (*pt* **occurred**) ocur-rir, suceder; (*exist*) encontrarse. **it
~red to me that** se me ocurrió que.

**~rence** /ɔ'kʌrəns/ n suceso m, acontecimiento m

**ocean** /'əʊʃn/ n océano m

**o'clock** /ɔ'klɒk/ adv. **it is 7 ~** son las siete

**octagon** /'ɒktəgən/ n octágono m

**octane** /'ɒkteɪn/ n octano m

**octave** /'ɒktɪv/ n octava f

**October** /ɒk'təʊbə(r)/ n octubre m

**octopus** /'ɒktəpəs/ n (pl **-puses**) pulpo m

**oculist** /'ɒkjʊlɪst/ n oculista m & f

**odd** /ɒd/ a (-er, -est) extraño, raro; ⟨number⟩ impar; ⟨one of pair⟩ sin pareja; ⟨occasional⟩ poco frecuente; ⟨left over⟩ sobrante. **fifty-~** unos cincuenta, cincuenta y pico. **the ~ one out** la excepción f. **~ity** n ⟨thing⟩ curiosidad f; ⟨person⟩ excéntrico m. **~ly** adv extrañamente. **~ly enough** por extraño que parezca. **~ment** /'ɒdmənt/ n retazo m. **~s** /ɒdz/ npl probabilidades fpl; ⟨in betting⟩ apuesta f. **~s and ends** retazos mpl. **at ~s** de punta, de malas

**ode** /əʊd/ n oda f

**odious** /'əʊdɪəs/ a odioso

**odour** /'əʊdə(r)/ n olor m. **~less** a inodoro

**of** /əv, ɒv/ prep de. **a friend ~ mine** un amigo mío. **how kind ~ you** es Vd muy amable

**off** /ɒf/ adv lejos; ⟨light etc⟩ apagado; ⟨tap⟩ cerrado; ⟨food⟩ pasado. ● prep de, desde; ⟨away from⟩ fuera de; ⟨distant from⟩ lejos de. **be better ~** estar mejor. **be ~** marcharse. **day ~** n día m de asueto, día m libre

**offal** /'ɒfl/ n menudos mpl, asaduras fpl

**off: ~beat** a insólito. **~ chance** n posibilidad f remota. **~ colour** a indispuesto

**offen|ce** /ɔ'fens/ n ofensa f; ⟨illegal act⟩ delito m. **take ~ce** ofenderse. **~d** /ɔ'fend/ vt ofender. **~der** n delincuente m & f. **~sive** /ɔ'fensɪv/ a ofensivo; ⟨disgusting⟩ repugnante. ● n ofensiva f

**offer** /'ɒfə(r)/ vt ofrecer. ● n oferta f. **on ~** en oferta

**offhand** /ɒf'hænd/ a ⟨casual⟩ desenvuelto; ⟨brusque⟩ descortés. ● adv de improviso

**office** /'ɒfɪs/ n oficina f; ⟨post⟩ cargo m

**officer** /'ɒfɪsə(r)/ n oficial m; ⟨policeman⟩ policía f, guardia m; ⟨of organization⟩ director m

**official** /ɔ'fɪʃl/ a & n oficial (m). **~ly** adv oficialmente

**officiate** /ɔ'fɪʃɪeɪt/ vi oficiar. **~ as** desempeñar las funciones de

**officious** /ɔ'fɪʃəs/ a oficioso

**offing** /'ɒfɪŋ/ n. **in the ~** en perspectiva

**off: ~licence** n tienda f de bebidas alcohólicas. **~load** vt descargar. **~putting** a ⟨disconcerting, fam⟩ desconcertante; ⟨repellent⟩ repugnante. **~set** /'ɒfset/ vt (pt -set, pres p -setting) contrapesar. **~shoot** /'ɒfʃuːt/ n retoño m; ⟨fig⟩ ramificación f. **~side** /ɒf'saɪd/ a ⟨sport⟩ fuera de juego. **~spring** /'ɒfsprɪŋ/ n invar progenie f. **~stage** a entre bastidores. **~white** a blancuzco, color hueso

**often** /'ɒfn/ adv muchas veces, con frecuencia, a menudo. **how ~?** ¿cuántas veces?

**ogle** /'əʊgl/ vt comerse con los ojos

**ogre** /'əʊgə(r)/ n ogro m

**oh** /əʊ/ int ¡oh!, ¡ay!

**oil** /ɔɪl/ n aceite m; ⟨petroleum⟩ petróleo m. ● vt lubricar. **~field** /'ɔɪlfiːld/ n yacimiento m petrolífero. **~painting** n pintura f al óleo. **~rig** /'ɔɪlrɪg/ n plataforma f de perforación. **~skins** /'ɔɪlskɪnz/ npl chubasquero m. **~y** a aceitoso; ⟨food⟩ grasiento

**ointment** /'ɔɪntmənt/ n ungüento m

**OK** /əʊ'keɪ/ int ¡vale!, ¡de acuerdo! ● a bien; ⟨satisfactory⟩ satisfactorio. ● adv muy bien

**old** /əʊld/ a (-er, -est) viejo; ⟨not modern⟩ anticuado; ⟨former⟩ antiguo. **how ~ is she?** ¿cuántos años tiene? **she is ten years ~** tiene diez años. **of ~** de antaño. **~ age** n vejez f. **~fashioned** a anticuado. **~ maid** n solterona f. **~world** a antiguo

**oleander** /əʊlɪ'ændə(r)/ n adelfa f

**olive** /'ɒlɪv/ n ⟨fruit⟩ aceituna f; ⟨tree⟩ olivo m. ● a de oliva; ⟨colour⟩ aceitunado

**Olympic** /ɔ'lɪmpɪk/ a olímpico. **~s** npl, **~ Games** npl Juegos mpl Olímpicos

**omelette** /'ɒmlɪt/ n tortilla f, tortilla f de huevos (Mex)

**om|en** /'əʊmen/ n agüero m. **~inous** /'ɒmɪnəs/ a siniestro

**omi|ssion** /ɔ'mɪʃn/ n omisión f. **~t** /ɔ'mɪt/ vt (pt **omitted**) omitir

**omnipotent** /ɒm'nɪpətənt/ a omnipotente

**on** /ɒn/ *prep* en, sobre. ~ **foot** a pie. ~ **Monday** el lunes. ~ **Mondays** los lunes. ~ **seeing** al ver. ~ **the way** de camino. ● *adv* (*light etc*) encendido; (*put on*) puesto, poco natural; (*machine*) en marcha; (*tap*) abierto. ~ **and off** de vez en cuando. ~ **and** ~ sin cesar. **and so** ~ y así sucesivamente. **be** ~ **at** (*fam*) criticar. **go** ~ continuar. **later** ~ más tarde

**once** /wʌns/ *adv* una vez; (*formerly*) antes. ● *conj* una vez que. **at** ~ en seguida. ~**over** *n* (*fam*) ojeada *f*

**oncoming** /ˈɒnkʌmɪŋ/ *a* que se acerca; (*traffic*) que viene en sentido contrario, de frente

**one** /wʌn/ *a* & *n* uno (*m*). ● *pron* uno. ~ **another** el uno al otro. ~ **by** ~ uno a uno. ~ **never knows** nunca se sabe. **the blue** ~ el azul. **this** ~ éste. ~**off** *a* (*fam*) único

**onerous** /ˈɒnərəs/ *a* oneroso

**one**: ~**self** /wʌnˈself/ *pron* (*subject*) uno mismo; (*object*) se; (*after prep*) sí (mismo). **by** ~**self** solo. ~**sided** *a* unilateral. ~**way** *a* (*street*) de dirección única; (*ticket*) de ida

**onion** /ˈʌnɪən/ *n* cebolla *f*

**onlooker** /ˈɒnlʊkə(r)/ *n* espectador *m*

**only** /ˈəʊnlɪ/ *a* único. ~ **son** *n* hijo *m* único. ● *adv* sólo, solamente. ~ **just** apenas. ~ **too** de veras. ● *conj* pero, sólo que

**onset** /ˈɒnset/ *n* principio *m*; (*attack*) ataque *m*

**onslaught** /ˈɒnslɔːt/ *n* ataque *m* violento

**onus** /ˈəʊnəs/ *n* responsabilidad *f*

**onward(s)** /ˈɒnwəd(z)/ *a* & *adv* hacia adelante

**onyx** /ˈɒnɪks/ *n* ónice *f*

**ooze** /uːz/ *vt/i* rezumar

**opal** /ˈəʊpl/ *n* ópalo *m*

**opaque** /əʊˈpeɪk/ *a* opaco

**open** /ˈəʊpən/ *a* abierto; (*free to all*) público; (*undisguised*) manifiesto; (*question*) discutible; (*view*) despejado. ~ **sea** *n* alta mar *f*. ~ **secret** *n* secreto *m* a voces. **O**~ **University** *n* Universidad *f* a Distancia. **half**-~ *a* medio abierto. **in the** ~ *n* al aire libre. ● *vt/i* abrir. ~**ended** *a* abierto. ~**er** /ˈəʊpənə(r)/ *n* (*for tins*) abrelatas *m invar*; (*for bottles with caps*) abrebotellas *m invar*; (*corkscrew*) sacacorchos *m invar*. **eye**-~**er** *n* (*fam*) revelación *f*. ~**ing** /ˈəʊpənɪŋ/ *n* abertura *f*; (*beginning*)

principio *m*; (*job*) vacante *m*. ~**ly** /ˈəʊpənlɪ/ *adv* abiertamente. ~**minded** *a* imparcial

**opera** /ˈɒprə/ *n* ópera *f*. ~**glasses** *npl* gemelos *mpl* de teatro

**operate** /ˈɒpəreɪt/ *vt* hacer funcionar. ● *vi* funcionar; (*medicine etc*) operar. ~ **on** (*med*) operar a

**operatic** /ɒpəˈrætɪk/ *a* operístico

**operation** /ɒpəˈreɪʃn/ *n* operación *f*; (*mec*) funcionamiento *m*. **in** ~ en vigor. ~**al** /ɒpəˈreɪʃnl/ *a* operacional

**operative** /ˈɒpərətɪv/ *a* operativo; (*law etc*) en vigor

**operator** *n* operario *m*; (*telephonist*) telefonista *m* & *f*

**operetta** /ɒpəˈretə/ *n* opereta *f*

**opinion** /əˈpɪnɪən/ *n* opinión *f*. **in my** ~ a mi parecer. ~**ated** *a* dogmático

**opium** /ˈəʊpɪəm/ *n* opio *m*

**opponent** /əˈpəʊnənt/ *n* adversario *m*

**opportun|e** /ˈɒpətjuːn/ *a* oportuno. ~**ist** /ɒpəˈtjuːnɪst/ *a* oportunista *m* & *f*. ~**ity** /ɒpəˈtjuːnətɪ/ *n* oportunidad *f*

**oppos|e** /əˈpəʊz/ *vt* oponerse a. ~**ed to** en contra de. **be** ~**ed to** oponerse a. ~**ing** *a* opuesto

**opposite** /ˈɒpəzɪt/ *a* opuesto; (*facing*) de enfrente. ● *n* contrario *m*. ● *adv* enfrente. ● *prep* enfrente de. ~ **number** *n* homólogo *m*

**opposition** /ɒpəˈzɪʃn/ *n* oposición *f*; (*resistence*) resistencia *f*

**oppress** /əˈpres/ *vt* oprimir. ~**ion** /-ʃn/ *n* opresión *f*. ~**ive** *a* (*cruel*) opresivo; (*heat*) sofocante. ~**or** *n* opresor *m*

**opt** /ɒpt/ *vi*. ~ **for** elegir. ~ **out** negarse a participar

**optic|al** /ˈɒptɪkl/ *a* óptico. ~**ian** /ɒpˈtɪʃn/ *n* óptico *m*

**optimis|m** /ˈɒptɪmɪzəm/ *n* optimismo *m*. ~**t** /ˈɒptɪmɪst/ *n* optimista *m* & *f*. ~**tic** /-ˈmɪstɪk/ *a* optimista

**optimum** /ˈɒptɪməm/ *n* lo óptimo, lo mejor

**option** /ˈɒpʃn/ *n* opción *f*. ~**al** /ˈɒpʃənl/ *a* facultativo

**opulen|ce** /ˈɒpjʊləns/ *n* opulencia *f*. ~**t** /ˈɒpjʊlənt/ *a* opulento

**or** /ɔː(r)/ *conj* o; (*before Spanish o- and* ho-) u; (*after negative*) ni. ~ **else** si no, o bien

**oracle** /ˈɒrəkl/ *n* oráculo *m*

**oral** /'ɔːrəl/ a oral. ● n (*fam*) examen m oral

**orange** /'ɒrɪndʒ/ n naranja f; (*tree*) naranjo m; (*colour*) color m naranja. ● a de color naranja. ~**ade** n naranjada f

**orator** /'ɒrətə(r)/ n orador m

**oratorio** /ɒrə'tɔːrɪəʊ/ n (pl -os) oratorio m

**oratory** /'ɒrətrɪ/ n oratoria f

**orb** /ɔːb/ n orbe m

**orbit** /'ɔːbɪt/ n órbita f. ● vt orbitar

**orchard** /'ɔːtʃəd/ n huerto m

**orchestra** /'ɔːkɪstrə/ n orquesta f. ~l /-'kestrəl/ a orquestal. ~**te** /'ɔː kɪstreɪt/ vt orquestar

**orchid** /'ɔːkɪd/ n orquídea f

**ordain** /ɔː'deɪn/ vt ordenar

**ordeal** /ɔː'diːl/ n prueba f dura

**order** /'ɔːdə(r)/ n orden m; (*com*) pedido m. in ~ that para que. in ~ to para. ● vt (*command*) mandar; (*com*) pedir

**orderly** /'ɔːdəlɪ/ a ordenado. ● n asistente m & f

**ordinary** /'ɔːdɪnrɪ/ a corriente; (*average*) medio; (*mediocre*) ordinario

**ordination** /ɔːdɪ'neɪʃn/ n ordenación f

**ore** /ɔː(r)/ n mineral m

**organ** /'ɔːgən/ n órgano m

**organic** /ɔː'gænɪk/ a orgánico

**organism** /'ɔːgənɪzəm/ n organismo m

**organist** /'ɔːgənɪst/ n organista m & f

**organization** /ɔːgənaɪ'zeɪʃn/ n organización f. ~**e** /'ɔːgənaɪz/ vt organizar. ~**er** n organizador m

**orgasm** /'ɔːgæzəm/ n orgasmo m

**orgy** /'ɔːdʒɪ/ n orgía f

**Orient** /'ɔːrɪənt/ n Oriente m. ~**al** /-'entl/ a & n oriental (m & f)

**orientate** /'ɔːrɪənteɪt/ vt orientar. ~**ion** /-'teɪʃn/ n orientación f

**orifice** /'ɒrɪfɪs/ n orificio m

**origin** /'ɒrɪdʒɪn/ n origen m. ~**al** /ə'rɪdʒənl/ a original. ~**ality** /-'nælətɪ/ n originalidad f. ~**ally** adv originalmente. ~**ate** /ə'rɪdʒɪneɪt/ vi. ~**ate from** provenir de. ~**ator** n autor m

**ormolu** /'ɔːməluː/ n similor m

**ornament** /'ɔːnəmənt/ n adorno m. ~**al** /-'mentl/ a de adorno. ~**ation** /-en'teɪʃn/ n ornamentación f

**ornate** /ɔː'neɪt/ a adornado; ⟨*style*⟩ florido

**ornithology** /ɔːnɪ'θɒlədʒɪ/ n ornitología f

**orphan** /'ɔːfn/ n huérfano m. ● vt dejar huérfano. ~**age** n orfanato m

**orthodox** /'ɔːθədɒks/ a ortodoxo. ~**y** n ortodoxia f

**orthopaedic** /ɔːθə'piːdɪk/ a ortopédico. ~**s** n ortopedia f

**oscillate** /'ɒsɪleɪt/ vi oscilar

**ossify** /'ɒsɪfaɪ/ vt osificar. ● vi osificarse

**ostensible** /ɒs'tensɪbl/ a aparente. ~**y** adv aparentemente

**ostentation** /ɒsten'teɪʃn/ n ostentación f. ~**ious** a ostentoso

**osteopath** /'ɒstɪəpæθ/ n osteópata m & f. ~**y** /-'ɒpəθɪ/ n osteopatía f

**ostracize** /'ɒstrəsaɪz/ vt excluir

**ostrich** /'ɒstrɪtʃ/ n avestruz m

**other** /'ʌðə(r)/ a & n & pron otro (m). ~ **than** de otra manera que. the ~ **one** el otro. ~**wise** /'ʌðəwaɪz/ adv de otra manera; (*or*) si no

**otter** /'ɒtə(r)/ n nutria f

**ouch** /aʊtʃ/ int ¡ay!

**ought** /ɔːt/ v aux deber. I ~ **to see it** debería verlo. he ~ **to have done it** debería haberlo hecho

**ounce** /aʊns/ n onza f (= 28.35 gr.)

**our** /'aʊə(r)/ a nuestro. ~**s** /'aʊəz/ poss pron el nuestro, la nuestra, los nuestros, las nuestras. ~**selves** /aʊə'selvz/ pron (*subject*) nosotros mismos, nosotras mismas; (*reflexive*) nos; (*after prep*) nosotros (mismos), nosotras (mismas)

**oust** /aʊst/ vt expulsar, desalojar

**out** /aʊt/ adv fuera; ⟨*light*⟩ apagado; (*in blossom*) en flor; (*in error*) equivocado. ~**-and**—a cien por cien. ~ **of date** anticuado; (*not valid*) caducado. ~ **of doors** fuera. ~ **of order** estropeado; (*sign*) no funciona. ~ **of pity** por compasión. ~ **of place** fuera de lugar; (*fig*) inoportuno. ~ **of print** agotado. ~ **of sorts** indispuesto. ~ **of stock** agotado. ~ **of tune** desafinado. ~ **of work** parado, desempleado. be ~ equivocarse. be ~ **of** quedarse sin. be ~ **to** estar resuelto a. **five** ~ **of six** cinco de cada seis. **made** ~ **of** hecho de

**outbid** /aʊt'bɪd/ vt (pt -bid, pres p -bidding) ofrecer más que

**outboard** /'aʊtbɔːd/ a fuera borda

**outbreak** /'aʊtbreɪk/ n (*of anger*) arranque m; (*of war*) comienzo m; (*of disease*) epidemia f

**outbuilding** /'aʊtbɪldɪŋ/ n dependencia f

**outburst** /'aʊtbɜːst/ n explosión f

**outcast** /'aʊtkɑːst/ n paria m & f

**outcome** /'aʊtkʌm/ n resultado m

**outcry** /'aʊtkraɪ/ n protesta f

**outdated** /aʊt'deɪtɪd/ a anticuado

**outdo** /aʊt'duː/ vt (pt -did, pp -done) superar

**outdoor** /'aʊtdɔː(r)/ a al aire libre. ~s /-'dɔːz/ adv al aire libre

**outer** /'aʊtə(r)/ a exterior

**outfit** /'aʊtfɪt/ n equipo m; (clothes) traje m. ~ter n camisero m

**outgoing** /'aʊtɡəʊɪŋ/ a ⟨minister etc⟩ saliente; (sociable) abierto. ~s npl gastos mpl

**outgrow** /aʊt'ɡrəʊ/ vt (pt -grew, pp -grown) crecer más que ⟨person⟩; hacerse demasiado grande para ⟨clothes⟩. **he's ~n his trousers** le quedan pequeños los pantalones

**outhouse** /'aʊthaʊs/ n dependencia f

**outing** /'aʊtɪŋ/ n excursión f

**outlandish** /aʊt'lændɪʃ/ a extravagante

**outlaw** /'aʊtlɔː/ n proscrito m. ● vt proscribir

**outlay** /'aʊtleɪ/ n gastos mpl

**outlet** /'aʊtlet/ n salida f

**outline** /'aʊtlaɪn/ n contorno m; (summary) resumen m. ● vt trazar; (describe) dar un resumen de

**outlive** /aʊt'lɪv/ vt sobrevivir a

**outlook** /'aʊtlʊk/ n perspectiva f

**outlying** /'aʊtlaɪɪŋ/ a remoto

**outmoded** /aʊt'məʊdɪd/ a anticuado

**outnumber** /aʊt'nʌmbə(r)/ vt sobrepasar en número

**outpatient** /'aʊtpeɪʃnt/ n paciente m externo

**outpost** /'aʊtpəʊst/ n avanzada f

**output** /'aʊtpʊt/ n producción f

**outrage** /'aʊtreɪdʒ/ n ultraje m. ● vt ultrajar. ~ous /aʊt'reɪdʒəs/ a escandaloso, atroz

**outright** /'aʊtraɪt/ adv completamente; (at once) inmediatamente; (frankly) francamente. ● a completo; ⟨refusal⟩ rotundo

**outset** /'aʊtset/ n principio m

**outside** /'aʊtsaɪd/ a & n exterior (m). /aʊt'saɪd/ adv fuera. ● prep fuera de. ~r /aʊt'saɪdə(r)/ n forastero m; (in race) caballo m no favorito

**outsize** /'aʊtsaɪz/ a de tamaño extraordinario

**outskirts** /'aʊtskɜːts/ npl afueras fpl

**outspoken** /aʊt'spəʊkn/ a franco. **be ~** no tener pelos en la lengua

**outstanding** /aʊt'stændɪŋ/ a excepcional; (not settled) pendiente; (conspicuous) sobresaliente

**outstretched** /aʊt'stretʃt/ a extendido

**outstrip** /aʊt'strɪp/ vt (pt -stripped) superar

**outward** /'aʊtwəd/ a externo; ⟨journey⟩ de ida. ~ly adv por fuera, exteriormente. ~(s) adv hacia fuera

**outweigh** /aʊt'weɪ/ vt pesar más que; (fig) valer más que

**outwit** /aʊt'wɪt/ vt (pt -witted) ser más listo que

**oval** /'əʊvl/ a oval(ado). ● n óvalo m

**ovary** /'əʊvərɪ/ n ovario m

**ovation** /əʊ'veɪʃn/ n ovación f

**oven** /'ʌvn/ n horno m

**over** /'əʊvə(r)/ prep por encima de; (across) al otro lado de; (during) durante; (more than) más de. ~ **and above** por encima de. ● adv por encima; (ended) terminado; (more) más; (in excess) de sobra. ~ **again** otra vez. ~ **and** ~ una y otra vez. ~ **here** por aquí. ~ **there** por allí. **all** ~ por todas partes

**over...** /'əʊvə(r)/ pref sobre..., super...

**overall** /əʊvər'ɔːl/ a global; ⟨length, cost⟩ total. ● adv en conjunto. /'əʊvərɔːl/ n, ~s npl mono m

**overawe** /əʊvər'ɔː/ vt intimidar

**overbalance** /əʊvə'bæləns/ vt hacer perder el equilibrio. ● vi perder el equilibrio

**overbearing** /əʊvə'beərɪŋ/ a dominante

**overboard** /'əʊvəbɔːd/ adv al agua

**overbook** /əʊvə'bʊk/ vt aceptar demasiadas reservaciones para

**overcast** /əʊvə'kɑːst/ a nublado

**overcharge** /əʊvə'tʃɑːdʒ/ vt (fill too much) sobrecargar; (charge too much) cobrar demasiado

**overcoat** /'əʊvəkəʊt/ n abrigo m

**overcome** /əʊvə'kʌm/ vt (pt -came, pp -come) superar, vencer. **be ~ by** estar abrumado de

**overcrowded** /əʊvə'kraʊdɪd/ a atestado (de gente)

**overdo** /əʊvə'duː/ vt (pt -did, pp -done) exagerar; (culin) cocer demasiado

**overdose** /'əʊvədəʊs/ n sobredosis f

**overdraft** /'əʊvədrɑːft/ n giro m en descubierto

**overdraw** /əʊvə'drɔː/ vt (pt **-drew**, pp **-drawn**) girar en descubierto. **be ~n** tener un saldo deudor

**overdue** /əʊvə'djuː/ a retrasado; (belated) tardío; (bill) vencido y no pagado

**overestimate** /əʊvər'estɪmeɪt/ vt sobrestimar ● vi

**overflow** /əʊvə'fləʊ/ vi desbordarse. /'əʊvəfləʊ/ n (excess) exceso m; (outlet) rebosadero m

**overgrown** /əʊvə'grəʊn/ a demasiado grande; (garden) cubierto de hierbas

**overhang** /əʊvə'hæŋ/ vt (pt **-hung**) sobresalir por encima de; (fig) amenazar. ● vi sobresalir. /'əʊvəhæŋ/ n saliente f

**overhaul** /əʊvə'hɔːl/ vt revisar. /'əʊvəhɔːl/ n revisión f

**overhead** /əʊvə'hed/ adv por encima. /'əʊvəhed/ a de arriba. ~s npl gastos mpl generales

**overhear** /əʊvə'hɪə(r)/ vt (pt **-heard**) oír por casualidad

**overjoyed** /əʊvə'dʒɔɪd/ a muy contento. **he was** ~ rebosaba de alegría

**overland** /'əʊvəlænd/ a terrestre. ● adv por tierra

**overlap** /əʊvə'læp/ vt (pt **-lapped**) traslapar. ● vi traslaparse

**overleaf** /əʊvə'liːf/ adv a la vuelta. **see** ~ véase al dorso

**overload** /əʊvə'ləʊd/ vt sobrecargar

**overlook** /əʊvə'lʊk/ vt dominar; (building) dar a; (forget) olvidar; (oversee) inspeccionar; (forgive) perdonar

**overnight** /əʊvə'naɪt/ adv por la noche, durante la noche; (fig, instantly) de la noche a la mañana. **stay** ~ pasar la noche. ● a de noche

**overpass** /'əʊvəpɑːs/ n paso m a desnivel, paso m elevado

**overpay** /əʊvə'peɪ/ vt. (pt **-paid**) pagar demasiado

**overpower** /əʊvə'paʊə(r)/ vt subyugar; dominar (opponent); (fig) abrumar. ~ing a abrumador

**overpriced** /əʊvə'praɪst/ a demasiado caro

**overrate** /əʊvə'reɪt/ vt supervalorar

**overreach** /əʊvə'riːtʃ/ vr. ~ **o.s.** extralimitarse

**overreact** /əʊvərɪ'ækt/ vi reaccionar excesivamente

**overrid|e** /əʊvə'raɪd/ vt (pt **-rode**, pp **-ridden**) pasar por encima de. ~ing a dominante

**overripe** /'əʊvəraɪp/ a pasado, demasiado maduro

**overrule** /əʊvə'ruːl/ vt anular; denegar (claim)

**overrun** /əʊvə'rʌn/ vt (pt **-ran**, pp **-run**, pres p **-running**) invadir; exceder (limit)

**overseas** /əʊvə'siːz/ a de ultramar. ● adv al extranjero, en ultramar

**oversee** /əʊvə'siː/ vt (pt **-saw**, pp **-seen**) vigilar. ~r /'əʊvəsɪə(r)/ n supervisor m

**overshadow** /əʊvə'ʃædəʊ/ vt (darken) sombrear; (fig) eclipsar

**overshoot** /əʊvə'ʃuːt/ vt (pt **-shot**) excederse. ~ **the mark** pasarse de la raya

**oversight** /'əʊvəsaɪt/ n descuido m

**oversleep** /əʊvə'sliːp/ vi (pt **-slept**) despertarse tarde. **I overslept** se me pegaron las sábanas

**overstep** /əʊvə'step/ vt (pt **-stepped**) pasar de. ~ **the mark** pasarse de la raya

**overt** /'əʊvɜːt/ a manifiesto

**overtak|e** /əʊvə'teɪk/ vt/i (pt **-took**, pp **-taken**) sobrepasar; (auto) adelantar. ~ing n adelantamiento m

**overtax** /əʊvə'tæks/ vt exigir demasiado

**overthrow** /əʊvə'θrəʊ/ vt (pt **-threw**, pp **-thrown**) derrocar. /'əʊvəθrəʊ/ n derrocamiento m

**overtime** /'əʊvətaɪm/ n horas fpl extra

**overtone** /'əʊvətəʊn/ n (fig) matiz m

**overture** /'əʊvətjʊə(r)/ n obertura f. ~s npl (fig) propuestas fpl

**overturn** /əʊvə'tɜːn/ vt/i volcar

**overweight** /əʊvə'weɪt/ a demasiado pesado. **be** ~ pesar demasiado, ser gordo

**overwhelm** /əʊvə'welm/ vt aplastar; (with emotion) abrumar. ~ing a aplastante; (fig) abrumador

**overwork** /əʊvə'wɜːk/ vt hacer trabajar demasiado. ● vi trabajar demasiado. ● n trabajo m excesivo

**overwrought** /əʊvə'rɔːt/ a agotado, muy nervioso

**ovulation** /ɒvjʊ'leɪʃn/ n ovulación f

**ow|e** /əʊ/ vt deber. ~ing a debido. ~ing to a causa de

**owl** /aʊl/ n lechuza f, búho m

**own** /əʊn/ a propio. **get one's** ~ **back** (fam) vengarse. **hold one's** ~

mantenerse firme, saber defenderse. **on one's ~** por su cuenta. ● *vt* poseer, tener. ● *vi.* **~ up (to)** *(fam)* confesar. **~er** *n* propietario *m*, dueño *m*. **~ership** *n* posesión *f*; *(right)* propiedad *f*

**ox** /ɒks/ *n* (*pl* **oxen**) buey *m*

**oxide** /'ɒksaɪd/ *n* óxido *m*

**oxygen** /'ɒksɪdʒən/ *n* oxígeno *m*

**oyster** /'ɔɪstə(r)/ *n* ostra *f*

# P

**p** /piː/ *abbr* (*pence*, *penny*) penique(s) (*m*(*pl*))

**pace** /peɪs/ *n* paso *m*. ● *vi.* **~ up and down** pasearse de aquí para allá. **~-maker** *n* (*runner*) el que marca el paso; (*med*) marcapasos *m invar*. **keep ~ with** andar al mismo paso que

**Pacific** /pə'sɪfɪk/ *a* pacífico. ● *n.* **~ (Ocean)** (Océano *m*) Pacífico *m*

**pacif|ist** /'pæsɪfɪst/ *n* pacifista *m* & *f*. **~y** /'pæsɪfaɪ/ *vt* apaciguar

**pack** /pæk/ *n* fardo *m*; (*of cards*) baraja *f*; (*of hounds*) jauría *f*; (*of wolves*) manada *f*; (*large amount*) montón *m*. ● *vt* empaquetar; hacer (*suitcase*); (*press down*) apretar. ● *vi* hacer la maleta. **~age** /'pækɪdʒ/ *n* paquete *m*. ● *vt* empaquetar. **~age deal** *n* acuerdo *m* global. **~age tour** *n* viaje *m* organizado. **~ed lunch** *n* almuerzo *m* frío. **~ed out** (*fam*) de bote en bote. **~et** /'pækɪt/ *n* paquete *m*. **send ~ing** echar a paseo

**pact** /pækt/ *n* pacto *m*, acuerdo *m*

**pad** /pæd/ *n* almohadilla *f*; (*for writing*) bloc *m*; (*for ink*) tampón *m*; (*flat*, *fam*) piso *m*. ● *vt* (*pt* **padded**) rellenar. **~ding** *n* relleno *m*. ● *vi* andar a pasos quedos. **launching ~** plataforma *f* de lanzamiento

**paddle**[1] /'pædl/ *n* canalete *m*

**paddle**[2] /'pædl/ *vi* mojarse los pies

**paddle-steamer** /'pædlstiːmə(r)/ *n* vapor *m* de ruedas

**paddock** /'pædək/ *n* recinto *m*; (*field*) prado *m*

**paddy** /'pædɪ/ *n* arroz *m* con cáscara. **~field** *n* arrozal *m*

**padlock** /'pædlɒk/ *n* candado *m*. ● *vt* cerrar con candado

**paediatrician** /piːdɪə'trɪʃn/ *n* pediatra *m* & *f*

**pagan** /'peɪgən/ *a* & *n* pagano (*m*)

**page**[1] /peɪdʒ/ *n* página *f*. ● *vt* paginar

**page**[2] /peɪdʒ/ *n* (*in hotel*) botones *m invar*. ● *vt* llamar

**pageant** /'pædʒənt/ *n* espectáculo *m* (histórico). **~ry** *n* boato *m*

**pagoda** /pə'gəʊdə/ *n* pagoda *f*

**paid** /peɪd/ *see* pay. ● *a.* **put ~ to** (*fam*) acabar con

**pail** /peɪl/ *n* cubo *m*

**pain** /peɪn/ *n* dolor *m*. **~ in the neck** (*fam*) ⟨*persona*⟩ pesado *m*; ⟨*thing*⟩ lata *f*. **be in ~** tener dolores. **~s** *npl* (*effort*) esfuerzos *mpl*. **be at ~s** esmerarse. ● *vt* doler. **~ful** /'peɪnfl/ *a* doloroso; (*laborious*) penoso. **~killer** *n* calmante *m*. **~less** *a* indoloro. **~staking** /'peɪnzteɪkɪŋ/ *a* esmerado

**paint** /peɪnt/ *n* pintura *f*. ● *vt/i* pintar. **~er** *n* pintor *m*. **~ing** *n* pintura *f*

**pair** /peə(r)/ *n* par *m*; (*of people*) pareja *f*. **~ of trousers** pantalón *m*, pantalones *mpl*. ● *vi* emparejarse. **~ off** emparejarse

**pajamas** /pə'dʒɑːməz/ *npl* pijama *m*

**Pakistan** /pɑːkɪ'stɑːn/ *n* el Pakistán *m*. **~i** *a* & *n* paquistaní (*m* & *f*)

**pal** /pæl/ *n* (*fam*) amigo *m*

**palace** /'pælɪs/ *n* palacio *m*

**palat|able** /'pælətəbl/ *a* sabroso; (*fig*) aceptable. **~e** /'pælət/ *n* paladar *m*

**palatial** /pə'leɪʃl/ *a* suntuoso

**palaver** /pə'lɑːvə(r)/ *n* (*fam*) lío *m*

**pale**[1] /peɪl/ *a* (**-er**, **-est**) pálido; ⟨*colour*⟩ claro. ● *vi* palidecer

**pale**[2] /peɪl/ *n* estaca *n*

**paleness** /'peɪlnɪs/ *n* palidez *f*

**Palestin|e** /'pælɪstaɪn/ *n* Palestina *f*. **~ian** /-'stɪnɪən/ *a* & *n* palestino (*m*)

**palette** /'pælɪt/ *n* paleta *f*. **~-knife** *n* espátula *f*

**pall**[1] /pɔːl/ *n* paño *m* mortuorio; (*fig*) capa *f*

**pall**[2] /pɔːl/ *vi.* **~ (on)** perder su sabor (para)

**pallid** /'pælɪd/ *a* pálido

**palm** /pɑːm/ *n* palma *f*. ● *vt.* **~ off** encajar (**on** a). **~ist** /'pɑːmɪst/ *n* quiromántico *m*. **P~ Sunday** *n* Domingo *m* de Ramos

**palpable** /'pælpəbl/ *a* palpable

**palpitat|e** /'pælpɪteɪt/ *vi* palpitar. **~ion** /-'teɪʃn/ *n* palpitación *f*

**paltry** /'pɔːltrɪ/ *a* (**-ier**, **-iest**) insignificante

**pamper** /'pæmpə(r)/ *vt* mimar

**pamphlet** /'pæmflɪt/ n folleto m

**pan** /pæn/ n cacerola f; (for frying) sartén f; (of scales) platillo m; (of lavatory) taza f

**panacea** /pænə'sɪə/ n panacea f

**panache** /pæ'næʃ/ n brío m

**pancake** /'pænkeɪk/ n hojuela f, crêpe f

**panda** /'pændə/ n panda m. ~ car n coche m de la policía

**pandemonium** /pændɪ'məʊnɪəm/ n pandemonio m

**pander** /'pændə(r)/ vi. ~ to complacer

**pane** /peɪn/ n (of glass) vidrio m

**panel** /'pænl/ n panel m; (group of people) jurado m. ~ling n paneles mpl

**pang** /pæŋ/ n punzada f

**panic** /'pænɪk/ n pánico m. ● vi (pt **panicked**) ser preso de pánico. ~-stricken a preso de pánico

**panoram|a** /pænə'rɑːmə/ n panorama m. ~ic /-'ræmɪk/ a panorámico

**pansy** /'pænzɪ/ n pensamiento m; (effeminate man, fam) maricón m

**pant** /pænt/ vi jadear

**pantechnicon** /pæn'teknɪkən/ n camión m de mudanzas

**panther** /'pænθə(r)/ n pantera f

**panties** /'pæntɪz/ npl bragas fpl

**pantomime** /'pæntəmaɪm/ n pantomima f

**pantry** /'pæntrɪ/ n despensa f

**pants** /pænts/ npl (man's underwear, fam) calzoncillos mpl; (woman's underwear, fam) bragas fpl; (trousers, fam) pantalones mpl

**papa|cy** /'peɪpəsɪ/ n papado m. ~l a papal

**paper** /'peɪpə(r)/ n papel m; (newspaper) periódico m; (exam) examen m; (document) documento m. on ~ en teoría. ● vt empapelar, tapizar (LAm). ~back /'peɪpəbæk/ a en rústica. ● n libro m en rústica. ~clip n sujetapapeles m invar, clip m. ~weight /'peɪpəweɪt/ n pisapapeles m invar. ~work n papeleo m, trabajo m de oficina

**papier mâché** /pæpɪeɪ'mæʃeɪ/ n cartón m piedra

**par** /pɑː(r)/ n par f; (golf) par m. feel below ~ no estar en forma. on a ~ with a la par con

**parable** /'pærəbl/ n parábola f

**parachut|e** /'pærəʃuːt/ n paracaídas m invar. ● vi lanzarse en paracaídas. ~ist n paracaidista m & f

**parade** /pə'reɪd/ n desfile m; (street) paseo m; (display) alarde m. ● vi desfilar. ● vt hacer alarde de

**paradise** /'pærədaɪs/ n paraíso m

**paradox** /'pærədɒks/ n paradoja f. ~ical /-'dɒksɪkl/ a paradójico

**paraffin** /'pærəfɪn/ n queroseno m

**paragon** /'pærəgən/ n dechado m

**paragraph** /'pærəgrɑːf/ n párrafo m

**parallel** /'pærəlel/ a paralelo. ● n paralelo m; (line) paralela f. ● vt ser paralelo a

**paraly|se** /'pærəlaɪz/ vt paralizar. ~sis /pə'rælɪsɪs/ n (pl -ses /-siːz/) parálisis f. ~tic /pærə'lɪtɪk/ a & n paralítico (m)

**parameter** /pə'ræmɪtə(r)/ n parámetro m

**paramount** /'pærəmaʊnt/ a supremo

**paranoia** /pærə'nɔɪə/ n paranoia f

**parapet** /'pærəpɪt/ n parapeto m

**paraphernalia** /pærəfə'neɪlɪə/ n trastos mpl

**paraphrase** /'pærəfreɪz/ n paráfrasis f. ● vt parafrasear

**paraplegic** /pærə'pliːdʒɪk/ n parapléjico m

**parasite** /'pærəsaɪt/ n parásito m

**parasol** /'pærəsɒl/ n sombrilla f

**paratrooper** /'pærətruːpə(r)/ n paracaidista m

**parcel** /'pɑːsl/ n paquete m

**parch** /pɑːtʃ/ vt resecar. be ~ed tener mucha sed

**parchment** /'pɑːtʃmənt/ n pergamino m

**pardon** /'pɑːdn/ n perdón m; (jurid) indulto m. I beg your ~! ¡perdone Vd! I beg your ~? ¿cómo?, ¿mande? (Mex). ● vt perdonar

**pare** /peə(r)/ vt cortar ‹nails›; (peel) pelar, mondar

**parent** /'peərənt/ n (father) padre m; (mother) madre f; (source) origen m. ~s npl padres mpl. ~al /pə'rentl/ a de los padres

**parenthesis** /pə'renθəsɪs/ n (pl -theses /-siːz/) paréntesis m invar

**parenthood** /'peərənthʊd/ n paternidad f, maternidad f

**Paris** /'pærɪs/ n París m

**parish** /'pærɪʃ/ n parroquia f; (municipal) municipio m. ~ioner /pə'rɪʃənə(r)/ n feligrés m

**Parisian** /pə'rɪzɪən/ a & n parisino (m)

**parity** /'pærətɪ/ n igualdad f

**park** /pɑːk/ *n* parque *m*. ● *vt/i* aparcar. ~ **oneself** *vr* (*fam*) instalarse

**parka** /ˈpɑːkə/ *n* anorak *m*

**parking-meter** /ˈpɑːkɪŋmiːtə(r)/ *n* parquímetro *m*

**parliament** /ˈpɑːləmənt/ *n* parlamento *m*. **~ary** /-ˈmentrɪ/ *a* parlamentario

**parlour** /ˈpɑːlə(r)/ *n* salón *m*

**parochial** /pəˈrəʊkɪəl/ *a* parroquial; (*fig*) pueblerino

**parody** /ˈpærədɪ/ *n* parodia *f*. ● *vt* parodiar

**parole** /pəˈrəʊl/ *n* libertad *f* bajo palabra, libertad *f* provisional. **on ~** libre bajo palabra. ● *vt* liberar bajo palabra

**paroxysm** /ˈpærəksɪzəm/ *n* paroxismo *m*

**parquet** /ˈpɑːkeɪ/ *n*. ~ **floor** *n* parqué *m*

**parrot** /ˈpærət/ *n* papagayo *m*

**parry** /ˈpærɪ/ *vt* parar; (*avoid*) esquivar. ● *n* parada *f*

**parsimonious** /pɑːsɪˈməʊnɪəs/ *a* parsimonioso

**parsley** /ˈpɑːslɪ/ *n* perejil *m*

**parsnip** /ˈpɑːsnɪp/ *n* pastinaca *f*

**parson** /ˈpɑːsn/ *n* cura *m*, párroco *m*

**part** /pɑːt/ *n* parte *f*; (*of machine*) pieza *f*; (*of serial*) entrega *f*; (*in play*) papel *m*; (*side in dispute*) partido *m*. **on the ~ of** por parte de. ● *adv* en parte. ● *vt* separar. ~ **with** *vt* separarse de. ● *vi* separarse

**partake** /pɑːˈteɪk/ *vt* (*pt* -**took**, *pp* -**taken**) participar. ~ **of** compartir

**partial** /ˈpɑːʃl/ *a* parcial. **be ~ to** ser aficionado a. **~ity** /-ɪˈælətɪ/ *n* parcialidad *f*. **~ly** *adv* parcialmente

**participa|nt** /pɑːˈtɪsɪpənt/ *n* participante *m* & *f*. **~te** /pɑːˈtɪsɪpeɪt/ *vi* participar. **~tion** /-ˈpeɪʃn/ *n* participación *f*

**participle** /ˈpɑːtɪsɪpl/ *n* participio *m*

**particle** /ˈpɑːtɪkl/ *n* partícula *f*

**particular** /pəˈtɪkjʊlə(r)/ *a* particular; (*precise*) meticuloso; (*fastidious*) quisquilloso. ● *n*. **in ~** especialmente. **~ly** *adv* especialmente. **~s** *npl* detalles *mpl*

**parting** /ˈpɑːtɪŋ/ *n* separación *f*; (*in hair*) raya *f*. ● *a* de despedida

**partisan** /pɑːtɪˈzæn/ *n* partidario *m*

**partition** /pɑːˈtɪʃn/ *n* partición *f*; (*wall*) tabique *m*. ● *vt* dividir

**partly** /ˈpɑːtlɪ/ *adv* en parte

**partner** /ˈpɑːtnə(r)/ *n* socio *m*; (*sport*) pareja *f*. **~ship** *n* asociación *f*; (*com*) sociedad *f*

**partridge** /ˈpɑːtrɪdʒ/ *n* perdiz *f*

**part-time** /pɑːtˈtaɪm/ *a* & *adv* a tiempo parcial

**party** /ˈpɑːtɪ/ *n* reunión *f*, fiesta *f*; (*group*) grupo *m*; (*pol*) partido *m*; (*jurid*) parte *f*. ~ **line** *n* (*telephone*) línea *f* colectiva

**pass** /pɑːs/ *vt* pasar; (*in front of*) pasar por delante de; (*overtake*) adelantar; (*approve*) aprobar ⟨*exam, bill, law*⟩; hacer ⟨*remark*⟩; pronunciar ⟨*judgement*⟩. ~ **down** transmitir. ~ **over** pasar por alto de. ~ **round** distribuir. ~ **through** pasar por; (*cross*) atravesar. ~ **up** (*fam*) dejar pasar. ● *vi* pasar; (*in exam*) aprobar. ~ **away** morir. ~ **out** (*fam*) desmayarse. ● *n* (*permit*) permiso *m*; (*in mountains*) puerto *m*, desfiladero *m*; (*sport*) pase *m*; (*in exam*) aprobado *m*. **make a ~ at** (*fam*) hacer proposiciones amorosas a. **~able** /ˈpɑːsəbl/ *a* pasable; ⟨*road*⟩ transitable

**passage** /ˈpæsɪdʒ/ *n* paso *m*; (*voyage*) travesía *f*; (*corridor*) pasillo *m*; (*in book*) pasaje *m*

**passenger** /ˈpæsɪndʒə(r)/ *n* pasajero *m*

**passer-by** /pɑːsəˈbaɪ/ *n* (*pl* **passers-by**) transeúnte *m* & *f*

**passion** /ˈpæʃn/ *n* pasión *f*. **~ate** *a* apasionado. **~ately** *adv* apasionadamente

**passive** /ˈpæsɪv/ *a* pasivo. **~ness** *n* pasividad *f*

**passmark** /ˈpɑːsmɑːk/ *n* aprobado *m*

**Passover** /ˈpɑːsəʊvə(r)/ *n* Pascua *f* de los hebreos

**passport** /ˈpɑːspɔːt/ *n* pasaporte *m*

**password** /ˈpɑːswɜːd/ *n* contraseña *f*

**past** /pɑːst/ *a* & *n* pasado (*m*). **in times ~** en tiempos pasados. **the ~ week** *n* la semana *f* pasada. ● *prep* por delante de; (*beyond*) más allá de. ● *adv* por delante. **drive ~** pasar en coche. **go ~** pasar

**paste** /peɪst/ *n* pasta *f*; (*adhesive*) engrudo *m*. ● *vt* (*fasten*) pegar; (*cover*) engrudar. **~board** /ˈpeɪstbɔːd/ *n* cartón *m*. ~ **jewellery** *n* joyas *fpl* de imitación

**pastel** /ˈpæstl/ *a* & *n* pastel (*m*)

**pasteurize** /ˈpæstʃəraɪz/ *vt* pasteurizar

**pastiche** /pæˈstiːʃ/ *n* pastiche *m*

**pastille** /'pæstɪl/ n pastilla f

**pastime** /'pɑːstaɪm/ n pasatiempo m

**pastoral** /'pɑːstərəl/ a pastoral

**pastr|ies** npl pasteles mpl, pastas fpl. ~y /'peɪstrɪ/ n pasta f

**pasture** /'pɑːstʃə(r)/ n pasto m

**pasty**[1] /'pæstɪ/ n empanada f

**pasty**[2] /'peɪstɪ/ a pastoso; (pale) pálido

**pat**[1] /pæt/ vt (pt patted) dar palmaditas en; acariciar ⟨dog etc⟩. ● n palmadita f; (of butter) porción f

**pat**[2] /pæt/ adv en el momento oportuno

**patch** /pætʃ/ n pedazo m; (period) período m; (repair) remiendo m; (piece of ground) terreno m. **not a ~ on** (fam) muy inferior a. ● vt remendar. ~ **up** arreglar. ~**work** n labor m de retazos; (fig) mosaico m. ~y a desigual

**pâté** /'pæteɪ/ n pasta f, paté m

**patent** /'peɪtnt/ a patente. ● n patente f. ● vt patentar. ~ **leather** n charol m. ~**ly** adv evidentemente

**patern|al** /pə'tɜːnl/ a paterno. ~**ity** /pə'tɜːnətɪ/ n paternidad f

**path** /pɑːθ/ n (pl -s /pɑːðz/) sendero m; (sport) pista f; (of rocket) trayectoria f; (fig) camino m

**pathetic** /pə'θetɪk/ a patético, lastimoso

**pathology** /pə'θɒlədʒɪ/ n patología f

**pathos** /'peɪθɒs/ n patetismo m

**patien|ce** /'peɪʃns/ n paciencia f. ~**t** /'peɪʃnt/ a & n paciente (m & f). ~**tly** adv con paciencia

**patio** /'pætɪəʊ/ n (pl -os) patio m

**patriarch** /'peɪtrɪɑːk/ n patriarca m

**patrician** /pə'trɪʃn/ a & n patricio (m)

**patriot** /'pætrɪət/ n patriota m & f. ~**ic** /-'ɒtɪk/ a patriótico. ~**ism** n patriotismo m

**patrol** /pə'trəʊl/ n patrulla f. ● vt/i patrullar

**patron** /'peɪtrən/ n (of the arts etc) mecenas m & f; (customer) cliente m & f; (of charity) patrocinador m. ~**age** /'pætrənɪdʒ/ n patrocinio m; (of shop etc) clientela f. ~**ize** vt ser cliente de; (fig) tratar con condescendencia

**patter**[1] /'pætə(r)/ n (of steps) golpeteo m; (of rain) tamborileo m. ● vi correr con pasos ligeros; ⟨rain⟩ tamborilear

**patter**[2] /'pætə(r)/ (speech) jerga f; (chatter) parloteo m

**pattern** /'pætn/ n diseño m; (model) modelo m; (sample) muestra f; (manner) modo m; (in dressmaking) patrón m

**paunch** /pɔːntʃ/ n panza f

**pauper** /'pɔːpə(r)/ n indigente m & f, pobre m & f

**pause** /pɔːz/ n pausa f. ● vi hacer una pausa

**pave** /peɪv/ vt pavimentar. ~ **the way for** preparar el terreno para

**pavement** /'peɪvmənt/ n pavimento m; (at side of road) acera f

**pavilion** /pə'vɪlɪən/ n pabellón m

**paving-stone** /'peɪvɪŋstəʊn/ n losa f

**paw** /pɔː/ n pata f; (of cat) garra f. ● vi tocar con la pata; ⟨person⟩ manosear

**pawn**[1] /pɔːn/ n (chess) peón m; (fig) instrumento m

**pawn**[2] /pɔːn/ vt empeñar. ● n. **in ~** en prenda. ~**broker** /'pɔːnbrəʊkə(r)/ n prestamista m & f. ~**shop** n monte m de piedad

**pawpaw** /'pɔːpɔː/ n papaya f

**pay** /peɪ/ vt (pt paid) pagar; prestar ⟨attention⟩; hacer ⟨compliment, visit⟩. ~ **back** devolver. ~ **cash** pagar al contado. ~ **in** ingresar. ~ **off** pagar. ~ **out** pagar. ● vi pagar; (be profitable) rendir. ● n paga f. **in the ~ of** al servicio de. ~**able** /'peɪəbl/ a pagadero. ~**ment** /'peɪmənt/ n pago m. ~**off** n (sl) liquidación f; (fig) ajuste m de cuentas. ~**roll** /'peɪrəʊl/ n nómina f. ~ **up** pagar

**pea** /piː/ n guisante m

**peace** /piːs/ n paz f. ~ **of mind** tranquilidad f. ~**able** a pacífico. ~**ful** /'piːsfl/ a tranquilo. ~**maker** /'piːsmeɪkə(r)/ n pacificador m

**peach** /piːtʃ/ n melocotón m, durazno m (LAm); (tree) melocotonero m, duraznero m (LAm)

**peacock** /'piːkɒk/ n pavo m real

**peak** /piːk/ n cumbre f; (maximum) máximo m. ~ **hours** npl horas fpl punta. ~**ed cap** n gorra f de visera

**peaky** /'piːkɪ/ a pálido

**peal** /piːl/ n repique m. ~**s of laughter** risotadas fpl

**peanut** /'piːnʌt/ n cacahuete m, maní m (Mex). ~**s** (sl) una bagatela f

**pear** /peə(r)/ n pera f; (tree) peral m

**pearl** /pɜːl/ n perla f. ~**y** a nacarado

**peasant** /'peznt/ n campesino m

**peat** /piːt/ n turba f

**pebble** /'pebl/ n guijarro m

**peck** /pek/ *vt* picotear; (*kiss, fam*) dar un besito a. ● *n* picotazo *m*; (*kiss*) besito *m*. **~ish** /'pekɪʃ/ *a*. be **~ish** (*fam*) tener hambre, tener gazuza (*fam*)

**peculiar** /pɪ'kjuːlɪə(r)/ *a* raro; (*special*) especial. **~ity** /-'ærətɪ/ *n* rareza *f*; (*feature*) particularidad *f*

**pedal** /'pedl/ *n* pedal *m*. ● *vi* pedalear

**pedantic** /pɪ'dæntɪk/ *a* pedante

**peddle** /'pedl/ *vt* vender por las calles

**pedestal** /'pedɪstl/ *n* pedestal *m*

**pedestrian** /pɪ'destrɪən/ *n* peatón *m*. ● *a* de peatones; (*dull*) prosaico. **~ crossing** *n* paso *m* de peatones

**pedigree** /'pedɪgriː/ *n* linaje *m*; (*of animal*) pedigrí *m*. ● *a* ⟨*animal*⟩ de raza

**pedlar** /'pedlə(r)/ *n* buhonero *m*, vendedor *m* ambulante

**peek** /piːk/ *vi* mirar a hurtadillas

**peel** /piːl/ *n* cáscara *f*. ● *vt* pelar ⟨*fruit, vegetables*⟩. ● *vi* pelarse. **~ings** *npl* peladuras *fpl*, monda *f*

**peep**[1] /piːp/ *vi* mirar a hurtadillas. ● *n* mirada *f* furtiva

**peep**[2] /piːp/ ⟨*bird*⟩ piar. ● *n* pío *m*

**peep-hole** /'piːphəʊl/ *n* mirilla *f*

**peer**[1] /pɪə(r)/ *vi* mirar. **~ at** escudriñar

**peer**[2] /pɪə(r)/ *n* par *m*, compañero *m*. **~age** *n* pares *mpl*

**peev|ed** /piːvd/ *a* (*sl*) irritado. **~ish** /'piːvɪʃ/ *a* picajoso

**peg** /peg/ *n* clavija *f*; (*for washing*) pinza *f*; (*hook*) gancho *m*; (*for tent*) estaca *f*. **off the ~** de percha. ● *vt* (*pt* **pegged**) fijar ⟨*precios*⟩. **~ away at** afanarse por

**pejorative** /pɪ'dʒɒrətɪv/ *a* peyorativo, despectivo

**pelican** /'pelɪkən/ *n* pelícano *m*. **~ crossing** *n* paso *m* de peatones (con semáforo)

**pellet** /'pelɪt/ *n* pelotilla *f*; (*for gun*) perdigón *m*

**pelt**[1] /pelt/ *n* pellejo *m*

**pelt**[2] /pelt/ *vt* tirar. ● *vi* llover a cántaros

**pelvis** /'pelvɪs/ *n* pelvis *f*

**pen**[1] /pen/ *n* (*enclosure*) recinto *m*

**pen**[2] /pen/ *n* (*for writing*) pluma *f*, estilográfica *f*; (*ball-point*) bolígrafo *m*

**penal** /'piːnl/ *a* penal. **~ize** *vt* castigar. **~ty** /'penltɪ/ *n* castigo *m*; (*fine*)

multa *f*. **~ty kick** *n* (*football*) penalty *m*

**penance** /'penəns/ *n* penitencia *f*

**pence** /pens/ *see* **penny**

**pencil** /'pensl/ *n* lápiz *m*. ● *vt* (*pt* **pencilled**) escribir con lápiz. **~sharpener** *n* sacapuntas *m invar*

**pendant** /'pendənt/ *n* dije *m*, medallón *m*

**pending** /'pendɪŋ/ *a* pendiente. ● *prep* hasta

**pendulum** /'pendjʊləm/ *n* péndulo *m*

**penetrat|e** /'penɪtreɪt/ *vt/i* penetrar. **~ing** *a* penetrante. **~ion** /-'treɪʃn/ *n* penetración *f*

**penguin** /'peŋgwɪn/ *n* pingüino *m*

**penicillin** /penɪ'sɪlɪn/ *n* penicilina *f*

**peninsula** /pə'nɪnsjʊlə/ *n* península *f*

**penis** /'piːnɪs/ *n* pene *m*

**peniten|ce** /'penɪtəns/ *n* penitencia *f*. **~t** /'penɪtənt/ *a & n* penitente (*m & f*). **~tiary** /penɪ'tenʃərɪ/ *n* (*Amer*) cárcel *m*

**pennant** /'penənt/ *n* banderín *m*

**penn|iless** /'penɪlɪs/ *a* sin un céntimo. **~y** /'penɪ/ *n* (*pl* **pennies** *or* **pence**) penique *m*

**pension** /'penʃn/ *n* pensión *f*; (*for retirement*) jubilación *f*. ● *vt* pensionar. **~able** *a* con derecho a pensión; ⟨*age*⟩ de la jubilación. **~er** *n* jubilado *m*. **~ off** jubilar

**pensive** /'pensɪv/ *a* pensativo

**pent-up** /pent'ʌp/ *a* reprimido; (*confined*) encerrado

**pentagon** /'pentəgən/ *n* pentágono *m*

**Pentecost** /'pentɪkɒst/ *n* Pentecostés *m*

**penthouse** /'penthaʊs/ *n* ático *m*

**penultimate** /pen'ʌltɪmət/ *a* penúltimo

**penury** /'penjʊərɪ/ *n* penuria *f*

**peony** /'piːənɪ/ *n* peonía *f*

**people** /'piːpl/ *npl* gente *f*; (*citizens*) pueblo *m*. **~ say** se dice. **English ~** los ingleses *mpl*. **my ~** (*fam*) mi familia *f*. ● *vt* poblar

**pep** /pep/ *n* vigor *m*. ● *vt*. **~ up** animar

**pepper** /'pepə(r)/ *n* pimienta *f*; (*vegetable*) pimiento *m*. ● *vt* sazonar con pimienta. **~y** *a* picante. **~corn**

/'pepəkɔːn/ *n* grano *m* de pimienta. **∼corn rent** *n* alquiler *m* nominal

**peppermint** /'pepəmɪnt/ *n* menta *f*; (*sweet*) pastilla *f* de menta

**pep talk** /'peptɔːk/ *n* palabras *fpl* animadoras

**per** /pɜː(r)/ *prep* por. **∼ annum** al año. **∼ cent** por ciento. **∼ head** por cabeza, por persona. **ten miles ∼ hour** diez millas por hora

**perceive** /pə'siːv/ *vt* percibir; (*notice*) darse cuenta de

**percentage** /pə'sentɪdʒ/ *n* porcentaje *m*

**percepti|ble** /pə'septəbl/ *a* perceptible. **∼on** /pə'sepʃn/ *n* percepción *f*. **∼ve** *a* perspicaz

**perch**[1] /pɜːtʃ/ *n* (*of bird*) percha *f*. ● *vi* posarse

**perch**[2] /pɜːtʃ/ (*fish*) perca *f*

**percolat|e** /'pɜːkəleɪt/ *vt* filtrar. ● *vi* filtrarse. **∼or** *n* cafetera *f*

**percussion** /pə'kʌʃn/ *n* percusión *f*

**peremptory** /pə'remptərɪ/ *a* perentorio

**perennial** /pə'renɪəl/ *a & n* perenne (*m*)

**perfect** /'pɜːfɪkt/ *a* perfecto. /pə'fekt/ *vt* perfeccionar. **∼ion** /pə'fekʃn/ *n* perfección *f*. **to ∼ion** a la perfección. **∼ionist** *n* perfeccionista *m & f*. **∼ly** /'pɜːfɪktlɪ/ *adv* perfectamente

**perforat|e** /'pɜːfəreɪt/ *vt* perforar. **∼ion** /-'reɪʃn/ *n* perforación *f*

**perform** /pə'fɔːm/ *vt* hacer, realizar; representar (*play*); desempeñar (*role*); (*mus*) interpretar. **∼ an operation** (*med*) operar. **∼ance** *n* ejecución *f*; (*of play*) representación *f*; (*of car*) rendimiento *m*; (*fuss, fam*) jaleo *m*. **∼er** *n* artista *m & f*

**perfume** /'pɜːfjuːm/ *n* perfume *m*

**perfunctory** /pə'fʌŋktərɪ/ *a* superficial

**perhaps** /pə'hæps/ *adv* quizá(s), tal vez

**peril** /'perəl/ *n* peligro *m*. **∼ous** *a* arriesgado, peligroso

**perimeter** /pə'rɪmɪtə(r)/ *n* perímetro *m*

**period** /'pɪərɪəd/ *n* período *m*; (*lesson*) clase *f*; (*gram*) punto *m*. ● *a* de (la) época. **∼ic** /-'ɒdɪk/ *a* periódico. **∼ical** /pɪərɪ'ɒdɪkl/ *n* revista *f*. **∼ically** /-'ɒdɪklɪ/ *adv* periódico

**peripher|al** /pə'rɪfərəl/ *a* periférico. **∼y** /pə'rɪfərɪ/ *n* periferia *f*

**periscope** /'perɪskəʊp/ *n* periscopio *m*

**perish** /'perɪʃ/ *vi* perecer; (*rot*) estropearse. **∼able** *a* perecedero. **∼ing** *a* (*fam*) glacial

**perjur|e** /'pɜːdʒə(r)/ *vr*. **∼e o.s.** perjurarse. **∼y** *n* perjurio *m*

**perk**[1] /pɜːk/ *n* gaje *m*

**perk**[2] /pɜːk/ *vt/i*. **∼ up** *vt* reanimar. ● *vi* reanimarse. **∼y** *a* alegre

**perm** /pɜːm/ *n* permanente *f*. ● *vt* hacer una permanente a

**permanen|ce** /'pɜːmənəns/ *n* permanencia *f*. **∼t** /'pɜːmənənt/ *a* permanente. **∼tly** *adv* permanentemente

**permea|ble** /'pɜːmɪəbl/ *a* permeable. **∼te** /'pɜːmɪeɪt/ *vt* penetrar; (*soak*) empapar

**permissible** /pə'mɪsəbl/ *a* permisible

**permission** /pə'mɪʃn/ *n* permiso *m*

**permissive** /pə'mɪsɪv/ *a* indulgente. **∼ness** *n* tolerancia *f*. **∼ society** *n* sociedad *f* permisiva

**permit** /pə'mɪt/ *vt* (*pt* **permitted**) permitir. /'pɜːmɪt/ *n* permiso *m*

**permutation** /pɜːmjuː'teɪʃn/ *n* permutación *f*

**pernicious** /pə'nɪʃəs/ *a* pernicioso

**peroxide** /pə'rɒksaɪd/ *n* peróxido *m*

**perpendicular** /pɜːpən'dɪkjʊlə(r)/ *a & n* perpendicular (*f*)

**perpetrat|e** /'pɜːpɪtreɪt/ *vt* cometer. **∼or** *n* autor *m*

**perpetua|l** /pə'petʃʊəl/ *a* perpetuo. **∼te** /pə'petʃʊeɪt/ *vt* perpetuar. **∼tion** /-'eɪʃn/ *n* perpetuación *f*

**perplex** /pə'pleks/ *vt* dejar perplejo. **∼ed** *a* perplejo. **∼ing** *a* desconcertante. **∼ity** *n* perplejidad *f*

**persecut|e** /'pɜːsɪkjuːt/ *vt* perseguir. **∼ion** /-'kjuːʃn/ *n* persecución *f*

**persever|ance** /pɜːsɪ'vɪərəns/ *n* perseverancia *f*. **∼e** /pɜːsɪ'vɪə(r)/ *vi* perseverar, persistir

**Persian** /'pɜːʃn/ *a* persa. **the ∼ Gulf** *n* el golfo *m* Pérsico. ● *n* persa (*m & f*); (*lang*) persa *m*

**persist** /pə'sɪst/ *vi* persistir. **∼ence** *n* persistencia *f*. **∼ent** *a* persistente; (*continual*) continuo. **∼ently** *adv* persistentemente

**person** /'pɜːsn/ *n* persona *f*

**personal** /'pɜːsənl/ *a* personal

**personality** /pɜːsə'nælətɪ/ *n* personalidad *f*; (*on TV*) personaje *m*

**personally** /'pɜːsənəlɪ/ *adv* personalmente; (*in person*) en persona

**personify** /pə'sɒnɪfaɪ/ *vt* person-
ificar

**personnel** /pɜːsə'nel/ *n* personal *m*

**perspective** /pə'spektɪv/ *n* perspectiva *f*

**perspicacious** /pɜːspɪ'keɪʃəs/ *a*
perspicaz

**perspir|ation** /pɜːspə'reɪʃn/ *n* sudor
*m*. ~e /pəs'paɪə(r)/ *vi* sudar

**persua|de** /pə'sweɪd/ *vt* persuadir.
~sion *n* persuasión *f*. ~sive
/pə'sweɪsɪv/ *a* persuasivo. ~sively
*adv* de manera persuasiva

**pert** /pɜːt/ *a* (*saucy*) impertinente;
(*lively*) animado

**pertain** /pə'teɪn/ *vi*. ~ to relacionarse con

**pertinent** /'pɜːtɪnənt/ *a* pertinente.
~ly *adv* pertinentemente

**pertly** /'pɜːtlɪ/ *adv* impertinent-
emente

**perturb** /pə'tɜːb/ *vt* perturbar

**Peru** /pə'ruː/ *n* el Perú *m*

**perus|al** /pə'ruːzl/ *n* lectura *f* cui-
dadosa. ~e /pə'ruːz/ *vt* leer
cuidadosamente

**Peruvian** /pə'ruːvɪən/ *a* & *n* peruano
(*m*)

**perva|de** /pə'veɪd/ *vt* difundirse por.
~sive *a* penetrante

**perver|se** /pə'vɜːs/ *a* (*stubborn*)
terco; (*wicked*) perverso. ~sity *n*
terquedad *f*; (*wickedness*) per-
versidad *f*. ~sion *n* perversión *f*. ~t
/pə'vɜːt/ *vt* pervertir. /'pɜːvɜːt/ *n*
pervertido *m*

**pessimis|m** /'pesɪmɪzəm/ *n* pes-
imismo *m*. ~t /'pesɪmɪst/ *n* pesimista *m* & *f*. ~tic /-'mɪstɪk/ *a*
pesimista

**pest** /pest/ *n* insecto *m* nocivo, plaga
*f*; (*person*) pelma *m*; (*thing*) lata *f*

**pester** /'pestə(r)/ *vt* importunar

**pesticide** /'pestɪsaɪd/ *n* pesticida *f*

**pet** /pet/ *n* animal *m* doméstico;
(*favourite*) favorito *m*. ● *a* preferido. ● *vt* (*pt* petted) acariciar

**petal** /'petl/ *n* pétalo *m*

**peter** /'piːtə(r)/ *vi*. ~ out (*supplies*)
agotarse; (*disappear*) desparecer

**petite** /pə'tiːt/ *a* (*of woman*) chiquita

**petition** /pɪ'tɪʃn/ *n* petición *f*. ● *vt*
dirigir una petición a

**pet name** /'petneɪm/ *n* apodo *m*
cariñoso

**petrify** /'petrɪfaɪ/ *vt* petrificar. ● *vi*
petrificarse

**petrol** /'petrəl/ *n* gasolina *f*. ~eum
/pɪ'trəʊlɪəm/ *n* petróleo *m*. ~ gauge

*n* indicador *m* de nivel de gasolina.
~ **pump** *n* (*in car*) bomba *f* de gasolina; (*at garage*) surtidor *m* de gasolina. ~ **station** *n* gasolinera *f*. ~
**tank** *n* depósito *m* de gasolina

**petticoat** /'petɪkəʊt/ *n* enaguas *fpl*.

**pett|iness** /'petɪnɪs/ *n* mezquindad *f*.
~y /'petɪ/ *a* (-ier, -iest) insignificante; (*mean*) mezquino. ~y
**cash** *n* dinero *m* para gastos
menores. ~y **officer** *n* suboficial *m*
de marina

**petulan|ce** /'petjʊləns/ *n* irri-
tabilidad *f*. ~t /'petjʊlənt/ *a*
irritable

**pew** /pjuː/ *n* banco *m* (de iglesia)

**pewter** /'pjuːtə(r)/ *n* peltre *m*

**phallic** /'fælɪk/ *a* fálico

**phantom** /'fæntəm/ *n* fantasma *m*

**pharmaceutical** /fɑːmə'sjuːtɪkl/ *a*
farmacéutico

**pharmac|ist** /'fɑːməsɪst/ *n* far-
macéutico *m*. ~y /'fɑːməsɪ/ *n* farmacia *f*

**pharyngitis** /færɪn'dʒaɪtɪs/ *n* far-
ingitis *f*

**phase** /feɪz/ *n* etapa *f*. ● *vt*. ~ in
introducir progresivamente. ~ out
retirar progresivamente

**PhD** *abbr* (*Doctor of Philosophy*) *n*
Doctor *m* en Filosofía

**pheasant** /'feznt/ *n* faisán *m*

**phenomenal** /fɪ'nɒmɪnl/ *a*
fenomenal

**phenomenon** /fɪ'nɒmɪnən/ *n* (*pl*
-ena) fenómeno *m*

**phew** /fjuː/ *int* ¡uy!

**phial** /'faɪəl/ *n* frasco *m*

**philanderer** /fɪ'lændərə(r)/ *n* mariposón *m*

**philanthrop|ic** /fɪlən'θrɒpɪk/ *a* fil-
antrópico. ~ist /fɪ'lænθrəpɪst/ *n* fil-
ántropo *m*

**philatel|ist** /fɪ'lætəlɪst/ *n* filatelista *m*
& *f*. ~y /fɪ'lætəlɪ/ *n* filatelia *f*

**philharmonic** /fɪlhɑː'mɒnɪk/ *a*
filarmónico

**Philippines** /'fɪlɪpiːnz/ *npl* Filipinas
*fpl*

**philistine** /'fɪlɪstaɪn/ *a* & *n* filisteo
(*m*)

**philosoph|er** /fɪ'lɒsəfə(r)/ *n* filósofo
*m*. ~ical /-ə'sɒfɪkl/ *a* filosófico. ~y
/fɪ'lɒsəfɪ/ *n* filosofía *f*

**phlegm** /flem/ *n* flema *f*. ~atic
/fleg'mætɪk/ *a* flemático

**phobia** /'fəʊbɪə/ *n* fobia *f*

**phone** /fəʊn/ *n* (*fam*) teléfono *m*.
● *vt/i* llamar por teléfono. ~ **back**

⟨*caller*⟩ volver a llamar; ⟨*person called*⟩ llamar. ~ **box** *n* cabina *f* telefónica

**phonetic** /fə'netɪk/ *a* fonético. ~**s** *n* fonética *f*

**phoney** /'fəʊnɪ/ *a* (**-ier**, **-iest**) (*sl*) falso. ● *n* (*sl*) farsante *m* & *f*

**phosphate** /'fɒsfeɪt/ *n* fosfato *m*

**phosphorus** /'fɒsfərəs/ *n* fósforo *m*

**photo** /'fəʊtəʊ/ *n* (*pl* **-os**) (*fam*) fotografía *f*, foto *f* (*fam*)

**photocopy** /'fəʊtəʊkɒpɪ/ *n* fotocopia *f*. ● *vt* fotocopiar

**photogenic** /fəʊtəʊ'dʒenɪk/ *a* fotogénico

**photograph** /'fəʊtəgrɑːf/ *n* fotografía *f*. ● *vt* hacer una fotografía de, sacar fotos de. ~**er** /fə'tɒgrəfə(r)/ *n* fotógrafo *m*. ~**ic** /-'græfɪk/ *a* fotográfico ~**y** /fə'tɒgrəfɪ/ *n* fotografía *f*

**phrase** /freɪz/ *n* frase *f*, locución *f*, expresión *f*. ● *vt* expresar. ~**book** *n* libro *m* de frases

**physical** /'fɪzɪkl/ *a* físico

**physician** /fɪ'zɪʃn/ *n* médico *m*

**physic|ist** /'fɪzɪsɪst/ *n* físico *m*. ~**s** /'fɪzɪks/ *n* física *f*

**physiology** /fɪzɪ'ɒlədʒɪ/ *n* fisiología *f*

**physiotherap|ist** /fɪzɪəʊ'θerəpɪst/ *n* fisioterapeuta *m* & *f*. ~**y** /fɪzɪəʊ'θerəpɪ/ *n* fisioterapia *f*

**physique** /fɪ'ziːk/ *n* constitución *f*, (*appearance*) físico *m*

**pian|ist** /'pɪənɪst/ *n* pianista *m* & *f*. ~**o** /pɪ'ænəʊ/ *n* (*pl* **-os**) piano *m*

**piccolo** /'pɪkələʊ/ *n* flautín *m*, píccolo *m*

**pick**[1] /pɪk/ (*tool*) pico *m*

**pick**[2] /pɪk/ *vt* escoger; recoger ⟨*flowers etc*⟩; forzar ⟨*a lock*⟩; (*dig*) picar. ~ **a quarrel** buscar camorra. ~ **holes in** criticar. ● *n* (*choice*) selección *f*; (*the best*) lo mejor. ~ **on** *vt* (*nag*) meterse con. ~ **out** *vt* escoger; (*identify*) identificar; destacar ⟨*colour*⟩. ~ **up** *vt* recoger; (*lift*) levantar; (*learn*) aprender; adquirir ⟨*habit, etc*⟩; obtener ⟨*information*⟩; contagiarse de ⟨*illness*⟩. ● *vi* mejorar; (*med*) reponerse

**pickaxe** /'pɪkæks/ *n* pico *m*

**picket** /'pɪkɪt/ *n* (*striker*) huelguista *m* & *f*; (*group of strikers*) piquete *m*; (*stake*) estaca *f*. ~ **line** *n* piquete *m*. ● *vt* vigilar por piquetes. ● *vi* estar de guardia

**pickle** /'pɪkl/ *n* (*in vinegar*) encurtido *m*; (*in brine*) salmuera *f*. **in a ~**

(*fam*) en un apuro. ● *vt* encurtir. ~**s** *npl* encurtido *m*

**pick**: ~**pocket** /'pɪkpɒkɪt/ *n* ratero *m*. ~**up** *n* (*sl*) ligue *m*; (*truck*) camioneta *f*; (*stylus-holder*) fonocaptor *m*, brazo *m*

**picnic** /'pɪknɪk/ *n* comida *f* campestre. ● *vi* (*pt* **picnicked**) merendar en el campo

**pictorial** /pɪk'tɔːrɪəl/ *a* ilustrado

**picture** /'pɪktʃə(r)/ *n* (*painting*) cuadro *m*; (*photo*) fotografía *f*; (*drawing*) dibujo *m*; (*beautiful thing*) preciosidad *f*; (*film*) película *f*; (*fig*) descripción *f*. **the ~s** *npl* el cine *m*. ● *vt* imaginarse; (*describe*) describir

**picturesque** /pɪktʃə'resk/ *a* pintoresco

**piddling** /'pɪdlɪŋ/ *a* (*fam*) insignificante

**pidgin** /'pɪdʒɪn/ *a*. ~ **English** *n* inglés *m* corrompido

**pie** /paɪ/ *n* empanada *f*; (*sweet*) pastel *m*, tarta *f*

**piebald** /'paɪbɔːld/ *a* pío

**piece** /piːs/ *n* pedazo *m*; (*coin*) moneda *f*; (*in game*) pieza *f*. **a ~ of advice** un consejo *m*. **a ~ of news** una noticia *f*. **take to ~s** desmontar. ● *vt*. ~ **together** juntar. ~**meal** /'piːsmiːl/ *a* gradual; (*unsystematic*) poco sistemático. —*adv* poco a poco. ~**work** *n* trabajo *m* a destajo

**pier** /pɪə(r)/ *n* muelle *m*

**pierc|e** /pɪəs/ *vt* perforar. ~**ing** *a* penetrante

**piety** /'paɪətɪ/ *n* piedad *f*

**piffl|e** /'pɪfl/ *n* (*sl*) tonterías *fpl*. ~**ing** *a* (*sl*) insignificante

**pig** /pɪg/ *n* cerdo *m*

**pigeon** /'pɪdʒɪn/ *n* paloma *f*; (*culin*) pichón *m*. ~**hole** *n* casilla *f*

**pig**: ~**gy** /'pɪgɪ/ *a* (*greedy, fam*) glotón. ~**gy-back** *adv* a cuestas. ~**gy bank** *n* hucha *f*. ~**headed** *a* terco

**pigment** /'pɪgmənt/ *n* pigmento *m*. ~**ation** /-'teɪʃn/ *n* pigmentación *f*

**pig**: ~**skin** /'pɪgskɪn/ *n* piel *m* de cerdo. ~**sty** /'pɪgstaɪ/ *n* pocilga *f*

**pigtail** /'pɪgteɪl/ *n* (*plait*) trenza *f*

**pike** /paɪk/ *n invar* (*fish*) lucio *m*

**pilchard** /'pɪltʃəd/ *n* sardina *f*

**pile**[1] /paɪl/ *n* (*heap*) montón *m*. ● *vt* amontonar. ~ **it on** exagerar. ● *vi* amontonarse. ~ **up** *vt* amontonar. ● *vi* amontonarse. ~**s** /paɪlz/ *npl* (*med*) almorranas *fpl*

**pile**[2] /paɪl/ *n* (*of fabric*) pelo *m*

**pile-up** /'paɪlʌp/ *n* accidente *m* múltiple

**pilfer** /'pɪlfə(r)/ *vt/i* hurtar. ∼**age** *n*, ∼**ing** *n* hurto *m*

**pilgrim** /'pɪlgrɪm/ *n* peregrino. ∼**age** *n* peregrinación *f*

**pill** /pɪl/ *n* píldora *f*

**pillage** /'pɪlɪdʒ/ *n* saqueo *m*. ● *vt* saquear

**pillar** /'pɪlə(r)/ *n* columna *f*. ∼**box** *n* buzón *m*

**pillion** /'pɪlɪən/ *n* asiento *m* trasero. **ride** ∼ ir en el asiento trasero

**pillory** /'pɪlərɪ/ *n* picota *f*

**pillow** /'pɪləʊ/ *n* almohada *f*. ∼**case** /'pɪləʊkeɪs/ *n* funda *f* de almohada

**pilot** /'paɪlət/ *n* piloto *m*. ● *vt* pilotar. ∼**light** *n* fuego *m* piloto

**pimp** /pɪmp/ *n* alcahuete *m*

**pimple** /'pɪmpl/ *n* grano *m*

**pin** /pɪn/ *n* alfiler *m*; (*mec*) perno *m*. ∼**s and needles** hormigueo *m*. ● *vt* (*pt* **pinned**) prender con alfileres; (*hold down*) enclavijar; (*fix*) sujetar. ∼ **s.o. down** obligar a uno a que se decida. ∼ **up** fijar

**pinafore** /'pɪnəfɔː(r)/ *n* delantal *m*. ∼ **dress** *n* mandil *m*

**pincers** /'pɪnsəz/ *npl* tenazas *fpl*

**pinch** /pɪntʃ/ *vt* pellizcar; (*steal*, *sl*) hurtar. ● *vi* ⟨*shoe*⟩ apretar. ● *n* pellizco *m*; (*small amount*) pizca *f*. **at a** ∼ en caso de necesidad

**pincushion** /'pɪnkʊʃn/ *n* acerico *m*

**pine**[1] /paɪn/ *n* pino *m*

**pine**[2] /paɪn/ *vi*. ∼ **away** consumirse. ∼ **for** suspirar por

**pineapple** /'paɪnæpl/ *n* piña *f*, ananás *m*

**ping** /pɪŋ/ *n* sonido *m* agudo. ∼**pong** /'pɪŋpɒŋ/ *n* pimpón *m*, ping-pong *m*

**pinion** /'pɪnjən/ *vt* maniatar

**pink** /pɪŋk/ *a & n* color (*m*) de rosa

**pinnacle** /'pɪnəkl/ *n* pináculo *m*

**pin:** ∼**point** *vt* determinar con precisión *f*. ∼**stripe** /'pɪnstraɪp/ *n* raya *f* fina

**pint** /paɪnt/ *n* pinta *f* (= *0.57 litre*)

**pin-up** /'pɪnʌp/ *n* (*fam*) fotografía *f* de mujer

**pioneer** /paɪə'nɪə(r)/ *n* pionero *m*. ● *vt* ser el primero, promotor de, promover

**pious** /'paɪəs/ *a* piadoso

**pip**[1] /pɪp/ *n* (*seed*) pepita *f*

**pip**[2] /pɪp/ (*time signal*) señal *f*

**pip**[3] /pɪp/ (*on uniform*) estrella *f*

**pipe** /paɪp/ *n* tubo *m*; (*mus*) caramillo *m*; (*for smoking*) pipa *f*. ● *vt* conducir por tuberías. ∼**down** (*fam*) bajar la voz, callarse. ∼**cleaner** *n* limpiapipas *m invar*. ∼**dream** *n* ilusión *f*. ∼**line** /'paɪplaɪn/ *n* tubería *f*; (*for oil*) oleoducto *m*. **in the** ∼**line** en preparación *f*. ∼**r** *n* flautista *m & f*

**piping** /'paɪpɪŋ/ *n* tubería *f*. ∼ **hot** muy caliente, hirviendo

**piquant** /'piːkənt/ *a* picante

**pique** /piːk/ *n* resentimiento *m*

**pira**|**cy** /'paɪərəsɪ/ *n* piratería *f*. ∼**te** /'paɪərət/ *n* pirata *m*

**pirouette** /pɪrʊ'et/ *n* pirueta *f*. ● *vi* piruetear

**Pisces** /'paɪsiːz/ *n* (*astr*) Piscis *m*

**pistol** /'pɪstl/ *n* pistola *f*

**piston** /'pɪstən/ *n* pistón *m*

**pit** /pɪt/ *n* foso *m*; (*mine*) mina *f*; (*of stomach*) boca *f*. ● *vt* (*pt* **pitted**) marcar con hoyos; (*fig*) oponer. ∼ **o.s. against** medirse con

**pitch**[1] /pɪtʃ/ *n* brea *f*

**pitch**[2] /pɪtʃ/ (*degree*) grado *m*; (*mus*) tono *m*; (*sport*) campo *m*. ● *vt* lanzar; armar ⟨*tent*⟩. ∼ **into** (*fam*) atacar. ● *vi* caerse; ⟨*ship*⟩ cabecear. ∼ **in** (*fam*) contribuir. ∼**ed battle** *n* batalla *f* campal

**pitch-black** /pɪtʃ'blæk/ *a* oscuro como boca de lobo

**pitcher** /'pɪtʃə(r)/ *n* jarro *m*

**pitchfork** /'pɪtʃfɔːk/ *n* horca *f*

**piteous** /'pɪtɪəs/ *a* lastimoso

**pitfall** /'pɪtfɔːl/ *n* trampa *f*

**pith** /pɪθ/ *n* (*of orange, lemon*) médula *f*; (*fig*) meollo *m*

**pithy** /'pɪθɪ/ *a* (**-ier, -iest**) conciso

**piti**|**ful** /'pɪtɪfl/ *a* lastimoso. ∼**less** *a* despiadado

**pittance** /'pɪtns/ *n* sueldo *m* irrisorio

**pity** /'pɪtɪ/ *n* piedad *f*; (*regret*) lástima *f*. ● *vt* compadecerse de

**pivot** /'pɪvət/ *n* pivote *m*. ● *vt* montonar sobre un pivote. ● *vi* girar sobre un pivote; (*fig*) depender (**on** de)

**pixie** /'pɪksɪ/ *n* duende *m*

**placard** /'plækɑːd/ *n* pancarta *f*; (*poster*) cartel *m*

**placate** /plə'keɪt/ *vt* apaciguar

**place** /pleɪs/ *n* lugar *m*; (*seat*) asiento *m*; (*post*) puesto *m*; (*house, fam*) casa *f*. **take** ∼ tener lugar. ● *vt* poner, colocar; (*remember*) recordar; (*identify*) identificar. **be**

~d (*in race*) colocarse. ~mat *n* salvamanteles *m invar*. ~ment /'pleɪsmənt/ *n* colocación *f*

placid /'plæsɪd/ *a* plácido

plagiari|sm /'pleɪdʒərɪzm/ *n* plagio *m*. ~ze /'pleɪdʒəraɪz/ *vt* plagiar

plague /pleɪg/ *n* peste *f*; (*fig*) plaga *f*. ● *vt* atormentar

plaice /pleɪs/ *n invar* platija *f*

plaid /plæd/ *n* tartán *m*

plain /pleɪn/ *a* (-er, -est) claro; (*simple*) sencillo; (*candid*) franco; (*ugly*) feo. in ~ clothes en traje de paisano. ● *adv* claramente. ● *n* llanura *f*. ~ly *adv* claramente; (*frankly*) francamente; (*simply*) sencillamente. ~ness *n* claridad *f*; (*simplicity*) sencillez *f*

plaintiff /'pleɪntɪf/ *n* demandante *m* & *f*

plait /plæt/ *vt* trenzar. ● *n* trenza *f*

plan /plæn/ *n* proyecto *m*; (*map*) plano *m*. ● *vt* (*pt* planned) planear, proyectar; (*intend*) proponerse

plane¹ /pleɪn/ *n* (*tree*) plátano *m*

plane² /pleɪn/ *n* (*level*) nivel *m*; (*aviat*) avión *m*. ● *a* plano

plane³ /pleɪn/ *n* (*tool*) cepillo m. ● *vt* cepillar

planet /'plænɪt/ *n* planeta *m*. ~ary *a* planetario

plank /plæŋk/ *n* tabla *f*

planning /'plænɪŋ/ *n* planificación *f*. family ~ *n* planificación familiar. town ~ *n* urbanismo *m*

plant /plɑːnt/ *n* planta *f*; (*mec*) maquinaria *f*; (*factory*) fábrica *f*. ● *vt* plantar; (*place in position*) colocar. ~ation /plɑːn'teɪʃn/ *n* plantación *f*

plaque /plæk/ *n* placa *f*

plasma /'plæzmə/ *n* plasma *m*

plaster /'plɑːstə(r)/ *n* yeso *m*; (*adhesive*) esparadrapo *m*; (*for setting bones*) escayola *f*. ~ of Paris *n* yeso *m* mate. ● *vt* enyesar; (*med*) escayolar (*broken bone*); (*cover*) cubrir (with de). ~ed *a* (*fam*) borracho

plastic /'plæstɪk/ *a* & *n* plástico (*m*)

Plasticine /'plæstɪsiːn/ *n* (P) pasta *f* de modelar, plastilina *f* (P)

plastic surgery /plæstɪk'sɜːdʒərɪ/ *n* cirugía *f* estética

plate /pleɪt/ *n* plato *m*; (*of metal*) chapa *f*; (*silverware*) vajilla *f* de plata; (*in book*) lámina *f*. ● *vt* (*cover with metal*) chapear

plateau /'plætəʊ/ *n* (*pl* plateaux) *n* meseta *f*

plateful /'pleɪtfl/ *n* (*pl* -fuls) plato *m*

platform /'plætfɔːm/ *n* plataforma *f*; (*rail*) andén *m*

platinum /'plætɪnəm/ *n* platino *m*

platitude /'plætɪtjuːd/ *n* tópico *m*, perogrullada *f*, lugar *m* común

platonic /plə'tɒnɪk/ *a* platónico

platoon /plə'tuːn/ *n* pelotón *m*

platter /'plætə(r)/ *n* fuente *f*, plato *m* grande

plausible /'plɔːzəbl/ *a* plausible; (*person*) convincente

play /pleɪ/ *vt* jugar; (*act role*) desempeñar el papel de; tocar (*instrument*). ~ safe no arriesgarse. ~ up to halagar. ● *vi* jugar. ~ed out agotado. ● *n* juego *m*; (*drama*) obra *f* de teatro. ~ on words *n* juego *m* de palabras. ~ down *vt* minimizar. ~ on *vt* aprovecharse de. ~ up (*fam*) causar problemas. ~act *vi* hacer la comedia. ~boy /'pleɪbɔɪ/ *n* calavera *m*. ~er *n* jugador *m*; (*mus*) músico *m*. ~ful *a* juguetón. ~fully *adv* jugando; (*jokingly*) en broma. ~ground /'pleɪgraʊnd/ *n* parque *m* de juegos infantiles; (*in school*) campo *m* de recreo. ~group *n* jardín *m* de la infancia. ~ing /'pleɪɪŋ/ *n* juego *m*. ~ing-card *n* naipe *m*. ~ing-field *n* campo *m* de deportes. ~mate /'pleɪmeɪt/ *n* compañero *m* (de juego). ~pen *n* corralito *m*. ~thing *n* juguete *m*. ~wright /'pleɪraɪt/ *n* dramaturgo *m*

plc /piːel'siː/ *abbr* (*public limited company*) S.A., sociedad *f* anónima

plea /pliː/ *n* súplica *f*; (*excuse*) excusa *f*; (*jurid*) defensa *f*

plead /pliːd/ *vt* (*jurid*) alegar; (*as excuse*) pretextar. ● *vi* suplicar; (*jurid*) abogar. ~ with suplicar

pleasant /'pleznt/ *a* agradable

pleas|e /pliːz/ *int* por favor. ● *vt* agradar, dar gusto a. ● *vi* agradar; (*wish*) querer. ~e o.s. hacer lo que quiera. do as you ~e haz lo que quieras. ~ed *a* contento. ~ed with satisfecho de. ~ing *a* agradable

pleasur|e /'pleʒə(r)/ *n* placer *m*. ~able *a* agradable

pleat /pliːt/ *n* pliegue *m*. ● *vt* hacer pliegues en

plebiscite /'plebɪsɪt/ *n* plebiscito *m*

plectrum /'plektrəm/ *n* plectro *m*

pledge /pledʒ/ *n* prenda *f*; (*promise*) promesa *f*. ● *vt* empeñar; (*promise*) prometer

plent|iful /'plentɪfl/ *a* abundante. ~y /'plentɪ/ *n* abundancia *f*. ~y (of) muchos (de)

**pleurisy** /'plʊərəsɪ/ *n* pleuresía *f*

**pliable** /'plaɪəbl/ *a* flexible

**pliers** /'plaɪəz/ *npl* alicates *mpl*

**plight** /plaɪt/ *n* situación *f* (difícil)

**plimsolls** /'plɪmsəlz/ *npl* zapatillas *fpl* de lona

**plinth** /plɪnθ/ *n* plinto *m*

**plod** /plɒd/ *vi* (*pt* **plodded**) caminar con paso pesado; (*work hard*) trabajar laboriosamente. **~der** *n* empollón *m*

**plonk** /plɒŋk/ *n* (*sl*) vino *m* peleón

**plop** /plɒp/ *n* paf *m*. ● *vi* (*pt* **plopped**) caerse con un paf

**plot** /plɒt/ *n* complot *m*; (*of novel etc*) argumento *m*; (*piece of land*) parcela *f*. ● *vt* (*pt* **plotted**) tramar; (*mark out*) trazar. ● *vi* conspirar

**plough** /plaʊ/ *n* arado *m*. ● *vt/i* arar. **~ through** avanzar laboriosamente por

**ploy** /plɔɪ/ *n* (*fam*) estratagema *f*, truco *m*

**pluck** /plʌk/ *vt* arrancar; depilarse (*eyebrows*); desplumar (*bird*); recoger (*flowers*). **~ up courage** hacer de tripas corazón. ● *n* valor *m*. **~y** *a* (**-ier, -iest**) valiente

**plug** /plʌg/ *n* tapón *m*; (*elec*) enchufe *m*; (*auto*) bujía *f*. ● *vt* (*pt* **plugged**) tapar; (*advertise, fam*) dar publicidad a. **~ in** (*elec*) enchufar

**plum** /plʌm/ *n* ciruela *f*; (*tree*) ciruelo *m*

**plumage** /'pluːmɪdʒ/ *n* plumaje *m*

**plumb** /plʌm/ *a* vertical. ● *n* plomada *f*. ● *adv* verticalmente; (*exactly*) exactamente. ● *vt* sondar

**plumb|er** /'plʌmə(r)/ *n* fontanero *m*. **~ing** *n* instalación *f* sanitaria, instalación *f* de cañerías

**plume** /pluːm/ *n* pluma *f*

**plum job** /plʌm'dʒɒb/ *n* (*fam*) puesto *m* estupendo

**plummet** /'plʌmɪt/ *n* plomada *f*. ● *vi* caer a plomo, caer en picado

**plump** /plʌmp/ *a* (**-er, -est**) rechoncho. ● *vt*. **~ for** elegir. **~ness** *n* gordura *f*

**plum pudding** /plʌm'pʊdɪŋ/ *n* budín *m* de pasas

**plunder** /'plʌndə(r)/ *n* (*act*) saqueo *m*; (*goods*) botín *m*. ● *vt* saquear

**plung|e** /plʌndʒ/ *vt* hundir; (*in water*) sumergir. ● *vi* zambullirse; (*fall*) caer. ● *n* salto *m*. **~er** *n* (*for sink*) desatascador *m*; (*mec*) émbolo *m*. **~ing** *a* (*neckline*) bajo, escotado

**plural** /'plʊərəl/ *a & n* plural (*m*)

**plus** /plʌs/ *prep* más. ● *a*. positivo. ● *n* signo *m* más; (*fig*) ventaja *f*. **five ~** más de cinco

**plush** /plʌʃ/ *n* felpa *f*. ● *a* de felpa, afelpado; (*fig*) lujoso. **~y** *a* lujoso

**plutocrat** /'pluːtəkræt/ *n* plutócrata *m & f*

**plutonium** /pluː'təʊnjəm/ *n* plutonio *m*

**ply** /plaɪ/ *vt* manejar (*tool*); ejercer (*trade*). **~ s.o. with drink** dar continuamente de beber a uno. **~wood** *n* contrachapado *m*

**p.m.** /piː'em/ *abbr* (*post meridiem*) de la tarde

**pneumatic** /njuː'mætɪk/ *a* neumático

**pneumonia** /njuː'məʊnjə/ *n* pulmonía *f*

**PO** /piː'əʊ/ *abbr* (*Post Office*) oficina *f* de correos

**poach** /pəʊtʃ/ *vt* escalfar (*egg*); cocer (*fish etc*); (*steal*) cazar en vedado. **~er** *n* cazador *m* furtivo

**pocket** /'pɒkɪt/ *n* bolsillo *m*; (*of air, resistance*) bolsa *f*. **be in ~** salir ganado. **be out of ~** salir perdiendo. ● *vt* poner en el bolsillo. **~book** *n* (*notebook*) libro *m* de bolsillo; (*purse, Amer*) cartera *f*; (*handbag, Amer*) bolso *m*. **~money** *n* dinero *m* para los gastos personales

**pock-marked** /'pɒkmɑːkt/ *a* (*face*) picado de viruelas

**pod** /pɒd/ *n* vaina *f*

**podgy** /'pɒdʒɪ/ *a* (**-ier, -iest**) rechoncho

**poem** /'pəʊɪm/ *n* poesía *f*

**poet** /'pəʊɪt/ *n* poeta *m*. **~ess** *n* poetisa *f*. **~ic** /-'etɪk/ *a*, **~ical** /-'etɪkl/ *a* poético. **P~ Laureate** *n* poeta laureado. **~ry** /'pəʊɪtrɪ/ *n* poesía *f*

**poignant** /'pɔɪnjənt/ *a* conmovedor

**point** /pɔɪnt/ *n* punto *m*; (*sharp end*) punta *f*; (*significance*) lo importante; (*elec*) toma *f* de corriente. **good ~s** cualidades *fpl*. **to the ~** pertinente. **up to a ~** hasta cierto punto. **what is the ~?** ¿para qué?, ¿a qué fin? ● *vt* (*aim*) apuntar; (*show*) indicar. **~ out** señalar. ● *vi* señalar. **~-blank** *a & adv* a boca de jarro, a quemarropa. **~ed** /'pɔɪntɪd/ *a* puntiagudo; (*fig*) mordaz. **~er** /'pɔɪntə(r)/ *n* indicador *m*; (*dog*) perro *m* de muestra; (*clue, fam*) indicación *f*. **~less** /'pɔɪntlɪs/ *a* inútil

**poise** /pɔɪz/ n equilibrio m; (elegance) elegancia f, (fig) aplomo m. ~d a en equilibrio. ~d for listo para

**poison** /'pɔɪzn/ n veneno m. ● vt envenenar. ~ous a venenoso; (chemical etc) tóxico

**poke** /pəʊk/ vt empujar; atizar (fire). ~ fun at burlarse de. ~ out asomar (head). ● vi hurgar; (pry) meterse. ~ about fisgonear. ● n empuje m

**poker**[1] /'pəʊkə(r)/ n atizador m

**poker**[2] /'pəʊkə(r)/ (cards) póquer m. ~-face n cara f inmutable

**poky** /'pəʊkɪ/ a (-ier, -iest) estrecho

**Poland** /'pəʊlənd/ n Polonia f

**polar** /'pəʊlə(r)/ a polar. ~ bear n oso m blanco

**polarize** /'pəʊləraɪz/ vt polarizar

**Pole** /pəʊl/ polaco m

**pole**[1] /pəʊl/ n palo m; (for flag) asta f

**pole**[2] /pəʊl/ (geog) polo m. ~-star n estrella f polar

**polemic** /pə'lemɪk/ a polémico. ● n polémica f

**police** /pə'liːs/ n policía f. ● vt vigilar. ~man /pə'liːsmən/ n (pl -men) policía m, guardia m. ~ record n antecedentes mpl penales. ~ state n estado m policíaco. ~ station n comisaría f. ~woman /-wʊmən/ n (pl -women) mujer m policía

**policy**[1] /'pɒlɪsɪ/ n política f

**policy**[2] /'pɒlɪsɪ/ (insurance) póliza f (de seguros)

**polio(myelitis)** /'pəʊlɪəʊ(maɪə'laɪtɪs)/ n polio(mielitis) f

**polish** /'pɒlɪʃ/ n (for shoes) betún m; (for floor) cera f; (for nails) esmalte m de uñas; (shine) brillo m; (fig) finura f. nail ~ esmalte m de uñas. ● vt pulir; limpiar (shoes); encerar (floor). ~ off despachar. ~ed a pulido; (manner) refinado. ~er n pulidor m; (machine) pulidora f

**Polish** /'pəʊlɪʃ/ a & n polaco (m)

**polite** /pə'laɪt/ a cortés. ~ly adv cortésmente. ~ness n cortesía f

**politic|al** /pə'lɪtɪkl/ a político. ~ian /pɒlɪ'tɪʃn/ n político m. ~s /'pɒlətɪks/ n política f

**polka** /'pɒlkə/ n polca f. ~ dots npl diseño m de puntos

**poll** /pəʊl/ n elección f; (survey) encuesta f. ● vt obtener (votes)

**pollen** /'pɒlən/ n polen m

**polling-booth** /'pəʊlɪŋbuːð/ n cabina f de votar

**pollut|e** /pə'luːt/ vt contaminar. ~ion /-ʃn/ n contaminación f

**polo** /'pəʊləʊ/ n polo m. ~-neck n cuello m vuelto

**poltergeist** /'pɒltəgaɪst/ n duende m

**polyester** /pɒlɪ'estə(r)/ n poliéster m

**polygam|ist** /pə'lɪgəmɪst/ n polígamo m. ~ous a polígamo. ~y /pə'lɪgəmɪ/ n poligamia f

**polyglot** /'pɒlɪglɒt/ a & n políglota (m & f)

**polygon** /'pɒlɪgən/ n polígono m

**polyp** /'pɒlɪp/ n pólipo m

**polystyrene** /pɒlɪ'staɪriːn/ n poliestireno m

**polytechnic** /pɒlɪ'teknɪk/ n escuela f politécnica

**polythene** /'pɒlɪθiːn/ n polietileno m. ~ bag n bolsa f de plástico

**pomegranate** /'pɒmɪgrænɪt/ n (fruit) granada f

**pommel** /'pʌml/ n pomo m

**pomp** /pɒmp/ n pompa f

**pompon** /'pɒmpɒn/ n pompón m

**pompo|sity** /pɒm'pɒsətɪ/ n pomposidad f. ~us /'pɒmpəs/ a pomposo

**poncho** /'pɒntʃəʊ/ n (pl -os) poncho m

**pond** /pɒnd/ n charca f; (artificial) estanque m

**ponder** /'pɒndə(r)/ vt considerar. ● vi reflexionar. ~ous /'pɒndərəs/ a pesado

**pong** /pɒŋ/ n (sl) hedor m. ● vi (sl) apestar

**pontif|f** /'pɒntɪf/ n pontífice m. ~ical /-'tɪfɪkl/ a pontifical; (fig) dogmático. ~icate /pɒn'tɪfɪkeɪt/ vi pontificar

**pontoon** /pɒn'tuːn/ n pontón m. ~ bridge n puente m de pontones

**pony** /'pəʊnɪ/ n poni m. ~-tail n cola f de caballo. ~-trekking n excursionismo m en poni

**poodle** /'puːdl/ n perro m de lanas, caniche m

**pool**[1] /puːl/ n charca f; (artificial) estanque m. (swimming-) ~ n piscina f

**pool**[2] /puːl/ (common fund) fondos mpl comunes; (snooker) billar m americano. ● vt aunar. ~s npl quinielas fpl

**poor** /pʊə(r)/ a (-er, -est) pobre; (not good) malo. be in ~ health estar mal de salud. ~ly a (fam) indispuesto. ● adv pobremente; (badly) mal

**pop**[1] /pɒp/ n ruido m seco; (of bottle) taponazo m. ● vt (pt **popped**) hacer reventar; (put) poner. ~ **in** vi entrar; (visit) pasar por. ~ **out** vi saltar; (person) salir un rato. ~ **up** vi surgir, aparecer

**pop**[2] /pɒp/ a (popular) pop invar. ● n (fam) música f pop. ~ **art** n arte m pop

**popcorn** /'pɒpkɔ:n/ n palomitas fpl

**pope** /pəʊp/ n papa m

**popgun** /'pɒpgʌn/ n pistola f de aire comprimido

**poplar** /'pɒplə(r)/ n chopo m

**poplin** /'pɒplɪn/ n popelina f

**poppy** /'pɒpɪ/ n amapola f

**popular** /'pɒpjʊlə(r)/ a popular. ~**ity** /-'lærətɪ/ n popularidad f. ~**ize** vt popularizar

**populat|e** /'pɒpjʊleɪt/ vt poblar. ~**ion** /-'leɪʃn/ n población f; (number of inhabitants) habitantes mpl

**porcelain** /'pɔ:səlɪn/ n porcelana f

**porch** /pɔ:tʃ/ n porche m

**porcupine** /'pɔ:kjʊpaɪn/ n puerco m espín

**pore**[1] /pɔ:(r)/ n poro m

**pore**[2] /pɔ:(r)/ vi. ~ **over** estudiar detenidamente

**pork** /pɔ:k/ n cerdo m

**porn** /pɔ:n/ n (fam) pornografía f. ~**ographic** /-ə'græfɪk/ a pornográfico. ~**ography** /pɔ:'nɒgrəfɪ/ n pornografía f

**porous** /'pɔ:rəs/ a poroso

**porpoise** /'pɔ:pəs/ n marsopa f

**porridge** /'pɒrɪdʒ/ n gachas fpl de avena

**port**[1] /pɔ:t/ n puerto m; (porthole) portilla f. ~ **of call** puerto de escala

**port**[2] /pɔ:t/ (naut, left) babor m. ● a de babor

**port**[3] /pɔ:t/ (wine) oporto m

**portable** /'pɔ:təbl/ a portátil

**portal** /'pɔ:tl/ n portal m

**portent** /'pɔ:tent/ n presagio m

**porter** /'pɔ:tə(r)/ n portero m; (for luggage) mozo m. ~**age** n porte m

**portfolio** /pɔ:t'fəʊljəʊ/ n (pl -os) cartera f

**porthole** /'pɔ:thəʊl/ n portilla f

**portico** /'pɔ:tɪkəʊ/ n (pl -oes) pórtico m

**portion** /'pɔ:ʃn/ n porción f. ● vt repartir

**portly** /'pɔ:tlɪ/ a (-ier, -iest) corpulento

**portrait** /'pɔ:trɪt/ n retrato m

**portray** /pɔ:'treɪ/ vt retratar; (represent) representar. ~**al** n retrato m

**Portug|al** /'pɔ:tjʊgl/ n Portugal m. ~**uese** /-'gi:z/ a & n portugués (m)

**pose** /pəʊz/ n postura f. ● vt colocar; hacer (question); plantear (problem). ● vi posar. ~ **as** hacerse pasar por. ~**r** /'pəʊzə(r)/ n pregunta f difícil

**posh** /pɒʃ/ a (sl) elegante

**position** /pə'zɪʃn/ n posición f; (job) puesto m; (status) rango m. ● vt colocar

**positive** /'pɒzətɪv/ a positivo; (real) verdadero; (certain) seguro. ● n (foto) positiva f. ~**ly** adv positivamente

**possess** /pə'zes/ vt poseer. ~**ion** /pə'zeʃn/ n posesión f. **take** ~**ion of** tomar posesión de. ~**ions** npl posesiones fpl; (jurid) bienes mpl. ~**ive** /pə'zesɪv/ a posesivo. ~**or** n poseedor m

**possib|ility** /pɒsə'bɪlətɪ/ n posibilidad f. ~**le** /'pɒsəbl/ a posible. ~**ly** adv posiblemente

**post**[1] /pəʊst/ n (pole) poste m. ● vt fijar (notice)

**post**[2] /pəʊst/ (place) puesto m

**post**[3] /pəʊst/ (mail) correo m. ● vt echar (letter). **keep s.o.** ~**ed** tener a uno al corriente

**post...** /pəʊst/ pref post

**post:** ~**age** /'pəʊstɪdʒ/ n franqueo m. ~**al** /'pəʊstl/ a postal. ~**al order** n giro m postal. ~**box** n buzón m. ~**card** /'pəʊstka:d/ n (tarjeta f) postal f. ~**code** n código m postal

**post-date** /pəʊst'deɪt/ vt poner fecha posterior a

**poster** /'pəʊstə(r)/ n cartel m

**poste restante** /pəʊst'resta:nt/ n lista f de correos

**posteri|or** /pɒ'stɪərɪə(r)/ a posterior. ● n trasero m. ~**ty** /pɒs'terətɪ/ n posteridad f

**posthumous** /'pɒstjʊməs/ a póstumo. ~**ly** adv después de la muerte

**post:** ~**man** /'pəʊstmən/ n (pl -men) cartero m. ~**mark** /'pəʊstma:k/ n matasellos m invar. ~**master** /'pəʊstma:stə(r)/ n administrador m de correos. ~**mistress** /'pəʊstmɪstrɪs/ n administradora f de correos

**post-mortem** /'pəʊstmɔ:təm/ n autopsia f

**Post Office** /'pəʊstɒfɪs/ n oficina f de correos, correos mpl

**postpone** /pəʊst'pəʊn/ vt aplazar. **~ment** n aplazamiento m
**postscript** /'pəʊstskrɪpt/ n posdata f
**postulant** /'pɒstjʊlənt/ n postulante m & f
**postulate** /'pɒstjʊleɪt/ vt postular
**posture** /'pɒstʃə(r)/ n postura f. ● vi adoptar una postura
**posy** /'pəʊzɪ/ n ramillete m
**pot** /pɒt/ n (for cooking) olla f; (for flowers) tiesto m; (marijuana, sl) mariguana f. **go to ~** (sl) echarse a perder. ● vt (pt potted) poner en tiesto
**potassium** /pə'tæsjəm/ n potasio m
**potato** /pə'teɪtəʊ/ n (pl -oes) patata f, papa f (LAm)
**pot:** **~belly** n barriga f. **~boiler** n obra f literaria escrita sólo para ganar dinero
**poten|cy** /'pəʊtənsɪ/ n potencia f. **~t** /'pəʊtnt/ a potente; (drink) fuerte
**potentate** /'pəʊtənteɪt/ n potentado m
**potential** /pəʊ'tenʃl/ a & n potencial (m). **~ity** /-ʃɪ'ælətɪ/ n potencialidad f. **~ly** adv potencialmente
**pot-hole** /'pɒthəʊl/ n caverna f; (in road) bache m. **~r** n espeleólogo m
**potion** /'pəʊʃn/ n poción f
**pot:** **~ luck** n lo que haya. **~shot** n tiro m al azar. **~ted** /'pɒtɪd/ see pot. ● a (food) en conserva
**potter**[1] /'pɒtə(r)/ n alfarero m
**potter**[2] /'pɒtə(r)/ vi hacer pequeños trabajos agradables, no hacer nada de particular
**pottery** /'pɒtərɪ/ n cerámica f
**potty** /'pɒtɪ/ a (-ier, -iest) (sl) chiflado. ● n orinal m
**pouch** /paʊtʃ/ n bolsa f pequeña
**pouffe** /puːf/ n (stool) taburete m
**poulterer** /'pəʊltərə(r)/ n pollero m
**poultice** /'pəʊltɪs/ n cataplasma f
**poultry** /'pəʊltrɪ/ n aves fpl de corral
**pounce** /paʊns/ vi saltar, atacar de repente. ● n salto m, ataque m repentino
**pound**[1] /paʊnd/ n (weight) libra f (= 454g); (money) libra f (esterlina)
**pound**[2] /paʊnd/ n (for cars) depósito m
**pound**[3] /paʊnd/ vt (crush) machacar; (bombard) bombardear. ● vi golpear; (heart) palpitar; (walk) ir con pasos pesados
**pour** /pɔː(r)/ vt verter. **~ out** servir (drink). ● vi fluir; (rain) llover a cántaros. **~ in** (people) entrar en

tropel. **~ing rain** n lluvia f torrencial. **~ out** (people) salir en tropel
**pout** /paʊt/ vi hacer pucheros. ● n puchero m, mala cara f
**poverty** /'pɒvətɪ/ n pobreza f
**powder** /'paʊdə(r)/ n polvo m; (cosmetic) polvos mpl. ● vt polvorear; (pulverize) pulverizar. **~ one's face** ponerse polvos en la cara. **~ed** a en polvo. **~y** a polvoriento
**power** /'paʊə(r)/ n poder m; (elec) corriente f; (energy) energía f; (nation) potencia f. **~ cut** n apagón m. **~ed** a con motor. **~ed by** impulsado por. **~ful** a poderoso. **~less** a impotente. **~station** n central f eléctrica
**practicable** /'præktɪkəbl/ a practicable
**practical** /'præktɪkl/ a práctico. **~ joke** n broma f pesada. **~ly** adv prácticamente
**practi|ce** /'præktɪs/ n práctica f; (custom) costumbre f; (exercise) ejercicio m; (sport) entrenamiento m; (clients) clientela f. **be in ~ce** (doctor, lawyer) ejercer. **be out of ~ce** no estar en forma. **in ~ce** (in fact) en la práctica; (on form) en forma. **~se** /'præktɪs/ vt hacer ejercicios en; (put into practice) poner en práctica; (sport) entrenarse en; ejercer (profession). ● vi ejercitarse; (professional) ejercer. **~sed** a experto
**practitioner** /præk'tɪʃənə(r)/ n profesional m & f. **general ~** médico m de cabecera. **medical ~** médico m
**pragmatic** /præg'mætɪk/ a pragmático
**prairie** /'preərɪ/ n pradera f
**praise** /preɪz/ vt alabar. ● n alabanza f. **~worthy** a loable
**pram** /præm/ n cochecito m de niño
**prance** /prɑːns/ vi (horse) hacer cabriolas; (person) pavonearse
**prank** /præŋk/ n travesura f
**prattle** /'prætl/ vi parlotear. ● n parloteo m
**prawn** /prɔːn/ n gamba f
**pray** /preɪ/ vi rezar. **~er** /preə(r)/ n oración f. **~ for** rogar
**pre..** /priː/ pref pre...
**preach** /priːtʃ/ vt/i predicar. **~er** n predicador m
**preamble** /priː'æmbl/ n preámbulo m

**pre-arrange** /priːəˈreɪndʒ/ vt arreglar de antemano. ~**ment** n arreglo m previo

**precarious** /prɪˈkeərɪəs/ a precario. ~**ly** adv precariamente

**precaution** /prɪˈkɔːʃn/ n precaución f. ~**ary** a de precaución; (preventive) preventivo

**precede** /prɪˈsiːd/ vt preceder

**preceden|ce** /ˈpresɪdəns/ n precedencia f. ~**t** /ˈpresɪdənt/ n precedente m

**preceding** /prɪˈsiːdɪŋ/ a precedente

**precept** /ˈpriːsept/ n precepto m

**precinct** /ˈpriːsɪŋkt/ n recinto m. **pedestrian** ~ zona f peatonal. ~**s** npl contornos mpl

**precious** /ˈpreʃəs/ a precioso. ● adv (fam) muy

**precipice** /ˈpresɪpɪs/ n precipicio m

**precipitat|e** /prɪˈsɪpɪteɪt/ vt precipitar. /prɪˈsɪpɪtət/ n precipitado m. ● a precipitado. ~**ion** /-ˈteɪʃn/ n precipitación f

**precipitous** /prɪˈsɪpɪtəs/ a escarpado

**précis** /ˈpreɪsiː/ n (pl précis /-siːz/) resumen m

**precis|e** /prɪˈsaɪs/ a preciso; (careful) meticuloso. ~**ely** adv precisamente. ~**ion** /-ˈsɪʒn/ n precisión f

**preclude** /prɪˈkluːd/ vt (prevent) impedir; (exclude) excluir

**precocious** /prɪˈkəʊʃəs/ a precoz. ~**ly** adv precozmente

**preconce|ived** /priːkənˈsiːvd/ a preconcebido. ~**ption** /-ˈsepʃn/ n preconcepción f

**precursor** /priːˈkɜːsə(r)/ n precursor m

**predator** /ˈpredətə(r)/ n animal m de rapiña. ~**y** a de rapiña

**predecessor** /ˈpriːdɪsesə(r)/ n predecesor m, antecesor m

**predestin|ation** /prɪdestɪˈneɪʃn/ n predestinación f. ~**e** /priːˈdestɪn/ vt predestinar

**predicament** /prɪˈdɪkəmənt/ n apuro m

**predicat|e** /ˈpredɪkət/ n predicado m. ~**ive** /prɪˈdɪkətɪv/ a predicativo

**predict** /prɪˈdɪkt/ vt predecir. ~**ion** /-ʃn/ n predicción f

**predilection** /priːdɪˈlekʃn/ n predilección f

**predispose** /priːdɪˈspəʊz/ vt predisponer

**predomina|nt** /prɪˈdɒmɪnənt/ a predominante. ~**te** /prɪˈdɒmɪneɪt/ vi predominar

**pre-eminent** /priːˈemɪnənt/ a preeminente

**pre-empt** /priːˈempt/ vt adquirir por adelantado, adelantarse a

**preen** /priːn/ vt limpiar, arreglar. ~ o.s. atildarse

**prefab** /ˈpriːfæb/ n (fam) casa f prefabricada. ~**ricated** /-ˈfæbrɪkeɪtɪd/ a prefabricado

**preface** /ˈprefəs/ n prólogo m

**prefect** /ˈpriːfekt/ n monitor m; (official) prefecto m

**prefer** /prɪˈfɜː(r)/ vt (pt preferred) preferir. ~**able** /ˈprefrəbl/ a preferible. ~**ence** /ˈprefrəns/ n preferencia f. ~**ential** /-əˈrenʃl/ a preferente

**prefix** /ˈpriːfɪks/ n (pl -ixes) prefijo m

**pregnan|cy** /ˈpregnənsɪ/ n embarazo m. ~**t** /ˈpregnənt/ a embarazada

**prehistoric** /priːhɪˈstɒrɪk/ a prehistórico

**prejudge** /priːˈdʒʌdʒ/ vt prejuzgar

**prejudice** /ˈpredʒʊdɪs/ n prejuicio m; (harm) perjuicio m. ● vt predisponer; (harm) perjudicar. ~**d** a parcial

**prelate** /ˈprelət/ n prelado m

**preliminar|ies** /prɪˈlɪmɪnərɪz/ npl preliminares mpl. ~**y** /prɪˈlɪmɪnərɪ/ a preliminar

**prelude** /ˈpreljuːd/ n preludio m

**pre-marital** /priːˈmærɪtl/ a prematrimonial

**premature** /ˈpremətjʊə(r)/ a prematuro

**premeditated** /priːˈmedɪteɪtɪd/ a premeditado

**premier** /ˈpremɪə(r)/ a primero. ● n (pol) primer ministro

**première** /ˈpremɪə(r)/ n estreno m

**premises** /ˈpremɪsɪz/ npl local m. **on the** ~ en el local

**premiss** /ˈpremɪs/ n premisa f

**premium** /ˈpriːmɪəm/ n premio m. **at a** ~ muy solicitado

**premonition** /priːməˈnɪʃn/ n presentimiento m

**preoccup|ation** /priːɒkjʊˈpeɪʃn/ n preocupación f. ~**ied** /-ˈɒkjʊpaɪd/ a preocupado

**prep** /prep/ n deberes mpl

**preparation** /prepəˈreɪʃn/ n preparación f. ~**s** npl preparativos mpl

**preparatory** /prɪ'pærətrɪ/ a preparatorio. ~ **school** n escuela f primaria privada

**prepare** /prɪ'peə(r)/ vt preparar. ● vi prepararse. ~d **to** dispuesto a

**prepay** /pri:'peɪ/ vt (pt -paid) pagar por adelantado

**preponderance** /prɪ'pɒndərəns/ n preponderancia f

**preposition** /prepə'zɪʃn/ n preposición f

**prepossessing** /pri:pə'zesɪŋ/ a atractivo

**preposterous** /prɪ'pɒstərəs/ a absurdo

**prep school** /'prepsku:l/ n escuela f primaria privada

**prerequisite** /pri:'rekwɪzɪt/ n requisito m previo

**prerogative** /prɪ'rɒgətɪv/ n prerrogativa f

**Presbyterian** /prezbɪ'tɪərɪən/ a & n presbiteriano (m)

**prescri|be** /prɪ'skraɪb/ vt prescribir; (med) recetar. ~**ption** /-'ɪpʃn/ n prescripción f; (med) receta f

**presence** /'prezns/ n presencia f; (attendance) asistencia f. ~ **of mind** presencia f de ánimo

**present**[1] /'preznt/ a & n presente (m & f). **at** ~ actualmente. **for the** ~ por ahora

**present**[2] /'preznt/ n (gift) regalo m

**present**[3] /prɪ'zent/ vt presentar; (give) obsequiar. ~ **s.o. with** obsequiar a uno con. ~**able** a presentable. ~**ation** /prezn'teɪʃn/ n presentación f; (ceremony) ceremonia f de entrega

**presently** /'prezntlɪ/ adv dentro de poco

**preserv|ation** /prezə'veɪʃn/ n conservación f. ~**ative** /prɪ'zɜ:vətɪv/ n preservativo m. ~**e** /prɪ'zɜ:v/ vt conservar; (maintain) mantener; (culin) poner en conserva. ● n coto m; (jam) confitura f

**preside** /prɪ'zaɪd/ vi presidir. ~ **over** presidir

**presiden|cy** /'prezɪdənsɪ/ n presidencia f. ~**t** /'prezɪdənt/ n presidente m. ~**tial** /-'denʃl/ a presidencial

**press** /pres/ vt apretar; exprimir (fruit etc); (insist on) insistir en; (iron) planchar. **be** ~**ed for** tener poco. ● vi apretar; (time) apremiar; (fig) urgir. ~ **on** seguir adelante. ● n presión f; (mec, newspapers)

prensa f; (printing) imprenta f. ~ **conference** n rueda f de prensa. ~ **cutting** n recorte m de periódico. ~**ing** /'presɪŋ/ a urgente. ~**stud** n automático m. ~**up** n plancha f

**pressure** /'preʃə(r)/ n presión f. ● vt hacer presión sobre. ~**cooker** n olla f a presión. ~ **group** n grupo m de presión

**pressurize** /'preʃəraɪz/ vt hacer presión sobre

**prestig|e** /pre'sti:ʒ/ n prestigio m. ~**ious** /pre'stɪdʒəs/ a prestigioso

**presum|ably** /prɪ'zju:məblɪ/ adv presumiblemente, probablemente. ~**e** /prɪ'zju:m/ vt presumir. ~**e** (**up)on** vi abusar de. ~**ption** /-'zʌmpʃn/ n presunción f. ~**ptuous** /prɪ'zʌmptʃʊəs/ a presuntuoso

**presuppose** /pri:sə'pəʊz/ vt presuponer

**preten|ce** /prɪ'tens/ n fingimiento m; (claim) pretensión f; (pretext) pretexto m. ~**d** /prɪ'tend/ vt/i fingir. ~**d to** (lay claim) pretender

**pretentious** /prɪ'tenʃəs/ a pretencioso

**pretext** /'pri:tekst/ n pretexto m

**pretty** /'prɪtɪ/ a (-ier, -iest) bonito, lindo (esp LAm); (person) guapo

**prevail** /prɪ'veɪl/ vi predominar; (win) prevalecer. ~ **on** persuadir

**prevalen|ce** /'prevələns/ n costumbre f. ~**t** /'prevələnt/ a extendido

**prevaricate** /prɪ'værɪkeɪt/ vi despistar

**prevent** /prɪ'vent/ vt impedir. ~**able** a evitable. ~**ion** /-ʃn/ n prevención f. ~**ive** a preventivo

**preview** /'pri:vju:/ n preestreno m, avance m

**previous** /'pri:vɪəs/ a anterior. ~ **to** antes de. ~**ly** adv anteriormente, antes

**pre-war** /pri:'wɔ:(r)/ a de antes de la guerra

**prey** /preɪ/ n presa f; (fig) víctima f. **bird of** ~ n ave f de rapiña. ● vi. ~ **on** alimentarse de; (worry) atormentar

**price** /praɪs/ n precio m. ● vt fijar el precio de. ~**less** a inapreciable; (amusing, fam) muy divertido. ~**y** a (fam) caro

**prick** /prɪk/ vt/i pinchar. ~ **up one's ears** aguzar las orejas. ● n pinchazo m

**prickl|e** /'prɪkl/ n (bot) espina f; (of animal) púa f; (sensation) picor m. **~y** a espinoso; ⟨animal⟩ lleno de púas; ⟨person⟩ quisquilloso

**pride** /praɪd/ n orgullo m. **~ of place** n puesto m de honor. ● vr. **~ o.s. on** enorgullecerse de

**priest** /priːst/ n sacerdote m. **~hood** n sacerdocio m. **~ly** a sacerdotal

**prig** /prɪg/ n mojigato m. **~gish** a mojigato

**prim** /prɪm/ a **(primmer, primmest)** estirado; (prudish) gazmoño

**primarily** /'praɪmərɪli/ adv en primer lugar

**primary** /'praɪmərɪ/ a primario; (chief) principal. **~ school** n escuela f primaria

**prime**¹ /praɪm/ vt cebar ⟨gun⟩; (prepare) preparar; aprestar ⟨surface⟩

**prime**² /praɪm/ a principal; (first rate) excelente. **~ minister** n primer ministro m. ● n. **be in one's ~** estar en la flor de la vida

**primer**¹ /'praɪmə(r)/ n (of paint) primera mano f

**primer**² /'praɪmə(r)/ (book) silabario m

**primeval** /praɪ'miːvl/ a primitivo

**primitive** /'prɪmɪtɪv/ a primitivo

**primrose** /'prɪmrəʊz/ n primavera f

**prince** /prɪns/ n príncipe m. **~ly** a principesco. **~ss** /prɪn'ses/ n princesa f

**principal** /'prɪnsəpl/ a principal. ● n (of school etc) director m

**principality** /prɪnsɪ'pælətɪ/ n principado m

**principally** /'prɪnsɪpəlɪ/ adv principalmente

**principle** /'prɪnsəpl/ n principio m. **in ~** en principio. **on ~** por principio

**print** /prɪnt/ vt imprimir; (write in capitals) escribir con letras de molde. ● n (of finger, foot) huella f; (letters) caracteres mpl; (of design) estampado m; (picture) grabado m; (photo) copia f. **in ~** ⟨book⟩ disponible. **out of ~** agotado. **~ed matter** n impresos mpl. **~er** /'prɪntə(r)/ n impresor m; (machine) impresora f. **~ing** n tipografía f. **~out** n listado m

**prior** /'praɪə(r)/ n prior m. ● a anterior. **~ to** antes de

**priority** /praɪ'ɒrətɪ/ n prioridad f

**priory** /'praɪərɪ/ n priorato m

**prise** /praɪz/ vt apalancar. **~ open** abrir por fuerza

**prism** /'prɪzəm/ n prisma m

**prison** /'prɪzn/ n cárcel m. **~er** n prisionero m; (in prison) preso m; (under arrest) detenido m. **~ officer** n carcelero m

**pristine** /'prɪstiːn/ a prístino

**privacy** /'prɪvəsɪ/ n intimidad f; (private life) vida f privada. **in ~** en la intimidad

**private** /'praɪvət/ a privado; (confidential) personal; ⟨lessons, house⟩ particular; ⟨ceremony⟩ en la intimidad. ● n soldado m raso. **in ~** en privado; (secretly) en secreto. **~ eye** n (fam) detective m privado. **~ly** adv en privado; (inwardly) interiormente

**privation** /praɪ'veɪʃn/ n privación f

**privet** /'prɪvɪt/ n alheña f

**privilege** /'prɪvəlɪdʒ/ n privilegio m. **~d** a privilegiado

**privy** /'prɪvɪ/ a. **~ to** al corriente de

**prize** /praɪz/ n premio m. ● a ⟨idiot etc⟩ de remate. ● vt estimar. **~fighter** n boxeador m profesional. **~giving** n reparto m de premios. **~winner** n premiado m

**pro** /prəʊ/ n. **~s and cons** el pro m y el contra m

**probab|ility** /prɒbə'bɪlətɪ/ n probabilidad f. **~le** /'prɒbəbl/ a probable. **~ly** adv probablemente

**probation** /prə'beɪʃn/ n prueba f; (jurid) libertad f condicional. **~ary** a de prueba

**probe** /prəʊb/ n sonda f; (fig) encuesta f. ● vt sondar. ● vi. **~ into** investigar

**problem** /'prɒbləm/ n problema m. ● a difícil. **~atic** /-'mætɪk/ a problemático

**procedure** /prə'siːdʒə(r)/ n procedimiento m

**proceed** /prə'siːd/ vi proceder. **~ing** n procedimiento m. **~ings** /prə'siːdɪŋz/ npl (report) actas fpl; (jurid) proceso m

**proceeds** /'prəʊsiːdz/ npl ganancias fpl

**process** /'prəʊses/ n proceso m. **in ~ of** en vías de. **in the ~ of time** con el tiempo. ● vt tratar; revelar ⟨photo⟩. **~ion** /prə'seʃn/ n desfile m

**proclaim** /prə'kleɪm/ vt proclamar. **~mation** /prɒklə'meɪʃn/ n proclamación f

**procrastinate** /prəʊ'kræstɪneɪt/ *vi* aplazar, demorar, diferir

**procreation** /prəʊkrɪ'eɪʃn/ *n* procreación *f*

**procure** /prə'kjʊə(r)/ *vt* obtener

**prod** /prɒd/ *vt* (*pt* **prodded**) empujar; (*with elbow*) dar un codazo a. • *vi* dar con el dedo. • *n* empuje *m*; (*with elbow*) codazo *m*

**prodigal** /'prɒdɪgl/ *a* pródigo

**prodigious** /prə'dɪdʒəs/ *a* prodigioso

**prodigy** /'prɒdɪdʒɪ/ *n* prodigio *m*

**produce** /prə'dju:s/ *vt* (*show*) presentar; (*bring out*) sacar; poner en escena ‹*play*›; (*cause*) causar; (*manufacture*) producir. /'prɒdju:s/ *n* productos *mpl*. **~er** /prə'dju:sə(r)/ *n* productor *m*; (*in theatre*) director *m*

**product** /'prɒdʌkt/ *n* producto *m*. **~ion** /prə'dʌkʃn/ *n* producción *f*; (*of play*) representación *f*

**productiv|e** /prə'dʌktɪv/ *a* productivo. **~ity** /prɒdʌk'tɪvətɪ/ *n* productividad *f*

**profan|e** /prə'feɪn/ *a* profano; (*blasphemous*) blasfemo. **~ity** /-'fænətɪ/ *n* profanidad *f*

**profess** /prə'fes/ *vt* profesar; (*pretend*) pretender

**profession** /prə'feʃn/ *n* profesión *f*. **~al** *a & n* profesional (*m & f*)

**professor** /prə'fesə(r)/ *n* catedrático *m*; (*Amer*) profesor *m*

**proffer** /'prɒfə(r)/ *vt* ofrecer

**proficien|cy** /prə'fɪʃənsɪ/ *n* competencia *f*. **~t** /prə'fɪʃnt/ *a* competente

**profile** /'prəʊfaɪl/ *n* perfil *m*

**profit** /'prɒfɪt/ *n* (*com*) ganancia *f*; (*fig*) provecho *m*. • *vi*. **~ from** sacar provecho de. **~able** *a* provechoso

**profound** /prə'faʊnd/ *a* profundo. **~ly** *adv* profundamente

**profus|e** /prə'fju:s/ *a* profuso. **~ely** *adv* profusamente. **~ion** /-ʒn/ *n* profusión *f*

**progeny** /'prɒdʒənɪ/ *n* progenie *f*

**prognosis** /prɒg'nəʊsɪs/ *n* (*pl* **-oses**) pronóstico *m*

**program(|me)** /'prəʊgræm/ *n* programa *m*. • *vt* (*pt* **programmed**) programar. **~mer** *n* programador *m*

**progress** /'prəʊgres/ *n* progreso *m*, progresos *mpl*; (*development*) desarrollo *m*. **in ~** en curso. /prə'gres/ *vi* hacer progresos; (*develop*) desarrollarse. **~ion** /prə'greʃn/ *n* progresión *f*

**progressive** /prə'gresɪv/ *a* progresivo; (*reforming*) progresista. **~ly** *adv* progresivamente

**prohibit** /prə'hɪbɪt/ *vt* prohibir. **~ive** /-bətɪv/ *a* prohibitivo

**project** /prə'dʒekt/ *vt* proyectar. • *vi* (*stick out*) sobresalir. /'prɒdʒekt/ *n* proyecto *m*

**projectile** /prə'dʒektaɪl/ *n* proyectil *m*

**projector** /prə'dʒektə(r)/ *n* proyector *m*

**proletari|an** /prəʊlɪ'teərɪən/ *a & n* proletario (*m*). **~at** /prəʊlɪ'teərɪət/ *n* proletariado *m*

**prolif|erate** /prə'lɪfəreɪt/ *vi* proliferar. **~eration** /-'reɪʃn/ *n* proliferación *f*. **~ic** /prə'lɪfɪk/ *a* prolífico

**prologue** /'prəʊlɒg/ *n* prólogo *m*

**prolong** /prə'lɒŋ/ *vt* prolongar

**promenade** /prɒmə'nɑːd/ *n* paseo *m*; (*along beach*) paseo *m* marítimo. • *vt* pasear. • *vi* pasearse. **~ concert** *n* concierto *m* (que forma parte de un festival de música clásica en Londres, en que no todo el público tiene asientos)

**prominen|ce** /'prɒmɪnəns/ *n* prominencia *f*; (*fig*) importancia *f*. **~t** /'prɒmɪnənt/ *a* prominente; (*important*) importante; (*conspicuous*) conspicuo

**promiscu|ity** /prɒmɪ'skju:ətɪ/ *n* libertinaje *m*. **~ous** /prə'mɪskjʊəs/ *a* libertino

**promis|e** /'prɒmɪs/ *n* promesa *f*. • *vt/i* prometer. **~ing** *a* prometedor; ‹*person*› que promete

**promontory** /'prɒməntrɪ/ *n* promontorio *m*

**promot|e** /prə'məʊt/ *vt* promover. **~ion** /-'məʊʃn/ *n* promoción *f*

**prompt** /prɒmpt/ *a* pronto; (*punctual*) puntual. • *adv* en punto. • *vt* incitar; apuntar ‹*actor*›. **~er** *n* apuntador *m*. **~ly** *adv* puntualmente. **~ness** *n* prontitud *f*

**promulgate** /'prɒmlgeɪt/ *vt* promulgar

**prone** /prəʊn/ *a* echado boca abajo. **~ to** propenso a

**prong** /prɒŋ/ *n* (*of fork*) diente *m*

**pronoun** /'prəʊnaʊn/ *n* pronombre *m*

**pronounc|e** /prə'naʊns/ *vt* pronunciar; (*declare*) declarar. **~ement** *n* declaración *f*. **~ed**

/prə'naʊnst/ *a* pronunciado; (*noticeable*) marcado

**pronunciation** /prənʌnsɪ'eɪʃn/ *n* pronunciación *f*

**proof** /pruːf/ *n* prueba *f*; (*of alcohol*) graduación *f* normal. ● *a*. ~ **against** a prueba de. ~**reading** *n* corrección *f* de pruebas

**prop¹** /prɒp/ *n* puntal *m*; (*fig*) apoyo *m*. ● *vt* (*pt* **propped**) apoyar. ~ **against** (*lean*) apoyar en

**prop²** /prɒp/ (*in theatre, fam*) accesorio *m*

**propaganda** /prɒpə'gændə/ *n* propaganda *f*

**propagat|e** /'prɒpəgeɪt/ *vt* propagar. ● *vi* propagarse. ~**ion** /-'geɪʃn/ *n* propagación *f*

**propel** /prə'pel/ *vt* (*pt* **propelled**) propulsar. ~**ler** /prə'pelə(r)/ *n* hélice *f*

**propensity** /prə'pensətɪ/ *n* propensión *f*

**proper** /'prɒpə(r)/ *a* correcto; (*suitable*) apropiado; (*gram*) propio; (*real, fam*) verdadero. ~**ly** *adv* correctamente

**property** /'prɒpətɪ/ *n* propiedad *f*; (*things owned*) bienes *mpl*. ● *a* inmobiliario

**prophe|cy** /'prɒfəsɪ/ *n* profecía *f*. ~**sy** /'prɒfɪsaɪ/ *vt/i* profetizar. ~**t** /'prɒfɪt/ *n* profeta *m*. ~**tic** /prə'fetɪk/ *a* profético

**propitious** /prə'pɪʃəs/ *a* propicio

**proportion** /prə'pɔːʃn/ *n* proporción *f*. ~**al** *a*, ~**ate** *a* proporcional

**propos|al** /prə'pəʊzl/ *n* propuesta *f*. ~**al of marriage** oferta *f* de matrimonio. ~**e** /prə'pəʊz/ *vt* proponer. ● *vi* hacer una oferta de matrimonio

**proposition** /prɒpə'zɪʃn/ *n* proposición *f*; (*project, fam*) asunto *m*

**propound** /prə'paʊnd/ *vt* proponer

**proprietor** /prə'praɪətə(r)/ *n* propietario *m*

**propriety** /prə'praɪətɪ/ *n* decoro *m*

**propulsion** /prə'pʌlʃn/ *n* propulsión *f*

**prosaic** /prə'zeɪk/ *a* prosaico

**proscribe** /prə'skraɪb/ *vt* proscribir

**prose** /prəʊz/ *n* prosa *f*

**prosecut|e** /'prɒsɪkjuːt/ *vt* procesar; (*carry on*) proseguir. ~**ion** /-'kjuːʃn/ *n* proceso *m*. ~**or** *n* acusador *m*. **Public P~or** fiscal *m*

**prospect** /'prɒspekt/ *n* vista *f*; (*expectation*) perspectiva *f*. /prə'spekt/ *vi* prospectar

**prospective** /prə'spektɪv/ *a* probable; (*future*) futuro

**prospector** /prə'spektə(r)/ *n* prospector *m*, explorador *m*

**prospectus** /prə'spektəs/ *n* prospecto *m*

**prosper** /'prɒspə(r)/ *vi* prosperar. ~**ity** /-'sperətɪ/ *n* prosperidad *f*. ~**ous** /'prɒspərəs/ *a* próspero

**prostitut|e** /'prɒstɪtjuːt/ *n* prostituta *f*. ~**ion** /-'tjuːʃn/ *n* prostitución *f*

**prostrate** /'prɒstreɪt/ *a* echado boca abajo; (*fig*) postrado

**protagonist** /prə'tægənɪst/ *n* protagonista *m & f*

**protect** /prə'tekt/ *vt* proteger. ~**ion** /-ʃn/ *n* protección *f*. ~**ive** /prə'tektɪv/ *a* protector. ~**or** *n* protector *m*

**protégé** /'prɒtɪʒeɪ/ *n* protegido *m*. ~**e** *n* protegida *f*

**protein** /'prəʊtiːn/ *n* proteína *f*

**protest** /'prəʊtest/ *n* protesta *f*. **under** ~ bajo protesta. /prə'test/ *vt/i* protestar. ~**er** *n* (*demonstrator*) manifestante *m & f*

**Protestant** /'prɒtɪstənt/ *a & n* protestante (*m & f*)

**protocol** /'prəʊtəkɒl/ *n* protocolo *m*

**prototype** /'prəʊtətaɪp/ *n* prototipo *m*

**protract** /prə'trækt/ *vt* prolongar

**protractor** /prə'træktə(r)/ *n* transportador *m*

**protrude** /prə'truːd/ *vi* sobresalir

**protuberance** /prə'tjuːbərəns/ *n* protuberancia *f*

**proud** /praʊd/ *a* orgulloso. ~**ly** *adv* orgullosamente

**prove** /pruːv/ *vt* probar. ● *vi* resultar. ~**n** *a* probado

**provenance** /'prɒvənəns/ *n* procedencia *f*

**proverb** /'prɒvɜːb/ *n* proverbio *m*. ~**ial** /prə'vɜːbɪəl/ *a* proverbial

**provide** /prə'vaɪd/ *vt* proveer. ● *vi*. ~ **against** precaverse de. ~ **for** (*allow for*) prever; mantener (*person*). ~**d** /prə'vaɪdɪd/ *conj*. ~ (**that**) con tal que

**providen|ce** /'prɒvɪdəns/ *n* providencia *f*. ~**t** *a* providente. ~**tial** /prɒvɪ'denʃl/ *a* providencial

**providing** /prə'vaɪdɪŋ/ *conj*. ~ **that** con tal que

**provinc|e** /'prɒvɪns/ *n* provincia *f*; (*fig*) competencia *f*. ~**ial** /prə'vɪnʃl/ *a* provincial

**provision** /prəˈvɪʒn/ n provisión f; (*supply*) suministro m; (*stipulation*) condición f. ∼s npl comestibles mpl

**provisional** /prəˈvɪʒənl/ a provisional. ∼ly adv provisionalmente

**proviso** /prəˈvaɪzəʊ/ n (pl -os) condición f

**provo|cation** /prɒvəˈkeɪʃn/ n provocación f. ∼cative /-ˈvɒkətɪv/ a provocador. ∼ke /prəˈvəʊk/ vt provocar

**prow** /praʊ/ n proa f

**prowess** /ˈpraʊɪs/ n habilidad f; (*valour*) valor m

**prowl** /praʊl/ vi merodear. ● n ronda f. be on the ∼ merodear. ∼er n merodeador m

**proximity** /prɒkˈsɪmətɪ/ n proximidad f

**proxy** /ˈprɒksɪ/ n poder m. by ∼ por poder

**prude** /pruːd/ n mojigato m

**pruden|ce** /ˈpruːdəns/ n prudencia f. ∼t /ˈpruːdənt/ a prudente. ∼tly adv prudentemente

**prudish** /ˈpruːdɪʃ/ a mojigato

**prune**[1] /pruːn/ n ciruela f pasa

**prune**[2] /pruːn/ vt podar

**pry** /praɪ/ vi entrometerse

**psalm** /sɑːm/ n salmo m

**pseudo...** /ˈsjuːdəʊ/ pref seudo...

**pseudonym** /ˈsjuːdənɪm/ n seudónimo m

**psychiatr|ic** /saɪkɪˈætrɪk/ a psiquiátrico. ∼ist /saɪˈkaɪətrɪst/ n psiquiatra m & f. ∼y /saɪˈkaɪətrɪ/ n psiquiatría f

**physic** /ˈsaɪkɪk/ a psíquico

**psycho-analys|e** /saɪkəʊˈænəlaɪz/ vt psicoanalizar. ∼is /saɪkəʊˈnæləsɪs/ n psicoanálisis m. ∼t /-ɪst/ n psicoanalista m & f

**psycholog|ical** /saɪkəˈlɒdʒɪkl/ a psicológico. ∼ist /saɪˈkɒlədʒɪst/ n psicólogo m. ∼y /saɪˈkɒlədʒɪ/ n psicología f

**psychopath** /ˈsaɪkəpæθ/ n psicópata m & f

**pub** /pʌb/ n bar m

**puberty** /ˈpjuːbətɪ/ n pubertad f

**pubic** /ˈpjuːbɪk/ a pubiano, púbico

**public** /ˈpʌblɪk/ a público

**publican** /ˈpʌblɪkən/ n tabernero m

**publication** /pʌblɪˈkeɪʃn/ n publicación f

**public house** /pʌblɪkˈhaʊs/ n bar m

**publicity** /pʌbˈlɪsətɪ/ n publicidad f

**publicize** /ˈpʌblɪsaɪz/ vt publicar, anunciar

**publicly** /ˈpʌblɪklɪ/ adv públicamente

**public school** /pʌblɪkˈskuːl/ n colegio m privado; (*Amer*) instituto m

**public-spirited** /pʌblɪkˈspɪrɪtɪd/ a cívico

**publish** /ˈpʌblɪʃ/ vt publicar. ∼er n editor m. ∼ing n publicación f

**puck** /pʌk/ n (*ice hockey*) disco m

**pucker** /ˈpʌkə(r)/ vt arrugar. ● vi arrugarse

**pudding** /ˈpʊdɪŋ/ n postre m; (*steamed*) budín m

**puddle** /ˈpʌdl/ n charco m

**pudgy** /ˈpʌdʒɪ/ a (-ier, -iest) rechoncho

**puerile** /ˈpjʊəraɪl/ a pueril

**puff** /pʌf/ n soplo m; (*for powder*) borla f. ● vt/i soplar. ∼ at chupar (*pipe*). ∼ out apagar (*candle*); (*swell up*) hinchar. ∼ed a (*out of breath*) sin aliento. ∼ pastry n hojaldre m. ∼y /ˈpʌfɪ/ a hinchado

**pugnacious** /pʌgˈneɪʃəs/ a belicoso

**pug-nosed** /ˈpʌgnəʊzd/ a chato

**pull** /pʊl/ vt tirar de; sacar (*tooth*); torcer (*muscle*). ∼ a face hacer una mueca. ∼ a fast one hacer una mala jugada. ∼ down derribar (*building*). ∼ off quitarse; (*fig*) lograr. ∼ one's weight poner de su parte. ∼ out sacar. ∼ s.o.'s leg tomarle el pelo a uno. ∼ up (*uproot*) desarraigar; (*reprimand*) reprender. ● vi tirar (at de). ∼ away (*auto*) alejarse. ∼ back retirarse. ∼ in (*enter*) entrar; (*auto*) parar. ∼ o.s. together tranquilizarse. ∼ out (*auto*) salirse. ∼ through recobrar la salud. ∼ up (*auto*) parar. ● n tirón m; (*fig*) atracción f; (*influence*) influencia f. give a ∼ tirar

**pulley** /ˈpʊlɪ/ n polea f

**pullover** /ˈpʊləʊvə(r)/ n jersey m

**pulp** /pʌlp/ n pulpa f; (*for paper*) pasta f

**pulpit** /ˈpʊlpɪt/ n púlpito m

**pulsate** /ˈpʌlseɪt/ vi pulsar

**pulse** /pʌls/ n (*med*) pulso m

**pulverize** /ˈpʌlvəraɪz/ vt pulverizar

**pumice** /ˈpʌmɪs/ n piedra f pómez

**pummel** /ˈpʌml/ vt (pt pummelled) aporrear

**pump**[1] /pʌmp/ n bomba f; ● vt sacar con una bomba; (*fig*) sonsacar. ∼ up inflar

**pump**[2] /pʌmp/ (*plimsoll*) zapatilla f de lona; (*dancing shoe*) escarpín m

**pumpkin** /ˈpʌmpkɪn/ n calabaza f

**pun** /pʌn/ n juego m de palabras

**punch**[1] /pʌntʃ/ vt dar un puñetazo a; (*perforate*) perforar; hacer ⟨hole⟩. ● n puñetazo m; (*vigour, sl*) empuje m; (*device*) punzón m

**punch**[2] /pʌntʃ/ (*drink*) ponche m

**punch**: ~**drunk** a aturdido a golpes. ~ **line** n gracia f. ~**up** n riña f

**punctilious** /pʌŋkˈtɪlɪəs/ a meticuloso

**punctual** /ˈpʌŋktʃʊəl/ a puntual. ~**ity** /-ˈælətɪ/ n puntualidad f. ~**ly** adv puntualmente

**punctuat|e** /ˈpʌŋktʃʊeɪt/ vt puntuar. ~**ion** /-ˈeɪʃn/ n puntuación f

**puncture** /ˈpʌŋktʃə(r)/ n (*in tyre*) pinchazo m. ● vt pinchar. ● vi pincharse

**pundit** /ˈpʌndɪt/ n experto m

**pungen|cy** /ˈpʌndʒənsɪ/ n acritud f; (*fig*) mordacidad f. ~**t** /ˈpʌndʒənt/ a acre; ⟨remark⟩ mordaz

**punish** /ˈpʌnɪʃ/ vt castigar. ~**able** a castigable. ~**ment** n castigo m

**punitive** /ˈpjuːnɪtɪv/ a punitivo

**punk** /pʌŋk/ a (*music, person*) punk

**punnet** /ˈpʌnɪt/ n canastilla f

**punt**[1] /pʌnt/ n (*boat*) batea f

**punt**[2] /pʌnt/ vi apostar. ~**er** n apostante m & f

**puny** /ˈpjuːnɪ/ a (**-ier, -iest**) diminuto; (*weak*) débil; (*petty*) insignificante

**pup** /pʌp/ n cachorro m

**pupil**[1] /ˈpjuːpl/ n alumno m

**pupil**[2] /ˈpjuːpl/ n (*of eye*) pupila f

**puppet** /ˈpʌpɪt/ n títere m

**puppy** /ˈpʌpɪ/ n cachorro m

**purchase** /ˈpɜːtʃəs/ vt comprar. ● n compra f. ~**r** n comprador m

**pur|e** /ˈpjʊə(r)/ a (**-er, -est**) puro. ~**ely** adv puramente. ~**ity** n pureza f

**purée** /ˈpjʊəreɪ/ n puré m

**purgatory** /ˈpɜːgətrɪ/ n purgatorio m

**purge** /pɜːdʒ/ vt purgar. ● n purga f

**purif|ication** /pjʊərɪfɪˈkeɪʃn/ n purificación f. ~**y** /ˈpjʊərɪfaɪ/ vt purificar

**purist** /ˈpjʊərɪst/ n purista m & f

**puritan** /ˈpjʊərɪtən/ n puritano m. ~**ical** /-ˈtænɪkl/ a puritano

**purl** /pɜːl/ n (*knitting*) punto m del revés

**purple** /ˈpɜːpl/ a purpúreo, morado. ● n púrpura f

**purport** /pəˈpɔːt/ vt. ~ **to be** pretender ser

**purpose** /ˈpɜːpəs/ n propósito m; (*determination*) resolución f. **on** ~ a propósito. **to no** ~ en vano. ~**built** a construido especialmente. ~**ful** a (*resolute*) resuelto. ~**ly** adv a propósito

**purr** /pɜː(r)/ vi ronronear

**purse** /pɜːs/ n monedero m; (*Amer*) bolso m, cartera f (*LAm*). ● vt fruncir

**pursu|e** /pəˈsjuː/ vt perseguir, seguir. ~**er** n perseguidor m. ~**it** /pəˈsjuːt/ n persecución f; (*fig*) ocupación f

**purveyor** /pəˈveɪə(r)/ n proveedor m

**pus** /pʌs/ n pus m

**push** /pʊʃ/ vt empujar; apretar ⟨button⟩. ● vi empujar. ● n empuje m; (*effort*) esfuerzo m; (*drive*) dinamismo m. **at a** ~ en caso de necesidad. **get the** ~ (*sl*) ser despedido. ~ **aside** vt apartar. ~ **back** vt hacer retroceder. ~ **off** vi (*sl*) marcharse. ~ **on** vi seguir adelante. ~ **up** vt levantar. ~**button telephone** n teléfono m de teclas. ~**chair** n sillita f con ruedas. ~**ing** /ˈpʊʃɪŋ/ a ambicioso. ~**over** n (*fam*) cosa f muy fácil, pan comido. ~**y** a (*pej*) ambicioso

**puss** /pʊs/ n minino m

**put** /pʊt/ vt (*pt* put, *pres p* putting) poner; (*express*) expresar; (*say*) decir; (*estimate*) estimar; hacer ⟨question⟩. ~ **across** comunicar; (*deceive*) engañar. ~ **aside** poner aparte. ~ **away** guardar. ~ **back** devolver; retrasar ⟨clock⟩. ~ **by** guardar; ahorrar ⟨money⟩. ~ **down** depositar; (*suppress*) suprimir; (*write*) apuntar; (*kill*) sacrificar. ~ **forward** avanzar. ~ **in** introducir; (*submit*) presentar. ~ **in for** pedir. ~ **off** aplazar; (*disconcert*) desconcertar. ~ **on** (*wear*) ponerse; cobrar ⟨speed⟩; encender ⟨light⟩. ~ **one's foot down** mantenerse firme. ~ **out** (*extinguish*) apagar; (*inconvenience*) incomodar; extender ⟨hand⟩; (*disconcert*) desconcertar. ~ **to sea** hacerse a la mar. ~ **through** (*phone*) comunicar. ~ **up** levantar; subir ⟨price⟩; alojar ⟨guest⟩. ~ **up with** soportar. **stay** ~ (*fam*) no moverse

**putrefy** /ˈpjuːtrɪfaɪ/ vi pudrirse

**putt** /pʌt/ n (*golf*) golpe m suave

**putty** /ˈpʌtɪ/ n masilla f

**put-up** /ˈpʊtʌp/ a. ~ **job** n confabulación f

**puzzl|e** /'pʌzl/ n enigma m; (*game*) rompecabezas m invar. ● vt dejar perplejo. ● vi calentarse los sesos. **~ing** a incomprensible; (*odd*) curioso

**pygmy** /'pɪgmɪ/ n pigmeo m

**pyjamas** /pə'dʒɑːməz/ npl pijama m

**pylon** /'paɪlɒn/ n pilón m

**pyramid** /'pɪrəmɪd/ n pirámide f

**python** /'paɪθn/ n pitón m

# Q

**quack**[1] /kwæk/ n (*of duck*) graznido m

**quack**[2] /kwæk/ (*person*) charlatán m. **~ doctor** n curandero m

**quadrangle** /'kwɒdræŋgl/ n cuadrilátero m; (*court*) patio m

**quadruped** /'kwɒdruped/ n cuadrúpedo m

**quadruple** /'kwɒdrʊpl/ a & n cuádruplo (m). ● vt cuadruplicar. **~t** /-plət/ n cuatrillizo m

**quagmire** /'kwægmaɪə(r)/ n ciénaga f; (*fig*) atolladero m

**quail** /kweɪl/ n codorniz f

**quaint** /kweɪnt/ a (-er, -est) pintoresco; (*odd*) curioso

**quake** /kweɪk/ vi temblar. ● n (*fam*) terremoto m

**Quaker** /'kweɪkə(r)/ n cuáquero (m)

**qualification** /kwɒlɪfɪ'keɪʃn/ n título m; (*requirement*) requisito m; (*ability*) capacidad f; (*fig*) reserva f

**qualif|ied** /'kwɒlɪfaɪd/ a cualificado; (*limited*) limitado; (*with degree, diploma*) titulado. **~y** /'kwɒlɪfaɪ/ vt calificar; (*limit*) limitar. ● vi sacar el título; (*sport*) clasificarse; (*fig*) llenar los requisitos

**qualitative** /'kwɒlɪtətɪv/ a cualitativo

**quality** /'kwɒlɪtɪ/ n calidad f; (*attribute*) cualidad f

**qualm** /kwɑːm/ n escrúpulo m

**quandary** /'kwɒndrɪ/ n. **in a ~** en un dilema

**quantitative** /'kwɒntɪtətɪv/ a cuantitativo

**quantity** /'kwɒntɪtɪ/ n cantidad f

**quarantine** /'kwɒrəntiːn/ n cuarentena f

**quarrel** /'kwɒrəl/ n riña f. ● vi (*pt* **quarrelled**) reñir. **~some** a pendenciero

**quarry**[1] /'kwɒrɪ/ n (*excavation*) cantera f

**quarry**[2] /'kwɒrɪ/ n (*animal*) presa f

**quart** /kwɔːt/ n (poco más de un) litro m

**quarter** /'kwɔːtə(r)/ n cuarto m; (*of year*) trimestre m; (*district*) barrio m. **from all ~s** de todas partes. ● vt dividir en cuartos; (*mil*) acuartelar. **~s** npl alojamiento m

**quartermaster** /'kwɔːtəmɑːstə(r)/ n intendente m

**quarter: ~final** n cuarto m de final. **~ly** a trimestral. ● adv cada tres meses

**quartet** /kwɔː'tet/ n cuarteto m

**quartz** /kwɔːts/ n cuarzo m. ● a (*watch etc*) de cuarzo

**quash** /kwɒʃ/ vt anular

**quasi..** /'kweɪsaɪ/ pref cuasi...

**quaver** /'kweɪvə(r)/ vi temblar. ● n (*mus*) corchea f

**quay** /kiː/ n muelle m

**queasy** /'kwiːzɪ/ a (*stomach*) delicado

**queen** /kwiːn/ n reina f. **~ mother** n reina f madre

**queer** /kwɪə(r)/ a (-er, -est) extraño; (*dubious*) sospechoso; (*ill*) indispuesto. ● n (*sl*) homosexual m

**quell** /kwel/ vt reprimir

**quench** /kwentʃ/ vt apagar; sofocar (*desire*)

**querulous** /'kwerʊləs/ a quejumbroso

**query** /'kwɪərɪ/ n pregunta f. ● vt preguntar; (*doubt*) poner en duda

**quest** /kwest/ n busca f

**question** /'kwestʃən/ n pregunta f; (*for discussion*) cuestión f. **in ~** en cuestión. **out of the ~** imposible. **without ~** sin duda. ● vt preguntar; (*police etc*) interrogar; (*doubt*) poner en duda. **~able** /'kwestʃənəbl/ a discutible. **~ mark** n signo m de interrogación. **~naire** /kwestʃə'neə(r)/ n cuestionario m

**queue** /kjuː/ n cola f. ● vi (*pres p* **queuing**) hacer cola

**quibble** /'kwɪbl/ vi discutir; (*split hairs*) sutilizar

**quick** /kwɪk/ a (-er, -est) rápido. **be ~!** ¡date prisa! ● adv rápidamente. ● n. **to the ~** en lo vivo. **~en** /'kwɪkən/ vt acelerar. ● vi acelerarse. **~ly** adv rápidamente. **~sand** /'kwɪksænd/ n arena f movediza. **~tempered** a irascible

**quid** /kwɪd/ *n invar* (*sl*) libra *f*
(esterlina)

**quiet** /'kwaɪət/ *a* (**-er, -est**) tranquilo;
(*silent*) callado; (*discreet*) discreto.
● *n* tranquilidad *f*. **on the ~** a
escondidas. **~en** /'kwaɪətn/ *vt* calmar. ● *vi* calmarse. **~ly** *adv* tranquilamente; (*silently*) silenciosamente; (*discreetly*) discretamente.
**~ness** *n* tranquilidad *f*

**quill** /kwɪl/ *n* pluma *f*

**quilt** /kwɪlt/ *n* edredón *m*. ● *vt*
acolchar

**quince** /kwɪns/ *n* membrillo *m*

**quinine** /kwɪ'niːn/ *n* quinina *f*

**quintessence** /kwɪn'tesns/ *n* quintaesencia *f*

**quintet** /kwɪn'tet/ *n* quinteto *m*

**quintuplet** /'kwɪntjuːplət/ *n* quin-
tillizo *m*

**quip** /kwɪp/ *n* ocurrencia *f*

**quirk** /kwɜːk/ *n* peculiaridad *f*

**quit** /kwɪt/ *vt* (*pt* **quitted**) dejar. ● *vi*
abandonar; (*leave*) marcharse;
(*resign*) dimitir. **~ doing** (*cease*,
*Amer*) dejar de hacer

**quite** /kwaɪt/ *adv* bastante; (*completely*) totalmente; (*really*) verdaderamente. **~ (so)!** ¡claro! **~ a
few** bastante

**quits** /kwɪts/ *a* a la par. **call it ~**
darlo por terminado

**quiver** /'kwɪvə(r)/ *vi* temblar

**quixotic** /kwɪk'sɒtɪk/ *a* quijotesco

**quiz** /kwɪz/ *n* (*pl* **quizzes**) serie *f* de
preguntas; (*game*) concurso *m*. ● *vt*
(*pt* **quizzed**) interrogar. **~zical**
/'kwɪzɪkl/ *a* burlón

**quorum** /'kwɔːrəm/ *n* quórum *m*

**quota** /'kwəʊtə/ *n* cuota *f*

**quot|ation** /kwəʊ'teɪʃn/ *n* cita *f*;
(*price*) presupuesto *m*. **~ation
marks** *npl* comillas *fpl*. **~e** /kwəʊt/
*vt* citar; (*com*) cotizar. ● *n* (*fam*) cita
*f*; (*price*) presupuesto *m*. **in ~es** *npl*
entre comillas

**quotient** /'kwəʊʃnt/ *n* cociente *m*

# R

**rabbi** /'ræbaɪ/ *n* rabino *m*

**rabbit** /'ræbɪt/ *n* conejo *m*

**rabble** /'ræbl/ *n* gentío *m*. **the ~** (*pej*)
el populacho *m*

**rabi|d** /'ræbɪd/ *a* feroz; (*dog*) rabioso.
**~es** /'reɪbiːz/ *n* rabia *f*

**race**[1] /reɪs/ *n* carrera *f*. ● *vt* hacer
correr (*horse*); acelerar (*engine*).
● *vi* (*run*) correr, ir corriendo;
(*rush*) ir de prisa

**race**[2] /reɪs/ (*group*) raza *f*

**race: ~course** /'reɪskɔːs/ *n* hipódromo *m*. **~horse** /'reɪshɔːs/ *n*
caballo *m* de carreras. **~riots**
/'reɪsraɪəts/ *npl* disturbios *mpl*
raciales. **~track** /'reɪstræk/ *n* hipódromo *m*

**racial** /'reɪʃl/ *a* racial. **~ism** /-ɪzəm/
*n* racismo *m*

**racing** /'reɪsɪŋ/ *n* carreras *fpl*. **~ car**
*n* coche *m* de carreras

**racis|m** /'reɪsɪzəm/ *n* racismo *m*. **~t**
/'reɪsɪst/ *a & n* racista (*m & f*)

**rack**[1] /ræk/ *n* (*shelf*) estante *m*; (*for
luggage*) rejilla *f*; (*for plates*) escu-
rreplatos *m invar*. ● *vt*. **~ one's
brains** devanarse los sesos

**rack**[2] /ræk/. *n*. **go to ~ and ruin** quedarse en la ruina

**racket**[1] /'rækɪt/ *n* (*for sports*) raqueta

**racket**[2] /'rækɪt/ (*din*) alboroto *m*;
(*swindle*) estafa *f*. **~eer** /-ə'tɪə(r)/ *n*
estafador *m*

**raconteur** /rækɒn'tɜː/ *n* anecdotista
*m & f*

**racy** /'reɪsɪ/ *a* (**-ier, -iest**) vivo

**radar** /'reɪdɑː(r)/ *n* radar *m*

**radian|ce** /'reɪdɪəns/ *n* resplandor
*m*. **~t** /'reɪdɪənt/ *a* radiante. **~tly**
*adv* con resplandor

**radiat|e** /'reɪdɪeɪt/ *vt* irradiar. ● *vi*
divergir. **~ion** /-'eɪʃn/ *n* radiación *f*.
**~or** /'reɪdɪeɪtə(r)/ *n* radiador *m*

**radical** /'rædɪkl/ *a & n* radical (*m*)

**radio** /'reɪdɪəʊ/ *n* (*pl* **-os**) radio *f*. ● *vt*
transmitir por radio

**radioactiv|e** /reɪdɪəʊ'æktɪv/ *a* radi-
activo. **~ity** /-'tɪvətɪ/ *n* radi-
actividad *f*

**radiograph|er** /reɪdɪ'ɒgrəfə(r)/ *n*
radiógrafo *m*. **~y** *n* radiografía *f*

**radish** /'rædɪʃ/ *n* rábano *m*

**radius** /'reɪdɪəs/ *n* (*pl* **-dii** /-dɪaɪ/)
radio *m*

**raffish** /'ræfɪʃ/ *a* disoluto

**raffle** /'ræfl/ *n* rifa *f*

**raft** /rɑːft/ *n* balsa *f*

**rafter** /'rɑːftə(r)/ *n* cabrio *m*

**rag**[1] /ræg/ *n* andrajo *m*; (*for wiping*)
trapo *m*; (*newspaper*) periodicucho
*m*. **in ~s** (*person*) andrajoso;
(*clothes*) hecho jirones

**rag**[2] /ræg/ *n* (*univ*) festival *m* estu-
diantil; (*prank*, *fam*) broma *f*

pesada. ● *vt* (*pt* **ragged**) (*sl*) tomar el pelo a

**ragamuffin** /'rægəmʌfın/ *n* granuja *m*, golfo *m*

**rage** /reɪdʒ/ *n* rabia *f*; (*fashion*) moda *f*. ● *vi* estar furioso; (*storm*) bramar

**ragged** /'rægɪd/ *a* (*person*) andrajoso; (*clothes*) hecho jirones; (*edge*) mellado

**raid** /reɪd/ *n* (*mil*) incursión *f*; (*by police*, *etc*) redada *f*; (*by thieves*) asalto *m*. ● *vt* (*mil*) atacar; (*police*) hacer una redada en; (*thieves*) asaltar. **~er** *n* invasor *m*; (*thief*) ladrón *m*

**rail**[1] /reɪl/ *n* barandilla *f*; (*for train*) riel *m*; (*rod*) barra *f*. **by ~** por ferrocarril

**rail**[2] /reɪl/ *vi*. **~ against**, **~ at** insultar

**railing** /'reɪlɪŋ/ *n* barandilla *f*; (*fence*) verja *f*

**rail‖road** /'reɪlrəʊd/ *n* (*Amer*), **~way** /'reɪlweɪ/ *n* ferrocarril *m*. **~way-man** *n* (*pl* **-men**) ferroviario *m*. **~way station** *n* estación *f* de ferrocarril

**rain** /reɪn/ *n* lluvia *f*. ● *vi* llover. **~bow** /'reɪnbəʊ/ *n* arco *m* iris. **~coat** /'reɪnkəʊt/ *n* impermeable *m*. **~fall** /'reɪnfɔːl/ *n* precipitación *f*. **~water** *n* agua *f* de lluvia. **~y** /'reɪnɪ/ *a* (**-ier**, **-iest**) lluvioso

**raise** /reɪz/ *vt* levantar; (*breed*) criar; obtener (*money etc*); hacer (*question*); plantear (*problem*); subir (*price*). **~ one's glass to** brindar por. **~ one's hat** descubrirse. ● *n* (*Amer*) aumento *m*

**raisin** /'reɪzn/ *n* (*uva f*) pasa *f*

**rake**[1] /reɪk/ *n* rastrillo *m*. ● *vt* rastrillar; (*search*) buscar en. **~ up** remover

**rake**[2] /reɪk/ *n* (*man*) calavera *m*

**rake-off** /'reɪkɒf/ *n* (*fam*) comisión *f*

**rally** /'rælɪ/ *vt* reunir; (*revive*) reanimar. ● *vi* reunirse; (*in sickness*) recuperarse. ● *n* reunión *f*; (*recovery*) recuperación *f*; (*auto*) rallye *m*

**ram** /ræm/ *n* carnero *m*. ● *vt* (*pt* **rammed**) (*thrust*) meter por la fuerza; (*crash into*) chocar con

**rambl‖e** /'ræmbl/ *n* excursión *f* a pie. ● *vi* ir de paseo; (*in speech*) divagar. **~e on** divagar. **~er** *n* excursionista *m* & *f*. **~ing** *a* (*speech*) divagador

**ramification** /ræmɪfɪ'keɪʃn/ *n* ramificación *f*

**ramp** /ræmp/ *n* rampa *f*

**rampage** /ræm'peɪdʒ/ *vi* alborotarse. /'ræmpeɪdʒ/ *n*. **go on the ~** alborotarse

**rampant** /'ræmpənt/ *a*. **be ~** (*disease etc*) estar extendido

**rampart** /'ræmpɑːt/ *n* muralla *f*

**ramshackle** /'ræmʃækl/ *a* desvencijado

**ran** /ræn/ *see* **run**

**ranch** /rɑːntʃ/ *n* hacienda *f*

**rancid** /'rænsɪd/ *a* rancio

**rancour** /'ræŋkə(r)/ *n* rencor *m*

**random** /'rændəm/ *a* hecho al azar; (*chance*) fortuito. ● *n*. **at ~** al azar

**randy** /'rændɪ/ *a* (**-ier**, **-iest**) lujurioso, cachondo (*fam*)

**rang** /ræŋ/ *see* **ring**[2]

**range** /reɪndʒ/ *n* alcance *m*; (*distance*) distancia *f*; (*series*) serie *f*; (*of mountains*) cordillera *f*; (*extent*) extensión *f*; (*com*) surtido *m*; (*open area*) dehesa *f*; (*stove*) cocina *f* económica. ● *vi* extenderse; (*vary*) variar

**ranger** /'reɪndʒə(r)/ *n* guardabosque *m*

**rank**[1] /ræŋk/ *n* posición *f*, categoría *f*; (*row*) fila *f*; (*for taxis*) parada *f*. **the ~ and file** la masa *f*. ● *vt* clasificar. ● *vi* clasificarse. **~s** *npl* soldados *mpl* rasos

**rank**[2] /ræŋk/ *a* (**-er**, **-est**) exuberante; (*smell*) fétido; (*fig*) completo

**rankle** /'ræŋkl/ *vi* (*fig*) causar rencor

**ransack** /'rænsæk/ *vt* registrar; (*pillage*) saquear

**ransom** /'rænsəm/ *n* rescate *m*. **hold s.o. to ~** exigir rescate por uno; (*fig*) hacer chantaje a uno. ● *vt* rescatar; (*redeem*) redimir

**rant** /rænt/ *vi* vociferar

**rap** /ræp/ *n* golpe *m* seco. ● *vt/i* (*pt* **rapped**) golpear

**rapacious** /rə'peɪʃs/ *a* rapaz

**rape** /reɪp/ *vt* violar. ● *n* violación *f*

**rapid** /'ræpɪd/ *a* rápido. **~ity** /rə'pɪdətɪ/ *n* rapidez *f*. **~s** /'ræpɪdz/ *npl* rápido *m*

**rapist** /'reɪpɪst/ *n* violador *m*

**rapport** /ræ'pɔː(r)/ *n* armonía *f*, relación *f*

**rapt** /ræpt/ *a* (*attention*) profundo. **~ in** absorto en

**raptur‖e** /'ræptʃə(r)/ *n* éxtasis *m*. **~ous** *a* extático

**rare**[1] /reə(r)/ *a* (**-er**, **-est**) raro

**rare**[2] /reə(r)/ *a* (*culin*) poco hecho

**rarefied** /'reərɪfaɪd/ *a* enrarecido

**rarely** /'reəlı/ *adv* raramente

**rarity** /'reərətı/ *n* rareza *f*

**raring** /'reərıŋ/ *a* (*fam*). ~ **to** impaciente por

**rascal** /'rɑːskl/ *n* tunante *m & f*

**rash**[1] /ræʃ/ *a* (**-er, -est**) imprudente, precipitado

**rash**[2] /ræʃ/ *n* erupción *f*

**rasher** /'ræʃə(r)/ *n* loncha *f*

**rash|ly** /'ræʃlı/ *adv* imprudentemente, a la ligera. ~**ness** *n* imprudencia *f*

**rasp** /rɑːsp/ *n* (*file*) escofina *f*

**raspberry** /'rɑːzbrı/ *n* frambuesa *f*

**rasping** /'rɑːspıŋ/ *a* áspero

**rat** /ræt/ *n* rata *f*. ● *vi* (*pt* **ratted**). ~ **on** (*desert*) desertar; (*inform on*) denunciar, chivarse

**rate** /reıt/ *n* (*ratio*) proporción *f*; (*speed*) velocidad *f*; (*price*) precio *m*; (*of interest*) tipo *m*. **at any** ~ de todas formas. **at the** ~ **of** (*on the basis of*) a razón de. **at this** ~ así. ● *vt* valorar; (*consider*) considerar; (*deserve, Amer*) merecer. ● *vi* ser considerado. ~**able value** *n* valor *m* imponible. ~**payer** /'reıtpeıə(r)/ *n* contribuyente *m & f*. ~**s** *npl* (*taxes*) impuestos *mpl* municipales

**rather** /'rɑːðə(r)/ *adv* mejor dicho; (*fairly*) bastante; (*a little*) un poco. ● *int* claro. **I would** ~ **not** prefiero no

**ratif|ication** /rætıfı'keıʃn/ *n* ratificación *f*. ~**y** /'rætıfaı/ *vt* ratificar

**rating** /'reıtıŋ/ *n* clasificación *f*; (*sailor*) marinero *m*; (*number, TV*) índice *m*

**ratio** /'reıʃıəʊ/ *n* (*pl* **-os**) proporción *f*

**ration** /'ræʃn/ *n* ración *f*. ● *vt* racionar

**rational** /'ræʃənəl/ *a* racional. ~**ize** /'ræʃənəlaız/ *vt* racionalizar

**rat race** /'rætreıs/ *n* lucha *f* incesante para triunfar

**rattle** /'rætl/ *vi* traquetear. ● *vt* (*shake*) agitar; (*sl*) desconcertar. ● *n* traqueteo *m*; (*toy*) sonajero *m*. ~ **off** (*fig*) decir de corrida

**rattlesnake** /'rætlsneık/ *n* serpiente *f* de cascabel

**ratty** /'rætı/ *a* (**-ier, -iest**) (*sl*) irritable

**raucous** /'rɔːkəs/ *a* estridente

**ravage** /'rævıdʒ/ *vt* estragar. ~**s** /'rævıdʒız/ *npl* estragos *mpl*

**rave** /reıv/ *vi* delirar; (*in anger*) enfurecerse. ~ **about** entusiasmarse por

**raven** /'reıvn/ *n* cuervo *m*. ● *a* ⟨*hair*⟩ negro

**ravenous** /'rævənəs/ *a* voraz; ⟨*person*⟩ hambriento. **be** ~ morirse de hambre

**ravine** /rə'viːn/ *n* barranco *m*

**raving** /'reıvıŋ/ *a*. ~ **mad** loco de atar. ~**s** *npl* divagaciones *fpl*

**ravish** /'rævıʃ/ *vt* (*rape*) violar. ~**ing** *a* (*enchanting*) encantador

**raw** /rɔː/ *a* (**-er, -est**) crudo; (*not processed*) bruto; ⟨*wound*⟩ en carne viva; (*inexperienced*) inexperto; ⟨*weather*⟩ crudo. ~ **deal** *n* tratamiento *m* injusto, injusticia *f*. ~ **materials** *npl* materias *fpl* primas

**ray** /reı/ *n* rayo *m*

**raze** /reız/ *vt* arrasar

**razor** /'reızə(r)/ *n* navaja *f* de afeitar; (*electric*) maquinilla *f* de afeitar

**Rd** *abbr* (*Road*) C/, Calle *f*

**re**[1] /riː/ *prep* con referencia a. ● *pref* re...

**re**[2] /reı/ *n* (*mus, second note of any musical scale*) re *m*

**reach** /riːtʃ/ *vt* alcanzar; (*extend*) extender; (*arrive at*) llegar a; (*achieve*) lograr; (*hand over*) pasar, dar. ● *vi* extenderse. ● *n* alcance *m*; (*of river*) tramo *m* recto. **within** ~ **of** al alcance de; (*close to*) a corta distancia de

**react** /rı'ækt/ *vi* reaccionar. ~**ion** /rı'ækʃn/ *n* reacción *f*. ~**ionary** *a & n* reaccionario (*m*)

**reactor** /rı'æktə(r)/ *n* reactor *m*

**read** /riːd/ *vt* (*pt* **read** /red/) leer; (*study*) estudiar; (*interpret*) interpretar. ● *vi* leer; ⟨*instrument*⟩ indicar. ● *n* (*fam*) lectura *f*. ~ **out** *vt* leer en voz alta. ~**able** *a* interesante, agradable; (*clear*) legible. ~**er** /'riːdə(r)/ *n* lector *m*. ~**ership** *n* lectores *m*

**readi|ly** /'redılı/ *adv* (*willingly*) de buena gana; (*easily*) fácilmente. ~**ness** /'redınıs/ *n* prontitud *f*. **in** ~**ness** preparado, listo

**reading** /'riːdıŋ/ *n* lectura *f*

**readjust** /riːə'dʒʌst/ *vt* reajustar. ● *vi* readaptarse (**to** a)

**ready** /'redı/ *a* (**-ier, -iest**) listo, preparado; (*quick*) pronto. ~**-made** *a* confeccionado. ~ **money** *n* dinero *m* contante. ~ **reckoner** *n* baremo *m*. **get** ~ preparase

**real** /rıəl/ *a* verdadero. ● *adv* (*Amer, fam*) verdaderamente. ~ **estate** *n* bienes *mpl* raíces

**realis|m** /'rɪəlɪzəm/ n realismo m. ∼t /'rɪəlɪst/ n realista m & f. ∼tic /-'lɪstɪk/ a realista. ∼tically /-'lɪstɪklɪ/ adv de manera realista

**reality** /rɪ'ælətɪ/ n realidad f

**realiz|ation** /rɪəlaɪ'zeɪʃn/ n comprensión f; (com) realización f. ∼e /'rɪəlaɪz/ vt darse cuenta de; (fulfil, com) realizar

**really** /'rɪəlɪ/ adv verdaderamente

**realm** /relm/ n reino m

**ream** /riːm/ n resma f

**reap** /riːp/ vt segar; (fig) cosechar

**re:** ∼appear /riːə'pɪə(r)/ vi reaparecer. ∼appraisal /riːə'preɪzl/ n revaluación f

**rear**[1] /rɪə(r)/ n parte f de atrás. ● a posterior, trasero

**rear**[2] /rɪə(r)/ vt (bring up, breed) criar. ∼ one's head levantar la cabeza. ● vi ⟨horse⟩ encabritarse. ∼ up ⟨horse⟩ encabritarse

**rear:** ∼admiral n contraalmirante m. ∼guard /'rɪəgɑːd/ n retaguardia f

**re:** ∼arm /riː'ɑːm/ vt rearmar. ● vi rearmarse. ∼arrange /riːə'reɪndʒ/ vt arreglar de otra manera

**reason** /'riːzn/ n razón f, motivo m. **within** ∼ dentro de lo razonable. ● vi razonar

**reasonable** /'riːzənəbl/ a razonable

**reasoning** /'riːznɪŋ/ n razonamiento m

**reassur|ance** /riːə'ʃʊərəns/ n promesa f tranquilizadora; (guarantee) garantía f. ∼e /riːə'ʃʊə(r)/ vt tranquilizar

**rebate** /'riːbeɪt/ n reembolso m; (discount) rebaja f

**rebel** /'rebl/ n rebelde m & f. /rɪ'bel/ vi (pt rebelled) rebelarse. ∼lion n rebelión f. ∼lious a rebelde

**rebound** /rɪ'baʊnd/ vi rebotar; (fig) recaer. /'riːbaʊnd/ n rebote m. **on the** ∼ (fig) por reacción

**rebuff** /rɪ'bʌf/ vt rechazar. ● n desaire m

**rebuild** /riː'bɪld/ vt (pt rebuilt) reconstruir

**rebuke** /rɪ'bjuːk/ vt reprender. ● n reprensión f

**rebuttal** /rɪ'bʌtl/ n refutación f

**recall** /rɪ'kɔːl/ vt (call s.o. back) llamar; (remember) recordar. ● n llamada f

**recant** /rɪ'kænt/ vi retractarse

**recap** /'riːkæp/ vt/i (pt recapped) (fam) resumir. ● n (fam) resumen m

**recapitulat|e** /riːkə'pɪtʃʊleɪt/ vt/i resumir. ∼ion /-'leɪʃn/ n resumen m

**recapture** /riː'kæptʃə(r)/ vt recobrar; (recall) hacer revivir

**reced|e** /rɪ'siːd/ vi retroceder. ∼ing a ⟨forehead⟩ huidizo

**receipt** /rɪ'siːt/ n recibo m. ∼s npl (com) ingresos mpl

**receive** /rɪ'siːv/ vt recibir. ∼r /-ə(r)/ n (of stolen goods) perista m & f; (of phone) auricular m

**recent** /'riːsnt/ a reciente. ∼ly adv recientemente

**receptacle** /rɪ'septəkl/ n recipiente m

**reception** /rɪ'sepʃn/ n recepción f; (welcome) acogida f. ∼ist n recepcionista m & f

**receptive** /rɪ'septɪv/ a receptivo

**recess** /rɪ'ses/ n hueco m; (holiday) vacaciones fpl; (fig) parte f recóndita

**recession** /rɪ'seʃn/ n recesión f

**recharge** /riː'tʃɑːdʒ/ vt cargar de nuevo, recargar

**recipe** /'resəpɪ/ n receta f

**recipient** /rɪ'sɪpɪənt/ n recipiente m & f; (of letter) destinatario m

**reciprocal** /rɪ'sɪprəkl/ a recíproco

**reciprocate** /rɪ'sɪprəkeɪt/ vt corresponder a

**recital** /rɪ'saɪtl/ n (mus) recital m

**recite** /rɪ'saɪt/ vt recitar; (list) enumerar

**reckless** /'reklɪs/ a imprudente. ∼ly adv imprudentemente. ∼ness n imprudencia f

**reckon** /'rekən/ vt/i calcular; (consider) considerar; (think) pensar. ∼ on (rely) contar con. ∼ing n cálculo m

**reclaim** /rɪ'kleɪm/ vt reclamar; recuperar ⟨land⟩

**reclin|e** /rɪ'klaɪn/ vi recostarse. ∼ing a acostado; ⟨seat⟩ reclinable

**recluse** /rɪ'kluːs/ n solitario m

**recogni|tion** /rekəg'nɪʃn/ n reconocimiento m. **beyond** ∼tion irreconocible. ∼ze /'rekəgnaɪz/ vt reconocer

**recoil** /rɪ'kɔɪl/ vi retroceder. ● n (of gun) culatazo m

**recollect** /rekə'lekt/ vt recordar. ∼ion /-ʃn/ n recuerdo m

**recommend** /rekə'mend/ vt recomendar. ∼ation /-'deɪʃn/ n recomendación f

**recompense** /'rekəmpens/ *vt*
recompensar. ● *n* recompensa *f*
**reconcil|e** /'rekənsaɪl/ *vt* reconciliar
⟨*people*⟩; conciliar ⟨*facts*⟩. **~e o.s.**
resignarse (**to** a). **~iation**
/-sɪlɪ'eɪʃn/ *n* reconciliación *f*
**recondition** /ri:kən'dɪʃn/ *vt* reacon-
dicionar, arreglar
**reconnaissance** /rɪ'kɒnɪsns/ *n*
reconocimiento *m*
**reconnoitre** /rekə'nɔɪtə(r)/ *vt* (*pres p*
**-tring**) (*mil*) reconocer. ● *vi* hacer
un reconocimiento
**re: ~consider** /ri:kən'sɪdə(r)/ *vt*
volver a considerar. **~construct** /ri:
kən'strʌkt/ *vt* reconstruir. **~con-
struction** /-ʃn/ *n* reconstrucción *f*
**record** /rɪ'kɔːd/ *vt* (*in register*) registrar; (*in diary*) apuntar; (*mus*)
grabar. /'rekɔːd/ *n* (*file*) docu-
mentación *f*, expediente *m*; (*mus*)
disco *m*; (*sport*) récord *m*. **off the ~**
en confianza. **~er** /rɪ'kɔːdə(r)/ *n*
registrador *m*; (*mus*) flauta *f* dulce.
**~ing** *n* grabación *f*. **~player** *n*
tocadiscos *m invar*
**recount** /rɪ'kaʊnt/ *vt* contar,
relatar, referir
**re-count** /ri:'kaʊnt/ *vt* recontar. /'ri:
kaʊnt/ *n* (*pol*) recuento *m*
**recoup** /rɪ'kuːp/ *vt* recuperar
**recourse** /rɪ'kɔːs/ *n* recurso *m*. **have
~ to** recurrir a
**recover** /rɪ'kʌvə(r)/ *vt* recuperar.
● *vi* reponerse. **~y** *n* recuperación *f*
**recreation** /rekrɪ'eɪʃn/ *n* recreo *m*.
**~al** *a* de recreo
**recrimination** /rɪkrɪmɪ'neɪʃn/ *n*
recriminación *f*
**recruit** /rɪ'kruːt/ *n* recluta *m*. ● *vt*
reclutar. **~ment** *n* reclutamiento *m*
**rectang|le** /'rektæŋgl/ *n* rectángulo
*m*. **~ular** /-'tæŋgjʊlə(r)/ *a* rectan-
gular
**rectif|ication** /rektɪfɪ'keɪʃn/ *n* recti-
ficación *f*. **~y** /'rektɪfaɪ/ *vt* rectificar
**rector** /'rektə(r)/ *n* párroco *m*; (*of
college*) rector *m*. **~y** *n* rectoría *f*
**recumbent** /rɪ'kʌmbənt/ *a* recos-
tado
**recuperat|e** /rɪ'kuːpəreɪt/ *vt* re-
cuperar. ● *vi* reponerse. **~ion**
/-'reɪʃn/ *n* recuperación *f*
**recur** /rɪ'kɜː(r)/ *vi* (*pt* **recurred**) repe-
tirse. **~rence** /rɪ'kʌrɪns/ *n* repetición *f*. **~rent** /rɪ'kʌrənt/ *a* repetido
**recycle** /ri:'saɪkl/ *vt* reciclar
**red** /red/ *a* (**redder, reddest**) rojo.
● *n* rojo. **in the ~** ⟨*account*⟩ en

descubierto. **~breast** /'redbrest/ *n*
petirrojo *m*. **~brick** /'redbrɪk/ *a*
⟨*univ*⟩ de reciente fundación. **~den**
/'redn/ *vt* enrojecer. ● *vi* enro-
jecerse. **~dish** *a* rojizo
**redecorate** /ri:'dekəreɪt/ *vt* pintar
de nuevo
**rede|em** /rɪ'diːm/ *vt* redimir. **~em-
ing quality** *n* cualidad *f* com-
pensadora. **~mption** /-'dempʃn/ *n*
redención *f*
**redeploy** /ri:dɪ'plɔɪ/ *vt* disponer de
otra manera; (*mil*) cambiar de
frente
**red: ~handed** *a* en flagrante. **~
herring** *n* (*fig*) pista *f* falsa. **~hot** *a*
al rojo; ⟨*news*⟩ de última hora
**Red Indian** /red'ɪndjən/ *n* piel *m* & *f*
roja
**redirect** /ri:daɪ'rekt/ *vt* reexpedir
**red: ~letter day** *n* día *m* señalado,
día *m* memorable. **~ light** *n* luz *f*
roja. **~ness** *n* rojez *f*
**redo** /ri:'duː/ *vt* (*pt* **redid**, *pp* **redone**)
rehacer
**redouble** /rɪ'dʌbl/ *vt* redoblar
**redress** /rɪ'dres/ *vt* reparar. ● *n*
reparación *f*
**red tape** /red'teɪp/ *n* (*fig*) papeleo *m*
**reduc|e** /rɪ'djuːs/ *vt* reducir. ● *vi*
reducirse; (*slim*) adelgazar. **~tion**
/'dʌkʃn/ *n* reducción *f*
**redundan|cy** /rɪ'dʌndənsɪ/ *n* super-
fluidad *f*; (*unemployment*) desempleo *m*. **~t** /rɪ'dʌndənt/ *a* superfluo.
**be made ~t** perder su empleo
**reed** /ri:d/ *n* caña *f*; (*mus*) lengüeta *f*
**reef** /ri:f/ *n* arrecife *m*
**reek** /ri:k/ *n* mal olor *m*. ● *vi*. **~ (of)**
apestar a
**reel** /ri:l/ *n* carrete *m*. ● *vi* dar vueltas; (*stagger*) tambalearse. ● *vt*. **~
off** (*fig*) enumerar
**refectory** /rɪ'fektərɪ/ *n* refectorio *m*
**refer** /rɪ'fɜː(r)/ *vt* (*pt* **referred**)
remitir. ● *vi* referirse. **~ to** referirse a; (*consult*) consultar
**referee** /refə'riː/ *n* árbitro *m*; (*for
job*) referencia *f*. ● *vi* (*pt* **refereed**)
arbitrar
**reference** /'refrəns/ *n* referencia *f*.
**~ book** *n* libro *m* de consulta. **in ~
to, with ~ to** en cuanto a; (*com*)
respecto a
**referendum** /refə'rendəm/ *n* (*pl*
**-ums**) referéndum *m*
**refill** /ri:'fɪl/ *vt* rellenar. /'ri:fɪl/ *n*
recambio *m*

**refine** /rɪ'faɪn/ vt refinar. **~d** a refinado. **~ment** n refinamiento m; (tec) refinación f. **~ry** /-ərɪ/ n refinería f

**reflect** /rɪ'flekt/ vt reflejar. ● vi reflejar; (think) reflexionar. **~ upon** perjudicar. **~ion** /-ʃn/ n reflexión f; (image) reflejo m. **~ive** /rɪ'flektɪv/ a reflector; (thoughtful) pensativo. **~or** n reflector m

**reflex** /'ri:fleks/ a & n reflejo (m)

**reflexive** /rɪ'fleksɪv/ a (gram) reflexivo

**reform** /rɪ'fɔ:m/ vt reformar. ● vi reformarse. ● n reforma f. **~er** n reformador m

**refract** /rɪ'frækt/ vt refractar

**refrain**[1] /rɪ'freɪn/ n estribillo m

**refrain**[2] /rɪ'freɪn/ vi abstenerse (from de)

**refresh** /rɪ'freʃ/ vt refrescar. **~er** /rɪ'freʃə(r)/ a (course) de repaso. **~ing** a refrescante. **~ments** npl (food and drink) refrigerio m

**refrigerat|e** /rɪ'frɪdʒəreɪt/ vt refrigerar. **~or** n nevera f, refrigeradora f (LAm)

**refuel** /ri:'fju:əl/ vt/i (pt refuelled) repostar

**refuge** /'refju:dʒ/ n refugio m. take **~** refugiarse. **~e** /refjʊ'dʒi:/ n refugiado m

**refund** /rɪ'fʌnd/ vt reembolsar. /'ri:fʌnd/ n reembolso m

**refurbish** /ri:'fɜ:bɪʃ/ vt renovar

**refusal** /rɪ'fju:zl/ n negativa f

**refuse**[1] /rɪ'fju:z/ vt rehusar. ● vi negarse

**refuse**[2] /'refju:s/ n basura f

**refute** /rɪ'fju:t/ vt refutar

**regain** /rɪ'geɪn/ vt recobrar

**regal** /'ri:gl/ a real

**regale** /rɪ'geɪl/ vt festejar

**regalia** /rɪ'geɪlɪə/ npl insignias fpl

**regard** /rɪ'gɑ:d/ vt mirar; (consider) considerar. as **~s** en cuanto a. ● n mirada f; (care) atención f; (esteem) respeto m. **~ing** prep en cuanto a. **~less** /rɪ'gɑ:dlɪs/ adv a pesar de todo. **~less of** sin tener en cuenta. **~s** npl saludos mpl. kind **~s** npl recuerdos mpl

**regatta** /rɪ'gætə/ n regata f

**regency** /'ri:dʒənsɪ/ n regencia f

**regenerate** /rɪ'dʒenəreɪt/ vt regenerar

**regent** /'ri:dʒənt/ n regente m & f

**regime** /reɪ'ʒi:m/ n régimen m

**regiment** /'redʒɪmənt/ n regimiento m. **~al** /-'mentl/ a del regimiento. **~ation** /-en'teɪʃn/ n reglamentación f rígida

**region** /'ri:dʒən/ n región f. in the **~ of** alrededor de. **~al** a regional

**register** /'redʒɪstə(r)/ n registro m. ● vt registrar; matricular (vehicle); declarar (birth); certificar (letter); facturar (luggage); (indicate) indicar; (express) expresar. ● vi (enrol) inscribirse; (fig) producir impresión. **~ office** n registro m civil

**registrar** /redʒɪ'strɑ:(r)/ n secretario m del registro civil; (univ) secretario m general

**registration** /redʒɪ'streɪʃn/ n registración f; (in register) inscripción f; (of vehicle) matrícula f

**registry** /'redʒɪstrɪ/ n. **~ office** n registro m civil

**regression** /rɪ'greʃn/ n regresión f

**regret** /rɪ'gret/ n pesar m. ● vt (pt regretted) lamentar. I **~ that** siento (que). **~fully** adv con pesar. **~table** a lamentable. **~tably** adv lamentablemente

**regular** /'regjʊlə(r)/ a regular; (usual) habitual. ● n (fam) cliente m habitual. **~ity** /-'lærətɪ/ n regularidad f. **~ly** adv regularmente

**regulat|e** /'regjʊleɪt/ vt regular. **~ion** /-'leɪʃn/ n arreglo m; (rule) regla f

**rehabilitat|e** /ri:hə'bɪlɪteɪt/ vt rehabilitar. **~ion** /-'teɪʃn/ n rehabilitación f

**rehash** /ri:'hæʃ/ vt volver a presentar. /'ri:hæʃ/ n refrito m

**rehears|al** /rɪ'hɜ:sl/ n ensayo m. **~e** /rɪ'hɜ:s/ vt ensayar

**reign** /reɪn/ n reinado m. ● vi reinar

**reimburse** /ri:ɪm'bɜ:s/ vt reembolsar

**reins** /reɪnz/ npl riendas fpl

**reindeer** /'reɪndɪə(r)/ n invar reno m

**reinforce** /ri:ɪn'fɔ:s/ vt reforzar. **~ment** n refuerzo m

**reinstate** /ri:ɪn'steɪt/ vt reintegrar

**reiterate** /ri:'ɪtəreɪt/ vt reiterar

**reject** /rɪ'dʒekt/ vt rechazar. /'ri:dʒekt/ n producto m defectuoso. **~ion** /'dʒekʃn/ n rechazamiento m, rechazo m

**rejoic|e** /rɪ'dʒɔɪs/ vi regocijarse. **~ing** n regocijo m

**rejoin** /rɪ'dʒɔɪn/ vt reunirse con; (answer) replicar. **~der** /rɪ'dʒɔɪndə(r)/ n réplica f

**rejuvenate** /rɪ'dʒuːvəneɪt/ vt rejuvenecer

**rekindle** /riː'kɪndl/ vt reavivar

**relapse** /rɪ'læps/ n recaída f. ● vi recaer; (into crime) reincidir

**relate** /rɪ'leɪt/ vt contar; (connect) relacionar. ● vi relacionarse (to con). ~**d** a emparentado; ‹ideas etc› relacionado

**relation** /rɪ'leɪʃn/ n relación f; (person) pariente m & f. ~**ship** n relación f; (blood tie) parentesco m; (affair) relaciones fpl

**relative** /'relətɪv/ n pariente m & f. ● a relativo. ~**ly** adv relativamente

**relax** /rɪ'læks/ vt relajar. ● vi relajarse. ~**ation** /riːlæk'seɪʃn/ n relajación f; (rest) descanso m; (recreation) recreo m. ~**ing** a relajante

**relay** /'riːleɪ/ n relevo m. ~ (**race**) f carrera ' f de relevos. /rɪ'leɪ/ vt retransmitir

**release** /rɪ'liːs/ vt soltar; poner en libertad ‹prisoner›; lanzar ‹bomb›; estrenar ‹film›; (mec) desenganchar; publicar ‹news›; emitir ‹smoke›. ● n liberación f; (of film) estreno m; (record) disco m nuevo

**relegate** /'relɪgeɪt/ vt relegar

**relent** /rɪ'lent/ vi ceder. ~**less** a implacable; (continuous) incesante

**relevan|ce** /'relɪvəns/ n pertinencia f. ~**t** /'relɪvənt/ a pertinente

**reliab|ility** /rɪlaɪə'bɪlətɪ/ n fiabilidad f. ~**le** /rɪ'laɪəbl/ a seguro; ‹person› de fiar; (com) serio

**relian|ce** /rɪ'laɪəns/ n dependencia f; (trust) confianza f. ~**t** a confiado

**relic** /'relɪk/ n reliquia f. ~**s** npl restos mpl

**relie|f** /rɪ'liːf/ n alivio m; (assistance) socorro m; (outline) relieve m. ~**ve** /rɪ'liːv/ vt aliviar; (take over from) relevar

**religio|n** /rɪ'lɪdʒən/ n religión f. ~**us** /rɪ'lɪdʒəs/ a religioso

**relinquish** /rɪ'lɪŋkwɪʃ/ vt abandonar, renunciar

**relish** /'relɪʃ/ n gusto m; (culin) salsa f. ● vt saborear. **I don't ~ the idea** no me gusta la idea

**relocate** /riːləʊ'keɪt/ vt colocar de nuevo

**reluctan|ce** /rɪ'lʌktəns/ n desgana f. ~**t** /rɪ'lʌktənt/ a mal dispuesto. **be ~t to** no tener ganas de. ~**tly** adv de mala gana

**rely** /rɪ'laɪ/ vi. ~ **on** contar con; (trust) fiarse de; (depend) depender

**remain** /rɪ'meɪn/ vi quedar. ~**der** /rɪ'meɪndə(r)/ n resto m. ~**s** npl restos mpl; (left-overs) sobras fpl

**remand** /rɪ'mɑːnd/ vt. ~ **in custody** mantener bajo custodia. ● n. **on ~** bajo custodia

**remark** /rɪ'mɑːk/ n observación f. ● vt observar. ~**able** a notable

**remarry** /riː'mærɪ/ vi volver a casarse

**remedial** /rɪ'miːdɪəl/ a remediador

**remedy** /'remədɪ/ n remedio m. ● vt remediar

**rememb|er** /rɪ'membə(r)/ vt acordarse de. ● vi acordarse. ~**rance** n recuerdo m

**remind** /rɪ'maɪnd/ vt recordar. ~**er** n recordatorio m; (letter) notificación f

**reminisce** /remɪ'nɪs/ vi recordar el pasado. ~**nces** npl recuerdos mpl. ~**nt** /remɪ'nɪsnt/ a. **be ~nt of** recordar

**remiss** /rɪ'mɪs/ a negligente

**remission** /rɪ'mɪʃn/ n remisión f; (of sentence) reducción f de condena

**remit** /rɪ'mɪt/ vt (pt remitted) perdonar; enviar ‹money›. ● vi moderarse. ~**tance** n remesa f

**remnant** /'remnənt/ n resto m; (of cloth) retazo m; (trace) vestigio m

**remonstrate** /'remənstreɪt/ vi protestar

**remorse** /rɪ'mɔːs/ n remordimiento m. ~**ful** a lleno de remordimiento. ~**less** a implacable

**remote** /rɪ'məʊt/ a remoto; (slight) leve; ‹person› distante. ~ **control** n mando m a distancia. ~**ly** adv remotamente. ~**ness** n lejanía f; (isolation) aislamiento m, alejamiento m; (fig) improbabilidad f

**remov|able** /rɪ'muːvəbl/ a movible; (detachable) de quita y pon, separable. ~**al** n eliminación f; (from house) mudanza f. ~**e** /rɪ'muːv/ vt quitar; (dismiss) despedir; (get rid of) eliminar; (do away with) suprimir

**remunerat|e** /rɪ'mjuːnəreɪt/ vt remunerar. ~**ion** /-'reɪʃn/ n remuneración f. ~**ive** a remunerador

**Renaissance** /rə'neɪsəns/ n Renacimiento m

**rend** /rend/ vt (pt rent) rasgar

**render** /'rendə(r)/ vt rendir; (com) presentar; (mus) interpretar; prestar ⟨help etc⟩. ~ing n (mus) interpretación f

**rendezvous** /'rɒndɪvuː/ n (pl -vous /-vuːz/) cita f

**renegade** /'renɪgeɪd/ n renegado

**renew** /rɪ'njuː/ vt renovar; (resume) reanudar. ~able a renovable. ~al n renovación f

**renounce** /rɪ'naʊns/ vt renunciar a; (disown) repudiar

**renovat|e** /'renəveɪt/ vt renovar. ~ion /-'veɪʃn/ n renovación f

**renown** /rɪ'naʊn/ n fama f. ~ed a célebre

**rent**[1] /rent/ n alquiler m. ● vt alquilar

**rent**[2] /rent/ see rend

**rental** /rentl/ n alquiler m

**renunciation** /rɪnʌnsɪ'eɪʃn/ n renuncia f

**reopen** /riː'əʊpən/ vt reabrir. ● vi reabrirse. ~ing n reapertura f

**reorganize** /riː'ɔːgənaɪz/ vt reorganizar

**rep**[1] /rep/ n (com, fam) representante m & f

**rep**[2] /rep/ (theatre, fam) teatro m de repertorio

**repair** /rɪ'peə(r)/ vt reparar; remendar ⟨clothes, shoes⟩. ● n reparación f; (patch) remiendo m. in good ~ en buen estado

**repartee** /repɑː'tiː/ n ocurrencias fpl

**repatriat|e** /riː'pætrɪeɪt/ vt repatriar. ~ion /-'eɪʃn/ n repatriación f

**repay** /riː'peɪ/ vt (pt repaid) reembolsar; pagar ⟨debt⟩; (reward) recompensar. ~ment n reembolso m, pago m

**repeal** /rɪ'piːl/ vt abrogar. ● n abrogación f

**repeat** /rɪ'piːt/ vt repetir. ● vi repetir(se). ● n repetición f. ~edly /rɪ'piːtɪdlɪ/ adv repetidas veces

**repel** /rɪ'pel/ vt (pt repelled) repeler. ~lent a repelente

**repent** /rɪ'pent/ vi arrepentirse. ~ance n arrepentimiento m. ~ant a arrepentido

**repercussion** /riːpə'kʌʃn/ n repercusión f

**reperto|ire** /'repətwɑː(r)/ n repertorio m. ~ry /'repətrɪ/ n repertorio m. ~ry (theatre) n teatro m de repertorio

**repetit|ion** /repɪ'tɪʃn/ n repetición f. ~ious /-'tɪʃəs/ a, ~ive /rɪ'petətɪv/ a que se repite; (dull) monótono

**replace** /rɪ'pleɪs/ vt reponer; (take the place of) sustituir. ~ment n sustitución f; (person) sustituto m. ~ment part n recambio m

**replay** /'riːpleɪ/ n (sport) repetición f del partido; (recording) repetición f inmediata

**replenish** /rɪ'plenɪʃ/ vt reponer; (refill) rellenar

**replete** /rɪ'pliːt/ a repleto

**replica** /'replɪkə/ n copia f

**reply** /rɪ'plaɪ/ vt/i contestar. ● n respuesta f

**report** /rɪ'pɔːt/ vt anunciar; (denounce) denunciar. ● vi presentar un informe; (present o.s.) presentarse. ● n informe m; (schol) boletín m; (rumour) rumor m; (newspaper) reportaje m; (sound) estallido m. ~age /repɔː'tɑːʒ/ n reportaje m. ~edly adv según se dice. ~er /rɪ'pɔːtə(r)/ n reportero m, informador m

**repose** /rɪ'pəʊz/ n reposo m

**repository** /rɪ'pɒzɪtrɪ/ n depósito m

**repossess** /riːpə'zes/ vt recuperar

**reprehen|d** /reprɪ'hend/ vt reprender. ~sible /-səbl/ a reprensible

**represent** /reprɪ'zent/ vt representar. ~ation /-'teɪʃn/ n representación f. ~ative /reprɪ'zentətɪv/ a representativo. ● n representante m & f

**repress** /rɪ'pres/ vt reprimir. ~ion /-ʃn/ n represión f. ~ive a represivo

**reprieve** /rɪ'priːv/ n indulto m; (fig) respiro m. ● vt indultar; (fig) aliviar

**reprimand** /'reprɪmɑːnd/ vt reprender. ● n represión f

**reprint** /'riːprɪnt/ n reimpresión f; (offprint) tirada f aparte. /riː'prɪnt/ vt reimprimir

**reprisal** /rɪ'praɪzl/ n represalia f

**reproach** /rɪ'prəʊtʃ/ vt reprochar. ● n reproche m. ~ful a de reproche, reprobador. ~fully adv con reproche

**reprobate** /'reprəbeɪt/ n malvado m; (relig) réprobo m

**reproduc|e** /riːprə'djuːs/ vt reproducir. ● vi reproducirse. ~tion /-'dʌkʃn/ n reproducción f. ~tive /-'dʌktɪv/ a reproductor

**reprove** /rɪ'pruːv/ vt reprender

**reptile** /'reptaɪl/ n reptil m

**republic** /rɪ'pʌblɪk/ n república f.
~**an** a & n republicano (m)
**repudiate** /rɪ'pju:dɪeɪt/ vt repudiar;
(refuse to recognize) negarse a
reconocer
**repugnan|ce** /rɪ'pʌgnəns/ n repug-
nancia f. ~**t** /rɪ'pʌgnənt/ a
repugnante
**repuls|e** /rɪ'pʌls/ vt rechazar,
repulsar. ~**ion** /-ʃn/ n repulsión f.
~**ive** a repulsivo
**reputable** /'repjʊtəbl/ a acreditado,
de confianza, honroso
**reputation** /repjʊ'teɪʃn/ n reputación f
**repute** /rɪ'pju:t/ n reputación f. ~**d**
/-ɪd/ a supuesto. ~**dly** adv según se
dice
**request** /rɪ'kwest/ n petición f. ● vt
pedir. ~ **stop** n parada f
discrecional
**require** /rɪ'kwaɪə(r)/ vt requerir;
(need) necesitar; (demand) exigir.
~**d** a necesario. ~**ment** n requisito
m
**requisite** /'rekwɪzɪt/ a necesario.
● n requisito m
**requisition** /rekwɪ'zɪʃn/ n requi-
sición f. ● vt requisar
**resale** /'ri:seɪl/ n reventa f
**rescind** /rɪ'sɪnd/ vt rescindir
**rescue** /'reskju:/ vt salvar. ● n salvamento m. ~**r** /-ə(r)/ n salvador m
**research** /rɪ'sɜ:tʃ/ n investigación f.
● vt investigar. ~**er** n investigador
m
**resembl|ance** /rɪ'zembləns/ n pare-
cido m. ~**e** /rɪ'zembl/ vt parecerse a
**resent** /rɪ'zent/ vt resentirse por.
~**ful** a resentido. ~**ment** n resentimiento m
**reservation** /rezə'veɪʃn/ n reserva f;
(booking) reservación f
**reserve** /rɪ'zɜ:v/ vt reservar. ● n
reserva f; (in sports) suplente m & f.
~**d** a reservado
**reservist** /rɪ'zɜ:vɪst/ n reservista m
& f
**reservoir** /'rezəvwɑ:(r)/ n embalse m;
(tank) depósito m
**reshape** /ri:'ʃeɪp/ vt formar de
nuevo, reorganizar
**reshuffle** /ri:'ʃʌfl/ vt (pol)
reorganizar. ● n (pol) reorganiza-
ción f
**reside** /rɪ'zaɪd/ vi residir
**residen|ce** /'rezɪdəns/ n residencia f.
~**ce permit** n permiso m de residencia. **be in** ~**ce** (doctor etc)

interno. ~**t** /'rezɪdənt/ a & n resi-
dente (m & f). ~**tial** /rezɪ'denʃl/ a
residencial
**residue** /'rezɪdju:/ n residuo m
**resign** /rɪ'zaɪn/ vt/i dimitir. ~ **o.s. to**
resignarse a. ~**ation** /rezɪg'neɪʃn/ n
resignación f; (from job) dimisión f.
~**ed** a resignado
**resilien|ce** /rɪ'zɪlɪəns/ n elasticidad f;
(of person) resistencia f. ~**t**
/rɪ'zɪlɪənt/ a elástico; (person)
resistente
**resin** /'rezɪn/ n resina f
**resist** /rɪ'zɪst/ vt resistir. ● vi resistirse. ~**ance** n resistencia f.
~**ant** a resistente
**resolut|e** /'rezəlu:t/ a resuelto. ~**ion**
/-'lu:ʃn/ n resolución f
**resolve** /rɪ'zɒlv/ vt resolver. ~ **to do**
resolverse a hacer. ● n resolución f.
~**d** a resuelto
**resonan|ce** /'rezənəns/ n resonancia
f. ~**t** /'rezənənt/ a resonante
**resort** /rɪ'zɔ:t/ vi. ~ **to** recurrir a.
● n recurso m; (place) lugar m turístico. **in the last** ~ como último
recurso
**resound** /rɪ'zaʊnd/ vi resonar. ~**ing**
a resonante
**resource** /rɪ'sɔ:s/ n recurso m. ~**ful**
a ingenioso. ~**fulness** n ingeniosi-
dad f
**respect** /rɪ'spekt/ n (esteem) respeto
m; (aspect) respecto m. **with** ~ **to**
con respecto a. ● vt respetar
**respectab|ility** /rɪspektə'bɪlətɪ/ n
respetabilidad f. ~**le** /rɪ'spektəbl/ a
respetable. ~**ly** adv respetable-
mente
**respectful** /rɪ'spektfl/ a respetuoso
**respective** /rɪ'spektɪv/ a respectivo.
~**ly** adv respectivamente
**respiration** /respə'reɪʃn/ n respiración f
**respite** /'respaɪt/ n respiro m, tregua
f
**resplendent** /rɪ'splendənt/ a
resplandeciente
**respon|d** /rɪ'spɒnd/ vi responder.
~**se** /rɪ'spɒns/ n respuesta f; (reaction) reacción f
**responsib|ility** /rɪspɒnsə'bɪlətɪ/ n
responsabilidad f. ~**le** /rɪ'spɒnsəbl/
a responsable; (job) de responsabilidad. ~**ly** adv con formalidad
**responsive** /rɪ'spɒnsɪv/ a que reac-
ciona bien. ~ **to** sensible a
**rest**[1] /rest/ vt descansar; (lean)
apoyar; (place) poner, colocar. ● vi

descansar; (*lean*) apoyarse. ● *n*
descanso *m*; (*mus*) pausa *f*
**rest²** /rest/ *n* (*remainder*) resto *m*, lo
demás; (*people*) los demás, los otros
*mpl*. ● *vi* (*remain*) quedar
**restaurant** /'rest∂rɒnt/ *n* restaurante *m*
**restful** /'restfl/ *a* sosegado
**restitution** /restɪ'tjuːʃn/ *n* resti-
tución *f*
**restive** /'restɪv/ *a* inquieto
**restless** /'restlɪs/ *a* inquieto. ~**ly**
*adv* inquietamente. ~**ness** *n*
inquietud *f*
**restor|ation** /rest∂'reɪʃn/ *n* restau-
ración *f*. ~**e** /rɪ'stɔː(r)/ *vt*
restablecer; restaurar (*building*);
(*put back in position*) reponer;
(*return*) devolver
**restrain** /rɪ'streɪn/ *vt* contener. ~
**o.s.** contenerse. ~**ed** *a* (*moderate*)
moderado; (*in control of self*) comedido. ~**t** *n* restricción *f*; (*moderation*) moderación *f*
**restrict** /rɪ'strɪkt/ *vt* restringir.
~**ion** /-ʃn/ *n* restricción *f*. ~**ive**
/rɪ'strɪktɪv/ *a* restrictivo
**result** /rɪ'zʌlt/ *n* resultado *m*. ● *vi*. ~
**from** resultar de. ~ **in** dar como
resultado
**resume** /rɪ'zjuːm/ *vt* reanudar. ● *vi*
continuar
**résumé** /'rezjʊmeɪ/ *n* resumen *m*
**resumption** /rɪ'zʌmpʃn/ *n* continuación *f*
**resurgence** /rɪ'sɜːdʒ∂ns/ *n* resur-
gimiento *m*
**resurrect** /rez∂'rekt/ *vt* resucitar.
~**ion** /-ʃn/ *n* resurrección *f*
**resuscitat|e** /rɪ'sʌsɪteɪt/ *vt* resu-
citar. ~**ion** /-'teɪʃn/ *n* resucitación *f*
**retail** /'riːteɪl/ *n* venta *f* al por menor.
● *a* & *adv* al por menor. ● *vt* vender
al por menor. ● *vi* venderse al por
menor. ~**er** *n* minorista *m* & *f*
**retain** /rɪ'teɪn/ *vt* retener; (*keep*)
conservar
**retainer** /rɪ'teɪn∂(r)/ *n* (*fee*) anticipo
*m*
**retaliat|e** /rɪ'tælɪeɪt/ *vi* desquitarse.
~**ion** /-'eɪʃn/ *n* represalias *fpl*
**retarded** /rɪ'tɑːdɪd/ *a* retrasado
**retentive** /rɪ'tentɪv/ *a* (*memory*)
bueno
**rethink** /riː'θɪŋk/ *vt* (*pt* **rethought**)
considerar de nuevo
**reticen|ce** /'retɪsns/ *n* reserva *f*. ~**t**
/'retɪsnt/ *a* reservado, callado
**retina** /'retɪn∂/ *n* retina *f*

**retinue** /'retɪnjuː/ *n* séquito *m*
**retir|e** /rɪ'taɪ∂(r)/ *vi* (*from work*) ju-
bilarse; (*withdraw*) retirarse; (*go to
bed*) acostarse. ● *vt* jubilar. ~**ed** *a*
jubilado. ~**ement** *n* jubilación *f*.
~**ing** /rɪ'taɪ∂rɪŋ/ *a* reservado
**retort** /rɪ'tɔːt/ *vt/i* replicar. ● *n* réplica *f*
**retrace** /riː'treɪs/ *vt* repasar. ~
**one's steps** volver sobre sus pasos
**retract** /rɪ'trækt/ *vt* retirar. ● *vi*
retractarse
**retrain** /riː'treɪn/ *vt* reciclar,
reeducar
**retreat** /rɪ'triːt/ *vi* retirarse. ● *n* retirada *f*; (*place*) refugio *m*
**retrial** /rɪ'traɪ∂l/ *n* nuevo proceso *m*
**retribution** /retrɪ'bjuːʃn/ *n* justo *m*
castigo
**retriev|al** /rɪ'triːvl/ *n* recuperación *f*.
~**e** /rɪ'triːv/ *vt* (*recover*) recuperar;
(*save*) salvar; (*put right*) reparar.
~**er** *n* (*dog*) perro *m* cobrador
**retrograde** /'retr∂greɪd/ *a* retrógrado
**retrospect** /'retr∂spekt/ *n* retros-
pección *f*. **in** ~ retrospectivamente. ~**ive** /-'spektɪv/ *a* retrospectivo
**return** /rɪ'tɜːn/ *vi* volver; (*reappear*)
reaparecer. ● *vt* devolver; (*com*)
declarar; (*pol*) elegir. ● *n* vuelta *f*;
(*com*) ganancia *f*; (*restitution*) devo-
lución *f*. ~ **of income** *n* declaración
*f* de ingresos. **in** ~ **for** a cambio de.
**many happy** ~**s!** ¡feliz cumpleaños!
~**ing** /rɪ'tɜːnɪŋ/ *a*. ~**ing officer** *n*
escrutador *m*. ~ **match** *n* partido *m*
de desquite. ~ **ticket** *n* billete *m* de
ida y vuelta. ~**s** *npl* (*com*) ingresos
*mpl*
**reunion** /riː'juːnɪ∂n/ *n* reunión *f*
**reunite** /riːjuː'naɪt/ *vt* reunir
**rev** /rev/ *n* (*auto*, *fam*) revolución *f*.
● *vt/i*. ~ (**up**) (*pt* **revved**) (*auto*,
*fam*) acelerar(se)
**revamp** /riː'væmp/ *vt* renovar
**reveal** /rɪ'viːl/ *vt* revelar. ~**ing** *a*
revelador
**revel** /'revl/ *vi* (*pt* **revelled**) jaranear.
~ **in** deleitarse en. ~**ry** *n* juerga *f*
**revelation** /rev∂'leɪʃn/ *n* revelación
*f*
**revenge** /rɪ'vendʒ/ *n* venganza *f*;
(*sport*) desquite *m*. **take** ~
vengarse. ● *vt* vengar. ~**ful** *a* vin-
dicativo, vengativo
**revenue** /'rev∂njuː/ *n* ingresos *mpl*

**reverberate** /rɪ'vɜːbəreɪt/ vi ⟨light⟩ reverberar; ⟨sound⟩ resonar
**revere** /rɪ'vɪə(r)/ vt venerar
**reverence** /'revərəns/ n reverencia f
**reverend** /'revərənd/ a reverendo
**reverent** /'revərənt/ a reverente
**reverie** /'revərɪ/ n ensueño m
**revers** /rɪ'vɪə/ n (pl **revers** /rɪ'vɪəz/) n solapa f
**revers|al** /rɪ'vɜːsl/ n inversión f. **~e** /rɪ'vɜːs/ a inverso. ● n contrario m; (back) revés m; (auto) marcha f atrás. ● vt invertir; anular ⟨decision⟩; (auto) dar marcha atrás a. ● vi (auto) dar marcha atrás
**revert** /rɪ'vɜːt/ vi. **~ to** volver a
**review** /rɪ'vjuː/ n repaso m; (mil) revista f; (of book, play, etc) crítica f. ● vt analizar ⟨situation⟩; reseñar ⟨book, play, etc⟩. **~er** n crítico m
**revile** /rɪ'vaɪl/ vt injuriar
**revis|e** /rɪ'vaɪz/ vt revisar; (schol) repasar. **~ion** /-ɪʒn/ n revisión f; (schol) repaso m
**reviv|al** /rɪ'vaɪvl/ n restablecimiento m; (of faith) despertar m; (of play) reestreno m. **~e** /rɪ'vaɪv/ vt restablecer; resucitar ⟨person⟩. ● vi restablecerse; ⟨person⟩ volver en sí
**revoke** /rɪ'vəʊk/ vt revocar
**revolt** /rɪ'vəʊlt/ vi sublevarse. ● vt dar asco a. ● n sublevación f
**revolting** /rɪ'vəʊltɪŋ/ a asqueroso
**revolution** /revə'luːʃn/ n revolución f. **~ary** a & n revolucionario (m). **~ize** vt revolucionar
**revolve** /rɪ'vɒlv/ vi girar
**revolver** /rɪ'vɒlvə(r)/ n revólver m
**revolving** /rɪ'vɒlvɪŋ/ a giratorio
**revue** /rɪ'vjuː/ n revista f
**revulsion** /rɪ'vʌlʃn/ n asco m
**reward** /rɪ'wɔːd/ n recompensa f. ● vt recompensar. **~ing** a remunerador; (worthwhile) que vale la pena
**rewrite** /riːˈraɪt/ vt (pt **rewrote**, pp **rewritten**) escribir de nuevo; (change) redactar de nuevo
**rhapsody** /'ræpsədɪ/ n rapsodia f
**rhetoric** /'retərɪk/ n retórica f. **~al** /rɪ'tɒrɪkl/ a retórico
**rheumati|c** /ruː'mætɪk/ a reumático. **~sm** /'ruːmətɪzəm/ n reumatismo m
**rhinoceros** /raɪ'nɒsərəs/ n (pl **-oses**) rinoceronte m
**rhubarb** /'ruːbɑːb/ n ruibarbo m
**rhyme** /raɪm/ n rima f; (poem) poesía f. ● vt/i rimar

**rhythm** /'rɪðəm/ n ritmo m. **~ic(al)** /'rɪðmɪk(l)/ a rítmico
**rib** /rɪb/ n costilla f. **—vt** (pt **ribbed**) (fam) tomar el pelo a
**ribald** /'rɪbld/ a obsceno, verde
**ribbon** /'rɪbən/ n cinta f
**rice** /raɪs/ n arroz m. **~ pudding** n arroz con leche
**rich** /rɪtʃ/ a (-er, -est) rico. ● n ricos mpl. **~es** npl riquezas fpl. **~ly** adv ricamente. **~ness** n riqueza f
**rickety** /'rɪkətɪ/ a (shaky) cojo, desvencijado
**ricochet** /'rɪkəʃeɪ/ n rebote m. ● vi rebotar
**rid** /rɪd/ vt (pt **rid**, pres p **ridding**) librar (of de). **get ~ of** deshacerse de. **~dance** /'rɪdns/ n. **good ~dance!** ¡qué alivio!
**ridden** /'rɪdn/ see **ride**. ● a (infested) infestado. **~ by** (oppressed) agobiado de
**riddle**[1] /'rɪdl/ n acertijo m
**riddle**[2] /'rɪdl/ vt acribillar. **be ~d with** estar lleno de
**ride** /raɪd/ vi (pt **rode**, pp **ridden**) (on horseback) montar; (go) ir (en bicicleta, a caballo etc). **take s.o. for a ~** (fam) engañarle a uno. ● vt montar a ⟨horse⟩; ir en ⟨bicycle⟩; recorrer ⟨distance⟩. ● n (on horse) cabalgata f; (in car) paseo m en coche. **~r** /-ə(r)/ n (on horse) jinete m; (cyclist) ciclista m & f; (in document) cláusula f adicional
**ridge** /rɪdʒ/ n línea f, arruga f; (of mountain) cresta f; (of roof) caballete m
**ridicul|e** /'rɪdɪkjuːl/ n irrisión f. ● vt ridiculizar. **~ous** /rɪ'dɪkjʊləs/ a ridículo
**riding** /'raɪdɪŋ/ n equitación f
**rife** /raɪf/ a difundido. **~ with** lleno de
**riff-raff** /'rɪfræf/ n gentuza f
**rifle**[1] /'raɪfl/ n fusil m
**rifle**[2] /'raɪfl/ vt saquear
**rifle-range** /'raɪflreɪndʒ/ n campo m de tiro
**rift** /rɪft/ n grieta f; (fig) ruptura f
**rig**[1] /rɪg/ vt (pt **rigged**) aparejar. ● n (at sea) plataforma f de perforación. **~ up** vt improvisar
**rig**[2] /rɪg/ vt (pej) amañar
**right** /raɪt/ a (correct, fair) exacto, justo; (morally) bueno; (not left) derecho; (suitable) adecuado. ● n (entitlement) derecho m; (not left) derecha f; (not evil) bien m. **~ of**

**way** *n* (*auto*) prioridad *f*. **be in the ~**
tener razón. **on the ~** a la derecha.
**put ~** rectificar. ● *vt* enderezar;
(*fig*) corregir. ● *adv* a la derecha;
(*directly*) derecho; (*completely*)
completamente; (*well*) bien. **~**
**away** *adv* inmediatamente. **~**
**angle** *n* ángulo *m* recto
**righteous** /'raɪtʃəs/ *a* recto; (*cause*)
justo
**right: ~ful** /'raɪtfl/ *a* legítimo.
**~fully** *adv* legítimamente. **~hand**
**man** *n* brazo *m* derecho. **~ly** *adv*
justamente. **~ wing** *a* (*pol*) *n*
derechista
**rigid** /'rɪdʒɪd/ *a* rígido. **~ity**
/-'dʒɪdɪtɪ/ *n* rigidez *f*
**rigmarole** /'rɪgmərəʊl/ *n* galimatías
*m invar*
**rig|orous** /'rɪgərəs/ *a* riguroso.
**~our** /'rɪgə(r)/ *n* rigor *m*
**rig-out** /'rɪgaʊt/ *n* (*fam*) atavío *m*
**rile** /raɪl/ *vt* (*fam*) irritar
**rim** /rɪm/ *n* borde *m*; (*of wheel*) llanta
*f*; (*of glasses*) montura *f*. **~med** *a*
bordeado
**rind** /raɪnd/ *n* corteza *f*; (*of fruit*) cáscara *f*
**ring¹** /rɪŋ/ *n* (*circle*) círculo *m*; (*circle
of metal etc*) aro *m*; (*on finger*) anillo
*m*; (*on finger with stone*) sortija *f*;
(*boxing*) cuadrilátero *m*; (*bullring*)
ruedo *m*, redondel *m*, plaza *f*; (*for
circus*) pista *f*. ● *vt* rodear
**ring²** /rɪŋ/ *n* (*of bell*) toque *m*; (*tinkle*)
tintineo *m*; (*telephone call*) llamada
*f*. ● *vt* (*pt* **rang**, *pp* **rung**) hacer
sonar; (*telephone*) llamar por teléfono. **~ the bell** tocar el timbre. ● *v*
sonar. **~ back** *vt/i* volver a llamar.
**~ off** *vi* colgar. **~ up** *vt* llamar por
teléfono
**ring: ~leader** /'rɪŋliːdə(r)/ *n* cabecilla *f*. **~ road** *n* carretera *f* de
circunvalación
**rink** /rɪŋk/ *n* pista *f*
**rinse** /rɪns/ *vt* enjuagar. ● *n* acla-
rado *m*; (*of dishes*) enjuague *m*; (*for
hair*) reflejo *m*
**riot** /'raɪət/ *n* disturbio *m*; (*of colours*) profusión *f*. **run ~** desen-
frenarse. ● *vi* amotinarse. **~er** *n*
amotinador *m*. **~ous** *a* tumultuoso
**rip** /rɪp/ *vt* (*pt* **ripped**) rasgar. ● *vi*
rasgarse. **let ~** (*fig*) soltar. ● *n* ras-
gadura *f*. **~ off** *vt* (*sl*) robar. **~cord**
*n* (*of parachute*) cuerda *f* de
abertura

**ripe** /raɪp/ *a* (**-er, -est**) maduro. **~n**
/'raɪpən/ *vt/i* madurar. **~ness** *n*
madurez *f*
**rip-off** /'rɪpɒf/ *n* (*sl*) timo *m*
**ripple** /'rɪpl/ *n* rizo *m*; (*sound*) murmullo *m*. ● *vt* rizar. ● *vi* rizarse
**rise** /raɪz/ *vi* (*pt* **rose**, *pp* **risen**)
levantarse; (*rebel*) sublevarse;
(*river*) crecer; (*prices*) subir. ● *n* subida *f*; (*land*) altura *f*; (*increase*)
aumento *m*; (*to power*) ascenso *m*.
**give ~ to** ocasionar. **~r** /-ə(r)/ *n*.
**early ~r** *n* madrugador *m*
**rising** /'raɪzɪŋ/ *n* (*revolt*) sublevación *f*. ● *a* (*sun*) naciente. **~**
**generation** *n* nueva generación *f*
**risk** /rɪsk/ *n* riesgo *m*. ● *vt* arriesgar.
**~y** *a* (**-ier, -iest**) arriesgado
**risqué** /'riːskeɪ/ *a* subido de color
**rissole** /'rɪsəʊl/ *n* croqueta *f*
**rite** /raɪt/ *n* rito *m*
**ritual** /'rɪtʃʊəl/ *a* & *n* ritual (*m*)
**rival** /'raɪvl/ *a* & *n* rival (*m*). ● *vt* (*pt*
**rivalled**) rivalizar con. **~ry** *n* rivalidad *f*
**river** /'rɪvə(r)/ *n* río *m*
**rivet** /'rɪvɪt/ *n* remache *m*. ● *vt*
remachar. **~ing** *a* fascinante
**Riviera** /rɪvɪ'erə/ *n*. **the (French) ~**
la Costa *f* Azul. **the (Italian) ~** la
Riviera *f* (Italiana)
**rivulet** /'rɪvjʊlɪt/ *n* riachuelo *m*
**road** /rəʊd/ *n* (*in town*) calle *f*;
(*between towns*) carretera *f*, (*way*)
camino *m*. **on the ~** en camino.
**~hog** *n* conductor *m* descortés.
**~house** *n* albergue *m*. **~map** *n*
mapa *m* de carreteras. **~side**
/'rəʊdsaɪd/ *n* borde *m* de la carretera. **~ sign** *n* señal *f* de tráfico.
**~way** /'rəʊdweɪ/ *n* calzada *f*.
**~works** *npl* obras *fpl*. **~worthy**
/'rəʊdwɜːðɪ/ *a* (*vehicle*) seguro
**roam** /rəʊm/ *vi* vagar
**roar** /rɔː(r)/ *n* rugido *m*; (*laughter*)
carcajada *f*. ● *vt/i* rugir. **~ past**
(*vehicles*) pasar con estruendo. **~**
**with laughter** reírse a carcajadas.
**~ing** /'rɔːrɪŋ/ *a* (*trade etc*) activo
**roast** /rəʊst/ *vt* asar; tostar (*coffee*).
● *vi* asarse; (*person, coffee*) tostarse.
● *a* & *n* asado (*m*). **~ beef** *n* rosbif *m*
**rob** /rɒb/ *vt* (*pt* **robbed**) robar; asaltar (*bank*). **~ of** privar de. **~ber** *n*
ladrón *m*; (*of bank*) atracador *m*.
**~bery** *n* robo *m*
**robe** /rəʊb/ *n* manto *m*; (*univ etc*)
toga *f*. **bath-~** *n* albornoz *m*
**robin** /'rɒbɪn/ *n* petirrojo *m*

**robot** /'rəʊbɒt/ n robot m, autómata m

**robust** /rəʊ'bʌst/ a robusto

**rock**[1] /rɒk/ n roca f; (*boulder*) peñasco m; (*sweet*) caramelo m en forma de barra; (*of Gibraltar*) peñón m. **on the ~s** (*drink*) con hielo; (*fig*) arruinado. **be on the ~s** (*marriage etc*) andar mal

**rock**[2] /rɒk/ vt mecer; (*shake*) sacudir. ● vi mecerse; (*shake*) sacudirse. ● n (*mus*) música f rock

**rock**: **~-bottom** a (*fam*) bajísimo. **~ery** /'rɒkərɪ/ n cuadro m alpino, rocalla f

**rocket** /'rɒkɪt/ n cohete m

**rock**: **~ing-chair** n mecedora f. **~ing-horse** n caballo m de balancín. **~y** /'rɒkɪ/ a (-ier, -iest) rocoso; (*fig, shaky*) bamboleante

**rod** /rɒd/ n vara f; (*for fishing*) caña f; (*metal*) barra f

**rode** /rəʊd/ *see* **ride**

**rodent** /'rəʊdnt/ n roedor m

**rodeo** /rə'deɪəʊ/ n (*pl* -os) rodeo m

**roe**[1] /rəʊ/ n (*fish eggs*) hueva f

**roe**[2] /rəʊ/ (*pl* **roe**, *or* **roes**) (*deer*) corzo m

**rogu|e** /rəʊg/ n pícaro m. **~ish** a picaresco

**role** /rəʊl/ n papel m

**roll** /rəʊl/ vt hacer rodar; (*roll up*) enrollar; (*flatten lawn*) allanar; aplanar (*pastry*). ● vi rodar; (*ship*) balancearse; (*on floor*) revolcarse. **be ~ing (in money)** (*fam*) nadar (en dinero). ● n rollo m; (*of ship*) balanceo m; (*of drum*) redoble m; (*of thunder*) retumbo m; (*bread*) panecillo m; (*list*) lista f. **~ over** vi (*turn over*) dar una vuelta. **~ up** vt enrollar; arremangar (*sleeve*). ● vi (*fam*) llegar. **~-call** n lista f

**roller** /'rəʊlə(r)/ n rodillo m; (*wheel*) rueda f; (*for hair*) rulo m, bigudí m. **~-coaster** n montaña f rusa. **~-skate** n patín m de ruedas

**rollicking** /'rɒlɪkɪŋ/ a alegre

**rolling** /'rəʊlɪŋ/ a ondulado. **~-pin** n rodillo m

**Roman** /'rəʊmən/ a & n romano (m). **~ Catholic** a & n católico (m) (romano)

**romance** /rəʊ'mæns/ n novela f romántica; (*love*) amor m; (*affair*) aventura f

**Romania** /rəʊ'meɪnɪə/ n Rumania f. **~n** a & n rumano (m)

**romantic** /rəʊ'mæntɪk/ a romántico. **~ism** n romanticismo m

**Rome** /'rəʊm/ n Roma f

**romp** /rɒmp/ vi retozar. ● n retozo m

**rompers** /'rɒmpəz/ npl pelele m

**roof** /ruːf/ n techo m, tejado m; (*of mouth*) paladar m. ● vt techar. **~-garden** n jardín m en la azotea. **~-rack** n baca f. **~-top** n tejado m

**rook**[1] /rʊk/ n grajo m

**rook**[2] /rʊk/ (*in chess*) torre f

**room** /ruːm/ n cuarto m, habitación f; (*bedroom*) dormitorio m; (*space*) sitio m; (*large hall*) sala f. **~y** a espacioso; (*clothes*) holgado

**roost** /ruːst/ n percha f. ● vi descansar. **~er** n gallo m

**root**[1] /ruːt/ n raíz f. **take ~** echar raíces. ● vt hacer arraigar. ● vi echar raíces, arraigarse

**root**[2] /ruːt/ vt/i. **~ about** vi hurgar. **~ for** vi (*Amer, sl*) alentar. **~ out** vt extirpar

**rootless** /'ruːtlɪs/ a desarraigado

**rope** /rəʊp/ n cuerda f. **know the ~s** estar al corriente. ● vt atar. **~ in** vt agarrar

**rosary** /'rəʊzərɪ/ n (*relig*) rosario m

**rose**[1] /rəʊz/ n rosa f; (*nozzle*) roseta f

**rose**[2] /rəʊz/ *see* **rise**

**rosé** /'rəʊzeɪ/ n (*vino m*) rosado m

**rosette** /rəʊ'zet/ n escarapela f

**roster** /'rɒstə(r)/ n lista f

**rostrum** /'rɒstrəm/ n tribuna f

**rosy** /'rəʊzɪ/ a (-ier, -iest) rosado; (*skin*) sonrosado

**rot** /rɒt/ vt (*pt* **rotted**) pudrir. ● vi pudrirse. ● n putrefacción f; (*sl*) tonterías fpl

**rota** /'rəʊtə/ n lista f

**rotary** /'rəʊtərɪ/ a giratorio, rotativo

**rotat|e** /rəʊ'teɪt/ vt girar; (*change round*) alternar. ● vi girar; (*change round*) alternarse. **~ion** /-∫n/ n rotación f

**rote** /rəʊt/ n. **by ~** maquinalmente, de memoria

**rotten** /'rɒtn/ a podrido; (*fam*) desagradable

**rotund** /rəʊ'tʌnd/ a redondo; (*person*) regordete

**rouge** /ruːʒ/ n colorete m

**rough** /rʌf/ a (-er, -est) áspero; (*person*) tosco; (*bad*) malo; (*ground*) accidentado; (*violent*) brutal; (*approximate*) aproximado; (*diamond*) bruto. ● adv duro. **~ copy** n, **~ draft** n borrador m. ● n (*ruffian*) matón *m*. ● *vt*. ~ **it** vivir sin comodidades. ~ **out** *vt* esbozar

**roughage** /'rʌfidʒ/ *n* alimento *m* indigesto, afrecho *m*; (*for animals*) forraje *m*

**rough**: **~-and-ready** *a* improvisado. **~-and-tumble** *n* riña *f*. **~ly** *adv* toscamente; (*more or less*) más o menos. **~ness** *n* aspereza *f*; (*lack of manners*) incultura *f*; (*crudeness*) tosquedad *f*

**roulette** /ru:'let/ *n* ruleta *f*

**round** /raʊnd/ *a* (**-er, -est**) redondo. ● *n* círculo *m*; (*slice*) tajada *f*; (*of visits, drinks*) ronda *f*; (*of competition*) vuelta *f*; (*boxing*) asalto *m*. ● *prep* alrededor de. ● *adv* alrededor. ~ **about** (*approximately*) aproximadamente. **come ~ to, go ~ to** (*a friend etc*) pasar por casa de. ● *vt* redondear; doblar ‹*corner*›. ~ **off** *vt* terminar. ~ **up** *vt* reunir; redondear ‹*price*›

**roundabout** /'raʊndəbaʊt/ *n* tiovivo *m*; (*for traffic*) glorieta *f*. ● *a* indirecto

**rounders** /'raʊndəz/ *n* juego *m* parecido al béisbol

**round**: **~ly** *adv* (*bluntly*) francamente. ~ **trip** *n* viaje *m* de ida y vuelta. **~-up** *n* reunión *f*; (*of suspects*) redada *f*

**rous|e** /raʊz/ *vt* despertar. **~ing** *a* excitante

**rout** /raʊt/ *n* derrota *f*. ● *vt* derrotar

**route** /ru:t/ *n* ruta *f*; (*naut, aviat*) rumbo *m*; (*of bus*) línea *f*

**routine** /ru:'ti:n/ *n* rutina *f*. ● *a* rutinario

**rov|e** /rəʊv/ *vt/i* vagar (por). **~ing** *a* errante

**row**[1] /rəʊ/ *n* fila *f*

**row**[2] /rəʊ/ *n* (*in boat*) paseo *m* en bote (de remos). ● *vi* remar

**row**[3] /raʊ/ *n* (*noise, fam*) ruido *m*; (*quarrel*) pelea *f*. ● *vi* (*fam*) pelearse

**rowdy** /'raʊdɪ/ *a* (**-ier, -iest**) *n* ruidoso

**rowing** /'rəʊɪŋ/ *n* remo *m*. **~boat** *n* bote *m* de remos

**royal** /'rɔɪəl/ *a* real. **~ist** *a* & *n* monárquico (*m*). **~ly** *adv* magníficamente. **~ty** /'rɔɪəltɪ/ *n* familia *f* real; (*payment*) derechos *mpl* de autor

**rub** /rʌb/ *vt* (*pt* **rubbed**) frotar. ~ **it in** insistir en algo. ● *n* frotamiento *m*. ~ **off on s.o.** *vi* pegársele a uno. ~ **out** *vt* borrar

**rubber** /'rʌbə(r)/ *n* goma *f*. ~ **band** *n* goma *f* (elástica). ~ **stamp** *n* sello *m* de goma. **~-stamp** *vt* (*fig*) aprobar maquinalmente. **~y** *a* parecido al caucho

**rubbish** /'rʌbɪʃ/ *n* basura *f*; (*junk*) trastos *mpl*; (*fig*) tonterías *fpl*. **~y** *a* sin valor

**rubble** /'rʌbl/ *n* escombros *m*; (*small*) cascajo *m*

**ruby** /'ru:bɪ/ *n* rubí *m*

**rucksack** /'rʌksæk/ *n* mochila *f*

**rudder** /'rʌdə(r)/ *n* timón *m*

**ruddy** /'rʌdɪ/ *a* (**-ier, -iest**) rubicundo; (*sl*) maldito

**rude** /ru:d/ *a* (**-er, -est**) descortés, mal educado; (*improper*) indecente; (*brusque*) brusco. **~ly** *adv* con descortesía. **~ness** *n* descortesía *f*

**rudiment** /'ru:dɪmənt/ *n* rudimento *m*. **~ary** /-'mentrɪ/ *a* rudimentario

**rueful** /'ru:fl/ *a* triste

**ruffian** /'rʌfɪən/ *n* rufián *m*

**ruffle** /'rʌfl/ *vt* despeinar ‹*hair*›; arrugar ‹*clothes*›. ● *n* (*frill*) volante *m*, fruncido *m*

**rug** /rʌg/ *n* tapete *m*; (*blanket*) manta *f*

**Rugby** /'rʌgbɪ/ *n*. ~ **(football)** *n* rugby *m*

**rugged** /'rʌgɪd/ *a* desigual; (*landscape*) accidentado; (*fig*) duro

**ruin** /'ru:ɪn/ *n* ruina *f*. ● *vt* arruinar. **~ous** *a* ruinoso

**rule** /ru:l/ *n* regla *f*; (*custom*) costumbre *f*; (*pol*) dominio *m*. **as a ~** por regla general. ● *vt* gobernar; (*master*) dominar; (*jurid*) decretar; (*decide*) decidir. ~ **out** *vt* descartar. **~d paper** *n* papel *m* rayado

**ruler** /'ru:lə(r)/ *n* (*sovereign*) soberano *m*; (*leader*) gobernante *m* & *f*; (*measure*) regla *f*

**ruling** /'ru:lɪŋ/ *a* ‹*class*› dirigente. ● *n* decisión *f*

**rum** /rʌm/ *n* ron *m*

**rumble** /'rʌmbl/ *vi* retumbar; ‹*stomach*› hacer ruidos. ● *n* retumbo *m*; (*of stomach*) ruido *m*

**ruminant** /'ru:mɪnənt/ *a* & *n* rumiante (*m*)

**rummage** /'rʌmɪdʒ/ *vi* hurgar

**rumour** /'ru:mə(r)/ *n* rumor *m*. ● *vt*. **it is ~ed that** se dice que

**rump** /rʌmp/ *n* (*of horse*) grupa *f*; (*of fowl*) rabadilla *f*. ~ **steak** *n* filete *m*

**rumpus** /'rʌmpəs/ *n* (*fam*) jaleo *m*

**run** /rʌn/ *vi* (*pt* **ran**, *pp* **run**, *pres p* **running**) correr; (*flow*) fluir; (*pass*) pasar; ⟨*function*⟩ funcionar; ⟨*melt*⟩ derretirse; ⟨*bus etc*⟩ circular; ⟨*play*⟩ representarse (continuamente); ⟨*colours*⟩ correrse; (*in election*) presentarse. ● *vt* tener ⟨*house*⟩; ⟨*control*⟩ dirigir; correr ⟨*risk*⟩; (*drive*) conducir; (*pass*) pasar; (*present*) presentar; forzar ⟨*blockade*⟩. ～ **a temperature** tener fiebre. ● *n* corrida *f*, carrera *f*; (*journey*) viaje *m*; (*outing*) paseo *m*, excursión *f*; (*distance travelled*) recorrido *m*; (*ladder*) carrera *f*; (*ski*) pista *f*; (*series*) serie *f*. **at a** ～ corriendo. **have the** ～ **of** tener a su disposición. **in the long** ～ a la larga. **on the** ～ de fuga. ～ **across** *vt* toparse con ⟨*friend*⟩. ～ **away** *vi* escaparse. ～ **down** *vi* bajar corriendo; ⟨*clock*⟩ quedarse sin cuerda. ● *vt* (*auto*) atropellar; (*belittle*) denigrar. ～ **in** *vt* rodar ⟨*vehicle*⟩. ● *vi* entrar corriendo. ～ **into** *vt* toparse con ⟨*friend*⟩; (*hit*) chocar con. ～ **off** *vt* tirar ⟨*copies etc*⟩. ～ **out** *vi* salir corriendo; ⟨*liquid*⟩ salirse; (*fig*) agotarse. ～ **out of** quedar sin. ～ **over** *vt* (*auto*) atropellar. ～ **through** *vt* traspasar; (*revise*) repasar. ～ **up** *vt* hacerse ⟨*bill*⟩. ● *vi* subir corriendo. ～ **up against** tropezar con ⟨*difficulties*⟩. ～**away** /'rʌnəweɪ/ *a* fugitivo; ⟨*success*⟩ decisivo; ⟨*inflation*⟩ galopante. ● *n* fugitivo *m*. ～ **down** *a* ⟨*person*⟩ agotado. ～**down** *n* informe *m* detallado

**rung**[1] /rʌŋ/ *n* (*of ladder*) peldaño *m*

**rung**[2] /rʌŋ/ *see* **ring**

**run:** ～**ner** /'rʌnə(r)/ *n* corredor *m*; (*on sledge*) patín *m*. ～**ner bean** *n* judía *f* escarlata. ～**ner-up** *n* subcampeón *m*, segundo *m*. ～**ning** /'rʌnɪŋ/ *n* (*race*) carrera *f*. **be in the** ～**ning** tener posibilidades de ganar. ● *a* en marcha; ⟨*water*⟩ corriente; ⟨*commentary*⟩ en directo. **four times** ～**ning** cuatro veces seguidas. ～**ny** /'rʌnɪ/ *a* líquido; ⟨*nose*⟩ que moquea. ～**of-the-mill** *a* ordinario. ～**up** *n* período *m* que precede. ～**way** /'rʌnweɪ/ *n* pista *f*

**rupture** /'rʌptʃə(r)/ *n* ruptura *f*; (*med*) hernia *f*. ● *vt/i* quebrarse

**rural** /'rʊərəl/ *a* rural

**ruse** /ruːz/ *n* ardid *m*

**rush**[1] /rʌʃ/ *n* (*haste*) prisa *f*; (*crush*) bullicio *m*. ● *vi* precipitarse. ● *vt* apresurar; (*mil*) asaltar

**rush**[2] /rʌʃ/ *n* (*plant*) junco *m*

**rush-hour** /'rʌʃaʊə(r)/ *n* hora *f* punta

**rusk** /rʌsk/ *n* galleta *f*, tostada *f*

**russet** /'rʌsɪt/ *a* rojizo. ● *n* (*apple*) manzana *f* rojiza

**Russia** /'rʌʃə/ *n* Rusia *f*. ～**n** *a* & *n* ruso (*m*)

**rust** /rʌst/ *n* orín *m*. ● *vt* oxidar. ● *vi* oxidarse

**rustic** /'rʌstɪk/ *a* rústico

**rustle** /'rʌsl/ *vt* hacer susurrar; (*Amer*) robar. ～ **up** (*fam*) preparar. ● *vi* susurrar

**rust:** ～**proof** *a* inoxidable. ～**y** *a* (**-ier, -iest**) oxidado

**rut** /rʌt/ *n* surco *m*. **in a** ～ en la rutina de siempre

**ruthless** /'ruːθlɪs/ *a* despiadado. ～**ness** *n* crueldad *f*

**rye** /raɪ/ *n* centeno *m*

# S

**S** *abbr* (*south*) sur *m*

**sabbath** /'sæbəθ/ *n* día *m* de descanso; (*Christian*) domingo *m*; (*Jewish*) sábado *m*

**sabbatical** /sə'bætɪkl/ *a* sabático

**sabot|age** /'sæbətɑːʒ/ *n* sabotaje *m*. ● *vt* sabotear. ～**eur** /-'tɜː(r)/ *n* saboteador *m*

**saccharin** /'sækərɪn/ *n* sacarina *f*

**sachet** /'sæʃeɪ/ *n* bolsita *f*

**sack**[1] /sæk/ *n* saco *m*. **get the** ～ (*fam*) ser despedido. ● *vt* despedir. ～**ing** *n* arpillera *f*; (*fam*) despido *m*

**sack**[2] /sæk/ *vt* (*plunder*) saquear

**sacrament** /'sækrəmənt/ *n* sacramento *m*

**sacred** /'seɪkrɪd/ *a* sagrado

**sacrifice** /'sækrɪfaɪs/ *n* sacrificio *m*. ● *vt* sacrificar

**sacrileg|e** /'sækrɪlɪdʒ/ *n* sacrilegio *m*. ～**ious** /-'lɪdʒəs/ *a* sacrílego

**sacrosanct** /'sækrəʊsæŋkt/ *a* sacrosanto

**sad** /sæd/ *a* (**sadder, saddest**) triste. ～**den** /'sædn/ *vt* entristecer

**saddle** /'sædl/ *n* silla *f*. **be in the** ～ (*fig*) tener las riendas. ● *vt* ensillar ⟨*horse*⟩. ～ **s.o. with** (*fig*) cargar a uno con. ～**bag** *n* alforja *f*

**sad:** ～**ly** *adv* tristemente; (*fig*) desgraciadamente. ～**ness** *n* tristeza *f*

**sadis|m** /'seɪdɪzəm/ *n* sadismo *m*. ～**t** /'seɪdɪst/ *n* sádico *m*. ～**tic** /sə'dɪstɪk/ *a* sádico

**safari** /sə'fɑːrɪ/ n safari m

**safe** /seɪf/ a (**-er**, **-est**) seguro; (out of danger) salvo; (cautious) prudente. ~ **and sound** sano y salvo. ● n caja f fuerte. ~ **deposit** n caja f de seguridad. ~**guard** /'seɪfgɑːd/ n salvaguardia f. ● vt salvaguardar. ~**ly** adv sin peligro; (in safe place) en lugar seguro. ~**ty** /'seɪftɪ/ n seguridad f. ~**ty belt** n cinturón m de seguridad. ~**ty-pin** n imperdible m. ~**ty-valve** n válvula f de seguridad

**saffron** /'sæfrən/ n azafrán m

**sag** /sæg/ vi (pt **sagged**) hundirse; (give) aflojarse

**saga** /'sɑːgə/ n saga f

**sage**[1] /seɪdʒ/ n (wise person) sabio m. ● a sabio

**sage**[2] /seɪdʒ/ n (herb) salvia f

**sagging** /'sægɪŋ/ a hundido; (fig) decaído

**Sagittarius** /sædʒɪ'teərɪəs/ n (astr) Sagitario m

**sago** /'seɪgəʊ/ n sagú m

**said** /sed/ see **say**

**sail** /seɪl/ n vela f; (trip) paseo m (en barco). ● vi navegar; (leave) partir; (sport) practicar la vela; (fig) deslizarse. ● vt manejar ⟨boat⟩. ~**ing** n (sport) vela f. ~**ing-boat** n, ~**ing-ship** n barco m de vela. ~**or** /'seɪlə(r)/ n marinero m

**saint** /seɪnt, before name sənt/ n santo m. ~**ly** a santo

**sake** /seɪk/ n. **for the** ~ **of** por, por el amor de

**salacious** /sə'leɪʃəs/ a salaz

**salad** /'sæləd/ n ensalada f. ~ **bowl** n ensaladera f. ~ **cream** n mayonesa f. ~**dressing** n aliño m

**salar|ied** /'sælərɪd/ a asalariado. ~**y** /'sælərɪ/ n sueldo m

**sale** /seɪl/ n venta f; (at reduced prices) liquidación f. **for** ~ (sign) se vende. **on** ~ en venta. ~**able** /'seɪləbl/ a vendible. ~**sman** /'seɪlzmən/ n (pl **-men**) vendedor m; (in shop) dependiente m; (traveller) viajante m. ~**swoman** n (pl **-women**) vendedora f; (in shop) dependienta f

**salient** /'seɪlɪənt/ a saliente, destacado

**saliva** /sə'laɪvə/ n saliva f

**sallow** /'sæləʊ/ a (**-er**, **-est**) amarillento

**salmon** /'sæmən/ n invar salmón m. ~ **trout** n trucha f salmonada

**salon** /'sælɒn/ n salón m

**saloon** /sə'luːn/ n (on ship) salón m; (Amer, bar) bar m; (auto) turismo m

**salt** /sɔːlt/ n sal f. ● a salado. ● vt salar. ~**cellar** n salero m. ~**y** a salado

**salutary** /'sæljʊtrɪ/ a saludable

**salute** /sə'luːt/ n saludo m. ● vt saludar. ● vi hacer un saludo

**salvage** /'sælvɪdʒ/ n salvamento m; (goods) objetos mpl salvados. ● vt salvar

**salvation** /sæl'veɪʃn/ n salvación f

**salve** /sælv/ n ungüento m

**salver** /'sælvə(r)/ n bandeja f

**salvo** /'sælvəʊ/ n (pl **-os**) salva f

**same** /seɪm/ a igual (as que); (before noun) mismo (as que). **at the** ~ **time** al mismo tiempo. ● pron. **the** ~ el mismo, la misma, los mismos, las mismas. **do the** ~ **as** hacer como. ● adv. **the** ~ de la misma manera. **all the** ~ de todas formas

**sample** /'sɑːmpl/ n muestra f. ● vt probar ⟨food⟩

**sanatorium** /sænə'tɔːrɪəm/ n (pl **-ums**) sanatorio m

**sanctify** /'sæŋktɪfaɪ/ vt santificar

**sanctimonious** /sæŋktɪ'məʊnɪəs/ a beato

**sanction** /'sæŋkʃn/ n sanción f. ● vt sancionar

**sanctity** /'sæŋktətɪ/ n santidad f

**sanctuary** /'sæŋktʃʊərɪ/ n (relig) santuario m; (for wildlife) reserva f; (refuge) asilo m

**sand** /sænd/ n arena f. ● vt enarenar. ~**s** npl (beach) playa f

**sandal** /'sændl/ n sandalia f

**sand:** ~**castle** n castillo m de arena. ~**paper** /'sændpeɪpə(r)/ n papel m de lija. ● vt lijar. ~**storm** /'sændstɔːm/ n tempestad f de arena

**sandwich** /'sænwɪdʒ/ n bocadillo m, sandwich m. ● vt. ~**ed between** intercalado

**sandy** /'sændɪ/ a arenoso

**sane** /seɪn/ a (**-er**, **-est**) ⟨person⟩ cuerdo; ⟨judgement, policy⟩ razonable. ~**ly** adv sensatamente

**sang** /sæŋ/ see **sing**

**sanitary** /'sænɪtrɪ/ a higiénico; ⟨system etc⟩ sanitario. ~ **towel** n, ~ **napkin** n (Amer) compresa f (higiénica)

**sanitation** /sænɪ'teɪʃn/ n higiene f; (drainage) sistema m sanitario

**sanity** /'sænɪtɪ/ n cordura f; (fig) sensatez f

**sank** /sæŋk/ see **sink**

**Santa Claus** /'sæntəklɔːz/ n Papá m Noel

**sap** /sæp/ n (in plants) savia f. ● vt (pt **sapped**) agotar

**sapling** /'sæplɪŋ/ n árbol m joven

**sapphire** /'sæfaɪə(r)/ n zafiro m

**sarcas|m** /'sɑːkæzəm/ n sarcasmo m. **~tic** /-'kæstɪk/ a sarcástico

**sardine** /sɑː'diːn/ n sardina f

**Sardinia** /sɑː'dɪnɪə/ n Cerdeña f. **~n** a & n sardo (m)

**sardonic** /sɑː'dɒnɪk/ a sardónico

**sash** /sæʃ/ n (over shoulder) banda f; (round waist) fajín m. **~window** n ventana f de guillotina

**sat** /sæt/ see **sit**

**satanic** /sə'tænɪk/ a satánico

**satchel** /'sætʃl/ n cartera f

**satellite** /'sætəlaɪt/ n & a satélite (m)

**satiate** /'seɪʃɪeɪt/ vt saciar

**satin** /'sætɪn/ n raso m. ● a de raso; (like satin) satinado

**satir|e** /'sætaɪə(r)/ n sátira f. **~ical** /sə'tɪrɪkl/ a satírico. **~ist** /'sætərɪst/ n satírico m. **~ize** /'sætəraɪz/ vt satirizar

**satisfaction** /sætɪs'fækʃn/ n satisfacción f

**satisfactor|ily** /sætɪs'fæktərɪlɪ/ adv satisfactoriamente. **~y** /sætɪs'fæktərɪ/ a satisfactorio

**satisfy** /'sætɪsfaɪ/ vt satisfacer; (convince) convencer. **~ing** a satisfactorio

**satsuma** /sæt'suːmə/ n mandarina f

**saturat|e** /'sætʃəreɪt/ vt saturar, empapar. **~ed** a saturado, empapado. **~ion** /-'reɪʃn/ n saturación f

**Saturday** /'sætədeɪ/ n sábado m

**sauce** /sɔːs/ n salsa f; (cheek) descaro m. **~pan** /'sɔːspən/ n cazo m

**saucer** /'sɔːsə(r)/ n platillo m

**saucy** /'sɔːsɪ/ a (-ier, -iest) descarado

**Saudi Arabia** /saʊdɪə'reɪbɪə/ n Arabia f Saudí

**sauna** /'sɔːnə/ n sauna f

**saunter** /'sɔːntə(r)/ vi deambular, pasearse

**sausage** /'sɒsɪdʒ/ n salchicha f

**savage** /'sævɪdʒ/ a salvaje; (fierce) feroz; (furious, fam) rabioso. ● n salvaje m & f. ● vt atacar. **~ry** n ferocidad f

**sav|e** /seɪv/ vt salvar; ahorrar (money, time); (prevent) evitar. ● n (football) parada f. ● prep salvo, con excepción de. **~er** n ahorrador m. **~ing** n ahorro m. **~ings** npl ahorros mpl

**saviour** /'seɪvɪə(r)/ n salvador m

**savour** /'seɪvə(r)/ n sabor m. ● vt saborear. **~y** a (appetizing) sabroso; (not sweet) no dulce. ● n aperitivo m (no dulce)

**saw**[1] /sɔː/ see **see**[1]

**saw**[2] /sɔː/ n sierra f. ● vt (pt **sawed**, pp **sawn**) serrar. **~dust** /'sɔːdʌst/ n serrín m. **~n** /sɔːn/ see **saw**

**saxophone** /'sæksəfəʊn/ n saxófono m

**say** /seɪ/ vt/i (pt **said** /sed/) decir; rezar (prayer). **I ~!** ¡no me digas! ● n. **have a ~** expresar una opinión; (in decision) tener voz en capítulo. **have no ~** no tener ni voz ni voto. **~ing** /'seɪɪŋ/ n refrán m

**scab** /skæb/ n costra f; (blackleg, fam) esquirol m

**scaffold** /'skæfəʊld/ n (gallows) cadalso m, patíbulo m. **~ing** /'skæfəldɪŋ/ n (for workmen) andamio m

**scald** /skɔːld/ vt escaldar; calentar (milk etc). ● n escaldadura f

**scale**[1] /skeɪl/ n escala f

**scale**[2] /skeɪl/ n (of fish) escama f

**scale**[3] /skeɪl/ vt (climb) escalar. **~ down** vt reducir (proporcionalmente)

**scales** /skeɪlz/ npl (for weighing) balanza f, peso m

**scallop** /'skɒləp/ n venera f; (on dress) festón m

**scalp** /skælp/ n cuero m cabelludo. ● vt quitar el cuero cabelludo a

**scalpel** /'skælpəl/ n escalpelo m

**scamp** /skæmp/ n bribón m

**scamper** /'skæmpə(r)/ vi. **~ away** marcharse corriendo

**scampi** /'skæmpɪ/ npl gambas fpl grandes

**scan** /skæn/ vt (pt **scanned**) escudriñar; (quickly) echar un vistazo a; (radar) explorar. ● vi (poetry) estar bien medido

**scandal** /'skændl/ n escándalo m; (gossip) chismorreo m. **~ize** /'skændəlaɪz/ vt escandalizar. **~ous** a escandaloso

**Scandinavia** /skændɪ'neɪvɪə/ n Escandinavia f. **~n** a & n escandinavo (m)

**scant** /skænt/ a escaso. **~ily** adv insuficientemente. **~y** /'skæntɪ/ a (-ier, -iest) escaso

**scapegoat** /'skeɪpgəʊt/ n cabeza f de turco

**scar** /skɑ:(r)/ n cicatriz f. ● vt (pt **scarred**) dejar una cicatriz en. ● vi cicatrizarse

**scarc|e** /skeəs/ a (-er, -est) escaso. **make o.s.** ~**e** (fam) mantenerse lejos. ~**ely** /'skeəslɪ/ adv apenas. ~**ity** n escasez f

**scare** /skeə(r)/ vt asustar. **be** ~**d** tener miedo. ● n susto m. ~**crow** /'skeəkrəʊ/ n espantapájaros m invar. ~**monger** /'skeəmʌŋgə(r)/ n alarmista m & f

**scarf** /skɑ:f/ n (pl **scarves**) bufanda f; (over head) pañuelo m

**scarlet** /'skɑ:lət/ a escarlata f. ~ **fever** n escarlatina f

**scary** /'skeərɪ/ a (-ier, -iest) que da miedo

**scathing** /'skeɪðɪŋ/ a mordaz

**scatter** /'skætə(r)/ vt (throw) esparcir; (disperse) dispersar. ● vi dispersarse. ~**brained** a atolondrado. ~**ed** a disperso; (occasional) esporádico

**scatty** /'skætɪ/ a (-ier, -iest) (sl) atolondrado

**scavenge** /'skævɪndʒ/ vi buscar (en la basura). ~**r** /-ə(r)/ n (vagrant) persona f que busca objetos en la basura

**scenario** /sɪ'nɑ:rɪəʊ/ n (pl -os) argumento; (of film) guión m

**scen|e** /si:n/ n escena f; (sight) vista f; (fuss) lío m. **behind the** ~**es** entre bastidores. ~**ery** /'si:nərɪ/ n paisaje m; (in theatre) decorado m. ~**ic** /'si:nɪk/ a pintoresco

**scent** /sent/ n olor m; (perfume) perfume m; (trail) pista f. ● vt presentir; (make fragrant) perfumar

**sceptic** /'skeptɪk/ n escéptico m. ~**al** a escéptico. ~**ism** /-sɪzəm/ n escepticismo m

**sceptre** /'septə(r)/ n cetro m

**schedule** /'ʃedjuːl, 'skedjuːl/ n programa f; (timetable) horario m. **behind** ~ con retraso. **on** ~ sin retraso. ● vt proyectar. ~**d flight** n vuelo m regular

**scheme** /ski:m/ n proyecto m; (plot) intriga f. ● vi hacer proyectos; (pej) intrigar. ~**r** n intrigante m & f

**schism** /'sɪzəm/ n cisma m

**schizophrenic** /skɪtsə'frenɪk/ a & n esquizofrénico (m)

**scholar** /'skɒlə(r)/ n erudito m. ~**ly** a erudito. ~**ship** n erudición f; (grant) beca f

**scholastic** /skə'læstɪk/ a escolar

**school** /skuːl/ n escuela f; (of univ) facultad f. ● a (age, holidays, year) escolar. ● vt enseñar; (discipline) disciplinar. ~**boy** /'skuːlbɔɪ/ n colegial m. ~**girl** /-gɜːl/ n colegiala f. ~**ing** n instrucción f. ~**master** /'skuːlmɑːstə(r)/ n (primary) maestro m; (secondary) profesor m. ~**mistress** n (primary) maestra f; (secondary) profesora f. ~**teacher** n (primary) maestro m; (secondary) profesor m

**schooner** /'skuːnə(r)/ n goleta f; (glass) vaso m grande

**sciatica** /saɪ'ætɪkə/ n ciática f

**scien|ce** /'saɪəns/ n ciencia f. ~**ce fiction** n ciencia f ficción. ~**tific** /-'tɪfɪk/ a científico. ~**tist** /'saɪəntɪst/ n científico m

**scintillate** /'sɪntɪleɪt/ vi centellear

**scissors** /'sɪsəz/ npl tijeras fpl

**sclerosis** /sklə'rəʊsɪs/ n esclerosis f

**scoff** /skɒf/ vt (sl) zamparse. ● vi. ~ **at** mofarse de

**scold** /skəʊld/ vt regañar. ~**ing** n regaño m

**scone** /skɒn/ n (tipo m de) bollo m

**scoop** /skuːp/ n paleta f; (news) noticia f exclusiva. ● vt. ~ **out** excavar. ~ **up** recoger

**scoot** /skuːt/ vi (fam) largarse corriendo. ~**er** /'skuːtə(r)/ n escúter m; (for child) patinete m

**scope** /skəʊp/ n alcance m; (opportunity) oportunidad f

**scorch** /skɔːtʃ/ vt chamuscar. ~**er** n (fam) día m de mucho calor. ~**ing** a (fam) de mucho calor

**score** /skɔ:(r)/ n tanteo m; (mus) partitura f; (twenty) veintena f; (reason) motivo m. **on that** ~ en cuanto a eso. ● vt marcar; (slash) rayar; (mus) instrumentar; conseguir (success). ● vi marcar un tanto; (keep score) tantear. ~ **over s.o.** aventajar a. ~**r** /-ə(r)/ n tanteador m

**scorn** /skɔːn/ n desdén m. ● vt desdeñar. ~**ful** a desdeñoso. ~**fully** adv desdeñosamente

**Scorpio** /'skɔːpɪəʊ/ n (astr) Escorpión m

**scorpion** /'skɔːpɪən/ n escorpión m

**Scot** /skɒt/ n escocés m. ~**ch** /skɒtʃ/ a escocés. ● n güisqui m

**scotch** /skɒtʃ/ vt frustrar; (suppress) suprimir

**scot-free** /skɒt'friː/ a impune; (gratis) sin pagar

**Scot:** ~**land** /'skɒtlənd/ n Escocia f.
~**s** a escocés. ~**sman** n escocés m.
~**swoman** n escocesa f. ~**tish** a
escocés

**scoundrel** /'skaʊndrəl/ n canalla f

**scour** /'skaʊə(r)/ vt estregar;
(search) registrar. ~**er** n estropajo
m

**scourge** /skɜːdʒ/ n azote m

**scout** /skaʊt/ n explorador m. **Boy
S**~ explorador m. • vi. ~ **(for)**
buscar

**scowl** /skaʊl/ n ceño m. • vi fruncir
el entrecejo

**scraggy** /'skrægɪ/ a (-ier, -iest)
descarnado

**scram** /skræm/ vi (sl) largarse

**scramble** /'skræmbl/ vi (clamber)
gatear. ~ **for** pelearse para
obtener. • vt revolver ⟨eggs⟩. • n
(difficult climb) subida f difícil;
(struggle) lucha f

**scrap** /skræp/ n pedacito m; (fight,
fam) pelea f. • vt (pt scrapped) desechar. ~**book** n álbum m de recortes. ~**s** npl sobras fpl

**scrape** /skreɪp/ n raspadura f; (fig)
apuro m. • vt raspar; (graze)
arañar; (rub) frotar. • vi. ~
**through** lograr pasar; aprobar por
los pelos ⟨exam⟩. ~ **together**
reunir. ~**r** /-ə(r)/ n raspador m

**scrap:** ~ **heap** n montón m de
deshechos. ~**iron** n chatarra f

**scrappy** /'skræpɪ/ a fragmentario,
pobre, de mala calidad

**scratch** /skrætʃ/ vt rayar; (with nail
etc) arañar; rascar ⟨itch⟩. • vi
arañar. • n raya f; (from nail etc)
arañazo m. **start from** ~ empezar
sin nada, empezar desde el principio. **up to** ~ al nivel requerido

**scrawl** /skrɔːl/ n garrapato m. • vt/i
garrapatear

**scrawny** /'skrɔːnɪ/ a (-ier, -iest)
descarnado

**scream** /skriːm/ vt/i gritar. • n grito
m

**screech** /skriːtʃ/ vi gritar; ⟨brakes
etc⟩ chirriar. • n grito m; (of brakes
etc) chirrido m

**screen** /skriːn/ n pantalla f; (folding)
biombo m. • vt (hide) ocultar; (protect) proteger; proyectar ⟨film⟩;
seleccionar ⟨candidates⟩

**screw** /skruː/ n tornillo m. • vt atornillar. ~**driver** /'skruːdraɪvə(r)/ n
destornillador m. ~ **up** atornillar;
entornar ⟨eyes⟩; torcer ⟨face⟩; (ruin,

sl) arruinar. ~**y** /'skruːɪ/ a (-ier,
-iest) (sl) chiflado

**scribble** /'skrɪbl/ vt/i garrapatear.
• n garrapato m

**scribe** /skraɪb/ n copista m & f

**script** /skrɪpt/ n escritura f; (of film
etc) guión m

**Scriptures** /'skrɪptʃəz/ npl Sagradas
Escrituras fpl

**script-writer** /'skrɪptraɪtə(r)/ n
guionista m & f

**scroll** /skrəʊl/ n rollo m (de
pergamino)

**scrounge** /skraʊndʒ/ vt/i obtener
de gorra; (steal) birlar. ~**r** /-ə(r)/ n
gorrón m

**scrub** /skrʌb/ n (land) maleza f;
(clean) fregado m. • vt/i (pt
scrubbed) fregar

**scruff** /skrʌf/ n. **the** ~ **of the neck** el
cogote m

**scruffy** /'skrʌfɪ/ a (-ier, -iest)
desaliñado

**scrum** /skrʌm/ n, **scrummage**
/'skrʌmɪdʒ/ n (Rugby) melée f

**scrup|le** /'skruːpl/ n escrúpulo m.
~**ulous** /-a scrupu-
loso. ~**ulously** adv escrupulosa-
mente

**scrutin|ize** /'skruːtɪnaɪz/ vt escu-
driñar. ~**y** /'skruːtɪnɪ/ n examen m
minucioso

**scuff** /skʌf/ vt arañar ⟨shoes⟩

**scuffle** /'skʌfl/ n pelea f

**scullery** /'skʌlərɪ/ n trascocina f

**sculpt** /skʌlpt/ vt/i esculpir. ~**or** n
escultor m. ~**ure** /-tʃə(r)/ n escul-
tura f. • vt/i esculpir

**scum** /skʌm/ n espuma f; (people,
pej) escoria f

**scurf** /skɜːf/ n caspa f

**scurrilous** /'skʌrɪləs/ a grosero

**scurry** /'skʌrɪ/ vi correr

**scurvy** /'skɜːvɪ/ n escorbuto m

**scuttle**[1] /'skʌtl/ n cubo m del carbón

**scuttle**[2] /'skʌtl/ vt barrenar ⟨ship⟩

**scuttle**[3] /'skʌtl/ vi. ~ **away** correr,
irse de prisa

**scythe** /saɪð/ n guadaña f

**SE** abbr (south-east) sudeste m

**sea** /siː/ n mar m. **at** ~ en el mar;
(fig) confuso. **by** ~ por mar.
~**board** /'siːbɔːd/ n litoral m.
~**farer** /'siːfeərə(r)/ n marinero m.
~**food** /'siːfuːd/ n mariscos mpl.
~**gull** /'siːgʌl/ n gaviota f. ~**horse**
n caballito m de mar, hipocampo m

**seal**[1] /siːl/ n sello m. • vt sellar. ~
**off** acordonar ⟨area⟩

**seal**[2] /siːl/ (*animal*) foca *f*

**sea level** /ˈsiːlevl/ *n* nivel *m* del mar

**sealing-wax** /ˈsiːlɪŋwæks/ *n* lacre *m*

**sea lion** /ˈsiːlaɪən/ *n* león *m* marino

**seam** /siːm/ *n* costura *f*; (*of coal*) veta *f*

**seaman** /ˈsiːmən/ *n* (*pl* **-men**) marinero *m*

**seamy** /ˈsiːmɪ/ *a*. **the ~ side** *n* el lado *m* sórdido, el revés *m*

**seance** /ˈseɪɑːns/ *n* sesión *f* de espiritismo

**sea**: **~plane** /ˈsiːpleɪn/ *n* hidroavión *f*. **~port** /ˈsiːpɔːt/ *n* puerto *m* de mar

**search** /sɜːtʃ/ *vt* registrar; (*examine*) examinar. ● *vi* buscar. ● *n* (*for sth*) búsqueda *f*; (*of sth*) registro *m*. **in ~ of** en busca de. **~ for** buscar. **~ing** *a* penetrante. **~party** *n* equipo *m* de salvamento. **~light** /ˈsɜːtʃlaɪt/ *n* reflector *m*

**sea**: **~scape** /ˈsiːskeɪp/ *n* marina *f*. **~shore** *n* orilla *f* del mar. **~sick** /ˈsiːsɪk/ *a* mareado. **be ~sick** marearse. **~side** /ˈsiːsaɪd/ *n* playa *f*

**season** /ˈsiːzn/ *n* estación *f*; (*period*) temporada *f*. ● *vt* (*culin*) sazonar; secar (*wood*). **~able** *a* propio de la estación. **~al** *a* estacional. **~ed** /ˈsiːznd/ *a* (*fig*) experto. **~ing** *n* condimento *m*. **~-ticket** *n* billete *m* de abono

**seat** /siːt/ *n* asiento *m*; (*place*) lugar *m*; (*of trousers*) fondillos *mpl*; (*bottom*) trasero *m*. **take a ~** sentarse. ● *vt* sentar; (*have seats for*) tener asientos para. **~-belt** *n* cinturón *m* de seguridad

**sea**: **~urchin** *n* erizo *m* de mar. **~weed** /ˈsiːwiːd/ *n* alga *f*. **~worthy** /ˈsiːwɜːðɪ/ *a* en estado de navegar

**secateurs** /ˈsekətɜːz/ *npl* tijeras *fpl* de podar

**sece|de** /sɪˈsiːd/ *vi* separarse. **~ssion** /-eʃn/ *n* secesión *f*

**seclu|de** /sɪˈkluːd/ *vt* aislar. **~ded** *a* aislado. **~sion** /-ʒn/ *n* aislamiento *m*

**second**[1] /ˈsekənd/ *a* & *n* segundo (*m*). **on ~ thoughts** pensándolo bien. ● *adv* (*in race etc*) en segundo lugar. ● *vt* apoyar. **~s** *npl* (*goods*) artículos *mpl* de segunda calidad; (*more food, fam*) otra porción *f*

**second**[2] /sɪˈkɒnd/ *vt* (*transfer*) trasladar temporalmente

**secondary** /ˈsekəndrɪ/ *a* secundario. **~ school** *n* instituto *m*

**second**: **~best** *a* segundo. **~class** *a* de segunda clase. **~hand** *a* de segunda mano. **~ly** *adv* en segundo lugar. **~rate** *a* mediocre

**secre|cy** /ˈsiːkrəsɪ/ *n* secreto *m*. **~t** /ˈsiːkrɪt/ *a* & *n* secreto (*m*). **in ~t** en secreto

**secretar|ial** /sekrəˈteərɪəl/ *a* de secretario. **~iat** /sekrəˈteərɪət/ *n* secretaría *f*. **~y** /ˈsekrətrɪ/ *n* secretario *m*. **S~y of State** ministro *m*: (*Amer*) Ministro *m* de Asuntos Exteriores

**secrete** /sɪˈkriːt/ *vt* (*med*) secretar. **~ion** /-ʃn/ *n* secreción *f*

**secretive** /ˈsiːkrɪtɪv/ *a* reservado

**secretly** /ˈsiːkrɪtlɪ/ *adv* en secreto

**sect** /sekt/ *n* secta *f*. **~arian** /-ˈteərɪən/ *a* sectario

**section** /ˈsekʃn/ *n* sección *f*; (*part*) parte *f*

**sector** /ˈsektə(r)/ *n* sector *m*

**secular** /ˈsekjʊlə(r)/ *a* seglar

**secur|e** /sɪˈkjʊə(r)/ *a* seguro; (*fixed*) fijo. ● *vt* asegurar; (*obtain*) obtener. **~ely** *adv* seguramente. **~ity** /sɪˈkjʊərətɪ/ *n* seguridad *f*; (*for loan*) garantía *f*, fianza *f*

**sedate** /sɪˈdeɪt/ *a* sosegado

**sedat|ion** /sɪˈdeɪʃn/ *n* sedación *f*. **~ive** /ˈsedətɪv/ *a* & *n* sedante (*m*)

**sedentary** /ˈsedntrɪ/ *a* sedentario

**sediment** /ˈsedɪmənt/ *n* sedimento *m*

**seduc|e** /sɪˈdjuːs/ *vt* seducir. **~er** /-ə(r)/ *n* seductor *m*. **~tion** /sɪˈdʌkʃn/ *n* seducción *f*. **~tive** /-tɪv/ *a* seductor

**see**[1] /siː/ ● *vt* (*pt* **saw**, *pp* **seen**) ver; (*understand*) comprender; (*notice*) notar; (*escort*) acompañar. **~ing that** visto que. **~ you later!** ¡hasta luego! ● *vi* ver; (*understand*) comprender. **~ about** ocuparse de. **~ off** despedirse de. **~ through** llevar a cabo; descubrir el juego de (*person*). **~ to** ocuparse de

**see**[2] /siː/ *n* diócesis *f*

**seed** /siːd/ *n* semilla *f*; (*fig*) germen *m*; (*tennis*) preseleccionado *m*. **~ling** *n* plantón *m*. **go to ~** granar; (*fig*) echarse a perder. **~y** /ˈsiːdɪ/ *a* (**-ier, -iest**) sórdido

**seek** /siːk/ *vt* (*pt* **sought**) buscar. **~ out** buscar

**seem** /siːm/ *vi* parecer. **~ingly** *adv* aparentemente

**seemly** /ˈsiːmlɪ/ *a* (**-ier, -iest**) correcto

**seen** /siːn/ *see* see¹
**seep** /siːp/ *vi* filtrarse. ∼**age** *n* filtración *f*
**see-saw** /'siːsɔː/ *n* balancín *m*
**seethe** /siːð/ *vi* (*fig*) hervir. **be seething with anger** estar furioso
**see-through** /'siːθruː/ *a* transparente
**segment** /'seɡmənt/ *n* segmento *m*; (*of orange*) gajo *m*
**segregat|e** /'seɡrɪɡeɪt/ *vt* segregar. ∼**ion** /-'ɡeɪʃn/ *n* segregación *f*
**seiz|e** /siːz/ *vt* agarrar; (*jurid*) incautarse de. ∼**e on** *vi* valerse de. ∼**e up** *vi* (*tec*) agarrotarse. ∼**ure** /'siːʒə(r)/ *n* incautación *f*; (*med*) ataque *m*
**seldom** /'seldəm/ *adv* raramente
**select** /sɪ'lekt/ *vt* escoger; (*sport*) seleccionar. ● *a* selecto; (*exclusive*) exclusivo. ∼**ion** /-ʃn/ *n* selección *f*. ∼**ive** *a* selectivo
**self** /self/ *n* (*pl* **selves**) sí mismo. ∼**-addressed** *a* con su propia dirección. ∼**-assurance** *n* confianza *f* en sí mismo. ∼**-assured** *a* seguro de sí mismo. ∼**-catering** *a* con facilidades para cocinar. ∼**-centred** *a* egocéntrico. ∼**-confidence** *n* confianza *f* en sí mismo. ∼**-confident** *a* seguro de sí mismo. ∼**-conscious** *a* cohibido. ∼**-contained** *a* independiente. ∼**-control** *n* dominio *m* de sí mismo. ∼**-defence** *n* defensa *f* propia. ∼**-denial** *n* abnegación *f*. ∼**-employed** *a* que trabaja por cuenta propia. ∼**-esteem** *n* amor *m* propio. ∼**-evident** *a* evidente. ∼**-government** *n* autonomía *f*. ∼**-important** *a* presumido. ∼**-indulgent** *a* inmoderado. ∼**-interest** *n* interés *m* propio. ∼**ish** /'selfɪʃ/ *a* egoísta. ∼**ishness** *n* egoísmo *m*. ∼**less** /'selflɪs/ *a* desinteresado. ∼**-made** *a* rico por su propio esfuerzo. ∼**-opinionated** *a* intransigente; (*arrogant*) engreído. ∼**-pity** *n* compasión *f* de sí mismo. ∼**-portrait** *n* autorretrato *m*. ∼**-possessed** *a* dueño de sí mismo. ∼**-reliant** *a* independiente. ∼**-respect** *n* amor *m* propio. ∼**-righteous** *a* santurrón. ∼**-sacrifice** *n* abnegación *f*. ∼**-satisfied** *a* satisfecho de sí mismo. ∼**-seeking** *a* egoísta. ∼**-service** *a* & *n* autoservicio (*m*). ∼**-styled** *a* sedicente, llamado. ∼**-sufficient** *a* independiente. ∼**-willed** *a* terco
**sell** /sel/ *vt* (*pt* **sold**) vender. **be sold on** (*fam*) entusiasmarse por. **be sold**

out estar agotado. ● *vi* venderse. ∼**-by date** *n* fecha *f* de caducidad. ∼ off *vt* liquidar. ∼ up *vt* vender todo. ∼**er** *n* vendedor *m*
**Sellotape** /'seləteɪp/ *n* (*P*) (papel *m*) celo *m*, cinta *f* adhesiva
**sell-out** /'selaʊt/ *n* (*betrayal*, *fam*) traición *f*
**semantic** /sɪ'mæntɪk/ *a* semántico. ∼**s** *n* semántica *f*
**semaphore** /'seməfɔː(r)/ *n* semáforo *m*
**semblance** /'sembləns/ *n* apariencia *f*
**semen** /'siːmən/ *n* semen *m*
**semester** /sɪ'mestə(r)/ *n* (*Amer*) semestre *m*
**semi...** /'semɪ/ *pref* semi...
**semi|breve** /'semɪbriːv/ *n* semibreve *f*, redonda *f*. ∼**circle** /'semɪsɜːkl/ *n* semicírculo *m*. ∼**circular** /-'sɜːkjʊlə(r)/ *a* semicircular. ∼**colon** /semɪ'kəʊlən/ *n* punto *m* y coma. ∼**detached** /semɪdɪ'tætʃt/ *a* ⟨*house*⟩ adosado. ∼**final** /semɪ'faɪnl/ *n* semifinal *f*
**seminar** /'semɪnɑː(r)/ *n* seminario *m*
**seminary** /'semɪnərɪ/ *n* (*college*) seminario *m*
**semiquaver** /'semɪkweɪvə(r)/ *n* (*mus*) semicorchea *f*
**Semit|e** /'siːmaɪt/ *n* semita *m* & *f*. ∼**ic** /sɪ'mɪtɪk/ *a* semítico
**semolina** /semə'liːnə/ *n* sémola *f*
**senat|e** /'senɪt/ *n* senado *m*. ∼**or** /-ətə(r)/ *n* senador *m*
**send** /send/ *vt/i* (*pt* **sent**) enviar. ∼ away despedir. ∼ away for pedir (por correo). ∼ for enviar a buscar. ∼ off for pedir (por correo). ∼ up (*fam*) parodiar. ∼**er** *n* remitente *m*. ∼**-off** *n* despedida *f*
**senil|e** /'siːnaɪl/ *a* senil. ∼**ity** /sɪ'nɪlətɪ/ *n* senilidad *f*
**senior** /'siːnɪə(r)/ *a* mayor; (*in rank*) superior; ⟨*partner etc*⟩ principal. ● *n* mayor *m* & *f*. ∼ citizen *n* jubilado *m*. ∼**ity** /-'ɒrətɪ/ *n* antigüedad *f*
**sensation** /sen'seɪʃn/ *n* sensación *f*. ∼**al** *a* sensacional
**sense** /sens/ *n* sentido *m*; (*common sense*) juicio *m*; (*feeling*) sensación *f*. **make** ∼ *vt* tener sentido. **make** ∼ **of** comprender. ∼**less** *a* insensato; (*med*) sin sentido
**sensibilities** /sensɪ'bɪlətɪz/ *npl* susceptibilidad *f*. ∼**ibility** /sensɪ'bɪlətɪ/ *n* sensibilidad *f*

**sensible** /'sensəbl/ *a* sensato; *‹cloth-ing›* práctico

**sensitiv|e** /'sensɪtɪv/ *a* sensible; *(touchy)* susceptible. **~ity** /-'tɪvətɪ/ *n* sensibilidad *f*

**sensory** /'sensərɪ/ *a* sensorio

**sensual** /'senʃʊəl/ *a* sensual. **~ity** /-'ælətɪ/ *n* sensualidad *f*

**sensuous** /'sensʊəs/ *a* sensual

**sent** /sent/ *see* **send**

**sentence** /'sentəns/ *n* frase *f*; *(jurid)* sentencia *f*; *(punishment)* condena *f*. ● *vt.* **~ to** condenar a

**sentiment** /'sentɪmənt/ *n* sentimiento *m*; *(opinion)* opinión *f*. **~al** /sentɪ'mentl/ *a* sentimental. **~ality** /-'tælətɪ/ *n* sentimentalismo *m*

**sentry** /'sentrɪ/ *n* centinela *f*

**separable** /'sepərəbl/ *a* separable

**separate¹** /'sepərət/ *a* separado; *(independent)* independiente. **~ly** *adv* por separado. **~s** *npl* coordinados *mpl*

**separat|e²** /'sepəreɪt/ *vt* separar. ● *vi* separarse. **~ion** /-'reɪʃn/ *n* separación *f*. **~ist** /'sepərətɪst/ *n* separatista *m & f*

**September** /sep'tembə(r)/ *n* se(p)tiembre *m*

**septic** /'septɪk/ *a* séptico. **~ tank** *n* fosa *f* séptica

**sequel** /'si:kwəl/ *n* continuación *f*; *(consequence)* consecuencia *f*

**sequence** /'si:kwəns/ *n* sucesión *f*; *(of film)* secuencia *f*

**sequin** /'si:kwɪn/ *n* lentejuela *f*

**serenade** /serə'neɪd/ *n* serenata *f*. ● *vt* dar serenata a

**seren|e** /sɪ'ri:n/ *a* sereno. **~ity** /-enətɪ/ *n* serenidad *f*

**sergeant** /'sɑ:dʒənt/ *n* sargento *m*

**serial** /'sɪərɪəl/ *n* serial *m*. ● *a* de serie. **~ize** *vt* publicar por entregas

**series** /'sɪərɪ:z/ *n* serie *f*

**serious** /'sɪərɪəs/ *a* serio. **~ly** *adv* seriamente; *(ill)* gravemente. **take ~ly** tomar en serio. **~ness** *n* seriedad *f*

**sermon** /'sɜ:mən/ *n* sermón *m*

**serpent** /'sɜ:pənt/ *n* serpiente *f*

**serrated** /sɪ'reɪtɪd/ *a* serrado

**serum** /'sɪərəm/ *n* (*pl* **-a**) suero *m*

**servant** /'sɜ:vənt/ *n* criado *m*; *(fig)* servidor *m*

**serve** /sɜ:v/ *vt* servir; *(in the army etc)* prestar servicio; cumplir *‹sentence›*. **~ as** servir de. **~ its purpose** servir para el caso. **it ~s you right** ¡bien te lo mereces! ¡te está bien

merecido! ● *vi* servir. ● *n* *(in tennis)* saque *m*

**service** /'sɜ:vɪs/ *n* servicio *m*; *(maintenance)* revisión *f*. **of ~ to** útil a. ● *vt* revisar *‹car etc›*. **~able** /'sɜ:vɪsəbl/ *a* práctico; *(durable)* duradero. **~ charge** *n* servicio *m*. **~man** /'sɜ:vɪsmən/ *n* (*pl* **-men**) militar *m*. **~s** *npl* *(mil)* fuerzas *fpl* armadas. **~ station** *n* estación *f* de servicio

**serviette** /sɜ:vɪ'et/ *n* servilleta *f*

**servile** /'sɜ:vaɪl/ *a* servil

**session** /'seʃn/ *n* sesión *f*; *(univ)* curso *m*

**set** /set/ *vt* (*pt* **set**, *pres p* **setting**) poner; poner en hora *‹clock etc›*; fijar *‹limit etc›*; *(typ)* componer. **~ fire to** pegar fuego a. **~ free** *vt* poner en libertad. ● *vi* *‹sun›* ponerse; *‹jelly›* cuajarse. ● *n* serie *f*; *(of cutlery etc)* juego *m*; *(tennis)* set *m*; *(TV, radio)* aparato *m*; *(of hair)* marcado *m*; *(in theatre)* decorado *m*; *(of people)* círculo *m*. ● *a* fijo. **be ~ on** estar resuelto a. **~ about** *vi* empezar a. **~ back** *vt* *(delay)* retardar; *(cost, sl)* costar. **~ off** *vi* salir. ● *vt* *(make start)* poner en marcha; hacer estallar *‹bomb›*. **~ out** *vi* *(declare)* declarar; *(leave)* salir. **~ sail** salir. **~ the table** poner la mesa. **~ up** *vt* establecer. **~back** *n* revés *m*. **~ square** *n* escuadra *f* de dibujar

**settee** /se'ti:/ *n* sofá *m*

**setting** /'setɪŋ/ *n* *(of sun)* puesta *f*; *(of jewel)* engaste *m*; *(in theatre)* escenario *m*; *(typ)* composición *f*. **~lotion** *n* fijador *m*

**settle** /'setl/ *vt* *(arrange)* arreglar; *(pay)* pagar; fijar *‹date›*; calmar *‹nerves›*. ● *vi* *(come to rest)* posarse; *(live)* instalarse. **~ down** calmarse; *(become orderly)* sentar la cabeza. **~ for** aceptar. **~ up** ajustar cuentas. **~ment** /'setlmənt/ *n* establecimiento *m*; *(agreement)* acuerdo *m*; *(com)* liquidación *f*; *(place)* colonia *f*. **~r** /-ə(r)/ *n* colonizador *m*

**set:** **~to** *n* pelea *f*. **~up** *n* *(fam)* sistema *m*

**seven** /'sevn/ *a & n* siete *(m)*. **~teen** /sevn'ti:n/ *a & n* diecisiete *(m)*. **~teenth** *a & n* decimoséptimo *(m)*. **~th** *a & n* séptimo *(m)*. **~tieth** *a & n* setenta *(m)*, septuagésimo *(m)*. **~ty** /'sevntɪ/ *a & n* setenta *(m)*

**sever** /'sevə(r)/ vt cortar; (fig) romper

**several** /'sevrəl/ a & pron varios

**severance** /'sevərəns/ n (breaking off) ruptura f

**sever|e** /sɪ'vɪə(r)/ a (-er, -est) severo; (violent) violento; (serious) grave; (weather) riguroso. **~ely** adv severamente; (seriously) gravemente. **~ity** /-'verətɪ/ n severidad f; (violence) violencia f; (seriousness) gravedad f

**sew** /səʊ/ vt/i (pt sewed, pp sewn, or sewed) coser

**sew|age** /'suːɪdʒ/ n aguas fpl residuales. **~er** /'suːə(r)/ n cloaca f

**sewing** /'səʊɪŋ/ n costura f. **~-machine** n máquina f de coser

**sewn** /səʊn/ see **sew**

**sex** /seks/ n sexo m. **have ~** tener relaciones sexuales. ● a sexual. **~ist** /'seksɪst/ a & n sexista (m & f)

**sextet** /seks'tet/ n sexteto m

**sexual** /'seksʊəl/ a sexual. **~ intercourse** n relaciones fpl sexuales. **~ity** /-'ælətɪ/ n sexualidad f

**sexy** /'seksɪ/ a (-ier, -iest) excitante, sexy, provocativo

**shabb|ily** /'ʃæbɪlɪ/ adv pobremente; (act) mezquinamente. **~iness** n pobreza f; (meanness) mezquindad f. **~y** /'ʃæbɪ/ a (-ier, -iest) (clothes) gastado; (person) pobremente vestido; (mean) mezquino

**shack** /ʃæk/ n choza f

**shackles** /'ʃæklz/ npl grillos mpl, grilletes mpl

**shade** /ʃeɪd/ n sombra f; (of colour) matiz m; (for lamp) pantalla f. **a ~ better** un poquito mejor. ● vt dar sombra a

**shadow** /'ʃædəʊ/ n sombra f. **S~ Cabinet** n gobierno m en la sombra. ● vt (follow) seguir. **~y** a (fig) vago

**shady** /'ʃeɪdɪ/ a (-ier, -iest) sombreado; (fig) dudoso

**shaft** /ʃɑːft/ n (of arrow) astil m; (mec) eje m; (of light) rayo m; (of lift, mine) pozo m

**shaggy** /'ʃægɪ/ a (-ier, -iest) peludo

**shak|e** /ʃeɪk/ vt (pt shook, pp shaken) sacudir; agitar (bottle); (shock) desconcertar. **~e hands with** estrechar la mano a. ● vi temblar. **~e off** vi deshacerse de. ● n sacudida f. **~e-up** n reorganización f. **~y** /'ʃeɪkɪ/ a (-ier, -iest) tembloroso; (table etc) inestable; (unreliable) incierto

**shall** /ʃæl/ v, aux (first person in future tense). **I ~ go** iré. **we ~ see** veremos

**shallot** /ʃə'lɒt/ n chalote m

**shallow** /'ʃæləʊ/ a (-er, -est) poco profundo; (fig) superficial

**sham** /ʃæm/ n farsa f; (person) impostor m. ● a falso; (affected) fingido. ● vt (pt shammed) fingir

**shambles** /'ʃæmblz/ npl (mess, fam) desorden m total

**shame** /ʃeɪm/ n vergüenza f. **what a ~!** ¡qué lástima! ● vt avergonzar. **~-faced** /'ʃeɪmfeɪst/ a avergonzado. **~ful** a vergonzoso. **~fully** adv vergonzosamente. **~less** a desvergonzado

**shampoo** /ʃæm'puː/ n champú m. ● vt lavar

**shamrock** /'ʃæmrɒk/ n trébol m

**shandy** /'ʃændɪ/ n cerveza f con gaseosa, clara f

**shan't** /ʃɑːnt/ = **shall not**

**shanty** /'ʃæntɪ/ n chabola f. **~ town** n chabolas fpl

**shape** /ʃeɪp/ n forma f. ● vt formar; determinar (future). ● vi formarse. **~ up** prometer. **~less** a informe. **~ly** /'ʃeɪplɪ/ a (-ier, -iest) bien proporcionado

**share** /ʃeə(r)/ n porción f; (com) acción f. **go ~s** compartir. ● vt compartir; (divide) dividir. ● vi participar. **~ in** participar en. **~holder** /'ʃeəhəʊldə(r)/ n accionista m & f. **~-out** n reparto m

**shark** /ʃɑːk/ n tiburón m; (fig) estafador m

**sharp** /ʃɑːp/ a (-er, -est) (knife etc) afilado; (pin etc) puntiagudo; (pain, sound) agudo; (taste) acre; (sudden, harsh) brusco; (well defined) marcado; (dishonest) poco escrupuloso; (clever) listo. ● adv en punto. **at seven o'clock ~** a las siete en punto. ● n (mus) sostenido m. **~en** /'ʃɑːpn/ vt afilar; sacar punta a (pencil). **~ener** n (mec) afilador m; (for pencils) sacapuntas m invar. **~ly** adv bruscamente

**shatter** /'ʃætə(r)/ vt hacer añicos; (upset) perturbar. ● vi hacerse añicos. **~ed** a (exhausted) agotado

**shav|e** /ʃeɪv/ vt afeitar. ● vi afeitarse. ● n afeitado m. **have a ~e** afeitarse. **~en** a (face) afeitado; (head) rapado. **~er** n maquinilla f (de afeitar). **~ing-brush** n brocha f de afietar. **~ing-cream** n crema f de afeitar

**shawl** /ʃɔːl/ n chal m

**she** /ʃiː/ pron ella. ● n hembra f

**sheaf** /ʃiːf/ n (pl **sheaves**) gavilla f

**shear** /ʃɪə(r)/ vt (pp **shorn**, or **sheared**) esquilar. **~s** /ʃɪəz/ npl tijeras fpl grandes

**sheath** /ʃiːθ/ n (pl **-s** /ʃiːðz/) vaina f; (contraceptive) condón m. **~e** /ʃiːð/ vt envainar

**shed**[1] /ʃed/ n cobertizo m

**shed**[2] /ʃed/ vt (pt **shed**, pres p **shedding**) perder; derramar (tears); despojarse de (clothes). **~ light on** aclarar

**sheen** /ʃiːn/ n lustre m

**sheep** /ʃiːp/ n invar oveja f. **~dog** n perro m pastor. **~ish** /ʃiːpɪʃ/ a vergonzoso. **~ishly** adv tímidamente. **~skin** /ʃiːpskɪn/ n piel f de carnero, zamarra f

**sheer** /ʃɪə(r)/ a puro; (steep) perpendicular; (fabric) muy fino. ● adv a pico

**sheet** /ʃiːt/ n sábana f; (of paper) hoja f; (of glass) lámina f; (of ice) capa f

**sheikh** /ʃeɪk/ n jeque m

**shelf** /ʃelf/ n (pl **shelves**) estante m. **be on the ~** quedarse para vestir santos

**shell** /ʃel/ n concha f; (of egg) cáscara f; (of building) casco m; (explosive) proyectil m. ● vt desgranar (peas etc); (mil) bombardear. **~fish** /ʃelfɪʃ/ n invar (crustacean) crustáceo m; (mollusc) marisco m

**shelter** /ʃeltə(r)/ n refugio m, abrigo m. ● vt abrigar; (protect) proteger; (give lodging to) dar asilo a. ● vi abrigarse. **~ed** a (spot) abrigado; (life etc) protegido

**shelv|e** /ʃelv/ vt (fig) dar carpetazo a. **~ing** /ʃelvɪŋ/ n estantería f

**shepherd** /ʃepəd/ n pastor m. ● vt guiar. **~ess** /-'des/ n pastora f. **~'s pie** n carne f picada con puré de patatas

**sherbet** /ʃɜːbət/ n (Amer, water-ice) sorbete m

**sheriff** /ʃerɪf/ n alguacil m, sheriff m

**sherry** /ʃerɪ/ n (vino m de) jerez m

**shield** /ʃiːld/ n escudo m. ● vt proteger

**shift** /ʃɪft/ vt cambiar; cambiar de sitio (furniture etc); echar (blame etc). ● n cambio m; (work) turno m;

(workers) tanda f. **make ~** arreglárselas. **~less** /ʃɪftlɪs/ a holgazán

**shifty** /ʃɪftɪ/ a (-ier, -iest) taimado

**shilling** /ʃɪlɪŋ/ n chelín m

**shilly-shally** /ʃɪlɪʃælɪ/ vi titubear

**shimmer** /ʃɪmə(r)/ vi rielar, relucir. ● n luz f trémula

**shin** /ʃɪn/ n espinilla f

**shine** /ʃaɪn/ vi (pt **shone**) brillar. ● vt sacar brillo a. **~ on** dirigir (torch). ● n brillo m

**shingle** /ʃɪŋgl/ n (pebbles) guijarros mpl

**shingles** /ʃɪŋglz/ npl (med) herpes mpl & fpl

**shiny** /ʃaɪnɪ/ a (-ier, -iest) brillante

**ship** /ʃɪp/ n buque m, barco m. ● vt (pt **shipped**) transportar; (send) enviar; (load) embarcar. **~building** /ʃɪpbɪldɪŋ/ n construcción f naval. **~ment** n envío m. **~per** n expedidor m. **~ping** n envío m; (ships) barcos mpl. **~shape** /ʃɪpʃeɪp/ adv & a en buen orden, en regla. **~wreck** /ʃɪprek/ n naufragio m. **~wrecked** a naufragado. **be ~wrecked** naufragar. **~yard** /ʃɪpjɑːd/ n astillero m

**shirk** /ʃɜːk/ vt esquivar. **~er** n gandul m

**shirt** /ʃɜːt/ n camisa f. **in ~sleeves** en mangas de camisa. **~y** /ʃɜːtɪ/ a (sl) enfadado

**shiver** /ʃɪvə(r)/ vi temblar. ● n escalofrío m

**shoal** /ʃəʊl/ n banco m

**shock** /ʃɒk/ n sacudida f; (fig) susto m; (elec) descarga f; (med) choque m. ● vt escandalizar. **~ing** a escandaloso; (fam) espantoso. **~ingly** adv terriblemente

**shod** /ʃɒd/ see **shoe**

**shodd|ily** /ʃɒdɪlɪ/ adv mal. **~y** /ʃɒdɪ/ a (-ier, -iest) mal hecho, de pacotilla

**shoe** /ʃuː/ n zapato m; (of horse) herradura f. ● vt (pt **shod**, pres p **shoeing**) herrar (horse). **be well shod** estar bien calzado. **~horn** /ʃuːhɔːn/ n calzador m. **~lace** n cordón m de zapato. **~maker** /ʃuːmeɪkə(r)/ n zapatero m. **~ polish** n betún m. **~string** n. **on a ~string** con poco dinero. **~tree** n horma f

**shone** /ʃɒn/ see **shine**

**shoo** /ʃuː/ vt ahuyentar

**shook** /ʃʊk/ see **shake**

**shoot** /ʃuːt/ vt (pt **shot**) disparar; rodar (film). ● vi (hunt) cazar. ● n (*bot*) retoño *m*; (*hunt*) cacería *f*. ∼ **down** *vt* derribar. ∼ **out** *vi* (*rush*) salir disparado. ∼ **up** ⟨*prices*⟩ subir de repente; (*grow*) crecer. ∼**ing-range** *n* campo *m* de tiro

**shop** /ʃɒp/ *n* tienda *f*; (*work-shop*) taller *m*. **talk** ∼ hablar de su trabajo. ● *vi* (*pt* **shopping**) hacer compras. ∼ **around** buscar el mejor precio. **go** ∼**ping** ir de compras. ∼ **assistant** *n* dependiente *m*. ∼**keeper** /ʃɒpkiːpə(r)/ *n* tendero *m*. ∼**lifter** *n* ratero *m* (de tiendas). ∼**lifting** *n* ratería *f* (de tiendas). ∼**per** *n* comprador *m*. ∼**ping** /ʃɒpɪŋ/ *n* compras *fpl*. ∼**ping bag** *n* bolsa *f* de la compra. ∼**ping centre** *n* centro *m* comercial. ∼ **steward** *n* enlace *m* sindical. ∼**window** *n* escaparate *m*

**shore** /ʃɔː(r)/ *n* orilla *f*

**shorn** /ʃɔːn/ *see* **shear**

**short** /ʃɔːt/ *a* (**-er, -est**) corto; (*not lasting*) breve; ⟨*person*⟩ bajo; (*curt*) brusco. **a** ∼ **time ago** hace poco. **be** ∼ **of** necesitar. **Mick is** ∼ **for Michael** Mick es el diminutivo de Michael. ● *adv* (*stop*) en seco. ∼ **of doing** a menos que no hagamos. ● *n*. **in** ∼ en resumen. ∼**age** /ʃɔːtɪdʒ/ *n* escasez *f*. ∼**bread** /ʃɔːtbred/ *n* galleta *f* de mantequilla. ∼**change** *vt* estafar, engañar. ∼ **circuit** *n* cortocircuito *m*. ∼**coming** /ʃɔːtkʌmɪŋ/ *n* deficiencia *f*. ∼ **cut** *n* atajo *m*. ∼**en** /ʃɔːtn/ *vt* acortar. ∼**hand** /ʃɔːthænd/ *n* taquigrafía *f*. ∼**hand typist** *n* taquimecanógrafo *m*, taquimeca *f* (*fam*). ∼**lived** *a* efímero. ∼**ly** /ʃɔːtlɪ/ *adv* dentro de poco. ∼**s** *npl* pantalón *m* corto. ∼**sighted** *a* miope. ∼**tempered** *a* de mal genio

**shot** /ʃɒt/ *see* **shoot**. ● *n* tiro *m*; (*person*) tirador *m*; (*photo*) foto *f*; (*injection*) inyección *f*. **like a** ∼ como una bala; (*willingly*) de buena gana. ∼**gun** *n* escopeta *f*

**should** /ʃʊd, ʃəd/ *v, aux*. **I** ∼ **go** debería ir. **I** ∼ **have seen him** debiera haberlo visto. **I** ∼ **like** me gustaría. **if he** ∼ **come** si viniese

**shoulder** /ʃəʊldə(r)/ *n* hombro *m*. ● *vt* cargar con ⟨*responsibility*⟩; llevar a hombros ⟨*burden*⟩. ∼**blade** *n* omóplato *m*. ∼**strap** *n* correa *f* del hombro; (*of bra etc*) tirante *m*

**shout** /ʃaʊt/ *n* grito *m*. ● *vt/i* gritar. ∼ **at s.o.** gritarle a uno. ∼ **down** hacer callar a gritos

**shove** /ʃʌv/ *n* empujón. *m*. ● *vt* empujar; (*put, fam*) poner. ● *vi* empujar. ∼ **off** *vi* (*fam*) largarse

**shovel** /ʃʌvl/ *n* pala *f*. ● *vt* (*pt* **shovelled**) mover con la pala

**show** /ʃəʊ/ *vt* (*pt* **showed**, *pp* **shown**) mostrar; (*put on display*) exponer; poner ⟨*film*⟩. ● *vi* (*be visible*) verse. ● *n* demostración *f*; (*exhibition*) exposición *f*; (*ostentation*) pompa *f*; (*in theatre*) espectáculo *m*; (*in cinema*) sesión *f*. **on** ∼ expuesto. ∼ **off** *vt* lucir; (*pej*) ostentar. ● *vi* presumir. ∼ **up** *vi* destacar; (*be present*) presentarse. ● *vt* (*unmask*) desenmascarar. ∼**case** *n* vitrina *f*. ∼**down** *n* confrontación *f*

**shower** /ʃaʊə(r)/ *n* chaparrón *m*; (*of blows etc*) lluvia *f*; (*for washing*) ducha *f*. **have a** ∼ ducharse. ● *vi* ducharse. ● *vt*. ∼ **with** colmar de. ∼**proof** /ʃaʊəpruːf/ *a* impermeable. ∼**y** *a* lluvioso

**show**: ∼**jumping** *n* concurso *m* hípico. ∼**manship** /ʃəʊmənʃɪp/ *n* teatralidad *f*, arte *f* de presentar espectáculos

**shown** /ʃəʊn/ *see* **show**

**show**: ∼**off** *n* fanfarrón *m*. ∼**place** *n* lugar *m* de interés turístico. ∼**room** /ʃəʊruːm/ *n* sala *f* de exposición *f*

**showy** /ʃəʊɪ/ *a* (**-ier, -iest**) llamativo; ⟨*person*⟩ ostentoso

**shrank** /ʃræŋk/ *see* **shrink**

**shrapnel** /ʃræpnəl/ *n* metralla *f*

**shred** /ʃred/ *n* pedazo *m*; (*fig*) pizca *f*. ● *vt* (*pt* **shredded**) hacer tiras; (*culin*) cortar en tiras. ∼**der** *n* desfibradora *f*, trituradora *f*

**shrew** /ʃruː/ *n* musaraña *f*; (*woman*) arpía *f*

**shrewd** /ʃruːd/ *a* (**-er, -est**) astuto. ∼**ness** *n* astucia *f*

**shriek** /ʃriːk/ *n* chillido *m*. ● *vt/i* chillar

**shrift** /ʃrɪft/ *n*. **give s.o. short** ∼ despachar a uno con brusquedad

**shrill** /ʃrɪl/ *a* agudo

**shrimp** /ʃrɪmp/ *n* camarón *m*

**shrine** /ʃraɪn/ *n* (*place*) lugar *m* santo; (*tomb*) sepulcro *m*

**shrink** /ʃrɪŋk/ *vt* (*pt* **shrank**, *pp* **shrunk**) encoger. ● *vi* encogerse; (*draw back*) retirarse; (*lessen*) disminuir. ∼**age** *n* encogimiento *m*

**shrivel** /ʃrɪvl/ *vi* (*pt* **shrivelled**) (*dry up*) secarse; (*become wrinkled*) arrugarse

**shroud** /ʃraʊd/ n sudario m; (fig) velo m. ● vt (veil) velar

**Shrove** /ʃrəʊv/ n. ~ **Tuesday** n martes m de carnaval

**shrub** /ʃrʌb/ n arbusto m

**shrug** /ʃrʌg/ vt (pt **shrugged**) encogerse de hombros. ● n encogimiento m de hombros

**shrunk** /ʃrʌŋk/ see **shrink**

**shrunken** /'ʃrʌŋkən/ a encogido

**shudder** /'ʃʌdə(r)/ vi estremecerse. ● n estremecimiento m

**shuffle** /'ʃʌfl/ vi arrastrar los pies. ● vt barajar ⟨cards⟩. ● n arrastramiento m de los pies; (of cards) barajadura f

**shun** /ʃʌn/ vt (pt **shunned**) evitar

**shunt** /ʃʌnt/ vt apartar, desviar

**shush** /ʃʊʃ/ int ¡chitón!

**shut** /ʃʌt/ vt (pt shut, pres p **shutting**) cerrar. ● vi cerrarse. ~ **down** cerrar. ~ **up** vt cerrar; (fam) hacer callar. ● vi callarse. ~**down** n cierre m. ~**ter** /'ʃʌtə(r)/ n contraventana f; (photo) obturador m

**shuttle** /'ʃʌtl/ n lanzadera f; (train) tren m de enlace. ● vt transportar. ● vi ir y venir. ~**cock** /'ʃʌtlkɒk/ n volante m. ~ **service** n servicio m de enlace

**shy** /ʃaɪ/ a (-er, -est) tímido. ● vi (pt **shied**) asustarse. ~ **away from** huir. ~**ness** n timidez f

**Siamese** /saɪə'miːz/ a siamés

**sibling** /'sɪblɪŋ/ n hermano m, hermana f

**Sicil|ian** /sɪ'sɪljən/ a & n siciliano (m). ~**y** /'sɪsɪlɪ/ n Sicilia f

**sick** /sɪk/ a enfermo; ⟨humour⟩ negro; (fed up, fam) harto. be ~ (vomit) vomitar. be ~ of (fig) estar harto de. feel ~ sentir náuseas. ~**en** /'sɪkən/ vt dar asco. ● vi caer enfermo. be ~**ening for** incubar

**sickle** /'sɪkl/ n hoz f

**sick:** ~**ly** /'sɪklɪ/ a (-ier, -iest) enfermizo; ⟨taste, smell etc⟩ nauseabundo. ~**ness** /'sɪknɪs/ n enfermedad f. ~**room** n cuarto m del enfermo

**side** /saɪd/ n lado m; (of river) orilla f; (of hill) ladera f; (team) equipo m; (fig) parte f. ~ **by** ~ uno al lado del otro. on the ~ (sideline) como actividad secundaria; (secretly) a escondidas. ● a lateral. ● vi. ~ **with** tomar el partido de. ~**board** /'saɪdbɔːd/ n aparador m. ~**boards** npl, ~**burns** npl (sl) patillas fpl.

~**car** n sidecar m. ~**effect** n efecto m secundario. ~**light** /'saɪdlaɪt/ n luz f de posición. ~**line** /'saɪdlaɪn/ n actividad f secundaria. ~**long** /-lɒŋ/ a & adv de soslayo. ~**road** n calle f secundaria. ~**saddle** n silla f de mujer. **ride** ~**saddle** adv a mujeriegas. ~**show** n atracción f secundaria. ~**step** vt evitar. ~**track** vt desviar del asunto. ~**walk** /'saɪdwɔːk/ n (Amer) acera f, vereda f (LAm). ~**ways** /'saɪdweɪz/ a & adv de lado. ~**whiskers** npl patillas fpl

**siding** /'saɪdɪŋ/ n apartadero m

**sidle** /'saɪdl/ vi avanzar furtivamente. ~ **up to** acercarse furtivamente

**siege** /siːdʒ/ n sitio m, cerco m

**siesta** /sɪ'estə/ n siesta f

**sieve** /sɪv/ n cernedor m. ● vt cerner

**sift** /sɪft/ vt cerner. ● vi. ~ **through** examinar

**sigh** /saɪ/ n suspiro. ● vi suspirar

**sight** /saɪt/ n vista f; (spectacle) espectáculo m; (on gun) mira f. **at** (first) ~ a primera vista. **catch** ~ **of** vislumbrar. **lose** ~ **of** perder de vista. **on** ~ a primera vista. **within** ~ **of** (near) cerca de. ● vt ver, divisar. ~**seeing** /'saɪtsiːɪŋ/ n visita f turística. ~**seer** /-ə(r)/ n turista m & f

**sign** /saɪn/ n señal f. ● vt firmar. ~ **on**, ~ **up** vt inscribir. ● vi inscribirse

**signal** /'sɪgnəl/ n señal f. ● vt (pt **signalled**) comunicar; hacer señas a ⟨person⟩. ~**box** n casilla f del guardavía. ~**man** /'sɪgnəlmən/ n (pl -men) guardavía f

**signatory** /'sɪgnətrɪ/ n firmante m & f

**signature** /'sɪgnətʃə(r)/ n firma f. ~ **tune** n sintonía f

**signet-ring** /'sɪgnɪtrɪŋ/ n anillo m de sello

**significan|ce** /sɪg'nɪfɪkəns/ n significado m. ~**t** /sɪg'nɪfɪkənt/ a significativo; (important) importante. ~**tly** adv significativamente

**signify** /'sɪgnɪfaɪ/ vt significar. ● vi (matter) importar, tener importancia

**signpost** /'saɪnpəʊst/ n poste m indicador

**silen|ce** /'saɪləns/ n silencio m. ● vt hacer callar. ~**cer** /-ə(r)/ n silenciador m. ~**t** /'saɪlənt/ a silencioso;

⟨*film*⟩ mudo. **~tly** *adv* silenciosamente

**silhouette** /ˈsɪluːˈet/ *n* silueta *f*. ● *vt*. **be ~d** perfilarse, destacarse (**against** contra)

**silicon** /ˈsɪlɪkən/ *n* silicio *m*. **~ chip** *n* pastilla *f* de silicio

**silk** /sɪlk/ *n* seda *f*. **~en** *a*, **~y** *a* ⟨*of silk*⟩ de seda; (*like silk*) sedoso. **~worm** *n* gusano *m* de seda

**sill** /sɪl/ *n* antepecho *m*; (*of window*) alféizar *m*; (*of door*) umbral *m*

**silly** /ˈsɪlɪ/ *a* (**-ier, -iest**) tonto. ● *n*. **~billy** (*fam*) tonto *m*

**silo** /ˈsaɪləʊ/ *n* (*pl* **-os**) silo *m*

**silt** /sɪlt/ *n* sedimento *m*

**silver** /ˈsɪlvə(r)/ *n* plata *f*. ● *a* de plata. **~ plated** *a* bañado en plata, plateado. **~side** /ˈsɪlvəsaɪd/ *n* (*culin*) contra *f*. **~smith** /ˈsɪlvəsmɪθ/ *n* platero *m*. **~ware** /ˈsɪlvəweə(r)/ *n* plata *f*. **~ wedding** *n* bodas *fpl* de plata. **~y** *a* plateado; ⟨*sound*⟩ argentino

**simil|ar** /ˈsɪmɪlə(r)/ *a* parecido. **~arity** /-ɪˈlærətɪ/ *n* parecido *m*. **~arly** *adv* de igual manera

**simile** /ˈsɪmɪlɪ/ *n* símil *m*

**simmer** /ˈsɪmə(r)/ *vt/i* hervir a fuego lento; (*fig*) hervir. **~ down** calmarse

**simpl|e** /ˈsɪmpl/ *a* (**-er, -est**) sencillo; ⟨*person*⟩ ingenuo. **~e-minded** *a* ingenuo. **~eton** /ˈsɪmpltən/ *n* simplón *m*. **~icity** /-ˈplɪsetɪ/ *n* secillez *f*. **~ification** /-ɪˈkeɪʃn/ *n* simplificación *f*. **~ify** /ˈsɪmplɪfaɪ/ *vt* simplificar. **~y** *adv* sencillamente; (*absolutely*) absolutamente

**simulat|e** /ˈsɪmjʊleɪt/ *vt* simular. **~ion** /-ˈleɪʃn/ *n* simulación *f*

**simultaneous** /sɪmlˈteɪnɪəs/ *a* simultáneo. **~ly** *adv* simultáneamente

**sin** /sɪn/ *n* pecado *m*. ● *vi* (*pt* **sinned**) pecar

**since** /sɪns/ *prep* desde. ● *adv* desde entonces. ● *conj* desde que; (*because*) ya que

**sincer|e** /sɪnˈsɪə(r)/ *a* sincero. **~ely** *adv* sinceramente. **~ity** /-ˈserətɪ/ *n* sinceridad *f*

**sinew** /ˈsɪnjuː/ *n* tendón *m*. **~s** *npl* músculos *mpl*

**sinful** /ˈsɪnfl/ *a* pecaminoso; (*shocking*) escandaloso

**sing** /sɪŋ/ *vt/i* (*pt* **sang**, *pp* **sung**) cantar

**singe** /sɪndʒ/ *vt* (*pres p* **singeing**) chamuscar

**singer** /ˈsɪŋə(r)/ *n* cantante *m & f*

**singl|e** /ˈsɪŋgl/ *a* único; (*not double*) sencillo; (*unmarried*) soltero; ⟨*bed, room*⟩ individual. ● *n* (*tennis*) juego *m* individual; (*ticket*) billete *m* sencillo. ● *vt*. **~e out** escoger; (*distinguish*) distinguir. **~e-handed** *a & adv* sin ayuda. **~e-minded** *a* resuelto

**singlet** /ˈsɪŋglɪt/ *n* camiseta *f*

**singly** /ˈsɪŋglɪ/ *adv* uno a uno

**singsong** /ˈsɪŋsɒŋ/ *a* monótono. ● *n*. **have a ~** cantar juntos

**singular** /ˈsɪŋgjʊlə(r)/ *n* singular *f*. ● *a* singular; (*uncommon*) raro; ⟨*noun*⟩ en singular. **~ly** *adv* singularmente

**sinister** /ˈsɪnɪstə(r)/ *a* siniestro

**sink** /sɪŋk/ *vt* (*pt* **sank**, *pp* **sunk**) hundir; perforar ⟨*well*⟩; invertir ⟨*money*⟩. ● *vi* hundirse; ⟨*patient*⟩ debilitarse. ● *n* fregadero *m*. **~ in** *vi* penetrar

**sinner** /ˈsɪnə(r)/ *n* pecador *m*

**sinuous** /ˈsɪnjʊəs/ *a* sinuoso

**sinus** /ˈsaɪnəs/ *n* (*pl* **-uses**) seno *m*

**sip** /sɪp/ *n* sorbo *m*. ● *vt* (*pt* **sipped**) sorber

**siphon** /ˈsaɪfən/ *n* sifón *m*. *vt*. **~ out** sacar con sifón

**sir** /sɜː(r)/ *n* señor *m*. **S~** *n* (*title*) sir *m*

**siren** /ˈsaɪərən/ *n* sirena *f*

**sirloin** /ˈsɜːlɔɪn/ *n* solomillo *m*, lomo *m* bajo

**sirocco** /sɪˈrɒkəʊ/ *n* siroco *m*

**sissy** /ˈsɪsɪ/ *n* hombre *m* afeminado, marica *m*, mariquita *m*; (*coward*) gallina *m & f*

**sister** /ˈsɪstə(r)/ *n* hermana *f*; (*nurse*) enfermera *f* jefe. **S~ Mary** Sor María. **~-in-law** *n* (*pl* **~s-in-law**) cuñada *f*. **~ly** *a* de hermana; (*like sister*) como hermana

**sit** /sɪt/ *vt* (*pt* **sat**, *pres p* **sitting**) sentar. ● *vi* sentarse; ⟨*committee etc*⟩ reunirse. **be ~ting** estar sentado. **~ back** *vi* (*fig*) relajarse. **~ down** *vi* sentarse. **~ for** *vi* presentarse a ⟨*exam*⟩; posar para ⟨*portrait*⟩. **~ up** *vi* enderezarse; (*stay awake*) velar. **~-in** *n* ocupación *f*

**site** /saɪt/ *n* sitio *m*. **building ~** *n* solar *m*. ● *vt* situar

**sit: ~ting** *n* sesión *f*; (*in restaurant*) turno *m*. **~ting-room** *n* cuarto *m* de estar

**situat|e** /'sɪtjʊeɪt/ vt situar. **~ed** a situado. **~ion** /-'eɪʃn/ n situación f; (job) puesto m

**six** /sɪks/ a & n seis (m). **~teen** /sɪk'stiːn/ a & n dieciséis (m). **~teenth** a & n decimosexto (m). **~th** a & n sexto (m). **~tieth** a & n sesenta (m), sexagésimo (m). **~ty** /'sɪkstɪ/ a & n sesenta (m)

**size** /saɪz/ n tamaño m; (of clothes) talla f; (of shoes) número m; (extent) magnitud f. ● vt. **~ up** (fam) juzgar. **~able** a bastante grande

**sizzle** /'sɪzl/ vi crepitar

**skate¹** /skeɪt/ n patín m. ● vi patinar. **~board** /'skeɪtbɔːd/ n monopatín m. **~r** n patinador m

**skate²** /skeɪt/ n invar (fish) raya f

**skating** /'skeɪtɪŋ/ n patinaje m. **~rink** n pista f de patinaje

**skein** /skeɪn/ n madeja f

**skelet|al** /'skelɪtl/ a esquelético. **~on** /'skelɪtn/ n esqueleto m. **~on staff** n personal m reducido

**sketch** /sketʃ/ n esbozo m; (drawing) dibujo m; (in theatre) pieza f corta y divertida. ● vt esbozar. ● vi dibujar. **~y** /'sketʃɪ/ a (-ier, -iest) incompleto

**skew** /skjuː/ n. **on the ~** sesgado

**skewer** /'skjuːə(r)/ n broqueta f

**ski** /skiː/ n (pl skis) esquí m. ● vi (pt skied, pres p skiing) esquiar. **go ~ing** ir a esquiar

**skid** /skɪd/ vi (pt skidded) patinar. ● n patinazo m

**ski: ~er** n esquiador m. **~ing** n esquí m

**skilful** /'skɪlfl/ a diestro

**ski-lift** /'skiːlɪft/ n telesquí m

**skill** /skɪl/ n destreza f, habilidad f. **~ed** a hábil; (worker) cualificado

**skim** /skɪm/ vt (pt skimmed) espumar; desnatar (milk); (glide over) rozar. **~ over** vt rasar. **~ through** vi hojear

**skimp** /skɪmp/ vt escatimar. **~y** /'skɪmpɪ/ a (-ier, -iest) insuficiente; (skirt, dress) corto

**skin** /skɪn/ n piel f. ● vt (pt skinned) despellejar; pelar (fruit). **~-deep** a superficial. **~-diving** n natación f submarina. **~flint** /'skɪnflɪnt/ n tacaño m. **~ny** /'skɪnɪ/ a (-ier, -iest) flaco

**skint** /skɪnt/ a (sl) sin una perra

**skip¹** /skɪp/ vi (pt skipped) vi saltar; (with rope) saltar a la comba. ● vt saltarse. ● n salto m

**skip²** /skɪp/ n (container) cuba f

**skipper** /'skɪpə(r)/ n capitán m

**skipping-rope** /'skɪpɪŋrəʊp/ n comba f

**skirmish** /'skɜːmɪʃ/ n escaramuza f

**skirt** /skɜːt/ n falda f. ● vt rodear; (go round) ladear

**skirting-board** /'skɜːtɪŋbɔːd/ n rodapié m, zócalo m

**skit** /skɪt/ n pieza f satírica

**skittish** /'skɪtɪʃ/ a juguetón; (horse) nervioso

**skittle** /'skɪtl/ n bolo m

**skive** /skaɪv/ vi (sl) gandulear

**skivvy** /'skɪvɪ/ n (fam) criada f

**skulk** /skʌlk/ vi avanzar furtivamente; (hide) esconderse

**skull** /skʌl/ n cráneo m; (remains) calavera f. **~cap** n casquete m

**skunk** /skʌŋk/ n mofeta f; (person) canalla f

**sky** /skaɪ/ n cielo m. **~blue** a & n azul (m) celeste. **~jack** /'skaɪdʒæk/ vt secuestrar. **~jacker** n secuestrador m. **~light** /'skaɪlaɪt/ n tragaluz m. **~scraper** /'skaɪskreɪpə(r)/ n rascacielos m invar

**slab** /slæb/ n bloque m; (of stone) losa f; (of chocolate) tableta f

**slack** /slæk/ a (-er, -est) flojo; (person) negligente; (period) de poca actividad. ● n (of rope) parte f floja. ● vt aflojar. ● vi aflojarse; (person) descansar. **~en** /'slækən/ vt aflojar. ● vi aflojarse; (person) descansar. **~en (off)** vt aflojar. **~ off** (fam) aflojar

**slacks** /slæks/ npl pantalones mpl

**slag** /slæg/ n escoria f

**slain** /sleɪn/ see **slay**

**slake** /sleɪk/ vt apagar

**slam** /slæm/ vt (pt slammed) golpear; (throw) arrojar; (criticize, sl) criticar. **~ the door** dar un portazo. ● vi cerrarse de golpe. ● n golpe m; (of door) portazo m

**slander** /'slɑːndə(r)/ n calumnia f. ● vt difamar. **~ous** a calumnioso

**slang** /slæŋ/ n jerga f, argot m. **~y** a vulgar

**slant** /slɑːnt/ vt inclinar; presentar con parcialidad (news). ● n inclinación f; (point of view) punto m de vista

**slap** /slæp/ vt (pt slapped) abofetear; (on the back) dar una palmada; (put) arrojar. ● n bofetada f; (on back) palmada f. ● adv de lleno. **~dash**

/'slæpdəʃ/ a descuidado. ~happy a (fam) despreocupado; (dazed, fam) aturdido. ~stick /'slæpstɪk/ n payasada f. ~up a (sl) de primera categoría
slash /slæʃ/ vt acuchillar; (fig) reducir radicalmente. ● n cuchillada f
slat /slæt/ n tablilla f
slate /sleɪt/ n pizarra f. ● vt (fam) criticar
slaughter /'slɔːtə(r)/ vt masacrar; matar (animal). ● n carnicería f; (of animals) matanza f. ~house /'slɔːtəhaʊs/ n matadero m
Slav /slɑːv/ a & n eslavo (m)
slave /sleɪv/ n esclavo m. ● vi trabajar como un negro. ~e-driver n negrero m. ~ery /-ərɪ/ n esclavitud f. ~ish /'sleɪvɪʃ/ a servil
Slavonic /slə'vɒnɪk/ a eslavo
slay /sleɪ/ vt (pt slew, pp slain) matar
sleazy /'sliːzɪ/ a (-ier, -iest) (fam) sórdido
sledge /sledʒ/ n trineo m. ~hammer n almádena f
sleek /sliːk/ a (-er, -est) liso, brillante; (elegant) elegante
sleep /sliːp/ n sueño m. go to ~ dormirse. ● vi (pt slept) dormir. ● vt poder alojar. ~er n durmiente m & f; (on track) traviesa f; (berth) coche-cama m. ~ily adv soñolientamente. ~ing-bag n saco m de dormir. ~ing-pill n somnífero m. ~less a insomne. ~lessness n insomnio m. ~walker n sonámbulo m. ~y /'sliːpɪ/ a (-ier, -iest) soñoliento. be ~y tener sueño
sleet /sliːt/ n aguanieve f. ● vi caer aguanieve
sleeve /sliːv/ n manga f; (for record) funda f. up one's ~ en reserva. ~less a sin mangas
sleigh /sleɪ/ n trineo m
sleight /slaɪt/ n. ~ of hand prestidigitación f
slender /'slendə(r)/ a delgado; (fig) escaso
slept /slept/ see sleep
sleuth /sluːθ/ n investigador m
slew¹ /sluː/ see slay
slew² /sluː/ vi (turn) girar
slice /slaɪs/ n lonja f; (of bread) rebanada f; (of sth round) rodaja f; (implement) paleta f. ● vt cortar; rebanar (bread)
slick /slɪk/ a liso; (cunning) astuto. ● n. (oil)~ capa f de aceite

slide /slaɪd/ vt (pt slid) deslizar. ● vi resbalar. ~e over pasar por alto de. ● n resbalón m; (in playground) tobogán m; (for hair) pasador m; (photo) diapositiva f; (fig, fall) baja f. ~e-rule n regla f de cálculo. ~ing a corredizo. ~ing scale n escala f móvil
slight /slaɪt/ a (-er, -est) ligero; (slender) delgado. ● vt ofender. ● n desaire m. ~est a mínimo. not in the ~est en absoluto. ~ly adv un poco
slim /slɪm/ a (slimmer, slimmest) delgado. ● vi (pt slimmed) adelgazar
slime /slaɪm/ n légamo m, lodo m, fango m
slimness /'slɪmnɪs/ n delgadez f
slimy /'slaɪmɪ/ a legamoso, fangoso, viscoso; (fig) rastrero
sling /slɪŋ/ n honda f; (toy) tirador; (med) cabestrillo m. ● vt (pt slung) lanzar
slip /slɪp/ vt (pt slipped) deslizar. ~ s.o.'s mind olvidársele a uno. ● vi deslizarse. ● n resbalón m; (mistake) error m; (petticoat) combinación f; (paper) trozo m. ~ of the tongue n lapsus m linguae. give the ~ to zafarse de, dar esquinazo a. ~ away vi escabullirse. ~ into vi ponerse (clothes). ~ up vi (fam) equivocarse
slipper /'slɪpə(r)/ n zapatilla f
slippery /'slɪpərɪ/ a resbaladizo
slip: ~-road n rampa f de acceso. ~shod /'slɪpʃɒd/ a descuidado. ~up n (fam) error m
slit /slɪt/ n raja f; (cut) corte m. ● vt (pt slit, pres p slitting) rajar; (cut) cortar
slither /'slɪðə(r)/ vi deslizarse
sliver /'slɪvə(r)/ n trocito m; (splinter) astilla f
slobber /'slɒbə(r)/ vi babear
slog /slɒg/ vt (pt slogged) golpear. ● vi trabajar como un negro. ● n golpetazo m; (hard work) trabajo m penoso
slogan /'sləʊgən/ n eslogan m
slop /slɒp/ vt (pt slopped) derramar. ● vi derramarse. ~s npl (fam) agua f sucia
slope /sləʊp/ vi inclinarse. ● vt inclinar. ● n declive m, pendiente m. ~ing a inclinado
sloppy /'slɒpɪ/ a (-ier, -iest) (wet) mojado; (food) líquido; (work)

descuidado; ⟨person⟩ desaliñado; (fig) sentimental

**slosh** /slɒʃ/ vi (fam) chapotear. ● vt (hit, sl) pegar

**slot** /slɒt/ n ranura f. ● vt (pt slotted) encajar

**sloth** /sləʊθ/ n pereza f

**slot-machine** /'slɒtməʃiːn/ n distribuidor m automático; (for gambling) máquina f tragaperras

**slouch** /slaʊtʃ/ vi andar cargado de espaldas; (in chair) repanchigarse

**Slovak** /'sləʊvæk/ a & n eslovaco (m). ~ia /sləʊ'vækɪə/ n Eslovaquia f

**slovenl|iness** /'slʌvnlɪnɪs/ n despreocupación f. ~y /'slʌvnlɪ/ a descuidado

**slow** /sləʊ/ a (-er, -est) lento. be ~ ⟨clock⟩ estar atrasado. in ~ motion a cámara lenta. ● adv despacio. ● vt retardar. ● vi ir más despacio. ● down, ~ up vt retardar. ● vi ir más despacio. ~coach /'sləʊkəʊtʃ/ n tardón m. ~ly adv despacio. ~ness n lentitud f

**sludge** /slʌdʒ/ n fango m; (sediment) sedimento m

**slug** /slʌg/ n babosa f; (bullet) posta f. ~gish /'slʌgɪʃ/ a lento

**sluice** /sluːs/ n (gate) compuerta f; (channel) canal m

**slum** /slʌm/ n tugurio m

**slumber** /'slʌmbə(r)/ n sueño m. ● vi dormir

**slump** /slʌmp/ n baja f repentina; (in business) depresión f. ● vi bajar repentinamente; (flop down) dejarse caer pesadamente; (collapse) desplomarse

**slung** /slʌŋ/ see sling

**slur** /slɜː(r)/ vt/i (pt slurred) articular mal. ● n dicción f defectuosa; (discredit) calumnia f

**slush** /slʌʃ/ n nieve f medio derretida; (fig) sentimentalismo m. ~ fund n fondos mpl secretos para fines deshonestos. ~y a ⟨road⟩ cubierto de nieve medio derretida

**slut** /slʌt/ n mujer f desaseada

**sly** /slaɪ/ a (slyer, slyest) (crafty) astuto; (secretive) furtivo. ● n. on the ~ a escondidas. ~ly adv astutamente

**smack**[1] /smæk/ n golpe m; (on face) bofetada f. ● adv (fam) de lleno. ● vt pegar

**smack**[2] /smæk/ vi. ~ of saber a; (fig) oler a

**small** /smɔːl/ a (-er, -est) pequeño. ● n. the ~ of the back la región f lumbar. ~ ads npl anuncios mpl por palabras. ~ change n cambio m. ~holding /'smɔːlhəʊldɪŋ/ n parcela f. ~pox /'smɔːlpɒks/ n viruela f. ~ talk n charla f. ~time a (fam) de poca monta

**smarmy** /'smɑːmɪ/ a (-ier, -iest) (fam) zalamero

**smart** /smɑːt/ a (-er, -est) elegante; (clever) inteligente; (brisk) rápido. ● vi escocer. ~en /'smɑːtn/ vt arreglar. ● vi arreglarse. ~en up vi arreglarse. ~ly adv elegantemente; (quickly) rápidamente. ~ness n elegancia f

**smash** /smæʃ/ vt romper; (into little pieces) hacer pedazos; batir ⟨record⟩. ● vi romperse; (collide) chocar (into con). ● n (noise) estruendo m; (collision) choque m; (com) quiebra f. ~ing /'smæʃɪŋ/ a (fam) estupendo

**smattering** /'smætərɪŋ/ n conocimientos mpl superficiales

**smear** /smɪə(r)/ vt untar (with de); (stain) manchar (with de); (fig) difamar. ● n mancha f; (med) frotis m

**smell** /smel/ n olor m; (sense) olfato m. ● vt/i (pt smelt) oler. ~y a maloliente

**smelt**[1] /smelt/ see smell

**smelt**[2] /smelt/ vt fundir

**smile** /smaɪl/ n sonrisa f. ● vi sonreír(se)

**smirk** /smɜːk/ n sonrisa f afectada

**smite** /smaɪt/ vt (pt smote, pp smitten) golpear

**smith** /smɪθ/ n herrero m

**smithereens** /smɪðə'riːnz/ npl añicos mpl. smash to ~ hacer añicos

**smitten** /'smɪtn/ see smite. ● a encaprichado (with por)

**smock** /smɒk/ n blusa f, bata f

**smog** /smɒg/ n niebla f con humo

**smok|e** /sməʊk/ n humo m. ● vt/i fumar. ~eless a sin humo. ~er /-ə(r)/ n fumador m. ~e-screen n cortina f de humo. ~y a ⟨room⟩ lleno de humo

**smooth** /smuːð/ a (-er, -est) liso; ⟨sound, movement⟩ suave; ⟨sea⟩ tranquilo; ⟨manners⟩ zalamero. ● vt alisar; (fig) allanar. ~ly adv suavemente

**smote** /sməʊt/ see smite

**smother** /'smʌðə(r)/ *vt* sofocar; (*cover*) cubrir

**smoulder** /'sməuldə(r)/ *vi* arder sin llama; (*fig*) arder

**smudge** /smʌdʒ/ *n* borrón *m*, mancha *f*. ● *vt* tiznar. ● *vi* tiznarse

**smug** /smʌg/ *a* (**smugger, smuggest**) satisfecho de sí mismo

**smuggl|e** /'smʌgl/ *vt* pasar de contrabando. **~er** *n* contrabandista *m* & *f*. **~ing** *n* contrabando *m*

**smug:** **~ly** *adv* con suficiencia. **~ness** *n* suficiencia *f*

**smut** /smʌt/ *n* tizne *m*; (*mark*) tiznajo *m*. **~ty** *a* (**-ier, -iest**) tiznado; (*fig*) obsceno

**snack** /snæk/ *n* tentempié *m*. **~bar** *n* cafetería *f*

**snag** /snæg/ *n* problema *m*; (*in cloth*) rasgón *m*

**snail** /sneɪl/ *n* caracol *m*. **~'s pace** *n* paso *m* de tortuga

**snake** /sneɪk/ *n* serpiente *f*

**snap** /snæp/ *vt* (*pt* **snapped**) (*break*) romper; castañetear (*fingers*). ● *vi* romperse; ⟨*dog*⟩ intentar morder; (*say*) contestar bruscamente; ⟨*whip*⟩ chasquear. **~ at** ⟨*dog*⟩ intentar morder; (*say*) contestar bruscamente. ● *n* chasquido *m*; (*photo*) foto *f*. ● *a* instantáneo. **~ up** *vt* agarrar. **~py** /'snæpɪ/ *a* (**-ier, -iest**) (*fam*) rápido. **make it ~py!** (*fam*) ¡date prisa! **~shot** /'snæpʃɒt/ *n* foto *f*

**snare** /sneə(r)/ *n* trampa *f*

**snarl** /snɑːl/ *vi* gruñir. ● *n* gruñido *m*

**snatch** /snætʃ/ *vt* agarrar; (*steal*) robar. ● *n* arrebatamiento *m*; (*short part*) trocito *m*; (*theft*) robo *m*

**sneak** /sniːk/ *n* soplón *m*. ● *vi*. **~ in** entrar furtivamente. **~ out** salir furtivamente

**sneakers** /'sniːkəz/ *npl* zapatillas *fpl* de lona

**sneak|ing** /'sniːkɪŋ/ *a* furtivo. **~y** *a* furtivo

**sneer** /snɪə(r)/ *n* sonrisa *f* de desprecio. ● *vi* sonreír con desprecio. **~ at** hablar con desprecio a

**sneeze** /sniːz/ *n* estornudo *m*. ● *vi* estornudar

**snide** /snaɪd/ *a* (*fam*) despreciativo

**sniff** /snɪf/ *vt* oler. ● *vi* aspirar por la nariz. ● *n* aspiración *f*

**snigger** /'snɪgə(r)/ *n* risa *f* disimulada. ● *vi* reír disimuladamente

**snip** /snɪp/ *vt* (*pt* **snipped**) tijeretear. ● *n* tijeretada *f*; (*bargain, sl*) ganga *f*

**snipe** /snaɪp/ *vi* disparar desde un escondite. **~r** /ə(r)/ *n* tirador *m* emboscado, francotirador *m*

**snippet** /'snɪpɪt/ *n* retazo *m*

**snivel** /'snɪvl/ *vi* (*pt* **snivelled**) lloriquear. **~ling** *a* llorón

**snob** /snɒb/ *n* esnob *m*. **~bery** *n* esnobismo *m*. **~bish** *a* esnob

**snooker** /'snuːkə(r)/ *n* billar *m*

**snoop** /snuːp/ *vi* (*fam*) curiosear

**snooty** /'snuːtɪ/ *a* (*fam*) desdeñoso

**snooze** /snuːz/ *n* sueñecito *m*. ● *vi* echarse un sueñecito

**snore** /snɔː(r)/ *n* ronquido *m*. ● *vi* roncar

**snorkel** /'snɔːkl/ *n* tubo *m* respiratorio

**snort** /snɔːt/ *n* bufido *m*. ● *vi* bufar

**snout** /snaʊt/ *n* hocico *m*

**snow** /snəʊ/ *n* nieve *f*. ● *vi* nevar. **be ~ed under with** estar inundado por. **~ball** /'snəʊbɔːl/ *n* bola *f* de nieve. **~drift** *n* nieve amontonada. **~drop** /'snəʊdrɒp/ *n* campanilla *f* de invierno. **~fall** /'snəʊfɔːl/ *n* nevada *f*. **~flake** /'snəʊfleɪk/ *n* copo *m* de nieve. **~man** /'snəʊmæn/ *n* (*pl* **-men**) muñeco *m* de nieve. **~plough** *n* quitanieves *m invar*. **~storm** /'snəʊstɔːm/ *n* nevasca *f*. **~y** *a* ⟨*place*⟩ de nieves abundantes; ⟨*weather*⟩ con nevadas seguidas

**snub** /snʌb/ *vt* (*pt* **snubbed**) desairar. ● *n* desaire *m*. **~-nosed** /'snʌbnəʊzd/ *a* chato

**snuff** /snʌf/ *n* rapé *m*. ● *vt* despabilar ⟨*candle*⟩. **~ out** apagar ⟨*candle*⟩

**snuffle** /'snʌfl/ *vi* respirar ruidosamente

**snug** /snʌg/ *a* (**snugger, snuggest**) cómodo; (*tight*) ajustado

**snuggle** /'snʌgl/ *vi* acomodarse

**so** /səʊ/ *adv* (*before a or adv*) tan; (*thus*) así. ● *conj* así que. **~ am I** yo tambien. **~ as to** para. **~ far** *adv* (*time*) hasta ahora; (*place*) hasta aquí. **~ far as I know** que yo sepa. **~ long!** (*fam*) ¡hasta luego! **~ much** tanto. **~ that** *conj* para que. **and ~ forth, and ~ on** y así sucesivamente. **if ~** si es así. **I think ~** creo que sí. **or ~** más o menos

**soak** /səʊk/ *vt* remojar. ● *vi* remojarse. **~ in** penetrar. **~ up** absorber. **~ing** *a* empapado. ● *n* remojón *m*

**so-and-so** /'səʊənsəʊ/ *n* fulano *m*

**soap** /səʊp/ n jabón m. ● vt enjabonar. ~ **powder** n jabón en polvo. ~**y** a jabonoso

**soar** /sɔː(r)/ vi elevarse; ⟨price etc⟩ ponerse por las nubes

**sob** /sɒb/ n sollozo m. ● vi (pt **sobbed**) sollozar

**sober** /ˈsəʊbə(r)/ a sobrio; ⟨colour⟩ discreto

**so-called** /ˈsəʊkɔːld/ a llamado, supuesto

**soccer** /ˈsɒkə(r)/ n (fam) fútbol m

**sociable** /ˈsəʊʃəbl/ a sociable

**social** /ˈsəʊʃl/ a social; (sociable) sociable. ● n reunión f. ~**ism** /-zəm/ n socialismo m. ~**ist** /ˈsəʊʃəlɪst/ a & n socialista m & f. ~**ize** /ˈsəʊʃəlaɪz/ vt socializar. ~**ly** adv socialmente. ~ **security** n seguridad f social. ~ **worker** n asistente m social

**society** /səˈsaɪətɪ/ n sociedad f

**sociolog|ical** /səʊsɪəˈlɒdʒɪkl/ a sociológico. ~**ist** n sociólogo m. ~**y** /səʊsɪˈɒlədʒɪ/ n sociología f

**sock**[1] /sɒk/ n calcetín m

**sock**[2] /sɒk/ vt (sl) pegar

**socket** /ˈsɒkɪt/ n hueco m; (of eye) cuenca f; (wall plug) enchufe m; (for bulb) portalámparas m invar, casquillo m

**soda** /ˈsəʊdə/ n sosa f; (water) soda f. ~**water** n soda f

**sodden** /ˈsɒdn/ a empapado

**sodium** /ˈsəʊdɪəm/ n sodio m

**sofa** /ˈsəʊfə/ n sofá m

**soft** /sɒft/ a (-er, -est) blando; ⟨sound, colour⟩ suave; (gentle) dulce, tierno; (silly) estúpido. ~ **drink** n bebida f no alcohólica. ~ **spot** n debilidad f. ~**en** /ˈsɒfn/ vt ablandar; (fig) suavizar. ● vi ablandarse; (fig) suavizarse. ~**ly** adv dulcemente. ~**ness** n blandura f; (fig) dulzura f. ~**ware** /ˈsɒftweə(r)/ n programación f, software m

**soggy** /ˈsɒgɪ/ a (-ier, -iest) empapado

**soh** /səʊ/ n (mus, fifth note of any musical scale) sol m

**soil**[1] /sɔɪl/ n suelo m

**soil**[2] /sɔɪl/ vt ensuciar. ● vi ensuciarse

**solace** /ˈsɒləs/ n consuelo m

**solar** /ˈsəʊlə(r)/ a solar. ~**ium** /səˈleərɪəm/ n (pl -a) solario m

**sold** /səʊld/ see **sell**

**solder** /ˈsɒldə(r)/ n soldadura f. ● vt soldar

**soldier** /ˈsəʊldʒə(r)/ n soldado m. ● vi. ~ **on** (fam) perseverar

**sole**[1] /səʊl/ n (of foot) planta f; (of shoe) suela f

**sole**[2] /səʊl/ (fish) lenguado m

**sole**[3] /səʊl/ a único, solo. ~**ly** adv únicamente

**solemn** /ˈsɒləm/ a solemne. ~**ity** /səˈlemnətɪ/ n solemnidad f. ~**ly** adv solemnemente

**solicit** /səˈlɪsɪt/ vt solicitar. ● vi importunar

**solicitor** /səˈlɪsɪtə(r)/ n abogado m; (notary) notario m

**solicitous** /səˈlɪsɪtəs/ a solícito

**solid** /ˈsɒlɪd/ a sólido; ⟨gold etc⟩ macizo; (unanimous) unánime; ⟨meal⟩ sustancioso. ● n sólido m. ~**arity** /sɒlɪˈdærətɪ/ n solidaridad f. ~**ify** /səˈlɪdɪfaɪ/ vt solidificar. ● vi solidificarse. ~**ity** /səˈlɪdətɪ/ n solidez f. ~**ly** adv sólidamente. ~**s** npl alimentos mpl sólidos

**soliloquy** /səˈlɪləkwɪ/ n soliloquio m

**solitaire** /sɒlɪˈteə(r)/ n solitario m

**solitary** /ˈsɒlɪtrɪ/ a solitario

**solitude** /ˈsɒlɪtjuːd/ n soledad f

**solo** /ˈsəʊləʊ/ n (pl -os) (mus) solo m. ~**ist** n solista m & f

**solstice** /ˈsɒlstɪs/ n solsticio m

**soluble** /ˈsɒljʊbl/ a soluble

**solution** /səˈluːʃn/ n solución f

**solvable** a soluble

**solve** /sɒlv/ vt resolver

**solvent** /ˈsɒlvənt/ a & n solvente (m)

**sombre** /ˈsɒmbə(r)/ a sombrío

**some** /sʌm/ a alguno; (a little) un poco de. ~ **day** algún día. ~ **two hours** unas dos horas. **will you have** ~ **wine?** ¿quieres vino? ● pron algunos; (a little) un poco. ~ **of us** algunos de nosotros. **I want** ~ quiero un poco. ● adv (approximately) unos. ~**body** /ˈsʌmbədɪ/ pron alguien. ● n personaje m. ~**how** /ˈsʌmhaʊ/ adv de algún modo. ~**how or other** de una manera u otra. ~**one** /ˈsʌmwʌn/ pron alguien. ● n personaje m

**somersault** /ˈsʌməsɔːlt/ n salto m mortal. ● vi dar un salto mortal

**some**: ~**thing** /ˈsʌmθɪŋ/ pron algo m. ~**thing like** algo como; (approximately) cerca de. ~**time** /ˈsʌmtaɪm/ a ex. ● adv algún día; (in past) durante. ~**time last summer** a (durante) el verano pasado. ~**times** /ˈsʌmtaɪmz/ adv de vez en cuando, a veces. ~**what** /ˈsʌmwɒt/ adv algo, un poco. ~**where** /ˈsʌmweə(r)/ adv en alguna parte

**son** /sʌn/ n hijo m

**sonata** /sə'nɑːtə/ n sonata f

**song** /sɒŋ/ n canción f. **sell for a ~** vender muy barato. **~book** n cancionero m

**sonic** /'sɒnɪk/ a sónico

**son-in-law** /'sʌnɪnlɔː/ n (pl **sons-in-law**) yerno m

**sonnet** /'sɒnɪt/ n soneto m

**sonny** /'sʌnɪ/ n (fam) hijo m

**soon** /suːn/ adv (-er, -est) pronto; (in a short time) dentro de poco; (early) temprano. **~ after** poco después. **~er or later** tarde o temprano. **as ~ as** en cuanto; **as ~ as possible** lo antes posible. **I would ~er not go** prefiero no ir

**soot** /sʊt/ n hollín m

**sooth|e** /suːð/ vt calmar. **~ing** a calmante

**sooty** /'sʊtɪ/ a cubierto de hollín

**sophisticated** /sə'fɪstɪkeɪtɪd/ a sofisticado; (complex) complejo

**soporific** /sɒpə'rɪfɪk/ a soporífero

**sopping** /'sɒpɪŋ/ a. **~ (wet)** empapado

**soppy** /'sɒpɪ/ a (-ier, -iest) (fam) sentimental; (silly, fam) tonto

**soprano** /sə'prɑːnəʊ/ n (pl **-os**) (voice) soprano m; (singer) soprano f

**sorcerer** /'sɔːsərə(r)/ n hechicero m

**sordid** /'sɔːdɪd/ a sórdido

**sore** /sɔː(r)/ a (-er, -est) que duele, dolorido; (distressed) penoso; (vexed) enojado. ● n llaga f. **~ly** /'sɔːlɪ/ adv gravemente. **~ throat** n dolor m de garganta. **I've got a ~ throat** me duele la garganta

**sorrow** /'sɒrəʊ/ n pena f, tristeza f. **~ful** a triste

**sorry** /'sɒrɪ/ a (-ier, -ier) arrepentido; (wretched) lamentable; (sad) triste. **be ~** sentirlo; (repent) arrepentirse. **be ~ for s.o.** (pity) compadecerse de uno. **~!** ¡perdón!, ¡perdone!

**sort** /sɔːt/ n clase f; (person, fam) tipo m. **be out of ~s** estar indispuesto; (irritable) estar de mal humor. ● vt clasificar. **~ out** (choose) escoger; (separate) separar; resolver (problem)

**so-so** /'səʊsəʊ/ a & adv regular

**soufflé** /'suːfleɪ/ n suflé m

**sought** /sɔːt/ see **seek**

**soul** /səʊl/ n alma f. **~ful** /'səʊlfl/ a sentimental

**sound**[1] /saʊnd/ n sonido m; ruido m. ● vt sonar; (test) sondar. ● vi sonar; (seem) parecer (**as if** que)

**sound**[2] /saʊnd/ a (-er, -est) sano; (argument etc) lógico; (secure) seguro. **~ asleep** profundamente dormido

**sound**[3] /saʊnd/ (strait) estrecho m

**sound barrier** /'saʊndbærɪə(r)/ n barrera f del sonido

**soundly** /'saʊndlɪ/ adv sólidamente; (asleep) profundamente

**sound: ~proof** a insonorizado. **~track** n banda f sonora

**soup** /suːp/ n sopa f. **in the ~** (sl) en apuros

**sour** /'saʊə(r)/ a (-er, -est) agrio; (cream, milk) cortado. ● vt agriar. ● vi agriarse

**source** /sɔːs/ n fuente f

**south** /saʊθ/ n sur m. ● a del sur. ● adv hacia el sur. **S~ Africa** n África f del Sur. **S~ America** n América f (del Sur), Sudamérica f. **S~ American** a & n sudamericano (m). **~east** n sudeste m. **~erly** /'sʌðəlɪ/ a sur; (wind) del sur. **~ern** /'sʌðən/ a del sur, meridional. **~erner** n meridional m. **~ward** a sur; ● adv hacia el sur. **~wards** adv hacia el sur. **~west** n sudoeste m

**souvenir** /suːvə'nɪə(r)/ n recuerdo m

**sovereign** /'sɒvrɪn/ n & a soberano (m). **~ty** n soberanía f

**Soviet** /'səʊvɪət/ a (history) soviético. **the ~ Union** n la Unión f Soviética

**sow**[1] /səʊ/ vt (pt **sowed**, pp **sowed** or **sown**) sembrar

**sow**[2] /saʊ/ n cerda f

**soya** /'sɔɪə/ n. **~ bean** n soja f

**spa** /spɑː/ n balneario m

**space** /speɪs/ n espacio m; (room) sitio m; (period) período m. ● a (research etc) espacial. ● vt espaciar. **~out** espaciar. **~craft** /'speɪskrɑːft/ n, **~ship** n nave f espacial. **~suit** n traje m espacial

**spacious** /'speɪʃəs/ a espacioso

**spade** /speɪd/ n pala f. **~s** npl (cards) picos mpl, picas fpl; (in Spanish pack) espadas fpl. **~work** /'speɪdwɜːk/ n trabajo m preparatorio

**spaghetti** /spə'getɪ/ n espaguetis mpl

**Spain** /speɪn/ n España f

**span**[1] /spæn/ n (of arch) luz f; (of time) espacio m; (of wings) envergadura f. ● vt (pt **spanned**) extenderse sobre

**span**[2] /spæn/ see **spick**

**Spaniard** /'spænjəd/ n español m

**spaniel** /'spænjəl/ *n* perro *m* de aguas

**Spanish** /'spænɪʃ/ *a & n* español (*m*)

**spank** /spæŋk/ *vt* dar un azote a. **~ing** *n* azote *m*

**spanner** /'spænə(r)/ *n* llave *f*

**spar** /spɑ:(r)/ *vi* (*pt* **sparred**) entrenarse en el boxeo; (*argue*) disputar

**spare** /speə(r)/ *vt* salvar; (*do without*) prescindir de; (*afford to give*) dar; (*use with restraint*) escatimar. ● *a* de reserva; (*surplus*) sobrante; ⟨*person*⟩ enjuto; ⟨*meal etc*⟩ frugal. **~ (part)** *n* repuesto *m*. **~ time** *n* tiempo *m* libre. **~ tyre** *n* neumático *m* de repuesto

**sparing** /'speərɪŋ/ *a* frugal. **~ly** *adv* frugalmente

**spark** /spɑ:k/ *n* chispa *f*. ● *vt*. **~ off** (*initiate*) provocar. **~ing-plug** *n* (*auto*) bujía *f*

**sparkl|e** /'spɑ:kl/ *vi* centellear. ● *n* centelleo *m*. **~ing** *a* centelleante; ⟨*wine*⟩ espumoso

**sparrow** /'spærəʊ/ *n* gorrión *m*

**sparse** /spɑ:s/ *a* escaso; ⟨*population*⟩ poco denso. **~ly** *adv* escasamente

**spartan** /'spɑ:tn/ *a* espartano

**spasm** /'spæzəm/ *n* espasmo *m*; (*of cough*) acceso *m*. **~odic** /spæz'mɒdɪk/ *a* espasmódico

**spastic** /'spæstɪk/ *n* víctima *f* de parálisis cerebral

**spat** /spæt/ *see* **spit**

**spate** /speɪt/ *n* avalancha *f*

**spatial** /'speɪʃl/ *a* espacial

**spatter** /'spætə(r)/ *vt* salpicar (**with** de)

**spatula** /'spætjʊlə/ *n* espátula *f*

**spawn** /spɔ:n/ *n* hueva *f*. ● *vt* engendrar. ● *vi* desovar

**speak** /spi:k/ *vt/i* (*pt* **spoke**, *pp* **spoken**) hablar. **~ for** *vi* hablar en nombre de. **~ up** *vi* hablar más fuerte. **~er** /'spi:kə(r)/ *n* (*in public*) orador *m*; (*loudspeaker*) altavoz *m*. **be a Spanish ~er** hablar español

**spear** /spɪə(r)/ *n* lanza *f*. **~head** /'spɪəhed/ *n* punta *f* de lanza. ● *vt* (*lead*) encabezar. **~mint** /'spɪəmɪnt/ *n* menta *f* verde

**spec** /spek/ *n*. **on ~** (*fam*) por si acaso

**special** /'speʃl/ *a* especial. **~ist** /'speʃəlɪst/ *n* especialista *m & f*. **~ity** /-ɪ'ælətɪ/ *n* especialidad *f*. **~ization** /-'zeɪʃn/ *n* especialización *f*. **~ize** /'speʃəlaɪz/ *vi* especializarse.

**~ized** *a* especializado. **~ty** *n* especialidad *f*. **~ly** *adv* especialmente

**species** /'spi:ʃi:z/ *n* especie *f*

**specif|ic** /spə'sɪfɪk/ *a* específico. **~ically** *adv* específicamente. **~ication** /-ɪ'keɪʃn/ *n* especificación *f*; (*details*) descripción *f*. **~y** /'spesɪfaɪ/ *vt* especificar

**specimen** /'spesɪmɪn/ *n* muestra *f*

**speck** /spek/ *n* manchita *f*; (*particle*) partícula *f*

**speckled** /'spekld/ *a* moteado

**specs** /speks/ *npl* (*fam*) gafas *fpl*, anteojos *mpl* (*LAm*)

**spectac|le** /'spektəkl/ *n* espectáculo *m*. **~les** *npl* gafas *fpl*, anteojos *mpl* (*LAm*). **~ular** /spek'tækjʊlə(r)/ *a* espectacular

**spectator** /spek'teɪtə(r)/ *n* espectador *m*

**spectre** /'spektə(r)/ *n* espectro *m*

**spectrum** /'spektrəm/ *n* (*pl* -**tra**) espectro *m*; (*of ideas*) gama *f*

**speculat|e** /'spekjʊleɪt/ *vi* especular. **~ion** /-'leɪʃn/ *n* especulación *f*. **~ive** /-lətɪv/ *a* especulativo. **~or** *n* especulador *m*

**sped** /sped/ *see* **speed**

**speech** /spi:tʃ/ *n* (*faculty*) habla *f*; (*address*) discurso *m*. **~less** *a* mudo

**speed** /spi:d/ *n* velocidad *f*; (*rapidity*) rapidez *f*; (*haste*) prisa *f*. ● *vi* (*pt* **sped**) apresurarse. (*pt* **speeded**) (*drive too fast*) ir a una velocidad excesiva. **~ up** *vt* acelerar. ● *vi* acelerarse. **~boat** /'spi:dbəʊt/ *n* lancha *f* motora. **~ily** *adv* rápidamente. **~ing** *n* exceso *m* de velocidad. **~ometer** /spi:'dɒmɪtə(r)/ *n* velocímetro *m*. **~way** /'spi:dweɪ/ *n* pista *f*; (*Amer*) autopista *f*. **~y** /'spi:dɪ/ *a* (-**ier**, -**iest**) rápido

**spell**[1] /spel/ *n* (*magic*) hechizo *m*

**spell**[2] /spel/ *vt/i* (*pt* **spelled** *or* **spelt**) escribir; (*mean*) significar. **~ out** *vt* deletrear; (*fig*) explicar. **~ing** *n* ortografía *f*

**spell**[3] /spel/ (*period*) período *m*

**spellbound** /'spelbaʊnd/ *a* hechizado

**spelt** /spelt/ *see* **spell**[2]

**spend** /spend/ *vt* (*pt* **spent**) gastar; pasar ⟨*time etc*⟩; dedicar ⟨*care etc*⟩. ● *vi* gastar dinero. **~thrift** /'spendθrɪft/ *n* derrochador *m*

**spent** /spent/ *see* **spend**

**sperm** /spɜ:m/ *n* (*pl* **sperms** *or* **sperm**) esperma *f*

**spew** /spju:/ *vt/i* vomitar

**spher|e** /sfɪə(r)/ n esfera f. **~ical** /'sferɪkl/ a esférico

**sphinx** /sfɪŋks/ n esfinge f

**spice** /spaɪs/ n especia f; (fig) sabor m

**spick** /spɪk/ a. **~ and span** impecable

**spicy** /'spaɪsɪ/ a picante

**spider** /'spaɪdə(r)/ n araña f

**spik|e** /spaɪk/ n (of metal etc) punta f. **~y** a puntiagudo; ⟨person⟩ quisquilloso

**spill** /spɪl/ vt (pt spilled or spilt) derramar. ● vi derramarse. **~ over** desbordarse

**spin** /spɪn/ vt (pt spun, pres p spinning) hacer girar; hilar ⟨wool etc⟩. ● vi girar. ● n vuelta f; (short drive) paseo m

**spinach** /'spɪnɪdʒ/ n espinacas fpl

**spinal** /'spaɪnl/ a espinal. **~ cord** n médula f espinal

**spindl|e** /'spɪndl/ n (for spinning) huso m. **~y** a larguirucho

**spin-drier** /spɪn'draɪə(r)/ n secador m centrífugo

**spine** /spaɪn/ n columna f vertebral; (of book) lomo m. **~less** a (fig) sin carácter

**spinning** /'spɪnɪŋ/ n hilado m. **~top** n trompa f, peonza f. **~wheel** n rueca f

**spin-off** /'spɪnɒf/ n beneficio m incidental; (by-product) subproducto m

**spinster** /'spɪnstə(r)/ n soltera f; (old maid, fam) solterona f

**spiral** /'spaɪərəl/ a espiral, helicoidal. ● n hélice f. ● vi (pt spiralled) moverse en espiral. **~ staircase** n escalera f de caracol

**spire** /'spaɪə(r)/ n (archit) aguja f

**spirit** /'spɪrɪt/ n espíritu m; (boldness) valor m. **in low ~s** abatido. ● vt. **~ away** hacer desaparecer. **~ed** /'spɪrɪtɪd/ a animado, fogoso. **~lamp** n lamparilla f de alcohol. **~level** n nivel m de aire. **~s** npl (drinks) bebidas fpl alcohólicas

**spiritual** /'spɪrɪtjʊəl/ a espiritual. ● n canción f religiosa de los negros. **~ualism** /-zəm/ n espiritismo m. **~ualist** /'spɪrɪtjʊəlɪst/ n espiritista m & f

**spit**[1] /spɪt/ vt (pt spat or spit, pres p spitting) escupir. ● vi escupir; (rain) lloviznar. ● n esputo m; (spittle) saliva f

**spit**[2] /spɪt/ (for roasting) asador m

**spite** /spaɪt/ n rencor m. **in ~ of** a pesar de. ● vt fastidiar. **~ful** a rencoroso. **~fully** adv con rencor

**spitting image** /spɪtɪŋ'ɪmɪdʒ/ n vivo retrato m

**spittle** /spɪtl/ n saliva f

**splash** /splæʃ/ vt salpicar. ● vi esparcirse; ⟨person⟩ chapotear. ● n salpicadura f; (sound) chapoteo m; (of colour) mancha f; (drop, fam) gota f. **~ about** vi chapotear. **~ down** vi ⟨spacecraft⟩ amerizar

**spleen** /spli:n/ n bazo m; (fig) esplín m

**splendid** /'splendɪd/ a espléndido

**splendour** /'splendə(r)/ n esplendor m

**splint** /splɪnt/ n tablilla f

**splinter** /'splɪntə(r)/ n astilla f. ● vi astillarse. **~ group** n grupo m disidente

**split** /splɪt/ vt (pt split, pres p splitting) hender, rajar; rajar; (divide) dividir; (share) repartir. **~ one's sides** caerse de risa. ● vi partirse; (divide) dividirse. **~ on s.o.** (sl) traicionar. ● n hendidura f; (tear) desgarrón m; (quarrel) ruptura f; (pol) escisión f. **~ up** vi separarse. **~ second** n fracción f de segundo

**splurge** /splɜ:dʒ/ vi (fam) derrochar

**splutter** /'splʌtə(r)/ vi chisporrotear; ⟨person⟩ farfullar. ● n chisporroteo m; (speech) farfulla f

**spoil** /spɔɪl/ vt (pt spoilt or spoiled) estropear, echar a perder; (ruin) arruinar; (indulge) mimar. ● n botín m. **~s** npl botín m. **~sport** n aguafiestas m invar

**spoke**[1] /spəʊk/ see speak

**spoke**[2] /spəʊk/ n (of wheel) radio m

**spoken** /spəʊkən/ see speak

**spokesman** /'spəʊksmən/ n (pl -men) portavoz m

**spong|e** /spʌndʒ/ n esponja f. ● vt limpiar con una esponja. ● vi. **~e on** vivir a costa de. **~e-cake** n bizcocho m. **~er** /-ə(r)/ n gorrón m. **~y** a esponjoso

**sponsor** /'spɒnsə(r)/ n patrocinador m; (surety) garante m. ● vt patrocinar. **~ship** n patrocinio m

**spontane|ity** /spɒntə'neɪɪtɪ/ n espontaneidad f. **~ous** /spɒn'teɪnjəs/ a espontáneo. **~ously** adv espontáneamente

**spoof** /spu:f/ n (sl) parodia f

**spooky** /'spu:kɪ/ a (-ier, -iest) (fam) escalofriante

**spool** /spuːl/ n carrete m; (of sewing-machine) canilla f

**spoon** /spuːn/ n cuchara f. ~**fed** a (fig) mimado. ~**feed** vt (pt -**fed**) dar de comer con cuchara. ~**ful** n (pl -**fuls**) cucharada f

**sporadic** /spəˈrædɪk/ a esporádico

**sport** /spɔːt/ n deporte m; (amusement) pasatiempo m; (person, fam) persona f alegre, buen chico m, buena chica f. **be a good** ~ ser buen perdedor. • vt lucir. ~**ing** a deportivo. ~**ing chance** n probabilidad f de éxito. ~**s car** n coche m deportivo. ~**s coat** n chaqueta f de sport. ~**sman** /ˈspɔːtsmən/ n, (pl -**men**) ~**swoman** /ˈspɔːtswʊmən/ n (pl -**women**) deportista m & f

**spot** /spɒt/ n mancha f; (pimple) grano m; (place) lugar m; (in pattern) punto m; (drop) gota f; (a little, fam) poquito m. **in a** ~ (fam) en un apuro. **on the** ~ en el lugar; (without delay) en el acto. • vt (pt spotted) manchar; (notice, fam) observar, ver. ~ **check** n control m hecho al azar. ~**less** a inmaculado. ~**light** /ˈspɒtlaɪt/ n reflector m. ~**ted** a moteado; ⟨cloth⟩ a puntos. ~**ty** a (-**ier**, -**iest**) manchado; ⟨skin⟩ con granos

**spouse** /spaʊz/ n cónyuge m & f

**spout** /spaʊt/ n pico m; (jet) chorro m. **up the** ~ (ruined, sl) perdido. • vi chorrear

**sprain** /spreɪn/ vt torcer. • n torcedura f

**sprang** /spræŋ/ see **spring**

**sprat** /spræt/ n espadín m

**sprawl** /sprɔːl/ vi ⟨person⟩ repanchigarse; ⟨city etc⟩ extenderse

**spray** /spreɪ/ n (of flowers) ramo m; (water) rociada f; (from sea) espuma f; (device) pulverizador m. • vt rociar. ~**gun** n pistola f pulverizadora

**spread** /spred/ vt (pt spread) (stretch, extend) extender; untar ⟨jam etc⟩; difundir ⟨idea, news⟩. • vi extenderse; ⟨disease⟩ propagarse; ⟨idea, news⟩ difundirse. • n extensión f; (paste) pasta f; (of disease) propagación f; (feast, fam) comilona f. ~**eagled** a con los brazos y piernas extendidos

**spree** /spriː/ n. **go on a** ~ (have fun, fam) ir de juerga

**sprig** /sprɪg/ n ramito m

**sprightly** /ˈspraɪtlɪ/ a (-**ier**, -**iest**) vivo

**spring** /sprɪŋ/ n (season) primavera f; (device) muelle m; (elasticity) elasticidad f; (water) manantial m. • a de primavera. • vt (pt sprang, pp sprung) hacer inesperadamente. • vi saltar; (issue) brotar. ~ **from** vi provenir de. ~ **up** vi surgir. ~**board** n trampolín m. ~**time** n primavera f. ~**y** a (-**ier**, -**iest**) elástico

**sprinkl|e** /ˈsprɪŋkl/ vt salpicar; (with liquid) rociar. • n salpicadura f; (of liquid) rociada f. ~**ed with** salpicado de. ~**er** /-ə(r)/ n regadera f. ~**ing** /ˈsprɪŋklɪŋ/ n (fig, amount) poco m

**sprint** /sprɪnt/ n carrera f. • vi correr. ~**er** n corredor m

**sprite** /spraɪt/ n duende m, hada f

**sprout** /spraʊt/ vi brotar. • n brote m. **(Brussels)** ~**s** npl coles fpl de Bruselas

**spruce** /spruːs/ a elegante

**sprung** /sprʌŋ/ see **spring**. • a de muelles

**spry** /spraɪ/ a (spryer, spryest) vivo

**spud** /spʌd/ n (sl) patata f, papa f (LAm)

**spun** /spʌn/ see **spin**

**spur** /spɜː(r)/ n espuela f; (stimulus) estímulo m. **on the** ~ **of the moment** impulsivamente. • vt (pt spurred). ~ **(on)** espolear; (fig) estimular

**spurious** /ˈspjʊərɪəs/ a falso. ~**ly** adv falsamente

**spurn** /spɜːn/ vt despreciar; (reject) rechazar

**spurt** /spɜːt/ vi chorrear; (make sudden effort) hacer un esfuerzo repentino. • n chorro m; (effort) esfuerzo m repentino

**spy** /spaɪ/ n espía m & f. • vt divisar. • vi espiar. ~ **out** vt reconocer. ~**ing** n espionaje m

**squabble** /ˈskwɒbl/ n riña f. • vi reñir

**squad** /skwɒd/ n (mil) pelotón m; (of police) brigada f; (sport) equipo m

**squadron** /ˈskwɒdrən/ n (mil) escuadrón m; (naut, aviat) escuadrilla f

**squalid** /ˈskwɒlɪd/ a asqueroso; (wretched) miserable

**squall** /skwɔːl/ n turbión m. • vi chillar. ~**y** a borrascoso

**squalor** /ˈskwɒlə(r)/ n miseria f

**squander** /ˈskwɒndə(r)/ vt derrochar

**square** /skweə(r)/ n cuadrado m; (open space in town) plaza f; (for drawing) escuadra f. ● a cuadrado; (not owing) sin deudas, iguales; (honest) honrado; ⟨meal⟩ satisfactorio; (old-fashioned, sl) chapado a la antigua. **all ~** iguales. ● vt (settle) arreglar; (math) cuadrar. ● vi (agree) cuadrar. **~ up to** enfrentarse con. **~ly** adv directamente

**squash** /skwɒʃ/ vt aplastar; (suppress) suprimir. ● n apiñamiento m; (drink) zumo m; (sport) squash m. **~y** a blando

**squat** /skwɒt/ vi (pt **squatted**) ponerse en cuclillas; (occupy illegally) ocupar sin derecho. ● n casa f ocupada sin derecho. ● a (dumpy) achaparrado. **~ter** /-ə(r)/ n ocupante m & f ilegal

**squawk** /skwɔːk/ n graznido m. ● vi graznar

**squeak** /skwiːk/ n chillido m; (of door etc) chirrido m. ● vi chillar; ⟨door etc⟩ chirriar. **~y** a chirriador

**squeal** /skwiːl/ n chillido m. ● vi chillar. **~ on** (inform on, sl) denunciar

**squeamish** /ˈskwiːmɪʃ/ a delicado; (scrupulous) escrupuloso. **be ~ about snakes** tener horror a las serpientes

**squeeze** /skwiːz/ vt apretar; exprimir ⟨lemon etc⟩; (extort) extorsionar (**from** de). ● vi (force one's way) abrirse paso. ● n estrujón m; (of hand) apretón m. **credit ~** n restricción f de crédito

**squelch** /skweltʃ/ vi chapotear. ● n chapoteo m

**squib** /skwɪb/ n (firework) buscapiés m invar

**squid** /skwɪd/ n calamar m

**squiggle** /ˈskwɪgl/ n garabato m

**squint** /skwɪnt/ vi ser bizco; (look sideways) mirar de soslayo. ● n estrabismo m

**squire** /ˈskwaɪə(r)/ n terrateniente m

**squirm** /skwɜːm/ vi retorcerse

**squirrel** /ˈskwɪrəl/ n ardilla f

**squirt** /skwɜːt/ vt arrojar a chorros. ● vi salir a chorros. ● n chorro m

**St** abbr (saint) /sənt/ S, San(to); (street) C/, Calle f

**stab** /stæb/ vt (pt **stabbed**) apuñalar. ● n puñalada f; (pain) punzada f; (attempt, fam) tentativa f

**stabili|ty** /stəˈbɪlətɪ/ n estabilidad f. **~ze** /ˈsteɪbɪlaɪz/ vt estabilizar. **~zer** /-ə(r)/ n estabilizador m

**stable**[1] /ˈsteɪbl/ a (-er, -est) estable

**stable**[2] /ˈsteɪbl/ n cuadra f. ● vt poner en una cuadra. **~boy** n mozo m de cuadra

**stack** /stæk/ n montón m. ● vt amontonar

**stadium** /ˈsteɪdjəm/ n estadio m

**staff** /stɑːf/ n (stick) palo m; (employees) personal m; (mil) estado m mayor; (in school) profesorado m. ● vt proveer de personal

**stag** /stæg/ n ciervo m. **~-party** n reunión f de hombres, fiesta f de despedida de soltero

**stage** /steɪdʒ/ n (in theatre) escena f; (phase) etapa f; (platform) plataforma f. **go on the ~** hacerse actor. ● vt representar; (arrange) organizar. **~-coach** n (hist) diligencia f. **~ fright** n miedo m al público. **~-manager** n director m de escena. **~ whisper** n aparte m

**stagger** /ˈstægə(r)/ vi tambalearse. ● vt asombrar; escalonar ⟨holidays etc⟩. ● n tambaleo m. **~ing** a asombroso

**stagna|nt** /ˈstægnənt/ a estancado. **~te** /stægˈneɪt/ vi estancarse. **~tion** /-ˈʃn/ n estancamiento m

**staid** /steɪd/ a serio, formal

**stain** /steɪn/ vt manchar; (colour) teñir. ● n mancha f; (liquid) tinte m. **~ed glass window** n vidriera f de colores. **~less** /ˈsteɪnlɪs/ a inmaculado. **~less steel** n acero m inoxidable. **~ remover** n quitamanchas m invar

**stair** /steə(r)/ n escalón m. **~s** npl escalera f. **flight of ~s** tramo m de escalera. **~case** /ˈsteəkeɪs/ n, **~way** n escalera f

**stake** /steɪk/ n estaca f; (for execution) hoguera f; (wager) apuesta f; (com) intereses mpl. **at ~** en juego. ● vt estacar; (wager) apostar. **~ a claim** reclamar

**stalactite** /ˈstæləktaɪt/ n estalactita f

**stalagmite** /ˈstæləgmaɪt/ n estalagmita f

**stale** /steɪl/ a (-er, -est) no fresco; ⟨bread⟩ duro; ⟨smell⟩ viciado; ⟨news⟩ viejo; (uninteresting) gastado. **~mate** /ˈsteɪlmeɪt/ n (chess) ahogado m; (deadlock) punto m muerto

**stalk**[1] /stɔːk/ n tallo m

**stalk²** /stɔ:k/ *vi* andar majestuosamente. ● *vt* seguir; *‹animal›* acechar

**stall¹** /stɔ:l/ *n* (*stable*) cuadra *f*; (*in stable*) casilla *f*; (*in theatre*) butaca *f*; (*in market*) puesto *m*; (*kiosk*) quiosco *m*

**stall²** /stɔ:l/ *vt* parar *‹engine›*. ● *vi* *‹engine›* pararse; (*fig*) andar con rodeos

**stallion** /'stæljən/ *n* semental *m*

**stalwart** /'stɔ:lwət/ *n* partidario *m* leal

**stamina** /'stæmɪnə/ *n* resistencia *f*

**stammer** /'stæmə(r)/ *vi* tartamudear. ● *n* tartamudeo *m*

**stamp** /stæmp/ *vt* (*with feet*) patear; (*press*) estampar; poner un sello en *‹envelope›*; (*with rubber stamp*) sellar; (*fig*) señalar. ● *vi* patear. ● *n* sello *m*; (*with foot*) patada *f*; (*mark*) marca *f*, señal *f*. ~ **out** (*fig*) acabar con

**stampede** /stæm'pi:d/ *n* desbandada *f*; (*fam*) pánico *m*. ● *vi* huir en desorden

**stance** /stɑ:ns/ *n* postura *f*

**stand** /stænd/ *vi* (*pt* **stood**) estar de pie; (*rise*) ponerse de pie; (*be*) encontrarse; (*stay firm*) permanecer; (*pol*) presentarse como candidato (**for** en). ~ **to reason** ser lógico. ● *vt* (*endure*) soportar; (*place*) poner; (*offer*) ofrecer. ~ **a chance** tener una posibilidad. ~ **one's ground** mantenerse firme. **I'll** ~ **you a drink** te invito a una copa. ● *n* posición *f*, postura *f*; (*mil*) resistencia *f*; (*for lamp etc*) pie *m*, sostén *m*; (*at market*) puesto *m*; (*booth*) quiosco *m*; (*sport*) tribuna *f*. ~ **around** no hacer nada. ~ **back** retroceder. ~ **by** *vi* estar preparado. ● *vt* (*support*) apoyar. ~ **down** *vi* retirarse. ~ **for** *vt* representar. ~ **in for** suplir a. ~ **out** destacarse. ~ **up** *vi* ponerse de pie. ~ **up for** defender. ~ **up to** *vt* resistir a

**standard** /'stændəd/ *n* norma *f*; (*level*) nivel *m*; (*flag*) estandarte *m*. ● *a* normal, corriente. **~ize** *vt* uniformar. ~ **lamp** *n* lámpara *f* de pie. **~s** *npl* valores *mpl*

**stand:** **~by** *n* (*person*) reserva *f*; (*at airport*) lista *f* de espera. **~in** *n* suplente *m* & *f*. **~ing** /'stændɪŋ/ *a* de pie; (*upright*) derecho. ● *n* posición *f*; (*duration*) duración *f*. **~offish** *a* (*fam*) frío. **~point** /'stændpɔɪnt/ *n*

punto *m* de vista. **~still** /'stændstɪl/ *n*. **at a ~still** parado. **come to a ~still** pararse

**stank** /stæŋk/ *see* **stink**

**staple¹** /'steɪpl/ *a* principal

**staple²** /'steɪpl/ *n* grapa *f*. ● *vt* sujetar con una grapa. **~r** /-ə(r)/ *n* grapadora *f*

**star** /stɑ:/ *n* (*incl cinema, theatre*) estrella *f*; (*asterisk*) asterisco *m*. ● *vi* (*pt* **starred**) ser el protagonista

**starboard** /'stɑ:bəd/ *n* estribor *m*

**starch** /stɑ:tʃ/ *n* almidón *m*; (*in food*) fécula *f*. ● *vt* almidonar. **~y** *a* almidonado; (*food*) feculento; (*fig*) formal

**stardom** /'stɑ:dəm/ *n* estrellato *m*

**stare** /steə(r)/ *n* mirada *f* fija. ● *vi*. ~ **at** mirar fijamente

**starfish** /'stɑ:fɪʃ/ *n* estrella *f* de mar

**stark** /stɑ:k/ *a* (**-er, -est**) rígido; (*utter*) completo. ● *adv* completamente

**starlight** /'stɑ:laɪt/ *n* luz *f* de las estrellas

**starling** /'stɑ:lɪŋ/ *n* estornino *m*

**starry** /'stɑ:rɪ/ *a* estrellado. **~-eyed** *a* (*fam*) ingenuo, idealista

**start** /stɑ:t/ *vt* empezar; poner en marcha *‹machine›*; (*cause*) provocar. ● *vi* empezar; (*jump*) sobresaltarse; (*leave*) partir; *‹car etc›* arrancar. ● *n* principio *m*; (*leaving*) salida *f*; (*sport*) ventaja *f*; (*jump*) susto *m*. **~er** *n* (*sport*) participante *m* & *f*; (*auto*) motor *m* de arranque; (*culin*) primer plato *m*. **~ing-point** *n* punto *m* de partida

**startle** /'stɑ:tl/ *vt* asustar

**starv|ation** /stɑ:'veɪʃn/ *n* hambre *f*. **~e** /stɑ:v/ *vt* hacer morir de hambre; (*deprive*) privar. ● *vi* morir de hambre

**stash** /stæʃ/ *vt* (*sl*) esconder

**state** /steɪt/ *n* estado *m*; (*grand style*) pompa *f*. **S~** *n* Estado *m*. **be in a ~** estar agitado. ● *vt* declarar; expresar *‹views›*; (*fix*) fijar. ● *a* del Estado; (*schol*) público; (*with ceremony*) de gala. **~less** *a* sin patria

**stately** /'steɪtlɪ/ *a* (**-ier, -iest**) majestuoso

**statement** /'steɪtmənt/ *n* declaración *f*; (*account*) informe *m*. **bank ~** *n* estado *m* de cuenta

**stateroom** /'steɪtrʊm/ *n* (*on ship*) camarote *m*

**statesman** /'steɪtsmən/ *n* (*pl* **-men**) estadista *m*

**static** /'stætɪk/ *a* inmóvil. **~s** *n* estática *f*; (*rad*, *TV*) parásitos *mpl* atmosféricos, interferencias *fpl*

**station** /'steɪʃn/ *n* estación *f*; (*status*) posición *f* social. ● *vt* colocar; (*mil*) estacionar

**stationary** /'steɪʃənərɪ/ *a* estacionario

**stationer** /'steɪʃənə(r)/ *n* papelero *m*. **~'s (shop)** *n* papelería *f*. **~y** *n* artículos *mpl* de escritorio

**station-wagon** /'steɪʃnwægən/ *n* furgoneta *f*

**statistic** /stə'tɪstɪk/ *n* estadística *f*. **~al** /stə'tɪstɪkl/ *a* estadístico. **~s** /stə'tɪstɪks/ *n* (*science*) estadística *f*

**statue** /'stætʃuː/ *n* estatua *f*. **~sque** /-ʊ'esk/ *a* escultural. **~tte** /-ʊ'et/ *n* figurilla *f*

**stature** /'stætʃə(r)/ *n* talla *f*, estatura *f*

**status** /'steɪtəs/ *n* posición *f* social; (*prestige*) categoría *f*; (*jurid*) estado *m*

**statut|e** /'stætʃuːt/ *n* estatuto *m*. **~ory** /-ʊtrɪ/ *a* estatutario

**staunch** /stɔːnʃ/ *a* (**-er, -est**) leal. **~ly** *adv* lealmente

**stave** /'steɪv/ *n* (*mus*) pentagrama *m*. ● *vt*. **~ off** evitar

**stay** /steɪ/ *n* soporte *m*, sostén *m*; (*of time*) estancia *f*; (*jurid*) suspensión *f*. ● *vi* quedar; (*spend time*) detenerse; (*reside*) alojarse. ● *vt* matar ‹*hunger*›. **~ the course** terminar. **~ in** quedar en casa. **~ put** mantenerse firme. **~ up** no acostarse. **~ing-power** *n* resistencia *f*

**stays** /steɪz/ *npl* (*old use*) corsé *m*

**stead** /sted/ *n*. **in s.o.'s ~** en lugar de uno. **stand s.o. in good ~** ser útil a uno

**steadfast** /'stedfɑːst/ *a* firme

**stead|ily** /'stedɪlɪ/ *adv* firmemente; (*regularly*) regularmente. **~y** /'stedɪ/ *a* (**-ier, -iest**) firme; (*regular*) regular; (*dependable*) serio

**steak** /steɪk/ *n* filete *m*

**steal** /stiːl/ *vt* (*pt* **stole**, *pp* **stolen**) robar. **~ the show** llevarse los aplausos. **~ in** *vi* entrar a hurtadillas. **~ out** *vi* salir a hurtadillas

**stealth** /stelθ/ *n*. **by ~** sigilosamente. **~y** *a* sigiloso

**steam** /stiːm/ *n* vapor *m*; (*energy*) energía *f*. ● *vt* (*cook*) cocer al vapor; empañar ‹*window*›. ● *vi* echar vapor. **~ ahead** (*fam*) hacer progresos. **~ up** *vi* ‹*glass*› empañar.

**~engine** *n* máquina *f* de vapor. **~er** /'stiːmə(r)/ *n* (*ship*) barco *m* de vapor. **~roller** /'stiːmrəʊlə(r)/ *n* apisonadora *f*. **~y** *a* húmedo

**steel** /stiːl/ *n* acero *m*. ● *vt*. **~ o.s.** fortalecerse. **~ industry** *n* industria *f* siderúrgica. **~ wool** *n* estropajo *m* de acero. **~y** *a* acerado; (*fig*) duro, inflexible

**steep** /stiːp/ *a* (**-er, -est**) escarpado; ‹*price*› (*fam*) exorbitante. ● *vt* (*soak*) remojar. **~ed in** (*fig*) empapado de

**steeple** /'stiːpl/ *n* aguja *f*, campanario *m*. **~chase** /'stiːpltʃeɪs/ *n* carrera *f* de obstáculos

**steep:** **~ly** *adv* de modo empinado. **~ness** *n* lo escarpado

**steer** /stɪə(r)/ *vt* guiar; gobernar ‹*ship*›. ● *vi* (*in ship*) gobernar. **~ clear of** evitar. **~ing** *n* (*auto*) dirección *f*. **~ing-wheel** *n* volante *m*

**stem** /stem/ *n* tallo *m*; (*of glass*) pie *m*; (*of word*) raíz *f*; (*of ship*) roda *f*. ● *vt* (*pt* **stemmed**) detener. ● *vi*. **~ from** provenir de

**stench** /stentʃ/ *n* hedor *m*

**stencil** /'stensl/ *n* plantilla *f*; (*for typing*) cliché *m*. ● *vt* (*pt* **stencilled**) estarcir

**stenographer** /ste'nɒɡrəfə(r)/ *n* (*Amer*) estenógrafo *m*

**step** /step/ *vi* (*pt* **stepped**) ir. **~ down** retirarse. **~ in** entrar; (*fig*) intervenir. **~ up** *vt* aumentar. ● *n* paso *m*; (*surface*) escalón *m*; (*fig*) medida *f*. **in ~** (*fig*) de acuerdo con. **out of ~** (*fig*) en desacuerdo con. **~brother** /'stepbrʌðə(r)/ *n* hermanastro *m*. **~daughter** *n* hijastra *f*. **~father** *n* padrastro *m*. **~ladder** *n* escalera *f* de tijeras. **~mother** *n* madrastra *f*. **~ping-stone** /'stepɪŋstəʊn/ *n* pasadera *f*; (*fig*) escalón *m*. **~sister** *n* hermanastra *f*. **~son** *n* hijastro *m*

**stereo** /'sterɪəʊ/ *n* (*pl* **-os**) cadena *f* estereofónica. ● *a* estereofónico. **~phonic** /sterɪəʊ'fɒnɪk/ *a* estereofónico. **~type** /'sterɪəʊtaɪp/ *n* estereotipo *m*. **~typed** *a* estereotipado

**steril|e** /'steraɪl/ *a* estéril. **~ity** /stə'rɪlətɪ/ *n* esterilidad *f*. **~ization** /-'zeɪʃn/ *n* esterilización *f*. **~ize** /'sterɪlaɪz/ *vt* esterilizar

**sterling** /'stɜːlɪŋ/ *n* libras *fpl* esterlinas. ● *a* ‹*pound*› esterlina; (*fig*) excelente. **~ silver** *n* plata *f* de ley

**stern**[1] /stɜːn/ n (of boat) popa f

**stern**[2] /stɜːn/ a (-er, -est) severo. **~ly** adv severamente

**stethoscope** /'steθəskəʊp/ n estetoscopio m

**stew** /stjuː/ vt/i guisar. ● n guisado m. **in a ~** (fam) en un apuro

**steward** /stjʊəd/ n administrador m; (on ship, aircraft) camarero m. **~ess** /-'des/ n camarera f; (on aircraft) azafata f

**stick** /stɪk/ n palo m; (for walking) bastón m; (of celery etc) tallo m. ● vt (pt stuck) (glue) pegar; (put, fam) poner; (thrust) clavar; (endure, sl) soportar. ● vi pegarse; (remain, fam) quedarse; (jam) bloquearse. **~ at** (fam) perseverar en. **~ out** sobresalir; (catch the eye, fam) resaltar. **~ to** aferrarse a; cumplir (promise). **~ up for** (fam) defender. **~er** /'stɪkə(r)/ n pegatina f. **~ing-plaster** n esparadrapo m. **~in-the-mud** n persona f chapada a la antigua

**stickler** /'stɪklə(r)/ n. **be a ~ for** insistir en

**sticky** /'stɪkɪ/ a (-ier, -iest) pegajoso; (label) engomado; (sl) difícil

**stiff** /stɪf/ a (-er, -est) rígido; (difficult) difícil; (manner) estirado; (drink) fuerte; (price) subido; (joint) tieso; (muscle) con agujetas. **~en** /'stɪfn/ vt poner tieso. **~ly** adv rígidamente. **~ neck** n torticolis f. **~ness** n rigidez f

**stifle** /'staɪfl/ vt sofocar. **~ing** a sofocante

**stigma** /'stɪgmə/ n (pl -as) estigma m. (pl **stigmata** /'stɪgmətə/) (relig) estigma m. **~tize** vt estigmatizar

**stile** /staɪl/ n portillo m con escalones

**stiletto** /stɪ'letəʊ/ n (pl -os) estilete m. **~ heels** npl tacones mpl aguja

**still**[1] /stɪl/ a inmóvil; (peaceful) tranquilo; (drink) sin gas. ● n silencio m. ● adv todavía; (nevertheless) sin embargo

**still**[2] /stɪl/ (apparatus) alambique m

**still**: **~born** a nacido muerto. **~ life** n (pl -s) bodegón m. **~ness** n tranquilidad f

**stilted** /'stɪltɪd/ a artificial

**stilts** /stɪlts/ npl zancos mpl

**stimul|ant** /'stɪmjʊlənt/ n estimulante m. **~ate** /'stɪmjʊleɪt/ vt estimular. **~ation** /-'leɪʃn/ n estímulo m. **~us** /'stɪmjʊləs/ n (pl -li /-laɪ/) estímulo m

**sting** /stɪŋ/ n picadura f; (organ) aguijón m. ● vt/i (pt stung) picar

**sting|iness** /'stɪndʒɪnɪs/ n tacañería f. **~y** /'stɪndʒɪ/ a (-ier, -iest) tacaño

**stink** /stɪŋk/ n hedor m. ● vi (pt stank or stunk, pp stunk) oler mal. ● vt. **~ out** apestar (room); ahuyentar (person). **~er** /-ə(r)/ n (sl) problema m difícil; (person) mal bicho m

**stint** /stɪnt/ n (work) trabajo m. ● vi. **~ on** escatimar

**stipple** /'stɪpl/ vt puntear

**stipulat|e** /'stɪpjʊleɪt/ vt/i estipular. **~ion** /-'leɪʃn/ n estipulación f

**stir** /stɜː(r)/ vt (pt stirred) remover, agitar; (mix) mezclar; (stimulate) estimular. ● vi moverse. ● n agitación f; (commotion) conmoción f

**stirrup** /'stɪrəp/ n estribo m

**stitch** /stɪtʃ/ n (in sewing) puntada f; (in knitting) punto m; (pain) dolor m de costado; (med) punto m de sutura. **be in ~es** (fam) desternillarse de risa. ● vt coser

**stoat** /stəʊt/ n armiño m

**stock** /stɒk/ n (com, supplies) existencias fpl; (com, variety) surtido m; (livestock) ganado m; (lineage) linaje m; (finance) acciones fpl; (culin) caldo m; (plant) alhelí m. **out of ~** agotado. **take ~** (fig) evaluar. **~ a corriente**; (fig) trillado. ● vt abastecer (with de). ● vi. **~ up** abastecerse (with de). **~broker** /'stɒkbrəʊkə(r)/ n corredor m de bolsa. **S~ Exchange** n bolsa f. **well-~ed** a bien provisto

**stocking** /'stɒkɪŋ/ n media f

**stock**: **~-in-trade** /stɒkɪntreɪd/ n existencias fpl. **~ist** /'stɒkɪst/ n distribuidor m. **~pile** /'stɒkpaɪl/ n reservas fpl. ● vt acumular. **~still** a inmóvil. **~taking** n (com) inventario m

**stocky** /'stɒkɪ/ a (-ier, -iest) achaparrado

**stodg|e** /stɒdʒ/ n (fam) comida f pesada. **~y** a pesado

**stoic** /'stəʊɪk/ n estoico. **~al** a estoico. **~ally** adv estoicamente. **~ism** /-sɪzəm/ n estoicismo m

**stoke** /stəʊk/ vt alimentar. **~r** /'stəʊkə(r)/ n fogonero m

**stole**[1] /stəʊl/ see **steal**

**stole**[2] /stəʊl/ n estola f

**stolen** /'stəʊlən/ see **steal**

**stolid** /'stɒlɪd/ a impasible. **~ly** adv impasiblemente

**stomach** /'stʌmək/ n estómago m.
● vt soportar. ~-ache n dolor m de
estómago

**ston|e** /stəʊn/ n piedra f; (med) cál-
culo m; (in fruit) hueso m; (weight,
pl **stone**) peso m de 14 libras (=
6,348 kg). ● a de piedra. ● vt apedrear; deshuesar (fruit). ~e-deaf a
sordo como una tapia. ~emason
/'stəʊnmeɪsn/ n albañil m. ~ework
/'stəʊnwɜːk/ n cantería f. ~y a pe-
dregoso; (like stone) pétreo

**stood** /stʊd/ see **stand**

**stooge** /stuːdʒ/ n (in theatre) compañero m; (underling) lacayo m

**stool** /stuːl/ n taburete m

**stoop** /stuːp/ vi inclinarse; (fig)
rebajarse. ● n. **have a** ~ ser cargado de espaldas

**stop** /stɒp/ vt (pt **stopped**) parar;
(cease) terminar; tapar ⟨a leak etc⟩;
(prevent) impedir; (interrupt) interrumpir. ● vi pararse; (stay, fam)
quedarse. ● n (bus etc) parada f;
(gram) punto m; (mec) tope m. ~
**dead** vi pararse en seco. ~cock
/'stɒpkɒk/ n llave f de paso. ~gap
/'stɒpgæp/ n remedio m provisional.
~(-over) n escala f. ~page
/'stɒpɪdʒ/ n parada f; (of work) paro
m; (interruption) interrupción f.
~per /'stɒpə(r)/ n tapón m. ~press
n noticias fpl de última hora. ~
**light** n luz f de freno. ~watch n
cronómetro m

**storage** /'stɔːrɪdʒ/ n alma-
cenamiento m. ~ **heater** n acu-
mulador m. **in cold** ~ almacenaje m
frigorífico

**store** /stɔː(r)/ n provisión f; (shop,
depot) almacén m; (fig) reserva f. **in**
~ en reserva. **set** ~ **by** dar importancia a. ● vt (for future) poner en
reserva; (in warehouse) almacenar.
~ **up** vt acumular

**storeroom** /'stɔːruːm/ n despensa f

**storey** /'stɔːrɪ/ n (pl **-eys**) piso m

**stork** /stɔːk/ n cigüeña f

**storm** /stɔːm/ n tempestad f; (mil)
asalto m. ● vi rabiar. ● vt (mil) asaltar. ~y a tempestuoso

**story** /'stɔːrɪ/ n historia f; (in newspaper) artículo m; (fam) mentira f,
cuento m. ~**teller** n cuentista m & f

**stout** /staʊt/ a (-er, -est) (fat) gordo;
(brave) valiente. ● n cerveza f
negra. ~ness n corpulencia f

**stove** /stəʊv/ n estufa f

**stow** /stəʊ/ vt guardar; (hide) esconder. ● vi. ~ **away** viajar de polizón.
~**away** /'stəʊəweɪ/ n polizón m

**straddle** /'strædl/ vt estar a
horcajadas

**straggl|e** /'strægl/ vi rezagarse. ~y
a desordenado

**straight** /streɪt/ a (-er, -est) derecho,
recto; (tidy) en orden; (frank)
franco; ⟨drink⟩ solo, puro; ⟨hair⟩
lacio. ● adv derecho; (direct) directamente; (without delay)
inmediatamente. ~ **on** todo recto.
~ **out** sin vacilar. **go** ~ enmendarse. ● n recta f. ~ **away**
inmediatamente. ~en /'streɪtn/ vt
enderezar. ● vi enderezarse.
~forward /streɪt'fɔːwəd/ a franco;
(easy) sencillo. ~forwardly adv
francamente. ~ness n rectitud f

**strain**¹ /streɪn/ n (tension) tensión f;
(injury) torcedura f. ● vt estirar;
(tire) cansar; (injure) torcer; (sieve)
colar

**strain**² /streɪn/ n (lineage) linaje m;
(streak) tendencia f

**strained** /streɪnd/ a forzado; ⟨re-
lations⟩ tirante

**strainer** /-ə(r)/ n colador m

**strains** /streɪnz/ npl (mus) acordes
mpl

**strait** /streɪt/ n estrecho m. ~jacket
n camisa f de fuerza. ~laced a
remilgado, gazmoño. ~s npl apuro
m

**strand** /strænd/ n (thread) hebra f;
(sand) playa f. ● vi ⟨ship⟩ varar. **be**
~ed quedarse sin recursos

**strange** /streɪndʒ/ a (-er, -est)
extraño, raro; (not known) desconocido; (unaccustomed) nuevo. ~ly
adv extrañamente. ~ness n extra-
ñeza f. ~r /'streɪndʒə(r)/ n desconocido m

**strang|le** /'strængl/ vt estrangu-
lar; (fig) ahogar. ~lehold
/'strænglhəʊld/ n (fig) dominio m
completo. ~ler /-ə(r)/ n estrangulador m. ~ulation /strængjʊ'leɪʃn/
n estrangulación f

**strap** /stræp/ n correa f; (of garment)
tirante m. ● vt (pt **strapped**) atar
con correa; (flog) azotar

**strapping** /'stræpɪŋ/ a robusto

**strata** /'strɑːtə/ see **stratum**

**strat|agem** /'strætədʒəm/ n estra-
tagema f. ~egic /strə'tiːdʒɪk/ a
estratégico. ~egically adv es-
tratégicamente. ~egist n estratega

*m & f.* **~egy** /'strætədʒɪ/ *n* estrategia *f*

**stratum** /'strɑːtəm/ *n* (*pl* **strata**) estrato *m*

**straw** /strɔː/ *n* paja *f.* **the last ~** el colmo

**strawberry** /'strɔːbərɪ/ *n* fresa *f*

**stray** /streɪ/ *vi* vagar; (*deviate*) desviarse (**from** de). ● *a* ⟨*animal*⟩ extraviado, callejero; (*isolated*) aislado. ● *n* animal *m* extraviado, animal *m* callejero

**streak** /striːk/ *n* raya *f*; (*of madness*) vena *f.* ● *vi* moverse como un rayo. **~y** *a* (**-ier, -iest**) rayado; ⟨*bacon*⟩ entreverado

**stream** /striːm/ *n* arroyo *m*; (*current*) corriente *f*; (*of people*) desfile *m*; (*schol*) grupo *m.* ● *vi* correr. **~ out** *vi* ⟨*people*⟩ salir en tropel

**streamer** /'striːmə(r)/ *n* (*paper*) serpentina *f*; (*flag*) gallardete *m*

**streamline** /'striːmlaɪn/ *vt* dar línea aerodinámica a; (*simplify*) simplificar. **~d** *a* aerodinámico

**street** /striːt/ *n* calle *f.* **~car** /'striːtkɑː/ *n* (*Amer*) tranvía *m.* **~ lamp** *n* farol *m.* **~ map** *n*, **~ plan** *n* plano *m*

**strength** /streŋθ/ *n* fuerza *f*; (*of wall etc*) solidez *f.* **on the ~ of** a base de. **~en** /'streŋθn/ *vt* reforzar

**strenuous** /'strenjʊəs/ *a* enérgico; (*arduous*) arduo; (*tiring*) fatigoso. **~ly** *adv* enérgicamente

**stress** /stres/ *n* énfasis *f*; (*gram*) acento *m*; (*mec, med, tension*) tensión *f.* ● *vt* insistir en

**stretch** /stretʃ/ *vt* estirar; (*extend*) extender; (*exaggerate*) forzar. **~ a point** hacer una excepción. ● *vi* estirarse; (*extend*) extenderse. ● *n* estirón *m*; (*period*) período *m*; (*of road*) tramo *m.* **at a ~** seguido; (*in one go*) de un tirón. **~er** /'stretʃə(r)/ *n* camilla *f*

**strew** /struː/ *vt* (*pt* **strewed,** *pp* **strewn** *or* **strewed**) esparcir; (*cover*) cubrir

**stricken** /'strɪkən/ *a.* **~ with** afectado de

**strict** /strɪkt/ *a* (**-er, -est**) severo; (*precise*) estricto, preciso. **~ly** *adv* estrictamente. **~ly speaking** en rigor

**stricture** /'strɪktʃə(r)/ *n* crítica *f*; (*constriction*) constricción *f*

**stride** /straɪd/ *vi* (*pt* **strode,** *pp* **stridden**) andar a zancadas. ● *n* zancada

**strident** /'straɪdnt/ *a* estridente

**strife** /straɪf/ *n* conflicto *m*

**strike** /straɪk/ *vt* (*pt* **struck**) golpear; encender ⟨*match*⟩; encontrar ⟨*gold etc*⟩; ⟨*clock*⟩ dar. ● *vi* golpear; (*go on strike*) declararse en huelga; (*be on strike*) estar en huelga; (*attack*) atacar; ⟨*clock*⟩ dar la hora. ● *n* (*of workers*) huelga *f*; (*attack*) ataque *m*; (*find*) descubrimiento *m.* **on ~** en huelga. **~ off,** **~ out** tachar. **~ up a friendship** trabar amistad. **~r** /'straɪkə(r)/ *n* huelguista *m & f*

**striking** /'straɪkɪŋ/ *a* impresionante

**string** /strɪŋ/ *n* cuerda *f*; (*of lies, pearls*) sarta *f.* **pull ~s** tocar todos los resortes. ● *vt* (*pt* **strung**) (*thread*) ensartar. **~ along** (*fam*) engañar. **~ out** extender(se). **~ed** *a* (*mus*) de cuerda

**stringen|cy** /'strɪndʒənsɪ/ *n* rigor *m.* **~t** /'strɪndʒənt/ *a* riguroso

**stringy** /'strɪŋɪ/ *a* fibroso

**strip** /strɪp/ *vt* (*pt* **stripped**) desnudar; (*tear away, deprive*) quitar; desmontar ⟨*machine*⟩. ● *vi* desnudarse. ● *n* tira *f.* **~ cartoon** *n* historieta *f*

**stripe** /straɪp/ *n* raya *f*; (*mil*) galón *m.* **~d** *a* a rayas, rayado

**strip:** **~ light** *n* tubo *m* fluorescente. **~per** /-ə(r)/ *n* artista *m & f* de striptease. **~tease** *n* número *m* del desnudo, striptease *m*

**strive** /straɪv/ *vi* (*pt* **strove,** *pp* **striven**). **~ to** esforzarse por

**strode** /strəʊd/ *see* **stride**

**stroke** /strəʊk/ *n* golpe *m*; (*in swimming*) brazada *f*; (*med*) apoplejía *f*; (*of pen etc*) rasgo *m*; (*of clock*) campanada *f*; (*caress*) caricia *f.* ● *vt* acariciar

**stroll** /strəʊl/ *vi* pasearse. ● *n* paseo *m*

**strong** /strɒŋ/ *a* (**-er, -est**) fuerte. **~box** *n* caja *f* fuerte. **~hold** /'strɒŋhəʊld/ *n* fortaleza *f*; (*fig*) baluarte *m.* **~ language** *n* palabras *fpl* fuertes, palabras *fpl* subidas de tono. **~ly** *adv* (*greatly*) fuertemente; (*with energy*) enérgicamente; (*deeply*) profundamente. **~ measures** *npl* medidas *fpl* enérgicas. **~-minded** *a* resuelto. **~room** *n* cámara *f* acorazada

**stroppy** /'strɒpɪ/ *a* (*sl*) irascible

**strove** /strəʊv/ *see* **strive**

**struck** /strʌk/ *see* **strike**. ~ **on** (*sl*) entusiasta de

**structur|al** /'strʌktʃərəl/ *a* estructural. ~**e** /'strʌktʃə(r)/ *n* estructura *f*

**struggle** /'strʌgl/ *vi* luchar. ~ **to one's feet** levantarse con dificultad. ● *n* lucha *f*

**strum** /strʌm/ *vt/i* (*pt* **strummed**) rasguear

**strung** /strʌŋ/ *see* **string**. ● *a.* ~ **up** (*tense*) nervioso

**strut** /strʌt/ *n* puntal *m*; (*walk*) pavoneo *m*. ● *vi* (*pt* **strutted**) pavonearse

**stub** /stʌb/ *n* cabo *m*; (*counterfoil*) talón *m*; (*of cigarette*) colilla *f*; (*of tree*) tocón *m*. ● *vt* (*pt* **stubbed**). ~ **out** apagar

**stubble** /'stʌbl/ *n* rastrojo *m*; (*beard*) barba *f* de varios días

**stubborn** /'stʌbən/ *a* terco. ~**ly** *adv* tercamente. ~**ness** *n* terquedad *f*

**stubby** /'stʌbɪ/ *a* (**-ier, -iest**) achaparrado

**stucco** /'stʌkəʊ/ *n* (*pl* **-oes**) estuco *m*

**stuck** /stʌk/ *see* **stick**. ● *a* (*jammed*) bloqueado; (*in difficulties*) en un apuro. ~ **on** (*sl*) encantado con. ~**up** *a* (*sl*) presumido

**stud**[1] /stʌd/ *n* tachón *m*; (*for collar*) botón *m*. ● *vt* (*pt* **studded**) tachonar. ~**ded with** sembrado de

**stud**[2] /stʌd/ *n* (*of horses*) caballeriza *f*

**student** /'stjuːdənt/ *n* estudiante *m & f*

**studied** /'stʌdɪd/ *a* deliberado

**studio** /'stjuːdɪəʊ/ *n* (*pl* **-os**) estudio *m*. ~ **couch** *n* sofá *m* cama. ~ **flat** *n* estudio *m* de artista

**studious** /'stjuːdɪəs/ *a* estudioso; (*studied*) deliberado. ~**ly** *adv* estudiosamente; (*carefully*) cuidadosamente

**study** /'stʌdɪ/ *n* estudio *m*; (*office*) despacho *m*. ● *vt/i* estudiar

**stuff** /stʌf/ *n* materia *f*, sustancia *f*; (*sl*) cosas *fpl*. ● *vt* rellenar; disecar ‹*animal*›; (*cram*) atiborrar; (*block up*) tapar; (*put*) meter de prisa. ~**ing** *n* relleno *m*

**stuffy** /'stʌfɪ/ *a* (**-ier, -iest**) mal ventilado; (*old-fashioned*) chapado a la antigua

**stumbl|e** /'stʌmbl/ *vi* tropezar. ~**e across**, ~**e on** tropezar con. ● *n*

tropezón *m*. ~**ing-block** *n* tropiezo *m*, impedimento *m*

**stump** /stʌmp/ *n* cabo *m*; (*of limb*) muñón *m*; (*of tree*) tocón *m*. ~**ed** /stʌmpt/ *a* (*fam*) perplejo. ~**y** /'stʌmpɪ/ *a* (**-ier, -iest**) achaparrado

**stun** /stʌn/ *vt* (*pt* **stunned**) aturdir; (*bewilder*) pasmar. ~**ning** *a* (*fabulous, fam*) estupendo

**stung** /stʌŋ/ *see* **sting**

**stunk** /stʌŋk/ *see* **stink**

**stunt**[1] /stʌnt/ *n* (*fam*) truco *m* publicitario

**stunt**[2] /stʌnt/ *vt* impedir el desarrollo de. ~**ed** *a* enano

**stupefy** /'stjuːpɪfaɪ/ *vt* dejar estupefacto

**stupendous** /stjuː'pendəs/ *a* estupendo. ~**ly** *adv* estupendamente

**stupid** /'stjuːpɪd/ *a* estúpido. ~**ity** /-'pɪdətɪ/ *n* estupidez *f*. ~**ly** *adv* estúpidamente

**stupor** /'stjuːpə(r)/ *n* estupor *m*

**sturd|iness** /'stɜːdɪnɪs/ *n* robustez *f*. ~**y** /'stɜːdɪ/ *a* (**-ier, -iest**) robusto

**sturgeon** /'stɜːdʒən/ *n* (*pl* **sturgeon**) esturión *m*

**stutter** /'stʌtə(r)/ *vi* tartamudear. ● *n* tartamudeo *m*

**sty**[1] /staɪ/ *n* (*pl* **sties**) pocilga *f*

**sty**[2] /staɪ/ *n* (*pl* **sties**) (*med*) orzuelo *m*

**styl|e** /staɪl/ *n* estilo *m*; (*fashion*) moda *f*. **in** ~ con todo lujo. ● *vt* diseñar. ~**ish** /'staɪlɪʃ/ *a* elegante. ~**ishly** *adv* elegantemente. ~**ist** /'staɪlɪst/ *n* estilista *m & f*. **hair** ~**ist** *n* peluquero *m*. ~**ized** /'staɪlaɪzd/ *a* estilizado

**stylus** /'staɪləs/ *n* (*pl* **-uses**) aguja *f* (de tocadiscos)

**suave** /swɑːv/ *a* (*pej*) zalamero

**sub...** /sʌb/ *pref* sub...

**subaquatic** /sʌbə'kwætɪk/ *a* subacuático

**subconscious** /sʌb'kɒnʃəs/ *a & n* subconsciente (*m*). ~**ly** *adv* de modo subconsciente

**subcontinent** /sʌb'kɒntɪnənt/ *n* subcontinente *m*

**subcontract** /sʌbkən'trækt/ *vt* subcontratar. ~**or** /-ə(r)/ *n* subcontratista *m & f*

**subdivide** /sʌbdɪ'vaɪd/ *vt* subdividir

**subdue** /səb'djuː/ *vt* dominar ‹*feelings*›; sojuzgar ‹*country*›. ~**d** *a* (*depressed*) abatido; ‹*light*› suave

**subhuman** /sʌb'hjuːmən/ *a* infrahumano

**subject** /'sʌbdʒɪkt/ *a* sometido. ~ **to**
sujeto a. ● *n* súbdito *m*; (*theme*)
asunto *m*; (*schol*) asignatura *f*;
(*gram*) sujeto *m*; (*of painting, play,
book etc*) tema *m*. /səb'dʒekt/ *vt*
sojuzgar; (*submit*) someter. ~**ion**
/-ʃn/ *n* sometimiento *m*

**subjective** /səb'dʒektɪv/ *a* subjetivo.
~**ly** *adv* subjetivamente

**subjugate** /'sʌbdʒʊgeɪt/ *vt* subyugar

**subjunctive** /səb'dʒʌŋktɪv/ *a* & *n*
subjuntivo (*m*)

**sublet** /sʌb'let/ *vt* (*pt* **sublet**, *pres p*
**subletting**) subarrendar

**sublimat|e** /'sʌblɪmeɪt/ *vt* sublimar.
~**ion** /-'meɪʃn/ *n* sublimación *f*

**sublime** /sə'blaɪm/ *a* sublime. ~**ly**
*adv* sublimemente

**submarine** /sʌbmə'ri:n/ *n* submarino *m*

**submerge** /səb'mɜ:dʒ/ *vt* sumergir.
● *vi* sumergirse

**submi|ssion** /səb'mɪʃn/ *n* sumisión
*f*. ~**ssive** /-sɪv/ *a* sumiso. ~**t**
/səb'mɪt/ *vt* (*pt* **submitted**) someter.
● *vi* someterse

**subordinat|e** /sə'bɔ:dɪnət/ *a* & *n*
subordinado (*m*). /sə'bɔ:dɪneɪt/ *vt*
subordinar. ~**ion** /-'neɪʃn/ *n* subor-
dinación *f*

**subscri|be** /səb'skraɪb/ *vi* suscribir.
~**be to** suscribir (*fund*); (*agree*)
estar de acuerdo con; abonarse a
⟨*newspaper*⟩. ~**ber** /-ə(r)/ *n* abon-
ado *m*. ~**ption** /-rɪpʃn/ *n* sus-
cripción *f*

**subsequent** /'sʌbsɪkwənt/ *a* subsiguiente. ~**ly** *adv* posteriormente

**subservient** /səb'sɜ:vjənt/ *a* servil

**subside** /səb'saɪd/ *vi* ⟨*land*⟩ hundirse; ⟨*flood*⟩ bajar; ⟨*storm, wind*⟩
amainar. ~**nce** *n* hundimiento *m*

**subsidiary** /səb'sɪdɪərɪ/ *a* subsi-
diario. ● *n* (*com*) sucursal *m*

**subsid|ize** /'sʌbsɪdaɪz/ *vt* sub-
vencionar. ~**y** /'sʌbsədɪ/ *n* sub-
vención *f*

**subsist** /səb'sɪst/ *vi* subsistir. ~**ence**
*n* subsistencia *f*

**subsoil** /'sʌbsɔɪl/ *n* subsuelo *m*

**subsonic** /sʌb'sɒnɪk/ *a* subsónico

**substance** /'sʌbstəns/ *n* substancia *f*

**substandard** /sʌb'stændəd/ *a*
inferior

**substantial** /səb'stænʃl/ *a* sólido;
⟨*meal*⟩ substancial; (*considerable*)
considerable. ~**ly** *adv* considerablemente

**substantiate** /səb'stænʃɪeɪt/ *vt*
justificar

**substitut|e** /'sʌbstɪtju:t/ *n* sub-
stituto *m*. ● *vt/i* substituir. ~**ion**
/-'tju:ʃn/ *n* substitución *f*

**subterfuge** /'sʌbtəfju:dʒ/ *n* subterfugio *m*

**subterranean** /sʌbtə'reɪnjən/ *a*
subterráneo

**subtitle** /'sʌbtaɪtl/ *n* subtítulo *m*

**subtle** /'sʌtl/ *a* (**-er, -est**) sutil. ~**ty**
*n* sutileza *f*

**subtract** /səb'trækt/ *vt* restar. ~**ion**
/-ʃn/ *n* resta *f*

**suburb** /'sʌbɜ:b/ *n* barrio *m*. **the** ~**s**
las afueras *fpl*. ~**an** /sə'bɜ:bən/ *a*
suburbano. ~**ia** /sə'bɜ:bɪə/ *n* las afueras *fpl*

**subvention** /səb'venʃn/ *n* sub-
vención *f*

**subver|sion** /səb'vɜ:ʃn/ *n* sub-
versión *f*. ~**sive** /səb'vɜ:sɪv/ *a* sub-
versivo. ~**t** /səb'vɜ:t/ *vt* subvertir

**subway** /'sʌbweɪ/ *n* paso *m* subterráneo; (*Amer*) metro *m*

**succeed** /sək'si:d/ *vi* tener éxito. ● *vt*
suceder a. ~ **in doing** lograr hacer.
~**ing** *a* sucesivo

**success** /sək'ses/ *n* éxito *m*. ~**ful** *a*
que tiene éxito; (*chosen*) elegido

**succession** /sək'seʃn/ *n* sucesión *f*. **in**
~ sucesivamente, seguidos

**successive** /sək'sesɪv/ *a* sucesivo.
~**ly** *adv* sucesivamente

**successor** /sək'sesə(r)/ *n* sucesor *m*

**succinct** /sək'sɪŋkt/ *a* sucinto

**succour** /'sʌkə(r)/ *vt* socorrer. ● *n*
socorro *m*

**succulent** /'sʌkjʊlənt/ *a* suculento

**succumb** /sə'kʌm/ *vi* sucumbir

**such** /sʌtʃ/ *a* tal. ● *pron* los que, las
que; (*so much*) tanto. **and** ~ y tal.
● *adv* tan. ~ **a big house** una casa
tan grande. ~ **and** ~ tal o cual. ~
**as it is** tal como es. ~**like** *a* (*fam*)
semejante, de ese tipo

**suck** /sʌk/ *vt* chupar; sorber
⟨*liquid*⟩. ~ **up** absorber. ~ **up to** (*sl*)
dar coba a. ~**er** /'sʌkə(r)/ *n* (*plant*)
chupón *m*; (*person, fam*) primo *m*

**suckle** /'sʌkl/ *vt* amamantar

**suction** /'sʌkʃn/ *n* succión *f*

**sudden** /'sʌdn/ *a* repentino. **all of a**
~ de repente. ~**ly** *adv* de repente.
~**ness** *n* lo repentino

**suds** /sʌds/ *npl* espuma *f* (de jabón)

**sue** /su:/ *vt* (*pres p* **suing**) demandar
(**for** por)

**suede** /sweɪd/ *n* ante *m*

**suet** /'suːɪt/ n sebo m

**suffer** /'sʌfə(r)/ vt sufrir; (tolerate) tolerar. ● vi sufrir. ~ance /'sʌfərəns/ n. on ~ance por tolerancia. ~ing n sufrimiento m

**suffic|e** /sə'faɪs/ vi bastar. ~iency /sə'fɪʃənsɪ/ n suficiencia f. ~ient /sə'fɪʃnt/ a suficiente; (enough) bastante. ~iently adv suficientemente, bastante

**suffix** /'sʌfɪks/ n (pl -ixes) sufijo m

**suffocat|e** /'sʌfəkeɪt/ vt ahogar. ● vi ahogarse. ~ion /-'keɪʃn/ n asfixia f

**sugar** /'ʃʊɡə(r)/ n azúcar m & f. ● vt azucarar. ~-bowl n azucarero m. ~ lump n terrón m de azúcar. ~y a azucarado.

**suggest** /sə'dʒest/ vt sugerir. ~ible /sə'dʒestɪbl/ a sugestionable. ~ion /-tʃən/ n sugerencia f; (trace) traza f. ~ive /sə'dʒestɪv/ a sugestivo. be ~ive of evocar, recordar. ~ively adv sugestivamente

**suicid|al** /suːɪ'saɪdl/ a suicida. ~e /'suːɪsaɪd/ n suicidio m; (person) suicida m & f. commit ~e suicidarse

**suit** /suːt/ n traje m; (woman's) traje m de chaqueta; (cards) palo m; (jurid) pleito m. ● vt convenir; (clothes) sentar bien a; (adapt) adaptar. be ~ed for ser apto para. ~ability n conveniencia f. ~able a adecuado. ~ably adv convenientemente. ~case /'suːtkeɪs/ n maleta f, valija f (LAm)

**suite** /swiːt/ n (of furniture) juego m; (of rooms) apartamento m; (retinue) séquito m

**suitor** /'suːtə(r)/ n pretendiente m

**sulk** /sʌlk/ vi enfurruñarse. ~s npl enfurruñamiento m. ~y a enfurruñado

**sullen** /'sʌlən/ a resentido. ~ly adv con resentimiento

**sully** /'sʌlɪ/ vt manchar

**sulphur** /'sʌlfə(r)/ n azufre m. ~ic /-'fjʊərɪk/ a sulfúrico. ~ic acid n ácido m sulfúrico

**sultan** /'sʌltən/ n sultán m

**sultana** /sʌl'tɑːnə/ n pasa f gorrona

**sultry** /'sʌltrɪ/ a (-ier, -iest) (weather) bochornoso; (fig) sensual

**sum** /sʌm/ n suma f. ● vt (pt summed). ~ up resumir (situation); (assess) evaluar

**summar|ily** /'sʌmərɪlɪ/ adv sumariamente. ~ize vt resumir. ~y /'sʌmərɪ/ a sumario. ● n resumen m

**summer** /'sʌmə(r)/ n verano m. ~-house n glorieta f, cenador m. ~time n verano m. ~ time n hora f de verano. ~y a veraniego

**summit** /'sʌmɪt/ n cumbre f. ~ conference n conferencia f cumbre

**summon** /'sʌmən/ vt llamar; convocar (meeting, s.o. to meeting); (jurid) citar. ~ up armarse de. ~s /'sʌmənz/ n llamada f; (jurid) citación f. ● vt citar

**sump** /sʌmp/ n (mec) cárter m

**sumptuous** /'sʌmptjʊəs/ a suntuoso. ~ly adv suntuosamente

**sun** /sʌn/ n sol m. ● vt (pt sunned). ~ o.s. tomar el sol. ~bathe /'sʌnbeɪð/ vi tomar el sol. ~beam /'sʌnbiːm/ n rayo m de sol. ~burn /'sʌnbɜːn/ n quemadura f de sol. ~burnt a quemado por el sol

**sundae** /'sʌndeɪ/ n helado m con frutas y nueces

**Sunday** /'sʌndeɪ/ n domingo m. ~ school n catequesis f

**sun:** ~dial /'sʌndaɪl/ n reloj m de sol. ~down /'sʌndaʊn/ n puesta f del sol

**sundry** /'sʌndrɪ/ a diversos. all and ~ todo el mundo. sundries npl artículos mpl diversos

**sunflower** /'sʌnflaʊə(r)/ n girasol m

**sung** /sʌŋ/ see sing

**sun-glasses** /'sʌnɡlɑːsɪz/ npl gafas fpl de sol

**sunk** /sʌŋk/ see sink. ~en /'sʌŋkən/ ● a hundido

**sunlight** /'sʌnlaɪt/ n luz f del sol

**sunny** /'sʌnɪ/ a (-ier, -iest) (day) de sol; (place) soleado. it is ~ hace sol

**sun:** ~rise /'sʌnraɪz/ n amanecer m, salida f del sol. ~-roof n techo m corredizo. ~set /'sʌnset/ n puesta f del sol. ~shade /'sʌnʃeɪd/ n quitasol m, sombrilla f; (awning) toldo m. ~shine /'sʌnʃaɪn/ n sol m. ~spot /'sʌnspɒt/ n mancha f solar. ~stroke /'sʌnstrəʊk/ n insolación f. ~tan n bronceado m. ~tanned a bronceado. ~tan lotion n bronceador m

**sup** /sʌp/ vt (pt supped) sorber

**super** /'suːpə(r)/ a (fam) estupendo

**superannuation** /suːpərænjʊ'eɪʃn/ n jubilación f

**superb** /suː'pɜːb/ a espléndido. ~ly adv espléndidamente

**supercilious** /suːpə'sɪlɪəs/ a desdeñoso

**superficial** /suːpə'fɪʃl/ a superficial. ~ity /-ɪ'ælətɪ/ n superficialidad f. ~ly adv superficialmente

**superfluous** /suːˈpɜːfluəs/ a superfluo

**superhuman** /suːpəˈhjuːmən/ a sobrehumano

**superimpose** /suːpərɪmˈpəʊz/ vt sobreponer

**superintend** /suːpərɪnˈtend/ vt vigilar. ~**ence** n dirección f. ~**ent** n director m; (of police) comisario m

**superior** /suːˈpɪərɪə(r)/ a & n superior (m). ~**ity** /-ˈɒrətɪ/ n superioridad f

**superlative** /suːˈpɜːlətɪv/ a & n superlativo (m)

**superman** /ˈsuːpəmæn/ n (pl -men) superhombre m

**supermarket** /ˈsuːpəmɑːkɪt/ n supermercado m

**supernatural** /suːpəˈnætʃrəl/ a sobrenatural

**superpower** /ˈsuːpəpaʊə(r)/ n superpotencia f

**supersede** /suːpəˈsiːd/ vt reemplazar, suplantar

**supersonic** /suːpəˈsɒnɪk/ a supersónico

**superstitio|n** /suːpəˈstɪʃn/ n superstición f. ~**us** a supersticioso

**superstructure** /ˈsuːpəstrʌktʃə(r)/ n superestructura f

**supertanker** /ˈsuːpətæŋkə(r)/ n petrolero m gigante

**supervene** /suːpəˈviːn/ vi sobrevenir

**supervis|e** /ˈsuːpəvaɪz/ vt supervisar. ~**ion** /-ˈvɪʒn/ n supervisión f. ~**or** /-zə(r)/ n supervisor m. ~**ory** a de supervisión

**supper** /ˈsʌpə(r)/ n cena f

**supplant** /səˈplɑːnt/ vt suplantar

**supple** /sʌpl/ a flexible. ~**ness** n flexibilidad f

**supplement** /ˈsʌplɪmənt/ n suplemento m. ● vt completar; (increase) aumentar. ~**ary** /-ˈmentərɪ/ a suplementario

**suppl|ier** /səˈplaɪə(r)/ n suministrador m; (com) proveedor m. ~**y** /səˈplaɪ/ vt proveer; (feed) alimentar; satisfacer ⟨a need⟩. ~**y with** abastecer de. ● n provisión f, suministro m. ~**y and demand** oferta f y demanda

**support** /səˈpɔːt/ vt sostener; (endure) soportar, aguantar; (fig) apoyar. ● n apoyo m; (tec) soporte m. ~**er** /-ə(r)/ n soporte m; (sport) seguidor m, hincha m & f. ~**ive** a alentador

**suppos|e** /səˈpəʊz/ vt suponer; (think) creer. **be ~ed to** deber. **not be ~ed to** (fam) no tener permiso para, no tener derecho a. ~**edly** adv según cabe suponer; (before adjective) presuntamente. ~**ition** /sʌpəˈzɪʃn/ n suposición f

**suppository** /səˈpɒzɪtərɪ/ n supositorio m

**suppress** /səˈpres/ vt suprimir. ~**ion** n supresión f. ~**or** /-ə(r)/ n supresor m

**suprem|acy** /suːˈpreməsɪ/ n supremacía f. ~**e** /suːˈpriːm/ a supremo

**surcharge** /ˈsɜːtʃɑːdʒ/ n sobreprecio m; (tax) recargo m

**sure** /ʃʊə(r)/ a (-er, -est) seguro, cierto. **make ~** asegurarse. ● adv (Amer, fam) ¡claro! **~ enough** efectivamente. ~**footed** a de pie firme. ~**ly** adv seguramente

**surety** /ˈʃʊərətɪ/ n garantía f

**surf** /sɜːf/ n oleaje m; (foam) espuma f

**surface** /ˈsɜːfɪs/ n superficie f. ● a superficial, de la superficie. ● vt (smoothe) alisar; (cover) recubrir (with de). ● vi salir a la superficie; (emerge) emerger. **~ mail** n por vía marítima

**surfboard** /ˈsɜːfbɔːd/ n tabla f de surf

**surfeit** /ˈsɜːfɪt/ n exceso m

**surfing** /ˈsɜːfɪŋ/ n, **surf-riding** /ˈsɜːfraɪdɪŋ/ n surf m

**surge** /sɜːdʒ/ vi ⟨crowd⟩ moverse en tropel; ⟨waves⟩ encresparse. ● n oleada f; (elec) sobretensión f

**surgeon** /ˈsɜːdʒən/ n cirujano m

**surgery** /ˈsɜːdʒərɪ/ n cirugía f; (consulting room) consultorio m; (consulting hours) horas fpl de consulta

**surgical** /ˈsɜːrdʒɪkl/ a quirúrgico

**surl|iness** /ˈsɜːlɪnɪs/ n aspereza f. ~**y** /ˈsɜːlɪ/ a (-ier, -iest) áspero

**surmise** /səˈmaɪz/ vt conjeturar

**surmount** /səˈmaʊnt/ vt superar

**surname** /ˈsɜːneɪm/ n apellido m

**surpass** /səˈpɑːs/ vt sobrepasar, exceder

**surplus** /ˈsɜːpləs/ a & n excedente (m)

**surpris|e** /səˈpraɪz/ n sorpresa f. ● vt sorprender. ~**ing** a sorprendente. ~**ingly** adv asombrosamente

**surrealis|m** /səˈrɪəlɪzəm/ n surrealismo m. ~**t** n surrealista m & f

**surrender** /səˈrendə(r)/ vt entregar. ● vi entregarse. ● n entrega f; (mil) rendición f

**surreptitious** /sʌrəpˈtɪʃəs/ a clandestino

**surrogate** /ˈsʌrəgət/ n substituto m

**surround** /səˈraʊnd/ vt rodear; (mil) cercar. ● n borde m. ~ing a circundante. ~ings npl alrededores mpl

**surveillance** /sɜːˈveɪləns/ n vigilancia f

**survey** /ˈsɜːveɪ/ n inspección f; (report) informe m; (general view) vista f de conjunto. /səˈveɪ/ vt examinar, inspeccionar; (inquire into) hacer una encuesta de. ~or n topógrafo m, agrimensor

**surviv|al** /səˈvaɪvl/ n supervivencia f. ~e /səˈvaɪv/ vt/i sobrevivir. ~or /-ə(r)/ n superviviente m & f

**susceptib|ility** /səsɛptəˈbɪlətɪ/ n susceptibilidad f. ~le /səˈsɛptəbl/ a susceptible. ~le to propenso a

**suspect** /səˈspɛkt/ vt sospechar. /ˈsʌspɛkt/ a n sospechoso (m)

**suspend** /səˈspɛnd/ vt suspender. ~er /səsˈpɛndə(r)/ n liga f. ~er belt n liguero m. ~ers npl (Amer) tirantes mpl

**suspense** /səˈspɛns/ n incertidumbre f; (in film etc) suspense m

**suspension** /səˈspɛnʃn/ n suspensión f. ~ bridge n puente m colgante

**suspicion** /səˈspɪʃn/ n sospecha f; (trace) pizca f

**suspicious** /səˈspɪʃəs/ a desconfiado; (causing suspicion) sospechoso

**sustain** /səˈsteɪn/ vt sostener; (suffer) sufrir

**sustenance** /ˈsʌstɪnəns/ n sustento m

**svelte** /svɛlt/ a esbelto

**SW** abbr (south-west) sudoeste m

**swab** /swɒb/ n (med) tapón m

**swagger** /ˈswægə(r)/ vi pavonearse

**swallow**[1] /ˈswɒləʊ/ vt/i tragar. ● n trago m. ~ up tragar; consumir (savings etc)

**swallow**[2] /ˈswɒləʊ/ n (bird) golondrina f

**swam** /swæm/ see **swim**

**swamp** /swɒmp/ n pantano m. ● vt inundar; (with work) agobiar. ~y a pantanoso

**swan** /swɒn/ n cisne m

**swank** /swæŋk/ n (fam) ostentación f. ● vi (fam) fanfarronear

**swap** /swɒp/ vt/i (pt swapped) (fam) (inter)cambiar. ● n (fam) (inter)cambio m

**swarm** /swɔːm/ n enjambre m. ● vi ⟨bees⟩ enjambrar; (fig) hormiguear

**swarthy** /ˈswɔːðɪ/ a (-ier, -iest) moreno

**swastika** /ˈswɒstɪkə/ n cruz f gamada

**swat** /swɒt/ vt (pt swatted) aplastar

**sway** /sweɪ/ vi balancearse. ● vt (influence) influir en. ● n balanceo m; (rule) imperio m

**swear** /sweə(r)/ vt/i (pt swore, pp sworn) jurar. ~ by (fam) creer ciegamente en. ~word n palabrota f

**sweat** /swɛt/ n sudor m. ● vi sudar

**sweat|er** /ˈswɛtə(r)/ n jersey m. ~shirt n sudadera f

**swede** /swiːd/ n naba f

**Swede** /swiːd/ n sueco m

**Sweden** /ˈswiːdn/ n Suecia f

**Swedish** /ˈswiːdɪʃ/ a & n sueco (m)

**sweep** /swiːp/ vt (pt swept) barrer; deshollinar ⟨chimney⟩. ~ the board ganar todo. ● vi barrer; ⟨road⟩ extenderse; (go majestically) moverse majestuosamente. ● n barrido m; (curve) curva f; (movement) movimiento m; (person) deshollinador m. ~ away vt barrer. ~ing a ⟨gesture⟩ amplio; ⟨changes etc⟩ radical; ⟨statement⟩ demasiado general. ~stake /ˈswiːpsteɪk/ n lotería f

**sweet** /swiːt/ a (-er, -est) dulce; (fragrant) fragante; (pleasant) agradable. have a ~ tooth ser dulcero. ● n caramelo m; (dish) postre m. ~bread /ˈswiːtbrɛd/ n lechecillas fpl. ~en /ˈswiːtn/ vt endulzar. ~ener /-ə(r)/ n dulcificante m. ~heart /ˈswiːthɑːt/ n amor m. ~ly adv dulcemente. ~ness n dulzura f. ~ pea n guisante m de olor

**swell** /swɛl/ vt (pt swelled, pp swollen or swelled) hinchar; (increase) aumentar. ● vi hincharse; (increase) aumentarse; ⟨river⟩ crecer. ● a (fam) estupendo. ● n (of sea) oleaje m. ~ing n hinchazón m

**swelter** /ˈswɛltə(r)/ vi sofocarse de calor

**swept** /swɛpt/ see **sweep**

**swerve** /swɜːv/ vi desviarse

**swift** /swɪft/ a (-er, -est) rápido. ● n (bird) vencejo m. ~ly adv rápidamente. ~ness n rapidez f

**swig** /swɪg/ vt (pt swigged) (fam) beber a grandes tragos. ● n (fam) trago m

**swill** /swɪl/ *vt* enjuagar; (*drink*) beber a grandes tragos. ● *n* (*food for pigs*) bazofia *f*

**swim** /swɪm/ *vi* (*pt* **swam**, *pp* **swum**) nadar; ⟨*room, head*⟩ dar vueltas. ● *n* baño *m*. **~mer** *n* nadador *m*. **~ming-bath** *n* piscina *f*. **~mingly** /'swɪmɪŋlɪ/ *adv* a las mil maravillas. **~ming-pool** *n* piscina *f*. **~ming-trunks** *npl* bañador *m*. **~suit** *n* traje *m* de baño

**swindle** /'swɪndl/ *vt* estafar. ● *n* estafa *f*. **~r** /-ə(r)/ *n* estafador *m*

**swine** /swaɪn/ *npl* cerdos *mpl*. ● *n* (*pl* **swine**) (*person, fam*) canalla *m*

**swing** /swɪŋ/ *vt* (*pt* **swung**) balancear. ● *vi* oscilar; ⟨*person*⟩ balancearse; (*turn round*) girar. ● *n* balanceo *m*, vaivén *m*; (*seat*) columpio *m*; (*mus*) ritmo *m*. **in full ~** en plena actividad. **~ bridge** *n* puente *m* giratorio

**swingeing** /'swɪndʒɪŋ/ *a* enorme

**swipe** /swaɪp/ *vt* golpear; (*snatch, sl*) birlar. ● *n* (*fam*) golpe *m*

**swirl** /swɜːl/ *vi* arremolinarse. ● *n* remolino *m*

**swish** /swɪʃ/ *vt* silbar. ● *a* (*fam*) elegante

**Swiss** /swɪs/ *a & n* suizo (*m*). **~ roll** *n* bizcocho *m* enrollado

**switch** /swɪtʃ/ *n* (*elec*) interruptor *m*; (*change*) cambio *m*. ● *vt* cambiar; (*deviate*) desviar. **~ off** (*elec*) desconectar; apagar ⟨*light*⟩. **~ on** (*elec*) encender; arrancar ⟨*engine*⟩. **~back** /'swɪtʃbæk/ *n* montaña *f* rusa. **~board** /'swɪtʃbɔːd/ *n* centralita *f*

**Switzerland** /'swɪtsələnd/ *n* Suiza *f*

**swivel** /'swɪvl/ ● *vi* (*pt* **swivelled**) girar

**swollen** /'swəʊlən/ *see* **swell**. ● *a* hinchado

**swoon** /swuːn/ *vi* desmayarse

**swoop** /swuːp/ *vi* ⟨*bird*⟩ calarse; ⟨*plane*⟩ bajar en picado. ● *n* calada *f*; (*by police*) redada *f*

**sword** /sɔːd/ *n* espada *f*. **~fish** /'sɔːdfɪʃ/ *n* pez *m* espada

**swore** /swɔː(r)/ *see* **swear**

**sworn** /swɔːn/ *see* **swear**. ● *a* ⟨*enemy*⟩ jurado; ⟨*friend*⟩ leal

**swot** /swɒt/ *vt/i* (*pt* **swotted**) (*schol, sl*) empollar. ● *n* (*schol, sl*) empollón *m*

**swum** /swʌm/ *see* **swim**

**swung** /swʌŋ/ *see* **swing**

**sycamore** /'sɪkəmɔː(r)/ *n* plátano *m* falso

**syllable** /'sɪləbl/ *n* sílaba *f*

**syllabus** /'sɪləbəs/ *n* (*pl* **-buses**) programa *m* (de estudios)

**symbol** /'sɪmbl/ *n* símbolo *m*. **~ic(al)** /-'bɒlɪk(l)/ *a* simbólico. **~ism** *n* simbolismo *m*. **~ize** *vt* simbolizar

**symmetr|ical** /sɪ'metrɪkl/ *a* simétrico. **~y** /'sɪmətrɪ/ *n* simetría *f*

**sympath|etic** /sɪmpə'θetɪk/ *a* comprensivo; (*showing pity*) compasivo. **~ize** /-aɪz/ *vi* comprender; (*pity*) compadecerse (**with** de). **~izer** *n* (*pol*) simpatizante *m & f*. **~y** /'sɪmpəθɪ/ *n* comprensión *f*; (*pity*) compasión *f*; (*condolences*) pésame *m*. **be in ~y with** estar de acuerdo con

**symphon|ic** /sɪm'fɒnɪk/ *a* sinfónico. **~y** /'sɪmfənɪ/ *n* sinfonía *f*

**symposium** /sɪm'pəʊzɪəm/ *n* (*pl* **-ia**) simposio *m*

**symptom** /'sɪmptəm/ *n* síntoma *m*. **~atic** /-'mætɪk/ *a* sintomático

**synagogue** /'sɪnəgɒg/ *n* sinagoga *f*

**synchroniz|ation** /sɪŋkrənaɪ'zeɪʃn/ *n* sincronización *f*. **~e** /'sɪŋkrənaɪz/ *vt* sincronizar

**syncopat|e** /'sɪŋkəpeɪt/ *vt* sincopar. **~ion** /-'peɪʃn/ *n* síncopa *f*

**syndicate** /'sɪndɪkət/ *n* sindicato *m*

**syndrome** /'sɪndrəʊm/ *n* síndrome *m*

**synod** /'sɪnəd/ *n* sínodo *m*

**synonym** /'sɪnənɪm/ *n* sinónimo *m*. **~ous** /-'nɒnɪməs/ *a* sinónimo

**synopsis** /sɪ'nɒpsɪs/ *n* (*pl* **-opses** /-siːz/) sinopsis *f*, resumen *m*

**syntax** /'sɪntæks/ *n* sintaxis *f invar*

**synthesi|s** /'sɪnθəsɪs/ *n* (*pl* **-theses** /-siːz/) síntesis *f*. **~ze** *vt* sintetizar

**synthetic** /sɪn'θetɪk/ *a* sintético

**syphilis** /'sɪfɪlɪs/ *n* sífilis *f*

**Syria** /'sɪrɪə/ *n* Siria *f*. **~n** *a & n* sirio (*m*)

**syringe** /'sɪrɪndʒ/ *n* jeringa *f*. ● *vt* jeringar

**syrup** /'sɪrəp/ *n* jarabe *m*, almíbar *m*; (*treacle*) melaza *f*. **~y** *a* almibarado

**system** /'sɪstəm/ *n* sistema *m*; (*body*) organismo *m*; (*order*) método *m*. **~atic** /-ə'mætɪk/ *a* sistemático. **~atically** /-ə'mætɪklɪ/ *adv* sistemáticamente. **~s analyst** *n* analista *m & f* de sistemas

# T

**tab** /tæb/ *n* (*flap*) lengüeta *f*; (*label*) etiqueta *f*. **keep ~s on** (*fam*) vigilar
**tabby** /'tæbɪ/ *n* gato *m* atigrado
**tabernacle** /'tæbənækl/ *n* tabernáculo *m*
**table** /'teɪbl/ *n* mesa *f*; (*list*) tabla *f*. **~ of contents** índice *m*. ● *vt* presentar; (*postpone*) aplazar. **~cloth** *n* mantel *m*. **~mat** *n* salvamanteles *m invar*. **~spoon** /'teɪblspu:n/ *n* cucharón *m*, cuchara *f* sopera. **~spoonful** *n* (*pl* **-fuls**) cucharada *f*
**tablet** /'tæblɪt/ *n* (*of stone*) lápida *f*; (*pill*) tableta *f*; (*of soap etc*) pastilla *f*
**table tennis** /'teɪbltenɪs/ *n* tenis *m* de mesa, ping-pong *m*
**tabloid** /'tæblɔɪd/ *n* tabloide *m*
**taboo** /tə'bu:/ *a & n* tabú (*m*)
**tabulator** /'tæbjʊleɪtə(r)/ *n* tabulador *m*
**tacit** /'tæsɪt/ *a* tácito
**taciturn** /'tæsɪtɜːn/ *a* taciturno
**tack** /tæk/ *n* tachuela *f*; (*stitch*) hilván *m*; (*naut*) virada *f*; (*fig*) línea *f* de conducta. ● *vt* sujetar con tachuelas; (*sew*) hilvanar. **~ on** añadir. ● *vi* virar
**tackle** /'tækl/ *n* (*equipment*) equipo *m*; (*football*) placaje *m*. ● *vt* abordar ⟨*problem etc*⟩; (*in rugby*) hacer un placaje a
**tacky** /'tækɪ/ *a* pegajoso; (*in poor taste*) vulgar, de pacotilla
**tact** /tækt/ *n* tacto *m*. **~ful** *a* discreto. **~fully** *adv* discretamente
**tactic|al** /'tæktɪkl/ *a* táctico. **~s** /'tæktɪks/ *npl* táctica *f*
**tactile** /'tæktaɪl/ *a* táctil
**tact: ~less** *a* indiscreto. **~lessly** *adv* indiscretamente
**tadpole** /'tædpəʊl/ *n* renacuajo *m*
**tag** /tæg/ *n* (*on shoe-lace*) herrete *m*; (*label*) etiqueta *f*. ● *vt* (*pt* **tagged**) poner etiqueta a; (*trail*) seguir. ● *vi*. **~ along** (*fam*) seguir
**tail** /teɪl/ *n* cola *f*. **~s** *npl* (*tailcoat*) frac *m*; (*of coin*) cruz *f*. ● *vt* (*sl*) seguir. ● *vi*. **~ off** disminuir. **~-end** *n* extremo *m* final, cola *f*
**tailor** /'teɪlə(r)/ *n* sastre *m*. ● *vt* confeccionar. **~-made** *n* hecho a la medida. **~-made for** (*fig*) hecho para
**tailplane** /'teɪlpleɪn/ *n* plano *m* de cola

**taint** /teɪnt/ *n* mancha *f*. ● *vt* contaminar
**take** /teɪk/ *vt* (*pt* **took**, *pp* **taken**) tomar, coger (*not LAm*), agarrar (*esp LAm*); (*contain*) contener; (*capture*) capturar; (*endure*) aguantar; (*require*) requerir; tomar ⟨*bath*⟩; dar ⟨*walk*⟩; (*carry*) llevar; (*accompany*) acompañar; presentarse para ⟨*exam*⟩; sacar ⟨*photo*⟩; ganar ⟨*prize*⟩. **~ advantage of** aprovechar. **~ after** parecerse a. **~ away** quitar. **~ back** retirar ⟨*statement etc*⟩. **~ in** achicar ⟨*garment*⟩; (*understand*) comprender; (*deceive*) engañar. **~ off** quitarse ⟨*clothes*⟩; (*mimic*) imitar; (*aviat*) despegar. **~ o.s. off** marcharse. **~ on** (*undertake*) emprender; contratar ⟨*employee*⟩. **~ out** (*remove*) sacar. **~ over** tomar posesión de; (*assume control*) tomar el poder. **~ part** participar. **~ place** tener lugar. **~ sides** tomar partido. **~ to** dedicarse a; (*like*) tomar simpatía a ⟨*person*⟩; (*like*) aficionarse a ⟨*thing*⟩. **~ up** dedicarse a ⟨*hobby*⟩; (*occupy*) ocupar; (*resume*) reanudar. **~ up with** trabar amistad con. **be ~n ill** ponerse enfermo. ● *n* presa *f*; (*photo, cinema, TV*) toma *f*
**takings** /'teɪkɪŋz/ *npl* ingresos *mpl*
**take: ~-off** *n* despegue *m*. **~-over** *n* toma *f* de posesión
**talcum** /'tælkəm/ *n*. **~ powder** *n* (polvos *mpl* de) talco (*m*)
**tale** /teɪl/ *n* cuento *m*
**talent** /'tælənt/ *n* talento *m*. **~ed** *a* talentoso
**talisman** /'tælɪzmən/ *n* talismán *m*
**talk** /tɔːk/ *vt/i* hablar. **~ about** hablar de. **~ over** discutir. ● *n* conversación *f*; (*lecture*) conferencia *f*. **small ~** charla *f*. **~ative** *a* hablador. **~er** *n* hablador *m*; (*chatterbox*) parlanchín *m*. **~ing-to** *n* reprensión *f*
**tall** /tɔːl/ *a* (**-er, -est**) alto. **~ story** *n* (*fam*) historia *f* inverosímil. **that's a ~ order** *n* (*fam*) eso es pedir mucho
**tallboy** /'tɔːlbɔɪ/ *n* cómoda *f* alta
**tally** /'tælɪ/ *n* tarja *f*; (*total*) total *m*. ● *vi* corresponder (**with** a)
**talon** /'tælən/ *n* garra *f*
**tambourine** /tæmbə'riːn/ *n* pandereta *f*
**tame** /teɪm/ *a* (**-er, -est**) ⟨*animal*⟩ doméstico; ⟨*person*⟩ dócil; (*dull*) insípido. ● *vt* domesticar; domar

⟨*wild animal*⟩. **~ly** *adv* dócilmente. **~r** /-ə(r)/ *n* domador *m*

**tamper** /'tæmpə(r)/ *vi.* **~ with** manosear; (*alter*) alterar, falsificar

**tampon** /'tæmpɒn/ *n* tampón *m*

**tan** /tæn/ *vt* (*pt* **tanned**) curtir ⟨*hide*⟩; ⟨*sun*⟩ broncear. ● *vi* ponerse moreno. ● *n* bronceado *m*. ● *a* (*colour*) de color canela

**tandem** /'tændəm/ *n* tándem *m*

**tang** /tæŋ/ *n* sabor *m* fuerte; (*smell*) olor *m* fuerte

**tangent** /'tændʒənt/ *n* tangente *f*

**tangerine** /tændʒə'riːn/ *n* mandarina *f*

**tangibl|e** /'tændʒəbl/ *a* tangible. **~y** *adv* perceptiblemente

**tangle** /'tæŋgl/ *vt* enredar. ● *vi* enredarse. ● *n* enredo *m*

**tango** /'tæŋgəʊ/ *n* (*pl* -**os**) tango *m*

**tank** /tæŋk/ *n* depósito *m*; (*mil*) tanque *m*

**tankard** /'tæŋkəd/ *n* jarra *f*, bock *m*

**tanker** /'tæŋkə(r)/ *n* petrolero *m*; (*truck*) camión *m* cisterna

**tantaliz|e** /'tæntəlaɪz/ *vt* atormentar. **~ing** *a* atormentador; (*tempting*) tentador

**tantamount** /'tæntəmaʊnt/ *a.* **~ to** equivalente a

**tantrum** /'tæntrəm/ *n* rabieta *f*

**tap**[1] /tæp/ *n* grifo *m*. **on ~** disponible. ● *vt* explotar ⟨*resources*⟩; interceptar ⟨*phone*⟩

**tap**[2] /tæp/ *n* (*knock*) golpe *m* ligero. ● *vt* (*pt* **tapped**) golpear ligeramente. **~dance** *n* zapateado *m*

**tape** /teɪp/ *n* cinta *f*. ● *vt* atar con cinta; (*record*) grabar. **have sth ~d** (*sl*) comprender perfectamente. **~measure** *n* cinta *f* métrica

**taper** /'teɪpə(r)/ *n* bujía *f*. ● *vt* ahusar. ● *vi* ahusarse. **~ off** disminuir

**tape: ~ recorder** *n* magnetofón *m*, magnetófono *m*. **~ recording** *n* grabación *f*

**tapestry** /'tæpɪstrɪ/ *n* tapicería *f*; (*product*) tapiz *m*

**tapioca** /tæpɪ'əʊkə/ *n* tapioca *f*

**tar** /tɑː(r)/ *n* alquitrán *m*. ● *vt* (*pt* **tarred**) alquitranar

**tard|ily** /'tɑːdɪlɪ/ *adv* lentamente; (*late*) tardíamente. **~y** /'tɑːdɪ/ *a* (-**ier**, -**iest**) (*slow*) lento; (*late*) tardío

**target** /'tɑːgɪt/ *n* blanco *m*; (*fig*) objetivo *m*

**tariff** /'tærɪf/ *n* tarifa *f*

**tarmac** /'tɑːmæk/ *n* pista·*f* de aterrizaje. **T~** *n* (*P*) macadán *m*

**tarnish** /'tɑːnɪʃ/ *vt* deslustrar. ● *vi* deslustrarse

**tarpaulin** /tɑː'pɔːlɪn/ *n* alquitranado *m*

**tarragon** /'tærəgən/ *n* estragón *m*

**tart**[1] /tɑːt/ *n* pastel *m*; (*individual*) pastelillo *m*

**tart**[2] /tɑːt/ *n* (*sl*, *woman*) prostituta *f*, fulana *f* (*fam*). ● *vt.* **~ o.s. up** (*fam*) engalanarse

**tart**[3] /tɑːt/ *a* (-**er**, -**est**) ácido; (*fig*) áspero

**tartan** /'tɑːtn/ *n* tartán *m*, tela *f* escocesa

**tartar** /'tɑːtə(r)/ *n* tártaro *m*. **~ sauce** *n* salsa *f* tártara

**task** /tɑːsk/ *n* tarea *f*. **take to ~** reprender. **~ force** *n* destacamento *m* especial

**tassel** /'tæsl/ *n* borla *f*

**tast|e** /teɪst/ *n* sabor *m*, gusto *m*; (*small quantity*) poquito *m*. ● *vt* probar. ● *vi.* **~e of** saber a. **~eful** *a* de buen gusto. **~eless** *a* soso; (*fig*) de mal gusto. **~y** *a* (-**ier**, -**iest**) sabroso

**tat** /tæt/ *see* **tit**[2]

**tatter|ed** /'tætəd/ *a* hecho jirones. **~s** /'tætəz/ *npl* andrajos *mpl*

**tattle** /'tætl/ *vi* charlar. ● *n* charla *f*

**tattoo**[1] /tæ'tuː/ *n* (*mil*) espectáculo *m* militar

**tattoo**[2] /tæ'tuː/ *vt* tatuar. ● *n* tatuaje *m*

**tatty** /'tætɪ/ *a* (-**ier**, -**iest**) gastado, en mal estado

**taught** /tɔːt/ *see* **teach**

**taunt** /tɔːnt/ *vt* mofarse de. **~ s.o. with sth** echar algo en cara a uno. ● *n* mofa *f*

**Taurus** /'tɔːrəs/ *n* (*astr*) Tauro *m*

**taut** /tɔːt/ *a* tenso

**tavern** /'tævən/ *n* taberna *f*

**tawdry** /'tɔːdrɪ/ *a* (-**ier**, -**iest**) charro

**tawny** /'tɔːnɪ/ *a* bronceado

**tax** /tæks/ *n* impuesto *m*. ● *vt* imponer contribuciones a ⟨*person*⟩; gravar con un impuesto ⟨*thing*⟩; (*fig*) poner a prueba. **~able** *a* imponible. **~ation** /-'seɪʃn/ *n* impuestos *mpl*. **~collector** *n* recaudador *m* de contribuciones. **~free** *a* libre de impuestos

**taxi** /'tæksɪ/ *n* (*pl* -**is**) taxi *m*. ● *vi* (*pt* **taxied**, *pres p* **taxiing**) ⟨*aircraft*⟩ rodar por la pista. **~ rank** *n* parada *f* de taxis

**taxpayer** /'tækspeɪə(r)/ n contribuyente m & f

**te** /tiː/ n (mus, seventh note of any musical scale) si m

**tea** /tiː/ n té m. **~bag** n bolsita f de té. **~break** n descanso m para el té

**teach** /tiːtʃ/ vt/i (pt **taught**) enseñar. **~er** n profesor m; (primary) maestro m. **~in** n seminario m. **~ing** n enseñanza f. ● a docente. **~ing staff** n profesorado m

**teacup** /'tiːkʌp/ n taza f de té

**teak** /tiːk/ n teca f

**tea-leaf** /'tiːliːf/ n hoja f de té

**team** /tiːm/ n equipo m; (of horses) tiro m. ● vi. **~ up** unirse. **~work** n trabajo m en equipo

**teapot** /'tiːpɒt/ n tetera f

**tear**[1] /teə(r)/ vt (pt **tore**, pp **torn**) rasgar. ● vi rasgarse; (run) precipitarse. **~ apart** n rasgón m. **~ apart** desgarrar. **~ o.s. away** separarse

**tear**[2] /tɪə(r)/ n lágrima f. **in ~s** llorando

**tearaway** /'teərəweɪ/ n gamberro m

**tear** /tɪə(r)/: **~ful** a lloroso. **~gas** n gas m lacrimógeno

**tease** /tiːz/ vt tomar el pelo a; cardar ⟨cloth etc⟩. ● n guasón m. **~r** /-ə(r)/ n (fam) problema m difícil

**tea**: **~set** n juego m de té. **~spoon** /'tiːspuːn/ n cucharilla f. **~spoonful** n (pl -**fuls**) (amount) cucharadita f

**teat** /tiːt/ n (of animal) teta f; (for bottle) tetilla f

**tea-towel** /'tiːtaʊəl/ n paño m de cocina

**technical** /'teknɪkl/ a técnico. **~ity** n /-'kælətɪ/ n detalle m técnico. **~ly** adv técnicamente

**technician** /tek'nɪʃn/ n técnico m

**technique** /tek'niːk/ n técnica f

**technolog|ist** /tek'nɒlədʒɪst/ n tecnólogo m. **~y** /tek'nɒlədʒɪ/ n tecnología f

**teddy bear** /'tedɪbeə(r)/ n osito m de felpa, osito m de peluche

**tedious** /'tiːdɪəs/ a pesado. **~ly** adv pesadamente

**tedium** /'tiːdɪəm/ n aburrimiento m

**tee** /tiː/ n (golf) tee m

**teem** /tiːm/ vi abundar; (rain) llover a cántaros

**teen|age** /'tiːneɪdʒ/ a adolescente; (for teenagers) para jóvenes. **~ager** /-ə(r)/ n adolescente m & f, joven m & f. **~s** /tiːnz/ npl. **the ~s** la adolescencia f

**teeny** /'tiːnɪ/ a (-**ier**, -**iest**) (fam) chiquito

**teeter** /'tiːtə(r)/ vi balancearse

**teeth** /tiːθ/ see **tooth**. **~e** /tiːð/ vi echar los dientes. **~ing troubles** npl (fig) dificultades fpl iniciales

**teetotaller** /tiː'təʊtələ(r)/ n abstemio m

**telecommunications** /telɪkəmjuːnɪ'keɪʃnz/ npl telecomunicaciones fpl

**telegram** /'telɪgræm/ n telegrama m

**telegraph** /'telɪgrɑːf/ n telégrafo m. ● vt telegrafiar. **~ic** /-'græfɪk/ a telegráfico

**telepath|ic** /telɪ'pæθɪk/ a telepático. **~y** /tɪ'lepəθɪ/ n telepatía f

**telephon|e** /'telɪfəʊn/ n teléfono m. ● vt llamar por teléfono. **~e booth** n cabina f telefónica. **~e directory** n guía f telefónica. **~e exchange** n central f telefónica. **~ic** /-'fɒnɪk/ a telefónico. **~ist** /tɪ'lefənɪst/ n telefonista m f

**telephoto** /telɪ'fəʊtəʊ/ a. **~ lens** n teleobjetivo m

**teleprinter** /'telɪprɪntə(r)/ n teleimpresor m

**telescop|e** /'telɪskəʊp/ n telescopio m. **~ic** /-'kɒpɪk/ a telescópico

**televis|e** /'telɪvaɪz/ vt televisar. **~ion** /'telɪvɪʒn/ n televisión f. **~ion set** n televisor m

**telex** /'teleks/ n télex m. ● vt enviar por télex

**tell** /tel/ vt (pt **told**) decir; contar ⟨story⟩; (distinguish) distinguir. ● vi (produce an effect) tener efecto; (know) saber. **~ off** vt reprender. **~er** /'telə(r)/ n (in bank) cajero m

**telling** /'telɪŋ/ a eficaz

**tell-tale** /'telteɪl/ n soplón m. ● a revelador

**telly** /'telɪ/ n (fam) televisión f, tele f (fam)

**temerity** /tɪ'merətɪ/ n temeridad f

**temp** /temp/ n (fam) empleado m temporal

**temper** /'tempə(r)/ n (disposition) disposición f; (mood) humor m; (fit of anger) cólera f; (of metal) temple m. **be in a ~** estar de mal humor. **keep one's ~** contenerse. **lose one's ~** enfadarse, perder la paciencia. ● vt templar ⟨metal⟩

**temperament** /'tempramənt/ n temperamento m. **~al** /-'mentl/ a caprichoso

**temperance** /'tempərəns/ n moderación f

**temperate** /'tempərət/ a moderado; ‹climate› templado

**temperature** /'temprɪtʃə(r)/ n temperatura f. **have a ~** tener fiebre

**tempest** /'tempɪst/ n tempestad f. **~uous** /-'pestjʊəs/ a tempestuoso

**temple**[1] /'templ/ n templo m

**temple**[2] /'templ/ (anat) sien f

**tempo** /'tempəʊ/ n (pl **-os** or **tempi**) ritmo m

**temporar|ily** /'tempərərəlı/ adv temporalmente. **~y** /'tempərəri/ a temporal, provisional

**tempt** /tempt/ vt tentar. **~ s.o. to** inducir a uno a. **~ation** /-'teɪʃn/ n tentación f. **~ing** a tentador

**ten** /ten/ a & n diez (m)

**tenable** /'tenəbl/ a sostenible

**tenaci|ous** /tɪ'neɪʃəs/ a tenaz. **~ty** /-æsətɪ/ n tenacidad f

**tenan|cy** /'tenənsɪ/ n alquiler m. **~t** /'tenənt/ n inquilino m

**tend**[1] /tend/ vi. **~ to** tener tendencia a

**tend**[2] /tend/ vt cuidar

**tendency** /'tendənsɪ/ n tendencia f

**tender**[1] /'tendə(r)/ a tierno; (painful) dolorido

**tender**[2] /'tendə(r)/ n (com) oferta f. **legal ~** n curso m legal. ● vt ofrecer, presentar

**tender:** **~ly** adv tiernamente. **~ness** n ternura f

**tendon** /'tendən/ n tendón m

**tenement** /'tenəmənt/ n vivienda f

**tenet** /'tenɪt/ n principio m

**tenfold** /'tenfəʊld/ a diez veces mayor, décuplo. ● adv diez veces

**tenner** /'tenə(r)/ n (fam) billete m de diez libras

**tennis** /'tenɪs/ n tenis m

**tenor** /'tenə(r)/ n tenor m

**tens|e** /tens/ a (**-er**, **-est**) tieso; (fig) tenso. ● n (gram) tiempo m. ● vi. **~ up** tensarse. **~eness** n, **~ion** /'tenʃn/ n tensión f

**tent** /tent/ n tienda f, carpa f (LAm)

**tentacle** /'tentəkl/ n tentáculo m

**tentative** /'tentətɪv/ a provisional; (hesitant) indeciso. **~ly** adv provisionalmente; (timidly) tímidamente

**tenterhooks** /'tentəhʊks/ npl. **on ~** en ascuas

**tenth** /tenθ/ a & n décimo (m)

**tenuous** /'tenjʊəs/ a tenue

**tenure** /'tenjʊə(r)/ n posesión f

**tepid** /'tepɪd/ a tibio

**term** /tɜːm/ n (of time) período m; (schol) trimestre m; (word etc) término m. ● vt llamar. **~s** npl condiciones fpl; (com) precio m. **on bad ~s** en malas relaciones. **on good ~s** en buenas relaciones

**terminal** /'tɜːmɪnl/ a terminal, final. ● n (rail) estación f terminal; (elec) borne m. (**air**) **~** n término m, terminal m

**terminat|e** /'tɜːmɪneɪt/ vt terminar. ● vi terminarse. **~tion** /-'neɪʃn/ n terminación f

**terminology** /tɜːmɪ'nɒlədʒɪ/ n terminología f

**terrace** /'terəs/ n terraza f; (houses) hilera f de casas. **the ~s** npl (sport) las gradas fpl

**terrain** /tə'reɪn/ n terreno m

**terrestrial** /tɪ'restrɪəl/ a terrestre

**terribl|e** /'terəbl/ a terrible. **~y** adv terriblemente

**terrier** /'terɪə(r)/ n terrier m

**terrific** /tə'rɪfɪk/ a (excellent, fam) estupendo; (huge, fam) enorme. **~ally** adv (fam) terriblemente; (very well) muy bien

**terrify** /'terɪfaɪ/ vt aterrorizar. **~ing** a espantoso

**territor|ial** /terɪ'tɔːrɪəl/ a territorial. **~y** /'terɪtrɪ/ n territorio m

**terror** /'terə(r)/ n terror m. **~ism** /-zəm/ n terrorismo m. **~ist** /'terərɪst/ n terrorista m & f. **~ize** /'terəraɪz/ vt aterrorizar

**terse** /tɜːs/ a conciso; (abrupt) brusco

**test** /test/ n prueba f; (exam) examen m. ● vt probar; (examine) examinar

**testament** /'testəmənt/ n testamento m. **New T~** Nuevo Testamento. **Old T~** Antiguo Testamento

**testicle** /'testɪkl/ n testículo m

**testify** /'testɪfaɪ/ vt atestiguar. ● vi declarar

**testimon|ial** /testɪ'məʊnɪəl/ n certificado m; (of character) recomendación f. **~y** /'testɪmənɪ/ n testimonio m

**test:** **~ match** n partido m internacional. **~tube** n tubo m de ensayo, probeta f

**testy** /'testɪ/ a irritable

**tetanus** /'tetənəs/ n tétanos m invar

**tetchy** /'tetʃɪ/ a irritable

**tether** /'teðə(r)/ vt atar. ● n. **be at the end of one's ~** no poder más

**text** /tekst/ n texto m. **~book** n libro m de texto

**textile** /'tekstaɪl/ a & n textil (m)

**texture** /'tekstʃə(r)/ n textura f

**Thai** /taɪ/ a & n tailandés (m). **~land** n Tailandia f

**Thames** /temz/ n Támesis m

**than** /ðæn, ðən/ conj que; (with numbers) de

**thank** /θæŋk/ vt dar las gracias a, agradecer. **~ you** gracias. **~ful** /'θæŋkfl/ a agradecido. **~fully** con gratitud; (happily) afortunadamente. **~less** /'θæŋklɪs/ a ingrato. **~s** npl gracias fpl. **~s!** (fam) ¡gracias! **~s to** gracias a

**that** /ðæt, ðət/ a (pl those) ese, aquel, esa, aquella. ● pron (pl those) ése, aquél, ésa, aquélla. **~ is** es decir. **~'s it!** ¡eso es! **~ is why** por eso. **is ~ you?** ¿eres tú? **like ~** así. ● adv tan. ● rel pron que; (with prep) el que, la que, el cual, la cual. ● conj que

**thatch** /θætʃ/ n techo m de paja. **~ed** a con techo de paja

**thaw** /θɔː/ vt deshelar. ● vi deshelarse; ‹snow› derretirse. ● n deshielo m

**the** /ðə, ðiː/ def art el, la, los, las. **at ~** al, a la, a los, a las. **from ~** del, de la, de los, de las. **to ~** al, a la, a los, a las. ● adv. **all ~ better** tanto mejor

**theatr|e** /'θɪətə(r)/ n teatro m. **~ical** /-'ætrɪkl/ a teatral

**theft** /θeft/ n hurto m

**their** /ðeə(r)/ a su, sus

**theirs** /ðeəz/ poss pron (el) suyo, (la) suya, (los) suyos, (las) suyas

**them** /ðem, ðəm/ pron (accusative) los, las; (dative) les; (after prep) ellos, ellas

**theme** /θiːm/ n tema m. **~ song** n motivo m principal

**themselves** /ðəm'selvz/ pron ellos mismos, ellas mismas; (reflexive) se; (after prep) sí mismos, sí mismas

**then** /ðen/ adv entonces; (next) luego, después. **by ~** para entonces. **now and ~** de vez en cuando. **since ~** desde entonces. ● a de entonces

**theolog|ian** /θɪə'ləʊdʒən/ n teólogo m. **~y** /θɪ'ɒlədʒɪ/ n teología f

**theorem** /'θɪərəm/ n teorema m

**theor|etical** /θɪə'retɪkl/ a teórico. **~y** /'θɪərɪ/ n teoría f

**therap|eutic** /θerə'pjuːtɪk/ a terapéutico. **~ist** n terapeuta m & f. **~y** /'θerəpɪ/ n terapia f

**there** /ðeə(r)/ adv ahí, allí. **~ are** hay. **~ he is** ahí está. **~ is** hay. **~ it is** ahí está. **down ~** ahí abajo. **up ~** ahí arriba. ● int ¡vaya! **~, ~!** ¡ya, ya! **~abouts** adv por ahí. **~after** adv después. **~by** adv por eso. **~fore** /'ðeəfɔː(r)/ adv por lo tanto.

**thermal** /'θɜːml/ a termal

**thermometer** /θə'mɒmɪtə(r)/ n termómetro m

**thermonuclear** /θɜːməʊ'njuːklɪə(r)/ a termonuclear

**Thermos** /'θɜːməs/ n (P) termo m

**thermostat** /'θɜːməstæt/ n termostato m

**thesaurus** /θɪ'sɔːrəs/ n (pl -ri /-raɪ/) diccionario m de sinónimos

**these** /ðiːz/ a estos, estas. ● pron éstos, éstas

**thesis** /'θiːsɪs/ n (pl theses /-siːz/) tesis f

**they** /ðeɪ/ pron ellos, ellas. **~ say that** se dice que

**thick** /θɪk/ a (-er, -est) espeso; (dense) denso; (stupid, fam) torpe; (close, fam) íntimo. ● adv espesamente, densamente. ● n. **in the ~ of** en medio de. **~en** /'θɪkən/ vt espesar. ● vi espesarse

**thicket** /'θɪkɪt/ n matorral m

**thick: ~ly** adv espesamente, densamente. **~ness** n espesor m

**thickset** /θɪk'set/ a fornido

**thick-skinned** /θɪk'skɪnd/ a insensible

**thief** /θiːf/ n (pl thieves) ladrón m

**thiev|e** /θiːv/ vt/i robar. **~ing** a ladrón

**thigh** /θaɪ/ n muslo m

**thimble** /'θɪmbl/ n dedal m

**thin** /θɪn/ a (thinner, thinnest) delgado; ‹person› flaco; (weak) débil; (fine) fino; (sparse) escaso. ● adv ligeramente. ● vt (pt thinned) adelgazar; (dilute) diluir. **~ out** hacer menos denso. ● vi adelgazarse; (diminish) disminuir

**thing** /θɪŋ/ n cosa f. **for one ~** en primer lugar. **just the ~** exactamente lo que se necesita. **poor ~!** ¡pobrecito! **~s** npl (belongings) efectos mpl; (clothing) ropa f

**think** /θɪŋk/ vt (pt thought) pensar, creer. ● vi pensar (about, of en); (carefully) reflexionar; (imagine) imaginarse. **~ better of it** cambiar de idea. **I ~ so** creo que sí. **~ over** vt pensar bien. **~ up** vt idear,

inventar. **~er** *n* pensador *m*.
**~tank** *n* grupo *m* de expertos

**thin:** **~ly** *adv* ligeramente. **~ness** *n*
delgadez *f*; (*of person*) flaqueza *f*

**third** /θɜːd/ *a* tercero. ● *n* tercio *m*,
tercera parte *f*. **~rate** *a* muy
inferior. **T~ World** *n* Tercer Mundo
*m*

**thirst** /θɜːst/ *n* sed *f*. **~y** *a* sediento.
**be ~y** tener sed

**thirteen** /θɜː'tiːn/ *a & n* trece (*m*).
**~th** *a & n* decimotercero (*m*)

**thirt|ieth** /'θɜːtɪəθ/ *a & n* trigésimo
(*m*). **~y** /'θɜːtɪ/ *a & n* treinta (*m*)

**this** /ðɪs/ *a* (*pl* **these**) este, esta. **~
one** éste, ésta. ● *pron* (*pl* **these**)
éste, ésta, esto. **like ~** así

**thistle** /'θɪsl/ *n* cardo *m*

**thong** /θɒŋ/ *n* correa *f*

**thorn** /θɔːn/ *n* espina *f*. **~y** *a*
espinoso

**thorough** /'θʌrə/ *a* completo; (*deep*)
profundo; (*cleaning etc*) a fondo;
(*person*) concienzudo

**thoroughbred** /'θʌrəbred/ *a* de pura
sangre

**thoroughfare** /'θʌrəfeə(r)/ *n* calle *f*.
**no ~** prohibido el paso

**thoroughly** /'θʌrəlɪ/ *adv*
completamente

**those** /ðəʊz/ *a* esos, aquellos, esas,
aquellas. ● *pron* ésos, aquéllos,
ésas, aquéllas

**though** /ðəʊ/ *conj* aunque. ● *adv* sin
embargo. **as ~** como si

**thought** /θɔːt/ *see* **think**. ● *n* pensamiento *m*; (*idea*) idea *f*. **~ful** /'θɔː
tfl/ *a* pensativo; (*considerate*)
atento. **~fully** *adv* pensativamente;
(*considerately*) atentamente. **~less**
/'θɔːtlɪs/ *a* irreflexivo; (*inconsiderate*) desconsiderado

**thousand** /'θaʊznd/ *a & n* mil (*m*).
**~th** *a & n* milésimo (*m*)

**thrash** /θræʃ/ *vt* azotar; (*defeat*)
derrotar. **~ out** discutir a fondo

**thread** /θred/ *n* hilo *m*; (*of screw*)
rosca *f*. ● *vt* ensartar. **~ one's way**
abrirse paso. **~bare** /'θredbeə(r)/ *a*
raído

**threat** /θret/ *n* amenaza *f*. **~en**
/'θretn/ *vt/i* amenazar. **~ening** *a*
amenazador. **~eningly** *adv* de
modo amenazador

**three** /θriː/ *a & n* tres (*m*). **~fold** *a*
triple. ● *adv* tres veces. **~some**
/'θriːsəm/ *n* conjunto *m* de tres
personas

**thresh** /θreʃ/ *vt* trillar

**threshold** /'θreʃhəʊld/ *n* umbral *m*

**threw** /θruː/ *see* **throw**

**thrift** /θrɪft/ *n* economía *f*, ahorro *m*.
**~y** *a* frugal

**thrill** /θrɪl/ *n* emoción *f*. ● *vt*
emocionar. ● *vi* emocionarse;
(*quiver*) estremecerse. **be ~ed with**
estar encantado de. **~er** /'θrɪlə(r)/
*n* (*book*) libro *m* de suspense; (*film*)
película *f* de suspense. **~ing** *a*
emocionante

**thrive** /θraɪv/ *vi* prosperar. **~ing** *a*
próspero

**throat** /θrəʊt/ *n* garganta *f*. **have a
sore ~** dolerle la garganta

**throb** /θrɒb/ *vi* (*pt* **throbbed**) palpitar; (*with pain*) dar punzadas; (*fig*)
vibrar. ● *n* palpitación *f*; (*pain*)
punzada *f*; (*fig*) vibración *f*. **~bing**
(*pain*) punzante

**throes** /θrəʊz/ *npl*. **in the ~ of** en
medio de

**thrombosis** /θrɒm'bəʊsɪs/ *n* trombosis *f*

**throne** /θrəʊn/ *n* trono *m*

**throng** /θrɒŋ/ *n* multitud *f*

**throttle** /'θrɒtl/ *n* (*auto*) acelerador
*m*. ● *vt* ahogar

**through** /θruː/ *prep* por, a través de;
(*during*) durante; (*by means of*) por
medio de; (*thanks to*) gracias a.
● *adv* de parte a parte, de un lado
a otro; (*entirely*) completamente; (*to
the end*) hasta el final. **be ~** (*finished*) haber terminado. ● *a* (*train
etc*) directo

**throughout** /θruː'aʊt/ *prep* por
todo; (*time*) en todo. ● *adv* en todas
partes; (*all the time*) todo el tiempo

**throve** /θrəʊv/ *see* **thrive**

**throw** /θrəʊ/ *vt* (*pt* **threw**, *pp*
**thrown**) arrojar; (*baffle etc*)
desconcertar. **~ a party** (*fam*) dar
una fiesta. ● *n* tiro *m*; (*of dice*) lance
*m*. **~ away** *vt* tirar. **~ over** *vt* abandonar. **~ up** *vi* (*vomit*) vomitar. **~a-
way** *a* desechable

**thrush** /θrʌʃ/ *n* tordo *m*

**thrust** /θrʌst/ *vt* (*pt* **thrust**) empujar;
(*push in*) meter. ● *n* empuje *m*. **~
(up)on** imponer a

**thud** /θʌd/ *n* ruido *m* sordo

**thug** /θʌg/ *n* bruto *m*

**thumb** /θʌm/ *n* pulgar *m*. **under the
~ of** dominado por. ● *vt* hojear
(*book*). **~ a lift** hacer autostop. **~in-
dex** *n* uñeros *mpl*

**thump** /θʌmp/ *vt* golpear. ● *vi*
(*heart*) latir fuertemente. ● *n* por-
razo *m*; (*noise*) ruido *m* sordo

**thunder** /'θʌndə(r)/ n trueno m. ● vi tronar. ~ **past** pasar con estruendo. ~**bolt** /'θʌndəbəʊlt/ n rayo m. ~**clap** /'θʌndəklæp/ n trueno m. ~**storm** /'θʌndəstɔːm/ n tronada f. ~**y** a con truenos

**Thursday** /'θɜːzdeɪ/ n jueves m

**thus** /ðʌs/ adv así

**thwart** /θwɔːt/ vt frustrar

**thyme** /taɪm/ n tomillo m

**thyroid** /'θaɪrɔɪd/ n tiroides m invar

**tiara** /tɪ'ɑːrə/ n diadema f

**tic** /tɪk/ n tic m

**tick**[1] /tɪk/ n tictac m; (mark) señal f, marca f; (instant, fam) momentito m. ● vi hacer tictac. ● vt. ~ (**off**) marcar. ~ **off** vt (sl) reprender. ~ **over** vi (of engine) marchar en vacío

**tick**[2] /tɪk/ n (insect) garrapata f

**tick**[3] /tɪk/ n. **on** ~ (fam) a crédito

**ticket** /'tɪkɪt/ n billete m, boleto m (LAm); (label) etiqueta f; (fine) multa f. ~**collector** n revisor m. ~**office** n taquilla f

**tickl|e** /'tɪkl/ vt hacer cosquillas a; (amuse) divertir. ● n cosquilleo m. ~**ish** /'tɪklɪʃ/ a cosquilloso; (problem) delicado. **be** ~**ish** tener cosquillas

**tidal** /'taɪdl/ a de marea. ~ **wave** n maremoto m

**tiddly-winks** /'tɪdlɪwɪŋks/ n juego m de pulgas

**tide** /taɪd/ n marea f; (of events) curso m. ● vt. ~ **over** ayudar a salir de un apuro

**tidings** /'taɪdɪŋz/ npl noticias fpl

**tid|ily** /'taɪdɪlɪ/ adv en orden; (well) bien. ~**iness** n orden m. ~**y** /'taɪdɪ/ a (**-ier, -iest**) ordenado; (amount, fam) considerable. ● vt/i. ~**y** (**up**) ordenar. ~**y o.s. up** arreglarse

**tie** /taɪ/ vt (pres p **tying**) atar; hacer ⟨a knot⟩; (link) vincular. ● vi (sport) empatar. ● n atadura f; (necktie) corbata f; (link) lazo m; (sport) empate m. ~ **in with** relacionar con. ~ **up** atar; (com) inmovilizar. **be** ~**d up** (busy) estar ocupado

**tier** /tɪə(r)/ n fila f; (in stadium etc) grada f; (of cake) piso m

**tie-up** /'taɪʌp/ n enlace m

**tiff** /tɪf/ n riña f

**tiger** /'taɪgə(r)/ n tigre m

**tight** /taɪt/ a (**-er, -est**) ⟨clothes⟩ ceñido; (taut) tieso; ⟨control etc⟩ riguroso; ⟨knot, nut⟩ apretado; (drunk, fam) borracho. ● adv bien; (shut) herméticamente. ~ **corner** n (fig)

apuro m. ~**en** /'taɪtn/ vt apretar. ● vi apretarse. ~**fisted** a tacaño. ~**ly** adv bien; (shut) herméticamente. ~**ness** n estrechez f. ~**rope** /'taɪtrəʊp/ n cuerda f floja. ~**s** /taɪts/ npl leotardos mpl

**tile** /taɪl/ n (decorative) azulejo m; (on roof) teja f; (on floor) baldosa f. ● vt azulejar; tejar ⟨roof⟩; embaldosar ⟨floor⟩

**till**[1] /tɪl/ prep hasta. ● conj hasta que

**till**[2] /tɪl/ n caja f

**till**[3] /tɪl/ vt cultivar

**tilt** /tɪlt/ vt inclinar. ● vi inclinarse. ● n inclinación f. **at full** ~ a toda velocidad

**timber** /'tɪmbə(r)/ n madera f (de construcción); (trees) árboles mpl

**time** /taɪm/ n tiempo m; (moment) momento m; (occasion) ocasión f; (by clock) hora f; (epoch) época f; (rhythm) compás m. ~ **off** tiempo libre. **at** ~**s** a veces. **behind the** ~**s** anticuado. **behind** ~ atrasado. **for the** ~ **being** por ahora. **from** ~ **to** ~ de vez en cuando. **have a good** ~ divertirse, pasarlo bien. **in a year's** ~ dentro de un año. **in no** ~ en un abrir y cerrar de ojos. **in** ~ a tiempo; (eventually) con el tiempo. **on** ~ a la hora, puntual. ● vt elegir el momento; cronometrar ⟨race⟩. ~ **bomb** n bomba f de tiempo. ~**honoured** a consagrado. ~**lag** n intervalo m

**timeless** /'taɪmlɪs/ a eterno

**timely** /'taɪmlɪ/ a oportuno

**timer** /'taɪmə(r)/ n cronómetro m; (culin) avisador m; (with sand) reloj m de arena; (elec) interruptor m de reloj

**timetable** /'taɪmteɪbl/ n horario m

**time zone** /'taɪmzəʊn/ n huso m horario

**timid** /'tɪmɪd/ a tímido; (fearful) miedoso. ~**ly** adv tímidamente

**timing** /'taɪmɪŋ/ n medida f del tiempo; (moment) momento m; (sport) cronometraje m

**timorous** /'tɪmərəs/ a tímido; (fearful) miedoso. ~**ly** adv tímidamente

**tin** /tɪn/ n estaño m; (container) lata f. ~ **foil** n papel m de estaño. ● vt (pt **tinned**) conservar en lata, enlatar

**tinge** /tɪndʒ/ vt teñir (**with** de); (fig) matizar (**with** de). ● n matiz m

**tingle** /'tɪŋgl/ vi sentir hormigueo; (with excitement) estremecerse

**tinker** /'tɪŋkə(r)/ n hojalatero m.
● vi. ~ **(with)** jugar con; (repair)
arreglar

**tinkle** /'tɪŋkl/ n retintín m; (phone
call, fam) llamada f

**tin**: ~**ned** a en lata. ~**ny** a metálico.
~**opener** n abrelatas m invar. ~
**plate** n hojalata f

**tinpot** /'tɪnpɒt/ a (pej) inferior

**tinsel** /'tɪnsl/ n oropel m

**tint** /tɪnt/ n matiz m

**tiny** /'taɪnɪ/ a (-ier, -iest) diminuto

**tip**¹ /tɪp/ n punta f

**tip**² /tɪp/ vt (pt tipped) (tilt) inclinar;
(overturn) volcar; (pour) verter● vi
inclinarse; (overturn) volcarse. ● n
(for rubbish) vertedero m. ~ **out**
verter

**tip**³ /tɪp/ vt (reward) dar una propina a. ~ **off** advertir. ● n (reward)
propina f; (advice) consejo m

**tip-off** /'tɪpɒf/ n advertencia f

**tipped** /tɪpt/ a (cigarette) con filtro

**tipple** /'tɪpl/ vi beborrotear. ● n
bebida f alcohólica. **have a** ~ tomar
una copa

**tipsy** /'tɪpsɪ/ a achispado

**tiptoe** /'tɪptəʊ/ n. **on** ~ de puntillas

**tiptop** /'tɪptɒp/ a (fam) de primera

**tirade** /taɪ'reɪd/ n diatriba f

**tire** /'taɪə(r)/ vt cansar. ● vi
cansarse. ~**d** /'taɪəd/ a cansado. ~**d**
**of** harto de. ~**d out** agotado. ~**less**
a incansable

**tiresome** /'taɪəsəm/ a (annoying)
fastidioso; (boring) pesado

**tiring** /'taɪərɪŋ/ a cansado

**tissue** /'tɪʃuː/ n tisú m; (handkerchief) pañuelo m de papel. ~**paper** n papel m de seda

**tit**¹ /tɪt/ n (bird) paro m

**tit**² /tɪt/ n. ~ **for tat** golpe por golpe

**titbit** /'tɪtbɪt/ n golosina f

**titillate** /'tɪtɪleɪt/ vt excitar

**title** /'taɪtl/ n título m. ~**d** a con título nobiliario. ~**deed** n título m de
propiedad. ~**role** n papel m
principal

**tittle-tattle** /'tɪtltætl/ n cháchara f

**titular** /'tɪtjʊlə(r)/ a nominal

**tizzy** /'tɪzɪ/ n (sl). **get in a** ~ ponerse
nervioso

**to** /tuː, tə/ prep a; (towards) hacia;
(in order to) para; (according to)
según; (as far as) hasta; (with times)
menos; (of) de. **give it** ~ **me** dámelo.
**I don't want to** no quiero. **twenty**
~ **seven** (by clock) las siete menos
veinte. ● adv. **push** ~, **pull** ~

cerrar. ~ **and fro** adv de aquí para
allá

**toad** /təʊd/ n sapo m

**toadstool** /'təʊdstuːl/ n seta f
venenosa

**toast** /təʊst/ n pan m tostado, tostada f; (drink) brindis m. **drink a** ~
**to** brindar por. ● vt brindar por.
~**er** n tostador m de pan

**tobacco** /tə'bækəʊ/ n tabaco m.
~**nist** n estanquero m. ~**nist's shop**
n estanco m

**to-be** /tə'biː/ a futuro

**toboggan** /tə'bɒgən/ n tobogán m

**today** /tə'deɪ/ n & adv hoy (m). ~
**week** dentro de una semana

**toddler** /'tɒdlə(r)/ n niño m que
empieza a andar

**toddy** /'tɒdɪ/ n ponche m

**to-do** /tə'duː/ n lío m

**toe** /təʊ/ n dedo m del pie; (of shoe)
punta f. **big** ~ dedo m gordo (del
pie). **on one's** ~**s** (fig) alerta. ● vt.
~ **the line** conformarse. ~**hold** n
punto m de apoyo

**toff** /tɒf/ n (sl) petimetre m

**toffee** /'tɒfɪ/ n caramelo m

**together** /tə'geðə(r)/ adv junto, juntos; (at same time) a la vez. ~ **with**
junto con. ~**ness** n compañerismo
m

**toil** /tɔɪl/ vi afanarse. ● n trabajo m

**toilet** /'tɔɪlɪt/ n servicio m, retrete m;
(grooming) arreglo m, tocado m.
~**paper** n papel m higiénico. ~**ries**
/'tɔɪlɪtrɪz/ npl artículos mpl de tocador. ~ **water** n agua f de Colonia

**token** /'təʊkən/ n señal f; (voucher)
vale m; (coin) ficha f. ● a simbólico

**told** /təʊld/ see **tell**. ● a. **all** ~ con
todo

**tolerabl|e** /'tɒlərəbl/ a tolerable;
(not bad) regular. ~**y** adv
pasablemente

**toleran|ce** /'tɒlərəns/ n tolerancia f.
~**t** /'tɒlərənt/ a tolerante. ~**tly** adv
con tolerancia

**tolerate** /'tɒləreɪt/ vt tolerar

**toll**¹ /təʊl/ n peaje m. **death** ~
número m de muertos. **take a heavy**
~ dejar muchas víctimas

**toll**² /təʊl/ vi doblar, tocar a muerto

**tom** /tɒm/ n gato m (macho)

**tomato** /tə'mɑːtəʊ/ n (pl ~**oes**)
tomate m

**tomb** /tuːm/ n tumba f, sepulcro m

**tomboy** /'tɒmbɔɪ/ n marimacho m

**tombstone** /'tuːmstəʊn/ n lápida f
sepulcral

**tom-cat** /'tɒmkæt/ *n* gato *m* (macho)

**tome** /təʊm/ *n* librote *m*

**tomfoolery** /tɒm'fuːlərɪ/ *n* payasadas *fpl*, tonterías *fpl*

**tomorrow** /tə'mɒrəʊ/ *n* & *adv* mañana (*f*). **see you ~!** ¡hasta mañana!

**ton** /tʌn/ *n* tonelada *f* (= *1,016 kg*). **~s of** (*fam*) montones de. **metric ~** tonelada *f* (métrica) (= *1,000 kg*)

**tone** /təʊn/ *n* tono *m*. ● *vt*. **~ down** atenuar. **~ up** tonificar ⟨*muscles*⟩. ● *vi*. **~ in** armonizar. **~deaf** *a* que no tiene buen oído

**tongs** /tɒŋz/ *npl* tenazas *fpl*; (*for hair, sugar*) tenacillas *fpl*

**tongue** /tʌŋ/ *n* lengua *f*. **~ in cheek** *adv* irónicamente. **~tied** *a* mudo. **get ~tied** trabársele la lengua. **~twister** *n* trabalenguas *m invar*

**tonic** /'tɒnɪk/ *a* tónico. ● *n* (*tonic water*) tónica *f*; (*med, fig*) tónico *m*. **~ water** *n* tónica *f*

**tonight** /tə'naɪt/ *adv* & *n* esta noche (*f*); (*evening*) esta tarde (*f*)

**tonne** /tʌn/ *n* tonelada *f* (métrica)

**tonsil** /'tɒnsl/ *n* amígdala *f*. **~litis** /-'laɪtɪs/ *n* amigdalitis *f*

**too** /tuː/ *adv* demasiado; (*also*) también. **~ many** *a* demasiados. **~ much** *a* & *adv* demasiado

**took** /tʊk/ *see* **take**

**tool** /tuːl/ *n* herramienta *f*. **~bag** *n* bolsa *f* de herramientas

**toot** /tuːt/ *n* bocinazo *m*. ● *vi* tocar la bocina

**tooth** /tuːθ/ *n* (*pl* **teeth**) diente *m*; (*molar*) muela *f*. **~ache** /'tuːθeɪk/ *n* dolor *m* de muelas. **~brush** /'tuːθbrʌʃ/ *n* cepillo *m* de dientes. **~comb** /'tuːθkəʊm/ *n* peine *m* de púa fina. **~less** *a* desdentado, sin dientes. **~paste** /'tuːθpeɪst/ *n* pasta *f* dentífrica. **~pick** /'tuːθpɪk/ *n* palillo *m* de dientes

**top¹** /tɒp/ *n* cima *f*; (*upper part*) parte *f* de arriba; (*upper surface*) superficie *f*; (*lid, of bottle*) tapa *f*; (*of list*) cabeza *f*. **from ~ to bottom** de arriba abajo. **on ~ (of)** encima de; (*besides*) además. ● *a* más alto; (*in rank*) superior, principal; (*maximum*) máximo. **~ floor** *n* último piso *m*. ● *vt* (*pt* **topped**) cubrir; (*exceed*) exceder. **~ up** *vt* llenar

**top²** /tɒp/ *n* (*toy*) trompa *f*, peonza *f*

**top: ~ hat** *n* chistera *f*. **~heavy** *a* más pesado arriba que abajo

**topic** /'tɒpɪk/ *n* tema *m*. **~al** /'tɒpɪkl/ *a* de actualidad

**top: ~less** /'tɒplɪs/ *a* ⟨*bather*⟩ con los senos desnudos. **~most** /'tɒpməʊst/ *a* (el) más alto. **~notch** *a* (*fam*) excelente

**topography** /tə'pɒɡrəfɪ/ *n* topografía *f*

**topple** /'tɒpl/ *vi* derribar; (*overturn*) volcar

**top secret** /tɒp'siːkrɪt/ *a* sumamente secreto

**topsy-turvy** /tɒpsɪ'tɜːvɪ/ *adv* & *a* patas arriba

**torch** /tɔːtʃ/ *n* lámpara *f* de bolsillo; (*flaming*) antorcha *f*

**tore** /tɔː(r)/ *see* **tear¹**

**toreador** /'tɒrɪədɔː(r)/ *n* torero *m*

**torment** /'tɔːment/ *n* tormento *m*. /tɔː'ment/ *vt* atormentar

**torn** /tɔːn/ *see* **tear¹**

**tornado** /tɔː'neɪdəʊ/ *n* (*pl* **-oes**) tornado *m*

**torpedo** /tɔː'piːdəʊ/ *n* (*pl* **-oes**) torpedo *m*. ● *vt* torpedear

**torpor** /'tɔːpə(r)/ *n* apatía *f*

**torrent** /'tɒrənt/ *n* torrente *m*. **~ial** /tə'renʃl/ *a* torrencial

**torrid** /'tɒrɪd/ *a* tórrido

**torso** /'tɔːsəʊ/ *n* (*pl* **-os**) torso *m*

**tortoise** /'tɔːtəs/ *n* tortuga *f*. **~shell** *n* carey *m*

**tortuous** /'tɔːtjʊəs/ *a* tortuoso

**torture** /'tɔːtʃə(r)/ *n* tortura *f*, tormento *m*. ● *vt* atormentar. **~r** /-ə(r)/ *n* atormentador *m*, verdugo *m*

**Tory** /'tɔːrɪ/ *a* & *n* (*fam*) conservador (*m*)

**toss** /tɒs/ *vt* echar; (*shake*) sacudir. ● *vi* agitarse. **~ and turn** (*in bed*) revolverse. **~ up** echar a cara o cruz

**tot¹** /tɒt/ *n* nene *m*; (*of liquor, fam*) trago *m*

**tot²** /tɒt/ *vt* (*pt* **totted**). **~ up** (*fam*) sumar

**total** /'təʊtl/ *a* & *n* total (*m*). ● *vt* (*pt* **totalled**) sumar

**totalitarian** /təʊtælɪ'teərɪən/ *a* totalitario

**total: ~ity** /təʊ'tælətɪ/ *n* totalidad *f*. **~ly** *adv* totalmente

**totter** /'tɒtə(r)/ *vi* tambalearse. **~y** *a* inseguro

**touch** /tʌtʃ/ *vt* tocar; (*reach*) alcanzar; (*move*) conmover. ● *vi* tocarse. ● *n* toque *m*; (*sense*) tacto *m*; (*contact*) contacto *m*; (*trace*) pizca *f*. **get in ~ with** ponerse en contacto con. **~ down** ⟨*aircraft*⟩ aterrizar. **~ off**

disparar ⟨gun⟩; (fig) desencadenar. ~ on tratar levemente. ~ up retocar. ~-and-go a incierto, dudoso

**touching** /'tʌtʃɪŋ/ a conmovedor

**touchstone** /'tʌtʃstəʊn/ n (fig) piedra f de toque

**touchy** /'tʌtʃɪ/ a quisquilloso

**tough** /tʌf/ a (-er, -est) duro; (strong) fuerte, resistente. ~en /'tʌfn/ vt endurecer. ~ness n dureza f; (strength) resistencia f

**toupee** /'tuːpeɪ/ n postizo m, tupé m

**tour** /tʊə(r)/ n viaje m; (visit) visita f; (excursion) excursión f; (by team etc) gira f. ● vt recorrer; (visit) visitar

**touris|m** /'tʊərɪzəm/ n turismo m. ~t /'tʊərɪst/ n turista m & f. ● a turístico. ~t office n oficina f de turismo

**tournament** /'tɔːnəmənt/ n torneo m

**tousle** /'taʊzl/ vt despeinar

**tout** /taʊt/ vi. ~ (for) solicitar. ● n solicitador m

**tow** /təʊ/ vt remolcar. ● n remolque m. on ~ a remolque. with his family in ~ (fam) acompañado por su familia

**toward(s)** /tə'wɔːd(z)/ prep hacia

**towel** /'taʊəl/ n toalla f. ~ling n (fabric) toalla f

**tower** /'taʊə(r)/ n torre f. ● vi. ~ above dominar. ~ block n edificio m alto. ~ing a altísimo; ⟨rage⟩ violento

**town** /taʊn/ n ciudad f, pueblo m. go to ~ (fam) no escatimar dinero. ~ hall n ayuntamiento m. ~ planning n urbanismo m

**tow-path** /'təʊpɑːθ/ n camino m de sirga

**toxi|c** /'tɒksɪk/ a tóxico. ~n /'tɒksɪn/ n toxina f

**toy** /tɔɪ/ n juguete m. ● vi. ~ with jugar con ⟨object⟩; acariciar ⟨idea⟩. ~shop n juguetería f

**trac|e** /treɪs/ n huella f; (small amount) pizca f. ● vt seguir la pista de; (draw) dibujar; (with tracing-paper) calcar; (track down) encontrar. ~ing n calco m. ~ing-paper n papel m de calcar

**track** /træk/ n huella f; (path) sendero m; (sport) pista f; (of rocket etc) trayectoria f; (rail) vía f. keep ~ of vigilar. make ~s (sl) marcharse. ● vt seguir la pista de. ~ down vt localizar. ~ suit n traje m de deporte, chandal m

**tract**[1] /trækt/ n (land) extensión f; (anat) aparato m

**tract**[2] /trækt/ n (pamphlet) opúsculo m

**traction** /'trækʃn/ n tracción f

**tractor** /'træktə(r)/ n tractor m

**trade** /treɪd/ n comercio m; (occupation) oficio m; (exchange) cambio m; (industry) industria f. ● vt cambiar. ● vi comerciar. ~ in (give in part-exchange) dar como parte del pago. ~ mark n marca f registrada. ~r /-ə(r)/ n comerciante m & f. ~sman /'treɪdzmən/ n (pl -men) (shop-keeper) tendero m. ~ union n sindicato m. ~ unionist n sindicalista m & f. ~ wind n viento m alisio

**trading** /'treɪdɪŋ/ n comercio m. ~ estate n zona f industrial

**tradition** /trə'dɪʃn/ n tradición f. ~al a tradicional. ~alist n tradicionalista m & f. ~ally adv tradicionalmente

**traffic** /'træfɪk/ n tráfico m. ● vi (pt **trafficked**) comerciar (in en). ~-lights npl semáforo m. ~ warden n guardia m, controlador m de tráfico

**trag|edy** /'trædʒɪdɪ/ n tragedia f. ~ic /'trædʒɪk/ a trágico. ~ically adv trágicamente

**trail** /treɪl/ vi arrastrarse; (lag) rezagarse. ● vt (track) seguir la pista de. ● n estela f; (track) pista f; (path) sendero m. ~er /'treɪlə(r)/ n remolque m; (film) avance m

**train** /treɪn/ n tren m; (of dress) cola f; (series) sucesión f; (retinue) séquito m. ● vt adiestrar; (sport) entrenar; educar ⟨child⟩; guiar ⟨plant⟩; domar ⟨animal⟩. ● vi adiestrarse; (sport) entrenarse. ~ed a (skilled) cualificado; (doctor) diplomado. ~ee n aprendiz m. ~er n (sport) entrenador m; (of animals) domador m. ~ers mpl zapatillas fpl de deporte. ~ing n instrucción f; (sport) entrenamiento m

**traipse** /treɪps/ vi (fam) vagar

**trait** /treɪ(t)/ n característica f, rasgo m

**traitor** /'treɪtə(r)/ n traidor m

**tram** /træm/ n tranvía m

**tramp** /træmp/ vt recorrer a pie. ● vi andar con pasos pesados. ● n (vagrant) vagabundo m; (sound) ruido m de pasos; (hike) paseo m largo

**trample** /'træmpl/ *vt/i* pisotear. ~ **(on)** pisotear

**trampoline** /'træmpəli:n/ *n* trampolín *m*

**trance** /trɑːns/ *n* trance *m*

**tranquil** /'træŋkwɪl/ *a* tranquilo. ~**lity** /-'kwɪlətɪ/ *n* tranquilidad *f*

**tranquillize** /'træŋkwɪlaɪz/ *vt* tranquilizar. ~**r** /-ə(r)/ *n* tranquilizante *m*

**transact** /træn'zækt/ *vt* negociar. ~**ion** /-ʃn/ *n* transacción *f*

**transatlantic** /trænzət'læntɪk/ *a* transatlántico

**transcend** /træn'send/ *vt* exceder. ~**ent** *a* sobresaliente

**transcendental** /trænsen'dentl/ *a* trascendental

**transcribe** /træns'kraɪb/ *vt* transcribir; grabar ⟨*recorded sound*⟩

**transcript** /'trænskrɪpt/ *n* copia *f*. ~**ion** /-ɪpʃn/ *n* transcripción *f*

**transfer** /træns'fɜː(r)/ *vt* (*pt* **transferred**) trasladar; calcar ⟨*drawing*⟩. ● *vi* trasladarse. ~ **the charges** (*on telephone*) llamar a cobro revertido. /'trænsfɜː(r)/ *n* traslado *m*; (*paper*) calcomanía *f*. ~**able** *a* transferible

**transfigur|ation** /trænsfɪgjʊ'reɪʃn/ *n* transfiguración *f*. ~**e** /træns'fɪgə(r)/ *vt* transfigurar

**transfix** /træns'fɪks/ *vt* traspasar; (*fig*) paralizar

**transform** /træns'fɔːm/ *vt* transformar. ~**ation** /-ə'meɪʃn/ *n* transformación *f*. ~**er** /-ə(r)/ *n* transformador *m*

**transfusion** /træns'fjuːʒn/ *n* transfusión *f*

**transgress** /træns'gres/ *vt* traspasar, infringir. ~**ion** /-ʃn/ *n* transgresión *f*; (*sin*) pecado *m*

**transient** /'trænzɪənt/ *a* pasajero

**transistor** /træn'zɪstə(r)/ *n* transistor *m*

**transit** /'trænsɪt/ *n* tránsito *m*

**transition** /træn'zɪʒn/ *n* transición *f*

**transitive** /'trænsɪtɪv/ *a* transitivo

**transitory** /'trænsɪtrɪ/ *a* transitorio

**translat|e** /trænz'leɪt/ *vt* traducir. ~**ion** /-ʃn/ *n* traducción *f*. ~**or** /-ə(r)/ *n* traductor *m*

**translucen|ce** /trænz'luːsns/ *n* traslucidez *f*. ~**t** /trænz'luːsnt/ *a* traslúcido

**transmission** /trænz'mɪʃn/ *n* transmisión *f*

**transmit** /trænz'mɪt/ *vt* (*pt* **transmitted**) transmitir. ~**ter** /-ə(r)/ *n*

transmisor *m*; (*TV, radio*) emisora *f*

**transparen|cy** /træns'pærənsɪ/ *n* transparencia *f*; (*photo*) diapositiva *f*. ~**t** /træns'pærənt/ *a* transparente

**transpire** /træn'spaɪə(r)/ *vi* transpirar; (*happen, fam*) suceder, revelarse

**transplant** /træns'plɑːnt/ *vt* trasplantar. /'trænsplɑːnt/ *n* trasplante *m*

**transport** /træn'spɔːt/ *vt* transportar. /'trænspɔːt/ *n* transporte *m*. ~**ation** /-'teɪʃn/ *n* transporte *m*

**transpos|e** /træn'spəʊz/ *vt* transponer; (*mus*) transportar. ~**ition** /-pə'zɪʃn/ *n* transposición *f*; (*mus*) transporte *m*

**transverse** /'trænzvɜːs/ *a* transverso

**transvestite** /trænz'vestaɪt/ *n* travestido *m*

**trap** /træp/ *n* trampa *f*. ● *vt* (*pt* **trapped**) atrapar; (*jam*) atascar; (*cut off*) bloquear. ~**door** /'træpdɔː(r)/ *n* trampa *f*; (*in theatre*) escotillón *m*

**trapeze** /trə'piːz/ *n* trapecio *m*

**trappings** /'træpɪŋz/ *npl* (*fig*) atavíos *mpl*

**trash** /træʃ/ *n* pacotilla *f*; (*refuse*) basura *f*; (*nonsense*) tonterías *fpl*. ~**can** *n* (*Amer*) cubo *m* de la basura. ~**y** *a* de baja calidad

**trauma** /'trɔːmə/ *n* trauma *m*. ~**tic** /-'mætɪk/ *a* traumático

**travel** /'trævl/ *vi* (*pt* **travelled**) viajar. ● *vt* recorrer. ● *n* viajar *m*. ~**ler** /-ə(r)/ *n* viajero *m*. ~**ler's cheque** *n* cheque *m* de viaje. ~**ling** *n* viajar *m*

**traverse** /træ'vɜːs/ *vt* atravesar, recorrer

**travesty** /'trævɪstɪ/ *n* parodia *f*

**trawler** /'trɔːlə(r)/ *n* pesquero *m* de arrastre

**tray** /treɪ/ *n* bandeja *f*

**treacher|ous** *a* traidor; (*deceptive*) engañoso. ~**ously** *adv* traidoramente. ~**y** /'tretʃərɪ/ *n* traición *f*

**treacle** /'triːkl/ *n* melaza *f*

**tread** /tred/ *vi* (*pt* **trod**, *pp* **trodden**) andar. ~ **on** pisar. ● *vt* pisar. ● *n* (*step*) paso *m*; (*of tyre*) banda *f* de rodadura. ~**le** /'tredl/ *n* pedal *m*. ~**mill** /'tredmɪl/ *n* rueda *f* de molino; (*fig*) rutina *f*

**treason** /'triːzn/ *n* traición *f*

**treasure** /'treʒə(r)/ *n* tesoro *m*. ● *vt* apreciar mucho; (*store*) guardar

**treasur|er** /'treʒərə(r)/ n tesorero m. **~y** /'treʒərɪ/ n tesorería f. **the T~y** n el Ministerio m de Hacienda

**treat** /triːt/ vt tratar; (consider) considerar. ● **s.o.** invitar a uno. ● n placer m; (present) regalo m

**treatise** /'triːtɪz/ n tratado m

**treatment** /'triːtmənt/ n tratamiento m

**treaty** /'triːtɪ/ n tratado m

**treble** /'trebl/ a triple; ‹clef› de sol; ‹voice› de tiple. ● vt triplicar. ● vi triplicarse. ● n tiple m & f

**tree** /triː/ n árbol m

**trek** /trek/ n viaje m arduo, caminata f. ● vi (pt **trekked**) hacer un viaje arduo

**trellis** /'trelɪs/ n enrejado m

**tremble** /'trembl/ vi temblar

**tremendous** /trɪ'mendəs/ a tremendo; (huge, fam) enorme. **~ly** adv tremendamente

**tremor** /'tremə(r)/ n temblor m

**tremulous** /'tremjʊləs/ a tembloroso

**trench** /trentʃ/ n foso m, zanja f; (mil) trinchera f. **~ coat** n trinchera f

**trend** /trend/ n tendencia f; (fashion) moda f. **~setter** n persona f que lanza la moda. **~y** a (-ier, -iest) (fam) a la última

**trepidation** /trepɪ'deɪʃn/ n inquietud f

**trespass** /'trespəs/ vi. **~ on** entrar sin derecho; (fig) abusar de. **~er** /-ə(r)/ n intruso m

**tress** /tres/ n trenza f

**trestle** /'tresl/ n caballete m. **~table** n mesa f de caballete

**trews** /truːz/ npl pantalón m

**trial** /'traɪəl/ n prueba f; (jurid) proceso m; (ordeal) prueba f dura. **~ and error** tanteo m. **be on ~** estar a prueba; (jurid) ser procesado

**triang|le** /'traɪæŋgl/ n triángulo m. **~ular** /-'æŋgjʊlə(r)/ a triangular

**trib|al** /'traɪbl/ a tribal. **~e** /traɪb/ n tribu f

**tribulation** /trɪbjʊ'leɪʃn/ n tribulación f

**tribunal** /traɪ'bjuːnl/ n tribunal m

**tributary** /'trɪbjʊtrɪ/ n (stream) afluente m

**tribute** /'trɪbjuːt/ n tributo m. **pay ~ to** rendir homenaje a

**trice** /traɪs/ n. **in a ~** en un abrir y cerrar de ojos

**trick** /trɪk/ n trampa f; engaño m; (joke) broma f; (at cards) baza f; (habit) manía f. **do the ~** servir. **play a ~ on** gastar una broma a. ● vt engañar. **~ery** /'trɪkərɪ/ n engaño m

**trickle** /'trɪkl/ vi gotear. **~ in** (fig) entrar poco a poco. **~ out** (fig) salir poco a poco

**trickster** /'trɪkstə(r)/ n estafador m

**tricky** /'trɪkɪ/ a delicado, difícil

**tricolour** /'trɪkələ(r)/ n bandera f tricolor

**tricycle** /'traɪsɪkl/ n triciclo m

**trident** /'traɪdənt/ n tridente m

**tried** /traɪd/ see **try**

**trifl|e** /'traɪfl/ n bagatela f; (culin) bizcocho m con natillas, jalea, frutas y nata. ● vi. **~e with** jugar con. **~ing** a insignificante

**trigger** /'trɪgə(r)/ n (of gun) gatillo m. ● vt. **~ (off)** desencadenar

**trigonometry** /trɪgə'nɒmɪtrɪ/ n trigonometría f

**trilby** /'trɪlbɪ/ n sombrero m de fieltro

**trilogy** /'trɪlədʒɪ/ n trilogía f

**trim** /trɪm/ a (**trimmer**, **trimmest**) arreglado. ● vt (pt **trimmed**) cortar; recortar ‹hair etc›; (adorn) adornar. ● n (cut) recorte m; (decoration) adorno m; (state) estado m. **in ~** en buen estado; (fit) en forma. **~ming** n adorno m. **~mings** npl recortes mpl; (decorations) adornos mpl; (culin) guarnición f

**trinity** /'trɪnɪtɪ/ n trinidad f. **the T~** la Trinidad

**trinket** /'trɪŋkɪt/ n chuchería f

**trio** /'triːəʊ/ n (pl -os) trío m

**trip** /trɪp/ vt (pt **tripped**) hacer tropezar. ● vi tropezar; (go lightly) andar con paso ligero. ● n (journey) viaje m; (outing) excursión f; (stumble) traspié m. **~ up** vi tropezar. ● vt hacer tropezar

**tripe** /traɪp/ n callos mpl; (nonsense, sl) tonterías fpl

**triple** /'trɪpl/ a triple. ● vt triplicar. ● vi triplicarse. **~ts** /'trɪplɪts/ npl trillizos mpl

**triplicate** /'trɪplɪkət/ a triplicado. **in ~** por triplicado

**tripod** /'traɪpɒd/ n trípode m

**tripper** /'trɪpə(r)/ n (on day trip etc) excursionista m & f

**triptych** /'trɪptɪk/ n tríptico m

**trite** /traɪt/ a trillado

**triumph** /'traɪʌmf/ *n* triunfo *m*. ● *vi* trinufar (**over** sobre). **~al** /-'ʌmfl/ *a* triunfal. **~ant** /-'ʌmfnt/ *a* triunfante

**trivial** /'trɪvɪəl/ *a* insignificante. **~ity** /-'ælətɪ/ *n* insignificancia *f*

**trod, trodden** /trɒd, trɒdn/ *see* **tread**

**trolley** /'trɒlɪ/ *n* (*pl* **-eys**) carretón *m*. **tea ~** *n* mesita *f* de ruedas. **~bus** *n* trolebús *m*

**trombone** /trɒm'bəʊn/ *n* trombón *m*

**troop** /truːp/ *n* grupo *m*. ● *vi*. **~ in** entrar en tropel. **~ out** salir en tropel. ● *vt*. **~ing the colour** saludo *m* a la bandera. **~er** *n* soldado *m* de caballería. **~s** *npl* (*mil*) tropas *fpl*

**trophy** /'trəʊfɪ/ *n* trofeo *m*

**tropic** /'trɒpɪk/ *n* trópico *m*. **~al** *a* tropical. **~s** *npl* trópicos *mpl*

**trot** /trɒt/ *n* trote *m*. **on the ~** (*fam*) seguidos. ● *vi* (*pt* **trotted**) trotar. **~ out** (*produce, fam*) producir

**trotter** /'trɒtə(r)/ *n* (*culin*) pie *m* de cerdo

**trouble** /'trʌbl/ *n* problema *m*; (*awkward situation*) apuro *m*; (*inconvenience*) molestia *f*; (*conflict*) conflicto *m*; (*med*) enfermedad *f*; (*mec*) avería *f*. **be in ~** estar en un apuro. **make ~** armar un lío. **take ~** tomarse la molestia. ● *vt* (*bother*) molestar; (*worry*) preocupar. ● *vi* molestarse; (*worry*) preocuparse. **be ~d about** preocuparse por. **~maker** *n* alborotador *m*. **~some** *a* molesto

**trough** /trɒf/ *n* (*for drinking*) abrevadero *m*; (*for feeding*) pesebre *m*; (*of wave*) seno *m*; (*atmospheric*) mínimo *m* de presión

**trounce** /traʊns/ *vt* (*defeat*) derrotar; (*thrash*) pegar

**troupe** /truːp/ *n* compañía *f*

**trousers** /'traʊzəz/ *npl* pantalón *m*; pantalones *mpl*

**trousseau** /'truːsəʊ/ *n* (*pl* **-s** /-əʊz/) ajuar *m*

**trout** /traʊt/ *n* (*pl* **trout**) trucha *f*

**trowel** /'traʊəl/ *n* (*garden*) desplantador *m*; (*for mortar*) paleta *f*

**truant** /'truːənt/ *n*. **play ~** hacer novillos

**truce** /truːs/ *n* tregua *f*

**truck**[1] /trʌk/ *n* carro *m*; (*rail*) vagón *m*; (*lorry*) camión *m*

**truck**[2] /trʌk/ *n* (*dealings*) trato *m*

**truculent** /'trʌkjʊlənt/ *a* agresivo

**trudge** /trʌdʒ/ *vi* andar penosamente. ● *n* caminata *f* penosa

**true** /truː/ *a* (**-er, -est**) verdadero; (*loyal*) leal; (*genuine*) auténtico; (*accurate*) exacto. **come ~** realizarse

**truffle** /'trʌfl/ *n* trufa *f*; (*chocolate*) trufa *f* de chocolate

**truism** /'truːɪzəm/ *n* perogrullada *f*

**truly** /'truːlɪ/ *adv* verdaderamente; (*sincerely*) sinceramente; (*faithfully*) fielmente. **yours ~** (*in letters*) le saluda atentamente

**trump** /trʌmp/ *n* (*cards*) triunfo *m*. ● *vt* fallar. **~ up** inventar

**trumpet** /'trʌmpɪt/ *n* trompeta *f*. **~er** /-ə(r)/ *n* trompetero *m*, trompeta *m* & *f*

**truncated** /trʌŋ'keɪtɪd/ *a* truncado

**truncheon** /'trʌntʃən/ *n* porra *f*

**trundle** /'trʌndl/ *vt* hacer rodar. ● *vi* rodar

**trunk** /trʌŋk/ *n* tronco *m*; (*box*) baúl *m*; (*of elephant*) trompa *f*. **~-call** *n* conferencia *f*. **~-road** *n* carretera *f* (nacional). **~s** *npl* bañador *m*

**truss** /trʌs/ *n* (*med*) braguero *m*. **~ up** *vt* (*culin*) espetar

**trust** /trʌst/ *n* confianza *f*; (*association*) trust *m*. **on ~** a ojos cerrados; (*com*) al fiado. ● *vi* confiar. **~ to** confiar en. ● *vt* confiar en; (*hope*) esperar. **~ed** *a* leal

**trustee** /trʌ'stiː/ *n* administrador *m*

**trust: ~ful** *a* confiado. **~fully** *adv* confiadamente. **~worthy** *a*, **~y** *a* digno de confianza

**truth** /truːθ/ *n* (*pl* **-s** /truːðz/) verdad *f*. **~ful** *a* veraz; (*true*) verídico. **~fully** *adv* sinceramente

**try** /traɪ/ *vt* (*pt* **tried**) probar; (*be a strain on*) poner a prueba; (*jurid*) procesar. **~ on** *vt* probarse (*garment*). **~ out** *vt* probar. ● *vi* probar. **~ for** *vi* intentar conseguir. ● *n* tentativa *f*, prueba *f*; (*rugby*) ensayo *m*. **~ing** *a* difícil; (*annoying*) molesto. **~out** *n* prueba *f*

**tryst** /trɪst/ *n* cita *f*

**T-shirt** /'tiːʃɜːt/ *n* camiseta *f*

**tub** /tʌb/ *n* tina *f*; (*bath, fam*) baño *m*

**tuba** /'tjuːbə/ *n* tuba *f*

**tubby** /'tʌbɪ/ *a* (**-ier, -iest**) rechoncho

**tube** /tjuːb/ *n* tubo *m*; (*rail, fam*) metro *m*. **inner ~** *n* cámara *f* de aire

**tuber** /'tjuːbə(r)/ *n* tubérculo *m*

**tuberculosis** /tjuːbɜːkjʊ'ləʊsɪs/ *n* tuberculosis *f*

**tub|ing** /'tjuːbɪŋ/ n tubería f, tubos mpl. **~ular** a tubular

**tuck** /tʌk/ n pliegue m. ● vt plegar; (put) meter; (put away) remeter; (hide) esconder. **~ up** vt arropar ⟨child⟩. ● vi. **~ in(to)** (eat, sl) comer con buen apetito. **~shop** n confitería f

**Tuesday** /'tjuːzdeɪ/ n martes m

**tuft** /tʌft/ n (of hair) mechón m; (of feathers) penacho m; (of grass) manojo m

**tug** /tʌg/ vt (pt tugged) tirar de; (tow) remolcar. ● vi tirar fuerte. ● n tirón m; (naut) remolcador m. **~of-war** n lucha f de la cuerda; (fig) tira m y afloja

**tuition** /tjuːˈɪʃn/ n enseñanza f

**tulip** /'tjuːlɪp/ n tulipán m

**tumble** /'tʌmbl/ vi caerse. **~ to** (fam) comprender. ● n caída f

**tumbledown** /'tʌmbldaʊn/ a ruinoso

**tumble-drier** /tʌmbl'draɪə(r)/ n secadora f (eléctrica con aire de salida)

**tumbler** /'tʌmblə(r)/ n (glass) vaso m

**tummy** /'tʌmɪ/ n (fam) estómago m

**tumour** /'tjuːmə(r)/ n tumor m

**tumult** /'tjuːmʌlt/ n tumulto m. **~uous** /-'mʌltjʊəs/ a tumultuoso

**tuna** /'tjuːnə/ n (pl tuna) atún m

**tune** /tjuːn/ n aire m. **be in ~** estar afinado. **be out of ~** estar desafinado. ● vt afinar; sintonizar ⟨radio, TV⟩; (mec) poner a punto. ● vi. **~ in (to)** ⟨radio, TV⟩ sintonizarse. **~ up** afinar. **~ful** a melodioso. **~r** /-ə(r)/ n afinador m; (radio, TV) sintonizador m

**tunic** /'tjuːnɪk/ n túnica f

**tuning-fork** /'tjuːnɪŋfɔːk/ n diapasón m

**Tunisia** /tjuːˈnɪzɪə/ n Túnez m. **~n** a & n tunecino (m)

**tunnel** /'tʌnl/ n túnel m. ● vi (pt tunnelled) construir un túnel en

**turban** /'tɜːbən/ n turbante m

**turbid** /'tɜːbɪd/ a túrbido

**turbine** /'tɜːbaɪn/ n turbina f

**turbo-jet** /'tɜːbəʊdʒet/ n turborreactor m

**turbot** /'tɜːbət/ n rodaballo m

**turbulen|ce** /'tɜːbjʊləns/ n turbulencia f. **~t** /'tɜːbjʊlənt/ a turbulento

**tureen** /tjʊˈriːn/ n sopera f

**turf** /tɜːf/ n (pl turfs or turves) césped m; (segment) tepe m. **the ~** n

las carreras fpl de caballos. ● vt. **~ out** (sl) echar

**turgid** /'tɜːdʒɪd/ a ⟨language⟩ pomposo

**Turk** /tɜːk/ n turco m

**turkey** /'tɜːkɪ/ n (pl -eys) pavo m

**Turk|ey** /'tɜːkɪ/ f Turquía f. **T~ish** a & n turco (m)

**turmoil** /'tɜːmɔɪl/ n confusión f

**turn** /tɜːn/ vt hacer girar, dar vueltas a; volver ⟨direction, page, etc⟩; cumplir ⟨age⟩; dar ⟨hour⟩; doblar ⟨corner⟩; (change) cambiar; (deflect) desviar. **~ the tables** volver las tornas. ● vi girar, dar vueltas; (become) hacerse; (change) cambiar. ● n vuelta f; (in road) curva f; (change) cambio m; (sequence) turno m; (of mind) disposición f; (in theatre) número m; (fright) susto m; (of illness, fam) ataque m. **bad ~** mala jugada f. **good ~** favor m. **in ~** a su vez. **out of ~** fuera de lugar. **to a ~** (culin) en su punto. **~ against** vt volverse en contra de. **~ down** vt (fold) doblar; (reduce) bajar; (reject) rechazar. **~ in** vt entregar. ● vi (go to bed, fam) acostarse. **~ off** vt cerrar ⟨tap⟩; apagar ⟨light, TV, etc⟩. ● vi desviarse. **~ on** vt abrir ⟨tap⟩; encender ⟨light etc⟩; (attack) atacar; (attract, fam) excitar. **~ out** vt expulsar; apagar ⟨light etc⟩; (produce) producir; (empty) vaciar. ● vi (result) resultar. **~ round** vi dar la vuelta. **~ up** vi aparecer. ● vt (find) encontrar; levantar ⟨collar⟩; poner más fuerte ⟨gas⟩. **~ed-up** a ⟨nose⟩ respingona. **~ing** /'tɜːnɪŋ/ n vuelta f; (road) bocacalle f. **~ing-point** n punto m decisivo.

**turnip** /'tɜːnɪp/ n nabo m

**turn: ~out** n (of people) concurrencia f; (of goods) producción f. **~over** /'tɜːnəʊvə(r)/ n (culin) empanada f; (com) volumen m de negocios; (of staff) rotación f. **~pike** /'tɜːnpaɪk/ n (Amer) autopista f de peaje. **~stile** /'tɜːnstaɪl/ n torniquete m. **~table** /'tɜːnteɪbl/ n plataforma f giratoria; (on record-player) plato m giratorio. **~up** n (of trousers) vuelta f

**turpentine** /'tɜːpəntaɪn/ n trementina f

**turquoise** /'tɜːkwɔɪz/ a & n turquesa (f)

**turret** /'tʌrɪt/ *n* torrecilla *f*; (*mil*) torreta *f*

**turtle** /'tɜːtl/ *n* tortuga *f* de mar. **~neck** *n* cuello *m* alto

**tusk** /tʌsk/ *n* colmillo *m*

**tussle** /'tʌsl/ *vi* pelearse. ● *n* pelea *f*

**tussock** /'tʌsək/ *n* montecillo *m* de hierbas

**tutor** /'tjuːtə(r)/ *n* preceptor *m*; (*univ*) director *m* de estudios, profesor *m*. **~ial** /tjuː'tɔːrɪəl/ *n* clase *f* particular

**tuxedo** /tʌk'siːdəʊ/ *n* (*pl* **-os**) (*Amer*) esmoquin *m*

**TV** /tiː'viː/ *n* televisión *f*

**twaddle** /'twɒdl/ *n* tonterías *fpl*

**twang** /twæŋ/ *n* tañido *m*; (*in voice*) gangueo *m*. ● *vt* hacer vibrar. ● *vi* vibrar

**tweed** /twiːd/ *n* tela *f* gruesa de lana

**tweet** /twiːt/ *n* piada *f*. ● *vi* piar

**tweezers** /'twiːzəz/ *npl* pinzas *fpl*

**twel|fth** /twelfθ/ *a & n* duodécimo (*m*). **~ve** /twelv/ *a & n* doce (*m*)

**twent|ieth** /'twentɪəθ/ *a & n* vigésimo (*m*). **~y** /'twentɪ/ *a & n* veinte (*m*)

**twerp** /twɜːp/ *n* (*sl*) imbécil *m*

**twice** /twaɪs/ *adv* dos veces

**twiddle** /'twɪdl/ *vt* hacer girar. **~ one's thumbs** (*fig*) no tener nada que hacer. **~ with** jugar con

**twig**[1] /twɪg/ *n* ramita *f*

**twig**[2] /twɪg/ *vt/i* (*pt* **twigged**) (*fam*) comprender

**twilight** /'twaɪlaɪt/ *n* crepúsculo *m*

**twin** /twɪn/ *a & n* gemelo (*m*)

**twine** /twaɪn/ *n* bramante *m*. ● *vt* torcer. ● *vi* enroscarse

**twinge** /twɪndʒ/ *n* punzada *f*; (*fig*) remordimiento *m* (de conciencia)

**twinkle** /'twɪŋkl/ *vi* centellear. ● *n* centelleo *m*

**twirl** /twɜːl/ *vt* dar vueltas a. ● *vi* dar vueltas. ● *n* vuelta *f*

**twist** /twɪst/ *vt* torcer; (*roll*) enrollar; (*distort*) deformar. ● *vi* torcerse; (*coil*) enroscarse; (*road*) serpentear. ● *n* torsión *f*; (*curve*) vuelta *f*; (*of character*) peculiaridad *f*

**twit**[1] /twɪt/ *n* (*sl*) imbécil *m*

**twit**[2] /twɪt/ *vt* (*pt* **twitted**) tomar el pelo a

**twitch** /twɪtʃ/ *vt* crispar. ● *vi* crisparse. ● *n* tic *m*; (*jerk*) tirón *m*

**twitter** /'twɪtə(r)/ *vi* gorjear. ● *n* gorjeo *m*

**two** /tuː/ *a & n* dos (*m*). **in ~ minds** indeciso. **~-faced** *a* falso, insincero. **~-piece (suit)** *n* traje *m* (de dos piezas). **~some** /'tuːsəm/ *n* pareja *f*. **~-way** *a* (*traffic*) de doble sentido

**tycoon** /taɪ'kuːn/ *n* magnate *m*

**tying** /'taɪŋ/ *see* **tie**

**type** /taɪp/ *n* tipo *m*. ● *vt/i* escribir a máquina. **~-cast** *a* (*actor*) encasillado. **~script** /'taɪpskrɪpt/ *n* texto *m* escrito a máquina. **~writer** /'taɪpraɪtə(r)/ *n* máquina *f* de escribir. **~written** /-ɪtn/ *a* escrito a máquina, mecanografiado

**typhoid** /'taɪfɔɪd/ *n*. **~ (fever)** fiebre *f* tifoidea

**typhoon** /taɪ'fuːn/ *n* tifón *m*

**typical** /'tɪpɪkl/ *a* típico. **~ly** *adv* típicamente

**typify** /'tɪpɪfaɪ/ *vt* tipificar

**typi|ng** /'taɪpɪŋ/ *n* mecanografía *f*. **~st** *n* mecanógrafo *m*

**typography** /taɪ'pɒgrəfɪ/ *n* tipografía *f*

**tyran|nical** /tɪ'rænɪkl/ *a* tiránico. **~nize** *vi* tiranizar. **~ny** /'tɪrənɪ/ *n* tiranía *f*. **~t** /'taɪərənt/ *n* tirano *m*

**tyre** /'taɪə(r)/ *n* neumático *m*, llanta *f* (*Amer*)

# U

**ubiquitous** /juː'bɪkwɪtəs/ *a* omnipresente, ubicuo

**udder** /'ʌdə(r)/ *n* ubre *f*

**UFO** /'juːfəʊ/ *abbr* (*unidentified flying object*) OVNI *m*, objeto *m* volante no identificado

**ugl|iness** /'ʌglɪnɪs/ *n* fealdad *f*. **~y** /'ʌglɪ/ *a* (**-ier, -iest**) feo

**UK** /juː'keɪ/ *abbr* (*United Kingdom*) Reino *m* Unido

**ulcer** /'ʌlsə(r)/ *n* úlcera *f*. **~ous** *a* ulceroso

**ulterior** /ʌl'tɪərɪə(r)/ *a* ulterior. **~ motive** *n* segunda intención *f*

**ultimate** /'ʌltɪmət/ *a* último; (*definitive*) definitivo; (*fundamental*) fundamental. **~ly** *adv* al final; (*basically*) en el fondo

**ultimatum** /ʌltɪ'meɪtəm/ *n* (*pl* **-ums**) ultimátum *m* invar

**ultra...** /'ʌltrə/ *pref* ultra...

**ultramarine** /ʌltrəmə'riːn/ *n* azul *m* marino

**ultrasonic** /ʌltrə'sɒnɪk/ *a* ultrasónico

**ultraviolet** /ˌʌltrə'vaɪələt/ a ultravioleta a invar

**umbilical** /ʌm'bɪlɪkl/ a umbilical. ~ **cord** n cordón m umbilical

**umbrage** /'ʌmbrɪdʒ/ n resentimiento m. **take** ~ ofenderse (**at** por)

**umbrella** /ʌm'brelə/ n paraguas m invar

**umpire** /'ʌmpaɪə(r)/ n árbitro m. ● vt arbitrar

**umpteen** /'ʌmptiːn/ a (sl) muchísimos. ~**th** a (sl) enésimo

**UN** /juː'en/ abbr (United Nations) ONU f, Organización f de las Naciones Unidas

**un...** /ʌn/ pref in..., des..., no, poco, sin

**unabated** /ʌnə'beɪtɪd/ a no disminuido

**unable** /ʌn'eɪbl/ a incapaz (**to** de). **be** ~ **to** no poder

**unabridged** /ʌnə'brɪdʒd/ a íntegro

**unacceptable** /ʌnək'septəbl/ a inaceptable

**unaccountabl|e** /ʌnə'kaʊntəbl/ a inexplicable. ~**y** adv inexplicablemente

**unaccustomed** /ʌnə'kʌstəmd/ a insólito. **be** ~ **to** a no estar acostumbrado a

**unadopted** /ʌnə'dɒptɪd/ a (of road) privado

**unadulterated** /ʌnə'dʌltəreɪtɪd/ a puro

**unaffected** /ʌnə'fektɪd/ a sin afectación, natural

**unaided** /ʌn'eɪdɪd/ a sin ayuda

**unalloyed** /ʌnə'lɔɪd/ a puro

**unanimous** /juː'nænɪməs/ a unánime. ~**ly** adv unánimemente

**unannounced** /ʌnə'naʊnst/ a sin previo aviso; (unexpected) inesperado

**unarmed** /ʌn'ɑːmd/ a desarmado

**unassuming** /ʌnə'sjuːmɪŋ/ a modesto, sin pretensiones

**unattached** /ʌnə'tætʃt/ a suelto; (unmarried) soltero

**unattended** /ʌnə'tendɪd/ a sin vigilar

**unattractive** /ʌnə'træktɪv/ a poco atractivo

**unavoidabl|e** /ʌnə'vɔɪdəbl/ a inevitable. ~**y** adv inevitablemente

**unaware** /ʌnə'weə(r)/ a ignorante (**of** de). **be** ~ **of** ignorar. ~**s** /-eəz/ adv desprevenido

**unbalanced** /ʌn'bælənst/ a desequilibrado

**unbearabl|e** /ʌn'beərəbl/ a inaguantable. ~**y** adv inaguantablemente

**unbeat|able** /ʌn'biːtəbl/ a insuperable. ~**en** a no vencido

**unbeknown** /ʌnbɪ'nəʊn/ a desconocido. ~ **to** (fam) sin saberlo yo

**unbelievable** /ʌnbɪ'liːvəbl/ a increíble

**unbend** /ʌn'bend/ vt (pt unbent) enderezar. ● vi (relax) relajarse. ~**ing** a inflexible

**unbiased** /ʌn'baɪəst/ a imparcial

**unbidden** /ʌn'bɪdn/ a espontáneo; (without invitation) sin ser invitado

**unblock** /ʌn'blɒk/ vt desatascar

**unbolt** /ʌn'bəʊlt/ vt desatrancar

**unborn** /ʌn'bɔːn/ a no nacido todavía

**unbounded** /ʌn'baʊndɪd/ a ilimitado

**unbreakable** /ʌn'breɪkəbl/ a irrompible

**unbridled** /ʌn'braɪdld/ a desenfrenado

**unbroken** /ʌn'brəʊkən/ a (intact) intacto; (continuous) continuo

**unburden** /ʌn'bɜːdn/ vt. ~ **o.s.** desahogarse

**unbutton** /ʌn'bʌtn/ vt desabotonar, desabrochar

**uncalled-for** /ʌn'kɔːldfɔː(r)/ a fuera de lugar; (unjustified) injustificado

**uncanny** /ʌn'kænɪ/ a (-ier, -iest) misterioso

**unceasing** /ʌn'siːsɪŋ/ a incesante

**unceremonious** /ʌnserɪ'məʊnɪəs/ a informal; (abrupt) brusco

**uncertain** /ʌn'sɜːtn/ a incierto; (changeable) variable. **be** ~ **whether** no saber exactamente si. ~**ty** n incertidumbre f

**unchang|ed** /ʌn'tʃeɪndʒd/ a igual. ~**ing** a inmutable

**uncharitable** /ʌn'tʃærɪtəbl/ a severo

**uncivilized** /ʌn'sɪvɪlaɪzd/ a incivilizado

**uncle** /'ʌŋkl/ n tío m

**unclean** /ʌn'kliːn/ a sucio

**unclear** /ʌn'klɪə(r)/ a poco claro

**uncomfortable** /ʌn'kʌmfətəbl/ a incómodo; (unpleasant) desagradable. **feel** ~ no estar a gusto

**uncommon** /ʌn'kɒmən/ a raro. ~**ly** adv extraordinariamente

**uncompromising** /ʌn'kɒmprəmaɪzɪŋ/ a intransigente

**unconcerned** /ʌnkən'sɜːnd/ a indiferente

**unconditional** /ˌʌnkən'dɪʃənl/ a incondicional. **∼ly** adv incondicionalmente

**unconscious** /ʌn'kɒnʃəs/ a inconsciente; (med) sin sentido. **∼ly** adv inconscientemente

**unconventional** /ˌʌnkən'venʃənl/ a poco convencional

**uncooperative** /ˌʌnkəʊ'ɒpərətɪv/ a poco servicial

**uncork** /ʌn'kɔːk/ vt descorchar, destapar

**uncouth** /ʌn'kuːθ/ a grosero

**uncover** /ʌn'kʌvə(r)/ vt descubrir

**unctuous** /'ʌŋktjʊəs/ a untuoso; (fig) empalagoso

**undecided** /ˌʌndɪ'saɪdɪd/ a indeciso

**undeniabl|e** /ˌʌndɪ'naɪəbl/ a innegable. **∼y** adv indiscutiblemente

**under** /'ʌndə(r)/ prep debajo de; (less than) menos de; (in the course of) bajo, en. ● adv debajo, abajo. **∼ age** a menor de edad. **∼ way** adv en curso; (on the way) en marcha

**under...** pref sub...

**undercarriage** /'ʌndəkærɪdʒ/ n (aviat) tren m de aterrizaje

**underclothes** /'ʌndəkləʊðz/ npl ropa f interior

**undercoat** /'ʌndəkəʊt/ n (of paint) primera mano f

**undercover** /ˌʌndə'kʌvə(r)/ a secreto

**undercurrent** /'ʌndəkʌrənt/ n corriente f submarina; (fig) tendencia f oculta

**undercut** /'ʌndəkʌt/ vt (pt **undercut**) (com) vender más barato que

**underdeveloped** /ˌʌndədɪ'veləpt/ a subdesarrollado

**underdog** /'ʌndədɒg/ n perdedor m. **the ∼s** npl los de abajo

**underdone** /ˌʌndə'dʌn/ a (meat) poco hecho

**underestimate** /ˌʌndər'estɪmeɪt/ vt subestimar

**underfed** /ˌʌndə'fed/ a desnutrido

**underfoot** /ˌʌndə'fʊt/ adv bajo los pies

**undergo** /'ʌndəgəʊ/ vt (pt **-went**, pp **-gone**) sufrir

**undergraduate** /ˌʌndə'grædjʊət/ n estudiante m & f universitario (no licenciado)

**underground** /ˌʌndə'graʊnd/ adv bajo tierra; (in secret) clandestinamente. /'ʌndəgraʊnd/ a subterráneo; (secret) clandestino. ● n metro m

**undergrowth** /'ʌndəgrəʊθ/ n maleza f

**underhand** /'ʌndəhænd/ a (secret) clandestino; (deceptive) fraudulento

**underlie** /ˌʌndə'laɪ/ vt (pt **-lay**, pp **-lain**, pres p **-lying**) estar debajo de; (fig) estar a la base de

**underline** /ˌʌndə'laɪn/ vt subrayar

**underling** /'ʌndəlɪŋ/ n subalterno m

**underlying** /ˌʌndə'laɪŋ/ a fundamental

**undermine** /ˌʌndə'maɪn/ vt socavar

**underneath** /ˌʌndə'niːθ/ prep debajo de. ● adv por debajo

**underpaid** /ˌʌndə'peɪd/ a mal pagado

**underpants** /'ʌndəpænts/ npl calzoncillos mpl

**underpass** /'ʌndəpɑːs/ n paso m subterráneo

**underprivileged** /ˌʌndə'prɪvɪlɪdʒd/ a desvalido

**underrate** /ˌʌndə'reɪt/ vt subestimar

**undersell** /ˌʌndə'sel/ vt (pt **-sold**) vender más barato que

**undersigned** /'ʌndəsaɪnd/ a abajo firmante

**undersized** /ˌʌndə'saɪzd/ a pequeño

**understand** /ˌʌndə'stænd/ vt/i (pt **-stood**) entender, comprender. **∼able** a comprensible. **∼ing** /ˌʌndə'stændɪŋ/ a comprensivo. ● n comprensión f; (agreement) acuerdo m

**understatement** /ˌʌndə'steɪtmənt/ n subestimación f

**understudy** /'ʌndəstʌdɪ/ n sobresaliente m & f (en el teatro)

**undertake** /ˌʌndə'teɪk/ vt (pt **-took**, pp **-taken**) emprender; (assume responsibility) encargarse de

**undertaker** /'ʌndəteɪkə(r)/ n empresario m de pompas fúnebres

**undertaking** /ˌʌndə'teɪkɪŋ/ n empresa f; (promise) promesa f

**undertone** /'ʌndətəʊn/ n. **in an ∼** en voz baja

**undertow** /'ʌndətəʊ/ n resaca f

**undervalue** /ˌʌndə'væljuː/ vt subvalorar

**underwater** /ˌʌndə'wɔːtə(r)/ a submarino. ● adv bajo el agua

**underwear** /'ʌndəweə(r)/ n ropa f interior

**underweight** /'ʌndəweɪt/ a de peso insuficiente. **be ∼** estar flaco

**underwent** /ˌʌndə'went/ see **undergo**

**underworld** /'ʌndəwɜːld/ n (crim-
inals) hampa f

**underwrite** /ʌndə'raɪt/ vt (pt -wrote,
pp -written) (com) asegurar. ~r
/-ə(r)/ n asegurador m

**undeserved** /ʌndɪ'zɜːvd/ a inmerecido

**undesirable** /ʌndɪ'zaɪərəbl/ a indeseable

**undeveloped** /ʌndɪ'veləpt/ a sin
desarrollar

**undies** /'ʌndɪz/ npl (fam) ropa f
interior

**undignified** /ʌn'dɪgnɪfaɪd/ a indecoroso

**undisputed** /ʌndɪs'pjuːtɪd/ a incontestable

**undistinguished** /ʌndɪs'tɪŋgwɪʃt/ a
mediocre

**undo** /ʌn'duː/ vt (pt -did, pp -done)
deshacer; (ruin) arruinar; reparar
⟨wrong⟩. leave ~ne dejar sin hacer

**undoubted** /ʌn'daʊtɪd/ a indudable. ~ly adv indudablemente

**undress** /ʌn'dres/ vt desnudar. ● vi
desnudarse

**undue** /ʌn'djuː/ a excesivo

**undulat|e** /'ʌndjʊleɪt/ vi ondular.
~ion /-'leɪʃn/ n ondulación f

**unduly** /ʌn'djuːlɪ/ adv excesivamente

**undying** /ʌn'daɪɪŋ/ a eterno

**unearth** /ʌn'ɜːθ/ vt desenterrar

**unearthly** /ʌn'ɜːθlɪ/ a sobrenatural;
(impossible, fam) absurdo. ~ hour
n hora intempestiva

**uneas|ily** /ʌn'iːzɪlɪ/ adv inquieta-
mente. ~y /ʌn'iːzɪ/ a incómodo;
(worrying) inquieto

**uneconomic** /ʌniːkə'nɒmɪk/ a poco
rentable

**uneducated** /ʌn'edjʊkeɪtɪd/ a inculto

**unemploy|ed** /ʌnɪm'plɔɪd/ a
parado, desempleado; (not in use)
inutilizado. ~ment n paro m,
desempleo m

**unending** /ʌn'endɪŋ/ a interminable, sin fin

**unequal** /ʌn'iːkwəl/ a desigual

**unequivocal** /ʌnɪ'kwɪvəkl/ a
inequívoco

**unerring** /ʌn'ɜːrɪŋ/ a infalible

**unethical** /ʌn'eθɪkl/ a sin ética,
inmoral

**uneven** /ʌn'iːvn/ a desigual

**unexceptional** /ʌnɪk'sepʃənl/ a
corriente

**unexpected** /ʌnɪk'spektɪd/ a
inesperado

**unfailing** /ʌn'feɪlɪŋ/ a inagotable;
(constant) constante; (loyal) leal

**unfair** /ʌn'feə(r)/ a injusto. ~ly adv
injustamente. ~ness n injusticia f

**unfaithful** /ʌn'feɪθfl/ a infiel. ~ness
n infidelidad f

**unfamiliar** /ʌnfə'mɪlɪə(r)/ a desconocido. be ~ with desconocer

**unfasten** /ʌn'fɑːsn/ vt desabrochar
⟨clothes⟩; (untie) desatar

**unfavourable** /ʌn'feɪvərəbl/ a des-
favorable

**unfeeling** /ʌn'fiːlɪŋ/ a insensible

**unfit** /ʌn'fɪt/ a inadecuado, no apto;
(unwell) en mal estado físico;
(incapable) incapaz

**unflinching** /ʌn'flɪntʃɪŋ/ a resuelto

**unfold** /ʌn'fəʊld/ vt desdoblar; (fig)
revelar. ● vi (view etc) extenderse

**unforeseen** /ʌnfɔː'siːn/ a imprevisto

**unforgettable** /ʌnfə'getəbl/ a inolvidable

**unforgivable** /ʌnfə'gɪvəbl/ a imperdonable

**unfortunate** /ʌn'fɔːtʃənət/ a desgraciado; (regrettable) lamentable. ~ly
adv desgraciadamente

**unfounded** /ʌn'faʊndɪd/ a infundado

**unfriendly** /ʌn'frendlɪ/ a poco amis-
toso, frío

**unfurl** /ʌn'fɜːl/ vt desplegar

**ungainly** /ʌn'geɪnlɪ/ a desgarbado

**ungodly** /ʌn'gɒdlɪ/ a impío. ~ hour
n (fam) hora f intempestiva

**ungrateful** /ʌn'greɪtfl/ a desagradecido

**unguarded** /ʌn'gɑːdɪd/ a indefenso;
(incautious) imprudente, incauto

**unhapp|ily** /ʌn'hæpɪlɪ/ adv infeliz-
mente; (unfortunately) desgraciadamente. ~iness n tristeza f. ~y
/ʌn'hæpɪ/ a (-ier, -iest) infeliz, triste;
(unsuitable) inoportuno. ~y with
insatisfecho de ⟨plans etc⟩

**unharmed** /ʌn'hɑːmd/ a ileso, sano y
salvo

**unhealthy** /ʌn'helθɪ/ a (-ier, -iest)
enfermizo; (insanitary) malsano

**unhinge** /ʌn'hɪndʒ/ vt desquiciar

**unholy** /ʌn'həʊlɪ/ a (-ier, -iest) impío;
(terrible, fam) terrible

**unhook** /ʌn'hʊk/ vt desenganchar

**unhoped** /ʌn'həʊpt/ a. ~ for
inesperado

**unhurt** /ʌn'hɜːt/ a ileso

**unicorn** /'juːnɪkɔːn/ n unicornio m

**unification** /ju:nɪfɪ'keɪʃn/ n unificación f

**uniform** /'ju:nɪfɔ:m/ a & n uniforme (m). ~ity /-'fɔ:mətɪ/ n uniformidad f. ~ly adv uniformemente

**unify** /'ju:nɪfaɪ/ vt unificar

**unilateral** /ju:nɪ'lætərəl/ a unilateral

**unimaginable** /ʌnɪ'mædʒɪnəbl/ a inconcebible

**unimpeachable** /ʌnɪm'pi:tʃəbl/ a irreprensible

**unimportant** /ʌnɪm'pɔ:tnt/ a insignificante

**uninhabited** /ʌnɪn'hæbɪtɪd/ a inhabitado; (abandoned) despoblado

**unintentional** /ʌnɪn'tenʃənl/ a involuntario

**union** /'ju:njən/ n unión f; (trade union) sindicato m. ~ist n sindicalista m & f. U~ Jack n bandera f del Reino Unido

**unique** /ju:'ni:k/ a único. ~ly adv extraordinariamente

**unisex** /'ju:nɪseks/ a unisex(o)

**unison** /'ju:nɪsn/ n. in ~ al unísono

**unit** /'ju:nɪt/ n unidad f; (of furniture etc) elemento m

**unite** /ju:'naɪt/ vt unir. ● vi unirse. **U~d Kingdom (UK)** n Reino m Unido. **U~d Nations (UN)** n Organización f de las Naciones Unidas (ONU). **U~d States (of America) (USA)** n Estados mpl Unidos (de América) (EE.UU.)

**unity** /'ju:nɪtɪ/ n unidad f; (fig) acuerdo m

**univers|al** /ju:nɪ'vɜ:sl/ a universal. ~e /'ju:nɪvɜ:s/ n universo m

**university** /ju:nɪ'vɜ:sətɪ/ n universidad f. ● a universitario

**unjust** /ʌn'dʒʌst/ a injusto

**unkempt** /ʌn'kempt/ a desaseado

**unkind** /ʌn'kaɪnd/ a poco amable; (cruel) cruel. ~ly adv poco amablemente. ~ness n falta f de amabilidad; (cruelty) crueldad f

**unknown** /ʌn'nəʊn/ a desconocido

**unlawful** /ʌn'lɔ:fl/ a ilegal

**unleash** /ʌn'li:ʃ/ vt soltar; (fig) desencadenar

**unless** /ʌn'les, ən'les/ conj a menos que, a no ser que

**unlike** /ʌn'laɪk/ a diferente; (not typical) impropio de. ● prep a diferencia de. ~lihood n improbabilidad f. ~ly /ʌn'laɪklɪ/ a improbable

**unlimited** /ʌn'lɪmɪtɪd/ a ilimitado

**unload** /ʌn'ləʊd/ vt descargar

**unlock** /ʌn'lɒk/ vt abrir (con llave)

**unluck|ily** /ʌn'lʌkɪlɪ/ adv desgraciadamente. ~y /ʌn'lʌkɪ/ a (-ier, -iest) desgraciado; (number) de mala suerte

**unmanly** /ʌn'mænlɪ/ a poco viril

**unmanned** /ʌn'mænd/ a no tripulado

**unmarried** /ʌn'mærɪd/ a soltero. ~ mother n madre f soltera

**unmask** /ʌn'mɑ:sk/ vt desenmascarar. ● vi quitarse la máscara

**unmentionable** /ʌn'menʃənəbl/ a a que no se debe aludir

**unmistakabl|e** /ʌnmɪ'steɪkəbl/ a inconfundible. ~y adv claramente

**unmitigated** /ʌn'mɪtɪgeɪtɪd/ a (absolute) absoluto

**unmoved** /ʌn'mu:vd/ a (fig) indiferente (by a), insensible (by a)

**unnatural** /ʌn'nætʃərəl/ a no natural; (not normal) anormal

**unnecessar|ily** /ʌn'nesəsərɪlɪ/ adv innecesariamente. ~y /ʌn'nesəsərɪ/ a innecesario

**unnerve** /ʌn'nɜ:v/ vt desconcertar

**unnoticed** /ʌn'nəʊtɪst/ a inadvertido

**unobtainable** /ʌnəb'teɪnəbl/ a inasequible; (fig) inalcanzable

**unobtrusive** /ʌnəb'tru:sɪv/ a discreto

**unofficial** /ʌnə'fɪʃl/ a no oficial. ~ly adv extraoficialmente

**unpack** /ʌn'pæk/ vt desempaquetar (parcel); deshacer (suitcase). ● vi deshacer la maleta

**unpalatable** /ʌn'pælətəbl/ a desagradable

**unparalleled** /ʌn'pærəleld/ a sin par

**unpick** /ʌn'pɪk/ vt descoser

**unpleasant** /ʌn'pleznt/ a desagradable. ~ness n lo desagradable

**unplug** /ʌn'plʌg/ vt (elec) desenchufar

**unpopular** /ʌn'pɒpjʊlə(r)/ a impopular

**unprecedented** /ʌn'presɪdentɪd/ a sin precedente

**unpredictable** /ʌnprɪ'dɪktəbl/ a imprevisible

**unpremeditated** /ʌnprɪ'medɪteɪtɪd/ a impremeditado

**unprepared** /ʌnprɪ'peəd/ a no preparado; (unready) desprevenido

**unprepossessing** /ʌnpri:pə'zesɪŋ/ a poco atractivo

**unpretentious** /ʌnprɪ'tenʃəs/ a sin pretensiones, modesto

**unprincipled** /ʌn'prɪnsɪpld/ *a* sin principios

**unprofessional** /ʌnprə'feʃənəl/ *a* contrario a la ética profesional

**unpublished** /ʌn'pʌblɪʃt/ *a* inédito

**unqualified** /ʌn'kwɒlɪfaɪd/ *a* sin título; ⟨fig⟩ absoluto

**unquestionabl|e** /ʌn'kwestʃənəbl/ *a* indiscutible. **~y** *adv* indiscutiblemente

**unquote** /ʌn'kwəʊt/ *vi* cerrar comillas

**unravel** /ʌn'rævl/ *vt* (*pt* **unravelled**) desenredar; deshacer ⟨knitting etc⟩. ● *vi* desenredarse

**unreal** /ʌn'rɪəl/ *a* irreal. **~istic** *a* poco realista

**unreasonable** /ʌn'riːzənəbl/ *a* irrazonable

**unrecognizable** /ʌnrekəg'naɪzəbl/ *a* irreconocible

**unrelated** /ʌnrɪ'leɪtɪd/ *a* ⟨facts⟩ inconexo, sin relación; ⟨people⟩ no emparentado

**unreliable** /ʌnrɪ'laɪəbl/ *a* ⟨person⟩ poco formal; ⟨machine⟩ poco fiable

**unrelieved** /ʌnrɪ'liːvd/ *a* no aliviado

**unremitting** /ʌnrɪ'mɪtɪŋ/ *a* incesante

**unrepentant** /ʌnrɪ'pentənt/ *a* impenitente

**unrequited** /ʌnrɪ'kwaɪtɪd/ *a* no correspondido

**unreservedly** /ʌnrɪ'zɜːvɪdlɪ/ *adv* sin reserva

**unrest** /ʌn'rest/ *n* inquietud *f*; ⟨pol⟩ agitación *f*

**unrivalled** /ʌn'raɪvld/ *a* sin par

**unroll** /ʌn'rəʊl/ *vt* desenrollar. ● *vi* desenrollarse

**unruffled** /ʌn'rʌfld/ ⟨person⟩ imperturbable

**unruly** /ʌn'ruːlɪ/ *a* indisciplinado

**unsafe** /ʌn'seɪf/ *a* peligroso; ⟨person⟩ en peligro

**unsaid** /ʌn'sed/ *a* sin decir

**unsatisfactory** /ʌnsætɪs'fæktərɪ/ *a* insatisfactorio

**unsavoury** /ʌn'seɪvərɪ/ *a* desagradable

**unscathed** /ʌn'skeɪðd/ *a* ileso

**unscramble** /ʌn'skræmbl/ *vt* descifrar

**unscrew** /ʌn'skruː/ *vt* destornillar

**unscrupulous** /ʌn'skruːpjʊləs/ *a* sin escrúpulos

**unseat** /ʌn'siːt/ *vt* ⟨pol⟩ quitar el escaño a

**unseemly** /ʌn'siːmlɪ/ *a* indecoroso

**unseen** /ʌn'siːn/ *a* inadvertido. ● *n* ⟨translation⟩ traducción *f* a primera vista

**unselfish** /ʌn'selfɪʃ/ *a* desinteresado

**unsettle** /ʌn'setl/ *vt* perturbar. **~d** *a* perturbado; ⟨weather⟩ variable; ⟨bill⟩ por pagar

**unshakeable** /ʌn'ʃeɪkəbl/ *a* firme

**unshaven** /ʌn'ʃeɪvn/ *a* sin afeitar

**unsightly** /ʌn'saɪtlɪ/ *a* feo

**unskilled** /ʌn'skɪld/ *a* inexperto. **~ worker** *n* obrero *m* no cualificado

**unsociable** /ʌn'səʊʃəbl/ *a* insociable

**unsolicited** /ʌnsə'lɪsɪtɪd/ *a* no solicitado

**unsophisticated** /ʌnsə'fɪstɪkeɪtɪd/ *a* sencillo

**unsound** /ʌn'saʊnd/ *a* defectuoso, erróneo. **of ~ mind** demente

**unsparing** /ʌn'speərɪŋ/ *a* pródigo, ⟨cruel⟩ cruel

**unspeakable** /ʌn'spiːkəbl/ *a* indecible

**unspecified** /ʌn'spesɪfaɪd/ *a* no especificado

**unstable** /ʌn'steɪbl/ *a* inestable

**unsteady** /ʌn'stedɪ/ *a* inestable; ⟨hand⟩ poco firme; ⟨step⟩ inseguro

**unstinted** /ʌn'stɪntɪd/ *a* abundante

**unstuck** /ʌn'stʌk/ *a* suelto. **come ~** despegarse; ⟨fail, fam⟩ fracasar

**unstudied** /ʌn'stʌdɪd/ *a* natural

**unsuccessful** /ʌnsək'sesfʊl/ *a* fracasado. **be ~** no tener éxito, fracasar

**unsuitable** /ʌn'suːtəbl/ *a* inadecuado; (*inconvenient*) inconveniente

**unsure** /ʌn'ʃʊə(r)/ *a* inseguro

**unsuspecting** /ʌnsə'spektɪŋ/ *a* confiado

**unthinkable** /ʌn'θɪŋkəbl/ *a* inconcebible

**untid|ily** /ʌn'taɪdɪlɪ/ *adv* desordenadamente. **~iness** *n* desorden *m*. **~y** /ʌn'taɪdɪ/ *a* (**-ier, -iest**) desordenado; ⟨person⟩ desaseado

**untie** /ʌn'taɪ/ *vt* desatar

**until** /ən'tɪl, ʌn'tɪl/ *prep* hasta. ● *conj* hasta que

**untimely** /ʌn'taɪmlɪ/ *a* inoportuno; (*premature*) prematuro

**untiring** /ʌn'taɪərɪŋ/ *a* incansable

**untold** /ʌn'təʊld/ *a* incalculable

**untoward** /ʌntə'wɔːd/ *a* (*inconvenient*) inconveniente

**untried** /ʌn'traɪd/ *a* no probado

**untrue** /ʌn'truː/ *a* falso

**unused** /ʌn'juːzd/ *a* nuevo. /ʌn'juːst/ *a*. **~ to** no acostumbrado a

**unusual** /ʌn'juːʒʊəl/ a insólito; (*exceptional*) excepcional. ~**ly** adv excepcionalmente

**unutterable** /ʌn'ʌtərəbl/ a indecible

**unveil** /ʌn'veɪl/ vt descubrir; (*disclose*) revelar

**unwanted** /ʌn'wɒntɪd/ a superfluo; ⟨child⟩ no deseado

**unwarranted** /ʌn'wɒrəntɪd/ a injustificado

**unwelcome** /ʌn'welkəm/ a desagradable; ⟨guest⟩ inoportuno

**unwell** /ʌn'wel/ a indispuesto

**unwieldy** /ʌn'wiːldɪ/ a difícil de manejar

**unwilling** /ʌn'wɪlɪŋ/ a no dispuesto. **be** ~ no querer. ~**ly** adv de mala gana

**unwind** /ʌn'waɪnd/ vt (*pt* **unwound**) desenvolver. ● vi desenvolverse; (*relax*, *fam*) relajarse

**unwise** /ʌn'waɪz/ a imprudente

**unwitting** /ʌn'wɪtɪŋ/ a inconsciente; (*involuntary*) involuntario. ~**ly** adv involuntariamente

**unworthy** /ʌn'wɜːðɪ/ a indigno

**unwrap** /ʌn'ræp/ vt (*pt* **unwrapped**) desenvolver, deshacer

**unwritten** /ʌn'rɪtn/ a no escrito; ⟨agreement⟩ tácito

**up** /ʌp/ adv arriba; (*upwards*) hacia arriba; (*higher*) más arriba; (*out of bed*) levantado; (*finished*) terminado. ~ **here** aquí arriba. ~ **in** (*fam*) versado en, fuerte en. ~ **there** allí arriba. ~ **to** hasta. **be one** ~ **on** llevar la ventaja a. **be** ~ **against** enfrentarse con. **be** ~ **to** tramar ⟨plot⟩; (*one's turn*) tocar a; a la altura de ⟨task⟩; (*reach*) llegar a. **come** ~ subir. **feel** ~ **to it** sentirse capaz. **go** ~ subir. **it's** ~ **to you** depende de tí. **what is** ~? ¿qué pasa? ● prep arriba; (*on top of*) en lo alto de. ● vt (*pt* **upped**) aumentar. ● n. ~**s and downs** npl altibajos mpl

**upbraid** /ʌp'breɪd/ vt reprender

**upbringing** /'ʌpbrɪŋɪŋ/ n educación f

**update** /ʌp'deɪt/ vt poner al día

**upgrade** /ʌp'greɪd/ vt ascender ⟨person⟩; mejorar ⟨equipment⟩

**upheaval** /ʌp'hiːvl/ n trastorno m

**uphill** /'ʌphɪl/ a ascendente; (*fig*) arduo. ● adv /ʌp'hɪl/ cuesta arriba. **go** ~ subir

**uphold** /ʌp'həʊld/ vt (*pt* **upheld**) sostener

**upholster** /ʌp'həʊlstə(r)/ vt tapizar. ~**er** /-rə(r)/ n tapicero m. ~**y** n tapicería f

**upkeep** /'ʌpkiːp/ n mantenimiento m

**up-market** /ʌp'mɑːkɪt/ a superior

**upon** /ə'pɒn/ prep en; (*on top of*) encima de. **once** ~ **a time** érase una vez

**upper** /'ʌpə(r)/ a superior. ~ **class** n clases fpl altas. ~ **hand** n dominio m, ventaja f. ~**most** a (el) más alto. ● n (*of shoe*) pala f

**uppish** /'ʌpɪʃ/ a engreído

**upright** /'ʌpraɪt/ a derecho; ⟨piano⟩ vertical. ● n montante m

**uprising** /'ʌpraɪzɪŋ/ n sublevación f

**uproar** /'ʌprɔː(r)/ n tumulto m. ~**ious** /-'rɔːrɪəs/ a tumultuoso

**uproot** /ʌp'ruːt/ vt desarraigar

**upset** /ʌp'set/ vt (*pt* **upset**, *presp* **upsetting**) trastornar; desbaratar ⟨plan etc⟩; (*distress*) alterar. /'ʌpset/ n trastorno m

**upshot** /'ʌpʃɒt/ n resultado m

**upside-down** /ʌpsaɪd'daʊn/ adv al revés; (*in disorder*) patas arriba. **turn** ~ volver

**upstairs** /ʌp'steəz/ adv arriba. /'ʌpsteəz/ a de arriba

**upstart** /'ʌpstɑːt/ n arribista m & f

**upstream** /'ʌpstriːm/ adv río arriba; (*against the current*) contra la corriente

**upsurge** /'ʌpsɜːdʒ/ n aumento m; (*of anger etc*) arrebato m

**uptake** /'ʌpteɪk/ n. **quick on the** ~ muy listo

**uptight** /'ʌptaɪt/ a (*fam*) nervioso

**up-to-date** /ʌptə'deɪt/ a al día; ⟨news⟩ de última hora; (*modern*) moderno

**upturn** /'ʌptɜːn/ n aumento m; (*improvement*) mejora f

**upward** /'ʌpwəd/ a ascendente. ● adv hacia arriba. ~**s** adv hacia arriba

**uranium** /jʊ'reɪnɪəm/ n uranio m

**urban** /'ɜːbən/ a urbano

**urbane** /ɜː'beɪn/ a cortés

**urbanize** /'ɜːbənaɪz/ vt urbanizar

**urchin** /'ɜːtʃɪn/ n pilluelo m

**urge** /ɜːdʒ/ vt incitar, animar. ● n impulso m. ~ **on** animar

**urgen|cy** /'ɜːdʒənsɪ/ n urgencia f. ~**t** /'ɜːdʒənt/ a urgente. ~**tly** adv urgentemente

**urin|ate** /'jʊərɪneɪt/ vi orinar. ~**e** /'jʊərɪn/ n orina f

**urn** /ɜːn/ *n* urna *f*

**Uruguay** /jʊərəgwaɪ/ *n* el Uruguay *m*. **~an** *a* & *n* uruguayo (*m*)

**us** /ʌs, əs/ *pron* nos; (*after prep*) nosotros, nosotras

**US(A)** /juːesˈeɪ/ *abbr* (*United States* (*of America*)) EE.UU., Estados *mpl* Unidos

**usage** /ˈjuːzɪdʒ/ *n* uso *m*

**use** /juːz/ *vt* emplear. /juːs/ *n* uso *m*, empleo *m*. **be of ~** servir. **it is no ~** es inútil, no sirve para nada. **make ~ of** servirse de. **~ up** agotar, consumir. **~d** /juːzd/ *a* ⟨*clothes*⟩ gastado. /juːst/ *pt*. **he ~d to say** decía, solía decir. ● *a*. **~d to** acostumbrado a. **~ful** /ˈjuːsfl/ *a* útil. **~fully** *adv* útilmente. **~less** *a* inútil; ⟨*person*⟩ incompetente. **~r** /-zə(r)/ *n* usuario *m*

**usher** /ˈʌʃə(r)/ *n* ujier *m*; (*in theatre etc*) acomodador *m*. ● *vt*. **~ in** hacer entrar. **~ette** *n* acomodadora *f*

**USSR** *abbr* (*history*) (*Union of Soviet Socialist Republics*) URSS

**usual** /ˈjuːʒʊəl/ *a* usual, corriente; (*habitual*) acostumbrado, habitual. **as ~** como de costumbre, como siempre. **~ly** *adv* normalmente. **he ~ly wakes up early** suele despertarse temprano

**usurer** /ˈjuːʒərə(r)/ *n* usurero *m*

**usurp** /juːˈzɜːp/ *vt* usurpar. **~er** /-ə(r)/ *n* usurpador *m*

**usury** /ˈjuːʒərɪ/ *n* usura *f*

**utensil** /juːˈtensl/ *n* utensilio *m*

**uterus** /ˈjuːtərəs/ *n* útero *m*

**utilitarian** /juːtɪlɪˈteərɪən/ *a* utilitario

**utility** /juːˈtɪlətɪ/ *n* utilidad *f*. **public ~** *n* servicio *m* público. ● *a* utilitario

**utilize** /ˈjuːtɪlaɪz/ *vt* utilizar

**utmost** /ˈʌtməʊst/ *a* extremo. ● *n*. **one's ~** todo lo posible

**utter**[1] /ˈʌtə(r)/ *a* completo

**utter**[2] /ˈʌtə(r)/ *vt* (*speak*) pronunciar; dar ⟨*sigh*⟩; emitir ⟨*sound*⟩. **~ance** *n* expresión *f*

**utterly** /ˈʌtəlɪ/ *adv* totalmente

**U-turn** /ˈjuːtɜːn/ *n* vuelta *f*


# V

**vacan|cy** /ˈveɪkənsɪ/ *n* (*job*) vacante *f*; (*room*) habitación *f* libre. **~t** *a* libre; (*empty*) vacío; ⟨*look*⟩ vago

**vacate** /vəˈkeɪt/ *vt* dejar

**vacation** /vəˈkeɪʃn/ *n* (*Amer*) vacaciones *fpl*

**vaccin|ate** /ˈvæksɪneɪt/ *vt* vacunar. **~ation** /-ˈneɪʃn/ *n* vacunación *f*. **~e** /ˈvæksiːn/ *n* vacuna *f*

**vacuum** /ˈvækjʊəm/ *n* (*pl* **-cuums** or **-cua** ) vacío *m*. **~ cleaner** *n* aspiradora *f*. **~ flask** *n* termo *m*

**vagabond** /ˈvægəbɒnd/ *n* vagabundo *m*

**vagary** /ˈveɪgərɪ/ *n* capricho *m*

**vagina** /vəˈdʒaɪnə/ *n* vagina *f*

**vagrant** /ˈveɪgrənt/ *n* vagabundo *m*

**vague** /veɪg/ *a* (**-er, -est**) vago; ⟨*outline*⟩ indistinto. **be ~ about** no precisar. **~ly** *adv* vagamente

**vain** /veɪn/ *a* (**-er, -est**) vanidoso; (*useless*) vano, inútil. **in ~** en vano. **~ly** *adv* vanamente

**valance** /ˈvæləns/ *n* cenefa *f*

**vale** /veɪl/ *n* valle *m*

**valentine** /ˈvæləntaɪn/ *n* (*card*) tarjeta *f* del día de San Valentín

**valet** /ˈvælɪt, ˈvæleɪ/ *n* ayuda *m* de cámara

**valiant** /ˈvælɪənt/ *a* valeroso

**valid** /ˈvælɪd/ *a* válido; ⟨*ticket*⟩ valedero. **~ate** *vt* dar validez a; (*confirm*) convalidar. **~ity** /-ˈɪdətɪ/ *n* validez *f*

**valley** /ˈvælɪ/ *n* (*pl* **-eys**) valle *m*

**valour** /ˈvælə(r)/ *n* valor *m*

**valuable** /ˈvæljʊəbl/ *a* valioso. **~s** *npl* objetos *mpl* de valor

**valuation** /væljʊˈeɪʃn/ *n* valoración *f*

**value** /ˈvæljuː/ *n* valor *m*; (*usefulness*) utilidad *f*. **face ~** *n* valor *m* nominal; (*fig*) significado *m* literal. ● *vt* valorar; (*cherish*) apreciar. **~ added tax (VAT)** *n* impuesto *m* sobre el valor añadido (IVA). **~d** *a* (*appreciated*) apreciado, estimado. **~r** /-ə(r)/ *n* tasador *m*

**valve** /vælv/ *n* válvula *f*

**vampire** /ˈvæmpaɪə(r)/ *n* vampiro *m*

**van** /væn/ *n* furgoneta *f*; (*rail*) furgón *m*

**vandal** /ˈvændl/ *n* vándalo *m*. **~ism** /-əlɪzəm/ *n* vandalismo *m*. **~ize** *vt* destruir

**vane** /veɪn/ *n* (*weathercock*) veleta *f*; (*naut, aviat*) paleta *f*

**vanguard** /ˈvænɡɑːd/ *n* vanguardia *f*

**vanilla** /vəˈnɪlə/ *n* vainilla *f*

**vanish** /ˈvænɪʃ/ *vi* desaparecer

**vanity** /ˈvænɪtɪ/ *n* vanidad *f*. **~ case** *n* neceser *m*

**vantage** /'vɑːntɪdʒ/ n ventaja f. ~ **point** n posición f ventajosa

**vapour** /'veɪpə(r)/ n vapor m

**variable** /'veərɪəbl/ a variable

**varian|ce** /'veərɪəns/ n. **at** ~**ce** en desacuerdo. ~**t** /'veərɪənt/ a diferente. ● n variante m

**variation** /veərɪ'eɪʃn/ n variación f

**varicoloured** /'veərɪkʌləd/ a multicolor

**varied** /'veərɪd/ a variado

**varicose** /'værɪkəʊs/ a varicoso. ~ **veins** npl varices fpl

**variety** /və'raɪətɪ/ n variedad f. ~ **show** n espectáculo m de variedades

**various** /'veərɪəs/ a diverso. ~**ly** adv diversamente

**varnish** /'vɑːnɪʃ/ n barniz m; (for nails) esmalte m. ● vt barnizar

**vary** /'veərɪ/ vt/i variar. ~**ing** a diverso

**vase** /vɑːz, Amer veɪs/ n jarrón m

**vasectomy** /və'sektəmɪ/ n vasectomía f

**vast** /vɑːst/ a vasto, enorme. ~**ly** adv enormemente. ~**ness** n inmensidad f

**vat** /væt/ n tina f

**VAT** /viːeɪ'tiː/ abbr (value added tax) IVA m, impuesto m sobre el valor añadido

**vault** /vɔːlt/ n (roof) bóveda f; (in bank) cámara f acorazada; (tomb) cripta f; (cellar) sótano m; (jump) salto m. ● vt/i saltar

**vaunt** /vɔːnt/ vt jactarse de

**veal** /viːl/ n ternera f

**veer** /vɪə(r)/ vi cambiar de dirección; (naut) virar

**vegetable** /'vedʒɪtəbl/ a vegetal. ● n legumbre m; (greens) verduras fpl

**vegetarian** /vedʒɪ'teərɪən/ a & n vegetariano (m)

**vegetate** /'vedʒɪteɪt/ vi vegetar

**vegetation** /vedʒɪ'teɪʃn/ n vegetación f

**vehemen|ce** /'viːəməns/ n vehemencia f. ~**t** /'viːəmənt/ a vehemente. ~**tly** adv con vehemencia

**vehicle** /'viːɪkl/ n vehículo m

**veil** /veɪl/ n velo m. **take the** ~ hacerse monja. ● vt velar

**vein** /veɪn/ n vena f; (mood) humor m. ~**ed** a veteado

**velocity** /vɪ'lɒsɪtɪ/ n velocidad f

**velvet** /'velvɪt/ n terciopelo m. ~**y** a aterciopelado

**venal** /'viːnl/ a venal. ~**ity** /-'nælətɪ/ n venalidad f

**vendetta** /ven'detə/ n enemistad f prolongada

**vending-machine** /'vendɪŋ məʃiːn/ n distribuidor m automático

**vendor** /'vendə(r)/ n vendedor m

**veneer** /və'nɪə(r)/ n chapa f; (fig) barniz m, apariencia f

**venerable** /'venərəbl/ a venerable

**venereal** /və'nɪərɪəl/ a venéreo

**Venetian** /və'niːʃn/ a & n veneciano (m). **v~ blind** n persiana f veneciana

**vengeance** /'vendʒəns/ n venganza f. **with a** ~ (fig) con creces

**venison** /'venɪzn/ n carne f de venado

**venom** /'venəm/ n veneno m. ~**ous** a venenoso

**vent** /vent/ n abertura f; (for air) respiradero m. **give** ~ **to** dar salida a. ● vt hacer un agujero en; (fig) desahogar

**ventilat|e** /'ventɪleɪt/ vt ventilar. ~**ion** /-'leɪʃn/ n ventilación f. ~**or** /-ə(r)/ n ventilador m

**ventriloquist** /ven'trɪləkwɪst/ n ventrílocuo m

**venture** /'ventʃə(r)/ n empresa f (arriesgada). **at a** ~ a la ventura. ● vt arriesgar. ● vi atreverse

**venue** /'venjuː/ n lugar m (de reunión)

**veranda** /və'rændə/ n terraza f

**verb** /vɜːb/ n verbo m

**verbal** /'vɜːbl/ a verbal. ~**ly** adv verbalmente

**verbatim** /vɜː'beɪtɪm/ adv palabra por palabra, al pie de la letra

**verbose** /vɜː'bəʊs/ a prolijo

**verdant** /'vɜːdənt/ a verde

**verdict** /'vɜːdɪkt/ n veredicto m; (opinion) opinión f

**verge** /vɜːdʒ/ n borde m. ● vt. ~ **on** acercarse a

**verger** /'vɜːdʒə(r)/ n sacristán m

**verif|ication** /verɪfɪ'keɪʃn/ n verificación f. ~**y** /'verɪfaɪ/ vt verificar

**veritable** /'verɪtəbl/ a verdadero

**vermicelli** /vɜːmɪ'tʃelɪ/ n fideos mpl

**vermin** /'vɜːmɪn/ n sabandijas fpl

**vermouth** /'vɜːməθ/ n vermut m

**vernacular** /və'nækjʊlə(r)/ n lengua f; (regional) dialecto m

**versatil|e** /'vɜːsətaɪl/ a versátil. ~**ity** /-'tɪlətɪ/ n versatilidad f

**verse** /vɜːs/ n estrofa f; (poetry) poesías fpl; (of Bible) versículo m

**versed** /vɜːst/ a. ~ **in** versado en
**version** /'vɜːʃn/ n versión f
**versus** /'vɜːsəs/ prep contra
**vertebra** /'vɜːtɪbrə/ n (pl **-brae** /-briː /) vértebra f
**vertical** /'vɜːtɪkl/ a & n vertical (f). ~**ly** adv verticalmente
**vertigo** /'vɜːtɪɡəʊ/ n vértigo m
**verve** /vɜːv/ n entusiasmo m, vigor m
**very** /'verɪ/ adv muy. ~ **much** muchísimo. ~ **well** muy bien. **the ~ first** el primero de todos. ● a mismo. **the ~ thing** exactamente lo que hace falta
**vespers** /'vespəz/ npl vísperas fpl
**vessel** /'vesl/ n (receptacle) recipiente m; (ship) buque m; (anat) vaso m
**vest** /vest/ n camiseta f; (Amer) chaleco m. ● vt conferir. ~**ed interest** n interés m personal; (jurid) derecho m adquirido
**vestige** /'vestɪdʒ/ n vestigio m
**vestment** /'vestmənt/ n vestidura f
**vestry** /'vestrɪ/ n sacristía f
**vet** /vet/ n (fam) veterinario m. ● vt (pt vetted) examinar
**veteran** /'vetərən/ n veterano m
**veterinary** /'vetərɪnərɪ/ a veterinario. ~ **surgeon** n veterinario m
**veto** /'viːtəʊ/ n (pl **-oes**) veto m. ● vt poner el veto a
**vex** /veks/ vt fastidiar. ~**ation** /-'seɪʃn/ n fastidio m. ~**ed question** n cuestión f controvertida. ~**ing** a fastidioso
**via** /'vaɪə/ prep por, por vía de
**viab|ility** /vaɪə'bɪlətɪ/ n viabilidad f. ~**le** /'vaɪəbl/ a viable
**viaduct** /'vaɪədʌkt/ n viaducto m
**vibrant** /'vaɪbrənt/ a vibrante
**vibrat|e** /vaɪ'breɪt/ vt/i vibrar. ~**ion** /-ʃn/ n vibración f
**vicar** /'vɪkə(r)/ n párroco m. ~**age** /-rɪdʒ/ n casa f del párroco
**vicarious** /vɪ'keərɪəs/ a indirecto
**vice**[1] /vaɪs/ n vicio m
**vice**[2] /vaɪs/ n (tec) torno m de banco
**vice...** /'vaɪs/ pref vice...
**vice   versa** /vaɪsɪ'vɜːsə/  .adv viceversa
**vicinity** /vɪ'sɪnɪtɪ/ n vecindad f. **in the ~ of** cerca de
**vicious** /'vɪʃəs/ a (spiteful) malicioso; (violent) atroz. ~ **circle** n círculo m vicioso. ~**ly** adv cruelmente
**vicissitudes** /vɪ'sɪsɪtjuːdz/ npl vicisitudes fpl

**victim** /'vɪktɪm/ n víctima f. ~**ization** /-aɪ'zeɪʃn/ n persecución f. ~**ize** vt victimizar
**victor** /'vɪktə(r)/ n vencedor m
**Victorian** /vɪk'tɔːrɪən/ a victoriano
**victor|ious** /vɪk'tɔːrɪəs/ a victorioso. ~**y** /'vɪktərɪ/ n victoria f
**video** /'vɪdɪəʊ/ a video. ● n (fam) magnetoscopio m. ~ **recorder** n magnetoscopio m. ~**tape** n videocassette f
**vie** /vaɪ/ vi (pres p **vying**) rivalizar
**view** /vjuː/ n vista f; (mental survey) visión f de conjunto; (opinion) opinión f. **in my** ~ a mi juicio. **in** ~ **of** en vista de. **on** ~ expuesto. **with a** ~ **to** con miras a. ● vt ver; (visit) visitar; (consider) considerar. ~**er** /-ə(r)/ n espectador m; (TV) televidente m & f. ~**finder** /'vjuːfaɪndə(r)/ n visor m. ~**point** /'vjuːpɔɪnt/ n punto m de vista
**vigil** /'vɪdʒɪl/ n vigilia f. ~**ance** n vigilancia f. ~**ant** a vigilante. **keep** ~ velar
**vigo|rous** /'vɪɡərəs/ a vigoroso. ~**ur** /'vɪɡə(r)/ n vigor m
**vile** /vaɪl/ a (base) vil; (bad) horrible; (weather, temper) de perros
**vilif|ication** /vɪlɪfɪ'keɪʃn/ n difamación f. ~**y** /'vɪlɪfaɪ/ vt difamar
**village** /'vɪlɪdʒ/ n aldea f. ~**r** /-ə(r)/ n aldeano m
**villain** /'vɪlən/ n malvado m; (in story etc) malo m. ~**ous** a infame. ~**y** n infamia f
**vim** /vɪm/ n (fam) energía f
**vinaigrette** /vɪnɪ'ɡret/ n. ~ **sauce** n vinagreta f
**vindicat|e** /'vɪndɪkeɪt/ vt vindicar. ~**ion** /-'keɪʃn/ n vindicación f
**vindictive** /vɪn'dɪktɪv/ a vengativo. ~**ness** n carácter m vengativo
**vine** /vaɪn/ n vid f
**vinegar** /'vɪnɪɡə(r)/ n vinagre m. ~**y** a (person) avinagrado
**vineyard** /'vɪnjəd/ n viña f
**vintage** /'vɪntɪdʒ/ n (year) cosecha f. ● a (wine) añejo; (car) de época
**vinyl** /'vaɪnɪl/ n vinilo m
**viola** /vɪ'əʊlə/ n viola f
**violat|e** /'vaɪəleɪt/ vt violar. ~**ion** /-'leɪʃn/ n violación f
**violen|ce** /'vaɪələns/ n violencia f. ~**t** /'vaɪələnt/ a violento. ~**tly** adv violentamente
**violet** /'vaɪələt/ a & n violeta (f)
**violin** /'vaɪəlɪn/ n violín m. ~**ist** n violinista m & f

**VIP** /viːaɪˈpiː/ *abbr* (*very important person*) personaje *m*
**viper** /ˈvaɪpə(r)/ *n* víbora *f*
**virgin** /ˈvɜːdʒɪn/ *a & n* virgen (*f*). ~**al** *a* virginal. ~**ity** /vəˈdʒɪnətɪ/ *n* virginidad *f*
**Virgo** /ˈvɜːgəʊ/ *n* (*astr*) Virgo *f*
**viril|e** /ˈvɪraɪl/ *a* viril. ~**ity** /-ˈrɪlətɪ/ *n* virilidad *f*
**virtual** /ˈvɜːtʃʊəl/ *a* verdadero. **a** ~ **failure** prácticamente un fracaso. ~**ly** *adv* prácticamente
**virtue** /ˈvɜːtʃuː/ *n* virtud *f*. **by** ~ **of, in** ~ **of** en virtud de
**virtuoso** /vɜːtjʊˈəʊzəʊ/ *n* (*pl* -**si** /-ziː/) virtuoso *m*
**virtuous** /ˈvɜːtʃʊəs/ *a* virtuoso
**virulent** /ˈvɪrʊlənt/ *a* virulento
**virus** /ˈvaɪərəs/ *n* (*pl* -**uses**) virus *m*
**visa** /ˈviːzə/ *n* visado *m*, visa *f* (*LAm*)
**vis-a-vis** /viːzaːˈviː/ *adv* frente a frente. ● *prep* respecto a; (*opposite*) en frente de
**viscount** /ˈvaɪkaʊnt/ *n* vizconde *m*. ~**ess** *n* vizcondesa *f*
**viscous** /ˈvɪskəs/ *a* viscoso
**visib|ility** /vɪzɪˈbɪlətɪ/ *n* visibilidad *f*. ~**le** /ˈvɪzɪbl/ *a* visible. ~**ly** *adv* visiblemente
**vision** /ˈvɪʒn/ *n* visión *f*; (*sight*) vista *f*. ~**ary** /ˈvɪʒənərɪ/ *a & n* visionario (*m*)
**visit** /ˈvɪzɪt/ *vt* visitar; hacer una visita a ⟨*person*⟩. ● *vi* hacer visitas. ● *n* visita *f*. ~**or** *n* visitante *m & f*; (*guest*) visita *f*; (*in hotel*) cliente *m & f*
**visor** /ˈvaɪzə(r)/ *n* visera *f*
**vista** /ˈvɪstə/ *n* perspectiva *f*
**visual** /ˈvɪʒʊəl/ *a* visual. ~**ize** /ˈvɪʒʊəlaɪz/ *vt* imaginar(se); (*foresee*) prever. ~**ly** *adv* visualmente
**vital** /ˈvaɪtl/ *a* vital; (*essential*) esencial
**vitality** /vaɪˈtælətɪ/ *n* vitalidad *f*
**vital:** ~**ly** /ˈvaɪtəlɪ/ *adv* extremadamente. ~**s** *npl* órganos *mpl* vitales. ~ **statistics** *npl* (*fam*) medidas *fpl*
**vitamin** /ˈvɪtəmɪn/ *n* vitamina *f*
**vitiate** /ˈvɪʃɪeɪt/ *vt* viciar
**vitreous** /ˈvɪtrɪəs/ *a* vítreo
**vituperat|e** /vɪˈtjuːpəreɪt/ *vt* vituperar. ~**ion** /-ˈreɪʃn/ *n* vituperación *f*
**vivaci|ous** /vɪˈveɪʃəs/ *a* animado, vivo. ~**ously** *adv* animadamente. ~**ty** /-ˈvæsətɪ/ *n* viveza *f*

**vivid** /ˈvɪvɪd/ *a* vivo. ~**ly** *adv* intensamente; (*describe*) gráficamente. ~**ness** *n* viveza *f*
**vivisection** /vɪvɪˈsekʃn/ *n* vivisección *f*
**vixen** /ˈvɪksn/ *n* zorra *f*
**vocabulary** /vəˈkæbjʊlərɪ/ *n* vocabulario *m*
**vocal** /ˈvəʊkl/ *a* vocal; (*fig*) franco. ~**ist** *n* cantante *m & f*
**vocation** /vəʊˈkeɪʃn/ *n* vocación *f*. ~**al** *a* profesional
**vociferate** /vəˈsɪfəreɪt/ *vt/i* vociferar. ~**ous** *a* vociferador
**vogue** /vəʊg/ *n* boga *f*. **in** ~ de moda
**voice** /vɔɪs/ *n* voz *f*. ● *vt* expresar
**void** /vɔɪd/ *a* vacío; (*not valid*) nulo. ~ **of** desprovisto de. ● *n* vacío *m*. ● *vt* anular
**volatile** /ˈvɒlətaɪl/ *a* volátil; ⟨*person*⟩ voluble
**volcan|ic** /vɒlˈkænɪk/ *a* volcánico. ~**o** /vɒlˈkeɪnəʊ/ *n* (*pl* -**oes**) volcán *m*
**volition** /vəˈlɪʃn/ *n*. **of one's own** ~ de su propia voluntad
**volley** /ˈvɒlɪ/ *n* (*pl* -**eys**) (*of blows*) lluvia *f*; (*of gunfire*) descarga *f* cerrada
**volt** /vəʊlt/ *n* voltio *m*. ~**age** *n* voltaje *m*
**voluble** /ˈvɒljʊbl/ *a* locuaz
**volume** /ˈvɒljuːm/ *n* volumen *m*; (*book*) tomo *m*
**voluminous** /vəˈljuːmɪnəs/ *a* voluminoso
**voluntar|ily** /ˈvɒləntərəlɪ/ *adv* voluntariamente. ~**y** /ˈvɒləntərɪ/ *a* voluntario
**volunteer** /vɒlənˈtɪə(r)/ *n* voluntario *m*. ● *vt* ofrecer. ● *vi* ofrecerse voluntariamente; (*mil*) alistarse como voluntario
**voluptuous** /vəˈlʌptjʊəs/ *a* voluptuoso
**vomit** /ˈvɒmɪt/ *vt/i* vomitar. ● *n* vómito *m*
**voracious** /vəˈreɪʃəs/ *a* voraz
**vot|e** /vəʊt/ *n* voto *m*; (*right*) derecho *m* de votar. ● *vi* votar. ~**er** /-ə(r)/ *n* votante *m & f*. ~**ing** *n* votación *f*
**vouch** /vaʊtʃ/ *vi*. ~ **for** garantizar
**voucher** /ˈvaʊtʃə(r)/ *n* vale *m*
**vow** /vaʊ/ *n* voto *m*. ● *vi* jurar
**vowel** /ˈvaʊəl/ *n* vocal *f*
**voyage** /ˈvɔɪɪdʒ/ *n* viaje *m* (en barco)
**vulgar** /ˈvʌlgə(r)/ *a* vulgar. ~**ity** /-ˈgærətɪ/ *n* vulgaridad *f*. ~**ize** *vt* vulgarizar

**vulnerab|ility** /vʌlnərə'bɪlətɪ/ n vulnerabilidad f. **~le** /'vʌlnərəbl/ a vulnerable

**vulture** /'vʌltʃə(r)/ n buitre m

**vying** /'vaɪɪŋ/ see vie

# W

**wad** /wɒd/ n (pad) tapón m; (bundle) lío m; (of notes) fajo m; (of cotton wool etc) bolita f

**wadding** /'wɒdɪŋ/ n relleno m

**waddle** /'wɒdl/ vi contonearse

**wade** /weɪd/ vt vadear. ● vi. **~ through** abrirse paso entre; leer con dificultad ⟨book⟩

**wafer** /'weɪfə(r)/ n barquillo m; (relig) hostia f

**waffle**[1] /'wɒfl/ n (fam) palabrería f. ● vi (fam) divagar

**waffle**[2] /'wɒfl/ n (culin) gofre m

**waft** /wɒft/ vt llevar por el aire. ● vi flotar

**wag** /wæg/ vt (pt wagged) menear. ● vi menearse

**wage** /weɪdʒ/ n. **~s** npl salario m. ● vt. **~ war** hacer la guerra. **~r** /'weɪdʒə(r)/ n apuesta f. ● vt apostar

**waggle** /'wægl/ vt menear. ● vi menearse

**wagon** /'wægən/ n carro m; (rail) vagón m. **be on the ~** (sl) no beber

**waif** /weɪf/ n niño m abandonado

**wail** /weɪl/ vi lamentarse. ● n lamento m

**wainscot** /'weɪnskət/ n revestimiento m, zócalo m

**waist** /weɪst/ n cintura f. **~band** n cinturón m

**waistcoat** /'weɪstkəʊt/ n chaleco m

**waistline** /'weɪstlaɪn/ n cintura f

**wait** /weɪt/ vt/i esperar; (at table) servir. **~ for** esperar. **~ on** servir. ● n espera f. **lie in ~** acechar

**waiter** /'weɪtə(r)/ n camarero m

**wait**: **~ing-list** n lista f de espera. **~ing-room** n sala f de espera

**waitress** /'weɪtrɪs/ n camarera f

**waive** /weɪv/ vt renunciar a

**wake**[1] /weɪk/ vt (pt woke, pp woken) despertar. ● vi despertarse. ● n velatorio m. **~ up** vt despertar. ● vi despertarse

**wake**[2] /weɪk/ n (naut) estela f. **in the ~ of** como resultado de, tras

**waken** /'weɪkən/ vt despertar. ● vi despertarse

**wakeful** /'weɪkfl/ a insomne

**Wales** /weɪlz/ n País m de Gales

**walk** /wɔːk/ vi andar; (not ride) ir a pie; (stroll) pasearse. ~ **out** salir; ⟨workers⟩ declararse en huelga. ~ **out on** abandonar. ● vt andar por ⟨streets⟩; llevar de paseo ⟨dog⟩. ● n paseo m; (gait) modo m de andar; (path) sendero m. ~ **of life** clase f social. **~about** /'wɔːkəbaʊt/ n (of royalty) encuentro m con el público. **~er** /-ə(r)/ n paseante m & f

**walkie-talkie** /wɔːkɪ'tɔːkɪ/ n transmisor-receptor m portátil

**walking** /'wɔːkɪŋ/ n paseo m. **~stick** n bastón m

**Walkman** /'wɔːkmən/ n (P) estereo m personal, Walkman m (P), magnetófono m de bolsillo

**walk**: **~out** n huelga f. **~over** n victoria f fácil

**wall** /wɔːl/ n (interior) pared f; (exterior) muro m; (in garden) tapia f; (of city) muralla f. **go to the ~** fracasar. **up the ~** (fam) loco. ● vt amurallar ⟨city⟩

**wallet** /'wɒlɪt/ n cartera f, billetera f (LAm)

**wallflower** /'wɔːlflaʊə(r)/ n alhelí m

**wallop** /'wɒləp/ vt (pt walloped) (sl) golpear con fuerza. ● n (sl) golpe m fuerte

**wallow** /'wɒləʊ/ vi revolcarse

**wallpaper** /'wɔːlpeɪpə(r)/ n papel m pintado

**walnut** /'wɔːlnʌt/ n nuez f; (tree) nogal m

**walrus** /'wɔːlrəs/ n morsa f

**waltz** /wɔːls/ n vals m. ● vi valsar

**wan** /wɒn/ a pálido

**wand** /wɒnd/ n varita f

**wander** /'wɒndə(r)/ vi vagar; (stroll) pasearse; (digress) divagar; ⟨road, river⟩ serpentear. ● n paseo m. **~er** /-ə(r)/ n vagabundo m. **~lust** /'wɒndəlʌst/ n pasión f por los viajes

**wane** /weɪn/ vi menguar. ● n. **on the ~** disminuyendo

**wangle** /'wæŋgl/ vt (sl) agenciarse

**want** /wɒnt/ vt querer; (need) necesitar; (require) exigir. ● vi. ~ **for** carecer de. ● n necesidad f; (lack) falta f; (desire) deseo m. **~ed** a ⟨criminal⟩ buscado. **~ing** a (lacking) falto de. **be ~ing** carecer de

**wanton** /'wɒntən/ a (licentious) lascivo; (motiveless) sin motivo

**war** /wɔː(r)/ n guerra f. **at ~** en guerra

**warble** /'wɔːbl/ vt cantar trinando.
● vi gorjear. ● n gorjeo m. ~r /-ə(r)/
n curruca f

**ward** /wɔːd/ n (in hospital) sala f; (of
town) barrio m; (child) pupilo m.
● vt. ~ off parar

**warden** /'wɔːdn/ n guarda m

**warder** /'wɔːdə(r)/ n carcelero m

**wardrobe** /'wɔːdrəʊb/ n armario m;
(clothes) vestuario m

**warehouse** /'weəhaʊs/ n almacén m

**wares** /weəz/ npl mercancías fpl

**war**: ~fare /'wɔːfeə(r)/ n guerra f.
~head /'wɔːhed/ n cabeza f
explosiva

**warily** /'weərɪlɪ/ adv cautelosamente

**warlike** /'wɔːlaɪk/ a belicoso

**warm** /wɔːm/ a (-er, -est) caliente;
(hearty) caluroso. **be** ~ ⟨person⟩
tener calor. **it is** ~ hace calor. ● vt.
~ (up) calentar; recalentar ⟨food⟩;
(fig) animar. ● vi. ~ (up) calentarse; (fig) animarse. ~ **to** tomar
simpatía a ⟨person⟩; ir entu-
siasmándose por ⟨idea etc⟩.
~-blooded a de sangre caliente.
~-hearted a simpático. ~ly adv
(heartily) calurosamente

**warmonger** /'wɔːmʌŋgə(r)/ n beli-
cista m & f

**warmth** /wɔːmθ/ n calor m

**warn** /wɔːn/ vt avisar, advertir.
~ing n advertencia f; (notice) aviso
m. ~ off (advise against) aconsejar
en contra de; (forbid) impedir

**warp** /wɔːp/ vt deformar; (fig) pervertir. ● vi deformarse

**warpath** /'wɔːpɑːθ/ n. **be on the** ~
buscar camorra

**warrant** /'wɒrənt/ n autorización f;
(for arrest) orden f. ● vt justificar.
~-officer n suboficial m

**warranty** /'wɒrəntɪ/ n garantía f

**warring** /'wɔːrɪŋ/ a en guerra

**warrior** /'wɒrɪə(r)/ n guerrero m

**warship** /'wɔːʃɪp/ n buque m de
guerra

**wart** /wɔːt/ n verruga f

**wartime** /'wɔːtaɪm/ n tiempo m de
guerra

**wary** /'weərɪ/ a (-ier, -iest) cauteloso

**was** /wəz, wɒz/ see **be**

**wash** /wɒʃ/ vt lavar; (flow over)
bañar. ● vi lavarse. ● n lavado m;
(dirty clothes) ropa f sucia; (wet
clothes) colada f; (of ship) estela f.
**have a** ~ lavarse. ~ **out** vt enjuagar; (fig) cancelar. ~ **up** vi fregar

los platos. ~**able** a lavable. ~-**basin**
n lavabo m. ~**ed-out** a (pale) pálido;
(tired) rendido. ~**er** /'wɒʃə(r)/ n
arandela f; (washing-machine) lavadora f. ~**ing** /'wɒʃɪŋ/ n lavado m;
(dirty clothes) ropa f sucia; (wet
clothes) colada f. ~**ing-machine** n
lavadora f. ~**ing-powder** n jabón m
en polvo. ~**ing-up** n fregado m;
(dirty plates etc) platos mpl para fregar. ~**out** n (sl) desastre m.
~-**room** n (Amer) servicios mpl.
~-**stand** n lavabo m. ~-**tub** n tina f
de lavar

**wasp** /wɒsp/ n avispa f

**wastage** /'weɪstɪdʒ/ n desperdicios
mpl

**waste** /weɪst/ ● a de desecho; ⟨land⟩
yermo. ● n derroche m; (rubbish)
desperdicio m; (of time) pérdida f.
● vt derrochar; (not use) desperdiciar; perder ⟨time⟩. ● vi. ~ **away**
consumirse. ~-**disposal unit** n trituradora f de basuras. ~**ful** a dis-
pendioso; ⟨person⟩ derrochador.
~-**paper basket** n papelera f. ~s npl
tierras fpl baldías

**watch** /wɒtʃ/ vt mirar; (keep an eye
on) vigilar; (take heed) tener cuidado con; ver ⟨TV⟩. ● vi mirar; (keep
an eye on) vigilar. ● n vigilancia f;
(period of duty) guardia f; (time-
piece) reloj m. **on the** ~ alerta. ~
**out** vi tener cuidado. ~-**dog** n perro
m guardián; (fig) guardián m. ~**ful**
a vigilante. ~-**maker**
/'wɒtʃmeɪkə(r)/ n relojero m. ~-**man**
/'wɒtʃmən/ n (pl -**men**) vigilante m.
~-**tower** n atalaya f. ~-**word**
/'wɒtʃwɜːd/ n santo m y seña

**water** /'wɔːtə(r)/ n agua f. **by** ~ (of
travel) por mar. **in hot** ~ (fam) en
un apuro. ● vt regar ⟨plants etc⟩;
(dilute) aguar, diluir. ● vi ⟨eyes⟩ llorar. **make s.o.'s mouth** ~ hacérsele
la boca agua. ~ **down** vt diluir; (fig)
suavizar. ~-**closet** n wáter m. ~-**colour** n acuarela f. ~-**course** /'wɔːtəkɔː
s/ n arroyo m; (artificial) canal m.
~-**cress** /'wɔːtəkres/ n berro m. ~-**fall**
/'wɔːtəfɔːl/ n cascada f. ~-**ice** n sorbete m. ~**ing-can** /'wɔːtərɪŋkæn/ n
regadera f. ~-**lily** n nenúfar m.
~-**line** n línea f de flotación. ~-**logged** /'wɔːtəlɒgd/ a saturado de agua,
empapado. ~ **main** n cañería f principal. ~ **melon** n sandía f. ~-**mill** n
molino m de agua. ~ **polo** n polo m

acuático. **~power** n energía f hidráulica. **~proof** /'wɔːtəpruːf/ a & n impermeable (m); ⟨watch⟩ sumergible. **~shed** /'wɔːtəʃed/ n punto m decisivo. **~skiing** n esquí m acuático. **~softener** n ablandador m de agua. **~tight** /'wɔːtətaɪt/ a hermético, estanco; (fig) irrecusable. **~way** n canal m navegable. **~wheel** n rueda f hidráulica. **~wings** npl flotadores mpl. **~works** /'wɔːtəwɜːks/ n sistema m de abastecimiento de agua. **~y** /'wɔːtərɪ/ a acuoso; ⟨colour⟩ pálido; ⟨eyes⟩ lloroso

**watt** /wɒt/ n vatio m

**wave** /weɪv/ n onda f; (of hand) señal f; (fig) oleada f. ● vt agitar; ondular ⟨hair⟩. ● vi (signal) hacer señales con la mano; ⟨flag⟩ flotar. **~band** /'weɪvbænd/ n banda f de ondas. **~length** /'weɪvleŋθ/ n longitud f de onda

**waver** /'weɪvə(r)/ vi vacilar

**wavy** /'weɪvɪ/ a (-ier, -iest) ondulado

**wax**[1] /wæks/ n cera f. ● vt encerar

**wax**[2] /wæks/ vi ⟨moon⟩ crecer

**wax: ~en** a céreo. **~work** /'wækswɜːk/ n figura f de cera. **~y** a céreo

**way** /weɪ/ n camino m; (distance) distancia f; (manner) manera f, modo m; (direction) dirección f; (means) medio m; (habit) costumbre f. **be in the ~** estorbar. **by the ~** a propósito. **by ~ of** a título de, por. **either ~** de cualquier modo. **in a ~** en cierta manera. **in some ~s** en ciertos modos. **lead the ~** mostrar el camino. **make ~** dejar paso a. **on the ~** en camino. **out of the ~** remoto; (extraordinary) fuera de lo común. **that ~** por allí. **this ~** por aquí. **under ~** en curso. **~bill** n hoja f de ruta. **~farer** /'weɪfeərə(r)/ n viajero m. **~ in** n entrada f

**waylay** /weɪ'leɪ/ vt (pt -laid) acechar; (detain) detener

**way: ~ out** n salida f. **~out** a ultramoderno, original. **~s** npl costumbres fpl. **~side** /'weɪsaɪd/ n borde m del camino

**wayward** /'weɪwəd/ a caprichoso

**we** /wiː/ pron nosotros, nosotras

**weak** /wiːk/ a (-er, -est) débil; ⟨liquid⟩ aguado, acuoso; (fig) flojo. **~en** vt debilitar. **~kneed** a irresoluto. **~ling** /'wiːklɪŋ/ n persona f débil. **~ly** adv débilmente. ● a enfermizo. **~ness** n debilidad f

**weal** /wiːl/ n verdugón m

**wealth** /welθ/ n riqueza f. **~y** a (-ier, -iest) rico

**wean** /wiːn/ vt destetar

**weapon** /'wepən/ n arma f

**wear** /weə(r)/ vt (pt wore, pp worn) llevar; (put on) ponerse; tener ⟨expression etc⟩; (damage) desgastar. ● vi desgastarse; (last) durar. ● n uso m; (damage) desgaste m; (clothing) ropa f. **~ down** vt desgastar; agotar ⟨opposition etc⟩. **~ off** vi desaparecer. **~ on** vi ⟨time⟩ pasar. **~ out** vt desgastar; (tire) agotar. **~able** a que se puede llevar. **~ and tear** desgaste m

**wear|ily** /'wɪərɪlɪ/ adv cansadamente. **~iness** n cansancio m. **~isome** /'wɪərɪsəm/ a cansado. **~y** /'wɪərɪ/ a (-ier, -iest) cansado. ● vt cansar. ● vi cansarse. **~y of** cansarse de

**weasel** /'wiːzl/ n comadreja f

**weather** /'weðə(r)/ n tiempo m. **under the ~** (fam) indispuesto. ● a meteorológico. ● vt curar ⟨wood⟩; (survive) superar. **~beaten** a curtido. **~cock** /'weðəkɒk/ n, **~vane** n veleta f

**weave** /wiːv/ vt (pt wove, pp woven) tejer; entretejer ⟨story etc⟩; entrelazar ⟨flowers etc⟩. **~ one's way** abrirse paso. ● n tejido m. **~r** /-ə(r)/ n tejedor m

**web** /web/ n tela f; (of spider) telaraña f; (on foot) membrana f. **~bing** n cincha f

**wed** /wed/ vt (pt wedded) casarse con; ⟨priest etc⟩ casar. ● vi casarse. **~ded to** (fig) unido a

**wedding** /'wedɪŋ/ n boda f. **~cake** n pastel m de boda. **~ring** n anillo m de boda

**wedge** /wedʒ/ n cuña f; (space filler) calce m. ● vt acuñar; (push) apretar

**wedlock** /'wedlɒk/ n matrimonio m

**Wednesday** /'wenzdeɪ/ n miércoles m

**wee** /wiː/ a (fam) pequeñito

**weed** /wiːd/ n mala hierba f. ● vt desherbar. **~killer** n herbicida m. **~ out** vt eliminar. **~y** a ⟨person⟩ débil

**week** /wiːk/ n semana f. **~day** /'wiːkdeɪ/ n día m laborable. **~end** n fin m de semana. **~ly** /'wiːklɪ/ a semanal. ● n semanario m. ● adv semanalmente

**weep** /wiːp/ vi (pt wept) llorar. **~ing willow** n sauce m llorón

**weevil** /'wiːvɪl/ n gorgojo m

**weigh** /weɪ/ vt/i pesar. **~ anchor** levar anclas. **~ down** vt (fig) oprimir. **~ up** vt pesar; (fig) considerar

**weight** /weɪt/ n peso m. **~less** a ingrávido. **~lessness** n ingravidez f. **~lifting** n halterofilia f, levantamiento m de pesos. **~y** a (**-ier, -iest**) pesado; (influential) influyente

**weir** /wɪə(r)/ n presa f

**weird** /wɪəd/ a (**-er, -est**) misterioso; (bizarre) extraño

**welcome** /'welkəm/ a bienvenido. **~ to do** libre de hacer. **you're ~e!** (after thank you) ¡de nada! ● n bienvenida f; (reception) acogida f. ● vt dar la bienvenida a; (appreciate) alegrarse de

**welcoming** /'welkəmɪŋ/ a acogedor

**weld** /weld/ vt soldar. ● n soldadura f. **~er** n soldador m

**welfare** /'welfeə(r)/ n bienestar m; (aid) asistencia f social. **W~ State** n estado m benefactor. **~ work** n asistencia f social

**well¹** /wel/ adv (**better, best**) bien. **~ done!** ¡bravo! **as ~** también. **as ~ as** tanto... como. **be ~** estar bien. **do ~** (succeed) tener éxito. **very ~** muy bien. ● a bien. ● int bueno; (surprise) ¡vaya! **~ I never!** ¡no me digas!

**well²** /wel/ n pozo m; (of staircase) caja f

**well: ~-appointed** a bien equipado. **~-behaved** a bien educado. **~-being** n bienestar m. **~-bred** a bien educado. **~-disposed** a benévolo. **~-groomed** a bien aseado. **~-heeled** a (fam) rico

**wellington** /'welɪŋtən/ n bota f de agua

**well: ~-knit** a robusto. **~-known** a conocido. **~-meaning** a, **~ meant** a bienintencionado. **~ off** a acomodado. **~-read** a culto. **~-spoken** a bienhablado. **~-to-do** a rico. **~-wisher** n bienqueriente m & f

**Welsh** /welʃ/ a & n galés (m). **~ rabbit** n pan m tostado con queso

**welsh** /welʃ/ vi. **~ on** no cumplir con

**wench** /wentʃ/ n (old use) muchacha f

**wend** /wend/ vt. **~ one's way** encaminarse

**went** /went/ see **go**

**wept** /wept/ see **weep**

**were** /wɜː(r), wə(r)/ see **be**

**west** /west/ n oeste m. **the ~** el Occidente m. ● a del oeste. ● adv hacia el oeste, al oeste. **go ~** (sl) morir. **W~ Germany** n Alemania f Occidental. **~erly** a del oeste. **~ern** a occidental. ● n (film) película f del Oeste. **~erner** /-ənə(r)/ n occidental m & f. **W~ Indian** a & n antillano (m). **W~ Indies** npl Antillas fpl. **~ward** a, **~ward(s)** adv hacia el oeste

**wet** /wet/ a (**wetter, wettest**) mojado; (rainy) lluvioso, de lluvia; (person, sl) soso. **~ paint** recién pintado. **get ~** mojarse. ● vt (pt **wetted**) mojar, humedecer. **~ blanket** n aguafiestas m & f invar. **~ suit** n traje m de buzo

**whack** /wæk/ vt (fam) golpear. ● n (fam) golpe m. **~ed** /wækt/ a (fam) agotado. **~ing** a (huge, sl) enorme. ● n paliza f

**whale** /weɪl/ n ballena f. **a ~ of a** (fam) maravilloso, enorme

**wham** /wæm/ int ¡zas!

**wharf** /wɔːf/ n (pl **wharves** or **wharfs**) muelle m

**what** /wɒt/ a el que, la que, lo que, los que, las que; (in questions & exclamations) qué. ● pron lo que; (interrogative) qué. **~ about going?** ¿si fuésemos? **~ about me?** ¿y yo? **~ for?** ¿para qué? **~ if?** ¿y si? **~ is it?** ¿qué es? **~ you need** lo que te haga falta. ● int ¡cómo! **~ a fool!** ¡qué tonto!

**whatever** /wɒt'evə(r)/ a cualquiera. ● pron (todo) lo que, cualquier cosa que

**whatnot** /'wɒtnɒt/ n chisme m

**whatsoever** /wɒtsəʊ'evə(r)/ a & pron = **whatever**

**wheat** /wiːt/ n trigo m. **~en** a de trigo

**wheedle** /'wiːdl/ vt engatusar

**wheel** /wiːl/ n rueda f. **at the ~** al volante. **steering-~** n volante m. ● vt empujar ‹bicycle etc›. ● vi girar. **~ round** girar. **~barrow** /'wiːlbærəʊ/ n carretilla f. **~chair** /'wiːltʃeə(r)/ n silla f de ruedas

**wheeze** /wiːz/ vi resollar. ● n resuello m

**when** /wen/ adv cuándo. ● conj cuando

**whence** /wens/ adv de dónde

**whenever** /wen'evə(r)/ adv en cualquier momento; (every time that) cada vez que

**where** /weə(r)/ adv & conj donde;
(interrogative) dónde. ~ are you
going? ¿adónde vas? ~ are you
from? ¿de dónde eres?

**whereabouts** /'weərəbaʊts/ adv
dónde. ● n paradero m

**whereas** /weər'æz/ conj por cuanto;
(in contrast) mientras (que)

**whereby** /weə'baɪ/ adv por lo cual

**whereupon** /weərə'pɒn/ adv
después de lo cual

**wherever** /weər'evə(r)/ adv (in
whatever place) dónde (diablos).
● conj dondequiera que

**whet** /wet/ vt (pt **whetted**) afilar;
(fig) aguzar

**whether** /'weðə(r)/ conj si. ~ you
like it or not que te guste o no te
guste. **I don't know** ~ **she will like it**
no sé si le gustará

**which** /wɪtʃ/ a (in questions) qué. ~
one cuál. ~ one of you cuál de
vosotros. ● pron (in questions) cuál;
(relative) que; (object) el cual, la
cual, lo cual, los cuales, las cuales

**whichever** /wɪtʃ'evə(r)/ a cualquier.
● pron cualquiera que, el que, la
que

**whiff** /wɪf/ n soplo m; (of smoke)
bocanada f; (smell) olorcillo m

**while** /waɪl/ n rato m. ● conj mientras; (although) aunque. ● vt. ~
away pasar ‹time›

**whilst** /waɪlst/ conj = **while**

**whim** /wɪm/ n capricho m

**whimper** /'wɪmpə(r)/ vi lloriquear.
● n lloriqueo m

**whimsical** /'wɪmzɪkl/ a caprichoso;
(odd) extraño

**whine** /waɪn/ vi gimotear. ● n gimo-
teo m

**whip** /wɪp/ n látigo m; (pol) oficial m
disciplinario. ● vt (pt **whipped**) azotar; (culin) batir; (seize) agarrar.
~cord n tralla f. ~ped cream n
nata f batida. ~ping-boy
/'wɪpɪŋbɔɪ/ n cabeza f de turco.
~round n colecta f. ~ up (incite)
estimular

**whirl** /wɜːl/ vt hacer girar rápidamente. ● vi girar rápidamente;
(swirl) arremolinarse. ● n giro m;
(swirl) remolino m. ~pool /'wɜːlpuː
l/ n remolino m. ~wind /'wɜːlwɪnd/
n torbellino m

**whirr** /wɜː(r)/ n zumbido m. ● vi
zumbar

**whisk** /wɪsk/ vt (culin) batir. ● n
(culin) batidor m. ~ away llevarse

**whisker** /'wɪskə(r)/ n pelo m. ~s npl
(of man) patillas fpl; (of cat etc)
bigotes mpl

**whisky** /'wɪskɪ/ n güisqui m

**whisper** /'wɪspə(r)/ vt decir en voz
baja. ● vi cuchichear; ‹leaves etc›
susurrar. ● n cuchicheo m; (of
leaves) susurro m; (rumour) rumor
m

**whistle** /'wɪsl/ n silbido m; (instrument) silbato m. ● vi silbar. ~-stop
n (pol) breve parada f (en gira
electoral)

**white** /waɪt/ a (-er, -est) blanco. go
~ ponerse pálido. ● n blanco; (of
egg) clara f. ~bait /'waɪtbeɪt/ n (pl
~bait) chanquetes mpl. ~ coffee n
café m con leche. ~collar worker n
empleado m de oficina. ~ elephant
n objeto m inútil y costoso

**Whitehall** /'waɪthɔːl/ n el gobierno m
británico

**white**: ~ horses n cabrillas fpl.
~hot a ‹metal› candente. ~ lie n
mentirijilla f. ~n vt/i blanquear.
~ness n blancura f. W~ Paper n
libro m blanco. ~wash /'waɪtwɒʃ/ n
jalbegue m; (fig) encubrimiento m.
● vt enjalbegar; (fig) encubrir

**whiting** /'waɪtɪŋ/ n (pl **whiting**)
(fish) pescadilla f

**whitlow** /'wɪtləʊ/ n panadizo m

**Whitsun** /'wɪtsn/ n Pentecostés m

**whittle** /'wɪtl/ vt. ~ (down) tallar;
(fig) reducir

**whiz** /wɪz/ vi (pt **whizzed**) silbar;
(rush) ir a gran velocidad. ~ past
pasar como un rayo. ~kid n (fam)
joven m prometedor, promesa f

**who** /huː/ pron que, quien; (interrogative) quién; (particular person)
el que, la que, los que, las que

**whodunit** /huː'dʌnɪt/ n (fam) novela
f policíaca

**whoever** /huː'evə(r)/ pron quien-
quera que; (interrogative) quién
(diablos)

**whole** /həʊl/ a entero; (not broken)
intacto. ● n todo m, conjunto m;
(total) total m. as a ~ en conjunto.
on the ~ por regla general. ~heart-
ed a sincero. ~meal a integral

**wholesale** /'həʊlseɪl/ n venta f al por
mayor. ● a & adv al por mayor. ~r
/-ə(r)/ n comerciante m & f al por
mayor

**wholesome** /'həʊlsəm/ a saludable

**wholly** /'həʊlɪ/ adv completamente

**whom** /hu:m/ *pron* que, a quien; (*interrogative*) a quién

**whooping cough** /'hu:pɪŋkɒf/ *n* tos *f* ferina

**whore** /hɔ:(r)/ *n* puta *f*

**whose** /hu:z/ *pron* de quién. ● *a* de quién; (*relative*) cuyo

**why** /waɪ/ *adv* por qué. ● *int* ¡toma!

**wick** /wɪk/ *n* mecha *f*

**wicked** /'wɪkɪd/ *a* malo; (*mischievous*) travieso; (*very bad, fam*) malísimo. **~ness** *n* maldad *f*

**wicker** /'wɪkə(r)/ *n* mimbre *m & f.* ● *a* de mimbre. **~work** *n* artículos *mpl* de mimbre

**wicket** /'wɪkɪt/ *n* (*cricket*) rastrillo *m*

**wide** /waɪd/ *a* (**-er, -est**) ancho; (*fully opened*) de par en par; (*far from target*) lejano; ⟨*knowledge etc*⟩ amplio. ● *adv* lejos. **far and ~** por todas partes. **~ awake** *a* completamente despierto; (*fig*) despabilado. **~ly** *adv* extensamente; (*believed*) generalmente; (*different*) muy. **~n** *vt* ensanchar

**widespread** /'waɪdspred/ *a* extendido; (*fig*) difundido

**widow** /'wɪdəʊ/ *n* viuda *f.* **~ed** *a* viudo. **~er** *n* viudo *m.* **~hood** *n* viudez *f*

**width** /wɪdθ/ *n* anchura *f.* **in ~** de ancho

**wield** /wi:ld/ *vt* manejar; ejercer (*power*)

**wife** /waɪf/ *n* (*pl* **wives**) mujer *f,* esposa *f*

**wig** /wɪg/ *n* peluca *f*

**wiggle** /'wɪgl/ *vt* menear. ● *vi* menearse

**wild** /waɪld/ *a* (**-er, -est**) salvaje; (*enraged*) furioso; ⟨*idea*⟩ extravagante; (*with joy*) loco; (*random*) al azar. ● *adv* en estado salvaje. **run ~** crecer en estado salvaje. **~s** *npl* regiones *fpl* salvajes

**wildcat** /'waɪldkæt/ *a.* **~ strike** *n* huelga *f* salvaje

**wilderness** /'wɪldənɪs/ *n* desierto *m*

**wild**: **~fire** /'waɪldfaɪ(r)/ *n.* **spread like ~fire** correr como un reguero de pólvora. **~goose chase** *n* empresa *f* inútil. **~life** /'waɪldlaɪf/ *n* fauna *f.* **~ly** *adv* violentamente; (*fig*) locamente

**wilful** /'wɪlfʊl/ *a* intencionado; (*self-willed*) terco. **~ly** *adv* intencionadamente; (*obstinately*) obstinadamente

**will¹** /wɪl/ *v aux.* **~ you have some wine?** ¿quieres vino? **he ~ be** será. **you ~ be back soon, won't you?** volverás pronto, ¿no?

**will²** /wɪl/ *n* voluntad *f;* (*document*) testamento *m*

**willing** /'wɪlɪŋ/ *a* complaciente. **~ to** dispuesto a. **~ly** *adv* de buena gana. **~ness** *n* buena voluntad *f*

**willow** /'wɪləʊ/ *n* sauce *m*

**will-power** /'wɪlpaʊə(r)/ *n* fuerza *f* de voluntad

**willy-nilly** /wɪlɪ'nɪlɪ/ *adv* quieras que no

**wilt** /wɪlt/ *vi* marchitarse

**wily** /'waɪlɪ/ *a* (**-ier, -iest**) astuto

**win** /wɪn/ *vt* (*pt* **won**, *pres p* **winning**) ganar; (*achieve, obtain*) conseguir. ● *vi* ganar. ● *n* victoria *f.* **~ back** *vt* reconquistar. **~ over** *vt* convencer

**wince** /wɪns/ *vi* hacer una mueca de dolor. **without wincing** sin pestañear. ● *n* mueca *f* de dolor

**winch** /wɪntʃ/ *n* cabrestante *m.* ● *vt* levantar con el cabrestante

**wind¹** /wɪnd/ *n* viento *m;* (*in stomach*) flatulencia *f.* **get the ~ up** (*sl*) asustarse. **get ~ of** enterarse de. **in the ~** en el aire. ● *vt* dejar sin aliento

**wind²** /waɪnd/ *vt* (*pt* **wound**) (*wrap around*) enrollar; dar cuerda a ⟨*clock etc*⟩. ● *vi* ⟨*road etc*⟩ serpentear. **~ up** *vt* dar cuerda a ⟨*watch, clock*⟩; (*provoke*) agitar, poner nervioso; (*fig*) terminar, concluir

**wind** /wɪnd/: **~bag** *n* charlatán *m.* **~cheater** *n* cazadora *f*

**winder** /'waɪndə(r)/ *n* devanador *m;* (*of clock, watch*) llave *f*

**windfall** /'wɪndfɔ:l/ *n* fruta *f* caída; (*fig*) suerte *f* inesperada

**winding** /'waɪndɪŋ/ *a* tortuoso

**wind instrument** /'wɪndɪnstrəmənt/ *n* instrumento *m* de viento

**windmill** /'wɪndmɪl/ *n* molino *m* (de viento)

**window** /'wɪndəʊ/ *n* ventana *f;* (*in shop*) escaparate *m;* (*of vehicle, booking-office*) ventanilla *f.* **~box** *n* jardinera *f.* **~dresser** *n* escaparatista *m & f.* **~shop** *vi* mirar los escaparates

**windpipe** /'wɪndpaɪp/ *n* tráquea *f*

**windscreen** /'wɪndskri:n/ *n,* **windshield** *n* (*Amer*) parabrisas *m invar.* **~ wiper** *n* limpiaparabrisas *m invar*

**wind** /wɪnd/: **~swept** a barrido por el viento. **~y** a (**-ier, -iest**) ventoso, de mucho viento. **it is ~y** hace viento

**wine** /waɪn/ n vino m. **~cellar** n bodega f. **~glass** n copa f. **~grower** n vinicultor m. **~growing** n vinicultura f. • a vinícola. **~ list** n lista f de vinos. **~tasting** n cata f de vinos

**wing** /wɪŋ/ n ala f; (auto) aleta f. **under one's ~** bajo la protección de uno. **~ed** a alado. **~er** /-ə(r)/ n (sport) ala m & f. **~s** npl (in theatre) bastidores mpl

**wink** /wɪŋk/ vi guiñar el ojo; ⟨light etc⟩ centellear. • n guiño m. **not to sleep a ~** no pegar ojo

**winkle** /'wɪŋkl/ n bígaro m

**win:** **~ner** /-ə(r)/ n ganador m. **~ning-post** n poste m de llegada. **~ning smile** n sonrisa f encantadora. **~nings** npl ganancias fpl

**winsome** /'wɪnsəm/ a atractivo

**wint|er** /'wɪntə(r)/ n invierno m. • vi invernar. **~ry** a invernal

**wipe** /waɪp/ vt limpiar; (dry) secar. • n limpión m. **give sth a ~** limpiar algo. **~ out** (cancel) cancelar; (destroy) destruir; (obliterate) borrar. **~ up** limpiar; (dry) secar

**wire** /'waɪə(r)/ n alambre m; (elec) cable m; (telegram, fam) telegrama m

**wireless** /'waɪəlɪs/ n radio f

**wire** netting /waɪə'netɪŋ/ n alambrera f, tela f metálica

**wiring** n instalación f eléctrica

**wiry** /'waɪərɪ/ a (**-ier, -iest**) ⟨person⟩ delgado

**wisdom** /'wɪzdəm/ n sabiduría f. **~ tooth** n muela f del juicio

**wise** /waɪz/ a (**-er, -est**) sabio; (sensible) prudente. **~crack** /'waɪzkræk/ n (fam) salida f. **~ly** adv sabiamente; (sensibly) prudentemente

**wish** /wɪʃ/ n deseo m; (greeting) saludo m. **with best ~es** (in letters) un fuerte abrazo. • vt desear. **~ on** (fam) encajar a. **~ s.o. well** desear buena suerte a uno. **~bone** n espoleta f (de las aves). **~ful** a deseoso. **~ful thinking** n ilusiones fpl

**wishy-washy** /'wɪʃɪwɒʃɪ/ a soso; ⟨person⟩ sin convicciones, falto de entereza

**wisp** /wɪsp/ n manojito m; (of smoke) voluta f, (of hair) mechón m

**wisteria** /wɪs'tɪərɪə/ n glicina f

**wistful** /'wɪstfl/ a melancólico

**wit** /wɪt/ n gracia f; (person) persona f chistosa; (intelligence) ingenio m. **be at one's ~s' end** no saber qué hacer. **live by one's ~s** vivir de expedientes, vivir del cuento

**witch** /wɪtʃ/ n bruja f. **~craft** n brujería f. **~doctor** n hechicero m

**with** /wɪð/ prep con; (cause, having) de. **be ~ it** (fam) estar al día, estar al tanto. **the man ~ the beard** el hombre de la barba

**withdraw** /wɪð'drɔː/ vt (pt **withdrew**, pp **withdrawn**) retirar. • vi apartarse. **~al** n retirada f. **~n** a ⟨person⟩ introvertido

**wither** /'wɪðə(r)/ vi marchitarse. • vt (fig) fulminar

**withhold** /wɪð'həʊld/ vt (pt **withheld**) retener; (conceal) ocultar (from a)

**within** /wɪð'ɪn/ prep dentro de. • adv dentro. **~ sight** a la vista

**without** /wɪð'aʊt/ prep sin

**withstand** /wɪð'stænd/ vt (pt **~stood**) resistir a

**witness** /'wɪtnɪs/ n testigo m; (proof) testimonio m. • vt presenciar; firmar como testigo ⟨document⟩. **~box** n tribuna f de los testigos

**witticism** /'wɪtɪsɪzəm/ n ocurrencia f

**wittingly** /'wɪtɪŋlɪ/ adv a sabiendas

**witty** /'wɪtɪ/ a (**-ier, -iest**) gracioso

**wives** /waɪvz/ see **wife**

**wizard** /'wɪzəd/ n hechicero m. **~ry** n hechicería f

**wizened** /'wɪznd/ a arrugado

**wobb|le** /'wɒbl/ vi tambalearse; ⟨voice, jelly, hand⟩ temblar; ⟨chair etc⟩ balancearse. **~y** a ⟨chair etc⟩ cojo

**woe** /wəʊ/ n aflicción f. **~ful** a triste. **~begone** /'wəʊbɪɡɒn/ a desconsolado

**woke, woken** /wəʊk, 'wəʊkən/ see **wake**[1]

**wolf** /wʊlf/ n (pl **wolves**) lobo m. **cry ~** gritar al lobo. • vt zamparse. **~whistle** n silbido m de admiración

**woman** /'wʊmən/ n (pl **women**) mujer f. **single ~** soltera f. **~ize** /'wʊmənaɪz/ vi ser mujeriego. **~ly** a femenino

**womb** /wuːm/ n matriz f

**women** /'wɪmɪn/ npl see **woman**. **~folk** /'wɪmɪnfəʊk/ npl mujeres fpl.

~'s **lib** n movimiento m de liberación de la mujer

**won** /wʌn/ see **win**

**wonder** /'wʌndə(r)/ n maravilla f; (*bewilderment*) asombro m. **no** ~ no es de extrañarse (**that** que). ● vi admirarse; (*reflect*) preguntarse

**wonderful** /'wʌndəfl/ a maravilloso. ~**ly** adv maravillosamente

**won't** /wəʊnt/ = **will not**

**woo** /wu:/ vt cortejar

**wood** /wʊd/ n madera f; (*for burning*) leña f; (*area*) bosque m; (*in bowls*) bola f. **out of the** ~ (*fig*) fuera de peligro. ~**cutter** /'wʊdkʌtə(r)/ n leñador m. ~**ed** a poblado de árboles, boscoso. ~**en** a de madera. ~**land** n bosque m

**woodlouse** /'wʊdlaʊs/ n (*pl* -**lice**) cochinilla f

**woodpecker** /'wʊdpekə(r)/ n pájaro m carpintero

**woodwind** /'wʊdwɪnd/ n instrumentos mpl de viento de madera

**woodwork** /'wʊdwɜ:k/ n carpintería f; (*in room etc*) maderaje m

**woodworm** /'wʊdwɜ:m/ n carcoma f

**woody** /'wʊdɪ/ a leñoso

**wool** /wʊl/ n lana f. **pull the** ~ **over s.o.'s eyes** engañar a uno. ~**len** a de lana. ~**lens** npl ropa f de lana. ~**ly** a (-**ier**, -**iest**) de lana; (*fig*) confuso. ● n jersey m

**word** /wɜ:d/ n palabra f; (*news*) noticia f. **by** ~ **of mouth** de palabra. **have** ~**s with** reñir con. **in** ~ en una palabra. **in other** ~**s** es decir. ● vt expresar. ~**ing** n expresión f, términos mpl. ~**perfect** a. **be** ~**perfect** saber de memoria. ~ **processor** n procesador m de textos. ~**y** a prolijo

**wore** /wɔ:(r)/ see **wear**

**work** /wɜ:k/ n trabajo m; (*arts*) obra f. ● vt hacer trabajar; manejar ‹*machine*›. ● vi trabajar; ‹*machine*› funcionar; ‹*student*› estudiar; ‹*drug etc*› tener efecto; (*be successful*) tener éxito. ~ **in** introducir(se). ~ **off** desahogar. ~ **out** vt resolver; (*calculate*) calcular; elaborar ‹*plan*›. ● vi (*succeed*) salir bien; (*sport*) entrenarse. ~ **up** vt desarrollar. ● vi excitarse. ~**able** /'wɜ:kəbl/ a (*project*) factible. ~**aholic** /wɜ:kə'hɒlɪk/ n trabajador m obsesivo. ~**ed up** a agitado. ~**er** /'wɜ:-

kə(r)/ n trabajador m; (*manual*) obrero m

**workhouse** /'wɜ:khaʊs/ n asilo m de pobres

**work**: ~**ing** /'wɜ:kɪŋ/ a ‹*day*› laborable; ‹*clothes etc*› de trabajo. ● n (*mec*) funcionamiento m. **in** ~**ing order** en estado de funcionamiento. ~**ing class** n clase f obrera. ~**ing-class** a de la clase obrera. ~**man** /'wɜ:kmən/ n (*pl* -**men**) obrero m. ~**manlike** /'wɜ:kmənlaɪk/ a concienzudo. ~**manship** n destreza f. ~**s** npl (*building*) fábrica f; (*mec*) mecanismo m. ~**shop** /'wɜ:kʃɒp/ n taller m. ~**to-rule** n huelga f de celo

**world** /wɜ:ld/ n mundo m. **a** ~ **of** enorme. **out of this** ~ maravilloso. ● a mundial. ~**ly** a mundano. ~**wide** a universal

**worm** /wɜ:m/ n lombriz f; (*grub*) gusano m. ● vi. ~ **one's way** insinuarse. ~**eaten** a carcomido

**worn** /wɔ:n/ see **wear**. ● a gastado. ~**out** a gastado; ‹*person*› rendido

**worr|ied** /'wʌrɪd/ a preocupado. ~**ier** /-ə(r)/ n aprensivo m. ~**y** /'wʌrɪ/ vt preocupar; (*annoy*) molestar. ● vi preocuparse. ● n preocupación f. ~**ying** a inquietante

**worse** /wɜ:s/ a peor. ● adv peor; (*more*) más. ● n lo peor. ~**n** vt/i empeorar

**worship** /'wɜ:ʃɪp/ n culto m; (*title*) señor, su señoría. ● vt (*pt* **worshipped**) adorar

**worst** /wɜ:st/ a (el) peor. ● adv peor. ● n lo peor. **get the** ~ **of it** llevar la peor parte

**worsted** /'wʊstɪd/ n estambre m

**worth** /wɜ:θ/ n valor m. ● a. **be** ~ valer. **it is** ~ **trying** vale la pena probarlo. **it was** ~ **my while** (me) valió la pena. ~**less** a sin valor. ~**while** /'wɜ:θwaɪl/ a que vale la pena

**worthy** /'wɜ:ðɪ/ a meritorio; (*respectable*) respetable; (*laudable*) loable

**would** /wʊd/ v aux. ~ **you come here please?** ¿quieres venir aquí? ~ **you go?** ¿irías tú? **he** ~ **come if he could** vendría si pudiese. **I** ~ **come every day** (*used to*) venía todos los días. **I** ~ **do it** lo haría yo. ~**be** a supuesto

**wound**[1] /wu:nd/ n herida f. ● vt herir

**wound**[2] /waʊnd/ see **wind**[2]

**wove, woven** /wəʊv, 'wəʊvn/ *see* **weave**

**wow** /waʊ/ *int* ¡caramba!

**wrangle** /'ræŋgl/ *vi* reñir. ● *n* riña *f*

**wrap** /ræp/ *vt* (*pt* **wrapped**) envolver. **be ~ped up in** (*fig*) estar absorto en. ● *n* bata *f*; (*shawl*) chal *m*. **~per** /-ə(r)/ *n*, **~ping** *n* envoltura *f*

**wrath** /rɒθ/ *n* ira *f*. **~ful** *a* iracundo

**wreath** /ri:θ/ *n* (*pl* **-ths** /-ðz/) guirnalda *f*; (*for funeral*) corona *f*

**wreck** /rek/ *n* ruina *f*; (*sinking*) naufragio *m*; (*remains of ship*) buque *m* naufragado. **be a nervous ~** tener los nervios destrozados. ● *vt* hacer naufragar; (*fig*) arruinar. **~age** *n* restos *mpl*; (*of building*) escombros *mpl*

**wren** /ren/ *n* troglodito *m*

**wrench** /rentʃ/ *vt* arrancar; (*twist*) torcer. ● *n* arranque *m*; (*tool*) llave *f* inglesa

**wrest** /rest/ *vt* arrancar (**from** a)

**wrestl|e** /'resl/ *vi* luchar. **~er** /-ə(r)/ *n* luchador *m*. **~ing** *n* lucha *f*

**wretch** /retʃ/ *n* desgraciado *m*; (*rascal*) tunante *m & f*. **~ed** *a* miserable; (*weather*) horrible, de perros; (*dog etc*) maldito

**wriggle** /'rɪgl/ *vi* culebrear. **~ out of** escaparse de. **~ through** deslizarse por. ● *n* serpenteo *m*

**wring** /rɪŋ/ *vt* (*pt* **wrung**) retorcer. **~ out of** (*obtain from*) arrancar. **~ing wet** empapado

**wrinkle** /'rɪŋkl/ *n* arruga *f*. ● *vt* arrugar. ● *vi* arrugarse

**wrist** /rɪst/ *n* muñeca *f*. **~watch** *n* reloj *m* de pulsera

**writ** /rɪt/ *n* decreto *m* judicial

**write** /raɪt/ *vt*/*i* (*pt* **wrote**, *pp* **written**, *pres p* **writing**) escribir. **~ down** *vt* anotar. **~ off** *vt* cancelar; (*fig*) dar por perdido. **~ up** *vt* hacer un reportaje de; (*keep up to date*) poner al día. **~off** *n* pérdida *f* total. **~r** /-ə(r)/ *n* escritor *m*; (*author*) autor *m*. **~up** *n* reportaje *m*; (*review*) crítica *f*

**writhe** /raɪð/ *vi* retorcerse

**writing** /'raɪtɪŋ/ *n* escribir *m*; (*handwriting*) letra *f*. **in ~** por escrito. **~s** *npl* obras *fpl*. **~paper** *n* papel *m* de escribir

**written** /'rɪtn/ *see* **write**

**wrong** /rɒŋ/ *a* incorrecto; (*not just*) injusto; (*mistaken*) equivocado. **be ~** no tener razón; (*be mistaken*)

**equivocarse**. ● *adv* mal. **go ~** equivocarse; (*plan*) salir mal; (*car etc*) estropearse. ● *n* injusticia *f*; (*evil*) mal *m*. **in the ~** equivocado. ● *vt* ser injusto con. **~ful** *a* injusto. **~ly** *adv* mal; (*unfairly*) injustamente

**wrote** /rəʊt/ *see* **write**

**wrought** /rɔ:t/ *a*. **~ iron** *n* hierro *m* forjado

**wrung** /rʌŋ/ *see* **wring**

**wry** /raɪ/ *a* (**wryer, wryest**) torcido; (*smile*) forzado. **~ face** *n* mueca *f*

# X

**xenophobia** /zenə'fəʊbɪə/ *n* xenofobia *f*

**Xerox** /'zɪərɒks/ *n* (*P*) fotocopiadora *f*. **xerox** *n* fotocopia *f*

**Xmas** /'krɪsməs/ *n abbr* (*Christmas*) Navidad *f*, Navidades *fpl*

**X-ray** /'eksreɪ/ *n* radiografía *f*. **~s** *npl* rayos *mpl* X. ● *vt* radiografiar

**xylophone** /'zaɪləfəʊn/ *n* xilófono *m*

# Y

**yacht** /jɒt/ *n* yate *m*. **~ing** *n* navegación *f* a vela

**yam** /jæm/ *n* ñame *m*, batata *f*

**yank** /jæŋk/ *vt* (*fam*) arrancar violentamente

**Yankee** /'jæŋkɪ/ *n* (*fam*) yanqui *m & f*

**yap** /jæp/ *vi* (*pt* **yapped**) (*dog*) ladrar

**yard**[1] /jɑ:d/ *n* (*measurement*) yarda *f* (= *0.9144 metre*)

**yard**[2] /jɑ:d/ *n* patio *m*; (*Amer, garden*) jardín *m*

**yardage** /'jɑ:dɪdʒ/ *n* metraje *m*

**yardstick** /'jɑ:dstɪk/ *n* (*fig*) criterio *m*

**yarn** /jɑ:n/ *n* hilo *m*; (*tale, fam*) cuento *m*

**yashmak** /'jæʃmæk/ *n* velo *m*

**yawn** /jɔ:n/ *vi* bostezar. ● *n* bostezo *m*

**year** /jɪə(r)/ *n* año *m*. **be three ~s old** tener tres años. **~book** *n* anuario *m*. **~ling** /'jɜ:lɪŋ/ *n* primal *m*. **~ly** *a* anual. ● *adv* anualmente

**yearn** /'jɜ:n/ *vi*. **~ for** anhelar. **~ing** *n* ansia *f*

**yeast** /ji:st/ *n* levadura *f*

**yell** /jel/ *vi* gritar. ● *n* grito *m*

**yellow** /'jeləʊ/ a & n amarillo (m). ∼**ish** a amarillento

**yelp** /jelp/ n gañido m. ● vi gañir

**yen** /jen/ n muchas ganas fpl

**yeoman** /'jəʊmən/ n (pl -men). **Y**∼ **of the Guard** alabardero m de la Casa Real

**yes** /jes/ adv & n sí (m)

**yesterday** /'jestədeɪ/ adv & n ayer (m). **the day before** ∼ anteayer m

**yet** /jet/ adv todavía, aún; (already) ya. **as** ∼ hasta ahora. ● conj sin embargo

**yew** /ju:/ n tejo m

**Yiddish** /'jɪdɪʃ/ n judeoalemán m

**yield** /ji:ld/ vt producir. ● vi ceder. ● n producción f; (com) rendimiento m

**yoga** /'jəʊgə/ n yoga m

**yoghurt** /'jɒgət/ n yogur m

**yoke** /jəʊk/ n yugo m; (of garment) canesú m

**yokel** /'jəʊkl/ n patán m, palurdo m

**yolk** /jəʊk/ n yema f (de huevo)

**yonder** /'jɒndə(r)/ adv a lo lejos

**you** /ju:/ pron (familiar form) tú, vos (Arg), (pl) vosotros, vosotras, ustedes (LAm); (polite form) usted, (pl) ustedes; (familiar, object) te, (pl) os, les (LAm); (polite, object) le, la, (pl) les; (familiar, after prep) ti, (pl) vosotros, vosotras, ustedes (LAm); (polite, after prep) usted, (pl) ustedes. **with** ∼ (familiar) contigo, (pl) con vosotros, con vosotras, con ustedes (LAm); (polite) con usted, (pl) con ustedes; (polite reflexive) consigo. **I know** ∼ te conozco, le conozco a usted. **you can't smoke here** aquí no se puede fumar

**young** /jʌŋ/ a (-er, -est) joven. ∼ **lady** n señorita f. ∼ **man** n joven m. **her** ∼ **man** (boyfriend) su novio m. **the** ∼ npl los jóvenes mpl; (of animals) la cría f. ∼**ster** /'jʌŋstə(r)/ n joven m

**your** /jɔ:(r)/ a (familiar) tu, (pl) vuestro; (polite) su

**yours** /jɔ:z/ poss pron (el) tuyo, (pl) (el) vuestro, el de ustedes (LAm); (polite) el suyo. **a book of** ∼**s** un libro tuyo, un libro suyo. **Y**∼**s faithfully**, **Y**∼**s sincerely** le saluda atentamente

**yourself** /jɔ:'self/ pron (pl **yourselves**) (familiar, subject) tú mismo, tú misma, (pl) vosotros mismos, vosotras mismas, ustedes mismos (LAm), ustedes mismas (LAm); (polite, subject) usted mismo, usted misma, (pl) ustedes mismos, ustedes mismas, usted mismo, usted misma, (pl) ustedes mismos, ustedes mismas, (pl) os, se (LAm); (polite, object) se; (familiar, after prep) ti, (pl) vosotros, vosotras, ustedes (LAm); (polite, after prep) sí

**youth** /ju:θ/ n (pl **youths** /ju:ðz/) juventud f; (boy) joven m; (young people) jóvenes mpl. ∼**ful** a joven, juvenil. ∼**hostel** n albergue m para jóvenes

**yowl** /jaʊl/ vi aullar. ● n aullido m

**Yugoslav** /'ju:gəslɑ:v/ a & n yugoslavo (m). ∼**ia** /-'slɑ:vɪə/ n Yugoslavia f

**yule** /ju:l/ n, **yule-tide** /'ju:ltaɪd/ n (old use) Navidades fpl

# Z

**zany** /'zeɪnɪ/ a (-ier, -iest) estrafalario

**zeal** /zi:l/ n celo m

**zealot** /'zelət/ n fanático m

**zealous** /'zeləs/ a entusiasta. ∼**ly** /'zeləslɪ/ adv con entusiasmo

**zebra** /'zebrə/ n cebra f. ∼ **crossing** n paso m de cebra

**zenith** /'zenɪθ/ n cenit m

**zero** /'zɪərəʊ/ n (pl -os) cero m

**zest** /zest/ n gusto m; (peel) cáscara f

**zigzag** /'zɪgzæg/ n zigzag m. ● vi (pt **zigzagged**) zigzaguear

**zinc** /zɪŋk/ n cinc m

**Zionis|m** /'zaɪənɪzəm/ n sionismo m. ∼**t** n sionista m & f

**zip** /zɪp/ n cremallera f. ● vt. ∼ **(up)** cerrar (la cremallera)

**Zip code** /'zɪpkəʊd/ n (Amer) código m postal

**zip fastener** /zɪp'fɑ:snə(r)/ n cremallera f

**zircon** /'zɜ:kən/ n circón m

**zither** /'zɪðə(r)/ n cítara f

**zodiac** /'zəʊdɪæk/ n zodiaco m

**zombie** /'zɒmbɪ/ n (fam) autómata m & f

**zone** /zəʊn/ n zona f

**zoo** /zu:/ n (fam) zoo m, jardín m zoológico. ∼**logical** /zəʊə'lɒdʒɪkl/ a zoológico

**zoolog|ist** /zəʊ'ɒlədʒɪst/ n zoólogo m. ∼**y** /zəʊ'ɒlədʒɪ/ n zoología f

**zoom** /zu:m/ vi ir a gran velocidad. ∼ **in** (photo) acercarse rápidamente. ∼ **past** pasar zumbando. ∼ **lens** n zoom m

**Zulu** /'zu:lu:/ n zulú m & f

# Numbers · Números

| English | | Spanish |
|---|---|---|
| zero | 0 | cero |
| one (first) | 1 | uno (primero) |
| two (second) | 2 | dos (segundo) |
| three (third) | 3 | tres (tercero) |
| four (fourth) | 4 | cuatro (cuarto) |
| five (fifth) | 5 | cinco (quinto) |
| six (sixth) | 6 | seis (sexto) |
| seven (seventh) | 7 | siete (séptimo) |
| eight (eighth) | 8 | ocho (octavo) |
| nine (ninth) | 9 | nueve (noveno) |
| ten (tenth) | 10 | diez (décimo) |
| eleven (eleventh) | 11 | once (undécimo) |
| twelve (twelfth) | 12 | doce (duodécimo) |
| thirteen (thirteenth) | 13 | trece (decimotercero) |
| fourteen (fourteenth) | 14 | catorce (decimocuarto) |
| fifteen (fifteenth) | 15 | quince (decimoquinto) |
| sixteen (sixteenth) | 16 | dieciséis (decimosexto) |
| seventeen (seventeenth) | 17 | diecisiete (decimoséptimo) |
| eighteen (eighteenth) | 18 | dieciocho (decimoctavo) |
| nineteen (nineteenth) | 19 | diecinueve (decimonoveno) |
| twenty (twentieth) | 20 | veinte (vigésimo) |
| twenty-one (twenty-first) | 21 | veintiuno (vigésimo primero) |
| twenty-two (twenty-second) | 22 | veintidós (vigésimo segundo) |
| twenty-three (twenty-third) | 23 | veintitrés (vigésimo tercero) |
| twenty-four (twenty-fourth) | 24 | veinticuatro (vigésimo cuarto) |
| twenty-five (twenty-fifth) | 25 | veinticinco (vigésimo quinto) |
| twenty-six (twenty-sixth) | 26 | veintiséis (vigésimo sexto) |
| thirty (thirtieth) | 30 | treinta (trigésimo) |
| thirty-one (thirty-first) | 31 | treinta y uno (trigésimo primero) |
| forty (fortieth) | 40 | cuarenta (cuadragésimo) |
| fifty (fiftieth) | 50 | cincuenta (quincuagésimo) |
| sixty (sixtieth) | 60 | sesenta (sexagésimo) |
| seventy (seventieth) | 70 | setenta (septuagésimo) |
| eighty (eightieth) | 80 | ochenta |

| | | (octogésimo) |
|---|---|---|
| ninety (ninetieth) | 90 | noventa (nonagésimo) |
| a/one hundred (hundredth) | 100 | cien (centésimo) |
| a/one hundred and one (hundred and first) | 101 | ciento uno (centésimo primero) |
| two hundred (two hundredth) | 200 | doscientos (ducentésimo) |
| three hundred (three hundredth) | 300 | trescientos (tricentésimo) |
| four hundred (four hundredth) | 400 | cuatrocientos (cuadringentésimo) |
| five hundred (five hundredth) | 500 | quinientos (quingentésimo) |
| six hundred (six hundredth) | 600 | seiscientos (sexcentésimo) |
| seven hundred (seven hundredth) | 700 | setecientos (septingentésimo) |
| eight hundred (eight hundredth) | 800 | ochocientos (octingentésimo) |
| nine hundred (nine hundredth) | 900 | novecientos (noningentésimo) |
| a/one thousand (thousandth) | 1000 | mil (milésimo) |
| two thousand (two thousandth) | 2000 | dos mil (dos milésimo) |
| a/one million (millionth) | 1,000,000 | un millón (millonésimo) |

# Spanish Verbs · Verbos españoles

Regular verbs:

in **-ar** (*e.g.* comprar)
*Present;* compr|o, ~as, ~a, ~amos,
~áis, ~an
*Future:* comprar|é, ~ás, ~á,
~emos, ~éis, ~án
*Imperfect:* compr|aba, ~abas, ~aba,
~ábamos, ~abais, ~aban
*Preterite:* compr|é, ~aste, ~ó,
~amos, ~asteis, ~aron
*Present subjunctive:* compr|e, ~es,
~e, ~emos, ~éis, ~en
*Imperfect subjunctive:* compr|ara,
~aras ~ara, ~áramos, ~arais,
~aran
compr|ase, ~ases, ~ase,
~ásemos, ~aseis, ~asen
*Conditional:* comprar|ía, ~ías, ~ía,
~íamos, ~íais, ~ían
*Present participle:* comprando
*Past participle:* comprado
*Imperative:* compra, comprad

in **-er** (*e.g.* beber)
*Present:* beb|o, ~es, ~e, ~emos,
~éis, ~en
*Future:* beber|é, ~ás, ~á, ~emos,
~éis, ~án
*Imperfect:* beb|ía, ~ías, ~ía,
~íamos, ~íais, ~ían
*Preterite:* beb|í, ~iste, ~ió, ~imos,
~isteis, ~ieron
*Present subjunctive:* beb|a, ~as, ~a,
~amos, ~áis, ~an
*Imperfect subjunctive:* beb|iera,
~ieras, ~iera, ~iéramos, ~ierais,
~ieran
beb|iese, ~ieses, ~iese,
~iésemos, ~ieseis, ~iesen
*Conditional:* beber|ía, ~ías, ~ía,
~íamos, ~íais, ~ían
*Present participle:* bebiendo
*Past participle:* bebido
*Imperative:* bebe, bebed

in **-ir** (*e.g.* vivir)
*Present:* viv|o, ~es, ~e, ~imos, ~ís,
~en
*Future:* vivir|é, ~ás, ~á, ~emos,
~éis, ~án
*Imperfect:* viv|ía, ~ias, ~ía, ~íamos,
~íais, ~ían
*Preterite:* viv|í, ~iste, ~ió, ~imos,
~isteis, ~ieron

*Present subjunctive:* viv|a, ~as, ~a,
~amos, ~áis, ~an
*Imperfect subjunctive:* viv|iera,
~ieras, ~iera, ~iéramos, ~ierais,
~ieran
viv|iese, ~ieses, ~iese,
~iésemos, ~ieseis, ~iesen
*Conditional:* vivir|ía, ~ías, ~ía,
~íamos, ~íais, ~ían
*Present participle:* viviendo
*Past participle:* vivido
*Imperative:* vive, vivid


Irregular verbs:

[1] **cerrar**
*Present:* cierro, cierras, cierra,
cerramos, cerráis, cierran
*Present subjunctive:* cierre, cierres,
cierre, cerremos, cerréis, cierren
*Imperative:* cierra, cerrad


[2] **contar, mover**
*Present:* cuento, cuentas, cuenta,
contamos, contáis, cuentan
muevo, mueves, mueve,
movemos, movéis, mueven
*Present subjunctive:* cuente, cuentes,
cuente, contemos, contéis,
cuenten
mueva, muevas mueva,
movamos, mováis, muevan
*Imperative:* cuenta, contad mueve,
moved


[3] **jugar**
*Present:* juego, juegas, juega,
jugamos, jugáis, juegan
*Preterite:* jug|ué, jugaste, jugó,
jugamos, jugasteis, jugaron
*Present subjunctive:* juegue, juegues,
juegue, juguemos, juguéis,
jueguen


[4] **sentir**
*Present:* siento, sientes, siente,
sentimos, sentís, sienten
*Preterite:* sentí, sentiste, sintió,
sentimos, sentisteis, sintieron
*Present subjunctive:* sienta, sientas,
sienta, sintamos, sintáis, sientan
*Imperfect subjunctive:* sint|iera,
~ieras, ~iera, ~iéramos, ~ierais,
~ieran

sint|iese, ~ieses, ~iese,
~iésemos, ~ieseis, ~iesen
*Present participle:* sintiendo
*Imperative:* siente, sentid

**[5] pedir**
*Present:* pido, pides, pide, pedimos,
pedís, piden
*Preterite:* pedí, pediste, pidió,
pedimos, pedisteis, pidieron
*Present subjunctive:* pid|a, ~as, ~a,
~amos, ~áis, ~an
*Imperfect subjunctive:* pid|iera,
~ieras, ~iera, ~iéramos, ~ierais,
~ieran
pid|iese, ~ieses, ~iese,
~iésemos, ~ieseis, ~iesen
*Present participle:* pidiendo
*Imperative:* pide, pedid

**[6] dormir**
*Present:* duermo, duermes, duerme,
dormimos, dormís, duermen
*Preterite:* dormí, dormiste, durmió,
dormimos, dormisteis, durmieron
*Present subjunctive:* duerma,
duermas, duerma, durmamos,
durmáis, duerman
*Imperfect subjunctive:* durm|iera,
~ieras, ~iera, ~iéramos, ~ierais,
~ieran
durm|iese, ~ieses, ~iese,
~iésemos, ~ieseis, ~iesen
*Present participle:* durmiendo
*Imperative:* duerme, dormid

**[7] dedicar**
*Preterite:* dediqué, dedicaste, dedicó,
dedicamos, dedicasteis, dedicaron
*Present subjunctive:* dediqu|e, ~ues,
~e, ~emos, ~éis, ~en

**[8] delinquir**
*Present:* delinco, delinques,
delinque, delinquimos, delinquís,
delinquen
*Present subjunctive:* delinc|a, ~as,
~a, ~amos, ~áis, ~an

**[9] vencer, esparcir**
*Present:* venzo, vences, vence,
vencemos, vencéis, vencen
esparzo, esparces, esparce,
esparcimos, esparcís, esparcen
*Present subjunctive:* venz|a, ~as,
~a, ~amos, ~áis, ~an esparz|a,
~as, ~a, ~amos, ~áis, ~an

**[10] rechazar**
*Preterite:* rechacé, rechazaste,
rechazó, rechazamos,
rechazasteis, rechazaron
*Present subjunctive:* rechac|e, ~es,
~e, ~emos, ~éis, ~en

**[11] conocer, lucir**
*Present:* conozco, conoces, conoce,
conocemos, conocéis, conocen
luzco, luces, luce, lucimos, lucís,
lucen
*Present subjunctive:* conozc|a, ~as,
~a, ~amos, ~áis, ~an luzc|a,
~as, ~a, ~amos, ~áis, ~an

**[12] pagar**
*Preterite:* pagué, pagaste, pagó,
pagamos, pagasteis, pagaron
*Present subjunctive:* pagu|e, ~es,
~e, ~emos, ~éis, ~en

**[13] distinguir**
*Present:* distingo, distingues,
distingue, distinguimos,
distinguís, distinguen
*Present subjunctive:* disting|a, ~as,
~a, ~amos, ~áis, ~an

**[14] acoger, afligir**
*Present:* acojo, acoges, acoge,
acogemos, acogéis, acogen
aflijo, afliges, aflige, afligimos,
afligís, afligen
*Present subjunctive:* acoj|a, ~as, ~a,
~amos, ~áis, ~an
aflij|a, ~as, ~a, ~amos, ~áis,
~an

**[15] averiguar**
*Preterite:* averigüé, averiguaste,
averiguó, averiguamos,
averiguasteis, averiguaron
*Present subjunctive:* averigü|e, ~es,
~e, ~emos, ~éis, ~en

**[16] agorar**
*Present:* agüero, agüeras, agüera,
agoramos, agoráis, agüeran
*Present subjunctive:* agüere,
agüeres, agüere, agoremos,
agoréis, agüeren
*Imperative:* agüera, agorad

**[17] huir**
*Present:* huyo, huyes, huye, huimos,
huís, huyen

*Preterite:* huí, huiste, huyó, huimos,
huisteis, huyeron
*Present subjunctive:* huy|a, ~as, ~a,
~amos, ~áis, ~an
*Imperfect subjunctive:* huy|era,
~eras, ~era, ~éramos, ~erais,
~eran
huy|ese, ~eses, ~ese, ~ésemos,
~eseis, ~esen
*Present participle:* huyendo

**[18] creer**
*Preterite:* creí, creíste, creyó,
creímos, creísteis, creyeron
*Imperfect subjunctive:* crey|era,
~eras, ~era, ~éramos, ~erais,
~eran
crey|ese, ~eses, ~ese, ~ésemos,
~eseis, ~esen
*Present participle:* creyendo
*Past participle:* creído

**[19] argüir**
*Present:* arguyo, arguyes, arguye,
argüimos, argüís, arguyen
*Preterite:* argüí, argüiste, arguyó,
argüimos, argüisteis, arguyeron
*Present subjunctive:* arguy|a, ~as,
~a, ~amos, ~áis, ~an
*Imperfect subjunctive:* arguy|era,
~eras, ~era, ~éramos, ~erais,
~eran
arguy|ese, ~eses, ~ese,
~ésemos, ~eseis, ~esen
*Present participle:* arguyendo
*Imperative:* arguye, argüid

**[20] vaciar**
*Present:* vacío, vacías, vacía,
vaciamos, vaciáis, vacían
*Present subjunctive:* vacíe, vacíes,
vacíe, vaciemos, vaciéis, vacíen
*Imperative:* vacía, vaciad

**[21] acentuar**
*Present:* acentúo, acentúas, acentúa,
acentuamos, acentuáis, acentúan
*Present subjunctive:* acentúe,
acentúes, acentúe, acentuemos,
acentuéis, acentúen
*Imperative:* acentúa, acentuad

**[22] ateñer, engullir**
*Preterite:* atañ|í, ~aste, ~ó, ~amos,
~asteis, ~eron engull|í ~iste,
~ó, ~imos, ~isteis, ~eron
*Imperfect subjunctive:* atañ|era,
~eras, ~era, ~éramos, ~erais,

~eran
atañ|ese, ~eses, ~ese, ~ésemos,
~eseis, ~esen
engull|era, ~eras, ~era,
~éramos, ~erais, ~eran
engull|ese, ~eses, ~ese,
~ésemos, ~eseis, ~esen
*Present participle:* atañendo
engullendo

**[23] aislar, aullar**
*Present:* aíslo, aíslas, aísla, aislamos,
aisláis, aíslan
aúllo, aúllas, aúlla, aullamos
aulláis, aúllan
*Present subjunctive:* aísle, aísles,
aísle, aislemos, aisléis, aíslen
aúlle, aúlles, aúlle, aullemos,
aulléis, aúllen
*Imperative:* aísla, aislad
aúlla, aullad

**[24] abolir, garantir**
*Present:* abolimos, abolís
garantimos, garantís
*Present subjunctive:* not used
*Imperative:* abolid
garantid

**[25] andar**
*Preterite:* anduv|e, ~iste, ~o,
~imos, ~isteis, ~ieron
*Imperfect subjunctive:* anduv|iera,
~ieras, ~iera, ~iéramos, ~ierais,
~ieran
anduv|iese, ~ieses, ~iese,
~iésemos, ~ieseis, ~iesen

**[26] dar**
*Present:* doy, das, da, damos, dais,
dan
*Preterite:* di, diste, dio, dimos,
disteis, dieron
*Present subjunctive:* dé, des, dé,
demos, deis, den
*Imperfect subjunctive:* diera, dieras,
diera, diéramos, dierais, dieran
diese, dieses, diese, diésemos,
dieseis, diesen

**[27] estar**
*Present:* estoy, estás, está, estamos,
estáis, están
*Preterite:* estuv|e, ~iste, ~o, ~imos,
~isteis, ~ieron
*Present subjunctive:* esté, estés, esté,
estemos, estéis, estén

*Imperfect subjunctive:* estuv|iera,
~ieras, ~iera, ~iéramos, ~ierais,
~ieran
estuv|iese, ~ieses, ~iese,
~iésemos, ~ieseis, ~iesen
*Imperative:* está, estad

**[28] caber**
*Present:* quepo, cabes, cabe,
cabemos, cabéis, caben
*Future:* cabr|é, ~ás, ~á, ~emos,
~éis, ~án
*Preterite:* cup|e, ~iste, ~o, ~imos,
~isteis, ~ieron
*Present subjunctive:* quep|a, ~as,
~a, ~amos, ~áis, ~an
*Imperfect subjunctive:* cup|iera,
~ieras, ~iera, ~iéramos, ~ierais,
~ieran
cup|iese, ~ieses, ~iese,
~iésemos, ~ieseis, ~iesen
*Conditional:* cabr|ía, ~ías, ~ía,
~íamos, ~íais, ~ían

**[29] caer**
*Present:* caigo, caes, cae, caemos,
caéis, caen
*Preterite:* caí, caiste, cayó, caímos,
caísteis, cayeron
*Present subjunctive:* caig|a, ~as, ~a,
~amos, ~áis, ~an
*Imperfect subjunctive:* cay|era,
~eras, ~era, ~éramos, ~erais,
~eran
cay|ese, ~eses, ~ese, ~ésemos,
~eseis, ~esen
*Present participle:* cayendo
*Past participle:* caído

**[30] haber**
*Present:* he, has, ha, hemos, habéis,
han
*Future:* habr|é ~ás, ~á, ~emos,
~éis, ~án
*Preterite:* hub|e, ~iste, ~o, ~imos,
~isteis, ~ieron
*Present subjunctive:* hay|a, ~as,
~amos, ~áis, ~an
*Imperfect subjunctive:* hub|iera,
~ieras, ~iera, ~iéramos, ~ierais,
~ieran
hub|iese, ~ieses, ~iese,
~iésemos, ~ieseis, ~iesen
*Conditional:* habr|ía, ~ías, ~ía,
~íamos, ~íais, ~ían
*Imperative:* habe, habed

**[31] hacer**

*Present:* hago, haces, hace, hacemos,
hacéis, hacen
*Future:* har|é, ~ás, ~á, ~emos,
~éis, ~án
*Preterite:* hice, hiciste, hizo, hicimos,
hicisteis, hicieron
*Present subjunctive:* hag|a, ~as, ~a,
~amos, ~áis, ~an
*Imperfect subjunctive:* hic|iera,
~ieras, ~iera, ~iéramos, ~ierais,
~ieran
hic|iese, ~ieses, ~iese, ~iésemos,
~ieseis, ~iesen
*Conditional:* har|ía, ~ías, ~ía,
~íamos, ~íais, ~ían
*Past participle:* hecho
*Imperative:* haz, haced

**[32] placer**
*Preterite:* plació/plugo
*Present subjunctive:* plazca
*Imperfect subjunctive:*
placiera/pluguiera
placiese/pluguiese

**[33] poder**
*Present:* puedo, puedes, puede,
podemos, podéis, pueden
*Future:* podr|é, ~ás, ~á, ~emos,
~éis, ~án
*Preterite:* pud|e, ~iste, ~o, ~imos,
~isteis, ~ieron
*Present subjunctive:* pueda, puedas,
pueda, podamos, podáis, puedan
*Imperfect subjunctive:* pud|iera,
~ieras, ~iera, ~iéramos, ~ierais,
~ieran
pud|iese, ~ieses, ~iese,
~iésemos, ~ieseis, ~iesen
*Conditional:* podr|ía, ~ías, ~ía,
~íamos, ~íais, ~ían
*Past participle:* pudiendo

**[34] poner**
*Present:* pongo, pones, pone,
ponemos, ponéis, ponen
*Future:* pondr|é, ~ás, ~á, ~emos,
~éis, ~án
*Preterite:* pus|e, ~iste, ~o, ~imos,
~isteis, ~ieron
*Present subjunctive:* pong|a, ~as,
~a, ~amos, ~áis, ~an
*Imperfect subjunctive:* pus|iera,
~ieras, ~iera, ~iéramos, ~ierais,
~ieran
pus|iese, ~ieses, ~iese,
~iésemos, ~ieseis, ~iesen

*Conditional:* pondría, ~ías, ~ía,
~íamos, ~íais, ~ían
*Past participle:* puesto
*Imperative:* pon, poned

**[35] querer**
*Present:* quiero, quieres, quiere,
queremos, queréis, quieren
*Future:* querré, ~ás, ~á, ~emos,
~éis, ~án
*Preterite:* quise, ~iste, ~o, ~imos,
~isteis, ~ieron
*Present subjunctive:* quiera, quieras,
quiera, queramos, queráis,
quieran
*Imperfect subjunctive:* quisiera,
~ieras, ~iera, ~iéramos, ~ierais,
~ieran
quisiese, ~ieses, ~iese,
~iésemos, ~ieseis, ~iesen
*Conditional:* querría, ~ías, ~ía,
~íamos, ~íais, ~ían
*Imperative:* quiere, quered

**[36] raer**
*Present:* raigo/rayo, raes, rae,
raemos, raéis, raen
*Preterite:* raí, raíste, rayó, raímos,
raísteis, rayeron
*Present subjunctive:* raiga, ~as, ~a,
~amos, ~áis, ~an
raya, ~as, ~a, ~amos, ~áis, ~an
*Imperfect subjunctive:* rayera,
~eras, ~era, ~éramos, ~erais,
~eran
rayese, ~eses, ~ese, ~ésemos,
~eseis, ~esen
*Present participle:* rayendo
*Past participle:* raído

**[37] roer**
*Present:* roo/roigo/royo, roes, roe,
roemos, roéis, roen
*Preterite:* roí, roíste, royó, roímos,
roísteis, royeron
*Present subjunctive:* roa/roiga/roya,
roas, roa, roamos, roáis, roan
*Imperfect subjunctive:* royera,
~eras, ~era, ~éramos, ~erais,
~eran
royese, ~eses, ~ese, ~ésemos,
~eseis, ~esen
*Present participle:* royendo
*Past participle:* roído

**[38] saber**
*Present:* sé, sabes, sabe, sabemos,
sabéis, saben

*Future:* sabré, ~ás, ~á, ~emos,
~éis, ~án
*Preterite:* supe, ~iste, ~o, ~imos,
~isteis, ~ieron
*Present subjunctive:* sepa, ~as, ~a,
~amos, ~áis, ~an
*Imperfect subjunctive:* supiera,
~ieras, ~iera, ~iéramos, ~ierais,
~ieran
supiese, ~ieses, ~iese,
~iésemos, ~ieseis, ~iesen
*Conditional:* sabría, ~ías, ~ía,
~íamos, ~íais, ~ían

**[39] ser**
*Present:* soy, eres, es, somos, sois,
son
*Imperfect:* era, eras, era, éramos,
erais, eran
*Preterite:* fui, fuiste, fue, fuimos,
fuisteis, fueron
*Present subjunctive:* sea, ~as, ~a,
~amos, ~áis, ~an
*Imperfect subjunctive:* fuera, ~eras,
~era, ~éramos, ~erais, ~eran
fuese, ~eses, ~ese, ~ésemos,
~eseis, ~esen
*Imperative:* sé, sed

**[40] tener**
*Present:* tengo, tienes, tiene,
tenemos, tenéis, tienen
*Future:* tendré, ~ás, ~á, ~emos,
~éis, ~án
*Preterite:* tuve, ~iste, ~o, ~imos,
~isteis, ~ieron
*Present subjunctive:* tenga, ~as, ~a,
~amos, ~áis, ~an
*Imperfect subjunctive:* tuviera,
~ieras, ~iera, ~iéramos, ~ierais,
~ieran
tuviese, ~ieses, ~iese,
~iésemos, ~ieseis, ~iesen
*Conditional:* tendría, ~ías, ~ía,
~íamos, ~íais, ~ían
*Imperative:* ten, tened

**[41] traer**
*Present:* traigo, traes, trae, traemos,
traéis, traen
*Preterite:* traje, ~iste, ~o, ~imos,
~isteis, ~eron
*Present subjunctive:* traiga, ~as,
~a, ~amos, ~áis, ~an
*Imperfect subjunctive:* trajera,
~eras, ~era, ~éramos, ~erais,
~eran

traj|ese, ~eses, ~ese, ~ésemos,
~eseis, ~esen
*Present participle:* trayendo
*Past participle:* traído

**[42] valer**
*Present:* valgo, vales, vale, valemos,
valéis, valen
*Future:* vald|ré, ~ás, ~á, ~emos,
~éis, ~án
*Present subjunctive:* valg|a, ~as, ~a,
~amos ~áis, ~an
*Conditional:* vald|ría, ~ías, ~ía,
~íamos, ~íais, ~ían
*Imperative:* val/vale, valed

**[43] ver**
*Present:* veo, ves, ve, vemos, véis,
ven
*Imperfect:* ve|ía, ~ías, ~ía, ~íamos,
~iais, ~ían
*Preterite:* vi, viste, vio, vimos,
visteis, vieron
*Present subjunctive:* ve|a, ~as, ~a,
~amos, ~áis, ~an
*Past participle:* visto

**[44] yacer**
*Present:* yazco/yazgo/yago, yaces,
yace, yacemos, yacéis, yacen
*Present subjunctive:*
yazca/yazga/yaga, yazcas,
yazca, yazcamos, yazcáis, yazcan
*Imperative:* yace/yaz, yaced

**[45] asir**
*Present:* asgo, ases, ase, asimos, asís,
asen
*Present subjunctive:* asg|a, ~as, ~a,
~amos, ~áis, ~an

**[46] decir**
*Present:* digo, dices, dice, decimos,
decís, dicen
*Future:* dir|é, ~ás, ~á, ~emos,
~éis, ~án
*Preterite:* dij|e, ~iste, ~o, ~imos,
~isteis, ~eron
*Present subjunctive:* dig|a, ~as, ~a,
~amos, ~áis, ~an
*Imperfect subjunctive:* dij|era,
~eras, ~era, ~éramos, ~erais,
~eran
dij|ese, ~eses, ~ese, ~ésemos,
~eseis, ~esen
*Conditional:* dir|ía, ~ías, ~ía,
~íamos, ~íais, ~ían
*Present participle:* dicho

*Imperative:* di, decid

**[47] reducir**
*Present:* reduzco, reduces, reduce,
reducimos, reducís, reducen
*Preterite:* reduj|e, ~iste, ~o, ~imos,
~isteis, ~eron
*Present subjunctive:* reduzc|a, ~as,
~a, ~amos, ~áis, ~an
*Imperfect subjunctive:* reduj|era,
~eras, ~era, ~éramos, ~erais,
~eran
reduj|ese, ~eses, ~ese, ~ésemos,
~eseis, ~esen

**[48] erguir**
*Present:* irgo, irgues, irgue,
erguimos, erguís, irguen
yergo, yergues, yergue, erguimos,
erguís, yerguen
*Preterite:* erguí, erguiste, irguió,
erguimos, erguisteis, irguieron
*Present subjunctive:* irg|a, ~as, ~a,
~amos, ~áis, ~an
yerg|a, ~as, ~a, ~amos, ~áis,
~an
*Imperfect subjunctive:* irgu|iera,
~ieras, ~iera, ~iéramos, ~ierais,
~ieran
irgu|iese, ~ieses, ~iese,
~iésemos, ~ieseis, ~iesen
*Present participle:* irguiendo
*Imperative:* irgue/yergue, erguid

**[49] ir**
*Present:* voy, vas, va, vamos, vais,
van
*Imperfect:* iba, ibas, iba, íbamos,
ibais, iban
*Preterite:* fui, fuiste, fue, fuimos,
fuisteis, fueron
*Present subjunctive:* vay|a, ~as, ~a,
~amos, ~áis, ~an
*Imperfect subjunctive:* fu|era, ~eras,
~era, ~éramos, ~erais, ~eran
fu|ese, ~eses, ~ese, ~ésemos,
~eseis, ~esen
*Present participle:* yendo
*Imperative:* ve, id

**[50] oír**
*Present:* oigo, oyes, oye, oímos, oís,
oyen
*Preterite:* oí, oíste, oyó, oímos, oísteis,
oyeron
*Present subjunctive:* oig|a, ~as, ~a,
~amos, ~áis, ~an

*Imperfect subjunctive:* oy|era, ~**eras,**
~**era,** ~**éramos,** ~**erais,** ~**eran**
oy|ese, ~**eses,** ~**ese,** ~**ésemos,**
~**eseis,** ~**esen**
*Present participle:* oyendo
*Past participle:* oído
*Imperative:* oye, oíd

[51] **reír**
*Present:* río, ríes, ríe, reímos, reís,
ríen
*Preterite:* reí, reíste, rió, reímos,
reísteis, rieron
*Present subjunctive:* ría, rías, ría,
riamos, riáis, rían
*Present participle:* riendo
*Past participle:* reído
*Imperative:* ríe, reíd

[52] **salir**
*Present:* salgo, sales, sale, salimos,
salís, salen
*Future:* saldr|é, ~**ás,** ~**á,** ~**emos,**
~**éis,** ~**án**

*Present subjunctive:* salg|a, ~**as,** ~**a,**
~**amos,** ~**áis,** ~**an**
*Conditional:* saldr|ía, ~**ías,** ~**ía,**
~**íamos,** ~**íais,** ~**ían**
*Imperative:* sal, salid

[53] **venir**
*Present:* vengo, vienes, viene,
venimos, venís, vienen
*Future:* vendr|é, ~**ás,** ~**á,** ~**emos,**
~**éis,** ~**án**
*Preterite:* vin|e, ~**iste,** ~**o,** ~**imos,**
~**isteis,** ~**ieron**
*Present subjunctive:* veng|a, ~**as,**
~**a,** ~**amos,** ~**áis,** ~**an**
*Imperfect subjunctive:* vin|iera,
~**ieras,** ~**iera,** ~**iéramos,** ~**ierais,**
~**ieran**
vin|iese, ~**ieses,** ~**iese,**
~**iésemos,** ~**ieseis,** ~**iesen**
*Conditional:* vendr|ía, ~**ías,** ~**ía,**
~**íamos,** ~**íais,** ~**ían**
*Present participle:* viniendo
*Imperative:* ven, venid

# Verbos Irregulares Ingleses

| Infinitivo | Pretérito | Participio pasado |
|---|---|---|
| arise | arose | arisen |
| awake | awoke | awoken |
| be | was | been |
| bear | bore | borne |
| beat | beat | beaten |
| become | became | become |
| befall | befell | befallen |
| beget | begot | begotten |
| begin | began | begun |
| behold | beheld | beheld |
| bend | bent | bent |
| beset | beset | beset |
| bet | bet, betted | bet, betted |
| bid | bade, bid | bidden, bid |
| bind | bound | bound |
| bite | bit | bitten |
| bleed | bled | bled |
| blow | blew | blown |
| break | broke | broken |
| breed | bred | bred |
| bring | brought | brought |
| broadcast | broadcast(ed) | broadcast |
| build | built | built |
| burn | burnt, burned | burnt, burned |
| burst | burst | burst |
| buy | bought | bought |
| cast | cast | cast |
| catch | caught | caught |
| choose | chose | chosen |
| cleave | clove, cleft, cleaved | cloven, cleft, cleaved |
| cling | clung | clung |
| clothe | clothed, clad | clothed, clad |
| come | came | come |
| cost | cost | cost |
| creep | crept | crept |
| crow | crowed, crew | crowed |
| cut | cut | cut |
| deal | dealt | dealt |
| dig | dug | dug |
| do | did | done |
| draw | drew | drawn |
| dream | dreamt, dreamed | dreamt, dreamed |
| drink | drank | drunk |
| drive | drove | driven |
| dwell | dwelt | dwelt |
| eat | ate | eaten |
| fall | fell | fallen |
| feed | fed | fed |
| feel | felt | felt |
| fight | fought | fought |
| find | found | found |

| *Infinitivo* | *Pretérito* | *Participio pasado* |
|---|---|---|
| flee | fled | fled |
| fling | flung | flung |
| fly | flew | flown |
| forbear | forbore | forborne |
| forbid | forbad(e) | forbidden |
| forecast | forecast(ed) | forecast(ed) |
| foresee | foresaw | foreseen |
| foretell | foretold | foretold |
| forget | forgot | forgotten |
| forgive | forgave | forgiven |
| forsake | forsook | forsaken |
| freeze | froze | frozen |
| gainsay | gainsaid | gainsaid |
| get | got | got |
| give | gave | given |
| go | went | gone |
| grind | ground | ground |
| grow | grew | grown |
| hang | hung, hanged | hung, hanged |
| have | had | had |
| hear | heard | heard |
| hew | hewed | hewn, hewed |
| hide | hid | hidden |
| hit | hit | hit |
| hold | held | held |
| hurt | hurt | hurt |
| inlay | inlaid | inlaid |
| keep | kept | kept |
| kneel | knelt | knelt |
| knit | knitted, knit | knitted, knit |
| know | knew | known |
| lay | laid | laid |
| lead | led | led |
| lean | leaned, leant | leaned, leant |
| leap | leaped, leapt | leaped, leapt |
| learn | learned, learnt | learned, learnt |
| leave | left | left |
| lend | lent | lent |
| let | let | let |
| lie | lay | lain |
| light | lit, lighted | lit, lighted |
| lose | lost | lost |
| make | made | made |
| mean | meant | meant |
| meet | met | met |
| mislay | mislaid | mislaid |
| mislead | misled | misled |
| misspell | misspelt | misspelt |
| mistake | mistook | mistaken |
| misunderstand | misunderstood | misunderstood |
| mow | mowed | mown |
| outbid | outbid | outbid |
| outdo | outdid | outdone |
| outgrow | outgrew | outgrown |
| overcome | overcame | overcome |

| Infinitivo | Pretérito | Participio pasado |
|---|---|---|
| overdo | overdid | overdone |
| overhang | overhung | overhung |
| overhear | overheard | overheard |
| override | overrode | overridden |
| overrun | overran | overrun |
| oversee | oversaw | overseen |
| overshoot | overshot | overshot |
| oversleep | overslept | overslept |
| overtake | overtook | overtaken |
| overthrow | overthrew | overthrown |
| partake | partook | partaken |
| pay | paid | paid |
| prove | proved | proved, proven |
| put | put | put |
| quit | quitted, quit | quitted, quit |
| read /ri:d/ | read /red/ | read /red/ |
| rebuild | rebuilt | rebuilt |
| redo | redid | redone |
| rend | rent | rent |
| repay | repaid | repaid |
| rewrite | rewrote | rewritten |
| rid | rid | rid |
| ride | rode | ridden |
| ring | rang | rung |
| rise | rose | risen |
| run | ran | run |
| saw | sawed | sawn, sawed |
| say | said | said |
| see | saw | seen |
| seek | sought | sought |
| sell | sold | sold |
| send | sent | sent |
| set | set | set |
| sew | sewed | sewn, sewed |
| shake | shook | shaken |
| shear | sheared | shorn, sheared |
| shed | shed | shed |
| shine | shone | shone |
| shoe | shod | shod |
| shoot | shot | shot |
| show | showed | shown, showed |
| shrink | shrank | shrunk |
| shut | shut | shut |
| sing | sang | sung |
| sink | sank | sunk |
| sit | sat | sat |
| slay | slew | slain |
| sleep | slept | slept |
| slide | slid | slid |
| sling | slung | slung |
| slit | slit | slit |
| smell | smelt, smelled | smelt, smelled |
| smite | smote | smitten |
| sow | sowed | sown, sowed |
| speak | spoke | spoken |

| *Infinitivo* | *Pretérito* | *Participio pasado* |
|---|---|---|
| speed | speeded, sped | speeded, sped |
| spell | spelt, spelled | spelt, spelled |
| spend | spent | spent |
| spill | spilt, spilled | spilt, spilled |
| spin | spun | spun |
| spit | spat | spat |
| split | split | split |
| spoil | spoilt, spoiled | spoilt, spoiled |
| spread | spread | spread |
| spring | sprang | sprung |
| stand | stood | stood |
| steal | stole | stolen |
| stick | stuck | stuck |
| sting | stung | stung |
| stink | stank, stunk | stunk |
| strew | strewed | strewn, strewed |
| stride | strode | stridden |
| strike | struck | struck |
| string | strung | strung |
| strive | strove | striven |
| swear | swore | sworn |
| sweep | swept | swept |
| swell | swelled | swollen, swelled |
| swim | swam | swum |
| swing | swung | swung |
| take | took | taken |
| teach | taught | taught |
| tear | tore | torn |
| tell | told | told |
| think | thought | thought |
| thrive | thrived, throve | thrived, thriven |
| throw | threw | thrown |
| thrust | thrust | thrust |
| tread | trod | trodden, trod |
| unbend | unbent | unbent |
| undergo | underwent | undergone |
| understand | understood | understood |
| undertake | undertook | undertaken |
| undo | undid | undone |
| upset | upset | upset |
| wake | woke, waked | woken, waked |
| waylay | waylaid | waylaid |
| wear | wore | worn |
| weave | wove | woven |
| weep | wept | wept |
| win | won | won |
| wind | wound | wound |
| withdraw | withdrew | withdrawn |
| withhold | withheld | withheld |
| withstand | withstood | withstood |
| wring | wrung | wrung |
| write | wrote | written |